Communications
in Computer and Information Science 345

Editorial Board

Simone Diniz Junqueira Barbosa
Pontifical Catholic University of Rio de Janeiro (PUC-Rio),
Rio de Janeiro, Brazil
Phoebe Chen
La Trobe University, Melbourne, Australia
Alfredo Cuzzocrea
ICAR-CNR and University of Calabria, Italy
Xiaoyong Du
Renmin University of China, Beijing, China
Joaquim Filipe
Polytechnic Institute of Setúbal, Portugal
Orhun Kara
TÜBİTAK BİLGEM and Middle East Technical University, Turkey
Tai-hoon Kim
Konkuk University, Chung-ju, Chungbuk, Korea
Igor Kotenko
St. Petersburg Institute for Informatics and Automation
of the Russian Academy of Sciences, Russia
Dominik Ślęzak
University of Warsaw and Infobright, Poland
Xiaokang Yang
Shanghai Jiao Tong University, China

T0180908

Jingsheng Lei   Fu Lee Wang   Mo Li
Yuan Luo (Eds.)

Network Computing and Information Security

Second International Conference, NCIS 2012
Shanghai, China, December 7-9, 2012
Proceedings

 Springer

Volume Editors

Jingsheng Lei
Shanghai University of Electric Power
School of Computer and Information Engineering
Shanghai 200090, China
E-mail: jshlei@shiep.edu.cn

Fu Lee Wang
Caritas Institute of Higher Education
18 Chui Ling Road, Tseung Kwan O, Hong Kong, China
E-mail: pwang@cihe.edu.hk

Mo Li
Nanyang Technological University (NTU)
School of Computer Engineering
Computer Science Division
50 Nanyang Avenue, Singapore
E-mail: limo@ntu.edu.sg

Yuan Luo
Shanghai Jiao Tong University
Department of Computer Science and Engineering
Shanghai 200030, China
E-mail: luoyuan@cs.sjtu.edu.cn

ISSN 1865-0929   e-ISSN 1865-0937
ISBN 978-3-642-35210-2   e-ISBN 978-3-642-35211-9
DOI 10.1007/978-3-642-35211-9
Springer Heidelberg Dordrecht London New York

Library of Congress Control Number: 2012952316

CR Subject Classification (1998): D.4.6, C.2.1, C.2.4, C.4, H.3.4

© Springer-Verlag Berlin Heidelberg 2012
This work is subject to copyright. All rights are reserved, whether the whole or part of the material is
concerned, specifically the rights of translation, reprinting, re-use of illustrations, recitation, broadcasting,
reproduction on microfilms or in any other way, and storage in data banks. Duplication of this publication
or parts thereof is permitted only under the provisions of the German Copyright Law of September 9, 1965,
in its current version, and permission for use must always be obtained from Springer. Violations are liable
to prosecution under the German Copyright Law.
The use of general descriptive names, registered names, trademarks, etc. in this publication does not imply,
even in the absence of a specific statement, that such names are exempt from the relevant protective laws
and regulations and therefore free for general use.

Typesetting: Camera-ready by author, data conversion by Scientific Publishing Services, Chennai, India

Printed on acid-free paper

Springer is part of Springer Science+Business Media (www.springer.com)

Preface

The 2012 International Conference on Network Computing and Information Security (NCIS 2012) was held in Shanghai, China during December 7–9, 2012. NCIS 2012 received 517 submissions from 10 countries and regions. After rigorous reviews, 104 high-quality papers were selected for publication in the NCIS 2012 proceedings. The acceptance rate was 20.11%.

The aim of NCIS 2012 was to bring together researchers working in many different areas of network computing and information security to foster the exchange of new ideas and promote international collaboration. In addition to the large number of submitted papers, there were several internationally well-known keynote speakers.

On behalf of the Organizing Committee, we thank Shanghai University of Electric Power for its sponsorship and logistics support. We also thank the members of the Organizing Committee and the Program Committee for their hard work. We are very grateful to the keynote speakers, session chairs, reviewers, and student helpers. Last but not least, we thank all the authors and participants for the great contributions that made this conference possible.

December 2012

Jingsheng Lei
Fu Lee Wang
Mo Li
Yuan Luo

Organization

Organizing Committee

General Co-chairs

Hao Zhang   Shanghai University of Electric Power, China
Yunhao Liu   Tsinghua University, China

Program Committee Co-chairs

Mo Li   Nanyang Technological University, Singapore
Yuan Luo   Shanghai Jiao Tong University, China

Steering Committee Chair

Jingsheng Lei   Shanghai University of Electric Power, China

Local Arrangement Co-chairs

Junjie Yang   Shanghai University of Electric Power, China
Haizhou Du   Shanghai University of Electric Power, China

Proceedings Co-chairs

Fu Lee Wang   Caritas Institute of Higher Education,
                                Hong Kong
Ting Jin   Fudan University, China

Sponsorship Chair

Zhiyu Zhou   Zhejiang Sci-Tech University, China

Program Committee

Habtamu Abie	Norwegian Computing Center, Norway
Xianbin Cao	Beihang University, China
Ai Chen	Chinese Academy of Sciences, China
Guihai Chen	Nanjing University, China
Hanhua Chen	Huazhong University of Science and Technology, China
Shiping Chen	CSIRO ICT Centre Australia, Australia
Yanling Chen	Norwegian University of Science and Technology, Norway
Qi Cheng	Oklahoma State University, USA
Rui Chu	National University of Defence Technology, China
Tasos Dagiuklas	Technological Educational Institute (TEI) of Mesolonghi, Greece
Guojun Dai	Hangdian University, China
Xiaolei Dong	Shanghai Jiao Tong University, China
Junzhao Du	Xidian University, China
Jun Gao	Peking University, China
Yu Gu	Singapore University of Technology and Design, Singapore
Deke Guo	National University of Defence Technology, China
Yuan He	HKUST, Hong Kong
Feng Hong	Ocean University of China, China
Chunming Hu	Beihang University, China
Yixin Jiang	Tsinghua University, China
Athanasios Kakarountas	Technological Educational Institute of the Ionian Islands, Greece
Haibin Kan	Fudan University, China
Dong Seong Kim	Duke University, USA
Hui Li	Peking University, China
Yong Li	Beijing Jiaotong University, China
Xiaofei Liao	Huazhong University of Science and Technology, China
Shan Lin	Temple University, USA
Kebin Liu	HKUST, Hong Kong
Nan Liu	Southeast University, China
Shengli Liu	Shanghai Jiao Tong University, China
Yunhuai Liu	Chinese Academy of Sciences, China
Zihui Liu	Beijing Institute of Technology, China
Li Lu	University of Electronic Science and Technology of China, China

Xiaoqiang Lu	Chinese Academy of Sciences, China
Xucheng Luo	University of Electronic Science and Technology of China, China
Huadong Ma	Beijing University of Posts and Telecommunications, China
Yanwei Pang	Tianjin University, China
Longjiang Qu	National University of Defense Technology, China
Slim Rekhis	University of Carthage, Tunisia
Weisong Shi	Wayne State University, USA
Lingyang Song	Peking University, China
Zhou Su	Waseda University, Japan
Hailong Sun	Beihang University, China
Chunming Tang	Guangzhou University, China
Zhiguo Wan	Tsinghua University, China
Jilong Wang	Tsinghua University, China
Lei Wang	Dalian University of Technology, China
Xin Wang	Fudan University, China
Yang Wang	Peking University, China
Chuliang Weng	Shanghai Jiao Tong University, China
Hejun Wu	Sun Yat-Sen University, China
Xiaobin Wu	Nanjing University, China
Shutao Xia	Tsinghua University, China
Bin Xiao	Hong Kong Polytechnic University, Hong Kong
Gaogang Xie	Chinese Academy of Sciences, China
Bin Xu	Tsinghua University, China
Guangtao Xue	Shanghai Jiao Tong University, China
Pingkun Yan	Philips Research, The Netherlands
Panlong Yang	Nanjing Institute of Communication Engineering, China
Zheng Yang	HKUST, Hong Kong
Lihua Yin	Chinese Academy of Sciences, China
Mei Yu	Tianjin University, China
Sherali Zeadally	University of the District of Columbia, USA
Dian Zhang	HKUST, Hong Kong
Fangguo Zhang	Sun Yat-Sen University, China
Jin Zhang	HKUST, Hong Kong
Yan Zhang	Simula Research Laboratory, University of Oslo, Norway
Zhifang Zhang	Chinese Academy of Sciences, China

Feng Zhao	Huazhong University of Science and Technology, China
Xibin Zhao	Tsinghua University, China
Huiyu Zhou	Queen's University Belfast, UK
Yanmin Zhu	Shanghai Jiao Tong University, China
Xinjian Zhuo	Beijing University of Posts and Telecom, China
Deqing Zou	Huazhong University of Science and Technology, China

Table of Contents

Cloud Computing

Communication and Information Systems

Design and Analysis of Cryptographic Algorithms

Information Hiding and Watermarking

Intelligent Networked Systems

Multimedia Computing and Intelligence

Network and Wireless Network Security

Network Communication

Parallel and Distributed Systems

Security Modeling and Architectures

Sensor Network

Signal and Information Processing

Virtualization Techniques and Applications

Wireless Network

On the Isomorphism Classes of Elliptic Curves with 2-Torsion Points

Hongfeng Wu[1] and Rongquan Feng[2]

[1] College of Sciences North China University of Technology Beijing 100144, China
whfmath@gmail.com
[2] LMAM, School of Mathematical Sciences Peking University Beijing 100871, China
fengrq@math.pku.edu.cn

Abstract. This paper presents explicit formulas for the number of isomorphism classes of elliptic curves with 2-torsion points over finite fields. These results also can be used in the elliptic curve cryptosystems and classification problems.

Keywords: elliptic curve, cryptography, isomorphism classes, finite field.

1   Introduction

Elliptic curves have been studied in some branch of mathematics such as algebraic geometry and number theory. Elliptic curve cryptosystems were proposed by Miller (1986) and by Koblitz (1987) which rely on the difficulty of discrete logarithmic problem based on elliptic curves. Elliptic curve cryptography has some advantage with respect to other cryptosystems such as RSA and cryptosystem based on multiplicative groups of finite fields. Lack of sub-exponential algorithms for solving discrete logarithm problem based on elliptic curves is the main advantage of this system. One of the main operations in elliptic curves cryptosystem is the scalar multiplication. The speed of scalar multiplication plays an important role in the efficiency of the whole system. Elliptic curves can be represented in different forms. To obtain faster scalar multiplications, various forms of elliptic curves have been extensively studied in the last two decades. Some important elliptic curve families include twisted Jacobi intersections [5, 7], Edward curves [2, 3, 6], Jacobi quartic [4, 5], Montgomery curves etc. Details of the previous works can be found in [1-3]. In order to choose appropriate elliptic curves in cryptography one should know isomorphism classes of elliptic curves. Some formulae about the number of isomorphism classes of general elliptic curves over a finite field can be found in literatures. For example, Schoof presented the number of isomorphism classes of elliptic curves over the finite field $\mathbb{F}_q$ in [11], Menezes presented the number of isomorphism classes of elliptic curves of the forms $y^2 = x^3 + ax + b$ over the finite field $\mathbb{F}_q$ in [9]. A 2-torsion point in an elliptic curve means a point of order 2, that is, a point $P \in E(\mathbb{F}_q)$, $P \neq O$ and $2P = O$. The elliptic curves over finite fields with 2-torsion points can be divided into two families:

J. Lei et al. (Eds.): NCIS 2012, CCIS 345, pp. 1–7, 2012.
© Springer-Verlag Berlin Heidelberg 2012

elliptic curves with only one 2-torsion point and curves with three 2-torsion points. Note that all the Jacobi intersections curves, Edward curves, Jacobi quartics curves admit at least one 2-torsion point. Therefore, it is an interesting and important problem to enumerate the isomorphism classes of elliptic curves with 2-torsion points over finite fields.

In this paper, we give the explicit formulae for the number of isomorphism classes of elliptic curves with 2-torsion points over finite fields. These results can be used in the elliptic curve cryptosystems and classification problems. This paper is organized as follows. We give some preliminaries in Section 2. In Section 3 we present the explicit formulae for the number of isomorphism classes.

2   Preliminaries

A curve means a projective variety of dimension 1. There are several ways to define elliptic curves. In this paper, an irreducible curve is said to be an elliptic curve if it is birationally equivalent to a non-singular plane cubic curve. It is well-known that every elliptic curve E over a field K can be written as a Weierstrass equation

$$E : Y^2 + a_1 XY + a_3 Y = X^3 + a_2 X^2 + a_4 X + a_6$$

with coefficients $a_1, a_2, a_3, a_4, a_6 \in K$. The discriminant $\Delta(E)$ and the j-invariant $j(E)$ of E are defined as

$$\Delta(E) = -b_2^2 b_8 - 8b_4^3 - 27b_6^2 + 9b_2 b_4 b_6 \text{ and } j(E) = (b_2^2 - 24b_4)^3 / \Delta(E), \text{ where}$$

$$\begin{cases} b_2 = a_1^2 + 4a_2, \\ b_4 = 2a_4 + a_1 a_3, \\ b_6 = a_3^2 + 4a_6, \\ b_8 = a_1^2 a_6 - a_1 a_3 a_4 + 4a_2 a_6 + a_2 a_3^2 - a_4^2. \end{cases}$$

Two projective varieties V_1 and V_2 are isomorphic if there exist morphisms $\phi : V_1 \to V_2$ and $\varphi : V_2 \to V_1$ such that $\varphi \circ \phi$ and $\phi \circ \varphi$ are the identity maps on V_1 and V_2 respectively. Two elliptic curves (E_1, O_1) and (E_2, O_2) are said to be isomorphic if there exist morphisms ϕ, φ such that E_1 and E_2 are isomorphic as projective varieties and $\phi(O_1) = O_2$ and $\varphi(O_2) = O_1$. Now Let

$$E_1 : Y^2 + a_1 XY + a_3 Y = X^3 + a_2 X^2 + a_4 X + a_6$$

and

$$E_2 : Y^2 + a'_1 XY + a'_3 Y = X^3 + a'_2 X^2 + a'_4 X + a'_6$$

be two elliptic curves defined over K. It is known [12] that E_1 and E_2 are isomorphic over $\overline{K}$ if and only if $j(E_1) = j(E_2)$, where $\overline{K}$ is the algebraic closure of K. However [12], let L be an extension of K, then E_1 and E_2 are isomorphic over L if and only if there exist $u, r, s, t \in L$ and $u \neq 0$ such that the change of variables

$(X, Y) \to (u^2 X + r, u^3 Y + u^2 sX + t)$ maps the equation of E_1 to the equation of E_2. For two simplified equations E_1 and E_2 with $a_1 = a_3 = a'_1 = a'_3 = 0$, they are isomorphic over L if and only if there exists $u, r \in L$ and $u \neq 0$ such that [9]

$$\begin{cases} u^2 a'_2 = a_2 + 3r, \\ u^4 a'_4 = a_4 + 2ra_2 + 3r^2, \\ u^6 a'_6 = a_6 + ra_4 + r^2 a_2 + r^3. \end{cases}$$

3   Enumeration

Let E be an elliptic curve with one order 2 point. By moving this point to $(0,0)$, it can be changed to the form $E_{a,b} : y^2 = x^3 + ax^2 + bx$ with $a, b \in \mathbb{F}_q$. By addition formula, $P \in E(\mathbb{F}_q)$ is a point of order 2 if and only if the y-coordinate equals to 0. Thus, elliptic curve E has three points of order 2 if and only if the equation of E can be written as $T_{a,b} : y^2 = x(x-a)(x-b)$ with $a, b \in \mathbb{F}_q$.

Every elliptic curve is isomorphic to a Legendre curve $E_\lambda : y^2 = x(x-1)(x-\lambda)$ over an algebraic closed field. The result of isomorphism classes of Legendre curves defined over finite fields can be found in [8]. In order to enumerate the $\mathbb{F}_q$-isomorphism classes of elliptic curve with 2-torsion points, it is sufficient to enumerate the $\mathbb{F}_q$-isomorphism classes of elliptic curve families $y^2 = x(x-a)(x-b)$ and $y^2 = x(x^2 + ax + b)$ with a, b run through the finite field $\mathbb{F}_q$. It is well known [9] that the number of elliptic curves which are $\mathbb{F}_q$-isomorphic to $y^2 = x^3 + ax + b$ equals to

$$\begin{cases} \dfrac{q-1}{6}, & a = 0, q \equiv 1 \bmod 3 \\[2mm] \dfrac{q-1}{4}, & b = 0, q \equiv 1 \bmod 4 \\[2mm] \dfrac{q-1}{2}, & others. \end{cases}$$

The j-invariant of $E_{a,b}$ is $\dfrac{256(a^2-3b)^3}{b^2(a^2-4b)}$. Note that $j(E_{a,b})=0$ if and only if $a^2=3b$ and $j(E_{a,b})=1728$ if and only if $a(2a^2-9b)=0$ since $E_{a,b}$ is isomorphic to $y^2=x^3-27(a^2-3b)x+27a(2a^2-9b)$. Every point of order 2 admits such a change. Hence, when $E_{a,b}$ has only one point of order 2, the number of elliptic curves which is $\mathbb{F}_q$-isomorphic to $E_{a,b}$ equals to

$$
\begin{cases}
\dfrac{q-1}{6}, & \text{if } j=0 \text{ and } q \equiv 1 \bmod 3, \\[3mm]
\dfrac{q-1}{4}, & \text{if } j=1728 \text{ and } q \equiv 1 \bmod 4, \\[3mm]
\dfrac{q-1}{2}, & \text{others.}
\end{cases}
$$

When $E_{a,b}$ has three order 2 points, the number of elliptic curves which is $\mathbb{F}_q$-isomorphic to $E_{a,b}$ equals to

$$
\begin{cases}
\dfrac{q-1}{2}, & \text{if } j=0 \text{ and } q \equiv 1 \bmod 3, \\[3mm]
\dfrac{3(q-1)}{4}, & \text{if } j=1728 \text{ and } q \equiv 1 \bmod 4, \\[3mm]
\dfrac{3(q-1)}{2}, & \text{others.}
\end{cases}
$$

The number of elliptic curves with three order 2 points equals to $\dfrac{(q-1)(q-2)}{2}$ since they admit the normal forms $y^2=x(x-a)(x-b),\ a,b\neq 0, a\neq b$. Hence the number of elliptic curves with only one order 2 point equals to

$$
q(q-1)-\frac{(q-1)(q-2)}{2}-(q-1)=\frac{q(q-1)}{2}.
$$

The number of elliptic curves $E_{a,b}: y^2=x^3+ax^2+bx$ with $j(E_{a,b})=0$ equals to $q-1$ since $j(E_{a,b})=0$ if and only if $a^2=3b$. Thus, if it includes three order 2 points then $a^2 - 4b = -b$ is a square element in the finite field. Therefore, -3 is a square element too in the field. Hence, if the j-invariant $j(E_{a,b}) = 0$, then the number of elliptic curves $E_{a,b} : y^2 = x^3 + ax^2 + bx$ with three order 2 points equals to $(q-1)$ if $q \equiv 1 \bmod 3$ and equals to 0 if $q \equiv 2 \bmod 3$ .Similarly, for the curve $E_{a,b}$, $j(E_{a,b}) = 1728$ if and only if $a(9b - 2a^2) = 0$, i.e., $b = 2(a/3)^2$. Therefore, the number of elliptic curves $E_{a,b} : y^2 = x^3 + ax^2 + bx$ with $j = 1728$ equals to $(q-1) + (q-1) = 2(q-1)$. Thus, if $E_{a,b}$ has three order 2 points then $a^2 - 4b$ is a square element in $\mathbb{F}_q$. Since $9b = 2a^2$ from $j = 1728$, therefore $a^2 - 4b = b/2 = (a/3)^2$. Thus, the number of elliptic curves $E_{a,b} : y^2 = x^3 + ax^2 + bx$ with three order 2 points equals to $3(q-1)/2$ when $j = 1728$. Hence, the number of elliptic curves $E_{a,b} : y^2 = x^3 + ax^2 + bx$ which hold three order 2 points with $j(E_{a,b}) \neq 0,1728$ equals to

$$
\begin{cases}
\dfrac{(q-1)(q-7)}{2}, & \text{if } q \equiv 1 \bmod 3, \\
\dfrac{(q-1)(q-5)}{2}, & \text{if } q \equiv 2 \bmod 3.
\end{cases}
$$

By the above argument, the number of $\mathbb{F}_q$-isomorphism classes of elliptic curves $B_{a,b} : y^2 = x(x-a)(x-b)$ defined over $\mathbb{F}_q$ equals to

$$
\frac{q-1}{\dfrac{q-1}{2}} + \frac{\dfrac{3(q-1)}{2}}{\dfrac{3(q-1)}{4}} + \frac{\dfrac{(q-1)(q-7)}{2}}{\dfrac{3(q-1)}{2}} = \frac{q+5}{3},
$$

When $q \equiv 1 \bmod 12$. By similar computation, we have the following theorem.

Theorem 1: Let $\mathbb{F}_q$ be the finite field with q elements and characteristic > 3. Then the number of $\mathbb{F}_q$-isomorphism classes of $y^2 = x(x-a)(x-b)$ defined over $\mathbb{F}_q$ with $ab(a-b) \neq 0$ is

$$\begin{cases} \dfrac{q+5}{3}, & if \ q \equiv 1 \bmod 12, \\[2mm] \dfrac{q+1}{3}, & if \ q \equiv 5 \bmod 12, \\[2mm] \dfrac{q+2}{3}, & if \ q \equiv 7 \bmod 12, \\[2mm] \dfrac{q-2}{3}, & if \ q \equiv 11 \bmod 12. \end{cases}$$

Similarly, the number of curves with only one 2-torsion point and $j = 0$ equals to

$$\begin{cases} 0, & if \ q \equiv 1 \bmod 3, \\ q-1, & if \ q \equiv 2 \bmod 3. \end{cases}$$

The number of curves with only one 2-torsion point and $j = 1728$ equals to $(q-1)/2$. The number of curves with only one 2-torsion point and $j \neq 0, 1728$ equals to

$$\begin{cases} \dfrac{(q-1)^2}{2}, & if \ q \equiv 1 \bmod 3, \\[3mm] \dfrac{(q-1)(q-3)}{2}, & if \ q \equiv 2 \bmod 3. \end{cases}$$

Using the similar method as above, we have the following theorem.

Theorem 2: Let $\mathbb{F}_q$ be the finite field with q elements and characteristic > 3. Then the number of $\mathbb{F}_q$-isomorphism classes of curves $y^2 = x(x^2 + ax + b)$ with only one 2-torsion point defined over $\mathbb{F}_q$ is

$$\begin{cases} q+1, & if \ q \equiv 1, 5 \bmod 12, \\ q, & if \ q \equiv 7, 11 \bmod 12. \end{cases}$$

Summing up the numbers in Theorems 1 and 2, we get the number of isomorphism classes of elliptic curves with at least one 2-torsion point in the following theorem.

Theorem 3: Let $\mathbb{F}_q$ be the finite field with q elements and characteristic > 3. Let N_q denote the number of $\mathbb{F}_q$-isomorphism classes of elliptic curves defined over $\mathbb{F}_q$ with at least one 2-torsion point. Then

$$N_q = \begin{cases} \dfrac{4q+8}{3}, & \textit{if } q \equiv 1 \bmod 12, \\[2mm] \dfrac{4q+4}{3}, & \textit{if } q \equiv 5 \bmod 12, \\[2mm] \dfrac{4q+2}{3}, & \textit{if } q \equiv 7 \bmod 12, \\[2mm] \dfrac{4q-2}{3}, & \textit{if } q \equiv 11 \bmod 12. \end{cases}$$

Acknowledgments. This work is supported by the National Natural Science Foundation of China (No. 11101002 and No. 10990011) and by the science research startup foundation of North China University of Technology.

References

1. Bernstein, D., Lange, T.: Explicit-Formula Database, http://www.hyperelliptic.org/EFD
2. Bernstein, D.J., Birkner, P., Joye, M., Lange, T., Peters, C.: Twisted Edwards Curves. In: Vaudenay, S. (ed.) AFRICACRYPT 2008. LNCS, vol. 5023, pp. 389–405. Springer, Heidelberg (2008)
3. Bernstein, D.J., Lange, T.: Faster Addition and Doubling on Elliptic Curves. In: Kurosawa, K. (ed.) ASIACRYPT 2007. LNCS, vol. 4833, pp. 29–50. Springer, Heidelberg (2007)
4. Billet, O., Joye, M.: The Jacobi Model of an Elliptic Curve and Side-Channel Analysis. In: Fossorier, M.P.C., Høholdt, T., Poli, A. (eds.) AAECC 2003. LNCS, vol. 2643, pp. 34–42. Springer, Heidelberg (2003)
5. Chudnovsky, D.V., Chudnovsky, G.V.: Sequences of numbers generated by addition in formal groups and new primality and factorization tests. Advances in Applied Mathematics 7, 385–434 (1986)
6. Edwards, H.M.: A normal form for elliptic curves. Bull. Amer. Math. Soc. 44, 393–422 (2007)
7. Feng, R., Nie, M., Wu, H.: Twisted Jacobi Intersections Curves. In: Kratochvíl, J., Li, A., Fiala, J., Kolman, P. (eds.) TAMC 2010. LNCS, vol. 6108, pp. 199–210. Springer, Heidelberg (2010)
8. Wu, H., Feng, R.: On the isomorphism classes of Legendre elliptic curves over finite fields. Sci. China Math. 54(9), 1885–1890 (2011)
9. Menezes, A.J.: Elliptic Curve Public Key Cryptosystems. Kluwer Academic Publishers (1993)
10. Miller, V.S.: Use of Elliptic Curves in Cryptography. In: Williams, H.C. (ed.) CRYPTO 1985. LNCS, vol. 218, pp. 417–426. Springer, Heidelberg (1986)
11. Schoof, R.: Nonsigular plane cubic curves over finite field. J. Combine Theory Ser. A 46, 183–211 (1987)
12. Silverman, J.H.: The Arithmetic of Elliptic Curves. GTM, vol. 106. Springer, Berlin (1986)

Template-Based and Second-Order Differential Power Analysis Attacks on Masking

Huilin Yin[1] and Ruiying Zhao[2]

[1] Dept. of Electronics and Information in CDHK, Tongji University, SipingRd.1239, 200092
Shanghai, China
yinhuilin@tongji.edu.cn
[2] Shanghai Information Security Testing Evaluation and Certification Center, Lujiabang 1308,
200011 Shanghai, China
zhaory@shtec.gov.cn

Abstract. In this paper we discuss the security of masked implementations. As an effective countermeasure against first-order DPA (Differential power analysis) attacks, masking works because the randomly masked intermediate values cause a power consumption that is not predictable by the attacker. We perform and analyze the template-based DPA and second-order DPA attacks on the scenario that the input values and output values of the AES SubBytes operation are concealed by the same mask-value. The experimental results confirm that, the masked implementation can be attacked by template-based DPA attacks and second-order DPA attacks.

Keywords: Side-channel attack, Differential Power Analysis (DPA), Masking, Template-based DPA, Second-Order DPA.

1   Introduction

In power analysis attacks, the attacker attempts to reveal secret information on basis of the cryptographic device's power consumption. Power analysis attacks work because the cryptographic devices' power consumption depends on the executed cryptographic algorithms' intermediate values. Hence, the goal of countermeasures against such attacks is to make the power consumption independent of those intermediate values [2]. Masking is one of the countermeasures that has been extensively discussed in the scientific community. In a masked implementation, each intermediate value is concealed by a random value that is called mask. The mask is generated inside the cryptographic device and is not known by the attacker. Masking prevents DPA attacks because the randomly masked intermediate values cause a power consumption that is not predictable by the attacker. The masks are added at the very beginning of the algorithm to the plaintext. During the execution of the algorithm, all intermediate values stay masked and the masks are modified by the operations in the algorithm. But it has turned out that virtually every masking scheme can be attacked [2].

J. Lei et al. (Eds.): NCIS 2012, CCIS 345, pp. 8–14, 2012.
© Springer-Verlag Berlin Heidelberg 2012

This paper is organized as follows. In Sect.2, we first focus on the description of general principle of template-based DPA and then we perform and analyze the template-based DPA on masked AES SubBytes operation. In Sect.3, we explain the pre-processing and second-order DPA on masked AES SubBytes operation. In Sect.4, we have the conclusion.

2   Template-Based DPA on Masked AES SubBytes Operation

2.1   General Principle of Template-Based DPA Attacks

The key concept of template attack is to store the probability distribution of leaking information for each device state. Signal classification techniques are subsequently used to assign a captured trace from a device to one device state. That is to say, template attacks consist of two phases: the first phase template building, in which the characterization takes place, and the second phase template matching, in which the characterization is used for an attack[2].There is no essential difference between the application of a template-based DPA attack to an unmasked and to a masked implementation[3].

2.1.1   Template Building

According to the statistical analysis of power traces, power traces can be characterized by a multivariate normal distribution defined by a mean vector and a covariance matrix $(\mathbf{m}, \mathbf{C})$. On the device, we execute the sequences of instructions with different data $d_i\,(i = 1,...,D)$ and keys $k_j\,(j = 1,...,K)$ (D and K is the number of all data and all keys respectively) in order to record the resulting power consumption. Then, we group together the traces corresponding to a pair of (d_i, k_j), and estimate the mean vector and the covariance matrix of the multivariate normal distribution. As a result, we obtain a template for every pair of data and key (d_i, k_j) :

$h_{d_i,k_j} = (\mathbf{m}, \mathbf{C})_{d_i,k_j}$. There are different ways to build templates besides the template for pairs of data and key, such as the template for intermediate values and the template with power models. The choice of the strategy depends on the known information of the device.

2.1.2   Template Matching

2.1.2.1   Template Matching for One Given Trace. The probability density function of the multivariate normal distribution with the tuple $(\mathbf{m}, \mathbf{C})_{d_i,k_j}$ and the power trace

$\mathbf{t}$ can be evaluated as follows:

$$p(\mathbf{t};(\mathbf{m},\mathbf{C})_{d_i,k_j}) = \frac{\exp(-\frac{1}{2}\cdot(\mathbf{t}-\mathbf{m})'\cdot\mathbf{C}^{-1}\cdot(\mathbf{t}-\mathbf{m}))}{\sqrt{(2\cdot\pi)^T\cdot\det(\mathbf{C})}} \tag{1}$$

The probabilities $p(\mathbf{t};(\mathbf{m},\mathbf{C})_{d_1,k_1}),...,p(\mathbf{t};(\mathbf{m},\mathbf{C})_{d_D,k_K})$ measure how well the templates fit to a given trace $\mathbf{t}$. Matching a given trace $\mathbf{t}$ with the template h_{d_i,k_j} means that we use equation (1) to calculate the probability $p(\mathbf{t}/k_j)$. According to the maximum-likelihood decision rule, the highest probability is associated with the correct key.

2.1.2.2   Template Matching for Multiple Power Traces. Often there is just not enough information available in a single trace to attack the device successfully. We need multiple power traces $\mathbf{T}$. The task of the attack is to determine $p(k_j/\mathbf{T})$, which means the probability that, given the matrix $\mathbf{T}$, the key of device equals k_j. According to Bayes' theorem, we have

$$p(k_j/\mathbf{T}) = \frac{(\prod_{i=1}^{D} p(\mathbf{t}_i^{'}/k_j))\cdot p(k_j)}{\sum_{l=1}^{K}((\prod_{i=1}^{D} p(\mathbf{t}_i^{'}/k_l))\cdot p(k_l))} \tag{2}$$

The probability for each key is identical, i.e. $p(k_j) = 1/K$.

The probabilities $p(\mathbf{t}_i^{'}/k_j)$ equal the probability density function $p(\mathbf{t}_i^{'};h_{d_i,k_j})$, which can be calculated with equation (1).

2.2   Implementation of the Template-Based DPA Attack on Masked AES SubBytes Operation

In our scenario, the input values and output values of the AES SubBytes operation are concealed by the same mask-value. The power traces come from the Oswald's OpenSCA[5]. Firstly, we select the interesting points to reduce the dimension of the templates. Then we build the templates with Hamming-weight power model. Finally, we calculate the probability for each key and find the correct key.

2.2.1   Interesting Points Finding
The size of the covariance matrix grows quadratically with the number of points in the trace. So we choose the interesting points, what contain the most characterization information, to constitute templates. We assume that we know where to match the

templates and we work only with the interesting points. In our scenario, we have 12 interesting points.

2.2.2 Templates with Hamming-Weight Model Building

We attack the SubBytes input and output, hence we compute them for all possible combinations of key and mask. For the hypothetical power consumption, we apply Hamming-weight (HW) function to the both intermediate values. For each intermediate value, there are nine Hamming weights 0,...,8. So we have 81 HW- templates $h_{i,j}$ for the input with HW i and the output with HW j. Each template includes the mean vector $\mathbf{m}$ and the covariance matrix $\mathbf{C}$. For example, $h_{4,7} = [\mathbf{m}_{4,7}, \mathbf{C}_{4,7}]$ means the template for the input-HW 4 and the output-HW 7 and $h_{9,3} = [\mathbf{m}_{9,3}, \mathbf{C}_{9,3}]$ means the template for the input-HW 9 and the output-HW 3.

$\mathbf{m}_{4,7}$= [-43.05, -34.69, -51.25, -52.13, -43.01, -38.05, -47.72, -52.81,-34.28,-51.57,-58.40, -60.87] .

$\mathbf{m}_{9,3}$=[-37.25, -28.50, -37.00, -41.50,-33.25, -28.25, -46.00, -51.00, -35.00, -50.50, -58.00,-64.25] .

2.2.3 Templates Matching and the Correct Key Finding

We calculate the probability of how the templates fit to the given power traces and determine the correct key. Fig.1 shows the probability corresponding to all 256 keys. The key 185 leads to the highest probability 0.9988 and the correct key is 185. Almost all the incorrect key hypotheses have the probability zero.

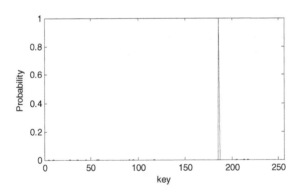

Fig. 1. Result of the template-based attack

3   Second-Order DPA on Masked AES SubBytes Operation

3.1   Principle of Second-Order DPA Attacks

A higher-order DPA attack is defined by Kocher et al.[1] as a DPA attack that combines one or more samples within a single power trace. In a higher-order DPA attack, the attacker calculates joint statistical properties of the power consumption at multiple sample times within the power signals. In [4], the definition of an nth-order DPA attack is given as follows: An nth-order DPA attack makes use of n different samples in the power consumption signal that correspond to n different intermediate values calculated during the execution of an algorithm. Countermeasures that prevent first-order DPA attacks may not be effective against higher-order attacks. Second-order DPA attacks work in the same way as first-order DPA attacks except that they some-times require preprocessing the power traces [2].

3.2   Implementation of Second-Order DPA on Masked AES SubBytes Operation

3.2.1   Preprocessing

The preprocessing prepares the power traces for the DPA attack. In the preprocessing step, we apply a preprocessing function $pre()$ to each power trace. We choose the two masked intermediate values u_m and v_m. Typically, the exact time when these two masked values are computed is unknown. So, we can only guess an interval $I = t_{r+1}, \ldots, t_{r+l}$ of the power trace, which likely contains the two values u_m and v_m. We apply the preprocessing function to all combinations of points in this interval. Several types of preprocessing functions have been discussed in the literature. Mes-serger [4] has proposed the absolute-difference function. The different preprocessing functions lead to different correlation coefficients in the DPA. Which preprocessing function is the best depends on the power model of the device. The absolute-difference function is a good choice for the Hamming weight power model.

3.2.2   DPA Attacks on Preprocessed Traces

The second-order DPA attack follows the same five-step process as a first-order DPA attack.

- *Select intermediate value.* We are interested in the input values and output values of the AES SubBytes operation, which are concealed by the same mask-value. We attack the XOR of the two values.
- *Acquire traces.* The measured traces are preprocessed, using the absolute-difference function.
- *Compute intermediate value.* We compute XOR (before_sbox, after_sbox) for each key hypothesis as follows:

$$u_{i,j} = d_i \oplus k_j \tag{3}$$

$$v_{i,j} = S(d_i \oplus k_j) \tag{4}$$

$$\omega_{i,j} = u_{i,j} \oplus v_{i,j} = (d_i \oplus k_j) \oplus S(d_i \oplus k_j) \tag{5}$$

- *Compute hypothetical power consumption.* We apply Hamming-Weight function to intermediate values and the hypothetical power consumption is calculated as follows:

$$h_{i,j} = HW(\omega_{i,j}) = HW((d_i \oplus k_j) \oplus S(d_i \oplus k_j)) \qquad (6)$$

- *Compute correlation of hypothetical power consumption and preprocessed measurement-traces.* The correct key is 185 and the maximal correlation is 0.24. Fig.2 shows the correlation traces of all hypothetical keys. It can be observed that only one trace (of the correct key) has significant peaks. Fig.3 shows only the correlation trace of the correct key.

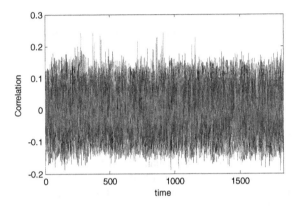

Fig. 2. DPA correlation of all hypothetical keys

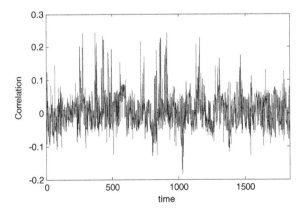

Fig. 3. DPA correlation of the correct key

4   Conclusion

In this paper, we have presented the template-based DPA attack and the second-order DPA attack on masked AES SubBytes operation. The experimental results confirm that, masking by itself is insufficient to protect masked smart card implementation against power analysis attacks. The combination of countermeasures, such as combination of masking and randomization of operations, should be analyzed to increase the resistance against power analysis attacks.

References

1. Kocher, P.C., Jaffe, J., Jun, B.: Differential Power Analysis. In: Wiener, M. (ed.) CRYPTO 1999. LNCS, vol. 1666, pp. 388–397. Springer, Heidelberg (1999)
2. Mangard, S., Oswald, E., Popp, T.: Power Analysis Attacks – Revealing the Secrets of Smart Cards. Springer (2007)
3. Oswald, E., Mangard, S.: Template Attacks on Masking—Resistance Is Futile. In: Abe, M. (ed.) CT-RSA 2007. LNCS, vol. 4377, pp. 243–256. Springer, Heidelberg (2006)
4. Messerges, T., Koc, C., Christof, P.: Using Second-Order Power Analysis to Attack DPA Resistant Software. In: Paar, C., Koç, Ç.K. (eds.) CHES 2000. LNCS, vol. 1965, pp. 238–251. Springer, Heidelberg (2000)
5. http://opensca.sourceforge.net/
6. Herbst, C., Oswald, E., Mangard, S.: An AES Smart Card Implementation Resistant to Power Analysis Attacks. In: Zhou, J., Yung, M., Bao, F. (eds.) ACNS 2006. LNCS, vol. 3989, pp. 239–252. Springer, Heidelberg (2006)
7. Chari, S., Rao, J.R., Rohatgi, P.: Template Attacks. In: Kaliski Jr., B.S., Koç, Ç.K., Paar, C. (eds.) CHES 2002. LNCS, vol. 2523, pp. 13–28. Springer, Heidelberg (2003)

Design and Implementation of Linux File Mandatory Access Control

Liye Tian[1,2], Xing Rong[3,2], and Tingting Liu[3]

[1] Naval Aeronautical and Astronautical University, Yantai, China
[2] College of Computer Science and Technology, Beijing University of Technology, Beijing, China
[3] Institute of Electronic Technology, PLA Information Engineering University, Zhengzhou, China
new.tianli@163.com

Abstract. To control file access in Linux, Linux Security Module (LSM) and Virtual Filesystem are analyzed. Based on the LSM security field & hooks, a file mandatory access control system is designed and implemented on Linux2.6.26. This system meets GB17859-1999's requirements by preserving subject and object labels. Kernel hooks are widely used in the system to get labels and judge if an access is legal. In a simplified environment the system is tested, test result shows that the system is able to complete file mandatory access control according to security policy.

Keywords: linux security module, virtual filesystem, mandatory access control.

1 Introduction

According to Chinese national criteria "Classified criteria for security protection of computer information system (GB17859-1999)", all information systems above level 3 are called high security level computer information system, which are required to carry out the security function-mandatory access control [1]. These systems set subject and object labels for processes, files, segments, devices, etc.[2], they also preserve a group of mandatory access control rules in them. Using LSM to achieve file mandatory access control is discussed in this paper.

2 LSM Mechanism

Linux originator Linus Torvalds announced a variable accessing control unit—Flask at Linux kernel2.5 summit meeting in 2001 Feb. Then he realized it's necessary to add a bottom layer access control mechanism to popular version of Linux kernel, in which any specific security policy can be loaded as a loadable kernel module. Soon afterwards WireX launched this project, it was named as LSM.

Nowadays, LSM becomes a part of stable kernel2.6, and it is accepted as a security standard. Each Linux release version provides LSM to user freely. LSM doesn't interfere with POSIX.1e capabilities, and modifies few of kernel source codes. LSM is

J. Lei et al. (Eds.): NCIS 2012, CCIS 345, pp. 15–22, 2012.
© Springer-Verlag Berlin Heidelberg 2012

effective, when we need to use a security policy, we load its kernel module, when we need another, load another. Patch is totally unnecessary.

2.1   LSM Architecture

LSM defined and carried out a general security frame work, supplied standard interfaces for security module developer. LSM itself doesn't provide any security function, but provides some basic structures such as security fields and interface functions which are needed by security modules. Security modules are developed based on these structures, and security modules provide security function after they are inserted into kernel[3].

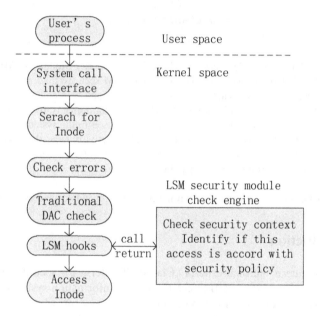

Fig. 1. LSM process

As shown in Figure 1, when a user's process call system interface, the system will search for required resource, with errors check and traditional DAC check. After both check are passed, LSM hooks check it again to identify if this access is accord with security policy in this module. Legal accesses are allowed to access required resources, while illegal ones are banned with an error return [4].

2.2   LSM Implementation

LSM is implemented by the following 5 modifications of Linux kernel[5].

1) Adding a security field to certain kernel data structures. In Linux source codes, task_struct(process), inode(pipe, file, socket), linux_binprm(program), file(files opened by process), super_block(file system) are appended with a security field.

```
#ifdef CONFIG_SECURITY
void *security;
#endif
```

Security module and inner kernel objects are connected through this void pointer. The structure that pointed by this pointer is defined by developer according to demand.

2) Inserting some security hooks call at key points in source codes. LSM provides a series of hooks to manage kernel objects. On another hand, LSM provides several calls of hooks to judge accesses to these objects. The calls of these 2 kinds' hooks are both implemented through a global security_operations type struct: security_ops. In this struct hooks are separated into several groups by different kernel objects, and it also contains system top level hook.

3) A common security system call sys_security() is added. Its 3 parameters are unsigned int id, unsigned int call, unsigned long*args. The meaning of parameters is defined by developer.

4) Provide functions to register and unregister a kernel module as a security module. When a security policy module is needed we must use the function register_security() to register it to LSM frame work. This function setups a global security_ops, makes kernel inquires about security policy to this module's hooks. Onec a security module is loaded, it becomes the policy center of the system, and it will not be covered by the subsequent module until it is unregistered by the function unregister_security(). After a module is unregistered, hooks are replaced by default ones, of which most are doing nothing. LSM supports multi security modules but the latter module should be registered to the former one by function mod_reg_security(), and mod_unreg_security() for unregister.

5) Transplant most of capabilities into a selectable security module.

3   Design and Implementation of File Mandatory Access Control

3.1   Analysis of Linux Filesystem and Common File Model

The Virtual Filesystem(VFS) is used in Linux, You can transparently mount disks or partitions that host file formats used by Windows, or other Unix systems. For example, Disk-based filesystems: Ext2, Ext3, NTFS, System V, HFS. Network filesystems: NFS, CIFS, NCP. Special filesystems: /proc. The VFS is an abstraction layer between the application program and the filesystem implementations[6]. VFS handles all system calls related to a standard Unix filesystem. Its main strength is providing a common interface to several kinds of filesystems. If a user's program access two different filesystem /floppy/test and /tmp/test, it only need to interact with VFS by means of generic system calls, the VFS will interact with specific filesystems.

The key idea behind the VFS consists of introducing a common file model capable of representing all supported filesystems. The common file model consists of superblock object, inode object, file object, dentry object.

Superblock stores information concerning a mounted filesystem. For disk-based filesystems, this object usually corresponds to a filesystem control block stored on disk. Inode stores general information about a specific file. Each inode object is associated with an inode number, which uniquely identifies the file within the filesystem. File stores information about the interaction between an opened file and a process. This information exists only in kernel memory during the period when a process has the file open. Dentry stores information about the linking of a directory entry with the corresponding file. Each disk-based filesystem stores this information in its own particular way on disk.

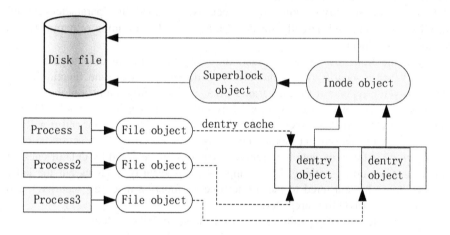

Fig. 2. Interaction between processes and VFS objects

Figure 2 illustrates with an example how processes interact with files. Three different processes have opened the same file, two of them using the same hard link. In this case, each of the three processes uses its own file object, while only one dentry objects are required for each hard link. Both dentry objects refer to the same inode object, which identifies the superblock object and, together with the latter, the common disk file. These objects are what we are going to mark.

3.2   Linux Processes

Processes are often called tasks or threads in the Linux source code. User's process does everything for user, so it is regarded as subject in our system. Each process associates with a process descriptor, in which saves the process's priority, state, and its address space. Process descriptor is task_struct structure, it is complicated, and some of the key members are listed here.

```
struct task_struct {
  volatile long state;
  atomic_t usage;
  struct list_head tasks;
  struct mm_struct *mm, *active_mm;
  void *security;
……}
```

3.3   Policy and Design

In high security level computer information system, mandatory access control is necessary. MAC builds an ordered system environment, keeps illegal accesses away. Before executing, kinks of user's program are stored in filesystem in the form of file. Therefore, doing mandatory access control to files also controls user's power and executable operations.

Entities of a system are divided into subjects and objects in the process of access. In this paper subject is user's process, and object is file. They are assigned to several different security levels, operations that can be done from a subject to an object are read, write, or execute, etc. In our protosystem we simplify problems to: subject and object has only two security levels 0 and 1, and subject can r or w a object. In a simplified policy, legal operations are: 0r0, 0w0, 0r1, 0w1, 1w1, 1r1, illegal operations are: 1w0, 1r0.

The mandatory access control mechanism in protosystem contains three functional parts. First, while the system is booting, the security module ergods all objects mentioned in section A, label them with subject or object label. Second, when a user create or open a new file, label it with compatible label by hooks. Third, after labeling subjects and objects is completed, permit or forbid a access in file related hooks according to security policy.

3.4   Important Structures and Codes

Subject label structure:

```
typedef struct tagsubject_label
{
  char entity_class;
  V_String * name;
  UINT16 entity_type;
  DOMAIN_LABEL sub_label;
  int level;
} SUB_LABEL;
```

entity_class: indicates a subject or object, this variable is setup for transferring parameters of functions.
name: the name of the entity, a variablelength string.

entity_type: type of the entity, for instance, file, user, role, device, etc.
sub_label: indicates domain of a subject.
level: security level of a subject.

Object label structure:

```
typedef struct tagobject_label
{
  char entity_class;
  V_String * name;
  UINT16 entity_type;
  UINT16 entity_flags;
  DOMAIN_LABEL obj_label;
  Void * sec_info;
}OBJ_LABEL;
```

Besides the same members to subject, object contains
    entity_flags: object data store flag, indicates object's special store method, for instance, encryption, verify, read only, compress, etc.

Key code for ergod all subjects:

```
do{
  currmnt=list_entry(temp,struct vfsmount, mnt_list);
  currsb=currmnt->mnt_sb;
  my_marksb(mountpoint,currsb);
  mark_allinode_of_sb(currsb);
  temp=temp->next;
  }while(temp!=list);
```

Key code for ergod all objects:

```
for_each_process(tasks)
  {mark(tasks->security);
  }
```

To label new files and processes is simple, we could assign a structure to void *security in hooks. Besides hooks provided by LSM, such as inode_alloc_security, sb_alloc_security, we also setup customized hook inodesecdata_install.
The function of judging is completed in hooks inode_permission, file_permission. The whole process see Figure 3.
    After coding of hooks is finished, put them in security_operation:

```
static struct security_operations my_ops={
.inode_permission=my_inode_permission,
......};
```

When the security module is initializing, register these hooks by register_security(&my_ops).

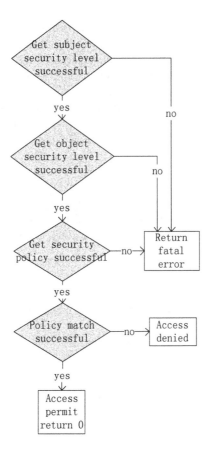

Fig. 3. Access control flow

4   Test and Conclusion

The system is tested as follow.

1) add a link of compiled security module to /etc/rc3.d, when the system is booting, mark all file related objects with a security level 0, mark all process related objects with a security level 0.

2) after booting is finished, mark all user's process with a security level 1 by hooks, mark all new created or open file with a security level 1 by hooks.

3) create a new file /home/test by vi/vim, write characters char in this file, save and exit vi/vim.

4) type a command: cat /home/test

system echo: char
type a command: cat /var/log/messages
system echo: Access denied!

LSM is a kernel level flexible common access control framework. It provides several functions, so that access control could be structured and modular. With the help of LSM, programmers just pay attention to establishing security policy and implementing a security function, but no need to pay attention to bottom layer code.

In this paper a Linux file mandatory access control system is developed based on LSM of Linux kernel2.6.26. Test result indicates this security module behaves well. What to be done next is to divide multi security levels according to actual situation, and to establish more reasonable and powerful security policy.

Acknowledgment. This paper's work is supported by: National Key Basic Research Program (973) Project, 2007CB311100. Doctoral foundation of BJUT, X0007999200902. PhD. Start-up Fund of Beijing University of Technology. Opening project of State Key Laboratory of Information Security (Institute of Software, Chinese Academy of Sciences). China Postdoctoral Science Foundation, 20090461461.

References

1. Classified criteria for security protection of computer information system. Chinese national criteria, GB17859-1999 (1999)
2. Changxiang, S.: Information Security Introduction. Publishing House of Electronics Industry, Beijing (2009)
3. Zhengping, L., Guoqing, W., Huanguo, Z.: Research on LSM Access Control. Computer Engineering 30(13), 23–25 (2004)
4. Weipeng, L., Jun, H., Huijun, L., Yi, L.: Mandatory Access Control Mechanism of Executable Program Under LSM. Computer Engineering 34(7), 160–162 (2008)
5. Li, W.: Research and Implementation of Enhanced Access Control Technology Based on Linux. Master's thesis of PLA Information Engineering University (2008)
6. Daniel, P.B., Marco, C.: Understanding the Linux Kernel, 3rd edn. O'Reilly (2005)

Design and Application of Fine-Grained Access Control Model[*]

Xuelian Xie[1], Haibo Yang[2], and Lanyou Li[1]

[1] Office of Information Construction and Management , Nanjing Institute of Technology,
Nanjing 211167, China
[2] Nanjing Institute of Industry Technology, Nanjing Jiangsu, 210098 China
`xie_xue_lian@126.com, {yhb4507,lilanyou}@163.com`

Abstract. This paper   provides a method of constructing mandatory access control model from role-based access control model, which produces a new fine-grained access control model,named EDFFAC model.The EDFFAC model includes two sub-models: D-EDFFAC model and R-EDFFAC model ,which are respectively compatible with discretionary access control (DAC) and role-based access control(RBAC) in relational database systems. Based on the EDFFAC model, the analysis methods are presented and the corresponding checking me-chanism is implemented. Then the researches on inference problems in database systems with fine-grained access control are conducted. At last, using the access strategy and scope relation of SQL as an example, the analysis process of application is shown.

Keywords: fine-grained access control model, inference controlling, query modification.

1   Introduction

With the increasingly complex requirements of database security, in recent years da-tabase access control has aroused widespread concern. The basic purpose of access control is to prevent unauthorized users from accessing the system and the legitimate users from illegally using system resources. Access control limits the visitors and executable procedures operated, which is a key technology and the most effective means of database system security.

Traditional database access control model can be divided into three categories: Discretionary Access Control(DAC)[1],Mandatory Access Control (MAC) [2]and Role-Based Access Control(RBAC)[3].

Traditional database access control model is to be regarded as coarse-grained access control, as well as that its authorized particle is the entire database table or view rather than tuples or elements. Especially in the web-oriented system, in order to provide flexible privacy protection methods to satisfy the security requirements, it is

---

[*] Youth research fund of Nanjing Institute of Technology(QKJA2011011).

of great significance to research on fine-grained access control[4-5]. Here is an example.

Bank system allows customers to check their account information, but they can not view the information of other customers; however, bank tellers can be able to query account information of all the customers, but they can not view their personal address information. This is a fine-grained Access Control case.

Extended Double-Filters-based Fine-grained Access Control model supports not only the closed access control policy, but also the open access control policy, namely it supports fine-grained negative authorization and multiple fine-grained access control policies, which improves the expressive power of database access control policy, thereby to reduce the burden of the security administrator in order to ensure that the system performance within the acceptable range.

2   Fine-Grained Access Control Policy Description

Description methods of fine-grained access control policies can be divided into three categories, a view-based approach, a predicate-based approach and a datalog-based approach.

2.1   View-Based Approach

We can describe the method through view about access control permissions in view-based approach. View describes the information which can be accessed by users in database. It is different from the view of traditional SQL statement supported. As well, the users can not directly access the base tables but view in the traditional SQL .However, the view here allow users to directly access the base tables.

(1)INGRES-based access control

Processor Stonebraker and wong introduced the method of implementing fine-grained access control based on INGRES view access control. We describe the user's access rights through the view and to use the query modification technology to achieve fine grained access control. The basic meaning of query modification is to modify and execute the SQL statement dynamically and transparently to ensure that users can not access the information which didn't be allowed.

(2) Motro-based access control

Processor Motro proposed a query modification algorithm which is similar to INGRES. When a user submits a query statement Q, it is also regarded as a view. When the view Q is derived by the security set view V, the Q is allowed to be accessed; When the view is not derived but the sub-view set of Q is derived by the security set view V, the sub-view is allowed to be accessed. Its downside is that there are some problems such as the disjoint sub-view produced by the algorithm. Then, the logical structure returned by the algorithm is adapted to the user's expectations. For example, a query is expected to return the ancestral structure with three attributes, but it returned two attributes, which is not acceptable, that is, a query is expected to return to the ancestral structure with three attributes, but the real return may only contain two properties, which means this application is not acceptable .

2.2   Predicate-Based Approach

The most representative predicate-based approach is the Oracle Virtual Private Database (VPD). Fine-grained access control policy returns the SQL predicate through the policy function definition. In order to achieve the fine-grained access control policy function ,we bind the policy function with the base table or view. However, the description of the fine-grained access control security policy proposed by Oracle VPD is so complex that it is poor in availability and scalability.

2.3   Datalog-Based Approach

Processor B.Purevji etc. proposed the fine-grained access control policy such as datalog-based approach. Using the Authorization Description Language (ADL) ,he made the description of the fine-grained access control. In order to solve the safety analysis problem of fine-grained access control policy, we provide the datalog rule-based description of methods. The flaw is that it can not be directly used in DBMS, and we must convert to enable its effect in the general DBMS further.

3   EDFFAC Model

3.1   Concepts and symbols

The concepts and symbols of fine-gained access control are shown in the following table.

$R(A_1,A_2,...,A_n)$ shows the database relation (base table or view).

$R^*=\{ A_1,A_2,...,A_n \}$ shows the collections set of the all the properties of the relation R

$S=\{s_1,s_2,...,s_m\}$ shows the subject collection set of database ,the subject is the user or role of database

$U=\{ u_1,u_2,...,u_k\}$ shows the user collection set of database

$RL=\{ r_1,r_2,...,r_k\}$ shows the role collection set of database

$O=\{ o_1,o_2,...,o_n\}$ shows the object collection set of database

$AC=\{select,\ insert,\ update,\ delete\}$ shows the operations collection set

$FIL=\{fil_1,fil_2,...fil_n\}$shows the filter collection set,and $filk\in$ FIL shows one filter. The tuple is regarded as the input parameters,and the false, true or error as the output parameters of fitlers. Most of all, the filter plays an important role mainly to used to describe and determine data accessibility on EDFFAC model.

$PFIL=\{pfil_1,pfil_2,...,pfil_m\}$shows the filter policy collection set. Any one policy filter $pfil_i$ is a tuple named $<al\_pfil_i,pr\_pfil_i>$,in which $al\_pfil_i\in$ FIL, $pr\_pfil_i\in$ FIL,and al_pfil_i allows the filter, while pr_pfili prohibits the filter.

Table 1. The concepts and symbols of fine-grained access control table

Symbol	Concept
R	Relations (base table or view)
R*	Collection set of properties of the relation R
S	Subject (user or role)
U	User
RL	Role
O	Object (the base table or view)
AC	Access control
FIL	Set of filters
PFIL	Set of policy filters
F	Policy function
P	Privilege of update collection
l	Privilege of reading & select
w	Privilege of writing & insert
e	Privilege of edit &update
d	Privilege of delete

3.2   EDFFAC Model

(1) D-EDFFAC model

D-EDFFAC model expands from the DAC model, its formal definition is as follows:

1. U, O, FIL, F, AC, respectively represents a collection set of users, a collection set of object, a collection set of filters, a collection set of policy functions, a collection set of operations;

2. $RO = \{(O, f_o) \mid o \in O, f_o \in F\}$ is the collection set of constrained objects;

3. $ROP = \{(r_o, a) \mid r_o \in RO, a \in AC\}$ is the collection set of constrained   object privileges;

4. $ROPAU \subseteq U \times ROP$ shows the relationship between the constrained object privileges and the users.

In D-EDFFAC model, a constrained object ro is the tuple of (o, f_o), where o is the relationship and f_o is the policy function. Policy function f_o specifies policy filters for all the attributes of relations o in order to specify what data of o allowed to be accessed. Each policy filter function contains the allowed filter and prohibited filter respectively to support to allow the policy and prohibit policy.

(2) R-EDFFAC model

R-EDFFAC model expands from the RBAC model, which formal define as follows:

1. U,RL,O,FIL,F,AC respectively represents a collection set of users, a collection set of roles, a collection set of object, a collection set of filters, a collection set of policy functions, a collection set of operations;

2. $RO = \{(O, f_o) \mid o \in O, f_o \in F\}$ is the collection set of constrained objects;

3. $ROP = \{(r_o, a) \mid r_o \in RO, a \in AC\}$ is the collection set of constrained object privileges;

4.ROPAR $\subseteq$ RL $\times$ ROP shows the relationship between the constrained object privileges and the roles.

5. P={(o,l),(o,w),(o,e),(o,d)|o$\in$O}is the collection set of update privilege. It can obtain the privilege through DBA.

In D-EDFFAC model, a constrained object ro is the tuple of (o, f_o), where o is the relationship and f_o is the policy function.

3.3   Updating Operations Inference Controlling of EDFFAC Model

In the DAC DBMS , assume the existence of the base table book (id, name, price, isbn),and its owner is Tom. Tom grants the update operation authorization to the Lily but query authorization. That is to say that it does not allow Lily to query any information from the book table. However, Lily is allowed to execute update operation on the book table. Assume that there is a tuple of (2, Systems Analysis & Design, 30,978-7-115-18696-6). When Lily executes the update statement sql=" UPDATE book SET price=89 WHERE id=2 and name=' Systems Analysis & Design ' " and the system returns the successful implementation result of system. Meanwhile, Lily may infer the price of ' Systems Analysis & Design ' is 89. We can call it inference controlling because of the information leakages by the update operations. When the database system supports fine-grained access control, the update operation inference controlling becomes more complex.

Security Policy Conditions: We can label it the R_s and R_u according to the u users' query and update operations in relation R through EDFFAC policy. If the following security conditions are met, the R_s and R_u meet the security conditions,where t_u and t_s are corresponding to the R_s and R_u tuples.

Condition 1: if $\exists A_i \in R.^*, t_u[A_i] = t[A_i]$,then $\forall A_j \in R.^*, t_s[A_j] = t[A_j]$;

Condition 2: $\forall A \in R.^*, t_s[A] = \Phi_u$

Condition 1 and **Condition 2** are complementary, and be met any one of them, the two conditions will be met. If allowed to update some attribute value of tuple t, the meaning of Condition 1 is to be allowed to query all the attribute value of tuple t. Meanwhile, there is no existing information which is not allowed to query in tuple t because it is to be allowed to view entire tuple t. Any update operation result does not cause the disclosure of information in tuple t. When the **Condition 2** is met , any attribute value is not allowed to be updated, then all the updated operation in tuple t have been the failure result. Therefore, the results of any updated operation will not cause leakage of the tuple t. So,when the security conditions are met, any updated operation executed by user u relation to R of the tuple t does not cause disclosure information, which is safe. When security conditions are not met, there will be an updated statement and its result relies on the information which is not allowed to view. When the DFFAC policy in relation R meet the security conditions, the result of any updated operation does not cause the disclosure of information in R. The tuple of relation R is affected by the database state, it needs to ensure that EDFFAC policy is safe in any database state of relation R.

3.4   EDFFAC Model Query Modification Algorithm

Fine-grained access control algorithm is based on Key Attribute of Query Modifcation Algorithm[6].

Key Attributes: For any query statement Q, R is the relation of Q. For any attribute $A \in R.^{*}$, if A belongs to the WHERE sub-statement of Q, A is called the key attributes of the query statement Q and the relation R.

Step1: Create a temporary view for each relation of the query statement. For query Q, according to the key attributes of each relation, then, we obtain the fine-grained access control filter policy corresponding to the key attributes. Assume that the query statement is R_j corresponding to the key attributes of Ai_1, Ai_2, ... of Ai_m. The EDFFAC policy is $p = (s, (o, f_o), select)$, in which o is the relation of R_j, then R_i 's corresponding temporary view is as follows:

(SELECT * FROM R_i WHERE ((f_o (Ai_1, allow) and not f_o (Ail, prohibit)) and (f_o (Ai_2, allow) and not f_o (Ai_2, prohibit)) and ... and (f_o (Ai_m, allow) and not f_o (Ai_m, prohibit)))

Step2: Using the temporary view to replace the relation to the corresponding query statement.

Step3: Using the CASE statement to modify each attribute of the query SELECT_LIST sub-statement.

The KAB query modification algorithm is as follows. If the user submits a query Q which consists of n relations and m query sub-statement , the time complexity of the KAB algorithm is O (mn).

Input: the query statement Q, EDFFAC policy P=(s,(f_o),select)`

Output: the modified query statement Q '

CASE1 : Q="SELECT Ai_1,Ai_2,...., Ai_k from R WHERE conds" ,which R.*={ $A_1, A_2,...,A_n$ }

Step1: key attributes: BA ={$Ab_1, Ab_2,...,Ab_j$}

Step2: construct temporary view of R '

(SELECT * FROM R_i WHERE (($fo(Ab_1$,allow) and not f_o (Ab_1,prohibit)) and (f_o (Ab_2,allow) and not f_o (Ab_2,prohibit)) and ... and(f_o(Ab_j,allow) and not f_o (Ab_j,prohibit)))

step3: get all the attributes of the query statement Q in the SELECT_LIST: SL = {Ai_1, ..., Ai_k}, and use 'CASE' statement to modify the attributes of the SL and obtain the final modified query Q '=

SELECT CASE WHEN $fo(Ai_1$,allow) and not f_o (Ai_1,prohibit) THEN Ai_1 ELSE NULL AS Ai_1,...., CASE WHEN $fo(Ai_k$,allow) and not f_o (Ai_k,prohibit) THEN Ai_k ELSE NULL AS Ai_k, FROM R' WHERE conds;

CASE2: Q="SELECT Ai_1,Ai_2,...,Ai_k FROM $R_1,R_2,...,R_m$ WHERE conds";

step1: Get the temporary view R' with the step1 and step2 of CASE1 according to each relation R_i (i [1 ... m]).

step2: Get all the attributes of the query statement in the SELECT_LIST: SL = {Ai$_1$, ..., Ai$_k$}, and use 'CASE' statement to modify the attributes of the SL and obtain the final modified query Q '.

CASE3: The query statement Q which contains query sub-statement Qs.

step1: Using the temporary view from step1 and step2 of CASE1 to replace the relation to Qs.

step2: use 'CASE' statement to modify the attributes of the Q SELECT_LIST and obtain the final modified query Q '.

4   Conclusion

EDFFAC model has the following advantages:

The EDFAAC model supports fine-grained access control refused authorization, and it gets up to the element level. Therefore, the ability to support fine-grained authorization special case and temporary authorization special security requirements has expanded to improve the expressive power of database access control policy.

EDFFAC model has made a close connection with the database access control model. DAC model and RBAC model is widely used in the database system. And EDFFAC model has expanded from the DAC model and the RBAC model, which makes it compatible with the existing components and easy management and maintenance to access control policies of database system.

References

1. Sandhu, R., Samarati, P.: Access Control: Principles and Practice. IEEE Communications Magazine 32(9), 40–48 (1994)
2. Bell, D.E., LaPadula, L.J.: Seeure Computer Systems:Unified Exposition and Multics Interpretation. Technical RePort MTR-2997 The Mitre Corp. Bedford Mass (1976)
3. Wedde, H.F., Lischka, M.: Role-Based Access Control in Ambient and Remote Space. In: Proceedings of the 9th ACM Symposium on Access Control Models and Technologies(SACMAT 2004), New York, USA, pp. 21–30 (2004)
4. Jain, U.: Seminar Report Fine-grained Access Control in Databases. Technical Report KReSIT IIT Bombay (2004)
5. Chaudhuri, S., Dutta, T., Sudarshan, S.: Fine Grained Authorization through Predicated Grants. In: Proceedings of the 23rd International Conference on Data Engineering (ICDE), Istanbul, Turkey, pp. 1174–1183. IEEE Computer Society, Washington, DC (2007)
6. Shi, J.: Research on Fine-Grained Access Control in Relational Databases.The doctorial dissertation of Huazhong University of Science and Technology (May 2010)

Intel SYSRET Privilege Escalation Vulnerability Analysis[*]

Yong Wang, Xiuxia Tian, Jianping Xu, Shuai Chen, and Heng Yang

Department of Computer Science and Technology, Shanghai University of Electric Power,
Pingliang Road. 2103,
200090 Shanghai, China
wy616@126.com

Abstract. Intel SYSTET privilege escalation vulnerability CVE-2012-0217 is recently discovered, which can escalate user privilege ring 3 to kernel system ring 0 and affect many operating systems, such as Intel x64-based versions of Windows 7 and Windows Server 2008 R2. We compared the SYSRET instruction difference between AMD instruction system and Intel instruction system. And summarized the Intel SYSRET privilege escalation procedure according to windows privilege rings structure, IA-32, IA-64 memory model, Intel IA-64 SYSCALL and SYSRET instructions. In the end we discussed CVE-2012-0217 vulnerability as SYSRET privilege escalation.

Keywords: Privilege Escalation, vulnerability, CVE-2012-0217.

1 Introduction

CVE-2012-0217 vulnerability is harmful to some 64-bit operating system and virtualization software. As the SYSCALL and SYSRET of AMD instruction are used in Intel CPU, the difference between AMD instruction system and Intel system, some program can escalate the user ring 3 privilege to system kernel ring 0 privilege. Once the vulnerability is used by hacker program, it's very dangerous for affected operating system.

The affected operating systems are Intel x64-based versions of Windows 7 and Windows Server 2008 R2. Systems with AMD or ARM-based CPUs are not affected by this vulnerability [18].

Preventing privilege escalation [1,5] is very important issue for system security, the CVE-2012-0217 vulnerability is from the AMD instruction system [2]. The SYSCALL and SYSRET instruction are used in operating system virtualization [3,8]. The Intel SYSRET instruction privilege escalation [4, 6,7, 9] is summarized.

---

[*] This work is supported by State Key Laboratory of Information Security (Institute of Software, Chinese Academy of Sciences) (04-02-1), Shanghai Education Commission Innovation Foundation (11YZ192), Shanghai Science and Technology Commission Key Program (11511504400) and National Nature Science Foundation of China under Grant (60903188). Natural science foundation of Shanghai City (NO.12ZR1411900).

J. Lei et al. (Eds.): NCIS 2012, CCIS 345, pp. 30–37, 2012.
© Springer-Verlag Berlin Heidelberg 2012

1.1   Privilege Rings

Microprocessor has several levels privilege from ring 0 to ring 3. Ring 0 is the kernel level for operating system with most privileges. Ring 3 is the application level for user with limited privileges. The program in ring 0 can directly access ring 3, otherwise ring 3 can't use ring 0 privilege [10].

The privilege rings of CPU and operating system difference illustrated in Fig. 1.

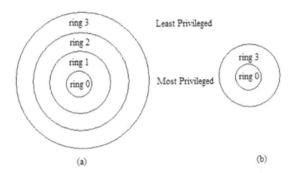

Fig. 1. Privilege rings provide more CPU (*left Fig.*) modes than operating system used (*right Fig*). Windows XP only has ring 0 for kernel mode and ring 3 for user mode. Device drivers always run in kernel mode.

1.2   Privilege Escalation

Malware usually use privilege escalation to get system kernel privilege use application program.

- Many windows services run on kernel privilege. As cmd.exe is a system service with kernel privilege, Windows XP or Windows Vista has privilege escalation via CMD console hack [1,9,10].
- The Intel SYSRET privilege escalation happens in CVE-2012-0217 vulnerability. The SYSRET instruction is defined by AMD with SYSCALL instruction in Sept. 1997 and revised in May 1998. The SYSRET instruction is the return instruction in conjunction with SYSCALL. The SYSRET in Intel 64-32 instruction set means return from fast system call. Hacker will access to operating system memory via SYSRET privilege escalation [1,11].
- IOS Jailbreak is removing the privilege limitations imposed by IOS operating system by breaking digital rights management, which includes iPhone, iPad. IOS jailbreak tools allow users to gain kernel privilege of IOS.
- Web shell is a type of privilege escalation script program, which belongs to cross zone script hack. Hacker upload web shell program into web server by user privilege, yet when the script program the hacker get administrator privilege. The hacker can download any web and change web contents. The cross zone script hack is a

permit low privilege zone script get system privilege zone under web vulnerability [1, 9, 10].

2   Memory Models

2.1   IA-32 Bits Memory Models

IA-32 bits CPU architecture has three memory models: flat, segmented and real address mode:

- **Real-address memory model** -- The real address mode use linear address space divided into equal 64K bytes sized segments. The model is used in Intel 8086, 8088 and 80286. The physical address space is from 0 to 2^{20}-1 (1M) bytes [12].
- physical address=16 * segment + offset
- **Flat memory model** -- Flat memory model is also named linear memory model. The address space is from 0 to 2^{32}-1. All code, data, extra and stack segments are all in same address linear space. The flat memory model is always used in 32 bits assembly language [12].
- **Segmented memory model** --Although physical address in segmented memory model has segment and offset similar to real-address model, the each segment can be as large as 2^{32}-1 bytes. All the segments are mapped into the linear address space [12].
- **Paging and virtual memory model** – When the operating system enable the paging memory model, physical linear address space is divided into pages which are mapped to virtual memory. The application program is transparent to virtual memory and mapped as needed into physical linear address. When the operating system disabled the paging memory model, the linear memory is directly into physical linear address space as the flat or segmented memory model. The paging and virtual memory model can get greater address space than 4G bytes [12].

2.2   IA-64 Bits Memory Model

IA-64 bits memory is linear address space from 0 to 264-1. However, Intel CPU support less than 64-bit as physical address space through the paging mechanism. The IA-64 bit mode use flat virtual space for code, data, and OS kernel [12].

User model virtual memory address space limits for supported 64-bit releases of Windows is 8T bytes With IMAGE_FILE_LARGE_ADDRESS_AWARE set. The limit on 64-bit win7 ultimate is 192GB, Windows Server 2008 R2 datacenter 2TB.

IA-64 define 128 general integer registers from r0 to r127, 128 float point registers from f0 to f127, and 8 branch registers from b0 to b7 for function call linkage and return. Region register r32-r35 are the input registers, r36-r40 are the local variable registers, and r41-r46 are the output registers. Region register also used in virtual memory translation.

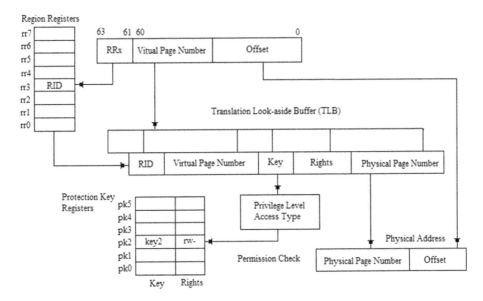

Fig. 2. Bit 61 to bit 63 of virtual address pointer to region registers identifiers (RIDs). Translation Look-aside Buffer (TLB) contains RIDs with virtual page number (VPN) key, rights, and physical page number. The key in TLB is used in permission check. The protection key registers store TLB key and rights. Physical address is according to the TLB physical page number and virtual address offset [16].

3   SYSCALL and SYSRET

3.1   SYSCALL

SYSCALL is fast call to privilege level 0 system procedures for operating system designers [11]. Intel updates for 64-bit registers IA32_STAR (64-bit mode), IA32_LSTAR (64-bit mode), IA32_CSTAR (64-bit mode), IA32_SFMASK (64-bit mode) for SYSCALL and SYSRET.

The following C function describes the SYSCALL instruction logic procedure in Intel 64-bit architecture.

```
VOID SYSCALL()
{
   If( (IA32_EFER.SCE!=1)||(IA32_EFER.LMA!=1)||(CS.L!=1))
           /*
*Not in 64-bit mode or SYSCALL/SYSRET not *enabled in
IA32_EFER. Legacy mode and compatibility mode are dis-
abled.*/
   THEN
           #UD;  /* #UD exception */
      FI;
```

```
    RCX=RIP;            /* save RIP for SYSCALL return */
    RIP=LSTAR_MSR; /* load a new RIP from LSTAR_MSR */
    R11=EFLAGS;        /* save EFLAGS to R11 */
    EFLAGS = (EFLAGS MASKED BY IA32_FMASK)
/* IA32_FMASK value C000_0084) */
    CPL=0;
/* processor set CS register, limit base is 0H */
    CS.SEL = IA32_STAR_MSR[47:32];
    CS.DPL = 0;
    CS.BASE = 0;
    CS.LIMIT = 0xFFFFF;
    CS.GRANULAR = 1;
/* processor set SS register, limit base is 0H   */
    SS.SEL = IA32_STAR_MSR[47:32] + 8;
    SS.DPL = 0;
    SS.BASE = 0;
    SS.LIMIT = 0xFFFFF;
    SS.GRANULAR = 1;
}[13].
```

3.2   SYSRET

SYSRET executes a fast return to privilege level 3 user code from system procedures executing at protections levels 0. The base and limit address of CS and SS segment registers remain the same for all processes, including the operating system [11,13].

The following C function describes the SYSRET instruction logic procedure in Intel 64-bit architecture.

```
VOID SYSRET()
{
  IF ((CS.L!=1)||(IA32_EFER.LMA!=1)||(IA32_EFER.SCE!=1))
/* Not in 64-Bit Mode or SYSCALL/SYSRET not enabled in
   IA32_EFER , System call extension is disalbe*/
  THEN #UD;   /* do exception ud*/
     FI;
  IF (CPL != 0) /* CPL !=0 */
  THEN #GP(0);
     FI;
  IF (RCX != CANONICAL_ADDRESS)
  THEN #GP(0);
     FI;
  IF (OPERAND_SIZE = 64)
  THEN    /* Return to 64-Bit Mode */
     EFLAGS = R11;
     CPL = 0x3; /* CPL = 3*/
     CS.SEL = IA32_STAR[63:48] + 16;
/*sets the CS selector value to MSR */
     CS.PL = 0x3;
     SS.SEL = IA32_STAR[63:48] + 8;
```

```
    SS.PL = 0x3;
    RIP = RCX; /* copy RCX to RIP for return*/
  ELSE    /* Return to Compatibility Mode by Osize32 */
    EFLAGS =R11;
    CPL =0x3; /* CPL = 3*/
    CS.SEL = IA32_STAR[63:48] ;
    CS.PL = 0x3;
    SS.SEL = IA32_STAR[63:48] + 8;
/* keep descriptors in the GDT/LDT that correspond to se-
lectors */
    SS.PL = 0x3;
    EIP = ECX;
    FI;
}[13].
```

4   SYSRET Privilege Escalation

4.1   CVE-2012-0217 Vulnerability Impacts

Rafal Wojtczuk reported CVE-2012-0217, The Xen Security team recently disclosed a vulnerability, Xen Security Advisory 7 (CVE-2012-0217), which would allow guest administrators to escalate to hypervisor-level privileges.

Xen's blog post The Intel SYSRET privilege escalation methods [9, 17]. This CVE-2012-0217 vulnerability only affects Intel x64-based versions of Windows 7 and Windows Server 2008 R2. Systems with AMD or ARM-based CPUs are not affected by this vulnerability [18].

Table 1. Vulnerability Summary for CVE-2012-0217

Impact	Impact Type	OS Types affected
CVSS v2 Base Score:7.2	unauthorized disclosure	Windows 7 Gold and SP1
Impact Subscore: 10.0	unauthorized modification;	FreeBSD before 9.0-RELEASE-p3
Exploitability Subscore: 3.9	disruption of service	Windows Server 2008 R2 and R2 SP1
Access Complexity: Low		NetBSD 6.0 Beta and earlier
Authentication: Not re-		Citrix XenServer 6.0.2 and earlier
quired to exploit		Oracle Solaris 11 and earlier

4.2   CVE-2012-0217 SYSRET Privilege Escalation

CVE-2012-0217 vulnerability is the SYSRET instruction difference between the AMD and Intel CPU. SYSCALL and SYSRET designed by AMD. Intel also issued these instructions for IA-64 OS system. [9]

iZsh debug FreeBSD under VMware fusion on Mac OSX through listening port 8864. And load the FreeBSD's kernel symbols in gdb7.4.1. Then triggering the vulnerability by allocating a page before the non-canonical address boundary, calling an syscall using the SYSCALL instruction. After SYSCALL restores, SYSRET instruction executes. The next instruction is still in kernel privilege ring 0 [17].

Once SYSRET can't return privilege ring 3, the kernel privilege ring 0 can give the hacker the chance to execute arbitrary code. iZsh also give shell code using the SYSRET instruction [17].

Dunlapg post a paper on the Intel SYSRET privilege escalation, the paper shows that 64-bit versions of NetBSD, FreeBSD, and Windows 7 are vulnerable [9].

5   Results Analysis

CVE-2012-0217 vulnerability is posted in Microsoft security bulletin MS12-042 on Windows kernel cloud allowing elevation of privilege. The affected systems are composed of Windows XP SP3, Windows Server 2003 SP2, Windows 7 for x64-based system and Windows Server 2008 R2 for X64-based Systems. As the Intel SYSRET instruction vulnerability, it's hard job to cope with the CVE-2012-0217 vulnerability immediately [9].

References

1. Niels, P., Markus, F., Peter, H.: Preventing Privilege Escalation. In: Proceedings of the 12th Conference on USENIX Security Symposium, SSYM 2003, vol. 12, p. 16 (2003)
2. Toshiyuki, M.: Kernel korner: kernel mode Linux for AMD64. J. Linux Journal 205, 136 (2005)
3. Keith, A., Ole, A.: A comparison of software and hardware techniques for x86 virtualization. In: Proceedings of the 12th International Conference on Architectural Support for Programming Languages and Operating Systems, ASPLOS-XII, pp. 1–12 (2006)
4. Arvind, S., Mark, L., Ning, Q., Adrian, P.: SecVisor: a tiny hypervisor to provide lifetime kernel code integrity for commodity OSes. In: Proceedings of Twenty-First ACM SIGOPS Symposium on Operating Systems Principles, SOSP 2007, pp. 335–350 (2007)
5. Sven, B., Lucas, D., Alexandra, D., Thomas, F., Ahmad-Reza, S., Bhargava, S.: POSTER: The Quest for Security against Privilege Escalation Attacks on Android. In: Proceedings of the 18th ACM Conference on Computer and Communications Security, CCS 2011, pp. 741–743 (2011)
6. Peter, F., Angela, D.B., Ashvin, G.: Comprehensive kernel instrumentation via dynamic binary translation. In: Proceedings of the Seventeenth International Conference on Architectural Support for Programming Languages and Operating Systems, ASPLOS 2012, pp. 135–146 (2012)
7. Avadh, P., Furat, A., Shunfei, C., Kanad, G.: MARSS: a full system simulator for multi-core x86 CPUs. In: Proceedings of the 48th Design Automation Conference, DAC 2011, pp. 1050–1055 (2011)
8. John, R.L., Peter, D., Kanad, G.: SymCall: symbiotic virtualization through VMM-to-guest upcalls. In: Proceedings of the 7th ACM SIGPLAN/SIGOPS International Conference on Virtual Execution Environments, VEE 2011, pp. 193–204 (2011)
9. The Intel SYSRET privilege escalation, http://blog.xen.org/index.php/2012/06/13/the-intel-sysret-privilege-escalation/

10. Privilege escalation,
    http://en.wikipedia.org/wiki/Privilege_escalation
11. AMD Application Note, SYSCALL and SYSRET Instruction Specification
12. Intel, Intel® 64 and IA-32 Architectures Software Developer's Manual Vol.1: Basic Architecture
13. Intel, Intel® 64 and IA-32 Architectures Software Developer's Manual Vol. 2 (2A & 2B): Instruction Set Reference, A-Z
14. Jean, G.: Embedded X86 Programming: Protected Mode, Protection and Segmentation, Paging, http://home.swipnet.se/smaffy/ asm/info/embedded_pmode.pdf
15. IA-64 Architecture, http://www.linuxclustersinstitute.org/ conferences/archive/2000/PDF/Tutorial_IA-64.pdf
16. Jerry, H., Dale, M., Jonathan, R., Hewlett, P., Allan, K., Hans, M., Rumi, Z.: Introduction The IA-64 Architecture, pp. 12–23. IEEE (2000)
17. iZsh: CVE-2012-0217: Intel's sysret Kernel Privilege Escalation (on FreeBSD), http://fail0verflow.com/blog/2012/ cve-2012-0217-intel-sysret-freebsd.html
18. CVE-2012-0217,
    http://cve.mitre.org/cgi-bin/cvename.cgi?name=CVE-2012-0217

Analysis of Cloud Security and a Reliable Transmission Based on UDP

Dixin Su[1] and Zhiping Zhou[1,2]

[1] School of Internet of Things, Jiangnan University, Wuxi, 214122, China
[2] Jiangnan institute of Smart Energy, Wuxi, 214122, China
sudixin@gmail.com, zzp-wx@163.com

Abstract. Cloud computing is a new concept which has broad prospect in personal applications and business area, but the security issues are not resolved. According to the cloud computing system, this paper analyzes and summarizes it then presents a solution to the Cloud Security by a reliable transmission protocol based on UDP. It introduces the fundamental principle and emphasizes the confirming and retransmission mechanism. In the End, the paper analyzes the protocol.

Keywords: UDP, Cloud Security, Data Loss, Data Retransmission.

1 Introduction

Since the concept "cloud computing" came out in 2007, great changes have taken place in the field of IT around the world by the reason that it make up the traditional mode's shortages ,the lack of cost savings and system scalability. Whether from individual application level or business level, cloud computing has a broad prospect. However, its security issues still need to be solved.

Cloud computing has many security issues, such as the lack of a unified standards, the identification of service providers' authorities and the security of information storage [1-2]. At present, the various cloud computing providers have the different standards for the internal structure. In addition, the way to protect information security and backup is different, either. Consequently, on the one hand service providers should establish a set of protection mechanisms according to their own circumstances. On the other hand, authentication between users and service provider is a major security problem [3-4].This problem can be solved by unified authentication protocol and this paper presents an improved protocol to resolve cloud computing security.

Because cloud computing has high-speed computing power and its scale is large, the protocol "Radius"(Remote Authentication Dial In User Service) [5] is chosen as the authentication protocol between the user and the ISP which provides centralized Authentication, Authorization, and Accounting (AAA) management for computers to connect and use a network service. Radius protocol is relatively simple, easy to be managed, and in most cases able to meet the needs of the current network applications. In addition, Radius using UDP as transport so that it makes the authentication

J. Lei et al. (Eds.): NCIS 2012, CCIS 345, pp. 38–44, 2012.
© Springer-Verlag Berlin Heidelberg 2012

quickly ,easy and reduces the pressure of the certification process. So a conclusion can be drawn is that all characters Radius has is the requirements of cloud computing. But the loss of UDP packet can not be ignored, and this paper would present an improved UDP protocol to solve this problem [6].

2   The Improved Protocol

2.1   UDP Protocol

Up to now there are two reliable transport protocols based on UDP protocol. One way is to mark each UDP with a unique number before UDP header .At this condition when receiver receives a UDP packet, the acknowledgment message with related number will be sent to the sender [7]. Although this improvement is on optimizing the reliability of data transmission, it will spend a lot of time in processing and produce a large number of acknowledgment messages which lead to reduce efficiency. The other one is to send just a confirmation of UDP packet received within the time interval and packet count. The confirmation will make sure that the serial numbers before the packet number has been received, and after a period the sender will send the lost packet. In this mechanism, although transmission speed is faster and it occupies the low bandwidth, but the sender is always in a passive position that it only resend UDP packets which did not be received within the specified time. On this basis, the new improved protocol can make the sender retransmit packets automatically and the receiver also takes the initiative to request retransmission [8].

2.2   Fundamental Principle of the Protocol

The improved protocol makes the UDP data section begin with 6 bytes for reliable data transmission, including 2 bytes ID, 2 bytes of the lost packet's number, 2 bytes of the number of acknowledgment packet. The 2 bytes ID gives each UDP packet unique number used to identify the packet. And the number of lost packet suggests that the receiver did not receive the packet and ask to resend it, 0 by default. The number of acknowledgment packet is to confirm that the serial numbers before it are received. In order to confirm and retransmit packets, we should use a queue to restore the packets which do not receive acknowledgments and a buffer zone to resend packets. When a packet is sent, at the same time it will be stored in the buffer zone until the sender receive the corresponding acknowledgement. (Fig. 1).

16 bits ID	16 bits ID of lost packet	16 bits ID of confirmed packet
data		

Fig. 1. UDP structure

As a conclusion, the fundamental principle is as follows. a. when each confirmation is received, the serial packets located in the former of the queue will be confirmed (including the confirmation itself) [9].b. The UDP packets which have been identified will be removed form buffer. c. If the queue is full, only to send UDP packet to buffer. d. Each packet in the queue has a timer .when the time turn to 0 , the packet will automatically be resent. The whole mechanism relies on the confirming mechanism and retransmission mechanism.

2.3   Confirmation of Packets

The protocol has different priority confirming mechanisms. These three mechanisms are used in combination to achieve packet confirmation.

The first one is respective confirmation. When the sender and receiver communicate by the improved UDP protocol, every packet with acknowledgment number can take confirming message to each other. And if the confirmation with the biggest number is sent, it suggests that packets less than the number are confirmed. (Fig. 2)

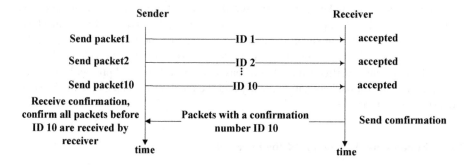

Fig. 2. Respective confirmation

The second one is inserting confirmation by time. Once a UDP packet is received, the receiver will check a timer for inserted confirmed. If not start, then turn on it. When the timer expires and there is not the other confirming mechanisms working, then sending acknowledgment message to the sender. In the meanwhile, the timer turns back to 0. (Fig. 3)

Fig. 3. Insert confirmation by timer

The third one is inserting confirmation by count. When the sender and receiver communicate by using the improved UDP protocol, they record the numbers of UDP packets received by using a counter. If the counter achieves the predetermined value and there is no other confirming mechanisms working, then sending acknowledgment message to each other and the counter turns back to 0.(Fig. 4)

Fig. 4. Insert confirmation by counter

These three mechanisms have different priorities that the respective confirmation has the higher priority than the others. Generally, the protocol uses confirmation by count and confirmation by time in combination. And the respective confirmation is used often, but no matter which mechanisms are chosen the timer and counter will turn back to 0.

2.4   Retransmission of packets

(1) Automatic retransmission mechanism. Communication parties maintain timer for each packet in the queue they send. The timer is used to retransmit packet. When the

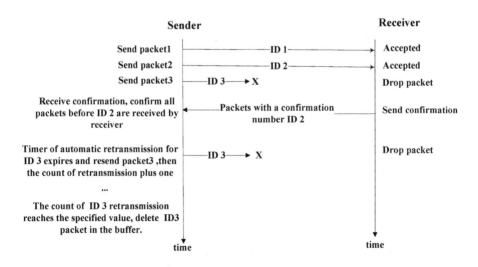

Fig. 5. Automatic retransmission

time expires and the party does not receive confirmation from the opposite one, the packet will be sent again. In addition, timer turns back and the counter of resending add one. But if the number of retransmission reaches the target count, then packets stored in the UDP buffer will be removed and the counter and timer of retransmission will also be set to 0. (Fig. 5.)

(2) Retransmission request mechanism. When the sender and receiver communicate by using the improved UDP protocol, the receiver can inform the sender to resend the lost packet by 2 bytes of the lost packet's ID. Once the message is received, sender will respond immediately.After that the count of retransmission plus one and timer will be put back to 0. (Fig. 6)

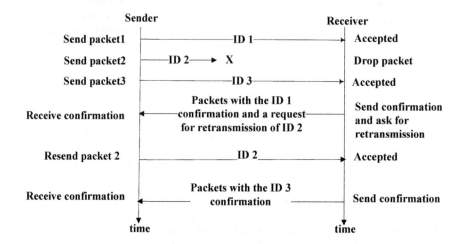

Fig. 6. Request for retransmission

2.5   Dealing with the Disorder of Packets

Most of time the packets received are out of order. However, the confirming and re-transmission mechanism are based on the order of packets. As a result, a method should be established to make the packets which are received sort from small to large. In general, dealing with the out order of packets and requesting for retransmission are used in combination.

2.6   Setting of Timers

There are different kinds of timers mentioned above. Like the timer for inserting con-firmation, and for automatic retransmission. Although the setting of various timers is different, it is interrelated. The timer for automatic retransmission is started when UDP packet is sent. What should be noticed is that automatic retransmission works just after receiver inserts at least two confirmation by timer. From the above, a conclusion can be drawn is that the length of timer for automatic retransmission should be larger than the timer for inserting confirmation to prevent from dropping a confirmation.

3   Analysis of Protocol

The improved protocol is suitable for most applications which need to take into account the reliability and efficiency. Since only occupy data portion six bytes, the protocol is simply controlled, flexible and easy to use.

Contrast to the first way that once the receiver gets a UDP packet then sends a confirmation,   the improved one will not only enhance the reliability of data transmission but also avoid spending a lot of time to identify and occupy smaller bandwidth by selective retransmission. In the meantime, compared with the second way that improve reliability by sending just a confirmation of UDP packet within the time interval and packet count, on the one hand the improved one increase efficiency, on the other hand which characters of the protocol stand out is that it makes the sender take an active part in communication instead of resending packets just when timer expires. Receiver asking to retransmit the lost packets can avoid the sender resend all packets within the specified time. This method achieves equality between the two communication parties.

However, although the improved protocol solves the problem of dropping packets and achieves equality between the two communication parties, but it still has several disadvantages as follows.

(1) Each time a UDP packet is sent, it only can ask a request of retransmission because it just contains a packet's number (ID) that require to resend. In this case if there are a lot of requests for retransmission, then the packets will be sent one by one. For example, the receiver loses totally N packets, so before the automatic retransmission works it will ask a request at least N times.

(2) Each packet is equipped with timer used for retransmission so that it increases workload. In the improved UDP protocol each UDP packet has a retransmission timer .When the communication parties send a large number of packets to each other , the system will produce corresponding timers. And it leads to heavy workload. In addition, there are other several types of timers which are interrelated. As a consequence the time configuration makes system more complicated.

(3) Requirement for large UDP buffer. Due to the large number of UDP packets, the protocol needs a larger UDP buffer and confirmation queue (the longest confirmation queue is totally $2 \wedge 16$ and the protocol has $2 \wedge 16$ buffer units).

4   Conclusion

In order to solve the problem of UDP packet loss, this paper presents a reliable transmission protocol based on UDP. It introduces the fundamental principle and emphasizes a variety of confirming and retransmission mechanisms which ensure the reliability of the protocol. It is reliable like TCP and continues to have the advantages of common UDP like sample, efficient. Using the protocol in Authentication,

Authorization and Accounting between cloud computing service provider and user is more secure and reliable. However, it has some shortcomings and how to modify the shortages would be the important task in the future.

References

1. Zhang, J.: Survey of research progress on cloud computing. Application Research of Computers 27(2), 431–433 (2010)
2. Chen, O., Deng, O.: Cloud computing and its key techniques. Application Research of Computers 29(9), 2562–2567 (2009)
3. Fauzi, A.A.C., Noraziah, A.: On Cloud Computing Security Issues, Pahang (2012)
4. Chen, D., Huang, X., Ren, X.: Analysis of Cloud Computing and Cloud Security. Computer Technology and Development 20(2), 99–102 (2010)
5. Zhang, Q., Yu, Z., Li, R.: Analysis and Compare of Protocols for AAA Service. Application Research of Computers 2, 296–301 (2007)
6. Boulevard, W.: RFC793-transmission control Protocol [S/OL](1981–09), http://www.faqs.Org/rfc793.html
7. Fu, Y., Lu, J.: Research on and realization of a UDP—based reliable data transfer protocol. Study on Optical Communications 5, 17–19 (2009)
8. Velten, D., Hinden, R., Sax, J.: RFC908-reliable data protocol [S/OL] (1984-07), http://www.faqs.Org/rfcs/rfc908.html
9. Wang, Y.: Research and application of reliable data transmission technique based on UDP. Computer Engineering and Applications 46(3), 105–108 (2010)

A Survey of Passive Image Forensics

Weimin Wei, Liping Sun, Dongjie Tang, Yan Zhao, and Hongjiao Li

School of Computer and Information Engineering, Shanghai University of Electric Power,
Shanghai, 200090, China
weiweimin@hotmail.com

Abstract. Over the past years, digital images have been widely used in the Internet and many other applications. As image processing techniques are developing rapidly, tampering digital images without leaving any obvious traces becomes easier and easier. Passive image forensics is a technology of detecting image authenticity and source without relying on any pre-extraction or pre-embedded information. According to the forensics characteristics used by image authentication, the techniques of passive image forensics for authenticity detection are divided into three categories: techniques based on the traces left by the process of image forgery, techniques based on the consistency of imaging equipment, and techniques based on the statistical characteristics of natural images. The basic characteristics of typical methods are summarized in detail for each category. Passive image forensics has become a hot topic with broad prospect in multimedia security.

Keywords: image forgery, tampering identification, digital watermark, passive image forensics.

1 Introduction

In the analog world, an image (a photograph) has generally been accepted as a "proof of occurrence" of the depicted event. In today's digital age, the creation and manipulation of digital images is made simple by digital processing tools that are easily and widely available. As a consequence, seeing is no longer believing. A new passive image forensics (PIF) has evolved quickly during the last few years. Unlike the signature-based or watermark-based methods, the new technology does not need any signature generated or watermark embedded in advance. It assumes that different imaging devices or processing tools would introduce different inherent patterns into the output images. These underlying patterns are consistent in the original images and would be altered after some kind of manipulations. Thus, they can be used as evidence for image source identification and alteration detection.

PIF research aims at uncovering underlying facts about an image. For example PIF techniques look for authoritative answers to questions such as [1]: Is this image an "original" image or was it created by cut and paste operations from different images? Does this image truly represent the original scene or was it digitally tampered to deceive the viewer? What is the processing history of the image? What parts of the image

J. Lei et al. (Eds.): NCIS 2012, CCIS 345, pp. 45–55, 2012.
© Springer-Verlag Berlin Heidelberg 2012

has undergone processing and up to what extent? Was the image acquired by a source manufactured by vendor X or vendor Y? Did this image originate from source X as claimed?

Thus, PIF can be divided into several parts: 1) Image authenticity identification, judging whether or not digital images experience any form of alteration after obtaining it, is also called anti-fake detection. 2) Identification of image source, judging which device generates the image (digital camera, scanner, camera in mobile phone, computer, and etc.). Owing to the different characteristics of the device, there must be some different inherent patterns in the generated images. So, identification of image source can analyze and extract the characteristics which can distinguish the origin of the image and then establish the characteristic database in order to serve for identification [2]. Technologies for source identification can also be used in authenticity identification. 3) Forensics steganalysis, technique aims to prove the tampering towards the integrity of the image. Differing from steganalysis, forensics steganalysis does not only find whether or not there is secret information hidden in the image, but it also requires extract the hiding information as evidence to use it in a court of law. Nowadays, the study of forensics steganalysis focuses on finding hiding information while not extracting it. Future research on the steganalysis should go further to make sure the methods, embedded software, keywords, and etc. in order to extract the hiding information correctly [3]. This paper focusses on the relevant technology of image authenticity identification.

2   The Primary Methods of Passive Image Forensics

PIF was based on a hypothesis that brilliant tampering can make tampering trace invisible while inherent statistical characteristics of the image have been changed. According to the hypothesis, Hany Farid grouped this technique into five categories [4]: 1) pixel-based techniques that detect statistical anomalies introduced at the pixel level; 2) format-based techniques that leverage the statistical correlations introduced by a specific lossy compression scheme; 3) camera-based techniques that exploit artifacts introduced by the camera lens, sensor, or on-chip post-processing; 4) physically based techniques that explicitly model and detect anomalies in the three-dimensional interaction between physical objects, light, and the camera; and 5) geometric-based techniques that make measurements of objects in the world and their positions relative to the camera.

According to the forensics characteristics used by image authentication, the techniques of PIF for authenticity detection are divided into three categories [5]: 1) Techniques based on the traces left by the process of image forgery; these characteristics might be deviation features, blur degree, similarity and so on. Nowadays, current methods on this field including copy-move detecting, resampling, double JPEG, lighting inconsistencies, blurring estimation and etc. 2) Techniques based on the consistency of imaging equipment, which introduces many strong distinguishable characteristics during image collecting. They are consistent in the entire image. So, this consistency can be used to image forgery detecting and tampering locating. The current research methods include color filter-array aberration, sensor noise pattern, chromatic aberration, consistency detecting and etc. 3) Techniques based on the statistical characteristics of natural images, It points out a series of characteristics which are allergic to the tampering firstly. Then, find whether the image tampered through compare the characteristics value and reference value. These methods mostly depend on categorizer to draw a conclusion. Current methods use characteristics for image forensics, such as higher order statistics, image quality metrics, binary similarity measures, higher order wavelet statistics, and etc.

2.1   Techniques Based on the Traces Left by the Process of Image Forgery

1) Copy-move

Copy-move detecting is referred to that the tampering content comes from other parts of the same image [6]. The parts used to copy and cover mostly are irregular areas, such as grass, flowers, trees, gravels and architects. This kind of image tampering, in spite of processing the tampering image probably, will make the tampering image share some same areas with the original image. Thus, the best way to detect this is to search the resemblances in the image through a brute force search. Nowadays, advanced methods mostly inherit this thought. They divide the image into overlapping squares and then search and match each square. Its computing efficiency can also be improved by searching and matching the characteristics of the image instead of the areas [7-10]. But, this behavior will lead to false alert for those real images which have recurred resembling contents. In order to make tampering images hard to be detected, falsifiers also make advantage of some feather cutting or some modifiers to erase tampering traces.

2) Resampling

When a part of an image is copied into other locations in the same image or another image, tampering contents should experience a series of handling like scaling, spinning and so on to find an appropriate size and direction for erasing tampering trace. Thus, such actions tend to leave resampling trace. Even though these traces cannot arouse doubts in visual, the pixels always have a periodic linear relation with other pixels around them. We can detect whether or not these images have been altered. Currently, image resampling detecting can be generally divided into two categories. The first category is Bayesian posterior probability iterative estimation based-on expectation maximization (EM); the other category is periodical detecting method.

EM algorithm, belonging to a kind of iterative methods, primarily aims to solve maximumlikelihood estimator problem with uncompleted data. In PIF, resampling based-on EM was firstly proposed by Popescu [11]. The core of detecting algorithm is estimating the posteriori probability of interpolation in each pixel. Without considering strong noise, this algorithm can effectively detect whether or not the image has experienced scaling and rotating operations while cannot judge the degree of such operations. Kirchner put forward another quick EM algorithm [12] without using iterative algorithm, which improves the algorithm efficiency. In general, EM algorithm can only judge whether or not the image experienced resampling operations while cannot make sure the degree of this action. Consequently, EM algorithm is unable to estimate resampling factor.

Gallagher [13] finds that the variance of the second derivative of an interpolated signal has a periodicity equal to the sampling rate of the original signal. Practically, this characteristic can be exploited to determine whether a given image has been created by a low-order interpolator and the rate of interpolation factor can be estimated. On that basis, Mahdian introduces Radon alteration, putting forward an algorithm of which can judge rotation angles qualitatively [14]. Prasad also use the periodicity of second derivative to find the traces of imaging scaling [15]. It sets the points which have changed to 1 and the remaining to 0. Then, the periodicity character can be found by analyzing the spectrum. However, this method only can judge resampling operation qualitatively. According to Nearest-neighbor and bilinear interpolation can present stronger periodicity for first order derivative and second order derivative respectively, Suwendi brought up a detecting algorithm [16] to distinguish Nearest-neighbor and bilinear interpolation, which can estimate image scaling factors while less precise than the algorithm mentioned in the literature [13].

3) Double JPEG

When combining many JPEG images into a new one, tampering images experienced twice JPEG coding which means that some contents will twice be quantified by different DCT coefficient quantification. It will cause some characteristics abnormal in image. Thus, this kind of double JPEG compressions will make the histogram of DCT factor produce periodical models. It can offer passive forensics clues [17]. Farid presents a method that detecting the JPEG combining image in pixel level [18]. First, compress the JPEG combining image which to be tested with different quality factors. Then, compare it with the original image. Tampering areas can be distinguished by Kolmogorov-Smirnov statistical tools. What should be pointed out is that double compress just can be served as a kind of clue to find the tampering images rather than confirm that the image must be tampering.

4) Lighting inconsistencies

When combining objects from different images into one image, it tends to be very difficult to adjust the light condition of one object to match the others completely since it needs to re-establish light environment like shadows. Johnson presents a method [19] that the light direction of image can be estimated by the edging pixels of the object. If there is more than one light direction in an image, it can be considered that the image is combined. Subsequently, Johnson presents a new method [20] to extend the light source environment detecting method into multiple light source environment detecting method. Furthermore, they present another way by identifying reflected light from people's eyes to estimate the light direction or light condition [21]. The inconsistencies can be used to reveal tampering trace of images especially detecting portraits. Supposing that the geometrical shapes of objects in the image is known, Mahajan puts forward a new way to detect the lighting transfer and image consistency without estimating light source [22].

5) Blurring estimation

In order to produce a seamless doctored face, applying blurring is inevitable. Other than face replacement, skin smoothing and panorama are also blurring involved digital image tampering. Blurring is a very common process in digital image manipulation; it could be used to reduce the degree of discontinuity or to remove unwanted defects, ultimately, it is used to generate plausible digital image forensics. Hence if an additional blurring process applied on an image is detectable, possible fraud can be exposed even in a credible image. From the fundamentals of frequency domain knowledge about the mathematical model, Hsiao and Pei develop a scheme to detect blur regions for general images then modify it for identifying digital forensics [23]. In general, if a digital image undergoes a copy-paste type of forgery, average blurriness value of the forged region is expected to be different as compared to the non-tampered parts of the image. The method of estimating blurriness value of an image is based on the regularity properties of wavelet transform coefficients which involve measuring the decay of wavelet transform coefficients across scales [24].

2.2   Techniques Based on the Consistency of Imaging Equipment

1) CFA interpolation

Detecting the inherent feature caused by imaging device is one of the major means in passive forensic. In most cases, colored images made by middle and low level cameras are gained by a single sensor combined with CFA (Color Filter Array). The most common CFA is Bayer matrix which is composed of red sensors, green sensors and blue sensors in a certain order. Thus, only one color component intensity can be got in any location while the other two color component intensitys are obtained through the interpolation from the surrounding sensors.

Different cameras often use different CFA interpolation, such as bilinear, bicubic, smooth hue transition, median, gradient-based, and adaptive color plane etc. Popescu uses a simplified linear model to express the periodical relevance of CFA interpolation and then uses EM algorithm to qualify and estimate the relevance in the image [25]. But forgers also can simulate interpolation operations to make the relevance reappear in order to invalidate detecting method. Long and Huang consider that it is too simple to use a linear module to express CFA interpolating rule. They put forward that mean square error model can be used to describe spatial relevance among image pixels brought by CFA interpolations [26]. Then, get a coefficient matrix through each color channel based on this model and reduce the dimensions of the coefficient matrix with PCA and send the coefficient matrix whose dimensions reduced by PCA into BP neural network with forward feedback for detecting images. Swaminathan considers that most tampering operations can be approximated to linear or non-linear combinations. Thus, they offered a deconvolution algorithm to detect the following operations [27] after gaining the image so as to detect the authenticity of images. In conclusion, the methods mentioned above can effectively distinguish CFA interpolating images and non-interpolating images. And it is also effective in the situations that images being compressed or additive noise etc [28]. But if forger sampling CFA or interpolate again, this method will lose efficacy. Nowadays, there are many papers about based-on CFA interpolation detecting technology published. However, Fo-veonTM X3 imaging sensor can obtain three basic colors from each pixel. Detecting methods for this situation need further research.

2) Camera response function

Photometric methods in computer vision require calibration of the camera's radiometric response. Lin presents a method that using the edge pixel of different colors deduces CRF (camera response function) [29]. If the contents of different colors come from different original images, the gained CRF will include some anomalous characteristics which are different from normal CRF. And then, it can be confirmed that the image experienced synthesis processing [30]. For a given image, Hsu and Chang identify suspicious splicing areas, compute the geometry invariants from the pixels within each region, and then estimate the camera response function (CRF) from these geometry invariants [31].

3) Pattern noise

Images produced by different type cameras include different pattern noise. If the pattern noise of an area is different from other areas, it can be considered that this area is added artificially [32]. But if the forger is very skillful with possessing relevant imaging device and large number of relevant images, it is still possible to eliminate or add specific pattern noise.

4) Gamma correction

The luminance non-linearity introduced by many imaging devices can often be described by a simple point-wise operation (gamma correction). Farid presents a technique for blindly estimating the amount of gamma correction in the absence of any calibration information or knowledge of the imaging device [33]. The basic approach exploits the fact that gamma correction introduces specific higher-order correlations in the frequency domain. These correlations can be detected using tools from polyspectral analysis. The amount of gamma correction is then estimated by minimizing these correlations.

5) Lens distortions

Virtually all imaging devices introduce some amount of geometric lens distortion. Farid and Popescu presents a technique for blindly removing these distortions in the absence of any calibration information or explicit knowledge of the imaging device [35]. The basic approach exploits the fact that lens distortion introduces specific higher-order correlations in the frequency domain. These correlations can be detected using tools from polyspectral analysis [34].

6) Chromatic aberration

Virtually all optical imaging systems introduce a variety of aberrations into an image. Chromatic aberration, for example, results from the failure of an optical system to perfectly focus light of different wavelengths. Lateral chromatic aberration manifests itself, to a first-order approximation, as an expansion/contraction of color channels with respect to one another. When tampering with an image, this aberration is often disturbed and fails to be consistent across the image. Johnson and Farid describe a computational technique for automatically estimating lateral chromatic aberration and show its efficacy in detecting digital tampering [36].

2.3   Techniques Based on the Statistical Characteristics of Natural Images

This kind of method extracts a series of reference threshold values which are sensitive to the tampering images through analyzing a large number of photographic images and tampering images, such as the pixel average, RGB correlation, and wavelet statistical characteristic and so on. Then discover the changed parts through comparing the characteristic value of the image which to be tested with the reference value to judge whether the image tempered. This kind of method usually uses categorizer like SVM (Support Vector Machine) and needs large number of image samples to practice.

1) Hany Farid Group: Method based-on higher-order wavelet statistics
Computer graphics rendering software is capable of generating highly photorealistic images that can be impossible to differentiate from photographic images. Lyu uses wavelet analysis based-on QMF (Quadrature Mirror Filter) to distinguish them [37]. The first four order statistics (mean, variance, skewness, and kurtosis) of the subband coefficient histograms at each orientation, scale, and color channel are collected. The best performance was 27.6% correctly classified photographic images, with a 1.4% false-negative rate. Then, Lyu adds LAH (Local Angular Harmonic) and extracts phase statistical characteristic based-on rotation-invariant [38] in the model mentioned before. It improves categorized accuracy of photographic images to 74.3%.

2) Shih-Fu Chang Group: Method based-on higher-order statistics
Bicoherence is a normalized bispectrum, i.e., the third order correlation of three harmonically related Fourier frequencies of a signal which is wildly used in human speech synthesis. Ng and his group use bicoherence features for image splicing detection passively [39]. Unfortunately, the result cannot achieve the original expectations. Only 62% images are detected correctly. Then they add three new characteristics: magnitude and phase features, prediction discrepancy, and edge percentage [40]. After SVM categorizing, the accuracy increases to 72%. Nevertheless, this algorithm demands that the image is only splicing without any other operations.

3) Nasir Memon Group: method base-on image quality metrics
A doctored image (or the least parts of it) would have undergone some image processing operations like scaling, rotation, brightness adjustment etc. Based on this fact, Nasir Memon and his group use IQMS (image quality metrics) in steganographic to judge image tampering. They propose a novel way of measuring the distortion between two images, one being the original and the other processed. The measurements are used as features in classifier design [41]. Experiments show that the average of categorized accurate rates of brightness adjustment, contrast enhancement and mixed sequential processing can reach 74%.

The correlation between the bit-planes as well the binary texture characteristics within the bit planes will differ between an original and a doctored image. This change in the intrinsic characteristics of the image can be monitored via the quantal-spatial moments of the bit-planes. Binary Similarity Measures (BSM) are used as features in classifier design. Experiments show that the linear classifiers based on BSM features can detect with satisfactory reliability most of the image doctoring executed via Photoshop tool [42]. Its accuracy rate can reach to 75.5%. Soon afterwards, they combine IQMs, BSMs and HOWS (higher order wavelet statistics) into a complex forensics characteristic set [43] whose categorized effect is much more excellent than a single characteristic. However, the corresponding calculating complexity is improved to the great extent.

3   Research Actuality of PIF

Technology of passive image forensics has developed drastically during recent years, especially for the research institutes in America. Hany Farid and his group [44] in Dartmouth University have attained great achievements in resampling [11], lighting inconsistency [19-21], Gamma correction [33], lens distortion [35], chromatic aberration [36], source image identification [37], double JPEG [18], etc.

Jessica Fridrich and her group [45] in Binghamton University offer a forensics steganalysis method [3] based on steganalysis used in detecting steganography and passive image forensics to justify whether the hidden information in the image. The key of their research lies in identifying the origin of cameras [2] by considering the pattern noise of a digital camera as 'shell marks'. And they also use DCT quantified [9] to solve copy-move detecting problem.

Min Wu and her group in Maryland University [46] analyze and detect spatial filter, double JPEG, resampling, brightness adjustment and so on through the DCT factor relevance of different JPEG image areas [47]. In addition, they can use blind deconvolution technology to simulate imaging process in order to obtain a series of filtering operations [48].

Shih-fu Chang and his group in Columbia University[49] collect evidence[31] for variant images made by different cameras through researching the specific signal processing methods in imaging process, such as CCD lens distortion correction, white balance, Gamma correction and pattern noise etc. They also use bicoherence analysis to detect splicing tampering images [40]. And they establish an online Columbia TrustFoto system [50]. It makes use of image acquisition device, object geometry model and surface property model and the combination of the three to detect whether the images are photographic images or photorealistic images.

Nasir Memon and his group [1] in Polytechnic University put forward that use three categories (IQMs, HOWS, BSMs) of forensic features and discuss the design of classifiers between doctored and original images [41-43].

In practical application aspect, Farid and his group launched two detecting tools for Adobe Systems Incorporated. One of them called "clone detector" which can make sure whether a part of an image is copied from other parts. The other one called "truth dots" which can analyze whether a part of pixels are lost [51]. In the first of October, 2009, Chinese government launched a public safety industry norm called GA/T832-2009, in which technological standard for imaging standard was included which regulated the technological demands of forensic facilities, imaging modes and the form of exchanged information.

4   Conclusions

During recent years, digital media passive forensics has been paid more and more attention in many international famous issues and conferences. In 2005, IEEE launched a new academic periodical called Transaction on Information Forensics and Security. Many international sessions like ACM Multimedia and Security Workshop, International Information Hiding Workshop, International Workshop on Digital Watermarking and Digital Forensics Research Workshop hold the relevant seminars predicting the importance and frontier of passive image forensics.

In general, the research on PIF has a long way to go because of two aspects as followed; one hand, some aspects must be based on some specific conditions while variant tampering images cannot cater to them; thus we must launch other new methods which can be applied everywhere; on the other hand, some methods tend to be effective for simple distortions but ineffective for complex ones. Consequently, we can achieve a lot in this field.

Acknowledgements. The authors are grateful for the anonymous reviewers who made constructive comments. This work was supported by the Natural Science Foundation of Shanghai (11ZR1414300), and the Innovation Program of Shanghai Municipal Education Commission (11YZ194, 12YZ146).

References

1. Sencar, H.T., Memnon, N.: Overview of State-of-the-Art in Digital Image Forensics. Statistical Science and Interdisciplinary Research. World Scientific Press (2008)
2. Lukáš, J., Fridrich, J., Goljan, M.: Digital Camera Identification from Sensor Pattern Noise. IEEE Trans. on Information Forensics and Security 1(2), 205–214 (2006)
3. Fridrich, J., Goljan, M., et al.: Forensic Steganalysis, Determining the Stego Key in Spatial Domain Steganography. In: Proc. of Security, Steganography, and Watermarking of Multimedia Contents, San Jose, USA, vol. 5681, pp. 631–642 (2005)
4. Farid, H.: Image Forgery Detection. IEEE Signal Processing Magazine 26(2), 16–25 (2009)
5. Qiong, W., Guohui, L., et al.: A Survey of Blind Digital Image Forensics Technology for Authenticity Detection. ACTA Automatica Sinica 34(12), 1458–1466 (2008)
6. Mahdian, B., Saic, S.: Detection of Copy-Move Forgery Using a Method Based on Blur Moment Invariants. Forensic Science International 171(2), 180–189 (2007)
7. Luo, W., Huang, J., Qiu, G.: Robust Detection of Region-Duplication Forgery in Digital Image. In: 18th Int. Conf. on Pattern Recognition, Hong Kong, pp. 746–749 (2006)
8. Popescu, A.C., Farid, H.: Exposing Digital Forgeries by Detecting Duplicated Image Regions. TR2004-515, Dartmouth College (2004)
9. Fridrich, J., Soukal, D., Lukáš, J.: Detection of Copy-Move Forgery in Digital Images. In: Proc. Digital Forensic Research Workshop, Cleveland (2003)
10. Weimin, W., Shuozhong, W., et al.: Estimation of Image Rotation Angle Using Interpolation-Related Spectral Signatures with Application to Blind Detection of Image Forgery. IEEE Transactions on Information Forensics and Security 5(3), 507–517 (2010)

11. Popescu, A.C., Farid, H.: Exposing Digital Forgeries by Detecting Traces of Resampling. IEEE Trans. on Signal Processing 53(2), 758–767 (2005)
12. Kirchner, M.: Fast and Reliable Resampling Detection by Spectral Analysis of Fixed Linear Predictor Residue. In: Proc. 10th ACM Workshop on Multimedia and Security, pp. 11–20 (2008)
13. Gallagher, A.C.: Detection of Linear and Cubic Interpolation in JPEG Compressed Images. In: CRV 2005, Washington, USA, pp. 65–72 (2005)
14. Mahdian, B., Saic, S.: Blind Authentication Using Periodic Properties of Interpolation. IEEE Trans. on Information Forensics and Security 3(3), 529–538 (2008)
15. Prasad, S., Ramakrishnan, K.: On Resampling Detection and its Application to Detect Image Tampering. In: IEEE Int. Conf. on Multimedia and Expo., pp. 1325–1328 (2006)
16. Suwendi, A., Allebach, J.P.: Nearest-neighbor and Bilinear Resampling Factor Estimation to Detect Blockiness or Blurriness of an Image. Journal of Electronic Imaging 17(2), 23005 (2008)
17. Fridrich, J., Lukáš, J.: Estimation of Primary Quantization Matrix in Double Compressed JPEG Images. In: Proc. Digital Forensic Research Workshop, Cleveland, pp. 1–17 (2003)
18. Farid, H.: Exposing Digital Forgeries from JPEG Ghosts. IEEE Trans. on Information Forensics and Security 4(1), 154–160 (2009)
19. Johnson, M.K., Farid, H.: Exposing Digital Forgeries by Detecting Inconsistencies in Lighting. In: ACM Multimedia and Security Workshop, New York (2005)
20. Johnson, M.K., Farid, H.: Exposing Digital Forgeries in Complex Lighting Environments. IEEE Trans. on Information Forensics Security 3(2), 450–461 (2007)
21. Johnson, M.K., Farid, H.: Exposing Digital Forgeries Through Specular Highlights on the Eye. In: Furon, T., Cayre, F., Doërr, G., Bas, P. (eds.) IH 2007. LNCS, vol. 4567, pp. 311–325. Springer, Heidelberg (2008)
22. Mahajan, D., Ramamoorthi, R., Curless, B.: A Theory of Frequency Domain Invariants, Spherical Harmonic Identities for BRDF/Lighting Transfer and Image Consistency. IEEE Trans. on Pattern Analysis and Machine Intelligence 30(2), 1–14 (2008)
23. Hsiao, D., Pei, S.: Detecting Digital Tampering by Blur Estimation. In: 1st Int. Workshop on Systematic Approaches to Digital Forensic Engineering, Taipei, pp. 264–278 (2005)
24. Sutcu, Y., Coskun, B., et al.: Tamper Detection Based On Regularity of Wavelet Transform Coefficients. In: IEEE Int. Conf. on Image Processing, San Antonio, TX, USA, pp. 397–400 (2007)
25. Popescu, A.C., Farid, H.: Exposing Digital Forgeries in Color Filter Array Interpolated Images. IEEE Trans. on Signal Processing 53(10), 3948–3959 (2005)
26. Long, Y.J., Huang, Y.Z.: Image Based Source Camera Identification Using Demosaicking. In: 8th Workshop on Multimedia Signal Processing, Victoria, pp. 419–424 (2006)
27. Swaminathan, A., et al.: Image Tampering Identification Using Blind Deconvolution. In: IEEE Int. Conf. on Image Processing, Atlanta, pp. 2311–2314 (2006)
28. Cao, H., Kot, A.C.: Accurate Detection of Demosaicing Regularity for Digital Image Forensics. IEEE Trans. on Information Forensics and Security 4(4), 899–910 (2009)
29. Lin, S., et al.: Radiometric Calibration from a Single Image. In: IEEE Computer Society Conf. on Computer Vision and Pattern Recognition, vol. 2, pp. 938–945 (2004)
30. Lint, Z., Wang, R., et al.: Detecting Doctored Images Using Camera Response Normality and Consistency. In: IEEE Computer Society Conf. on Computer Vision and Pattern Recognition, vol. 1, pp. 1087–1092 (2005)
31. Hsu, Y., Chang, S.: Detecting Image Splicing Using Geometry Invariants and Camera Characteristics Consistency. In: IEEE Int. Conf. on Multimedia and Expo., Toronto, pp. 549–552 (2006)

32. Lukáš, J., Fridrich, J., Goljan, M.: Detecting Digital Image Forgeries Using Sensor Pattern Noise. In: Security, Steganography, and Watermarking of Multimedia Contents, 60720Y1-11, San Jose (2006)
33. Farid, H.: Blind Inverse Gamma Correction. IEEE Trans. on Image Processing 10(10), 1428–1433 (2001)
34. Weng, J.: Camera Calibration with Distortion Models and Accuracy Evaluation. IEEE Trans. on Pattern Analysis and Machine Intelligence 14(10), 965–979 (1992)
35. Farid, H., Popescu, A.C.: Blind Removal of Lens Distortions. J. of the Optical Society of America 18(9), 2072–2078 (2001)
36. Johnson, M.K., Farid, H.: Exposing Digital Forgeries Through Chromatic Aberration. In: Proc. 8th Workshop on Multimedia and Security, vol. 6072, pp. 48–55 (2006)
37. Lyu, S., Farid, H.: How Realistic Is Photorealistic? IEEE Trans. on Signal Processing 53(2), 845–850 (2005)
38. Lyu, S.: Natural Image Statistics for Digital Image Forensics. Department of Computer Science, Dartmouth College (2005)
39. Ng, T., Chang, S.: A Model for Image Splicing. In: IEEE Int. Conf. on Image Processing, vol. 2, pp. 1169–1172 (2004)
40. Ng, T., Chang, S., Sun, Q.: Blind Detection of Photomontage Using Higher Order Statistics. In: IEEE Int. Symposium on Circuits and Systems, Canada, pp. V688–V691 (2004)
41. Avcibas, I., Bayram, S., et al.: A Classifier Design for Detecting Image Manipulations. In: Proc. 2004 Int. Conf. on Image Processing, Singapore, pp. 2645–2648 (2004)
42. Bayram, S., et al.: Image Manipulation Detection with Binary Similarity Measures. In: Proc. 13th European Signal Processing Conf., Antalya, pp. 752–755 (2005)
43. Bayram, S., Avcibas, I., et al.: Image Manipulation Detection. Journal of Electronic Imaging 15(4), 41102 (2006)
44. Farid, H.: Image Forgery Detection. IEEE Signal Processing Magazine 26(2), 16–25 (2009)
45. Fridrich, J.: Digital Image Forensics. IEEE Signal Processing Magazine 26(2), 26–37 (2009)
46. Swaminathan, A., Wu, M., Liu, K.J.: Component Forensics (Theory, Methodologies, and Applications). IEEE Signal Processing Magazine 26(2), 38–48 (2009)
47. Swaminathan, A., et al.: Nonintrusive Component Forensics of Visual Sensors Using Output Images. IEEE Trans. on Information Forensics and Security 2(1), 91–106 (2007)
48. Swaminathan, A., Wu, M., Liu, K.J.: Image Tampering Identification Using Blind Deconvolution. In: IEEE Int. Conf. on Image Processing, Atlanta, pp. 2311–2314 (2006)
49. Ng, T., Chang, S.: Identifying and Prefiltering Images. IEEE Signal Processing Magazine 26(2), 49–58 (2009)
50. TrustFoto Homepage, http://www.ee.columbia.edu/ln/dvmm/trustfoto/
51. Hany Farid Homepage, http://www.cs.dartmouth.edu/farid/press/washingtonpost07.html

A Novel Fast η-Adapt Slide Window Elliptic Curve Cryptography Algorithm

Hongxia Shi[1] and Yi Ouyang[2]

[1] School of Economics and Management, Zhejiang University of Science & Technology
SHX602@163.com
[2] College of Computer and Information Engineering, Zhejiang Gongshang University
oyy@mail.zjgsu.edu.cn

Abstract. Elliptic Curve Cryptography (ECC) as a research hotspot in public key cryptography. In this paper, we proposed a novel fast η-adapt slide window Elliptic Curve Cryptography algorithm to set up the software validation process. This paper introduces a novel fast η-adapt slide window of the elliptic curve cryptosystem. The innovation of this paper is a fast algorithm for elliptic curve one of the key - elliptic curve slide window size generation algorithm, given an opportunity to generate KP. Using Fast Adaptive sliding window ECC algorithm: η-adapt slide window algorithm to shorten the point addition computing time, we built a software validation System . The experiment shows that the results are excellent.

Keywords: ECC, Digital Private Credentials, adapt slide window, Credential Issue Protocol.

1 Introduction

Elliptic Curve Cryptography (ECC) is a research hotspot in public key cryptography. In public key cryptography each user or the device taking part in the communication generally have a pair of keys, a public key and a private key, and a set of operations associated with the keys to do the cryptographic operations. Only the particular user knows the private key whereas the public key is distributed to all users taking part in the communication[1].

Digital Private Credentials[2], one of the important privacy preserving technique, allow user to disclose only a specific portion of the credential. This avoids leakage of important data. It can be presented in such a manner that it leaves no (or partial) evidence of the disclosed information. To help organizations against misuse of credentials, it also provides features like unforgeability and non-repudiation.

This paper introduces a novel fast η-adapt slide window of the elliptic curve cryptosystem. The innovation of this paper is a fast algorithm for elliptic curve one of the key - elliptic curve slide window size generation algorithm, given an opportunity to generate KP.

J. Lei et al. (Eds.): NCIS 2012, CCIS 345, pp. 56–62, 2012.
© Springer-Verlag Berlin Heidelberg 2012

In this paper we implement a protocol of digital private credentials based on fast elliptic curve arithmetic. First we start with the discussion of elliptic curve cryptography. Then we define the system set up and how group parameters are chosen. Credential Issue and Credential Show protocol are discussed in sections 4 and 5 respectively. We perform security and efficiency analysis of the protocol. It is followed by the conclusion and future work in the last section.

2   Elliptic Curve Arithmetic

In this paper, we use the protocol of private credentials[3] in terms of Elliptic Curve Cryptography.

2.1   Elliptic Curve Cryptography

The mathematical operations of ECC is defined over the elliptic curve y2 = x3 + ax + b, where 4a3 + 27b2 $\neq$ 0. Each value of the 'a' and 'b' gives a different elliptic curve. All points (x, y) which satisfies the above equation plus a point at infinity lies on the elliptic curve. The public key is a point in the curve and the private key is a random number. The public key is obtained by multiplying the private key with the generator point G in the curve. One main advantage of ECC is its small key size. A 160-bit key in ECC is considered to be as secured as 1024-bit key in RSA.[3,4]

The security of ECC depends on the difficulty of Elliptic Curve Discrete Logarithm Problem (ECDLP). Let P and Q be the two points on the curve such that kP = Q, where k is a scalar and is called elliptic curve discrete logarithm of Q to the base P. Given P and Q, it is computationally infeasible to obtain k, if k is sufficiently large.

2.2   Fast Adaptive Sliding Window ECC Algorithm: η-Adapt Slide Window Algorithm

In this paper, we use a generalization of ECC function,binary algorithem.The basic algorithms in a fast scalar multiplication algorithm is a double-add method, the integer k in binary notation, and then add points, point doubling operator.

Let

$$K = \sum_{j=0}^{l-1} k_j 2^j \tag{1}$$

where $k_j \in \{0,1\}$,then

$$KP = \sum_{j=0}^{l-1} k_j 2^j p$$

$$= \sum_{j=0}^{l-1} (k_j p) 2^j \qquad (2)$$

$$= 2(...2(k_{l-1} p + k_{l-2} p))...) + k_0 p$$

```
Input: postive n and P.
Output: nP
Let n = n_{i-1}n_{i-2}...n_0 is binary form ,where n_{i-1} = 1 and n_k ∈ {0,1}
R=0
for j=i-1 to 0
R=2R
if( n_j == 1 ) then R=R+P
endfor
return R;
```

Adaptive sliding window algorithm is actually a dynamic search window technology. The basic idea is to skip two consecutive continuous window for 0 bits using point doubling each time to find the window, starting left to right, encountered the maximum window w then adjust the size of window to $w_t = \alpha w_{t-1} + (1-\alpha)b$,where a as regulatory factor, b is the number of consecutive skipped 0.Making is expected to count only the odd values within the window, saving storage space. Point operation speed of the first times faster than a common point and the speed, we can reduce the number of points plus or times point algorithm optimization.

Let k n is the binary bits,W is the time window, w is too long, and is expected to count a long time, the best situation for n-1 multiplying the worst n-1 multiplier n-1 times of large numbers

W is too short degenerate into a binary algorithm.

η-Adapt Slide Window Algorithm

```
input k, P
output:KP
1 Initial computing: P_j = jP
2. R=0 and j=l-1,i=d
3. while(j>=0)
{
   if(ki==0) then t=0;u=0;
else
   Find the maxiam t<=w,and Q ← 2^t Q
If( u ≠ 0 )  Q ← Q+P
i=i-t
   }
```

```
Return Q
```

For example(w is the window's length):
    ...0000<u>110110000</u>11111111110   w=9
    ...0000<u>110110000</u>11111111110   w=9-4=5
    the computing time equal to :4 point doubling + 5 point doubling +1 point addition +4 point doubling.
    ...0000<u>11011000</u>011111111100   w=8
    ...0000<u>11011000</u>011111111100   w=8-4=4
    the computing time equal to :4 point doubling + 4 point doubling +1 point addition +1 point doubling+1 point addition+4 point doubling
    ...0000<u>11011000</u>011111111100   w=8
    ...0000<u>11011000</u>011111111100   w=8-3=5
    the computing time equal to :4 point doubling + 5 point doubling +1 point addition +4 point doubling

3   Software validation System Set-Up

The protocol uses the concept of restrictive blind signature[4], where the signing authority does not exactly get to know the message that is signed. To avoid misuse of the signature, the signature may contain some message indicating what the signature stands for. This message is included in the message M which is known to the signer as well as the user. Let Eq(a,b) be the elliptic curve where q is a prime. P be a point on the curve whose order is a very large prime n so that nP = O.

3.1   Certification Authority

Throughout the system, CA issues the private credentials to the users and user shows these credentials to the verifiers. Each CA has a public key and a private key. A private key consists of (y0, y2, ... , yl-1) where yi ($0 \le i \le$ l-1) are randomly selected from Z* n.. It then publishes the value of the public key as (H0, P1, P2... Pl-1) whereH0 = y0P , P1 = y1P, P2 = y2P, ... , Pl-1 = yl-1P.

3.2   Digital Private Credentials Based on Fast Elliptic Curve Arithmetic.

Let Eq(a,b) be the elliptic curve where q is a prime. P be a point on the curve whose order is a very large prime n so that nP = O.User maintains a secret value α which is chosen at random from Z*n . He also chooses attributes x1, x2, ... , xl from Zn.

3.3   Credential Issue Protocol

In Credential Issue Protocol, CA certifies user's attributes x1, x2, ... , xl if they are valid. To maintain unlinkability between the credential issued and the credential being verified, CA does not get to know the exact signature he makes on the attributes. At the end of the protocol CA signs H', the signature being (u',v').The software of the author (also known as the signature process) produced by the following method, the processing flowchart as fig.1.

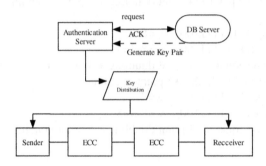

Fig. 1. The Credential Issue Protocal Processing flowchart

```
1 Select an elliptic curve of Ep (a, b), and the basis point
G.
2. Select the private key k (k <n, n is the order of G), the
use of point G calculated public key K = kG.
3. Generates a random integer r (r <n), calculate the point
R = rG;
4. User name and point R coordinate values x, y as parameters,
the calculation of the SHA (Secure Hash Algorithm Secure Hash
Algorithm, similar to MD5) value of the Hash = SHA (username,
x, y);
5. Computing sn≡r - Hash * k (mod n).
6. Let sn and Hash serial number as the user name's serial
number.
```

The software validation process is as follows: (there are elliptic curve Ep (a, b), and the basis points G, the public key K).

```
Step 1.From the user to enter the serial number, extract the
sn and the Hash;
Step 2. computing the point R≡sn*G+Hash*K ( mod p ), if sn
and Hash are correct, then the value of R equal to the software
of the midpoint of the signature process R (x, y) coordinates
for sn≡r-Hash*k (mod n) ,so
sn*G + Hash*K =(r-Hash*k)*G+Hash*K
=rG-Hash*kG+Hash*K
=rG- Hash*K+ Hash*K
=rG=R ;
```

```
Step 3.User name and point R coordinate values x, y as a
parameter to calculate H = SHA (username, x, y);
Step 4. If H = Hash then registration successful else
registration failed.
```

4   Conclusion

Elliptic curve cryptography is a new cryptosystem to adapt to future communications technologies and information security technology development, it is a significant advantage in computational speed and storage space, it has become a research hotspot in the public-key cryptosystem. In fact, the elliptic curve cryptographic algorithms, there are several places to be completed calculation, the main future research directions in three aspects [5,6]:

(1) To quickly select a safe elliptic curve.

(2) To effectively calculate the order of the elliptic curve. The core step is to select a secure elliptic curve calculation on the elliptic curve order, effective algorithm for computing elliptic curve order is also an extremely important part of secure elliptic curve cryptosystem.

(3) In the elliptic curve cryptosystem, elliptic curve groups point multiplier accounts for a large proportion of the whole operation, its efficiency related to the efficiency of the implementation of the entire system.

This paper introduces a novel fast η-adapt slide window of the elliptic curve cryptosystem. The innovation of this paper is a fast algorithm for elliptic curve one of the key - elliptic curve slide window size generation algorithm, given an opportunity to generate KP.Using Fast Adaptive sliding window ECC algorithm: η-adapt slide window algorithm to shorten the point addition computing time, we built a software validation System . The experiment shows that the results are excellent.

Acknowledges. This work is supported by the Scientific Research Fund of Science Technology Department of Zhejiang Province of China (Grand No. 2011C24008 and No. 2012C23121).

References

1. Boneh, D., DeMillo, R.A., Lipton, R.J.: On the importance of eliminating errors in cryptographic computations. Journal of Cryptology 14(2), 101–119 (2001)
2. Ciet, M., Joye, M.: Elliptic Curve Cryptosystems in the Presence of Permanent and Transient Faults. Designs, Codes and Cryptography 36, 33–43 (2005)
3. Hess, F.: The GHS Attack Revisited. In: Biham, E. (ed.) EUROCRYPT 2003. LNCS, vol. 2656, pp. 374–387. Springer, Heidelberg (2003)

4. Jao, D., Yoshida, K.: Boneh-Boyen Signatures and the Strong Diffie-Hellman Problem. In: Shacham, H., Waters, B. (eds.) Pairing 2009. LNCS, vol. 5671, pp. 1–16. Springer, Heidelberg (2009)
5. Galbraith, S.D., Lin, X., Scott, M.: Endomorphisms for Faster Elliptic Curve Cryptography on a Large Class of Curves. In: Joux, A. (ed.) EUROCRYPT 2009. LNCS, vol. 5479, pp. 518–535. Springer, Heidelberg (2009)
6. Hankerson, D., Karabina, K., Menezes, A.J.: Analyzing the Galbraith-Lin-Scott point multiplication method for elliptic curves over binary fields. IEEE Transactions on Computers 58, 1411–1420 (2009)

Application of Neural Network and Cluster Analysis in Anomaly Detection

Xudong Wu[1,*], Bingxiang Liu[2], and Yingxi Li[1]

[1] Jiangxi Ceramic & Art Institute, Jingdezhen, 333000, China
[2] Jingdezhen Ceramic Institute, Jingdezhen, 333403, China
wxd20077@126.com

Abstract. This paper, taking the applying data of financial subsidy for agriculture development as an example, makes use of cluster analysis to set anomalous points detection data stream on the basis of data source and finds the most possible fields which may cause abnormal records; then uses neural network and cluster analysis method respectively to analyze and compare the abnormal records for finding out the data likely carrying the humbug, which could be consulted by management department when making decisions.

Keywords: abnormal detection, neural network, cluster.

1 Introduction

Anomalous data are data which centralize and depart from the most other data. Anomaly detection could be described as this: give some data objects and the expected number of anomalous data, then find out the obvious differences and suddenness or several former objects which are different from the other data. The application areas of anomalous data include: detecting humbugs and analyzing risks in areas of telecom, insurance, and bank; digging out criminal actions in e-business; forecasting disaster weather; analyzing income tax records from different groups and finding anomalous models and trends in revenues; deducing who is likely to be suspect in safety-checking departments such as CIQ and civil aviation; spying the price-disguising in applying to customs; setting up the marketing schemes; studying the consuming- behaviors among those who spend little and who spend much; looking for the anomalous reactions produced by medical treatment schemes and medicine in medical research; examining intruding in computers; construing athletes' results; effectively reducing the wrong words-inputting when applying anomalous detection to text editor.

---

* Corresponding author.

J. Lei et al. (Eds.): NCIS 2012, CCIS 345, pp. 63–69, 2012.
© Springer-Verlag Berlin Heidelberg 2012

2   Theory Analyses

2.1   Abnormal Detection Based on Cluster

There are two ways of abnormal detection based on cluster. The first is abnormal detection to static state, specifically, to cluster the data, calculate the outlier factors of objects or clusters, then confirm that those objects or objects in clusters which remain with carrying big outlier factors are abnormity; the second is abnormal detection to dynamic state, this is to say, to use the way of abnormal detection to static state to build up abnormal detection models, detect the abnormity according to the similitude degree between the objects and models gotten.

The way of abnormal detection based on cluster is made up of two stages. The first is using one-pass clustering algorithm to cluster the data; the second is to calculate to outlier factors, rank the clusters in term of abnormal factors, at last ascertain the abnormal cluster, namely, abnormal objects.

Algorithm could be described as following:

The fist stage, cluster: cluster the data collection D, get the result

$$C = \{C_1, C_2, ..., C_K\}$$

The second stage, ascertaining the abnormal cluster: calculate the outlier factors $OF(C_i)$ in each cluster $C_i(1 \leq i \leq k)$, then reorder the $C_i(1 \leq i \leq k)$ according to $OF(C_i)$ in decreasing order, finally educe the smallest b under meeting the

condition: $\dfrac{\sum\limits_{i=1}^{b}|C_i|}{|D|} \geq \varepsilon(0 < \varepsilon < 3)$. Mark the cluster $C_1, C_2, ..., C_b$ as "outlier"(

Every object is considered to be abnormal); mark $C_{b+1}, C_{b+2}, ..., C_k$ as "normal"(Every object is considered to be normal).

2.2   Neural Network

Neural network, sometimes called multilayer perceptron, essentially speaking, is simplification model formed by the mode of mind's dealing with information. It works through simulating a great number of inter-connective simple disposing cells, which seem like the nonfigurative edition of nerve cells. The categories of neural network models include: perceptron, radial basis function network, probability neural network, broad-sense regress neural network, Hopfield neural network, Elman network, self-organizing feature mapping network, adaptive resonance theory network and so on. The most commonly used neural network model is BP three layer network model, which is constituted by input layer, hidden layer and output layer. Each crunode is connected. Weight value represents the connection strength of connecting every layer cell, which is gradually changing as the study to network.

3   The Experiment Process

3.1   Using the Abnormal Detection to Set Up Data Stream

Pretreating the application data of financial subsidy for agriculture development as figure 1:

Fig. 1. Data pretreatment

Data collection includes 9 fields: ID, unique identifier; name, name of applicant; geographical location (middle part / north / southwest/southeast); the quality of the field; rainfall, the rainfall of the field during every year; field earning, declared yearly field earning; main crops, corn/ wheat/potato/rapeseed ; the type of application, the type of financial subsidy applied; requisition sum, the sum of financial subsidy applied.

Using "clementine" data mining software and quickly setting up the flow chart as the following figure 2:

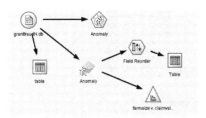

Fig. 2. Anomalous points detection flow   **Fig. 3.** Anomalous points detection result

Abnormal records could be quickly screened out by anomalous points detecting nodes; the detection result is displayed as figure 3. Abnormal detection is founded on cluster method. Through establishing abnormal points detection model to produce "$0-Anomaly" fields, latent abnormal records are showed. Then the holistic abnormal exponential value of each record is computed; at the same time, the three fields of claimtype, maincrop and region, the most probably causing abnormal records, emerge from the equity combinations. From the requisition sum, the sizes of fields are protracted; meanwhile, "$0-Anomaly" fields are attached to check the abnormal records. Figure 4 and figure 5 are charts of anomalous points dispersive points, which show the biggest, the smallest requisition and other requisition.

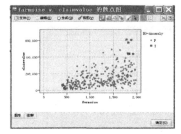 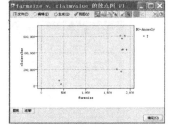

Fig. 4. Dispersive points   **Fig. 5.** Dispersive points

In abnormal detection models, non-abnormal records are chosen to give up and latent abnormal records tagged are listed; then the holistic abnormal exponential value of each record is also listed, and the equity combinations and the fields of most probably causing abnormal records are standing out, as figure 6:

	Id	$0-Anomaly	$0-AnomalyIndex	$0-PeerGroup	$0-Field-1	$0-FieldImpact-1	$0-Field-2	$0-FieldImpact-2
1	id633	T	1.600	2	claimvalue	0.358	farminco.	0.275
2	id647	T	1.403	2	farminco...	0.334	claimvalue	0.181
3	id654	T	1.495	2	rainfall	0.322	maincrop	0.181
4	id703	T	1.358	1	rainfall	0.233	region	0.219
5	id704	T	1.427	2	farminco...	0.267	maincrop	0.190
6	id736	T	1.604	2	claimvalue	0.404	farminco.	0.233
7	id752	T	1.770	2	claimvalue	0.391	farminco.	0.155
8	id791	T	1.366	1	maincrop	0.238	rainfall	0.163
9	id913	T	1.641	1	region	0.181	landquality	0.160
10	id983	T	1.350	2	region	0.167	maincrop	0.166

Fig. 6. Abnormal data records

3.2   Using Neural Network to Carry through Analyzing

To keep on analyzing, exploration chart could be used to investigate the data, then help to create assumed conditions which are useful for modeling. As abnormal fields hereinbefore belong to the requisition type of 'claimtype", the type of humbug existing in data may be that one field appears synchronously more than one piece of financial subsidy application form. To find out the repeating applying, distribution chart is the tool to check. As figure 7 and figure 8 exhibit: farmers, name=618 and name=777, hand in more than one piece of financial subsidy application form; before analyzing the data, repeating applying should be eliminated.

Fig. 7. Applied fields distribution   **Fig. 8.** Eliminated data

According to each field's characters applied for subsidy, the language of CLEM in "Clementine" can be brought to educe the new fields; by the size of the fields, the types of main crops and the agrotype, the expected income of this field is evaluated, which is presented as figure 9 and 10:

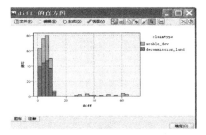

Fig. 9. Income difference histogram   **Fig. 10.** Chosen data

Figure 9 is an income difference histogram of expected income and real income. By this histogram, it is obvious to see the warp existing in the types of applying. There is a big warp in the type named as " arable_dev" financial subsidy. As figure 10, the record whose applying type is named as " arable_dev" is chosen to train neural network. One could mount the direction of the applied sum " claimvalue" field as output and other fields as input variable, then use BP neural network to train results, which is showed as figure 11:

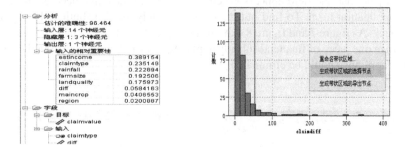

Fig. 11. Neural network training chart   **Fig. 12.** Claimdiff straight cube chart

The training results show that expected applying sum basically match real applying sum in most cases. For showing the differences between the real applying sum and the pre-evaluated applying sum, another Claimdff fields (which are similar to the income difference fields educed previously) are educed to produce Claimdff straight cube chart. This chart reveals the applicants whose applying sums are bigger than the pre-evaluated applying sum. The chart is figure 12.

Lining out areas in straight cube chart produces a selecting node to further investigate those applicants whose Claimdiff values are comparatively more than 50%, as figure 13:

	id	name	region	farmsize	claimdiff	rainfall	landquality	farmincc
1	id613	name613	southeast	440	76.792	86	3	115544.
2	id627	name627	southeast	500	61.578	93	3	102720.
3	id628	name628	southeast	880	112.780	15	5	70439.
4	id773	name773	midlands	500	117.633	15	7	56220.
5	id896	name896	southeast	1120	85.263	15	5	81314.
6	id897	name897	midlands	580	129.410	27	4	60611.
7	id899	name899	north	480	69.459	35	5	81809.

Fig. 13. The abnormal data record of neural network training

3.3   Using Cluster Method to Analysis

Using cluster method to analysis the abnormal data records, as figure 14:

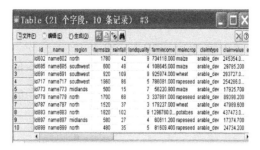

Fig. 14. The abnormal data record based on cluster method

4   Conclusion

Anomalous detection is a research hotspot in the area of data mining. It could be a method of data filtrating that can avoid the mistakes in the later period of data mining; but also could be considered as a technology of data mining, combined with other arithmetic model to be applied to fault diagnosing, computer network inbreak checking, business humbug detecting and so on. Therefore, studying efficient and exact anomaly detection method has important significance and practical value. This paper uses two models, neural network and anomalous detection, to analyze and compare the abnormal data, then further analyzes the data of applying for subsidy, finally finds out the probably existing humbug. The experimental results prove the validity and feasibility of the two methods, and provide a very effective data detection method for the management department.

References

1. Li, H.: The Application of One Improved Cluster Method in Abnormal Detection. Microelectronics and Computer (08), 66–69 (2010)
2. Zhoujunlin: Distributed No-supervising Anomaly Detection Based on Models Sharing. The Transaction in Zhengzhou University (01), 89–92 (2010)
3. Zhaoliangdong: One Abnormal Detection Method Based on Improved BP Neural Network. Micro-computer Information (28), 216–218 (2010)
4. Chenbin, Chensongcan: Anomaly Detection Overview. Transaction in Shandong University (06), 13–22 (2009)

Clustering System Call Arguments for Remote Attestation

Hongjiao Li, Xiuxia Tian, Weimin Wei, and Chaochao Sun

School of Computer and Information Engineering, Shanghai University of Electric Power,
Shanghai, 200090
hjli@shiep.edu.cn

Abstract. In trusted computing, remote attestation is an essential feature to determine the trustworthiness of a remote platform by analyzing its integrity. In this paper, we present a new paradigm that leverages clustering system call arguments for integrity measurement and reporting in remote attestation. The major contribution of this paper is two-folds: (1) We introduce a clustering process to characterize system call arguments. (2) We introduce model verification for efficient trust reporting. Our proposed technique is evaluated on a real world dataset extracted from a Linux System. The results show that different clustering algorithms can achieve different average accuracy while introduce low overheads.

Keywords: Remote Attestation, System Call Arguments, Clustering.

1 Introduction

In distributed computing environments, it is crucial to measure whether a remote party runs buggy, malicious application codes or is improperly configured. Remote attestation techniques have been proposed for this purpose by analyzing the integrity of a remote system to determine its trustworthiness. Typical attestation mechanisms are designed based on the following steps. First, an attestation requester (attester) sends a challenge to a target system (attestee), which responds with the evidence of the integrity of its hardware and software components. Second, the attester derives runtime properties of the attestee and determines the trustworthiness of the attestee. Finally and optionally, the attester returns an attestation result, such as integrity status, to the attestee.

Various attestation approaches and techniques have been proposed. Integrity Measurement Architecture (IMA) [1] is an implementation of TCG [2] approach to provide verifiable evidence with respect to the current runtime state of a measured system. Moreover, several attestation methods have been introduced to address privacy properties [3], system behaviors [4], and information flow model [5-6]. System call sequence-based remote attestation [7-9] is a new avenue in remote attestation research and will lead to several new and improved techniques of remotely verifying the behavior of a platform in a flexible and scalable manner. In this paper, we focus on clustering system call arguments for efficient and accurate remote attestation. The main contributions of our work are: (1) We introduce a clustering process to create correlations among different arguments of the same system call to achieve better characterization. Therefore, the clustering step aims to capture relationships among the values of

J. Lei et al. (Eds.): NCIS 2012, CCIS 345, pp. 70–78, 2012.
© Springer-Verlag Berlin Heidelberg 2012

various arguments (e.g., to create correlations among some filenames and specific opening modes). (2) In remote attestation, it is necessary to measure system call sequences on a remote platform and reporting them to the challenger in an efficient and trustworthy manner. We introduce a model verification method to fulfill efficient integrity verification process.

This paper is organized as follows. Section 2 briefly overviews exist system call sequence-based remote attestation mechanisms. Section 3 describes leveraging system call arguments clustering for integrity measurement and reporting. In Section 4 we elaborate and compare the evaluation results using different clustering algorithms. Section 5 concludes this paper.

2   Related Works on System Call Sequenced-Based Remote Attestation

In traditional security research, such as intrusion detection systems (ids), some of the most successful behavior measurement techniques revolve around the concept of sequences of system calls originating from an application [10-12]. In the context of remote attestation, measurement of behavior through system calls has been studied previously. Gu et al. [7-8] have proposed the use of measuring the set of system calls made by a target application at runtime and comparing them with the benchmark. The benchmark is obtained by statically analyzing the calls made by a pristine copy of the application, either through source code analysis or a disassembly process in case the source is not available. The method has a lot of potential but has several limitations: reporting all system calls made by a process to a remote platform is a serious bottle-neck. The number of calls made by a typical mail server, for example, may easily reach several million within the span of a few days' uptime [13]. Tamleek Ali et al [9] present a new approach which allows the modeling of an application's behavior through stochastic models of machine learning. The paper details the process of how to use sequences of system calls as a metric for stochastic models to predict the trustworthi-ness of a target application. Experiments show that the method is feasible and effective in identifying malicious behavior. Consequently, the mechanism is a flexible attestation mechanism to measure the dynamic behavior of a target application.

It is remarkable that none of above works have utilized other features of system calls, such as, system call arguments or the return values of system calls. This is due to the inherent complexity of the task, but undoubtedly system call arguments contain a wide range of information that can be useful for remote attestation. Such information in system call arguments can be further utilized for increasing accuracy and robustness.

3   Leveraging System Call Arguments Clustering for Remote Attestation

Figure 1 shows our proposed system call sequence-based remote attestation architec-ture. There are two aspects of this architecture: 1) Trusted measurement and reporting mechanisms at the target platform; 2) Verification mechanisms at the challenger end. Our paper focuses on the first aspect.

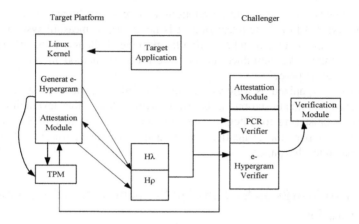

Fig. 1. System Call Sequenced-based Remote Attestattion

3.1   System Call Sequence Capturing

Capturing critical system calls made by an executable is a fairly trivial task. We implemented this logging mechanism in the following steps:

(1) The system call **Strace** is used to monitor specified process, and store the data to file, at the same time, calculate the related information about each system call, such as system call name, system call arguments, execution time, times and error numbers , etc.

(2) In [9], it is pointed out that including the scarcely used system calls in the dataset significantly reduced the accuracy of the model. We therefore use occurring time in **Strace** to find the most-often used system calls. Also, in our implementation, we are interested in logging certain system calls that we identify as being critical according to its dangerous level, it allows the users to specify critical system calls with respect the two factors from Table 1.

Table 1. System Call Level

dangerous level	system call
heavy	chmod, chown, chown32, fchmod, fchown, fchown32, lchown, lchown32, link, mknod, mount, open, rename, symlink, unlink
middle	close, creat, dup2, flock, ftruncate, ftruncate64, ioctl, mkdir, nfsservctl, quotactl, rmdir, truncate, truncate64, umount, umount2
mild	chdir, chroot, fchdrir, fcntl, fcntl64, fsync, llseek, lseek, newselect, poll, pread, putpmsg, pwrite, read, readv, sendfile, umask, utime, afs_syscall, write, writev
safe	other system calls

(3) Our system call sequence representation scheme is an improved Hypergram, proposed by Mehdi et al. [11], called e-Hypergram. The e-Hypergram is a structure reflecting short sequences of system calls associated with its arguments in a k–dimensional hyperspace, where k is equal to the number of unique system calls. Therefore, each dimension represents one type of system call associating its arguments that need to be measured.

For each program, the e-Hypergram is initialized to lie at the origin of the hypercube of k dimensions. The process of e-Hypergram generating is the same as Hypergram. The difference is that on the occurrence of each system call i: the system call associated with its arguments are stored. After the process has terminated, we cluster system call arguments along each dimension.

3.2   Clustering System Call Arguments

In the context of remote attestation, we applied a hierarchical clustering algorithm to find, for each system call, sub-clusters of invocation with similar arguments; we are interested in creating models on these clusters, and not on the general system call, in order to better capture integrity normal and deviations.

The core step in creating a good clustering is of course the definition of the distance among different sets of arguments. We proceed by comparing corresponding argu-ments in the calls, and for each couple of arguments, we compute

$$d_a = \begin{cases} K(.)+\alpha(i)\delta(i) \\ 0 \end{cases} \qquad \begin{array}{l} if \dots the \dots elements \dots are \dots differnent \\ otherwise \end{array}$$

Where $K(.)$ is a fixed quantity that creates a "step" between different elements, while the second term is the real distance between the arguments $\delta(i)$, normalized by a pa-rameter $\alpha(.)$. Note that above formula is a template: the use of (.) denotes that such variables are parametric with respect to the type of argument; how $K(.)$, $\alpha(.)$ and $\delta(i)$ are computed will be detailed below for each type of argument. The distance between two different system calls, i and j, is computed as the sum of distances among corres-ponding arguments $D(i,j) = \sum_{a \in A} d_a$ (where A is the set of system call arguments).

As stated, at least four different types of arguments are passed to system calls: pathnames and filenames, discrete numeric values, arguments passed to programs for execution, users and group identifiers (UIDs and GIDs).   For each type of argument, it is necessary to design a representative model and an appropriate distance function as the method proposed in [14].

●   **Path Names and Filenames.** Pathnames and filenames are very frequently used in system calls. They have complex structures, rich of useful information and, there-fore, difficult to model properly. The first interesting information is commonality of the path, since files residing in the same branch of the file system are usually more similar than the ones in different branches.

Usually, inside a path, the first and last directories carry the most significance. If the filename has a similar structure to other filenames, this is indicative: for instance, common prefixes in the filename, such as the prefix lib, or common suffixes such as the extensions. We choose to reuse a very simple model --the directory tree depth. This is easy to compute and experimentally lead to fairly good results even if very simple.

● **Discrete Numeric Values.** Discrete numeric values, such as flags, opening modes, and so forth are usually chosen from a limited set. Therefore, we can store all of them along with a discrete probability. Since in this case two values can only be equal or different, we set up a binary distance model for clustering, where the distance between x and y is

$$d_a = \begin{cases} Kdisc \\ 0 \end{cases} \qquad \begin{matrix} x \neq y \\ x = y \end{matrix}$$

and K_{disc}, as usual, is a configuration parameter.

● **Execution Argument.** The execution argument (i.e., the arguments passed to the execve syscall) is difficult to model, but we found the length to be an extremely effective indicator of similarity of use. Therefore, we set up a binary distance model, where the distance between x and y is

$$d_a = \begin{cases} K \, arg \\ 0 \end{cases} \qquad \begin{matrix} |x| \neq |y| \\ |x| = |y| \end{matrix}$$

denoting with |x| the length of x and with K_{arg} a configuration parameter. In this way, arguments with the same length are clustered together. For each cluster, we compute the minimum and maximum values of the length of arguments.

● **UID or GID.** Many arguments express UIDs or GIDs, so we developed an ad hoc model for user and group identifiers. Our reasoning is that all these discrete values have three different meanings: UID 0 is reserved to the super-user; low values usually are for system special users, while real users have UIDs and GIDs above a threshold (usually 1,000). So, we divided the input space into these three groups and computed the distance for clustering using the following formula:

$$d_a = \begin{cases} Kuid \\ 0 \end{cases}_, \qquad \begin{matrix} if..belonging..to..differnent..groups \\ if..belonging..to..the..same..group \end{matrix}$$

and K_{uid}, as usual, is a user-defined parameter. Since UIDs are limited in number, they are preserved for testing, without associating a discrete probability to them. The probability for a new input to belong to the model is 1 if the UID belongs to the learned set and 0 otherwise.

3.3   System Call Arguments Measurement and Reporting

For system call arguments, integrity measurement is performed along each dimension. In each of these routines, we call a measurement function that calculates the values of system call arguments associated with originating executable. The hash of clusters computed and the hash of its representative models are extended into PCR-11. The task of reporting the measured e-Hypergram is far from trivial. Transmitting such a huge log over a network readily becomes a bottleneck for any remote attestation technique. On the other hand, if the complete log is not reported, the value of the PCR cannot be verified simply from the PCR_quote structure. The novelty of our approach is that the verification utilizes the hash of clusters, and the representative models of clustering process. For this purpose, we introduce the concept of model verification. For each dimension, the hash of clusters, and representative model and its appropriate distance function are utilized to fulfill the verification. When an attestation request is received, a piece of trusted code within kernel space performs verification of the e-Hypergram log created during the measurement process. We call this log for system call arguments local verification (H_λ). Hashes of entries in H_λ are aggregated in the same manner as the PCR_extend operation of the TPM. The aggregated value is compared with the expected value retrieved from the PCR_quote operation over PCR to ensure that none of the entries in H_λ has been tampered with. This process is termed as system call arguments verification of H_λ.

Upon successful verification, the final values of e-Hypergram associated with each process are stored in another log file termed as e-Hypergram log for remote verification ($H\rho$). With each entry in $H\rho$, PCR-12 is extended with the hash of the entry. Thus, $H\rho$ contains one entry per process thus significantly reducing the size of the log. Finally, $H\rho$ and PCR_quote over PCR-12 is returned to the challenger where it can be verified and validated.

4   Experiments and Evaluation

4.1   Data Clustering Under Weka

In order to ensure that our results can be reproduced, we have utilized the traces of system calls available in the datasets provided by UNM [11]. We take Stide [10] input format system call sequences and a mapping process to generate e-Hypergram. It allows the user to specify critical system calls. The e-Hypergram produced is used to train the stochastic model based on different machine learning techniques. We generate training data from the UNM datasets for *ftp* process. After dataset has been collected and transformed, we use the popular Wikato Environment for Knowledge Analysis (Weka) tool [15].

4.2   Results and Discussions

To verify the effectiveness of our clustering method for remote attestation, we do experiments from following aspects.

4.2.1   Clustering Results for Different Clustering Algorithm

We use a single connection method in hierarchical aggregation algorithms, including: Nearest neighbor, Furthest neighbor, Between groups average, Ward method and K-means algorithm (which is a classification clustering algorithm), using the collected datasets, perform randomized 20 times the clustering experiments, comparison of results list in Table 2.

Table 2. Clustering Results for different clustering algorithms

Algorithms	Average accuracy of running 20 cycles (%)
Nearest neighbor	67
Furthest neighbor	83
Between groups average	72.7
Ward method	86.3
K-means	80.60

Table 2 shows the average accuracy values for different clustering algorithms. It can be concluded that the Nearest neighbor and Between groups average algorithms performed relatively poorly in this scenario. Furthest neighbor, Ward method and K-means algorithms provide better results than these two. Using Ward method algorithm, we were able to achieve the highest average accuracy of 86.3.

4.2.2   Running Times for Clustering System Call Arguments

One of the main hurdles in making a remote attestation with system call arguments possible can be its processing overhead. Clustering system call arguments introduce different time complexity. There is need to consider the difference between different clustering algorithms.

Table 3. Running times for different clustering algorithms

Algorithms	Average running times with clustering arguments (s)
Nearest neighbor	1.5731025
Furthest neighbor	1.5243585
Between groups average	1.4926595
Ward method	2.299265
K-means	0.002832

Table 3 shows the running times for different clustering algorithms. On the whole, the running times of clustering algorithms are not long. By comparison, The Ward method algorithm takes the longest time to fulfill clustering process; The Furthest neighbor and Between groups average algorithms make little difference in running times. Compared with hierarchical aggregation algorithms, we found that the classification clustering algorithm K-means performs the best.

5   Conclusions

System call arguments can improve accuracy in remote attestation research and will lead to several new and improved techniques of remotely verifying the behavior of a platform in a flexible and scalable manner. In this paper, we have discussed clustering system call arguments for remote attestation. We have presented the implementation details and compared the experiment results under different clustering algorithms with respect to system call arguments. End results show that different clustering algorithms can achieve different AUC. The overhead introduced by clustering is low. The next step is to use the verification results to predict levels of trustworthiness of the target platform.

Acknowledgments. This paper is supported by the Innovation Program of Shanghai Municipal Education Commission under Grant No. 11YZ194 and No. 12YZ146, No. 12YZ147; Natural Science Foundation of Shanghai under Grant No. 11ZR1414300 ; the Key Technologies R&D Program of Shanghai Science and Technology Commission under Grant No. 10dz1501000.

References

[1] Sailer, R., Zhang, X., Jaeger, T., van Doorn, L.: Design and Implementation of a TCG-based Integrity Measurement Architecture. In: Proceedings of the 13th Conference on USENIX Security Symposium, SSYM 2004 (2004)

[2] Trusted Computing Group, TCG Specification Architecture Overview – Specification Revision 1.2 (April 2004), https://www.trustedcomputinggroup.org

[3] Chen, L., Landfermann, R., Löhr, H., Rohe, M., Sadeghi, A.-R.: A Protocol for Property-Based Attestation. In: Proceedings of the 1st ACM Workshop on Scalable Trusted Computing, NovaScotia Canada, pp. 7–16 (2006)

[4] Haldar, V., Chandra, D., Franz, M.: Semantic Remote Attestation: a Virtual Machine Directed Approach to Trusted Computing. In: USENIX Conference on Virtual Machine Research and Technology Symposium (2004)

[5] Jaeger, T., Sailer, R., Shankar, U.: PRIMA: Policy-Reduced Integrity Measurement Architecture. In: ACM SACMAT (2006)

[6] Xu, W., Zhang, X., Hu, H., Ahn, G.-J., Seifert, J.-P.: Remote Attestation with Domain-based Integrity Model and Policy Analysis. IEEE Transactions on Dependable and Secure Computing, 61 (2011)

[7] Gu, L., Ding, X., Deng, R., Xie, B., Mei, H.: Remote Attestation on Program Execution. In: Proceedings of the 2008 ACM Workshop on Scalable Trusted Computing, STC 2008. ACM, New York (2008)

[8] Gu, L., Cheng, Y., Ding, X., Deng, R., Guo, Y., Shao, W.: Remote Attestation on Function Execution. In: Proceedings of the 2009 International Conference on Trusted Systems, Trust 2009 (2009)

[9] Ali, T., Nauman, M., Zhang, X.: On Leveraging Stochastic Models for Remote Attestation. In: Chen, L., Yung, M. (eds.) INTRUST 2010. LNCS, vol. 6802, pp. 290–301. Springer, Heidelberg (2011)

[10] Forrest, S., Hofmeyr, S., Somayaji, A., Longstaff, T.: A Sense of Self for Unix Processes. In: IEEE Symposium on Security and Privacy, pp. 120–128 (1996)

[11] Mehdi, B., Ahmed, F., Khayyam, S., Farooq, M.: Towards a Theory of Generalizing System Call Representation For In-Execution Malware Detection. In: Proceedings of the IEEE International Conference on Communications, ICC 2010 (2010)

[12] Mutz, D., Robertson, W., Vigna, G., Kemmerer, R.A.: Exploiting Execution Context for the Detection of Anomalous System Calls. In: Kruegel, C., Lippmann, R., Clark, A. (eds.) RAID 2007. LNCS, vol. 4637, pp. 1–20. Springer, Heidelberg (2007)

[13] University of New Mexico: Computer Immune Systems -Datasets, http://www.cs.unm.edu/~immsec/systemcalls.html (accessed May 2010)

[14] Maggi, F., Matteucci, M., Zanero, S.: Detecting Intrusions through System Call Sequence and Argument Analysis. IEEE Transactions on Dependable and Secure Computing 7(4), 381–394 (2010)

[15] Hall, M., Frank, E., Holmes, G., Pfahringer, B., Reutemann, P., Witten, I.: The WEKA data mining software: An update. ACM SIGKDD Explorations Newsletter 11(1), 10–18 (2009)

Document Selective Protection Based on Third Service Framework

Mei Xue, Zhongxiong Yuan, and Jing Li

School of Computer and Information Science, Shanghai University of Electric Power, China
{qq.snow,yzx19700701}@163.com, lijing@shiep.edu.cn

Abstract. In this paper we present a selective protection solution based on the third service framework to achieve partial content protection in one document, which has the capability of enforcing diverse access control policies on different parts in addition to ensuring content confidentiality, integrity and non-repudiation. The approach we proposed has the flexibility of a more fine-grained content protection and lifecycle tracking capability compared with the nowadays DRM techniques. At the end of this paper we set up a prototype system which demonstrates our approach is feasible and can achieve the security of selective protection in one document.

Keywords: selective protection, third service provider, distributed document service, license service, tracking service.

1 Introduction

With the popularity and convenience of network connectivity in daily life, more and more individuals have the requirements to protect their digital documents, which are of valuable or sensitive [1]. The digital document is easy to spread, which leads content leakage to those illegal users. Actually the document is out of creator's control once users get the document, for they could juggle the content or send to other illegal users, all these damage the document creator's interests. In other scenario like OA system in the government or company, a file sent to multi-receivers who have diverse rights on different parts of one document, the sender has to prepare several different document versions for diverse receivers respectively.

In the above paradigms the critical problem to be resolved is to guarantee the digital document security, and what is more important is to afford the individuals the flexibility of selective protection, which enforces particular access control policies on different parts of one document so as to meet the creator's personal requirements, along with the lifecycle tracking capability to provide the document creator the document use map or distribution map.

The rest of this paper is organized in the following way: In Section 2, we review the related work of data protection methods and DRM. Section 3 proposes the third service provider framework. Section 4 discusses the selective protection in detail. We set up a prototype system in Section 5, and finally we conclude in Section 6.

J. Lei et al. (Eds.): NCIS 2012, CCIS 345, pp. 79–88, 2012.
© Springer-Verlag Berlin Heidelberg 2012

2   Related Work

A fundamental method of data protection in the area of information and network security is cryptography, which has been widely accepted as a traditional platform of data protection for decades. The application of cryptography is particularly prevalent in nowadays' information technology era [2]. Through the data encryption and decryption, the protection of data confidentiality and integrity are achieved.

The selective protection proposed in this paper is distinguished from the selective encryption [3][4],which are mainly applied in the field of secure multimedia communications, as the volume of multimedia data is huge to transmit and the cost will be overwhelmed if each packet is encrypted or decrypted. The focus we discuss in this paper is on how to protect the partial contents in one document.

Recent research has been extensively carried on the area of DRM [5][6][7], which is used to prevent the unauthorized users from accessing protected content. DRM employs several security techniques such as cryptography, watermark, and access control etc. to achieve the content security. The well-known foreign products are Windows RM [8] (Rights Management) released by Microsoft and Locklizard [9]. Windows RM solution allows information owners to encrypt a variety of electronic data (especially Microsoft Office 2003 applications) and set control policies on them. RM can be used to prevent illegal use of the document. Locklizard ensures the security of PDF documents, files, web pages, images, e-tutorials and software, and prevents them from copied, printed, and content shared. Domestic document security products are mainly two kinds: Founder Apabi system [10] and the forefront of cutting-edge computer technology Co., Ltd. Management System (eDocGuard) system [11].

Although nowadays DRM techniques protecting the document against the illegal users to some extent, but in the case the document creator is willing to share parts of the document instead of the whole document with the specified users and preferred to assign different access control policies on different parts respectively, they can't satisfy the need of content part protection. In addition, they can't track the whole distribution, which help the creator master his document flow so as to detect illegal user as soon as possible. In order to resolve the above problems with enough flexibility, we propose our selective protection scheme based on the third service Provider.

3   Our Proposed Third Service Provider Framework

Our framework is composed of three parts: Client Service Controller at Document Creator side, Client Service Controller at Document User side and Third Service Provider at Server side which includes three services specifically, as shown in Figure1. The Third Service Provider can integrate the three services into one Server or deploy them into different Servers.

–   Client Service Controller
The Client Service Controller should have the capabilities of implementing encapsulating the document into a protected form and restoring the protected form into its

original form at the client side based on the selective protection proposed in this paper, deriving the license from the Third Service Provider, controlling rights enforcement and querying the tracking information from the third service provider. The Client Service Controller could be implemented by software or hardware.

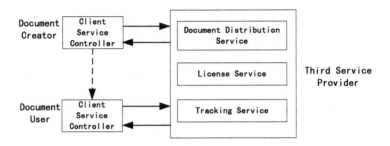

Fig. 1. The Third Service Provider Architecture

–   Document Distribution Service

Document Distribution Service is mainly for distributing the selective protection document. There are two distribution means for document creator: (1) sending it to the receiver directly through mails or other peer-to-peer service; (2) uploading and storing it at the Document Distribution Service which publishes the relevant information of the document for user to find and get his desired document. User also has two means to derive the protected document. Specifically, the document can be pushed to the receiver by the Document Distribution Service or pulled from Document Distribution Service alternatively as well. It's up to the design requirements.

–   License Service

License Service should have the capability of storing the personal access control policies defined by the document creator and issuing licenses to the requesting user. The access control policy in our framework is the criterion to permit user to access the protected content. It can be expressed as access rights list, that is, principal owns the right on resource if and only if he meets certain condition:

$$SR=<principal, resource, condition, right>$$

There are several tools to describe SR, such as Extensible Access Control Markup Language (XACML) [12], OASIS Rights Language Technical Committee [13], MPEG Rights Expression Language[14][15], Digital Property Rights Language (DPRL), Open eBook Forum (OeBF) [16], Extensible Rights Markup Language (XrML) [17], IEEE LTSC DREL Project (Digital Rights Expression Language), Open Digital Rights Language (ODRL) [18] .

Before the user implements his rights on the protected part of the document, he should acquire the license from the License Service.

- Tracking Service

Lifecycle tracking is of significance to control protected document distribution and its use, based on which the document creator could easily get the document distribution map and use map. Once security problem occurs in the protected document, it's easy to locate the source of illegal operation, which improves the situation of uncontrollable distribution to some extent. Meantime, the audit information from the lifecycle tracking provides the basis of statistics analysis for document and presents a series of market-related information of document (if the document is for business purpose).

The tracking capability requires the Client Service Provider has three functionalities (1) recording user's operation-related information at each step of document lifecycle (2) storing the tracking information (3) generating the audit information according to the corresponding tracking information. However, with the document widely distributed, the problem of tracking information expansion rises if storing all the tracking information into the Client Service Provider. Thereby, Tracking Service at the Third Service Provider is introduced to store and audit the tracking information. By storing the tracking information into Tracking Service at regular intervals, the Client Service Controller only keep the latest tracking information. When the creator needs the tracking information of document, they can get them from the Tracking Service through Client Service Controller.

IV. Our Selective Protection Approach

In our proposed approach, selective protection means that the document creator can decide the parts to be protected in the document and assign the access control policies on them. Therefore, a document after implemented our selective protection is composed of several selective protection parts and other unprotected parts. Each protection part is relatively independent entity which can employ different cryptography and have its own access control policy.

- **Selective Protection Form**

In our approach, the protected part is embedded into the document at the position of its original part. The ideal form for document after selective protection does not change its original file format (eg. file format of *.doc after protection is still *.doc). Figure 2 shows an ideal integrated document form after selective protection. FC denotes the unprotected part and G denotes the protected part.

| FC1 | G1 | FC2 · · · | Gn | FCm |

Fig. 2. An ideal integrated document form after selective protection

While the actual file format is modified due to the additional information added into the document to secure the document transmission security which can't be distinguished by the original document application. Therefore, the Client Service Controller should filter the additional information firstly and make use of the local document application to distinguish the embedded protection part from the unprotected parts and enforce control measures based on the predefined access control policy.

− Document XML Representation after Selective Protection

Based on the above analysis, a document contained two selective protection parts expressed in XML is as follows:

```
<FILE>
        <FreeContent>
        unprotected part
        </FreeContent>
        <Section>
         Selective protection part
        </Section>
        <FreeContent>
        unprotected part
        </FreeContent>
        <Section>
        Selective protection part
        </Section>
        <FreeContent>
        unprotected part
        </FreeContent>
    </FILE>
```

− **Integrated Selective Protection Document Produce Scheme**

The above XML representation provides us a reasonable structure of integrated protected parts with unprotected parts in a document, which is easy to extend to add the additional security information. Figure 3 shows the integrated selective protection document producing scheme:

The whole process of creating an integrated selective protection document is as follows:

(1) Document Creator divides a document into the parts to be protected and the parts unprotected $\left(\sum_i PCi + \sum_i FCi \right)$;

(2) Encrypt the PCi with KS, assign the PCi access control policy and additional copyright message, and combine the both into Gi.

(3) Repeat (2) until all desired content are protected, Combine all unprotected parts with all protected parts to get a new document protection form PF, $PF = \sum_i FC(i) +$

$\sum_i Gi$;

(4) Get the Hash value on PF as the information digest, and encrypt it with the KR as its signature.

(5) Combine the PF with the signature into WPF.

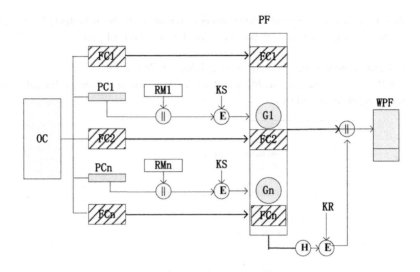

Fig. 3. The integrated document produce scheme

OC=Original Content   FCi=NO i Free Content   PCi=NO i Content to Protect
T=Protection Tag   ‖=Combination of two blocks   E=Encrypt
KS=Key   RMi=Use Rule & CopyRight Message for PCi
PF=Protected File   Gi=Selective Protection on Part i   H=Hash algorithm
KR=Private Key   WPF=Integrated Selective Protection File

- **Authorization and Authentication in Using Integrated Selective Protection Document**

In our selective protection approach, user can view the unprotected parts without acquiring any permission after received the selective protection document, while he should acquire the license before he implements rights (such as view) on the protected ones. One of the key points of our approach is all operations no matter on protected parts or unprotected parts should be performed under the Client Service Controller. The Third Service Provider enforces the authorization and authentication for user as well as an alternative distribution means. The basic steps of authentication and authorization process are as follows:

(1) Document creator creates an integrated selective protection document under the Client Service Controller.

(2) Document creator sends his access control policies assigned on specified protection parts to the License Service which stores these access control policies and issues license to the requesting user.

(3) Creator sends the protected document to the user through mails (or through Document Distribution Service).

(4) User views the unprotected parts of the document, if he wants to view one of the protected parts (Gi), he should send a request (REQ) encrypted with License Service Provider's (LS) public key(denoted as PK) to the LS through Client Service Controller (CSC).

$$
\text{CSC:} \quad E_{PK}(REQ(User| Di| Gi \mid View)) \Rightarrow LS
$$

(5) The License Service Provider (LS) decrypts the request (REQ) with its private key (SK), authenticates the user identity firstly (sometime may require the user to perform business payment if the creator distribute his document for business purpose), issues the license (LICS) to authorize the user his request rights based on the pre-submitted access policy on Gi, and then sends the LICS encrypted with user's public key (PK') to the CSC at the user side.

$$
\begin{aligned}
&\text{LS:} \quad D_{SK}(REQ(User| Di| Gi \mid View)) \\
&\text{LS:} \quad AUTH(User) \\
&\text{LS:} \quad LICS_{user}(Di|Gi|View| key) \\
&\text{LS:} \quad E_{PK'}(LICS_{user}) \Rightarrow CSC
\end{aligned}
$$

(6) The Client Service Controller (CSC) at the user side decrypts the license (LICS) with user's private key (SK'), and the user implements his rights on Gi within his right range under the Client Service Controller.

$$
\text{CSC:} \quad D_{SK'}(LICS_{user})
$$

− Security Analysis on Selective Protection

In our selective protection, we employ symmetric cryptography to encrypt the selective parts to achieve content confidentiality and define the access policies to ensure only the legal user can access the protection part within his right range under the Client Service Provider. Moreover, we employ public key system during the communication between the user and the License Service which prevents the Man-in-the-Middle attack. The Client Service Controller on the user side affirms the integrity and non-repudiation of the integrated selective protection document. Specifically, The Client Service Controller (1) decrypts the signature contained in the protected part with user private key; (2) Generate new Hash value based on the protected part, and compare it with the step(1) achieves; (3) If the two are equal, the integrated selective protection document is considered of integrity and non-repudiation after its transmission.

Although our approach provides a more fine-grained content protection which enforces different access control policies on selective protection parts in one document, it also has the symmetric cryptography's drawbacks: it's easier to be cracked compared with the asymmetry cryptography. Once the encrypting key leaked, the protected content could be accessed by other unauthorized user. In this case, the tracking service in our proposed framework is helpful to find the illegal access through the use map or distribution map.

4   Prototype System Experiment

Assuming the document distribution is in a government environment we designed a prototype system in which the document distribution is a mixture of mail-forwarding and deriving from a third server, and we employed the above discussed selective protection based on the Third Service Provider. Figure 4 shows making the access policy on the specified selective part and sequentially generating the selective protection part in a DOC file shown in figure5. Through the Client Service Controller the user acquires his license as shown in figure 6 and enforces his right (shown in figure 7) to view the specified selective protection part as shown in figure 8. Also, the document creator can view the use and distribution of the document as shown in figure 9.

Fig. 4. Make the access policy   **Fig. 5.** Generate the selective protection part

```
<RIGHTSGROUP name="Main Rights">
  <COMMENT>Rights description</COMMENT>
    <RIGHTSLIST>
      <VIEW>
        <ACCESS>
          <PRINCIPAL internal-id="5000">
            <ENABLINGBITS type="sealed-des-key">
              <VALUE                       encoding="base64"
              size="512">E75/0j...</VALUE>
            </ENABLINGBITS>
          </PRINCIPAL>
        </ACCESS>
      </VIEW>
    </RIGHTSLIST>
</RIGHTSGROUP>
```

Fig. 6. License

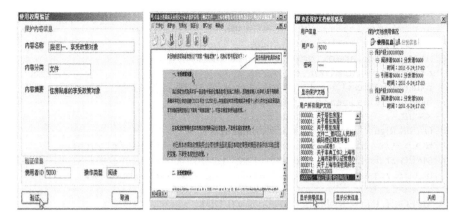

Fig. 7. Enforce rights **Fig. 8.** View the protected part **Fig. 9.** Track information

5 Conclusion

In this paper we put forward a selective protection solution to achieve partial content protection, which prevents the document creator from creating different versions for different user. The approach we proposed has flexibility of a more fine-grained content protection in addition to ensuring content confidentiality, integrity and non-repudiation compared with the nowadays DRM techniques. The prototype system demonstrates our approach is feasible to provide the user useful and reasonable choice when there's a selective protection requirement.

References

[1] Yague Mariernrna, I.: The digital information war. Online Information Review 31(1), 5–9 (2007)
[2] Jena, D., Panigrahy, S.K., Jena, S.K.: A novel and efficient cryptosystem for long message encryption. In: Proceedings of Int'l Conference on Industrial and Information Systems, pp. 7–9 (2009)
[3] Jun, L., Zou, L., Xie, C. (eds.) A two-way selective encryption algorithm for MPEG video. In: Proceedings of International Workshop on Networking, Architecture, and Storages (2006)
[4] Lian, S., Liu, Z., Ren, Z.: Secure advanced video coding based on selective encryption algorithms. IEEE Transactions on Consumer Electronics 52, 621–629 (2006)
[5] Rosenblatt, W., Trippe, W., Mooney, S.: Digital Rights Management: Business and Technology. M&T Books, New York (2002)
[6] Garnett, N.: Digital rights management, copyright, and napster. ACM SIGecom Exchanges 2(2), 1–5 (2001)
[7] Sander, T.: Golden Times for Digital Rights Management? In: Syverson, P.F. (ed.) FC 2001. LNCS, vol. 2339, pp. 55–65. Springer, Heidelberg (2002)

[8] http://www.microsoft.com/en-us/server-cloud/windows-server/active-directory-overview.aspx

[9] http://www.locklizard.com/

[10] http://www.apabi.cn/

[11] http://www.drm.net.cn/

[12] Extensible Access Control Markup Language (XACML) (2005), http://docs.oasis-open.org/xacml/2.0/XACML-2.0-OS-NORMATIVE.zip

[13] OASIS Rights Language Technical Committee, http://parallelwww.oasis-open.org/committees/rights/

[14] MPEG-21 ,Part 5: Rights Expression Language (REL), http://mpeg.telecomitalialab.com/standards/mpeg-21/mpeg-21.btm

[15] MPEG-21, Part 6: Rights Data Dictionary (RDD), http://mpeg.telecomitalialab.com/standards/mpeg-21/mpeg-21.Htm

[16] Open eBook Forum (OeBF), http://www.openebook.org/specifications/rrwgcoordinated.html

[17] ContentGuard Extensible Rights Markup Language (XrML) (2001), http://www.xrml.org/

[18] Open Digital Rights Language (ODRL) (2002), http://www.w3.org/TR/odrl/

Fine-Grain Trusted Storage and Transitivity Policy for Open Network Environment

Lin Zhang and Ruchuan Wang

College of Computer, Nanjing University of Posts and Telecommunications, Nanjing,
210003, China
zhangl@njupt.edu.cn

Abstract. Trusted system will be an important trend of the research in the field of security. The new architecture of trusted model is proposed for open network, which describes the trust-building processes from many ways. Fine-grain trusted storage structures are designed based on interaction ability and honesty capability, which are based on n history windows. On this condition, trusted transitivity tree based on honesty is studied, which enhances the rationality of the model. Then trusted path-searching policy is presented, which is based on depth-first traversal. Experimental results show that new trusted models conform to the social communication relations.

Keywords: open network, trust model, storage, transitivity.

1 Introduction

With the rapid development of computer and network technology, traditional security schemes have not met the needs of open network, such as grid, P2P, ad hoc and so on. For example, authentication[1], access control[2] and authorization[3] mechanisms are mostly based on identities and credentials and deployed in the relatively stable domains. At the same time they acquiesce that there are some trust relationships among nodes in open network in advance. But nodes in open network are abundant, distributed, dynamic and independent in a large degree. So it is necessary for us to integrate trust mechanism into traditional security schemes in order to make system be more believable and responsible.

Since Anderson presented the concept of trusted system in the 70s of 20th century, the trusted problem has been focused in the field of information system. About trusted terminal units, domestic scholars have studied a lot[4-6]. Most of them are discussing how to embed TPM(Trusted Platform Module) into terminal units better.

In addition, scholars have presented lots of trust models based on different mathematics methods for open network[7-10],such as probability, D-S evidence, fuzzy sets, cloud fuzzy etc. These researches have driven the development of trust model. But, there are some kinds of deficiency which must be noticed quietly for us.

(1) Trust models lay particular stress on the subjective factors, which will induce the trust evaluation results inaccuracy. This is, the requirement analysis of trusted

J. Lei et al. (Eds.): NCIS 2012, CCIS 345, pp. 89–97, 2012.
© Springer-Verlag Berlin Heidelberg 2012

system has not been all-round. It is necessary to conduct a new trusted framework for open network, which will consider both the subjective factors and the objective ones.

(2) About trust storage, the hash algorithm is usually applied into select the nodes which will place the information of trust. But little of literatures can give how to design the detailed storage structure in the selected nodes.

(3) Trust transitivity is an important problem among many key technologies. Present transitivity models are mostly based on trust value to transitive the indirect recommendation trust value, which lose sight of the importance of honesty of recommenders. In addition, trust transitivity algorithm or protocols are little introduced.

The rest of this paper is organized as follows. Section 2 outlines trusted framework for open network, followed by the trust model in Section 3, such as storage structure, transitivity tree and transitivity policy. Section 4 presents the experimental investigations. The conclusions are given in Section 5.

2   Framework of Trust Model for Open Network

Definition 1. Traditional secure mechanisms are labeled objective factors, such as PKI authentication, authorization, encryption technology, secure protocols and so on. They are mostly implemented in the relativity stable environment and based on the real credentials.

Definition 2. The current trust models put emphasis on judging whether the objector is trusted or not according to its historical experience information about objector's behaviors. It is mostly an idea. So we label it as subjective factor.

It is imperative for us to integrate the objective factors and subjective ones into trusted network architecture. The detailed trusted network framework can be shown in Fig.1.

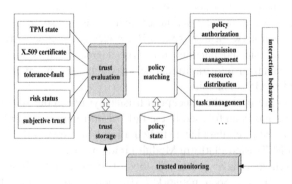

Fig. 1. Trusted network framework

Here, we study the construction scheme of trust model from 4 sides: hardware platform, software platform, objective secure factors and subjective ones. Thus, it can make trusted measurement consider multi-factors. For example, objective factors include TPM state, PKI certification, credibility and tolerance-fault of software, risk status message[12-13]. The subjective factor means the reputation and trust information based on node's behaviors.

Trust Evaluation: It will analyze the multiple subjectivity-objectivity factors, look these as its inputs and apply the appropriate evaluation arithmetic to compute the trusted degree of nodes.

Policy Matching: It will make a matching between the trust evaluation results and the policy state information. If it's successful, the trust requestor can access correlative resources. Otherwise, it is deemed the un-trusted node and is rejected.

Trust Monitoring: It will research the behavioral science of nodes in open network. It can trace the node's behaviors instantaneously and make a quick disposal on abnormal behavior, including the real time renewal on trusted state and so on, in order to make the system go forward in a virtuous way.

3   Fine-Grain Trust Model

3.1   Trusted Storage Structure

Accuracy: it is a field to express the direct interaction trust value. $accuracy \in [0,1]$.

Honesty: it expresses the fact degree of node's recommendation ability. $honesty \in [0,1]$.

Comparing with literatures[14-15], we are only concerned about the node's "accuracy" value if it is a direct trustee, and we only pay attention to its "honesty" value which represents the attitude of recommendation if it is a recommender.

Take node1 for example, the detailed storage structure about "honesty" can be shown in Tab.1.

Table 1. Storage structure of "honesty"

Node$_1$	honesty	honesty$_1$	t$_1$	honesty$_2$	t$_2$	...	honesty$_n$	t$_n$	Head
Node$_i$	0.85	0.87	time$_1$	0.6	time$_2$	...	0.7	time$_n$	3
Node$_j$									
......									

As we known, trust value of nodes can gradually reduce as time go. Of course, there are no exceptions for "honesty" and "accuracy". The late several interaction records can provide the essential reference points for the new computation of trust value. In our model, we apply n windows to record the latest n times interaction information. Here,

honesty$_i$: Value of honesty stored in the No. n windows.

t$_i$: Time of the No. n interaction.

Head : The tail hand of the n windows, which denotes the numbered window with the farthest interaction record.

honesty : The present value of "honesty", which is computed by referring to the history value of n windows abut "honesty" .

The same is the field of "accuracy".

Take "honesty" for example, for the n history records, their devotion to computation of node's trust value is very different. The farther history record is away from now, the smaller it plays a role in trusted computing. The same is the weighting factor. The formula of "honesty" is as follows.

$$honesty = \frac{\sum_{i=1}^{n} honesty_i * e^{-\frac{|t_i-t|}{\alpha_t}}}{\sum_{i=1}^{n} e^{-\frac{|t_i-t|}{\alpha_t}}} \tag{1}$$

$e^{-\frac{|t_i-t|}{\alpha_t}}$ denotes the time decrease degree. t is the present time, and α_t is a constant which is called time decrease factor.

3.2   Trusted Transitivity Tree

Most of literatures ignore the recommendation ability of nodes, that is, they think node's interaction capability is equal to recommendation ability. It is wrong.

In our model, we do not use trust degree("accuracy") to replace recommendation ability("honesty") any more. Fig.2 shows an instance of trust transitivity tree based on "accuracy" and "honesty".

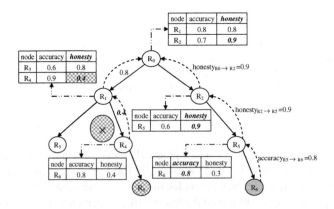

Fig. 2. A fine-grain trusted transitivity instance

Here, Node R_0 is trust requestor. He trusts node R_1 and R_2, and R_2 trusts node R_5 and so on. Let node R_6 be the service provider, then there are two transitivity paths. path$_1$: $R_0 \leftarrow R_1 \leftarrow R_4 \leftarrow R_6$; path$_2$: $R_0 \leftarrow R_2 \leftarrow R_5 \leftarrow R_6$. Additionally,

$accuracy_{R_i \rightarrow R_j}$: Direct trust value of R_j stored in the database of node R_i.

$honesty_{R_i \rightarrow R_j}$: Recommendation-honesty degree of R_j stored in the database of node R_i, which is also the history experience of node R_i.

$\Gamma_I(R_i, R_j)$: Recommendation trust value aggregated by R_i about object node R_j.
In literatures [14-15]:

$$\Gamma_I(R_0, R_6) = \frac{w(R_4)*accuracy_{R_4 \rightarrow R_6} + w(R_5)*accuracy_{R_5 \rightarrow R_6}}{w(R_4) + w(R_5)} \qquad (2)$$

$$w(R_4) = accuracy_{R_0 \rightarrow R_1} * accuracy_{R_1 \rightarrow R_4} \qquad (3)$$

$$w(R_5) = accuracy_{R_0 \rightarrow R_2} * accuracy_{R_2 \rightarrow R_5} \qquad (4)$$

The detailed problems from his model are as follows.

1) We can know from Fig.2 that the interaction trust value stored in node R_1 is 0.9 about R_4, that is, $accuracy_{R_1 \rightarrow R_4} = 0.9$. And the honesty ability of R_4 is 0.4, $honesty_{R_1 \rightarrow R_4} = 0.4$. In fact, path$_1$ is a invalid recommendation path because of the lower honesty ability of R_4. But literatures[14-15] had not made difference between the two abilities. It used the accuracy ability(0.9) taking the place of honesty one(0.4). So in his view this path is valid. In this case it is wrong.

2) We also can know form formula(2) that $\Gamma_I(R_0, R_6)$ will be $[accuracy_{R_4 \rightarrow R_6}, accuracy_{R_5 \rightarrow R_6}]$, that is $[0.8, 0.8]$. It is no doubt that $\Gamma_I(R_0, R_6)$ will be equal to 0.8 whatever the two recommendation paths are in this instance. This is surely unreasonable in fact. $accuracy_{R_5 \rightarrow R_6}$ will decrease with the extending of recommendation path (from R_6 to R_0).

In this paper we will make an improvement in trusted transitivity.
Take path$_2$: $R_0 \leftarrow R_2 \leftarrow R_5 \leftarrow R_6$ for example, let $RT_{R_6}^{R_2}$ be recommendation trust value about node R_6, which is provided by R_2. Then,

$$RT_{R_6}^{R_2} = honesty_{R_0 \rightarrow R_2} * honesty_{R_2 \rightarrow R_5} * accuracy_{R_5 \rightarrow R_6} \qquad (5)$$

If there is another recommendation path: $R_0 \leftarrow R_1 \leftarrow R_3 \leftarrow R_6$,its recommendation value is labeled $RT_{R_6}^{R_1}$, then the aggregated recommendation trust value $\Gamma_I(R_0, R_6)$ by this two paths is computed as follows:

$$\Psi_I(R_0, R_6) = \frac{honesty_{R_0 \to R_1} * RT_{R_6}^{R_1} + honesty_{R_0 \to R_2} * RT_{R_6}^{R_2}}{honesty_{R_0 \to R_1} + honesty_{R_0 \to R_2}} \tag{6}$$

If there are many paths, the computation method is the same.

3.3   Trusted Paths-Searching Policy

Let *cycle* mark the level of transitivity tree. The detailed trusted paths-searching policies are as follows:

Step 1: To open its trust records of user-node and start to search all transitivity paths aiming at every resource node in open network. At this time, $cycle = 1$.

Step 2: Trust requestor searches all of nodes which have made some interaction records before. If this node is object which we are searching, then going to Step 3 otherwise going to step 5.

Step 3: If $cycle = 1$, then there's a direct trust relationship between user and this node. It is necessary for us to store this direct trust value into data base of system and to search the next recommendation path continuatively with a breadth-first traversal method. Then going to step 2, otherwise going to step 4.

Step 4: There is a recommendation trust relationship. The recommendation path and recommendation trust value will be stored into data base. $cycle --$. The program will go to the upper level and search continuously. Then going to step 2.

Step 5: If this node has not further trust interaction records, then the current path is invalid. We must search the next node in the breadth-first traversal method sequentially, then going to step 2, otherwise going to step 6.

Step 6: If the honesty value of this node is greater than threshold of honesty, then going to step 7 otherwise going to step 10.

Step 7: If the length of recommendation path is greater than threshold of path length, then going to step 10, otherwise going to step 8.

Step 8: If this node has been found in the recommendation path, then going to step 10, otherwise going to step 9.

Step 9: This node can be selected as a valid recommendation node. And it will be taken down in the path. $cycle ++$. Then going on traverse and going to step 2.

Step 10: This path is invalid. If this node is not the final trust record, then continuing making a breadth-first traversal, going to step 2, otherwise going to the upper level and going on, $cycle --$, and going to step 2.

Step 11: To integrate the direct trust value and many recommendation trust value with the appropriate algorithm. Then the final trust value is acquired. The high-trust nodes will be selected to interact with user node.

4   Experimental Analysis

This paper puts emphasis on the fine-grain direct trust ability in trusted storage and transitivity mechanism. That is, having make a differentiation between accuracy ability and honesty capability. Take literatures[14-15] for example, they make accuracy ability be equal to honesty capability, it is incorrect. This will be validated in the following experiment.

We take Fig.2 as the context of experimentation. On the surface, There seems to be two transitivity paths: $path_1$ is $R_0 \leftarrow R_2 \leftarrow R_5 \leftarrow R_6$ and $path_2$ is $R_0 \leftarrow R_1 \leftarrow R_4 \leftarrow R_6$.

About $path_1$, Fig.3 shows the different transitivity process of the two trust models. Here, horizontal ordinate represents trust transitivity process from R_6 to R_0. Vertical ordinate describes the alterable condition of recommendation trust value during the course of the whole transitivity.

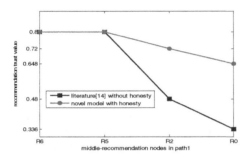

Fig. 3. Comparison diagram of models about $path_1$

It can be shown that recommendation trust value of the two models are also 0.8 at R_5. But these is a great change when trust value arrives at R_2 node. In literature [14], R_2 uses the low accuracy value of R_5 ($accuracy_{R_2 \rightarrow R_5} = 0.6$) replacing its high honesty value($honesty_{R_2 \rightarrow R_5} = 0.9$). Thus its trust value drops dramatically at R_2 (to be equal to 0.48). This is not correct in fact. While the trust attenuation of novel model is few because R_5 has a high recommendation capability. This fits the law of society-relationship development.

About $path_2$, Fig.4 shows the different results.

Here, recommendation trust value of the two models are also 0.8 at R_4. But it changes dramatically at R_1. In literature [14], R_1 uses the high accuracy value of R_4 ($accuracy_{R_1 \rightarrow R_4} = 0.9$) replacing its low honesty value($honesty_{R_1 \rightarrow R_4} = 0.4$). Thus its trust value is smoothing down a bit at R_2 (to be equal to 0.72). This is also wrong. In this paper, when honesty value of a node is less than 0.5, we regard it as an untrusted node and the corresponding transitivity-path is invalid. The novel model has made a correct judgement at R_1. Recommendation trust value, provided by R_4, is assessed by R_1 at zero. So the continuous searching is avoided on the basis of this condition.

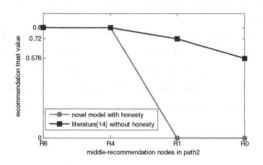

Fig. 4. Comparison diagram of models about $path_2$

5   Conclusions

In this paper, we have made an improvement on trust model. Firstly, a novel solving-sheme about trusted problem is put forword in open network environment. Secondly, recommendation ability ("honesty") is considered to take part in computing recommendation trust value. then, the correlate trust storage structure, trust transitivity tree and policy are introduced, which are all based on "accuracy" and "honesty". Finally, experimentation results show the novel model is rational and valid.

Acknowledgments. This work is supported by the Natural Science Foundation of Jiangsu Province (BK2011072); Science Foundation Project sponsored by NJUPT (NY209015).

References

1. Haiyan, W., Ruchuan, W.: CPK-based grid authentication: a step forward. The Journal of China Universities of Posts and Telecommunications 14(1), 26–31 (2007)
2. Jiangang, C., Ruchuan, W., Haiyan, W.: The extended RBAC model based on grid computing. The Journal of China Universities of Posts and Telecommunications 13(3), 93–97 (2006)
3. Yong, D., Jiangang, C., Ruchuan, W., Lin, Z.: Authorization delegation mechanism based trust level in grid computing. Journal on Communications 29(9), 10–17 (2008)
4. Edward, W.: Understanding trusted computing:Will its benefits outweigh its drawbacks? IEEE Security & Privacy 1(3), 60–62 (2003)
5. Zhuying, L., Xiaojie, L., Lin, L., Lei, S., Gang, X.: Security model research based on trusted computing in ad hoc network. China Communications 7, 1–10 (2011)
6. Junfeng, T., Ye, Z.: Trust shell based constitution model of trusted software. China Communications 7, 11–22 (2011)

7. Yuxing, S., Songhua, H., Lijun, C.: Bayesian Decision-Making Based Recommendation Trust Revision Model in Ad Hoc Networks. Journal of Software 20(9), 2574–2586 (2009)
8. Yu, B., Munindar, P.: An evidential model of distributed reputation management. In: AAMAS 2002, pp. 15–19 (2002)
9. Lin, Z., Ruchuan, W., Haiyan, W.: Trusted decision mechanism based on fuzzy logic for open network. Journal of Computers 3(12), 76–83 (2008)
10. Souxin, W., Li, Z., Hesong, L.: Evaluation approach of subjective trust based on cloud model. Journal of Software 21(6), 1341–1352 (2010)
11. Chuang, L., Xuhai, P.: Research on trustworthy networks. Chinese Journal of Computers 28(5), 751–758 (2005)
12. Mehmet, S.: Security Meter: A Practical Decision-Tree Model to Quantify Risk. IEEE Security & Privacy, 14–24 (2005)
13. Schechter, S.E.: Toward Econometric Models of the Security Risk from Remote Attacks. IEEE Security & Privacy, 40–44 (2005)
14. Xiaoyong, L., Xiaolin, G.: Cognitive model of dynamic trust forecasting. Journal of Software 21(1), 163–176 (2010)
15. Xiaoyong, L., Xiaolin, G., Juan, Z., Dapeng, F.: Novel Scalable Aggregation Algorithm of Feedback Trust Information. Journal of Xi'an Jiaotong University 41(8), 879–883 (2007)

A Deep Understanding of Cloud Computing Security

Hongjiao Li, Xiuxia Tian, Weimin Wei, and ChaoChao Sun

School of Computer and Information Engineering, Shanghai University of Electric Power,
Shanghai, P.R.C.
hjli@shiep.edu.cn

Abstract. In this paper, three typical definitions of cloud computing are listed. Security issues in cloud computing are analyzed. Novelties in cloud threat model, new problems and new research directions in cloud computing environment are also outlined.

Keywords: Cloud Computing, Cloud Security.

1   Introduction

Cloud computing is computing as it has long been the dream of a new infrastructure of this title, it is the most recent is rapidly into commercial reality. The overarching goal of Cloud Computing is to provide on-demand computing services with high reliability, scalability, and availability in distributed environments.   Up to date, there is no unified cloud computing definition, the representative definitions of industry and academia are the follows. In IBM technical white paper, Cloud Computing is defined as: the term used to describe both the cloud computing platform for a system or a type of application [1]. An early (less than one year old) effort at systematically framing cloud computing, "Above the Clouds: A Berkeley View of Cloud Computing," defined cloud computing to include application software delivered as services over the Internet, and the hardware and systems software in the datacenters that facilitate these services[2] . According to the definition of NIST, cloud Computing is a model for enabling ubiquitous, convenient, on-demand network access to a shared pool of configurable computing resources (e.g. networks, servers, storage, applications, and services) that can be rapidly provisioned and released with minimal management effort or service provider interaction[3].   Although above definitions are slightly different, it is foreseeable that the development of cloud computing will give Internet service providers, equipment manufacturers bring new development opportunities, will also work in people's lives and have a huge impact.

With the growing popularity of cloud computing, security issues, showing the importance of a gradual upward trend has become an important factor restricting the development. There comes an increasingly frequent cloud computing security incident. According to IDC's survey, 87.5% of users worry about security issues in cloud computing [4]. Obviously, security ranked first as the greatest challenge or issue of cloud computing. Gartner2009-year survey also stated that 70% of

J. Lei et al. (Eds.): NCIS 2012, CCIS 345, pp. 98–105, 2012.
© Springer-Verlag Berlin Heidelberg 2012

respondents believe that the recent CTO of cloud computing without the use of the primary reasons is that there is data security and privacy concern [5].

In this paper, we analyze the security requirements in cloud computing environment, detail the novelties in cloud threat model, present new problems and new research directions in cloud computing security. The remainder of this paper is organized as follows. In Section 2 security requirements of cloud computing security is analyzed. In Section 3, Novelties in the cloud threat model are described. New problems of cloud computing are detailed in Section 4. Section 5 details the new research directions for cloud computing security. Finally, the paper concludes in Section 6.

2   Security Issues in Cloud Computing

Arguably many of the incidents described as "cloud security" in fact just reflect traditional web application and data-hosting problems. The main part of the cloud computing security environment with other IT security controls is not different. The main security goal remains: confidentiality, integrity, availability, authentication, authorization and audit. However, compared with the traditional IT solutions, the use of cloud-based service model, operating modes and the cloud services technology, cloud computing may face different risks.

In cloud computing environment, many users participate in the cloud and they join or leave cloud dynamically. The number of user changes dynamically, as well as users use the different services, leading the user can not be classified. Other resources in the cloud computing environments are the same too. They should be able to deal with the changing dynamically. The cloud includes distributed users and resource from distributed local systems or organizes, which have different security policies. According to this reason, how to build a suitable relationship among them is a challenge. Also, Cloud computing environment is a virtualized environment, it can not be clearly defined boundaries to protect the device user, the traditional computing model can protected device user by dividing physical and logical security zones.

Therefore, in [6], it is pointed out that security issues to cloud computing include:

- Privacy Issues
- Data Ownership and Content Disclosure Issues
- Data Confidentiality
- Data Location
- Control Issues
- Regulatory and Legislative Compliance
- Forensic Evidence Issues
- Auditing Issues
- Business Continuity and Disaster Recovery Issues
- Trust Issues
- Security Policy Issues
- Emerging Threats to Cloud Computing

To date, most papers published on cloud security reflect continuations of established lines of security research, such as web security [7], data outsourcing and assurance [8], and virtual machines [9]. Below we discuss the new security aspects in cloud computing environment.

3   What's New in Cloud Computing Security?

3.1   Novelties in the Cloud Threat Model

New and unfamiliar threats to cloud computing are emerging. Examples include cross-virtual machine (VM) exploits, inter-processor exploits and cross-application vulnerability exploits. Although most of these widely publicized attacks to cloud computing are theoretical [10]. In [11, 12], it is argued that the cloud computing threat model includes several novel elements.

1. Data and software are not the only assets worth protecting. Activity patterns also need to be protected.
2. Business reputations also merit protection.
3. One must often accommodate a longer trust chain.
4. Competitive businesses can operate within the same cloud computing ecosystem.
5. Because cloud computing introduces a shared resource environment, unexpected side channels (passively observing information) and covert channels (actively sending data) can arise.

3.2   New Problems in Cloud Computing Security

There are also new problem areas in security that arise from cloud computing [11, 12]. These problems may only become apparent after the maturation and more widespread adoption of cloud computing as a technology.

1. Cheap data and data analysis.
2. For black hats, cloud computing offers a potentially more trustworthy alternative to botnets.
3. Another new issue comes from reputation fate-sharing, which has mixed consequences.
4. Mash-up authorization.
5. Cost-effective defense of availability.

4   New Research Directions in Cloud Computing Security

Combining the contemporary and historical viewpoints, we arrive at the position that many cloud computing security problems are not in fact new, but often will still require new solutions in terms of specific mechanisms. Existing contemporary works already explore many pertinent topics; we highlight here several areas that deserve more attention.

4.1   Multi-party Trust

The cloud computing system should also be able to provide services to users dynamically. This dynamic mechanism gives the user convenience to use the services and resources in the cloud computing environment. The participants, including users, local organized and distributed resources, should build trust relationships among the entities that will have mutual operation to each other. Participants need to organize dynamically to solve different problems. So the relationship among them changes dynamically too. Then the VO needs to establish dynamically the trust domain including the participants, such as the users and the resources, which span multiple organization or systems. Therefore, the root problem of cloud security is TRUST [13].

4.2   Mutual Audit-Ability

One important area that needs receive much attention is mutual audit-ability [12]. The auditing capabilities of most existing systems focus on one-way audit-ability. But in cloud computing, providers and users may need to demonstrate mutual trustworthiness, in a bilateral or multilateral fashion. Such audit-ability can have major benefits with regard to fate-sharing, such as enabling cloud providers in search and seizure incidents to demonstrate to law enforcement that they have turned over all relevant evidence, and prove to users that they turned over only the necessary evidence and nothing more.

Mutual audit-ability can also significantly assist with incident response and recovery, since both the cloud provider and the cloud user can be either the source or the target of an attack. Audit-ability also enables the attribution of blame in search and seizure incidents, which can prove vital so that law enforcement agencies do not overreach in carrying out their duties.

In cloud computing, it remains an open challenge to achieve thorough auditing without impairing performance. In short, mutual audit-ability needs significant work.

4.3   Always-Available Service

A subtle difficulty with understanding cloud computing threats arises from potentially inaccurate mental models of cloud computing as an always-available service [12].

Availability also needs to be considered in the context of an adversary whose goals are simply to sabotage activities. Increasingly, such adversaries are becoming realistic as political conflict is taken onto the web, and as the recent cyber attacks on Lithuania confirm. The damages are not only related to the losses of productivity, but extend to losses due to the degraded trust in the infrastructure, and potentially costly backup measures.

The cloud computing model encourages single points of failure. It is therefore important to develop methods for sustained availability (in the context of attack), and for recovery from attack. The latter could operate on the basis of minimization of losses, required service levels, or similar measures.

4.4   Virtualization Security [14]

When cloud computing is mentioned, virtualization technology is definitely referred to. In virtual environment, physical servers are consolidated to multiple virtual machine instances on virtualized servers. Virtualization technology introduced some specific security risks, for example, isolation problem. Virtualization actually takes full use of hardware resources, forming a relatively isolated virtual environment, but if you deploy properly, it will become a security threat.

In a virtualized environment, firewalls must be bidirectional and deployed on each VM instantiation. The management schema must be centralized to ensure that all VMs offer the same level of protection. Besides the security vulnerabilities, cloud providers must consider performance. Additionally, VMs and servers typically use the same OSs and software (including Web applications). Therefore, cloud computing makes the new challenges.

4.5   Data Security

Data security is another important research topic in cloud computing [5, 15].   Study of cloud computing security needs to focus on the analysis and solution of cloud computing service computing model, dynamic virtual management mode and multiple tenants sharing operation mode for data security and privacy protection challenges.

Since service providers typically do not have access to the physical security system of data centers, they must rely on the infrastructure provider to achieve full data security.

The infrastructure provider must achieve the following objectives: (i) confidentiality, for secure data access and transfer; (ii) audit-ability, for attesting whether security setting of applications has been tampered or not. Confidentiality is usually achieved using cryptographic protocols, whereas audit-ability can be achieved using remote attestation techniques.

4.6   Privacy

One area that is greatly affected by cloud computing is privacy, both in terms of legal compliance and user trust and this need to be considered at every phase of design. The key challenge for software engineers to design cloud services in such a way as to decrease privacy risk and to ensure legal compliance [16].

Privacy, including user data cannot be the unauthorized users to access, cannot be including service providers, other aspects have been clients of these data, and there are also many challenges. Privacy issues, may be more of a linkage problem, involves the legal problems, the individual's right to privacy includes service provider liability, an enterprise's business secrets and so on, and effective security solutions for the application of cloud computing plays a vital role in.

Because of privacy concerns, enterprises running clouds collecting data have felt increasing pressure to anonymize their data [11]. Another reason to anonymize data is to share data with other parties. Anonymizing data is another difficult problem.

4.7   Information-Centric Security

In order for enterprises to extend control to data in the cloud, we propose shifting from protecting data from the outside (system and applications which use the data) to protecting data from within. We call this approach of data and information protecting itself information-centric[11]. This self-protection requires intelligence be put in the data itself. Data needs to be self-describing and defending, regardless of its environment. Also, data needs to be encrypted and packaged with a usage policy. When accessed, data should consult its policy and attempt to re-create a secure environment using virtualization and reveal itself only if the environment is verified as trustworthy (using Trusted Computing). Information-centric security is a natural extension of the trend toward finer, stronger, and more usable data protection.

4.8   High-Assurance Remote Server Attestation [11]

Lack of transparency is a discouraging business from moving their data to the cloud. Data owners wish to audit how their data is being handled at the cloud, and in particular, ensure that their data is not being abused or leaked, or at least have an unalterable audit trail when it does happen.

A promising approach to address this problem is based on Trusted Computing. Imagine a trusted monitor installed at the cloud server that can monitor or audit the operations of the cloud server. The trusted monitor can provide "proofs of compliance" to the data owner, stating that certain access policies have not been violated. To ensure integrity of the monitor, Trusted Computing also allows secure bootstrapping of this monitor to run beside (and securely isolated from) the operating system and applications. The monitor can enforce access control policies and perform monitoring/auditing tasks. To produce a "proof of compliance", the code of the monitor is signed, as well as a "statement of compliance" produced by the monitor. When the data owner receives this proof of compliance, it can verify that the correct monitor code is run, and that the cloud server has complied with access control policies.

4.9   Privacy-Enhanced Business Intelligence

In cloud computing environment, there is a potential lack of control and transparency when a third party holds the data. A different approach to retaining control of data is to require the encryption of all cloud data. The problem is that encryption limits data use. In particular searching and indexing the data becomes problematic. Other cryptographic primitives, such as homographic encryption and Private Information Retrieval (PIR) perform computations on encrypted data without decrypting. As these cryptographic techniques are mature, they may open up new possibilities for cloud computing security.

4.10   Virtual Private Cloud

In research projects based on Trusted Computing and virtualization technology to enhance the security of cloud computing platform, the service provider in the public cloud computing platform can provide a virtual private cloud computing service; this will be an important developing direction. Without a doubt, virtual private cloud compared with public cloud will provide more value-added services. But the implementation method, virtual private cloud and virtual private network technology have great differences. For a virtual private cloud, the service providers need to realize the storage device and the CPU register as a non encryption protection. The tenant of the code and data in the cloud service providers to the memory and the CPU register in plaintext form is processed still get the confidentiality and integrity of protection to avoid other tenant or the attacker to steal. The Daoli project [17] provides a virtual private cloud computing service to ensure the confidentiality and integrity of user code and data, thus reducing cloud computing security risk.

5   Conclusions

Cloud computing is an emerging technology that offers unparalleled distributed computing resources at affordable infrastructure and operating costs.

In this paper, three representative definitions of cloud computing, IBM, Berkeley and NIST are explained. Although above definitions are slightly different, it can be understood that cloud computing is internet-based service model, in this way, the shared hardware, software resources and information can be provided to computers and other devices on demand.

With increasing employment of cloud computing, there comes increasingly frequent cloud computing security incidents. Novelties in the cloud threat model are emerged, and new problems aiming at cloud computing environment are also raised. Therefore, new research directions in cloud computing security need paid attention to.

Current work in the literature generally focuses only single aspects of the cloud security problem. There is a need for research that seeks to understand the ecosystem of threats.   .

Acknowledgment. This paper is supported by the Innovation Program of Shanghai Municipal Education Commission under Grant No. 11YZ194 and No. 12YZ146, No. 12YZ147; Natural Science Foundation of Shanghai under Grant No. 11ZR1414300 ; the Key Technologies R&D Program of Shanghai Science and Technology Commission under Grant No. 10dz1501000.

References

[1] http://www-900.ibm.com/ibm/ideasfromibm/cn/cloud/solutions/index.shtml

[2] Michael, A., Fox, A.: Above the Clouds: A Berkley View of Cloud Computing (February 10, 2009)

[3] The NIST Definition of Cloud Computing, version 15, by Peter Mell and Tim Grance, National Institute of Standards and Technology (NIST), Information Technology Laboratory (October 7, 2009), http://www.csrc.nist.gov

[4] International Data Corporation (2009), http://blogs.idc.com/ie/wpcontent/uploads/2009/12/idc_cloud_challenges_2009.jpg

[5] Feng, D.-G., Zhang, M., Zhang, Y., Xu, Z.: Research on Cloud Computing Security. Journal of Software 22(1), 71–82 (2011)

[6] Onwubiko, C.: Security Issues to Cloud Computing. In: Antonopoulos, N., Gillam, L. (eds.) Cloud Computing: Principles, Systems and Applications, Computer Communications and Networks, doi:10.1007/978-1-84996-241-4_1

[7] Biddle, R., van Oorschot, P.C., Patrick, A.S., Sobey, J., Whalen, T.: Browser interfaces and extended validation ssl certificates: an empirical study. In: Proceedings of the ACM Workshop on Cloud Computing Security, CCSW 2009 (2009)

[8] Bowers, K.D., Juels, A., Oprea, A.: Hail: a high-availability and integrity layer for cloud storage. In: Proceedings of the 16th ACM Conference on Computer and Communications Security, CCS 2009 (2009)

[9] Wei, J., Zhang, X., Ammons, G., Bala, V., Ning, P.: Managing security of virtual machine images in a cloud environment. In: Proceedings of the ACM Workshop on Cloud Computing Security, CCSW 2009 (2009)

[10] A Security Analysis of Cloud Computing, http://cloudcomputing.sys-con.com/node/1203943

[11] Amardeep Singh, Er., Monika Verma, Er.: Attacks and Security in Cloud Computing. International Journal of Advanced Engineering & Application, 300–302 (2011)

[12] Chen, A., Paxson, V., Katz, R.H.: What's New about Cloud Computing Security? Technical Report No. UCB/ EECS-2010-5

[13] Monsef, M., Gidado, N.: Trust and privacy concern in the Cloud. In: 2011 European Cup, IT Security for the Next Generation (2011)

[14] Kaufman, L.M.: Can Public-Cloud Security Meet Its Unique Challenges? IEEE Security & Privacy (July/August 2010)

[15] Zhang, Q., Cheng, L., Boutab, R.: Cloud computing: state-of-the-art and research challenges. Internet Serv. Appl. 1, 7–18 (2010), doi:10.1007/s13174-010-0007-6

[16] Krutz, R.L., Vines, R.D.: Cloud Security: A Comprehensive Guide to Secure Cloud Computing. Wiley Publishing, Inc., Canada, ISBN: 978-0-470-58987-8

[17] Li, D.: http://www.daoliproject.org

Study of Layers Construct for Data Mining Platform Based on Cloud Computing[*]

Yongzheng Lin

School of Information Science and Engineering, University of Jinan, Jinan, China

Abstract. AT the present time, data separately stored in network can't be mined efficiently, the layers construct for data mining platform based on cloud computing is put forward in this paper, and, all the function modules and the main designed methods are analyzed in details. The construct has been proved to be scientific and feasible by researches.

Keywords: cloud computing, data mining, layers construct, data reduction.

1   Introduction

With the application and development of the technology of computer network, especially the technology of cloud computing, more and more data was stored separately in different computers in network, the intense complexity to deal with such data has exceeded the limit of original data mining system and the scope of computing resources supplied by traditional single server. Thus, it's necessary for distributed computing technology to implement large scale parallel computing.

As upgrade of grid computing, cloud computing is a kind of calculation mode which can offer dynamic virtual resources to users via Internet[1], and is a computing platform which can offer dynamic resources pool, virtualization and high usability, and generally is used to design high performance program[2]. Although it is getting more and more popular to data mining by virtue of cloud platform, there are some heterogeneous and non-homogeneous data. Thus, it is necessary to firstly implement data reduction so as to visit heterogeneous and undefined data type, then to further design and achieve data mining system.

2   Architecture of Cloud Computing

Cloud computing can offer users a high-flexibility, high-reliability, transparent, safe bottom structure with friendly monitoring and maintenance interface, by which computing and memory resources could be distributed to users who needed, as is shown in figure 1. Thus, it is necessary for application based on this structure to get needful

---

[*] Sponsored by A Project of Shandong Province Education Science Program (ZK1101322B021) and Science Foundation of University of Jinan (XKY1020).

J. Lei et al. (Eds.): NCIS 2012, CCIS 345, pp. 106–112, 2012.
© Springer-Verlag Berlin Heidelberg 2012

resource according to respective interface rules. The cost is proportional to not the system throughput but the amount of resource used. As far as the realization of data mining based on cloud computing is concerned, users only need to pay close attention to the effectuation of service logic layer instead of the details of bottom platform and can run all kinds of algorithm by means of such cloud computing platform, then get the satisfied results by setting target response time.

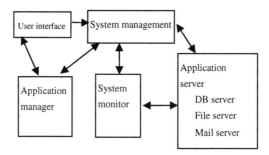

Fig. 1. Architecture of Cloud Computing

3   Brief Intreduction of Current Cloud Computing Platform

Since 2007, people have paid more and more attention to the research, discussion and relevant products. At present, cloud computing platforms, such as Google App Engine(GAE)[3]、 Amazon Elastic Computer Cloud(EC2)[4], have been so mature that they can offer preferable bottom architecture support for the realization of data mining system, which make it convenient to use computing resource on platform.

As a kind of cloud infrastructure service based on virtual server technology, Amazon Elastic Computer Cloud(EC2) devotes itself to providing large scale, reliable and elastic computing environment for users.

As a new generation of network program development platform based on cloud computing, Google App Engine(GAE) allows users to develop and run network application program on Google foundation frame, which could be easily built and maintained. Developers can easily get corresponding service only after unloading their application, so it is unnecessary to maintain servers.

4   Layers Construct for Data Mining Platform Based on Cloud Computing

During the process of designing data mining system based on cloud computing, hierarchical design thought is put forward, namely, the platform bottom-up is divided into: algorithm layer, task layer and user layer. As is shown in figure 2, each layer servers for its top layer, the bottommost layer provides cloud computing platform with application program interface, the topmost layer is user interface and opening interface which is used to share data set, call data cleaning and mining algorithms that can be easily integrated into user application to make platform more opening. Target system, which is built on cloud computing, can be used by users not only directly by means of all kinds of terminals but also indirectly by opening interfaces of other application programs. Users only pay more attention to adopting which algorithm to deal with data so as to get data mining results.

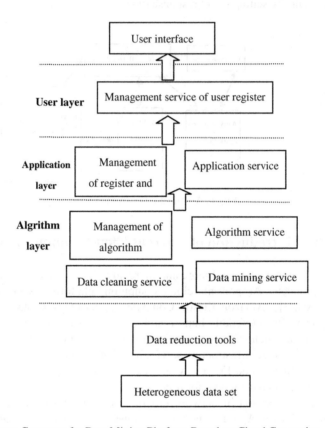

Fig. 2. Layers Construct for Data Mining Platform Based on Cloud Computing

4.1   Design of Data Rreduction Tools

As the object of data mining, data set is a set of same type data, and data set instance is an concrete data set which includes visiting address. The target of data reduction tools is to expand cloud computing platform so as to visit heterogeneous data and unidentified data. Therefore, data reduction tools can be called by data mining system to visit heterogeneous data.

Before accessing data set instance, users first   add a data set example definition file by management module of data reduction tool to describe the data set instance, and then use the definition file ID to call conventions tool data access module for data reading and writing. As is shown in figure 3.

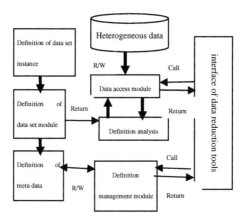

Fig. 3. Internal model of data reduction tools

Among them, the data access module provides reading service from data set, definition management module is answer for data definition service, data set definition service and registration and logout, definition analysis module include data analysis service, data set analysis service and data set instance service. The definition file, heterogeneous data sets and the relationship among them are described in figure 3, the arrow means calling.

Definition analysis module can achieve to visit heterogeneous datasets undefined data type by means of abstract and extended metadata definition, data set template definition and layer-by-layer abstract data set definition. Among them, the metadata definitions file, which store the definition of each data type, is maintained by service that is only open to the administrator, and provides atomic definition for data set template definition. Data set template file store user defined data set template, which is composed of data set definition service maintenance and data set registration service, and the actual data set corresponding and instantiation for data sets the instance file. Data set instance file is the basis of data access, by which data access component call service which select the specified data engine access to the specified location data, and return the meaning of data set used by various algorithms as parameters, that is to say, when the data set is accessed, the user can not only as usual get data content, and can obtain data set definition, which will eventually resolved to be various atomic data type combination which can be recognized by a variety of algorithm so as to achieve data layer abstract objective. Specific call process is as follows:

When user define data set, the system will examine whether the data set type defined is in data templates having already been defined or not by call data set definition service. If the template already exists, then simply call data set registration and cancellation of services the data set stored position and a data engine registration information to the data set example files, and when templates are not meeting the requirements, then call data set definition services, and use data analysis services provided by a data element definition to define the target data set template, at last call data set registration and cancellation of services.

4.2   Algorithm Layer

Algorithm layer achieve to call a variety of algorithms and manage interfaces by using uniform data source provided by next layer. According to the difference of three kinds of algorithm execution order and returning result, algorithms is separated as follows.

1) Data cleaning algorithm: calling corresponding interface according to preprocessing method which is implemented by the noise data set before data mining algorithms, data after being cleaned will be deposited through the data layer in cloud computing platform storage space for the next data mining.

2) Data mining algorithm: using data having been cleaned or other need not be cleaned data for data mining of unified call interface.

3) Visual algorithm: showing the results of data mining as tabular or graphic and other styles.

4) Algorithm registration and logout: Algorithm management module, which manage kinds of algorithms modules by means of plug-in units.

4.3   Application Layer

Application layer can describe data and   algorithms, which are involved in data mining process, and their relation and the order as task, moreover, can provide the call and the maintenance interface by application.

1)   Application service: provide call interface having been registered.

2)   Application registration and logout service: application management module, which manage various task definition files by way of plug-in units.

4.4   User Layer

User identity authentication and authorization function is   provided in this layer.

Services among layers mentioned above are described in the XML as the communication language and based on the representation of the state change of Web service form internal call to better support the scalability, and end with an open interface to open to the outside. The user may develop from any layer and   load the existing services into the system, which greatly enhances the system's openness and ease of use, and is preceded by a data mining platform architecture ever.

5   Design Key-Points

5.1   Plug-in Unit System Frame

The plug-in is a kind of program developed according to certain application development interface, whose structure is as shown in Figure 4. Each plug-in is composed of three parts: expansion point which provides service for upper layer, business logic layer, new extension point which calls the lower layer, the above three parts is composed of a charge module management binding package with various services. Bind package containing a service interface and various service interface which can return the service calling method and specification for upper the caller to be used to provide specific service parameter information. Bind package interface conforms to uniform standard, so that once the plug is placed on the platform specific directory, plug-ins can be dynamic identification and loaded. At the same time, the algorithm plug-in service interface function parameter is atomic data type combination mentioned before the current algorithm, that is to say, algorithm instead of a specific number, according to the specific arrangement of data to achieve specific, but to meet the algorithm under the premise of using the mentioned before abstract data to provide as much compatibility. Although the difficulty of algorithm realization   is relatively increased, but the algorithm greatly enhances the reusability, and can be used for other users on platform to deal with   various data processing.

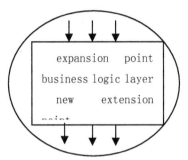

Fig. 4. Structure of Plug-in unit

5.2   Design of Open Interface

The function of open interface is convenient for other applications on data mining platform to use a variety of resources and services provided by data mining platform. In order to achieve high performance, simplicity, intuitive open interface, high scalability purposes, platform interface design is presented based on the REST (Representational State Transfer) [5] in this paper.

The resources in REST is not data, but the combinations of data and forms, and is classified into different resource because of their different forms of expression. All resources are uniquely identified by   URL (Uniform Resource Identifier). REST is based on the Http protocol, thus, any operation on resources is achieved by the Http protocol which put on an operational resources constraints in GET, POST, PUT, DELETE 4 method, just can realize creating , reading, updating, deleting and other operations.

6   Conclusion

Cloud computing is an computing platform that can   provide dynamic resource pools, virtualization and high-availability. Because of some problems ,such as the noise data and heterogeneous structure, data mining solutions by means of cloud computing have been put forward. In view of the above question, the layers construct for data mining platform based on cloud computing is put forward in this paper.

References

[1] Buyya, R., Yeo, C.S., Venugopal, S.: Market-Oriented Cloud Computing: Vision,Hype, and Reality for Delivering IT Services as Computing Utilities. In: Proceedings of the 2008 10th IEEE International Conference on High Performance Computing and Communications, pp. 5–13 (2008)

[2] Li, J., Zhang, J., Zhou, M.: Study of Enterprise Heterogeneous Data Integration Method Based on XML 28(9), 63–64 (2002)

[3] Chang, M.-F.: An Introduction to Cloud Computing Service Platform-Google App Engine. Computer and Communication 126, 24–33 (2008)

[4] Amazon Elastic Compute Cloud (EC2) (May 10, 2010),

[5] http://www.amazon.com/ec2/

[6] Richardson, L., Ruby, S.: Restful web services. O'Reilly (2007)

Cloud Task and Virtual Machine Allocation Strategy in Cloud Computing Environment

Xing Xu[1], Hao Hu[2], Na Hu[3], and Weiqin Ying[4]

[1] College of Information and Engineering, Jingdezhen Ceramic Institute, Jiangxi 333000, China
whuxx84@yahoo.com.cn
[2] Library of Huaihua University, Huaihua Hunan 418000, China
[3] Jingdezhen Ceramic Institute, Jingdezhen Jiangxi 333000, China
[4] School of Software, South China University of Technology, Guangzhou, China
yingweiqin@scut.edu.cn

Abstract. Targeted on cloud application services in cloud computing environment, a series of cloud task scheduling and virtual machine allocation strategies which are simple and easy to be implemented are put forward. There are five allocation strategies. They are the random allocation strategy, the full sequence allocation strategy, the sequence allocation strategy that the cloud tasks are sorted by the execution time before the tasks are assigned to the virtual machines by turns, the sequence allocation strategy that the virtual machines are sorted by the execution speed before the tasks are assigned to the virtual machines by turns and the greedy strategy that the load balancing is taken into account. The optimization objective is the total execution time of all tasks. Simulation and experimental analysis is operated on the simulation platform Cloudsim. Experimental results show that the time of the greedy strategy is the least, the time of the random strategy is the largest, and the time of the three sequence strategies are moderate.

Keywords: cloud computing, task allocation, greedy algorithm.

1   Introduction

Cloud computing [1] [2] [3] [4] is a new large-scale distributed computing paradigm and business is the main driving force in the cloud computing. Abstraction, virtualization, instantaneous deployment, broadband networks and other key technologies are applied in the cloud computing. It realizes intercommunication, interconnection and interoperability through Internet. In the form of a unified service (anything as a service), cloud computing uses the multi-terminal, multi-platform, multi-network for users to access a pay-as-you-go, dynamic configuration, flexibility expansion, low cost, high availability and reliability QoS (quality of service) service by the standard browser at any time and any place. The services include computing, storage, resource, and platform and so on. Cloud computing provides efficient solutions which to meet the demand of rapid increase of hardware cost, calculation

J. Lei et al. (Eds.): NCIS 2012, CCIS 345, pp. 113–120, 2012.
© Springer-Verlag Berlin Heidelberg 2012

storage capacity, services computing and the development of Web3.0. It more and more receives the attention of government, enterprises and research institutions.

Cloud task scheduling and virtual machine (VM) resource allocation optimization is an important, challenging and core component in the cloud application services and cloud computing systems. The efficiency of allocation directly affects the performance of the entire cloud application services. At present, many cloud vendors develop cloud computing applications according to their own infrastructure. The unified standards and constraints have not yet formed. Cloud computing job and task scheduling and resource management model is various. Li etc. proposed a task scheduling algorithm based on double-fitness genetic algorithm. Not only the total task completion time is the important criterion of the algorithm, but also the average completion time is the direct reference of the algorithm [5]. Xian etc. present dynamic scheduling algorithm based on the threshold. The algorithm achieves the flexible scheduling of tasks through dynamic scheduling between the virtual machine and effectively reduces the efficiency impact because of synchronization between the virtual machines [6]. For cloud computing service cluster resource scheduling and load balancing optimization problem, Liu etc. presented a cloud computing resource scheduling strategy based on the improved dynamic multi-swarm particle swarm optimization algorithm [7]. To solve the problem of VM resource scheduling in a cloud computing environment, Shailesh Sawant presents VM resource scheduling strategy that is based on genetic algorithm and focuses on system load balancing [8]. Aiming at the load balancing problem in VM resources scheduling, Gu etc present a scheduling strategy on load balancing of VM resources based on genetic algorithm[9]. A new allocation algorithm based on ant colony optimization was established to satisfy the property of cloud computing. When start, this algorithm first prognosticated the capability of the potential available resource nodes, then analyzed some factors such as network qualities or response times to acquire a set of optimal compute resources [10]. Combining with the immune clonal algorithm of rapid multi objective optimization, a heuristic cloud resource scheduling algorithm with application preference is proposed to solve the problem of high efficiency and effectiveness resource scheduling in cloud computing environments, the model of cloud resource scheduling is analyzed, the application preferences and the user utility of multi dimensional QoS is quantified, and the objective function of QoS is given. [11].

2   Allocation Strategy

In this section, five allocation strategies are presented, including one random allocation strategy, three sequence allocation strategies and one greedy allocation strategy.

2.1   The First Strategy

A set of cloud tasks are randomly assigned to one of a set of virtual machines. Because of random allocation, one or several virtual machines are assigned too many tasks and other virtual machines are allocated less tasks, and even some of the virtual machines don't implement any cloud task.

2.2   The Second Strategy

A group of cloud tasks are assigned to a virtual machine in sequence. When all the virtual machines are running tasks, the tasks are assigned to the virtual machines from the first virtual machine. The method is as far as possible to ensure that each virtual machine runs the same number of tasks in order to balance load.

2.3   The Third Strategy

In the actual situation, the instruction lengths of the cloud tasks are different. On the basis of the second strategy, firstly the cloud tasks are sorted according to the instruction lengths in descending order, and then the cloud tasks are assigned to a group of virtual machines in turn.

2.4   The Fourth Strategy

In the actual situation, the virtual machine execution speed is not the same. Based on the second strategy, the virtual machines are sorted in ascending order in terms of the execution speed, and then a set of cloud tasks are assigned to the virtual machines in order.

2.5   The Fifth Strategy

The cloud task execution time is equal to the task instruction length divided by the speed of execution of the virtual machine [4]. The other impact on the task execution time is not considered. In this context, the following conclusions can be drawn: If the execution time of a task on a virtual machine is the shortest, then the execution time on the other virtual machine is the shortest; if the execution speed of a virtual machine is the fastest, then the speed of this VM running any cloud task is faster than the other virtual machines'. The process of greedy strategy is as follows, and the flow chart is shown in Figure 1.

Step 1: sort the cloud task by instruction length in descending order;
Step 2: sort the virtual machine by execution speed in ascending order;
Step 3: define a time matrix to store the implementation time that a cloud task run on a virtual machine;
Step 4: attempt to assign the cloud task to the last column corresponding to the virtual machine, if the option is optimal relative to other options, then complete the allocation, otherwise the task is assigned to a virtual machine to make that the current result is the best;

Step 5: if a variety of allocation methods are currently the best results, the task is assigned to the virtual machine that have the least cloud task to realize a simple load balancing;

Step 6: if all the clouds tasks are assigned, then the algorithm stops, otherwise jump to Step 4.

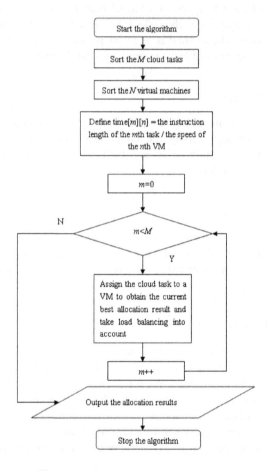

Fig. 1. The flow chart of the fifth strategy

3   Experiment and Simulation

CloudSim is a cloud computing simulation software developed by Gridbus project team and the grid Laboratory of the University of Melbourne in Australia. The Cloudsim can run on Windows and Linux systems, so it's cross-platform. And The Cloudsim supports cloud computing research and development. The newest version of the open source cloud computing simulation platform Cloudsim is 3.0. Cloudsim 3.0 is extended and developed to achieve the five scheduling algorithms proposed in the previous section. The platform is recompiled and the comparative analysis on the performance of the five allocation algorithms is operated. In the experiment, the number of the cloud task is ten and the number of the virtual machine is five. The length of the cloud task is 19365, 49809, 30218, 44157, 16754, 18336, 20045, 31493, 30727 and 31017, respectively. The speed of the virtual machine is 278,289,132,209 and 286, respectively. The experimental results are shown in Table 1 to Table 5. In the five tables, the first column is the number of cloud task; the second column is the number of virtual machines; the third column is the cloud task running time, the fourth column is the cloud task start time, the last column is the end time. Figure 2 is the time histogram that shows the total execution time of all tasks in five different allocation algorithms.

Table 1. Results of Random Allocation Strategy

Cloud Task NO	VM NO	Run Time	Start Time	Finish Time
4	4	58.58	0.1	58.68
0	1	67.01	0.1	67.11
5	3	87.73	0.1	87.83
9	4	108.45	58.68	167.13
3	1	152.79	67.11	219.9
7	1	108.97	219.9	328.87
1	2	377.34	0.1	377.44
2	2	228.92	377.44	606.36
6	2	151.86	606.36	758.22
8	2	232.78	758.22	991

Table 2. Results of the Full Sequence Allocation Strategy

Cloud Task NO	VM NO	Run Time	Start Time	Finish Time
4	4	58.58	0.1	58.68
0	0	69.66	0.1	69.76
5	0	65.96	69.76	135.71
9	4	108.45	58.68	167.13
1	1	172.35	0.1	172.45
3	3	211.28	0.1	211.38
2	2	228.92	0.1	229.02
6	1	69.36	172.45	241.8
8	3	147.02	211.38	358.39
7	2	238.58	229.02	467.6

From Table 1, it can be seen that because of random allocation four tasks are assigned to 2nd virtual machine, no task is assigned to number 0 virtual machine. These lead to load imbalance and the total completion time of ten tasks is the longest. From Tables 2 to 4, it can be seen that because of the sequential allocation, each virtual machine has two cloud tasks to run. The load is very balanced. The completion time of ten tasks in these three strategies is about half of random strategy. Strategy 3 and strategy 4 are the sequence allocation after sorting the cloud tasks and virtual machines. The longer cloud task is assigned to run at first; the faster virtual machine is used to run task at first. Comparing with strategy 2, the two strategies obtain a modest reduction in the run of total time. It can be confirmed from Table 2, to Table 4 and Figure 2. In the Table 5, the slowest virtual machine 2 is just assigned a task; the second fastest virtual machine, whose speed is less than 2% of the fastest virtual machine, is assigned three tasks; the other virtual machines are assigned two tasks. These moderately present loads balancing. The total running time of 10 tasks is only 283.16, and it is the shortest of the five strategies. Greedy allocation strategy realizes the optimal objective of the total running time.

Table 3. Results of the Cloud Tasks Sorting Sequence Allocation Strategy

Cloud Task NO	VM NO	Run Time	Start Time	Finish Time
8	4	107.44	0.1	107.54
9	3	148.4	0.1	148.5
3	1	152.79	0.1	152.89
4	4	58.58	107.54	166.11
1	0	179.17	0.1	179.27
6	1	69.36	152.89	222.25
5	3	87.73	148.5	236.23
7	2	238.58	0.1	238.68
2	0	108.7	179.27	287.96
0	2	146.7	238.68	385.38

Table 4. Results of the Virtual Machines Sorting Sequence Allocation Strategy

Cloud Task NO	VM NO	Run Time	Start Time	Finish Time
4	1	57.97	0.1	58.07
2	0	108.7	0.1	108.8
0	2	146.7	0.1	146.8
3	4	154.39	0.1	154.49
9	1	107.32	58.07	165.39
7	0	113.28	108.8	222.08
1	3	238.32	0.1	238.42
8	4	107.44	154.49	261.93
5	2	138.91	146.8	285.71
6	3	95.91	238.42	334.33

Table 5. Results of Greedy Allocation Strategy

Cloud Task NO	VM NO	Run Time	Start Time	Finish Time
7	0	113.28	0.1	113.38
9	3	148.4	0.1	148.5
3	4	154.39	0.1	154.49
1	1	172.35	0.1	172.45
8	0	110.53	113.38	223.91
6	4	70.09	154.49	224.58
2	2	228.92	0.1	229.02
5	3	87.73	148.5	236.23
0	1	67	172.45	239.45
4	4	58.58	224.58	283.16

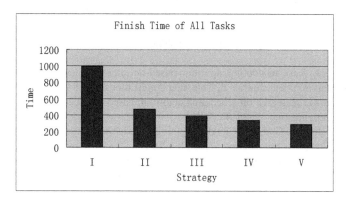

Fig. 2. Finish time of all tasks for different allocation strategy

4   Summary

In this article, the five kinds of cloud tasks and virtual machine scheduling allocation strategies are described.   The classes of Cloudsim are extended to implement customized scheduling and allocation strategies, and complete simulation of the scheduling algorithm, at last related tests and experiments proceed. The experimental results show that the greedy allocation strategy is the best, followed by three sequential allocation strategies, and random allocation strategy is the worst. The future research will focus on applying intelligence optimization algorithms to schedule cloud tasks and virtual machines.

Acknowledgments. This work was supported in part by the National Nature Science Foundation of China (61070009, 61165004, 61202313), the National Science and Technology Support Plan (2012BAH25F02), the Project of Jingdezhen Science and Technology Bureau (2011-1-47), the National Natural Science Foundation of Jiangxi Province (20122BAB211036, 20122BAB201044), and the Youth Science Foundation of Jiangxi Provincial Department of Education (GJJ12514), the Natural Science Foundation of Guangdong Province (S2011040002472), the Specialized Research Fund for the Doctoral Program of Higher Education (20110172120035), the Fundamental Research Funds for the Central Universities (2011ZM0107).

References

1. Buyya, R., Yeo, C., Venugopal, S., Broberga, J., Brandic, I.: Cloud computing and emerging IT platforms: vision, hype, and reality for delivering computing as the 5th utility. Future Generation Computer Systems 25, 599–616 (2009)
2. Armbrust, M., Fox, A., Griffith, R., Joseph, A., Katz, R., Konwinski, A., Lee, G., Patterson, D., Rabkin, A., Stoica, I., Zaharia, M.: A view of cloud Computing. Communications of the ACM 53, 50–58 (2010)
3. Foster, I., Zhao, Y., Raicu, I., Lu, S.: Cloud computing and grid computing 360 degree compared. In: Proc. of the Grid Computing Environments Workshop, pp. 1–10. IEEE Press, New York (2008)
4. Liu, P.: Cloud computing, 2nd edn. Publishing House of Electronics Industry, Beijing (2011)
5. Li, J., Peng, J.: Task scheduling algorithm based on improved genetic algorithm in cloud computing environment. Journal of Computer Applications 31, 184–186 (2011)
6. Xian, J., Yu, G.: Research on scheduling algorithm based on cloud computing. Computer and Digital Engineering 39, 39–42 (2011)
7. Liu, W., Zhang, M., Guo, W.: Cloud computing resource schedule strategy based on mpso algorithm. Computer Engineering 37, 43–45 (2011)
8. Sawant, S.: A Genetic Algorithm Scheduling Approach for Virtual Machine Resources in a Cloud Computing Environment, Master's Theses of San Jose State University, San Jose (2011)
9. Gu, J., Hu, J., Zhao, T., Sun, G.: A new resource scheduling strategy based on genetic algorithm in cloud computing environment. Journal of Computers 7, 42–52 (2012)
10. Hua, X., Zheng, J., Hu, W.: Ant colony optimization algorithm for computing resource allocation based on cloud computing environment. Journal of East China Normal University (Natural Science) 1, 127–134 (2010)
11. Sun, D., Chang, G., Li, F., Wang, C., Wang, X.: Optimizing Multi-Dimensional QoS Cloud Resource Scheduling by Immune Clonal with Preference. Acta Electronica Sinica 39, 1824–1831 (2011)

Method of Construct High Performance StaaS Infrastructure Base on Dynamic Request Data Supporting Cloud Computing

Hongyong Lu[1,2]

[1] Computer Science & Technology Department, Tongji University, No.1239 Siping Road, Shanghai 200092, China
[2] IBM China Systems & Technology Laboratory (CSTL), Building 10, 399 Ke Yuan Road, Shanghai 201203, China
hongyonglu@hotmail.com

Abstract. Cloud computing is one of the hottest topics in industry. High performance storage infrastructure is the basic, key component to support this, and it is also catch lots of attention from research to application. This paper mainly introduces a method to build up a novel Storage infrastructure to support Cloud Computing, the method named as IStaaSM (Intelligent Storage as a service with mixed products). IStaaSM grants storage infrastructure with self performance improvement ability in the environment with mixed storage products. This method analyzes regular pattern of user operations, identify hot data and migrate hot data to the storage product which has better performance to improve entire performance of storage infrastructure.

Keywords: Storage infrastructure, StaaS, IStaaSM, Cloud Computing, High Performance.

1 Introduction

Cloud Computing refers to the delivery of computing and storage capacity as a service to a heterogeneous community of end-recipients [1]. A cloud is a pool of virtualized computer resources. A cloud can: [2]

- Host a variety of different workloads, including batch-style back-end jobs and interactive, user-facing applications
- Allow workloads to be deployed and scaled-out quickly through the rapid provisioning of virtual machines or physical machines
- Support redundant, self-recovering, highly scalable programming models that allow workloads to recover from many unavoidable hardware/software failures
- Monitor resource use in real time to enable rebalancing of allocations when needed

In Nov. 2007 at Shanghai, IBM has unveiled its big plan about Cloud Computing which named "Blue Cloud". [3] After that, Cloud Computing becomes one of the hottest topics from research to application, and identified as a revolution to information

J. Lei et al. (Eds.): NCIS 2012, CCIS 345, pp. 121–129, 2012.
© Springer-Verlag Berlin Heidelberg 2012

and service delivery mechanism in information technology industry. More and more enterprises invests lot of resources in this area, includes IBM, Salesforce, Amazon, Microsoft and etc.

Cloud Computing provides possibility to enterprises on efficiency improvement of their IT hardware and software resources. It also provides possibility to let enterprises which are experts in IT technologies provide IT resources as service to others. Cloud Computing benefits service receivers with efficiency by on demand resource allocation, latest IT technologies, flexibility, reliability, low down capital expense and operation expense, human resource utilization. More and more enterprises and IT experts has desire to adopt Cloud Computing in near 5 years by the survey of developerWorks, IBM. [4] Cloud Computing provides lost of opportunities to both service provides and receivers.

2   Basic Cloud Computing Architecture

As Fig.1 displayed, hardware virtualization provides the foundation, there are three different layers with services in different levels.

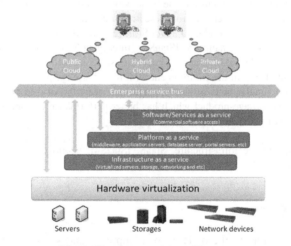

Fig. 1. Cloud computing architecture

- IaaS, Infrastructure as a service. This layer constructed based on servers, network devices, Storages and other kinds of hardware, and provides virtualized resources on demand. Virtualized resources include Virtual Machines, Servers, Storage, Load balancers, network...... By IaaS, users use provided interfaces to install operating system images, deploy applications, and maintain the OS and application software. IBM Cloud is an example. [5]
- PaaS, Platform as a service. The layer provides operating system and related services (just like middleware, execution runtime, database, and web server), related tools and developing languages. These services can be used by user to deploy their application to cloud. With this model, user focuses on application deployment and runtime configuration. EC2 (Elastic Compute Cloud) by Amazon is a typical PaaS cloud. [6]

- SaaS, Software as a service. In the model, cloud providers provide applications. User access needed application from clients or internet. Typical SaaS provides is Google Pack. Google Pack provides Calendar, Gmail, Google Talk, Docs and others through internet. [7]

According access restriction, there are three different cloud types. [9]

- Public cloud, providers provide available cloud applications, storage, and other resources to the general public.
- Private cloud is cloud only available for a single organization.
- Hybrid cloud is a composition of two clouds (private, public) that remains unique entities but is bound together, offering the benefits of multiple deployment models.

3   Intelligent Storage as a Service with Mixed Products (IStaaSM)

StaaS (Storage as a Service) is important part in Cloud Computing area. StaaS can be a standalone kind of SaaS / PaaS / IaaS; it is also can be the foundation of other kinds of SaaS / PaaS / IaaS.   Along with information explosion in new century, storage and related services becomes more and more popular, include StaaS.

Fig.2 displayed four layers of StaaS (Storage as a Service) architecture.

- Virtualization layer, responsible for virtualizes physical storage products to virtualized resources. Virtualized resources are foundation of resource allocation, management, and etc.
- VMM, Virtualization Management Monitor, responsible for manage virtualized resources and provide service under user's demand with user familiar style through VM.
- VM, Virtual Machine, style and method of service provision.
- Business Services, interfaces which user achieve needed service.

Virtualization layer is the key part; its performance determines the performance of whole architecture. Without efficient virtualization layer, the service provider needs either more hardware to fit user's demand or can't delivery service with quality.

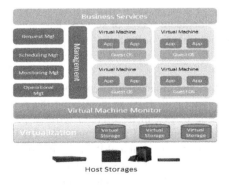

Fig. 2. Storage as Service Architecture

In current Cloud implementations, the hardware is virtualized in two different ways, single layer storage pool and multi layers storage pool. Total numbers of layers in virtualized resource pool make a distinction between these two ways.

- Single layer storage pool

The virtualized resources are located in a flat layer, and used randomly. This method is simple, and easy to manage. But the performance differential between different storage hardware is not considered, and this leads to performance wasting.

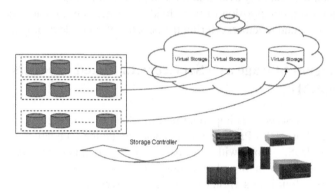

Fig. 3. Single layer storage pool

- Multi layers storage pool

Differential between different storage hardware has been considered, and service provider is trying to assign these resources to different kind of data according operation intensive. In this way, research and industry are focus on figure out how to assign operation intensive data with high performance resources. Currently, the mechanism used is static that means cloud implementer try to assign high performance resources at initial phase of cloud. It is hard to make adaption according user operation characteristics during operation phase of Cloud Computing systems.

IStaaSM enabled Cloud Computing infrastructure with intelligence on self performance improvement ability. The method analyzes user operations regularity and then move hot data to high performed hardware to improve performance of whole infrastructure.

With IStaaSM, there is dedicate server or servers (base on scale of Cloud Computing systems) which responsible to collect and maintain needed information and execute needed operations.

- Customization

This step indentifies the performance difference between storage products and establishes multi-layers storage pool. First is identifying the performance of each storage products. Three major ways can be used to retrieve performance of different storage products, information published by storage products vendor, trustable information published by 3rd part organization and IStaaSM performance method. IStaaSM performance method is part of IStaaSM, it submit read and write operations in different scales to determine performance of storage products. The second is establishing

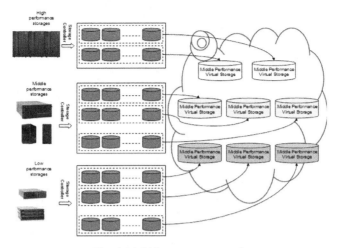

Fig. 4. Multi layers storage pool

virtualized storage pool. Cloud service provider input the number of vitalized resource layers, virtualized resource in different layers has different performance.

- Data Localization Map creation/Maintenance

Data Localization Map (DLP) is used to record data distribution in different virtualized resource layers. DLP represent current working state of virtualized resources. This step creates and maintains Data Localization Map.

- Hot Data Collection

This step executed during operation phase of Cloud Computing system, responsible for count data visit time in unit, and then calculate data hot level. Use scale number which nearest to data visit time as data hot level. The matrix which contains data hot level information for whole storage pool is called Data Operating Map (DOM). Use same scale criteria in first step, Fig.5 is an example of data visit time and it's DOM.

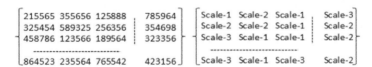

Fig. 5. Data visit time matrix and DOM example

- Dynamic Planning

For specific storage product, the performance is different in different situation. The first step is determining the loading ratio for specific storage product base on total loading ratio of storage pool. Loading ratio pointed means performance in different scale fixed. After that, data migration plan can be fixed base on provided profile. The profile contains priorities of data in different scales.

- Data Migration

This is last step that responsible for complete data migration and generate migration summary for reference and record.

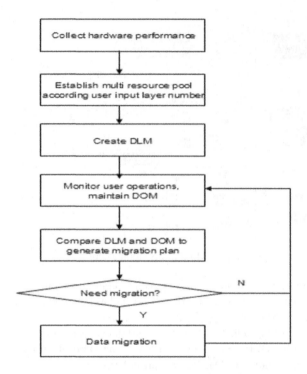

Fig. 6. Major steps of IStaaSM

4   Experiment and Future Work

To test and verify the effect of IStaaSM, this experiment simulates three different storage products to construct hardware fundamental. Three different storage products have different performance, following table contains performance information. To make experimental simple, the impact of data increasing and data load ratio to performance is not considered in this experiment. In the experimental, the time cost of 100GB / 200GB / 400GB will be calculated, recorded and compared.

Table 1. Simulated Storage devices in different performance

	Data Throughput
Storage 1	400MBps
Storage 2	200MBps
Storage 3	100MBps

4.1   Simulated Traditional StaaS System

In the simulated traditional StaaS system, the virtual storage has been distributed to different hardware randomly. And the distribution will not be changed during operation phase. The only way to make change of this is system re-construction. But reconstruction is costive and hard to accommodate to future. To make experiment result closer to real, simulated traditional StaaS system is constructed 10 times with same method. Each time, average of time cost of 100GB / 200GB / 400GB read and write is taken as final result.

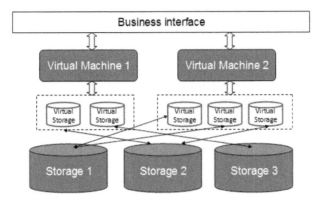

Fig. 7. Architecture of Simulated traditional StaaS system

Table 2. Experiment result in simulated traditional StaaS system

	Virtual Machine 1			Virtual Machine 2		
	100GB	200GB	400GB	100GB	200GB	400GB
1	666.67	1351.35	2580.65	546.45	1136.36	2127.66
2	578.03	1219.51	2325.58	617.28	1408.45	2259.89
3	473.93	956.94	1895.73	641.03	1136.36	2395.21
4	469.48	952.38	1716.74	529.10	1047.12	2020.20
5	529.10	1081.08	2127.66	500.00	956.94	1932.37
6	598.80	1183.43	2409.64	561.80	1092.90	2285.71
7	746.27	1282.05	2797.20	450.45	1069.52	1970.44
8	800.00	1492.54	2116.40	847.46	1626.02	3361.34
9	649.35	1408.45	2395.21	561.80	1041.67	2209.94
10	561.80	1098.90	3007.52	465.12	961.54	2020.20
Average	607.34	1202.66	2337.23	572.05	1147.69	2258.30

4.2   Simulated IStaaSM System

One server responsible for execute program to monitor usage of storages and execute programs to complete method of IStaaSM. The other server responsible for simulate requests. The different to experiment with traditional StaaS system, the IStaaSM system is constructed only once. After data operation completed, the system will refine the system with method which is brought up by this article automatically. After all steps which mentioned in Fig.6 completed, the data read and write will be repeat. New cost time will be calculated. Average of time cost of date read and write in each date scale is took as final result.

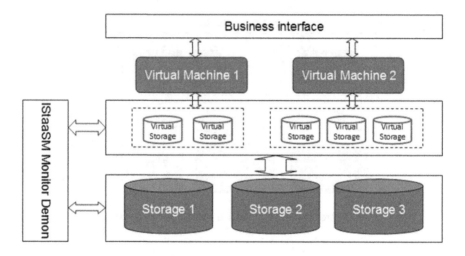

Fig. 8. Architecture of IStaaSM system

Table 3. Experiment result in IStaaSM system

	Virtual Machine 1			Virtual Machine 2		
	100GB	200GB	400GB	100GB	200GB	400GB
1	390.63	724.64	1877.93	321.54	787.40	1342.28
2	348.43	787.40	1503.76	353.36	662.25	1388.89
3	309.60	692.04	1632.65	427.35	823.05	1503.76
4	374.53	816.33	1731.60	411.52	754.72	1793.72
5	361.01	816.33	1581.03	347.22	754.72	1459.85
6	371.75	781.25	1709.40	369.00	711.74	1632.65
7	389.11	641.03	1503.76	331.13	719.42	1388.89
8	341.30	638.98	1639.34	335.57	781.25	1438.85
9	346.02	952.38	1286.17	452.49	671.14	1724.14
10	373.13	896.86	1342.28	331.13	787.40	1388.89
Average	360.55	774.72	1580.79	368.03	745.31	1506.19

5   Result and Future Work

IStaaSM endowed Storage as a Service system with intelligent on automatic performance enhancement. It runs in hardware virtualization layer of Cloud Computing Architecture. With IStaaSM, the performance of cloud system can has 30% to 50% improvement by average. The enhancement of IStaaSM can benefit industry, Cloud Computing provider and user.

The migration process needs a certain amount of hardware capacity, and amount resources which assigned to migration process impacts total time needed to complete whole process. In large scale of cloud system, the cost is huge. Simple, efficient data migration method can improve performance of IStaaSM system.

References

[1] http://en.wikipedia.org/wiki/Cloud_computing
[2] Boss, G., Malladi, P., Quan, D., Legregni, L., Hall, H.: Cloud computing. IBM White paper (2007), http://download.boulder.ibm.com/ibmdl/pub/software/dw/wes/hipods/Cloud_computing_wp_final_8Oct.pdf
[3] http://www-03.ibm.com/press/us/en/pressrelease/22613.wss
[4] O'Connell, M.: New developerWorks survey shows dominance of cloud computing and mobile application development. developerWorks, IBM, http://www.ibm.com/developerworks/aboutdw/2010survey-results/
[5] http://www-935.ibm.com/services/us/en/cloud-enterprise/index.html
[6] http://aws.amazon.com/
[7] http://tools.google.com/
[8] Kontio, M.: Architectural manifesto: An introduction to the possibilities (and risks) of cloud computing, http://www.ibm.com/developerworks/opensource/library/ar-archman10/index.html
[9] The NIST Definition of Cloud Computing. National Institute of Science and Technology (retrieved July 24, 2011)
[10] http://www.storageperformance.org

GIS Application Model Based on Cloud Computing

Linli Zhou, Rujing Wang, Chaoyuan Cui, and Chengjun Xie

Institute of Intelligent Machines, Chinese Academy of Sciences,
230031 Hefei, China
linlizhou@iim.ac.cn

Abstract. Cloud computing is a network-based computing model; it provides support for the upper cloud application environment by building a cloud computing infrastructure. The combination of GIS and cloud computing can provide new prospects for the development of information storage, processing and its application for the GIS. This paper presents a GIS application model based on cloud computing. The model which based on cloud computing, data storage and transparent user services uses GIS infrastructure and service facilities as the service support platform. It provides users with a stable, efficient and reliable service.

Keywords: Cloud Computing, GIS, Hadoop, GIS Services.

1 Introduction

IS applications mostly relates to the calculation of high-density data. GIS technology has been around for decades. With the maturity of the technology increases, more and more spatial data and non-spatial data have been applied. Increasingly advanced data collection technology also allows us to a rich variety of data from various data sources. At the same time, this trend brought the problem is that so vast amounts of data makes any single institution is difficult to be saved or processed. In addition, the GIS system of the location, the logical or physical data are mostly from the different computing institutions. GIS spatial analysis for these data is not only complex but also needs high computing power.

In order to share GIS data and computational results for those dispersed users in different physical locations, one scalable, low-cost computing platform such as cloud computing for GIS is essential. Various features of cloud computing is used to support various elements of the geospatial information including modeling storage and processing, etc. It can change the user-traditional GIS applications and construction mode. It can use geographic information resources more friendly, high efficiency and cost-effective.

This paper presents the application architecture of a cloud-based computing platform for the GIS system. First, we proposed an integrated model of cloud computing architecture of GIS applications; next give a typical example of application of cloud computing and application of GIS.

J. Lei et al. (Eds.): NCIS 2012, CCIS 345, pp. 130–136, 2012.
© Springer-Verlag Berlin Heidelberg 2012

2   Paper Preparation

Cloud computing-based GIS architecture will achieve a leap from single-to-LAN, Internet applications, meet the private and public cloud environments through a unified architecture, and realize the private cloud, public cloud integration, connectivity and interaction.

This technology can support the full application server, desktop, Web and mobile side, it can support a single point of release, automatic synchronization, frequency statistics, and automatic optimization, and support the cloud within the data migration between the migration of private-public cloud and the cloud center migration. Established model for this purpose called nGIS Servers application model, namely the multi-node GIS Servers.Fig.1 shows the architecture model:

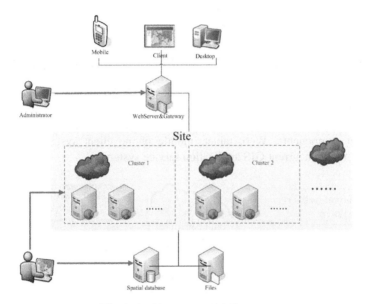

Fig. 1. Architecture model diagram

Model uses point to point, each GIS Server nodes are equal. So that the new model, even if accidental shoot down of a GIS Server node does not cause the entire map service stops running; Similarly, when the need to add a GIS Server node to the plug-in way to insert a node to improve the load capacity for the service . This loose, hot-pluggable architecture is the foundation to build a cloud GIS application.

Logically, the nGIS Servers nodes organize as a Site. The logical relationship of this model is simply summarized as follows: Site architecture unit; the Cluster logical unit to GIS services; GIS Server for the actual processing unit; GIS Instance for each GIS function processing container.

A series of data required by the running GIS Server was saved to the Site property. Such as: the cluster information, service information, service depends on the data, directory information and log information, and so on. GIS Server is based on this information in order to provide specific services.

A specific application of the GIS environment has only one site. Cluster is the logical unit of GIS services, it is a logical container for a specific service for a particular Cluster, hosted services, such as: Map Service, GP Service. Of course, the specific service capabilities were provided by the following GIS Server. A Cluster is not only carrying a service or a service, each Cluster can be for different types of multiple services to provide a container. The GIS Servers in the cluster has a perfect synergy to protect, such as: TCP poll, UDP broadcast heartbeat sensor.

GIS Server is the actual processing unit, there are multiple GIS Server nodes in a Cluster of logic, these GIS Server node load balancing logic function of the upper. The platform provides a variety of load balancing algorithms for different request, such as: intensive I / O, the long transaction type, high CPU type, it will automatically configure to a different load algorithm. GIS Server is a full-cached mode, so performance will be enhanced. The GIS Instance is the processing instance of the GIS Server which deals with specific functions.

3   Large-Scale Concurrent Cloud GIS Technology System

GIS services for cloud computing technology systems, including distributed storage service system, high-performance parallel processing systems, high availability application server system, high-concurrency Web server and other server-side system and desktop components, Web, tablet, mobile phone client system. Fig.2 shows Large-scale high concurrent GIS application service system:

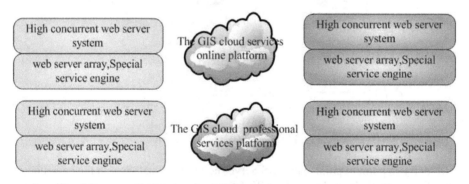

Fig. 2. Large-scale high concurrent GIS application service system diagram

The service system includes high concurrency and high-performance application services systems, highly efficient parallel processing system and the client, particularly mobile end system.

3.1   High Concurrency Map Service System

The map service system as GIS cloud services portal supports large-capacity, high concurrent user access; supports aggregate access to customized content and multi-map data resources; supports online failover mechanisms and off-site disaster recovery, backup emergency system; supports multiple geographically distributed architecture to achieve the trans regional load balancing. It be able to support large screen system, workstation, PC, tablet, mobile phones, car and even the smart TV and other equipment of the unified interaction and user collaboration; geospatial data fast security system, you can fast access to data across multiple networks.

3.2   High-Performance Application Service System

Cloud GIS application service system supports map editing, dynamic thematic maps, spatial query, spatial analysis and other online applications. Support for maps, images, 3D model, video, pictures, sound, and a variety of integrated space of mass associated with information storage and integrated management, support for geo-spatial information associated with dynamic integration; to support large-scale three-dimensional geospatial simulation, including large-scale three-dimensional scene fast rendering of large data, the load of high-detail true geospatial information and visualization of business systems integration; online development of customized support services, the expansion of services and client applications.

3.3   High-Efficiency Parallel Processing System

Cloud GIS parallel processing system with high-availability processing services technology architecture supports for distributed, parallel data processing, distributed deployment, and support processes visual design, the task of automatic segmentation and intelligent running, quick to support content publishing and based remote management of mobile terminals.

3.4   The Client and the Mobile Terminal System

Cloud of GIS client will be unprecedented rich and diverse technical requirements of diverse end devices to provide good support to maintain high performance, low-power operation, excellent device support and UI interactions, and efficient data compression and transmission technology, reliable transmission mechanism for technical support.

4   GIS Model Based on Open Source Cloud Computing Platform

Since the concept of cloud computing have been proposed, IT vendors launch their own cloud computing platform, Amazon AWS, Microsoft Windows Azure, IBM's Blue Cloud are typical representatives. But these platforms are commercial platform for people from the underlying research cloud computing, you cannot get more understanding. The open source cloud computing platform provides a more transparent system and structure of cloud computing, open source cloud computing platform for building cloud of GIS from the ground up development to solve the ineffective and inefficient calculated in GIS.

4.1   Open Source Cloud Computing Platform Hadoop

Hadoop is the most well-known open source cloud computing platform, analog and Google cloud computing technology. It is a distributed computing framework of the Apache open-source organization, a large number of low-cost hardware devices, composed of a cluster of computers to run the application, it provides a reliable interface for the application, it can build a high reliability and distributed system. Hadoop is a distributed file system which is mapping of simplification of the programming model, and distributed database (HBSE). The distributed file system is divided into the Namenode and Datanode node. Only one of which Namenode Datanodes can be many. Namenode responsible for responsible for maintaining the cluster metadata external to create, open, delete, and rename the file or directory function. Datanode store data, and is responsible for processing the data read and write requests. Datanode regularly reported to the Namenode news, to the Namenode and response messages to control Datanodes. The MapReduce of Hadoop has the Master / Slave structure. Master was Called Jobtracker, Slave was called Tasktracker, the user submits the calculation is called the Job, each Job, will be divided into several Tasks Jobtracker responsible for initiating, tracking, scheduling all the slaves. Fig.3 shows the HDFS structure diagram:

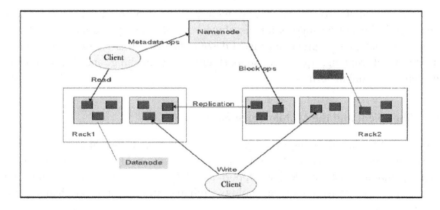

Fig. 3. HDFS structure diagram

4.2   The Hadoop-Based Cloud GIS

Hadoop platform for the cloud of GIS provides a stable platform. The Hadoop-based cloud GIS changed the original GIS system architecture, technical architecture can be divided into four layers: hardware infrastructure layer, resource layer of the virtualization platform layer of the Hadoop task management scheduling, cloud GIS management middleware layer and GIS cloud service layer. Fig.4 shows the Cloud GIS design model based on the Hadoop platform:

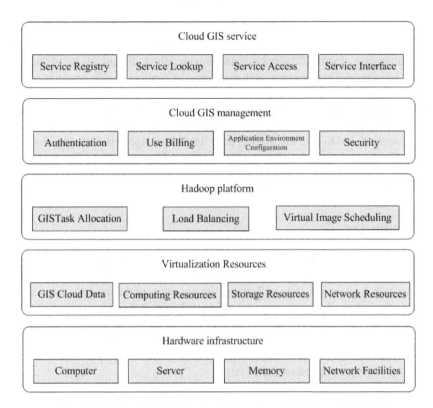

Fig. 4. The Cloud GIS design model based on the Hadoop platform

The bottom of the hardware infrastructure layer includes computers, networks, servers, storage, and so on. Hardware infrastructure to build cloud GIS necessary material conditions, the infrastructure can buy their own, can also be rented, leased services such as telecom operators, Amazon, IBM and other infrastructure, and then to build a GIS platform, software, content-level cloud GIS services.

Virtualization layer to build cloud GIS needs of a variety of software resources and hardware resources are abstracted as services. You can use the Microsoft SQL data services such as database via SOAP and REST standard interface uses Microsoft's cloud storage service.

Hadoop platform task scheduling layer uses the Hadoop cloud computing resource management, task scheduling on a number of GIS applications, and is responsible for GIS concurrent operation of the load balancing. MapReduce model deals with larger GIS data. Cloud GIS management is an essential part of the cloud GIS, clouds GIS management is mainly responsible for the cloud GIS user authentication, the use of GIS services, billing, application configuration, GIS data security. In cloud mode of GIS, GIS variety of applications and operating the network services in the form of user services, and billing in accordance with the use of time or traffic. The security of cloud of GIS can be encrypted over the network, separated by a firewall and other means of protection, to protect the safety of the cloud GIS facilities overall.

The cloud GIS service is on the top. The cloud can build GIS services to achieve the function. It can be aggregated according to the needs and business properties, can be re-customized cloud GIS services can dynamically scale stretching to meet the massive increase in applications and user need. Compute nodes or cells, can be replaced at any time. When a cloud cell has problem, new cloud cells can be gathered over to be replaced. It can provide an infinite number of ever-changing applications. Cloud GIS service layer GIS in a variety of functions packaged into a standard Web Services service, and to take the SOA system for the management and use. Cloud GIS foreign offers a variety of interfaces, can be achieved between the different resource aggregations. Cloud GIS external forms of service; users can use the cloud GIS services through the computer browser or cell phone.

5   Summary

At present, cloud computing has become a hot technology, and has the unprecedented attention. The emergence of cloud computing changes the existing IT infrastructure, the traditional desktop software will gradually transition to the network software, the software revolution of the new one is about to begin. The integration of GIS and mainstream IT technology was increasing quickly. GIS in large-scale, popular application trend has been very clear. The cloud computing model provides an excellent opportunity for the development of GIS. It will have a profound impact on spatial data mining and geospatial analysis.

Acknowledgments. This study is financially supported by the National Key Technology R&D Program of China (NO: 2012BAH20B02).

References

1. Lin, G., Fu, D., Zhu, J., Dasmalchi, G.: Cloud computing: It as a service IT Professional (2009)
2. Li, H., Sedayao, J., Hahn- Steichen, J., Jimison, E.: Developing an Enterprise Cloud Computing Strategy C - Intel Corporation (2009)
3. Dean, J., Ghemawat, S.: MapReduce:Simplified data processing on large clusters. In: Proc. of the 6th Symp. on Operating System
4. Ghemawat, S., Gobioff, H., Leung, S.: The Google file system. ACM SIGOPS Operating Systems Review, 29–43 (2003)
5. Barroso, L.A., Dean, J., Holzle, U.: Web Search for a Planet: The google Cluster Architecture. IEEE Micro. 23(2), 22–28 (2003)
6. Lin, C., Fu, D., Zhu, J., Dasmalchi, G.: Cloud computing: It as a serviceG - IT Professional (2009)
7. Heiser, J., Nicolett, M.: Accessing the Security Risks of Cloud Computing - Gartner Inc., Stamford (2008)
8. Li, H., Sedayao, J., Hahn-Steichen, J., Jimison, E.: Developing an Enterprise Cloud Computing Strategy, Intel Corporation (2009)
9. Aymerich, F.M., Fenu, G., Surcis, S.: An approach to a Cloud Computing network - Applications of Digital Information and Web (2008)

Development Framework for Cloud Services

Binh Minh Nguyen, Viet Tran, and Ladislav Hluchy

Institute of Informatics, Slovak Academy of Sciences,
Dubravska cesta 9, 845 07 Bratislava, Slovakia
{minh.ui,viet.ui,hluchy.ui}@savba.sk

Abstract. Cloud computing has seen a tremendous growth in the last five years. Along with the growth, many cloud types have been marketed. However, from the view of users, there are still barriers to exploit the cloud computing. Not only the migration into clouds is difficult, even so the development and deployment of new services from the beginning could be quite challenges. In this paper, we present a novel development framework for cloud services. Its design is based on abstraction approach and object-oriented programming technique, allowing cloud users to easily and rapidly develop and deploy their services. The approach also enables service migration and interoperability among the different clouds.

Keywords: cloud computing, service development, object-oriented programming, interoperability.

1 Introduction

With the advance of cloud technologies, the trend of developing and deploying applications in cloud environment also has appeared. There are economic as well as technological reasons why an application should be developed and deployed on the cloud. On the economic side, cloud computing can provide significant cost savings because of the increased utilization resulting from the pooling of resources (often virtualized). Otherwise, cloud computing enables rapid delivery of IT services, which increases business efficiency. On the operational side, manageability, performance, and scalability are the typical reasons why application developers consider cloud computing. However, this trend is being faced two challenges:

- The Platform as a Service (PaaS) type limits the developers to concrete platforms and Application Programming Interfaces (APIs).
- The Infrastructure as a Service (IaaS) type provides too low-level service.

In principle, PaaS clouds provide environments for hosting and API for implementing applications. The platforms will manage the execution of these applications and offer some advanced features like automatic scaling. However, for existing applications, PaaS may require rewriting completely the application codes using a dedicated platform what is not feasible for cloud developers. Furthermore, each platform can have different key features and API, what make moving the applications from a platform to another is practically impossible. Meanwhile, IaaS clouds provide

J. Lei et al. (Eds.): NCIS 2012, CCIS 345, pp. 137–147, 2012.
© Springer-Verlag Berlin Heidelberg 2012

resources (virtual machines, storage) as services where the users have full access to the resources and manipulate them directly. For instance, using IaaS, the users will log into virtual machines and directly execute some commands or modify some files in order to create their own development and deployment platform on the machines.

Easily realize that, while PaaS binds users into existing platforms, building applications on IaaS will be their choice to meet specific requirements. However, the use of IaaS is perceived as difficult with the users, requiring advance computer skills for the installation and usage [1], [2] and [3]. Specifically, to develop and deploy an application on an IaaS cloud, the users themselves have to carry out the following steps in turn:

1. Preparing virtual machine: the user selects a virtual machine image from repository to get provisioned and launched. Then, he or she configures the features of the virtual machine, including firewalls, persistent storage and so on.
2. Preparing platform on the virtual machine: if the software packages (e.g. web/app server/runtime, database server) are not installed, the user needs to install them.
3. Developing application: the user will develop the application on his or her platform.
4. Managing the virtual machine, platform, service: the final step is about managing the virtual machine, platform as well as service. For example, when there is an update or software pack on the OS, the IaaS provider will not automatically do it for the user.

Consequently, from the view of users, they need to have a solution which enables to simplify the development and deployment of appliances/services on IaaS clouds. The solution will allow the users to write cloud services, pack them and deliver the codes of the services for deployment on various clouds without any worry. The solution thus also provides the users with a single unified interface to overcome the incompatible API between the clouds. In this paper, we present the design and implementation of a novel development framework for cloud services. The foundation of the framework is an abstraction layer that provides cloud developers with a unified interface to support management of the entire service life cycle from development, through deployment to execution and operation over IaaS clouds. Based on the abstraction layer, the process of service development and deployment will be easier and simpler than the traditional approach. More importantly, the solution will overcome the problem of the centralized virtual machine manager, which allows the service migration and interoperability between different infrastructures.

2   Related Work

Although some cloud standardization efforts and open API abstractions have emerged, such as Open Virtualization Format (OVF) [4]; Open Cloud Computing Interface (OCCI) [5]; SimpleCloud API [6]; jCloud [7]; ApacheLibcloud [8]; DeltaCloud [9] and so on, but they have not yet brought any solution for service development and deployment issue in cloud environment. Typically, OVF allows reuse of a standard virtual machine image on diverse clouds. Thereby, services can move from a cloud to others along with the image. Besides OVF, another project is

OCCI that enables users to manage resources from different clouds via a single unified API. Unfortunately, both standards still require many efforts from users, who have to carry out a lot of the complex steps (identified in section 1) for developing and deploying their applications into the IaaS clouds. The reason is that these solutions have not provided a suitable programming model for the service development and deployment on the clouds. On the other hand, the standardizations force cloud providers to accept and support their products. Such scenario would face a very large impact on the cloud vendor competitiveness, as it requires the vendors to offer better quality services at lower prices without locking customers to rely on their resources.

Instead of these de-facto standards, the open API abstractions (e.g. SimpleCloud API, jCloud, ApacheLibcloud, DeltaCloud) also have been designed and implemented for managing resources from various clouds. The advantage of the API abstractions is independent of cloud vendors. However, like OCCI, these API also do not help users to develop and deploy applications more easily than the traditional way. The users still have to directly connect to the virtual machines, install and configure everything in order to prepare their own platforms. Currently, no API abstractions have provided functionalities for these tasks. In comparison with all projects above, our approach has differences and advantages in the following aspects:

- Support for service development and deployment - the layer provides users a development framework for developing and deploying services on various clouds. The layer also allows the customization and extension: developers can take developed appliances by others and customize/extend them to new capabilities without access to the original layer codes.
- Interoperability - developers can choose the target cloud infrastructure to deploy the services and manage them in a unified interface.
- Value-added providers - the framework will enable value-added providers in the way: services can deploy to available cloud infrastructures and deliver to users on requests.

3   Architecture Design

3.1   Design Idea

Most of IaaS providers offer a certain API, which enables developers to interact with cloud resources. In Fig. 1, the *current approach* describes the development and ldeployment of cloud-based appliances on IaaS clouds today. The developers have to develop and deploy their service in turn on every different cloud. It is difficult to realize because the developers must be familiarized with various APIs and operation system (OS). In this way, these services almost cannot migrate from a cloud to others. The use of our solution also is depicted with the *abstraction layer approach* in this figure. In which, the abstraction layer is the foundation of the development framework where developers can easily create new abstraction objects for their applications/services by inheriting the layer functionalities. The framework will allow extending/customizing existing abstractions layers (services) that created by other developers. Thus allowing the natural transition from IaaS via PaaS to SaaS that managed by the framework on different cloud infrastructures.

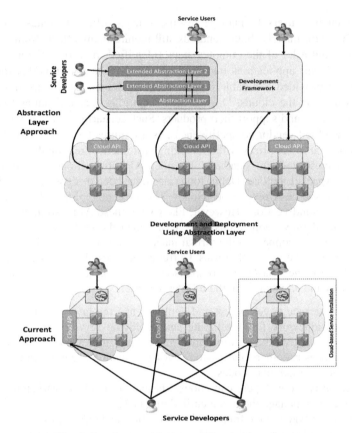

Fig. 1. Development framework for cloud services

In this direction, the abstraction layer will give a single unified interface with basic functionalities of virtual machine from various clouds. All applications/services using the framework will be built over the abstraction layer and inherit the interoperability from the layer. The layer does not require any additional modifications from existing cloud middlewares, so it does not require involvement of cloud providers. The abstraction layer will have the following features:

- Allowing developers to create cloud-based services by inheriting functionalities of the abstraction layer.
- Allowing developers to define and control what their users can do with the service via a clear interface. Limiting low-level access of users to virtual machines.
- Allowing developers to reuse simply existing code by other developers. Due to object-oriented programming (OOP), a developer can use the codes of other developers without detailed understanding inside the abstraction layer or preceding layers.
- Enabling the interoperability and migration of application between different clouds. The developed service can be deployed easily on various clouds without any obstacle.
- Allowing developers to backup their applications or data and restore whenever they need on suitable infrastructures.

3.2   Abstraction Layer Design

The abstraction layer has designed with several functions in order to manage and interact with virtual machines that belong to different clouds. These functions are divided into the following functionalities:

- Setting default: enables users to set which cloud will be used. This functionality only has `setDefault()` function.
- Provisioning: consists of `start()` and `stop()` function to create and terminate the virtual machines.
- Monitoring: gets actual information of the machines (memory use, IP address and so on) by `status()` function.
- Execution: runs user commands on the virtual machines by `execute()` function;
- Transfer: includes two functions named `put_data()` to upload and `get_data()` to download data to/from the virtual machines.
- Backup/Restoration: backup/restore machine configuration and user data into an image. The functionality involves `backup()` and `restore()` function.

To interact with various clouds, for each of the clouds, we have designed a driver, which used its specific API to manage virtual machines. Note that, the drivers do not need to implement all API functionalities that are provided by the cloud vendors. Each driver only use necessary functionalities to shape the abstraction layer functions, including `start()`, `stop()`, `status()`, `backup()` and `restore()`. The `setDefault()` function is call to set a driver (cloud) to use.

Otherwise, the execution and transfer functionality do not use any APIs because no APIs provide functionalities to carry out those operations. Thus the abstraction layer will abstract the connection and realization process and hide implementation details by the `execute()`, `put_data()` and `get_data()` function.

Through the abstract functions above, detailed interactions between the abstraction layer and different clouds will be hidden. Therefore, the users can manipulate multiple clouds at the same time under the unified interface irrespective of how each cloud works. The developers just inherit those functions to develop and deploy their services on the chosen cloud.

3.3   Inheritance and Software Layering of the Abstraction Layer

The developers can easily create new cloud service by using the abstraction layer. In Fig. 2, the developers only have to inherit the functions of the abstraction layer for developing their service functions. The functionalities of the service include:

- Initialization: the developer just call the `setDefault()` function of the abstraction layer to choose a cloud in order to deploy their service, then use `start()` function to create a virtual machine on the cloud. The developer can add commands to install software packages on newly created machine by the `execute()` function. He or she also can terminate the virtual machine that contains the service by the `stop()` function.

- Backup/Restoration: to create backup/restoration functions for the service, the developer will inherit the `backup()` and `restore()` function of the abstraction layer.
- Service functionalities: the developer can create several functionalities for their service. For examples, for database service, they can add a number of functions to import database, make query, and so on by inheriting the `execute()`, `get_data()` and `put_data()` function.

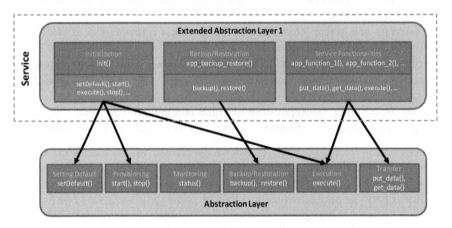

Fig. 2. Inheritance of the abstraction layer

In this way, users (distinguish from the developers) will use the service (extended abstraction layer 1) via its interface. The users would not require worrying about how the service deploys. Meanwhile, the developer can choose simply the target cloud to deploy their service without having to care about incompatible API because during the development and deployment, the developer does not use directly any middleware APIs. They only reuse the functions that are provided by the abstraction layer.

In addition, an extended abstraction layer, which has created by a developer, also can be used and extended further by other developers in the same way. Thus, the first developer defines the extended abstraction layer 1 with new functionalities on demand from his or her users. In other words, the extended layer 1 hid implementation details of the abstraction layer in its functionalities. Similarly, the later developers can also define functionalities for extended abstraction layer 2 over the layer 1 according to their users' needs by inheriting the layer 1 functionalities. As the result, each layer is practically a platform-as-a-service by itself, because the users can use the service via a clear interface provided by the previous developers. For example: a developer can create a LAMP (Linux-Apache-PHP-MySQL) layer that is equivalent to web-hosting platforms for his or her users. Another developer can use this LAMP layer to provide web applications (e.g. wiki, forum) without manipulating with the cloud infrastructures.

4   Implementation of the Abstraction Layer

The aim of the layer's implementation is to present. Currently, our abstraction layer has implemented for supporting three cloud systems: Eucalyptus 2.0.3 [10] (compatible with Amazon EC2 API [11]), OpenNebula 3.2.1 release [12] (using OCCI API specification) and OpenStack Compute (Essex release) [13]. As Python language [14], the abstraction layer has implemented as a class (Abstraction_Layer) which provides the functions for the manipulation with virtual machine (setDefault(), start(), stop(), status(), backup(), restore(), execute(), put_data() and get_data()). For each cloud infrastructure, we have respectively defined separate classes: Eucalyptus, OpenNebula and Openstack, which are the drivers of these clouds. Each the class uses the middleware-specific API and utility mechanisms (execution, transfer functionality) for the implementation. Structurally, the functions of the Abstraction_Layer class are derived from these separate classes. If we need to extend our implementation for a new cloud infrastructure (e.g. Rackspace [15]), the only thing we have to do is to create the new derived class (driver) for its specific middleware functions.

To use the Abstraction_Layer, we set vm variable as abstract object of a virtual machine. The abstraction layer functions like setDefault(), start(), stop(), ... will be called by the methods of vm variable i.e. vm.setDefault(), vm.start(), vm.stop() and so on. At that time, we choose a driver to use by calling the function vm.setDefault('driver_name'). Due to polymorphism of the object-oriented programming, vm.start() will be realized as Eucalyptus.start(), OpenNebula.start() or Openstack.start() according to the actual argument value of the setDefault() function. It means that the implementation of Abstraction_Layer and all its functions is independent from cloud middlewares. Similarly, users can execute, upload, download, ... by vm.execute(), vm.put_data(), vm.get_data(), ...

For example, the functions of the Abstraction_Layer class that are run one by one in Python interactive mode to select a cloud, create a virtual machine on the cloud, upload an application from local to the machine, install the application on the machine, download output file from the machine to local and terminate the machine, which look as follows:

```
vm = Abstraction_Layer()
vm.setDefault('Openstack')
vm.start()
vm.put_data('myapp.py')
vm.execute('. myapp.py')
vm.get_data('output.dat')
vm.stop()
```

The users of the abstraction layer can replace Openstack value in the vm.setDefault() above by OpenNebula or Eucalyptus to select other clouds. Default values of the methods are used whenever possible for the convenient use.

Sometime, the users only want to create a virtual machine for running their applications, they do not care about concrete image, or which type of instance should be used. The abstraction layer should not force the users to specify every parameter. For instance, to create a virtual machine, the command could be done fully in the form: vm.start('ami-XXXXX', 'large') or succinctly as follows: vm.start(). Then the virtual machine will be created with a default image and a default instance type. The users can get information about the created virtual machine simply if they want by running the following command: vm.status(). Note that the user authentication (information of cloud servers, usernames, passwords and key pairs) for using these clouds and the default parameters that have been already defined in a configuration file.

5   Example of the Service Development and Deployment

This section offers a description of the development and deployment process of a concrete service using the abstraction layer. From this description, service developers can themselves build their cloud-based services in the similar manner. Inspired by the fact that most users need a cloud database to store their data, a MySQL service on cloud has been built. Due to the functions of the abstraction layer, the service has been developed quickly and simply, allowing developers to deploy on the different supported clouds at the same time. The key features of this service are summarizes:

- Simple use: near-zero user efforts for installation, configuration and administration.
- Easy access: the user can connect the service with other applications like *phpMyAdmin* for management or use directly service via its functionalities.
- High availability and reliability, the service provides functionalities such as import/export data, backup/restore service.

The service functions have implemented by inheriting the existing functions of the abstraction layer. The service functions also are divided into three functionality groups like the Fig. 2. Each the group has implemented as a class. Thereof, the service program had three classes. Each class consists of specific service functions inside it. The initialization of the MySQL server, which has been programmed as follows:

```
class Init:
    global vm                            #set global for vm
    vm = Abstraction_Layer()
    vm.setDefault('driver_name')         #set cloud to use
    def START_VM(self):
        vm.start()
    def INSTALL_MYSQL(self, password):
        vm.execute('install_MySQL_command')
        ...
```

The backup and restoration functionality have been written shortly:

```
class Backup:
    def SERVICE_BACKUP(self):
        vm.backup()
    def SERVICE_RESTORE(self):
        vm.restore()
```

The database functionalities have been implemented as follows:

```
class Database_Commands:
    def MYSQL_COMMAND(self, MySQLstatements):
        vm.execute(MySQLstatements)
    def CREATE_DATABASE(self, database_name):
        vm.execute('MySQL_command_create_database')
    def IMPORT_DATABASE(self, database_name):
        vm.put_data(inputfile)
        vm.execute('MySQL_command_import_data')
    def EXPORT_DATABASE(self, database_name):
        vm.execute('MySQL_command_exports_data')
        vm.get_data(outputfile)
    ...
```

After the database service is developed, the MySQL service can be deployed simply by running commands:

```
service = Init()
service.START_VM()
service.INSTALL_MYSQL('user_password')
```

At this time, the cloud-based MySQL service could be linked to other applications (e.g. phpMyAdmin) with the following information: hostname (public IP address of the newly created virtual machine), username (root) and user password. The information will be displayed when the service.INSTALL_MYSQL() command finishes. Otherwise, after the deployment, users of the service also can use directly database server through the available functions that have been already developed above:

```
service = Database_Commands()
service.CREATE_DATABASE('blog')
service.MYSQL_COMMAND('GRANT ALL PRIVILEGES ...')
service.IMPORT_DATABASE(file)
...
```

To backup and restore whole service together with virtual machine, the users can run the commands:

```
service = Backup()
service.SERVICE_BACKUP()
service.SERVICE_RESTORE()
```

In this example, the database service is the extended abstraction layer 1 with its specific functions. We also can go further in using the abstraction layer to develop other appliances (e.g. web services, wiki pages, and forum) that are linked to this database service and thus will create the extended abstraction layer 2. The most important thing is that, the codes of extended layers can be deployed on any middleware by changing the name of target cloud in the setDefault() function. Thus, the abstraction layer enables the ability to move appliances among the different clouds without any obstacle.

6   Comparison with the Current Approach

Table 1 gives the comparison between the current and the abstraction layer approach in developing and deploying cloud services.

Table 1. Comparison between two approaches

	Current Approach	Abstraction Layer Approach
API knowledge requirement	Yes	No
Easy resource management	No	Yes
Easy software installation and configuration	No	Yes
OS skill requirement	Yes	No
Easy service development	No	Yes
Delivering service codes for the deployment on clouds	No	Yes
Backup and restoration	Yes - complex	Yes – simple

In the current approach, users are required having deep knowledge about various APIs and OSs in order to create virtual machines from different clouds, install and configure software packages on the machines. Furthermore, the current approach has not provided programming model for the service developers, what brings about the issue: there is no easy way for the developers to implement service utility functionalities on their user demands. Using current approach, the services can only deploy on a cloud and almost cannot move from the cloud to another. In addition, the backup and restoration is very complex via APIs. From the view of the developers, it is clear that the current approach causes many difficulties in developing and deploying services on various clouds at the same time.

Meanwhile, using the abstraction layer to develop and deploy services, the developers and users will gain many benefits rather than the current approach: first, the service developers only use the single unified interface of the abstraction layer without having to know about APIs of various cloud providers. Hence, the developers can easily manage and control resources (virtual machines) of different clouds. Second, the layer enables the ability of automatically installing and configuring software packages. Thus, to deploy developed services, the developers or users do not need to directly log into the instances and manually realize these complex operations. Therefore, they do not need to have OS skills. Third, due to the inheritance feature of the OOP, the developers can use the abstraction layer functions to develop easily the service utility functionalities for their users. Clearly, the services are practically PaaS or even SaaS with the users who just use the service functions without interacting directly with virtual machines. Next, the service codes are packed in files, which can be delivered for deployment on various clouds. During the deployment, the service developers will not face any trouble, including incompatible API and cloud systems. Finally, the backup and restoration functionalities are also simple to use. The users just run the intuitive service commands instead of using middleware APIs.

7   Conclusion

In this paper, we have presented the novel development framework for cloud services. The foundation of the framework is the abstraction layer. In our approach, the abstraction layer provides basic functionalities of virtual machine for each known cloud middlewares. Based on the layer, the process of service development and deployment will be easier and simpler than the traditional approach: developers will build their services by inheriting the existing functionalities of the abstraction layer without using any middleware APIs as well as directly connecting to the virtual machines. Thus, the developed services are independent of infrastructures and they can be deployed on the diverse clouds. In this way, the development framework enables the service interoperability, which is one of the invaluable features for cloud computing.

Acknowledgment. This work is supported by projects SMART II ITMS: 26240120029, CRISIS ITMS: 26240220060, VEGA No. 2/0054/12, CLAN No. APVV 0809-11.

References

1. Ramakrishnan, L., Jackson, K.R., Canon, S., Cholia, S., Shalf, J.: Defining Future Platform Requirements for e-Science Clouds. In: ACM Proceedings of the 1st ACM Symposium on Cloud Computing, pp. 101–106 (2009)
2. Goscinski, A., Brock, M.: Toward dynamic and attribute based publication, discovery and selection for cloud computing. Future Generation Computer Systems, 947–970 (2010)
3. Curry, R., Kiddle, C., Mirtchovski, A., Simmonds, R.: A Cloud-based Interactive Application Service. In: IEEE Proceedings of the Fifth International Conference on e-Science, pp. 102–109 (2009)
4. Open Virtualization Format, http://dmtf.org/sites/default/files/OVF%20Overview%20Document_2010.pdf
5. Metsch, T., Edmonds, A., Nyrén, R.: Open Cloud Computing Interface – Core. In: Open Grid Forum, OCCI-WG, Specification Document (2011), http://forge.gridforum.org/sf/go/doc16161
6. SimpleCloud API, http://simplecloud.org
7. jCloud, http://www.jclouds.org
8. ApacheLibcloud, http://libcloud.apache.org
9. DeltaCloud, http://deltacloud.apache.org
10. Nurmi, D., Wolski, R., Grzegorczyk, C., Obertelli, G., Soman, S., Youseff, L., Zagorodnov, D.: The Eucalyptus Open-Source Cloud-Computing System. In: IEEE Proceedings of the Ninth IEEE/ACM International Symposium on Cluster Computing and the Grid, pp. 124–131 (2011)
11. Amazon EC2 API, http://docs.amazonwebservices.com/AWSEC2/latest/APIReference/Welcome.html
12. Milojičić, D., Llorente, I.M., Montero, R.S.: OpenNebula: A Cloud management Tool. Journal IEEE Internet Computing 15(2), 11–14 (2011)
13. OpenStack, http://openstack.org
14. Python programming language, http://www.python.org
15. Rackspace Hosting cloud, http://www.rackspace.com

Research on Distributed File System with Hadoop

JunWu Xu[1] and JunLing Liang[2]

[1] Hubei Provincial Key Laboratory of Intelligent Robot Wuhan Institute of Technology
430073, China
[2] School of Automation, Wuhan University of Technology 430074, China

Abstract. This paper describes research in the use of Hadoop to develop applications.. This paper introduces the structure of Hadoop and describes the implementation of algorithms in our library. Hadoop is a top-level Apache project being built and used by a global community of contributors, written in the Java programming language. Yahoo! has been the largest contributor to the project, and uses Hadoop extensively across its businesses.

Keywords: JAVA, HBase, Hadoop, SSH.

1 What Is Hadoop?

Hadoop is a large-scale distributed batch processing infrastructure. While it can be used on a single machine, its true power lies in its ability to scale to hundreds or thousands of computers, each with several processor cores. Hadoop is also designed to efficiently distribute large amounts of work across a set of machines. every Hadoop-compatible filesystem should provide location awareness: the name of the rack (more precisely, of the network switch) where a worker node is. Hadoop applications can use this information to run work on the node where the data is, and, failing that, on the same rack/switch, so reducing backbone traffic. The Hadoop Distributed File System (HDFS) uses this when replicating data, to try to keep different copies of the data on different racks. The goal is to reduce the impact of a rack power outage or switch failure so that even if these events occur, the data may still be readable.

HDFS is the primary distributed storage used by Hadoop applications. A HDFS cluster primarily consists of a NameNode that manages the file system metadata and DataNodes that store the actual data. The HDFS Architecture Guide describes HDFS in detail. This user guide primarily deals with the interaction of users and administrators with HDFS clusters. The HDFS architecture diagram depicts basic interactions among NameNode, the DataNodes, and the clients. Clients contact NameNode for file metadata or file modifications and perform actual file I/O directly with the Data-Nodes.

The following are some of the salient features that could be of interest to many users.

J. Lei et al. (Eds.): NCIS 2012, CCIS 345, pp. 148–155, 2012.
© Springer-Verlag Berlin Heidelberg 2012

- Hadoop, including HDFS, is well suited for distributed storage and distributed processing using commodity hardware. It is fault tolerant, scalable, and extremely simple to expand. MapReduce, well known for its simplicity and applicability for large set of distributed applications, is an integral part of Hadoop.
- HDFS is highly configurable with a default configuration well suited for many installations. Most of the time, configuration needs to be tuned only for very large clusters.
- Hadoop is written in Java and is supported on all major platforms.
- Hadoop supports shell-like commands to interact with HDFS directly.
- The NameNode and Datanodes have built in web servers that makes it easy to check current status of the cluster.
- New features and improvements are regularly implemented in HDFS. The following is a subset of useful features in HDFS:

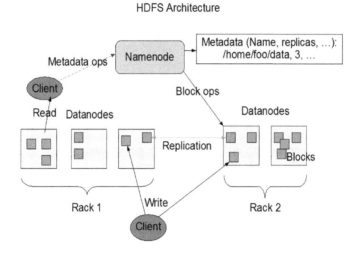

Fig. 1. HDFS Architecture

2   Hadoop Deployment

2.1   Configuration Details

Choose a logical name for this nameservice, for example "mycluster", and use this logical name for the value of this config option. The name you choose is arbitrary. It will be used both for configuration and as the authority component of absolute HDFS paths in the cluster.

Note: If you are also using HDFS Federation, this configuration setting should also include the list of other nameservices, HA or otherwise, as a comma-separated list.

```
<property>
  <name>dfs.federation.nameservices</name>
  <value>mycluster</value>
</property>
```

For both of the previously-configured NameNode IDs, set the full address and IPC port of the NameNode processs. Note that this results in two separate configuration options. For example:

```
<property>
  <name>dfs.namenode.rpc-address.mycluster.nn1</name>
  <value>machine1.example.com:8020</value>
</property>
<property>
  <name>dfs.namenode.rpc-address.mycluster.nn2</name>
  <value>machine2.example.com:8020</value>
</property>
```

Similarly to rpc-address above, set the addresses for both NameNodes' HTTP servers to listen on. For example:

```
<property>
  <name>dfs.namenode.http-address.mycluster.nn1</name>
  <value>machine1.example.com:50070</value>
</property>
<property>
  <name>dfs.namenode.http-address.mycluster.nn2</name>
  <value>machine2.example.com:50070</value>
</property>
```

2.2   Data Organization

HDFS is designed to support very large files. Applications that are compatible with HDFS are those that deal with large data sets. These applications write their data only once but they read it one or more times and require these reads to be satisfied at streaming speeds. HDFS supports write-once-read-many semantics on files. A typical block size used by HDFS is 64 MB. Thus, an HDFS file is chopped up into 64 MB chunks, and if possible, each chunk will reside on a different DataNode.

This is the basis for the communication protocol between the Map/Reduce framework and the streaming mapper/reducer. You can supply a Java class as the mapper and/or the reducer. The above example is equivalent to:

```
$HADOOP_HOME/bin/hadoop   jar $HADOOP_HOME/hadoop-streaming.jar \
    -input myInputDirs \
    -output myOutputDir \
    -mapper org.apache.hadoop.mapred.lib.IdentityMapper \
    -reducer /bin/wc
```

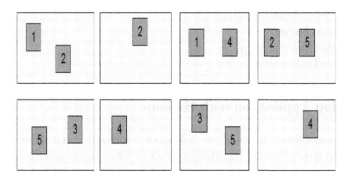

Block Replication

Namenode (Filename, numReplicas, block-ids, ...)
/users/sameerp/data/part-0, r:2, {1,3}, ...
/users/sameerp/data/part-1, r:3, {2,4,5}, ...

Datanodes

Fig. 2. A Blockreport contains a list of all blocks on a DataNode

(a) Specifying a Java Class as the Mapper/Reducer
You can supply a Java class as the mapper and/or the reducer.

```
$HADOOP_HOME/bin/hadoop   jar $HADOOP_HOME/hadoop-streaming.jar \
    -input myInputDirs \
    -output myOutputDir \
    -mapper org.apache.hadoop.mapred.lib.IdentityMapper \
    -reducer /bin/wc
```

You can specify stream.non.zero.exit.is.failure as true or false to make a streaming task that exits with a non-zero status to be Failure or Success respectively. By default, streaming tasks exiting with non-zero status are considered to be failed tasks.

(b) Packaging Files With Job Submissions

The executables do not need to pre-exist on the machines in the cluster; however, if they don't, you will need to use "-file" option to tell the framework to pack your executable files as a part of job submission. For example:

```
$HADOOP_HOME/bin/hadoop   jar $HADOOP_HOME/hadoop-streaming.jar \
     -input myInputDirs \
     -output myOutputDir \
     -mapper myPythonScript.py \
     -reducer /bin/wc \
    -file myPythonScript.py
```

In addition to executable files, you can also package other auxiliary files (such as dictionaries, configuration files, etc) that may be used by the mapper and/or the reducer. For example:

```
$HADOOP_HOME/bin/hadoop   jar $HADOOP_HOME/hadoop-streaming.jar \
     -input myInputDirs \
     -output myOutputDir \
     -mapper myPythonScript.py \
     -reducer /bin/wc \
     -file myPythonScript.py \
     -file myDictionary.txt
```

3   Develop Application with Hadoop

Our program needs three classes to run: a Mapper, a Reducer, and a Driver. The Driver tells Hadoop how to run the MapReduce process. The Mapper and Reducer operate on your data.

Right-click on the "src" folder under your project and select New * Other.... In the "Map/Reduce" folder on the resulting window, we can create Mapper, Reducer, and Driver classes based on pre-written stub code. Create classes named WordCountMapper, WordCountReducer, and WordCount that use the Mapper, Reducer, and Driver stubs respectively.

The code for each of these classes is shown here. You can copy this code into your files.

```
Listing 1 Source code
package org.myorg;

import java.io.IOException;
import java.util.*;
```

```java
import org.apache.hadoop.fs.Path;
import org.apache.hadoop.conf.*;
import org.apache.hadoop.io.*;
import org.apache.hadoop.mapred.*;
import org.apache.hadoop.util.*;

public class WordCount
{

    public static class Map extends MapReduceBase implements Map-
per<LongWritable, Text, Text, IntWritable> {
        private final static IntWritable one = new IntWritable(1);
        private Text word = new Text();

        public void map(LongWritable key, Text value, OutputCollector<Text,
IntWritable> output, Reporter reporter) throws IOException {
            String line = value.toString();
            StringTokenizer tokenizer = new StringTokenizer(line);
            while (tokenizer.hasMoreTokens())
            {
              word.set(tokenizer.nextToken());
                output.collect(word, one);
            }
        }
    }

    public static class Reduce extends MapReduceBase implements Reducer<Text,
IntWritable, Text, IntWritable> {
        public void reduce(Text key, Iterator<IntWritable> values, OutputCollec-
tor<Text, IntWritable> output, Reporter reporter) throws IOException {
            int sum = 0;
            while (values.hasNext())
            {
              sum += values.next().get();
            }
            output.collect(key, new IntWritable(sum));
        }
    }

    public static void main(String[] args) throws Exception
    {
        JobConf conf = new JobConf(WordCount.class);
        conf.setJobName("wordcount");
```

```
        conf.setOutputKeyClass(Text.class);
        conf.setOutputValueClass(IntWritable.class);

        conf.setMapperClass(Map.class);
        conf.setCombinerClass(Reduce.class);
        conf.setReducerClass(Reduce.class);

        conf.setInputFormat(TextInputFormat.class);
        conf.setOutputFormat(TextOutputFormat.class);

     FileInputFormat.setInputPaths(conf, new Path(args[0]));
     FileOutputFormat.setOutputPath(conf, new Path(args[1]));

        JobClient.runJob(conf);
     }
   }
```

(a) Run the application:

$ bin/hadoop   jar   /usr/joe/wordcount.jar   org.myorg.WordCount /usr/joe/wordcount/input /usr/joe/wordcount/output

(b) Output:

```
$ bin/hadoop dfs -cat /usr/joe/wordcount/output/part-00000
Bye 1
Goodbye 1
Hadoop 2
Hello 2
World 2
```

4   Conclusion

In this article, we   can use the Hadoop to develop application. Hadoop is specifically designed to have a very flat scalability curve. After a Hadoop program is written and functioning on ten nodes, very little--if any--work is required for that same program to run on a much larger amount of hardware. Orders of magnitude of growth can be managed with little re-work required for your applications.

References

1. Ghemawat, S., Gobioff, H., Leung, S.: The Google file system. In: Proc. of ACM Symposium on Operating Systems Principles, Lake George, NY, pp. 29–43 (October 2003)
2. Junqueira, F.P., Reed, B.C.: The life and times of a zookeeper. In: Proc. of the 28th ACM Symposium on Principles of Distributed Computing, Calgary, AB, Canada, August 10-12 (2009)

3. Carns, P.H., Ligon III, W.B., Ross, R.B., Thakur, R.: PVFS: A parallel file system for Linux clusters. In: Proc. of 4th Annual Linux Showcase and Conference, pp. 317–327 (2000)
4. Dean, J., Ghemawat, S.: MapReduce: Simplified Data Processing on Large Clusters. In: Proc. of the 6th Symposium on Operating Systems Design and Implementation, San Francisco CA (December 2004)
5. Weil, S., Brandt, S., Miller, E., Long, D., Maltzahn, C.: Ceph: A Scalable, High-Performance Distributed File System. In: Proc. of the 7th Symposium on Operating Systems Design and Implementation, Seattle, WA (November 2006)
6. Welch, B., Unangst, M., Abbasi, Z., Gibson, G., Mueller, B., Small, J., Zelenka, J., Zhou, B.: Scalable Performance of the Panasas Parallel file System. In: Proc. of the 6th USENIX Conference on File and Storage Technologies, San Jose, CA (February 2008)
7. Zhang, Z., Kulkarni, A., Ma, X., Zhou, Y.: Memory resource allocation for file system prefetching: from a supply chain management perspective. In: Proc. of the 4th ACM European Conf. on Computer Systems (EuroSys 2009), pp. 75–88. ACM Press, Germany (2009)
8. White, T.: Hadoop: The Definitive Guide. O'Reilly Media, Inc. (June 2009)
9. Dong, B., Zheng, Q., Qiao, M., Shu, J., Yang, J.: BlueSky Cloud Framework: An E-Learning Framework Embracing Cloud Computing. In: Jaatun, M.G., Zhao, G., Rong, C. (eds.) CloudCom 2009. LNCS, vol. 5931, pp. 577–582. Springer, Heidelberg (2009)
10. Soundararajan, G., Mihailescu, M., Amza, C.: Context-aware prefetching at the storage server. In: Proc. of the 2008 USENIX Annual Tech. Conf. (USENIX 2008), pp. 377–390. USENIX Association Press, Berkeley (2008)
11. Schmuck, F., Haskin, R.: GPFS: A Shared-Disk File System for Large Computing Clusters. In: Proc. of the 1st USENIX Conf. on File and Storage Technologies (FAST 2002), pp. 231–244. USENIX Association Press, Monterey (2002)
12. Ghemawat, S., Gobioff, H., Leung, S.-T.: The Google File System. In: Proc. of the 19th ACM Symp. on Operating Systems Principles (SOSP 2003), pp. 29–43. ACM Press, Lake (2003)
13. Li, M., Varki, E., Bhatia, S., Merchant, A.: TaP: Table-based Prefetching for Storage Caches. In: Proc. of the 6th USENIX Conf. on File and Storage Technologies (FAST 2008), pp. 81–96. USENIX Association Press, San Jose (2008)
14. Gill, B.S., Modha, D.S.: SARC: Sequential prefetching in adaptive replacement cache. In: Proc. of the 2005 USENIX Annual Tech. Conf. (USENIX 2005), pp. 293–308. USENIX Association Press, Anaheim (2005)
15. Gill, B.S., Bathen, L.A.D.: AMP: Adaptive Multistream Prefetching in a Shared Cache. In: Proc. of the 5th USENIX Conf. on File and Storage Technologies (FAST 2007), pp. 185–198. USENIX Association Press, San Jose (2007)

Requirement Uncertainty Analysis
for Service-Oriented Self-Adaptation Software

Wei Liu[1,2] and Zaiwen Feng[3]

[1] School of Computer Science and Engineering, Wuhan Institute of Technology,
Wuhan 430073, China
[2] Hubei Key Laboratory of Intelligence Robot
liuwei@mail.wit.edu.cn
[3] State Key Lab of Software Engineering (SKLSE), Wuhan University, Wuhan 430072, China
fengzw@whu.edu.cn

Abstract. While a few techniques have been developed to support the modeling and analysis of requirements for self-adaptive systems, limited attention has been paid to the description of service requirements and uncertainty in requirements of SoSAS. In this paper, we discussed the characteristics of service-oriented self-adaptation software. A context snapshot model to represent uncertainty is introduced in requirements with domain knowledge; and the context requirements to model user requirements and service requirements; and finally, propose means-c-end analysis to relate user and service requirement with context condition. We design and develop a support tool ConUSER to realize the uncertainty oriented requirement analysis.

Keywords: Self-adaptive software, Uncertainty, Context requirement.

1   Introduction

Service-oriented computing (SOC) [1] is a computing paradigm that utilizes services as fundamental elements for developing applications. Service-oriented software could realize dynamic aggregation of these resources to appease service customers requests. The development mode of service-oriented software is "Meet-in-the-Middle", which can be view from two perspectives: top-down presents requirement guiding and down-top realized service aggregation. This development mode determines that the requirements not only represent users' demand exactly and completely but also play as a foundation for aggregating service resources.

Software needs to dynamically adapt its behavior at run-time in response to changing conditions in the supporting computing, communication infrastructure, and in the surrounding environment [2]. Such self-adaptive software must become more versatile, flexible, resilient, dependable, robust, energy-efficient, recoverable, customizable, configurable, and self-optimizing by adapting to changing environment. Software engineering of service-oriented system could help software realizing the characters of self-adaptation. Through discovering, mining and customizing adapting

J. Lei et al. (Eds.): NCIS 2012, CCIS 345, pp. 156–163, 2012.
© Springer-Verlag Berlin Heidelberg 2012

service resources, a service oriented self-adaptation software (SoSAS) is able to modify its service behavior according to the changes in its continuing evolution requirement at runtime.

SoSAS requirement has the following features. On one hand, the requirement could replace the action of software architecture in traditional process of software design and development, which enable the requirements both represent the abstract users' demand and system design with web service characteristics, such as process (flow) of web service execution and service operation. However, whether object-oriented classical requirement models or widespread influence requirement models, both could not present the web service characteristics. On the other hand, the environment information of system is transforming implicit into explicit and the adaptation of system is transforming static into dynamic. This phenomenon induces uncertainty of system and the uncertainty demands dynamic adaptation of system. So the uncertainty should be view as a constituent in SoSAS requirement and that is different from functional requirements and non-functional requirements in elicitation and analysis technologies.

In order for these challenges to be met, a context-based model for self-adaptive software is proposed in this paper. Context aware technology in pervasive computing could provide a feasible research direct for uncertainty representation and modeling. Our proposal builds over a context snapshot model to represent uncertainty in requirement with domain knowledge and therefore it is expected to model user requirement and service requirement with domain goal and domain process. This paper proposes a context snapshot binding framework for modeling and analyzing requirements for service oriented self-adaptation software, called ConUSER. For illustration, the process is applied to an intelligent traffic software example, giving a first evidence for its benefits.

2   Service-Oriented Self-Adaptation Software

SOC based self-adaptive architecture facilitates the building of systems capable of dynamically adapting to varying environment for following reasons. First, a service is a reusable and independent building block that offers a particular functionality, so the architectures could be expediently modified to realize self-adaptive behavior. Second, SOC focuses on some aspect, such as the support for dynamic discovery, which are generally not explicit considerations of component-oriented architecture. Dynamic discovery could play an effective role when existing services can not satisfy the changing environment. Third, dynamic service composition has the potential to realize flexible and adaptable applications by properly selecting and combining components based on the user request and context. Therefore, the dynamic service composition is suitable for end-user applications in ubiquitous environments where available components are dynamic and expected users may vary.

SoSAS involves feedback processes with four key steps: service requirements collection, service requirements analyzation, service behavior decision and service adaptation evolution, as depicted in Fig.1. The feedback cycle starts with the collection of service users' context and relevant data from environment sensors. Some of the engineering questions are important to the engineering process are: What aspects of the environment should the self-adaptive system monitor? What is the relationship of environment data and service requirement elements? Next, the system analyzes the collected data for requirement. Some of the important questions here are: How to structuring and reasoning about the raw data? The analyzed data how to work as a crucial part in service requirements modeling? Next, the system makes a decision about how to adapt user context or environment changing. This step discusses the evolution condition of service requirement. Here, the important questions are: How to validate the state satisfies the evolution condition? How to evolution these evolution conditions to reduce evolution range? Finally, the system implements the decision. How to realize the service requirement adaptive action at runtime is the important question here.

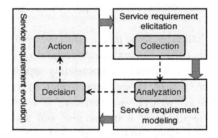

Fig. 1. Feedback processes of SoSAS

3   Requirements Uncertainty Representation

3.1   Expressing Uncertainty with Context

Requirement uncertainty means that requirements are not known until it is practically used, which results from software requirements creating an ill-defined problem[3]. Study on uncertainty in SoSAS requirement has some challenges: classification of these data for analyzation and refusing with service requirements; these data are viewed as dynamic domain knowledge for requirement modeling and evolution. Context-awareness technology in pervasive computing focusing on these challenges mentioned above could provide a solution for uncertainty representation and modeling in SoSAS.

Addressing the quite limited notions and early definitions of context, Dey provided the following general definition, which is probably the most widely accepted: "Context is any information that can be used to characterise the situation of an entity. An entity is a person, place, or object that is considered relevant to the interaction between the user and the application, including the user and the applications themselves" [4]. This definition emphasizes the interaction between the user and the system. Villegas et al. extending Dey's definition to propose an operational definition:

"Context is any information useful to characterize the state of individual entities and the relationships among them. This context information must be modeled in such a way that it can be preprocessed after its acquisition from the environment, classified according to the corresponding domain, handled to be provisioned based on the system's requirements, and maintained to support its dynamic evolution"[5].

The choice of context is due to its similarity and complementarily with uncertainty in requirement engineering for SoSAS: (i) states are persistent changing in both context and uncertainty; (ii) context and uncertainty have the ability to model the environment between user and system; (iii) context and uncertainty have relation with changing requirement. Hence, these points offer the possibility of using context to express uncertainty in the requirement phases of self-adaptation systems.

In special state, the uncertainty will be translated into certainty in self-adaptation software requirement. We can use context information in special state to record the certainties in a period of time.

3.2   Modeling Context Snapshot with Domain Knowledge

The context information keeping the same state in a period of time is named as context snapshot. Context snapshot can be characterized as static and dynamic. Static context snapshot keeps the same state in all the time, such as birthday of passenger. As self-adaptation software evolves with the environment change, the majority of context snapshot is dynamic.

The context snapshot in SoSAS requirement modeling includes two important functions. The first one is that the context snapshot will be used as refinement condition for user requirement modeling; and the second one is that it will be utilized as trigger event for service requirement implement. The task of context snapshot modeling includes classifying context factors and building influence relations. The factors are classified into explicit context and implicit context. The state values of explicit context are derived from context sensors, while the state value of implicit context is inferred from some state value.

A metamodel includes two parts: one is context snapshot metamodel in the right frame; the other is domain metamodel in the left frame. Base constructs for representing domain and context snapshot is defined as follows:

- Concept: declared abstract and only introduced for modeling concept property associations. Entity, Operation and Quality is concrete class of concept.
- ContextSnapshot: the state value of context factor keeps changeless in a period of time. ContextFactor and StateValue compose the context snapshot.
- ContextFactor: base construct for representing a group of entity as context knowledge. ComputingFactor (such as bandwidth and devices), UserFactor(such as the user's location and calendars) and PhysicalFactor (such as location, time, traffic conditions, and temperature) are concrete class of context factor. three main the three main context factor categories mentioned in [6] could be viewed as context information for requirement modeling.
- StateValue: is a conjunction of Predicate and Value. The value is classified into quantitative value (such as "180kbs"), and qualitative value (such as "medium").

- Profile: a set of context factors who have correlation.
- PolicyRule: an inference rule establishes generating regulation of implicit context snapshot. The content of policy rule is that several existing context snapshots educe a new context snapshot. The context snapshots appear in the same policy rule means having correlation and will be put in a profile.

Comparing with context model proposed to support context-aware applications, the modeling kernel is context snapshot but context concept. The context snapshot is the application object and the correlative context snapshots are modeled as profile.

The context snapshot is used as condition for goal refinement and traceability link, or precondition for process execution in requirement modeling. In our work, a rule markup language R2ML[7] as an interchange format for rules integrates the RuleML with the SWRL as well as the OCL. R2ML is utilized to describe the context snapshot for three main reasons follows: first, the adaptation rule are reaction rules (ECA rules) that follow the event-condition-action model; second, the conditions part of the rule is a conjunction of atoms and the atoms can be express context snapshots; third, the triggering event part of the rules specify the core concepts required for dynamic behavior of rules and provides the infrastructure for more detailed definition of this behavior.

The condition and precondition are a conjunction of context snapshots and it can be expressed with atoms, such as attribute atom and datatype predicate atom in R2ML as Fig.2.

```
1  <r2ml:conditions>
2   <r2ml:DatatypePredicateAtom r2ml:datatypePredicate="swrlb:lessThan">
3    <r2ml:dataArguments>
4     <r2ml:AttributeFunctionTerm r2ml:attribute="ex:CheckAvailability.travelExpenditure">
5      <r2ml:contextArgument>
6       <r2ml:ObjectVariable r2ml:name="chkAv" r2ml:class="ex:CheckAvailability"/>
7      </r2ml:contextArgument>
8     </r2ml:AttributeFunctionTerm>
9     <r2ml:AttributeFunctionTerm r2ml:attribute="ex:CheckAvailability.travelBudget">
10     <r2ml:contextArgument>
11      <r2ml:ObjectVariable r2ml:name="chkAv" r2ml:class="ex:CheckAvailability"/>
12     </r2ml:contextArgument>
13    </r2ml:AttributeFunctionTerm>
14   </r2ml:dataArguments>
15  </r2ml:DatatypePredicateAtom>
16  <r2ml:AttributionAtom r2ml:attribute="isEnough">
17   <r2ml:subject>
18    <r2ml:ObjectVariable r2ml:name="pessanger.Time"/>
19   </r2ml:subject>
20   <r2ml:dataValue>
21    <r2ml:TypedLiteral r2ml:lexicalValue="true" r2ml:datatype="xs:boolean"/>
22   </r2ml:dataValue>
23  </r2ml:AttributionAtom>
24 </r2ml:conditions>
```

Fig. 2. R2ML example of atoms

4   Uncertainty Requirement Analysis

Based on a goal-oriented user requirement model and a process-oriented service requirement model [8], we define a traceability link constructed between goal and process as an adapter. The traceability link is viewed as a critical feature for the model evolution . Context-based traceability link in our work is named means-c-end, which implies that a goal can be achieved via a process if and only if a context snapshot holds. Means-c-end analysis has two steps: linking goal and process model and constructing means-c-end (M-C-E).

Step one, linking goal and process model. Two types of link approaches are proposed namely *overlap relation* (OR) and *satisfaction relation* (SR). The former relation is created from goals to processes, while the latter relation is created from processes to goals.

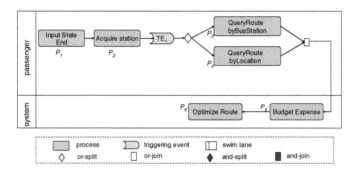

Fig. 3. Process model for city transportation system(part)

- Overlap rule. The rule is used to create overlap relations between goal and process with cues present. According to this rule, an overlap relation is created if the names of goals and processes can suggest such that, the entities are the same or as concepts have equivalent semantic, while the operations as concepts have similarity in domain model.
- Satisfaction rule. The rule is used to create satisfaction relations between goal and process with the effect of process and the related goal. The effect of process can related to the goal, which is a prerequisite for creating satisfaction relation.

For example, G_3^3 "Confirm station" and P_2 "Acquire station" have the same noun and similar verbs, so an overlap relation is created between them and denoted as OR(G_3^3, P_2). Ehe effect of P_3 represented as "taxiRouteGenerated" is related to G_4^3 whose name is "Generate taxi route". So satisfaction relation is denoting as SR(P_3, G_4^3).

Step two, constructing means-c-end. If a link is generated between a goal and a process and the goal is refined by context decomposition rule, then a means-c-end relation could be constructed from the supergoal and the process. It illuminates that the supergoal can be achieved via the process if and only if the condition holds. For instance, as mentioned above SR(P_3, G_4^3) and SR(P_4, G_4^4), while G_4^3 and G_4^4 are refined from G_3^4 by context decomposition rule, so means-c-end relation could be constructed from G_3^4 to P_3 and P_4, denoting as M-C-E(G_3^4, C_1, P_3) and M-C-E(G_3^4, C_2, P_4).

5   ConUSER Support Tool

In order to support the requirement editor and automatic analysis with context-based requirement representing and modeling techniques, we have developed prototype automated reasoning and analysis tool called ConUSER support tool. The whole structure of tool has two parts: requirement editor and requirement analyzer, as shown in Fig.4. Requirement editor module includes requirement model editor and R2ML editor. Requirement model editor had developed to strive to facilitate the requirement model construction process. ConUSER play some pivotal roles in the process of requirement modeling.

- The first step is to derive context snapshots and policy rule. Context snapshot editor is a kernel part of R2ML editor. The output of context snapshot editor consists of all context vocabularies, context snapshots and policy rules. Context vocabularies are described with R2ML vocabularies and context snapshots are described with R2ML atoms. Policy rules are created in R2ML editor. The output content is stored in a native XML database.
- The second step is to derive goal and process from user requirements. The requirements could be described by customer with a structure nature language SORL. SORL-based requirement elicitation approach enables common stakeholders to write requirements and employs semantic inducement to make correct, complete and consistent requirements. And then the SORL requirements could be translated into goals and processes.

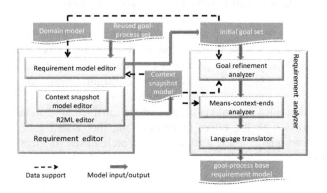

Fig. 4. Structure of ConUSER

- The third step is to construct goal-based requestors' requirement model and process-oriented provider's requirement model, which are refined and generated semi-automatically in requirement analyzer of ConUSER. The requestors' and provider's requirement model are constructed with a popular ontology language OWL. According to the three decomposition rules, goal refinement could be automatic via semantic inference with the assistant of domain-specific and context-specific knowledge model in goal refinement analyzer. And then, a process workflow is generated according to three widthways dependency relations proposed in [9].
- The last step is to analyze means-c-end. According to overlap rule and satisfaction rule, traceability link is constructed between goal and process. Means-c-end could be generated automatic in means-context-ends analyzer. The context snapshot represented with R2ML could be translated into OWL. The output of requirement analyzer in ConUSER is an OWL file, which represents the context-based requirement model.

6   Conclusion and Future Work

In this paper, we have developed a context snapshot fusion framework for modeling and analyzing requirements for service oriented self-adaptation software. The first technique is for using goal model to capture the user requirements and process model to capture service requirements. The second technique is for fusing context snapshot with user/service requirements that has to be implemented to enable the self-adaptation evolution of SoSAS. We have applied our framework on a scenario of a mobile information system of city transportation. We will work to discuss the self-adaptation evolution mechanism and develop our automated support tool.

Acknowledgments. Project supported by the National Natural Science Foundation of China under Grant (No. 60873024 and No.61272115), the Natural Science Foundation of Hubei Province (No.2010CDB08503), the Key Science Technology Research Project of Hubei Provincial Department of Education under Grant(No.D20121508), the Open Foundation of SKLSE(No. SKLSE-2010-08-25) and the Doctor foundation for Science Study Program of Wit (No.12096022).

References

[1] Huhns, M.N., Singh, M.P.: Service-oriented Computing: Key Concepts and Principles. Internet Computing IEEE 9(1), 75–81 (2005)
[2] McKinley, P.K., Sadjadi, S.M., Kasten, E.P., Cheng, B.H.C.: Composing adaptive software. IEEE Computer 37(7), 56–64 (2004)
[3] Bush, D., Finkelstein, A.: Requirements Stability Assessments Using Scenarios. In: Conference on Requirement Engineering, pp. 23–32. IEEE Computer Society Press, Los Alamitos (2003)
[4] Abowd, G.D., Dey, A.K., Brown, P.J., Davies, N., Smith, M., Steggles, P.: Towards a Better Understanding of Context and Context-Awareness. In: Gellersen, H.-W. (ed.) HUC 1999. LNCS, vol. 1707, pp. 304–307. Springer, Heidelberg (1999)
[5] Villegas, N.M., Müller, H.A.: Managing Dynamic Context to Optimize Smart Interactions and Services. In: Chignell, M., Cordy, J., Ng, J., Yesha, Y. (eds.) The Smart Internet. LNCS, vol. 6400, pp. 289–318. Springer, Heidelberg (2010)
[6] Buchholz, T., Küpper, A., Schiffers, M.: Quality of Context:What It Iis and why We Need It. In: 10th Workshop of the HP OpenView University Association (HPOVUA 2003), Geneva, Switzerland (2003)
[7] Wagner, G., et al.: R2ML: A General Approach for Marking up Rules. In: Bry, F., Fages, F., Marchiori, M., Ohlbach, H. (eds.) Dagstuhl Seminar Proceedings 05371 Principles and Practices of Semantic Web Reasoning (2005)
[8] Liu, W., Feng, Z.W.: Uncertainty Modeling of Self-adaptive Software Requirement. IJACT International Journal of Advancements in Computing Technology 4(11), 87–95 (2012)
[9] Liu, W., He, C.W., Zhang, K.: Domain Component-based Service Requirements Modeling and Analysis. In: The IEEE International Conference on Computational Intelligence and Software Engineering, Wuhan, China, pp. 1–5 (2009)

Optimization of Green Passive Optical Networks with Minimum Cost

Yongmin Qi[1], Xiaoqin Hu[1], Jia He[1], Qiliang Li[1], and Shilin Xiao[2]

[1] College of Communication Engineering, Hangzhou Dianzi University, Hangzhou, China
[2] State Key Lab of Advanced Optical Communication System & Networks,
Shanghai Jiao Tong University, China
ymqi@hdu.edu.cn

Abstract. We design green TDM-WDM hybrid PON networks to satisfy the increasing demand on broadband access. We develop a novel model and propose an effective strategy to minimize the cost and hence to save the cost of the upgrading PON networks. Mixed integer linear programming model is designed to upgrade the capacity of the networks by optimizing upgrading line-rates, add new wavelengths and the optimal splitter location based on the locations of the ONUs and the OLT. The studied case shows the attractive properties of our effective strategy.

Keywords: Passive optical network, Capacity upgrade, Minimum cost, Mixed integer linear programming (MILP).

1   Introduction

With the era of full-service, the demand of high-bandwidth business on video conferencing, high definition TV, online learning and interactive games was growing explosively [1]. The bandwidth in access networks has been steadily increasing since the 1990s, with an average growth of about 50% per year [2].The development of next-generation passive optical network technology has become research focus.

A PON is a point-to-multipoint structure of the optical access network, which is composed of one optical line terminal (OLT), one optical distribute network (ODN) and a number of optical Network Units (ONUs) [3]. The OLT belonging to the service node access network side device connects to the corresponding service node by the interface of the service node to complete the accessing of the access network service. ONUs as the user-side devices connect through the user-network interface with the user terminal, and provides a variety of bandwidth services to users connecting with the OLT. The ODN is composed of the optical fiber and optical splitter and other passive components without any electronic devices and electronic power supplies.

With the growth of communication traffic, capacity upgraded on the existing PON network is inevitable to reuse the legacy resources. It is expected that the two generations and more than two generations of PON systems can coexist in the same fiber-optic network. Then more attention was turned towards upgrading these line rates to

J. Lei et al. (Eds.): NCIS 2012, CCIS 345, pp. 164–171, 2012.
© Springer-Verlag Berlin Heidelberg 2012

upgrade current PON capacity [4] [5]. Besides, PON architectures basing on WDM technology allow adding new wavelengths to upgrade capacity [6]. To reduce the number of wavelength channels, TDM-WDM hybrid PON which makes it possible to support more than one wavelength allocated to each ONU can be implemented to increasing capacity [7]. Furthermore, Ref. [8] investigates the problem of network planning for PON deployment by considering two heuristic algorithms. But the two algorithms can not determine the optimal location of splitters so that the distance between the ONUs and an OLT and their associated splitter is not minimized. Authors in Ref. [9] formulate an optimization model to upgrade the capacity of PON network with minimum cost. However, the optimum position of the splitter is not taken into account. The optimum position can reduce the length of the total fiber, which is the sum of the feeder fiber lengths from each ONU and the OLT to the splitter. In another words, it can save the energy consumption of green PON networks and significantly reduce the fiber cost and the labor cost of trenching and laying the fiber which is expensive in general. In our research work, we target a green strategy to upgrade the capacity of the TDM-WDM hybrid PON by adding new wavelengths, upgrading the line rates and finding the optimum location of the splitter. We develop a novel model to optimize the cost of the green PON network, and hence to save the energy of the PON network. Extensive case study indicates that our green strategy is more effective than the single-step approach and the WDM approach in terms of cost saving and energy saving.

The rest of paper is organized as follows. Section 2 develops the MILP optimization model and proposes the strategy to upgrade capacity for green PON network and to find the optimal splitter location. Then, Section 3 involves the case study in detail. The comparison and analysis are presented in Section 4. Section 5 offers some conclusions on this study.

2   Problem Formulation and Optimization Model

Our method is a multi-step approach over several periods of time. It calculates the allocation of wavelengths and line rates in each period based on the growth in traffic demand and the cost savings. Furthermore, it finds the optimal location of splitter based on the minimum cost. We formulate an MILP model to obtain the optimal solution, which is as follows.

2.1   MILP Problem Formulation

Constants

$\mathbf{K}$:   set of line rates supported by the PON, which is denoted by $\{1, 2, ..., K\}$.

$\mathbf{N}$:   set of ONUs in the PON, which is denoted by $\{1, 2, ..., N\}$.

$\mathbf{L}$:   set of wavelengths that can be used in the PON, which is denoted by $\{1, 2, ..., L\}$.

R_k :   the value in Mbps of the k-th line rate, $k \in \mathbf{K}$.

θ :   the cost factor of the unit fiber.

γ: the labor cost to place the unit fiber.

x_0:   the abscissa of the OLT, which is assumed to be 0.

y_0:   the ordinate of the OLT, which is assumed to be 0.

x_i: the abscissa of the i-th ONU.

y_i: the ordinate of the i-th ONU.

α: the traffic growth factor.

n: the number of periods.

B_i: the initial guaranteed bandwidth for the i-th ONU (i.e., period 1) .

Variables

$p_{i,k,j}$:   binary variable that is 1 if the i-th ONU is operating on the j-th wavelength with the k-th line rate.

$c_{k,j}$:   binary variable that is 1 if the j-th wavelength is used with the k-th line rate.

$T_{k,j}$:   the cost to support the j-th wavelength with the k-th line rate at the OLT.

$U_{i,k,j}$:   the cost to support the j-th wavelength with the k-th line rate at the i-th ONU.

x_s: the abscissa of the splitter.

y_s: the ordinate of the splitter.

Objective

$$\min(\sum_{k=1}^{K}\sum_{i=1}^{N}\sum_{j=1}^{L}U_{i,k,j}p_{i,k,j} + \sum_{k=1}^{K}\sum_{j=1}^{L}T_{k,j}c_{k,j} + (\gamma+\theta)$$
$$(\sum_{i=1}^{N}\sqrt{(x_i-x_s)^2+(y_i-y_s)^2} + \sqrt{(x_s-x_0)^2+(y_s-y_0)^2})$$

(1)

The first term $\sum_{k=1}^{K}\sum_{i=1}^{N}\sum_{j=1}^{L}U_{i,k,j}p_{i,k,j}$ of Eq. (1) stands for the cost of all ONUs. The second term $\sum_{k=1}^{K}\sum_{j=1}^{L}T_{k,j}c_{k,j}$ of Eq. (1) is the cost of the OLT. Here, the cost of adding new transceivers is considered. The third term denotes the cost of fiber and the labor cost of trenching and laying the fiber to connect the splitter to the OLT and the ONUs.

Subject to

$$\sum_{k=1}^{K}c_{k,j}\leq 1, \quad \forall j\in L$$

(2)

$$\sum_{k=1}^{K}\sum_{j=1}^{L} p_{i,k,j} = 1, \quad \forall i \in \mathbf{N} \tag{3}$$

$$\sum_{k=1}^{K}\sum_{j=1}^{L} p_{i,k,j} R_k \geq B_i (1+\alpha)^n, \quad \forall i \in \mathbf{N} \tag{4}$$

$$\sum_{k=1}^{K} R_k c_{k,j} \geq \sum_{i=1}^{N}\sum_{k=1}^{K} B_i (1+\alpha)^n p_{i,k,j}, \quad \forall j \in \mathbf{L} \tag{5}$$

Eq. (2) prohibits more than one line rate over the same wavelength. Eq. (3) constraints that the i-th ONU uses one and only one wavelength and line rate. Eq. (4) ensures that the bandwidth of each ONU must be satisfied in each period. Eq. (5) guarantees the line rate of the j-th wavelength should be larger than or equal to the total bandwidth of the ONUs using the j-th wavelength.

2.2   Strategy of Pricing Factors

We will introduce the strategy of pricing factor in the following. $T_{k,j}$ and $U_{i,k,j}$ are decided by the previous period. Assuming that there are two line rates, e.g. $R_1 = 10000$ and $R_2 = 40000$, supported by the PON. There are three cases for $T_{k,j}$.

Case1: If the j-th wavelength is used in the current period, which was not used in the previous period. We set $T_{1,j} = 1$ and $T_{2,j} = 2.5$. $T_{1,j} = 1$ indicates the cost of the OLT to support the j-th wavelength with the line rate R_1 (i.e. 10Gbps). $T_{2,j} = 2.5$ indicates the cost of the OLT to support the j-th wavelength with the line rate R_2 (i.e. 40Gbps). It means the cost of the OLT to support low line rate less than high line rate.

Case2: If the j-th wavelength with R_1 used in the previous period is still used in current period, the cost of the OLT will be small because new investment will be not required. So, we set $T_{1,j} = 0.1$. On the other hand, if the j-th wavelength with R_2 is used in current period, the cost of the OLT will be large. Therefore, we set $T_{2,j} = 3$.

Case3: If the j-th wavelength with R_2 was used in the previous period, and the j-th wavelength with R_1 is used in current period, we set $T_{1,j} = 100$. It means that once high line rate was adopted in the previous period, the low line rate will be prohibited in the current period. If the j-th wavelength with R_2 used in the previous period is still used in current period, the cost of the OLT will be small because new investment will be not required. So, we set $T_{2,j} = 0.1$.

Similar to $T_{k,j}$, there are three cases for $U_{i,k,j}$.

Case1: If the j-th wavelength is used in the current period, which was not used in the previous period. We set $U_{i,1,j} = 1$ and $U_{i,2,j} = 2.5$.

Case2: If the j-th wavelength with R_1 used in the previous period is still used in current period, the cost of the i-th ONU will be small because new investment will be not required. So, we set $U_{i,1,j} = 0.01$. On the other hand, if the j-th wavelength with R_2 is used in current period, the cost of the i-th ONU will be large. Therefore, we set $U_{i,2,j} = 0.3$.

Case3: If the j-th wavelength with R_2 was used in the previous period, and the j-th wavelength with R_1 is used in current period, we set $U_{i,1,j} = 10$. It means that once high line rate was adopted in the previous period, the low line rate will be prohibited in the current period. If the j-th wavelength with R_2 used in the previous period is still used in current period, the cost of the i-th ONU will be small because new investment will be not required. So, we set $U_{i,2,j} = 0.01$.

3   Case Study

It is assumed that L= 5, and N= 20 in the PON network. In the PON network, ONUs 1-15 are buildings and ONUs 16-20 are home users. For ONUs 1-15, each wavelength can be used. For ONUs 16-20, only λ_1 can be used. We set $R_1 = 10000$, $R_2 = 40000$, and $\alpha = 0.5$. In period 1, the initial bandwidth of ONUs 1-15 and ONUs 16-20 are 600 Mbps and 100Mbps respectively and λ_1 is used in per ONU. Assuming that $\theta = 1$, $\gamma = 1.5$. The location of per ONU is generated at random.

In order to solve the optimization described in the previous section, simulation studies were carried out by CPLEX. We can get the optimum allocation of the wavelengths and the line rates shown in Table 1. On the other hand, the best location of the splitter is: $x_s = 37.81720$ and $y_s = 29.72240$.

In Table 1, the allocation of wavelength and the line rates is one of the cases. In the paper, we mainly consider the cost of transceivers. So if any ONU uses the wavelengths which are used in previous period, the cost of adding a new transceiver can be reduced in the current period. Similarly in the OLT it is also true. Namely if the j-th wavelength has been used at any ONU in the previous period, it does not require new investment when it is used in current period again.

In Table 1, the allocation of wavelength λ_1 at 10 Gbps in period 1 is known as initialization condition. In order to meet all the ONUs bandwidth requirements, at least 5 ONUs which can be selected arbitrarily should use a new wavelength λ_2 in period 2. Meanwhile, to reduce the cost of installing new transceivers, we should make full use of λ_1 at 10 Gbps. Similarly with the growing traffic in period 3, at least 2 ONUs of the OLT need use a new wavelength λ_3 at 10 Gbps and at least 7 ONUs of the OLT need use λ_2 at 10 Gbps. In order to reduce the total cost and to meet the demand on the capacity of PON network, the 5 ONUs which use λ_2 at 10 Gbps in period 2 should maintain the same in period 3. The results are shown in Table 1. Similarly, to meet the growing bandwidth requirements, at least 3 ONUs use λ_4 at 10 Gbps in period 4. To period 5 wavelengths with the line rate 10 Gbps can no longer meet the needs of the business, so a new wavelength λ_5 is added at 40 Gbps with the minimized cost for 4 ONUs.

Table 1. Wavelength allocation per ONU and period and the coordinates of per ONU

	(x_i, y_i)	Period 1	Period 2	Period 3	Period 4	Period 5
ONU 1	(11,15)	λ_1^*	λ_2	λ_2	λ_2	λ_2
ONU 2	(15,26)	λ_1	λ_2	λ_2	λ_2	λ_2
ONU 3	(17,64)	λ_1	λ_2	λ_2	λ_2	λ_2
ONU 4	(64,25)	λ_1	λ_2	λ_2	λ_2	$\boldsymbol{\lambda_5}$
ONU 5	(39,28)	λ_1	λ_2	λ_2	λ_3	λ_3
ONU 6	(54,17)	λ_1	λ_1	λ_2	λ_3	λ_3
ONU 7	(78,10)	λ_1	λ_1	λ_2	λ_4	λ_4
ONU 8	(10,75)	λ_1	λ_1	λ_3	λ_3	λ_3
ONU 9	(88,33)	λ_1	λ_1	λ_3	λ_3	$\boldsymbol{\lambda_5}$
ONU 10	(16,23)	λ_1	λ_1	λ_1	λ_4	λ_4
ONU 11	(82,40)	λ_1	λ_1	λ_1	λ_4	λ_4
ONU 12	(71,31)	λ_1	λ_1	λ_1	λ_1	$\boldsymbol{\lambda_5}$
ONU 13	(23,90)	λ_1	λ_1	λ_1	λ_1	$\boldsymbol{\lambda_5}$
ONU 14	(32,18)	λ_1	λ_1	λ_1	λ_1	λ_1
ONU 15	(26,29)	λ_1	λ_1	λ_1	λ_1	λ_1
ONU 16	(27,39)	λ_1	λ_1	λ_1	λ_1	λ_1
ONU 17	(33,36)	λ_1	λ_1	λ_1	λ_1	λ_1
ONU 18	(41,46)	λ_1	λ_1	λ_1	λ_1	λ_1
ONU 19	(57,38)	λ_1	λ_1	λ_1	λ_1	λ_1
ONU 20	(43,14)	λ_1	λ_1	λ_1	λ_1	λ_1

*Notation: λ_j means the j-th wavelength is assigned to their respective ONU with the line rate 10Gbps. Bold text means that the wavelength is assigned to their respective ONU with the line rate 40 Gbps.

4   Comparison of Results

Our method is a multi-step approach that considers five periods to optimize the allocation of wavelength and the line rates based on increasing capacity. We can compare this approach with single-step optimization. The single-step way is to optimize the allocation of wavelengths and the line rates according to our method based on the same input traffic of period 6. Besides, WDM technology is an approach to upgrade the capacity of PON network, which requires that each ONU needs a different wavelength.

Based on MILP model, we calculate the total cost of period 6 by a multi-step method. The result is 12.66. The single-step method which takes the allocation of period 1 as initial condition is applied. We obtain the result 14.07. For the WDM PON network, we can calculate the cost 40 according to the pricing factors and the same input traffic of period 6. Then the cost results of the three methods in period 6 are shown in the following picture.

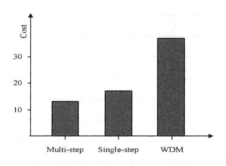

Fig. 1. Comparison of total cost of three approaches: multi-step, single-step, and WDM

The comparison of total cost of three approaches including multi-step, single-step, and WDM is shown in Fig. 1.

Table 2. The comparison of connected costs for 10 different positions

Positions(x_s, y_s)	Costs
(5.0,5.0)	2642.699
(5.0,10.0)	2511.448
(10.0,9.0)	2369.820
(13.8,25.6)	1938.657
(24.7,18.8)	1765.942
(33.5,26.0)	1533.206
(37.817,29.7224)	1485.240
(38.9,31.8)	1490.914
(45.9,49.0)	1797.877
(56.7,67.8)	2553.440

Furthermore, the location of splitter, i.e. x_s =37.81720 and y_s =29.72240, can minimize the lengths of the feeder fiber from each ONU and the OLT to the splitter. Minimizing the fiber lengths is further equivalent to saving the power consumption on the fiber and the total cost including the fiber cost and the labor cost of trenching and laying the fiber in the green PON network. We choose ten positions arbitrarily to compare their connected cost including the fiber cost and the labor cost with the optimal position. The comparison is presented in Table 2.

From the Table 2, we can see that the connected cost is minimum, when the splitter position is x_s =37.81720 and y_s =29.72240.

5   Conclusion

In this paper, we develop a MILP model which optimizes the allocation of wavelengths, the line rates of the ONUs and the optimal splitter location in the green PON network to satisfy the growing capacity and gain the minimum cost. The results show that our multi-step method to upgrade the PON capacity has less total cost than the other two approaches. Our strategy of upgrading a PON capacity reduces the wavelength channels supported by each ONU and the total number of wavelength within a period in the PON based on the increasing business. Furthermore, the fiber cost and the labor cost of interconnecting the splitter to the entire ONUs and the OLT is minimized.

Acknowledgments. This work was supported in part by the National Natural Science Foundation of China under Grant 60972032.

References

1. Shen, G., Li, J.: Cost minimization planning for Greenfield passive optical networks. J.Opt. Commun. Netw. 1(1), 17–29 (2009)
2. Eira, A., Pedro, J., Pires, J.: Optimized Design of Multistage Passive Optical Networks. J. Opt. Commun. Netw. 4(5), 402–411 (2012)
3. Chen, B., Shi, L., Gan, C.: Optimization Model and Simulation Analysis of Wavelength-shared WDM-PON. IEEE (2009)
4. Hajduczenia, M., Da Silva, H., Monteiro, P.: 10G EPON Development Process. In: Proc. Int. Conf. Transparent Optical Networks (ICTON), vol. 1, pp. 276–282 (July 2007)
5. Effenberger, F., Lin, H.: Backward Compatible Coexistence of PON Systems. In: Proc. OFC/NFOEC Conf. (2009)
6. Zhang, J., Ansari, N., Luo, Y., Effenberger, F., Ye, F.: Next-generation PONs: A Performance Investigation of Candidate Architectures for Next-generation Access Stage 1. IEEE Commun. Mag. 46(8), 49–57 (2009)
7. de Valicourt, G., Maké, D., Landreau, J., Lamponi, M., Duan, G.H., Chanclou, P., Brenot, R.: New RSOA Devices for Extended Reach and High Capacity Hybrid TDM/WDM -PON Networks. In: ECOC 2009, Vienna, Austria, September 20-24 (2009)
8. Kazovsky, L., Shaw, W., Gutierrez, D., Cheng, N., Wong, S.: Next Generation Optical Access Network. J. Lightwave Technol. 25(11), 3428–3442 (2007)
9. De Andrade, M., Tornatore, M., Sallent, S., Mukherjee, B.: Capacity Upgrade of Passive Optical Networks with Minimum Cost and System Disruption. In: International Conference on High Performance Switching and Routing, pp. 197–202 (2010)

Based on Wavelet Packet Transform and Embedded Web Technology of Buried Water Remote Monitoring System Design and Implementation

Zhengshu Yan

Ningbo City College of Vocational Technology,
Ningbo, China
yanzhengshu@nbcc.cn

Abstract. Because the city of groundwater in the pipeline laying is very extensive, but the lack of deeply buried underground pipeline station monitoring system, at the same time, originally using the direct method of leakage localization method is susceptible to noise interference, low precision. The article is aimed at these problems, research achievements at home and abroad on the basis of, to the negative pressure wave method as the main leakage detection method, and combining wavelet packet transform algorithm and the optimal wavelet packet algorithm of signal noise reduction, using sensor technology, communications technology, embedded web technology and database technology to design a remote management system for underground water pipeline realization of complex, pipeline leak detection and location and remote monitoring management.

Keywords: Wireless remote monitoring system, wavelet packet transform, uClinux, embedded WEB server.

1 Introduction

A lot of pipeline fault leakage is one of the most common, is due to the airtight pipeline pressure difference inside and outside of existence, the inner dielectric tube without permits the flow of the site, through the hole, such as capillary exudation, defects in leakage phenomenon. [1]The water pipe leak mainly adopts the 'Direct Method' on the leak location, but in the actual inspection process sensor getting information affected by environmental noise impact. This paper explores to improve the Negative Pressure Wave method as the main leakage detection method, and combining wavelet packet transform algorithm and the optimal wavelet packet algorithm of signal to reduce noise and obtain accurate leak signal. Through the design of matching remote monitoring system, monitor and manage the city water pipeline more accurately and effectively.

2 Underground Water Supply Pipeline Leakage Detection and Localization Algorithm Design

The pipeline leakage detection method based on negative pressure wave method, this method is through the pipe at both ends of the pressure difference changes to

J. Lei et al. (Eds.): NCIS 2012, CCIS 345, pp. 172–179, 2012.
© Springer-Verlag Berlin Heidelberg 2012

determine whether leakage occurs, through a conduit within the pressure difference, causes the liquid to leak department together, this process produces to the upstream and downstream generates negative pressure wave, according to the instantaneous pressure wave propagation to downstream time difference and gas velocity to calculate leakage point location.

Hypothesis: the whole L for underground water pipeline total length (m); X: leakage point to the conduit upstream sensor distance (m); in which T1, T2 when leakage occurs, the negative pressure wave to the upstream and downstream conduction time required (s); V pipeline pressure wave propagation velocity; ΔT, on the downstream sensor receives a pressure wave time difference; U, m / s for pipeline water flow speed. [2] Correction formula as below:

$$X = \frac{L(V - U) + (V^2 - U^2) \times \Delta T}{2V} \tag{1}$$

In order to suppress noise, through wavelet packet transform algorithm to detect the truth behind the strong noise signal edge, improve the monitoring accuracy of singular point.

2.1   Using the Wavelet Packet Transform Algorithm for Noise Reduction Optimization

Wavelet packet analysis is from the wavelet analysis extends out of a pair of signals are more detailed analysis and reconstruction method. Multi resolution analysis, $L^2(K)$ is a Orthogonal Function Systems, the system only on the orthogonal wavelet packet decomposition and reconstruction. Assumed $\varpi(t)$ is orthogonal scaling, $\partial(t)$ is corresponding orthogonal wavelet function, $\{V_k\}$ is spatial domain multi resolution generated by $\partial(t)$. Through the scale factor i, Hilbert space $L^2(K)$ is decomposed into all subspace (i∈Z) of the orthogonal sum .[3]

$$L^2(K) = \cdots \oplus W_{-1} \oplus W_0 \oplus W_1 \oplus W_2 \oplus \cdots \tag{2}$$

W_i as wavelet function $\Psi(t)$Closure (wavelet subspace), according to the binary fraction frequency subdivision, the scale space with a new subspace Ui unified characterization.

$$\begin{cases} U_i^0 = V_i, & i \in Z \\ U_i^1 = W_i, & i \in Z \end{cases} \tag{3}$$

Hilbert space orthogonal decomposition $V_{i+1} = V_i \oplus W_i$ can be replaced by U_i^n decomposition.

$$U_{i+1}^0 = U_i^0 \oplus U_i^1, \quad i \in Z \tag{4}$$

Assuming $u_n(t)$ fits following two scale equations as below:

$$\begin{cases} u_{2n}(t) = \sqrt{2} \sum_{k \in Z} h(k) u_n (2t - k) \\ u_{2n+1}(t) = \sqrt{2} \sum_{k \in Z} g(k) u_n (2t - k) \end{cases} \tag{5}$$

Because of $g(k) = (-1)^n h(1-k)$, When n = 0, the above two type is given:

$$\begin{cases} u_0(t) = \sum_{k \in Z} h_k u_0 (2t - k), \quad \mathrm{h}_k = \sqrt{2} h(k) \\ u_1(t) = \sum_{k \in Z} g_k u_0 (2t - k), \quad g_k = \sqrt{2} g(k) \end{cases} \tag{6}$$

Through the multi resolution analysis, $\varpi(t)$ and $\partial(t)$ meet the two-scale equation.

$$\begin{cases} \varpi(t) = \sum_{k \in Z} h_k \varpi(2t - k), \quad \{\mathrm{h}_k\}_{k \in Z} \in L^2 \\ \partial(t) = \sum_{k \in Z} g_k \partial(2t - k), \quad \{g_k\}_{k \in Z} \in L^2 \end{cases} \tag{7}$$

This kind of representation extension to n∈Z+ (a non-negative integer), the equivalent representation: [4]

$$U_{j+1}^n = U_j^{2n} \oplus U_j^{2n+1}, \quad j \in Z, n \in Z_+ \tag{8}$$

Set $g_j^n(t) \in U_j^n$, then

$$g_j^n(t) = \sum_l b_l^{j,n} \partial_n (2^j t - l) \tag{9}$$

Wavelet packet decomposition algorithm is as below:

$$\begin{cases} b_l^{j,2n} = \sum_k b_k^{j+1,n} a_{k-2l} \\ b_l^{j,2n+1} = \sum_k b_k^{j+1,n} c_{k-2l} \end{cases} \tag{10}$$

Using the wavelet packet transform formula between two scales (7), obtain wavelet packets reconstruction algorithm:

$$b_l^{j+1,n} = \sum_{l \in Z} b_k^{j,2n} p_{l-2k} + \sum_{l \in Z} b_k^{j,2n+1} q_{l-2k} \tag{11}$$

2.2   Optimal Wavelet Packet Selection

Optimal wavelet packet selection method can take the" best" choice problem is converted into a cost function minimization process. Optimal wavelet packet selection cost function is Shannon-Weaver entropy criterion, Discrete sequence of x(n) Shannon-Weaver entropy is defined as:

$$\varphi(x) = -\sum_i m(i) \log[m(i)] \tag{12}$$

Set $m(i) = \dfrac{|x(i)|^2}{\|x\|^2}$ then when m (i) =0, m (i) log[m(i)]=0:

$$\varphi(x) = \|x\|^{-2} \Phi(x) + \log(\|x\|^2) \tag{13}$$

In the above equation $\Phi(x)$ equal to $-\sum_i |x(i)|^2 \log(|x(i)|^2)$

According to the cost function, the optimal based search algorithm from the tree structure at the bottom, more child nodes of the parent node of entropy and entropy. If the parent node entropy is less than the nodes entropy sum,, so keep the parent node entropy; otherwise, use the child nodes entropy replaces parent node entropy to determine the best wavelet base.

3   Remote Monitoring System Design of Underground Pipeline

The system consists of Data acquisition, Data processing center system, Client system. The entire system network architecture as shown in Figure 1

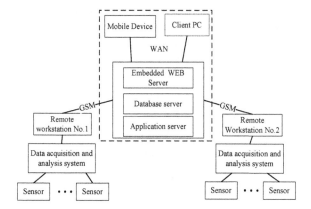

Fig. 1. Natural gas pipeline remote monitoring system architecture

1) Data Acquisition and Processing System
This part of the system from the main pipe sensor to obtain temperature, pressure and other parameters of the collection, at the same time the completion of these data of A / D conversion. The data is then sent to a link to the remote monitoring site PC, for further signal processing. Here is the basis of the whole system, every section of pipeline is a remote site management, this part of the system need higher stability and redundancy.

2) Central Data Processing System
This part includes the embedded Web server, Database server and the uClinux platform for the development of the application program.

3) Client System
Because the system uses the B/S structure, operation personnel needed by the remote server to complete the operation log. In order to improve the monitoring system security, design of multi user authentication service.

4   The Detailed Design of the System

4.1   Data Acquisition and Processing System Design

Due to obtain a variety of data from the pipeline, such as temperature, pressure, so in the pipeline laid in the sensor module which integrated HM30 and DS18B20 sensors to collect pressure and temperature data.

Information in the access to the computer before it has finished the A / D conversion. The computer through the AI interface data acquisition sensor, while the TC35 serial port and GPRS module link, in place of SIM card chip and corresponding set, rely on the GSM communication protocol for data automatic download and upload, at the same time the module to send and receive information encryption and decryption processing. [5]

4.2   Design and Implementation of Embedded Web Server

The embedded web server collects remote data of monitoring station via GSM network. Through the wavelet packet algorithm for noise reduction, calculate the leak location. At the same time for data storage and access security settings, the structure of the whole system as shown in figure 2.

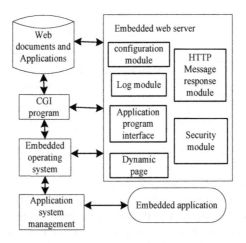

Fig. 2. Embedded web system structure diagram

1) Boa Server Configuration

To configure Boa, allowing it to support the execution of CGI programs. [6] First of all in the root file system / MNT / etc directory to establish a boa directory, modify the configuration file of boa server- boa.conf as below:

Change Group nogroup into 'Group 0', change ScriptAlias /cgi-bin/usr/lib/cgi-bin/ into ScriptAlias/cgi-bin/var/www/cgi-bin/ ,cgi-bin directory is for CGI script catalog.[7] Then in the file/mnt/etc creates a log file directory/var/log/boa, create an HTML document home directory /var/www, mime.types files will be copied to the /mnt/etc directory, create a CGI script directory/var/www/cgi-bin/. Finally use NFS tests Boa static HTML page whether normal access, CGI script whether normal operation. After configuration, recompile the kernel. The compiled kernel is downloaded to the hardware platform of ARM, start the uClinux operating system, IP configuration, run Boa Web Server, and then can be accessed through the browser webpage.

2) Central Database Design

The system database is based Microsoft SQL Server 2000. According to the system demands, design data Tables which include system parameter table, real-time data, history data table, the user table. Data table structure. Shown in Table 1:

Table 1. Database Function Table

Table name	Type	Function
Pipe_Info	System Parameter table	pipeline parameter information
S_Info	System Parameter table	sensor configuration information
R_Data	Real-time Data table	real-time monitoring data
H_ Data	History Data table	historical data
U_ Data	User table	user rights

4.3   Application Software Design Based on Embedded Web Server

Application software system consists of the following modules: parameter setting module, real-time information module, historical data module, fault statistics and video monitoring module, shown in Figure 3 below.

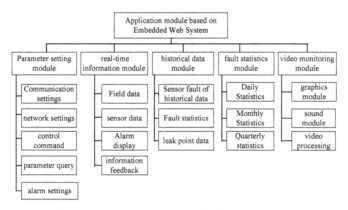

Fig. 3. Structure of system application modules

1) Parameter setting module

In this module, Administrator can set network parameters, inspection interval settings on line. Use inspection interval module to complete a pipeline inspection time settings, when setting the inspection time, at the same time to update a record in a database.

2) Real-time information module

In this module, Administrator can collect remote information by inputting line name, system of sensor number and other parameters.

3) Historical data module

History data inquiry module mainly uses ADOQuery control receives a user request, then by using the Open method to execute the query. In this module, use graphical display to show data.

4) Fault statistics

According to the different requirements of pipeline management company can be set according to the day, month or quarter statistics, through the fault types, time and other parameter settings, to select the best combination.

5) Video monitoring module

The video data receive module is based on security video surveillance system originally existed in the pipeline. In order to receive broadcast multiple images, in program implementation uses multi-thread technology, each thread to create a user interface window, and is responsible for one video stream is received and broadcast.

The main steps of implementation: (1)establish a connection to the Winsock, input connection server IP to send data to the server request (2) after receiving confirmation from the server information, start data receiving and display thread (3) According to the multicast address and port number, join the IP multicast group (4) decodes the video stream and play real timely.

4.4   Client Authentication Design

Because the embedded web system authentication mechanism is different from other kinds of server, so in this system, use Digest access authentication scheme.

When use the Digest access authentication, need modify the client response header and a list of parameter: WWW-Authenticate: Digest, realm='Embedded-WebServer', qop='auth', algorithm='MD5', stale='FALSE'. The server must ensure that each random number of response information is the unique.

After Web browsers receive feedback, enter the user name and password. According to requirements of parameter values list, do message digital signature. The authentication process is as shown in Figure4.

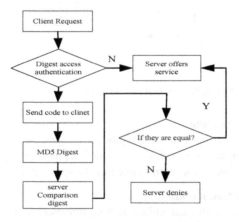

Fig. 4. Certification process flow diagram

Use MD5 algorithm to encrypt the message m, generate a summary of H (m). Then use encryption device E and the message digest encryption key k to get Ek (H (m)). Send the new request to the server, including the status line and request-header field, which must be included in the request header field Authorization. Server receives "response" message from the client, and gets the username and password from the encrypted password database. Authentication use the received message, signs after the start of entity authentication message digest H (m). Then compare the Web browser authentication message digest and signature of the embedded Web server to authenticate the message m to generate the signature Summary of equality. If equal the server resources, server processes the request of resources, otherwise deny the request.

After Web browser and embedded Web server finish Authentication message signature process, client authentication system will determine whether the user can login.

5   Conclusions

This system uses the wavelet packet algorithm to detect the pipes leakage location. Optimal wavelet packet algorithm is designed Based on the Shannon-Weaver entropy criterion to improve noise reduction effect and anti jamming ability. The system used wireless communication technology (GSM), PLC technology, bus technology, uCLinux server and embedded WEB technology. This system can be used for remote video monitoring, user authentication, data analysis and processing, can easily be ported the system to the mobile phone, PDA and mobile terminal. This system has better real-time, opening, expansibility and security performance. Provide new methods, and ideas for effective monitoring and management of City water pipeline network.

References

1. Hunaidi, O., Chu, W.T.: Acoustical characteristics of leak signals in plastic water distribution pipes. Applied Acoustic 58(3), 235–254 (1999)
2. Pinnington, R.J., Briscoe, A.R.: Externally applied sensor for ax-isymmetric waves in a fluid filled pipe. Journal of Sound and Vibration 173(4), 503–516 (1994)
3. Peng, Y.: Wavelet transform and engineering application. Science Press, Beijing (1999)
4. Cohen, A., Daubechies, I.: Orthonormal bases of compactly sup-ported wavelets III batter frequency resolution. SIAM Journal on Mathematical Analysis 24(2), 520–527 (1993)
5. Hong, L.: Implements Radio Data Transferring by TC35 Wireless Model. Telecom Engineering Technics and Standardization (3), 61–63 (2007)
6. Yang, D.-Q., Mei, D.-C., Zhang, Y., Liu, S.-J.: Dynamic Web Technology Based on Embedded ARM9 and Linux. Industrial Control Computer (8), 45–48 (2006)
7. Shi, F.-G., Duan, C.-X., Xiao, X.-H., Qian, T.-W.: The Research and Implementation of Embedded Web Server Based on Wireless Sensor Networks. Microcomputer Information (3), 148–150 (2011)

Primary Educational Resources Classification Study Based on Gagne Learning Classification Theory

Fan Yang, Jun Han[*], Jing Liu, Jun Tong, and Shuo Chen

Capital Normal University, Beijing 100048, China
{www.yangfan2007-47,fionaliujing}@163.com,
jameshan@vip.sina.com, {tongjun02.student,cskaoyandota}@sina.com

Abstract. Education resource management platform is based on certain norms and standards, collecting and managing a variety of media material resources and providing support services for teaching system. This paper mainly describes the classification of resources in primary education resource management platform, for some of the issues in primary school educational resources to analyze, and combination the Gagne learning classification theory proposed a new resource classification model from the perspective of learners.

Keywords: education resource management platform, educational resources, resource classification, learning classification theory, classification model.

1 Introduction

With the development of educational technology, in the form of networks as a medium for universal education has been widely promoted. The concept of "educational information" according to the national long-term education reform and development plan (2010-2020) ", provinces and cities nationwide construct education resource management platform to apply to students in different levels to use. At the same time, the classification of educational resources has become one of the key in the education resource management platform. How to improve the utilization of educational resources in this platform in primary education have also become problems to be solved. The article focus on the educational resources, analysing platform classification, and according to the classification theory of Gagne's learning come up with the optimization of resources in primary education resource management platform.

2 Functional and Structural Profiles of the Primary Education Resource Management Platform

Researching and summarizing a large number of primary education resource management platform, come to the basic structure of the general platform for document management system with a relational database to realize storage and management of educational information resources. The platform structure is shown in Fig. 1.[1]

---

[*] Corresponding author.

[1] Chen Xianghua, "Build Educational Resource Library Need to Address Key Issues" J. China Educational,2004, vol.1, pp.50-52.

J. Lei et al. (Eds.): NCIS 2012, CCIS 345, pp. 180–190, 2012.
© Springer-Verlag Berlin Heidelberg 2012

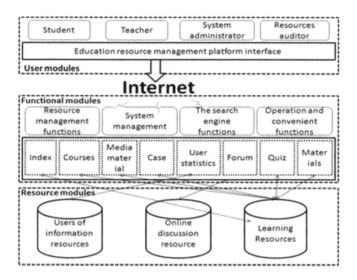

Fig. 1. The basic structure of the general primary education resource management platform

The platform is divided into three modules: user modules, function modules and resource modules. The following functions for each module in detail.

User modules: users are divided into primary education resource management platform: students, teachers, system administrators and resource auditors. User self-registration, when the registration is completed, you can use the resources in the platform. Unregistered users can browse the platform, but not to download and use within the platform resources.

Functional modules: divided into four major parts, including resource management functions, system management functions, search engine functions and convenient operation functions;

Resource management functions: including uploading and downloading of resources, resource classification, reviewing, finding, booking, storage, statistics, regularly updated features and so on;

System management functions: including system maintenance, system stability, security, portability and scalability. With access control and security control, do not have access may not use the related resources, and with a preliminary audit mechanism for uploading resources.

The search engine functions: primary education resource management platform contains a great number of information of educational resources. Users need to quickly and accurately find the resources, so they requested that the platform has a multi-stage retrieval mechanism to support a variety of retrieval methods parallel retrieval.

Operation and convenient functions: primary education resource management platform, users are mostly concentrated in the primary school students and teachers, so based on the user's characteristics and requirements of the interface is simple, beautiful, friendly, clear navigation, user-friendly.

Resource modules: including the user information database, online discussion resource library and learning resources library. User information repository used to store user information and usage, and to facilitate the utilization of statistical resources. Online discussion of the repository used to store the contents about message and forum to facilitate the learners to share learning experiences and teachers' guidance and help. Learning repository mainly storage teaching resources on platform for secondary learners.

Through the primary education resource management platform, users can upload a large number of learning resources, after processing, according to the different textbook versions, different disciplines and different file types to classify integration for the different needs of users. The purpose is to create a primary education resource management platform to achieve the construction of distributed resources, the orderly organization of resources and to maximize and improve resource utilization. While promoting the level of information for educators and learners, to improve the quality of education and learning.

3   The Overall Classification of Resources in Primary Education Resource Management Platform

By analyzing the different levels, different parts of the primary education resource management platform can be drawn that the majority of platform resources, showing the form of tree structure, the top-down model, by level of knowledge content, teaching resources be classified systematic. For example: Primary Resources Network, Beijing Educational Resources Network, and National Resources for Basic Education Network. At present, the classification of resources in primary education resource management platform is no uniform standard, according to the different types and angles can be divided into the following categories:

- According to the resource belongs to subject can be divided: Chinese, mathematics, English, art, music, morality, science, IT.
- According to the textbook version of the classification.
- According to the resource types can be divided into: The media material, including class text material, graphics (images) class material, video class material, audio-class material, animation class material; Gauge set, including the questions, a qualitative evaluation of gauge sets; Teaching and learning tools and templates, including instructional design software, learning tools and the template of teaching methods; Courseware including exercises, simulations, activities, experiments, online learning, visual aids, hands-on practice; literature and teaching cases.
- Can be divided based on the resource format: doc, ppt, swf, html, jpg, mp3, wav, wma, mpg, flv, wmv, rar, pdf, and so on.
- According to the manifestations of the resources can be divided into: electronic books, electronic journals, online databases, virtual libraries, encyclopedias, educational websites, virtual software, and other.
- According to the contents of the resource classification can be divided into chapters: Chapter 1 (Section I, section II, ...), the second chapter ...

- According to the topic of the resource classification can be divided into: such as: the language can be divided into (classical, prose, fiction ...)
- Resources to be classified according to the upload time, or click-through rate.
- According to the degree of openness of classification can be divided into: totally free, some fees and all fees.

Classification framework of existing educational resources focused on the present form of resources, the resources in accordance with the classification of the different classification of the system, but with subject-related knowledge accumulation is not conducive to the learner to accurately retrieve information. At the same time, primary education resource management platform provides a lot of redundant information. Resources are not as their quality that was presented to the learners, the most resource platforms in accordance with the level of click-through rate show the sequence of the resources, but the quality of the click-through rate is not directly proportional with the quality of the resource to a common problem in a lot of resource platforms. A large number of quality resources often appear in the final of all resources, and these resources just be ignored by the learner. At present, the utilization of resources in the resource management platform is low. The reason can be summarized as follows:

- Goals are not clear: Firstly, the resources in the primary education resource management platform to build is not clear, the builders mistakenly believe that a large number of learning resources uploaded to the Internet to create a resource platform, but lack of assessment of its effectiveness. Secondly, there are a large number of primary school online educational resources, a variety of types of resources, but the platform model is basically same, resulting in a lot of platform resources idle.
- Category problem: platform module design and category management are conducted in accordance with the ideas of the developers for the platform builders that lack of relevant teaching experience and theoretical knowledge, leading to the classification of resources is not easy to use. Classification method has been defined in the design of the platform of resources, different learners in the use of only in accordance with the classification of the previously defined to find related resources, and cannot be classified according to actual needs, resulting in a variety of resource library monotony and lacking of personality, and not from the actual needs of the development platform, naturally reduces the function of the repository.
- Integration issues: Each resource is relatively fragmented in the repository, which not be classified according to the actual value of the resource. To some extent increase the burden on the learner, while in the majority of primary education resources lack of educational resources portfolio function, namely: learners the resources required, long-term preservation, so that learners can learn repeatedly.
- Interface problems: Resources burdensome, irrational interface layout, mismanagement of resources. Causing learners to face a lot of resources are unable to start, will not be able to fully mobilize the enthusiasm of the learners, so cannot play the role of teaching resources library in the educational information.

- Re-use issues: Non-standard data definitions in the repository, bringing the resources of migration and management difficulties. The definition of data mostly according to the developer's understanding in existing library of educational resources and rarely based on internationally accepted standards or the relevant provisions. This does not have any built up on the basis of the primary reference standard repository, which is influence the aspects on the exchange and sharing of data, data migration and management.
- Resource Update issues: Part of the primary education resource management platform resources update slower and have lags. Therefore it will not help the learner grasp of new knowledge.
- Quality of the resources problem: The educational resources in the primary education resource management platform should not be to measure the "quantity" while ignoring the "quality" factors. The high-quality resources is an effective way to improve the utilization of resource management platform, one should be set up specifically responsible for the audit of resources, to ensure the quality of the resource.[2]

Through the analysis these seven problems can be divided into two categories: Firstly, the system function is imperfect. Secondly, the resource classification still have problems. Target is not clear, integration issues, resource reuse in the final analysis due to platform for building the initial system functions poorly defined and have flaws in the user's needs analysis survey. Interface issues, resource updates, resource quality problem is due to the resource classification issues derived from a series of questions. It is not difficult to find that resource classification is still a key issue in primary educational resources to improve the utilization of platform resources. Currently, the majority of the classification of the resource management platform ignored the feelings of the learners, so the classification of resources should from the perspective of learners and close contact with the learner's own characteristics, re-integrating the resources, so that learners can better to learn.

4   New Classification Model to Learn the Classification Theory Based on Gagne

The advantage of resources in primary education resource management platform is through visual stimulation to enhance learners' interest in the knowledge and enhance the independent learning ability, also provides a strong guarantee for the popularity of the "education information". The purpose of primary education resources is that students can quickly and accurately find the learning resources so that efficiently assist their learning. Gagne's learning Category theory provides a new perspective for resource classification. According to the revelation of the classification theory of Gagne's learning, learning resources can be classified as follows:

---

[2] Zhang Xianzeng and Chen Feng,"Design and Application of Teaching Resources Database Management System"J. China Educational,2003, vol.11, pp.51-52.

4.1   Classification Based on Gagne's Theory of Learning Level Guidance

Depending on the level of complexity of learning, Gagne proposed eight categories of learning. They are signal learning, stimulus - response learning (S-R learning), chain learning, verbal associative learning, discrimination learning, concept learning, rule learning, problem-solving learning. Gagne's classification is from simple to complex, from low level to high level. The first three types of learning are simple reaction, after five is a complex reaction. Later Gagne amends this classification, combining the first four categories of learning into one class, extending the concept of learning for the learning of specific concepts and definitions of the concept. The classification results: chain learning, discrimination learning, specific concept learning, definition of concept learning, rule learning, problem-solving learning.[3,4] According to Gagne's level of learning theory, combined with the personality traits of different ages educated in primary education. Can be presented from low grade to high grade resource classification that students in grade one and grade two in primary school mainly use chain learning, so we should provide image and animation resources to increase students' association and interests. Students in grade two and grade three mainly use discrimination learning, so we should give image, text and animation resources to enhance students' ability to observe and cultivate literacy and thinking awareness. Students in grade three and grade four mainly use specific concept learning and definition of concept learning, so we should provide text, image and operate resources to cultivate a sense of the phrase and abstract concepts concrete and improve students' ability. Students in grade three to grade six mainly use rule learning, so we should provide text, audio-visual and image resources to enable students to understand the rules, deepen students' learning the rules and abstract concepts concrete. Students in grade four to grade six mainly use problem-solving learning, so we should offer text resources to develop students' ability to solve problems.[5,6]

4.2   Classification of Learning Outcomes Based on Gagne's Theoretical

Gagne divide learning into five categories according to the learning outcomes: learning of verbal information, learning of intellectual skills, learning of cognitive strategies learning of attitude, learning of motor skill.[7]

Learning of verbal information is that students master the content of the speech information transfer or student learning outcomes based on verbal information

---

[3] Zhang Jiping and Liu Rihua,"The Revelation of The Gagne's Five Learning Classification Theory of School Education", J. nanchang Junior College, 2009, vol.1,pp.90-91.

[4] Gagne's learning outcomes classification theory, http://wenku.baidu.com/view/fee9f1d63186bceb19e8bb28.html DB/OL.

[5] Wang Lizhen."Analysis of Educational Resource Library and Construction Strategy", J. Chinese Modern Educational Equipment, 2006, vol.4.pp.89-92.

[6] Xu Xiaoxiong,"Robert Gagne Academic Thinking and The Revelation" , J. Ningbo University of Technology , Education and Science, 2009, vol.1.

[7] Sun Ying and Wu Leilei,"Digital Learning Rsource Cassification in Basic Education Study Based on Classification Theory of Learning Outcomes" J. Modern educational technology, 2008, vol18, pp.74-77.

expressed. This type of learning is usually organized, learners not only get the individual facts, but also give a lot of meaningful knowledge is based on certain teaching objectives. Both information learning and meaningful learning constitute a system of knowledge. To learn the knowledge of the language class, the learning of verbal information has played a prominent role. It is not only a necessary condition for further study, at the same time it also has a lot of practical significance in life, and verbal knowledge helps the expansion and extension of the thinking.

Learning of intellectual skills. Learning of verbal information to help students "what" questions; but the learning of intellectual skills to solve the problem of "how" to deal with the outside world of symbols and information. In all levels of learning are different intellectual skills. Gagne believes that the learning of each level of intellectual skills is based on the low-level intellectual skills have obtained. The most complex intellectual skills compose of many simple skills. Identify skills as a basic intellectual skill. In turn divided into different levels of learning and its contained different levels of complexity of mental operations: identify - concepts - rules - rules(problem solving). When students learn science class knowledge, intellectual skills play an important role. It can guide the thinking of the learners, so that students understand knowledge more clearly.[8]

Learning of cognitive strategies. The cognitive strategies are self-domination. The different between cognitive strategies and intellectual skills is the intellectual skills directed to the external environment of the learners', but cognitive strategies dominated learners own behavior in a specific environment. Simply speaking, cognitive strategies are learners used to "manage" their own learning process. Cognitive strategies of each individual according to the characteristics of the learner's own have more or less difference. Therefore, according to the characteristics of learners of different ages classified the resources for learners constructing their knowledge learning system plays an important role.

Learning of attitude. Attitude is the internal state by learning. This state affects the actions taken by individuals on certain things, people and events. The school's educational goals should include the cultivation of attitude, which from the various disciplines of learning, but more is obtained from internal and external activities and family. In numerous educational resources, video-based educational resources contribute to cultivate the learners' attitude.[9]

Learning of motor skill. Learning of motor skill, such as gymnastics skills, writing skills, drawing skills, to operate the instrument skills, is an integral part of the capacity. Classification from the learning outcomes of learning, helping students to learn and teachers to better organize the teaching, has more practical significance.

According to Gagne's learning outcomes, resources are divided into five types: memory resources, understand resources, improvement resources, emotional resources and operational resources. The corresponding relationship is shown in Table 1:[10,11]

---

[8] Shao Ruizhen,"Educational Psychology" M. Shanghai Education Press, 1983,pp.24-27.

[9] Wu Qinglin, "Cognitive Instructional Psychology", M. Shanghai Education Press, 2007.

[10] He Kekang, "The Nature of E-Learning ---- IT and Curriculum Integration" J. Educational study,2001, vol.1, pp.3-6.

[11] Li Pan, "The Revelation of Gagne Classification of Learning Outcomes Theory of Adult Learning", Adult Education College of Hebei University, J. 2010, vol.12.pp.30-31.

Table 1. New classification model is shown in table 1 above Gagne both learning theory of resources

Classification of learning outcomes	Type classification of resources
Learning of verbal information	Memory resources
Learning of intellectual skills	Understand resources
Learning of cognitive strategies	Improvement resources
Learning of attitude	Emotional resources
Learning of motor skill	Operational resources

Based on both learning theory on the resources of Gagne proposed new classification model shown in Fig. 2.[12,13]

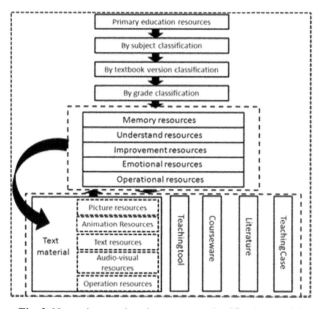

Fig. 2. New primary education resource classification model

---

[12] Wu Yonghong,"Construction and Application of School Education Resource Management Platform", J. Educational study, 2004, vol.11.pp.66-69.
[13] Wang Dechen, "The Study of Education Resource Management Platform",C. unpublished.

Based on the classification of resources in the existing primary education resource management platform, the teaching content of each grade is divided into five different dimensions: memory resources, understand resources, improvement resources, emotional resources and operational resources, and then refine the resources in each dimension.

For example, under the memory resources dimension in the first year of language teaching content, classified according to the chapter text material, education tools, templates, courseware, documentation and teaching cases, while need to take into account the learner's own characteristics, combined with learning level of classification theory, taking into account the form of resources for different age learners to classify integration of resources. For example: teaching resources in the first year should add more pictures, animation resources and reduce text type resources. The new classification model taking into account the learners' own characteristics, classified from the skills which learners want to acquire. A combination of two learning classifier theory, integrated with resource classification corresponding to the two theories to propose a new classification model. The model changes learners aimlessly to find resources in the past and provides a convenient way to find resources for learners.[14]

Classification of learning outcomes helps to set up teaching goals. Teaching goal boiled down to the Fifth learning results, to determine the goal of teaching students eventually master the learning results-oriented way to make teaching practice more targeted. First, to set goals for the students' final performance, simplify complicated Teaching goals; Second, teachers can be based on the teaching content belongs types of learning outcomes in instructional design.

In addition, teaching objectives Since Gagne classification learning outcomes makes more precise. Based on the learning results of classification, Gagne propose the "five ingredients goals" law to state teaching objectives. The five ingredients goal specifies the context of the behavior, the type of acquisition performance and the behavior of the object, the concrete actions of the students, as well as job-related tools, limit or special conditions. Using five ingredients target method design teaching objectives for each course or each lesson can get a detailed teaching plan, so as to make the teaching process to be precise.[15]

5   The Significance of the Learning Classification Theory of Resources in Primary Education Resources

5.1   For the Significance of Learners

Based on the classification theory of Gagne's learning and the needs of the learners' psychological and physiological Before learners' acquisition of knowledge have to

[14] Yu Shengquan and Zhu Lingyun, "Education Resources Technical Specifications of Architecture and Application Mode", J. China Educational, 2003, vol.3,pp.51-55.
[15] Yang Xiuwen and ZhaiJie,"Talking about Gagne's Classification of Learning Outcomes of The Impact on Teaching", J. Theory, 2011, vol.11, pp.278-279.

percept the learning outcomes of the requirements and clearly define learning objectives. The pre-perception can guide learners to select the appropriate method to master the learning content and provide a new way to find resources for learners.

5.2   For the Meaning of the Developer's

The developer can try a new resource-building mode. This mode can be applied to a variety of resource-based platform. Providing new ideas for developers and making development purposes clear. Breaking the traditional model which begin with the developer's own way of thinking and a single tree model classified. To improve the friendly interface, improve resource utilization.

5.3   For the Guiding Significance of the Primary Resource Classification Theory

On the one hand, according to Gagne theory of learning classification put forward new ideas in resource classification and add a theoretical basis and have some role in guiding the management of resources in the future of primary education resource management platform. Meanwhile, according to the resource classification more user-friendly, focusing on starting from the learner's point of view can help students to cultivate the ability of autonomous learning. On the other hand, contributing to the educational resources to construction norms established.

6   Conclusion

The learning classification theory from the view of the level of learners and the acquisition of skills combine with cognitive level and the skills required of learners at different stages, fully taking into account the subjectivity of students. The classification theory of learning applied to the classification of resources, not only is the classification of resources in a new way, which breaking the traditional classification model according to the textbook chapters, and also have meaning for the construction standards for educational resources. At present, facing a large number of educational resources emerge. To take a single resource classification model can meet the needs of learners no longer. How to reasonably allocate resources from the different needs of learners, thereby improving the utilization of resources, has become a focus of future research. Only by using the theory of learning classification model of combining with the previous classification can enable resources to be reasonably applied to the learners, and to facilitate better learning task. Therefore, the classification criteria of the specification resources, the integration of diverse classification, strengthen the construction of resource classification of the three aspects is the focus of future research.

References

1. Chen, X.: Build Educational Resource Library Need to Address Key Issues. J. China Educational 1, 50–52 (2004)
2. Zhang, X., Chen, F.: Design and Application of Teaching Resources Database Management System. J. China Educational 11, 51–52 (2003)
3. Zhang, J., Liu, R.: The Revelation of The Gagne's Five Learning Classification Theory of School Education. J. Nanchang Junior College 1, 90–91 (2009)
4. Gagne's learning outcomes classification theory DB/OL, http://wenku.baidu.com/view/fee9f1d63186bceb19e8bb28.html
5. Wang, L.: Analysis of Educational Resource Library and Construction Strategy. J. Chinese Modern Educational Equipment 4, 89–92 (2006)
6. Xu, X.: Robert Gagne Academic Thinking and The Revelation. J. Ningbo University of Technology, Education and Science 1 (2009)
7. Sun, Y., Wu, L.: Digital Learning Rsource Cassification in Basic Education Study Based on Classification Theory of Learning Outcomes. J. Modern Educational Technology 18, 74–77 (2008)
8. Shao, R.: Educational Psychology, pp. 24–27. Shanghai Education Press (1983)
9. Wu, Q.: Cognitive Instructional Psychology. Shanghai Education Press (2007)
10. He, K.: The Nature of E-Learning —— IT and Curriculum Integration. J. Educational Study 1, 3–6 (2001)
11. Pan, L.: The Revelation of Gagne Classification of Learning Outcomes Theory of Adult Learning. Adult Education College of Hebei University J. 12, 30–31 (2010)
12. Wu, Y.: Construction and Application of School Education Resource Management Platform. J. Educational Study 11, 66–69 (2004)
13. Wang, D.: The Study of Education Resource Management Platform (unpublished)
14. Yu, S., Zhu, L.: Education Resources Technical Specifications of Architecture and Application Mode. China Educational 3, 51–55 (2003)
15. Yang, X., Zhai, J.: Talking about Gagne's Classification of Learning Outcomes of The Impact on Teaching. J. Theory 11, 278–279 (2011)

A Special Subject Database in CALIS Project: Database of Local Resources in the Northwestern Guangxi[*]

Bo Zhou, Wenliang Liu, and Cuiyun Qui[**]

Hechi University, No.42 Longjiang Road, Yizhou City, Guangxi, China
zhoubo1114@163.com, liuwenliang@hotmail.com, hcxycy@126.com

Abstract. The paper mainly demonstrates the constructional scheme of database of local resources in the northwestern Guangxi in the project of special subject database in national colleges. It includes the overall goal, constructional thought, constructional content, developmental environment, organizational management, operational management and expected outcomes. The paper aims to provide a complete conference for the implementation of the database of local resources in the northwestern Guangxi and make the proceeding preparations for the daily maintenance and further extension.

Keywords: local resources, CALIS, information service, database.

1 Introduction

Special database in national colleges is one of models of CALIS (China Academic Library & Information System) [1] construction. It follows the constructional idea: constructing dispersedly, retrieving systematically, sharing resources and serving nationally, which supports the digital construction of unique and scarce resources. It also supports mining and rearranging of primary digital resources in network. It continues to support the construction of special database with the preliminary achievements, subject characteristics, local characteristics and distinctive national characteristics. The construction of the database adopts the way of organizing and managing intensively, constructing database comparatively systematically, constructing database apart by the engaging schools and supervising and guiding by the experts. The effect of the construction of CALIS special database [2, 3] is shown in Fig. 1, which is made up of two levels: the special database of local resources and the special database of national resources, which form the set of unified metadata and the structure of distributed object data. Both the special database of local resources and the special database of national resources all follow the same standards and norms. The mechanism of information sharing and information exchange between the two levels forms under the unified system framework, which makes the system open and portable.

---

[*] This research was financially supported by the Scientific Research Fund of Guangxi Provincial Education Department (No. 201202ZD082).

[**] Corresponding author.

J. Lei et al. (Eds.): NCIS 2012, CCIS 345, pp. 191–197, 2012.
© Springer-Verlag Berlin Heidelberg 2012

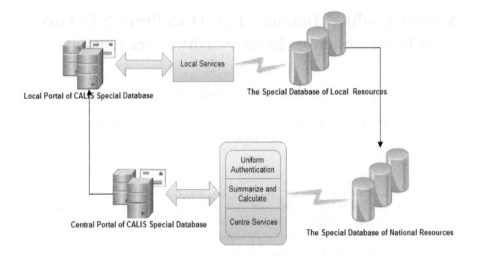

Fig. 1. Construction of CALIS special database

The northern Guangxi, centering on Hechi city, has history, culture, nature and ecological resources with strong local and national characteristics. It has such social functions as preserving outstanding minority and local historical culture, serving areas and the economical development. Using the opportunity of obtaining the constructional scheme of CALIS special database and based on the advantages in geography, academy in university and information service organizations in the aspect of characteristics resources, technology, human resources, constructing local resources database in the northwestern Guangxi should be developed so as to preserve and inherit excellent national minority culture and local culture, promoting the research, development and utilization of culture, history, natural and ecological resources in northwestern Guangxi, supporting social and economical development in northwestern Guangxi and the discipline construction of local colleges and improving the level of scientization, standardization and scaling of the construction of special database of information service organization in western minority areas, which are with great significance in melting into the sharing system of the national resources. Such databases have been constructed by many organizations as Chaoshan Documentation Database [4], Kazakh Cultural Features Database [5], Zhe-Merchant Characteristic Database [6] etc.

2   Constructional Foundation of the Database of Local Resources in the Northwestern Guangxi

2.1   The Foundation of Document Reserve

Thematic database of local document in the northwestern Guangxi has been established, which includes more than two thousands kinds of information as history, humanities, economy in the northwestern Guangxi. In the database, the information about the culture of Liu Sanjie folk song is comparatively systematic and the relating information collated in 2009 is included in the research database of Liu Sanjie [7]. The organization has ordered 1600 newspapers, newly purchases over 30000 copies every year and orders 14 Chinese and foreign language databases, whose types cover electronic journals, theses, conference papers, electronic information and newspapers. These resources are the solid data base of constructing special database.

2.2   The Foundation of Existing Special Database

Since 2005 the construction of the special database in the northwestern of Guangxi has begun. Universal database software has been successively used to develop 7 special databases. So far, there are more than 4000 articles of data and more than 4000 kinds of data to be input into the database. The construction of special database has good basis. The data having been put into database has been indexed basically according to metadata standard of the CALIS special database and the data is migrated and conversed easily.

2.3   The Foundation of Talents

During the process of more than 6 years of the construction of the special database, the qualified personnel who are capable of constructing and managing large-scale database have been trained. The subject and professional structure of the project team member are reasonable, which can meet the needs of the professional knowledge for the staff. Project director and part of the project members have the experience of presiding over and completing the various academic subjects or project development and they have the rich project management experience. Most of the members should have the experience of processing document information or information service automation and they are skilled in literature digitization, database maintenance, document indexing, indexing and other project related technical work.

2.4   The Foundation of Hardware Devices

The server and constructional and management system of information resources have been purchased in 2009 to comprehensively upgrade the platform of software and hardware in the process of developing special database of the information service institutions. The school attaches importance to the network, digitalization of information services. The information service institution, as a main mode of school network, build the disk array based SAN with 5TB capacity, whose network has reached the GPA, and   who reaches the desktop at the rate of 100MB/1000MB,. The development and application of special database should have a certain base of equipment and network.

2.5   The Foundation of Cooperative Network

The cooperation between school and the local area is emphasized. It has the better relationship of cooperation with such institutes as the local information service organization, Autonomous Science and Technology Information Institute and Hechi Science and Technology Information Institute in the aspects of literature collection, resource sharing and technical cooperation. When constructing special database, these collaboration networks should be used and they should be brought their superiority into full play to ensure completing the project.

2.6   The Foundation of Disciplinary Research

Such three key existing laboratories and research centers in colleges in Guangxi as Research and Development Laboratory in the northwestern Guangxi, Research center of Minority Intangible Cultural Heritage in the northwestern Guangxi and Base of literary Creation and Talents Training , such two key disciplines as literature and art and applied chemistry in colleges in Guangxi and the two research institutes, the culture Research Center for Hongshui River, Literature College in the northwestern Guangxi, Research Institute for Silkworm have formed the pattern of building key laboratories and Key disciplines. The academic resources as relevant rich research results and talents are solid foundations for the construction of special database.

3   Constructional Content

The database of local resources in the northwestern Guangxi includes many databases such as the database of minority culture in the northwestern Guangxi, the database of local history in the northwestern Guangxi, the database of art in the northwestern Guangxi, the database of nature and ecosystem in the northwestern Guangxi. The database collects all documents in the northwestern Guangxi in the aspects of history, humanities, the nature, economy, society. It includes such contents as history, geography, politics, economy, language, nationality, religion, meteorology, literature, art, customs, natural resources, science and technology and education in the northwestern Guangxi. It will highlight minority culture, local history, local arts, local nature and ecological resources. Documents collected in the database is not limited to the carrier and form of publication, including such literature types as information services, newspapers, journals, theses, conference proceedings, patent literature, standard literature, technical data, research reports, pictures, videos, audios, monuments, files, manuscripts, genealogies, music, cyber resources as well as such forms of publication as open publication, internal publications, folk, personal publications

3.1   Database of Local History

The database mainly reflects the conflicts between Han cultures and minority cultures, the historical process of ethnic fusion as well as revolutionary struggles of the people under the leadership of the party in the northwestern Guangxi. It records historical celebrities in the northwestern Guangxi and such important historical events as the moving of Zhejiang University westward to Yizhou. The characteristics of the database are such relevant records in modern journals in the northwestern Guangxi as Wei Baqun, Hongqijun, Baise uprising in Baise, Donglan Agricultural Movement Institute and guerrillas.

3.2   Database of Minority Culture

The database fully reflects the special cultures of the seven minorities in the northwestern Guangxi and systematically collects the related research data and research achievements of the seven minorities. The characteristics of the database are: the culture of the songs of Liu Sanjie, the culture of drums of Zhuang minority, the most representative and influential national cultures and Yifan Festival , the national minority intangible cultural heritage in northwestern Guangxi. The database includes such documents as academic papers, monographs, cyber source images, audios and videos. Rare and unique documents include folk song books, plays, original ecological folk song video, manuscripts, pictures etc.

3.3   Database of Art in the Northwestern Guangxi

Database mainly reflects the writers in the northwest of Guangxi, research results of the writers and the works closely related with the Northwestern Guangxi as well as of the language, writing and folklore in the northwestern Guangxi.

The characteristics of the database are research of the writers in the northwestern of Guangxi, research of Huang Tingjian and research of folklore in the northwest of Guangxi. The database includes: the research data of more than 30 writers in the northwestern Guangxi representing Dongxi, Ping Yiping, Guizi and Lan Huaichang; literature creation, research of the works and the calligraphy and works of Huang Tingjian; folk literature, literature research, reviews, history of folk literature in the northwestern Guangxi; data of dialect research in the northwestern Guangxi.

3.4   Database of Nature and Ecosystem in the Northwestern Guangxi

The contents of database are resources for long living in the northwestern Guangxi (such as resources for long living in Bama county), environment (such as Karst, rocky desertification, biodiversity), minerals (such as indium, antimony, tin, zinc), industry, biomass resource, Chinese herbal medicine, agriculture (such as the silkworm, green food) and the relevant research monographs, theses, standards, patents, achievements of science and technology of its development and use.

4   Conclusion

The unique digital characteristic literature resources in the northwest Guangxi formed after the construction of the database of local resources literature in the northwestern

Guangxi, which can protect and inherit excellent national minority cultures and local cultures, promote the research of the development and utilization of history, culture, nature and ecological resources in the northwestern Guangxi; support the development of society and economy in the northwestern Guangxi and the discipline construction of local university, improve the levels of science, standardization and scaling of the construction of special database in information service institutions in the western minority areas. By forming the database of characteristic resources, it can be integrated into the national resource sharing system so as to reduce the digital distance between developed areas and western regions.

The construction of the database of local resources literature in the northwestern Guangxi adopts a series of recommended related standards, format of metadata indexing, international and national standards of documents so as to achieve such functions as unified metadata retrieval and distributed full-text service of the database of local resources literature in the northwestern Guangxi to a certain degree.

Using the current domestic advanced and mature construction and management system platform of information resources to construct database of local resources literature in the northwestern Guangxi, the integration of the knowledge information resources has been achieved, collection, processing and content distribution and management of all kinds of local resources in the northwestern Guangxi have been fulfilled. Under the support of the intelligent search engine, content management and knowledge mining as well as full text retrieval service have been achieved.

Because of the better cooperation with the local organizations, it has the better relationship with the local information service organization, Autonomous Science and Technology Information Institute and Hechi Science and Technology Information Institute in the aspects of literature collection, resource sharing and technical cooperation. In the process of constructing the database of local resources literature in the northwestern Guangxi, strong force will be formed by using these cooperation networks and developing the unique advantage in the aspect of collecting data.

The construction of the database of local resources in the northwestern Guangxi follows the rule of CALIS resources sharing. The completed database, as the united constructional achievement of CALIS, provides the public free retrieval to CALIS organization, document transmission service in the way of CALIS document delivery services and document retrieval and the transmission of the original document delivery services based on Web.

Acknowledgments. The writing committee would like to thank Hechi University for its efforts in supplying laboratory and research instrument.

References

1. The basic technical specifications sub-simplified version of CALIS,
   `http://202.114.65.58/cms/resupload/1000000000000000000/`
   `001/calis_t2.doc`
2. Zhou, B., Liu, W., Liu, X.: Information Database for Mulam based on CALIS-standard. In: The 2012 Chinese Control and Decision Conference, pp. 4192–4195. IEEE Press (2012)

3. CALIS topics Information Center database, project profiles,
   `http://tsk.cadlis.edu.cn/tskopac/projectInfo.doc`
4. Que, B.: University Libraries Characteristic Special Subject Database Construction and Practice in CALIS Projects–Testing for the construction of "Chaoshan Documentation Database". Journal of Library Tribune 26, 14–16 (2006) (in Chinese)
5. Zhang, J., Jiang, X.: The Research in the Database Construction of Kazakh Cultural Features. Journal of Yili Normal University (Social Science Edition), 22–26 (2008) (in Chinese)
6. Gan, D.: The Topics and Significance of the Construction of Characteristic Database–Taking "Zhe-Merchant Characteristic Database" as an example. Journal of Library and Information Sciences in Agriculture 22, 43–45 (2010) (in Chinese)
7. Zhou, B.: Research on CALIS Standardized Reconstruction of the Special Bibliographic Database of Liu Sanjie with TPI. Journal of Hechi University 31, 101–105 (2011) (in Chinese)

The Design and Implementation of Automatic Drug Matching System

Xue Zhou, Lijian Chen, and ChaoMing Zhu

Xiaoshan Campus of Zhejiang Radio and Television University, Hangzhou, Zhejiang, China
48986103@qq.com

Abstract. Supervising and standardizing the price of drug as well as the quality has become a big problem for drug supervision departments. The system improves the study function for drug alias. The significant problem solved in this system is the Chinese Drug Match, and it will consider those problems about drug name abbreviation and alias. The system solves this problem with two tactics: the maximum matching method implement the word segmentation function with executing corporate with Chinese pinyin translate algorithm, and using the Levenshtein Distance method to compute the matching degree.

Keywords: Drugs matching, Word segmentation algorithm, Levenshtein Distance algorithm, Matching degree.

1 Introduction

There are now so many different drugs, and a large number of new drugs are being developed every day. Some drugs called the same name but produced in different companies. Sometimes different hospitals register one same drug in different aliases; while different doctors may use different abbreviations when prescribe the prescription and so on. In the hospital, doctors prescribe many prescriptions for patients every day, drug management and operational differences of different hospitals will cause that the same kinds of drugs in different hospitals have different prices. As the country's drug supervision departments, it should supervise and standardize the price of each drug as well as the quality. Above situations made the drug regulation complex and difficult, nowadays the regulation is completed by manual match, but it cost amount of man-power. How to decrease the difficulty when match drug and increase the matching efficiency is the most important function of this system. The job of this graduation design is to develop a drug prices matching system, it will solve those problems men-tioned. The system is designed for national drug supervision departments to test drug sales and to deal with large amounts of data information. National price system at different times have developed guidance sale price for each drug. Because the hospital sells lots of drugs every day, Supervision departments need regularly check up the records of drug sales of each hospital to determine the drug prices in the sales process. Through this powerful system, it makes drug supervision departments enable to com-plete this task well. The functions of the system include manage users, import drug records, search drugs, set threshold value, compute the matching degree, sort records, store aliases, judge acceptability and save results.

J. Lei et al. (Eds.): NCIS 2012, CCIS 345, pp. 198–204, 2012.
© Springer-Verlag Berlin Heidelberg 2012

2   Requirement Analysis

User management function is used to keep national drug price data secure. National drug prices are sensitive for public social, and it must restrict the number of users to manage these data. Only the administrator could operate this system and the number of user is restricted to one. It mainly supplies these functions as follows: register and login function, checking account and password in database function, checking information entered and feedback function, delete user account function. Import records files function is used to read records from excel files, and then insert these records into database. The administrator will have to choose type of records import before select excel file, including as follow: doctor records and national standard records. Save records into excel files function is used to store matching results after matching prices operation. Before creating stored file, the administrator must choose type of matching results follow as acceptable and unacceptable results.

Search records function is used to query records in database based on doctor record selected by administrator, and then list relative search results in standard list component. Searching function is based on the key words separated from drug name. Some drug may have aliases, and the system will query the alias table and get alias result set. All aliases will work similar with the drug name to get relative key word for selecting records in database. Calculate results function is used to help administrator to judge acceptability for doctor record selected based on the difference of prices. The function will check drug manufactory, format, matching degree and unit firstly and display relative attention dialog box based on all kinds of information stored in two records. Threshold management function is setting the lowest filter threshold, the system will filter records if the matching degree is lower than the threshold, and matching degree of all records listed in standard list component are high enough to pass the filter operation. Alias management function is used to store alias or synonym for selected drug name. It is also a self-study function to help increasing the matching accuracy. The administrator could judge drug name by himself and save it into database as the alias of doctor record which is selected before searching operation.

3   System Design

3.1   System Frame Design

System frame diagram composed by login frame, register frame and main frame. The login frame is consisted of two text fields and four buttons. The two text fields are used to input user account and relative password for login and deleting account functions. Button 'OK' is the login function trigger and displays the main frame if working success. 'Delete' is used to delete the administrator account after checking the correctness of inputted information. The button 'Register' is used to help the administrator register in this system. The register frame is consisted of five text field and two buttons. The system will collect administer data detail includes account, first name, last name and password from text fields. Button 'OK' is used to read data in text fields and insert into the database for completing register operation. The button 'Cancel' is used to close register system. The main frame is divided into six main components. Including Menu block, Hospital records list, Records information block, Standard records library, Acceptable results and Unacceptable results block. The Menu contains two menu buttons and several menu items, the Hospital records library display records stored in doctor table, the Records information block display all information of record selected by the administrator, including hospital record and relative standard record, the Standard records library display records queried from database, the Acceptable results block display results which could be accept and the Unacceptable results block display results that could not be accept. The following graph shows component relationship among these components, the arrow show data transmit direction between each part. As shown in Fig.1.

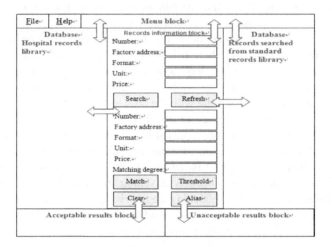

Fig. 1. System main frame diagram

3.2   System Components Description

The Menu block is a part of GUI design which includes import records and save result into excels files functions. The administrator should import both hospital and national standard drug records into the database before executing matching operation. Pressing the menu Item 'Import' which is hided in menu button 'File', and then the administrator chooses import type and the relative excel file for import records operation. After executing matching operation and get relative matching result, the administrator presses the menu Item 'Save as' hided in menu button 'File', and then store results as excel files. The Hospital records library displays all hospital drug records which are stored in the database. Every drug has lots of information, but only drug number and drug name will be displayed, the goal of this design is to save space and keep uniformity of record format. Other information of each record will be real-time displayed in the Records information block once the administrator selects any hospital record listed. The Standard records library is a part of GUI design and will list all search records. Before listing search results, the system will rank records based on the matching degree. The threshold value set by the administrator is used to filter records with excessive low matching degree, and the system will also filter records before list search records if the matching degree of current record is lower than the threshold value. Similar to the Hospital records library that the Standard records library will only display drug number and name of each record, while real-time display others in the Records information block if the administrator selects any search record. If there is no relative search record or matching result, the system will pop dialog box for displaying message. The Records information block is used to display hospital and standard records information details. The administrator could not read all information from the Hospital records library and Standard records library except the drug number and name, more information like manufactory address, drug format, unit, price and matching degree will be displayed in the Records information block. This block is close contact with the hospital and standard records library, it will real-time display details if the administrator selects any record which is listed in the Hospital or Standard records library. The Record information block is also a control platform for executing significant operations includes search results, set threshold value, match price and clean match result. The button 'Threshold' brings operation of setting threshold value. Pressing the button 'Search' after the administrator selects record listed in the Hospital records library, relative search result will be displayed in the Standard records library. If the user selects one of the search results and try to match price, the system will compute the agio between two prices and display result in the appropriate area. If the agio is acceptable, display matching result in the Acceptable results block, nevertheless display in the Unacceptable results block if agio exceed the permissible range. The Acceptable results block is a part of GUI design and is used to display results which the agio is acceptable. The result message will includes drug number, name and price of both hospital and standard records. The Unacceptable results block is also a part of GUI design and will display matching results which is similar with the Acceptable results block but the agio exceed the permissible range. The result message will includes drug number, name and price of both hospital and standard records.

3.3   Algorithm Design

(1) Word segmentation algorithm design. The system will use the maximum matching algorithm to separate Chinese words form a long string. The maximum matching method is one of the most popular structural segmentation algorithms for Chinese texts [1]. This method favors long words and is a greedy algorithm by design, hence, suboptimal. Segmentation will start from either end of the line. The basic idea of the algorithm is: First of all, establishing the Lexicon which contains all possible words. Segmenting a given word string s and get sub-character according to some established principles (forward or reverse), if the sub-string with the lexicon entries in a match, then the sub-string is a word, and continue to split up the remaining part until empty [2]; Otherwise the sub-string is not a word, then match the it the sub-string of s. Maximum

matching method is a widely used method of mechanical word segmentation method, where the "mechanical" because of the algorithm match rely solely on words in lexicon without AI [3]. The major advantage of maximum matching is its efficiency while its segmentation accuracy can be expected to lie around 95%. In this system, the lexicon will be separated to 23 sub-lexicons based on the Chinese pinyin and be classified to 2 main lexicon libraries called as follow: medicine library and normal library, that means the system will execute segmentation for drug name with medicine library, while using normal library if separate drug manufactory address. The 23 sub-lexicons could help system increase the matching efficiency by choosing relative automatically. The word segmentation algorithm will close cooperate with Chinese pinyin translation algorithm.

(2) Levenshtein Distance algorithm design. Levenshtein distance (LD) is a measure of the similarity between two strings, which we will refer to as the source string (s) and the target string (t). The distance is the number of deletions, insertions, or substitutions required to transform s into t. The greater the Levenshtein distance, the more different the strings are. The Levenshtein distance algorithm will be used when the system computes the matching degree accurately [4]. The steps as shown in Table 1. (3) Chinese pinyin translation algorithm design. This system separates lexicon to 23 sub-lexicons based on the Chinese pinyin. It will increase efficiency of executing word segmentation algorithm. The sub-lexicons are named from 'a' to 'z', so that the system should judge relative sub-lexicon before matching words listed in lexicon. The Chinese pinyin translation could pick up the first Chinese pinyin char of first Chinese char of a long Chinese string.

Step 1, the system pick up the first Chinese char from a long Chinese string, and then translate Chinese to Integer;

Step 2, query Hash database and pick up relative Chinese pinyin string array.

Step 3, the system will choose the first pinyin from pinyin array and pick up the first Chinese pinyin char as the result char.

Hash database will be stored as a local file in the project bag.

4   System Implementation

The whole program is written in Java under eclipse with jdk1.6.0_02 development environment[5]. Java is general-purpose, concurrent, class-based, and object-oriented, and is specifically designed to have as few implementation dependencies as possible. It is intended to let application developers "write once, run anywhere". All data are stored in MySQL as the database, so the user should install MySQL before running this program. Free-software projects that require a full-featured database management system often use MySQL. The user could download MySQL install file free in the Internet. The SQLyog Enterprise is powerful software that provides a GUI tools to manage MySQL databases, build database structure, and work with data records.

Table 1. 7 steps of Levenshtein Distance algorithm

Step	Description
1	Set n to be the length of s.Set m to be the length of t.
	If n = 0, return m and exit.If m = 0, return n and exit.
	Construct a matrix containing 0...m rows and 0...n columns.
2	Initialize the first row to 0...n.
	Initialize the first column to 0..m.
3	Examine each character of s (i from 1 to n).
4	Examine each character of t (j from 1 to m).
5	If s[i] equals t[j], the cost is 0.
	If s[i] doesn't equal t[j], the cost is 1.
6	Set cell d[i,j] of the matrix equal to the minimum of:
	a. The cell immediately above plus 1: d [i-1, j] + 1.
	b. The cell immediately to the left plus 1: d [i, j-1] + 1.
	c. The cell diagonally above and to the left plus the cost: d [i-1, j-1] + cost.
7	After the iteration steps (3, 4, 5, 6) are complete, the distance is found in cell d [n,m].

The User management function is based on the read, store and deletes operation to the database. If there is no user has already register as the administrator in this system, the register function could be allow to execute and will store information into the database. The system will check the database when the administrator try to login system or delete account. The user could login system or delete account successfully only if both account and password are correct. The Fig.2 shows the activity diagram of user management function.

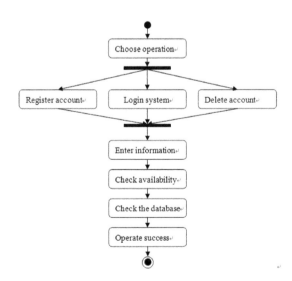

Fig. 2. The activity diagram of user management function

5   Summary

The system supply enough functions for national drug supervision departments to test drug sales. It is designed provide functions as follow: User management, Import records files, Save records into excel files, Search records, Sort records, Calculate results, Threshold management and Alias management. This system will use several algorithms like Word Segmentation algorithm, Levenshtein Distance algorithm and Chinese pinyin translate algorithm. This system provides a real-time display function that could real-time display all drug information once the mouse presses any record listed.

References

[1] Wong, P.-K., Chan, C.: Chinese Word Segmentation based on Maximum Matching and Word Binding Forc. The University of Hong Kong (1996)
[2] Gilleland, M.: Levenshtein Distance, in Three Flavors,
    http://www.merriampark.com
[3] Shawe-Taylor, J.: Fast string matching in a stationary ergodic sourc. University of London (1990)
[4] Boyer, R.S., Moore, J.S.: A fast string searching algorithm. Commun. ACM (1977)
[5] Hatcher, E., Gospodnetic, O.: Lucene in Action. Manning Publications (2005)

Asymmetric Encryption Scheme Based on Fingerprint Topological Transformation

Jianming Cui[1,2], Xiaojun Zhang[2], Guowei Yue[2], Hui Liu[2], and Zongsheng Lai[1]

[1] IMCS, East China Normal University, Shanghai, 200062, P.R. China
[2] Shandong University of Science and Technology, Qingdao, 266590, P.R. China
`cuijm399@163.com`

Abstract. This paper[1] proposes an asymmetric encryption scheme based on fingerprint minutiae. The topology remains unchanged during encryption with round transformation, displacement and rotation operation. Meanwhile, the validity and security is proved. When length of private key is k, the number of round transformation operations for brute-force method can arrive at 2^{2k}.

Keywords: Fingerprint minutiae, Round Transformation, Asymmetric encryption, Security.

1 Introduction

In recent years, network security is as urgent as time. It has become a trend in the field of information security using biological identification technology. Fingerprint is used widely because of its relatively stable, can not be copied or forged, not be easily lost or stolen, etc [1] [2]. Many fingerprint encryption methods and algorithms have been proposed gradually by researchers. But almost of all are constructed with symmetric encryption based on fingerprint minutiae information.

Diffie and Hellman proposed the idea of public-key cryptosystem in "New direction in cryptography"[3] in 1976. Based on the idea of constructing such a system, a variety of public-key cryptosystem based on different mathematical difficult problems have been proposed, such as the RSA public key cryptosystem [4], the security is built on top of the difficulty of large integer factorization; LGamal proposed LGamal method [5], its security depends on the DLP (discrete logarithm problem); elliptic curve cryptosystem (ECC) [6] [7] was proposed separately in 1985, whose security is based on the elliptic curve discrete logarithm problem. Asymmetric encryption system can be constructed a secure communication channel publicly by releasing the public key and hiding the private key. But it is difficult in selecting encryption key or process of encryption because it must deal with much more complex computation [8] [9], and biology minutiae of issuer was not involved in, it is make against for setting up faith channel based on identity of issuer.

---

[1] This paper is supported by Qingdao Science and Technology Development Project grants No. 11-2-4-6-(1)-jch.

J. Lei et al. (Eds.): NCIS 2012, CCIS 345, pp. 205–213, 2012.
© Springer-Verlag Berlin Heidelberg 2012

In this paper, an asymmetric encryption algorithm based on the equivalent transformation of fingerprint minutiae topological structure was presented. In the algorithm, the endpoint location data vector of fingerprint minutiae was regarded as the topological structure transformation object, the intersection location data vector was regarded as the private encryption key, and equivalent transformation of the object supports the encryption and decryption. The uniqueness of the fingerprint has solved the problem of identity authentication, and the biological character has realized the non-repudiation in electronic commerce.

Fingerprint feature minutiae consisted of endpoints and cross points can be extracted easily now. All of these endpoints and cross points constitute the fingerprint image point set topology. Combining with the traditional idea of asymmetric cryptography [10], this paper introduce an asymmetric encryption scheme with the method of topological transformation of the fingerprint minutiae topology.

2   Proposed Scheme

Assume that Alice and Bob communicate over an insecure channel, an eavesdropper, Eve, can see the whole communication and to inject her own messages in the channel. Where Bob is the decryption side and Alice is the encryption side.

2.1   Initial Settings

In an appropriate coordinate system, select all of representatives from the endpoints and cross points of the fingerprint image to constitute the vector matrix of fingerprint minutiae topology, which is set as $G[0] = (G[0]_{11}, G[0]_{12}, G[0]_{13}, \cdots G[0]_{nm})$, $G[0]_{ij} = (x_{ij}G[0]), y_{ij}G[0]), 1 \le i \le n, 1 \le j \le m$

This vector matrix is composed of two parts; one of is endpoints, set as $G[0_1]$,

$$G[0_1] = (G[0_1]_{11}, G[0_1]_{12}, G[0_1]_{13}, \cdots G[0_1]_{n_1 m_1})$$
$$G[0_1]_{ij} = (x_{ij}G[0_1]), y_{ij}G[0_1]), 1 \le i \le n_1, 1 \le j \le m_1$$

The other is cross points of the fingerprint image, set as $G[0_2]$,

$$G[0_2] = (G[0_2]_{11}, G[0_2]_{12}, G[0_2]_{13}, \cdots G[0_2]_{n2m2})$$
$$G[0_2] = (G[0_2]_{11}, G[0_2]_{12}, G[0_2]_{13}, \cdots G[0_2]_{n2m2})$$
$$G[0] = (G[0_1], G[0_2]) , \quad \text{where } n_1 m_1 + n_2 m_2 \le nm$$

2.2   Encryption and Decryption

A special operation, $\otimes$, is defined in encryption and decryption process, which is known as round transformation of the fingerprint minutiae topology, k_2, k_1 was set as private key of Bob and. Alice. $k_2 \otimes G[0]$, $k_1 \otimes G[0]$ denote the k_n round transformation to initial matrix vector of Bob and. Alice, respectively. Displacement and rotation transformation based on vector matrix constitute module operation, the XOR field operation of vector matrix element. The vector matrix element and its topological transformation are defined on a domain-based algebraic structure of the algebra system.

The domain of the fingerprint topology transformation is limited in Fig. 1 facility to operate. The flow of encryption and decryption is shown in Fig. 2.

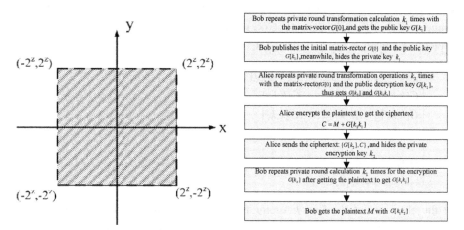

Fig. 1. Domain of the fingerprint topology transformation **Fig. 2.** Flow Of Encryption and Decryption

Bob can first obtain a vector matrix $G[0]$ of the fingerprint feature topology, and then select an appropriate key k_1 randomly as his decryption private key, calculate $G[k_1] = k_1 \otimes G[0]$, then send it to the Alice over an open channel.

When Alice receives $(G[0], G[k_1])$, she will select the appropriate size of the key k_2 as her encryption key, and it will calculate with Eq. 1.

$$G[k_2] = k_2 \otimes G[0] \tag{1}$$

$$G[k_2 k_1] = k_2 \otimes G[k_1] = (k_2 k_1) \otimes G[0] = \begin{bmatrix} G[k_2 k_1]_{11}, G[k_2 k_1]_{12}, \ldots, G[k_2 k_1]_{1m} \\ G[k_2 k_1]_{21}, G[k_2 k_1]_{22}, \ldots, G[k_2 k_1]_{2m} \\ \vdots \quad \vdots \quad , \cdots, \quad \vdots \\ G[k_2 k_1]_{n1}, G[k_2 k_1]_{n2}, \cdots, G[k_2 k_1]_{nm} \end{bmatrix}$$

$$= \begin{bmatrix} (x_{11}, y_{11}), (x_{12}, y_{12}), \ldots, (x_{1m}, y_{1m}) \\ (x_{21}, y_{21}), (x_{22}, y_{22}), \ldots, (x_{2m}, y_{2m}) \\ \vdots \quad , \quad \vdots \quad , \cdots, \quad \vdots \\ (x_{n1}, y_{n1}), (x_{n2}, y_{n2}), \cdots, (x_{nm}, y_{nm}) \end{bmatrix}$$

For the encrypted message M, it will be divide averagely group to $M_1, M_2, M_3, ..., M_h$, where $h \leq nm$. Get the abscissas of the vector h from vector matrix $G[k_2 k_1]$ to form a vector $(x_1', x_2', \cdots, x_h')$ with Eq. 2.

$$C_j = M_j + x_j', \text{ where } 1 \leq j \leq h \tag{2}$$

So it can get the cipher text $C = C_1 C_2 \cdots C_h$, and send $(C, G(k_2))$ over an open channel to Bob. When the data $(C, G(k_2))$ is sent from Alice, Bob will calculate with his private encryption key k_1 with Eq. 3.

$$
\begin{aligned}
G[k_1 k_2] &= k_1 \otimes G[k_2] = (k_1 k_2) \otimes G[0] \\
&= \begin{bmatrix}
G[k_1 k_2]_{11}, G[k_1 k_2]_{12}, ..., G[k_1 k_2]_{1m} \\
G[k_1 k_2]_{21}, G[k_1 k_2]_{22}, ..., G[k_1 k_1]_{2m} \\
\vdots \qquad \vdots \qquad , \cdots, \qquad \vdots \\
G[k_1 k_2]_{n1}, G[k_1 k_2]_{n2}, \cdots, G[k_1 k_2]_{nm}
\end{bmatrix} = \begin{bmatrix}
(x_{11}, y_{11}), (x_{12}, y_{12}), ..., (x_{1m}, y_{1m}) \\
(x_{21}, y_{21}), (x_{22}, y_{22}), ..., (x_{2m}, y_{2m}) \\
\vdots \quad , \quad \vdots \quad , \cdots, \quad \vdots \\
(x_{n1}, y_{n1}), (x_{n2}, y_{n2}), \cdots, (x_{nm}, y_{nm})
\end{bmatrix} \\
&= (k_2 k_1) \otimes G = G[k_2 k_1]
\end{aligned} \tag{3}
$$

Get the abscissas of the first h vector from vector matrix $G[k_1 k_2]$, form a vector $(x_1', x_2', \cdots, x_h')$, it can get the plaintext. Thus it can recovery the Alice's original encrypted message $M_1', M_2', M_3', ..., M_h'$ with Eq. 4.

$$M_j' = C_j - x_j', \text{where } 1 \leq j \leq h \tag{4}$$

Round Transformation. The round operation of the matrix of G vector is defined as the transformation of fingerprint minutiae topology. k times round of matrix of G vector operation is defined as the round computing in turn of $k, k-1, k-2, ..., 1$. If using the exhaustive attack method in the positive sequence, the key k needs 2^k round operation, while in the reverse sequence the key k needs $1 + 2 + ... 2^k = 2^k (2^k + 1) / 2$, approximately 2^{2k} round operation. The reverse sequence is better than the positive sequence on anti-attack. In the same anti-attack performance, the length of reverse sequence key is only half of the positive sequence key.

The one round transformation of $G[j]$ contains several times round operation, the results of each round transformation of $G[j]$ is denoted as $G[j+1]$. The number in each round operation ($MRNumber$) can be obtained with Eq. 5.

$$MRNumber[k-i] = (k-i)\%10 \tag{5}$$

Where $i = 0, 1, 2, \cdots, k$, while $MRNumber[k-i] < 3$, $MRNumber[k-i] = 3$. In order to facilitate implementation on hardware and software, the scope of the fingerprint minutiae topology limited within $[-2^k, 2^k] \times [-2^k, 2^k]$. To guarantee equivalent transformation, topological transformation operation is defined on a domain-based algebraic displacement and rotation.

Displacement Operation. Displacement is computed according to the quadrant where the fingerprint minutiae is located, suppose $1 \le i \le n$, $1 \le j \le m$; $f(G[j]_x)$ represents the XOR disperse computing of the abscissa of the different elements in the vector matrix $G[j]$, $f(G[j]_y)$ represents the XOR disperse computing of the ordinate of the different elements in the vector matrix $G[j]$.

When $x_{ij} > 2^z$, $m_x = 1$, When $x_{ij} < -2^z$, $m_x = -1$ m=-1, When $-2^z < x_{ij} < 2^z$, $n_x = 1$, otherwise $n_x = 0$. When $x_{ij} > 2^z$, $m_y = 1$, When $y_{ij} < -2^z$, $m_y = -1$, When $-2^z < y_{ij} < 2^z$, $n_y = 1$, otherwise $n_y = 0$; $dx = f(G[j]_x)\%P + \dfrac{(1+n_x)}{2}2^{z+1}m_x$, $dy = f(G[j]_y)\%P + \dfrac{(1+n_y)}{2}2^{z+1}m_y$.

When all the points in the initial vector matrix $G[j]$ do not meet the above conditions, if the round transformation key is even number, the displacement of the fingerprint minutiae points is $dx = f(G[j]_x)\%P$, $dy = f(G[j]_y)\%P$. If it is an odd number, the displacement of the fingerprint minutiae points is $dx = -f(G[j]_x)\%P$, $dy = -f(G[j]_y)\%P$.

According to the above calculated displacement, computing displacement of each element in the vector matrix $G[j]$ with Eq. 6

$$G[j]_{nm} \leftarrow G[j]_{nm} + (\Delta D)_{nm} \tag{6}$$

Where $G[j]_{nm}$ represents the initial vector matrix, $(\Delta D)_{nm}$ represents the displacement vector matrix and

$$(\Delta D)_{nm} = \begin{bmatrix} (dx,dy),(dx,dy),\cdots,(dx,dy) \\ (dx,dy),(dx,dy),\cdots,(dx,dy) \\ \vdots \quad \vdots \quad ,\cdots, \quad \vdots \\ (dx,dy),(dx,dy),\cdots,(dx,dy) \end{bmatrix}_{nm}$$

Rotation Operation. The topology of the fingerprint minutiae rotates to one central point, and this process can be divided into three steps.

(1) Define the central point(CP) of rotation

Let $x0 = G[j]_{x_s}$, $y0 = G[j]_{y_s}$ denote the CP of rotation when one of $G[j]$ rotates.

(2) Computing horizontal distance and vertical distance between each element in the vector matrix $G[j]$ and the CP of rotation with Eq. 7.

$$T_{nm} = G[j]_{nm} - (o)_{nm} \tag{7}$$

Where

$$(o)_{nm} = \begin{bmatrix} (G[j]_{x_5}, G[j]_{y_5}), (G[j]_{x_5}, G[j]_{y_5}), \cdots, (G[j]_{x_5}, G[j]_{y_5}) \\ (G[j]_{x_5}, G[j]_{y_5}), (G[j]_{x_5}), G[j]_{y_5}), \cdots, (G[j]x_{x_5}, G[j]_{y_5}) \\ \vdots \qquad \vdots \qquad , \cdots, \qquad \vdots \\ (G[j]_{x_5}, G[j]_{y_5}), (G[j]_{x_5}, G[j]_{y_5}), \cdots, (G[j]_{x_5}, G[j]_{y_5}) \end{bmatrix}_{nm}$$

(3) Computation of the rotation

When the vector matrix $G[j]$ of the fingerprint minutiae is in the first and third quadrants, the rotation factor $q = 1$, when the vector matrix $G[j]$ of the fingerprint minutiae is in other quadrants, the rotation factor $q = 0$. Thus the final result of the first round computing can be computed with Eq. 8.

$$G'[j]_{nm} = T_{nm} \cdot N_{nm} + (o)_{nm}$$

Where

$$N_{nm} = \begin{bmatrix} \begin{bmatrix} 0, & (-1)^q \\ (-1)^{q+1}, 0 \end{bmatrix} & & & \\ & \begin{bmatrix} 0, & (-1)^q \\ (-1)^{q+1}, 0 \end{bmatrix} & & \\ & & \ddots & \\ & & & \begin{bmatrix} 0, & (-1)^q \\ (-1)^{q+1}, 0 \end{bmatrix} \end{bmatrix}_{nm}$$ (8)

Let $G'[j]$ denote the initial vector matrix to carry on the next round computing, complete $MRNumber[k - j + 1]$ times round computing in order, get the result of the first round transformation that is, the initial vector matrix of the next round transformation. In accordance with the above round transformation process, the encryption and decryption both sides complete the encryption and decryption process though setting round transformation to k_2, k_1 of the initial matrix vector $G[0]$.

3   Program Analysis

3.1   Validity of the Proposed

Theorem 1 If Alice and Bob obey the rules of scheme, then Bob can get M successfully, namely, the scheme is successful.

Proof: If Alice and Bob obey the rules of scheme, Bob gets $(G[0], G[k_1])$ sent from Alice, and Alice obtain $(G[k_2], G[k_2 k_1])$ through K_2 times of round transformation operations. Alice sends $(C = encrypt(M), G(k_2))$ to Bob. When Bob receives $(C, G(k_2))$, he obtains $G[k_1 k_2]$ with K_1 times of round transformation operations of $G[k_2]$. If $G[k_2 k_1] = G[k_1 k_2])$, then Bob can recover M successfully. So, the validity can be proved with Eq. 9.

3.2   Security of the Proposed

Asymmetric public key security system is based mainly on the key security, rather than on the security of the cryptosystem algorithm. Although the proposed scheme doesn't like RSA or ECC is based on some math problems, this scheme can be proved to be safe with secret key and the limited computing power.

Theorem 2 When $G[0]$ is public, the probability of a successful attack on this program is $1/2^{|k|}$, where $|k|$ denotes the order of the key space of private round transformation.

$$
\begin{aligned}
G[k_2 k_1]_{nm} &= G[0]_{nm} \cdot \left(\left(\prod_{i=1}^{k_1} \prod_{h=1}^{M_i} N_{nm}^{1_{ih}} \right) \cdot \left(\prod_{j=1}^{k_2} \prod_{h=1}^{M_j} N_{nm}^{2_{jh}} \right) \right) + \sum_{i=1}^{k_1} \left((\Delta D_{nm}^{1_i} + o_{nm}^{1_i}) \cdot \prod_{h=1}^{M_i} N_{nm}^{1_{ih}} \right) \\
&\quad + \sum_{j=1}^{k_2} \left((\Delta D_{nm}^{2_j} + o_{nm}^{2_j}) \cdot \prod_{h=1}^{M_j} N_{nm}^{2_{jh}} \right) \\
&= G[0]_{nm} \cdot \left(\left(\prod_{j=1}^{k_2} \prod_{h=1}^{M_j} N_{nm}^{2_{jh}} \right) \cdot \prod_{i=1}^{k_1} \prod_{h=1}^{M_i} N_{nm}^{1_{ih}} \right) + \sum_{j=1}^{k_2} \left((\Delta D_{nm}^{2_j} + o_{nm}^{2_j}) \cdot \prod_{h=1}^{M_j} N_{nm}^{2_{jh}} \right) \\
&\quad + \sum_{i=1}^{k_1} \left((\Delta D_{nm}^{1_i} + o_{nm}^{1_i}) \prod_{h=1}^{k_1} N_{nm}^{1_{ih}} \right) \qquad = G[k_1 k_2])
\end{aligned}
\tag{9}
$$

Proof: Eve can obtain the public information relating to programs over an unsecure channel. The public information includes $G[0]$, round transformation results of $G[k_1]$ and $G[k_2]$ based on k_1 and k_2 of Bob and Alice, respectively. In addition, Eve can intercept ciphertext C. From the above, Eve needs to search key space of round transformation exhaustively to obtain k_1 and k_2. After that, Eve can compute $G[k_1 k_2]$ to get the encrypted message M. The probability of success is $1/2^{|k|}$. When key length is long enough, this probability is negligible.

Theorem 3 Assume a malicious attacker, Eve, has known some public information, he can analyze the process of encryption and decryption and get private round transformation key through round operation, and the computational complexity is an exponential polynomial.

Proof: Assume that Eve has known the decryption side of the initial matrix of the fingerprint minutia vector, $G[0]$ and $G[k_2]$. Based on the above, Eve tries to obtain k_2 of Bob.

Bob gets $G[k_2]$ by k_2 times round transformation on $G[0]$, one round transformation includes *MRNumber* times of round operation, which can be computed with Eq. 10.

$$
G'[0]_{nm} = G[0]_{nm} \cdot N_{nm} + ((\Delta D)_{nm} + (o)_{nm}) \cdot N_{nm} + (o)_{nm}
\tag{10}
$$

Bob complete one round operation of $G[0]$ with Eq. 11.

$$G[1]_{nm} = G[0]_{nm} \cdot \overbrace{N_{nm}^1 \cdot N_{nm}^2 \cdots N_{nm}^M}^{MRNumber[k_1]} + ((\Delta D)_{nm}^1 + (o)_{nm}^1) \cdot \overbrace{N_{nm}^1 \cdot N_{nm}^2 \cdots N_{nm}^M}^{MRNumber[k_1]}$$

$$+ ((\Delta D)_{nm}^2 + (o)_{nm}^2) \cdot \overbrace{N_{nm}^2 \cdots N_{nm}^M}^{MRNumber[k_1]-1} + \cdots + ((\Delta D)_{nm}^M + (o)_{nm}^M) \cdot N_{nm}^M + \qquad (11)$$

$$(o)_{nm}^1 \cdot \overbrace{N_{nm}^2 \cdots N_{nm}^M}^{MRNumber[k_1]-1} + (o)_{nm}^2 \cdot \overbrace{N_{nm}^3 \cdots N_{nm}^M}^{MRNumber[k_1]-2} + \cdots + (o)_{nm}^M$$

Bob completed the initial matrix vector transformation in one round of expressions with Eq. 11. Assume that g the minimum of *MRNumber* is MIN_M in every one round transformation operation. If malicious attacker, Eve, has known $G[0]$ and $G[k_2]$, computational complexity of k_2 is $O(G[0]^{MIN_M^{k_2}})$ at least. It can be seen that the computation of malicious attacker Eve displays exponential growth with increment of k_2. Thus malicious attacker's computational complexity is an exponential polynomial.

MIPS means million instructions per second, and a MIPS-year is equal to the number of steps processed for one year at one million instructions per second. It is generally accepted that 10^{12} MIPS years represents reasonable security at this time. When the key length is k, the total number of rounds transformation operation required for brute-force method is $1 + 2 + \ldots\ldots 2^k = 2^k(2^k+1)/2 \approx 2^{2k}$. Assume one computer can execute 1M instructions per second, then time of one round transformation operation is $t \approx 3.25*10^{-9}s$. To ensure the security of cryptosystem, then key length required $k = (\log_2(T/t))/2$, where T is the time to crack.

4   Summary

Compared with other public key cryptosystem, the program has the following advantages:(1) Includes the fingerprint minutia topology information of the issuer, it can be certified the reliability of the issuer.(2) The computational complexity is an exponential polynomial for malicious attacker's, so it has advantages of anti-attack performance.(3) Smaller memory space. The key length of this program is much smaller compared with other public key system.

References

1. Han, F., Hu, J., Yu, X., Wang, Y.: Fingerprint images encryption via multiscroll chaotic attractors. Applied Mathematics and Computation 185(2), 931–939 (2007)
2. Hong, L., Wan, Y., Jain: Fingerprint image enhancement: algorithm and performance evaluation. IEEE Transactions on Pattern Analysis and Machine Intelligence 20(8), 777–789 (2002)
3. Diffie-Hellman, W.: New direction in cryptography. IEEE Transaction on Information Theory 22(6), 644–654 (1976)
4. Rivest, R.L., Shamir, A., Adleman, L.: A method for obtaining digital signatures and public key crypto-systems. Communications of the ACM 21(2), 120–126 (1978)
5. Gamal, L.: A Public Key Cryptosystem and A Signature Scheme Based on Discrete Logarithms. IEEE Transactions on Information Theory 31(4), 469–472 (1985)

6. Koblitz, N.: Elliptic curve cryptosystems. Mathematics of Computation 48(177), 201–209 (1987)
7. Miller, V.S.: Use of Elliptic Curves in Cryptography. In: Williams, H.C. (ed.) CRYPTO 1985. LNCS, vol. 218, pp. 417–426. Springer, Heidelberg (1986)
8. Brown, G.E., Green, A.E.S.: American Journal of Physics 36(4), 371 (1968)
9. Smid, M.E., Branstad, D.K., NBS, Gaithersburg, M.D.: Data Encryptions Standard: past and future. Proceedings of the IEEE 76(5), 550–559 (1988)
10. Black, J., Rogaway, P., Shrimpton, T.: Encryption-Scheme Security in the Presence of Key-Dependent Messages. In: van der Hoek, A., Coen-Porisini, A. (eds.) SEM 2002. LNCS, vol. 2596, pp. 62–75. Springer, Heidelberg (2003)

A Kind of Digital Signature System Based on Linear Computing

Hai-ming Li

School of Computer and Information Engineering, Shanghai University of Electric Power,
Shanghai 201300, China

Abstract. In this paper, a kind of digital signature system is proposed. This method is based on the difficulty on getting the solutions of indefinite equations with integer coefficients in mathematical programming. It is a hard NP problem in computing. The signature system has random property like DSS so as to avoid forgery signature. Because only arithmetic plus and multiple operations are used, it is easy for hardware integration. This signature system can very suitably be used for digital signal processor development in DSP.

Keywords: Digital signature, Arithmetic coding, Secret keying problem.

1   Introduction

With the development of electronic commerce, digital signature technology has been more and more widespread and is given more attention. The protection of electronic information integrity, especially the protection of the completeness about important information, has become major issues of concern in the international community. The digital signature technology is a public key system, which guarantees correctness of the electronic data. The key system consists of a mathematical key pair. One is a private key that is used for electronic signature and also is called signature key. The other is a public key that is used for electronic signature verification and is known as secret key verification.

Ron Rivest, Adi Shamirh and Len Adleman proposed the first practical public key algorithm in 1978, which is the famous RSA that is based on the presumed difficulty of factoring large integers, the factoring problem[1]. A user of RSA creates and then publishes the product of two large prime numbers, along with an auxiliary value, as their public key. The prime factors must be kept secret. Anyone can use the public key to encrypt a message, but with currently published methods, if the public key is large enough, only someone with knowledge of the prime factors can feasibly decode the message. Once a fast integer factorization method is found, the system will collapse completely. The system is feasible both on digital signature and data encryption. The signature and encryption are symmetrical mutually inverse process. The patent of RSA is held by RSA Data Security Company, which was terminated in 2000. In fact many commercial products are now based on the system. However, the system has some fatal flaws. With the new achievements of the factorization of large

J. Lei et al. (Eds.): NCIS 2012, CCIS 345, pp. 214–220, 2012.
© Springer-Verlag Berlin Heidelberg 2012

numbers, the arithmetic digits used in the system becomes longer and longer. This leads to the difficulties of hardware development and hardware product development. The hardware life cycle is greatly reduced. In addition, the debate on the symmetry of its signature and encryption also leads to the failure that U.S. government avoided to put it into the digital signature standard.

Diffie–Hellman key exchange is a specific method of exchanging cryptographic keys. At present, it is the only method that can substitute RSA and transmitting the secret keys in open network. of the earliest practical examples of key exchange implemented within the field of cryptography[2]. The Diffie–Hellman key exchange method allows two parties that have no prior knowledge of each other to jointly establish a shared secret key over an insecure communications channel. D-H Method depends on the difficulty of the scattering logarithm problem which ensures its key safe. This key can then be used to encrypt subsequent communications using a symmetric key cipher.

The Diffie–Hellman key exchange method is as follows for shorts:

Suppose p is a very long prime number, a is an element of the domain. The two keys are generated as follows.

> ➤ SideA: select a random number v_A, $0 < v_A < p$
> ➤ SideA: let $u_A = \exp(v_A)$.
> ➤ SideB: select a random number v_B, $0 < v_B < p$
> ➤ SideB: let $u_B = \exp(v_B)$.
> ➤ SideA sends u_A to SideB; SideB sends u_B to SideA;
> ➤ SideA: compute $K = \exp(u_B)$; SideB: compute $K = \exp(u_A)$.

Where $\exp(x) = a^x \bmod p$. It can be easily proved that: K got by A and that got by B are identical. Therefore K can be shared between the two sides. The latest version of the famous software products of PGP uses this strategy other than RSA. It has been applied for data transfer between email users. The algorithm is considered more secure than RSA.

In 1984, Taher ElGamal proposed a new digital signature method to replace RSA. The ElGamal signature scheme is also based on the difficulty of computing discrete logarithms and introduced randomization safe practice to avoid the possibility that the signature is fabricated. Thus US government has adopted its amending form as a digital signature standard, which is known as DSS or DSA.

In recent years, knapsack problem, ellipse curve method and LUCAS function are adopted in the research of open key systems. However nearly all the open key systems based on the knapsack problem is cracked. The last two methods seem to be safer than RSA.

At present, most open key secure systems are based on the NP problems in number theory. But they have the common defects: the length of arithmetic digits is too long (often more than 1024 or 2048); this leads to the difficulties of hardware development and slowly running of software.

One kind of the digital signature method that based on the NP problems in integer matrix computing is introduced in this paper. Its hardware components are also described. It can be applied security fields such as cryptology and computer safety etc.

2   Finite Digital Signature Algorithm

The method is based on the difficulty of finding the solutions of linear indefinite equations with integer coefficients. It can be proved that the problem is a hard NP problem; this means that we can not find any algorithm to solve the problem in multinomial time.

According to this, we select three integer matrices A with N rows and M columns, B with M rows and N columns and C with N rows and N columns where AB=C. With regard to signature arithmetic, let B and C be public key and verification key. Let A be the secret key which cannot be public.

For any information x whose size is N, compute y=xA, y is the legal signature to x. if yB=xC then the legitimacy of signature information y can be verified. Otherwise y is illegal.

There exists a defect in this algorithm. With the increasing quantity of signature information, it is possible that the secret key may be cracked. For this reason, random mechanism is introduced in which some data in matrix A are random. In this way, the possible threats of solving A and fate signature by using enough information are avoided.

The operations this method involves are all integer arithmetic of 32 bit or 64 bit. If more delicate hardware design is adopted, even integral division operation can be avoided in this mechanism. Therefore it is very convenient to develop hardware products.

In the mechanism, an effective controlling algorithm of bit overflow needs to be applied whether 32 bit or 64 bit integer operations are used. It is applied to the bit overflow detection of all involved arithmetic operations.

The methods of secret key generation and signature verification are also given in the mechanism. It is achieved through a series of elementary transformation of matrices.

The finite digital signature algorithm is briefly described as follows:

- Input unsigned information x with length N.
- Use random method to generate integer matrix A with N rows and M columns and integer matrix B with M rows and N columns
- Compute C = AB, then C is N rows and N columns
- Let matrices B and C be public
- Compute y = xA

Then y is the signed information of x. It is very easy to verify the legitimacy of signature information y through simple computation whether yB is equal to xC .Thus matrices B and C are called verification secret keys. This method is relatively safe for finite signature applications. With the increasing quantity of signature information, it is possible that the secret key may be cracked through reverse computation using primitive information and signed information. A fate signature may be constructed using old true signatures because the signature process is linear. To solve this question, infinite digital signature method using elementary transformations of matrices and random matrices is proposed. It's safer and more flexible in application.

3   Infinite Digital Signature Algorithm

For convenience in description, we always have the assumption M=2N in this section. The assumption makes it easier that every block of matrix is the same size in matrix decomposition in the following.

According to the basic principle of matrix theory, every integer matrix can be transformed into diagonal matrix through elementary matrix transformations. Hence the signature matrix can be obtained from a series of elementary matrix transformations.

To construct signature matrix $A_{N \times M}$, $B_{M \times N}$ and $C_{N \times N}$, we use such simple matrix decomposition:

$$A = (A_1, A_2)$$
$$B = (B_1{}^T, B_2{}^T)^T$$
$$C = (C_1)$$

Such that every matrix block is N×N square matrix.

Where AB=C

Therefore we have

$$A_1B_1 + A_2B_2 = C_1 \tag{1}$$

To generate these matrices, we start with the diagonal matrices $D_A{}^1$, $D_B{}^1$, $D_A{}^2$, $D_B{}^2$, $D_C{}^1$, such that

$$D_A{}^1 D_B{}^1 + D_A{}^2 D_B{}^2 = D_C{}^1 \tag{2}$$

Assuming the above diagonal matrices are transformed into A, B and C after w left elementary transformations, denoted by $P_L{}^1$, $P_L{}^2$, ... $P_L{}^w$, t right elementary transformations, denoted by $P_r{}^1$, $P_r{}^2$, ... $P_r{}^t$ and s middle elementary transformations, denoted by $P_c{}^1$, $P_c{}^2$, ...$P_c{}^s$, we have

$$A = P_L{}^1 P_L{}^2 \ldots P_L{}^w \ (D_A{}^1, \ D_A{}^2) \ P_C{}^1 P_C{}^2 \ldots P_C{}^t \tag{3}$$

$$B = \underline{P_C}{}^t \ldots \underline{P_C}{}^2 \, \underline{P_C}{}^1 \ (D_B{}^1, \ D_B{}^2) \ P_r{}^1 \, P_r{}^1 \, \cdots P_r{}^s \tag{4}$$

$$C = P_L{}^1 \, P_L{}^2 \ldots P_L{}^w \ (C_1) \ P_r{}^1 \, P_r{}^2 \cdots P_r{}^s \tag{5}$$

Where, $\underline{P_c}{}^i$ is the inverse matrix of $P_c{}^i$, $i = 1 \ldots t$.

Let matrices B and C be public for verifying secret key. But every decomposing of A needs to be stored in order to be flexible in the signature mechanism. The above procedure can be described as follows algorithms.

Secret key generation algorithm:

> Use random method to generate diagonal matrices $D_A{}^1$, $D_B{}^1$
> Let $C_1 = D_A{}^1 D_B{}^1$, $D_B{}^2 = 0$
> Use random method to generate elementary transformation matrices $P_C{}^1, P_C{}^2, \ldots, P_C{}^t, P_L{}^1, P_L{}^2, \ldots, P_L{}^w, P_r{}^1, P_r{}^2, \cdots, P_r{}^s$

> ➤ Using (4) and (5), compute B and C, let B and C be public.
> ➤ Store the matrices as private secret key:D_A^{-1}, $P_C^1, P_C^2, ..., P_C^t$, $P_L^1, P_L^2, ..., P_L^w$

Using this secret key, following signature algorithm can be obtained.
  Infinite signature algorithm:

> ➤ Input unsigned information x with length N.
> ➤ Compute $u = xP_L^1 P_L^2 ... P_L^w D_A^{-1}$
> ➤ Generate a random number v of length N
> ➤ Compute $y = (u^T, v^T)^T P_C^1 P_C^2 ... P_C^t$

Then y is the signature information of x. It is very easy to verify the legitimacy of signature information y through simple computation whether yB is equal to xC.

  It's clear that the signature mechanism is very simple for computing. It makes a series of elementary transformation on the unsigned data, then generates a random vector and combines the results into a new vector. Finally the signed information is obtained through a series of elementary linear transformations.

4   Realization of the Signature Mechanism

The implementation of this method need the help of a physical entity, the entity may be a PC or a dedicated chip. This entity contains at least four components, namely ③ memory, ② central processing unit, ⑥ key generator and ⑦ randomizer as shown in Figure 1.

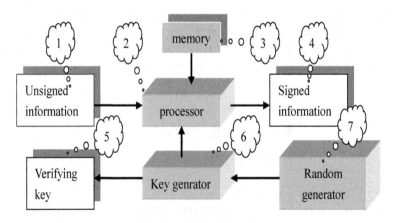

Fig. 1. Function Modal

  Memory ③ is used to store the dynamic data and processing code in computing process. Central processing unit ② performs operation code of the cryptosystem. so the system must at least contain one accumulator, one multiplier , a number of other functional registers and a physical interface to exchange data with the external memory. Because a key vector must be generated before the signature, a key generator ⑥ is needed in the process. Random numbers are used in the process, so there must be a random number generator ⑦ which can be either a physical device or a set of software. In the latter case, the physical device can be removed, but the the memory capacity and the amount of computing code need to be increased. In this signature system, the input is the plaintext message ①, the output is signature information ④ corresponding to the plaintext.

In the process of the signature device, plaintext message are done to generate a new vector combined with a random vector. The signature information is got by a series of elementary matrices transformation of the new vector. It only needs to calculate the product of two matrices and then compares the results in the process of verification in the device. In the encryption process, the computation is simply to calculate the product between vectors and matrices. In the decryption process, first a series of elementary matrix transformations are done, then a diagonal integer equations are solved, finally through a series of elementary matrix transformations, we get the plaintext message.

The process of key generator is as follows. Starting with a diagonal matrix, a series of random elementary linear transformations including left elementary transformations, middle elementary transformations and right elementary transformations are done, thus the signing key is obtained through output of the details in the corresponding transformation and the authentication key ⑤ is also got simultaneously through the output of two integer matrices.

5   Conclusions

The digital signature algorithm proposed in this paper has the following characteristics:

(1) The encryption algorithm and the authentication method are easy and not complicated. Since the algorithm involves only matrix operations, the generation and certification of digital signatures is quick and relatively easy.

(2) Signature forgery and repudiation can effectively be prevented. The complexity of the algorithm is strongly NP, and random numbers are also used. Therefore forged signatures are rarely possible by either using the existing digital signature to construct a new data packet, or using obtained data packet to forge a digital signature.

(3) To keep a backup of the digital signature in storage is realistic and practical.

Therefore, this system can be used as a specialized digital signature tool to ensure data integrity and security of electronic information. It will become a candidate for a competitive e-commerce security since its hardware design is simple and convenient.

References

[1] Coppersmith, D.: Small Solutions to Polynomial Equations, and Low Exponent RSA Vulnerabilities. Journal of Cryptology 10(4) (December 1997)
[2] Howard, P.G., Vitter, J.S.: Arithmetic Coding for data compression. Proc. IEEE 82(6) (1994)
[3] Lei, S.M.: Efficient multiplication-free arithmetic codes. IEEE Trans. Commun. 37(2) (1989)
[4] Jiang, J.: Novel design of arithmetic coding for data compression. IEEE Proc. Comput. Digit. 142(6) (1995)

Cryptanalysis and Improvement
of an Efficient Certificateless Signature Scheme

Chenhuang Wu[1,2], Xiaolin Lan[1], Jinhui Zhang[1], and Zhixiong Chen[1,2]

[1] Department of Mathematics, Putian University, Putian 351100, P.R. China
ptuwch@163.com, {ptulxl,ptzjh,ptczx}@126.com
[2] State Key Laboratory of Information Security, Institute of Software Chinese
Academy of Sciences, Beijing 100049, P.R. China

Abstract. In this paper, an efficient certificateless signature scheme which is recently proposed by Fengyin LI and Peiyu LIU, is analyzed but the scheme turns out to be insecure. Concretely, the proposed certificateless signature scheme can suffer from the public key replacement attack so that any one can forge a valid signature on any message. Then, to overcome this flaw, a comprehensive and improved scheme is proposed, whose security is based on the CDH assumption. Furthermore, the improved scheme can achieve the same trust level (Level 3) as that of the traditional PKI. In considering the precomputation, the efficiency of the improved scheme is almost the same as the original scheme.

Keywords: certificateless signature, cryptanalysis, public key replacement attack, CDH.

1 Introduction

In Asiacrypt 2003, AL-Riyami and Paterson introduced a new paradigm named Certificateless Public Key Cryptography (CL-PKC) [1], which removes the necessity of certificate to ensure the authentication of the user's public key in the traditional Certificate-Based Public Key Cryptography (CB-PKC)[2] and also overcomes the inherent key escrow problem in the Identity-Based Public Key Cryptography (IB-PKC)[3]. In CL-PKC, the trusted third party, named the KGC, first generates a partial private key from the user's identity and then delivers it to the user over a secure channel. Upon receiving the partial private key, the user selects a secret value and combines it with the partial private key to generate his private key. Moreover, the user also combines his secret value with the KGC's public parameters to generate his public key. From then on, CL-PKC draws more and more academics to do research on it for its noticeable advantages, such as [4 - 8], and so on.

Recently, LI and LIU proposed an efficient certificateless signature scheme from bilinear parings [9], whose security is proved on the hard assumptions of q-strong Diffie-Hellman problem and the Computational Diffie-Hellman (CDH) problem. However, we find that the signature scheme can suffer from the public key

J. Lei et al. (Eds.): NCIS 2012, CCIS 345, pp. 221–228, 2012.
© Springer-Verlag Berlin Heidelberg 2012

replacement attack so that any one can forge a valid signature on any message. Besides, the trust level of the signature scheme only achieves the level 2. (For detail about the "trust level" please refer to [10]). Finally, to overcome this attack, a comprehensive and improved scheme is proposed, whose security is based on the CDH assumption. Furthermore, by adjusting the steps in the signature scheme, the improved scheme can achieve the same trust level (Level 3) as that of the traditional PKI.

For the rest of this paper is organized as follows. In the next section, we will review some preliminaries required in this paper. In section 3, we review LI and LIU's efficient certificateless signature scheme. In section 4, the public key replacement attack is showed on LI and LIU's efficient certificateless signature scheme. In section 5, an improved signature scheme is proposed. Finally, we prove the improved scheme.

2   Preliminaries

Let G_1 and G_2 be additive and multiplicative cyclic groups of prime order q, respectively. Let P denote a generator in G_1. We assume that the discrete logarithm problems (DLP) in both G_1 and G_2 are hard.

2.1   Bilinear Pairings

Let $e : G_1 \times G_1 \to G_2$ be a map with following properties:

(1) **Bilinear:** For all $R, Q \in G_1$ and $a, b \in Z_q$, we have $e(aR, bQ) = e(R, Q)^{ab}$.

(2) **Non-degenerate:** $e(P, P) \neq 1_{G_2}$.

(3) **Computable:** There exists an efficient algorithm to compute $e(R, Q)$ for all $R, Q \in G_1$.

2.2   Complexity Assumptions

(1) Discrete Logarithm (DL) assumption.
Let G is a cyclic group generated by P with prime order q. Then, on inputs $y \in G$, there is no probabilistic polynomial time algorithm that outputs a value $x \in Z_q$ such that $y = xP$ with non-negligible probability.

(2) Computational Diffie-Hellman (CDH) assumption.
On inputs $(P, aP, bP) \in G_1^3$, where $a, b \in_R Z_q^*$ are random numbers, there is no probabilistic polynomial time algorithm that outputs the value abP with non-negligible probability.

3   Review of LI and LIU's Efficient Certificateless Signature Scheme

In this section, we review LI and LIU's efficient certificateless signature scheme in brief using the same notation as [9].

Let G_1 and G_2 be additive and multiplicative cyclic groups of prime order q, respectively. We assume that the discrete logarithm problems (DLP) in both G_1 and G_2 are hard. Let e be a bilinear pairing map. Let $H_1 : \{0,1\}^* \to G_1$ and $H_2 : \{0,1\}^* \to Z_q^*$ be two hash functions. These are used as a part of the system parameters generated by the KGC. Then, the efficient certificateless signature scheme is as follows:

- **Setup:** Given a security parameter k, the KGC chooses an arbitrary generator $P \in G_1$ and a random $s \in Z_q^*$, and sets $P_0 = sP$. Then the system parameters are set as $params = \langle G_1, G_2, e, q, P, P_0, H_1, H_2 \rangle$. The message space is $M = \{0,1\}^*$. The master secret key is $mk = s$.

- **Partial-Private-Key-Extract:** Given $params$, mk and a user Alice's identifier ID_A, the KGC computes $Q_A = H_1(ID_A) \in G_1$ and outputs a partial private key $D_A = sQ_A \in G_1$.

- **Set-Secret-Value:** Given $params$, the user Alice selects a random value $x_A \in Z_q^*$ as her secret value.

- **Set-Private-Key:** Given $params$ and the user the partial private key D_A, the user Alice generates her private key as $S_A = x_A D_A \in G_1$.

- **Set-Public-Key:** Given $params$ and the secret value x_A, the user Alice generates her public key as $P_A = x_A P_0 \in G_1$.

- **Sign:** Given $params$, ID_A, a message m and the private key S_A, the user Alice randomly chooses a $r \in Z_q^*$ and sets $U = rQ_A \in G_1$. Then she computes a signature $\sigma = (U, V)$ for the message m with $V = (r + h)S_A \in G_1$ and $h = H_2(m, U + P_A) \in Z_q^*$.

- **Verify:** Given a signature $\sigma = (U, V)$ for the message m, the signer's identity ID_A, and the signer's public key P_A, the verifier computes $h = H_2(m, U + P_A) \in Z_q^*$, and then checks whether or not the equation $e(P, V) = e(P_A, U + hQ_A)$ holds. If not, she rejects the signature. Otherwise, she accepts it.

4   Attack to LI and LIU's Efficient Certificateless Signature Scheme

In this section, we point out that LI and LIU's efficient certificateless signature scheme can suffer from the public key replacement attack so that any one can forge a valid signature on any message. The adversary forges a signature as follows:

- select a random value $l \in Z_q^*$, and replace the signer's public key as $P_A = lP$
- select a random element $U \in G_1$ and compute $h = H_2(m, U + P_A) \in Z_q^*$, where the message m is selected by the adversary as his wishes
- compute $V = l(U + hQ_A) \in G_1$, then $\sigma = (U, V)$ is the signature for the message m .

Obviously, $\sigma = (U, V)$ is a valid signature of the signer ID_A on the message m , whose public key is replaced by $P_A = lP$. We can notice that

$$e(P_A, U + hQ_A) = e(lP, U + hQ_A) = e(P, l(U + hQ_A)) = e(P, V) .$$

5   The Improvements of LI and LIU's Efficient Certificateless Signature Scheme

In this section, we give an improved scheme to overcome the above public key replacement attack.

- **Setup:** the same as the corresponding part in the original signature scheme above.
- **Set-Secret-Value:** the same as the corresponding part in the original signature scheme above.
- **Set-Public-Key:** Given *params* and the secret value x_A , the user Alice generates her public key as $PK_A = (P_{A1}, P_{A2})$, where $P_{A1} = x_A P_0 \in G_1, P_{A2} = x_A P \in G_1$. Then, Alice sends the public key $PK_A = (P_{A1}, P_{A2})$ to KGC.
- **Partial-Private-Key-Extract:** KGC verifies the public key of Alice by the equation $e(P, P_{A1}) = e(P_0, P_{A2})$ holds or not. If the above equation holds, KGC generates the partial private key for Alice by the following ways. Else, rejects. KGC computes $Q_A = H_1(ID_A, PK_A) \in G_1$ and outputs a partial private key $D_A = sQ_A \in G_1$. Then, KGC sends the partial private key D_A to Alice through secure channel.
- **Set-Private-Key:** the same as the corresponding part in the original signature scheme above.

- **Sign:** Given $params$, ID_A, a message m and the private key S_A, Alice randomly chooses a $r \in Z_q^*$ and sets $U = rQ_A \in G_1$. Then she computes a signature $\sigma = (U,V)$ for the message m with $V = (r+h)S_A \in G_1$ and $h = H_2(m,U + P_{A1}) \in Z_q^*$.

- **Verify:** Given a signature $\sigma = (U,V)$ for the message m, the signer's identity ID_A, and the signer's public key PK_A, the verifier verifies the signature in two steps:

  (1) To verify the validity of the public key of the Alice, the verifier computes the following equation: $e(P,P_{A1}) = e(P_0,P_{A2})$. If the equation above holds, then do the next step. Otherwise, it is showed that the public key is invalid. Then, refuse or contact with the signer for the true public key and then go on with the next step.

  (2) To verify the validity of the signature of the Alice, the verifier computes $h = H_2(m,U + P_{A1}) \in Z_q^*$, and then checks whether or not the equation $e(P,V) = e(P_{A1},U + hQ_A)$ holds. If not, she rejects the signature. Otherwise, she accepts it.

Remak: *We note that the first step is aimed to detect whether the public key of the signer is valid or not. Since the equation $e(P,P_{A1}) = e(P_0,P_{A2})$ is to ensure that the signer has the discrete logarithm knowledge of P_{A1} with P_0 (or P_{A2} with P). If the verifier verified the signature of the signer frequently, of course, from the next time he just did the second step directly. Thus, the efficiency of the improved scheme is almost the same as the original scheme.*

6   Security of the Improved Signature Scheme

It is well known that in certificateless cryptography there are two types of adversary: A_I and A_{II}. The adversary A_I, without the knowledge of the master key, is allowed to replace the user's public key. Reversely, the adversary A_{II}, with the knowledge of the master key, does not allow replacing the user's public key. Apparently, A_I is used to model an ordinary adversary, and A_{II} is used to model the KGC as an adversary. For details about of the security model in the certificateless signature, please refer to [6]. However, LI and LIU do not consider the above two types of adversary, but only with a short security analysis and get the result that the original scheme is based on the hard assumptions of q-strong Diffie-Hellman problem and the computational Diffie-Hellman problem. In the following part, we give a concrete security proof to the improved signature scheme. The result shows that the improved signature scheme can resist the two types of adversary (A_I and A_{II}) under the computational Diffie-Hellman assumption. Due to the space limitation, we only give sketch proof for the following theorems.

Theorem 1. The improved signature scheme above is correct.

Proof The correctness can easily be proved by straightforward calculating.

Theorem 2. The improved signature scheme above is unforgeable against the adversary A_I in the random oracle model under the CDH assumption.

Proof (sketch). As mentioned above, A_I can replace the public key of Alice. That is, we can assume that A_I knows the secret value x_A, but without the D_A. Actually, without the knowledge of D_A, A_I wants to construct (U,V) satisfying the above equation amount to forging a Hess signature. In [11], the security of Hess signature can be reduced to the CDH assumption.

Theorem 3. The improved signature scheme above is unforgeable against the adversary A_{II} in the random oracle model under the CDH assumption.

Proof (sketch). We know that the mater key is known to A_{II}. Thus, the target of A_{II} is to construct (U,V) satisfying the above equation. Then, we show that one can construct an algorithm $\Re$ that can solve the CDH problem by running A_{II} as a subroutine. The construction is as follows:

At the beginning, $\Re$ generate the system parameters. $\Re$ selects $s \in Z_q^*$ as the master secret key and sets $P_0 = sP$. Then, $\Re$ sends s and P_0 to A_{II}. We model the hash functions H_1, H_2 as random oracles which are operated by $\Re$. Hence, to perform as the random oracle, it needs to keep a list of the oracle queries that have been made. Let (P, aP, bP) is the input CDH challenge problem to $\Re$. Then, the purpose of $\Re$ is to output abP based on the forge signature ability of A_{II}. Without loss of generality, we assume that A_{II} may construct a signature on the identity ID^* and the message m^* with some probability. Then, the public key of ID^* is set as $PK_{ID^*} = (P_{ID^*1}, P_{ID^*2}) = (saP, aP)$.

When the simulation is started, the interaction with the hash oracle H_1 and H_2 are recorded in two lists of oracle queries, denoted by H_1 —List and H_2 —List, respectively. When A_{II} query to $\Re$ for $Q_{ID^*} = H_1(ID_{ID^*}, PK_{ID^*})$, $\Re$ sets $Q_{ID^*} = bP$. Then, by applying the forking technique [12], two forged signature on the same message m^* will be obtained, which are denoted by $(m^*, ID^*, PK_{ID^*}, U, V, h)$ and $(m^*, ID^*, PK_{ID^*}, U, V', h')$ satisfying $V \neq V'$ and $h \neq h'$. Thus, from $e(P,V) = e(P_A, U + hQ_A)$, $\Re$ can get the following equations

$$e(P,V) = e(aP, U + hbP) \text{ and } e(P,V') = e(aP, U + h'bP).$$

That is, $V = aU + habP$ and $V' = aU + h'abP$. Then, $\Re$ subtract the above two equations and get $abP = (h - h')^{-1}(V - V')$. Therefore, $\Re$ successfully obtains the solution of the CDH problem.

Theorem 4. The improved signature scheme above achieves the same trust level (Level 3) as that of the traditional PKI. However, the original signature scheme above only achieves the trust level 2.

Proof (sketch). In the improved signature scheme, if there are two valid signatures on two different public keys of the same user, respectively. It is sure that at least one public key is forged by the KGC. Because we have proved that a valid signature can be generated only by the one who has the knowledge of x_A and D_A together. We also note that the partial private key $D_A = sQ_A = sH_1(ID_A, PK_A)$, which actually is a signature on the (ID_A, PK_A) generated by the KGC. Obviously, only KGC can generate the two partial private keys. Therefore, the improved signature scheme achieves the level 3. However, in the original signature scheme, since $D_A = sQ_A = sH_1(ID_A)$ is only a signature on the ID_A generated by the KGC, which is unrelated to the public key PK_A. As a result, the two valid public keys may be generated by the signer himself or by the KGC which is indistinguishable, and then the original signature scheme above only achieves the trust level 2.

Acknowledgements. The paper is supported by the item of the National Natural Science Foundation of China (NO.61170246), the key item of Hercynian building for the colleges and universities service in Fujian Province (NO.2008HX03), the Open Funds of State Key Laboratory of Information Security (Chinese Academy of Sciences)(NO.01-01-1) and the item of the Education Committee of Fujian Province (NO.JA12291).

References

1. Al-Riyami, S.S., Paterson, K.G.: Certificateless Public Key Cryptography. In: Laih, C.-S. (ed.) ASIACRYPT 2003. LNCS, vol. 2894, pp. 452–473. Springer, Heidelberg (2003)
2. Gutmann, P.: PKI: It's not dead, just resting. IEEE Computer 35(8), 41–49 (2002)
3. Shamir, A.: Identity-Based Cryptosystems and Signature Schemes. In: Blakely, G.R., Chaum, D. (eds.) CRYPTO 1984. LNCS, vol. 196, pp. 47–53. Springer, Heidelberg (1985)
4. Hu, B.C., Wong, D.S., Zhang, Z., Deng, X.: Key Replacement Attack Against a Generic Construction of Certificateless Signature. In: Batten, L.M., Safavi-Naini, R. (eds.) ACISP 2006. LNCS, vol. 4058, pp. 235–246. Springer, Heidelberg (2006)
5. Huang, X., Susilo, W., Mu, Y., Zhang, F.: Certificateless designated verifier signature schemes. In: AINA 2006, vol. 2, pp. 15–19 (2006)
6. Zhang, Z., Wong, D.S., Xu, J., Feng, D.: Certificateless Public-Key Signature: Security Model and Efficient Construction. In: Zhou, J., Yung, M., Bao, F. (eds.) ACNS 2006. LNCS, vol. 3989, pp. 293–308. Springer, Heidelberg (2006)
7. Choi, K.Y., Park, J.H., Lee, D.H.: A new provably secure certificateless short signature scheme. Computers and Mathematics with Applications 61, 1760–1768 (2011)
8. Tso, R., Huang, X., Susilo, W.: Strongly secure certificateless short signatures. Journal of Systems and Software 6, 1409–1417 (2012)

9. Li, F., Liu, P.: An efficient certificateless signature scheme from bilinear parings. In: 2011 International Conference on Network Computing and Information Security, pp. 35–37 (2011)

10. Girault, M.: Self-certified Public Keys. In: Davies, D.W. (ed.) EUROCRYPT 1991. LNCS, vol. 547, pp. 490–497. Springer, Heidelberg (1991)

11. Hess, F.: Efficient Identity Based Signature Schemes Based on Pairings. In: Nyberg, K., Heys, H.M. (eds.) SAC 2002. LNCS, vol. 2595, pp. 310–324. Springer, Heidelberg (2003)

12. Pointcheval, D., Stern, J.: Security Proofs for Signature Schemes. In: Maurer, U.M. (ed.) EUROCRYPT 1996. LNCS, vol. 1070, pp. 387–398. Springer, Heidelberg (1996)

Robust Software Watermarking Scheme Using RC4 and HASH

Xiaoyan Sun[1], Maosheng Zhang[2], Xiaoshu Zhu[1], and Shuoming Li[3]

[1] School of Computer Science and Engineering, Yulin Normal University,
Yulin, 537000, Yulin, China
[2] School of Mathematics and Information, Yulin Normal University,
Yulin, 537000, Yulin, China
[3] Department of Electronic Engineering, Zhongshan Polytechnic,
Zhongshan, 528404, China
eterou@163.com

Abstract. In this paper, a novel software watermarking method using RC4 and Hash function is proposed. The method with good robust can be applied to protect and verify software copyright. The copyright information of ownership should be encrypted by RC4 stream cipher algorithm to ensure that the information is confidentiality, and prevent the information from forging. In order to avoid leaking the copyright information, the hash value is evaluated. Combining the PPCT and permutation encoding, even the code pointers have been attacked, this method will make use of the encrypted data or hash value to reconstruct the Dynamic diagram of the watermark information which was embedded in programs.

Keywords: software watermarking, robust, ownership, dynamic diagram.

1   Introduction

With the rapid development of network and universal popularization, the spread of digital products becomes more and more rapid. Thou it is conducive to the sharing of information, it leads to a serious challenges to the protection of intellectual property and in particular, causes great difficulties for software copyright protection. The quick spread of pirated softwares on network damages the rights of copyright holders seriously. when infringement of copyright cases happen, there is a common problem faced by all copyright holders that it is difficult for holders to put to the proof of ownership. Therefore, in addition to legal means, protecting intellectual property rights by technical means is very important for software developers. Software watermark is one of techniques to provide evidence against piracy.

Since Collberg presented dynamic software watermarking model in 1999[1], the software watermarking technology has achieved great development. There are a lot of software watermarking technologies appears, including classic software watermarking algorithms such as Davidson algorithm, Moskowitz algorithm, Stern algorithm,

J. Lei et al. (Eds.): NCIS 2012, CCIS 345, pp. 229–236, 2012.
© Springer-Verlag Berlin Heidelberg 2012

Arboit algorithm, Monden algorithm, Collberg-Thomborson algorithm and so on. However, the anti-attack capability of software watermarking is still a great challenge.

In this paper, a novel robust software watermarking system is proposed by combining planted plane cubic tree(PPCT) and permutation encoding. Due to the security of RC4 cryptosystem and one-way feature of hash function, the proposed system is secure and robust and is able to be used to verify the ownership of software.

2   Dynamic Graph Watermarking and Cryptogram Algorithms

2.1   Planted Plane Cubic Tree(PPCT)

PPCT is a binary tree with three additional features [2]:

(a) There is one extra node, whose degree is 1, called origin, which has a pointer to the root of the binary tree.
(b) Each leaf has a self-pointer and all leaves of the binary tree are linked into a circular linked list which includes the Origin.
(c) Every node in a PPCT has two outgoing pointers.

According to Catalan number theory[3] , a PPCT with n leaves (2n nodes) can represent any integer in the following formulation .

$$c(n) = \frac{1}{n} C_{2n-2}^{n-1} \tag{1}$$

Let c(n) be the number of PPCTs with n leaves. We can enumerate the PPCTs as shown in Figure 1.

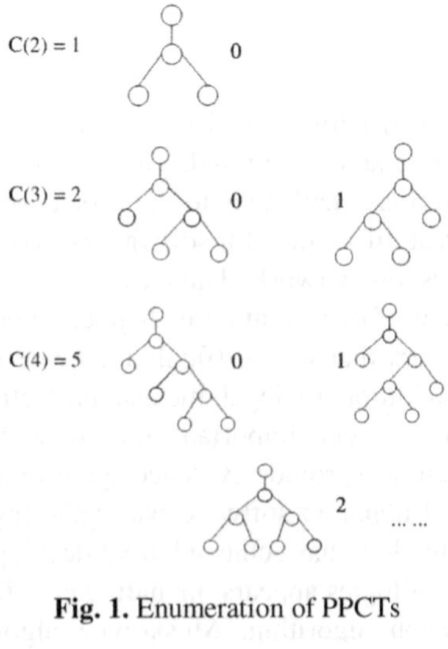

Fig. 1. Enumeration of PPCTs

2.2   Permutation Encoding

The structure of Permutation encoding is a Circular Linked List. The software watermark is represented with a permutation of the numbers <0,...,n-1>. For example, integer 1 can be represented by permutation <1, 2, 3, 5, 4> and 119 could be represented by <5, 4, 3, 2, 1>. The permutation <4, 5, 3, 1, 2> represents watermark number 29. Fig.2 shows a circular linked list for representing the watermark number 29. The 1st number 4 in the permutation is represented by a pointer from the 1st node to the 4th node in the diagram, and the last number 2 is represented by a pointer from the 5th node to the 2nd node. The representing range of permutation encoding with n nodes is n!-1[4].

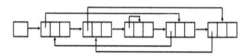

Fig. 2. Circular linked list for permutation

2.3   RC4 Algorithm

The RC4 cryptosystem is a nonlinear data table transformer sequence cryptosystem designed by RSA data security company[5].   Basing on a large data table, this system transforms data in the table into non-linear key sequences.   Though the length of the central map table S is random, it generally takes 256bits, which can be represented as S=(S0,S1,...,S255). Excepting table S, there are some other parameters in RC4 system, i.e. pointers I, J, in which both initial values are 0. The sequence T=< S0,S1,...,S255,I, J > is called states in RC4. New states are created by using non-linear transformations after flowing steps and finally the key k is outputted:

I=0, J=0 ;
I=I+1 mod 256;
J=J+SI mod 256;
swap SI and SJ;
The output function of RC4 are defined as follows :
h= SI+SJ mod 256;
k=Sh.

The key stream is generated by repeating the processes above. In encryption process, cipher texts are obtained by adding key streams and plain texts, while the plain texts are gotten by adding key streams and cipher texts.   The RC4 cryptosystem is widely used due to features such as simpleness, apparent nonlinearity and high efficiency [5, 6].

2.4   Hash Function

Hash function plays a key role in information security system. It is used in signature, integrality, identity authentication, dynamic password and so on[7]. Hash functions map variable-length messages M to fixed-length hash code h, which is a function value related to all bits in M. Hence, it is able to check errors in messages because the slight change of message will lead to tremendous changes in hash code. The basic applications of hash functions are listed below.

(a) Authentication

The sender generates the hash function of message M, and encrypts Hash(M) by using traditional cryptographic algorithm. And then, the encrypted information is appended to M. finally, the sender send messages to receiver. Based on the message M, the receiver recalculate hash function i.e. Hash(M) and compare this value with H(M) received from sender to estimate whether the message is authentic and integrated.

(b) Authentication and confidentiality

The sender generates the hash function of message M(Hash(M)) and appends hash value to M, and then encrypts the message and hash value and sends to receiver. After decrypting the received messages, receiver compares M with Hash(M) to confirm sender and information authentication. Due to the process of encryption, the hash function is able to provide identity authentication and confidentiality.

(c) Authentication and digital signature

Taking the advantage of public key cryptosystem, the sender generates hash function and the signature of hash value, and then sends these massages to receiver. The receiver verifies the signature to confirm authenticity. The sender is the only one who can generates the digital signature, so the verification process is able to confirm the sender and signature.

(d) authentication, signature and confidentiality

By combining public key cryptosystem and symmetric cryptography, hash function is able to provide confirmation of confidentiality, authentication and signature. The sender signs on the hash value of the message M with private key, and then encrypts M and signature with symmetric cryptography. The receiver decrypts messages from sender and verifies hash value [8].

Several constructions of hash functions have been proposed, based for example on DES[9, 10], or on RSA[9, 11]. MD series and SHA series, which are both based logical operations, are the most popular hash functions at present. There are three main techniques to design hash functions. (1) Straight construction. Lots of logical operations are used in this method to satisfy the security of hash function, rather than cryptography or other hypothesis. (2) Construction method based on block ciphers. Hash functions based on block ciphers is dependent on the security of ciphers. (3) Construction method based on difficulties of some mathematic problems such as factoring, discrete logarithm and so on. Hash functions based on this technic are secure under some reasonable hypothesis. In 2011, Dr.Wang presented a multivariate hash function based on the difficulty of multivariate polynomial equations over a finite field[12]. It is depicted in Fig.3.

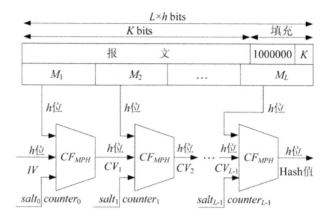

Fig. 3. Structure of hash function based on multivariate polynomial equations over a finite field

3   Hybrid Watermarking Using RC4 and Hash Function

One feature of the permutation encoding is high data rate, and PPCT has advantages of both binary tree and chain list, which makes it has good robustness, e.g. when the pointers of some nodes are modified, it can still be resumed effectively. However, its data rate is significantly low (≈0.5) [13]. In order to improve the performance of PPCT and permutation structure, this paper presents a better system combining HASH functions and RC4 algorithms.

The watermarking is composed of two parts: one is encrypted data N1 using RC4 algorithm and the other is hash value N2. According the registration information N0, the watermarking is computed as equation (2) and (3).

$$N_1 = RC4\ (N_0) \tag{2}$$

$$N_2 = HASH\ (N_0) \tag{3}$$

The integer N_1 is converted to PPCT diagram while N_2 is presented by permutation encoding with leaf nodes in PPCT. The right pointers in leaf nodes point to the next leaf node, and the permutation of left pointers represents N_2. The coding process is depicted in Fig.4.

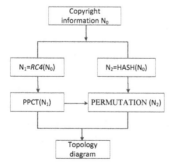

Fig. 4. Mechanism flow of hybrid watermarking algorithm

In the coding graph, nodes are the same with PPCT excepting leaf nodes. With every leaf node, left pointer is added to link the next node of the permutation. The in-degree and out-degree of left-most node are 2 and 3 respectively, while right-most node are 4 and 1, and other nodes are 3 and 2. That is, the degree of nodes which is used for permutation coding is 5, and the degree of none-leaf nodes in PPCT is 3. According to the degrees of nodes, permutation graph can be extracted easily. And then, PPCT is extracted with high efficiency. The structure of embedded and extracted processes are depicted in Fig.5

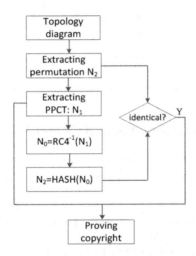

Fig. 5. Diagram of watermarking extracting

4   Performance

The proposed watermarking system is of good robustness because of the certainty of degrees of the nodes in PPCT, which is based on binary tree. Hash value is transformed to permutation graph, which is generated using leaf nodes. Combining PPCT and permutation graph, the system takes advantage of both good robustness of PPCT and high efficiency of permutation graph. Thus the attack resistance ability is significantly improved.

Thanks to the high efficiency and safety, the RC4 encoded watermarking information decreases the relevancy between the watermarking graph and original copyright information. Thus any unauthorized individual is unable to produce illegal faked productions even after obtaining the watermarking graph. At the meantime, utilizing the one-way and anti-collision features of hash function, and applying the PPCT leaf nodes structure to construct Hash number without adding new nodes can further improve system safety. As the Hash number doesn't carry any real watermarking information, attainting the intact watermarking or any one of PPCT and permutation graph is of no use to the potential attackers.

The right-owner identifies the ownership of software with high efficiency when copyright dispute has evolved if the watermarking inserted into program has not been modified. In case of watermarking is tampered, the rights-owner extracts PPCT to restore watermark to prove the copyright, or compare the hash value extracted from permutation graph with the hash value stored by right-owner and the identical of the two values denote ownership of the right. In conclusion, any one of the PPCT and permutation is able to be used to prove the copyright.

5   Conclusions

This paper introduced PPCT, permutation graphics, RC4 algorithm and Hash function at first. Based on the high efficiency and security of RC4 and the good collision-avoided and non-directionality of Hash functions, we present a hybrid software watermark Scheme combining PPCT and permutation graphics. The new scheme greatly enhanced the robustness of software watermark. The illegal activities such as forge the copyright owner are also avoided. On the basis of the exiting algorithms, the next stage of research work is to improve anti-attack capability of the core algorithm for software watermarking.

Acknowledgement. This research is supported by: The established Project by Educational Office of Guangxi (Grant Nos: 201106LX513; 201106LX516). Project of Yulin normal university (Grant Nos: 2012YJZD17; 2010YJQN18).

References

1. Smith, T.F., Waterman, M.S.: Identification of Common Molecular Subsequences. J. Mol. Biol. 147, 195–197 (1981)
2. Collberg, C., Thomborson, C.: Software watermarking: Models and dynamic embeddings. In: Proceedings of the 26th ACM SIGPLAN-SIGACT Symposium on Principles of Programming Languages, pp. 311–324. ACM, Texas (1999)
3. Palsberg, J., Krishnaswamy, S., Kwon, M., Ma, D., Shao, Q., Zhang, Y.: Experience with software watermarking. In: 16th Annual Conference on Computer Security Applications, ACSAC 2000, pp. 308–316. IEEE Computer Society Press (2000)
4. Goulden, I.P., Jackson, D.M.: Combinatorial enumeration. Dover Pubns, New York (2004)
5. Zhu, J., Yin, K., Liu, Y.: A Novel DGW Scheme Based on 2D_PPCT and Permutation. In: International Conference on Multimedia Information Networking and Security, MINES 2009, pp. 109–113. IEEE, Hubei (2009)
6. Rivest, R.L.: RSA Data Security 12, 9.2 (1992)
7. Yao, Y., Jiang, C., Wang, X.: Enhancing RC4 algorithm for WLAN WEP protocol. In: ontrol and Decision Conference (CCDC), pp. 3623–3627. Wuhan, China (2010)
8. Chuanhua, Z., Gemei, Z., Baohua, Z., Wei, W.: Study of One-way Hash Function to Digital Signature Technology. In: 2006 International Conference on Computational Intelligence and Security, pp. 1503–1506 (2006)
9. Hg, Z., Zy, W.: Introduction to Cryptography. Wuhan University Press, Wuhan (2009)

10. Davies, D.W., Price, W.L.: The application of digital signatures based on public key cryptosystems. National Physical Laboratory, Middlesex (1980)
11. Merkle, R.C.: One Way Hash Functions and DES. In: Brassard, G. (ed.) CRYPTO 1989. LNCS, vol. 435, pp. 428–446. Springer, Heidelberg (1990)
12. Girault, M.: Hash Functions Using Modulo-N Operations. In: Price, W.L., Chaum, D. (eds.) EUROCRYPT 1987. LNCS, vol. 304, pp. 217–226. Springer, Heidelberg (1988)
13. Wang, H.Z., Zhang, H.G., Yang, Y.: Design and Analysis of Multivariate Hash Function. Acta Electronica Sinica 39, 237–241 (2011)
14. Zhu, J.Q., Liu, Y.H., Lin, K.X.: A Novel Dynamic Graph Software Watermark Scheme. In: Proceedings of the 2009 First International Workshop on Education Technology and Computer Science, pp. 775–780. IEEE Computer Society, Washington, DC (2009)

A Novel Digital Watermarking Method Based on Lifting Wavelet Transform

Fei Xia, Hengzi Huang, Daogang Peng, and Hui Li

School of Electric & Automatic Engineering, Shanghai University of Electric Power
Shanghai, China
xiafei@shiep.edu.cn

Abstract. Wavelet transform based on lifting scheme called lifting wavelet transform. Lifting wavelet transform has some advantages, such as calculation speed, less memory, integer transform and other characteristics. To enhance the security of the watermark, a scrambling algorithm is adopted for the watermark image firstly. Then after a large number of simulation and performance analysis, one novel digital watermarking method based on lifting wavelet transform is proposed. Finally, the reconstructed image where watermark embedded has been testing a variety of attacks, including shear, compression, filtering, rotation, etc. The experimental results show that the imperceptibility and robustness of the method call be guaranteed.

Keywords: lifting scheme, wavelet transform, digital watermarking.

1 Introduction

In the new century, the Internet and digital media technology have rapid development. Compared with traditional media, digital media has great characters of improving the efficiency of the media information globalization. But digital technology development has also the disadvantages, such as the safety, security, piracy and optional manipulation. Compared with common media, digital is a kind of media, which is more convenient and open. Therefore, digital media copyright protection and information integrity guarantee has gradually become an important problem in digital technology. With the demand of information security, digital watermarking technology has rapid development and becomes the research hot spot. Because the present international watermark technology has not been formed unified standard, form a common follow standard has become common goal of the study of watermark. However, standard algorithm must have its advantages, generality and effectiveness, and to get the world identity, so forming standard is a difficult task. Because of the advantages of wavelet transform and future JPEG compression standard of popularization, the wavelet transform domain research watermark processing technology is the hot spot [1-6]. And in the field, it is the most likely standard watermarking algorithm. In this paper, a novel digital watermarking method based on lifting wavelet transform is proposed. Through watermarking algorithm design and simulation, the approach has the great meaning to achieve.

J. Lei et al. (Eds.): NCIS 2012, CCIS 345, pp. 237–243, 2012.
© Springer-Verlag Berlin Heidelberg 2012

2   Digital Watermarking

With the advent of the information age, especially the popularization of Internet, the information security protection has become an increasingly important issue. The current information security technology basically based in cryptography, whether the traditional key system or public key system, its protection way is to control access to the file, the file encryption, which allowed illegal users can't have any solution. But along with the computer processing capacity increasing rapidly, the method which increased key length to improve system intensive becomes more and more unsafe.

Digital watermarking is a kind of very close to the practical application of the data hiding technology. Embedded digital works of information must have the following basic characteristics can be called digital watermark.

1. Disguised in digital works embedding digital watermark which does not make obvious drop mass and to be felt.

2. Hidden the security of watermark information hiding place from the data rather than file and file format changes should not lead to the loss of the watermark data.

3. Robustness, it means after a variety of accidentally or intentionally signal processing, digital watermarking can still keep integrity or can still be accurate identification. Possible signal processing process including channel noise, filtering, digital and analog conversion, resampling, shear, displacement, dimension change and loss compression coding, etc.

3   Lifting Wavelet Transform

Lifting scheme is proposed by Sweldens and Daubechiiesa in the mid 1990'. Because based on the lifting scheme, the wavelet transform called lifting wavelet transform.

In lifting wavelet transform, wavelet is not produced necessarily by the expansion and shift of a certain mother wave. Their definition is very flexible, perhaps in one interval, may be in irregular grid. In 2 D space, lifting wavelet transform is more flexible and complex, which is not simply regularly divided into two dimensional plane, or may be defined in a surface, such as in one sphere. Another advantage of lifting scheme is that it can contain traditional wavelet. That is to say, all of the traditional wavelet can use lifting scheme structure out. Through the Eucliden algorithm, all the traditional wavelet can be obtained by lifting scheme of basic lift and dual decomposition. And using lifting scheme to realize wavelet filter has the following advantages. The operation is fast. It does not require additional memory. It can realize the integer wavelet transform.

Lifting wavelet transform has advantages of calculation speed and less memory. It can also realize the integer transform etc. The basic process can be divided into the three steps, including division, forecast and update. Through the two lift steps, forecast and update can realize signal separation between high frequency and low frequency. Because the signals are partial correlation, the point of the signal value can predict correctly through its adjacent signal value and the proper prediction operator. At the same time the error of the predictions is high frequency information. And this process is predicted link. The high frequency information in forecast link is to adjust signal next sampling to get low frequency information through the update operator. This process is update link.

4   Prepare of Watermark

In order to enhance the security of watermark, it typically requires the watermark scrambling process. Scrambling technology in image processing is increasingly important to the security and confidentiality of the information and develops a common image encryption technology. The early image scrambling technology is replacement location space for analog image. For a digital image, the scrambling process is not only performed in the spatial domain of the digital image, it can also be in the frequency domain of the image. Currently, the main considering digital image scrambling technologies are as follows. It includes Arnold transformation, magic square and Hilbert curve. In this paper, the Arnold transform is selected.

One binary watermark is designed. The image size is 64 * 64, which is shown in the Fig.1.

Fig. 1. Binary watermark image

Arnold algorithm [7] is used for scrambling digital watermark. The scrambling cycle is 1, 2,5,10 and 40 respectively. The watermark images after scrambling are shown in Fig.2.

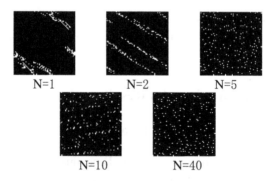

Fig. 2. Watermark image with different scrambling cycle

5   Digital Watermarking Algorithm

The watermarking embedding algorithm is as follows.

1. Selecting the binary watermark image which has certain significance, choosing the right key and scrambling watermark with Arnold algorithm. After scrambling, matrix of watermark is changed into a line vector.
2. To get a frequency sub-band diagram, s level lifting wavelet decomposition is done for the host image.
3. Determining a threshold T, searching importance coefficients on sub band, and establishing matrix to record the importance coefficient. If it is the importance coefficient, the corresponding position in the matrix is recorded as 1. Otherwise, it is 0.
4. According to the position of matrix, which records the importance of the coefficient, watermark information is embedded by the order of column cycle. If embedded binary watermarking information is 1, the record of matrix will be 2, which is the memory matrix.
5. According to the revised low frequency sub-band coefficient, s level reversed lifting wavelet transform is done for the reconstruction of the watermark image.

And watermark extraction algorithm is as follows.

1. S level lifting wavelet transform is carried for embed watermark image to get low frequency sub-band coefficient matrix.
6. According to the position of importance coefficient in memory matrix, relative calculation is made with the original image by column circulation.
7. Making watermark existence judgment. To judge watermark existence, setting a threshold T and calculating normalized cross-correlation. If there is a watermark, the step will be done. If there isn't a watermark, the extraction process will be stopped.
8. The extraction watermark image will be recovery into a matrix by column. According to the key and memory matrix, Arnold reverse scrambling is done to restore watermark image.

6   Algorithm Experimental Results

For testing the approach which is proposed in this paper, 512 * 512 Lena image is selected as the host image. And the watermark is a 64 * 64 binary image. Two-level lifting wavelet decomposition is used for Lena image. The reconstructed image embedded watermark and extracted watermark image are shown in Fig.3.

Fig. 3. The reconstructed image embedded watermark and extracted watermark image

It can be seen from the above simulation results that embedded watermark image with high imperceptibility. There is almost no difference between the two images. And the extraction of the watermark image is very clear. In the case of no attacks, the extracted watermark image is very close to the original watermark image. .

Next, we consider both geometric and non-geometric attacks. For geometric attacks, noise and cropping are used. For non-geometric attacks, filters and JPEG which is one of the most frequently used formats on the Internet are adopted. Some experimental results on extraction of copyright information image from the watermarked host image attacked by four kinds of common image processing attacks are shown in Fig.4. Four images of Fig. 4(a), Fig.4(c), Fig.4(e) and Fig.4(g) show respectively the watermarked host images with copyright information which are attacked by Gaussian noise, cropping, median filtering and compression. Moreover, other four images of Fig.4(b), Fig.4(d), Fig.4(f) and Fig.4(h) show the copyright information extracted from these watermarked host images. From Fig.4(b), Fig.4(d), Fig. 4(f) and Fig.4(h) show that the proposed watermarking scheme was robust to general attacks. That is to say, the proposed method can effectively resist attacks.

From Fig.4, we can see that these conventional attacked methods do not degraded the image quality of the copyright information so much. The proposed method discussed in this paper include robustness to the non-geometric attacks such as filters and compression, and also it is robust to geometrical attacks, for example, noise addition and cropping. Fig. 4 reveals that embedded copyright information can be robust enough to resist common image processing attacks and not be easily removable. The experimental results prove that our approach is feasibility in robustness.

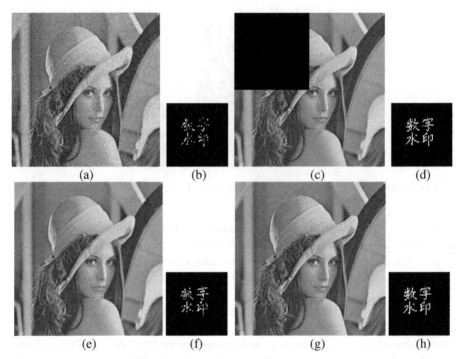

Fig. 4. The results of robustness simulation experiments (a) Watermarked image attacked by Gaussian noise; (b) Reconstruction of (a); (c) Watermarked image attacked by cropping; (d) Reconstruction of (c); (e) Watermarked image attacked by median filtering; (f) Reconstruction of (e); (g) Watermarked image attacked by JPEG compression; (h) Reconstruction of (g)

7   Conclusions

Lifting wavelet is the second generation wavelet transform. In order to strengthen the digital watermarking, the watermark algorithm based on the lifting wavelet transform has very strong robustness to   the loss compression, local clipping and filtering attack.

In this paper, a non-blind watermarking algorithm based on lifting wavelet transform is proposed. The embedded image watermark is carried into two lifting wavelet decomposition. According to the relationship of the importance coefficient, the binary watermark is embedded in the host images with an additional memory matrix. Through comparing the value of original image with the one of embedded watermark reconstructed image in every position and the memory matrix, the watermark can be extracted correctly. It can simultaneously meet the robustness and invisibility.

In all attacks, resistance against the filtering attack is the worst and resistance against the cropping attack is the best. Therefore, how to improve the robustness of the algorithm against filtering will be the focus of the further research.

References

1. Zhao, H., Wang, L., Wen, W.: Survey of Image Watermarking Based on DWT & DCT. Microcomputer Applications 29(1), 1–5 (2008)
2. Zhang, X., Zhang, G., Du, Y.: Multi-function Digital Watermark Based on Wavelet Transformation. Computer Engineering 34(18), 169–171 (2008)
3. Kishk, S., Javidi, B.: Information hiding technique with double phase encoding. Appl. Opt. 41(26), 5462–5470 (2002)
4. Kim, J.-Y., Kwon, S.-G., et al.: Adaptive digital watermarking based on wavelet transform using successive subband quantization and perceptual model. ITC-CSCC 2, 1240–1243 (2002)
5. Wu, D.: Research and Implement on Digital Watermark. China Science and Technology Information 11, 122 (2012)
6. Wu, Y.-K., Di, C.-H.: A Survey of Digital Watermarking Techniques. Journal of Liaoning University (Natural Sciences Edition) 37(3), 202–206 (2010)
7. Huang, J., Shi, Y.Q.: Reliable information bit hiding. IEEE Trans. Circuits and Systems for Video Technology 12(10), 916–920 (2002)

A New Practical Template Attack of AES

Yongbo Hu[1,2,3], Yeyang Zheng[3], and Jun Yu[1,2,3]

[1] ASIC and System State Key Lab., Fudan University, Shanghai, China
[2] Microelectronics of Fudan University, Shanghai, China
[3] Shanghai Fudan Microelectronics Group Co., Ltd., Shanghai
10212020016@fudan.edu.cn

Abstract. The author uses a new effective schedule of template attack method to attack 128 bit AES[7] successfully. This new method which includes only one type of template and several times of classification can access to the whole 128 bits key of AES theoretically. Moreover, the author also comes up with some improvements in order to use less memory and computing to make the attack more efficient.

Keywords: AES, template attack, SCA, PCA, correlation matrix.

1   Introduction

Since the first publication appearance in 1996[1], a probabilistic side-channel attack called template attack, is introduced [2], which is a really efficient attack method. AES algorithm is widely used nowadays. The side-channel attack (SCA) has been comprehensively studied by the cryptography community since the first publication written by Kocher [6]. A lot of countermeasures which lower the signal noise rate and make the side-channel information of the implementation independent of the key make the DPA/DEMA methods not possible anymore. However, the probabilistic side-channel attack [4] called template attack can efficient get the key of AES. The author proposed a total schedule of template attack for AES. And the author just needs one type of template and 128 times of classification to obtain the whole key of AES successfully. Moreover, the author also uses some details of improvements in order to make the template attack more efficient.

2   Template and Attack Schedule

2.1   The Template Introduction

The template we use is the hamming weight H [8] of each SBOX [7] of AES. H donates the number of '1' of a binary data. Hence, the hamming weight of our attack varies from zero to eight. And for a fully paralleled implementation of AES we need to establish 16 templates and if the implementation width of AES is L, the independent template number is L/8. in other words, we need to establish all the SBOX appeared in the implementation. Figure 1 shows the structure and template position of the first round of AES.

J. Lei et al. (Eds.): NCIS 2012, CCIS 345, pp. 244–249, 2012.
© Springer-Verlag Berlin Heidelberg 2012

$\{w\,(t,i)\,|\,1 \le i \le n\}$ donates the side-channel data and it is also called trace. n donates the number of trace. And let N be the point number of each trace. $\{P(i)\,|\,1 \le i \le n\}$ donates the total plaintexts which are random generated. Let K be the 128 bit key of fixed AES during the attack process.

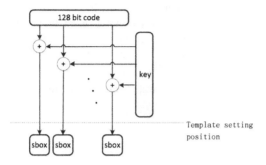

Fig. 1. the template setting position

2.2   Attack Schedule of AES

Suppose we have established the template introduced before and can do the classification successfully. The schedule of attack AES main includes 4 steps.

Step 1; 16 templates can be obtained by using 100000 traces which correspond to 100000 keys generated randomly to establish the templates of 16 SBOX.

Step 2; Sample series of traces which have the same input plaintext and an unknown key which we will obtain after the template attack. P_0 donates the plaintext. And after 16 times of classification we can obtain 16 hamming weight of the 16 SBOX.

$$\left\{ H_0 = H^i \,\middle|\, 1 \le i \le 16 \right\} \tag{2.1}$$

Step 3; change only one bit of plaintext P_0, P_1 donates the new plaintext. Use the first SBOX as an example. After the classifying task of the first SBOX, we have

$$
\begin{aligned}
H_{new} &= H\left(P_1[127:112] \oplus K[127:112] \right) \\
&= H\left(P[126:112] \oplus K[126:112] \right) + H\left(P_1[127] \oplus K[127] \right) \\
&= H\left(P[127:112] \oplus K[127:112] \right) \pm 1 \\
&= H^i \pm 1
\end{aligned}
\tag{2.2}
$$

$$if\left(H_{new} = H^i + 1 \right) \Rightarrow K[127] = P_0[127]$$

$$if\left(H_{new} = H^i - 1 \right) \Rightarrow K[127] = 1 - P_0[127]$$

Step 4; repeat step 3 for 128 times then the 128 bit keys of AES can be obtained.

3   Template Establish

In template attacks, the Gaussian noise model is considered. The establishing of template concludes 3 steps. Step1 is the preprocessing step which guarantees the alignment of the trace and also decreases the memory usage. Step2 is selecting points[1]. We use the PCA[3][5] method which will decrease the dimension of the data and also maintain the important information we need to build the template. Step3 calculates the multivariate Gaussian model which is the final template.

Actually, we have 9 different hamming weight (H) of each SBOX to be distinguished. And we use the first SBOX as an example. According to the hamming weight, the total n traces can be separated into to 9 different sets $\{W_i \mid 0 \le i \le 8\}$. Let $\{n_i \mid 0 \le i \le 8\}$ be the trace number for each hamming weight. And in order to build the templates clearly we pick one out of the trace sets. The vector of means can be computed as

$$\overline{W_i} = \frac{1}{n_i} \sum_{W \in W_i} W \tag{3.1}$$

Suppose the n_i traces form a matrix of $n_i \times N$. Let $\{X_i \mid 0 \le i \le N\}$ be the N columns of this matrix. Select two columns of this matrix X, Y. The empirical covariance of X, Y is defined as

$$COV(X,Y) = \frac{1}{N-1} \sum_{j=1}^{n_i} (X_j - \overline{X})(Y_j - \overline{Y}) \tag{3.2}$$

So the noise correlation matrix is computed as

$$CM(i,j) = COV(X_i, X_j) \tag{3.3}$$

For each of the trace set, a corresponding template is the pair $\left(\overline{W_i}, CM_i\right)$.

3.1   Preprocessing

The preprocessing step has a great influence for a successful attack. Actually we need to guarantee that all the traces are aligned precisely, because it seems difficult for us to align precisely sometimes. So after the alignment step, the author does an extra preprocessing before establishing the templates.

Let W be an original trace and k is a parameter that the attacker can choose independently. The preprocessing of a trace is computed as

$$W_{new} = zeros;$$
$$for\left(i = 0; i < N / k; i++\right)$$
$$for\left(j = 0; j < k; j++\right)$$
$$W_{new}(i) = W_{new}(i) + W(ki+j);$$

After this preprocessing, the signal misaligned for limited points can be aligned and also decrease the memory usage. The attacker needs to store a large number of traces which are used for establishing the template, typically $o(10^5)$. And the number of points of each curve is typically $o(10^4)$. This preprocessing can reduce the total memory usage to $1/k$.

3.2   PCA

In practice, the point number of each trace is very large, typically $o(10^4)$, and according to (3.3), the size of the CM is $N \times N$, this leads to large memory usage and complex computing. PCA is short for principal component analysis which is a standard statistical tool for decreasing the dimension of the matrix. PCA is to search a linear map which projects the high dimension matrix to low dimension and extracts the most important information from the initial matrix.

Use the 9 vectors of means $\{\overline{W}_i \mid 0 \le i \le 8\}$ computed before and calculate the correlation matrix according (3.3). Let M be the $N \times N$ correlation matrix. The singular value decomposition of M is computed as

$$M = U \times \Lambda \times V^T \left(UU^T = I, VV^T = I \right) \tag{3.4}$$

The linear projecting matrix is computed as

$$map = U\left(:,1:l\right) \times \sqrt{\Lambda\left(1:l,1:l\right)} \tag{3.5}$$

And all the trace W_i are projected to $W_i \times map^T$, the vector of means and the correlation matrix are projected to

$$\begin{aligned} \overline{W}_i\,' &= \overline{W}_i \times map^T \\ CM\,'_i &= map^T \times CM_i \times map \end{aligned} \tag{3.6}$$

And the entire variable can be projected to a new variable and the corresponding template $\left(\overline{W}_i\,', CM\,'_i \right)$ can be established successfully with less memory usage and computing for the classification.

4   Classification and Results

Pick one template $\left(\overline{W}_i, CM_i \right)$ as an example. The probability is computed as

$$p\left(W, \overline{W}_i, CM_i \right) = \frac{1}{(2\pi)^{l/2} \left| CM_i \right|^{0.5}} e^{-0.5\left(W - \overline{W}_i \right)^T CM_i^{-1}\left(W - \overline{W}_i \right)}$$

$$= e^{-0.5\left(W-\overline{W_i}\right)^T CM_i^{-1}\left(W-\overline{W_i}\right)-1/2\ln(2\pi)-0.5\ln\left(|CM_i|\right)}$$

$$= e^{p1}$$

(4.1)

So just need to compute $p1$ to estimate the probability which suppose that the trace W has a distribution of $\left(\overline{W_i}, CM_i\right)$. And the Bayes' theorem is used to calculate the probability when multiple classification traces used.

4.1   Bayes' Theorem Usage

Let $p\left(H_i|W_i\right)$ be the conditional probability which is based on the prior probability $p\left(H_i\right)$ and $p\left(W_i|H_i\right)$. The $p\left(H_i|W_i\right)$ is computed as

$$p\left(H_i|W_i\right) = \frac{p\left(W_i|H_i\right)p\left(H_i\right)}{\sum\limits_{i=1}^{9} p\left(W_i|H_i\right)p\left(H_i\right)}$$

(4.2)

And for the whole classification traces W , we can multiply the probability corresponding to the classification traces. $p\left(H_i\right)$ is set to $p\left(H_i|W_{i-1}\right)$ and the initial data of $p\left(H_i\right)$ is $\dfrac{c(i,n)}{256}$. Let N_w be the number of classification traces. So the final equation is

$$p\left(H_i|N_w\right) = \frac{\left(\prod\limits_{j=1}^{N_w} p\left(W_j|H_i\right)\right)p\left(H_i\right)}{\sum\limits_{i=1}^{9}\left(\prod\limits_{j=1}^{N_w} p\left(W_j|H_i\right)\right)p\left(H_i\right)}$$

(4.3)

And the probability of $p\left(W_j|H_i\right)$ is obtained when use the trace W_j to do the classification.

4.2   Attack Result

Figure 2 shows a template result for the first SBOX of AES. And the probability curve corresponding to right hamming weight is figured in red.

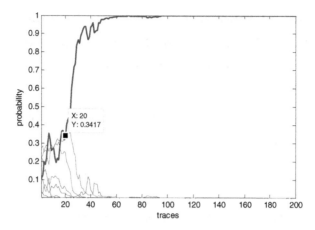

Fig. 2. The probability as a function of traces number

After several times of classification, the total Hamming weight $\left\{H_0 = H^i \middle| 1 \leq i \leq 16\right\}$ can be obtained. Then use the AES template attack schedule introduced before for 128 times. Then the whole 128 bit key can be obtained.

Actually, if each fixed plaintext needs 100 curves, the total traces number is 12800 in practical. And the computing complexity is very low because the classification is nearly the same operation.

And the templates for this AES attack are the model for different SBOX which depend on the width of the implementation. Compared with other work, this new method makes the attack easily and efficiently with regular computing and less memory usage.

References

1. Rechberger, C., Oswald, E.: Practical Template Attacks. In: Lim, C.H., Yung, M. (eds.) WISA 2004. LNCS, vol. 3325, pp. 440–456. Springer, Heidelberg (2005)
2. Kocher, P.C.: Timing Attacks on Implementations of Diffie-Hellman, RSA, DSS, and Other Systems. In: Koblitz, N. (ed.) CRYPTO 1996. LNCS, vol. 1109, pp. 104–113. Springer, Heidelberg (1996)
3. Jolliffe, I.T.: Principal Component Analysis, 2nd edn. Springer (2002)
4. Jacobs, I.S., Bean, C.P.: Fine particles, thin films and exchange anisotropy. In: Rado, G.T., Suhl, H. (eds.) Magnetism, vol. III, pp. 271–350. Academic, New York (1963) Template attacks
5. Archambeau, C., Peeters, E., Standaert, F.-X., Quisquater, J.-J.: Template Attacks in Principal Subspaces. In: Goubin, L., Matsui, M. (eds.) CHES 2006. LNCS, vol. 4249, pp. 1–14. Springer, Heidelberg (2006)
6. Kocher, P.C., Jaffe, J., Jun, B.: Differential Power Analysis. In: Wiener, M. (ed.) CRYPTO 1999. LNCS, vol. 1666, pp. 388–397. Springer, Heidelberg (1999)
7. Advanced Encryption Standard Development Effort (2000),
   http://www.nist.gov/aes
8. Brier, E., Clavier, C., Olivier, F.: Correlation Power Analysis with a Leakage Model. In: Joye, M., Quisquater, J.-J. (eds.) CHES 2004. LNCS, vol. 3156, pp. 16–29. Springer, Heidelberg (2004)

Multicasting of Images Resized Using Enhanced Seam Carving Technique in Hierarchical Group Communication

R. Pugalenthi[1], V.R. Rajasekar[2], U. Sakthi[1], and S. Preetham[3]

[1] Department of Computer Science and Engineering
St. Joseph's College of Engineering
Chennai -600119, Tamilnadu, India
{rpugalenthi1976,sakthi.ulaganathan}@gmail.com
[2] Department of Information Technology
Ministry of Higher Education, Sultanate of Oman
vrrsekar@yahoo.com
[3] CTS, Chennai, Tamilnadu, India
s.preetham89@rediffmail.com

Abstract. Multicast communication is a proficient method for delivery of multimedia data to a large group of users, with optimized network resources. Most of the commercial applications benefit from multicast, but however, requires a secure communication system in which data confidentiality, authentication and Quality of Service is achieved. In this paper, we propose an efficient mechanism for multicasting of resized images in hierarchical group communication, using enhanced seam carving technique. The proposed algorithm resizes the images without any lose in quality and distortion. These resized images are multicast to different users having different screen size and resolution and images are displayed without any compromise in the quality and thus the quality of service is achieved and improved. An experimental setup was implemented to verify the successfulness of the approach.

Keywords: Seam carving, Image resize, Wavelet Decomposition, Multicasting and Kerberos.

1 Introduction

Majority of the commercial applications that are used in internet are benefited from multicast communication [7] [12]. Multicasting is an efficient method for delivery of multimedia data to a large group of users and it can be used in many emerging services on the Internet. Examples of applications where only authorized users have access to data includes teleconferencing, video conferencing, DNS routers, news group, multiplayer games, massively parallel computing, database replication, name services, directory services, pay TV, real-time information update etc. Nowadays, the

J. Lei et al. (Eds.): NCIS 2012, CCIS 345, pp. 250–258, 2012.
© Springer-Verlag Berlin Heidelberg 2012

size of display panel of various users of a multicast group varies differently to satisfy several types of demands for consumer devices such as television, cellular phone, personal digital assistant, digital camera etc. Since these consumer devices have various screen sizes and resolutions, images are frequently resized to be displayed in each panel. Images are being resized for a very long time, there are many methods like re-sampling, cropping, scaling and conventional seam carving. The essential need is that important features need to be protected while fitting to different panels [4]. In this paper, we propose an enhanced seam carving technique for resizing images using wavelet decomposition technique. The resized images are multicast to devices which are having different screen size and resolution. Our experiment results show that the proposed technique is more efficient in terms of image quality.

2   Image Resizing Strategy

2.1   Seam Craving

Seam carving is an algorithm for image resizing that establishes the number of seams, which are connected paths of low energy pixels in an image in which seams are automatically removed to reduce image size or inserted to extend it [1]. This method involves calculation of an "importance" function or energy function. A vertical seam is a path of pixels connected from top to bottom in an image with one pixel in each row; horizontal seam is similar with the exception of the connection being from left to right. The "importance" function values a pixel by measuring its contrast with its neighbor pixels. This paper proposes a technique that can change the size of an image by gracefully carving-out or inserting pixels in different parts of the image. Seam carving uses an energy function defining the importance of pixels.

Fig. 1. First image shows original image, second shows the result of seam carving

For image reduction, seam selection ensures that while preserving the image structure, we remove more of the low energy pixels and fewer high energy ones. However, the conventional seam carving method exploits only the change of pixel intensities for the energy, the quality of the resized image can be severely distorted, when the intensities of background have more changes than those of main objects of interest [8]. To solve this problem, Hwang et al [1] introduced the saliency and face maps to obtain more accurate energy function considering human attention model in shown in Fig 1.

3   Improved Seam Craving for Image Resizing Using a Modified Energy Function

In [4], an improved seam carving using a modified energy function on wavelet decomposition is presented, a novel image resizing method. One of the drawbacks of conventional seam carving is, it selects the seam which is across the important contents depending on the layout and amount of the content and because of this image distortion will occur. The novel image resizing method [4] uses a modified energy function which imposes the two merits of wavelet decomposition, decomposing an image into different frequency sub-bands and scales pace representation of wavelet transforms [13]. The modified energy function which represents image features by utilizing wavelet coefficients and the quality of the image further enhanced by performing the conventional scaling based on the energy distribution. The weight consisting the sum of the wavelet coefficients in the Ith level is calculated as

$$\Phi_I(m,n) = \alpha \omega^I_{LH} + (1-\alpha)\omega^I_{HL} + \beta\, \omega^I_{HH} \qquad (1)$$

Where α and β are experimental constants. The modified energy function exploiting wavelet coefficients are obtained by

$$\partial(I(m,n)) = |\frac{\partial}{\partial x}I(m,n)| + |\frac{\partial}{\partial y}I(m,n)| + \sum_{l=1}^{L}\Phi_I(m,n)\cdot \qquad (2)$$

Experimental results shows [4] this method can achieve higher subjective image quality than existing methods including cropping, scaling, and conventional seam carving.

4   Wavelet Decomposition

A wavelet is a wave-like oscillation with amplitude that starts out at zero, increases, and then decreases back to zero. It can typically be visualized as a "brief oscillation" like one might see recorded by a seismograph or heart monitor. Wavelets can be implemented using a "shift, multiply and sum" technique called convolution. A wavelet transform is the representation of a function by wavelets. The wavelets are scaled and translated copies of a finite-length or fast decaying oscillating waveform. In the proposed technique, the energy function of the pixels is initially determined using the wavelet matrix, which are standard matrices available, through the process of convolution. Next the convoluted image is converted into an energy function. This is done in order to convert an image into a gray scale. After this, each pixel's energy is calculated and they are sorted in ascending order. The lowest eight connected pixel is taken and it is the lowest seam. For resizing, the lowest seam is added or removed to do the necessary resizing. Hence images are resized. The application of wavelets with reference to the quality of the image is described in [5] and [9]. The application of wavelet characteristics in neural networks in described in [2]. The main basic formula is the wavelet matrix and its value is given as follows. The vertical matrix is given as

$$\begin{vmatrix} 1 & 0 & -1 \\ 2 & 0 & -2 \\ 1 & 0 & -1 \end{vmatrix} \quad \text{similarly for horizontal matrix, the values are} \quad \begin{vmatrix} 1 & 2 & 1 \\ 0 & 0 & 0 \\ -1 & -2 & -1 \end{vmatrix}$$

These two matrices are convoluted with the original image both horizontally and vertically to get energy function which is edge detected. This edge detected image serves as a base for enhanced seam carving since it outlines areas which are important and areas which are not so important, Hence the contents of the image can be clearly distinguished from the background. From here we can proceed with conventional seam carving method i.e, to find out the seams and from there to find out the optimal seams and remove them to resize the original image. Then, according to the choice made by the server from vertical and horizontal seams, the optical seam is determined. The operation of the proposed system, enhanced seam carving technique is given in Fig 2.

Wavelet based transformation method decomposes images recursively at first which means decomposing the low frequency part of previous level. Let I_0 be a grayscale image decomposed by wavelet, and then the first level decomposition will be

$$I_0 = I_{LL1} + I_{LH1} + I_{HL1} + I_{HH1} \tag{3}$$

I_{LL1} represents the base image named Approximation- Low frequency parts. $I_{LH1}, I_{HL1}, I_{HH1}$ represents high frequency parts named Details. They represent Vertical, Horizontal and Diagonal Details. The base image named Approximations I_{LL1} will be decomposed at the second level. After first level decomposition, the second level decomposition will be

$$I_{LL1} = I_{LL2} + I_{LH2} + I_{HL2} + I_{HH2} \tag{4}$$

Recursively, n^{th} level decomposition will be

$$I_{LL(n-1)i} = I_{LLn} + I_{LHn} + I_{HLn} + I_{HHn} \quad n = 1,2,3... \tag{5}$$

So the nth decomposition will comprise 3n+1 sub-image sequences. Then the 3n+1 sub-sequences of nth level are fused applying different rules on low and high frequency parts. Finally inverse transformation will be taken to restore fused image, which will possess better quality. The entire process taking place in the pixels of the image is pictorially described in Fig 3.

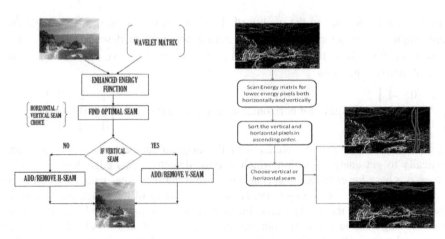

Fig. 2. Operation of the proposed system   **Fig. 3.** Seam carving process

5   Enhanced Energy Function

The proposed resizing method uses wavelet decomposition technique to provide improved results. The wavelet decomposition has two merits. The former is that the wavelet transforms decompose an image into different frequency sub bands, which is similar to the way the human visual system operates. The latter is that the scale space representation of wavelet transforms is so effective to represent image signals that they are widely used in the segmentation and classification of images.   In the proposed method, let I be an N X M images, we calculate the Enhanced Energy Function of the image using the formula

$$e\ (I\ (m,n)) = |\partial/\ \partial x\ I\ (m,n)| + |\partial/\ \partial y\ I\ (m,n)| \tag{6}$$

The Horizontal seam is defined as

$$S^{Y} = \left\{s_i^{\,y}\right\}_{i=1}^{N} = \left\{(y(i),i)\right\}_{i=1}^{N}, s.t. \forall \left| y(i) - y(i-1) \right| \le 1 \tag{7}$$

Where y is the mapping function such as $y:[1,\ldots M] \rightarrow [1,\ldots N]$.

Then optical seam in the Horizontal direction is selected from the seam in (7), which satisfies

$$S^{*} = \underset{S}{\arg\min}\ \sum_{i=1}^{N} e(I(s_i^{\,y})) \tag{8}$$

The vertical seam is obtained by same manner as (6)-(8).

6   Multicasting of Resized Images

In this section we discuss the basic architecture of authentication of users of multicast group, resizing of images and multicasting resized images in a hierarchical group communication. Let G be the set of all the members of group, we considered the group as a static group in which the members are constant. At the beginning of a multicast session, all users of the group G, has to join the group by providing multicast request and there credentials. All will be authenticated by the Authentication Server. In our implementation, authentication of users is done by using the Kerberos authentication protocol [6]. Once the authentication is completed, The requested images available in the Application Server will be sent to the members of the group G based on their request. Fig. 4, shows users with different screen size and resolution joined the group G. Before multicasting the images, based on the screen size and resolution of the user, images will be resized using enhanced seam carving technique. In order to identify the size and resolution of each user of the group G, application server will communicate the authentication server in which the information about all the users of the group G will be available including the screen size and resolution, which will be submitted to the Authentication Server during the authentication process. Application server then resizes the images based on the information provided by the authentication server. Thus the resized images will be multicast to the users. The topology of our implementation is shown in Fig. 4, which includes four homogenous networks and five multicast users. Application server is loaded with the enhanced seam carving technique and authentication server is implemented with Kerberos protocol for authentication.

7   Experimental Results

The performance of the proposed method was evaluated by testing several images. Test images are shrunken in the horizontal direction to compare the performance with the conventional seam carving and improved seam carving using a modified energy function based on wavelet decomposition [3]. Fig. 4 shows the comparison of image quality of each resizing method. Resized images will be multicast to various devices as shown in section VI, therefore resizing of images will be done by the application server based on the screen size and the resolution of the users of the multicast group. The information regarding the screen size and the resolution of the multicast users are stored in the database of application server. The quality of the image appears in the screen of the multicast users was improved.

(a)   (b)   (c)   (d)

Fig. 4. Example of test image (a) Original Image (b) Conventional seam carving (c) Result of improved seam carving [4] (d) Result of proposed method

Three metrics are used for comparing the performance of resizing algorithms. They are as follows. Quality Index (QI): Quality Index is high for a resizing strategy when the image does not lose its sharpness when it is enlarged [11]. Let $x = \{x_i \mid i = 1,2,...,N\}$ and $y = \{y_i \mid i = 1,2,...,N\}$ be the original and the test image signals, respectively. The proposed quality index is defined as [11].

$$Q = 4\sigma_{xy} \, x \, y \Big/ (\sigma_x^2 + \sigma_y^2)\left[(x)^2 + (y)^2\right] \tag{9}$$

$$x = 1/N \sum_{i=1}^{N} \overline{x_i} \quad , y = 1/N \sum_{i=1}^{N} \overline{y_i} \tag{10}$$

$$\sigma_x^2 = 1/N - 1\sum_{i=1}^{N}(x_i - \overline{x})^2 \quad \sigma_y^2 = 1/N - 1\sum_{i=1}^{N}(y_i - \overline{y})^2 \tag{11}$$

$$\sigma_{xy} = 1/N - 1\sum_{i=1}^{N}(x_i - \overline{x})(y_i - \overline{y}) \tag{12}$$

The dynamic range of Q is [-1,1]. The best value 1 is achieved if and only if $y_i = x_i$ for all i=1,2....N. This quality index models any distortions as a combination of three different factors. Loss of correlation, Mean distortion and Variance distortion. In order to understand this, we rewrite the definition of Q as a product of three components:

$$Q = \overline{\sigma_{xy}} / \sigma_x \sigma_y . 2xy/(x)^2 + (y)^2 . 2\sigma_x \sigma_y / \sigma_x^2 + \sigma_y^2 \tag{13}$$

The first component is the liner correlation coefficient between x and y, whose dynamic range is [-1,1]. The second component, with a value range of [0,1], measures how close the mean values are between x and y. It equals 1 if and only if x = y. The third component measures how similar the variances of the signal are. Its range of values is also [0, 1], where the best value 1 is achieved if and only if $\sigma_x = \sigma_y$.

Structured Similarity Index Metrics (SSIM): This involves measurement of image quality based on the initial uncompressed image [10]. It is calculated using the formula

$$SSIM = 4\sigma_{xy} x' y' / (\sigma x^2 + \sigma y^2)[x'^2 + y'^2]$$ (14)

$$MSSIM = 1/M\left(\sum SSIM(x_i, y_i)\right)$$ (15)

Where x' and y' are the reference images and σx and σy the images correlation coefficients. M is the number of local windows of the images.

Root Mean Square Error (RMSE): This is used to quantify the difference between an estimator and the true value of the quantity being estimated [11]. It is calculated using the formula

$$RMSE = \sqrt{\sum^m} \sum^n [I(i, j) - F(i, j)]^2 / N.M$$ (16)

Where i and j denotes the spatial position of pixels, M and N are the dimensions of the images. This is appropriate for a pair of images containing two resolutions.

8   Comparison Results

The table 1 portrays the efficiency of enhanced seam carving technique when the metrics QI, SSIM and RMSE are taken in to consideration. The QI value and SSIM value of the enhanced seam carving technique are high for seam carving technique compared to other resizing techniques, where as the RMSE is lower than other techniques. This proves that enhanced seam carving is more reliable than other methods. These values can be pragmatically estimated using MATLAB. From the above Table 1 a comparison graph is drawn below in Fig 5.

Table 1. Comparison Results

METHOD	QUALITY INDEX	SSIM	RMSE
E.SEAM	0.9904	0.6584	4.6401
UPSAMPLED	0.8374	0.4845	6.4091
CROPPING	0.7758	0.1522	7.3205

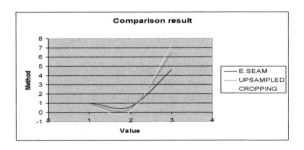

Fig. 5. Comparison of Enhance Seam Carving, Unsampled and Cropping

9   Conclusion

In this paper we have proposed a new approach for multicasting of images which are resized using enhanced seam carving technique, an effectual technique to resize multi-size images that utilizes wavelet decomposition technique. Experimental results show that the proposed method can achieve higher subjective image quality than the existing methods including resampling, cropping, scaling, and conventional seam carving. Current implementation includes only four homogenous networks and five multicast users, future work will focus on more number of users and heterogeneous networks with efficient rekeying approach for handling dynamic group of users, and also handling video and text data.

References

1. Hwang, D.-S., Chien, S.-Y.: Content-aware image resizing using perceptual seam carving with human attention model. In: Proceedings of IEEE International Conference on Multimedia and Expo., pp. 1029–1032 (August 2008)
2. Han, J.-W., Choi, K.-S., Wang, T.-S., Cheon, S.-H., Ko, S.-J.: Wavelet based seam carving for content-aware image resizing. In: Proceedings of 16th IEEE International Conference on Image Processing, pp. 345–348 (November 2009)
3. Conge, D.D., Kumar, M., Miller, R.L., Luo, J., Radha, H.: Improved seam carving for image resizing. In: Proceedings of IEEE Workshop on Signal Processing Systems, pp. 345–349 (October 2010)
4. Han, J.-W., Choi, K.-S., Wang, T.-S., Cheon, S.-H., Ko, S.-J.: Improved seam carving using a modified energy function based on wavelet decomposition. In: Proceedings of 13th IEEE International Symposium on Consumer Electronics, pp. 38–41 (May 2009)
5. Huang, K., Aviyente, S.: Wavelet feature selection for image classification. IEEE Transactions on Image Processing 17(9), 1709–1720 (2008)
6. Hu, D., Du, Z.: An improved Kerberos protocol based on fast RSA algorithm. In: Proceedings of IEEE International Conference on Information Theory and Information Security (ICITIS), pp. 274–278 (December 2010)
7. Leal, R.P., Martín, E.P., Cachinero, J.Á.: Internet TV Broadcast: What Next? In: Proceedings of IEEE International conference on Digital Telecommunications, pp. 71–74 (July 2009)
8. Avidan, S., Shamir, A.: Seam carving for content-aware image resizing. ACM Transactions on Graphics, 1–35 (July 2007)
9. Senthilkumar, S., Muttan, S.: Comparative Analysis on Remote Sensed Data Fusion. International Journal of Systemics, Cybermetics and Informatics (2009) ISSN 0973-4864
10. Wang, Z., Bovik, A.C.: A Universal Image Quality Index. IEEE Signal Processing Letters 9(3), 81–84 (2002)
11. Wang, Z., Bovik, A.C., Lu, L.: Why is Image Quality Assessment So Difficult? In: IEEE International Conference on Acoustics, Speech, & Signal Processing (May 2002)
12. Lu, Y., Li, X.: An Analytical Study of FairOM: A Fair Overlay Multicast Protocol for Internet-Scale Distributed Systems. In: Proceedings of IEEE International Workshop on Networking, Architecture and Storages, pp. 51–52 (August 2006)
13. Huang, K., Aviyente, S.: Wavelet feature selection for image classification. IEEE Transactions on Image Processing 17(9), 1707–1720 (2008)

A Relaxed Iterative Thresholding Reconstruction Algorithm Based on Compressed Sensing

Bingjie Li[*], Guangfei Li, Meng Ye, Mingfa Zheng, and Yuan Lv

School of Science, Air Force Engineering University, Xi'an, Shan xi, 710051
mingfazheng@126.com, leegf@sina.cn, mingfa103@163.com

Abstract. Based on the iterative hard thresholding (IHT) algorithm, this paper presents the relaxed iterative thresholding algorithm which is a modified algorithm of the conventional IHT algorithm. By introducing the relaxed factors, modifying the iterative formulae and proposing the relaxed algorithm correspondingly, we acquired the least number of iterations and error estimate required by the measurement matrices of satisfying the RIP. Compared with the IHT algorithm, the method presented in this paper not only has the advantages of keeping linear stability and clearly delimiting the upper limit of the number of iterations, but also obtains the same computational precision with the less number of iterations which saves the labor of calculation. Finally, taking the Hadamard orthogonal basis as sparse basis, the random Gaussian matrix as measurement matrix, we have verified the validity of the algorithm proposed above by experimental simulation.

Keywords: compressed sensing, measurement matrix, reconstruction algorithm, iterative hard thresholding algorithm.

1 Introduction

Many methods used for sparse reconstruction have been put forward. For example, Basis Pursuit Denoising (BPD) algorithm proposed for convex problem [1], Compressed Sensing Matching Pursuit (COSAMP) algorithm [2], Subspace Pursuit (SP) algorithm [3] and Iterative Hard Thresholding (IST/IHT) algorithm [4] and so on. These algorithms which have been improved on direction of search and output, offer the iterative rule and the terminate rule clearly and improve the precision of reconstruction. Compared with the BPD,COSAMP and SP algorithm, the IHT algorithm not only can be carried out under the same conditions of these algorithms, but also has the advantages of keeping linear stability and clearly delimiting the upper limit of the iterative times. Inspired by these before-mentioned literatures, this paper presents the relaxed iterative thresholding algorithm used for the sparse reconstruction problem in compressed sensing, which obtains the same computational precision with the less iterative times and plays down the complexity of calculation.

---

[*] Air Force Engineering University, Professor; Research field: Operations Research and Control Theory.

J. Lei et al. (Eds.): NCIS 2012, CCIS 345, pp. 259–267, 2012.
© Springer-Verlag Berlin Heidelberg 2012

2   Some Effective Reconstruction Algorithms

Compressed sensing is an emerging signal acquisition technique that enables signals to be sampled well below the Nyquist rate. We can assume a model as follow.

A signal f from an N dimensional Hilbert space is to be sampled. This is done by using M linear measurements $\{\langle f, \phi_n \rangle\}_n$, where $\langle f, \phi_n \rangle = \phi_n^T f$ is the scalar product and $\{\phi_n\}$ is a set of N dimensional vectors from the Hilbert space under consideration. Let X be the vector of elements x_i such that $f = \sum_{i=1}^{N} \psi_i x_i$ for some orthonormal basis ψ_i of the signal space. As f and x are equivalent, we will from now on assume that X is the signal. Let $\Theta \in R^{M \times N}$ be the matrix with entries $\langle \psi_i, \phi_j \rangle$ and let e be observation noise , so that the observation can be written as [11]

$$Y = \Theta X + e \tag{1}$$

It is underdetermined to resolve the problem of recovering X from Y because of $M < N$. To overcome this problem, we can assume X to be an exact K- sparse vector, i.e. a vector with not more than K non-zero entries, where $K < M$. So that the problem of recovering X can be translated as the following optimization problem

$$\min_{X : \|X\|_0 \leq K} \|Y - \Theta X\|_2 \tag{2}$$

Therefore, we are going to find that vector from all vectors X with no more than K non-zero elements, which minimizes the form $\|y - \Theta X\|_2$.

Generally speaking, problem (2) is an NP-HARD optimization problem. When the observation matrix Θ satisfies some conditions, this NP-HARD problem in the l_0 -norm can translate into an optimization to problem in the l_1 -norm.

$$\min \|\Theta X\|_1 \quad s.t. \quad Y = \Theta X$$

Only when the matrix Θ satisfies the Restricted Isometry Property (RIP), there exists a restricted isometry constant δ_K for which the following inequalities hold

$$(1 - \delta_k) \|X\|_2^2 \leq \|\hat{\Theta} X\|_2^2 \leq (1 + \delta_k) \|X\|_2^2 \tag{3}$$

for all vectors X with no more than K non-zero elements., where $\delta_K > 0$.

To analyse expediently, we introduce $\Theta = \dfrac{\hat{\Theta}}{1 + \delta_k}$ based on a re-scaled matrix, which satisfies the following asymmetric isometry property

$$(1 - \beta_K) \|X\|_2^2 \leq \|\Theta X\|_2^2 \leq \|X\|_2^2 \tag{4}$$

for all K -sparse X , where $\beta_K = 1 - \dfrac{1 - \delta_K}{1 + \delta_K}$.

$$\left\| \Theta X \right\|_2 \le \left\| X \right\|_2 + \frac{1}{\sqrt{K}} \left\| X \right\|_1 \tag{5}$$

The foundation of compressed sensing is that the signal X can be well approximated by a K-sparse vector. If We let X_k stand for the best K-term approximation to the vector X, then

Lemma 1. [2] Supposed we have a matrix Θ that satisfies the inequality $\left\| \Theta X_K \right\|_2 \le \left\| X_K \right\|_2$ for all K-sparse vectors. For such a matrix and for all vectors X, the following inequality holds

$$\left\| \Theta X \right\|_2 \le \left\| X \right\|_2 + \frac{1}{\sqrt{K}} \left\| X \right\|_1 \tag{6}$$

Lemma 2. [2] Given any vector X, consider the best K-term approximation to X, denoted by X_k. Define the error between X_k and X as $X_r = X - X_k$ and the error term $\tilde{e} = \Theta X_r + e$, such that $y = \Phi X + e = \Phi X_k + \tilde{e}$

When Θ satisfies RIP for sparsity K, then the norm of the error $\tilde{e}$ can be bounded by

$$\left\| \tilde{e} \right\|_2 \le \left\| X - X_K \right\|_2 + \frac{1}{\sqrt{K}} \left\| X - X_K \right\|_1 + \left\| e \right\|_2 \tag{7}$$

When Θ has a restricted isometry constant of $\delta_{2K} < 0.2$, the solution $X^* = \min_X \left\| X \right\|_1$ s.t $\left\| y - \Theta X \right\|_2 \le \varepsilon$ to the convex BPDN optimization problem obeys[5]

$$\left\| X^* - X \right\|_2 \le 8.5 \left[\frac{\left\| X - X_K \right\|_1}{\sqrt{K}} + \left\| e \right\|_2 \right] \tag{8}$$

The COSAMP arithmetic has the similar property to the SP arithmetic. If Θ has a restricted isometry constant of $\delta_{4k} \le 0.1$, then, after at most $6(K+1)$ iterations, COSAMP arithmetic would produce an approximation X^* that satisfies[2]

$$\left\| X^* - X \right\|_2 \le 20 \left[\left\| X - X_K \right\|_2 \right] + \frac{\left\| X - X_K \right\|_1}{\sqrt{K}} + \left\| e \right\|_2 \tag{9}$$

The Iterative Hard Thresholding algorithm (IHT) is the following iterative procedure. Let $X^{[0]} = 0$ and use the iteration[8]

$$X^{[n+1]} = H_K (X^{[n]} + \Theta^T (y - \Theta X^{[n]})) \tag{10}$$

where $H_k(X)$ is the non-linear operator that sets all but the largest K elements of X to zero. If such a set does not exit, a set can be selected either randomly or based on a predefined ordering of the elements. This algorithm not only has similar performance guarantees to Basis Pursuit De-Noising and CoSaMP, but also has the linearity stability property and need not calculate the reverse of matrix.

3   Relaxed Iterative Thresholding Reconstruction Algorithm

Let Θ_K be the sub-matrix of Θ and Θ_K contains only those columns maked up of the K largest coefficients in X. So that the best K-term approximation to X can be written as $\Theta_K^\dagger y$, where the "$\dagger$" signifies the Moor-penrose. By the lemma 1, the error estimate would be[2]

$$\left\| X - \Theta_K^\dagger y \right\|_2 \le \left(1 + \frac{1}{\sqrt{1-\beta_K}} \right) \left\| X - X_K \right\|_2 + \frac{1}{\sqrt{1-\beta_K}} \frac{\left\| X - X_K \right\|_1}{\sqrt{K}} + \frac{1}{\sqrt{1-\beta_K}} \left\| e \right\|_2 \quad (11)$$

let $r^{[n]} = X_K - X^{[n]}$,

$a^{[n+1]} = X^{[n]} + \Theta^T (y - \Theta X^{[n]}) = X^{[n]} + \Theta^T (\Theta X_K + \tilde{e} - \Theta X^{[n]})$,

$y^{[n+1]} = H_K(a^{[n+1]}), \quad \Gamma_K^* = \sup\{X_K\}$,

$\Gamma^n = \sup\{X^{[n]}\}, \quad B^{n+1} = \Gamma_K^* \cup \Gamma^{n+1}$

Actually, Γ_K^* is the set we are trying to identify, which with elements of the non-zero elements in the best K term approximation to X. Γ^n is the set associated with the K non-zero elements in iteration n and finally, B^n is the union of these two sets.

For all the sets Γ with $K = |\Gamma|$, based on the RIP of Θ we have the bounds[6]

$$\left\| \Theta_\Gamma^T y \right\|_2 \le \left\| y \right\|_2 \quad (12)$$

$$(1 - \beta_{|\Gamma|}) \left\| X_\Gamma \right\|_2 \le \left\| \Theta_\Gamma^T \Theta_\Gamma X_\Gamma \right\|_2 \le \left\| X_\Gamma \right\|_2 \quad (13)$$

Where Θ_Γ and X_Γ separately stand for the sub-matrices and sub-vectors of Θ, that's to say, the notation Θ_Γ and X_Γ contain only those columns with indices in the set Γ.

Lemma 3. [2, 7] If a matrix Θ satisfies RIP for sparsity K, then for all sets Γ with $|\Gamma| = K$ we have the bound

$$\left\| (I - \Theta_\Gamma^T \Theta_\Gamma) X_\Gamma \right\|_2 \le \beta_K \left\| X_\Gamma \right\|_2 \quad (14)$$

Lemma 4. [2, 8] If a matrix Θ satisfies RIP for sparsity K, then for any two disjoint sets Γ and Λ (i.e. $\Gamma \cap \Lambda = \varnothing$) for which $|\Gamma \cup \Lambda| = K$ we have the following inequality

$$\left\| \Theta_\Gamma^T \Theta_\Lambda X_\Lambda \right\|_2 \le \beta_K \left\| X_\Lambda \right\|_2 \quad (15)$$

The relaxed iterative thresholding reconstruction algorithm is the following iterative procedure. Let $X^{[0]} = 0$ and use the iteration

$$X^{[n+1]} = H_K(X^{[n]} + \varpi \, \Theta^T (y - \Theta X^{[n]})) \quad (16)$$

where relaxed factors $\varpi > 1$.

Theorem 1. Let X be any arbitrary vector, which is observed through a linear measurement system Θ that satisfies the restricted isometry property with $\beta_{3K} < 1/\sqrt{32}$. Given the noisy observation $y = \Theta X + e$, then after at most

$$\left\lceil \log_2\left(\frac{C\|X_K\|_2}{\|X - X_K\|_2 + \|X - X_K\|_1/\sqrt{K} + \|e\|_2} \right) \right\rceil \tag{17}$$

iterations, the relaxed iterative thresholding reconstruction algorithm calculates an approximate X^* that satisfies

$$\|X^* - X\|_2 \leq 7\left[\|X - X_K\|_2 + \frac{\|X - X_K\|_1}{\sqrt{K}} + \|e\|_2 \right] \tag{18}$$

where X_k is the best K-term approximation to X.

Proof. We should make the error satisfie the following inequation

$$\|X - X^{[n+1]}\|_2 \leq \|X - X_K\|_2 + \|X_K - X^{[n+1]}\|_2.$$

We now bound the right hand term using the triangle inequality

$$\|X_K - X^{[n+1]}\|_2 \leq \|X_{K,B^{n+1}} - a^{[n+1]}_{B^{n+1}}\|_2 + \|X^{[n+1]}_{B^{n+1}} - a^{[n+1]}_{B^{n+1}}\|_2$$

As showed in the above inequation, the error $X_K - X^{[n+1]}$ is supported on the set $B^{n+1} = \Gamma^*_K \cup \Gamma^{n+1}$. Furthermore, compared with X_K, $X^{[n+1]}$ is a better K-term approximation to $a^{[n+1]}_{B^{n+1}}$ so that $\|X^{[n+1]} - a^{[n+1]}_{B^{n+1}}\|_2 \leq \|X_K - a^{[n+1]}_{B^{n+1}}\|_2$. Therefore, we have

$$\|X_K - X^{[n+1]}\|_2 \leq 2\|X_{K,B^{n+1}} - a^{[n+1]}_{B^{n+1}}\|_2 \tag{19}$$

Thus the following inequation can be find from $a^{[n+1]}_{B^{n+1}}$

$$\|X_K - X^{[n+1]}\|_2 \leq 2\|X_{K,B^{n+1}} - X^{[n]}_{B^{n+1}} - \varpi\Theta^T_{B^{n+1}}\Theta r^{[n]} - \varpi\Theta^T_{B^{n+1}}\tilde{e}\|_2$$

$$\leq 2\|r^{[n]}_{B^{n+1}} - \varpi\Theta^T_{B^{n+1}}\Theta r^{[n]}\|_2 + 2\varpi\|\Theta^T_{B^{n+1}}\tilde{e}\|_2$$

$$= 2\|(I - \varpi\Theta^T_{B^{n+1}}\Theta_{B^{n+1}})r^{[n]}_{B^{n+1}} - \varpi\Theta^T_{B^{n+1}}\Theta_{B^n\backslash B^{n+1}}r^{[n]}_{B^n\backslash B^{n+1}}\|_2 + 2\varpi\|\Theta^T_{B^{n+1}}\tilde{e}\|_2$$

$$\leq 2\|(I - \varpi\Theta^T_{B^{n+1}}\Theta_{B^{n+1}})r^{[n]}_{B^{n+1}}\|_2 + 2\varpi\|\Theta^T_{B^{n+1}}\Theta_{B^n\backslash B^{n+1}}r^{[n]}_{B^n\backslash B^{n+1}}\|_2 + 2\varpi\|\Theta^T_{B^{n+1}}\tilde{e}\|_2$$

When the set $B^n\backslash B^{n+1}$ is disjoint from B^{n+1} and as $|B^n \cup B^{n+1}| \leq 3K$, we can make use of (4)、(12)、(14) and (15) and the fact that $\beta_{2K} \leq \beta_{3K}$

$$\left\|X_K - X^{[n+1]}\right\|_2 \le 2C\beta_{2K}\left\|r_{B^{n+1}}^{[n]}\right\|_2 + 2\varpi\beta_{3K}\left\|r_{B^n\setminus B^{n+1}}^{[n]}\right\|_2 + 2\varpi\|\tilde{e}\|_2 \le 2C\beta_{3K}\left(\left\|r_{B^{n+1}}^{[n]}\right\|_2 + \left\|r_{B^n\setminus B^{n+1}}^{[n]}\right\|_2\right) + 2\varpi\|\tilde{e}\|_2$$

Where $0 < C < 1$. Because $r_{B^{n+1}}^{[n]}$ and $r_{B^n\setminus B^{n+1}}^{[n]}$ are orthogonal , suggested by lemma 5 we can know that $\left\|X_K - X^{[n+1]}\right\|_2 \le 2\sqrt{2}C\beta_{3K}\left\|r^{[n]}\right\|_2 + 2\varpi\|\tilde{e}\|_2$

If we choose $\beta_{3K} < \dfrac{1}{\sqrt{32}}$, we have the bound

$$\left\|X_K - X^{[n+1]}\right\|_2 = \left\|r^{[n+1]}\right\|_2 < \frac{1}{2}C\left\|r^{[n]}\right\|_2 + 2\varpi\|\tilde{e}\|_2$$

so that $\left\|X_K - X^{[K]}\right\|_2 < 2^{-K}C\|X_K\|_2 + 4\varpi\|\tilde{e}\|_2$

and

$$\left\|X_K - X^{[n+1]}\right\|_2 \le 2^{-K}C\|X_K\|_2 + C\|(X - X_K)\|_2 + 4\varpi\|\tilde{e}\|_2$$

$$\le 2^{-K}C\|X_K\|_2 + (C + 4\varpi)\|(X - X_K)\|_2 + 4\frac{1}{\sqrt{K}}\varpi\|(X - X_K)\|_1 + 4\varpi\|e\|_2$$

Therefore, it assures that the error can be below any multiple c of $\|(X - X_K)\|_2 + \|(X - X_K)\|_1/\sqrt{K} + \|e\|_2$, as long as $c > C + 4\varpi$. For example, c =7 implies that we require that

$$2^{-K}C\|X_K\|_2 \le \|(X - X_K)\|_2 + \|(X - X_K)\|_1/\sqrt{K} + \|e\|_2$$

$$\Rightarrow 2^K \ge \frac{C\|X_K\|_2}{\|(X - X_K)\|_2 + \|(X - X_K)\|_1/\sqrt{K} + \|e\|_2} \Rightarrow 2^K \ge \frac{C\|X_K\|_2}{\|(X - X_K)\|_2 + \|(X - X_K)\|_1/\sqrt{K} + \|e\|_2}$$

$$\Rightarrow K \ge \left\lceil \log_2\left(\frac{C\|X_K\|_2}{\|X - X_K\|_2 + \|X - X_K\|_1/\sqrt{K} + \|e\|_2}\right)\right\rceil$$

i.e. that $\|X^* - X\|_2 \le 7\left[\|X - X_K\|_2 + \dfrac{\|X - X_K\|_1}{\sqrt{K}} + \|e\|_2\right]$

Then after at most $\left\lceil\log_2\left(\dfrac{C\|X_K\|_2}{\|X - X_K\|_2 + \|X - X_K\|_1/\sqrt{K} + \|e\|_2}\right)\right\rceil$ iterations, the

relaxed iterative thresholding reconstruction algorithm calculates an approximate X^* that satisfies $\|X^* - X\|_2 \le 7\left[\|X - X_K\|_2 + \dfrac{\|X - X_K\|_1}{\sqrt{K}} + \|e\|_2\right]$

Which completes the proof.

The upper limit of iterations is $\left\lceil \log_2 \left(\dfrac{\|X_K\|_2}{\|X - X_K\|_2 + \|X - X_K\|_1 / \sqrt{K} + \|e\|_2} \right) \right\rceil$ via

the IHT algorithm. By all appearances, the relaxed iterative thresholding reconstruction algorithm with the same rank of error estimate as the IHT algorithm requires fewer iterations than it because of $0 < C < 1$.

4   Example

Given a sparse signal X based on Hadamard orthogonal basis Ψ, the sparsity projection of signal X is s and the sparsity degree $K = 10$ (see in Fig.1,2).Let Gauss matrix as the measurement system $\tilde{\Phi}$ [9,10], where

$$\tilde{\Phi} \in R^{M \times N}, \tilde{\Phi}(i, j) = \frac{1}{\sqrt{M}} \phi_{ij}, \phi_{ij} \in N(0,1), \quad M = 8K, N = 256.$$

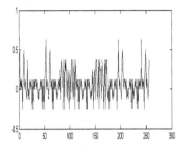
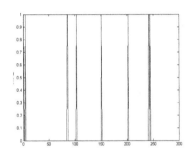

Fig. 1. Raw signal X   **Fig. 2.** Sparsity projection s

Via the iterative rule, let $\varpi = 3/2$, $s_{n+1} = H_K(s_n + \dfrac{3}{2}(A^{CS})^T(y - A^{CS}s_n))$, $s_0 = 0$

and end the iteration when $\|s_{n+1} - s_n\| \le 10^{-20}$, where $A^{CS} = \tilde{\Phi}\Psi$, $y = A^{CS}s$.

The matrix A^{CS} satisfies the restricted isometry property with $\delta_{10} \ge 0.9971$ via (2). Through   simulated experiment with the Matlab language, we can get the sparse projection of raw signal and reconstructed signal (see in Fig.3) with $M = 8K$.

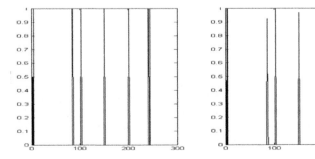

Fig. 3. The sparse projection of raw signal and reconstructed signal

We can get the reconstructed signal as follows(see in Fig.4),

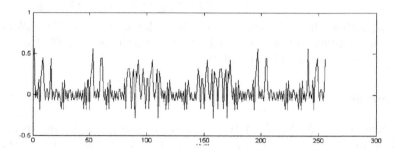

Fig. 4. The reconstructed signal

Defined $\|\hat{s} - s\|_2^2 / \|s\|_2^2$ as the relative error. After more simulated experiments, the reconstructed precision is 0.1058 with $M = 8K$, 0.1129 with $M = 10K$ and 0.1126 with $M = 128$,so that the reconstructed precision locates between 0.1 and 0.2 and is enough high.

5   Conclusions

This paper researchs the relaxed iterative thresholding algorithm whose main characteristic is faster constringency rate via introducing the relaxed factors.Under similar conditions on the restricted isometry constant, compared with the normal IHT,BPDN and COSAMP, the relaxed iterative thresholding algorithm requires fewer iterative times and obtains the appropriate calculated precision. In particular, all algorithms are guaranteed to recover a vector X from noisy measurements $y = \Phi X + e$ with similar error guarantees.

Acknowledgements. This work was financially supported by the Shanxi Province Science Foundations (SJ08A02).

References

1. Donoho, D.L.: Compressed Sensing. J. IEEE Trans. Information Theory 52, 1289–1306 (2006)
2. Needell, D., Tropp, J.: COSAMP: Iterative Signal Recovery From Complete and Inaccurate Samples. J. Appl. Comp. Harmonic Anal. 26, 301–321 (2009)
3. Dai, W., Milenkovic, O.: Subspace Pursuit for Compressive Sensing Signal Reconstruction. In: 2008 5th International Symposium on Turbo Codes and Related Topics, TURBOCODING, Lausanne, Switzerland, pp. 402–407 (2008)
4. Pope, G.: Compressive Sensing: a Summary of Reconstruction Algorithms. Eidgenössische Technische Hochschule, Zürich (2008)

5. Candes, E.: The Restricted Isometry Property and Its Implications for Compressed Sensing. J. Compte Rendus de l'Academiedes Sciences 346, 589–592 (2008)
6. Blumensath, T., Davies, M.E.: Iterative Thresholding for Sparse Approximationsl. J. Fourier Anal. Appl. 14, 629–654 (2008)
7. Blumensath, T., Davies, M.E.: Iterative Hard Thresholding for Compressed Sensing. J. Appl. Comp. Harmonic Anal. 27, 265–274 (2009)
8. Blumensath, T., Davies, M.E.: A Simple, Efficient and Near Optimal Algorithm for Compressed Sensing. In: Proceedings of the Int. Conf. on Acoustics, Speech and Signal Processing, pp. 3357–3360 (2009)
9. Raginsky, M., Willett, R.M.: Compressed Sensing Performance Bounds under Poisson Noise. J. IEEE Transactions on Signal Processing 58, 3990–4002 (2009)
10. Blanchard, J.D., Cartis, C., Tanner, J.: Decay Properties of Restricted Isometry Constants. J. IEEE Signal Processing 16, 572–575 (2009)
11. Blumensath, T., Davies, M.E.: Sampling Theorems for Signals from the Union of Finite-Dimensional Linear Subspaces. Submitted to IEEE Transactions on Information Theory (2008)

Multi-granule Association Rule Mining Based on Quantitative Concept Lattice

Dexing Wang, Qian Xie, Dongmei Huang, Hongchun Yuan, Hongyan Lu, and Jielong Xu

College of Information Technology, Shanghai Ocean University,
Shanghai 201306, China
{dxwang,dmhuang,hcyuan}@shou.edu.cn, Akaich2000@163.com

Abstract. It is important to mine different granule knowledge because high-level and more generational information is getting more interesting for users in knowledge discovery. As the main data reduction method, attribute-oriented induction (AOI) generally takes the simply statistical information from original databases into account, and it can only mine the knowledge with single attribute. However, in Hasse diagram of quantitative concept lattice, the generalization and specialization relationships between concepts can be expressed clearly, so it is easy to find attributes with the same cardinality in relational databases, as well as the appropriate thresholds. Association rule mining algorithm based on quantitative concept lattice can extract multi-granule knowledge in the multi-level and multi-attribute way. Therefore, different granule knowledge can be easily focused, and then the relationships of transforms between different granule knowledge can be discovered rapidly.

Keywords: Quantitative Concept Lattice, Multi-granule, Association Rule Mining, Knowledge Discovery.

1 Introduction

The scale of data shows an increasing trend in knowledge discovery. What people interested is the high-level and more generational information in the practical application of large-scale data, so it is very important to mine different granule knowledge. As an important method of knowledge discovery, data reduction is to focus different granule knowledge and discover the relationships of transforms between them. The typical data reduction method is AOI (attribute oriented induction) algorithm [1], and then LCHRL (learn characteristic rule) algorithm [2] was further proposed on the basis of AOI. Algorithms of GDBR (generalize database relation) [3] and FIGR (fast incremental generalization and re-generalization) [4] were proposed to improve the efficiency of the former two algorithms. In [5, 6], a dynamic programming algorithm based on AOI and a modified AOI algorithm combined with a simplified Boolean bit Karnaugh map were proposed respectively, and they both corrected the deficiencies of AOI.

J. Lei et al. (Eds.): NCIS 2012, CCIS 345, pp. 268–274, 2012.
© Springer-Verlag Berlin Heidelberg 2012

According to relevant domain knowledge [7, 9], AOI algorithm constructs its concept hierarchy tree, in which the concept level is expressed by single attribute, and there is only one generalization path from bottom to top for each attribute value, so these characters limit the ability of AOI algorithm on knowledge discovery, specific as follows: (1) For the threshold is difficult to set appropriately, the attribute induction results are always hard to meet users requirements. In particular, its results can not reach the appropriate concept level, on the one hand, the induction level may be too high to find useful information, on the other hand, it may be too low to reduce the data complexity; (2) These algorithms can not express the multi-level and multi-attribute relationships between attributes in the relational database, even if they can, the results will be very complex.

As a powerful tool of data analysis, concept lattice [8] has been widely used in knowledge discovery and data mining. Each node is called a concept, in which the extent represents all the object sets, and the intent represents attribute sets belonging to all the object sets. Concept lattice describes the relationship between objects and attributes, and with the Hasse diagram, it also clearly shows that the generalization and specialization relationship between concepts, so knowledge visualization is easy to realize. Quantitative concept lattice introduces equivalence relations into the intents of concept lattice, and it is built by quantifying the extents of concept lattice, so it contains all of the extent information.

This paper presents a novel multi-granule association rule mining method, that is the multi-granule association rule mining based on quantitative concept lattice. Compared with the AOI method, in Hasse diagram of quantitative concept lattice, we can clearly find the cardinality of the same attribute, as well as the appropriate thresholds users required. Quantitative concept lattice is a generalization-specialization relations hierarchical structure, and thus the final association rules are multi-level. Besides, its association rule mining involves more than one attribute, therefore the rules are multi-attribute.

For the association rules mining with multi-level and multi-attribute, it is very difficult to find strong association rules in the low-level data due to the sparsity of spatial data. While the strong association rules mined from the high-level concepts can finally provide knowledge users needed. Therefore, multi-level and multi-attribute association rule mining based on quantitative concept lattice is the multi-granule association rule mining.

2 Quantitative Concept Lattice

The detail description about concept lattice can be found in [8, 9, 10], here we only give some necessary basic notions of quantitative concept lattice.

Definition 1. *A context is defined as a triple $K=(O, D, R)$, where O is a set of objects, D is a set of attributes, and R is the binary relation between O and D, according to the inclusion relations between extents and intents, there is an unique ordered set that describes the structure of inherent lattice, which defines natural groupings and* *relationship descriptions between the objects and their attributes in the context, this structure is also known as (Galois) Concept Lattice (for short, CL).*

Definition 2. *Each pair such as (A, B) derived from the context is called a concept, where $A \in P(O)$, $B \in P(D)$, and $P(O)$, $P(D)$ are the power sets of O and D respectively, A and B create a connection in terms of the following properties: $A' = \{m \in D | \forall g \in A, gRm\}$, $B' = \{g \in O | \forall g \in B, gRm\}$, Where $A' = B$, $B' = A$, A is called the extent of concept, and B is called the intent, denoted as Extent(C) and Intent (C) respectively.*

Definition 3. *In a CL, partial order relation "<" between concept $C_1 = (A_1, B_1)$ and $C_2 = (A_2, B_2)$ is defined as $C_1 < C_2 \Leftrightarrow B_2 \subseteq B_1$, then C_1 is the sub-concept (son) of C_2, and C_2 is the sup-concept (father) of C_1, that is, the relation between C_2 and C_1 is the relation as that of father and son.*

If $C_1 < C_2$, there exists no a concept C = (A, B), such that satisfies $C_1 < C < C_2$, $C_1 < C_2$ is called a direct-sub-concept-direct-sup-concept-relation between C_1 and C_2, the Hasse diagram of concept lattice is generated according to the partial order relation: If $C_1 < C_2$ is a direct-sub-concept-direct-sup-concept, there exists an edge from C_2 to C_1.

Definition 4. *We call $C' = (|A|, B)$ is the quantitative concept of C = (A, B), and |A| is the cardinality of A. The lattice constituted by quantitative concepts is defined as Quantitative Concept Lattice (QCL).*

Quantitative concept lattice is just to quantify extents of concepts, and change representation forms of the extents. It can not change the structure of concept lattice, so it still applies to all the properties of concept lattice.

3   Multi-granule Association Rule Mining Algorithm Based on Quantitative Concept Lattice

3.1   Theorems and Algorithm of Multi-granule Association Rule Mining

For the concept C = (A, B) in quantitative concept lattice, the support of intent B can be described as Support $(B) = |A|/|U|$, in which |A| is the cardinality of C, and |U| is the cardinality of the universal set. For concepts $C_1 = (A_1, B_1)$ and $C_2 = (A_2, B_2)$, if C_1 is the sup-concept of C_2, the confidence of rule $B_1 \Rightarrow B_2 - B_1$ can be described as Confidence $= |A_2|/|A_1|$.

Theorem 1. *In quantitative concept lattice, if node C = (A, B) exists with m sup-concept nodes, namely $C_1 = (A_1, B_1)$, $C_2 = (A_2, B_2)...C_m = (A_m, B_m)$, then the association rule $t \Rightarrow B-t$ can be deduced when it satisfied $t \in \{B-B_1 \bigcup B_2...B_m\}$.*

Theorem 2. *If node C = (A, B) exists with two sup-concept nodes, namely $C_1 = (A_1, B_1)$, $C_2 = (A_2, B_2)$, then the association rule $t_1 t_2 \Rightarrow B-t_1 t_2$ can be deduced when it satisfied $\exists t_1 \in \{B_1 - B_1 \bigcap B_2\}$ and $\exists t_2 \in \{B_2 - B_1 \bigcap B_2\}$.*

(1) *If concepts C_1 and C_2 satisfy $C_2 \in sup\ (C_1)$, we can get the rule: $B_2 \Rightarrow B_1 \text{-} B_2$, its confidence is A_1/A_2. Otherwise, $B_1 \text{-} B_2 \Rightarrow B_2$, and its confidence is 100%.*

(2) *If concepts C_1 and C_2 do not satisfy $C_2 \in sup\ (C_1)$, and there are nonempty common maximum-sub-concept $C= (A, B)$, namely $C \in (max\text{-}sub\text{-}concept\ (C_1) \wedge max\text{-}sub\text{-}concept\ (C_2)) \wedge C \neq \varnothing$. Then the association rules between B_1 and B_2 can be obtained, namely $B_1 \Rightarrow B\text{-}B_1$, $B_2 \Rightarrow B\text{-}B_2$, and their confidences are A/A_1, A/A_2 respectively.*

The following steps introduce the algorithm of multi-granule association rule mining based on quantitative concept lattice.

Step 1. (1) Input the relational database D. Data discretization is the first work through classification or clustering, and then mark them to identify the category. Then delete the attributes that can not be reduced, and finally transform relational database into the decision table. (2) Input the minimum support threshold and the minimum confidence threshold;

Step 2. Construct the corresponding quantitative concept lattice according to the construction algorithm [11].

Step 3. Beginning with the top concept node, make a breath-first traversal downward to search for concept nodes. According to the theorems 1 and 2, output the association rules that satisfy the minimum support threshold and minimum confidence threshold.

3.2   Comparison and Analysis of the Algorithms

The construction algorithm of concept lattice was put forward in [11], n is the number of attributes, and its time complexity is $O\ (2^n)$. In good situation, it is actually $O\ (n^2)$ or $O\ (n)$, and in normal situation the result is $O\ (n^3)$. Quantitative concept lattice is built by quantifying the concept extents, so its time complexity of construction corresponds to concept lattice.

The time complexity of LCHR algorithm is $O\ (n \log n)$ as is analyzed in [2], and the time complexity of AOI algorithm is $O\ (np)$, where n is the number of tuples in relational database, p is the number of binary relations. The time complexity of GDBR algorithm and FIGR algorithm are both $O\ (n)$, which is smaller than the LCHR algorithm, and their space cost are both $O\ (p)$.

Multi-attribute induction based on AOI algorithm will always be confronted with the combinatorial explosion problem, while extracting association rules by quantitative concept lattice can avoid this problem. The time complexity of association rule mining based on quantitative concept lattice is $O\ (n + e)$, in which n is the number of concept nodes, and e is the number of edges between nodes. Its only defect is the time cost on construction of quantitative concept lattice. However, for large-scale databases, time spent on constructing the quantitative concept lattice is certain, but not linear growth.

4   An Example and Multi-granule Association Rule Mining

Use the recruitment and employment information in talent market for the experimental data. Construct the talents information table as shown in Table 1, to select important attribute data, and assess the quality of graduates.

Table 1. Talents Information Table

number	name	age	native place	city	major	college	quality
1	n_1	a_1	t_1	t	m_1	c_1	q_1
2	n_2	a_2	b_1	b	m_2	c_2	q_1
3	n_3	a_3	b_2	b	m_1	c_2	q_2
4	n_4	a_4	b_2	t	m_2	c_2	q_1
5	n_5	a_5	b_2	b	m_1	c_1	q_2
6	n_6	a_6	b_1	b	m_1	c_2	q_1

Remove attributes that can not be inducted, such as *name* and *age*. Construct the quantitative concept lattice of talents information, its Hasse diagram is shown in Fig.1.

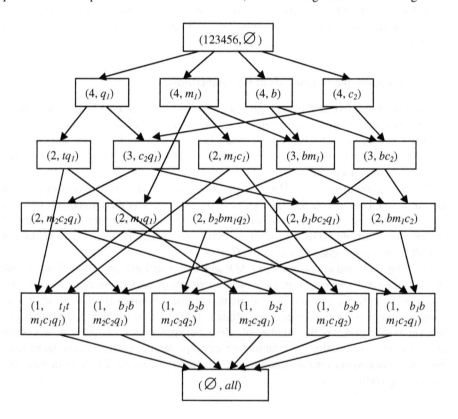

Fig. 1. Hasse diagram of quantitative concept lattice according to the talents information

In quantitative concept lattice, concepts $(2, b_2bm_1q_2)$ and $(2, b_1bc_2q_1)$ contain respectively the attributes b_1 and b_2, $b_1 \subset b$, $b_2 \subset b$, then attributes b_1 and b_2 can be inducted to b through generalization, namely the concept node $(4, b)$. For $b_2 \subset b$ in the line 4 of Table 1, the attribute of *city* becomes t but not b, so they are the cross-attributes. With the knowledge $\{b_1, b_2\} \subset \{b\}$, the AOI algorithm does not allow the cross-attributes to exist in the concept hierarchy tree. If the attribute $\{city\}$ is removed, we can only merge the records $\{2, 4\}$, and thus AOI algorithm can not realize these attribute induction.

The AOI method is based on attribute induction of the same concept level, while in practical application, some attributes refer to higher levels (coarse granule), and some attributes refer to lower levels (fine granule), so the knowledge included in these attributes is users needed. In Hasse diagram of quantitative concept lattice, different granule knowledge can be obtained visually. For example, concept $(4, b)$ is a coarse granule, and the fine granules including $(3, bm_1)$, $(3, bc_2)$ and $(2, bm_1c_2)$ can be obtained by specialization downward. Similarly, we can also get the coarse granules $(3, bm_1)$, $(3, bc_2)$ and $(4, b)$ by the generalization of concept $(2, bm_1c_2)$, and the rules of different granule users interested will be further extracted.

Association rule mining based on quantitative concept lattice is multi-level and multi-attribute, and supports and confidences of rules can be calculated directly from the extents of relative concept nodes. For concepts $(4, b)$, $(3, bm_1)$ and $(2, b_2bm_1q_2)$, there are the sub-concept-sup-concept relationships. According to the association rule mining algorithm based on quantitative concept lattice, we can get the association rules: $b \Rightarrow m_1$, $b \Rightarrow b_2m_1q_2$, $bm_1 \Rightarrow b_2q_2$, their supports from left to right are 3/6, 2/6, 2/6, and their confidences are 3/4, 2/4 and 2/3. Users can set the minimum support threshold and the minimum confidence threshold they needed, for example, 2/6 and 2/4, then we can output all the three rules.

For the association rule $b \Rightarrow m_1$, its support and confidence could be interpreted as: Support 3/6 shows that there are 3 individual living in city b, and majoring m_1 in 6 records. Confidence 3/4 shows that there are 3 individuals majoring m_1 in 4 individuals living in city b. Similarly, the support of association rule $bm_1 \Rightarrow b_2q_2$ is 2/6, which means two-sixths individuals living in city b, majoring m_1, with their native place b_2 and their quality of q_2. The confidence 2/3 also shows that for 3 individuals living in city b and majoring m_1, there are 2 individuals with their native place of b_2 and the quality of q_2. Thus the association rules extracted from quantitative concept lattice is multi-level, as well as multi-attribute, and the knowledge granule of rule $b \Rightarrow m_1$ is coarser than $bm_1 \Rightarrow b_2q_2$.

5   Conclusion

The association rule mining based on quantitative concept lattice can proceed in its Hasse diagram interactively. Compared with the knowledge discovery based on AOI algorithm, quantitative concept lattice is more vividly and concisely, so multiple relationships can be clearly expressed in the multi-level and multi-attribute way, and the transformation relationships between different granule knowledge can be further discovered. At the same time, we can also visually find attributes with the same cardinality. Support threshold and confidence threshold can be set as users needed, so multi-granule knowledge will be extracted easily.

Acknowledgement. This paper is supported by the national 973 program of China under grant No.2012CB316200 and the innovation program of shanghai municipal education commission under grant No. 12ZZ162.

References

1. Han, J., Cai, Y., Cercone, N.: Knowledge discovery in databases: An attribute-oriented approach. In: Proceedings of the18th VLDB Conference, Vancouver, British Columbia, Canada, pp. 547–559 (1992)
2. Han, J., Cai, Y., Cercone, N.: Data-driven discovery of quantitative rules in relation databases. IEEE Transactions on Knowledge and Data Engineering 5(1), 29–40 (1993)
3. Carter, C.L., Hamilton, H.J.: Performance evaluation of attribute-oriented algorithms for knowledge discovery from databases. In: Proceedings of 7th IEEE International Conference Tools with Artificial Intelligence, Washington, DC, pp. 486–489 (1995)
4. Carter, C.L., Hamilton, H.J.: Efficient attribute-oriented generalization for knowledge discovery from large databases. IEEE Transactions on Knowledge and Data Engineering 10(2), 193–208 (1998)
5. Chen, Y.L., Shen, C.C.: Mining generalized knowledge from ordered data through attribute-oriented induction techniques. European Journal of Operational Research 166(1), 221–245 (2005)
6. Huang, S.-M., Hsu, P.-Y., Wang, W.-C.: A Study on the Modified Attribute Oriented Induction Algorithm of Mining the Multi-value Attribute Data. In: Pan, J.-S., Chen, S.-M., Nguyen, N.T. (eds.) ACIIDS 2012, Part I. LNCS, vol. 7196, pp. 348–358. Springer, Heidelberg (2012)
7. Maggioni, L., Alexander, P.A.: Knowledge domains and domain learning. International Encyclopedia of Education, 255–264 (2010)
8. Wille, R.: Restructuring lattice theory: An approach based on hierarchies of concepts. In: Rival, I. (ed.) Ordered Sets, pp. 445–470. Reidel, Dordrecht (1982)
9. Wang, D.X., Hu, X.G., Liu, X.P., Wang, H.: Association rules mining on concept lattice using domain knowledge. In: IEEE Proceedings of the Fourth International Conference on Machine Learning and Cybernetics, Guangzhou, August 18-21, pp. 2151–2154 (2005)
10. Zhang, W.X., Ma, J.M., Fan, S.Q.: Variable threshold concept lattices. Information Sciences 177(22), 4883–4892 (2007)
11. Godin, R., Missaoui, R., Alcui, H.: Incremental concept formation algorithms based on Galois (concept) lattices. Computational Intelligence 11(2), 246–267 (1995)

Visual Scene Simulation to Civil Aviation Aircraft Approaching and Landing Using Dual Fuzzy Neural Network

Kaijun Xu

Department of Air Navigation, School of Flight Technology,
Civil Aviation Flight University of China
Guanghan, Sichuan, 618307, P.R. China
k_j_xu@163.com

Abstract. During the visual approach to landing of civil aviation aircraft, a human pilot bases control and timing of subsequent maneuvers mainly on the out-the-window view, as there is not sufficient time to read all instruments. The skill of making smooth and soft landings is acquired mainly through experience. Research has been done to identify the most important features in the visual scene for two phases of the visual approach to landing: glide slope tracking and the flare maneuver. In this paper we mainly focus on dual fuzzy neural network models and use this model to simulate the relationship between control and human input mathematically. By using the dual fuzzy neural network, a transparent model is obtained. Evaluation method for the pilot control is proposed to the networks and thus provided insight in the pilot's decision making process with respect to timing the flare maneuvers.

Keywords: Visual Scene Simulation, Dual Fuzzy Neural Network, Civil Aviation Aircraft, Approaching.

1   Introduction

With the increase of air traffic, the number of aircraft accidents has been increasing steadily. A large number of aircraft accidents have occurred during final approach and landing, and some of them could have been avoided if the pilot's control had been appropriate. Pilots' skills depend on their experience, which makes it difficult to make a guideline for control. Even if the pilot's skills seem sufficient under normal flight conditions, nobody knows whether the pilot can execute appropriate control in case of an emergency. Therefore, it is important to examine the pilot's potential control skill quantitatively, and the authors have developed an evaluation method for pilot control [1]. Furthermore, the knowledge of human pilot control strategy can also improve the performance of automatic control systems.

The subject of the analysis is the final landing control, because it is known as one of the most difficult maneuvers for airline pilots in normal operation. A characteristic maneuver at landing is the flare maneuver, which involves lifting of the nose to both

J. Lei et al. (Eds.): NCIS 2012, CCIS 345, pp. 275–280, 2012.
© Springer-Verlag Berlin Heidelberg 2012

land the aircraft on the main gear first and decrease the sink rate at the landing. A hard landing, which means landing with high sink rate, leads to damage of the airframe and passenger discomfort.

During the final landing phase, the information changes very rapidly, and the out-the-window-view (i.e., visual information) is the main information source for the pilot. In the flare maneuver, both estimation skill and control skill are required for a good landing, so the relationship between visual cues and pilot control was modeled using a dual fuzzy neural network (DFNN), which has been analyzed subsequently[2].

The research presented in this paper focuses on finding the visual scene a pilot uses, through analysis of scene and flight control data. A method is presented to construct a model of a human pilot which takes visual scene and generates longitudinal control actions during the visual approach to landing. This model is based on numerical data from real or simulated landings by human pilots. The model itself however is merely used to verify correspondence between the real pilot and the model. Of main interest are the structure and parameters of the resulting model, i.e., the driving inputs, internal relations and thresholds, as these give insight in the pilot's (subconscious) behavior.

This paper is structured as follows: Section 2 deals with the description of civil aviation aircraft landing control at visual approach. Then we will discuss the dual fuzzy neural network model in Section 3. In Section 4, our concept of the visual scene simulation to civil aviation aircraft will be presented. We mainly focus on the human pilot's subconscious behavior in the civil aviation aircraft visual scene approaching and landing. Finally, we conclude with a discussion and an outlook in Section 5.

2   Introduction Landing Control at Visual Approach

During a visual approach, the pilot can generally not afford to watch the instrument panel, so the visual information proves to be the main source for the pilot during the final landing phase. At that time, around the flare maneuver, the pilot has to obtain detailed information in real time in order to deal with varying flight situations. The closer the aircraft is to the airport, the more sensitive the visual information is, compared to the instrument panel. The optical flow of visual cues, such as the shape of runway or the position of the horizon, can be used to estimate the states of the landing airplane [3].

In the current study, the target of the analysis is twofold: glide slope tracking and the flare maneuver in the final landing phase. The image of the landing control is shown in Fig. 1.

The flare maneuver is a pitch-up control before touchdown. If the aircraft lands with the same high sink rate as that of approach, this will result in aircraft's damage and passenger discomfort. By pitch-up control, the sink rate is decreased and the aircraft can land on the main gear first. However, the timing of this flare maneuver is not constant and proper control should be applied depending on the situation.

The "implicit horizon" (distance between the horizon and the aim point, measured in the visual plane; $Y - H$ in Fig. 2) is often mentioned as an important cue

[4,5,6,7], especially for keeping the preferred glide slope. The position of the horizon (Y) is known to have a close relation to the pitch of the aircraft. The runway shape in general (also referred to as perspective), or specific cues like the perceived inclination angle of the runway edges (θ) and the apparent length or width of the runway are also mentioned in literature, but there is no consensus about their use [5,6,8,9].

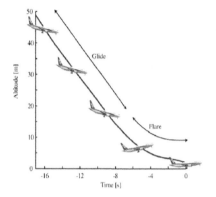

Fig. 1. The final approach to landing

Fig. 2. Implicit horizon- distance between the horizon and the aim point, measured in the visual plane

Fig. 2 shows an overview of the cues considered in this research. It must be kept in mind that the usage of cues varies through the phases of the landing [2], and that some cues are used as a trigger to commence a new phase.

3   Dual Fuzzy Neural Network Model

The use of dual fuzzy neural networks (DFNNs) is considered because of their close correspondence to human functioning and their generality and flexibility. As the main interest lies in the structure of the model, it is important to choose a model with high transparency, which is often a problem with NNs. To obtain a transparent network which can still be trained from data, the DFNN model proposed by Kaijun Xu and Yang Xu [10] is used as a transfer function in a NN framework. The DFNN and training procedure as described by Kaujun Xu [11] was implemented.

Dual fuzzy neural network model the biological nervous system, and consist of two same neural networks [10][11]. DFNN can make an appropriate nonlinear mapping of input/output data through a learning process. Neuron inter-connection weights are used to store the knowledge. The output of each network is calculated using the following expression.

Consider a nonlinear process given by:

$$\dot{x}_t = f(x_t, u_t) \tag{1}$$

Let us consider the following dynamic neural network to identify the nonlinear process Eq. (1):

$$\dot{\hat{x}}_t = A\hat{x}_t + W_t \phi(V_t \hat{x}_t) + U_t \tag{2}$$

$$\dot{x}_t = Ax_t + W^0 \phi(V^0 x_t) + U_t - \mu_t \tag{3}$$

The identified nonlinear system Eq. (1) can also be written as:

$$\dot{x}_t = Ax_t + W^* \phi(V^* x_t) + U_t - \tilde{f}_t \tag{4}$$

where $\tilde{f}_t$ is modeling error, V^* and W^* are set of weights chosen by the system identification agency.

The two fuzzy neural networks are presented:

$$\dot{\hat{x}}_\sigma = A_\sigma \hat{x}_\sigma + W_t^\sigma \phi_\sigma(V_t^\sigma \hat{x}_\sigma) + U_t \tag{5}$$

The neural network can be trained with the presence of a set of target examples or correct outputs, or with the presence of a mechanism that can provide corrections (a teacher), then the measure of error can be the sum of the squared errors as in the following:

$$e = \frac{1}{2} \sum_{i=1}^{N} (y_t(i) - y(i))^2 \tag{6}$$

4   Visual Scene Simulation

To find the cues a pilot is using when landing an airplane, a relation is sought between the available cues and the pilot's control. The current investigation only considers longitudinal motion (i.e., motion in the vertical plane) which limits the pilot control inputs to throttle setting and column deflection.

In order to analyze the pilot's control mathematically, a sensitivity analysis is applied to the DFNN models in this study. In the sensitivity analysis, the degree of change of the output is calculated for small changes of the inputs. The sensitivity can be calculated as follows:

$$s_{k,i} = \frac{\partial y_k^0}{\partial x_i} = \frac{\partial}{\partial x_i} \sum_{j=1}^{m} (w_{k,j}^0 y_j^h + b_k^0 / m) = \sum_{j=1}^{m} w_{k,j}^0 \frac{\partial y_j^h}{\partial x_i} = \sum_{j=1}^{m} w_{k,j}^0 w_{j,i}^h f \tag{7}$$

where, x_i is the i th input, and y_k^0 is the k th output. b_k^0 is the bias of the k th output, and f is an activation function in the hidden neurons.

In Fig. 3 and Fig. 4, the landings carried out in the MatLab simulator several different control strategies appeared to be used. The thick part of each line corresponds to the flare phase. The green [dark gray] line shows a "typical" landing, as described in the FAA Handbook. The red [black] line shows a strategy where the flare is mainly performed by decreasing the throttle.

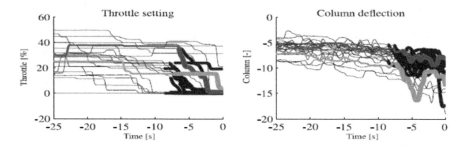

Fig. 3. Throttle setting and Column deflection

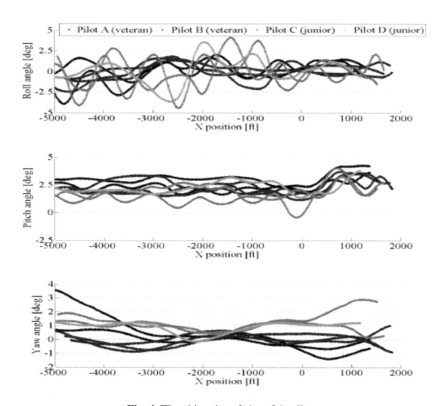

Fig. 4. Time histories of aircraft landing

5   Conclusion and Feature Works

The presented approach can reveal which visual cues a human pilot is using in the visual approach to landing. As landing skills are obtained through experience and pilots often can't explain "how" they fly, this information is valuable for trainee pilots who have not acquired enough skill yet. However, this knowledge also has various other applications such as the development of cockpit instruments, scene enhancement in bad weather approaches and improvement of simulator fidelity.

The key to constructing effective models to capture human pilot behavior in terms of vision based decision making and control, is to know which cues are used. Further identification of possible cues, representing them in suitable numerical variables, and knowing the limitations of the human visual system with respect to these cues is considered of great importance. Once this information is available, data mining or modeling such as the proposed method can reveal which cues are actually used and how. Future works are therefore considered in the field that connects aeronautics and psychophysics

Acknowledgement. This work is supported by the Open Foundation of Civil Aviation Flight University of China (Grant No.F2011KF04). Also be supported by Research Foundation of Civil Aviation Flight University of China (Grant No. J2011-04).

References

1. Suzuki, S., Sakamoto, Y., Sanematsu, Y., Takahara, H.: Analysis of Human Pilot Control Inputs using Neural Network. Journal of Aircraft 43(3), 793–796 (2006)
2. Mori, R., Suzuki, S., Sakamoto, Y., Takahara, H.: Analysis of Visual Cues during Landing Phase by using Neural Network Modeling. Journal of Aircraft 44(4), 2006–2011 (2007)
3. Gibson, J.J.: The Perception of the Visual World, Houghton Mifflin, Boston, MA (1950)
4. Airplane Flying Handbook, U.S. Department of Transportation, Federal Aviation Administration – Flight Standards Service, #FAA-H-8083-3A (2004)
5. Galanis, G., Jennings, A., Beckett, P.: Towards a general model of perception for simulation. In: SimTecT 1997, Canberra, pp. 21–26 (March 1997)
6. Lintern, G., Liu, Y.T.: Explicit and implicit horizons for simulated landing approaches. Human Factors 33(4), 401–417 (1991)
7. Naish, J.M.: Control information in visual flight. In: Seventh Annual Conference on Manual Control, NASA SP-281, pp. 167–176 (1972)
8. Hasbrook, A.H.: The approach and landing: cues and clues to a safe touchdown. Business and Commercial Aviation Magazine 37(5), 39–43 (1975)
9. Palmisano, S., Favelle, S., Prowse, G., Wadwell, R., Sachtler, B.: Investigation of visual flight cues for timing the initiation of the landing flare, Technical Report B2005/02121, Australian Transport Safety Bureau (June 2006)
10. Xu, K.J., Zou, L., Lai, J.J., Xu, Y.: An application of Dual-Fuzzy Neural-Networks to Design of Adaptive Fuzzy Controllers. In: The 3rd International Conference on Natural Computation (ICNC 2007) (2007)
11. Xu, K.J., Lai, J.J., Li, X.B., Pan, X.D., Xu, Y.: Adjustment strategy for a dual-fuzzy-neuro controller using genetic algorithms–application to gas-fired water heater. In: 8th International FLINS Conference On Computational Intelligence in Decision and Control (2008)

An Intelligent Knowledge Discovery Method Based on Genetic Algorithms and Conditional Probability

Da-zhai Yang[1,2], Chang-yong Liang[1], Guang-yun Si[3], and Wen-juan Cheng[4]

[1] School of Management at Hefei University of Technology, Hefei, China
[2] Economic and Information Commission of Hefei, Hefei, China
[3] Library of Anhui University, Hefei 230601, China
[4] School of Computer and Information at Hefei University of Technology, P.R. China
1078504976@qq.com, cyliang@163.com,
06075@ahu.edu.cn, ccheng@ah.edu.cn

Abstract. In this paper, we integrated genetic algorithm and conditional probability to build a novel retrieval method for knowledge discovery. Genetic algorithm and conditional probability are used to derive the weight of the attributes and improve traditional KNN respectively. Our method can be used for data mining issues with both continuous and discrete values of the characteristic attributes.

Keywords: knowledge management, data mining, genetic algorithm, conditional probability.

1   Introduction

Most of the previous related achievements are preliminary investigations and limited to presented an application framework or directly apply traditional KNN which is based on Euclidean or Hamming distance[1] [2]. Although traditional KNN has displayed its extraordinary performance in a large number of classifications, its advantage still consists in the retrieval problems which only contain continuous and logistic attributes[3].

Traditional KNN is effective in computing the distance among continuous values but not among discrete values. To discrete attributes, although traditional KNN still work by generally regarding them as logistic attributes, the results are not ideal. Taking the computing of the local similarity of a discrete attribute by traditional KNN for example, matching discrete attributes contribute maximally to the similarity while nonmatching attributes don't contribute at all. That means the difference of "high smooth" and "not smooth at all" is nondiscriminatory to that of "high smooth" and "middle". Obviously, that is unreasonable and unreliable. Hence, it is normal that this method does a poor job with discrete attributes. Meanwhile, weight plays an important role in knowledge discovery systems. It is an indispensable constituent part of knowledge retrieval. Generally, the weight has a significant influence on the results. However, experts' evaluation is still the most common way for weight determination in

J. Lei et al. (Eds.): NCIS 2012, CCIS 345, pp. 281–286, 2012.
© Springer-Verlag Berlin Heidelberg 2012

real-world knowledge reasoning systems. The weights from different expert groups may differ greatly, which probably has direct influence to retrieval results. Meanwhile, due to the complexity of the knowledge itself, it is not an easy work for experts to draw an appropriate weight. It is one of key tasks in this article to study how to decrease the impact of weights on reasoning results. For any of new approaches, the subjectivity of weight derivation must be considered to be reduced firstly. One of our aims is at a novel retrieval algorithm which is capable of improving the accuracy of knowledge matching in which both continuous values and discontinuous numbers are included.

Based on the above considerations, we research problem focuses on seeking a novel knowledge retrieval methods for the decision making problems with both continuous and discrete attributes in medical knowledge management. We integrated GA into conditional probability into and proposed a novel knowledge retrieval method named KRMGACP (Kase Retrieval Method based on Genetic Algorithm and Conditional Probability) to solve knowledge matching problem with both continuous and discrete attributes (logistic attributes included).In our method, the weight are derived by GA without experts' evaluation needed.

The paper is organized into four sections. The first section presents the study background, research problems and main content. The second section summarizes the extant literature on knowledge reasoning and its applications in the area of health care. The third section describes our research methods. The last section presents the conclusion and suggests an agenda for future research.

2   Literature Review

Why do the people need information or knowledge support for their decision making? As is known to all, not everyone has enough experience, knowledge or ability to make a correct decision, especially for inexperienced young people. Even to those experienced decision makers, they still need information support for making perfect decision. The informed discovery shows the physicians' decision ability is dependable to a great extent on the quality of the information they obtain. The valuable information will be helpful to improve physicians' ability of decision making and the accuracy of diagnosis. In the early stage, the decision support approaches mainly uses one-parameter model, such as linear discriminant analysis, logistic regression, and etc. The expensive mistakes of these approaches push researchers to look for other more accurate methods. Some of general data mining methods, such as decision tree, support vector machine (SVM), agent, theory of evidence theory, artificial neural network, Bayesian learning were used to resolve knowledge discovery problems[4]. There exist some limitations in these approaches. For example, the overfitting of Neural Network makes it generally only advantageous in classifications and hard to provide more detailed decision information for decision makers. In terms of decision tree, the global optimums are not always be returned by the heuristic algorithms (such as greedy algorithm).

As one of knowledge-based systems, the intelligent system based on KRMGACP can be used for special knowledge expression from historical records.

3   Methodologies

In this section, we describe the research design and methodology we employed to address the research questions. A novel retrieval method incorporating GA and conditional possibility, data set collected and experimental design are introduced respectively.

KNN based on Euclidean distance is the most popular retrieval algorithms and widely applied in various knowledge systems[5]. This method handles continuous attributes reasonably well, but it does a poor job with discrete attributes. Nonmatching discrete attributes contribute maximally to the distance while matching attributes don't contribute at all[6]. To the logistic attributes, it is suitable. However, to discrete attributes that are not logistic, the problem probably could emerge. To address this issue, Stanfill and Waltz[7] presented the value difference metric (VDM). In the VDM, conditional probabilities are used for the values of discrete attributes to refine the contribution of these attributes to the distance calculation.

After that, Wilson and Martinez introduced several new metrics based on the VDM: heterogeneous value difference metric (HVDM) which is similar to the similarity metric of Gower[8], interpolated VDM (IVDM) and windowed VDM (WDVM) which is a similar but more sophisticated version of IVDM. The IVDM and WDVM may be regarded as an extension of the VDM that takes into account continuous attributes by discretizing them to calculate sample probabilities[9].

By the basic idea of IVDM and WDVM, all the continuous attributes must be discrete for the calculation of sample probabilities. That is to say, it seems that they are still the approaches ready for discrete attributes in essence. One weakness of these methods is that the calculated similarity values may be changing with the extent of discretion to continuous attributes. That is to say, although the data set is the same, the retrieved results may be distinguished when different discretion extents are chosen. Another limitation is that the concept of weight in IVDM and WDVM is hard to be explained in real world specific research issue. It is not very easy to understand that the same attributes have different weights. Is there an effective approach that is able to handles both continuous and discrete attributes directly, without discretizing the continuous values? The answer is positive by our research results showed in following sections. In this paper, we integrated genetic algorithm and conditional probability into knowledge reasoning and proposed KRMGACP. As a novel knowledge retrieval method, KRMGACP is able to solve the similarity computation problems in which both continuous and discrete attributes are contained. Moreover, it is more appreciate to the custom of the people.

KRMGACP contains two sides of key technologies: weight determination approach and computing similarity method. In this article, GA is applied to the process of weight derivation and conditional probability is integrated with traditional Euclidean distance algorithms into computing similarity method.

Weight determination exists in various research problems in various fields[10]. Good weight derivation methods help to improve the accuracy of knowledge system. Generally, the research methods of weight determination may be divided into two broad categories: quantitative approaches and qualitative ones. There are fruitful achievements about weight determination methods, for example, J. Renauda, et al[11] used OWA operators to derive weight for industrial decision making problems. Another example is by Entropy method Zhi-hong Zou et al derive the weight for water quality research problem[12].

In traditional KNN, the default weight values of all the attributes are fixed to one. In practice, DELPHI and AHP are the most two commonly used approaches. In knowledge-based systems, there exists other methods for weight determination, such as linear programming, decision trees, analytic hierarchy process, genetic algorithms, and etc [13] [14], but all of them were studied in particular field or problems. Together with rigorous restrictions for use and other practical problems, it is for these methods to be popularized and have practical applications.

In this article, we proposed a weight derivation approach based on genetic algorithms and named GA-Weight. As global optimization techniques derived from the principles of natural selection and evolutionary theory, GAs have been theoretically and empirically proven to be robust search techniques. GAs are inspired on the principle of survival of the fittest, where the fittest individuals are selected to produce offspring for the next generation[15]. Their essence is "search algorithms based on the mechanics of natural selection and natural genetics". The GA used in this work was developed by Matlab.

KRMGACP contains a step of data normalization. All the attribute values are normalized to minimize the effects caused by technical variations, and as a result allow the data to be comparable before similarities are calculated. The detail of KRMGACP is described as follows.

$$
Dist = \begin{cases} \sum_{f=1}^{m} w_f |t_{kf} - x_{kf}| & when \ f \ continuous \\ \sum_{f=n-m}^{n} w_f D_{Local\text{-}Disc} & when \ f \ discrete(logistic \ included) \end{cases} \tag{1}
$$

$$
\begin{aligned}
S_{global} &= 1 - \left(\sum_{f=1}^{m} w_f |t_{kf} - x_{kf}| + \sum_{f=n-m}^{n} w_f * S_{Local\text{-}Disc} \right) \\
&= 1 - \left(\sum_{f=1}^{m} w_f |t_{kf} - x_{kf}| + \sum_{f=n-m}^{n} w_f * \sum_{f=n-m}^{n} q(t_f)\xi(t_f, x_{if}) \right)
\end{aligned} \tag{2}
$$

where,

$$
\xi(t_f, x_{if}) = \sum_{y \in Y} (P(y|t_f) - P(y|x_{if}))^2 \tag{3}
$$

In equation (3), $P(y|t_f)$ is the conditional probability of class label y given feature value t_f. $q(t_f)$ is calculated as follows:

$$q(t_f) = \sqrt{\sum_{y \in Y} P^2(y \mid t_f)}$$

(4)

A problem that claims attention, in equation (4), $q(t_f)$ is changing with the value of t_f, i.e. $q(t_f)$ which is dependent on t_f and y is not unique to a particular attribute of records. This does not fit the traditional definition of weight. Hence, $q(t_f)$ seems more like a probability factor rather than a weight variable.

4   Conclusion and Future Work

The primary objective of the study is to examine the role of knowledge discovery method in decision issues with continuous and logistic variables as well as a number of discrete attributes. We incorporated GA and conditional probability into the knowledge retrieval process and investigated that our method had better performance compared to conventional KNN and other commonly used classification methods. The future work is to conduct experiments to verify whether the proposed knowledge retrieval method incorporating GA and conditional probability has better performance in solving the problems with multiple discrete attributes, thus can be used to provide practical assistance during decision making. Based on the knowledge base, decision makers are able to draw a preliminary conclusion and then choose further alternatives and measures.

Acknowledgement. This study is financially support by the following foundations: Young Talents in Colleges of Anhui Province under Grant No. 2011SQRW107, National Natural Science Foundation of China under Grant No.70871032, Humanity and Social Science Foundation of Ministry of Education of China under Grant No. 09YJA630029, and the Hefei University of Technology 2011-2012 College Students Innovation Fund (with No. 60).

References

1. David, W., Paul, M., Rohit, R., Vivian, W.: Ensemble Strategies for a Medical Diagnostic Decision Support System: A Breast Cancer Diagnosis Application. European Journal of Operational Research 162, 532–551 (2005)
2. Bilska, A.O., Floyd, C.E.: Investigating Different Similarity Measures for a Knowledge-Based Classifier to Predict Breast Cancer. In: Proc. SPIE Med. Imaging, vol. 4322, pp. 1862–1866 (2001)
3. Cunningham, P.: A Taxonomy of Similarity Mechanisms for Knowledge-Based Reasoning. IEEE Transactions on Knowledge and Data Engineering 21, 1532–1543 (2008)
4. Tuan, Z.T., Chai, Q., Geok, S.N., Khalil, R.: Ovarian Cancer Diagnosis with Complementary Learning Fuzzy Neural Network. Artificial Intelligence in Medicine 43, 207–222 (2008)

5. Juan, M.C., Javier, B., Yanira, D.P., Dante, I.T.: Intelligent Environment for Monitoring Alzheimer Patients: Agent Technology for Health Care. Decision Support Systems 44, 382–396 (2008)
6. Schmidt, R., Gierl, L.: An Investigation of Retrieval Algorithms and Prototypes. Art Intelligence in Medicine 23, 171–186 (2001)
7. Stanfill, C., Waltz, D.L.: Toward Memory-Based Reasoning. Comm. ACM 29, 1213–1228 (1986)
8. Gower, J.C.: A General Coefficient of Similarity and Some of Its Properties. Biometrics 27, 857–874 (1971)
9. Wilson, D., Martinez, T.: Improved Heterogeneous Distance Functions. Artificial Intelligence Research 6, 1–34 (1997)
10. Renauda, J., Levratb, E., Fonteixc, C.: Weights Determination of OWA Operators by Parametric Identification. Mathematics and Computers in Simulation 77, 499–511 (2008)
11. Lu, Z., Frans, C., Paul, L.: Formalising Optimal Feature Weight Setting in Diagnosis as Linear Programming Problems. Knowledge-Based Systems 15, 391–398 (2002)
12. Fidelis, M.V., Lopes, H.S., Freitas, A.A.: Discovering Comprehensible Classification Rules with a Genetic Algorithm. In: Proc. of the 2000 Congress on Evolutionary Computation, vol. 1, pp. 805–810 (2000)
13. Goldberg, D.E.: Genetic Algorithms in Search. Optimization and Machine Learning. Addison-Wesley, Reading (1989)
14. Lu, Y., He, X., Du, J.J.: Malfunction Retrieval Algorithm Based on Grey System Theory. Computer Engineering of China 34, 28–32 (2003) (in Chinese)
15. Elter, M., Wendtland, R.S., Wittenberg, T.: The Prediction of Breast Cancer Biopsy Outcomes Using Two CAD Approaches That Both Emphasize an Intelligible Decision Process. Medical Physics 34, 4164–4172 (2007)

Brushless DC Motor Speed Control System Based on Fuzzy PID Controller

Guoqiang Cheng

Shengli Drilling Technology Research Institute of Sinopec, DongYing, China
cheng_gq@163.com

Abstract. For the further optimization of Brushless DC motor control performance, it is necessary to design suitable controller and the optimization of the parameters of the controller, in the production process control field, the PID control is still by far the most common control method. It has the advantages of simple structure, clear physical meanings of parameters, good control effect and strong robustness. On the analysis of the mathematical model of brushless DC motor and the control method. We can use fuzzy PID controller in brushless dc motor control while use of fuzzy control principle of PID parameters adjustment online. Moreover on the basis of Fuzzy Toolbox of MATLAB in application and Simulink for brushless dc motor speed control system was simulated. Experimental results show that the fuzzy PID control has better static and dynamic performance, control accuracy also rises greatly compared with the traditional PID control.

Keywords: Brushless DC motor, speed regulation, fuzzy PID control.

1 Introduction

Brush DC motor as the first motor is widely used in various areas of industrial and agricultural production, due to its wide, smooth, good speed performance, plays an important role in applications requiring speed control, but the mechanical reversing arrangement exists, limit their development and application. In 1978, the introduction of MAC classic brushless DC motor and its drive the launch of the electronic commutation, the brushless DC motor is really into the practical stage. More than 20 years, with the permanent magnet of new materials, microelectronic technology, automatic control technology and power electronics technology in particular, the development of high-power switching devices, the brushless motor has been considerable development.

Compared with the traditional control, fuzzy control can avoid the mathematical model (such as the equation of state, or transfer function), it seeks to processing of success and failure on a control problem and experience, summed up the experience from which to extract control rules with the construct system of multi-dimensional fuzzy conditional statements fuzzy language variable model, application of CRI, and other types of fuzzy reasoning method, you can control the amount of control requirements, we can say that fuzzy control is a control of the linguistic variables.

J. Lei et al. (Eds.): NCIS 2012, CCIS 345, pp. 287–294, 2012.
© Springer-Verlag Berlin Heidelberg 2012

2   The Working Principle and Mathematical Model of the Brushless DC Motor

2.1   The Working Principle of the Brushless DC Motor

General permanent magnet brushless DC motor is composed by the motor body (with the armature winding of the stator and permanent magnet rotor), position sensors and electronic commutation circuit three-part.

The electronic switch of brushless DC motor is used to control the sequence and timing of the power of the motor stator windings of each phase, mainly composed by power logic switching unit and a position sensor signal processing unit. Power logic switch unit is the core of the control circuit, its function is assigned to the power supply to a certain logical relationship to the winding of the brushless DC motor, so that the motor can produce the continuous torque. The order and time of the winding conduction depends on the rotor position from the position sensor signal. However, due to the signal generated by the position sensor generally can not be directly used to control the switching of power logic unit, after a certain amount of logic processing to control the logic switching unit. In summary, the composition of the brushless DC motor of the major components of the block diagram shown in Figure 1.

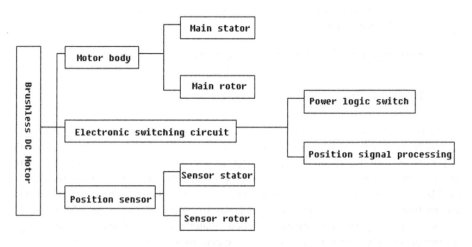

Fig. 1. Block diagram of Brushless DC motor

2.2   Brushless DC Motor Mathematical Model

In order to facilitate analysis of the mathematical model of the brushless DC motor and the electromagnetic torque and other characteristics, it is assumed that:

(1) Three-phase windings are completely symmetrical, the air-gap magnetic field is a square wave, the stator current and rotor magnetic field distribution are symmetrical;

(2) Ignore the impact of the alveolar, commutation process and armature reaction;

(3) The armature windings in the stator surface uniform and continuous distribution;

(4) The magnetic circuit is unsaturated, excluding the eddy current loss and hysteresis loss.

A complete mathematical model of the brushless DC motor system is shown in Figure 2.

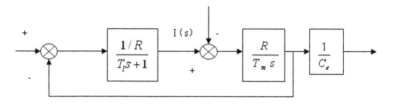

Fig. 2. The dynamic mathematical model of Brushless DC motor

Among them, T_i is the electromagnetic time constant of armature loop; T_m is drag system electromechanical time constant.

3   Fuzzy PID Controller Design

3.1   The Basic Principles of Fuzzy Control

Fuzzy control block diagram shown in Figure 3, the main difference is that the fuzzy control system with the usual computer control system using fuzzy controller.

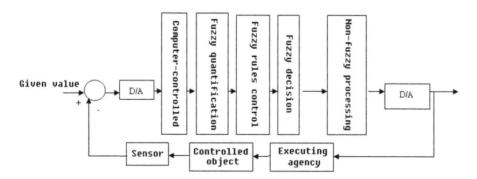

Fig. 3. The dynamic mathematical model of Brushless DC motor

In the deterministic control system, according to the number of input variables and output variables, it can be divided into the control system of the univariate and multivariate control systems. Fuzzy control system can also be a similar division of fuzzy control system for a single variable and multivariable fuzzy control system.

3.2   Speed Control System in the Fuzzy PID Controller Design

The speed of the brushless DC motor and the dynamic structure of the current double closed loop speed control system shown in Figure 4.

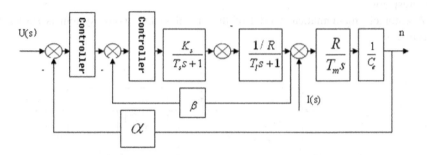

Fig. 4. The dynamic mathematical model of Brushless DC motor

The speed control system error e and error change ec as an input, the system is running continuously detect e and e_c, while taking advantage of fuzzy rules for fuzzy inference, query fuzzy matrix parameters to adjust to meet the e and ec at different times of the PID parameter self-tuning requirements. Namely the use of fuzzy rules have been built in line PID parameters amended so that the controlled object has good static and dynamic performance. Fuzzy PID control system structure shown in Figure 5.

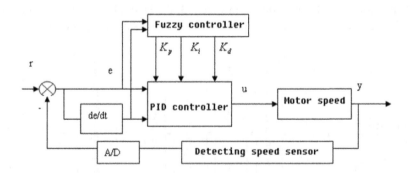

Fig. 5. The structure of fuzzy PID controller

In this paper fuzzy reasoning using Mamdani inference algorithm, and the defuzzification is the center of gravity method. Defuzzification output $\Delta K'p, \Delta K'i$, $\Delta K'd$. By the fuzzy control rules can be drawn from the surface shown in Figure 6 to Figure 8 shows the **output** control rules.

Table 1. Fuzzy control rule table

e	ec						
	NB	NM	NS	ZE	PS	PM	PB
NB	PB NB PS	PB NB NS	PM NM NB	PM NM NB	PS NS NB	ZE ZE NM	ZE ZE PS
NM	PB NB PS	PB NB NS	PM NM NB	PS NS NM	PS NS NM	ZE ZE NS	NS ZE ZE
NS	PM NB ZE	PM NM NS	PM NS NM	PS NS NM	ZE ZE NS	NS PS NS	NS PS ZE
ZE	PM NM ZE	PM NM NS	PS NS NS	ZE ZE NS	NS PS NS	NM PM ZE	NM PB ZE
PS	PS NM ZE	PS NS ZE	ZE ZE ZE	NS PS ZE	NS PS ZE	NM PM ZE	NM PB ZE
PM	PS ZE PB	ZE ZE NS	NS PS PS	NM PS PS	NM PM PS	NM PB PS	NB PB PB
PB	ZE ZE PB	ZE ZE PM	NM PS PM	NM PM PM	NM PM PS	NB PB PS	NB PB PB

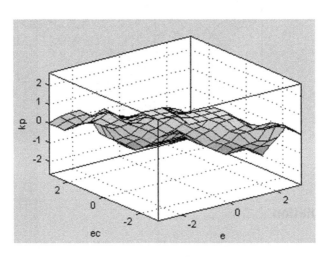

Fig. 6. The fuzzy reasoning output surface of K_p

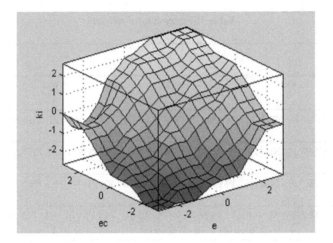

Fig. 7. The fuzzy reasoning output surface of K_i

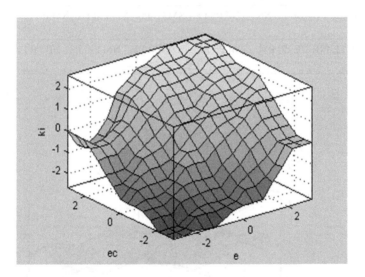

Fig. 8. The fuzzy reasoning output surface of K_d

4   Simulation

Brushless DC motor parameters are as follows: U_N=220V, I_N=136A, n_N== 1000r/min, the armature resistance R_a= 0.2Ω, allowing the overload factor λ= 1.5, deflector T_s= 0.00167s, the amplification factor K_s = 40, the total resistance of armature loop R = 0.5, total armature circuit inductance L = 15mH, mechanical and electrical time constant T_m= 1.18s, the armature circuit electromagnetic time T_l= 0.03s, the flywheel inertia of the motor shaft GD^2= 22.5N.M^2, the current feedback coefficient β= 0.05V / A, speed feedback coefficient α= 0.007V.min/r.

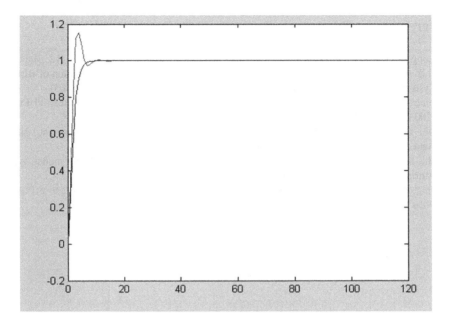

Fig. 9. Fuzzy PID control system step response

Use of system simulation module to build a simulation model of the traditional PID and fuzzy PID controller in Matlab / Simulink simulation before the first edited fuzzy inference system is embedded in the Fuzzy Logic Controller module.

It can be seen from the simulation results (Figure 9), fuzzy control regulation time is short, fast response, small overshoot, allowing the system to stabilize as soon as possible. Compared to pass a conventional PID control regulator, fuzzy PID control algorithm to control the brushless DC motor speed control system controllers can effectively improve the dynamic and static performance of the controlled object.

5   Conclusion

In this paper, the analysis of fuzzy PID controller and brushless DC motor mathematical model based on fuzzy PID controller used in the dual closed-loop speed control system of the brushless DC motor, and the basic module of the Matlab simulation tools build a brushless DC motor speed control system. The simulation results show that in the use of fuzzy PID controller, the torque ripple is small, the system is over-time, no overshoot, good stability, strong adaptability and robustness, and the model can be easily modify and replace function module, for future analysis of the motor and its control strategy offers a new method..

References

1. Long, S., Wang, P.: Fuzzy control rule adjustment. Fuzzy Mathematics 2, 105–112 (1982)
2. Ji, Z.-C., Shen, Y.-X., Jiang, J.-G.: A Novel Method for Modeling and Simulation of BLDC System Based on Matlab. Acta Simulata Systematica Sinica 12, 1745–1749 (2003)
3. Liu, J.: Advanced PID control and its MATLAB simulation. Electronic Industrial Press (2003)
4. Wu, B.-G., Ying, H.: Review of Fuzzy PID Control Techniques and Some Important Issues. Acta Automatica Sinica 27(4), 568–584 (2001)
5. Hu, S., Liu, S.: On the method of self-generating and selftuning control rule model. Acta Automatica Sinica 17(5), 606–610 (1991)
6. Guo, Q., Zhao, X.: Brushless DC motor principle and technology. China Electric Power Press, Beijing (2008)

Learning Sequent Patterns Discovery Scheme on Line

Chaoming Zhu[1], Lijian Chen[2], Xue Zhou[2], and Yuefeng Zheng[2]

[1] Zhejiang TV University Xiaoshan Academy, Hangzhou China
[2] Zhejiang University of Technology, Hangzhou China
Zhucm007@163.com

Abstract. How to establish an assistant learning environment on Internet has already been gained a great attention. The paper presents the learning sequent patterns discovery scheme. It is an effective web mining technique directing at huge data in learning sequence database, which can find out the relationship among these data actively and summarize the browsing pattern of every learner. The learning sequence patterns can help teachers to find out the relationship of each learning unit or the learning path most learners browse frequently in order to improve the structure of courses on Internet and learning efficient. From the experiments, it is obvious that the method is better than the others under the condition of same environment.

Keywords: Learning Sequent Patterns, Discovery Scheme, Web Mining, Assistant Learning.

1 Introduction

As the fast development of Internet, education on line can not only break the space restriction but make learners arrange class time freely. It combines learner's learning sequence with multi-evaluation to grasp efficiently the speed of learning. According to the present achievement, it has already been a trend in the future for learner to take the advantage of Internet to do some exploration on the structural learning freely [1].

Learning on line includes synchronous learning and non-synchronous learning; here we only discuss the non-synchronous learning. Non-synchronous learning affords classes on line; learners may enter the website of special subject learning courses by themselves and learn the relevant content in accordance with teacher's requirement on this special subject. The design of monographic practice emphasizes the truth and the topic integration, the activity design esteems the learner's independence, and the evaluation design takes both dynamic learning sequence and the quality of the best production into consideration. So it will be an important subject to provide a learning sequence tracking and administrating system, which make monographic learning on line more effective.

In administration on non-synchronous learning on Internet, tracking students' learning path always is one of the methods for teacher to acquire the students' learning states. The present Internet learning environment has provided some education administration function, the record system of learning sequence and the mechanism of data collecting. All of those could be used to collect the learners' data

J. Lei et al. (Eds.): NCIS 2012, CCIS 345, pp. 295–300, 2012.
© Springer-Verlag Berlin Heidelberg 2012

including how many times he or she browsed, when, the homepage and the content of the browse. Those data are called "learning sequent data". However, most of those records only provide behavior data of learners and cannot do some further analysis to find out some useful learning sequent patterns, those patterns may include the range of the units, the sequence of the unit the learners browse and the path they went through and so on. And the result we get by exploring the learners' browsing behavior can let the teacher know how did they visit those websites so that teachers are able to analyze the state of individual or the whole learners and find out some useful learning sequent patterns such as the relationship hidden in all kinds of learning elements, which help teachers improve the structure and the flow of those homepages [2].

In allusion to the process of mining on line learning sequential data, the writer takes the time restriction between two neighboring units or homepages during the browsing period. Mining sequential patterns mainly load the data into the main storage and do not read the database any more. So when the same learning unit appears in the different homepages during the learning process, it will produce a learning sequence patterns which does not exist, and the overmuch data cannot be load into the main storage and run totally. Inasmuch the learning sequent patterns in other mining sequential patterns [3][5][6] did not probe the time restriction between two neighboring units then became meaningless with the result that the two learning units are very far from each other. We can draw a conclusion that several methods mentioned are not suitable for mining the data of learning sequence under web circumstance. Although GPS put forward in [4] had think about the question of the space between two neighboring units and allow that there are the repeated learning units in learning sequence, it will become inefficiency for its several transferring from forward to backward sequence which may be needed in the process of looking for acute possible sequent patterns when the learning sequence is rather long.

In this paper, we proposed a discovery scheme which adapt to learning on the web called learning sequent patterns discovery scheme, LSPD scheme for short. This scheme going on as following: firstly, it collects the relevant data of learners such as homepages and the browsing time by using some track system and extracts everyone's browsing path pattern then divides into sessions (that is a series of browsing paths for every learner in certain period), called browsing sequence. The second step is starting sequential discovery pattern scheme. This scheme is based on the GSP algorithm, considering time constraints and sliding windows, put forward a more efficient way to avoid the choke point of forward and backward sequence. The learning sequent patterns got by this way could help teachers to realize the relationship in units and the frequent browsing path, by which improve the structure of the course and make learner get much progress.

2   Related Work

The definition of the sequential data discovery patterns is the question that how to find out the order of most people's sequent patterns in a sequence database. The research way of this question has two tropisms, one is based on I/O [3] [4][5][6], the other is based on memory [7][8], among them, [4] is the close relationship with our research work.

Agrawal &Srikant[3] are the first one who put forward this question, their algorithms are AprioriAll、 AprioriSome and DynamicSome. While sometimes the discovered patterns will become meaningless and redundant and waste more time when the space of two neighboring homepages are too short or too long. To overcome this shortcoming, Agrawal&Srikant introduce GSP [4], adding the concepts of taxonomies, time constraints and sliding windows and make the found data more effective. According to the experimental results, the speed is about 3~20 times as quick as AprioriAll. GSP algorithm includes two phases in looking for time-constrained sequences:

Forward phase: look forward all the subjects in the Ck sequence, when the space between two neighboring subjects is beyond the maximum of initialization, execute the backward phase.

Backward phase: trace from the present position where subject located in back to maximum, then look for the previous subject until regain all the sections and be sure that all the sections are within the maximum. Or find the first learning unit then come back to the backward phase. Repeat the two phases like this until the end.

Besides, some scholars like Chen; Park & Yu put forward the Full Scan (FS) and Selective Scan (SS) algorithm using the idea of DHP algorithm to reduce the number of the candidate k-sequences. FS algorithm has following steps, firstly, make LK represent all big K-reference sequence, and Ck represents an aggregate of candidate k-reference sequence. From database Df, we can get Li, and make a hash table to calculate every number in 2-refernce sequences. Then begin with K=2, we get Ck and Lk (K>=2) by turn. Ck is the result of Lk-i joining itself (means Lk-i $*$ Lk-i), the next step is reading database and calculating the frequency of every k-reference sequence aggregate in Ck, then get the Lk by checking whether the result surpass the minimum critical numerical value set in advance. The main difference of SS compared with FS is when C2 is rather small, C3' could get from C2 $*$ C2 instead of from L2 $*$ L2, if C3'is not bigger than C3,what's more,C2 and C3'can store in the storage at the same time, L2 and L3 could be found simultaneously next time. By doing this, we may save the reading time, and enhance the execution efficiency.

DSG algorithm uses graph to search the sequence patterns, during the whole process, it need read database only once. Although it reduces the practice of I/O, relatively increases the costs of much main storage (Yen&Chen, 1996). Reading only once may cause the problem that the subsequent sequences fail to store in database.

The methods above may fail to work in the main storage when met with huge database because of its limited container. In order to solve this problem, SPADE algorithm uses the concept of equivalence class and discomposes the original problem into several problems so that they can independently work in the main storage. SPADE algorithm reads database three times totally in the whole process.

As for those studies under web circumstance, their learning route may have repeated units, while DGS and SPADE both work in the main storage and may produce sequence patterns which do not exist in such situation. So it isn't applicable in mining sequence patterns like this. And other algorithms except GSP don't take the time restriction between two neighboring units. Basing on GSP algorithm, the writer introduces a useful learning sequent patterns discovery scheme.

3   Learning Sequent Patterns Discovery Scheme

To discover learner's browsing behavior under the circumstance of learning on the web, besides analyzing the learning path, we should think about the time of browsing. GSP has already take it into consideration, while it need several transferring movements from forward to backward sequence which may be needed in the process of looking for acute possible sequent patterns when the learner frequently do some traversal browsing in the same homepage or learning units. The newly proposed leaning sequent patterns discovery scheme (LSPC for short) is a more valuable scheme in this field.

The process includes two steps. The first step is finding out large 1-sequential patterns; the second step is deducing all large K-sequential patterns $\geqq 2)$, as shown in Fig.1.

$$L_1 = \{\text{Large 1-sequences}\};$$

For ($k = 2 ; L_{k-1} \neq 0 ; k = k+1$) do

$\quad C_k = $ set of candidate k-sequences;

For all learn-sequences ε in the database do increment

$\quad$ count of all $\alpha \in C_k$ contained in ε

$\quad L_k = \{ \alpha \in C_k \mid \alpha .sup \geq min\text{-}sup\} ;$

Set of all large sequence $= \cup_k L_k;$

Fig. 1. The process of LSPD

When candidate sequence comes out, we should discover some specific candidate sequences storing in the learning sequence and calculate their supported degree. Here is a quick scheme that need go through the learning sequence only once. Supposing d be a learning sequence, u = <A...Z> represents all the learning units on the web, and s = <s1...sn> is a candidate sequence. Firstly, we build a order list of learning units in u and store the list number corresponding to the every element in sequence into this order list, then transfer candidate sequence s to planar arrayed check list, the numbers in I lists mean the beginning browsing time of the anterior I elements in candidate sequence s. it has the merit of discover specific candidate sequences by gonging through the original learning sequence once and its shortcoming is that we must establish a order list having the index of candidate sequence s and store cost basing on check list.

The main process (as shown in Fig.2): firstly, judge whether the learning unit exist in order list before it read one element in learning sequence d, if yes, calculate the time slot between this unit and the previous one and check whether the result is in the range set before. If the result does not surpass the max-gap, please cover this counterpart of this unit in check list with previous list number, and store the beginning browsing time of this learning unit to the corresponding position in check list. Otherwise, do not store this unit and continue the next one if the previous unit does not exist or the time slot does not surpass the max-gap. Repeat above steps until the last unit in sequence s is discovered and meets all the conditions. We can draw a conclusion that there is candidate sequence s in the sequence d. the whole process will complete until learning sequence d is finish reading or candidate sequence s is discovered.

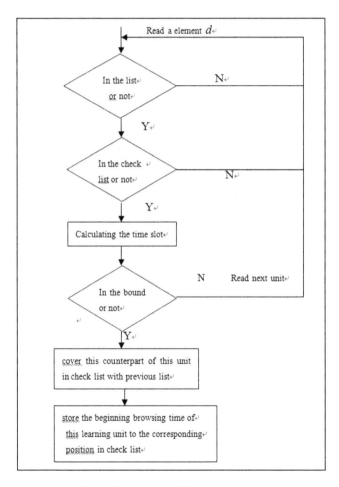

Fig. 2. The process of learning patterns

4   Summary

Getting to know the learners' browsing behavior under the web circumstance can not only supply the evidence to teacher for administration or to be the reference for learners, but also help design and update the structure of the website. In this article, directing the condition of learning on the web, the writer develops the learning sequence patterns discovery scheme basing on the GSP algorithm to find the most learners' learning sequence.

Acknowledgments. Project supported by Foundation of Zhejiang Educational Committee (No.Y201120121; No.Y201018954), Zhejiang Provincial Public Welfare Technology Applied Research Project (No.2011C21014), Zhejiang Provincial Natural Science Foundation of China (No.Y1101062), the Qianjiang Talent Project of Zhejiang Province (No. 2011R10087).

References

[1] Lee, C.-I., Ku, H.-K.: A Study of Personal Assistant Retrieval System for Elementary Student. In: The Sixth International Conference on Computers in Education, Beijing, China, October 14-17, pp. 628–633 (1998)

[2] Yan, T.W., Jacobesn, M., Hector, G.-M., Dayal, U.: From User Access Patterns to Dynamic Hypertext Linking. In: 5th International World Wide Web Conference (1996)

[3] Agrawal, R., Srikant, R.: Mining Sequence Patterns. In: Proceedings of the 11th International Conference on Data Engineering, March 6-10, pp. 3–10 (1995)

[4] Agrawal, R., Srikant, R.: Mining Sequential Patterns: Generalizations and Performance Improvements. In: Apers, P.M.G., Bouzeghoub, M., Gardarin, G. (eds.) EDBT 1996. LNCS, vol. 1057, pp. 3–17. Springer, Heidelberg (1996)

[5] Chen, M.-S., Park, J.-S., Yu, P.S.: Data Mining for Path Traversal Patterns in a Web Environment. In: Proceedings of the 16th International Conference on Distributed Computing Systems, May 27-30, pp. 385–392 (1996)

[6] Chen, M.-S., Park, J.-S., Yu, P.S.: Efficient Data Mining for Path Traversal Patterns. IEEE Transactions on Knowledge and Data Engineering 10(2), 209–221 (1998)

[7] Yen, S.-J., Chen, A.L.P.: An Efficient Approach to Discovering Knowledge from Large Database. In: PDIS, December 18-20, pp. 8–18 (1996)

[8] Zaki, M.J.: Efficient Enumeration of Frequent Sequences. In: CIKM, pp. 68–75 (1998)

Extension Control and Its Application Research in Power System

Xueqin Lu[1,*], Chen-ning Wu[1], and Xiangwu Xia[2]

[1] Department of Information and Control Engineering,
Shanghai University of Electric Power, Shanghai 200090, China
[2] Shanghai Research Institute of China Coal Technology &
Engineering Group Corp. Shanghai 200030, China
lvxueqin@shiep.edu.cn

Abstract. Extension is a new subject which solves contradictory problems. It studies the extensive possibility of things and the rules and methods of exploitation and innovation with formalized model. The extension control theory and method has provided the basis theory and method for people to solve the existent contradictory questions in the automatic control system such as stability, accuracy and speed. This paper briefly introduces the related basic concepts of extension control, such as the structure of canonical extension control, extension set of character status of basic extension controller, and general extension control algorithm, and so on. Also presents the extension application in power systems. The future work and prospect of development are described.

Keywords: Extension Set, Extension Control, Extension Algorithm, Power System, Extension Evaluation.

1 Introduction

Since the extension set theory presented in 1983 by Prof. Cai, which is a new kind of knowledge system for solving contradictory problem in the realistic world and based on matter-element and extension set [1][2]. The methodologies of extension theory have been widely utilized in various engineering applications, such as applying it in the applications of optimization, identification, pattern recognition, clustering and controller design, intelligent science, control, decision making, new product designing [3-4].

Extension Control, a concept and method of intelligent control, was established and developed on the basis of Extension Theory, which was originated from China [5]. The mathematics basis of traditional control, modern control and neural network control is L transform, status space analysis and neural network topology respectively, while that of extension control is extension set theory. In the recent years, many experts have carried out the corresponding research of the structure and algorithm of

---

* Corresponding author.

J. Lei et al. (Eds.): NCIS 2012, CCIS 345, pp. 301–306, 2012.
© Springer-Verlag Berlin Heidelberg 2012

extension controller. By now, the extension theory and extension engineering method have been entering into many research fields of extension control [7]-[10]. Unfortunately, the extension controller design lacks the information of needing control signal to develop the matter element. Furthermore, it is difficulty to find the transformation operator or something methodologies.

This paper briefly introduces the related basic concepts of extension control, such as the structure of canonical extension control, extension set of character status of basic extension controller, and general extension control algorithm, and so on. Also presents the extension application in power systems. The future work and prospect of development are described.

2   Proposed of Extension Control Method

In 1991, Li Jian proposed a new concept and method of intelligent control, denominated extension control [6], which basic idea is to solve control problem form the aspect of information transformation. It is to transform the control information into the eligible value range by using dependent degree to tune the output modification factors. Based on this idea, they set up the structure of extension controller is shown in Fig.1, which adopts dual-layer structure.

The basic extension controller consists of five parts: character selecting, character pattern identification, dependent degree identification, measure pattern identification and control algorithm. The basic extension controller is used for completing the main control function.

The upper-layer extension controller consists of database, repository, and manage of decision-making and information. Database and repository are used for saving the information of control process and expert knowledge respectively. As the basic extension controller's consummate and supplement, this upper-layer controller is used to optimize the basic control and reflect the transform of contradictory question, which is the extension control emphasized.

3   Extension Set of Basic Extension Controller

The basic extension controller adopts error e and error differential e as character values while the corresponding character status is S = (e,Δe). In order to calculate the dependent degree $K_{\tilde{X}}(S)$, the corresponding extension set $\tilde{X}$ about character status S= (e,Δe) of basic extension controller must be built first. Assumed that the allowable value ranges of error e and error differential Δe of control object are [-eom, eom] and [-Δeom, $\triangle$eom] respectively, the maximum extensible value range of error e and error differential Δe of control object are[-em, em] and [-Δem, $\triangle$em] respectively. So the extension set $\tilde{X}$ about character status S=(e, Δe) of basic extension controller can be represented in Fig. 2.

In fig. 2, assumed that character status of the original point is S 0 (0 ,0) , point S (e, Δe) is a character status of a random point in the coordinate plane.

Here defines that the distance from a random point of the coordinate plane to the original point of the coordinate plane is called status distance, written as D. Then from Fig. 2 it can get that the maximum status distance DO of classic domain, the maximum status distance Dm of extension domain, and the status distance DS of a random point of the coordinate plane can be represented by the following equations:

$$D_0 = \sqrt{e_{om}^2 + \Delta e_{om}^2} \tag{1}$$

$$D_m = \sqrt{e_m^2 + \Delta e_m^2} \tag{2}$$

$$D_s = \sqrt{e^2 + \Delta e^2} \tag{3}$$

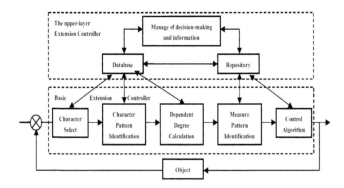

Fig. 1. The structure of canonical extension controller

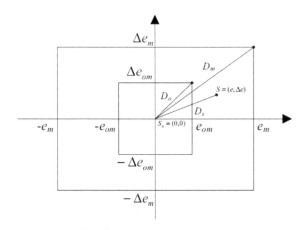

Fig. 2. The extension set $\tilde{X}$

4   The Improved Extension Control Algorithm of Extension Domain

Huang Ying et al [5] propose an improved extension control algorithm of extension domain.The output value u(t) can be given as follows:

$$u(t) = y(t)/k - \text{sgn}(e) \cdot K_{\tilde{X}}(S) \cdot u(t-1) \cdot p + \text{sgn}(e)D_s \cdot g \qquad (4)$$

where u(t) is the current output value; y(t) is the current sampling value of control object; k is the static gain; $K_{\tilde{X}}(S)$ is the dependent degree of character status S; u(t−1) is the last output value; Ds is the status distance. p and g are modification factors. In this equation, dependent degree $K_{\tilde{X}}(S)$ and status distance Ds are adopted to modify the output value u(t). sgn(e) is the symbol function of error shown in [5]

5   The Application of Extension Control in Power System

The extension control strategy is characterized by solving incompatibility during the control process[11][12]. It may be especially applied in control of a complex system not just characterized by nonlinearity like the power system[13].

Based on extension theory and conventional DGA(Dissolved Gas Analysis) three-ratio method, LI Zheng et al[15] proposed the extension set method to diagnose transformer fault. The matter-element models are established first for the three-ratio method. Then the extended relation functions(as shown in Fig. 3) of a point to an interval are offered, which are used to diagnose transformer faults.

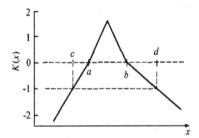
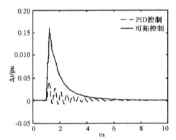

Fig. 3. Extended membership function

Fig. 4. Step response of two control methods

Aiming at the easily occurred incompatibility which leads to erroneous estimation, DU Lin et al established a transformer operational state assessment hierarchy index system, and proposed the corresponding model on the basis of the extension theory. The extension theory converts the multiobject assessment to single object assessment by combining qualitative and quantitative analysis methods to achieve a comprehensive assessment state. Moreover, the model also gives a definite method of classical domain in extension lever assessment to improve the assessment accuracy. The case analysis proves that the extension hierarchy assessment of power transformer is rational and effective.

A governor controller is designed by use of the extension control strategy to improve the dynamic performance of hydro-electric system. With the infinite-reservoir single-penstock hydro-governor infinite-bus system as the control object , a full hydro-machine-electric simulation model is established by integrating three models , i .e. , the elastic water hammer model of hydraulic system , the linearized hydro-turbine model, as well as the classical second-order model of synchronous generator[16]. Fig.4 shows, when the parameters are adjusted as appropriate, the conventional PID control system and the extenson control system all can achieve stable and no difference in status, but steady state time is longer with PID controller then extension controlle. the extension controller can significantly enhance the dynamic performance of hydro-generator governor.

Aiming at thesituation that the load forecasting of power system mais have certain errors , double extension gather-ype model and calculating way are put forward. The results of load forecasting demonst rate that the double extension gather-type model hase higher estimation accuracy.

6   Conclusions

The key-point of designing the extension controller is to find a systematic design approach under the developed structure of extension controller. Using the fuzzy controller architecture or heuristics approach to design the extension controller depends upon expert knowledge and experiences about the designed control system. In many situations, however, the skilled experts cannot give complete description about their control action according to system variables. For such cases, the same problem as the fuzzy controller arisen, the demanded system performance is not easily satisfied if we only depend upon the orientation of control common sense to design the extension controller.

Acknowledgements. This work was supported by Leading Academic Discipline Project of Shanghai Municipal Education Commission, Project Numbers: J51301.

References

[1] Wen, C.: Science Exploration 3(1), 83 (1983)
[2] Li, J., Wang, S.: Primary Research on Extension Control. In: Pro. of International Conference on Information and Systems, AMSE, Hangzhou, China, vol. (1), pp. 392–395 (1991)
[3] Chen, J.Y., Wong, C.: Stable Extension Control of Nonlinear Systems. In: IEEE International Conference on Systems, Man, and Cybernetics, pp. 2415–2418 (2000)

[4] Ying, H.: Extension control algorithm using extension set in control system. In: Third International Conference on Information Technology and Applications, vol. 1, pp. 407–410 (2005)

[5] Yang, G., Zhang, W., Huang, Y.: Computer and Information Science 2(1), 103–107 (2009) (in Chinese)

[6] Li, J., Wang, S.: Design of a Type of Extension Controller. In: Pro. of Theory and Application Workshop on Country Intelligent Control and Self-adaption Control, Xi An, China, pp. 90–97 (1993)

[7] Pan, D., Jin, Y.: Control Theory and Applications. China 13(3), 305–311 (1996) (in Chinese)

[8] Zhang, J., Yu, Y.: Guangdong Automation and Information Engineering (3), 5–7 (2000) (in Chinese)

[9] Yang, L., Wu, L., Aihua, H.: System Engineering Theory and its Implement (6), 126–130 (2000) (in Chinese)

[10] Chen, Z., Weng, Q.: Journal of Guangdong University of Technology 18(1), 38–41 (2001) (in Chinese)

[11] Cai, W., et al.: Extension Engineering. Science Press, Beijing (1997)

[12] Guan, F.-X.R., Wang, K.-J.: 38(7), 1146–1149 (2006)

[13] Zhu, H., Mölle, K.: A Concept on Dual Control of Mechanical Ventilation Based on the Extension Strategy. In: International Conference on Bioinformatics and Biomedical Engineering, pp. 1–4 (2010)

[14] Li, Z., Ma, H.: Electric Power Automation Equipment 24(11), 14–17 (2004) (in Chinese)

[15] Huang, W., Zhao, X., Wang, W.: Automation of Electric Power Systems 28(13), 45–49 (2004) (in Chinese)

[16] Wang, M., Liu, X., Yu, J.: Journal of Hysroelectric Engneering 28(4), 171–175, 186 (2009) (in Chinese)

Modified Information Retrieval Model Based on Markov Network

Jiali Zuo[1], Mingwen Wang[2], Jianyi Wan[2], Genxiu Wu[3], and Shuixiu Wu[2]

[1] School of Elementary Education, Jiangxi Normal University, Nanchang, China
August813cn@hotmail.com
[2] School of Computer and Information Engineering, Jiangxi Normal University,
Nanchang, China
mwwang@jxnu.edu.cn, wanjianyi@yahoo.com.cn,
wushuixiu@sina.com.cn
[3] School of Mathematics and Information Sciences, Jiangxi Normal University,
Nanchang, China
Wgx_nc@sina.com

Abstract. Information retrieval model is still can not achieve satisfactory performance. Many researches have shown that better term weighting method and model useful information in information retrieval can improve retrieval performance. In this paper we propose a modified information retrieval model based on Markov network, which model the related information using Markov network and use query information to modify term weighting, which can make the relevant document rank high. Experiment shows our model has better performance than baseline model.

Keywords: Markov network, term relationship, term weighting.

1 Introduction

Information retrieval model is central in information retrieval, which have been studied by many researches. But over the decade, no single retrieval model has proven to be most effective. Many reasons may cause poor retrieval performance, such as poor document representation and term independent assumption that taken by vector space model and unigram language model [1,6]. To obtain better performance, some researches focuses on better representation of information retrieval, which contains document and query representation. Other researches study the information retrieval model to model useful information to resolve term independent assumption.

As information retrieval is to retrieval a relevant document of a query and return to user. Actually, the process of retrieval is to measure the relevance degree of document and query, so the representation of document that to weight every term in document is of great importance, as tf and idf and BM25 has been proposed. On the other hand, there are two different useful information that can be used to resolve term independent assumption, semantic information and statistical information. Semantic information contains syntax, co-reference and named-entities[7]. A more common

J. Lei et al. (Eds.): NCIS 2012, CCIS 345, pp. 307–314, 2012.
© Springer-Verlag Berlin Heidelberg 2012

way is to use statistical information, such as term relationship mainly expressed using term co-occurrence. Some research add the relevant information into model directly[2,3,9.10], other studies focus on query expansion[11,12,13] or feedback [14,15,16].

From the linguistic point of view, we can find that the meaning of a term will be effect by its connection with other terms. As an example, when bank is connected with water, it means sloping land, and when it connected with money, its meaning is different. In information retrieval, a document relevant or not depend on the meaning of query terms. That is to say, the relevant degree of a document is decided by all the terms importance and its connection with each other.

In this paper we use Markov network to model term relationship. There are some successful applications of Markov network in information retrieval. Meltaz propose a Markov random model for term dependencies[5,15]. Different from these models, we use Markov network to model a document[17]. To get better term weighting and then improve retrieval performance, the model use query information to modify term importance.

The paper is organized as follows. In section 2 we give a brief introduction about Markov network and its application in information retrieval. Section 3 will introduce the information retrieval model we propose. Section 4 is about the experiments results, and the conclusions are given in the final section.

2   Information Retrieval Model Based on Markov Network

Markov network is a kind of undirected graphical model that can model complex problems especially for those that contains a great deal of variant. A Markov network consists of:

(1) A Markov network can be expressed as G(V, E) where V is a set of nodes of all the collection, and E is a set of edges between nodes representing dependencies between random variables.

(2) A set of functions $\Psi(c)$, each is a non-negative function assigned to a clique on the graph of.

The property of Markov network is any variable in the graph is independent of its non-neighbors given observed values for its neighbors.

The key problem of using Markov network in information retrieval is to construct a Markov network G representing D and Q, to estimate the joint distribution P over this graph, and then to use its value to measure the relevant of D and Q. According the Markov property, the joint distribution over the graph G can be factorized over the cliques of graph:

$$P_G(Q,D) = \frac{1}{Z} \prod_{c \in C(G)} \psi(c) \tag{1}$$

Where, D={t1,t2,…,tn} is a set of terms, Q is query node, C(G) is the set of cliques of graph G, and the functions Ψ(c) are referred to as factor potential or clique potential. Z normalizes the distribution and is hard to compute. For ranking purpose, we can infer that:

$$P_G(Q \mid D) \overset{rank}{=} \log P_G(Q \mid D) = \log \frac{P_G(Q, D)}{P_G(D)}$$

(2)

$$\overset{rank}{=} \log P_G(Q, D) \overset{rank}{=} \sum_{c \in C(G)} \log \psi(c)$$

In formula 2, the general formation of potential function Ψ(c)=exp(λ1, f(·)), and its definition is decided by the task and cliques what we consider. Feature function f(·) is real-valued feature function over cliques. In practice, feature function can take various forms and there also can define multiple potential functions for one clique.

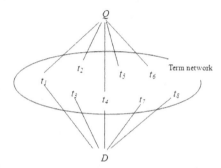

Fig. 1. Markov network information retrieval model

As shown in figure1, we just consider two kinds of cliques:C_{QT1} contains a query node Q and a term node that appear in the document, in which there is an edge between query node Q and term node t_i; C_{QTn} contains a query node Q and two or more term node $t_1…t_n$ (number of terms=n), in which there are edges between each two term nodes. In this paper, we set n=2. The reason that to construct these two cliques is that our study of information retrieval show information retrieval model should follow these two rules:

Rule 1. If a term t_i appears in both document and query, then this term is useful to retrieval.

Rule 2. If term t_i, t_j and t_k appear in both document and query, t_i and t_j have relationship, t_k has no relationship with other terms, then the contribution of these three terms to retrieval is different, and t_i and t_j should be more important than t_k. Actually, rule 1 is the match of single terms between document and query, which corresponds to clique C_{QT1}. Rule 2 is the contribution of query term relationship in document to query. From the table 2, we can see an edge is between query term node t_1 and t_2, which means these two nodes have term relationship and the importance of t_1 is increased as its relationship with t_2, and vice verse. Therefore, t_1 and t_2 is more important than t_4.

From the linguistic point of view, a term will be effected by its connection with other terms. In information retrieval, a document relevant or not depend on the meaning of terms in document and query. That is to say, the relevant degree of a document is decided by importance of all the terms that in query and documents and term relationship between terms.

Then the ranking function turns to be:

$$P_G(Q \mid D) \stackrel{rank}{=} \sum_{c \in QT_1} \lambda_1 f_{T_1}(c) + \sum_{c \in QT_2} \lambda_2 f_{T_2}(c) \tag{3}$$

Formula 3 show that the ranking function has two parts: the first factor is about QT1, which is the match of single query terms between query and document; the second factor is about QT2, which is the term relationship information. This two parts is weighted by λ1 and λ2 separately, where λ1 +λ2=1. If λ1 is much bigger, model performance is mainly influenced by term; if λ2 is bigger, model has more term relationship information. In extreme case, the model is general retrieval model when λ1 is set to be 0, and the model only consider term relationship when λ2 is set to be 1.

To measure term relationship, we use term co-occurrence in this paper:

$$\mathrm{Re}\, l_D(t_i, t_j) = p_D(t_i, t_j) \log \frac{p_D(t_i, t_j)}{p_D(t_i) p_D(t_j)} \tag{4}$$

Formula 4 shows that window of co-occurrence is defined as sentence. Other types of windows, such as paragraph can be used too. Actually, we can also consider some other methods including distance between terms or semantic relationship to compute term relationship, which will be discussed in the future work.

3   Modified Information Retrieval Model

As we mentioned before, the relevance degree of a document is defined by query terms it contains. If the weight of query term in a document is large, then it will increase the probability this document be judged relevant. In our Markov network information retrieval model, relevant degree of a document contains two parts: the weight of query term in document and query, and the term relationship of query terms in documents. So, a problem is that if a document does not contain any query term then the relevant degree of this document should be 0? It seems it is too simple to give its relevant degree 0, but its relevant degree should be simple than these documents that contain query terms. According to this, if the relevant degrees of documents that contain all query terms and documents that contain parts of query terms should be different, and latter one should be litter.

Intuitively, if a document A contains all the query terms, and meanwhile the other document B only contains a few of query terms, then document A should be more relevant. Especially in the case that query terms have ambiguity, ignore this difference may affect performance. Therefore, if a document only contains parts of query terms, the relevance degree of this document should be punished. As a example, if query contains '计算机' and '商店' and 'CPU' , document A contains all of three terms, document B only contains '计算机' and '商店', obviously document A should be more relevant, in other words the probability that A is relevant to query is greater than B. So, we define rule 3:

Rule 3 If Query Q contains term t_i, and t_j does not disappear in document, then the relevance degree of this document should be decreased.

According to this rule, we increase a clique in information retrieval model:

C_{QNI}: this clique contains query node Q and a term node t_i that is disconnected with Q, t_i is connected with Q.

After increased clique C_{QNI} to our information retrieval model, the ranking function turns to be:

$$P_G(Q \mid D) \overset{rank}{=} \sum_{c \in QT_1} \lambda_{T_1} f_{T_1}(c) + \sum_{c \in QT_2} \lambda_{T_2} f_{T_2}(c) + \sum_{c \in QN_1} \lambda_{N_1} f_{N_1}(c) \qquad (5)$$

In Formula 5, $\lambda_{T1} + \lambda_{T2} + \lambda_{NI} = 1$. The different between this formula from formula 3 is it contains a different part QN_1, which is the weighted by parameter λ_{NI}. This new part is to punish the document that contains only parts of query terms. If we set λ_{NI} to 0, the ranking function is equal to formula 3, and then the model turns to be the Markov network information retrieval model we described in Section 2. Actually, QN_1 is to use query information to modify the term importance.

4   Experiment and Analysis

In order to examine the performance of the model, we use a standard corpus Med with1033 documents and 30 queries, Cran with 1398 documents and 223 queries, Cisi with 1460 documents and 76 queries. We only use title of the queries, title and body of document in the experiment. The corpus is preprocessed as follows: all numbers and stopwords are removed, words are converted into lowercase, and word stemming is performing using the Porter stemmer.

4.1   Feature Selection

As feature selection is of great impact to retrieval performance, we use two kind of most used feature functions in this paper, which is Language models with Dirichlet smoothing[1,16] and BM25[17].

Feature function using Language models is:

$$f_1(c) = qtf_i \log[\frac{tf_{i,D} + \mu \frac{cf_i}{|C|}}{|D| + \mu}] \qquad (6)$$

Feature function using BM25 is:

$$f_1(c) = qtf_i \frac{(k_1 + 1)tf_{i,D}}{k_1\left((1-b)+b\dfrac{|D|}{|D|_{avg}}\right)+tf_{i,D}}$$

$$\log\frac{N - df_i + 0.5}{df_i + 0.5}$$

(7)

In these formulas, $tf_{i,D}$ and cf_i is the number of term t_i in document D and corpus C separately, df_i is the number of documents that t_i appears. $|C|$ and $|D|$ is the length of corpus and document. $|D|_{avg}$ means average document length in dataset. qtf_i is t_i count in query Q. μ, k_1 and b is the parameters of these two feature functions.

For the reason of space, we omit the details of f_2 and f_3 which are similar to f_1. Some other feature functions can also be used and will be discussed in our future work.

4.2   Experiment Results

Table 1 give the result of this model (noted by MMNR) comparing to baseline model and Markov network information retrieval model described in section 2 (noted by MNR). The result of this experiment makes us feel quite surprised is that the result of feature function of BM25 is rarely disappointed, even worse than baseline model. What is dramatic contrast to BM25 is that result of feature function of language model is satisfactory which is showed in table 1. According to the result and ranking function, the reason is:

(1)   The choice of feature function is of great impact to retrieval performance. The reason that the result of BM25 as feature function is rather poor may be the setting of f_{QNI} is not suited to the model. In contrast to it, the performance of language model as feature function is very good. As we analysis f_{QNI}, we find that its form like idf. As BM25 has information about idf, then f_{QNI} may increase too much idf information, which cause the weight of tf and document length decreased and affect model performance.

Table 1. Performance of modified information retrieval model based on Markov network comparing to other models

Model	Med			Cran			Cisi		
	MAP	P@10	P@20	MAP	P@10	P@20	MAP	P@10	P@20
Baseline (LM)	0.3825	0.4600	0.3850	0.2205	0.1726	0.1285	0.1256	0.1974	0.1553
MNR (LM)	0.4550	0.5757	0.4569	0.3047	0.2198	0.1532	0.1310	0.1907	0.1607
MMNR (LM)	0.5243	0.6414	0.4931	0.3109	0.2215	0.1646	0.1332	0.2037	0.1749

(2) When language model as feature function, idf and tf is combined and weight of f_{QNI} in this model is litter, then f_{QN} add enough but not too much idf information to the model, which improve retrieval performance.

(3) Improvements of MAP and P@10 are much better than P@20, which can be attributed to that MAP and P@10 is inclined to be high when relevant document is rank high. As this model decrease the relevant degree of documents that only contains parts of query terms, it can make the relevant document rank high and improve retrieval performance.

5   Conclusion

The paper proposes a modified information retrieval model based on Markov Network, in which relevant degree of a document contains two parts: the weight of query term in document and query, the term relationship of query terms in documents, and the punishment that documents only contain parts of query terms. As the model can make the relevant document rank high, it can improve retrieval performance. Experiment shows our model has better performance than baseline model.

Acknowledgement. This work was supported by the Nation Natural Science Foundation of China (NSFC) under Grant No.60963014, No.61272212 and No. 61163006 and Jiangxi Normal University Growing Foundation.

References

[1] Zhai, C.: Statistical Language Models for Information Retrieval: A Critical Review. Foundations and Trends in Information Retrieval 2, 137–215 (2008)

[2] Wang, X., Zhai, C.: Mining Term Association Patterns from Search Logs for Effective Query Reformulation. In: 17th ACM International Conference on Information and knowledge Management, pp. 479–488. ACM, New York (2008)

[3] Lease, M.: Natural Language Processing for Information Retrieval: the Time is Ripe (again). In: 2nd Ph.D. Workshop on Information and knowledge Management (PIKM 2007), pp. 1–8. ACM, New York (2007)

[4] Liu, S., Lin, F., Yu, C., Meng, W.: An Effective Approach to Document Retrieval via Utilizing Wordnet and Recognizing Phrases. In: 27th ACM Special Interest Group on Information Retrieval, pp. 266–272. ACM, New York (2004)

[5] Brants, T.: Natural Language Processing in Information Retrieval. In: 16th Meeting of Computational Linguistics in the Netherlands, pp. 1–13 (2003)

[6] Gao, J., Nie, J., Wu, G., Cao, G.: Dependence Language Model for Information Retrieval. In: 27th ACM Special Interest Group on Information Retrieval, pp. 170–177. ACM, New York (2004)

[7] Cao, G., Nie, J., Bai, J.: Integrating Word Relationships into Language Models. In: 28th ACM Special Interest Group on Information Retrieval, pp. 298–305. ACM, New York (2005)

[8] Karimzadehgan, M., Zhai, C.: Estimation of Statistical Translation Models Based on Mutual Information for Ad Hoc Information Retrieval. In: 33th ACM Special Interest Group on Information Retrieval, pp. 323–330. ACM, New York (2010)

[9] Bai, J., Song, D., Bruza, P., Nie, J., Cao, G.: Query Expansion Using Term Relationships in Language Models for Information Retrieval. In: 14th ACM International Conference on Information and Knowledge Management, pp. 688–695. ACM, New York (2005)

[10] Xu, J., Croft, W.: Query Expansion Using Local and Global Document Analysis. In: 19th ACM Special Interest Group on Information Retrieval, pp. 4–11. ACM, New York (1996)

[11] Lv, Y., Zhai, C.: Positional Relevance Model for Pseudo-Relevance Feedback. In: 33th ACM Special Interest Group on Information Retrieval, pp. 579–586. ACM, New York (2010)

[12] Dang, V., Croft, W.B.: Query Reformulation Using Anchor Text. In: 33th ACM International Conference on Web Search and Data Mining, pp. 41–50. ACM, New York (2010)

[13] Metzler, D., Croft, W.B.: A Markov Random Field Model for Term Dependencies. In: 27th ACM Special Interest Group on Information Retrieval, pp. 472–479. ACM, New York (2005)

[14] Metzler, D.: Automatic Feature Selection in the Markov Random Field Model for Information Retrieval. In: 16th ACM International Conference on Information and Knowledge Management, pp. 253–262. ACM, New York (2007)

[15] Metzler, D., Croft, W.B.: Latent Concept Expansion Using Markov Random Fields. In: 30th ACM Special Interest Group on Information Retrieval, pp. 311–318. ACM, New York (2007)

[16] Seo, J., Croft, W.B.: Geometric Representation for Multiple Documents. In: 33th ACM Special Interest Group on Information Retrieval, pp. 251–258. ACM, New York (2010)

[17] Zuo, J., Wang, M.: A Query Reformulation Model Using Markov Graphic Method. In: 2011 International Conference on Asian Language Processing, pp. 119–122. IEEE Computer Society, Los Alamitos (2011)

[18] Ponte, J.M., Croft, W.B.: A Language Modeling Approach to Information Retrieval. In: 21th ACM Special Interest Group on Information Retrieval, pp. 275–281. ACM, New York (1998)

[19] Iwayama, M., Fujii, A., Kando, N., Marukawa, Y.: An Empirical Study on Retrieval Models for Different Document Genres: Patents and Newspaper Ariticles. In: 26th ACM Special Interest Group on Information Retrieval, pp. 251–258. ACM, New York (2003)

Software Simulation of Lifts

Chong Wang, Hai-ming Li, and Jia-jia Ye

Computer and Information Engineering College, Shanghai University of Electric Power,
Shanghai 201300, China

Abstract. Lifts running modes are simulated in this paper. The simulating software is built by using Greenfoot platform and Java technology. The design of related classes is described through UML diagrams, which is created by Enterprise Architect tools. The related methods and basic interfaces are programmed by Java. The LSS(Lift Simulation Software) Model can be used for the strategies of energy saving of lifts.

Keywords: Lift, LSS, EA(Enterprise Architect), Java, UML.

1 Introduction

Modern high-rise business building in general are supporting the many sets of lifts, so how to arrange the lift operation mode, which can shorten people's average waiting time, ensure the normal use of the company employees, and can reduce the energy consumption, is one of the important contents for property management.

The LSS (Lift simulation software) use EA (Enterprise Architect) to design related classes, combining with relevant ideas of Software Engineering. It realizes the simulation of 10 floors and 3 lifts running state of the building, including start simulation, pause simulation and end simulation etc. Function. In dealing with people's request of take a lift in different floor, statistics the number of people in single ladder etc. Function.

2 Software Introduction

2.1 About Greenfoot

Greenfoot teaches object orientation with Java. Create 'actors' which live in 'worlds' to build games, simulations, and other graphical programs. The interface is a full IDE which includes project management, auto-completion, syntax highlighting, and other tools common to most IDEs. However the interface is designed to be simple and easy to use; built with beginners in mind. Greenfoot is used by thousands of institutions around the world. It provides easy transition into other environments, such as BlueJ and more professional IDEs.

J. Lei et al. (Eds.): NCIS 2012, CCIS 345, pp. 315–322, 2012.
© Springer-Verlag Berlin Heidelberg 2012

2.2   About Enterprise Architect(EA)

EA provides complete traceability from requirements, analysis and design models, through to implementation and deployment. And it provides powerful document generation and reporting tools with a full WYSIWYG template editor. Generate detailed reports with the information. Its Use Case Metrics capability makes it easy to assess relative project complexity, based on the number and type of use cases within the model, the type of project and capabilities of the development environment. With experience, use case metrics provide a great way to quickly assess the scope of a project.

3   The Process Principle of LSS

In the real condition, the operation of the lift is very complex and the lift control has been a hotspot among scholars both at home and abroad. It contains equipment manufacturing, intelligent control, sensing, software etc. technology. However, the primary task of the development process is to use the Software Engineering method abstract complex reality problem into model gradually.

Abstract process and development principle as shown in Fig.1, the project development process is designed to a three layers framework, according to the top-down development principles, the first layer is used to construct the entire building, and to hold the lift model; The second layer is used to deal with people's request of take a lift, and to monitor the event which is controlled through the passengers press the different button; The third is the running control of each lift and the processing of passengers request, and provides a set of classes and interface, in order to facilitate development mode to program. Each module realizes the function of each layer through the interaction between the classes gradually.

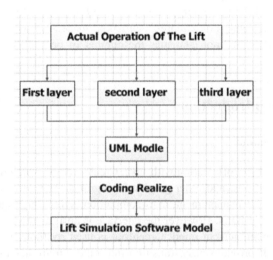

Fig. 1.

4   The Design of LSS

Combining with the actual conditions and the need of simulation software, the relationship between each abstract model of the whole goal is as shown in Fig.2, and the parameters, methods of each class, and their called relationship is as shown in Fig.3 below.

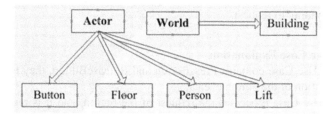

Fig. 2.

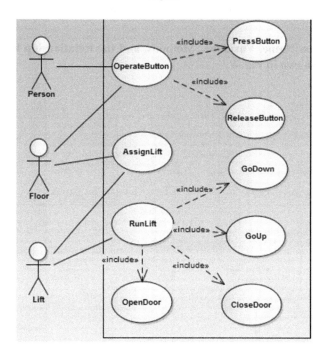

Fig. 3.

The LSS is developed on the Green Foot platform, which owns two basic kinds of operation, in which is World class including Building, Building extends from World. Another type of operation is Actor class, including: Button, Person, Floor, Lift, they all are inherited from Actor. Fig.3 shows the transferred message and called relationship between each class.

4.1   Use Case Diagram (Fig.3) Explanation

4.1.1   The Actor Explanation

The Person makes the request of take a lift, through selects the button;

The Floor receives the request of the Person, assigns the lift in response to the request of the passenger, and transmits the request message to the Lift, restore the state of the button;

The Lift receives message, and then transports the lift to the floor where the passenger is, responding to request.

4.1.2   The Use Case Explanation

OperateButton Use Case contains PressButton and ReleaseButton, they together constitute the operation of the button events;

AssignLift Use Case processes the request of the button, and it is responsible for assigning the lift to the target floor;

RunLift Use Case contains GoUp, GoDown, OpenDoor and CloseDoor four function, and it is used to realize the normal operation of the lift;

4.2   The Class Name, Variables, Methods, and the Relationship between Each other, Shown in Fig. 4

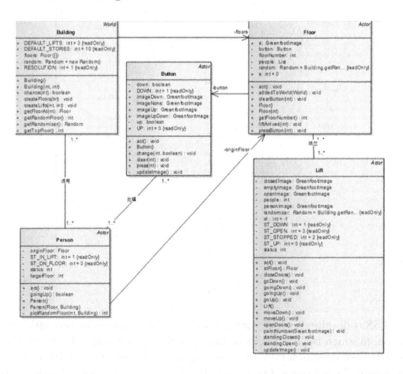

Fig. 4.

- **Building Class:** Loading software interface Lord background, providing the call method that loading the Lift and Floor elements to the main interface, and constituting the whole main body of the project;
- **Button Class:** Encapsulating the operation processing of press button and remove button, and loading the picture element on the main interface;
- **Floor Class:** Implementing the method of loading the Floor to the Building specifically, processing the request from the Button, and assigning the lift in response to request;
- **Person Class:** Implementing the method of loading the Person element to the Floor and Building specifically and making a request of take the lift;
- **Lift Class:** Receiving the assigned-lift message, running the lift to the floor according to the message, and taking passengers to the target floor;

5   The Implementation Of LSS

5.1   The Definition of Classes (Main Variables and Methods) as Follows

Class Building.java

```
public class Building extends World
begin
    final int DEFAULT_LIFTS = 3;// Set the default number
of lifts
    final int DEFAULT_STORIES = 10;// Sets the default
number of the floor
    private void createFloors(int numberOfFloors);//
Create all the floors in the building.
    private void createLifts(int numberOfLifts, int num-
berOfFloors);// Create all the lifts in the building.
end
```

Class Button.java

```
public class Button extends Actor
begin
    public void press(int direction);// Deal with press
the button
    public void clear(int direction);// Deal with remove
the button
    public void change(int direction, boolean onOff);//
Response press and remove button operation
end
```

Class Floor.java

```
public class Floor extends Actor
begin
    private List people;  // the people currently waiting
on this floor
```

```
    public Floor(int floorNumber);// Constructor of Floor
Class
    public void addedToWorld(World world);// Loading the
floor into the World, that is added to the interface of
the Lord
    public void pressButton(int direction);// Press a
button to call a lift to this floor.
    public void clearButton(int direction);// Release a
button after enter the lift
end
```

Class Person.java

```
public class Person extends Actor
begin
    private Floor originFloor;// Starting floor
    private int targetFloor;// Target floor
  public Person(Floor floor, Building building);// Added
the person to the Floor and Building
    private int pickRandomFloor(int currentFloor, Build-
ing building);// Choose a random floor number (but not
the current one).
end
```

Class Lift.java

```
public class Lift extends Actor
begin
    public void act();//Override act(),and judge the lift
state with up or down
    private void goingUp();//Deal with the request of the
rise
    private void goingDown();//Deal with the request of
the fall
    public void openDoors();//Open the lift door.
    public void closeDoors();//Close the lift door.
    private void paintNumber(GreenfootImage img);// Paint
the number of passengers onto the lift's image.
End
```

5.2   Two Important Processing

The number of passengers processing: In fact, the number of passengers who wants to take the lift on every floor is random. In this system, the number is assumed as randomly distributed. In order to simulate the realistic conditions, the system uses a random function to generate the number of passengers on each floor;

Passengers rise or fall request processing: In the actual case, the need of passengers who want to which floor is uncertain, but the rise or fall of the lift is opposite two operation, If we consider this state as a variable, and we can approximately assume that the distribution of the variable as a Bernoulli distribution. And in the system, we give rise a value of 0, fall a value of 1, and then assign each variables values of 0 or 1 through the variable named direction in the method invocation process, so as to realize the lift rise or fall;

5.3   Software Running Interfaces (Partial) Are Shown as in Fig.5

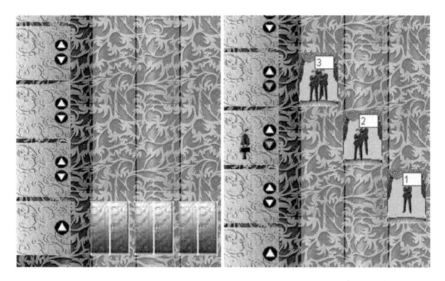

Fig. 5.

6   Conclusion

In the development process of this project, we use the top-down development method, divide it into several modules with the "divide and rule" thought, and gradually realize each module, layered realization. Thus regulates the software development process, and improves the efficiency of software development.

In the process of modeling, we abstract the complex problem into the simple model that can be realized through software. After obtaining multiple abstract objects, we construct each object corresponding operation on EA, so as to further improve the maneuverability of the model. In software coding process, we develop it on Greenfoot platform, make full use of its rich class library which helping to the realization of dynamic simulation software, so as to be able to develop simple, user-friendly LSS.

This LSS realizes the running state simulation of 10 floors with 3 lifts, and to some extent, it has simulated the actual operation of the lift successfully. At the same time, this software can be further extended, for example, it can be used to simulate the real lift power consumption, and to explore the energy saving mode of lift running. It owns some practical significance and economic significance.

References

1. Smith, T.F., Waterman, M.S.: Identification of Common Molecular Subsequences. J. Mol. Biol. 147, 195–197 (1981)
2. Ma, Z.: O-O Analysis and Design. China Machine Press (2011)
3. Booch, G., Rumbaugh, J., Jacobson, I.: The Unified Modeling Language User Guide, 2nd edn. Addison Wesley (2005)
4. Alani, A.F.: Performance Optimization of Knowledge-based Elevator Group Control System. In: Elevator Technology, vol. 6, IAEE, HK (1995)
5. Shiro, H.: New Elevator Group-control Method for Up-peak Periods. Int. of Systems Science (2003)
6. Markon, S., Kita, H., Nishikawa, Y.: Adaptive Optimal Elevator Group Control by Use of Neural Networks. Trans. of the Institute of Systems, Control, and Information Engineer. (1994)
7. Yasuhiro, O., Haruhiko, K., Sadaki, H., et al.: Elevator Group Control System Using Multi-agent System. Systems and Computers in Japan (2003)
8. Kim, C.B., Seong, K.A., Hyung, L.K., et al.: Design and Implementation of a Fuzzy Elevator GroupControl System. IEEE Trans. on Systems, Man and Cybernetics, Part A (1998)
9. Hirasawa, K., Kuzunuki, S., Iwasaka, T., et al.: Hall Call Assignment in Elevator Supervisory Control. The Trans. of IEEJ 2C (1979)
10. Lin, C.H., Fu, L.C.: PetriNet Based Dynamic Scheduling of an Elevator System. In: Proc. of IEEE Int Conf on Robotics and Automation, Minneapolis (1996)
11. Al Sharif, L.R.: New Concepts in Lift Traffic Analysis: The Inverse S-P Method. In: Proc. of ELEVCON 1992, Amsterdam (1992)
12. Daniel Liang, Y.: Introduction to Java Programming-Comprehensive Version, 6th edn. Prentice Hall (2008)
13. Pressman, R.S.: Software Engineering: A Practitioner's Approach, 6th edn. China Machine Press (2007)

Analysis on Power Flow of Distribution Network with DGs

Chen-ning Wu[*] and Xue-qin Lv[**]

School of Electric Power and Automation Engineering,
Shanghai University of Electric Power, Shanghai 200090, China

Abstract. Distributed generations are used more widely, so the problems of grid-connected become obvious. Power flow is the basic of studying power energy and the grid stability. This paper talks about the math model of distribution generations in power flow calculation based on different type. Then it introduces characteristics of classic distributed grid. Some power flow algorithms with DGs that applied wildly at present is expounded in details. It puts forward to advantages and shortcomings of each algorithm. The algorithm of solving PV nodes in back/forward sweep calculation is improved which is based on the power flow algorithm. The current value can be directly got by the amount of voltage change, and it doesn't need update reactive flow. The admittance matrix is derived that adapt small load and accurately handle the power flow in small load with DGs.

Keywords: distributed generation, power flow calculation, back/forward sweep, PV node.

1 Introduction

With the increasingly serious problem of the world's energy shortage, climate change and environmental pollution, the promotion and application of clean energy will be used more extensive. Recently years, China's renewable energy annual growth rate is 25%, and the rate of new distribution generations in energy support will develop from 7% to 15% in 2020[1].

Distributed generation is the system that has small scale, is placed near the load dispersed and can support power for users independently. Because of the trend of centralized power supply mode transition to the concentrated and dispersed power supply mode in global power industry, the DG must be an important development direction of global power industry in new century[2-3]. Due to DGs' power generation are low, so most of them are connected to distribution network or users directly to adjust the power peak and valley balance. Traditional distributed grid changes from single power source to multi-power-source when the DGs are connected into distribution network. It has a great impact on distribution network

---

[*] Interested in distribution network analysis with DG.
[**] Interested in power system stability and intelligent control.

J. Lei et al. (Eds.): NCIS 2012, CCIS 345, pp. 323–331, 2012.
© Springer-Verlag Berlin Heidelberg 2012

reconstruction, voltage distribution and relay protection. Because network reconstruction, failure treatment, reactive power optimization and state estimation and so on need the data of power flow, power flow became more important in distribution network with DGs. So establish the power flow calculation model and simulated with DGs will provide basis and reference in the study of DGs connecting into distribution grid[4-5]. DG usually can be defined for four node type: PV, PQ, PI, PQ(V). Wind generation can be as PQ node. Photovoltaic generation can be as PI node. Micro turbine usually can be as PV node. Double-fed asynchronous fan can be as PQ(V) node. Every node type has its typical algorithm in power flow calculation.

The traditional distribution network differs from the transmission system in the following aspects.

1) It is typically radial or weakly meshed.
2) Distribution lines usually have a larger R/X ratio.
3) There may be significant 3-phase unbalance including unbalanced loads and single-phase or 2-phase lines.

In connection with traits of distribution network, back/forward sweep has high calculation effective, fast iteration speed and simple program, so it is used widely in distribution network power flow calculation. But traditional back/forward sweep just solve slack and PQ node in system, it needs to modify the back/forward sweep algorithm when DGs connected in the distributed grid. Reference [6] improve the back/forward sweep, and proposes new node number process and weakly meshed grid, it uses the calculation method of reactive power compensation based on the sensitivity impedance matrix, but it doesn't consider the load affect. Normal DGs node type are modeling in reference [7], it proposes three-phase power flow algorithm in distribution network base on N-R method with DGs. Because of value of R/X is large, so N-R method has problem of difficult to convergence. In reference [8], back/forward sweep is used to solve radial distributed network power flow calculation, DGs are modeling as PQ and PV node type, but calculate speed and convergence speed is slow.

This paper proposes a new method to solve PV node in small load situation with DGs base on the back/forward sweep.

2   Modify Back/Forward Sweep Method of Distributed Grid

2.1   Theory Analysis

Recently, the back/forward sweep method of PV node in distributed grid is studied by some scholars. It uses the changing of voltage of PV node and the previous iteration voltage value to calculate the change of reactive power. Then it can update the reactive power of each PV nodes and PV node will change to PQ node, so the calculation will be easy. The method of updating reactive power has two types: sensitivity matrix method and power loss matrix method.

A typical distributed network shows in Fig.1, DGs are placed on the i-th node of the network. All the PV nodes voltages amplitude equal the line rated voltage, that's to say, the voltage are set up 1 p.u.

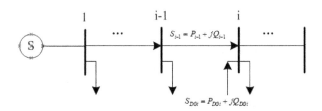

Fig. 1. Typical structure of distributed grid

At first, we assume that the voltage of root node is $U_1 \angle 0°$, the voltage amplitude of PV type distribution generation $U_i = U_{DG}$, $P_i = P_{DG}$, load power of the end node is $S_N = P_N + jQ_N$.

It also assume that the i node voltage of the k-th iteration is $U_i^{(k)}$, the current that flow into i node is $I_{i-1}^{(k)}$, so the current of DG is:

$$I_{DG}^{(k+1)} = \frac{S_{DGi}^{(k)}}{U_i^{(k)}} \tag{1}$$

The value of current $I_{i-1}^{(k)}$ is:

$$I_{i-1}^{(k+1)} = -I_{DG}^{(k+1)} + I_L^{(k+1)} + I_i^{(k+1)} \tag{2}$$

The k+1-th iteration voltage of i node is:

$$U_i^{(k+1)} = U_{i-1}^{(k+1)} - I_{i-1}^{(k+1)} Z_{i-1} \tag{3}$$

So the voltage change ΔU of two iterations can present by formula 4.

$$\Delta U = U_{DG} - U_i^{(k+1)} \tag{4}$$

Because $\Delta I = Y \Delta U$, so ΔI can be calculated directly by formula 4, and the next current value $I_i^{(k+2)}$ of PV node is:

$$I_i^{(k+2)} = I_i^{(k+1)} + \Delta I \tag{5}$$

So we can't correct the power.

In traditional method[8-9], there is:

$$\begin{bmatrix} X & R \\ -R & X \end{bmatrix} \begin{bmatrix} \Delta Q \\ \Delta P \end{bmatrix} = \begin{bmatrix} \Delta U \\ \Delta \delta \end{bmatrix} \quad (6)$$

$$X\Delta Q = \Delta U \quad (7)$$

ΔQ is calculated by (7), and update the next iteration reactive power. But the diagonal elements of X are sum of branch reactance of i-th PV type DGs to the first node. The non-diagonal elements of X are sum of branch reactance of two DGs. This algorithm doesn't concern the impact load on each node, because the load has impedance. If the load has low power, the result in that algorithm is not accurate.

In Fig.2, break up all PV nodes, so there is a break point in the network that the change of voltage is ΔU between two points. Because voltage per unit value is 1 in all PV nodes, the same to the root node, so the voltage difference between the point which connect to original radial network and the root node also is ΔU. Then the change in break point current is convert to calculate the current change between root node and PV node.

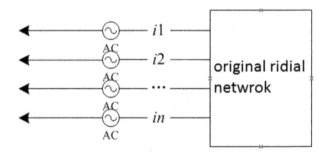

Fig. 2. Distributed grid with PV nodes

Node voltage equation is derived by Kirchhoff's current law, the change in current of one PV node(assume it is i node) is the sum current of all voltage amplitude constant node to the i node. The change current value between i node and root node is $\Delta I''_1$, and current changing other PV nodes is $\Delta I''_{i+1}$, ... $\Delta I''_{i+n}$, current flowing into the node is positive direction. So the sum change value of current of i node is:

$$\Delta I'_i = \Delta I''_1 + \Delta I''_{i+1} + \cdots \Delta I''_{i+n} \quad (8)$$

Among (8)

$$\Delta I''_1 = Y_{i1}\Delta U_1 \quad (9)$$

Y_{i1} is the equivalent admittance between root node and i node. All the load in the network change into admittance by formula $Y = \dfrac{S}{U^2}$.

The current change value between i+1 node and i node is

$$\Delta I''_{i+1} = Y_{i(i+1)} \Delta U_{i+1} \tag{10}$$

$Y_{i(i+1)}$ is the sum reactance between two PV type DGs.

Because there are n+1 constant voltage amplitude node that directly connect with i node, so it can be derived (11)

$$\begin{bmatrix} \Delta I'_i \\ \Delta I'_{i+1} \\ \vdots \\ \Delta I'_{i+n} \end{bmatrix} = \begin{bmatrix} Y_{ii} & -Y_{i(i+1)} & \cdots & -Y_{i(i+n)} \\ -Y_{(i+1)i} & Y_{(i+1)(i+1)} & \cdots & -Y_{(i+1)(i+n)} \\ \vdots & \vdots & \ddots & \vdots \\ -Y_{(i+n)i} & -Y_{(i+n)(i+1)} & \cdots & Y_{(i+n)(i+n)} \end{bmatrix} \begin{bmatrix} U_1 \\ U_{i+1} \\ \vdots \\ U_{i+n} \end{bmatrix} \tag{11}$$

Among it, $Y_{ii} = Y_{i1} + Y_{i(i+1)} + \cdots Y_{i(i+n)}$。

2.2   Calculation Step

Based on the basic theory that mentioned above, it uses matlab as simulink software. The step of back/forward sweep of distributed grid with PV type distribution generations shows below:

1) Read network parameters, and construct all PV node impedance matrix.

2) Set up the initial value of system parameter. The voltage per unit value of root node is 1. All the PV node voltage amplitude is 1, either. All nodes voltage per unit value of first iteration is 1.

3) Determine the place of PV type DGs.

4) Get the admittance matrix.

5) Update the current of each node, and using current type back/forward sweep to calculate voltage of all nodes.

6) Compare this iteration voltage amplitude with previous iteration voltage for all non-PV nodes, compare this iteration voltage with constant voltage for all PV nodes. If all value are less than given value ε, the go to step 8. If not, then go to step 7.

7) Calculate the current change value of PV node by $\Delta I = Y \Delta U$, then go to step 5.

8) Output the result of power flow.

3   Simulation Example

We use IEEE33 nodes system to simulate that shows in Fig.3. Standard power is 10MW, standard voltage is 12.66kV. The calculation accuracy ε is 10^{-4}.

In order to study the influence of power system with DGs and feasibility of algorithm, there are 8 programs in table1. Low load mode means the load value change into the original tenth at 7, 8, 24, 25 and 30 nodes.

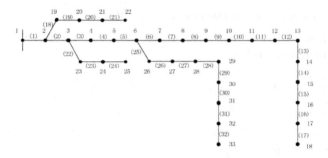

Fig. 3. Structure of IEEE33 nodes system

Table 1. Description of programs

	The node DGs connect
program 1	None of DG
program 2	16, 32 (P=200kW)
program 3	8, 27
program 4	Small load situation, 16, 32
program 5	Small load situation, 8, 27
program 6	16, 32 (traditional back/forward sweep)
program 7	16, 32 (small load situation with traditional algorithm)

The number of iterations and loss of the system of each program show in Table 2. Voltage curve of program 1-5 shows in Fig4.

Table 2. Number of iterations and loss of the system of each program

Node number	program1	program 2	program 3	program 4	program 5	program 6	program 7
Loss	3.3491	2.8830	3.1222	1.7391	1.9887	2.8963	2.4489
Number of iteration	4	5	5	5	4	5	5

It can conclude from the Fig.4 that each node voltage with DGs is significantly improved compared with none of DGs. The node which directly connects with DG has the highest voltage. So, for the real distribution power system, we can connect DGs to the nodes that have poor voltage level, so that improve the stability of power system.

Compared program 2 and program 3, it can conclude that when DGs are connected into the end of the system, it has better voltage level than connected into former nodes, and loss of system are lower, either. In small load situation, because of the total active and reactive power reduce greatly, so the voltage level and loss of system is better than normal load situation.

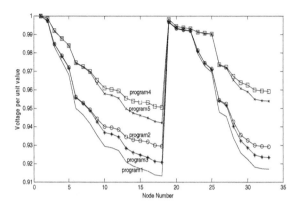

Fig. 4. Voltage per unit of program 1-5

The calculation result is almost same of program 2 and program 6 which is shown in Fig.5, it can prove this algorithm is correct.

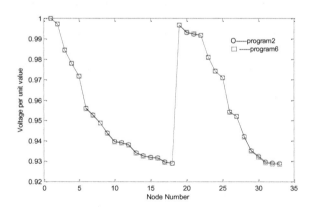

Fig. 5. Voltage curve of program2 and program6

We can see the number of iteration doesn't increase obviously when DGs connected into distributed grid from Table2, so the algorithm assure the calculation speed. In the small load situation, number of iteration is the same with situation without DGs. We can see the result of program 4 and program 7 has big difference

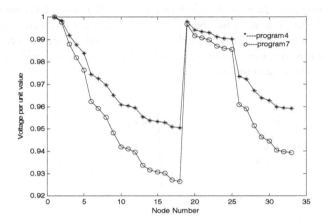

Fig. 6. Two algorithm compare in small load situation

from Fig.6. So, the traditional algorithm doesn't deal with small load situation much correctly, and it proves this algorithm can be applied in small load situation.

4   Conclusion

This paper talks about the math model of distribution generations in power flow calculation based on different type. Then it introduces characteristics of classic distributed grid. Some power flow algorithms with DGs that applied wildly at present is expounded in details. It puts forward to advantages and shortcomings of each algorithm. The algorithm of solving PV nodes in back/forward sweep calculation is improved which is based on the power flow algorithm. The current value can be directly got by the amount of voltage change, and it doesn't need update reactive flow. The admittance matrix is derived that adapt small load and accurately handle the power flow in small load with DGs.

References

[1] Coster, E.J., Myrzik, J.M.A., Kruimer, B., et al.: Integration Issues of Distributed Generation in Distribution Grids. Proceedings of the IEEE 99(1), 28–38 (2011)
[2] Zhang, L.-M., Tang, W., Zhao, Y.-J., et al.: Analysis of DG influences on system voltage and losses in distribution network. Power System Protection and Control 39(5), 91–96 (2011) (in Chinese)
[3] Chen, T.H., Chen, M.S., Hwang, K.J., Kotas, P., Chebli, E.: Distribution System Power Flow Analysis–A Rigid Approach. IEEE Transactions on Power Delivery 6(3), 1146–1152 (1991)
[4] Zhang, F., Cheng, C.S.: A Modified Newton Method for Radial Distribution System Fower Flow Analysis. IEEE Transactions on Power Systems 12(1), 389–397 (1997)

[5] Augugliaro, A., Dusonchet, L., Favuzza, S., et al.: A new backward/forward method for solving radial distribution networks with PV nodes. Electric Power System Research 78(3), 330–336 (2008)

[6] Dai, J., Wang, S., Zhu, J.-F.: Power flow method for weakly meshed distribution network with distributed generation. Power System Protection and Control 39(10), 37–41 (2011) (in Chinese)

[7] Wang, S.-X., Huang, L.-J., Wang, C.-S., et al.: Unbalanced three-phase power flow calculation for distributed power generation system. Electric Power Automation Equipment 27(8), 11–15 (2007) (in Chinese)

[8] Zhu, Y., Tmsovic, K.: Adaptive Power Flow Method for Distribution Systems with Dispersed Generation. IEEE Transactions on Power Delivery 17(3), 822–827 (2002)

Audio and Video Real Time Broadcast System Based on Android Platform

Jiaojiao Fu[1,2], Yumeng Zhang[1,2], and Hui Li[1,2,*]

[1] Shenzhen Key Lab of Cloud Computing & Application, Shenzhen Graduated School,
Peking University, Shenzhen, China 518055
[2] Engineering Lab of Converged Network Technology, Shenzhen Graduated School,
Peking University, Shenzhen, China 518055
`fujiaojiao@sz.pku.edu.cn, zhangyumeng06@gmail.com`
`lih64@pkusz.edu.cn`

Abstract. This paper describes how to design and complete an Audio and Video Real Time Broadcast System. Embedded devices based on Android OS are chosen as the recording terminal to get video and audio frames. The open source library Javacv is integrated for data processing, including encoding video into H.264 format and audio into AAC (Advanced Audio Coding) format, packing them into Flv (Flash Video) file and uploading the stream to Streaming Server with RTMP (Real Time Media Protocol) protocol through WiFi. Any equipment can get the contents through connecting the internet. This system has great significance for the promotion of embedded equipment and rapid information dissemination.

Keywords: Android, Real Time Broadcast, Streaming Server, RTMP, Javacv, H.264, AAC, Flv.

1 Introduction

Today, the rapid development of Internet and the popular use of mobile terminals make information transmission more convenient, timely and efficient, and truly meet the sharing needs of people. While video, since its formation, with its intuitive and vivid characteristics has become the first choice to accept and distribute news.

Android is an open source operating system based on Linux Kernel for mobile devices. It has five advantages: high opening, off operator restraint, self-defined application, easily use of the Google application and low price. Because of these, in the 5 years after its release, Android OS shares more than 59% in the global market, becoming the world's most popular intelligent mobile phone platform and expanding rapidly in the tablet market [1]. It provides very convenient software and hardware platforms for developers to design and test their applications. So, the selection of embedded devices based on Android OS for application development has great advantages.

---

* Corresponding author.

J. Lei et al. (Eds.): NCIS 2012, CCIS 345, pp. 332–339, 2012.
© Springer-Verlag Berlin Heidelberg 2012

This system will be very useful in information sharing for businesses and individuals. It will have a wide range of demands and application prospects in video conference, product promotion, sports events, live news broadcast and so on.

The remainder of the paper is organized as follows. Section 2 provides an overview of the system framework. Section 3 introduces the related concepts and the system's realization method. Section 4 shows the results, discusses the main problems encountered while debugging and gives the solutions. Section 5 summarizes the conclusions.

2   System Architecture Overview

Figure I illustrates the setup of the system implemented. The point of the arrow is the direction of the data flow.

Fig. 1. System Deployment Setup

Android mobile phone or tablet uses its own camera to record video and its own sound card to record audio. Android's architecture consists of 4 layers, from high to low respectively: Applications, Applications Framework, Libraries and Android Runtime, Linux Kernel. In Android, developers use Java as the development language. At the same time, in order to add support for the amount of original open source libraries, Android NDK can be used to let Java call the APIs written by C/C++. The key component is Android Runtime, which includes the core library for java programming and Dalvik virtual machine. Eclipse IDE is used for the development of Android application. Meanwhile, we also need to install Java Jdk, set java environment configuration, install Android SDK and ADT (Android development tools) plug-in. Eclipse IDE is an open-source software development tool that supports multiple languages, including Java. After connecting Android equipment and computer with USB interface or WiFi, we can debug the application, write the generated apk file into Android device and finally run it [2].

Streaming Server's main function is to receive and store streams form Android equipment and push them into the clients that ask for this service. The selected server is the Sewise Company's Streaming Media Server. It is a complete set of audio and video streaming platform, supporting audio and video streaming service (the audio encoding format must be AAC and the video encoding format must be H.264), using UDP and RTMP stream protocol, supporting two stream receiving modes-plug flow and push flow, providing interface for player and easily integrated into user's existing system and website platform [3].

3   System Implementation

3.1   Related Concepts

Javacv[4] based on GPLv2 protocol is an open source visual processing library. It is a group of jar packages for encapsulating commonly used computer vision libraries, including the interfaces of OpenCV, ffmpeg, libdc1394, OpenKinect, videoInput, ARToolKitPlus and so on. We can easily call these APIs through the class utility in Java platform including Android. Besides, Javacv also has hardware acceleration for full screen image display and can execute parallel code in multiple cores.

H.264(MPEG 4 Part 10)[5]defined by MPEG(Moving Picture Expert Group)of ISO and VCEG(Video Coding Expert Group)of ITU-TD, is the newest video coding standard. H.264/MPEG4-AVC has recently become one of the most popular video coding standard and has been applied to all common conferences, IPTV, HDTV and HD video storage.

AAC(Advanced Audio Coding)[6],is a kind of file compression format designed especially for audio data. Unlike mp3, it has used a new algorithm to code, which makes it more efficient and higher performance with lower price. In the condition of no significant drop of sound quality, using AAC format can let file more small.

Flv(Flash Video)[7]is a streaming media package format. It is developed with the introduction of FlashMX. The Flv file is very small and its loading is very fast, making network video viewing possible. It has efficiently solved the problem that after importing the video file into Flash, the exported SWF file is too large to use on the internet.

RTMP(Real Time Messaging Protocol)[8], which is over the TCP protocol or polling protocol HTTP, is the private protocol developed for audio, video and file data transmission between Flash player and server by Adobe Systems. RTMP is a container used to hold packages which can be data in AMF format and can also be Flv audio/video data. A single connection can transmit multiplexed network flow through different channels. All of the packages in the channels have fixed size, each of them contains a fixed length header and a body whose maximum length is 128 bytes.

3.2   Client Software

Figure 2 shows the relationship between Classes in the program. Class MainActivity is used to define User Interface. Class DataView is used to record, read, store audio and video data and set up necessary parameters. Class FFmpegFrameRecorder is used to encode audio and video data into the required format and pack them according to their time-stamps.

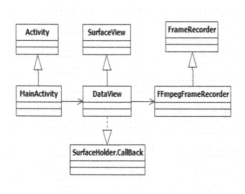

Fig. 2. Class diagram

Figure 3 is a flow chart of data processing. Briefly, the program is multi-threaded [9] with three threads: main thread, video recording and audio recording. The function of the main thread is to initialize the parameters, design user interface, control the whole program and process data; the video recording thread is to read and store every video frame for encoding; the audio recording thread is used to get audio data continually. Thread will run continuously and will not be interrupted unless there is a sentence to close it, so we can capture audio/video data with the two children threads.

3.3   Read Video Frame

Video frames are copied from camera to buffer with onPreviewFrame() method [10].The camera parameters have to be set before StartPreview(). One of the most important parameters is the preview frame rate, which is set to be 20f/s.

3.4   Read Audio Data

Audio data are read in another thread. In this way, we can record audio while video is recording and will not be influenced. The buffer size for audio data is set based on audio frequency, the number of channels and the encoding format. We read audio data into short type with read() function in Class AudioRecord.

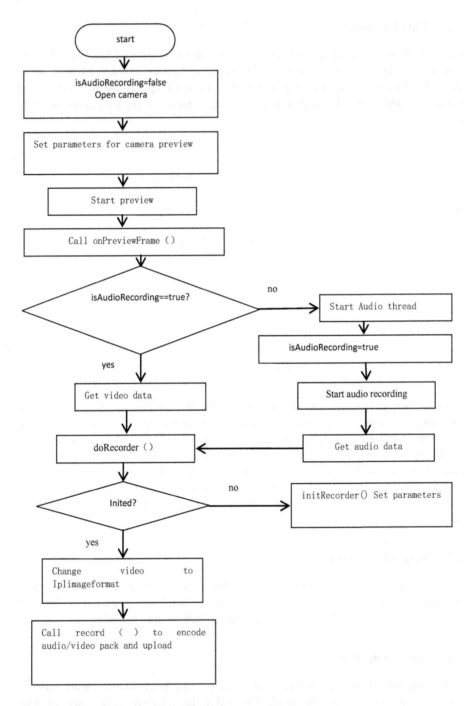

Fig. 3. Data Flow Chart

3.5   Parameter Initialization and Plug Flow

Related parameters need to be set before audio and video encoding. We have to convert the obtained video frame to Iplimage format, for the Iplimage data structure is used as the processing object in Opencv in FFmpegFrameRecorder.java.After audio and video encoding and packing, we use RTMP protocol for transmission. With the sentence:recorder=new FFmpegFrameRecorder
    ("rtmp://192.168.1.27:1935/livestream/12070660",width,height);   we   can   upload streams to the server specified in the first parameter.

3.6   Add Audio Support in Javacv

In FFmpegFrameRecorder.java, there is only support for video encoding and packing and no support for audio processing. Therefore, we need to change the abstract Class FrameRecorder and add the sentence: public abstract void record (Iplimage frame,short[] data) throws Exception. Audio data processing [11] should be added into FFmpegFrameRecorder.java, including setting AVCodecContext data structure for audio, encoding audio data and writing audio stream into the Flv package. In order to be played normally, audio and video time-stamps have to be calculated correctly. The calculation methods of audio and video time-stamp are identical.

3.7   Add H.264 Suport in Javacv

The video encoding format is very limited and there is no support for H.264 in Javacv. However, file compression is necessary to connect the server and let the stream transmit smoothly in the very limited network bandwidth. So, supporting for H.264 encoding format should be added in Javacv. The method is: firstly, recompile ffmpeg and libx264 [12]; then, add the generated libraries to the project; finally, set the parameters required by H.264 encoding.

4   Implementation Results and Discussion

After repeatedly debugging and improving, audio and video recorded by this system can form smooth pictures, clear voices and can be qualified for synchronous playback. In the process of debugging, several problems occurring and corresponding solutions are as follows. Firstly, the program closes automatically and gives the notice "system closed unexpectedly". The reason of this problem is that the initialization of the camera should not be in the function SurfaceChanged(). Secondly, the recorded file is achieved but its size is 0 KB. The solution is to add the permission for audio recording, video recording and external storage. Meanwhile, in order to push the stream to server, we also need to add internet connecting permission. Thirdly, the video plays too quickly after adding audio. The solution is to change the parameters for audio and video. According to tests, the parameters in different devices will have subtle differences, so it needs continuous adjustments with different terminal equipment. Figure 4 shows the recorded video and Figure 5 shows the result after pushing the stream to the server.

Fig. 4. Video Recording

Fig. 5. Upload to server

5   Conclusions

This paper describes a successful implementation of audio and video Real Time Broadcast System which uses Android Tablet as the audio and video capturing device and integrates Javacv for data processing. After testing, it is found that the recorded audio and video can be uploaded and distributed through WiFi on the limited network bandwidth. On the terminal, we can watch the real time broadcast smoothly with no sense of delay.

Acknowledgements. This work is supported by National Basic Research Program of China 2012CB315904, NSFC 61179028; Shenzhen Basic Research201005260234A, 201104210120A, Shenzhen Industry 201006110044A ; Guangdong Natural Science Fund 2011010000923.

References

1. http://baike.baidu.com/view/1241829.html
2. Jin, Y., Yao, S.: Android development entry. The people post and Telecommunications Press, Beijing (October 2009)
3. http://192.168.1.25/help/index.html
4. http://baike.baidu.com/view/6974524.html
5. Van der Auwera, G., David, P.T., Reisslein, M., Karam, L.: Traffic and Quality Characte;ization of Scalable Video StreamsEncoded with the H.264/AVC Scalable Video Coding Extension (May 2008)
6. http://baike.baidu.com/view/19772.html
7. http://baike.baidu.com/view/364757.html
8. http://www.adobe.com/devnet/rtmp.html
9. Gao, Y.: The Art of Java Programming. Tsinghua University Press, Beijing (2009)
10. She, Z., Chen, Y., Zheng, M., Chen, X., Guo, Z.: Google Android SDK Development Paradigm. The people post and Telecommunications Press, Beijing (June 2010)
11. http://www.oschina.net/code/explore/chromium.r67069/third_party/ffmpeg/patched-ffmpeg-mt/libavformat/output-example.c
12. http://stackoverflow.com/questions/8812827/build-ffmpeg-with-x264-for-android

Critical Chain Project Scheduling Problem Based on the Thermodynamic Particle Swarm Optimization Algorithm

Xing Xu[1], Hao Hu[2], Na Hu[3], and Weiqin Ying[4]

[1] College of Information and Engineering, Jingdezhen Ceramic Institute, Jiangxi 333000, China
whuxx84@yahoo.com.cn
[2] Library of Huaihua University, Huaihua Hunan 418000, China
[3] Jingdezhen Ceramic Institute, Jingdezhen Jiangxi 333000, China
[4] School of Software, South China University of Technology, Guangzhou, China
yingweiqin@scut.edu.cn

Abstract. For the project progress optimization problem, an improved particle swarm optimization algorithm based on thermodynamic mechanism is introduced and applied to the research and optimization of critical chain project scheduling. Experiments prove that the thermodynamic particle swarm optimization algorithm outperforms the basic particle optimization algorithm in solving such problems. The experimental results can serve as a theoretical guidance for administrators and decision-makers in enterprises to manage project administration in an overall and accurate way, take control of the project progress and guarantee the completion of a project on time.

Keywords: particle swarm optimization, thermodynamic, critical chain, project scheduling.

1 Introduction

Modern projects are increasingly complicated which require to be finished more efficiently within a shorter period and at a lower cost. Therefore, project plan and scheduling need higher feasibility, stability and accuracy. Theoretically speaking, project scheduling has a rich range of models, including flow-shop, job-shop and open-shop and other typical NP-hard problem in the field of job scheduling. These NP problems are difficult to be worked out by conventional algorithm [1]. As a typical swarm intelligence optimization algorithm, particle swarm optimization (PSO) is simple in principle, which owns both profound background of conventional evolutionary computation techniques and its own unique optimization performance. Since proposed, it has received extensive attention from scholars in the computation intelligence field [2]. While this algorithm has been widely applied to electricity, communication, industry and medical field, problems in practical application still emerge from time to time, which requires more and deeper theoretical research and application promotion of the particle swarm optimization algorithm. Project scheduling based on particle swarm optimization algorithm has become a frontier

J. Lei et al. (Eds.): NCIS 2012, CCIS 345, pp. 340–346, 2012.
© Springer-Verlag Berlin Heidelberg 2012

research topic both at home and abroad [3][4][5]. Critical chain project management is a new technique born from the combination of theory of constraints and project management techniques. It, as a completely new method, becomes a hot topic in project management and scheduling research [6][7][8][9]. In this way, this paper introduces thermodynamics and thermal motion mechanism into the design and analysis of particle swarm optimization algorithm, designs an improved particle swarm optimization algorithm integrating the thermal motion mechanism, and put forward, based on relevant theoretical study on critical chain, a new project scheduling optimization algorithm combining thermodynamic particle swarm optimization algorithm in order to give direction for project administration in enterprises.

2   Critical Chain

In 1997, Israel scientist Doctor Goldratt proposed a blank new project management method, i.e. critical chain project management (CCPM), which is an application and extension of theory of constraints (TOC) in the project management field. Critical chain method is a revised one based on the integration of Critical Path Method (CPM) and Program Evaluation and Review Technique (PERT). Conquering many theoretical and methodological shortcomings, it is simple in theory and operable in practice. Critical chain project management puts emphasis on taking into consideration the actual resource constraint, the dynamic administration in executing a project and the continual revision in project management operation in the designing of a project. It includes three types of buffer in project progress network: project buffer (PB), feeding buffer (FB), and resource buffer (RB), thus to eliminate the negative influence on project scheduling plan from uncertain factors and further to ensure successful operation in a dynamic environment of project plan which is programmed in a certain environment.

This paper has adopted the CCPM optimized model in reference [9], so as to shorten the project cycle and guarantee the stability of project plan by setting the project buffer and feeding buffer. The mathematical model is quoted as follows:

$$\min \ SFT_j \tag{1}$$

$$s.t. \ \ SST_i\text{-}SST_j \geq D \tag{2}$$

$$\sum_{j \in A_t} rjk \leq Rkt \ \ k=1,2,...,K;t=1,2,...,T \tag{3}$$

$$P(AFT_j \leq (SFT_j + PB)) \geq P_0 \tag{4}$$

where, SFT_j is the required time to finish Project j; SST_j is the planned to start j; At is the work aggregate during the time of t; and AFT_j is the actual time consumed to finish j. PB is the project buffer size and Po is the expected probability to be completed as planned. Formula (1) represents the minimized project period, formula (2) is the precedence relation constraint, formula (3) is the resource constraint. Formula (4) guarantees that probability to complete the project as planned exceeds the expected probability Po.

3   Particle Swarm Optimization Algorithms

3.1   Basic Particle Swarm Optimization Algorithm

Make an assumption that in a d-dimensional target search space, there is a swarm $S = \{X_1, X_2, \cdots X_N\}$ composed of N potential problem-solution particles, among which $X_i = (x_{i1}, x_{i2}, \cdots, x_{id}), i = 1, 2, \cdots, N$ represents the vector point of the d-dimensional space of No. i. $P_i = (p_{i1}, p_{i2}, \cdots, p_{id}), i = 1, 2, \cdots, N$ is used to record the best point that No. i can scan by itself, marked as pbest. In such as swarm group, there is at least one best numbered as g, and $P_g = (p_{g1}, p_{g2}, \cdots, p_{gd})$ is the best value marked as gbest and $g \in \{1, 2, \cdots, N\}$. Every particle has a velocity variable, and $v_i = (v_{i1}, v_{i2}, \cdots, v_{id}), i = 1, 2, \cdots N$ represents the velocity of No. i. The following formula can be used to update the velocity and position of each particle after the two best values are achieved.

$$v_{id}^{t+1} = v_{id}^t + R_1 c_1 (p_{id} - X_{id}^t) + R_2 c_2 (p_{gd} - X_{id}^t) \tag{5}$$

$$X_{id}^{t+1} = X_{id}^t + v_{id}^{t+1} \tag{6}$$

In formula (5) and (6), N is the total number of the particles in the swarm and i equals 1, 2,..., N.

t: the present times of the algorithm iteration.

v_{id}^t: the d-dimensional component of the velocity vector after particle i has been iterated for t times.

X_{id}^t: the d-dimensional component of the position vector after particle i has been iterated for t times.

P_{id}: the d-dimensional component of the best position of particle i.

P_{gd}: the d-dimensional component of the best position of swarm group.

R_1 and R_2 are two random numbers in the range of U(0,1).

c_1 and c_2 are learning factors, and usually $c_1 = c_2 = 2$.

In every dimension, particle has a maximized constraint velocity V_{max}. If the velocity in a certain dimension surpasses the pre-setting V_{max}, the velocity in that dimension will be set as V_{max}.

3.2   Improved Particle Swarm Optimization Algorithm

This paper has introduced molecular dynamic theory of statistical physics and designed a new PSO algorithm. The particle in this algorithm possesses attributes of speed and position in addition to an added acceleration attribute. This algorithm also defines the concept of swarm centroid.

Definition 1: Particle acceleration. Because the distance between molecules changes, the size and direction of F_i will change accordingly as F_i switches between repulsion and attraction. According to Newton's Second Law

$$a_i = F_i / m_i \tag{7}$$

The magnitude and direction of acceleration a_i will change as well. We ignore the magnitude of a_i, only take into account its direction. When F_i is mainly attraction, $a_i = 1$, and when F_i is mainly repulsion, $a_i = -1$.

Definition 2: Centroid. Swarm centroid refers to a hypothetical point when the quality of all particles focuses on one point. In an N-dimension space, the swarm centroid calculation formula is as follows:

$$X_{cen} = \sum x_i m_i / \sum m_i \tag{8}$$

Xi represents the coordinates of particle i in the swarm, m the quality of swarm particle. We can regard m_i as the weight of particle i. In practice, we can equal it to the fitness value of particle i. In this paper, we suppose that the quality of all particles is the same and equals 1. According to Definition 1 we redefine the formula of particle velocity update and position update:

$$v_{id}^{t+1} = \omega v_{id}^t + a_i [R_1 c_1 (P_{id} - X_{id}^t) + R_2 c_2 (p_{gd} - X_{id}^t)] \tag{9}$$

$$X_{id}^{t+1} = X_{id}^t + v_{id}^{t+1} \tag{10}$$

a_i is the acceleration speed of particles. Initially, the acceleration of all particles is a default 1. With the iterative algorithm, in accordance with the distance between particle I and centroid ($d(x_{cen}, x_i)$ is used to describe that distance for the sake of ease), we make constant adjustment of a_i (specific adjustment rules can be referred to in algorithm process). When $d(x_{cen}, x_i)$ is less than a threshold value d_l, the molecular force between particles and swarm centroid is mainly represented by repulsion, which drives particles away from swarm centroid to keep swarm diversity, which as a result benefits the global search of algorithm. When $d(x_{cen}, x_i)$ is more than a threshold value d_l, in order to ensure the algorithm convergence and strengthen the ability of local search of algorithm, molecular force is mainly represented by attraction, and attracts particles to fly toward swarm centroid.

The process of thermodynamics PSO is as follows:

Step1: Initialize a group of particles (swarm size as M), including position, speed and acceleration;

Step2: Assess the fitness value of each particle;

Step3: Update the optimal solution of particles and the current optimal solution of swarm;

Step4: If the algorithm convergence criteria meets or achieves maximum iterating times, follow Step7, otherwise do Step5;

Step5: for(i=0;i<M;i++)

{

if($a_i == +1$ && $d(x_{cen}, x_i) < d_l$) $a_i = -1$

if($a_i == -1$ && $d(x_{cen}, x_i) > d_h$) $a_i = +1$

Adjust particle velocity and position according to formula 9&10;

}

Step6: Fail to satisfy ending conditions, turn to Step2;

Step7: Output the algorithm to find the optimal solution and end the algorithm.

4   Experiments

Thermodynamic particle swarm optimization algorithm has been used to solve the problem of project management optimization scheduling based on critical chain. For the convenience to compare the experimental results, question of J301-1.SM in the international standard problem database PSPLIB presented in [9] has been taken as an example. The job information table content can be found in the above-mentioned literature. The algorithm is realized by using VC++ program. The parameters in thermodynamic particle swarm optimization algorithm can be referred in [10].

Table 1. Comparison of the experimental results among three algorithms

Experimental result	Basic PSO	Chaotic PSO	Thermodynamic PSO
Average operation time	5.8s	3.7s	3.9s
Average cycle span	47.8	43.5	43.4
Shortest cycle span	45.6	43.0	43.1

The algorithm performance examined includes the algorithm running time, average span of each cycle, and minimized cycle span. The algorithm has been operated randomly for 30 times and its results are illustrated in Table 1. The operational results show that the running time of the thermodynamic particle swarm optimization algorithm is shorter, the average cycle and minimized cycle is similar to that of chaotic particle swarm algorithm, but shorter than basic particle swarm algorithm, which thus is apparently beneficial for optimizing project and shortening project cycle. Thermodynamic particle swarm optimization algorithm is more advanced than basic particle swarm algorithm.

5   Conclusions

The writer has presented a discussion on that to shorten a project cycle, an improved particle swarm algorithm based on molecular force model is introduced and its experimental result has been compared with those derived from Basic PSO and Chaotic PSO respectively in solving critical chain project scheduling by the CCPM optimization model. The experimental results show that the performance of improved particle swarm algorithm is similar to that of chaotic particle swarm algorithm but much better than that of basic particle swarm algorithm, which proves the feasibility of thermodynamic particle swarm algorithm. Therefore, a comprehensive application of critical chain and thermodynamic particle swarm algorithm can be applied to solve the problems occurring in production scheduling in enterprises.

Acknowledgments. This work was supported in part by the National Nature Science Foundation of China (61070009, 61165004, 61202313), the National Science and Technology Support Plan (2012BAH25F02), the Project of Jingdezhen Science and Technology Bureau (2011-1-47), the National Natural Science Foundation of Jiangxi Province (20122BAB211036,20122BAB201044), and the Youth Science Foundation of Jiangxi Provincial Department of Education (GJJ12514), the Natural Science Foundation of Guangdong Province (S2011040002472), the Specialized Research Fund for the Doctoral Program of Higher Education (20110172120035), the Fundamental Research Funds for the Central Universities (2011ZM0107).

References

1. Liu, S.: Project scheduling theory and methods. China Machine Press, Beijing (2007)
2. Kennedy, J., Eberhart, R., Shi, Y.: Swarm Intelligence. Morgan Kaufmann Publishers, San Francisco (2001)
3. Wang, L., Liu, B.: Particle Swarm Optimization and Scheduling Algorithms. Tsinghua University Press, Beijing (2008)
4. Liu, Z.: Encoding of particle swarm optimization algorithm for scheduling problem. Journal of Wuhan University of Science and Technology 33, 99–104 (2010)

5. Ni, L., Duan, C., Jia, C.: Hybrid particle swarm optimization algorithm based on differential evolution for project scheduling problems. Application Research of Computers 28, 1286–1289 (2011)
6. Guo, Q., Li, H., Sai, Y.: The Analysis of Scheduling Optimization on Critical Chain Method for Multiple Projects. Industrial Engineering and Management 6, 41–45 (2008)
7. Wang, Z., Liu, Q., Yang, Y.: Research on Audit Project Progress Management Based on Critical Chain Method. Journal of Chongqing Technology and Business University (Natural Science Edition) 28, 275–280 (2011)
8. Ye, C., Pan, D., Pan, F.: Critical chain project management based on chaos particle swarm optimization. Application Research of Computers 28, 890–891 (2011)
9. Guo, F.: Research on multi-project scheduling based on particle swarm optimization and critical chain technologies. Huazhong University of Science and Technology PhD thesis, Wuhan (2010)
10. Xu, X., Li, Y., Jiang, D., Tang, M., Fang, S.: Improved particle swarm optimization algorithm based on theory of molecular motion. Journal of System Simulation 21, 1904–1907 (2009)

A Forgetting Scheme for Layered-Neurons Procedure

Shijiao Zhu

School of Computer and Information Engineering, Shanghai University of Electric Power,
Shanghai 200090, China
Zhusj707@hotmail.com

Abstract. In this paper, we propose a model of forgetting scheme for Neural Network by topologic. In general, parameters architecture is pre-defined for special problem and is not suitable for knowledge learning like human. Based on layered neurons architecture, we gave a ponn algorithm for constructive neural network which has properties of short-long learning procedure. Experimental result has demonstrated that the proposed model can store knowledge in terms of both short term and long term learning process.

1 Introduction

In order to simulate man's learning, neural network are proposed to process problems and have success applied into different fields [1]. In most cases, neural networks are defined architectures. We also notice that the early links between neural network and psychology have been largely weakened. This shift was accompanied by the increasing emphasis on statistical methods, such as SVM[2] method that require a large amount of data and learn far more slowly than human beings. The mathematical orientation of researchers is closely associated with an emphasis on approaches that find the best solution to problems, while human's solution is based on heuristics which usually produce acceptable results with little effort. One of human features is forgetting brain which evaluates data with different interest according to time [3]. We quoted the theory from psychology in the construction of artificial intelligence and gave a simulation framework of neuron's forgetting based on high-level cognition.

In the paper that follows, we begin with the definition what the forgetting brain mean in section 2. Next, the importance and evaluation of biases which is critical process of human brain are to be explained. A framework of the simulating schema of forgetting is discussed in section 3. In section 4, we give an example of the algorithm for the construction of dynamic neuron network and its application. Section 5 briefly summarizes the paper.

2 Model

Neurodegenerative disorders are characterized by extensive neuron death that leads to functional decline. It has been a commonly held notion that neuron death is restricted in normal aging. These disorders invariably reflect the following facts [3,4]: (i) major

J. Lei et al. (Eds.): NCIS 2012, CCIS 345, pp. 347–351, 2012.
© Springer-Verlag Berlin Heidelberg 2012

links are structurally disrupted through synapse loss and neuron death,(ii)there is selective vulnerability in respect to which neurons die and which are resistant to dege-
neration , and (iii) the symptoms of the particular neurodegenerative disorder follow
from the circuits connecting neurons that are disrupted and thus reflect the selective
vulnerability. According to above discussed, the forgetting procedure is the natural
property of brain for memory. Since knowledge has the supportive role of providing
information to select a representational or procedural interest, neuron will be recon-
structive and the information without biases will be forgotten. This biological principle shows the forgetting procedure of human brain in high lever cognition.

An interest data defines the bias of neuron learning. Typically, this produce is
evaluated with time and can be considered as a schema in the search space which is
defined by features, types, values and so on. For neuron learning, an interest data can
be characterized by several properties such as *strong* and *weak* strength in high dimension space. A strong strength means can be interested by the network and gives
neuron more priority, while the weak one less activity which will be in the edge of
forgetting. This is just the abstract assumption because any cognition of human can be
split into different sub-levels. From this black-box approach, the forgetting schema of
neurons in learning is simulated. While with the statistic point, this schema is impossible because more data are needed and the result is just a statistic value without the
learning process by data and time. It leaves the question for a practical implementation open, and the appropriate representational data interest and search heuristics with
more simple simulations are still required.

3   Forgetting Scheme

In more complexes, real-world domains, with potentially hundreds of features and
many sources of data, forgetting becomes even more critical: many old features can
be forgotten, but only those interesting data can be remembered or updated. And at
the same time, when learning, the recent data can be partly reminded instead of being
wholly forgotten at a time. Here we define the priority for the interest concept to construct neural network, which simulates the schema of man's forgetting.

Priority level of neuron determines the order of remembered data in the space of
concept by the representational interest. Neurons with high priority level will be re-
called effectively and perform judgment ahead of other neurons. Note that priority
level may interact: a learning procession and an interest date when inputting into
neuron.

For neural network with priority, we consider it as PONN (priority Ordered Neural
Network)[5] which is a dynamic neural network instead of fixed architecture neural
network. The neural constructive procedure can be described as:

For learning feature space, PONN can be initialized with few or empty hidden neurons. With the data learning, PONN analysis the data interactive relationship in high
dimension space and adjusts the priority of each neurons when adding or updating.
For reorganization process, PONN gives the result based on the input data and priorities of neuron in the network. The architecture can be described in figure1.

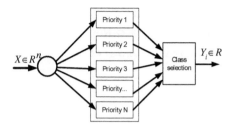

Fig. 1. The architecture of PONN

The output decision sequence of the PONN is symbolized as $O = \{o_1, o_2, ..., o_p\}$. The final output of network is Y_i where the i is class identification.

$$Y_i = \min\{i \mid Q(o_i) = 1\} \quad \text{Where } Q \text{ is mapping } y_i \rightarrow \{0,1\}.$$

For constructive algorithm, we use hype-ball neurons in hidden layers which the high priority level can be characterized the low priority number. The general algorithm can be described as:

Input: Feature space set $X = \{X_1, X_2, ..., X_m\} \subset \mathbb{R}^n$, and the target is $Y \in R$. Priority number k=1 neuron sets $\{\psi\}, D^{'} = \Phi$

Output: Priority Ordered Neural Network

Algorithm Start ：

```
While  X ≠ φ  do
For each  Xi in  X
→get max sub set ( Xi,sub ) of  Xi  and its  min Euclid
distance (d) of  Xj,i≠j
→use hype-ball neuron(ψ,d) to covering  Xi,sub ,and set
priority k to neuronψ
→add  Xi,sub to temp set D`
End of for
→set  X - D`  to  X , D` = Φ
k = k + 1
End while
```

For new coming data, PONN will update the priority number of neuron or add new neuron with a special priority. Here is the algorithm:

Input: new feature training

set $X'=\{X'_1,X'_2,...,X'_m\}\subset \mathbb{R}^n$, $Y\in R$. Already exist PONN

Output: Updated Priority Ordered Neural Network

Algorithm Start :

While $X'\neq \phi$ do

For each X'_i **in** X'

$\rightarrow$ get a consistent subset $X'_{i,sub}$ of X_i randomize, find whether has been covered by neurons of PONN

If covered($X'_{i,sub}$)

do nothing

else

   if(misclassified($X'_{i,sub}$))

   adjust covering space range of hyper-ball neuronψ and adjust its priority number to lower one.

else

   add new neuron with higher priority number k.

end if

end if

$\rightarrow$ add $X'_{i,sub}$ to temp set D

End of for

$\rightarrow$ set $X-D$ to X', $D=\Phi$

End while

For new samples inputting to the PONN, the priority level of hidden neurons is streng-thened or weakened which is similar to man's learning procedure. With this method, the older information is not destroyed (forgotten) when learning new data but can be partly fetched at any latest priority. For this updating and learning is only to adjust the special priority level of neurons, therefore, this method can process large data set with more effective heuristic algorithm. Next we will give an example of the methods.

4   Experimental Results

In experience, we use two sets: one is standard Benchmark set; another one is Lan-guage Identification with feature of MFCC. For class of Benchmark [6], number of training set 1 is 174 and training set 2 is 40,   and the number of its feature vector is 9. The number of testing set is 65. For the class of language, the MFCC features [7] of Chinese and English are selected with vector dimensional 496. The number of first training set 1 is 174 and following training set 2 is 40 and testing set is 300. The expe-riment based on 5-fold cross validation is performed to learn with training set 1 and then update PONN with training set 2. Table 1 has showed the result.

Table 1. The result of PONN for Train set 1 and Train set 2,where C. is Correct, E. is Error, R. is Refused,TR1 is Train set 1,and TR2 is Train set 2

Class	Number	C.Rate	E.Rate	R.Rate
Glass (TE=65)	TR1=174	52.831	47.619	0.0
	TR2= 40	80.952	19.048	0.0
Language Identification (TE=300)	TR1=411	70.769	23.077	6.154
	TR2= 89	86.154	13.846	0.0

From the table 1 we can notice that the whole learning ability is improved by new updating samples. PONN learns new data with keeping the older ones in a special priority level which does not destroy learned knowledge. We come to a conclusion that the short-term memory network by PONN is more similar to man's learning biological model.

5   Conclusion

In this paper, a forgetting scheme is designed for construct neural network. Based upon our model, dynamic network are constructed and can meeting samples learning procedure. The experimental results have demonstrated that our proposed scheme can present knowledge learning which has biological cognition basis, greater performances are expected, which can utilized to data learning with no architecture limit. Different learning layers should be made for further research.

References

[1] Galushkin, A.I.: Neural Network Theory. Springer, New York (2007)
[2] Widodo, A., Yang, B.-S.: Mechanical Systems and Signal Processing. Support Vector Machine in Machine Condition Monitoring and Fault Diagnosis 21(6), 2560–2574 (2007)
[3] O'Reilly, R.C.: Biologically Based Computational Models of High-Level Cognition. Science 314(6), 91–94 (2006)
[4] Morrison, J.H., Hof, P.R.: Life and Death of Neurons in the Aging Brain. Science 278(17), 412–419 (1997)
[5] Wang, S.J.: Bionic(topological)pattern recognition-A new model of pattern recognition theory and its applications. Acta Electron. Sinica 30(10), 1–4 (2002)
[6] Benchmark repository-A collection of artificial and real-world data sets, http://ww.ics.uci.edu/~mlearn/MLSummary.html
[7] Kim, H.K., Rose, R.C.: Cepstrum-domain acoustic feature compensation based on decomposition of speech and noise for ASR in noisy environments. IEEE Trans. Speech Audio Process. 11(5), 435–446 (2003)

A Cryptographic and Time-Constraint Access Control Scheme for Mobile Terminals

Jiazhu Dai, Chuan Zhang, and Zhilong Li

School of Computer Engineering and Science Shanghai University Shanghai 200072
daijz@shu.edu.cn,
zhangchuan210@163.com,
baron@shu.edu.com

Abstract. As more and more services and applications are used in the mobile phones, the sensitive data becomes more easily be leaked out. The simplest way is to encrypt the sensitive data, and only the user who has the key can decrypt the data, but, on doing this, the user can exposing the data repeatedly. Hence, we should not only restrict the people who can decrypt the sensitive data, but also restrict the time when the data can be exposed. The mobile phones are devices which have limited resources, their computing ability is limited, the operation on the phones should be simple as far as possible. In this paper, we put forward a cryptographic and time-constraint access control scheme for mobile terminals. We encrypt data with a method which similar to the digital envelopes technology, and it reduces the overload of calculation; use the hierarchical key assignment to reduce the process of key distribution; finally, according to the survival time of the data, the data will be deleted automatically, even the people who has the key, can't access the data after the survival time.

Keywords: security, encryption, sand box, hierarchical key assignment.

1   Introduction

With the communication technology becoming more mature, network communication bandwidth increasing and the operating system Android which is open-source is developing rapidly, the mobile terminals become widespread, the idea of mobile office gradually be applied to the real life. The chief question of the use and promotion of the mobile office is security. The most representative case is the use of the mobile police terminal, which has a great deal of sensitive data such as the Police Geographic Information System (PGIS). Hence, some method must be adopted to ensure that the data will not be disclosed illegally. For the problem, we should protect the security of the transmission data, and after the data has been stored in the phone, the user can only access data in a limited time, a certain period time latter, both the user and others will be unable to access the data.

As for the safety of transmitting data in the process of communications, encryption methods must be employed to prevent data from being eavesdropped. Frequently-used encryption algorithms, such as symmetric algorithms and public key encryption, they

J. Lei et al. (Eds.): NCIS 2012, CCIS 345, pp. 352–357, 2012.
© Springer-Verlag Berlin Heidelberg 2012

have some restrictions in mobile office. The symmetrical encryption algorithm has high efficiency but it very difficult to distribute and manage the key. The key of the public key encryption is easy to manage and transmit, however, the performance efficiency of the public key encryption is too low to encrypt big messages, and it requires the length of encrypted information piece should be less than the key. At present, there are a few studies for the data has been stored in mobile phones, after a certain time, it unable to access the data. [1, 2, 3, 4, 5, 6] present some methods to automatically delete data; after a period of time, so the users can't use them again, but these methods are not adjust to the mobile devices.

In this paper, we put forward a cryptographic and time-constraint access control scheme for mobile terminals. Namely, we develop a client on the mobile phone, it uses the technology of sand box, and the application runs in the sand box, ensuring the security of the data when it is in the process; we encrypt data with a method which similar to the digital envelopes technology, and it reduces the overload of calculation; owing to that some data has different layers such as the electronic map, we use the hierarchical key assignment to reduce the process of key distribution, namely, encrypt every layer data with different keys, the user who owns the top layer can be able to access the lower layer data; finally, according to the survival time of the data, the data will be deleted automatically, even the people who has the key, can't access the data after the survival time.

Structure of this paper is as follows. In section 2, we introduce the previous work related to delete data automatically. In section 3, we describe our solution to this problem. In section4, we will analyze the security and performance of the proposed solution and draw the conclusion. In section 5 we summarize our solution and outline the future work.

2   Related Works

In order to protect the sensitive data, we should ensure that they are deleted automatically without artificial operation. Academic puts forward some methods. In [1][4] authors proposed a solution named Vanish, it is a typical method, using the distributed hash table (DHT) to store data. DHT is a distributed storage method. Using its attribute we can ensure that the data have a certain life cycle, hence, data can be deleted automatically. This kind of method applies to the data distribution in network and cloud computing, however, owing to the DHT is scattered, we can't take it directly into use in the simple model of mobile terminals access servers, besides, researchers have shown how to use the Sybil attack in the DHTs to reconstruct the key, so, this method is not any more safety. In [2] author use the "state re-incarnation" to make the data no longer emerge again after a certain time. The thought is as following: after an application has received the data (containing sensitive data), record all of the input, when the life cycle of the sensitive data expired, the application will send back data (not including sensitive data) to access server, keeping the state consistent as before sending the data. However, the load of the communication is high and it increases the risk of leaking out the data when resending data to the serve. In [3][5] authors put forward that when the server sends data, specifying a future time point for the data, after the client has received the data, read this time point, and the data will be deleted automatically on that time point. This method requires synchronization operation, if the two parts have a different time or reside in different time-zones, even the combination of the both, the synchronous processing is very difficult.

3   System Model

Our goal is to design a security system model to realize the security of the sensitive data in the mobile terminals. The server is located in the trusted zone, hence it is absolutely security.

Our method is that we develop a client on the mobile phone, it uses the technology of sand box, and the application runs in the sand box, the transmitted data has a survival time, after the time, the data will be deleted automatically, ensuring the security of the data; besides, we encrypt data with a method which similar to the digital envelopes technology, and it not only guarantees the security of data transmission, but also reduces the overload of calculation; owing to that some data has different layers in real life, such as the electronic map in the PGIS, we use the hierarchical key assignment to reduce the process of key distribution, namely, encrypt every layer of the data with different keys, the user who owns the top layer can be able to access the lower layer data, reducing the process of key distribution and increasing the performance.

Specific security system model
Specific method is as follows: We develop a client on the mobile phone, it uses the technology of sand box, and the application runs in the sand box. The user of mobile phone needs to run the application to access data, therefore, he must login the client, before he enter into the client, a password K must be needed, and this password associates with the mark address of the phone, besides, there is a backup in the server, only the user inputs the correct password can he logs in to the client. On doing this can prevent the personnel beyond mobile phone user from logging in to the client, ensuring that even if the phone is lost, others can't access the data. In addition, when the mobile phone user changes the password, he must interact with the server, making the server have a backup password forever. After logging in to the client, the user can run the application, the mobile phone application will access the server to request the data, and the figure 1 shows the specific process.

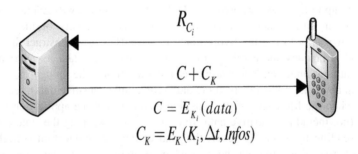

$$R_{C_i}$$

$$C + C_K$$

$$C = E_{K_i}(data)$$

$$C_K = E_K(K_i, \Delta t, Infos)$$

Fig. 1. Transfer Process

As above here, the specific process of the mobile phone application sends request to the server and downloads the data.

(1)   The mobile phone application sends request to the server to download data, and sends some access control information;

(2)   When the server has received some request information, some authentication must be handled, after that, according to the authority of mobile phone user and the request, using the method which similar to the digital envelope technology to encrypt data, concrete operation is as following: use the back-up key K which the server kept to encrypt the layered key K_i, a survival time of the data Δt (it is a different value according to the user's authority) and some other information Infos (it contains some information used for the hierarchical key assignment, and we will explain it in detail later), namely, $C_K = E_K(K_i, \Delta t, Infos)$, then use the key K_i to encrypt the transmitting data, namely: $C = E_{K_i}(data)$, and at last, send the encrypted data(C 、 C_K) to the phone;

(3)   After the mobile phone application has received the data, firstly, decrypt C_K with the key K, namely, $D_K(C_K) \longrightarrow (K_i, \Delta t, Infos)$. At this time, a timer which locates in the sand box begins to count down according to the survival time Δt, and after the time interval of Δt, all the data the application has received will be deleted automatically. Then, decrypt C with the key K_i, namely, $D_{K_i}(data) \longrightarrow data$. Owing to the data is stratified, if the data is the minimum hierarchical data, then the operation of decryption comes to the end, or else, according to the hierarchical key assignment, the key of the lower layer data can be exported by using the key K_i and Infos, and on this way, the lower layer data can be decrypted. The following explains how to realize the hierarchical key assignment.

As to some sensitive data is stratified in real life such as the electronic map in the PGIS, we want to reach the goal that the users who own the high layer data can access to lower layer data. According to [7, 8], we do some processing of the stratified data in the server, and design all layers of the data into a partial-order hierarchical tree, as following shows:

The tree consists of different layer node classes S = {C1, C2, ... Cn}. We note each level node as a class C_i ($1 \le i \le n$), and select a random key K_i for each level of node, for safety reasons, these keys could be automatically updated every a period of time. The symbol "$\preceq$"is partially ordered with a binary relation. The means of "$C_j \preceq C_i$" is that the class C_j has a security clearance lower than or equal to that of C_i. So C_i has the power to access the class C_j's resources. For each direct edge "$C_j \preceq C_i$", the server has a hierarchical relationship $r_{ij} = h\left(ID_i \| ID_j \| K_i\right) \oplus K_j$, ID_i/ID_j is the identity of class C_i/C_j respectively, $\|$ denotes the string concatenation, and $\oplus$

denotes the bit-wise XOR operation. So, the users who own the high level layered permission can get the key K_j of class C_j using the formula of $K_j = h\left(\text{ID}_i \| \text{ID}_j \| K_i\right) \oplus r_{ij}$, and can decrypt out the lower layer data. On doing this, we can implement the hierarchical key assignment.

If the phone application receives the data which is not the minimum hierarchical data, then some operations must be done. Using the current layered key K_i and the Infos which contains the identification of data layer ID_i, the identification of lower level than it layered ID_j and their directly hierarchical relationship r_{ij}, we can get the key K_j, namely, $K_j = h\left(\text{ID}_i \| \text{ID}_j \| K_i\right) \oplus r_{ij}$, and using the K_j, we will decrypt the data belongs to the layer of C_j. By performing the calculations similar to the above, we can decrypt all the lower layer data.

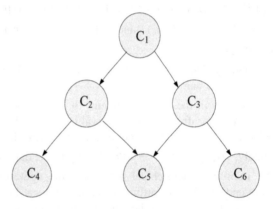

Fig. 2. An example of the partial-order hierarchical tree

4   Security and Performance Analysis

In this paper we use the technology of sand box to protect the security of the data and adopt the hierarchical tree to implement the hierarchical key assignment, reducing the key distribution. Our solution has the following advantages:

(1) Secure.
    a)   We reach the goal that only the legitimate user can access the sensitive data using the password, without the password, any one can't access the data.
    b)   The sensitive data can only be accessed in its survival time, after the survival time, even the legitimate user can not access the data.
(2) Performance.
    a)   We encrypt data with a method which similar to the digital envelopes technology, and it has lower computation overhead.
    b)   The technology of hierarchical key assignment is used, and it reduces the key distribution process, and the communication load is low.

5   Conclusion

In this paper we put forward a cryptographic and time-constraint access control scheme for mobile terminals. The scheme can protect the data stored in mobile terminals so that it only can be accessed in a limited time, and user who is granted to access higher layer data can get the lower layer data. Analysis shows that our solution is secure and has high performance. We will optimize the technology of sand box and have a test in the future.

Acknowledgements. The work of this paper is supported by Shanghai Key Subject Fund under grant NO:J50103 and Innovation Program of Shanghai Municipal Education Commission under grant NO:13YZ013.

References

1. Geambasu, Kohno, T., Levy, A., Levy, H.M.: Vanish: Increasing data privacy with self-destructing data. In: Proc. of the 18th USENIX Security Symposium (2009)
2. Kannan, J., Altekar, G., Maniatis, P., Chun, B.-G.: Making Programs Forget Enforcing Lifetime For Sensitive Data. In: Proceeding HotOS'13 Proceedings of the 13th USENIX Conference on Hot Topics in Operating Systems, pp. 23–23. USENIX Association, Berkeley (2011)
3. Popper, C., Basin, D., Capkun, S., Cremers, C.: Keeping data secret under full compromise using porter devices. In: Computer Security Applications Conference, pp. 241–250 (2010)
4. Yue, F., Wang, G., Liu, Q.: A Secure Self-Destructing Scheme for Electronic Data. euc. In: 2010 IEEE/IFIP International Conference on Embedded and Ubiquitous Computing, pp. 651–658 (2010)
5. Marforio, C.: Timed Data Deletion on Mobile Communication Devices (2010)
6. Wolchok, S., Hofmann, O.S., Heninger, N., Felten, E.W., Alex Halderman, J., Rossbach, C.J., Waters, B., Witchel, E.: Defeating Vanish with low-cost Sybil attacks against large DHTs. In: Proceedings of the 17th Network and Distributed System Security Symposium (NDSS). ISOC (2010)
7. Borders, K., Weele, E.V., Lau, B., Prakash, A.: Protecting Confidential Data on Personal Computers with Storage Capsules. In: Proc. Usenix Security (2009)
8. Chien, H.-Y.: Efficient Time-Bound Hierarchical Key Assignment Scheme. IEEE Trans. Knowledge and Data Eng. 16(10), 1302–1304 (2004)
9. Yang, R., Lin, C., Feng, F.: A Time and Mutable Attribute-Based Access Control Model. Journal of Computers 4(6), 510–518 (2009)
10. Nauman, M., Khan, S., Zhang, X.: Apex: Extending android permission model and enforcement with user-defined runtime constraints. In: ACM Symposium on Information, Computer and Communications Security, ASIACCS (2010)
11. Turkmen, F., Jung, E., Crispo, B.: Towards run-time verification in access control. In: IEEE International Symposium on Policies for Distributed Systems and Networks. IEEE (2011)
12. Google, http://www.google.com.hk/
13. Android, http://www.android.com/

A Distributed Multi-secret Sharing Scheme on the (t,n) Threshold

Guiqiang Chen[1,*], Huanwen Wang[2], Liqin Wang[3], and Yue Jin[3]

[1] Institute of Information Science and Engineering, Hebei North University,
Zhangjiakou, China
[2] Information Engineering, Zhangjiakou Vocational College of Technology,
Zhangjiakou, China
[3] Department of Electrical Engineering, Zhangjiakou Vocational College of Technology,
Zhangjiakou, China
guiqiangchen@yahoo.com.cn

Abstract. In the most present threshold multi-secret sharing scheme, there were some problems. For example, each participant's shadow was generated by the dealer, the fixed threshold, need of the secure channels, the fixed dealer or the secret center. To overcome these problems, a distributed multi-secret sharing scheme on the (t, n) threshold was proposed in this paper. This scheme has the following properties: 1) Each participant selects his shadow by himself; 2) There is no secure channel 3) There is no the fixed dealer, each participant may be dealer to distribute the multi-secret, and the multi-secret could be accomplished one time such as to distribute and to comeback and to update and to validate and so on operations;4) The participant could be dynamically added or deleted; 5) The efficient solutions against multiform cheating of any participant are proposed, therefore the proposed scheme has practicability and highly security.

Keywords: Multi-secret sharing, discrete logarithm, dynamic threshold, Lagrange interpolation formula.

1   Introduction

The multi-secret sharing is a very important direction of the cryptographic techniques. It is an important means of information security and data privacy. It is a basic tool for the design of security of cryptographic protocols, both in theory and in practice. It is very important in the communication key management and computer Network security. Since 1979 when Shamir[1] proposed a secret sharing scheme, the multi-secret sharing has been made very fruitful. The multi-secret sharing scheme [2-8] has the following advantages: 1) The participant only needs a secret share can share the many secrets; 2) It can prevent the fraud of the secret distribution and participants to a certain extent. However, it also has the following disadvantages: 1) each participant cannot choose the secret share; 2) it needs a secure channel of transmitting information between the secret distribution and the participants; 4) The threshold is

---

* Corresponding author.

J. Lei et al. (Eds.): NCIS 2012, CCIS 345, pp. 358–364, 2012.
© Springer-Verlag Berlin Heidelberg 2012

fixed; 5) Most of the multi-secret sharing is achieved by the multiple use of single secret sharing; 6) It can neither modify the other members of the secret share the premise, nor effectively add new members or delete old members; 7) It cannot meet the requirements of distributed computing. However, the actual applications in many cases require secret sharing scheme to meet the requirements of distributed computing. For example: in the wireless LAN communication, sensor networks and Ad.hoc network and other applications, users on the dispersed nodes to share information or digital key exchange secure communications can be well distributed secret sharing scheme solution. In 2006, He Bin [10] proposed a distributed shared program to meet the requirements of distributed computing based on the Chinese Remainder Theorem, but cannot compensate for other deficiencies. In order to address these deficiencies, based on the related literature [2-10] and research, using the discrete logarithm problem and the Lagrange interpolation formula, I propose a distributed dynamic multi-secret sharing scheme. The program has the following innovation: 1) Each participant selects his shadow by himself; 2) There is no secure channel 3) There is no the fixed dealer, each participant may be dealer to distribute the multi-secret, and the multi-secret could be accomplished one time such operations as to distribute and to comeback and to update and to validate and so on; 4) The participant could be dynamically added or deleted; and 5) The efficient solutions against multiform cheating of any participant are proposed, therefore the proposed scheme has practicability and highly security.

2   A Description of Multi-secret Sharing Scheme

The program consists of system initialization, the multi-secret distribution and multi-secret reconstruction of the three phase composition. First, some relevant definitions will be introduced.

Definition1: The multi-secret distributor $SD_j \{j = 1, 2, ..., n\}$ is the multi-secret sharing n participant $U_i \{i = 1, 2, ..., n\}$.

Definition 2: The bulletin board NB refers to the storage medium of the public parameters or data, the multi-secret sharing participants have access to the contents of the bulletin board, but Only the participants of the published parameters or data can modify the parameters or data of their own published in the bulletin board .

2.1   System Initialization

Step1: selecting the following parameters:

1). Selecting two large prime numbers for p and q, $2^{511} < p < 2^{512}, 2^{159} < q < 2^{160}$,and $q|p-1$;
2). The g being an order q generator in ;
3). A collision-free one-way hash function H (), and the $\{p, q, g, H()\}$ will be placed in the bulletin board NB;

Step2: After the $\{p,q,g,H()\}$ was announced in   the   system , each   participant U_i randomly   select an   integer x_i (said   the x_i is the secret share of the U_i) and

$2 <x_i <q-1$, and calculate, the each participant keep secret x_i, and the y_i is passed to the system. The system must ensure that all the participants have different y_i. If they have the same y_i, they should be required to re-select the secret share x_i and recalculate yi until they have different y_i.

Step3: from $[1, n]$ (n is the number of participants), each participant should select a different integer ID_i as its identity. The information of each participant U_i {ID_i, y_i} is disclosed on the bulletin board.

2.2   Multi-secret Distribution

Let $S=\{s_{jk}\}$ (where:$s_{jk} \in Z_p^*$, $j= 1,2, ..., n, k =1,2, ..., w_j$), which is the multi-secret set shared by n participants {$U_1, U_2, ..., U_n$}, the set $S_j = \{s_{j1}, s_{j2}, \cdots, s_{jw_j}\}$ (where: $j= 1, 2,...,n$) is the subset of the multi-secret set S, which are the participant j as the secret distributor SD_j distributes w_j secrets (where: $2(n+w_j)<p$), The secret distributor SD_j dynamically select threshold t_j (where $t_j \leq n$) according to the importance of multi-secret. It means that the threshold is different with the reconstruction of the multi-secret were distributed by the secret distributor SD_j. The secret distributor SD_j performs the following process with the secret subset S_j:

Step 1 : Randomly select an integer $r_j \in Z_p^*$, calculate $R_j = g^{r_j} \mod p$;

Step 2 : By $(ID_1, y_1^{r_j} \mod p)$, $(ID_2, y_2^{r_j} \mod p)$,..., $(ID_n, y_n^{r_j} \mod p)$, $(n+1, s_{j1})$, $(n+2, s_{j2})$,..., $(n+w_j, s_{jw_j})$ w_j+n point Lagrange interpolation formula to determine a (w_j+n-1)-order polynomial (refer with: Eq. 1).

$$f_j(x) = (\sum_{k=1}^{w_j} s_{jk} \prod_{l=1,l\neq k}^{w_j} \frac{x-(n+l)}{k-l} \prod_{i=1}^{n} \frac{x-ID_i}{(n+k)-ID_i} + \sum_{i=1}^{n} y_i^{r_j} \prod_{l=1,l\neq i}^{n} \frac{x-ID_l}{ID_i-ID_l} \prod_{k=1}^{w_j} \frac{x-(n+k)}{ID_i-(n+k)}) \mod p \quad (1)$$

Step3 : The secret distributor SD_j calculates { $f_j(n+w_j+1)$, $f_j(n+w_j+2)$,..., $f_j(n+w_j+(n+w_j-t_j))$ } common $(n+w_j-t_j)$ point value, and sharing of multi-secret $s_{jk} (k=1,2,\cdots,w_j)$ public information {$R_j, f_j(n+w_j+1), f_j(n+w_j+2)$,..., $f_j(n+w_j+(n+w_j-t_j))$ } published in the bulletin NB.

2.3   Multi-secret Reconstruction

Let W be the collection of members of t_j reconstruction of multi-secret in the U. Perform the following procedure:

Step 1: The participant $U_i \in W$ first obtained R_j from the bulletin board NB, and calculated: $A_{ji} = R_j^{x_i} \mod p$, and then randomly selected an integer $d_i \in Z_p^*$, and calculated: $C_{ji} = H(g, R_j, y_i, A_{ji}, g^{d_i}, R_j^{d_i})$, $B_{ji} = d_i + x_i C_{ji} \mod p$, and the {$A_{ji}, C_{ji}, B_{ji}$} will be safely sent to other member of W by the authentication encryption methods according to literature [9].

Step 2: After the $\{A_{ji},C_{ji},B_{ji}\}$ was received by other members U_i ($U_i \in W$) of the W, verify whether the equation $C_{ji} = H(g, R_j, y_i, A_{ji}, g^{B_{ji}} y_i^{-C_{ji}}, R_j^{B_{ji}} A_{ji}^{-C_{ji}})$ is valid. If it is valid, the $\{A_{ji},C_{ji},B_{ji}\}$ provided by U_i is effective. Otherwise U_i does not correctly calculate the $\{A_{ji},C_{ji},B_{ji}\}$, the retransmission is required until it's right or the appropriate error is handled.

Step 3: After all members $\{A_{ji},C_{ji},B_{ji}\}$ of the W were proven effective, the collection of multi-secret S_j and other public information as $\{f_j(n+w_j+1), f_j(n+w_j+2),...,$ $f_j(n+w_j+(n+w_j-t_j))\}$ a total of $(n+w_j-t_j)$ will be downloaded by U_i from the bulletin board NB, by (ID_i, A_{ji}) (where: $i \in W$, a total of t_j points), and $\{(n+w_j+1, f_j(n+w_j+1)), (n+w_j+2, f_j(n+w_j+2)),..., ((n+w_j+(n+w_j-t_j)), f_j(n+w_j+(n+w_j-t_j)))\}$, (a total of $n+w_j-t_j$ points)$\}$, If it is right to use (X_i, Y_i) $(i=1,2,...,n+w_j)$ to represent the $(n+w_j)$ value pairs, the multi-secrets s_{jk} can be restored by the Lagrange interpolation formula according to the expression. (refer with: Eq. 2)

$$s_{jk} = f_j(n+k) = \sum_{i=1}^{n+w_j} Y_i \prod_{l=1, l \neq i}^{n+w_j} \frac{(n+k-X_l)}{(X_i - X_l)} \mod p$$

(where:$j=1,2,...,n,k=1,2,...,w_j$) (2) .

3   The Characteristics Analysis

3.1   The Safety Analysis

1): For any multi-secret s_{jk} that will be reconstructed , any t_j participants jointly can restore the multi-secret s_{jk} . Known by the Lagrange interpolation formula, the polynomial $f_j(x)$ of $(n+w_j-1)$ order was reconstructed need to know the $(n+w_j)$ different points (X_i, Y_i) to satisfy the equation $Y_i = f_j(X_i)$. For multi-secret s_{jk}, Because of the secret distributor SD_j announced the $(n+w_j-t_j)$ values of the polynomial $f_j(x)$ that the participant cannot calculate, and need to the t_j values different from the opened value again, the polynomial $f_j(x)$ will be reconstructed . As a result, for multi-secret s_{jk}, the t_j $(ID_i, A_{ji} = R_j^{x_i} \mod p)$ data pairs of any t_j participants and the opened $(n+w_j-t_j)$ data pairs of the distribution together were able to recover the shared multi-secret s_{jk}. But less than t_j participants cannot get any information of multi-secret s_{jk}. We may assume that t_j-1 participants $U_1, U_2,..., U_{t_j-1}$ attempt to restore the multi-secret s_{jk}, must obtain the value of the other participant. For example, the value $R_j^{x_{t_j}} \mod p$ of the U_{t_j}, Known from $R_j^{x_{t_j}} \mod p = y_{t_j}^{r_j} \mod p = g^{x_{t_j} r_j} \mod p$, In addition to the secret distributor SD_j and participant U_{t_j}. Any remaining people cannot compute $R_j^{x_{t_j}} \mod p$, therefore $(U_{t_j}, R_j^{x_{t_j}} \bmod p)$ will not be achieved and it is impossible to use the Lagrange interpolation formula to calculate the s_{jk}.

2): The distributor SD_j and the other members cannot obtain secret share x_i in this scenario from the public information y_i of the participant U_i, because of the problem of computing discrete logarithm. On the other hand, the secret share of the participants x_i can be used multiple times, and it will not be compromised due to the reconstruction of the multi-secret of some distributor SD_j, for the attacker cannot calculate x_i from A_{ji}. It is faced with the problem of computing discrete logarithm to calculate x_i from $A_{ji} = R_j^{x_i} \bmod p = g^{x_i r_j} \bmod p$, In addition the attacker can not calculate x_i from $B_{ji}=d_i+x_iC_{ji} \bmod p$, because the equation has two unknowns elements.

3): Dishonest members tried to take advantage of the previous A_{ji} of other member, without cooperating with other $(t-1)$ members to reconstruct the secret. We may assume that he would like to use $\{A_{ji}^a, A_{ji}^b\}$ to reconstruct the multi-secret s_{jk}, Then $A_{ji}^c = A_{ji}^a A_{ji}^b = (g^{x_i})^{r_a+r_b} \bmod p$, That is, the attacker could find $r_c=r_a+r_b \bmod p$, it will be able to export $\{A_{ji}^c\}$ by $\{A_{ji}^a, A_{ji}^b\}$, but because of the r_j is randomly selected by the secret distributor SD, The probability of a successful attack of the attacker was only $1/2^{511}$ in the limited domain.

4): When the secret is reconstructed, the dishonest participant U_i with incorrect triples $\{A_{ji}, C_{ji}, B_{ji}\}$ attempts to verify the equation $C_{ji} = H(g, R_j, y_i, A_{ji}, g^{B_{ji}} y_i^{-C_{ji}}, R_j^{B_{ji}} A_{ji}^{-C_{ji}})$. Apparently it is senseless that the dishonest members of the participant U forged $\{C_{ji}\}$, it will only increase the difficulty of the attack. Because the value of C_{ji} has been computed originally by the participant U_i by choosing a number randomly. In order to pass the validation of the equation, the participant U_i can randomly select A_{ji} or B_{ji}, then calculate B_{ji} or A_{ji}, Thus it will be faced with the difficulty of discrete logarithm problem of one-way hash function inverse.

3.2   Add or Remove the Member

Before the multi-secret s_{jk} is restored, suppose there is another participant U_{n+1} must be added. First of all, the new member of U_{n+1} must choose his own secret share x_{n+1}, and calculate $y_{n+1} = g^{x_{n+1}} \bmod p$, distribute the y to the system. Second, the integer that it was not used by the other members in the set $[1, n+1]$ as an ID_{n+1} was assigned to the U_{n+1} by the system, and the (ID_{n+1}, y_{n+1}) was posted on the bulletin board. For multi-secret s_{jk} (where: $j=1, l+1, \ldots, n$) the secret dealer SD_j performed the $step1$ of the secret distribution phase again, and then a (w_j+n)-order polynomial $f_j(x)$ was constructed by $(ID_1, y_1^{r_j} \bmod p)$, $(ID_2, y_2^{r_j} \bmod p), \ldots$, $(ID_n, y_n^{r_j} \bmod p)$, $(ID_{n+1}, y_{n+1}^{r_j} \bmod p), (n+1+1, s_{j1}), (n+1+2, s_{j2}), \ldots, (n+1+w_j, s_{jw_j})$ total (w_j+n+1) points with the Lagrange interpolation formula. The last secret distributor announced the information $\{R_j, \quad f_j(n+1+w_j+1), f_j(n+1+w_j+2), \ldots, f_j(n+1+w_j+(n+w_j-t_j))$, $f_j(n+1+w_j+(n+1+w_j-t_j))\}$ of share secrets s_{jk} (where: $j=1, l+1, \ldots, n$) on the

Bulletin Board again, without having to modify any information of the other n participants, and the secret dealer SD_j need not establish a secure channel with the participants U_n also.

Before the multi-secret s_{jk} is restored, assume that the participant U_n was expelled for other reasons (or removed from, etc.). At this point the public information (ID_n, y_n) of the U_n will be deleted from the bulletin board by the secret dealer SD_j. For multi-secret $s_{jk}(j=l,l+1,\ldots,n)$, the secret distributor SD_j performed the *step1* of the secret distribution phase again, and then a (w_j+n-2)-order polynomial $f_j(x)$ was constructed by $(ID_1, y_1^{r_j} \bmod p), (ID_2, y_2^{r_j} \bmod p), \ldots, (ID_{n-1}, y_{n-1}^{r_j} \bmod p), (n-1+1,s_{j1}), (n-1+2,s_{j2}), \ldots, (n-1+w_j, s_{jw_j})$ total (w_j+n+1) points with the Lagrange interpolation formula. The last secret distributor announced the information $\{R_j, \ f_j(n-1+w_j+1), \ f_j(n-1+w_j+2), \ldots, f_j(n-1+w_j+(n-1+w_j-t_j)) \}$ of share secrets s_{jk} (where: $j=l, l+1, \ldots,n$) on the bulletin board again, without having to modify any information of the other n-1 participants.

According to the above analysis, even if the t_j participants were deleted (ie remove members reach a certain threshold) in the scheme, the multi-secret cannot be reconstructed by these members of the conspiracy before it is recovered. This shows that the scheme has a strong robustness.

3.3   Performance Analysis

In computational efficiency, each participant as the secret dealer can distribute the multi-secret, and the operation as distribution, restoration, update and verification etc can be finished once. It does not need a secure channel between the participants and the secret dealer. And it does not need to change the secret share of the other members when increasing or decreasing members. The overall computational complexity of this program decreases compared with the literature [10] program under the same multi-secret, Under the same security, it is more important in the ease implementation of the algorithm and the practicality of function. Therefore, it is closer to real life in the application.

4   Conclusion

It is the innovation of the author that a distributed dynamic threshold secret sharing scheme has been proposed on the discrete logarithm problem. The scheme has the following innovation: 1) Each participant selects his shadow by himself; 2) There is no secure channel 3) There is no the fixed dealer, each participant may be the dealer to distribute the multi-secret, and the multi-secret can be accomplished one time operations such as to distribute and to comeback and to update and to validate and so on; 4) The participant can be dynamically added or deleted; 5) The efficient solutions against multiform cheating of any participant are proposed, therefore the proposed scheme has practicability and highly security.

References

1. Tompa, M., Woll, H.: How to share a secret with cheaters. J. Cryptol. 1(1), 133–138 (1988)
2. Xing, H.M., Zhi, F.P., Ding, Y.: A Verifiable Multiple Secrets Sharing Scheme. Chinese of Journal Electronics 30(4), 540–543 (2002)
3. Harn, L.: Efficient sharing (broadcasting) of multiple secret. IEE Proc. Compute Digit. Tech. 143(3), 237–240 (1995)
4. Lin, T.Y., Wu, T.C. (t,n) threshold verifiable multi-secret sharing scheme based on factorization intractability and discrete logarithm modulo a composite problems. IEE Proc. Compute Digit. Tech. 146(5), 264–268 (1999)
5. Chang, T.Y., Hwang, M.S., Yang, W.P.: An improvement on the Lin wu (t, n) threshold verifiable multi-secret sharing scheme. Applied Mathematics and Computation 163(1), 169–178 (2005)
6. Xie, Q., Yu, X.-Y., Wang, J.-L.: A secure and Efficient (t,n) Multisecret Sharing Authenticating Scheme. Journal of Electronics & Information Technology 27(9), 1476–1478 (2005)
7. Gan, Y.-J., Cao, G.: A Cheat-proof Multi-secret Sharing Scheme Based on Factorization. Journal of the China Railway Society 26(4), 69–72 (2004)
8. Guo, Y., Gao, F., Ma, C.: Cheat-Proof Secret Share Schemes Based on Oneway Function. Microcomputer Information 36(12-3), 55–57 (2005)
9. Gan, Y.-J., Peng, Y.-Q., Xie, S.-Y., Zheng, X.-P.: Improvement of Publicly Verifiable Authenticated Encryption Scheme. Journal of Sichuan University (Engineering Science Edition) 37(3), 115–117 (2005)
10. He, B., Huang, J., Huang, G.-X., Tang, Y.: A new distributed and verifiable multi-secret sharing scheme. Microcomputer Information 22(12-3), 61–62 (2006)

Exploratory Study on Campus Network Security Solutions

Liang Wang

Shanghai Urban Management College, Shanghai China, 200232
civilwon@hotmail.com

Abstract. In the current wave of campus information technology development, the campus network information security has always been people's concerns. Among of them, how to protect the campus intranet from easily hack by external network and how to manage self-security of campus intranet is often a top priority. Therefore, this paper introduces a preliminary exploration of campus security solution from the point of view, such as: the security device structure design, ACL, VLAN, etc.

Keywords: Network Security, Campus Network, WIFI, Switch, Router.

1 Introduction

With the rapid development of computer networks, network applications have become an essential part of the informatization campus development. Teachers and students enjoy the various convenience brings from campus network. At the same time, it is also facing with a variety of intranet and internet security threats. Internet security has been basically completed during the initial construction of current network, it contains anti-attacking and anti-scanning device, like IPS, IDS, firewall, viruswall, etc. But the threats of campus intranet security include network attacks, data loss, hacking, virus, password tampering, ultra vires, and so on. Thus, the current campus intranet security management is much more difficult than the campus network's external interface management.

Therefore, the establishment of an effective system of internal network security is necessary. Depending on increasing the intranet security management device, setting security configuration for intranet firewall, setting security policy on the router and switch, etc., establish a complete network security system and measure and implement at every level.

2 Additional Internal Network Security Equipment

With the rapid development of computer network technology, more and more users to select different office work or telecommuting. By the campus net users, for example: the campus network users Mainly are teachers and students, the user if in scientific

J. Lei et al. (Eds.): NCIS 2012, CCIS 345, pp. 365–371, 2012.
© Springer-Verlag Berlin Heidelberg 2012

research, certainly will demand of campus net access anywhere at any time. And now use of WLAN, WIFI, etc wireless technology, that can at any time anywhere to connect the network. For the network managers, to meet the network users to access the network and their information and data`s security , server system`s security management, network access equipment safety management, business network security management became a top priority.

In the way of using WIFI or WLAN access the internal network or the Internet, the key way is often more vulnerable, WEP, WPA and other encryption methods can easily be cracked, so easy to make illegal user logs on to bring unauthorized access the internal network security issues.As the network managers in the remote access to users in the local area network within the permission to access can't make reasonable judgement. Thus, likely to cause the unauthorized access, and network internal purview division is often not clear enough, thus easy to bring visit instability and information data unsafety. At the same time, As the data in the transmission process, the data encryption and safety have not been effectively guarantee and be unable to guarantee the connection campus network of network security

As the hackers network technology development, previously adopted common server type key authentication has been unable to meet the current information security requirements. And therefore, to add the security equipment that making security access device between the user and equipment constitute a firewall permissions in order to achieve physical isolation, so that it can access more in line with requirements for safe access.

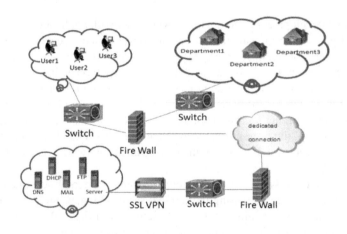

Fig. 1.

As fig 1, through the establishment of a special access program to arm mode SSL VPN device configuration management, and to determine the identity authentication system, then access through the deployment of appropriate safety equipment, physically isolated from the appropriate access for different identity of the user access to different application servers, business systems and using different resources.

Make user1, user2, user3 and department1, department2, department3 dedicated connection through the firewall switch access network. To access the campus network and effective resources within the campus network. Certification by the SSL VPN to ensure belong to different departments or different staff departments, according to the level obtained permission, you can access different servers, in order to prevent cross-authority access; access through the SSL VPN network management, can work effectively within the campus network to avoid the insecurity, which can further optimize the campus network management.

3   The Safety Switch Manager by the ACL

ACL is a list of instructions, mainly used in three-layer-switch or router. Access Control list determined to receive and send data packets, and according to the list of different rules, determined to send and receive data the amount of size.

In the same time create the ACL, you can list the details of the conditions determined by the address side, target, source, port, protocol and other conditions for details of management. Also, you can manage the current network traffic, enhance the efficiency of communication in order to avoid network congestion. Therefore, ACL can be used as a powerful tool for network control, can enhance network security, and to filter into and out of a router or switch interface layer packets.

In creating ACL,at the same time can list details condition, by the judge of IP address, target, the source, port, and the condition such as agreement to undertake detail management. At the same time, also can management the current network traffic, strengthen communication efficiency, in order to avoid the network congestion. Therefore, ACL also can serve as a powerful tool for network control, it can improve the security of network, and is used to filter the inflows and outflows router or three-3-layer switches interface packets.

3.1   Restrict Access to Single IP Address

As fig 2:In the ACL interface to receive or send data packets, the system will interface to determine the configuration of the ACL rules to determine whether to approve or reject, in order to achieve the purpose of access control, improve network security. Such as banning the IP address 10.20.30.0 network`s computer to access the 211.136.17.0 network`s computer.

Fig. 2.

ROUTER1
R1(config)#interface fastEthernet 1/1
R1(config-if)#ip address 10.20.30.1/24+2
R1(config)#interface fastEthernet 1/0
R1(config-if)#ip address 192.168.1.2/16+3
R1(config)#ip route 211.136.17.0 /24+4 fa1/0

ROUTER2
R2(config)#access-list 1 deny 10.20.30.0 0.0.0.255
R2(config)#access-list 1 per
R2(config)#access-list 1 permit any
R2(config)#interface fastEthernet 1/1
R2(config-if)#ip access-group 1 out

3.2   Through the Expansion of the ACL

As fig 2:Set the IP address ban access services. For example: banned IP address 10.20.30.0 network's computer access 211.136.17.0 network for the WWW service (namely prohibited access WEB page).

ROUTER1
R1(config)#interface fastEthernet 1/1
R1(config-if)#ip address 10.20.30.1 255.255.255.0
R1(config)#interface fastEthernet 1/0
R1(config-if)#ip address 192.168.1.2 255.255.0.0
R1(config)#ip route 211.136.17.0 255.255.255.0 fa1/0
ROUTER2
R2(config)#access-list 101 deny tcp 10.20.30 0.0.0.255 211.136.17.0 0.0.0.255 eq www
R2(config)#access-list 101 permit ip any any
R2(config)#interface fastEthernet 1/1
R2(config-if)#ip access-group 101 out

---

2 24=255.255.255.0
316=255.255.0.0
4 24=255.255.255.0

4   Use VLAN Technology for Local Area Network Security Management

VLAN--Virtual Local Area Network, it is a physical network in the IP address of the different user to logic division to different means broadcast domain, and can solve the network to the broadcast storm and safety and a kind of built agreement way.

The transmission of the data frames in Ethernet, under the premise of increased VLAN head a message, so as to determine the different working group and virtual network. Through the logic division, every VLAN is both independent individuals can also is an integral whole, the internal flow of data or broadcast traffic to the others and it won`t forwarding database, and can control the broadcast storm generation, at the same time also reduce the damage of virus attack , reduce the equipment management difficulty, improve the efficiency of the flow control, increase the security of the network. Meanwhile, as different VLAN can not communicate with each other to access another through the router must be achieved, which greatly enhanced the physical properties belong to different departments within the LAN part of the exchange of visits between the security.

4.1   VLAN advantages

4.1.1   To Prevent Broadcast Storms

Divided by the LAN VLAN, you can greatly reduce the network broadcast storm. When the VLAN appear in a segment of users a virus infection, its logic has been divided since the characteristics, resulting in no inter-VLAN communication segment in order to avoid affecting the entire internal network access.

4.1.2   High Efficiency and Low Cost

The network administrator for network management, property or requirement can be similar to the user, the user with a department divided into a VLAN. Similar properties as the needs of users also often similar, so after making the division of the VLAN greatly enhance the ease of management.

At the same time, the division of the VLAN, you can take advantage of the characteristics of the switch, the network link utilization greatly enhanced, in order to reduce costs.

4.1.3   To Increase the Adaptability and Flexibility of the Network

Through the VLAN management, the various categories of users, networks, demand combined into a variable as a whole at any time, the formation of virtual local area network, making network management has become very flexible and convenient it can be in a state of dynamic equilibrium .

4.2   By Using a VLAN Allows the Interconnection Network Can Be Safely

As fig 3 and fig 4 : Through the VLAN classification, can make the user originally belonged to a different port, but can belong to a VLAN, enabling secure network access. For example: switch set in the original division of the second floor there are two of the vlan office network, add a three-layer switch, vlan to achieve interoperability, in order to achieve security of the office network.

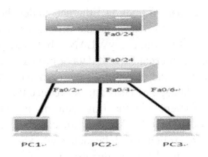

Fig. 3.

Name	Port	Ip	Netgate
PC1	Switch 1- fa0/2	10.1.1.2/24	10.1.1.1
PC2	Switch 1- fa0/4	10.1.1.3/24	10.1.1.1
PC3	Switch 1- fa0/6	10.1.2.2/24	10.1.2.1

Fig. 4.

layer switch configuration:
Switch1 (config) #   vlan 10
Switch1 (config) # interface range fa0/2,0/4
Switch1 (config-if) #swithport mode access vlan 10
Switch1 (config-if)exit
Switch1 (config) # vlan 20
Switch1 (config) # interface range fa0/2,0/46
Switch1 (config-if) #swithport mode access vlan 20
Switch1 (config-if)exit
Switch1(config)interface fa0/24
Switch1 (config-if) swithport mode trunk

Three-layer switch configuration :
Switch1 (config) # vlan 10
Switch1 (config) # interface vlan 10
Switch1 (config-if) #ip address 10.1.1.1 255.255.255.0
Switch1 (config) # vlan 20
Switch1 (config) # interface vlan 20
Switch1 (config-if) #ip address 10.1.2.1 255.255.255.0
Switch1(config)interface fa0/24
Switch1 (config-if) swithport mode trunk

5   Summary

With the rapid development of network technology and network complexity, high dependence on information systems, and other characteristics, these determine the current network security threats exist objectively, and the new network threats and network security solutions are also coming in thick and fast. The campus network information security is not only related to the campus network security, but also affects the whole society and the whole country's network information security in the current complex information environment. Therefore, effective management systems and security defense system are absolutely necessary. By adding the appropriate Network Secure Access audit devices, like SSL, VPN, and etc., within intranet, and using ACL, VLAN, etc. in the original device to tap its potential, gradually increase the campus network security and defense capability and further promote the network's safe, healthy, and rapid development.

References

1. Wang, S.Z., Liu, C.C.: To explore the safety of active network. Fuzhou Uuniversity (2009)
2. Yang, Y.: Network security theory and technology, pp. 76–89. People's posts and telecommunications publishing house (2003)
3. Wu, Y.: Network security technology research and application of the password vacuum electron technology, pp. 34–36 (2004)
4. Dong, L., Yun, L.: Public Key Infrastructure PKI and its API Mechanism. Northern Jiaotong University
5. Shi, P., Tian, H., Wang, Y.: Routing protocol security research. Xi'an University of Electronic Science and Technology

Research and Improvement of Adjustment Algorithm of Matching Rules of Intrusion Detection

Yan-Sen Zhou and Jin-Ran Yang

Department of Information Science and Technology, University of International Relations,
Beijing, China
{buptzhou,yangjinran211}@126.com

Abstract. Adjustment of Array sequence of matching rules can improve performance of network intrusion detection system. Firstly, This paper introduces static adjustment algorithm, which makes the most frequently used rules in the top of the list of rules, and reduces the frequency and time of following data packets; Secondly, two dynamic adjustment algorithms are designed and accomplished, which are algorithm of dynamic adjustment of matching rules based on variable sampling time T and algorithm of real-time adjustment based on matching trigger of feature event, the Former keeps the matching rule order consistent with the current network flow and adjust the sampling time T according to the number of network flow, the latter adopts three-step dynamical adjustment method to adjust rules sequence when intrusion happens. The experiment shows that the match performance of three-step dynamical adjustment algorithm has been significantly improved than other two adjust algorithms.

Keywords: real time, intrusion detection, matching rules, static adjust, dynamic adjust.

1 Introduction

The load of network intrusion detection system mainly depends on two factors, the network flow and the scale of rule database. In the terms of rule database itself, on one hand, the new attacks make the number of Intrusion rule increase; on the other hand, the continual upgrades and patches of the versions of Operating system and application services make these attacks invalid or decrease, so it will influence the performance of network intrusion detection system, if these old rules stay in the rule databases. In addition, as network attacks have a certain periodicity, one network attack often appears during some periods of time, while seldom during other time. For example, the original Array sequence is reserved and the rule of higher matching frequency is left behind. If there are N rules, then the following similar attacks also need be matched N times. If the N is very big, it will become the bottleneck of the detection system.

With the network flow increasing rapidly and exponential growth of the network attacks, if the array sequence of matching rule database isn't well adjusted, then detection engine load is so large that it may lead to the occurrence of omission. On the

J. Lei et al. (Eds.): NCIS 2012, CCIS 345, pp. 372–379, 2012.
© Springer-Verlag Berlin Heidelberg 2012

occasion that the scale of invasion of the rules can't be controlled, we can adjust the array sequence of matching rule database by putting the well-matched rules in the front of the rule databases. So, if we can make the matching rules corresponding the largest data flow in the network in the front of the rule row by array sequence adjustment of rule database of intrusion detection, we can also reduce the rule matching time of the similar subsequent data packets .Now there are two ways to adjust array sequence of rule database: static adjust and dynamic adjust.

2   Static Adjustment Algorithm of Matching Rule

2.1   Statistical Analysis of Static Adjustment Algorithm

Using Statistical analysis [3] algorithm to optimize the matching rules of network Intrusion detection refers to the algorithm which based on the used frequency within the stipulated period of time of intrusion detection matching rules. It dynamically adjusts the relative order of matching rules. As a result, it makes the most frequently used rules in the top of the list of rules, and it reduces the frequency and time of following data packets, thereby enhancing the performance of intrusion detection systems.

In order to adjust matching rules, it would be provided within a fixed time period T according to all historical data flow statistical analysis. All matching rules are based on historical data packets hit frequency. We sort the list of rules, so that the rules are matched at a high frequency in the front list of rules. Then next time, the time that matching the rule required the will be reduced. However, this method has obvious shortcomings. The order of matching the rules does not reflect the current network load conditions. It cannot adjust current network traffic rules which are more frequent to the top of rule database.

When we are implementing statistical analysis to adjust the order of matching rules, If the operation of intrusion detection is normal, we can set a statistical matching frequency fields in each rule, so that we can calculate period of time the number of times each rule is matched. Then we can sort according to the number of time. In order to reduce sorting time, we can use quick sort method. We can sacrifice space for time. In this way, after a period of time, we can adjust the order according to rule matching frequency. After the adjustment, frequency field values of all rules reset to 0.

The benefits of static statistical method are that changes of rule trees are based on statistics of a period of time. In this way, we can describe the basic network operation status more accurately and comprehensively. Efficiency of detection is improved effectively. What's more, computational burden of additional procedures to the system will not increase frequently. However, static adjustment algorithm of statistical analysis relies on analysis of the information on the alarm of a period of time. We resort after a period of time, so that the algorithm can't adapt the new matching rules caused by attack methods changing in time. The problem of time lag is serious. Before we change the rules, the detection of new attacks can't be optimized in time. To overcome the shortcomings of the algorithm, this system introduces a dynamic adjustment algorithm.

3   Dynamic Adjustment Algorithm

In order to make up the shortage of static adjust in delay performance, dynamic adjust algorithm is introduced .For the reason that it takes some time to adjust rule by static adjust, which can't indicate the characteristics of network intrusion behavior on that moment, while dynamic adjust can adjust to the changing network behavior quickly and adjust rules by another means. Now dynamic adjust mainly take two forms: based on variable sampling time T and based on the special events trigger.

3.1   Dynamic Adjustment of Matching Rules Based on Variable Sampling Time T

Using the Statistical analysis to optimize the intrusion detection methods, the key is whether the statistical data can reflect the real-time current network data flow. We should be as fast as possible so that the current order of pattern matching rules and the current network traffic type is consistent. Actually, when the sampling T is constant, the sensitivity of statistics has a direct relationship with the size of the current network flow. When the network flow is relatively great, we can get enough data to evaluate the development trend of network flow, so we should shorten the time on statistics to make the matching rules match the current network flow. otherwise, the rule array sequence may lag behind the current network flow. when the network flow is small relatively, and so is the T, we can't collect enough data, as a result, we can predict the development trend of network flow and then the adjusted order of filtering rules will not match the current network flow characteristics. On that occasion, we should lengthen the time T. Considering the two occasions, in order to keep the matching rule order Consistent with the current network flow, we should adjust the sampling time T according to the number of network flow. In this paper, the current network flow is stood for a flow factor F. Statistics time of unit T is inversely proportional to flow factor F.

1. Algorithm Description
In the following description, the D stands for intrusion detection default rules; R stands for other matching rules, stands for the number of rules, and r_1, r_2, ..., r_n stand for the rules in the set ; C $(r_i)(1 \leq i \leq n)$ stands for the number of packet matching the i(th) of the filter rules; C $(r_i)(1 \leq i \leq n)$ stands for the number of packet hitting the matching rules belonging to D; T0 Stands for the original sampling time; T_{new} Stands for the adjusted sampling time; F stands for the flow factor, F=the max handle flow of intrusion detection system/the current network flow($F \geq 1$),which is a variable inversely proportional to current network flow the size of a variable.

The detailed algorithm description is as follows:

(1) Initialization
Set $C(D) = 0$, $C(r_i) = 0$, and assume that when intrusion detection has just started, the order of filter rules is: $r_1, r_2, \cdots, r_n$, start a timer T_0 with the cycle of Initial time length;

(2) Match the rules and statistic the frequency of each rule.
When the intrusion detection system receives a packet, first, according to the agreement analysis, get the feature extraction of data packets. If the packet character match the number i rule, then counter corresponding to the rule increases by 1: $C(r_i)=C(r_i)+1$; if the packet matches none of the rules, then the counter corresponding to default rule D increases by 1: $C(D)=C(D)+1$

(3) Judge if the timer ends.
    If stopping timing, we should execute procedure (4) before restarting the timer, or go on with the procedure (2).

(4) Adjust the order of rules of set R, the operation should be conducted before the timer restarts.

Regard $C(r_i)$ as the key word,   rank the rules in R in descending order to obtain a new rule formation :$r1', r2', \cdots, rn'$. When the timer is reset, $C(r_i)$, $C(D)$ is cleared.

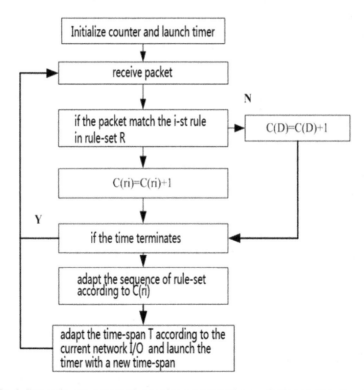

Fig. 1. Dynamic adjustment of matching rules based on variable sampling time T

(5)Adjust the T according to the current network flow.

When   F=the max handle flow of intrusion detection system / the current network flow, set $T_{new}=F*T_0$ and regard T_{new} as the new length of the timer. Then, restart the timer.

(6)Turn to procedure (3) and go on with matching rule by the new rule order.

3.2   Real-Time Adjustment Based on Matching Trigger of Feature Event

Dynamic adjustment of matching rules based on variable sampling time T makes it possible for the order of matching rule keep up with the characteristics of data flow in the network, but it's not real-time adjustment. In order to overcome algorithmic delay, make real-time adjustment possible, we should adopt real-time adjustment based on matching trigger of feature event.

The so called real-time adjustment based on matching trigger of feature event is to adjust certain sequence according to certain event trigger. That is, when the invasion network system functions normally, if certain rule is adjusted, then the whole sequence will change. Because the previous structure which adopts classification index in the rule set, in fact, each of the adjustments only direct for a subset, so the relevant adjustments will not affect the performance of test system performance.

The adjustment is applied to many test system. The most important is how to adjust it when certain rule is matched by certain event in the network. Some systems adopt "one step adjustment method", That is, the matched rule is set in the first position. The adjustment method can quickly keep up with the latest behavior of the network, but cause a huge changes of rule database. As a result, they affects the stability of the system; Some systems use "step by step adjustment method". When a rule is matched, the current matched rule will move forward one step. Although it can overcome the changes of "one step adjustment method", but the speed of rule change can't keep pace with changing behavior in network. In order to take into account the requirements of real-time and stability of the rule database, the system adopts three-step dynamical adjustment method, which requires add another field to the original rules to statistical frequency of matched rules.

The so called "three-step dynamical adjustment method" is that when the rule database matches certain rule, the current position value of matched rule is multiplied by 2/3, and then put the rule in the position calculated; If the similar attacks occurs again, the current position value is multiplied by 1/2. When the similar attacks occurs in the third , the rule matched is put in the first position. Thus, when the rule is matched by the same attacks three times, its array sequence is advanced to number 1. The rule rises very quickly, which accelerates the matching speed of the following similar attacks. What's more, with time passing by, the slow decrease tends to make the frequent-used attack pattern stable. After a long time, some invalid attacks and seldom used rules will be ranked at the tail of the rule database, which minimize the influence on matching.

In order to apply the three-step dynamical adjustment method, we should add a field that stands for the times to the rules, which can solve the problem of consecutive three matches attacks. There are four values in the field: 0, 1, and 2 and 3. The Algorithm flow chart is as follows:

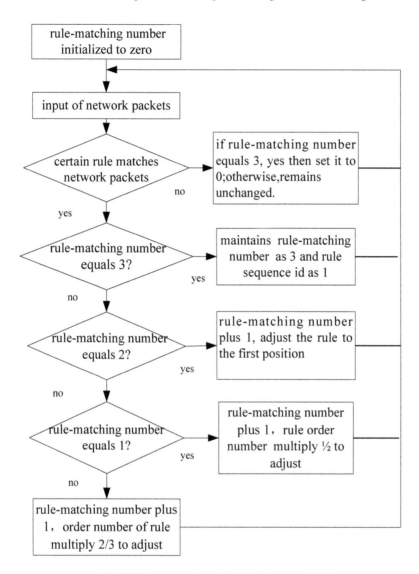

Fig. 2. Three-step dynamical adjustment method

In the Figure 2, when certain rule-matching number equals 3, the we will put it in the position 1; if the following attacks is still the same type, rule-matching number won't change, the rule order number is still 1, until the next attack doesn't match. When the attack of different type is matched by other rules, the top rule-matching number goes back to 1. However, the order number is still 1, till the attacks matched by one rule s successfully 3 times in the end. Then the original rule in the position 1 will move down by 1, becomes rank 2 and the new attack will become the rank 1; Then with the new rules have been arranged in the first serial number, serial number of the rules will be arranged in descending order, until precipitate to the end of the system rules.

As is seen, the algorithm not only ensures the relative stability of the rule matching option, but also keeps the matching rules of attacks of relative concentration in the time period of the day remains in the front position, which effectively improves the speed of matching rules.

4   Experimental Results

Three rule adjust algorithms are carried out in the following experimental environment: CPU Intel Core 2.80 GHz, memory 8G. The operating system is Windows 7 Professional. The test data used is provided by the MIT Lincoln Lab datasets.

In order to verify the impact of rules adjustment algorithm in rules matching, we use following experiment to compare performance. Experimental network uses the same parallel configuration structure and open-source intrusion detection system. It includes all rules (about 3000). It also records 10 groups of detection time (Unit: ms). Each group has 100 matching packets. Network speeds up in the testing process.

Table 1. Test results

group	1	2	3	4	5
Static adjustment	44.5	45.4	44.3	44.6	44.1
Variable sampling time	44.3	44.8	44.1	44.7	30.6
Three-step adjustment	45.4	44.1	43.8	30.8	29.9

group	6	7	8	9	10
Static adjustment	30.5	30.4	30.1	29.6	31.6
Variable sampling time	30.1	30.5	20.8	20.1	19.8
Three-step adjustment	29.1	20.1	19.8	19.3	11.7

Static adjustment changes the order of rules at a fixed time period. When group 6 packets come, we change the order of rules. Matching time reduced by nearly 10 ms. Using variable sampling time adjustment algorithm, the detection time Gradually reduces when network accelerates. The change of speed is higher than the static adjustment algorithm. Three-step dynamic adjustment algorithm adjusts every three group, and detection time continues to drop. These results indicate that static adjustments can't response to changes in network traffic in time, the average detection time is 36.5 ms. Variable sampling time adjustment algorithm can adjust rules sort in time based on network flow, the average detection time is 26.6 ms. Three-step dynamic adjustment algorithm can response to network changes in time, the average detection time is 23.5 ms. Therefore ,We can come to the conclusion that three-step dynamic adjustment algorithm has advantage in terms of detection time under the same circumstances.

5   Conclusion

There are many improved technologies in improving the efficiency of intrusion detection engine. The optimization of rules database is one of the main technologies. And researchers need to focus on it. We can reduce the range of each match by dividing rules database subset. We can adjust intrusion rules which frequently appear on the current network to the forefront position by using static and dynamic real-time adjustment. Then the number of rules for each match is reduced. By using this technology, we can provide some help in aspects of reducing the intrusion detection load. IDS designers who develop detection system can have a reference.

References

1. Jiang, J.: Intrusion detection of network security. Summary of Research. Learned Journal of Software 11(11), 1460–1466 (2000)
2. Ren, X.: Research and realization of method of improving rule matching speed of snort. Application of Computer 23(4), 59–61 (2003)
3. Yan, W.: Data Structure (C Language). Press of Tsinghua University, Beijing (2002)
4. Zhang, Y.: Course of Operating System of Computer, 3rd edn. Press of Tsinghua University, Beijing (2002)
5. Chen, T.: Optimization of rule set. Learned Journal of NEAI 20(6), 654–656 (2005)
6. Al-shaer, E., Hamed, H.: Design and Implementation of Firewall Policy Advisor-Tools.Technical Report CTI-techrep0801, School of Computer Science Telecommunications and Information Systems, Depaul University (August 2002)

Principal Component Analysis of Network Security Data Based on Projection Pursuit

Bin Wen and Guolong Chen[*]

College of Mathematics and Computer Sciences, Fuzhou University, Fuzhou 350108, China
{wenbin8901,fzucgl}@163.com

Abstract. In network security situation awareness system, the data are characterized by huge quantities, numerous features, redundancy, etc. These features may seriously impact the efficiency of situation evaluation and prediction. This paper proposes a principal component analysis algorithm based on projection pursuit (PP-PCA) to solve these problems. Combined with particle swarm optimization and exterior point penalty function, PP-PCA projects the data onto one-dimensional plane then figures out several composite indicators which play leading roles. The simulate experiment shows that it can overcome the redundancy and improve the efficiency of the situation evaluation and prediction.

Keywords: Projection Pursuit, Principal Component Analysis, Particle Swarm Optimization, Exterior Point Penalty Function.

1 Introduction

Network security situation awareness is the focus of the next generation network security technology [1]. It is a quantitative analysis method and fine measurement of the network security. To begin with it collects security elements, then understands their relations and evaluates the impacts, finally predicates the trends of the whole network. The NSSA system collects data from several kinds of network security system such as intrusion detection system, firewall and so on [2]. These log data are exceedingly huge data sets and have serious redundancy. For instance, the intrusions of DoS and Probe are mainly related to the features of flow; U2R and R2L are related to context properties. If we dispose these data immediately it will cost lots of time and the accuracy of the result can't be guaranteed. Therefore it is necessary to reduce the dimensions of the data and eliminate the irrelevant factors.

The major causes of these problems include excessive features, the construction of feature space, etc [3]. So many researchers address these problems by feature extraction method. Principal component analysis (PCA) is the well-known method for feature extraction [4]. PCA is a mathematical procedure that uses an orthogonal transformation to convert a set of observations of possibly correlated variables into a set of values of linearly uncorrelated variables called principal components.

---

[*] Corresponding author.

J. Lei et al. (Eds.): NCIS 2012, CCIS 345, pp. 380–387, 2012.
© Springer-Verlag Berlin Heidelberg 2012

This paper proposes a principal component analysis algorithm based on projection pursuit (PP-PCA). We apply the particle swarm optimization (PSO) to calculate the projection index and use the exterior point penalty function to handle the constraint conditions of PSO. The simulate experiment shows that it can overcome the redundancy and improve the efficiency of the situation evaluation and prediction.

There is some related research work on feature extraction of intrusion detection and network security system. Chebrolu S and others build up a feature selection model based on Bayesian Network and Classification and Regression Tree (CART) in [5]. It efficiently improves the detection performance. Opitz DW uses Genetic Algorithm to find a suitable feature subset and then classify with Neural Network in [6]. Tsymbal A and others construct a feature subset by using Stochastic Subspace method in [7].

2   Proposed Algorithm

2.1   Concept of PP-PCA

The main idea of PCA is that reconstructing a dataset of several uncorrelated indicators for original correlated indicators. Then take less numbers of the transformed indicators that contain the most information to replace the original indicators. Commonly we use linear combination to process reconstruction. The largest value of variance represents the largest amount of information. But the variance is an index representing the dispersibility of data. It describes the outline structure of data distribution in space and it is hard to describe the detail. The projection pursuit is a novel statistical approach to process high dimensional data [7]. It can overcome the curse of dimension. The main procedures of projection pursuit (PP) are show as follows. Firstly, construct a projection index [9]. Secondly, by calculating the projection index we can find projection directions that construct the low dimensional feature space which represents the most amounts of information for the original full data space. Finally, we can find an optimal projection direction which stands for the data structures or features of the original high dimensional data by maximizing or minimizing the projection index. In this sense, PCA is a special case of PP. By optimizing the designed projection index we can find out the detail or the local structure of data set.

Let sample $\{x(i, j) \mid i = 1, 2, ...n; j = 1, 2, ...p\}$ be p-dimensional observation data. The objective of projection pursuit is analysis of the structure and features of data by the one-dimensional projection of data. Let $a = \{a(1), a(2), a(3), ..., a(p)\}$ be p-dimensional unit vector. The one-dimensional projection value of data on direction a is defined as follows,

$$z(i) = \sum_{j=1}^{p} a(j)x(i, j) \qquad i = 1, 2, ...n .$$

(1)

The projection index is the function of $z(i)$, written as $Q(a)$. Then we need to minimize the index value, which is defined as follows,

$$Q(a_1) = \min(-\sum_{i=1}^{n} z(i) - Ez)^2 / (n-1), \qquad \sum_{j=1}^{p} a_1^2(j) = 1. \qquad (2)$$

Obviously, the index value $Q(a)$ is the largest eigenvalue of convariance matrix in PCA. And a_1 is the corresponding eigenvector to the largest eigenvalue. Then keeping on processing projection and calculate unit vector a_2 in the space perpendicular to a_1, where

$$Q(a_2) = \min(-\sum_{i=1}^{n} z(i) - Ez)^2 / (n-1), \qquad \sum_{j=1}^{p} a_2^2(j) = 1, a_2 \perp a_1. \qquad (3)$$

In the same way, we can extract several principal components which projection index values are greater than zero. Let d be the number of principal components, where $d \leq p$.

Calculate each principal component

$$F_{ii} = \sum_{j=1}^{p} a_{i\,j}^{'} x^{'}(i, j), \quad i = 1, 2, ..., n; \quad i^{'} = 1, 2, ..., d; \quad d \leq p. \qquad (4)$$

Through the above analysis, it shows that PP-PCA is an exploratory data analysis method. It searches the most efficient projection direction based on practical needs.

2.2   Particle Swarm Optimization

Particle swarm optimization is a kind of evolutionary algorithm proposed to solve objective optimization problem [10] [11]. PSO has been widely applied in many scientific fields, such as neural network training, fuzzy system control, wireless sensor network task scheduling, etc [12] [13]. Let search space be a p-dimensional space. The position of the particle i is represented with a position vector $x_i = (x_1, x_2, ..., x_p), i = 1, 2, ..., n$ and a velocity vector $v_i = (v_1, v_2, ..., v_p), i = 1, 2, ..., n$, where n is population size. The velocity and position of each particle are calculated according to (5) (6) (7)

$$v_{id} = w \times v_{id} + c_1 r_1 (p_{id} - x_{id}) + c_2 r_2 (p_{gd} - x_{id}). \qquad (5)$$

$$\begin{cases} v_{id} = v_{max}, & if \ v_{id} > v_{max} \\ v_{id} = -v_{max}, & if \ v_{id} < -v_{max} \end{cases} \tag{6}$$

$$x_{id} = x_{id} + v_{id} \tag{7}$$

Where w is the inertia weight, c_1 and c_2 are two positive constants called acceleration constants. r_1 and r_2 are random values between 0 and 1. v_{max} is a constant used to limit the velocities of the particles .

The fitness value of PSO is defined as the projection index value Q.

2.3   Exterior Point Penalty Function Method

Exterior point penalty function method, also known as exterior point method, is a typical algorithm to solve constraint optimization problem. There are some advantages of exterior point method, such as well convergence, easy to implement, wide application scope. How to handle the constraint conditions are the key when using PSO to solve constraint optimization problems [14]. When solving the equality constraint problem, the constraint violation function is defined as,

$$\Phi(x) = \sum_{l=1}^{m} |h_l(x)| . \tag{8}$$

Where $h_l(x)$ is lth equality constraint. If $\Phi(\breve{x}) \geq \varepsilon$ (ε is the accuracy), then particle $\breve{x}$ is infeasible solution. Let $\breve{x}$ be the initial point and use exterior point method to calculate the solution $\tilde{x}$ which satisfy the accuracy, then continue to optimize with PSO. The process of exterior point method can be summarized by following steps:

Step1: Assume $M_1 > 0, \varepsilon > 0, c \geq 0, k = 1$. Let initial point be $x^{(0)}$.

Step 2: Solve the unconstrained optimization problem

$$\min F(x, M_k) = f(x) + M_k \cdot \sum_{l=1}^{m} h_j^2(x) . \tag{9}$$

Where $x^{(k-1)}$ is the initial point. Assume the optimal solution to be $x^{(k)} = x(M_k)$.

Step 3: Let $T = \sum_{l=1}^{m} |h_l(x)|$.

Step 4: If $T < \varepsilon$, terminate iteration, output optimal value; otherwise let $M_{k+1} = c \cdot M_k, k = k + 1$, then skip to step 2.

2.4   PP-PCA Algorithm Description

According to the above analysis, the major steps of PP-PCA algorithm can be describe as follows:

Step 1: Set the current iterations $t = 1$. Set the swarm size to be N and search space dimension to be D. Generate the initial positions x_i^0 and velocities v_i^0. If a particle doesn't meet the constraint, let this particle to be the initial point and use exterior point method to renew this particle. Then calculate the fitness value Q.

Step 2: Set the best position of ith particle P_i to be its own value and set the P_g to be the best particle's position of the whole swarm.

Step 3: Update all particles according to the formulae. If there are some particles violate the constraints, use exterior point method to renew them.

Step 4: If the fitness value of current particle is better than P_i's, set P_i equal to it. If the fitness value of current particle is better than P_g's, set P_g equal to it.

Step 5: Let $t = t + 1$. If it meets the maximum iterations or it gets a expected fitness, skip to step 6, otherwise skip to step 3.

Step 6: If $Q > 0$, increase constraint conditions then skip to step 1, otherwise calculate each principal component and output them.

3   Analysis of Simulation Experiment

3.1   Data Preprocessing

In order to test and verify the effectiveness of this algorithm, we take KDD CUP 99 Data to be the dataset. Because of this dataset are very huge, we use 10 percents typical data to be experiment dataset.

In this extracted dataset each sample has 42 attributes. In first 41 attributes there are 9 discrete and 32 continuous attributes. The last one is the identity of attack categories. If often divides into 5 types, 4 attack types and 1 normal type. These 4 attack types are DoS, U2R, R2L and PRB.

In order to apply the algorithm we need to preprocess these data. Because of the algorithm can only process numeric, we need to serialize the discrete data and digitalize the character type data. For example, the attribute protocol_type contains these values: tcp, icmp, udp and others, and we transform its values into 1, 2, 3, and 4, respectively.

3.2   Data Preprocessing Analysis of Experiment Result

Verify the Effectiveness of PP-PCA Algorithm. We use the Waveform Database of Generator (version 2) Data Set, which comes from standard data set UCI, to verify the validity of the algorithm. This dataset contains 5000 instances and 40 continuous attributes. It is very similar to the KDD data.

Experiment 1: we use the J-48 method provided by Weka data mining tools to classify these data without any other data processing.

Experiment 2: we use the feature selection method based on Genetic Search, which is provided by Weka, select out a feature subset of 14 attributes, and then apply J-48 method.

Experiment 3: firstly we apply the PP-PCA method to select out 10 principal components of these data, and then use J-48 method to do classification.

In these 3 experiments above, we all use the 10-fold cross-validation method to calculate the accuracy rate of J-48 classification. The results show in table 1:

Table 1. Waveform Data Analysis

Dataset	Data Processing	Attribute Number	Accuracy
Waveform	none	40	75.08%
	Genetic Search	14	76.22%
	PP-PCA	10	85.22%

From the experiments results above, we can safely draw the conclusion that the PP-PCA not only can reduce the data dimensions but also can improve the classification accuracy rate.

PP-PCA on KDD Data. We extract 5000 instances from the 10 percents data which contains 2000 instances of normal, 2000 instances of DoS, 50 instances of U2R, 350 instances of R2L, 600 instances of Probe.

Firstly, we apply PP-PCA on these data, and then select 5 principal components. The proportions of each component are shown in the fig 1. According to the figure, we can see that the first 5 components make up about 89% and first 10 components about 96%.

Secondly we apply J-48 method on 5 selected components and 10 selected components, and then use 10-fold cross-validation to verify the classification accuracy. The results are shown in table 2.

We also can see the accuracy of each attack type from confusion matrix of Weka. It shows in table 3.

Thus we can pick out first 5 components to replace the original data which has 41 attributes.

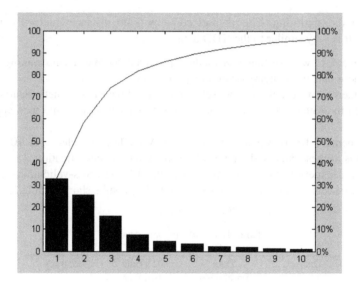

Fig. 1. Principal Components

Table 2. KDD Data Analysis

dataset	Data processing	Attribute number	accuracy
KDD CUP	PP-PCA	12	97%
99	PP-PCA	5	97.66%

Table 3. Accuracy of Each Attack

Attack type	Instance number	Accuracy
normal	2000	98.25%
Dos	2000	99%
U2R	50	66%
R2L	350	93.14%
Probe	600	96.5%

4   Conclusions

In this paper, PP-PCA algorithm is proposed to solve the high-dimensional and redundant problem of network security data. Combined PSO and exterior point penalty function method this algorithm can get several more concise and accurate principal components from the original dataset. The simulation comparison experiments show that the algorithm is efficient.

Acknowledgment. This research has been supported by the National Natural Science Foundation of China under Grant No. 61103175, the Key Project of Chinese Ministry of Education under Grant No.212086 and No.210110, the Key Project Development Foundation of Education Committee of Fujian province under Grand No. JA11011, the Technology Innovation Platform Project of Fujian Province under Grant No.2009J1007, the project development foundation of Fuzhou University under Grand No. 2010-XQ-21 and XRC-1037.

References

1. Bass, T., Gruber, D.: A Glimpse into the Future of Id (1999), http://www.usenix.org/publications/login/199929/features/future.html
2. Wang, H., Lai, J., Zhu, L., Liang, Y.: Survey of Network Situation Awareness System. Computer Science 33(10), 5–10 (2006)
3. Chulhee, L., David, L.: Feature extraction and classification algorithms for high dimensional data, TREE 93-1, Purdue University (1993)
4. Wang, J., Chang, C.: Independent Component Analysis-Based Dimensionality Reduction With Applications in Hyperspectral Image Analysis. IEEE - Transactions on Geoscience and Remote Sensing 44, 1586–1600 (2006)
5. Chebrolu, S., Abraham, A., Homas, J.P.: Feature deduction and ensemble design of intrusion detection systems. Computer & Security 24(4), 295–307 (2004)
6. Opitz, D.W.: Feature selection for ensembles. In: Proc. of the 16th National Conf. on Artificial Intelligence (AAAI), pp. 379–384. AAAI Press, Orlando (1999)
7. Tsymbal, A., Puuronen, S., Patterson, D.W.: Ensemble feature selection with the simple Bayesian classification. Information Fusion 4(2), 87–100 (2003)
8. Friedman, J.H., Tukey, J.W.: A Projection Pursuit Algorithm for Exploratory Data Analysis. IEEE Trans. on Computer 23(9), 881–890 (1974)
9. Huber, P.J.: Projection pursuit. Dept. of Statistics, Harvard University, Research report, number PJH-6 (1981)
10. Kennedy, J., Eberhart, R.C.: Particle swarm optimization. In: Proc. IEEE Int'l Conf. On Neural Networks, Piscataway, NJ, pp. 1942–1948 (1995)
11. Shi, Y.H., Eberhart, R.C.: A Modified Particle Swarm Optimizer. In: IEEE International Conference of Evolutionary Computation, pp. 69–73. IEEE, Piscataway (1998)
12. Guo, W.Z., Xiong, N.X., et al.: Design and Analysis of Self-Adapted Task Scheduling Strategies in Wireless Sensor Networks. Sensors 11(7), 6533–6554 (2011)
13. Guo, W.Z., Xiong, N.X., et al.: Distributed k-connected Fault-Tolerant Topology Control Algorithms with PSO in Future Autonomic Sensor Systems. International Journal of Sensor Networks 12(1), 53–62 (2012)
14. Gao, Y.L., Li, H.R.: Hybrid particle swarm algorithm of nonlinear constraint optimization problems. Mathematica Numerica Sinica 32(2), 135–146 (2010)

Multi-recipient Signcryption Algorithm for Communication of Mobile Ad Hoc Networks

Zhimin Li, Xin Xu, and Cunhua Li

School of Computer Engineering, Huaihai Institute of Technology, Jiangsu, China
{lizhimin1981,xinxu,ch.li}@gmail.com

Abstract. Since more and more applications of mobile ad hoc networks have been proposed, its communication security has become one of the biggest research challenges nowadays. In this paper, a new signcryption scheme was proposed which has multiple recipients. The proposed scheme is based on bilinear pairing and identity cryptography. The analysis results show that the scheme is provable secure in the random oracle model. Furthermore, it is significantly efficient as this scheme has less computation and storage requirements.

Keywords: Ad hoc networks, signcryption, provably secure, bilinear pairings, random oracle model.

1 Introduction

Mobile ad hoc network is a collection of autonomous nodes that communicate with each other by forming a multi-hop wireless network. As a new type of wireless communication networks, it has the following characters, no central control, changing in the topology dynamic, distributed management, resource-constrained. So there are more obstacles compared with the traditional fixed network in information authentication, confidentiality, integrity and anti-repudiation security maintenance. In this paper, we propose an Identity-based signcryption scheme that can be used in ad hoc networks. The proposed scheme has multiple recipients as group-oriented communication becomes more and more important in ad hoc networks, not only for network conference but also for dealing with malicious nodes. The scheme is proved to be secure that it is existentially unforgeable against adaptive chosen message attacks under the computational Diffie-Hellman assumption in the random oracle. We believe that our scheme is more suitable for ad hoc networks than previously proposed schemes.

In Section 2, we review some preliminaries required in this paper and describe the security and adversarial model. In Section 3, we propose a new Identity-based signcryption scheme. We analyze the proposed the scheme in Section 4. Finally, the conclusions are given in Section 5.

J. Lei et al. (Eds.): NCIS 2012, CCIS 345, pp. 388–394, 2012.
© Springer-Verlag Berlin Heidelberg 2012

2   Preliminaries

2.1   Bilinear Pairings and Diffie-Hellman Problem

Let G_1 be a cyclic additive group of prime order p and G_2 be a multiplicative group of the same prime order. Let $\hat{e}$: $G_1 \times G_1 \rightarrow G_2$ be a bilinear mapping with the following properties.

1. Bilinear: For all $P, Q \in G_1$, and $a, b \in Z_q^*$, $\hat{e}(aP, bQ) = \hat{e}(P, Q)^{ab}$,

2. Non-degenerate: $\hat{e}(Q, R) \neq 1$, for some $Q, R \in G_1$.
3. Computable: For any $P, Q \in G_1$, there is an efficient algorithm to compute $\hat{e}(P, Q)$.

The security of our scheme relies on the hardness of the computational Diffie-Hellman problem and computational bilinear Diffie-Hellman problem. So far, no algorithm is known to be able to solve any of them.

Definition 1. Let $(G_1, +)$ be generated by P, the computational Diffie-Hellman (CDH) problem in G_1 is to compute abP given aP, bP.

Definition 2. Given two groups G_1 and G_2 of the same prime order p, a bilinear mapping $\hat{e}$: $G_1 \times G_1 \rightarrow G_2$, a generator P of G_1, the computational bilinear Diffie-Hellman (CBDH) problem in $(G_1, G_2, \hat{e})$ is to compute $\hat{e}(P, P)^{abc}$, given (P, aP, bP, cP).

2.2   Security Notions

Malone-Lee [6] defined the security notions for Identity-based signcryption schemes. These notions are indistinguishability of Identity-based signcryption against adaptive chosen ciphertext attacks and unforgeability of Identity-based signcryption against adaptive chosen messages attacks. We modify his definitions slightly to adapt for our Identity-based signcryption scheme with multiple recipients.

Definition 3. An Identity-based signcryption scheme with multiple recipients is said to be indistinguishable against adaptive chosen ciphertext attacks (IND-IDSC-CCA2) if no polynomial bounded adversary has non-negligible advantage in the following game.

Setup: The challenger C runs the *Setup* algorithm with a security parameter 1^K and obtains public parameters *Params* and the master private key S. C sends *Params* to the adversary A and keeps S secret.

Phase I: The adversary A performs a polynomially bounded number of queries to C. The queries made by A may be adaptive, i.e. current query may depend on the answers to the previous queries. The various oracles and the queries made to these oracles are defined below:

1. Key extraction queries: A chooses an identity ID_i, C computes the corresponding private key $K_i = Extract(ID_i)$ and sends K_i to A.

2. Signcryption queries: A chooses identities ID_i and ID_{j1}, ID_{j2}, $\cdots$, ID_{jn} and a plaintext m. C computes $K_i = Extract(ID_i)$, generates the signcryption $\sigma = Signcrypt(m, K_i, (ID_{j1}, ID_{j2}, \cdots, ID_{jn}))$ and sends σ to A.

3. Unsigncryption queries: A chooses identity ID_i, one receiver identity ID_{jl}, $l \in_R \{1, \cdots, n\}$, and the signcryption σ. C generates the private key $K_{jl} = Extract(ID_{jl})$ and performs the unsigncryption of σ using K_{jl} and sends the result to A. The result of unsigncryption will be "invalid" if σ is not a valid signcryption. It returns the message m if σ is a valid signcryption.

Challenge: A chooses two plaintexts, m_0 and m_1 of equal length, the sender identity ID_i, the receiver identity ID_{j1}, ID_{j2}, $\cdots$, ID_{jn} and submits them to C. However, A should not have queried the private key corresponding to any ID_{jt}, $t \in_R \{1, \cdots, n\}$ in Phase I. C now chooses $b \in_R \{0, 1\}$ and computes $\sigma = Signcrypt(m_b, K_i, (ID_{j1}, ID_{j2}, \cdots, ID_{jn}))$ and sends σ to A.

Phase II: A is allowed to interact with C as in Phase-I with the following restrictions. A should not query the extract oracle for the private key corresponding to the receiver identity ID_{jt}, $t \in \{1, \cdots, n\}$. A should not query the unsigncrypt oracle with (σ, ID_i, ID_{jl}), $l \in_R \{1, \cdots, n\}$ as input, i.e. a query of the form $Unsigncrypt(\sigma, ID_i, ID_{jl})$, $l \in_R \{1, \cdots, n\}$ is not allowed.

Guess: Finally, A produces a bit b' and wins the game if $b' = b$.

The advantage of A in the above game is defined by $Adv(A) = |2Pr(b' = b) - 1|$, where $Pr(b' = b)$ denotes the probability that $b' = b$.

Definition 4. An Identity-based signcryption scheme with multiple recipients is said to be existentially unforgeable against adaptive chosen message attacks (EUF-CMA) if no polynomial bounded adversary has a non-negligible advantage in the following game.

Setup: The challenger C runs the Setup algorithm with security parameter 1^K and obtains public parameters *Params* and the master private key *S*. C sends *Params* to the adversary A and keeps *S* secret.

Training Phase: The adversary A performs a polynomially bounded number of queries adaptively as in Phase I of confidentiality game (IND-IDSC-CCA2).

Forgery: After a sufficient amount of training, A produces a signcryption (σ, ID_i, (ID_{j1}, ID_{j2}, $\cdots$, ID_{jn})) to C. Here, A should not have queried the private key of ID_i during the training phase and σ is not the output of $Signcrypt(m, ID_i, (ID_{j1}, ID_{j2}, \cdots, ID_{jn}))$ as input $m = Unsigncrypt(\sigma, ID_i, ID_{jl})$, $l \in_R \{1, \cdots, n\}$. A wins the game, if $Unsigncrypt(\sigma, ID_i, ID_{jl})$, $l \in_R \{1, \cdots, n\}$ is valid.

3   Concrete Scheme

In this section, we propose a new Identity-based signature scheme with multiple recipients which can be efficient used in ad hoc Networks.

Setup: Define G_1, G_2 and $\hat{e}$ as in previous section. Let H_1, H_2, H_3 and H_4 be four cryptographic hash functions where H_1: $\{0, 1\}^* \times G_1 \rightarrow G_1$, H_2: $\{0, 1\}^* \times G_1 \rightarrow G_1$, H_3: $\{0, 1\}^* \times G_1 \rightarrow G_1$, H_4: $G_2 \rightarrow \{0, 1\}^n$. Let P be a generator of G_1. E and D are a secure block cipher's encryption scheme and decryption scheme respectively with the length of cipher and key are both equal to n. PKG chooses a master secret key $S \in_R Z_q^*$, keeps S secret and computes $P_{pub} = SP$. The system's public parameters *Params* are $(G_1, G_2, q, P, P_{pub}, \hat{e}, H_1, H_2, H_3, H_4, E, D)$.

Extract: Given *Params*, to generate a secret key for a user with identity ID , PKG computes $K_{ID} = SQ_{ID}$, where $Q_{ID} = H_1(ID)$.

Signcrypt: To send a message m to users with identity $ID_{j1}, ID_{j2}, \cdots, ID_{jn}$, user A with identity ID_A follows the steps below. Firstly, choose $x \in_R Z_q^*$, $y \in_R \{0,1\}^n$, then compute $U = xP$, $\alpha_l = \hat{e}(P_{pub}, Q_{jl})^x$, for $l=1, 2, \cdots, n$, $\beta = H_2(m, U)$, $Z = E_y(m \| \beta)$, $r = H_3(Z, U, \beta)$, $V = xP_{pub} + rK_A$, $W_l = y \oplus H_4(\alpha_l)$, for $l=1, 2, \cdots, n$. The ciphertext is $\sigma = (Z\ U, V, W_1, W_2, \cdots, W_n, L)$, where L is a label including the informations how to associate the recipients.

Unsigncrypt: When receiving $\sigma' = (Z', U', V', W'_1, W'_2, \cdots, W'_n, L')$, user with Identity ID_{jl}, $l \in_R \{1, \cdots, n\}$ can verify the signature and derive the message by following the steps below. Firstly, find the correct W'_l according to L', then compute $\alpha'_l = \hat{e}(U', K_{jl})$, $y' = W'_l \oplus H_4(\alpha'_l)$, recover $m' \| \beta' = D_{y'}(Z')$ and c0ompute $r' = H_3(Z', U', \beta')$. At last, user accepts the message if and only if the equation holds, $\hat{e}(P, V') = \hat{e}(U', P_{pub})\hat{e}(P_{pub}, Q_A)^r$. Otherwise, output "Invalid".

4   Security Analysis

In this section, we analysis the security of the proposed scheme by using the definitions mentioned in Section 2.

Theorem 1 (Confidentiality). If their exists an adversary called A that is able to break the IND-IDSC-CCA2 security with an advantage ε, then there exists a distinguisher C that can solve the CBDH problem with advantage $O(\varepsilon)$.

Proof. The interaction between A and C can be viewed as a game given in definition 3. When C is provided with a random instance (P, aP, bP, cP) of the CBDH problem. C can use A as a subroutine and act as A's challenger in the IND-IDSC-CCA2 game to compute $\hat{e}(P, P)^{abc}$. In the proof, the hash functions are regarded as the random oracles. During the game, A will consult C for answers to the random oracles H_1, H_2, H_3 and H_4. C maintains lists L_1, L_2, L_3, L_4 respectively in storing the responses to the queries. These answers are randomly generated, but to maintain the consistency and to avoid collision.

Setup: For having the game with A, C chooses $P_{pub} = aP$ and gives A the system parameters $(G_1, G_2, q, P, P_{pub})$. Note that a is unknown to C, this value simulates the master secret key value for PKG in the game.

Phase I: During phase I, A is allowed to access the various oracles provided by C. A can get sufficient training before generating the forgery. The various oracles provided by C to A during training are as follows.

- **H_1 Oracle Queries (Ω_{H1}):** When this oracle is queried with ID_i by A, C responds as follows. C chooses a random number $i_R \in \{1, 2, \ldots, q_{H1}\}$, where q_{H1} is the maximum bounded number of allowed queries by A. At the i_R-th query, C answers by $H_1(ID_{iR}) = bP$, stores $(ID_{iR}, , bP)$ in list L_1. Otherwise, sets $Q_i = H_1(ID_i) = b_iP$, stores (ID_i, b_i, Q_i) in list L_1. C returns Q_i to A.

- **H_2 Oracle Queries (Ω_{H2}):** For a query with input (m_i, U_i), C performs the following. If (m_i, U_i, β_i) is available in list L_2, C returns β_i to A. Otherwise, C picks $\beta \in_R Z_q^*$ satisfying no vector $(\cdot, \cdot, \beta)$ exists in L_2, stores (m_i, U_i, β) in list L_2. Then, C returns β to A.

- **H_3 Oracle Queries (Ω_{H3}):** On a (Z_i, U_i, β_i) query, C checks whether there exists (Z_i, U_i, β_i, r_i) in L_3 or not. If such a tuple is found, C answers r_i, otherwise he chooses $r \in_R Z_q^*$, returns it as an answer to the query and puts the tuple (Z_i, U_i, β_i, r) into L_3.

  H_4 Oracle Queries (Ω_{H4}): On a α query, C checks whether there exists (α, w_i) in L_4 or not. If such a tuple is found, C answers w_i, otherwise he chooses $w \in_R \{0, 1\}^n$, returns it as an answer to the query and puts (α, w_i) into L_4.

- **Key extraction queries:** When A asks the secret key of user with identity ID_i, if $i = i_0$, then C fails and stops. Else, C computes $Q_i = \Omega_{H1}(ID_i)$, $K_i = aQ_i = b_iP_{pub}$. If $(ID_i, \cdot, Q_i)$ does not exists in the list L_1, C stores it in L_1. Then C returns K_i to A.

- **Signcryption queries:** A queries a signcryption for a plaintext m and identities ID_i and $(ID_{j1}, ID_{j2}, \cdots, ID_{jn})$. C has the following two cases to consider. Case1: $i \neq i_R$. C computes the private key S_i corresponding to ID_i by running the key extraction query algorithm. Then C answers the query by a call to Signcrypt(m, S_i, Q_j). Case 2: $i = i_R$. C chooses $r, x \in Z_q^*$, $y \in_R \{0,1\}^n$ and computes $U = xP - rQ_i$; $\alpha = \hat{e}(U, Q_{jl})$, $l=1, 2, \cdots, n$; $V = xP_1$. C runs the H_2 simulation algorithm to find $\beta = \Omega_{H2}(m, U)$; $Z = E_y(m\|\beta)$. C then checks if L_3 already contains a tuple (Z, U, β, r') with $r \neq r'$. In this case, C repeats the process with another random pair (x, r) until finding a tuple (m, U, k, r) whose first three elements do not appear in a tuple of the list L_3. When an appropriate pair (x, r) is found, the ciphertext $(Z, U, V, W_1, W_2, \cdots, W_n, L)$ appears to be valid from A's viewpoint.

- **Unsigncryption queries:** For an unsigncryption query, C has the following two cases to consider. Case 1: $j = i_R$. C always answers "invalid" to A. Case 2: $j \neq i_R$. C derives K_j from the key extraction algorithm, chooses $y \in_R \{0,1\}^n$, then C computes $\alpha_j = \hat{e}(U, K_j)$; $\beta = \Omega_{H2}(m, U)$; $m = D_y(C) \oplus \beta$; $r = \Omega_{H3}(C, U, \beta)$. C checks if $\hat{e}(P, V) = \hat{e}(U, P_1)\hat{e}(P, Q_A)^r$ holds. If the equation does not hold, C rejects the ciphertext. Otherwise C returns m to A.

Challenge Phase: At the end of Phase I interaction, A picks two messages (m_0, m_1) of equal length, the sender identity ID_S and the receivers identity $ID_{j1}, ID_{j2}, \cdots, ID_{jn}$, and submits to C. On getting this, C checks whether there exists $j_t = i_R$, $t=1, 2, \cdots, n$. If not, then we have the conclusion that C aborts. Otherwise, C chooses a random bit $t \in \{0, 1\}$ and generates the signcryption value of m_t as follows. C picks a random $x \in_R Z_q^*$, $y \in_R$

$\{0,1\}^n$, sets $U^*=aP$, computes $\beta^*=\Omega_{H2}(m_t, U^*)$; $Z^*= E_y(m \oplus \beta^*)$; $r^*=\Omega_{H3}(Z^*, U^*, \beta^*)$; $V = daP + r^*\Omega_{Extract}(ID_S)$, $W_l = y \oplus \Omega_{H4}(\alpha_l)$, $l=1, 2, \cdots, n$. C returns $\sigma^* = (Z^*, U^*, V^*, W_1, W_2, \cdots, W_n, L)$ as the challenge signcryption to A.

Phase-II: A interacts with C as in Phase-I, but with the following restrictions that A should not query the private key of ID_R and the unsigncryption of σ^* with ID_S as sender and receivers with $ID_{j1}, ID_{j2}, \cdots, ID_{jn}$. At the end of the interaction, A produces a bit t' for which he believes the relation $\sigma^* = \text{Signcrypt}(m_{t'}, K_S, ID_{jl})$, $t \in \{1,\cdots, n\}$ holds. At this moment, if $t = t'$, C outputs $\alpha_{iR} = \hat{e}(U^*, K_{iR}) = \hat{e}(aP, cbP) = \hat{e}(P, P)^{abc}$ as a solution of the CBDH problem, otherwise C stops and outputs "failure".

Probability Analysis: The probability of success of C can be measured by analyzing the various events that happen during the simulation. Assume $q_{H1}, q_{H2}, q_{H3}, q_{H4}, q_K, q_S, q_U$ are the maximum polynomial number of queries allowed to the oracles $\Omega_{H1}, \Omega_{H2}, \Omega_{H3}, \Omega_{H4}$, key extraction queries, signcryption queries and unsigncryption queries, respectively. The events in which C aborts the IND-IBSC-CCA2 game are list as follows. If A asked a key extraction query on ID_{i0} during the first stage, C fails. The probability for C not to fail in this event is $(q_{H_1} - q_K)/q_{H_1}$. Further, with a probability $1/(q_{H_1} - q_K)$, A chooses to be challenged using the receiver with identity ID_{i0}. Hence the probability that A's response is helpful to C is $1/q_{H_1}$.

Taking into account all the probabilities that C will not fail its simulation, the value of Adv(C) is calculated as follows.

$$\text{Adv(C)} = \varepsilon \frac{1}{C^n_{q_{H_1}}} \frac{1}{q_{H_2}} (1-q_S \frac{q_{H_2} + q_{H_3}}{2^{q_K}})(1 - \frac{q_{H_3} q_U}{2^{q_K}})$$

If the advantage ε of A to break the IND-IDSCMP-CCA2 game non-negligible, the probability of C solving CBDH problem is also non-negligible.   □

Theorem 2 (Unforgeability). If their exists an adversary called A that is able to break the EUF-CMA security with an advantage ε, then there exists a distinguisher C that can solve the CDH problem with advantage $O(\varepsilon)$.

The interaction between A and C can be viewed as a game given in definition 4. When C is provided with a random instance (P, aP, bP) of the CDH problem. C can use A as a subroutine and act as A's challenger in the EUF-CMA game to compute abP. During the game, A will consult C for answers to the random oracles H_1, H_2, H_3 and H_4. C maintains lists L_1, L_2, L_3, L_4 respectively in giving the responses to the queries. These answers are randomly generated, but to maintain the consistency and to avoid collision.

Setup: For having the game with A, C chooses $P_{pub} = aP$ and gives A the system parameters $(G_1, G_2, q, P, P_{pub})$. Note that a is unknown to C, this value simulates the master secret key value for the PKG in the game.

Training Phase: During this phase, A is allowed to access the various oracles provided by C. The various oracles provided by C to A during training are similar to the oracles described in phase I of Theorem 1.

Forgery Phase: After getting sufficient training, A submits the signcryption (ID_i, ID_{j1}, ID_{j2}, $\cdots$, ID_{jn}, σ) with the following restrictions that A has not ever queried the private key of ID_i and the unsigncryption of σ^*. If $i = i_0$ and σ is valid, C does the following. C retrieves r correspondingly from list $L3$, computes the value $abP = K_i = r^{-1}(V - xP_1)$, i.e., C obtains the solution to the CDH problem instance.

Probability Analysis: The probability of success of C can be measured by analyzing the various events that happen during the simulation. Assume q_{H1}, q_{H2}, q_{H3}, q_{H4}, q_K, q_S, q_U are the maximum polynomial number of queries allowed to the oracles Ω_{H1}, Ω_{H2}, Ω_{H3}, Ω_{H4}, key extraction queries, signcryption queries and unsigncryption queries, respectively. The events in which C aborts the EUF-CMA game are list as follows. If A asked a key extraction query on ID_{i0} during the first stage, C fails. The probability for C not to fail in this event is $(q_{H_1} - q_K)/q_{H_1}$. With a probability exactly $1/(q_{H_1} - q_K)$, A chooses to be challenged using the receiver with identity ID_{i0}. Hence the probability that A's response is helpful to C is $1/q_{H_1}$. We have the conclusion that if A can win the EUF-CMA game with an advantage ε, the value of Adv(C) is calculated as $\text{Adv(C)} = \varepsilon/q_{H_1}$. □

5   Conclusion

In this paper, we have proposed a provably secure Identity-based signature scheme that can be used in multiple recipients environment like group-oriented communication case. Under the assumption that the well known computational Diffie-Hellman problem is difficult, we have formally proved the security of the newly proposed scheme in the random oracle model.

References

1. Al-Riyami, S.S., Paterson, K.G.: CBE from CL-PKE: A Generic Construction and Efficient Schemes. In: Vaudenay, S. (ed.) PKC 2005. LNCS, vol. 3386, pp. 398–415. Springer, Heidelberg (2005)
2. Deng, H., Agrawal, D.P.: TIDS: threshold and identity-based security scheme for wireless ad hoc networks. Ad Hoc Networks 2(3), 291–307 (2004)
3. Galindo, D., Morillo, P., Ràfols, C.: Breaking Yum and Lee Generic Constructions of Certificate-Less and Certificate-Based Encryption Schemes. In: Atzeni, A.S., Lioy, A. (eds.) EuroPKI 2006. LNCS, vol. 4043, pp. 81–91. Springer, Heidelberg (2006)
4. Li, G., Han, W.: A New Scheme for Key Management in Ad Hoc Networks. In: Lorenz, P., Dini, P. (eds.) ICN 2005. LNCS, vol. 3421, pp. 242–249. Springer, Heidelberg (2005)
5. Malone-Lee, J.: Identity based signcryption. Cryptology ePrint Archive, Report 2002/098 (2002), http://eprint.iacr.org/2002/098
6. Yum, D.H., Lee, P.J.: Identity-Based Cryptography in Public Key Management. In: Katsikas, S.K., Gritzalis, S., López, J. (eds.) EuroPKI 2004. LNCS, vol. 3093, pp. 71–84. Springer, Heidelberg (2004)

A Survey of Research on Smart Grid Security

Lin Zhou[1,2] and Shiping Chen[1]

[1] University of Shanghai for Science and Technology,
[2] Shanghai University of Electric Power
200090 Shanghai, China
Zh046@189.cn

Abstract. Smart grid is the goal of China's power grid development, and the security problems can not be ignored during this period. In this paper, we focus on security risks both in computer network and industrial control network while moving to smart grid. We compared various research works related to these area, and emphasized the importance of SCADA system security. We summarized main attacks on SCADA system and analyzed different approaches to mitigate these threats. We highlighted some achievements of research in SCADA system security, also discussed some shortages of these research. Finally, we discussed the role of testbed in smart grid security research, and compared different testbeds in types and scales, approved their prominent effect in industrial control system security research.

Keywords: Smart Grid, SCADA Security, Information Security, Testbed.

1 Introduction to Smart Grid

The concept of smart grid has been taken out for a long time, and there are many definitions for it. The core of smart grid is to integrate every part in power grid system with information and communication technology[34], and smart grid is the goal and the future of power grid construction . Although the meaning of the smart grid is vary, but they all have the same theme: to build a smart system using mature computer network technology and information technology with advanced power grid control technology.

China has begun its power grid information project SG186 for a long time, many research and applications have been done during this period. The communication network for power grid has been built in many types, such as fiber communication, microwave communication, and satellite[9].

But after all of this job, we just finished the basic part of the smart grid, and we didn't reach the destination of building a robust smart grid. Many researches are focused on mixing information framework in power grid, making unified information platform, and there are still many questions need to be solved in information communication area, but we think the safety and reliability will be more important in a power grid.

In this paper, we discussed the security problems in smart grid, and we focused these security problems in information communication and industrial control system. The following parts of this paper is arranged as this: A review of study in information

J. Lei et al. (Eds.): NCIS 2012, CCIS 345, pp. 395–405, 2012.
© Springer-Verlag Berlin Heidelberg 2012

system security in power grid is discussed in section 2. The main security problems in SCADA system of power grid are shown in section 3, some methods for mitigation these problems are also mentioned. In section 4, we discussed the effect and meaning of a testbed in security research for SCADA system and information system. Finally, a discussion about the future work in section 5.

2   Information Security in Smart Grid

With the developing and wide using of computer network, we get more convenience in power grid operation and management, computer network also is a premise of intelligent power grid. But the security problems in computer network has been existed for a long time, and with the using of computer network in smart grid, the private, hidden communication network for power grid became more public, the power grid faces more and more threaten than before.

When we using information technology build a more intelligent system in power grid, all vulnerable along with information technology will be taken to power grid system, the problems such as protocol vulnerable, system bugs, attack on common network, all will be found in power grid environment. Many researches on security problems in smart grid are based on this concepts, they all start their work from the information security side, discuss the vulnerable in computer network and how these vulnerable affect smart grid. Understanding risks in public protocol clearly will be good for enforcing smart grid security, that's why we should do many works on information security.

After long time of study in information security, we can bring out the following risk type[3]:

- Spoofing —— gaining privilege by masquerades
- Tampering —— Intentional modification of the product so as to cause harm to the user
- Repudiation—— refute the validity of a contract or service level agreement
- Information Disclosure——disclosing the information to those who should not know
- Denial of Service—— make the resource unavailable to the intended users
- Elevation of Privilege—— increases for a higher role user access/privileges
- Phishing —— illegal access to protected data
- Cryptanalysis

All these problems have existed for many years in information system, and also been discussed for many years. In paper[1,4,5,7], the authors demonstrated their test result by using famous penetration tools, after making attacks, such as port scan, password cracking, SYN flood, on a computer network based power grid, they all can get the answer they want. We believe the result of test is the same with the list above, because these problems belong to protocols in computer network, they are not generated by the construction of smart grid.

To mitigate these risks we can install IDS system, use VPN channel, require encryption, authenticate users, and make protocol layer security (e.g. IPsec, TLS), we can find these typical methods were used in paper [1]. The author also told us that the problems like plain text transfer, unauthorized access, denial of service attack, will be solved after taking some of these methods. But the author only considered the information security problems in smart grid, because this is the way we use in computer network, it does fit the information network in smart grid, but it only gives us some common sense in information security and that's not the all for smart grid. The security policy we take from computer network maybe have some effect on information network in smart grid, and reduce some risk in it, but it cannot cover every part of smart grid. Smart grid is a hybrid system, and information network is only one section of it, so these security policy maybe not as good as they were in computer world.

In paper[2,3], we could find another typical idea. Besides the information security risk, they also cared the   particularity in smart grid. There are many differences between computer network and smart grid, not just in information security area. These are the main differences:

1) The performances of device are different
The devices in computer network have more powerful processor and big storage space; the devices in smart grid always get simple processor and no extra space. That means we can not install new functions on a smart grid device freely.

2) The architecture is different
Computer network has a layered architecture, and each layer has a simple function; smart grid is a Complex network, its component includes communication, control, transfer etc.

3) Different QoS request
We can restart computer or a network device when we need, but we cannot do this in a power grid.

According to these different, we must realize the particularity of the power grid side, and cannot only care the information security in smart grid. According to the paper[2], we can summarize main parts of a power grid in three level, as shown in figure 1.

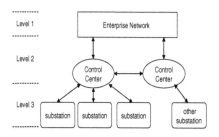
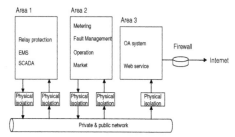

Fig. 1. Main section in a power grid   **Fig. 2.** Physical isolation in power grid

We have discussed many security problems about level 1 and given many mature methods for them, but we need some special efforts on level 2 and 3. A concept named 'security agent' was given in paper[2], that means a special equipment or module should be placed on critical area or critical device, to monitor the data flow in/out from them. The detail of this concept will be described in section 3.3.

A physical separation method is widely used by power grid in China. As shown in figure 2, every critical area is separated by a special hardware, the hardware can make diverse data communication in different direction.

In figure 2, different devices and system with different level are separated into different area, for the security of every area, physical isolation devices are used to implement one-way communication. And such communication is not directly based on public network protocol, some changes are made to ensure this separation also at logical level. This design of region isolation separating information networks and industrial control network, and mostly refused those security risks in traditional computer network out of the dedicated control network.

In this section, we can find that all the security policy for traditional network can be put into the smart grid environment directly, and these policy usually are discussed in a normal way, none of them is particularly designed for smart grid environment. But we must know that smart grid is not just another kind of information network. Moreover, some problems can be tolerated in the information system will become an accident in the industrial control system (e.g. restart).

3   Risk in SCADA System

Industrial control network is generally considered a private network, and it encounter less threaten from Internet than the computer network does. Smart grid combines common computer network and industrial control network together, the two network contact each other indirectly or directly, and this will inevitably brings risks in common network to the industrial control environment. On the other hand, we should notice the fact that with the developing of smart grid, the threaten on industrial control system begin to appear, and these threats show some different characteristics to common computer network.

In the major industrial control network, functions are widely based on supervisory control and data acquisition system (SCADA system). SCADA system integrates computer network, communication technology, microelectronics and automation technology. It is widely used in the electricity, petroleum, transportation and other industrial fields. It is an important part of critical infrastructure and also is serious to the national security.

SCADA system always has its own network, It is connected with dedicate data servers and operation workstations, operating PLC（Programmable Logic Controllers）、RTU (Remote Terminal Units）and IED（ Intelligent Electronic Devices）through HMI (Human Machine Interfaces)[8].

SCADA system is the central part of whole system in the smart grid, most control signal and feedback are relied on the SCADA system. According to the importance of the SCADA system, there are a lot of research attempts to explore the impact of today's network on the SCADA system, and the vulnerability of SCADA system.

On the other hand, the power grid in China is mostly physical separated from office network, this makes the external network can not directly access the internal network, so any kind of risk in office network can not reach the internal network. But this security strategy is not as safe as it looks like, the physical isolation does not mean completely safe. It is only isolated risks from the common computer network environment (e.g. office network, the Internet), but it can not prevent attacks targeted on the private network (industrialcontrol network).

In the past we would think that the SCADA system was a dedicated system and built on a dedicated communication network, had dedicated protocol. So risks from IT system will not threaten it, because this two system are not alike. However, after numerous researches, this idea is proved to be too optimistic.

3.1   Attacks on SCADA

In paper[4,7], the author try to warn us that we should not just pay more attention on office network and information security. The details of every private part in SCADA system cannot be ignored. Figure 3 shows a structure of SCADA system which is derived from figure 1, in this pure industrial control environment, there are still different risks that may exist in different area[7] .We can find them in these points:

- Network for SCADA components, operation workstations and servers
- Network in substation (wired or wireless)
- Communication network connecting SCADA and substation
- IEDs in substation

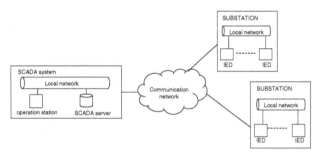

Fig. 3. Diagram of SCADA system

Perhaps the discussing on risk of SCADA system in paper[7] is just a theoretical analysis, or just an assumption, but researches in paper [1, 11, 13,24] demonstrated that, there are also various risks in a dedicated SCADA environment. The types of attacks on SCADA are summarized inTable 1.

Today many applications use TCP/IP based network to connect the SCADA system and remote substations or PLCs / RTUs due to the economy reason. The consequences of this is most attacks on TCP / IP network will be brought to the SCADA system, and may get illegal access to the SCADA system and launch attacks on it. Although SCADA system using private protocols, such as MODBUS, DNP3, or others, but these protocols are all open protocol, and can be exploited for vulnerable to make attacks.

To prove the risks in these special protocol, paper[11] tested some primary protocols in the SCADA system, and found many vulnerable in them. Table 2 shows the main conclusion of the research.

Table 1. Attacks on SCADA system

Attack field	Type	Methods	Influences or consequences
Outside attack	Communications hijacking or man-in-the-middle	Intercepting communications between slave and master	Performing illegal read/write to the MODBUS server; restart the server; complete shutdown of a section in the grid
	Wormhole	Malicious nodes work together to pass collected key data through its private channel	Changing the route in network (usually in Ad-hoc network) for data hacking or service Jamming
	Exploit	Connected to MTU or RTU via wireless link	Penetrating into the SCADA network, injecting false responses
Protocol vulnerable	Jamming	Jamming the Radio Frequency used by nodes	Affecting the availability of some parts of the network
	Replay	Changing authentication packets, Pretending the legal identification	spoofing security certification and making illegal access to the control system
	Spoofing	Changing the response to the master, reflecting normal operations	Control center remains unaware of the true state of the system fault
Physical attack	Destroying a node	Destroying a node by violence	The node will not be available
	Environment tampering	Making the node in an abnormal status	Master node receiving incorrect data from slaves
	Node displacement	change the location of the sensor nodes	Incorrect measurements, receive incorrect data
	Install new sensors	Making a malicious node accepted by the control system	Monitoring the physical system, and preparing for attack on the physical system
Inside attack	Sybil or Replication	Malicious node pretends to have multiple identities	Targeted more on wireless network or wireless sensors
	Denial of service	Collision in transmission; unfairness in using the channel	Exhausting a node's battery; jamming the communication channel
	Time-Synchronization	Destroying the synchronization Clock of a node	Jamming the normal communication between master and slave node
	Routing	Creating false route to degrade the availability; receiving more traffic for cryptanalysis	Key data leaking
	Response injection	Making wrong decisions with false responses	Influencing responses from RTU to MTU, stop links to SCADA system
	Command injection	Overwriting remote terminal register settings with false command	Influencing commands from MTU to RTU, also affecting the action of SCADA system
	Integrity	Changing actions of RTUs	Making system fault in end system, and causing economic loss or serious consequences

Table 2. Attacks on MODBUS and DNP3 protocol[11]

Protocol	Type	Method
MODBUS	DoS	Send server busy exceptions to the HMI
		Restart the MODBUS server
		Disable the server
		Set the server in listen only mode
		Using illegal packet size
	validity	Illegal commands sent from a compromised HMI
		Send command to shutdown the utility network
		Send command to clear register values
		Gain unauthorized access to data
	Communication hijacking or man-in-the-middle attack	Spoofing the communication between HMI and the MODBUS Server to send attacks to either device
DNP3	Jamming	Block field sensors from reporting data or events
	Spoofing	Cheating Master Control or HMI station
	DoS	Forcing PLC to execute an immediate restart
	man-in-the-middle attack	Modification of frames, and malicious function injection
	Regular attack	Device Scanning and Function Scanning

In paper[11], the author demonstrated the attacks listed in Table 2 with a testbed, that means launch an attack on SCADA system is not as difficult as we thought, and the protocol has no ability to protect itself. Furthermore, the entire SCADA system and its associated protocols are fragile, the consequences could be extremely serious when the system is attacked.

3.2   The End Point of Smart Grid

Smart meter is the end unit of smart grid, and it is directly connected with domestic user (or block user) . The AMR / AMI in smart grid makes the control center access data in these meters via wired or wireless network, and allow end-user interact with the center. But with the network function extending constantly, if we don't have certain protection on end unit, not only personal data and privacy of user will be disclosed, they may also be a path for invading the smart grid system through the AMR/AMI. We didn't expend this topic here, but there are many researches [25~29] discussed the possible risks existing in this area.

3.3   Analysis on Security Policy

In this section, we summarize different security approaches for smart grid security we just discussed and make some basic analysis.

Policy A : Cut out the Direct Connection between SCADA Network and Internet

Even if we can use firewall, IDS system or other security facilities in our network, but the attacks from the Internet still can have a chance to reach the SCADA system if there is a kind of connection leading to the Internet. The enterprise network do have the need of connecting to the SCADA system, so the best way to avoid outside attacks maybe the physical isolation. We should admit that, it can hardly make an attack on SCADA system directly through Internet, because of the physical isolation of network communication , as well as some private modification on TCP/IP packet . But we still can not say that there is no risk from the office network or the Internet. In the real world, SCADA center or master still using public communication system, so that can be one of the channels to invade, while there is no Internet connection[1,5]. We still need more researches on special methods for safe communication.

Policy B : Using IDS in SCADA System

We often use IDS system in our computer network for invasion warning. This approach maybe not suitable for SCADA environment. There is no IDS designed for SCADA system, and all facilities in SCADA system are relatively simpler than that in computer network, and they have no ability to run IDS. If some new IDS equipments and software are installed in the SCADA network, the using of new OS, software upgrading, and software patches will bring unknown risks to the SCADA system.

Policy C : Change the Critical Device and Enhance Safety of Key Area

For the convenient of system management and control, more and more SCADA system are connected using WAN. This also brings more risk to the SCADA system. We can find many possible entries to SCADA system through public communication network, and someone can invade the smart grid system through these entries[4, 47]. The best way to solve these problems is not using isolation only, we need to change those old equipments. When old SCADA / EMS system needs to be updated, that will be a good opportunity to enhance the whole system security, because the original equipments, system and designing are rarely consider security issues. The new equipment, new system design will fully meet security requirements and they can be integrated with security module or dedicated software. If the existed system and facilities must be reserved, security agent can be installed into the old system[4]. Security agent can be a module, a software, or a security switch, depend on the target facility it will protect and monitor. Security agent will hide the information of inner network, and monitor all the data packet pass the critical facilities.

In addition to these research on communication protocol and communication architecture, we should not neglect another important part: whether there is a backdoor in the hardware (e.g. chipset) for the SCADA system [33]. The famous "Stuxnet" virus in 2010 and this year's "flame" virus are all targeted on industrial control system, they remind us that there is no enough chip-level security research for the control system, we must pay more attention on this area in the future .

4   Testbed for Security Research

Experiments are often the best way to verify the theory. Lots of research use testbed as an experimental platform and research tool when they study problems of SCADA system security. We can roughly divide into two types of testbed based on papers[1, 5, 10], the simulation testbed and emulation testbed.

The simulation testbed is based on dedicated tools, using simulation modules and codes to solve some problems. In paper[1] the author wants to show a testbed which combined with simulation tools and SCADA hardware. This ideas can also be found in paper[5,10]. This kind of testbed are used for verifying different research idea by launching different attacks and the feedback from the testbed. Such a testbed is a laboratory tool, the same conclusion was made in paper[10], this kind testbed are suitable for research and pedagogy needs. But building this kind of testbed cannot meet the need of security requirements in smart grid or SCADA system, it lack the ability of information exchange between the different control system components[11].

Emulation testbed is more based on hardware and it is a comprehensive system. Due to the higher complexity and costs, this kind of testbed is often funded by government. National SCADA Test Bed Program (NSTB) was a very famous testbed project. It's almost a full scale electric power grid, it also include wireless testbed facility and cyber testbed. The scale of the testbed means it cannot be built by individual or some enterprises or several universities, but it is absolutely an ideal environment for testing any kind of problems in industrial control system. However, NSTB is not for public research, and it lacks the flexibility to explore different architectures, since it is primarily a physical system[10]. Another famous testbed is DETER. DETER is an Emulab-based security testbed. Many attacking and malware models and tools are available through DETER. It's a powerful emulation environment based on hardware facilities and ideal testbed for public research. But DETER is not especially designed for SCADA system, more often it is used for testing a new protocol against known attack modules[12].

5   Future Work

Research on security issues in smart grid is mostly focused on information security and the security problems in communication network of industrial control system, and such studies are mostly in a rough way. We cannot find some deeply research on SCADA system, especially on SCADA protocols. That maybe the future work on security problems in SCADA system and smart grid. On the other hand, we still cannot find some valuable research work on testbed in smart grid in China, so that will be part of our future research.

6   Conclusion

In this review we analyze the current research on security problems in smart grid. It shows that we should mainly focus on industrial control network security, rather than the security issues in traditional computer networks in smart grid. In addition, we stressed the research on security risks in industrial control system is still in an initial stage, and lack of deep study. We also emphasize that most researchers need suitable testbed for testing and verification in their work, which is also the lack part of recent research work in smart grid.

References

1. Giani, A., Karsai, G., Roosta, T., Shah, A., Sinopoli, B., Wiley, J.: A Testbed for Secure and Robust SCADA Systems. In: Proceedings of 14th IEEE Real-time and Embedded Technology and Applications Symposium (RTAS 2008), Saint Louis, MO (2008)
2. Wei, D., Lu, Y., Jafari, M., Skare, P., Rohde, K.: An Integrated Security System of Protecting Smart Grid against Cyber Attacks. In: Innovative Smart Grid Technologies (ISGT) Conference (2010)
3. Ray, P.D., Harnoor, R., Hentea, M.: Smart Power Grid Security: A Unified Risk Management Approach. In: 2010 Carnahan IEEE International Conference on Security Technology (ICCST), pp. 276–285 (2010)
4. Ericsson, G.N.: Cyber Security and Power System Communication—Essential Parts of a Smart Grid Infrastructure. IEEE Transactions on Power Delivery 25(3) (July 2010)
5. Gao, W., Morris, T., Reaves, B., Richey, D.: On SCADA Control System Command and Response Injection and Intrusion Detection. eCrime Researchers Summit (eCrime), 1–9, 18–20 (2010)
6. Dolezilek, D., Carson, K., Leech, K., Streett, K.: Secure SCADA and Engineering Access Communications: A Case Study of Private and Public Communication Link Security. In: 5th Annual Western Power Delivery Automation Conference (2003)
7. Björkman, G.: The VIKING Project– Towards more Secure SCADA Systems, http://www.cse.psu.edu/~smclaugh/cse598e-f11/papers/bjorkman.pdf
8. Nicholson, A., Webber, S., Dyer, S., Patel, T., Janicke, H.: SCADA security in the light of Cyber-Warfare. Computers & Security 31(4), 418–436 (2012)
9. Miao, X., Zhang, K., Tian, S.M., Li, J.Q., Yin, S.G., Zhao, Z.Y.: Information Communication System Supporting Smart Grid. Power System Technology 33(17) (2009)
10. Morris, T., Vaughn, R., Dandass, Y.S.: A Testbed for SCADA Control System Cybersecurity Research and Pedagogy. In: Proceedings of the Seventh Annual Workshop on Cyber Security and Information Intelligence Research, CSIIRW 2011, October 12-14. ACM (2011)
11. Mallouhi, M., Al-Nashif, Y., Cox, D., Chadaga, T., Hariri, S.: A Testbed for Analyzing Security of SCADA Control Systems (TASSCS). In: Innovative Smart Grid Technologies (ISGT), pp. 1–7. IEEE PES (2011)
12. Bergman, D.C., Jin, D., Nicol, D.M., Yardley, T.: The Virtual Power System Testbed and Inter-Testbed Integration. In: Proceedings of the 2nd Conference on Cyber Security Experimentation and Test, CSET 2009 (2009)
13. Cardenas, A.A., Roosta, T., Sastry, S.: Rethinking Security Properties, Threat Models, and the Design Space in Sensor Networks: A Case Study in SCADA Systems. Ad Hoc Networks 7(8), 1434–1447 (2009)
14. Boyer, W.F., McBride, S.A.: Study of Security Attributes of Smart Grid Systems – Current Cyber Security Issues. Idaho National Laboratory Critical Infrastructure Protection/Resilience Center (April 2009), http://www.inl.gov/technicalpublications/Documents/4235623.pdf
15. Jawurek, M., Johns, M.: Security Challenges of a Changing Energy Landscape. In: Securing Electronic Business Processes, ISSE 2010, pp. 249–259 (2011)
16. Lu, Z., Lu, X., Wang, W.Y., Wang, C.: Review and Evaluation of Security Threats on the Communication Networks in the Smart Grid. In: The 2010 Military Communications Conference (2010)

17. The Smart Grid Interoperability Panel–Cyber Security Working Group, NISTIR 7628, Guidelines for Smart Grid Cyber Security, vol.1(3) (2010)
18. Wright, A.K., Kalv, P., Sibery, R.: Interoperability and Security for Converged Smart Grid Networks. Grid-Interop Forum (2010)
19. Flick, T.: Hacking the Smart Grid. In: Black Hat USA Conf. Las Vegas, NV (2009)
20. Metke, A.R., Ekl, R.L.: Security Technology for Smart Grid Networks. IEEE Transactions on Smart Grid 1(1), 99–107 (2010)
21. Oman, P., Schweitzer, E.O., Roberts, J.: Safeguarding IEDS, Substations, and SCADA Systems Against Electronic Intrusions. In: 2001 Western Power Delivery Automation Conference (2001)
22. Liu, Y., Ning, P., Reiter, M.K.: False Data Injection Attacks Against State Estimation in Electric Power Grids. ACM Transactions on Information and System Security (TISSEC) 14(1) (2011)
23. Torchia, M.: Top 10 Considerations in Selecting a Distribution Area Network for Smart Grids. IDC Energy Insights (March 2011)
24. Hadley, M.D., Huston, K.A.: Secure SCADA Communication Protocol Performance Test Results. Pacific Northwest National Laboratory (August 2007)
25. Berthier, R., Sanders, W.H., Khurana, H.: Intrusion Detection for AMI: Requirements and Architectural Directions. In: 2010 First IEEE International Conference on Smart Grid Communications, SmartGridComm (2010)
26. Cleveland, F.M.: Cyber Security Issues for Advanced Metering Infrasttructure. In: Power and Energy Society General Meeting - Conversion and Delivery of Electrical Energy in the 21st Century (2008)
27. Bennett, C., Wicker, S.B.: Decreased Time Delay and Security Enhancement Recommendations for AMI Smart Meter Networks. In: Innovative Smart Grid Technologies, ISGT (2010)
28. Shein, R.: Security Measures For Advanced Metering Infrastructure Components. In: 2010 Asia-Pacific Power and Energy Engineering Conference (APPEEC), pp. 1–3 (2010)
29. McLaughlin, S., Podkuiko, D., McDaniel, P.: Energy Theft in the Advanced Metering Infrastructure. In: Rome, E., Bloomfield, R. (eds.) CRITIS 2009. LNCS, vol. 6027, pp. 176–187. Springer, Heidelberg (2010)
30. Flick, T., Morehouse, J.: Securing the Smart Grid– Next Generation Power Grid Security. Elsevier Inc. (2011)
31. Krutz, R.L.: Securing SCADA Systems. Wiley Publishing, Inc. (2006)
32. Fink, R.K., Spencer, D.F., Wells, R.A.: Lessons Learned from Cyber Security Assessments of SCADA and Energy Management Systems. Office of Electricity Delivery & Energy Reliability (September 2006)
33. Waksman, A., Sethumadhavan, S.: Silencing Hardware Backdoors. In: IEEE Symposium on Security and Privacy (May 2011)
34. Yang, D.C., Li, Y.: Study on the Structure and the Development Planning of Smart Grid in China. Power System Technology (December 2009)

Performance Analysis of the IEEE 802.16e Adaptive Cooperative ARQ Mechanism

Yong Jin[1,*] and Guang Wei Bai[2]

[1] Scholl of Computer Science & Engineering, Changshu Institute of Technology,
Changshu 215500, China
njutjinyong@yahoo.com.cn
[2] Department of Computer Science and Technology, Nanjing University of Technology,
Nanjing 210009, China
guangweibai@yahoo.com.cn

Abstract. This paper propose an adaptive cooperative ARQ mechanism based on the channel station of WiMAX networks, which could obtain high saturation throughput, real-time and reliable transmission at the same time. According to the principle and characteristics of conventional ARQ defined in IEEE 802.16e, a Markov chain model for analyzing the saturation throughput, packet error rate and average delay was built. An adaptive cooperative ARQ mechanism was established based on the Markov chain model. Additionally the above performance of the proposed scheme and the conventional ARQ would also be analyzed and discussed based on such model. The mathematical analysis show that the proposed mechanism could perform better in terms of saturation throughput, reliability and real time performance when compared with the conventional ARQ.

Keywords: WiMAX, IEEE 802.16e, Automatic Repeat reQuest (ARQ), Markov chain model, cooperative communication.

1 Introduction

With the development of accessing broadband Internet rapidly, IEEE 802.16e has been one of the most important standards of next generation wireless access technology of broadband metropolitan area networks[1], which has various advantages such as perfect standardization, high speed data transmission, wide service coverage, and so on. However, there is a severer conflict between limited resource and huge demand for data transmission in wireless communication system. Especially, data transmission over the disadvantageous wireless link condition is a big challenge [2] [3] due to the unreliable and dynamic characteristics of wireless networks, as well as high QoS requirements. Consequently, a robust, effective and reliable error control mechanism is necessary for wireless communication in such environment.

---

* This work is supported by the National Natural Science Foundation of China under Grant No. 61073197 and Scientific & Technological Support Project of Jiangsu Province under Grant No. BE2011186.

J. Lei et al. (Eds.): NCIS 2012, CCIS 345, pp. 406–413, 2012.
© Springer-Verlag Berlin Heidelberg 2012

The ARQ mechanism[4] uses a feedback channel for the confirmation of successful data delivery to request a retransmission of corrupted data, which is able to increase the throughput even if wireless channel state are getting worse. But the ARQ would increase the delay of packets due to the retransmission of former unsuccessfully received packets. The performance of IEEE 802.16e ARQ [5] depends on the setting of some parameters, which includes size of payload data carried in a frame, ARQ block size, PDU (Protocol Data Unit) size, limit of retransmission timeout timer, as well as packet acknowledgement type [6]. Simultaneously, Tykhomyrov *et al* [7] evaluate the ARQ performance for different parameters. Then Martikainen *et al* [8] analyzed the impact of PDU size on performance of the IEEE 802.16e networks with ARQ mechanism. The authors in [9] adjusted the PDU size according to the wireless channel state in order to obtain the best ARQ performance. On the other hand, cooperative communication provides a new way of introducing spatial diversity in wireless systems, where the mobile stations may not be able to support multiple antennas due to size or other constraints [10].

The rest of this paper is organized as follows. In the next section, the Markov chain model of conventional ARQ scheme is presented. The section 3 provides an overview on simulation model and contemplates the parameters applied in simulator. Besides the performance of conventional ARQ algorithm in WiMAX networks is also evaluated in the section 3. The section 4 presents the simulation results of the proposed scheme. Last section gives the conclusions.

2   Markov Chain Model of the Conventional ARQ

In the WiMAX network, we focuses on the evaluation of payload generated by ARQ procedure in the downlink direction by BS (see Fig. 1). In addition, we assume multihop communication between MS and BS using RSs (Relay Stations).

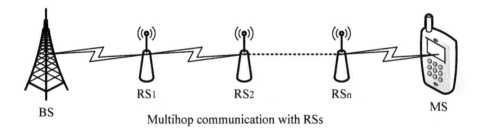

Fig. 1. Link level WiMAX networks topology

Each packet is transmitted over multihop communication. The probability of block error between two stations is the same over all hops. Therefore, the overall BLER of all hops between MS and BS is calculated according to the following formula:

$$BLER_{MS-BS} = 1 - (1 - BLER_{hop})^{N_{hops}} \tag{1}$$

Where $BLER_{hop}$ represents ARQ block error rate over each hop and N_{hops} is the number of overall hops between MS and BS. Note that $N_{hops} = n+1$, here n denotes the number of RSs in the wireless link.

Every data packet is divided into m frames. When frames are transmitted, some ARQ blocks in transmission may be error or lost, and then the sender will retransmit those ARQ blocks in different PDU. In IEEE 802.16e network, each frame generated either by MS or BS is segmented into PDUs, whose size is denoted by *PDUSize*. A PDU usually contains n blocks, which number is given by following equation:

$$n = \frac{S_{frame}}{PDUSize * S_{ARQ-block}} \tag{2}$$

Where S_{frame} is a total size of data frame, and similarly $S_{ARQ-block}$ represents a block size. Therefore, the state of each station is described by $\{j, b\}$, where j stands for the transmission stage, and b stands for the ARQ block sequence number and takes values $(1, 2, ... n)$.

$N(t)$ is defined as a random process representing the value of retransmission counter j at time t, where $1 \leq j \leq N_{max}$. $B(t)$ is defined as the random process representing the ARQ block, which is uniformly chosen in the range $(0,1,..., n)$. Above all, the bi-dimensional random process $\{N(t), B(t)\}$ is discrete-time Markov chain under the assumptions that the error probability of the wireless link and the BLER are both independent to the wireless communication procedure.

According to the Markov chain, we have the following transition rate between states:

$$\begin{cases} P\{j,k \mid j,k+1\} = 1 - BLER_{MS-BS} \\ P\{0,k \mid j,0\} = (1 - P_f) \\ P\{0,k \mid N_{max},0\} = (1 - P_f) \\ P\{j+1,k \mid j,k\} = BLER^j{}_{MS-BS} \end{cases} \tag{3}$$

Here, $P\{j_1,b_1 \mid j_0,b_0\} = P\{N(t)=j_1, B(t)=b_1 \mid N(t)=j_0, B(t)=b_0\}$. Let $b_{j,b} = \lim_{t \to \infty} P\{N(t)=j, B(t)=b\}$ be the stationary distribution of the Markov chain.

The ARQ block will be discarded if it has not been correctly received after having been retransmitted up to N_{max}. One frame would be transmitted successfully when the BSN (Block Sequence Number) of the current ARQ block is 1, the packet error rate P_W is given by the following equation.

$$P_W = 1 - (1 - (1 - (1 - BLER_{MS-BS}^{N_{max}})^{n*PDUSize})^{N_{max}+1})^m \tag{4}$$

Since the retransmission number of every ARQ block is different then the average retransmission number of every ARQ block is denoted by N_{avg}, which is expressed by equation (5).

$$N_{avg} = BLER_{MS-BS}(1-BLER_{MS-BS}) + 2*BLER_{MS-BS}^2(1-BLER_{MS-BS}) + \cdots + N_{max}BLER_{MS-BS}^{N_{max}}$$
$$= BLER_{MS-BS} + BLER_{MS-BS}^2 + \cdots + BLER_{MS-BS}^{N_{max}} \qquad (5)$$

So, average delay of transmitting one ARQ block T_{avg} is expressed by equation (6).

$$T_{avg} = T(1 + N_{avg}) = T\frac{1 - BLER_{MS-BS}^{N_{max}+1}}{1 - BLER_{MS-BS}} \qquad (6)$$

The delay of transmitting one ARQ block over the wireless link is denoted by T. In addition, we use the TCP-friendly rate control protocol [11] to ensure the fairness in channel bandwidth allocation to adjust to the variation of wireless channel. So, the saturation throughput with the TCP-friendly rate control is decided by equation (7).

$$S = \frac{S_{packet}}{T\sqrt{\frac{2P_w}{3}} + 4T\left(3\sqrt{\frac{3P_w}{8}}\right)P_w\left(1 + 32P_w^2\right)} \qquad (7)$$

3   Adaptive Cooperative ARQ in IEEE802.16e

3.1   System Model and Simulation Parameter

The simulation focuses on the evaluation of payload generated by the conventional ARQ procedure in the downlink direction by one user (see Table. 1).

Table 1. Simulation parameter settings for ARQ

Parameters	Value
Physical layer	OFDMa
BLER per hop [%]	1-5
N_{hops}	1-4
$S_{ARQ-block}$[bytes]	16, 32, 64, 128
$PDUSize$	1
Packet size[bytes]	1500
Transport protocol	TCP
ARQ ACK Types	Selective, Cumulative
Size of data in each DL frame [bytes]	1024
N_{max}	1~3
T [ms]	10

3.2   Performance Results of the Conventional ARQ

The performance analysis results of the conventional ARQ based on the Markov chain model are separated into some groups according to the $S_{ARQ-block}$ and N_{max}, in terms of the saturation throughput (see Fig. 2), average end to end delay (see Fig. 3) and packet error rate (see Fig. 4).

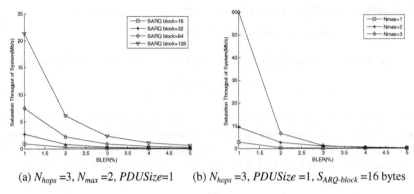

(a) N_{hops} =3, N_{max} =2, PDUSize=1   (b) N_{hops} =3, PDUSize =1, $S_{ARQ\text{-}block}$ =16 bytes

Fig. 2. Saturation throughput with the different $S_{ARQ\text{-}block}$ and N_{max}

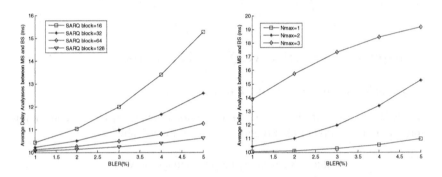

(a) N_{hops} =3, N_{max} =2, PDUSize=1   (b) N_{hops} =3, PDUSize =1, $S_{ARQ\text{-}block}$ =16 bytes

Fig. 3. Average delay with the different $S_{ARQ\text{-}block}$ and N_{max}

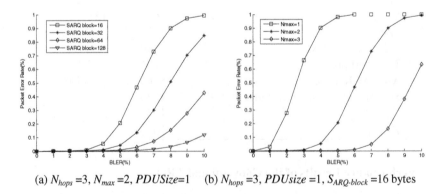

(a) N_{hops} =3, N_{max} =2, PDUSize=1   (b) N_{hops} =3, PDUsize =1, $S_{ARQ\text{-}block}$ =16 bytes

Fig. 4. Packet error rate with the different $S_{ARQ\text{-}block}$ and N_{max}

The impact of individual parameters observed from the previous figures on the efficiency of saturation throughput, average end to end delay and packet error rate can be summarized into the following conclusions:

(1) N_{hops}: the performance of conventional ARQ scheme is decreasing with higher number of hops since the reduction of the N_{hops} should be considered when the quality of the wireless link is poor.

(2) $S_{ARQ-block}$: the performance is improved significantly with larger $S_{ARQ-block}$; the level of this additional improvement is getting higher with BLER since the higher BLER increases the amount of packets not corrected by conventional ARQ.

(3) N_{max}: the improvement of a number of retransmissions on the saturation throughput and packet error rate is noticeable in most of scenarios; nevertheless the average end to end delay is largely increased with higher N_{max}.

(4) The value of N_{hops}, $S_{ARQ-block}$ and N_{max} could be adaptively adjusted based on the quality of the wireless link.

3.3   Adaptive Cooperative ARQ Algorithm

Here the proposed adaptive cooperation ARQ mechanism is used in every entity of the WiMAX networks, such as MS, BS and RSs.

Transmitter (MS or BS):

(1) TCP-friendly rate control protocol is used to ensure the fairness in channel bandwidth allocation and the smoothness of sending rate at all kinds of applications to adjust to the variation of wireless channel.

(2) At link layer, the value of N_{hops}, $S_{ARQ-block}$ and N_{max} are adjusted adaptively according to the BLER, which is obtained by the real measurement of the wireless channel.

(3) Selecting one relay station as the next hop receiver from RS1 to RSn based on the value of N_{hops} and BLER.

(4) OFDMa technology is used to transmission data at physical layer with AF relaying.

Cooperation communication (RSi ($1 \leq i \leq$ n):

(5) If RSi receives NACK in the next frame after transmission, the erroneous ARQ block would be retransmitted, which would be rearrange into the next PDU. If RSi does not receive any feedback within the time interval, then correspondent ARQ blocks will be retransmitted.

(6) The step (2), (3), (4) and (5) are executed at RSi until the frames are received successfully or dropped.

Receiver (BS or MS):

(7) If all the ARQ blocks are received without errors then the blocks have to be confirmed by Cumulative ACK. Otherwise NACK would be send to the transmitter.

4   Performance Evaluation

The performances of the proposed adaptive cooperative ARQ mechanism with AF relaying are evaluated by numerical analysis and discussed in this section as shown in Fig.5. The system model and simulation settings are illustrated in section 3.1.

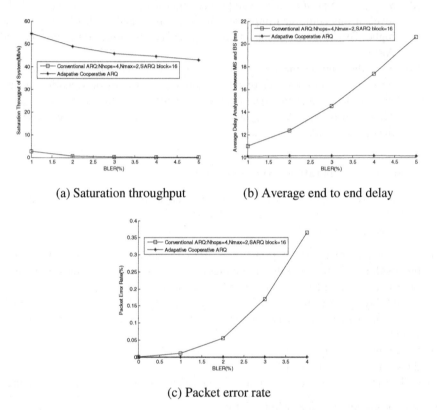

(a) Saturation throughput   (b) Average end to end delay

(c) Packet error rate

Fig. 5. Comparisons of performance between conventional ARQ and adaptive cooperative ARQ

Fig.5 compares the saturation throughput of system, packet error rate and average end to end delay between the conventional ARQ and the proposed mechanism. As can be observed from Fig.5, noticeable improvement is achieved by using the proposed ARQ mechanism instead of the conventional ARQ. Our investigations in both analytic and simulation approaches demonstrate that the adaptive cooperative mechanism provides a significant improvement in the reliability and the real-time performance of wireless transmission, with adapting to the fluctuation of the wireless network state dynamically.

5   Conclusion

This article analyzes the block error rate and communication performance of WiMAX systems with conventional ARQ of IEEE 802.16e using Markov chain model. Numerical results with the proposed analytical method have been presented and the characteristics of saturation throughput, average end to end delay and packet error rate with BLER has been summarized by the simulation results. On this basis, an adaptive cooperative ARQ mechanism with AF relaying was proposed. Our mathematical analyses and simulation results show that the proposed ARQ mechanism achieves better quality of wireless transmission comparing with conventional ARQ, in terms of saturation throughput, reliability and real-time performance on the receiving side of the WiMAX networks. Additionally, cooperative ARQ transmission can benefit from AF relaying system as a result of diversity gain, especially when the channel quality is not very good. Furthermore, the analytical Markov chain model can be extended to the systems with other ARQ schemes.

References

1. Air interface for fixed broadband wireless access systems - amendment for physical and medium access control layers for combined fixed and mobile operation in licensed bands. IEEE Standard 802.16e (December 2005)
2. Ian, F.A., Wang, X.D., Wang, W.L.: Wireless mesh networks: a survey. J. IEEE Communications Magazine 43(9), 445–487 (2005)
3. Ahmadi, S.: An overview of next-generation mobile WiMAX technology. J. IEEE Communications Magazine 47(6), 84–98 (2009)
4. Hang, L., Hairuo, M., Magda, E.Z., Sanjay, G.: Error control schemes for networks: an overview. J. Mobile Networks and Applications 2(2), 167–182 (1997)
5. Sayenko, A., Tykhomyrov, V., Martikainen, H., Alanen, O.: Performance Analysis of the IEEE 802.16 ARQ Mechanism. In: 10th ACM Symposium on Modeling, Analysis, and Simulation of Wireless and Mobile Systems, pp. 314–322. ACM Press, New York (2007)
6. Lee, B.G., Choi, S.: Broadband Wireless Access and Local Networks: Mobile WiMAX and WiFi. Artech House, USA (2008)
7. Tykhomyrov, V., Sayenko, A., Martikainen, H., Alanen, O., Hämäläinen, T.D.: Performance Evaluation of the IEEE 802.16 ARQ Mechanism. In: Koucheryavy, Y., Harju, J., Sayenko, A. (eds.) NEW2AN 2007. LNCS, vol. 4712, pp. 148–161. Springer, Heidelberg (2007)
8. Martikainen, H., Sayenko, A., Alanen, O., Tykhomyrov, V.: Optimal MAC PDU size in IEEE 802.16. In: 4th International Telecommunication Networking Workshop on QoS in Multiservice IP Networks, pp. 66–71 (2008)
9. Sengupta, S., Chatterjee, M., Ganguly, S., Izmailov, R.: Exploiting MAC Flexibility in WiMAX for Media Streaming. In: World of Wireless Mobile and Multimedia Networks, Taormina-Giardini Naxos, Italy, pp. 338–343 (2005)
10. Laneman, J.N., Tse, D.N.C., Wornell, G.W.: Cooperative diversity in wireless networks: efficient protocols and outage behavior. J. IEEE Transactions on Information Theory 50(12), 3062–3080 (2004)
11. Padhye, J.V., Firoiu, D., Towsley, J.K.: Modeling tcp throughput: A simple model and its empirical validation. In: The ACM SIGCOMM, pp. 303–314 (1998)

The Strategic Interaction Based on Public Goods Provision on Infinite Endogenous Plane Lattice

Ping Hu, Hong-Wei Gao[*], and Gui-Rong Wang

College of Mathematics, Qingdao University, Qingdao, China
qixiahuping@163.com,
gaosai@public.qd.sd.cn

Abstract. In this paper we consider the strategic interaction based on public goods provision and study equilibrium structures and the blinkers on infinite endogenous plane lattice. In contrast to other literatures, we emphasize the endogeneity of network, i.e., agents actively establish or delete links according to his benefits and interactive network is formed. The other key point is that the rule of network formation is the Bilateral-Bilateral rule. On the assumption, we use Netlogo simulations to verify the theoretical results.

Keywords: infinite plane lattice, public goods, strategic interaction, endogenous network, Netlogo simulation.

1   Introduction

The endogeneity of network is that the network environment is formed by means of agents actively establishing or deleting links according to his benefits. Because establishing or maintaining links requires labors or resources, the cost of links is essential. After network structure is formed, agents who have independent options interact according to some rules. In view of the locality of most economic interaction, any given economic agent only interacts with few agents and gathered information comes from interactive partners. So network structure is a plane lattice in this paper. On the assumption of endogenous network, we illustrate the interaction process and final equilibrium structures[1,2].

In the year 1993, Blume[3] studied related problems of strategic interaction on plane lattice. Each site on the 2-dimensional integer lattice is the address of one player. Each player interacts with only a few "neighboring players". However each player is indirectly connected to every other player in the population through a chain of neighborhood relations. Matthew O.Jackson & Alison Watts [4] and Sanjeev Goyal & Fernando Vega-Redondo[5] all examined endogenous networks and strategic interaction in games of coordination and powerful effects on results under the assumption of Bilateral rule and Unilateral rule respectively. Recent research includes the work of Fosco and Mengel[6]. They consider co-evolution of network and the choice of actions based on 2x2 Prisoner's Dilemma interaction game in Bilateral rule.

---

[*] Corresponding author.

J. Lei et al. (Eds.): NCIS 2012, CCIS 345, pp. 414–421, 2012.
© Springer-Verlag Berlin Heidelberg 2012

2   Games of Public Goods Provision

A typical example in Economics is the problem of public goods provision. As the publication of Paul Samuelson's pioneering literature[7,8] in 1954 and 1955, economists gradually accept the definition of Public Goods.

2.1   Notions and Concepts

In the plane lattice, each agent can establish links with his four neighbors. Player pays a cost f $(0 < f < 1)$ for establishing a link (a solid line) with one neighbor and then interacts with this player. If there is no link between two agents, they can't interact with each other. A player chooses an action C (providing public goods) or an action D (not providing public goods), while the cost of action C is e $(0 < e < 1)$. Generally speaking, agents prefer neighbors taking action C instead of himself taking action C when there are links. In general, choosing action C and paying the action cost are better than not taking action C in network at all.

In network g , let $N = \{1, 2, 3, \cdots\cdots, n, \cdots\}$ be the set of agents, assume the location of agent on infinite plane lattice is fixed. The set of actions is $A = \{C, D\}$ .For any $i, j \in N$, $g_{ij} \in \{0,1\}$, set the four neighbors of agent i is $i_k, k = 1, 2, 3, 4$ .We say player i establishes a link with agent i_k ,if $g_{ii_k} = 1$. Let $\bar{g}_{ij} = \max\{g_{ij}, g_{ji}\}$,note that $\bar{g}_{ij} = \bar{g}_{ji}$ for any $i, j \in N$ .The strategy of player i can be identified with $s_i = (g_i, a_i)$, where $g_i = (g_{i1}, \cdots, g_{i,i-1}, g_{i,i+1}, \cdots, g_{i,n}, \cdots)$ is the link decision by i and $a_i \in A$ is the action decision. The set of strategy of agent i is S_i , s_{-i} is the profile of agents strategies except agent i ,so $s_{-i} = (s_1, \cdots, s_{i-1}, s_{i+1}, \cdots, s_n, \cdots)$ .Let $N_i(g) = \{j \in N : \bar{g}_{ij} = 1\}$ be the set of interaction neighbors of agent i ,while $|N_i(g)|$ is its cardinality, the number of agents choosing action C (D)is $n_i(C)$ ($n_i(D)$),then $n_i(C) + n_i(D) = |N_i(g)| \leq 4$ .The payoff to agent i from choosing action C (D) is given by $\pi_i((g_i, C), s_{-i})$ ($\pi_i((g_i, D), s_{-i})$). $P(C)$ is the proportion of agents playing action C in network.

2.2   The Model

When agents interact with each other, if the agent or any his interaction neighbor chooses to provide public goods, both sides can obtain one unit of benefits, on the contrary, the benefits of two interaction agents are all zero as nobody provides public goods. The player chooses to provide should pay for the action cost $e \in (0,1)$.

Assume that link addition is bilateral, i.e., adding a link from player i to player i_k requires that both players i and i_k agree to add the link. And payoff is bilateral (if there is a link between two agents, they all have positive benefits), so the function of payoff is

$$\pi_i((g_i, C), s_{-i}) = n_i(C)(1 - e - \frac{f}{2}) + n_i(D)(1 - e - \frac{f}{2}) = |N_i(g)|(1 - e - \frac{f}{2})$$

$$\pi_i((g_i, D), s_{-i}) = n_i(C)(1 - \frac{f}{2}) + n_i(D)(-\frac{f}{2}) . \tag{1}$$

where $1 - e - \frac{f}{2} > 0$, $f < 2 - 2e$.

The payoff suggests that agents taking action C agree to establish links with four neighbors to interact and agents taking action D only agree to establish links with neighbors whose action is action C.

2.3   An Interaction Process

According to the combination of actions of agents and their neighbors, some possible local interaction structures on plane lattice are as follows:

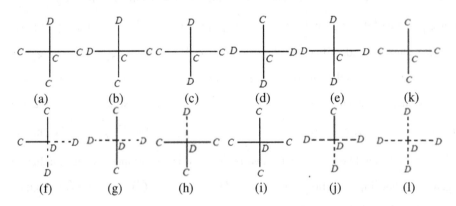

The center player i is the object we consider and the following is similar (a solid line means there is a link between two agents; conversely, there is no link between them).

Suppose four neighbors' strategies are fixed, we examine the change of strategy of agent i. If agent i chooses C, he will add links with four neighbors, so we only consider the action of agent i. In structure (a), for example, the payoff is $4(1 - e - \frac{f}{2})$ if the action is C; agent i changes his action to D and establishes links with agents whose action is C (now it is the structure(i)), the payoff is

$3(1-\dfrac{f}{2})$ .So if $4(1-e-\dfrac{f}{2})>3(1-\dfrac{f}{2})$,that is $f<2-8e$, structure (a) is stable for agent i ;if $f>2-8e$,he will change the strategy and choose the structure(i). And so on, for other 11 structures. Specially, (e) and (j) are always stable, but in structure (k) and (l), the strategy of agent i is unstable, (k) and (l) will become to (j) and (e) respectively. Note that the parameters e and f are the cost, so we assume $0<e<1$ 、 $0<f<1$.

According to the data in two tables, we can divide the parameter range of e and f and have four intervals: $0<f<2-8e$ $2-8e<f<2-4e$ $2-4e<f<2-\dfrac{8}{3}e$ and $2-\dfrac{8}{3}e<f<2-2e$ and four propositions.

3   Equilibrium Structure

Defination 1. On infinite endogenous plane lattice, agents play the interactive strategic game. We say a strategy profile $s^{*}=(s_{1}^{*},...,s_{i}^{*},...,s_{n}^{*},...)$ is a Nash equilibrium if, for all $s_{i}\in S_{i}$ and $i\in N$, $\pi_{i}(s_{i}^{*},s_{-i}^{*})\geq\pi_{i}(s_{i},s_{-i}^{*})$ .On the other hand, any agent can't unilaterally change his strategy (actions or links) to get a strictly higher payoff.

Defination 2. A network is said to be completely connected if for all $i\in N$ and $k=1,...,4$ such that $\overline{g_{ii_{k}}}=1$.

Defination 3. The set of strategy profiles $B=\{s^{1},s^{2},...,s^{m}\}$ is called a blinker, if the strategy profile in B emerges recurrently in some order in the interaction process.

For all Figures below, we shall assume that a solid line stands for a link between two players, the player of action C is indicated in blue color and person shape and the player of action D is indicated in red color and turtle shape.

We will pay more attention to the equilibrium network and blinkers. In fact, regardless of the range of parameter e and f , the strategies of links in equilibrium networks have the same features: if two agents of action D are neighbors, there is no link between; two neighboring agents will agree to establish a link in other cases. With respect to the action strategies, we have propositions below.

Proposition 3.1. In games of strategic interaction based on public goods provision on infinite endogenous plane lattice, if $0<f<2-8e$,then there are structure(a),(b),(c), (d),(e)and(j) in equilibrium networks and the features of action strategies are:

(i) if agent i chooses action C ,then $0\leq n_{i}(C)\leq 3$,

(ii) if agent i chooses action D ,then $n_{i}(C)=4$.

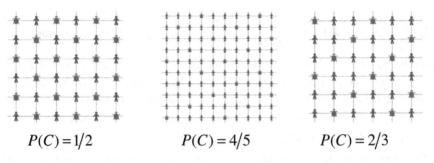

$$P(C) = 1/2 \qquad\qquad P(C) = 4/5 \qquad\qquad P(C) = 2/3$$

Fig. 1. Consists of (e),(j)   **Fig. 2.** Consists of (a),(j)   **Fig. 3.** Consists of (b),(j)

In this parameter range, we illustrate three possible equilibrium structures, as shown in Fig.1, Fig.2 and Fig.3.

As for the blinkers, in view of the capacity of this paper, only two regular blinkers, Fig.4 and Fig.5, are shown.

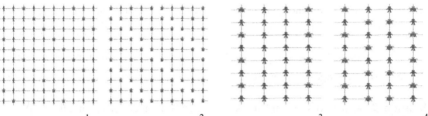

A strategy profile s^1 A strategy profile s^2 A strategy profile s^3 A strategy profile s^4

Fig. 4. Strategy profiles s^1 and s^2 compose the blinker $\{s^1, s^2\}$

Fig. 5. Strategy profiles s^3 and s^4 compose the blinker $\{s^3, s^4\}$

For agent i that chooses action C and $n_i(C)=4$ in strategy profile s^1, because $4(1-e-\frac{f}{2}) < 4(1-\frac{f}{2})$, he will change to action D in next stage, then the strategy profile s^2 is formed. But two neighbors of agent i also choose action D, it's better for agent i to choose action C again in later stage because $2(1-\frac{f}{2}) < 4(1-e-\frac{f}{2})$, then the strategy profile s^1 is formed. For links, agents of action C establish links with four neighbors no matter what action of the neighbor is; agents of action D only establish links with agents of action C, beginning the cycle. Note that we assume strategies of neighbors are fixed in the process of interaction before the agent changes the strategy; in other words, the best response of agent is myopic. It's a similar analysis for Fig.5.

For the blinker in Fig.5, the agent of action C will not change his action strategy if any one of neighbors chooses action D; the agent of action D will change the action strategy, choose action C and establish links unless actions of four neighbors are all C.

Proposition 3.2. In games of strategic interaction based on public goods provision on infinite endogenous plane lattice, if $2-8e < f < 2-4e$,then there are structure(b), (c),(d),(i),(e)and(j) in equilibrium networks and the features of action strategies are:

(i) if agent i chooses action C ,then $0 \leq n_i(C) \leq 2$,

(ii) if agent i chooses action D ,then $n_i(C)=3$ or $n_i(C)=4$.

Besides Fig.1 and Fig.3, Fig.6 is also an equilibrium structure and it's not completely connected. The regular blinker is Fig.7 except for Fig.4.

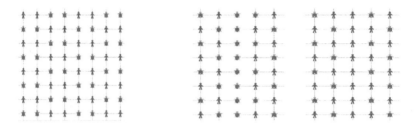

$$P(C) = 1/2$$

Fig. 6. Consists of (d),(i)

A strategy profile s^5 A strategy profile s^6

Fig. 7. Strategy profiles s^5 and s^6 compose the blinker $\{s^5, s^6\}$

For the blinker in Fig.7, if $2-8e < f < 2-4e$, the agent of action D in profile s^5 only has one neighbor whose action is C, then he will choose action C and add links with neighbors in next stage because $1 - \frac{f}{2} < 4(1 - e - \frac{f}{2})$. The agent of action C in profile s^6 will change to action D because $3(1 - \frac{f}{2}) > 4(1 - e - \frac{f}{2})$, and the cycle repeats.

Proposition 3.3. In games of strategic interaction based on public goods provision on infinite endogenous plane lattice, if $2-4e < f < 2 - \frac{8}{3}e$,then there are structure(d), (g),(h),(i),(e)and(j) in equilibrium networks and the features of action strategies are:

(i) if agent i chooses action C ,then $n_i(C)=0$ or $n_i(C)=1$,

(ii) if agent i chooses action D ,then $2 \leq n_i(C) \leq 4$.

In the parameter range, equilibrium structures include Fig.1, Fig.6 and Fig.8, Fig.6 and Fig.8 are not completely connected among them.

Need of the special note is that the blinker in Fig.9 differs from the regular blinkers in Fig.4,Fig.5 and Fig.7.It's only a Netlogo simulation experiment result among many blinkers and a combination of some regular blinkers. Same for Fig.11.

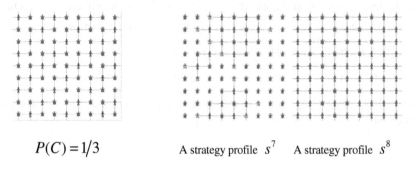

$P(C) = 1/3$ A strategy profile s^7 A strategy profile s^8

Fig. 8. Consists of (e),(g)   **Fig. 9.** Strategy profiles s^7 and s^8 compose the blinker $\{s^7, s^8\}$

Proposition 3.4. In games of strategic interaction based on public goods provision on infinite endogenous plane lattice, if $2-\dfrac{8}{3}e < f < 2-2e$,then there are structure(f),(g),(h),(i),(e)and(j) in equilibrium networks and the features of action strategies are:

(i) if agent i chooses action C ,then $n_i(D)=4$,

(ii) if agent i chooses action D ,then $1 \leq n_i(C) \leq 4$.

Equilibrium structures include Fig.1, Fig.8 and Fig.10, Fig.8 and Fig.10 are not completely connected among them. The blinker is as the Fig.11 shown.

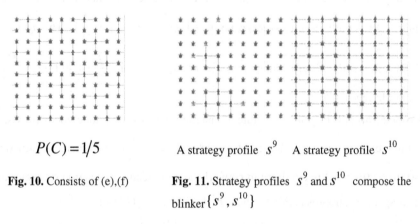

$P(C) = 1/5$ A strategy profile s^9 A strategy profile s^{10}

Fig. 10. Consists of (e),(f)   **Fig. 11.** Strategy profiles s^9 and s^{10} compose the blinker $\{s^9, s^{10}\}$

4   Conclusions

We study the agents in games of strategic interaction based on public goods provision on infinite endogenous plane lattice. Because the location of interactive agents is fixed, they can only interact with four neighbors at most. Another research direction is extending the interactive radius of agents. In the process of Netlogo simulation in this paper, the visual interface is formed by wrapping horizontally and vertically in order to satisfy the infinity of network as much as possible. We only examine the equilibrium structures in the Bilateral-Bilateral rule. In fact, we have discussed in the Unilateral-Unilateral rule in detail. But in view of the capacity of this paper, we will not repeat them here.

Acknowledgments. This work was supported by National Natural Science Foundation of China (70871064, 70971070, 71003057, 71171120), the International (Regional) Joint Research Program of China (71011120107), Natural Science Foundation of Shandong Province, China (ZR2010GQ001).

References

1. Gao, H.W., Yang, H.J., Wang, G.X., et al.: The existence theorem of absolute equilibrium about games on connected graph with state payoff vector. Science China-Mathematics 53(6), 1483–1490 (2010)
2. Goyal, S.: Learning in networks. In: Benhabib, J., Bisin, A., Jackson, M.O. (eds.) Handbook of Social Economics, vol. 1, pp. 679–727 (2011)
3. Blume, L.: The statistical mechanics of best-response strategy revision. Games and Economic Behavior 11, 111–145 (1995)
4. Jackson, M., Watts, A.: On the formation of interaction networks in social coordination games. Games and Economic Behavior 41, 265–291 (2002)
5. Goyal, S., Vega-Redondo, F.: Network formation and social Coordination. Games and Economic Behavior 50, 178–207 (2005)
6. Fosco, C., Mengel, F.: Cooperation through imitation and exclusion in networks. Journal of Economic Dynamics and Control 35(5), 641–658 (2011)
7. Samuelson, P.: The Pure Theory of Public Expenditure. The Review of Economics and Statistics 36, 387–389 (1954)
8. Samuelson, P.: Diagrammatic Exposition of a Theory of Public Expenditure. The Review of Economics and Statistics 37, 350–356 (1955)

Closed Circle DNA Model to QoS Routing for Ad Hoc Networks[*]

Zhi Yin[1,2,**], Mi Wen[1], and Chunming Ye[2]

[1] Department of Computer and Information Engineering,
Shanghai University of Electric Power, Shanghai 200090, China
[2] Business School, University of Shanghai for Science and Technology,
Shanghai 200093, China
yzzhizhi@163.com

Abstract. QoS routing problem is typical NP problem, we will adapt closed circle DNA model to resolve this problem. First, use three groups of DNA sequence to encode arc, cost and probe of each path; Second, use purposive ending technology to synthesize fixed jumping-off point and end point of all paths; third, filter out all minimal cost paths by inserting experiment and electrophoresis experiment; finally find the path with detect experiment. The process of algorithm's realization is straight forward; complexity of the algorithm is greatly reduced.

Keywords: QoS routing, model of closed circle DNA computing, DNA encoding, insert experiment, unidirectional links.

1 Introduction

Recently model of closed circle DNA computing is developed a kind of brand-new DNA computing model. Closed circle DNA molecule has flexible structure [1]. On the one hand, through the control access and delete the experiment adjust the chain long of closed circle DNA molecular, on the other hand, closed circle DNA and Double-stranded DNA, single-stranded DNA and DNA chip can mutual transformation each other.

Comparing with other DNA computing model, the flexibility structure of the close circle DNA computing model makes it have certain advantages. IN reference 3, DNA computing model can only find the feasible solution of QoS routing problem. The optimal solution still needs to use electronic computers to solve. This paper provides the model of mobile Ad Hoc network QoS routing problem. In this paper, first introduced the model of closed circle DNA computing, then for QoS routing problem, making the closed circle DNA computing encoding, designing the model of closed circle DNA computing to get the optimal solution directly, and without any increase in complexity algorithm to solve the QoS routing problem.

---

[*] Project supported by the National Nature Science Foundation of China (No. 60903188). and supported by the National Natural Science Foundation, China(No. 71271138), and the Humanities and Social Sciences Planning Fund of Ministry of Education (No.10YJA630187).
[**] Corresponding author.

J. Lei et al. (Eds.): NCIS 2012, CCIS 345, pp. 422–429, 2012.
© Springer-Verlag Berlin Heidelberg 2012

2   The Concept of Mobile Ad Hoc Network

In mobile Ad hoc network, literally it means "for a particular purpose or occasion". It uses wireless communication technology, and through the nodes forward network nodes with each other as its neighbor nodes router, to realize mobile Ad hoc network internal between host computer and internal and external host of communication between the hosts. Mobile Ad hoc network can work independently; can also connect with Internet or cellular wireless network. In the second case, mobile Ad hoc network is usually end subnet (stump network) in the form of existing network access. Considering the limitation of bandwidth and power, mobile Ad hoc network is not suitable for general as intermediate transmission network. It only allows produced in or destination is network internal node information in and out, and don't let other information through the network. Thus greatly reduced and the existing Internet mutual operation routing overhead. Fig 1 depicts a node by three of the Ad hoc working group on simple network.

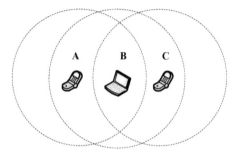

Fig. 1. A simple mobile Ad hoc network

3   QoS Routing Problem[2]

Assume that according to weighted directed graph $G=(V,E)$ express the communication network; V express the set of all network nodes among of graph G, E express the set of all links among of graph G, $n=|V|$ is node number of graph G, $s \in V$ is source node, $t \in |V - |s\|$ is destination node. For any of link $(s,t) \in E$, define three attributes: delay function $Delay(s,t)$, bandwidth function $Bandwidth(s,t)$, cost function $Cost(s,t)$. Assume that $p(s,t)$ express a path of node s to t, $e \in E$, then the path of the total delay function is defined as:

$$Delay(p(s,t)) = \sum_{e \in p(s,t)} Delay(e) \tag{1}$$

Bottleneck bandwidth function of the path $p(s,t)$ is defined as:

$$Bandwidth(p(s,t)) = \min\{Bandwidth(e)\} \qquad (2)$$

Cost function of the path $p(s,t)$ is defined as:

$$Cost(p(s,t)) = \sum_{e \in p(s,t)} Cost(e) \qquad (3)$$

QoS routing problem is to find a meet the following conditions of the path $p(s,t)$:Conditions 1 delay constraint: $Delay(p(s,t)) \le D$

Condition 2 bandwidth constraints: $Bandwidth(p(s,t)) \ge B$

Condition 3 cost constraints: among of the trees of satisfying condition 1 and condition 2, $Cost(p(s,t))$ is minimum.

According to this problem, before employ DNA computing, first, preprocesses the specific network model, that is remove the link of not meeting the requirements of the bandwidth, then the QOS routing question based on bandwidth and delay translate into the single delay constraint. The network as figure 1, link characteristics is described by triple elements: bandwidth, delay, cost. If a real-time business requirement $W_{min} = 2$ 、 $D_{max} = 8$, then after preprocessing. Node 1 is source node, and node 8 is destination node [3].

4   Model of Closed Circle DNA Computing and Biochemical Experiments

4.1   Model of Closed Circle DNA Computing

Basic closed circle DNA computing model requires that all closed circle DNA molecules at the same position have the same recognition sequence in the mixture This characteristic of DNA molecule structure extends mode of DNA encoding, widens the applied range of closed circle DNA computing model, and endows its biochemistry experiment with new contents: delete experiment or insert experiment can only change the chain length of some closed circle DNA molecules; group delete experiment is based on destroying cyclization of DNA molecules; group insert experiment is executed in different tubes simultaneously [4].

The closed circle DNA molecule contains $n+1$ position, where, the position of opening circle is in 0 positions, and its recognition sequence is r_0. The recognition sequence of other positions is $r_i (i = 1,2,\cdots,n)$, and its structure is $r_i = s_i t_i$, where, the position between s_i and t_i is recognition site of restriction endonucleases. Foreign DNA molecule of r_i is $p_{ij} (j = 1,2,\cdots,m)$, and its structure is $p_{ij} = t_i q_{ij} s_i$.

4.2   Biochemistry Experiments

Extended closed circle DNA computing model contains all biochemistry experiments of basic closed circle DNA computing model, group insert experiment, and group delete experiment. The following are analyses on group insert experiment and group delete experiment [5][6].

Group insert experiment: Foreign DNA molecule p_{ij} is inserted in recognition sequence r_i of closed circle DNA molecule. The process of its biochemistry operation is as follows. Restriction endonuclease corresponding to r_i is added into closed circle DNA mixture. Linear DNA molecule is generated after opening closed circle DNA molecule between s_i and t_i. After high performance liquid chromatography (HPLC) is done to delete restriction endonuclease, linear DNA mixture is divided into m groups, and the authors can get m kinds of test tubes; T4 DNA ligase and foreign DNA molecule p_{ij} are added into the j test tube ($j = 1, 2, \ldots, m$). Then closed circle DNA are formed again, where closed circle DNA adds a foreign DNA molecule p_{ij} between s_i and t_i. Finally all closed circle DNA molecules are mixed and HPLC is done to delete impurity.

Group delete experiment: By the action of various restriction endonucleases, all the closed circle DNA molecules which contain two or more recognition sites correspond these restriction endonucleases are deleted. The process of its biochemistry operation is as follows. First, by the action of various restriction endonucleases, closed circle DNA molecules are changed into linear DNA molecules. Then HPLC is done to delete restriction endonucleases. By the action of T4 DNA ligase, some of linear DNA molecules are turned into closed circle DNA molecules again, but the other part which has been cut into several segments cannot. Finally, gel electrophoresis experiment is done to delete linear DNA molecules and T4 DNA ligase.

5   Model of Closed Circle DNA Computing for QOS Routing

Step 1: Encoding for arc α_i ($i = 1, 2, \cdots, m$)

The first (arc) groups: $3'-\mu_i - 5'= \beta_i \gamma_i = p_i q_i, |\alpha_i| = 2|\beta_i| = 2|\gamma_i| = 6byte$

The second (cost) groups: $3'-k_i - 5'= q_i c_i p_i, |k_i| = |p_i| + |q_i| + |c_i| = 15 \times c_i - 6byte$

The third (probe) groups: $5'-k_i - 3'= q_i' c_i' p_i'$

The first group of coding representative arc α_i, μ_i is the enzymes recognition sequence [7]. The site between p_i and q_i is recognition sites. Then β_i and γ_i are on behalf of the arc of arrow tail and arrow top. The second group code represent the weight value of the arc α_i (namely cost). Considering that the single DNA molecule with the problem of easy to be broken along with increase length, when the weight value is 1, according to the node number choice the length 3bp. In order to ensure that the difference of the DNA code, when weight values greater than 1, a group of 15bp code are choose to representative a weight value. The third group code k_i' is complementary series of group code k_i . This part of the probe is marked fluorescent element for using to mark the experiment. t_0 is the open circle position of the code, for recognition sequence, t_0 :GGTCTC, The corresponding enzymes: Bsa I .The first group code is as table 1:

Table 1. The first group code

number	μ_1	μ_2	μ_3	μ_4	μ_5	μ_6
en-coding	GTGC AC	CCTA GG	ACCG GT	GGGC CC	ATTA AT	CTGA AG
enzymes	ApaL I	Avr I	Age I	Apa I	Ase I	Acu I
number	μ_7	μ_8	μ_9	μ_{10}	μ_{11}	μ_{12}
en-coding	GGAT CC	GAAG AC	GTAT CC	AGAT CT	ATGC AT	CTTG AG
en-zymes	BamH I	Bbs I	BciV I	Bgl I I	BfrB I	BpuE I

The second group encoding $3'-k_i -5'$:

$C_1 : 3'-ATC - 5'$ $C_2 : 3'-CAT - 5'$

$C_3 : 3'-ATCTACCACT\ TTCAACAT\ - 5'$

$C_4 : 3'-ATTACATACC\ CATTCATAAT\ CTAACCCTTC\ ATA - 5'$

$C_5 : 3'-CCACATTTCC\ AATAATCCCC\ TTATTAATCC\ ACA - 5'$

$C_6 : 3'-TAACAATTCA\ TTAACTAC\ - 5'$

$C_7 : 3'-TCC - 5'$ $C_8 : 3'-CCA - 5'$

$C_9 : 3'-ACATCACACT\ CATTACTATC\ ACCAAAATCT\ TTC - 5'$

$C_{10} : 3'-TACCCATTCA\ TCTAATCA\ - 5'$

$C_{11} : 3'-TCAACCAAAT\ CACTATCT\ - 5'$

$C_{12} : 3'-TCACCATTTC\ TCAACCAA\ - 5'$

Step 2: for the top of $V_1, V_n, V_k (k = 2,3, \cdots, n-1)$ Synthesis deck, just as table 2:

Step 3: The purpose of the termination technology, Synthesis all end to end chain between $V_1\ and\ V_n$

1. DNA molecules $t_0'\beta_j'$ of group deck R_1^1 is connected to $5'$ port by biotin molecules, and then fixed in a modified surface to product DNA chip. Port $3'$ of γ_i' and β_j of group deck of R_n^1 and R_1^2 , and port $5'$ of $\beta_i\gamma_i t_0$ active treatment respectively, make it's lose chemical activity.

2. DNA encoding of the first group of excessive coding (Remove the code of V_1 as end and V_n as top), Excessive deck group R_k , processed and excessive R_1^2 、 R_n^1 and R_n^2 , DNA molecular of chip mix fully. With the purpose of terminated

Table 2. The group of deck for top

Model of top group of deck	The group of deck for top
$R_1^1 = \{5'-t_0'\beta_j' - 3' \mid \alpha_i \text{ is out arc of } V_1\}$	$R_1^1 = \{t_0'\beta_1', t_0'\beta_3', t_0'\beta_4'\}$
$R_1^2 = \{3'-\beta_j - 5' \mid \alpha_j \text{ is out arc of } V_1\}$	$R_1^2 = \{\beta_1, \beta_3, \beta_4\}$
	$R_2 = \{\gamma_1'\beta_2'\}$
	$R_3 = \{\gamma_3'\beta_5', \gamma_3'\beta_7'\}$
$R_k = \{5'-\gamma_i'\beta_j' - 3' \left| \begin{array}{l} \alpha_i \text{ is enter arc of } V_k, \\ \alpha_i \text{ is out arc of } V_k \end{array}\right.\}$	$R_4 = \{\gamma_3'\beta_6', \gamma_2'\beta_{11}'\}$
	$R_5 = \{\gamma_4'\beta_8', \gamma_4'\beta_{10}', \gamma_5'\beta_8', \gamma_5'\beta_{10}', \gamma_6'\beta_8', \gamma_6'\beta_{10}'\}$
	$R_6 = \{\gamma_7'\beta_9'\}$
	$R_7 = \{\gamma_8'\beta_{12}', \gamma_9'\beta_{12}'\}$
$R_n^1 = \{5'-\gamma_i - 3' \mid \alpha_i \text{ is enter arc of } V_n\}$	$R_8^1 = \{\beta_{10}', \beta_{11}', \beta_{12}'\}$
$R_n^2 = \{3'-\beta_i\gamma_i t_0 - 5' \mid \alpha_i \text{ is top arc of } V_n\}$	$R_8^2 = \{\beta_{10}\gamma_{10}t_0, \beta_{11}\gamma_{11}t_0, \beta_{12}\gamma_{12}t_0\}$

technology, get double-stranded DNA. With T4DNA link enzyme hybrid reaction is happened. By high performance liquid chromatography to remove impurities, get an end to end chain from V_1 and V_n. The height of the reaction by the hybrid parallel, mixture represents all the set of this chain [8][9][10].

All synthesis closed circle DNA as follows:

$(\mu_1\mu_2\mu_{11}), (\mu_1\mu_2\mu_6\mu_{10}), (\mu_1\mu_2\mu_6\mu_8\mu_{12}), (\mu_4\mu_{10}), (\mu_4\mu_8\mu_{12}), (\mu_3\mu_5\mu_{10}), (\mu_3\mu_5\mu_8\mu_{12}), (\mu_3\mu_7\mu_9\mu_{12})$

Step 4 for all empowering chains (cost) and take the path of least cost

① set $i=1$

② Use enzymes corresponding μ_i to finish access the experiment, insert DNA fragments c_i

③ if $i=m$, then closed circle DNA open circle in t_0, finish gel electrophoresis experiment, take the shortest chain length DNA fragments, else $i=i+1$, turn into ②

After the access experiment, get experimental results as table 3:

Closed circle DNA open circle in t_0 and after electrophoresis experiment, get DNA of the shortest chain length $(\mu_1 c_1 \mu_1 \mu_2 c_2 \mu_2 \mu_{11} c_{11} \mu_{11})$, chain length is 66byte.

Step 5 Check all the least cost path

① Mixture sudden cooled from 95 °C to 68 °C, forming single DNA mixture. For port 5of the DNA molecules in mixture modified by "SH "base, and fixed in the wafer surface, made DNA chip. Set $i=1$.

Table 3. After the access experiment closed circle DNA and chain length

closed circle DNA	Chain length/ $(6 + \sum \mu_i + \sum \{(c_i - 1) \times 15 + 3\}) byte$
$(\mu_1 c_1 \mu_1 \mu_2 c_2 \mu_2 \mu_{11} c_{11} \mu_{11})$	66
$(\mu_1 c_1 \mu_1 \mu_2 c_2 \mu_2 \mu_6 c_6 \mu_6 \mu_{10} c_{10} \mu_{10})$	96
$(\mu_1 c_1 \mu_1 \mu_2 c_2 \mu_2 \mu_6 c_6 \mu_6 \mu_8 c_8 \mu_8 \mu_{12} c_{12} \mu_{12})$	111
$(\mu_4 c_4 \mu_4 \mu_{10} c_{10} \mu_{10})$	81
$(\mu_4 c_4 \mu_4 \mu_8 c_8 \mu_8 \mu_{12} c_{12} \mu_{12})$	96
$(\mu_3 c_3 \mu_3 \mu_5 c_5 \mu_5 \mu_{10} c_{10} \mu_{10})$	111
$(\mu_3 c_3 \mu_3 \mu_5 c_5 \mu_5 \mu_8 c_8 \mu_8 \mu_{12} c_{12} \mu_{12})$	126
$(\mu_3 c_3 \mu_3 \mu_7 c_7 \mu_7 \mu_9 c_9 \mu_9 \mu_{12} c_{12} \mu_{12})$	126

② Make mark probe and DNA chip fully mix; cooled from 95 °C to 68 °C, make hybrid reaction. And use 68 °C buffer fluids to rush not hybrid probe molecules. With the confocal laser microscopy scanning DNA chip, test hybrid results, record the DNA chip window. Have window place DNA molecular represents the paths of least cost have arc α_i, otherwise represent the path of least cost no arc α_i. Testing experiment results see table 4:

Analyzing the results, get the path of least cost by arc $\alpha_1, \alpha_2, \alpha_{11}$ composition. Corresponding node is the $V_1 \rightarrow V_2 \rightarrow V_4 \rightarrow V_8$.

Table 4. Testing experiment results

Probe number	1	2	3	4	5	6
experiment results	All bright	All bright	All not bright	All not bright	All not bright	All not bright
Probe number	7	8	9	10	11	12
experiment results	All not bright	All not bright	All not bright	All not bright	All bright	All not bright

6   Conclusions

Mobile Ad Hoc network QoS routing problem, this paper design corresponding model of closed circle DNA computing, and compared with other intelligent algorithm for the QoS routing problem, for large scale mobile Ad Hoc network , DNA computing is highly parallel when find the optimal solution . And improve the routing of the search speed; at the same time closed circle DNA can use again, and for the QoS routing problems can analyze the sensitivity and deal with more complex QoS routing problem.

References

1. Adleman, L.M.: Molecular computation of solutions to combinatorialproblems. Science 266(11), 1021–1024 (1994)
2. Zhou, K., Gao, Z., Xu, J.: An Algorithm of DNA Computing on 0-1 Planning Problem. Advances in Systems Science and Applications 5(4), 587–593 (2005)
3. Liu, W.: TSP problem based on DNA computing. Journal of Chemical Information and Computer Science 42(5), 1176–1178 (2002)
4. Zhou, K., Tong, X., Xu, J.: An algorithm of sticker DNA chip model on making spanning tree problem. In: Proc. of the Fifth International Conference on Machine Learning and Cybernetics, pp. 4287–4292 (2006)
5. Darehmiraki, M., MishmastNehi, H.: A surface-based DNA algorithm for the solving binary knapsack problem. Applied Mathematics and Computation 188(2), 1991–1994 (2007)
6. Zhou, K., Wang, Y., Liu, W., et al.: DNA algorithmof edge coloring problem on closed circle DNA. Journal of Huazhong University of Science and Technology (Nature Science) 34(9), 25–28 (2006)
7. Yin, Z., Ye, C.-M., Wen, M.: DNA Encoding Design Based on Minimal Free Energy. Computer Engineerand Application 1(4), 542–549 (2010)
8. Deaton, R., Murphy, R.C., Garzon, M., et al.: Good encodings for DNA-based solutions to combinatorial problems. In: Proc. 2nd Annual Meeting DNA Based Computing, pp. 247–258 (1996)
9. Shin, S.Y., Lee, I.H., Kim, D.: Multiobjective evolutionary optimization of DNA sequences for reliable DNA computing. IEEE Transaction on Evolutionary Computation 9(2), 143–158 (2005)
10. Khalid, N.K., Ibrahim, Z.: DNA Sequence Optimization Based on Continuous Particle Swarm Optimizationfor Reliable DNA Computing and DNA Nanotechnology. Journal of Computer Science 4(11), 942–950 (2008)

Research and Implementation of Embedded Remote Measurement and Control System Based on Industrial Ethernet

Hui Li, Hao Zhang, Daogang Peng, and Tianyu Chen

College of Electric Power and Automation Engineering
Shanghai University of Electric Power
Shanghai, China
elmerlee@163.com

Abstract. This paper mainly researches embedded data acquisition system and Industrial Ethernet communication system of equipment, and discusses design and implementation of embedded remote measurement and control system based on Industrial Ethernet. Using MagicARM2410 experiment platform as hardware platform and embedded Linux as software platform, this paper realizes an embedded remote measurement and control system based on Modbus/TCP Industrial Ethernet. The system accomplishes necessary supervisory and control tasks, as well as Modbus/TCP communication based on Qt's network module. It also can dynamically update data of client and server on friendly graphic user interface based on Qt.

Keywords: Industrial Ethernet, Modbus/TCP, Linux, Qt, MagicARM2410.

1 Introduction

Modern remote measurement and control system of equipment requires a variety of industrial equipments for remote monitoring, control and data transmission. On the other hand, enterprises require to achieve comprehensive and seamless information integration from field control layer to management layer, and to provide an open infrastructure. While current control system can not fully meet these requirements[1].

Industrial network is a key support system within production and manufacturing process, but its non-openness and non-compatibility has been the problems among its development process. In a long period of time, to form a control network, smart field devices and automation control devices rely on 4~20mA standard signal to communicate. As adapting to the decentralized, networked and intelligent features of industrial control systems, field bus systems have been a great development in these two decades. But in the industrial automation field, because of the lack of uniform international standards, in order to seize the world market, many manufacturers independently develop products. It leads to whether DCS or field bus are all standing at a party situation, and the products from different manufacturers are not compatible, and the cost of whole system is high, which no doubt greatly hinders the development of industrial automation and many new technologies.

J. Lei et al. (Eds.): NCIS 2012, CCIS 345, pp. 430–435, 2012.
© Springer-Verlag Berlin Heidelberg 2012

2   Presentation of Industrial Ethernet and Modbus/TCP

Ethernet-based industrial control networks have their advantages of high data transfer rate, high reliability, easy to maintenance, long-range transport and good interoperability. With the popularization and promotion of Internet technology, increasing of network communication rate and development of exchange technology, it gets the global users' support and hardware and software support, so as to rapidly develop and popularize. Therefore, Ethernet-based industrial control networks represent industrial control systems development trends. Modbus/TCP is a kind of Industrial Ethernet.

Modbus/TCP protocol defines how to use TCP/IP protocol to transmit Modbus messages[2]. This protocol is primarily used in the PLC, HMI, I/O modules and some Ethernet gateways which connected to other simple buses or I/O modules. In order to maintain continuous control of a separate transaction, it needs to encapsulate the transaction into a connection to ensure the servers identify, monitor or cancel the connections from the client without taking special measures.

Modbus/TCP protocol defines a bottom layer independent Protocol Data Unit (PDU), and introduces some additional areas in the Application Data Unit (ADU) on the map of a specific bus or network. The frame structure of Modbus/TCP is shown in Fig. 1.

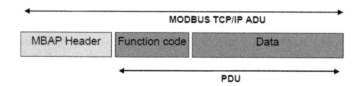

Fig. 1. Modbus/TCP Protocol Frame Structure

3   Presentation of Hardware and Software Platform

3.1   MagicARM2410 Experimental Platform

MagicARM2410 experimental platform is developed by Guangzhou Zhiyuan Electronics Co., Ltd. , which can use µC/OS-II, Linux and WinCE operating systems and support Qt, MiniGUI graphics systems. MagicARM2410 experimental platform uses S3C2410A microprocessor with ARM920T core, extending sufficient storage resources (SDRAM, NAND Flash, NOR Flash and E2PROM, etc.), supporting 10/100M Ethernet, USB bus, CAN bus, 8-inch 640×480 true color TFT LCD screen (touch screen) and using JTAG emulator to debug. It also retains PACK peripherals and GPIO output interfaces. Users can achieve almost all of the embedded experiments for teaching and developing[3].

3.2   Embedded Linux and Qt

Embedded Linux refers to cutting standard Linux to install in a small memory chip with a few KB or MB. It is suitable for specific embedded applications. In the current developed embedded systems, one half are using embedded Linux. In addition, in order to better adapt to the embedded development, based on standard Linux, embedded Linux still does some improvements.

Qt is a cross-platform C++ development tools. Sometimes it is known as C++ components toolbox. Qt is mainly used in the KDE desktop environment development. Software developed by Qt can compile and execute on any supported platform, without modifying the source code. The Qt platform can realize itself graphical interface style and other platform GUI style[4].

4   General Design of Modbus/TCP Server and Client

MagicARM2410 experimental platform uses embedded Linux and hardware devices to simulate field digital instrumentations. LED lights, step motor, DC motor and buzzer represent field equipments. A/D converters represent field A/D instruments. Server can control them through the drivers. Client via port 502 connects server, sending and receiving Modbus/TCP frames. Server programs are developed and debugged on the host computer in a cross-development environment. Successfully debugged programs will be written into the flash.

Server program executes in the embedded Linux of the experimental platform. It controls on-board equipments such as LEDs, stepper motor, DC motor, buzzer through the related drivers. According to this request, server needs to achieve the following objectives:

- Implementing Graphical User Interface (GUI) through inheriting QWidget class. The GUI contains buttons (QpushButton control), A/D conversion results (QLCDNumber control) and the tree status bar (QlistView control).
- Implementing Modbus/TCP server through inheriting QServerSocket class, and using Modbus/TCP port 502 for private listening.
- Implementing socket through inheriting QSocket class. Server sends Modbus/TCP response frame through writeBlock () method of QSocket class and connects readyRead() signal of QSocket class with data receiving function to implement data receiving.
- Using QFile class to store collected data.

Client program executes in the Qt/X11 of PC. It is responsible for sending control instructions, receiving, displaying and saving the A/D conversion results from   server in order to achieve centralized management and control of the entire network. According to this requirement, client needs to achieve the following objectives:

- Implementing Graphical User Interface (GUI) through inheriting QWidget class. The GUI contains buttons (QPushButton control), check boxes (QCheckBox control), A/D conversion results (QLCDNumber control), the status bar (QLabel control) and the upper-lower limit setting frame (QSpinBox control), etc. Program calls show() method of QWidget class to display GUI.

- Implementing Modbus/TCP client through inheriting QSocket class. Program uses connectToHost () method of Qsocket class to connect server port 502 and send Modbus/TCP request frames through writeBlock() method of Qsocket class. Similarly, it connects readyRead() signal of QSocket class with data receiving function to implement data receiving.
- As open(), close() and other methods belong to QWidget class conflict with the same methods of Linux unified IO interfaces, it needs to re-package the related driver methods.

5   Implementation of Measurement and Control System Based on Modbus/TCP

Socket provided by Qt fully uses class encapsulation mechanism. Users do not need to access various bottom structure operations. It uses Qt itself Signal/Slot mechanism to make program easier to understand. Qt provides four classes associated with Socket: QSocket, QServerSocket, QSocketDevice and QSocketNotifier. The system uses QSocket class and QServerSocket class.

Server reads A/D conversion results across related drivers. S3C2410A is built-in an 8 channel A/D converter with 10-bit resolution. Maximum conversion rate is 500kbit/s and non-linearity is 1 bit. A/D converter is a character device. Linux regards all devices as files. In order to use files, Linux provides unique file operation function interface. For example, operation function interface of the character device file is "file_operations" structure, defined in <linux/include/fs.h>. Program calls ioctl() function to achieve A/D conversion results.

Server also realizes the direct control of LEDs, step motor, DC motor and buzzer. When client receives Modbus/TCP control instructions of these devices, server calls the appropriate driver to implement LEDs light switch, step motor and DC motor start/stop switch and buzzer switch.

Client program defines two classes: one inherits from Client class of QDialog class to build a GUI; the other is Devmag class. The Devmag class repackages Linux standard IO operating functions such as open(), close() and ioctl() and provides the interface for calling these standard IO functions. The main reason to do so is QDialog class also includes these member functions. If these member functions are directly called in the client, it will cause SIGSEGV memory errors. Re-packaging these functions as Devmag class and regarding Devmag objects as members of Client class, through Devmag objects accessing standard IO interfaces, the memory errors will not occur. In addition, Client objects also contain QSocket object members to establish a connection with server, built with Client class.

The initial graphical interfaces of server and client are shown in Fig. 2. After reading A/D conversion results, the graphical interfaces of server and client are shown in Fig. 3.

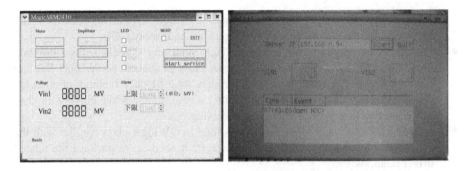

Fig. 2. (a) Initial Graphical Interface of Server   (b) Initial Graphical Interface of Client

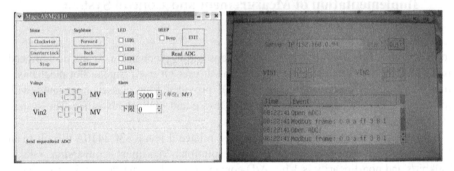

Fig. 3. (a) GUI of Server after Reading A/D Conversion   (b) GUI of Client after Reading A/D Conversion

Server program reads A/D converter every 0.1s. 2 channels A/D data store in member variables adc1, adc2 of server objects with dynamically refreshing. When a Modbus/TCP request comes from client to read the A/D conversion result, Server::revdata() calls Server::sendadc() and sends a Modbus/TCP response.

In the process of connecting to server, the related connection process will display as the form of logs in the main interface. After connection established, if there is a request, QSocket object will send readyRead() signal. The signal is binding with Client::revdata() slot. Within the Client::revdata() slot, after analyzing the request data read by Modbus/TCP, program will execute the appropriate actions based on the contents of the request, such as reading and writing coils and registers.

On the client graphical interface, there are some control buttons of LEDs, stepper motor, DC motor and buzzer. When these buttons are pressed, different signals will be sent. The corresponding slots, such as TcpClient::Beep() and TcpClient::LED(), will call Client::transmit() function to send Modbus/TCP request to server after receiving signals.

As a matter of fact, in this experiment, client plays a Modbus/TCP server's role, and server plays a Modbus/TCP client's role, while it doesn't impact implementing system functions indeed. On the graphical interface of server, users can read A/D conversion results, control LEDs, step motor, DC motor and buzzer. All of these are implemented by Modbus/TCP request and response.

6   Conclusion

This paper introduces the development process of industrial control network from fieldbus to Industrial Ethernet, and points out the position of Industrial Ethernet in the control system of equipment in future. It uses MagicARM2410 experiment platform, embedded Linux operating system and Qt graphics development tool to realize hardware and software development, and finally implements embedded remote measurement and control system based on Modbus/TCP Industrial Ethernet. In addition, this paper also discusses Modbus/TCP protocol and Client/Server implementation process, and analyzes the implementation process of communication between two sides. By realizing the application functions of Modbus/TCP client and server, it achieves embedded remote data acquisition and control of field equipments.

Acknowledgments. This work was supported by Shanghai Science and Technology Commission Key Program (No. 10250502000), Innovation Key Program of Shanghai Municipal Education Commission (No. 12ZZ177) and Innovation Program of Shanghai Municipal Education Commission (Grant No. 12YZ142).

References

1. Wang, R., Lei, B.: The Actuality and Development of Industrial Ethernet. Automation Panorama (4), 63–65 (2004)
2. Modbus Messaging on Tcp/Ip Implementation Guide V1.0b, Modbus-IDA (2006)
3. S3C2410A user's manual Revision 1.0. Samsung (2004)
4. Zhou, L., et al.: S3C2410 & Embedded Linux System Manuals. Beijing University of Aeronautics and Astronautics Press (2008)
5. Li, H., Zhang, H., Peng, D.: Design and Research of Embedded Data Processing Platform on Power Equipments. Journal of Information and Computational Science 5(4), 1875–1883 (2008)

Analysis of Time-Varying Characteristics of Internet End-to-End Network Delay*

Yonglei Yang, Wei Peng, Jingang Liu, and Lin Wang

School of Computer, National University of Defense Technology
Changsha, Hunan, 410073, China
{yangorzhu,taobao.qin}@gmail.com, wpeng@nudt.edu.cn,
wangxiaowang_cc@sina.com

Abstract. Network delay has great influence on application performance. It changes dynamically due to the instability of Internet routing and dynamic traffic load. Understanding the time-varying characteristics of Internet end-to-end network delay is important for network management and optimization. In this paper, we propose an analysis method by decomposing end-to-end delay into two components: basic delay and delay jitter. We propose an algorithm to extract the basic delay from a measured end-to-end delay time series. The algorithm is applied on a data set gathered by probing about 1000 destinations for one day. The statistical characteristics of basic delay are analyzed. The experimental results show that the intervals between two successive changes of basic delay follow the normal distribution approximately, which hints that the change of Internet end-to-end path may follow the same normal distribution, too. Our findings are helpful for improving network performance and detecting network anomalies.

Keywords: Internet, delay, measure, analysis, algorithm.

1   Introduction

Internet has undergone a fast growing during the last two decades and has become the biggest computer network which covers the whole world and plays a vital role in every field of human life. Many applications have been developed on the Internet, ranging from file transfer, email, web browsing to time-critical applications such as voice chatting, real-time games and Internet televisions Although some Internet applications are delay-tolerant, the performance of most applications is impact significantly by network delays. As an important parameter of network performance indicator, network delay plays a important role in providing quality-of-service (QoS) guarantee, traffic engineering, fault detection and network management. Through measurement and analysis of end-to-end Internet delay, its internal property and

---

* This work was supported in part by the National Natural Science Foundation of China under grant No.61070199, 61103188, 61103189 and 61100223, and Hunan Provincial Natural Science Foundation of China under grant No.11JJ7003.

J. Lei et al. (Eds.): NCIS 2012, CCIS 345, pp. 436–445, 2012.
© Springer-Verlag Berlin Heidelberg 2012

characteristics need be understood to predict the real time status of network, timely discover network failure events and improve the network service-providing capability of Internet service providers (ISPs). Meanwhile, many real-time applications, including voice chat and video conference, impose tight demands for network delay. For example, in voice chatting applications, if the network delay is too high, real-time transmission of voice data cannot be achieved, thus the application performance will be degraded significantly. Therefore, understanding the characteristics of Internet end-to-end network delay is important for improving application performance and network optimization.

Network delay can be analyzed by statistical methods. Statistical analysis can reflect the end-to-end delay change features in a certain period using real data collected from the Internet through some network measurement methods. Mathematical models can also be used to analyze network delay. Generally, there are three models: (1) time series model, which is widely used to predict the network delay through observing the previous delay data; (2) queuing model, which predicts network delay through the queue model in networks; (3) system identification model, which is mainly used to predict delay jitter by taking network as central nervous system.

Adopting time series model, this paper presents a method for analyzing the time-varying characteristics of Internet end-to-end network delay. The main idea of the method is to divide the end-to-end network delay into two parts: basic delay and delay jitter. An algorithm is proposed to extract basic delay from a delay time series. We use active measurement method to collect network delay data from the Internet and then apply the analysis method on the data set. The experimental results show that the intervals between two successive change of basic delay follows the normal distribution approximately. Such pattern reflects that the change of Internet end-to-end path may follow the same distribution, too. By this way, network real-time status can be learned, network events can be found and network anomaly can be detected so that network performance can be improved.

The rest of the paper is organized as follows. The related work is briefly introduced in section 2. The analysis method is proposed in section 3. Experiment settings and experimental results are shown in section 4. Finally, we give a conclusion in section 5.

2   Related Work

As an important indicator to measure network performance, network delay has been the focus and emphasis of research. In early works, Mills et al. used Ping to study the relationship between delay and different packet sizes and the retransmission timeout algorithm [1]. Bolot et al. deduced the delay interval approximation relation of adjacent packets through the use of Lindley repetition formula by measuring the delay and packet loss rate in Internet [2]. IETF performance indicator working group—IPPM (IP Performance Metrics) established standards and defined parameters describing network performance [3]. And then, the network delay is mainly based on the delay definition and measurement methods mentioned previously. Currently, international and domestic network delay measurement and research status are mainly made up of the following aspects.

IPPM Working Group [4] focuses on measuring and studying unidirectional delay, bi-directional delay and packet loss rate of network and defines network measuring indicators. IEPM [5] monitors the network physical link performance and measures bi-directional delay and packet loss rate of network through coordination of multiple measurement points. The Surveyor project group of ANS (Advanced Network & Service Inc) and the TTM project group of RIPE (Réseaux IP Européens) emphasize on the measurement and analysis of unidirectional delay of network. And the IPMON project [6] carried out by the American Sprint company adopts the clock synchronization technology based on GPS to measure network status, which makes the data including network delay be accurate to micro-second. Currently, much work have been done by the Internet measurement group of CAIDA [7].

Measurement tools are composed of active measurement tools, which play the dominant role, and passive measurement tools. The former includes traditional ping and traceroute tools, as well as measurement tools including pathchar, pchar, netprtf, Iperf, cing etc. Both Pathchar [8] and pchar [9] measure data including network delay and packet loss rate by using VPS to send ICMP messages; Netprtf and Iperf tools measure data including delay, delay jitter and batch transmission capacity trough TCP connection; Cing tool [10] calculates the unidirectional delay of every link by sending TTL limited messages to per-hop and extracting ICMP massages returned by router and eliminates the influence of clock skew through repetitive measurement.

Main topics in the research area of network delay include delay measurement methods and prediction techniques. Measurement methodology is mainly engaged in researching the influence of data packet size, data packet transmission rate, data packet transmission time interval and data packet transmission mode on delay measurement accuracy. Current research results show that random poisson distribution is prior to other data transmission modes, and more accurate data can be gained. Prediction research is mainly engaged in the intrinsic properties of network delay, including statistical prediction, which discovers the intrinsic features and disciplines through tremendous measurement of network delay data, and accurate prediction [11], which initiates predictive analysis based on analyzing network delay through network delay modeling and predicts the current network delay through applying the vector ARMA model to TCP retransmission timer.

3   Analysis Method

3.1   Basic Idea

As the important parameter influencing network performance, network end-to-end delay is composed of transmission delay, propagation delay, processing delay and queuing delay. Wherein, transmission delay is the time required to emit all data of a packet into the network. If a packet contains L bit data and the link transmission rate is R bits per second (bps), then the transmission delay is L/R. Propagation delay refers to the time from the first bit of one data message departing the router and reaching the next router, in which, if the length of a link is supposed to be d and transmission speed is v, then propagation delay is d/v. Processing delay refers to the time of the process that when the data message reaches the router, the router determines the re-transmission target interface and transmits the data message to the target interface through internal exchange system; and queuing delay refers to the time for the data message to queue for processing in the router.

It should be noted that the change of network end-to-end delay can be viewed both from the macroscopic level and the microscopic level. Thus, network end-to-end delay can be divided into two parts: basic delay and delay jitter. The basic delay reflects the overall trend of delay change in different time intervals, determined by network routing path and the average load on the path and represents macro-status change of network. Delay jitter reflects the instantaneous status change in a certain moment, influenced by instantaneous traffic burst and routing instability and represents the micro dynamics of network. Basic delay normally has a stable numerical value in a certain time range and delay jitter is very random with unstable numerical value. As shown in Fig.1, the figure in the left side is the measured end-to-end network delay and the one in the right includes the curves of decomposed basic delay and delay jitter. By this way, we can observe the dynamics of network both from the macro level and the micro level.

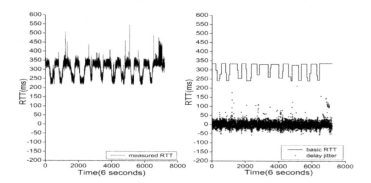

Fig. 1. Schematic Diagram of Delay Decomposition

In this paper, we focus on analyzing the time-varying properties of network basic delay. We conduct the analysis of basic delay with the measured network end-to-end delay data. The analysis procedure is stated as follows:

1) Choose the IP addresses to be probed and then measure the end-to-end network delay and collect the network delay data of different IP addresses;

2) Use an algorithm to decompose network delay into basic delay and delay jitter;

3) Analyze the network basic delay using some statistical methods.

3.2   Data Collection of Network Delay

Given the size and complexity of today's Internet, it is difficult to analyze end-to-end network delay. The distribution of destinations is important for improving the accuracy of analysis. In selection of IP addresses for measurement, attention must be paid with consideration of universality and representativeness. The universality refers to that the IP addresses to be measured must be chosen in a wide area covering the whole district, and the representativeness refers to that the IP addresses to be measured must be typical of a country or a region, which should embody the time-varying properties of network. And then, suitable measurement methods and tools should be chosen based on measurement requirements to accomplish data collection.

The measurement of network delay can be obtained through two measurement methods: active measurement and passive measurement. The former analyzes the contents of message time and sequence returned from the target node to obtain end-to-end network performance parameters through measuring the detection messages of ICMP, UDP and TCP transmitted from the node to the target node; and the passive measurement captures data header through monitoring one or more nodes of the network and analyzes the performance information including network delay and packet loss rate of the path between the measurement source and the destination node. Active measurement is flexible which can send messages for measuring according to the demands of different researchers, but network resources may be occupied, influencing network performance and incurring measurement errors. Therefore, in the process of measurement, the message size must be controlled to ensure the normal operation of network. Passive measurement is used to observe the network performance passively which will generate no influence on network performance, but the measurement point must be well chosen, and in the meantime, because of profound data stream passing nodes, capturing all data stream shall generate profound data stream. In this paper, active measurement method is adopted to obtain and measure network delay.

3.3   Algorithm for Network Delay Decomposition

According to the delay classification, we propose an algorithm for delay decomposition which divides network end-to-end delay into basic delay and delay jitter. The procedure of the algorithm is stated as follows.

Step 1: Optimize the data and exclude the highly fluctuating points (noise points). Suppose the average value of measurement delay in a certain delay sequence is x, the measurement value is x_i, $i = 1, 2, \cdots, N$, and the standard deviation is σ, which is defined as :

$$\sigma = \sqrt{\frac{\sum_{i=1}^{N} (x_i - \overline{x})^2}{(N-1)}} \tag{1}$$

Set the ratio of the data of $(\overline{x} - \sigma, \overline{x} + \sigma)$ in $x_1, x_2, \cdots, x_N$ as α. When α satisfies the value set, replace the point of $|x_i - \overline{x} > 2\sigma|$ with an average value.

Step 2: Data fitting. With reference to the data generated through optimization, set a parameter δ as the standard value to divide standard time. Firstly, set an initial time interval T, in which the maximum measurement delay is x_{max}, and the average value is $\bar{x}$. When $|x_{max} - \bar{x}| < 3\sigma$, use 3σ to replace Te-maxD. Then, when $|x_i - \bar{x}|/|x_{max} - \bar{x}|$ and the ratio between the number of data satisfying the conditions and the total data is more than $(1-\delta)$, x_i is replaced with $\bar{x}$. If the above two conditions are satisfied, the T value is reduced gradually till the set conditions are satisfied. Thirdly, when the average value between adjacent areas satisfies the following condition:

$$|\bar{x}_{k+1} - \bar{x}_k| < ((\bar{x}_{k+1} + \bar{x}_k)/2) * 5\%) \tag{2}$$

Then we integrate the adjacent intervals and replace $(\bar{x}_k + \bar{x}_{k+1})/2$ with average value.

Step 3: Optimize the time intervals. The time intervals extracted in step 2 are denoted as $T_1, T_2, \cdots, T_N$, and the corresponding average value as $\bar{x}_1, \bar{x}_2, \cdots, \bar{x}_N$. Take any two adjacent intervals T_i, T_{i+1}, the elements included in T_i are $x_{i1}, x_{i2}, \cdots, x_{is}$, the elements included in T_{i+1} are $x_{i+1,s+1}, x_{i+1,s+2}, \cdots, x_{i+1,s+t}$. The total number of elements of T_i and T_{i+1} is m=s+t, and the sum of their standard deviation is D.

$$D = \sqrt{\frac{\sum_{j=1}^{s}(x_{is} - \bar{x}_i)^2}{s}} + \sqrt{\frac{\sum_{k=1}^{t}(x_{i+1,s+k} - \bar{x}_{i+1})^2}{t}} \tag{3}$$

To optimize the time intervals, we dynamically change the set T_i and T_{i+1} by moving adjacent elements in T_i to T_{i+1} or vice verse. Thus, the size of T_i and T_{i+1} will change. The standard deviation of the interval is obtained after the sets change, produced a set of standard deviation as $\{D_1, D_2, \cdots, D_s, \cdots, D_t\}$, obtaining the minimum value, interval that corresponding to the minimum is the optimize interval. Calculate the new average value for the adjusted intervals according to the principle that the average value of adjacent intervals satisfies (2), and use $(\bar{x}_k + \bar{x}_{k+1})/2$ for final adjustment to determine the best location of each time segment, and then take the average value of delay measured in the corresponding time sequence as the basic delay and take the D-value between measured delay and basic delay as the delay jitter.

3.4   Statistical Analysis of Network Delay Data

In Internet, network end-to-end delay is determined by link bandwidth, routing protocol and network management strategy, network status etc., and in the case of taking no account of delay jitter, basic delay is thought to fluctuate up and down around a fixed interval in different intervals, so basic delay is assumed to comply with normal distribution which will be explained next.

Normal distribution, or Gaussian distribution is often used in the probability distribution of the fields like math, physics and engineering etc., the concept of which is: suppose there is probability distribution with the random variation X subjecting to a mathematical expectation μ and the standard deviation as σ^2, then its probability density function is displayed as normal distribution, recorded as $X \sim N(\mu, \sigma^2)$, wherein, expectation δ determines the location and standard deviation σ determines the range of distribution.

4   Experimental Analysis

4.1   Data Collection

Before measurement, 5000 domain names from different countries are collected. Then the domain names are translated to corresponding IP addresses by looking up into the domain name system (DNS). We randomly select a set of 1000 IP addresses from them, and probe the addresses every 6 seconds for 3 days and record the network delay and hop numbers. Fig.2 shows the geographical distribution of the probed 1000 IP addresses. Through the query QQ IP address database [12] and traceroute tool provided by Google, the location of IP addresses are inquired. Since real geographical locations of some addresses cannot be determined exactly, we use the capital locations to represent them.

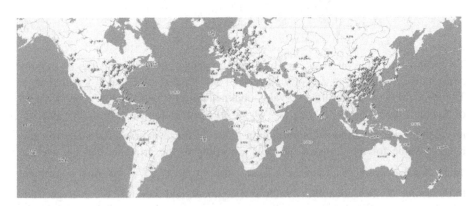

Fig. 2. Geographical Distribution of Probed Addresses

The Ping tool adopted in the paper successively sends Echo-Request detection messages of ICMP to the destinations, triggering the Echo-Response in the remote and then the delay and hop counts in the response messages are collected. Besides, the following improvements have been made to the measurement tool according to actual situations:

1) As there are many measurement addresses, data measurement cannot be done in the expected time, so the OpenMP (Open Multi-Processing) multithreading technology is adopted to set 20 threads to every procedure, and one thread probes one IP address to improve efficiency.

2) In measurement, 32-byte ICMP packets, and maximum round-trip delay is 1000ms. To ensure the accuracy of the measurement data, for the same IP address in 6-seconds interval , if one probing is failed, we will repeatedly probe until the probing is successful or for 3 times, and record the data.

4.2   Data Analysis

We probe the 1000 IP addresses every 6 second for 12 hours and obtain 7,200,000 data records for each destination. There are 59 IP addresses which could not be connected, so they are excluded in data analysis. The valid data accounts for 94.1%.

Delay Decomposition

Based on the data analysis method proposed in the paper, end-to-end network delay measurement and decomposition is conducted on the 941 IP addresses which are measured validly, and basic delay and delay jitter are drawn. In the analysis process, in order to reflect the real macro changing trend of end-to-end network delay and draw basic delay accurately, all the measurement data are decomposed and fitted through adjusting parameter α , changing range of time sequence t (increment during time intervals change) and parameter δ . In the experiment, α is set to be 50%, t=1000, and δ =38% to draw basic delay. Fig.3 is graphs formed from decomposition and fitting by respectively drawing data from Canada IP address of 24.137.192.2 and Germany IP address of 80.237.129.69. In graphs, the graph on the left side is end-to-end network measurement delay, and the one on the right is basic delay and delay jitter. It can be seen from the figures that through such data processing, the end-to-end network delay change in a certain period can be accurately reflected, dividing the measurement delay into basic delay and delay jitter, which is favorable for further analyzing.

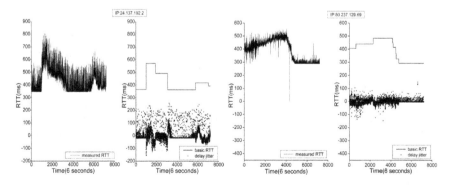

Fig. 3. Decomposition Results of Network Delay

Statistical Analysis of Basic Delay

With reference to the data to be analyzed, the Jarque-Bera provided by matlab is used to check function jbtest(X) and P-P graph is used to check whether basic delay is in conformity with normal distribution. Through Jarque-Bera and P-P graph verification, it is found that in the 941 IP addresses, the change of end-to-end network delay is in full conformity with normal distribution properties. Figures 4 respectively take the measured IP addresses of 80.81.194.31 (Germany) and 60.10.253.22 (Hebei, China) as examples. It can be seen from the figures that the curve displays as an approximately linear distribution, verifying that basic delay follows normal distribution.

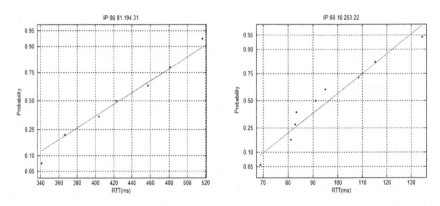

Fig. 4. Distribution of Basic Delay

It can be seen from what has been described above that decomposition of end-to-end network delay into basic delay and delay jitter and measurement and analysis of Internet data verify that, in the case of taking no account of delay jitter, basic delay follows normal distribution in a successive period.

5   Conclusion

Network delay is an important parameter reflecting network performance. To know the change of network status, a method to analyze the time-varying properties of network end-to-end delay is proposed in this paper. By improving the Ping measurement tools, we have measured 1000 IP addresses with a frequency of 6 seconds. Through the decomposition and fitting of the data, the statistical characteristics of basic delay are analyzed. The experimental results show that the intervals between two successive change of basic delay follows the normal distribution approximately, which hints that the change of Internet end-to-end path may follow the same normal distribution, too. Our findings are helpful for improving network performance and detecting network anomalies.

References

1. Mills, D.L.: Internet delay experiment. RFC-889 (1983)
2. Sanghi D., Agrawala A., Gudmundsson O., Jain B.: Experiment assessment of end-to-end behavior on Internet. In: Proc. IEEE INFOCOM 1993, pp. 867-874. IEEE, San Fransisco (1993)
3. IP Performance Metrics (2008), http://www.ietf.org/html.charters/ippm-charter.html
4. IPPM, http://www.advanced.rog/IPPM/
5. IEPM home page. Internet End-to-end Performance Monitoring (1998), http://www-iepm.slac.atanford.edu
6. Fraleigh, C., Moon, S., Lyles, B., et al.: Packet-level Traffic Measurement from the Sprint IP backbone. IEEE Network 17(6), 6–16 (2003)
7. CAIDA, http://www.caida.org/
8. Insolvibilie, G.: The Linux Socket Filter: Sniffing bytes over the networks. Linux Journal
9. Avinash, S., Ye, T., Superatik, B.: Connectionless port scan detection on the backbone. In: 25th IEEE International Performance, Computing and Communications Conference (2006)
10. Anagnostakis, K., Greenwald, G., Ryger, M.R.S.: Cing, measuring network-internal delays using only existing infrastructure. In: Proceedings of INFOCOM 2003: Twenty-Second Annual Joint Conference of the IEEE Computer and Communications Societies (2003)
11. Zhang, W.: Modeling and Research on Network Delay Predictability. Master Thesis, Beijing University of Technology (2007)
12. QQ IP address database, http://www.cz88.net/fox/ipdat.shtml

The Research of Agile Web Development Process and Quality Model

Jun Xie and Li Fang Xu

Information Engineering School of Nanchang University, Nanchang, China
xiejun@ncu.edu.cn, lucy19870814@163.com

Abstract. With the arrival of WEB2.0 age, the Web application presents explosive development. It is the key of Web development that whether we can meet the demands flexibly, develop quickly ,receive users' feedback swiftly and make adjustments fast (namely "Agile").This thesis is to research the agile Web development process and its quality model based on SSH framework, trying to find the balance point between rapid development of Web application systems and the improvement of the quality of Web application system so that we can develop Web application systems which can not only satisfy the demands quickly but also enhance the quality of Web application systems.

Keywords: Agile Web development, SSH framework, quality model, Web application.

1　Introduction

With the arrival of internet development craze which is marked with WEB2.0 and the quick increment of Internet usage, the developing methods based on Web engineering are drawing more and more attention which mainly is embodied in the differences between the development of Web application systems and traditional software. Being different from the traditional software engineering, web systems require quickly live, fast response and swiftly adapt to the changes so that it is not enough to apply the traditional engineering methods and technologies to system development based on the Web. Currently, in most circumstances, developing systems based on Web is arbitrary and lack systemic methods, process control and quality assurance. Therefore, it is very necessary and urgent to research the developing methods and quality assurance of Web engineering.

Web systems not only need to solve the business logics in itself, but also need to spend a lot of energy on other public parts, like users registering/logging on, users' passwords encryption, users management, pages requirements, data management, business objects management and so on. How can programmers concentrate on the systems' core business logics and how to avoid repetitive programming and a waste of resource to enhance the stability and effectiveness of the systems become the programmers' common problems. However, many kinds of Web frameworks can solve these problems and provide a proper programming pattern for software programmer

J. Lei et al. (Eds.): NCIS 2012, CCIS 345, pp. 446–452, 2012.
© Springer-Verlag Berlin Heidelberg 2012

so as to decrease the developing time of Web systems in large extent and brings a complete and high-quality strategy.

2   Introduction of MVC Pattern

MVC (Model-View-Controller) pattern is one of the software design patterns that are widely used at the present. It divides the software system into three different parts: model, view and controller which effectively separate the pages, business logic and business management so that it can lower the relationship among the inner components of software.

Meanwhile, model is to deal with data access and business management, view is to deal with the interaction between users and software and return the information users need while controller is to receive and response the users' asks and use model to deal with business and to return the result to the view [1].The process is as Fig.1.

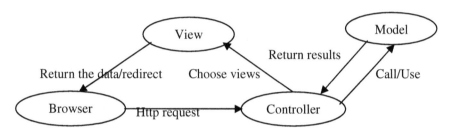

Fig. 1. MVC pattern

3   Introduction of SSH Framework

Struts, Spring and Hibernate are all light Web open-source frameworks based on J2EE developing platform which are different realizations of MVC design pattern.

3.1   Struts

Struts framework is a technology that puts many existed Web components together in certain ways (struts-config.xml) to make them work together to develop Web applications[2]. It provides a series of Struts taglibs in the view layer while ActionServlet and Action in controller layer. However, there is little referring to the model layer so that programmers can choose different ways to realize business functions according to the requirements. The Struts framework is as Fig.2.

Apart from the strong taglibs Struts framework provides, programmers also can define taglibs if they need. After doing some related configuration in file 'web.xml', programmers can import the taglibs into pages by using '<%@ include file="/taglibs.jsp" %>' so that it can be used repeatedly in many places and largely reduce the amount of code, making the pages simple and clear and also reduce the errors. Besides, with the development and extension of Struts frameworks and the appearance of Struts2,it will bring new chances to Web application development. So it can separate the pages and business logics by using Struts framework as the framework of view layer.

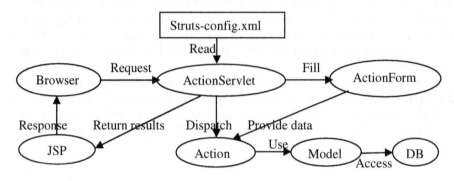

Fig. 2. Struts framework

3.2   Spring

Spring framework is a framework that provides one-top service for J2EE,whose core is IoC (Inversion of Control) or DI (Dependency of Injection) which can inject business objects for the whole application dynamically by the configuration file named applicationContext.xml ,consequently lowering the dependency level of objects in different layers. Apart from IoC, Spring AOP (Aspect-Oriented Programming) is another feature of Spring framework, which encapsulates the modules, such as permission, log, transaction management and the like that have little to do with the specific business operation but are often used, into repetitive part by using the interceptors [2].Therefore, using Spring framework as the framework of business logic layer can make the separation of business logic and business implementation.

3.3   Hibernate

Hibernate framework is a framework that lightly encapsulates JDBC, implements ORM framework and object-relation persistence and inquiry services. It becomes a bridge between application and database, making database operation more easy than before by reflecting the application objects and the relation between them to the tables and the relation between them in the database by using files named *.hbm.xml (* represents class name).Besides, it puts database connection information into the file named hibernate.cfg.xml so that programmers can switch data source only by changing the related configuration information in it, making it easy to transplant. So applying Hibernate framework to the persistent layer can separate business layer and database. Hibernate framework is as Fig.3.

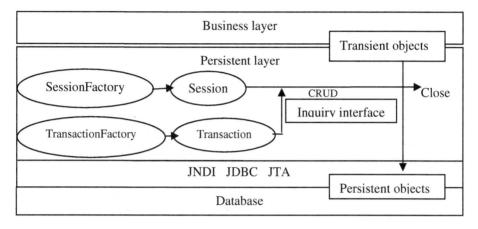

Fig. 3. Hibernate framework

4   Integration of SSH and Web Developing Process

4.1   Integration of Struts and Spring

Add spring plug-in to Struts. Add codes to the Struts configuration file named struts-config.xml as follows [3].

```
<plug-in
        className ="org.springframework.web.struts.ContextLoaderPlugIn">
        <set-property property="contextConfigLocation"
            value="/WEB-INF/applicationContext.xml"/>
</plug-in>
```

Delegating Action classes to Spring by setting the property named type in element <action> as "org.springframework.web.struts.DelegatingActionProxy" in file named struts-config.xml but adding the specific Action classes to Spring configuration file in form of bean .

Action proxy will search dynamically the bean whose value of property of name which is same as the value of the path property in the element <action> when Struts need to use a specific Action class to get the class.

4.2   Integration of Spring and Hibernate

Configure the Hibernate sessionFactory in the spring applicationContext.xml to make it in the management of spring. Register all the DAO to the spring configuration file in the form of bean which should be injected into the DAO property in related Action classes. There is no longer to configure the hibernate.cfg.xml.

All DAO share the same sessionFactory, letting each Hibernate DAO extend from Spring HibernateDaoSupport class to get a hibernateTemplate object [3] that encapsulates transaction and session from function-getHibernateTemplate().Then database can be accessed by using the object.

4.3   The Process of SSH Framework (Fig.4)

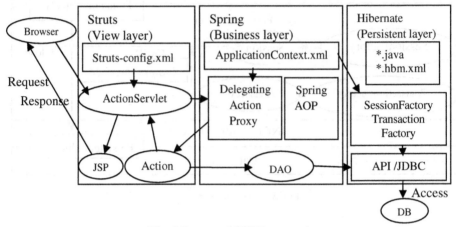

Fig. 4. Process of SSH Framework

4.4   Agile Web Developing Process Based on SSH

Apply SSH framework based on MVC design pattern to agile Web development, the process is as Fig.5.

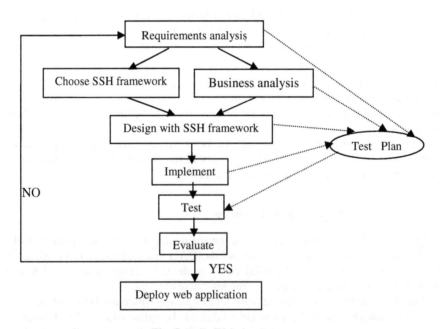

Fig. 5. Agile Web development

5   Analysis of Quality Model

Making Quality analysis of agile Web developing process based on SSH framework by using the six quality facts of ISO/IEC912 which are functionality, reliability, maintainability, development efficiency, workability and portability.

5.1   Functionality

Agile Web development is based on Struts, Spring and Hibernate which are mature frameworks and make a perfect combination. The requests that are sent by front pages can communicate with the database and implement the functional requirements of the application systems and can manage the errors in some extent. Besides, it provides friendly UI. Developers only need to add some related information to the configuration file then concentrate on business logic programming so that it can quickly meet the functional requirements from clients.

5.2   Reliability

It can keep all the application components in touch tightly by using configuration files which inject the required business objects for each component swiftly and stably in the runtime. So it ensures the efficiency when Web applications are running. Meanwhile, developers can do some modification to the frameworks used according to the demand to satisfy the developing requirements. Besides, the modification of a functional module may not influence others directly so that it can ensure the systems' stability and advance the reliability.

5.3   Maintainability

Because pages are write with taglibs and many pages use the same taglib, when errors appear or pages need to do some modification ,developers are only supported to modify the taglibs avoid modifying many pages which are good for maintenance in the long time. It enhances the maintainability and expandability by configuring the business objects or components to the configuration file in the form of bean in unified management. The encapsulation of JDBC makes it convenient to access and maintain the databases.

5.4   Development Efficiency

As Struts provides powerful taglibs, it realizes codes reuse and simplify the UI development so that it increases the developing efficiency largely. Spring provides AOP that extracts the enterprise services from the whole application and implements declaration call with the help of Interceptors which reduces the amount of codes largely and make the business logic simple and clear. Hibernate encapsulates specific database operation which can avoid writing large amount of similar SQL (inquiry, delete, update and so on) and is time-saving and high-efficiency.

5.5   Workability

Agile Web development adopts existed mature technologies to carry on, so the Web applications it develops are function-complete, less-error and easy-operating. Besides, systems provide friendly UI even when wrong operation happens so that Web applications are of good workability.

5.6   Portability

As Hibernate lightly encapsulates JDBC, developers need not to concentrate on the type of database and the specific database operation of the whole application, but only need to configure the related parameters in spring configuration file which can implement the switch between different databases and conveniently finish the transplant of databases.

6   Conclusions

This thesis simply introduces the MVC design pattern and the three prevalent light Web developing frameworks and integrates them in certain ways according to the requirements of high-speed developing and quick response and researches and analyses the developing process and its quality model. The Web development based on SSH implements MVC which lowers the degree of coupling between layers in large extent. Therefore, UI programmers, business logic programmers and database maintainers can focus their energy on their own work, making the developing process stable, fast and effective which in some extent reach the standard of agile Web development. Meanwhile, agile Web development pays attention to the developing participants and emphasizes on both the two-way communication between inner developing team and clients as well as the developing team itself which can quickly form feedback information and is good for the whole project development .However, each developing framework (including SSH) has its defects, so the research on the developing methods, developing process and quality model of agile Web developing will be meaningful to the whole Web development field.

Acknowledgements. This research was supported by Jiangxi Provincial Natural Science Fund Program (Project No. 20114BAB201047).

References

[1] Pu, T.: Struts framework and the process of Web application development. J. Liaoning Economics and Management Institute Journal 3, 53–54 (2008)
[2] Wang, J.: Deep explore of J2EE framework. Dongnan University Press, Jiangsu (2009)
[3] Liu, N.: Java EE project cases based on Eclipse Spring Struts Hibernate. People' Posts and Telecom Press, Beijing (2008)

Study on Nonlinear Parametrically Excited Vibration in Automatic Gauge Control System of the Rolling Mill

Ruicheng Zhang[1], Weiran An[2], and Pingping Yang[1]

[1] College of Electrical Engineering, Hebei United University, Hebei Tangshan 063009, China
[2] School of Automation Science and Electrical Engineering, Beijing University of Aeronautics and Astronautics, Beijing 100081, China
rchzhang@yahoo.com.cn

Abstract. The non-linear equation of the of the rolling mill automatic gauge control(AGC) system is derived based on analyzing the friction between roll and workpiece, the flexibility and the roll eccentricity force. By means of a multiple-scales method, the existence and stability of periodic solutions in a first-order approximation close to the main parametric resonance are investigated, and the frequency-response equation is provided. Bifurcations of the system and regions of chaotic solutions are found. It follows from the maximal Lyapunov exponent and Poincare map that vibration of the rolling system appear more complex with larger excitation amplitude.

Keywords: rolling mill, automatic gauge control(AGC), nonlinear vibration, parametric excitation, chaos.

1   Introduction

The rolling mill vibration phenomena often occur in the rolling process, which not only adversely affect the rolling surface smoothness, rolling accuracy, but also cause the damage of the rolling equipment. Therefore many scholars from domestic to foreign researched the mechanism and features from different perspectives. For example, Reference [1] established the self-excited vibration model of the rolling mill main drive system. Reference [2] found that leveling machine vibration phenomena caused by gear drive of the uncoiler and coiler drive system. Reference [3] established the model of the hot strip mill vertical vibration system and analyzed the self-excited vibration. Reference [4-5] studied on the nonlinear parametrically excited vibration of the plate mill. Reference [6] discussed the chaotic movement of the AGC control system, proposed a new explanation for this irregular movement phenomenon. However, reference [6] point out the system is chaos only according to the timing diagram and phase plane. The nonlinear vibration mechanism is not analysed. So the non-linear equation of the of the rolling mill automatic gauge control(AGC) system is derived. By means of a multiple-scales method, the existence and stability of periodic solutions in a first-order approximation close to the main parametric resonance are investigated, and the frequency-response equation is provided. Bifurcations of the

J. Lei et al. (Eds.): NCIS 2012, CCIS 345, pp. 453–461, 2012.
© Springer-Verlag Berlin Heidelberg 2012

system and regions of chaotic solutions are found. It follows from the maximal Lyapunov exponent and Poincare map that vibration of the rolling system appear more complex with larger excitation amplitude.

2   The Nonlinear Parametrically Excited Vibration Model of the AGC System

In the strip rolling mill, the rolling thickness variation is x, as shown in Figure 1. In the rolling process, the restoring force caused by the rolling thickness variation is conformed the spring equation, but the material resilience does not meet the Hooke law, and it belong to the physical nonlinear. Analysis as follows: In general, the elastic potential energy is taken the following more general form (only analyze one-dimensional movement):

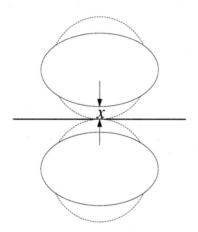

Fig. 1. Sketch map of eccentricity

$$U(x) = \frac{1}{2}kx^2 + \frac{1}{3}\lambda x^3 + \frac{1}{4}k_2 x^4 + \cdots$$

Where k, λ and k_2 are constant coefficients. So the resilience of the system is given as follow.

$$f = -\frac{dU}{dx} = -kx - \lambda x^2 - k_2 x^3 + \cdots$$

During rolling process, the elastic potential energy of roll system is symmetric, and the simple form is as follow:

$$U = \frac{1}{2}kx^2 + \frac{1}{4}k_2 x^4$$

Where, k_2 is usually a smaller coefficient compared with k. The resilience of this system is as follow:

$$f = -\frac{dU}{dx} = -kx - k_2 x^3$$

Within the arc of the roll and rolling contact, due to the combined effect of the friction coefficient and deformation resistance, the roll will be subject to the damping force and damping force is usually proportional to the velocity, $k_1 \dot{x}$ (k_1 is damping coefficient). In the rolling process, support roll suffer by cycle roll eccentricity force. For the deviation, rolling force can be expressed as [7]: (contains the fundamental and higher harmonic) $F = \sum_{i=1}^{\infty} F_i \cos(\omega_i t + \theta_i)$. Here considered the impact of fundamental,

According to Newton's second law, the motion differential equation of the support roll is given as (1):

$$\ddot{x} + \frac{k_1}{m_1}\dot{x} + \frac{k}{m_1}x + \frac{k_2}{m_1}x^3 - \frac{F}{m_1}\cos(\varpi t) = 0 \qquad (1)$$

Where: x is the eccentric displacement of supporting roller. k and k_2 are elastic deformation coefficient. k_1 is damping coefficient. F and ω are amplitude and angular frequency of the supporting roller eccentricity force, m_1 is the quality of the backup roll.

Introducing the non-dimensional time $\tau = \omega_0 t$, where $\omega_0 = \sqrt{k/m_1}$ and dependencies:

$$\varpi = \frac{\omega}{\omega_0}, \quad \mu = \frac{k_1 k}{2m_1 k_2}, \quad f = \frac{Fk}{m_1 k_2}, \quad \varepsilon = \frac{k_2}{k}$$

Dimensionless equation of motion can be written as

$$\ddot{x} + \omega_0^2 x + 2\varepsilon\mu\dot{x} + \varepsilon\omega_0^2 x^3 = \varepsilon f \cos(\varpi \tau) \qquad (2)$$

According to the non-linear vibration theory [8], the nonlinear vibration system may appear a variety of resonance phenomena, such as internal resonance, main parametric resonance, double resonance and so on. The following discussion is the situation $\varpi \approx \omega_0$, namely main parametric resonance.

3   Main Parametric Resonance Analysis of the AGC System

We anticipate a periodic solution of equation (2) using the multiple-scale-of –time method. For analytical calculations, ε is used as a small parameter. In the case of the main parametric resonance close to the first frequency of the free vibration, we can write

$$\varpi = \omega_0 + \varepsilon\sigma \qquad (3)$$

The original equation can be rewritten as

$$\ddot{x} + \omega_0^2 x = \varepsilon[-2\mu\dot{x} - \omega_0^2 x^3 + f \cos(\omega_0 + \varepsilon\sigma)\tau] \qquad (4)$$

Set solution as:

$$x = x_0(T_0, T_1) + x_1(T_0, T_1) \tag{5}$$

We define different time scales $T_n = \varepsilon^n t, n = 0, 1, 2, 3\cdots$, and think that these time scales are independent variables, so the nonlinear vibration $x(t, \varepsilon)$ is the function of each time, which can be written as:

$$x(t, \varepsilon) = \sum_{n=0}^{m} \varepsilon^n x_n(T_0, T_1, \cdots, T_m)$$

m is the highest order of the small parameter, which depend on the calculation precision. Time derivatives are expressed by the formulae:

$$\frac{d}{dt} = D_0 + \varepsilon D_1 + \cdots \varepsilon^m D_m = \sum_{n=0}^{m} \varepsilon^n D_n \tag{6}$$

$$\frac{d^2}{dt^2} = (D_0 + \varepsilon D_1 + \cdots + \varepsilon^m D_m)^2$$
$$= D_0^2 + 2\varepsilon D_0 D_1 + \varepsilon^2(D_1^2 + 2D_0 D_2) + \cdots \tag{7}$$

D_n is the partial differential operator symbol, which can be defined as:

$$D_n \xrightarrow{def} \frac{\partial}{\partial T_n} (n = 0, 1, \cdots, m)$$

Applying expressions (5) to equation (4), we obtain

$$D_0^2 x_0 + \omega_0^2 x_0 = 0 \tag{8}$$

$$D_0^2 x_1 + \omega_0^2 x_1 = -2D_0 D_1 x_0 - 2\mu D_0 x_0$$
$$- \omega_0^2 x_0^3 + f \cos(\omega_0 T_0 + \sigma T_1) \tag{9}$$

The solution of equation (8) may be presented in the form

$$x_0(T_0, T_1) = a(T_1)\cos[\omega_0 T_0 + \beta(T_1)]$$
$$= A(T_1)e^{j\omega_0 T_0} + cc \tag{10}$$

Where

$$A(T_1) = \frac{a(T_1)}{2}e^{j\beta(T_1)} \tag{11}$$

cc is the conjugate function of the former.

Substituting (10) into equation (9), we get

$$D_0^2 x_1 + \omega_0^2 x_1 = -[2j\omega_0(D_1 A + \mu A) + 3\omega_0^2 A^2 \bar{A}]e^{j\omega_0 T_0}$$
$$-\omega_0^2 A^3 e^{3j\omega_0 T_0} + \frac{f}{2}e^{j(\omega_0 T_0 + \sigma T_1)} + cc \tag{12}$$

The condition for the elimination of secular term leads to the relation:

$$2j\omega_0(D_1A+\mu A)+3\omega_0^2 A^2\overline{A}-\frac{f}{2}e^{j\sigma T_1}=0 \tag{13}$$

After substituting (11) into (13) and separating real and imaginary part, we find

$$\begin{cases} D_1 a = -\mu a + \dfrac{f}{2\omega_0}\sin(\sigma T_1 - \beta) \\[2mm] D_1\beta = \dfrac{3\omega_0}{8}a^2 - \dfrac{f}{2a\omega_0}\cos(\sigma T_1 - \beta) \end{cases} \tag{14}$$

This is the amplitude and phase of the first-order approximate solution, which should satisfy the differential equation of (10).we introduce

$$\varphi = \sigma T_1 - \beta \tag{15}$$

Transforming the equation (14) into the autonomous differential equations:

$$\begin{cases} D_1 a = -\mu a + \dfrac{f}{2\omega_0}\sin\varphi \\[2mm] D_1\varphi = \sigma - \dfrac{3\omega_0}{8}a^2 + \dfrac{f}{2a\omega_0}\cos\varphi \end{cases} \tag{16}$$

In order to determine the amplitude a_s and phase φ_s of stationary state solutions, make $D_1 a = 0, D_1\varphi = 0$,we can obtain that:

$$\begin{cases} \mu a_s = \dfrac{f}{2\omega_0}\sin\varphi_s \\[2mm] \sigma - \dfrac{3\omega_0}{8}a_s^2 = -\dfrac{f}{2a_s\omega_0}\cos\varphi_s \end{cases} \tag{17}$$

Using (3) and (17), we obtain an equation determining the amplitude of a periodic solution:

$$[\mu^2 + (\sigma - \frac{3\omega_0 a_s^2}{8})^2]a_s^2 = (\frac{f}{2\omega_0})^2 \tag{18}$$

Formula (18) is the equation of the amplitude-frequency curve.

The linearization of equation (16) at (α_s, φ_s) , we can get the autonomous differential equations of the disturbance Δa and $\Delta\varphi$:

$$\begin{cases} D_1\Delta a = -\mu\Delta a + \dfrac{f}{2\omega_0}\cos\varphi_s\Delta\varphi \\[2mm] D_1\Delta\varphi = -(\dfrac{3\omega_0 a_s}{4} + \dfrac{f}{2\omega_0 a_s^2}\cos\varphi_s)\Delta a \\[2mm] \qquad\quad - \dfrac{f}{2\omega_0 a_s}\sin\varphi_s\Delta\varphi \end{cases} \tag{19}$$

Canceling the φ_s in equation (17), we can get the characteristic equation:

$$
\det \begin{bmatrix} -\mu-\lambda & -a_s(\sigma-\dfrac{3\omega_0 a_s^2}{8}) \\ \dfrac{1}{a_s}(\sigma-\dfrac{9\omega_0 a_s^2}{8}) & -\mu-\lambda \end{bmatrix} = 0 \tag{20}
$$

Expanding the determinant, we obtain:

$$
\lambda^2 + 2\mu\lambda + \mu^2 + (\sigma-\frac{9\omega_0 a_s^2}{8})(\sigma-\frac{3\omega_0 a_s^2}{8}) = 0 \tag{21}
$$

When the damping $\mu > 0$, we can get the instability conditions of steady state solutions by the stability analysis:

$$
\mu^2 + (\sigma-\frac{9\omega_0 a_s^2}{8})(\sigma-\frac{3\omega_0 a_s^2}{8}) < 0 \tag{22}
$$

Instability conditions corresponds to a solution of the amplitude frequency response curve.

4   Numerical Simulation

In this system, the changes of parameters will have a direct impact and restricting to the vibration characteristics of the system. In a number of parameters, the angular frequency of the system is one of the important parameters. With the changing of angular frequency, we can observe that the system has different vibration characteristics.

Figure 2 shows that the phase plane diagram under the different value ϖ of the system (2), when ω_0=0.02, ε=0.02, μ=0.01, f=0.03[1]. The points of the phase plane diagram look like no rules, wandering, and never repeat the road they have traveled. Although phase trajectory is disorganized, it seems that they have internal law. We can not distinguish a periodic motion and non-periodic motion according to the phase trajectory. In this case, Poincare invented simpler description method. The name is called the Poincare section method. This method can be more easily determine whether the periodic motion or not, and we can judge the system appear chaos when there is the strange attractor.

Figure 3 shows the Poincare section diagram in the different values of ϖ of the system (2). According to the method of Poincare section [9]: when the Poincare section only have fixed point or a small number of discrete points, the motion of the system is periodic; when the Poincare section is a closed curve, the motion of the system is almost periodic; when Poincare section are a set of points, the vibration of the system is chaotic. Figure 3 shows the Poincare section diagram are stable image in the system, so we can get that the Figure 3 (a) is periodic, Figure 3 (b) is chaos.

In figure 4(a), we present the numerical results as a bifurcation diagram for the analysed system. Here we can see one regions of the discussed main parametric resonances for $\varpi \in [0.01, 0.05]$. However, we can not determine whether the system is chaotic vibration according to the bifurcation diagram. So we have calculated the maximal Lyapunov exponent in the region of excitation frequency $\varpi \in [0.01, 20]$.

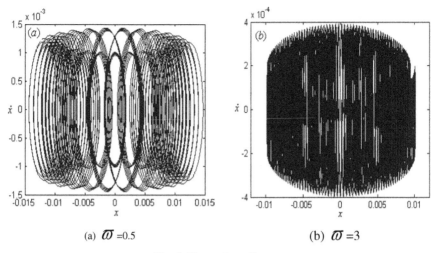

Fig. 2. Phase plane diagram

The exponent has been plotted in Figure 4(b). It can be seen from Figure 4 (b) the system (2) is chaotic motion when ϖ more than 0.0005 and less than 0.050624; the system (2) is periodic motion when ϖ more than 0.40149 and less than 0.55186, the system (2) is also chaotic motion when ϖ greater than 0.60199. The largest Lyapunov exponent is positive, in this region, the system occurred chaotic motion.

Thus, with the changing of ϖ, the movement forms of the AGC system gradually transform from the chaotic state to the periodic state, then get into the chaotic state, and then get to periodic motion, finally will get to the chaotic state. Therefore, the vibration system has a variety of nonlinear vibrations forms.

In actual production for the AGC system, when other parameters is fixed, we can adjust the roller eccentricity angular frequency, so that the movement forms of the AGC system are periodic motion, and avoid the system to produce chaotic motion, improve the control accuracy of the AGC system.

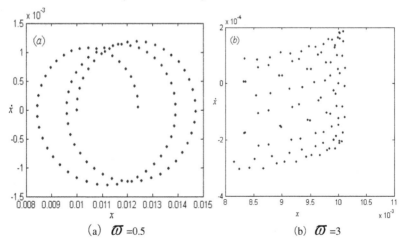

Fig. 3. Poincare section of the system

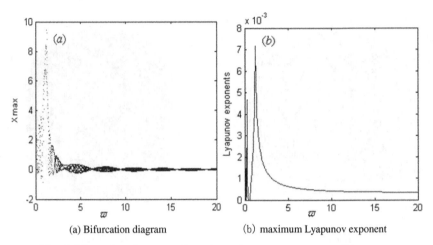

(a) Bifurcation diagram   (b) maximum Lyapunov exponent

Fig. 4. Bifurcation diagram and maximum Lyapunov exponent of the system

5   Conclusion

Aim at the AGC system may produce chaotic, especially under the influence of the roll eccentric angular frequency, some investigations have been developed. The results show that the roll eccentric angular frequency is an important parameter to affect the vibration characteristics of the system. We found that AGC system have a variety of nonlinear vibration forms, including periodic vibration and chaotic vibration. When the chaotic phenomena occur in the AGC system, we must give enough attention. When the system can not be run on periodic state using the traditional control methods, we can try to change the eccentricity angular frequency through adjusting the product speed. So we can improve the rolling accuracy through controlling chaos.With the improving of rolling requirements of the AGC system, the safety and reliability requirements are getting higher and higher. Research results have important significance to improve reliability and accuracy of the AGC system, which has a broad application prospects.

Acknowledgments. This work was supported by the Natural Science Foundation of Hebei Province (grant number: F2010000972).

References

1. Tao, Y., Wu, X.: plate mill self-excited vibration model. Mechanical design and Research 24(3), 116–120 (2008)
2. Bollinger, L.A.: Winding reel involvement in temper mill chatter. Iron and Steel Engineer 11, 27–29 (1994)
3. Zhang, H., Xiong, S.B., et al.: The hot strip mill modeling and simulation of the vertical vibration. China Mechanical Engineering 17(23), 2434–2438 (2006)

4. Jin, M., lan, L.F.: Hot strip mill self-excited vibration diagnosis and Vibration Analysis. Vibration, Testing and Diagnosis 26(4), 261–264 (2006)
5. Qi, M., Song, X.R., et al.: Plate rolling mill nonlinear parametrically excited vibration. Chongqing University Learned Journal 31(4), 393–396 (2008)
6. Zhang, L., Pengkai, X., Nan, T.C.: Hot rolling thickness control system in the chaotic phenomenon. Control Engineering 10(2), 173–175 (2003)
7. Liu, J., Sun, Y.K.: Hot strip rolling computer control. Machinery Industry Press (1997)
8. Chen, Y.S.: Nonlinear vibration. Higher Education Press, Beijing (2002)
9. Chen, Y.S.: Bifurcation and Chaos Theory of Nonlinear Vibration Systems. Higher Education Press, Beijing (1993)

Study on Self-excited Vibration
for Displacement Delayed Feedback System
in the Rolling Mill Main Drive System

Ruicheng Zhang, Pingping Yang, and Peipei Wang

College of Electrical Engineering, Hebei United University, Hebei Tangshan 063009, China
rchzhang@yahoo.com.cn

Abstract. The self-excited vibration model of the displacement delayed feedback system in the rolling mill main drive system is derived based on the friction torque caused by tension. The critical state between stability and instability is analyzed. Namely it is possibility that the system appear equal amplitude vibration. It can be seen that the displacement delayed feedback is equivalent to feedback of displacement and speed simultaneously, and it can changes the damping and stiffness at the same time. The stability of the displacement delayed feedback system in the rolling mill main drive is analyzed. A theoretical analysis of variable speed on vibration control was developed, and a simulator provided. The simulation results showed that variable speed was effective to suppress the self-excited vibration of the displacement delayed feedback system.

Keywords: rolling mill, main drive system, displacement delayed, self-excited vibration, suppress.

1   Introduction

The steel industry is an important pillar industry of China's national economy with the development of iron and steel industry, the number and stand-alone capacity of various types of the rolling mills and drag motor is increasing, which makes large rolling mill that is China's major steel equipment exist a variety of problems and safety hazards. The vibration of the rolling mill is the main problem, which is prevalent and looking forward to solve in the world of rolling mill production. There are a variety of vibrations [1], summed into two categories: one is the torsional vibration of the rolling mill main drive system; the other is the vertical vibration of the rolling mill.

The domestic and foreign scholars made many studies to solve the vibration problem in the rolling mill main drive system. Reference [2] and [3] established the vertical vibration model of the rolling mill main drive system and analyzed the self-excited vibration, reference [4] studied on third-octave-mode chatter on four-h cold rolling mills, reference [5] analyzed the self-excited vibration of the rolling mill main drive system. The impact of the nonlinear damping caused by the friction was considered as a major

J. Lei et al. (Eds.): NCIS 2012, CCIS 345, pp. 462–470, 2012.
© Springer-Verlag Berlin Heidelberg 2012

factor for the study on the self-excited vibration in the rolling mill main drive system in the before, but the practice showed that resistance moment caused by tension difference between the front and rear rolling mill rack, which caused displacement delayed feedback and the self-excited vibration in the rolling mill main drive system. So the self-excited vibration model of the displacement delayed feedback system in the rolling mill main drive system is derived, the stability of the self-excited vibration system is analyzed, it gives measures to avoid the self-excited vibration .The research results provide reference for vibration forecast ,vibration control and condition monitoring ,failure diagnosis of the steel production process.

2   The Model of the Displacement Delayed Feedback System in the Rolling Mill Main Drive

The rolling mill produce the self-excited vibration in the in production process. If connecting shaft of the rolling mill is uniform rotation, it simplifies the rolling mill main drive system as a concentrated mass of the mass-spring system [6] to further study the Self-excited vibration of the rolling mill drive system. Figure 1 is a mechanical model of the displacement delayed feedback system in the rolling mill main drive. In figure 1, k_1 is stiffness coefficient, c is damping coefficient, $T_{friction}$ is torque from friction changes, T_z is resistance moment caused by tension difference. θ is motional coordinate system, taking torque balance on the roll into consideration, it will have motional differential equation of roll:

$$J\ddot{\theta} + c\dot{\theta} + k_1\theta = -T_{fiction} - T_Z \tag{1}$$

In the formula (1), J is rotational inertia of the concentrated mass.

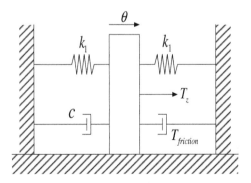

Fig. 1. The model of displacement delayed feedback system in the rolling mill main drive system

$T_{fiction}$ is described as formula (2):

$$T_{friction} = \mu P r_a \tag{2}$$

In the formula (2), μ is friction coefficient, P is rolling force.

Suppose friction factor μ between the roller and rolling fully obey the law of Coulomb drag, and friction factor has nothing to do with the relative velocity, $T_{fiction}$ is constant. The velocity feedback caused by stick-slip friction between the roller and rolling will not be discussed. The following only considers the situation of $T_{fiction}$ is constant.

Suppose rewinding roll has the same parameters, winding roll's response to the working roll has time delay τ when the vibration occurs, simultaneously, suppose $S_h = 0$.

According to the tension equation [7]:

$$\frac{dq_f}{dt} = \frac{E}{L}(v_f - v_2) = \frac{Er_a}{L}[\dot{\theta}(t-\tau) - \dot{\theta}(t)] \tag{3}$$

$$q_f = \frac{Er_a}{L}[\theta(t-\tau) - \theta(t)] + D_1 \tag{4}$$

$$\frac{dq_b}{dt} = \frac{E}{L}(v_1 - v_b) = \frac{Er_a(1-R)}{L}[\dot{\theta}(t) - \dot{\theta}(t-\tau)] \tag{5}$$

$$q_b = \frac{Er_a(1-R)}{L}[\theta(t) - \theta(t-\tau)] + D_2 \tag{6}$$

In the above formula, q_f, q_b are import and export tension; E is modulus of elasticity; L is spacing between two racks ; v_f, v_b are reel rate of rewinding roll; v_1, v_2 are import and export belt speed; t is time; D_1, D_2 are integration constants; R is reduction rate, $R = (y_1 - y_2)/y_1$, y_1, y_2 are entry and exit thickness of rolling.

The tension difference T_z caused by the resistance torque is described as formula (7):

$$T_z = (T_b v_1 - T_f v_2)/\dot{\theta} = T_b r_a \frac{y_2}{y_1} - T_f r_a = y_2 r_a B(q_b - q_f)$$
$$= \frac{(2-R)Er_a^2 y_2 B}{L}[\theta(t) - \theta(t-\tau)] + D_3 \tag{7}$$

In the formula (7), T_f, T_b are total import and export tension, B is rolling width, D_3 is integration constant.

$$t = 0, \ T_z = (T_b - T_f)r_a, t = 0, \ \theta(0) = \theta(-\tau)$$

Get initial conditions into the formula (7), it will have

$$T_z = \frac{(2-R)Er_a^2 y_2 B}{L}[\theta(t) - \theta(t-\tau)] + (T_b - T_f)r_a \tag{8}$$

Get the formula (2) and (8) into the formula (1),it will obtain motional differential equation of roll:

$$J\ddot{\theta} + c\dot{\theta} + k_1\theta = -T_{friction} - T_z$$
$$= -\mu \operatorname{Pr}_a - \frac{(2-R)Er_a^2 y_2 B}{L}[\theta(t) - \theta(t-\tau)] - (T_b - T_f)r_a \tag{9}$$

Omitting the impact of constant, it will have

$$J\ddot{\theta} + c\dot{\theta} + k_1\theta = -(2-R)Er_a^2 y_2 B[\theta(t) - \theta(t-\tau)]/L \tag{10}$$

$$\text{Suppose} \quad p = (2-R)Er_a^2 y_2 B/L \,, k = k_1 + p \tag{11}$$

Formula (10) can be changed into

$$J\ddot{\theta} + c\dot{\theta} + k\theta = p\theta(t-\tau) \tag{12}$$

Formula (12) is differential equations of displacement delayed feedback system in the rolling mill main drive system, or "time delay system".

3   Stability Analysis of the Displacement Delayed Feedback System

3.1   Stability Analysis

In the following, the critical state between stability and instability is analyzed, namely it is possibility of producing equal amplitude vibration.
Suppose

$$\theta(t) = a_0 \cos \omega t \tag{13}$$

Formula (13) can be changed into:

$$\dot{\theta}(t) = -a_0 \omega \sin \omega t$$

$$\begin{aligned}
\theta(t\text{-}\tau) &= a_0 \cos \omega(t\text{-}\tau) = a_0 \cos(\omega t\text{-}\varphi) \\
&= \cos\varphi(a_0 \cos \omega t) - \frac{1}{\omega}\sin\varphi(-\omega a_0 \sin \omega t)
\end{aligned} \tag{14}$$

In the above formula, ω is self-excited vibration frequency; $\varphi = \omega t$ is phase lag caused by the time delay; $\tau = L/v$, v is movement velocity of the rolling.
Formula (13) is substituted into the formula (14) and is marked:

$$k' = -p\cos\varphi \tag{15}$$

$$c' = (p\sin\varphi)/\omega \tag{16}$$

It will have:

$$p\theta(t\text{-}\tau) = -k'\theta(t) - c'\dot{\theta}(t) \tag{17}$$

Formula (17) is substituted into the formula (12) and it will have by transposition:

$$J\ddot{\theta} + (c+c')\dot{\theta} + (k+k')\theta = 0 \tag{18}$$

Formula (18) shows the damping of the system consists of two parts: one is the inherent damping of the vibration system with its damping coefficient is positive, known as " positive damping"; the other part is equivalent damping caused by the displacement delay feedback, formula (16) shows the damping coefficient c' can be positive or negative according to φ angle, while $180° < \varphi < 360°$, $\sin\varphi < 0$,so the equivalent damping coefficient is negative.

If the total damping coefficient (c + c ') is positive, then the vibrating system is stable. If the coefficient is large enough, it will enable (c + c ') <0, the total damping become negative, the system will be self-excited vibration because the instability occurs. Negative damping is actually a kind of "help", which not only dose not impede the vibration of the system, but also expand the vibration. Stiffness Coefficient of the system consists of two parts: the first part k is the stiffness of the vibrating body, generally which is positive; the second part is equivalent stiffness generated by the displacement feedback, which can be positive or negative. Equivalent stiffness can only be a slight increase or decrease of the total stiffness of the system, which is not essential influence on the characteristics of the system.

This shows the displacement delayed feedback is equivalent to the displacement and velocity feedback at the same time, which also changes the damping and stiffness of the system. Formula (15) and (16) were given equivalent stiffness coefficient and equivalent damping coefficient caused by the time delay feedback, it can get negative stiffness or negative damping according to the time delay τ , which caused static or dynamic instability.

3.2   The Impact of the Parameters on the System Stability

The influence of rolling parameters on the stability of rolling mill main drive system is analyzed. The equal amplitude vibration is studied simultaneously, which is critical state between stability and instability. In the formula (18) the total damping coefficient (c + c ') is as follows:

$$c + c' = c + p\sin\varphi / \omega = 0 \qquad (19)$$

Therefore it can be obtained critical parameter p_{cr} of the rolling system is the formula (20):

$$p_{cr} = -c\omega / \left[\sin(\omega L) / v\right] \qquad (20)$$

While $p > p_{cr}$, the total damping of the system is negative, self-excited vibration will occur. p_{cr} is also known as the "stability threshold".

Formula (18) can be changed into formula (21) on the condition that total damping is negative,

$$J\ddot{\theta} + (k + k')\theta = 0 \qquad (21)$$

The system can be changed into an equation of motion of free vibration without damping, its natural frequency ω is:

$$\omega = \sqrt{(k + k') / J} \qquad (22)$$

It can be also drawn as follows:

$$\omega^2 = \omega_n^2 + k'/J$$

In the above formula, ω is self-excited vibration frequency of the system; ω_n is natural frequency of the rolling mill itself.

It will have the stability equations of the system from formula (19) and formula (22):

$$c + p\sin(\omega L/v)/\omega = 0 \tag{23}$$

$$\omega^2 = \left[k_1 + p - p\cos(\omega L/v)\right]/J \tag{24}$$

4   Numerical Simulation

When the rolling mill structure and the dynamic characteristics of the rolling process is given, it can be obtained stability diagrams by the stability equations. The parameters of cold rolling mill with a 2030-type system are as follows:

$$J = 1542 kg \cdot m^2 , k_1 = 5.93 \times 10^6 N \cdot m / rad , \quad c = 50500 N \cdot m \cdot s / rad , L = 2m$$

The stability diagrams of the displacement delayed feedback system can be obtained by numerical simulation, which are shown in Figure 2. Figure 2(a) shows that in stability threshold (while $p = p_{cr}$), the relationship of the self-excited vibration frequency ω and the rolling velocity appears serrated. In figure 2(b), it is unstable region above the curve, it is stable region below the curve, simultaneously while $\sin(\omega L/v) = -1$ in the formula (20), it will have the minimum critical parameter of the rolling system $p_{cr,\min} = c\omega$, which is the rolling system parameter of the unconditional stable region, namely while $p < p_{cr,\min}$, the system are stable in any motional velocity of the rolling.

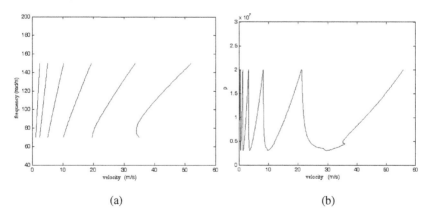

(a)   (b)

Fig. 2. The stability diagrams

5   Vibration Suppression

When damping coefficient of a vibration system is large enough, no matter how motivated it is, the vibration system will never be able to fully vibration. However, it is unrealistic that damping force is directly applied to the middle of the work roll and backup roll. To eliminate vibration, reference [8] provided a vibration-proof variable speed method for eliminating the fifth-octave vibration chatter in the rolling mill. So it is derived variable-speed method for the self-excited vibration of the displacement delayed feedback system in the rolling mill main drive system. Suppose damping coefficient is ignored in the formula (18), so the self-excited vibration frequency of the vibration system is:

$$\omega = \sqrt{\{k_1 + p[1 - \cos(\omega L / v)]\} / J} \tag{25}$$

It can be seen the vibration frequency of the mill can be changed by rolling motional velocity from equation (25). Therefore, torque of applying on the roll can be seen as an exciting force which is constant amplitude and frequency conversion at different speeds, so formula (12) can be simplified as:

$$J\ddot{\theta} + c\dot{\theta} + k\theta = T_0 \sin \omega_v t \tag{26}$$

In the formula (26), T_0 is the amplitude of the roll torque change; ω_v is angular frequency of frequency conversion, and $\omega_v = \omega_0 + \beta t$, β is frequency conversion velocity, ω_0 is initial angular frequency.

Formula (26) is made the Fourier transform, it will have:

$$Y(\omega) = |Y(\omega)| e^{i\phi(\omega)} \tag{27}$$

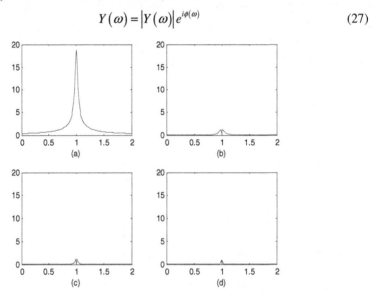

Fig. 3. The simulation results figure(vertical coordinates are $Y(\infty)\dfrac{k_1}{\pi T_0}$,abscissas are λ)

In the formula (27):

$$|Y(\omega)| = \frac{\dfrac{T_0}{k_1}\sqrt{\dfrac{\pi}{2\beta}}\left|\cos\left[\dfrac{\omega_0^2+(k_1/J)\lambda^2}{4\beta}+\dfrac{\pi}{4}\right]\right|}{\sqrt{(1-\lambda^2)^2+(2\xi\lambda)^2}}, \phi(\omega)=\frac{\omega_0\sqrt{k_1/J}\,\lambda}{2\beta}-\arctan\frac{2\xi\lambda}{1-\lambda^2}$$

$$\xi = c/c_c, c_c = 2\sqrt{Jk_1}, \lambda = \omega/\omega_n$$

In order to describe the effect of eliminating the flutter by variable-speed rolling, according to equation (27) a simulation is established to calculate the frequency response curve (Figure 3) for different β in the rolling mill main drive vibration system. The simulation parameters are $\xi = 0.02$, $\omega_n = 600\times2\pi(rad/s)$, $\omega_0 = 550\times2\pi(rad/s)$, $\beta = (0,1,5,10)\times2\pi\,(rad/s)$.

Simulation results showed the vibration response of frequency conversion excitation $\beta = 1\times2\pi$ in figure 3(b), $\beta = 5\times2\pi$ in figure 3(c) and $\beta = 10\times2\pi$ in figure 3(d) was significantly reduced, compared to the vibration response of the steady-state excitation with constant frequency in figure 3(a) $\beta = 0$. So variable speed can effectively reduce the vibration amplitude, which greatly slow down the development of vibration and effectively prevent flutter.

6   Conclusion

(1) The self-excited vibration model of the displacement delayed feedback system in the rolling mill main drive system is derived. The critical state between stability and instability is analyzed. Namely it is possibility that the system produce equal amplitude vibration. It can be seen that the displacement delayed feedback is equivalent to feedback of displacement and speed simultaneously, and it can changes the damping and stiffness at the same time.

(2) The rolling parameters of the unconditional stable region is derived by analyzing the influence of rolling parameters on the stability of the displacement delayed feedback system in the rolling mill main drive, namely while $p < P_{cr,min}$, the system are stable in any motional velocity of the rolling.

(3) The variable speed method can effectively reduce the vibration amplitude, which greatly slow down the development of vibration and effectively prevent flutter.

Acknowledgments. This work was supported by the Natural Science Foundation of Hebei Province (grant number: F2010000972).

References

1. Fang, W., Hong, D.: The Current Situation and Prospect of vertical vibration in the rolling mill. Steel Rolling 25(3), 45–47 (2008)
2. Chen, Y., Shi, T., Yang, S.: Study on Parametrically Excited Nonlinear Vibrations on 4-H Cold Rolling Mills. Chinese Journal of Mechanical Engineering 39(4), 56–60 (2003)
3. Zhang, H., Xiong, S., Wu, B.: Modeling and Simulation of vertical vibration of the hot strip mill. China Mechanical Engineering 17(23), 2434–2438 (2006)
4. Cheng, Y., Liu, S., Liao, G.: Study on third-octave chatter mechanismin on 4-H Cold Rolling Mills. Chinese Journal of Mechanical Engineering 39(6), 118–123 (2003)
5. Yang, Y., Wu, X.: Study on self-excited vibration model of Plate mill. Machine Design and Research 24(3), 116–120 (2008)
6. Li, H., Yang, W., Wen, B.: The Analysis of Self-excited Vibration in Mechanical System with Moving Boundary. Vibration and Shock 18(3), 1–4 (1999)
7. Ma, W., Xu, G., Yang, Y.: The deduce and research on tension formula in cold continuous rolling. Iron and Steel Research (3), 28–31 (2003)
8. Chen, Y., Li, W., Shi, T.: Study on fifth-octave regenerative chatter vibration mechanismin on 4-H Cold Rolling Mills. Journal of Science and Technology of Hua zhong University: Natural Science 31(5), 55–57 (2003)

Detection of Abnormal Nodes
in Clustered Control Systems Based
on Multiagent Group Prominence Analyses[*]

Yungui Zhang[1,2], Jiuchuan Jiang[3,**], Jingsheng Lei[4], and Wenyin Liu[3]

[1] School of Electrical Engineering and Automation, Harbin Institute of Technology,
Harbin, 150080, China
[2] Hybrid Process Industry Automation System and Equipment Technology State Key Lab,
Automation Research and Design Institute of Metallurgical Industry, Beijing, 100071, China
[3] Department of Computer Science, City University of Hong Kong, Hong Kong, China
[4] School of Computer and Information Engineering, Shanghai University of Electric Power,
Shanghai 200090, China
yunguizhang@263.net, jiangjiuchuan@163.com, jshlei@126.com,
csliuwy@cityu.edu.hk

Abstract. In now networked control systems, some nodes may be invaded and become abnormal which may tamper with the execution of tasks; especially, in clustered networked control systems, the nodes are hierarchical and hybrid, thus the detection of abnormal nodes is difficult. To deal with such problem, this paper uses the multiagent method to model and analyze the clustered control systems, where the cluster stations and control units are modeled as the coalition systems of hybrid agents. Based on the multiagent model, then the paper presents the concept of group prominence to measure the strategy characteristics of cluster stations and control units; finally, a model for detecting abnormal nodes based on multiagent group prominence analyses is presented, which can effectively improve the consistency of the system.

Keywords: Clustered Control Systems, Multiagent Modeling, Abnormal Nodes, Networked Control Systems, Group Prominence Analyses.

1 Introduction

The previous works on the control systems can be categorized into centralized and distributed approaches according to the control architectures [1]. Generally, the centralized control systems have poor reliability and scalability, thus which cannot be fitted for the current complex and dynamic control environments [2]. To overcome the drawbacks of centralized control systems, distributed approaches were presented in which there are no centralized controllers to control the whole system [3].

Nowadays, with the application of network technology into control systems, networked control systems were investigated in many related works [3][4]. The

---

[*] This work was supported by the National Natural Science Foundation of China (No. 61073189).
[**] Corresponding author.

J. Lei et al. (Eds.): NCIS 2012, CCIS 345, pp. 471–484, 2012.
© Springer-Verlag Berlin Heidelberg 2012

networked control system is a class of distributed control system which is implemented based on the network infrastructure; in networked control systems, there are many autonomous control or computing units which can be organized and communicated by the network structures. For the goodness of scalability and adaptability [5], networked control systems are frequently used in many industry and control areas.

To deal with the large scale situation of network control systems, group based hierarchical architecture is often used [6][17]; and, one special type of group based hierarchical architecture, clustering, is popular in real networked control systems. Clustering is particularly useful for applications that require scalability to thousands of nodes [7]; moreover, clustering can also reduce the complexity of system organization and the costs of communication. In clustered control systems, some control units with similar characteristics or monitoring objects are organized together to a cluster; in each cluster, there is a cluster station which takes charge of the actions of all control units within such cluster; the control units in the same cluster communicate with each other through the cluster station; the control units of different clusters communicate through the relay of their cluster stations. Therefore, in clustered control systems, there are two kinds of nodes: control units and cluster stations; the control units take charge of the tasks of monitoring and controlling the objects, and the cluster stations take charge of the management and communication of clusters.

Due to the openness of network, most networked control systems are vulnerable to network attacks nowadays [4]. With the attacks, some nodes in the control systems may be manipulated by intruders, which can be called abnormal nodes. The abnormal nodes may take some malicious actions, thus the systems cannot execute the control tasks well. Moreover, in real systems, there may be also some nodes which are in faulty, so those faulty nodes may be also abnormal and cannot execute the tasks correctly.

Therefore, detecting abnormal nodes is crucial for the security of networked control systems. Abnormal nodes detection is similar to the outlier detection; outlier detection has been used for centuries to detect and, where appropriate, remove anomalous observations from systems [8]. To detect the abnormal nodes, some classifier approaches are used in previous intrusion detection works, e.g., k-nearest neighbor classifier [9]. In summary, previous works on abnormality detection is often implemented by comparing each individual's strategy with the normalized strategy.

However, in clustered control systems, the hierarchical architectures are used and the behaviors of hybrid nodes are variable. Therefore, **how to find the abnormal nodes from those with hierarchical organization and hybrid actions is difficult**. To deal with such problem, this paper introduces the group prominence analysis method to analyze the abnormality of clusters. Considering the situation where there are many autonomous components in cluster stations and control units [10][11], this paper uses the multiagent method to model the cluster stations and control units; based on the multiagent modeling, then this paper uses the group analysis method on multiagent coalition system to detect the abnormal nodes in clustered control systems.

To the best of our knowledge, no studies have been conducted that address this problem using multiagent group prominence analyses. Therefore, the main contribution of this paper is that this paper uses the multiagent based group analysis method to detecting the abnormal nodes, which is more fitted for the clustering architecture of clustered control systems. The rest of this paper is organized as follows. In Section 2, we compare our work with the related work on the subject; in Section 3, we present the multiagent model for clustered control systems; in Section 4, we present the detection model of abnormal nodes in clustered control systems; finally, we discuss and conclude our paper in Section 5.

2   Related Work

Our research is related to modeling clustered networked control systems, security in networked control systems, behavior analyses in distributed systems. Generally, the related work can be categorized as follows.

2.1   Modeling Clustered Networked Control Systems

Nowadays, with the application of network technology into control systems, networked control systems were investigated in many related areas [3][4]. Networked control system is a class of distributed control system which is implemented based on the network infrastructure. For the goodness of scalability and adaptability [5], networked control systems are frequently used in reality. The clustered control system is a type of networked control systems, which is used to deal with the large scale situation and to reduce communication costs. Clustering architecture is often seen in sensor control network systems; for example, Younis et al. presents a hybrid energy efficient clustering model for sensor control networks, which increases system scalability and lifetime [7].

By comparing with the previous works on modeling clustered networked control systems, this paper uses hybrid multiagent coalition method to model the clustered control systems. In our model, the cluster stations and control units are respectively modeled by hybrid multiagent coalition sub-systems. With such modeling method, the hierarchy and heterogeneity of nodes in clustered control systems can be addressed well.

2.2   Security in Networked Control Systems

From the initialization research of networked control systems, safety is concerned in hazardous environments [4]. In the networked control systems, some nodes may be invaded due to the openness of networks; therefore, the security in networked control systems has been a very concerned subject in related areas. Creey and Byres analysed the security vulnerability of today's networked control networks [12]; Tsang and Kwong present a multi-agent IDS architecture that is designed for decentralized intrusion detection and prevention control in large switched networks [13]. Moreover, in fact many technologies in common internet intrusion detection systems can be also used in networked control systems; for example, Hegazy et al. describes a framework for intrusion detection using agent-based technology [14], which can also be used in networked control systems.

By comparing with the previous works on security in networked control systems, this paper concerns the abnormal nodes detection in clustered control systems with hybrid nodes. In the presented model, a multiagent group prominence analysis method is used which can be fitted for the hierarchy and clustering of nodes in clustered control systems.

2.3   Behavior Analyses in Multiagent Systems

Behavior analyses are often investigated in multiagent systems, through which we can justify the behavior model of agents. For example, Jiang and Xia presented a prominence convergence model [15] and a clustering communication model [16] for the situated multi-agent systems; Jiang and Hu presented a networked decision method to model the agents' behaviors in network structures [17]. Cao et al. presented an approach to extract and model system members and design a real-life OCAS system called financial trading rule automated development and evaluation [18]. Ohtsuki et al. presented a simple rule to model the evolution cooperation of multiagents in social networks [19]. In summary, in previous related works on behavior analyses of multiagent systems, they mainly consider the coordination among agents.

By comparing with the previous works, this paper uses the integrated strategies of varying agents within cluster stations and control units to model the behaviors of hybird nodes in clustered control systems. Our model can address the hybrid behaviors of nodes better than the previous works can.

3   Multiagent Modeling of Clustered Control Systems

3.1   On the Clustered Control Systems

Effective topology management in networked distributed control systems can increase the system scalability and lifetime, among which clustering is an effective topology control approach [7]. Clustering is particularly useful for applications that require scalability to large scale of control nodes. In clustered control systems, certain cluster stations are set in the networks and each cluster station takes charge of the control of some control units, which is similar to the structure of distributed blackboard architecture in multiagent systems [20].

Now we can describe the architecture of clustered control systems as follows: there are certain cluster stations and control units in the network; each cluster station manages some control units and takes charges of the task execution of those control units; control units do not communicate directly with each other but through their cluster stations; cluster stations can communicate with each other; control units monitor the objects and execute the control tasks. Fig.1 is an example of clustered control system, where there are six cluster stations and many control units (CUs). From Fig.1, we can see that each cluster station takes charge of some control units. Therefore, with the clustering, each control unit only needs to communicate with the cluster station, and each cluster station only needs to know its affiliated control units and other neighbor cluster stations in the network; therefore, such architecture is scalable to large scale of nodes.

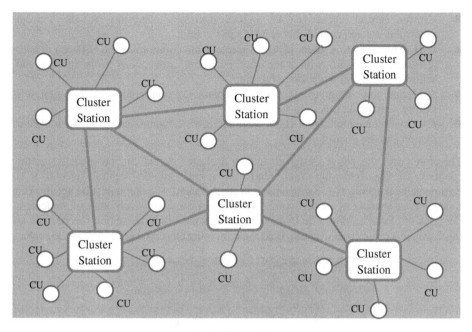

Fig. 1. Architecture of clustered control systems: this example includes six clusters; each cluster includes one cluster station and some control units; each cluster station takes charge the control of such cluster and communicates with other clusters

In real clustered control systems, the cluster stations and control units have some autonomous function components; therefore, now we can use the multiagent method to model the cluster stations and control units, shown as the following sections.

3.2 Multiagent Modeling for Cluster Stations

A cluster station and its affiliated control units can be regarded as a sub-system in the networked control system. A cluster station should manage the behaviors of the control units within its sub-system, and communicate with other clusters; moreover, people can directly communicate with and control the cluster stations. Therefore, we can design that the cluster station has the following functions:

- The cluster station can make decisions according to the current environments;
- The people can control and communicate with the cluster station;
- The cluster station can communicate with other cluster stations for coordination;
- The cluster station can communicate with the control units within the sub-systems and endow instructions.

An agent in the distributed system can be seen as a software component that can implement some tasks [11]. To implement the above functions, now we design that the cluster station contains the following software agents:

- Cluster central agent (CCA): makes decisions according to the current environments and controls the whole sub-system;
- C-H communication agent (CA_{C-H}): implements communication between cluster station and human, which includes receiving instructions from human and reporting status information to human;
- C-C communication agent (CA_{C-C}): implements communication between this cluster station and other cluster stations;
- C-U communication agent (CA_{C-U}): implements communication between cluster station and the control units.

Therefore, with the above designed agents, a cluster station can be modeled as the coalition of the following four kinds of agents: cluster central agents, C-H communication agents, C-C communication agents, and C-U communication agents. The four kinds of agents can act autonomously and cooperate with each other to implement the tasks of cluster station. The multiagent architecture of cluster station can be seen as Fig.2, where a centralized structure is adopted by using cluster central agent as the center.

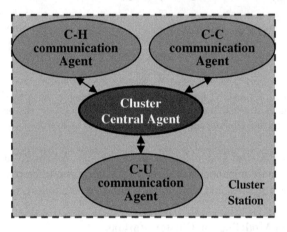

Fig. 2. The multiagent model of cluster station: this model includes four types of agents, which are CCA, CA_{C-H}, CA_{C-C}, and CA_{C-U}

3.3   Multiagent Modeling for Control Units

In clustered control systems, the control units are those who really execute the control tasks and control the objects. The control units should monitor the objects (such as production lines in plant control systems, sensing areas in sensor control systems, etc.) and control the behaviors of objects; moreover, the control units should communicate with the cluster station for receiving instructions or reporting status information. Therefore, we can design that each control unit has the following functions:

- The control unit can make decisions and execute control tasks according to the current environments and the instructions from cluster station.
- The control unit can communicate with the cluster station for reporting status information and receiving instructions.
- The control unit can monitor the objects.
- The control unit can execute the control operations on the objects.

To implement the above functions, we design that the control unit can contain the following software agents:

- Unit central agent (*UCA*): makes decisions according to the current environments and the instructions from cluster station, and manages other agents within the control unit;
- U-C communication agent (*CA_{U-C}*): implements communication between the control unit and the cluster station (which is factually conducted by the interaction between the U-C communication agent in control unit and C-U communication agent in cluster station);
- Monitor agent (*MA*): uses certain monitoring or sensing functions to monitor the objects;
- Execution agent (*EA*): implements the control operations on the objects, e.g., adjusting the velocity and direction of objects in a motion control system.

Therefore, with the above designed agents, a control unit can be modeled as the coalition of the following four kinds of agents: unit central agents, U-C communication agents, monitor agents, and execution agents. The four kinds of agents can act autonomously and cooperate with each other to implement the control tasks. The multiagent architecture of control unit can be seen as Fig.3, where a centralized structure is adopted by using unit central agent as the center.

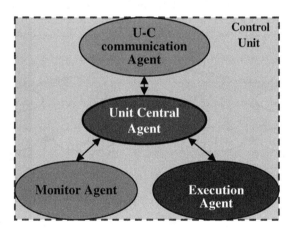

Fig. 3. The multiagent model of control unit: this model includes four types of agents, which are *UCA, CA_{U-C}, MA, and EA*

3.3   Multiagent Modeling for Clustered Control Systems

Therefore, with the multiagent modeling of cluster stations and control units, the clustered control system can be modeled as a hybrid multiagent coalition system. Based on our previous model for situated multiagent system [15], now we give the definition of the multiagent model for clustered control system, shown as follows.

Definition 1. A multiagent model for clustered control system can be described as a tuple $<Z, CS, CU, D_1, D_2, N>$, where:

1) Z denotes the geographical zone where the cluster stations and control units are situated. $Z=\{(x,y)\}|\delta_1\leq x\leq\delta_2,\ \gamma_1\leq y\leq\gamma_2\}$, where δ_1, δ_2, γ_1, γ_2 prescribe the scope of geographical zone.

2) $CS=\{CS_1, CS_2,\cdots, CS_n\}$ denotes the set of cluster stations, where n is the number of clusters; $CS_i=\{(CCA)_i, (CA_{C-H})_i, (CA_{C-C})_i, (CA_{C-U})_i\}$, $1\leq i\leq n$.

3) $CU=\{CU_1, CU_2,\cdots, CU_n\}$ denotes the set of control units, where n is the number of clusters, CU_i denotes the set of control units in the ith cluster (whose cluster station is CS_i). $CU_i=\{CU_{i1}, CU_{i2},\cdots, CU_{im}\}$, where m is the number of control units in the ith cluster; $CU_{ij}=\{(UCA)_{ij}, (CA_{U-C})_{ij}, (MA)_{ij}, (EA)_{ij}\}$, $1\leq j\leq m$.

4) D_1: $Z\times CS\rightarrow\{true, false\}$ is a mapping from the geographical localities to the cluster stations, which denotes the geographical distribution of the cluster stations, e.g., if the mapping value from (x,y) to CS_i is true, then it shows that there is an cluster station CS_i which locates at the place of (x,y).

5) D_2: $Z\times CU\rightarrow\{true, false\}$ is a mapping from the geographical localities to the control units, which denotes the geographical distribution of the control units, e.g., if the mapping value from (x,y) to CU_{ij} is true, then it shows that there is an control unit CU_{ij} which locates at the place of (x,y).

6) $N=<CS_i, CS_j>$, $1\leq i,j\leq n$, which denotes the interaction topology among cluster stations in the system.

For example, Fig.4 is a multiagent model for a clustered control system with two clusters; the first cluster has two control units, and the second cluster only has one control unit.

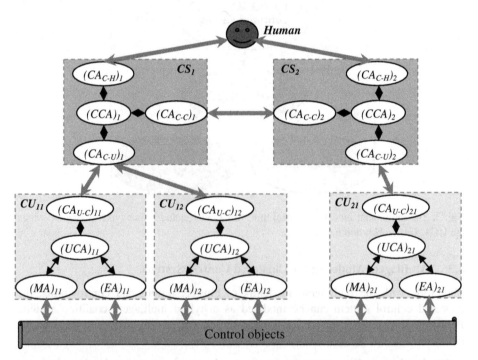

Fig. 4. A multiagent model for a clustered control system with two clusters, $C_1=\{CS_1, CU_{11}, CU_{12}\}$, $C2=\{CS_2, CU_{21}\}$

4   The Detection Model of Abnormal Nodes

Now we design the model for detecting abnormal nodes in clustered control systems. At first we define the prominence of control units and clusters; then, we present the detection model.

4.1   Prominence of Individual Control Units

Without loss of generality, we consider that an agent' strategy is prominent if it is higher than the average one in the system [15]. Now we design the prominence degree of agents in clustered control systems, shown as follows.

Definition 2. *Prominence degree of agent strategy.* Let $A(x)$ denote the set of agents with the type x and $s(x)_i$ be the strategy of agent $a(x)_i$, $a(x)_i \in A(x)$, then the prominence degree of agent $a(x)_i$ is defined as:

$$\lambda(x)_i = \frac{1}{\frac{1}{|A(x)|}\sum_{\forall a(x)_j \in A(x)} s(x)_j} \left(\left| s(x)_i - \frac{1}{|A(x)|}\sum_{\forall a(x)_j \in A(x)} s(x)_j \right| \right) \tag{1}$$

For example, the prominence degree of U-C communication agent $a(CA_{U-C})_i$ is:

$$\lambda(CA_{U-C})_i = \frac{\left| s(CA_{U-C})_i - \frac{1}{|A(CA_{U-C})|}\sum_{a(CA_{U-C})_j \in A(CA_{U-C})} s(CA_{U-C})_j \right|}{\frac{1}{|A(CA_{U-C})|}\sum_{a(CA_{U-C})_j \in A(CA_{U-C})} s(CA_{U-C})_j} \tag{2}$$

Definition 3. *The prominence degree of a control unit, CU_{ij} (i.e., the jth control unit in the ith cluster), is the weighted sum of all agents within it:*

$$\lambda_{CU_{ij}} = \alpha_1 \lambda(UCA)_{ij} + \alpha_2 \lambda(CA_{U-C})_{ij} + \alpha_3 \lambda(MA)_{ij} + \alpha_4 \lambda(EA)_{ij} \tag{3}$$

where $\alpha_1 + \alpha_2 + \alpha_3 + \alpha_4 = 1$.

4.2   Prominence of Clusters

The prominence of a cluster is determined by the ones of its station and control units.

Definition 4. *The prominence degree of a cluster station, CS_i, is the weighted sum of all agents within it:*

$$\lambda_{CS_i} = \beta_1 \lambda(CCA)_i + \beta_2 \lambda(CA_{C-H})_i + \beta_3 \lambda(CA_{C-C})_i + \beta_4 \lambda(CA_{C-U})_i \tag{4}$$

where $\beta_1+\beta_2+\beta_3+\beta_4=1$. The prominence of each agent is computed according to Definition 2.

Definition 5. Let there be a cluster, C_i, *the prominence degree of* C_i is the weighted sum of the average prominence degree of all control units within it and the prominence degree of its cluster station.

$$\lambda_{C_i} = \gamma_1 \lambda_{CS_i} + \gamma_2 \left(\frac{\sum_{\forall CU_{ij} \in CU_i} \lambda_{CU_{ij}}}{|CU_i|} \right) \quad (5)$$

where $|CU_i|$ denotes the number of all control units within cluster C_i, $\gamma_1+\gamma_2=1$.

4.3   The Model

In this paper, we mainly consider the situation of clustered control systems in monitoring environments, where the control units observe the objects in surrounding environments, such as sensor control systems [21]. Since there may be more than one control unit that monitors the same environment, the different control units may get different monitoring results. Therefore, to achieve the consistency of monitoring results, we can make the strategies of the same type of agents consistent [17][22]. The consistency of a set of control units can be measured by the average difference from each control unit's strategy to the average strategy.

Definition 6. Let there be a cluster, C_i; one of the control units within C_i is CU_{ij}. The consistency of CU_{ij} in cluster C_i, can be defined as follows.

The average strategy value of all unit central agents (UCA) in C_i is:

$$\overline{s(UCA)_i} = \frac{1}{|(UCA)_i|} \sum_{\forall a(UCA)_{ij} \in (UCA)_i} s(UCA)_{ij} \quad (6)$$

where $(UCA)_i$ is the set of all unit central agents in cluster C_i.

The average strategy value of all U-C communication agents (CA_{U-C}) in C_i is:

$$\overline{s(CA_{U-C})_i} = \frac{1}{|(CA_{U-C})_i|} \sum_{\forall a(CA_{U-C})_{ij} \in (CA_{U-C})_i} s(CA_{U-C})_{ij} \quad (7)$$

The average strategy value of all monitor agents (MA) in C_i is:

$$\overline{s(MA)_i} = \frac{1}{|(MA)_i|} \sum_{\forall a(MA)_{ij} \in (MA)_i} s(MA)_{ij} \quad (8)$$

The average strategy value of all execution agents (EA) in C_i is:

$$\overline{s(EA)}_i = \frac{1}{|(EA)_i|} \sum_{\forall a(EA)_{ij} \in (EA)_i} s(EA)_{ij} \tag{9}$$

Finally, now the consistency of CU_{ij} in C_i is defined as:

$$\mathbb{C}_i^j = \eta_1 \left(1 - \frac{\left| s(UCA)_{ij} - \overline{s(UCA)}_i \right|}{\overline{s(UCA)}_i} \right) + \eta_2 \left(1 - \frac{\left| s(CA_{U-C})_{ij} - \overline{s(CA_{U-C})}_i \right|}{\overline{s(CA_{U-C})}_i} \right)$$
$$+ \eta_3 \left(1 - \frac{\left| s(MA)_{ij} - \overline{s(MA)}_i \right|}{\overline{s(MA)}_i} \right) + \eta_4 \left(1 - \frac{\left| s(EA)_{ij} - \overline{s(EA)}_i \right|}{\overline{s(EA)}_i} \right) \tag{10}$$

where $\eta_1 + \eta_2 + \eta_3 + \eta_4 = 1$.

Similarly, now we can design the consistency of clusters within the whole system.

Definition 7. Let there be a cluster, C_i, whose station is CS_i. The consistency of C_i in the whole system is composed by two parts: the consistency of CS_i by comparing to other cluster stations in the system, and the consistency of all control units within C_i. The average strategy value of all cluster central agents (CCA) is:

$$\overline{s(CCA)} = \frac{1}{|CS|} \sum_{\forall a(CCA)_i \in CCA} s(CCA)_i \tag{11}$$

where $(CCA)_i$ is the cluster central agents in cluster C_i. $|CS|$ is the number of all cluster stations in the whole system.

The average strategy value of all C-H communication agents (CA_{C-H}) is:

$$\overline{s(CA_{C-H})} = \frac{1}{|CS|} \sum_{\forall a(CA_{C-H})_i \in CA_{C-H}} s(CA_{C-H})_i \tag{12}$$

The average strategy value of all C-C communication agents (CA_{C-C}) is:

$$\overline{s(CA_{C-C})} = \frac{1}{|CS|} \sum_{\forall a(CA_{C-C})_i \in CA_{C-C}} s(CA_{C-C})_i \tag{13}$$

The average strategy value of all C-U communication agents (CA_{C-U}) is:

$$\overline{s(CA_{C-U})} = \frac{1}{|CS|} \sum_{\forall a(CA_{C-U})_i \in CA_{C-U}} s(CA_{C-U})_i \tag{14}$$

Therefore, now the consistency of CS_i by comparing to other cluster stations in the system is:

$$\mathbb{C}(CS_i) = \delta_1 \left(1 - \frac{\left| s(CCA)_i - \overline{s(CCA)} \right|}{\overline{s(CCA)}} \right) + \delta_2 \left(1 - \frac{\left| s(CA_{C-H})_i - \overline{s(CA_{C-H})} \right|}{\overline{s(CA_{C-H})}} \right)$$
$$+ \delta_3 \left(1 - \frac{\left| s(CA_{C-C})_i - \overline{s(CA_{C-C})} \right|}{\overline{s(CA_{C-C})}} \right) + \delta_4 \left(1 - \frac{\left| s(CA_{C-U})_i - \overline{s(CA_{C-U})} \right|}{\overline{s(CA_{C-U})}} \right) \tag{15}$$

where $\delta_1 + \delta_2 + \delta_3 + \delta_4 = 1$.

Therefore, now we define the consistency of cluster C_i by integrating the consistency of all control units within C_i and the one of cluster station CS_i, shown as follows.

$$\mathbb{C}(C_i) = \mu_1 \left(\frac{1}{|CU_i|} \sum_{\forall CU_{ij} \in C_i} \mathbb{C}_i^j \right) + \mu_2 \mathbb{C}(CS_i) \tag{16}$$

where $\mu_1 + \mu_2 = 1$.

Finally, the consistency of the whole system is:

$$\mathbb{C} = \frac{1}{|C|} \sum_{C_i \in C} \mathbb{C}(C_i) = \frac{1}{|C|} \sum_{C_i \in C} \left(\mu_1 \left(\frac{1}{|CU_i|} \sum_{\forall CU_{ij} \in CU_i} \mathbb{C}_i^j \right) + \mu_2 \mathbb{C}(CS_i) \right) \tag{17}$$

where C is the set of all clusters in the system.

When there are no abnormal nodes in clustered control systems, the consistency of the system is relative higher. In this paper, we find out the most probable abnormal nodes step by step when the consistency is lower than the usual normal system consistency by computing the prominence degrees of each agent in the clusters. The detailed process is show as Algorithm 1.

Algorithm 1. Finding out the probable abnormal nodes when the consistency is much lower than the usual normal system consistency.

---

1) The usual normal system consistency is $\mathbb{NC}$;
2) Computing the consistency of the whole system according to Eq.(17), $\mathbb{C}$;
3) Computing the prominence degrees of all clusters according to Eq.(5);
4) While ($\mathbb{C} \le \mathbb{NC}$):
   4.1) Getting the set of remaining clusters by removing the nodes with the highest prominence degrees;
   4.2) Computing the consistency of the set of remaining clusters according to Eq.(17), $\mathbb{C}$;
5) End.

4.4   The Case Study

Now we make some case studies and numerical simulations to test the detection model. In the case studies and numerical simulations, we consider agents randomly distributed in a two-dimensional grid; the strategies of ordinary agents are randomly distributed in a limited scope $[0, \theta]$, and the strategy values of prominent agents are generally higher than θ, and there are 50% nodes are abnormal in each case. We make a series of case studies as follows: 1) at first we test the consistency (initial consistency); 2) we use Algorithm 1 to remove the abnormal nodes from the whole system; 4) we then test the new consistency (consistency after detection). The simulation results are shown as Fig.5, where the x-axis denotes the varying cases and the y-axis denotes the consistency. From Fig.5, we can see that after removing all of the abnormal nodes from system in each case, the consistencies increase to the usual

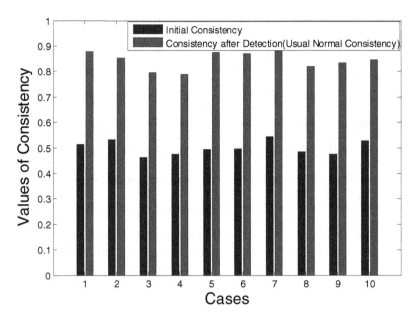

Fig. 5. Case studies and numerical simulation results

normal consistencies of the systems. Therefore, our detection model can effectively improve the consistency in all cases.

5   Conclusion

In networked control systems, the security is a very concerned issue. Clustered control system is one type of networked control systems, where nodes are hierarchical and hybrid. Therefore, traditional method for abnormality detection for single type of nodes cannot be applied well in clustered control systems. To deal with such problem, this paper presents a multiagent based method to model the nodes in clustered control systems which include cluster stations and control units. Based on the multiagent model, the paper presents the group prominence degree to measure the abnormality of cluster stations and control units. Finally, a model for detecting abnormal nodes based on group prominence analyses is presented, which can improve the consistency of nodes in the systems. In the future, we will concern about the application of our model in real large scale clustered control systems; moreover, the dynamic abnormality of nodes will also be considered.

References

1. Veillette, R.J.: Design of Reliable Control Systems. IEEE Transactions on Automatic Control 37(3), 290–304 (1992)
2. Fjuita, S., Lesser, V.R.: Centralized Task Distribution in The Presence of Uncertainty and Time Deadlines. In: Proceedings of the Second International Conference on Multiagent Systems (ICMAS 1996), Kyoto, Japan, December 10-13, pp. 87–94 (1996)

3. Lian, F.-L.: Network Design Consideration for Distributed Control Systems. IEEE Transactions on Control Systems Technology 10(2), 297–307 (2002)
4. Gupta, R.A., Chow, M.-Y.: Networked Control Systems: Overview and Research Trends. IEEE Transactions on Industrial Electronics 57(7), 2527–2535 (2010)
5. Wei, Z., Branicky, M.S., Phillips, S.M.: Stability of Networked Control Systems. IEEE Control Systems 21(1), 84–99 (2001)
6. Jones, A.T., McLean, C.R.: A Proposed Hierarchical Control Model for Automated Manufacturing Systems. Journal of Manufacturing Systems 5(1), 15–25 (1986)
7. Younis, O., Fahmy, S.: HEED: A Hybrid, Energy-Efficient Distributed Clustering Approach for Ad Hoc Sensor Networks. IEEE Transactions on Mobile Computing 3(4), 366–379 (2004)
8. Hodge, V., Austin, J.: A Survey of Outlier Detection Methodologies. Artificial Intelligence Review 22(2), 85–126 (2004)
9. Liao, Y., RaoVemuri, V.: Use of K-Nearest Neighbor Classifier for Intrusion Detection. Computers & Security 21(5), 439–448 (2002)
10. Jennings, N.R.: Controlling Cooperative Problem Solving in Industrial Multi-Agent Systems Using Joint Intentions. Artificial Intelligence 75(2), 195–240 (1995)
11. Brennan, R.W., Fletcher, M., Norrie, D.H.: An Agent-Based Approach to Reconfiguration of Real-Time Distributed Control Systems. IEEE Transactions on Robotics and Automation 18(4), 444–451 (2002)
12. Creery, A., Byres, E.J.: Industrial Cybersecurity for Power System and SCADA Networks-Be Secure. IEEE Industry Applications Magazine 13(4), 49–55 (2007)
13. Tsang, C.-H., Kwong, S.: Multi-Agent Intrusion Detection System in Industrial Network Using Ant Colony Clustering Approach and UnsupervisedFeature Extraction. In: Proceedings of the 2005 IEEE International Conference on Industrial Technology (ICIT 2005), Hong Kong, December 14-17, pp. 51–56 (2005)
14. Hegazy, I.M., Al-Arif, T., Fayed, Z.T., Faheem, H.M.: A Multi-Agent Based System for Intrusion Detection. IEEE Potential 22(4), 28–31 (2003)
15. Jiang, J.C., Xia, X.J.: Prominence Convergence in theCollective Synchronization of Situated Multi-Agents. Information Processing Letters 109(5), 278–285 (2009)
16. Jiang, J.C., Xia, Z.Y.: Cluster Partition-Based Communication of Multiagents: The Model and Analyses. Advances in Engineering Software 42(10), 807–814 (2011)
17. Jiang, Y., Hu, J., Lin, D.: Decision Making of Networked MultiagentSystems for Interaction Structures. IEEE Transactions on Systems, Man, and Cybernetics-Part A: Systems and Humans 41(6), 1107–1121 (2011)
18. Cao, L., Zhang, C., Zhou, M.C.: Engineering Open Complex Agent Systems: A Case Study. IEEE Transactions on Systems, Man and Cybernetics-Part C: Applications and Reviews 38(4), 483–496 (2008)
19. Ohtsuki, H., Hauert, C., Lieberman, E., Nowak, M.A.: A Simple Rule for The Evolution of Cooperation on Graphs and Social Networks. Nature 441, 502–505 (2006)
20. Jiang, Y., Jiang, J.C.: A Multi-Agent Coordination Model for The Variation of Underlying Network Topology. Expert Systems with Applications 29(2), 372–382 (2005)
21. Jiang, J.C., Lai, D.R., Zhang, Y.G., Lei, J.S.: A Tag-Based Solution for Data Sensing Conflicts in Multiple Sensing Agent Systems. Advances in Engineering Software 47(1), 170–177 (2012)
22. Jiang, Y., Hu, J.: Favor-based decision: A novel approach to modeling the strategy diffusion in causal multiagent societies. Expert Systems with Applications 38(4), 2974–2983 (2011)

Heterogeneous Clustering Computing Based on Parallel Task Distribution

Yi Lv[1] and Wenshi Chen[2]

[1] Office of Teaching Affairs, Liaoning University of Technology, Jinzhou, China
`lvyi@163.com`
[2] College of Electronics and Information Engineering, Liaoning University of Technology, Jinzhou, China
`lg_lx@126.com`

Abstract. To improve the computing efficiency of heterogeneous cluster, this paper presents a parallel task distribution approach for heterogeneous cluster. According to the computing power of each node in the cluster, the paper computes the weight of each node dynamically from the perspective of the predicated evaluation of system pressure. Then, the sub-task in each task period is distributed for each computing node in accordance with its weight, which can insure that each node can be assigned a rationale task and thus make a global optimum for the cluster. Experimental results demonstrated that the approach presented in this paper can guarantee the effective load of computing nodes and improve the service quality of cluster as well.

Keywords: Heterogeneous cluster, parallel computing, task distribution.

1 Introduction

In the situation of heterogeneous cluster, it may not achieve an ideally efficiency of computing power because of the difference between the processors in parallel computing. Moreover, because the computing ability and load of each node included in the heterogeneous cluster is different to each other, and even when the nodes in the computing of the load are close to one another at the beginning, but after some time, the load each node will be different, this will cause unbalance load distribution, which may lead to a serious failure of cluster computing.

In order to improve the computing efficiency of heterogeneous cluster, this paper presents a parallel task distribution approach for heterogeneous cluster. Specifically, based on the existing MPI task assignments model, this approach considers both the computing ability of each node in the cluster and the delay of communication in network.

The rest of this paper is organized as follows. Section 2 discusses the method of node computing ability evaluation. Section 3 presents the method for computing the number of ferry of task. Section 4 describes the method of task dynamic distribution for heterogeneous cluster. Section 5 shows the experimental results and the paper is concluded in Section 6.

J. Lei et al. (Eds.): NCIS 2012, CCIS 345, pp. 485–491, 2012.
© Springer-Verlag Berlin Heidelberg 2012

2   Evaluation of Node Computing Ability in Heterogeneous Cluster

Firstly, we consider the network circumstance. The node communication is adopted the asynchronous way, and only when the control section needs the data, the node load will be processed and the data will then be transferred. In this context, the pressure of network and data transmission will be minimized. In the context of different networks, the pressure of network transmission can be computed in different ways. In this paper, we take advantages of a disturbance factor--NET_M, which is a parameter in the actual network transmission and used to represent the actual transfer rate and ratio of network bandwidth.

Recently, a large number of load balance systems often use a task, scheduling load node, including CPU utilization, CPU_M, Memory utilization, MEM_M, and disk utilization, DISK_M, etc. Generally speaking, Node utilization, U, uses the experience weighting computing model. But for a computer with NFS and Linux, the main consideration is about memory and CPU operation, the information can be obtained by /proc file system (/proc/stat,/proc/meminfo) using the following formula,

$$U = \sqrt{CPU\_M^2 \times 0.2 + MEM\_M^2 \times 0.7 + NET\_M^2 \times 0.1} \tag{1}$$

In the formula (1), the experience is the relative parameter. However, after the node collects system efficiency regularly, the information will be sent to the master computer in accordance with task scheduling. But, in real applications when the master computer uses this information, they may have been "out-of-date", which may be different with the actual node utilization. So it is necessary to evaluate the computing power of nodes. Generally, two methods can be used-- moving average method and single exponential smoothing method for evaluating the node computing ability. The former is to average a large number of data, which needs a large number of data, and the evaluated results are relatively stable; while the latter uses the previous prediction data to take the place of prediction, mainly introducing a method of error constants to realize need for data. In this paper, we use the "minimum error square" as the rule of most proper combination prediction, setting up the model of it. And in this way, cluster computing is made to get the moving average and exponential smoothing weighting coefficients. Finally, the prediction efficiency of computing nodes can be obtained.

3   The Method for Computing the Number of Ferry of Task

In the context of parallel computing, parallel tasks relating to the number and size can be chosen on random, which means granularity of tasks arbitrarily small, independent task scheduling problem, are called the divisible load scheduling [1, 2]. In the fields of science and engineering, several real applications are consisting of a large number of independent tasks. In other words, these applications can be divided into any numbers and any sizes of the task block. So it is easy to make these applications paralleling directly. Especially in the master-slave mode, this type of application is also treated as divisible load. However, how to make the allocation rational, and in the computing process how to make the nodes and networks achieve the optimal balance are become to the key problems of such computing.

Under the given conditions, task allocation in heterogeneous cluster has the optimal solution, which means divisible load scheduling problem about the computing speed of the nodes, storage, and network environment in a different computer group is a complete N-P problem [3, 4, 5, 6]. Firstly, the task scheduling should be considered with the transmission delay, such as the UMR (Uniform Multi-Round) algorithm [7]. It discussed several rounds of scheduling framework in different computing environments, and obtained the almost optimal scheduling solution. But UMR considered only the task distribution and task processing stage and ignored the results of data return phase. Secondly, the task scheduling should be considered with the implementation of each phase of the tasks that are the task allocation, computing, and the results of all stages of processing. In the existing algorithms, the CAMR (Collection Aware Multi Round) [8] algorithm realized the alternate sending and receiving the results of computing. While computing, a processor returns to the previous stage of computing results and receives the data to be processed in the next stage, overlapping the information transfer and computation, thus reducing the overall application response time. However, this method ignores the communication delay. Finally, the task processing in the node status is not controllable, nor reliable, and simple computing node can not reflect the current capacity situation in the future. To the best of our knowledge, there is no model which can measure and predict the computing for evaluating the computing node

To solve the problems above, we propose a divisible load on arbitrary rounds of scheduling. The basic idea is that, firstly we estimate a round of scheduling, and then according to the load of computing nodes and computing power, make dynamic adjustment of the number of rounds. Its main features are as follows:

- According to the node and the power of computing load, it makes the evaluation. It can better reflect the function of nodes performance and reduce the stress of the network ;
- It uses non-blocking method to shorten the response time of master node and computing node;
- It tries to avoid the task process migration, only in zombie mode, makes the task node migration, and in storage, takes the NFS ways between tasks to minimize the pressure of communication between nodes;
- It takes the local computing on the task assignment and the node load, and uses the asynchronous communication to transmit data, with little competition among tasks.

4   The Method of Task Dynamic Distribution for Heterogeneous Cluster

We built a star form of computing platform consisting of a master node and four compute nodes. To an arbitrarily divisible task, compute nodes in the current round of processing the task received after the master node will return the resulting data. The master node use the serial transmission method to send and receive data, which means the same time sending and receiving operation can not overlap and do not participate in task processing. For any computing node, the computation time of sending and receiving data can be overlapped.

Algorithm structure is described as follows:

1. Set a load table; the table is generated by the node mode to compute the load;
2. According to Uniform Multi-Round model, determine the optimal scheduling algorithm for the number of rounds;
3. At the first time, using the greedy algorithm generates a scheduling program which is based on the priority of static load;
4. According to the estimated number of rounds, task assignments will be the best scheduling for using multiple distribution;
5. According to the load, clean up zombie nodes, regulate the node load, use NFS to initialize process migration, preserve the state, restart the process, and only process migration in the zombie nodes;
6. Collect all of nodes in the state of complete, make the whole collection, shut down your computer.

In terms of the speedup, a single computation of the compute nodes of the model work is still a subset of the whole calculation, so even in the worst case, the parallel program running time does not exceed a constant, and should be quite a serial program.

5   Experiment

From the above, we select a star platform as the experimental environment, a specific use of the Linux computer cluster environment of NFS based on MPICH.

This experiment uses the method of MPICH computer program based on Monte Carlo to compare the value of experimental data π, which is one of the statistical methods of a lot of random sampling and sample analysis, with experimental data obtained from the 101 to 1010.

In Table 1, the range of the actual 1010 computing sample is 1.410065508×109, but in the computing time less than 104, which means less than 1ms, the actual operation is not included in the data.

Table 2 shows the average load in the running time, of which the evaluation of load uses the percentage of available load.

Table 1. Experimental Data of Monte Carlo Method

Sample range	Value of π	Single computer mode(s)	Traditional single round of distribution (s)	Dynamic load balancing mode (s)
101	2.4	0.000	0.000	0.000
102	3.08	0.000	0.000	0.000
103	3.196	0.000	0.000	0.000
104	3.1496	0.000	0.000	0.000
105	3.14076	0.016	0.011	0.012
106	3.14234	0.187	0.096	0.093
107	3.1417	1.906	0.702	0.648
108	3.14158	18.828	6.815	5.931
109	3.14154	188.203	58.362	51.109
1010	3.14153	281.109	99.826	84.973

Table 2. Situation of Average load of Monte Carlo Method

Range of samples	Single computer mode (%)	Traditional single round of distribution (%)	Dynamic load balancing mode (%)
105	88.462	85.572	84.121
106	89.953	84.618	83.951
107	87.306	81.183	82.026
108	82.629	80.254	81.192
109	79.213	79.223	79.937
1010	73.438	77.920	78.425

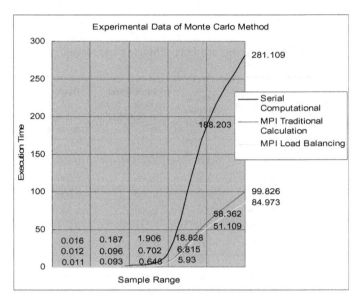

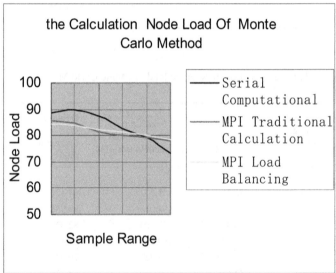

Fig. 1. The computing efficiency of MonteCarlo

It can be seen from the above method of dynamic load balancing is that the parallel computing can improve the capability of computing and reduce the computing time; and in the comparison of the load, the load balancing approach has increased the pressure on computing nodes and improved the utilization of computing nodes.

6   Conclusions

In order to improve the computing efficiency of heterogeneous cluster, this paper presents a parallel task distribution approach for heterogeneous cluster. According to the computing power of each node in the cluster, the paper computes the weight of each node dynamically from the perspective of the predicated evaluation of system pressure. Then, the sub-task in each task period is distributed for each computing node in accordance with its weight, which can insure that each node can be assigned a rationale task and thus make a global optimum for the cluster. Experimental results demonstrated that the approach presented in this paper can guarantee the effective load of computing nodes and improve the service quality of cluster as well.

References

1. Robertazzi, T.G.: Ten reasons to use divisible load theory. Computer 36(5), 63–66 (2003)
2. Beaumont, E., Legrand, A., Robert, Y.: Scheduling divisible workloads on heterogeneous platforms. Parallel Computing 29(9), 1121–1152 (2003)
3. Beaumont, E., Legrand, A.: Independentdivisible tasks scheduling on heterogeneous star-shaped platforms withlimited memory. In: Proceedings of the 13th Euromicro Conference on Parallel, Distributed and Network-based Processing, pp. 179–186. IEEE Computer Society Press, Los Alamitos (2005)
4. Legrand, A., Yang, Y., Casanova, H.: NP-completeness of thedivisible load scheduling problem on heterogeneous star platforms withaffine costs. In: CS 2005-0818. University of California, Berkeley (2005)
5. Bharadwaj, V., Ghose, D., Thomas, G., Robertazzi: Divisible load theory: a new paradigm for load scheduling in distributed systems. Cluster Computing 6(1), 123–161 (2003)
6. Drozdowski, M., Wolniewicz, P.: Divisible load scheduling in systems with limited memory. Cluster Computing 16(2), 52–68 (2003)
7. Yang, Y., Raadt, K., Cananova, H.: Multiround algorithms for scheduling dicisible loads. IEEE Transactions on Parallel and Distributed Systems 16(11), 1092–1102 (2005)
8. Zhao, M.Y., Zhang, T.W.: Multi-data assignment of three partion. Journal of Harbin University of Technology 40(5), 745–749 (2008)

Pedestrian Detection Based on Combining Classifier in Surveillance Video*

Yutang Wu, Xiaohua Wang, and Haihong Wu

Institute of Computer Application Technology, Hangzhou Dianzi University, Hangzhou, Zhejiang, 310018, China
wytsylar@163.com, wxh@cjlu.edu.cn, whh@hdu.edu.cn

Abstract. In the field of visual surveillance, pedestrian detection can be used in many situations, which is concerned by many researchers. In order to solve the problem of partial occlusion, a pedestrian detection method based on head-shoulders features is proposed. Firstly, the location of pedestrian can be obtained roughly by using vertical and horizontal projection characteristics of the foreground pixels in the slid windows combined with AdaBoost classifier. Secondly, we can obtain the head-shoulders content correctly by using the histogram of edge orient gradient characteristics combined with SVM. The experimental results indicate that the proposed method is effective to solve partial occlusion problem.

Keywords: pedestrian detection, head-shoulders features, AdaBoost, SVM.

1 Introduction

With the development of computer vision technologies, intelligent monitoring systems have been widely used, and pedestrian detection has become an important part of the intelligent monitoring systems. Unfortunately, there are many serious problems in detection process due to the pedestrian mutual occlusion, stance changes, the complex background, shadow and light factors. In recent years, many effective pedestrian detection methods are proposed by researchers. Viola et al. [2] constructed a fast pedestrian detector using Haar-like features and movement features combined with cascade AdaBoost classifier. Mikolajczyk et al. [3] proposed an upper limb detector based on the face, head and shoulders by using the joint direction-location histogram features. Ram et al. [5] and Lin [6] used the edgelet features to divide a whole people image into several parts. The characteristics of each divided part are detected individually and syncretized at last for final detection results. Papageorgious et al. [7] also proposed a body detector by using the improved Haar features and the polynomial SVM classifier.

---

* This research is supported in part by National Natural Science Fund (No.61202280) and Zhejiang Provincial Natural Science Fund (No.Y1110232).

J. Lei et al. (Eds.): NCIS 2012, CCIS 345, pp. 492–500, 2012.
© Springer-Verlag Berlin Heidelberg 2012

In order to improve the speed of pedestrian detection, Ma et al. [4] confirmed pedestrians' content through body image projection information obtained by the characteristics of projection histogram. Although this detection method is very fast, it cannot fully determine whether the detected results are pedestrians or not. Dalal et al. [1] proposed histogram of oriented gradient (HOG) features for pedestrian representation and adopted SVM as classification algorithm, which improved the accuracy of detection greatly. However, the feature dimension of this method is too high to meet the need of real-time application.

After analyzing lots of surveillance images, we can know the head and shoulders of pedestrian in the foreground of surveillance images are obvious and few occlusions occur when a pedestrian moves. Therefore, in this paper we consider and detect the head-shoulder part of pedestrian as the judgment evidence of pedestrian. This approach takes full advantage of the characteristics of pedestrian movement in the visual surveillance. For eliminating background complexity of the video sequence, we first extract the foreground pixels through background modeling, and then detect pedestrian in the foreground image. In our method, the horizontal and vertical projection features of the foreground are extracted, as well as the gradient histogram features, and then an effective combination of the AdaBoost classifier and SVM classifier is applied to perform object classification.

2   Our Proposed Method

2.1   The Basic Process of This Method

The process of this method can be divided into two parts: training phase and testing phase. Based on the acquired samples, both SVM and AdaBoost classifier model can be trained in the training phase. The main process of the detection can be described as follows: First of all, we do the background modeling and foreground detection from the input video sequence. By counting the number of foreground pixels in multi-scale sliding window, candidate regions of head-shoulder can be determined roughly. In the coarse detection, the projection characteristic is extracted from the candidate regions and then the cascade AdaBoost classifier is used to perform the initial recognition of head-shoulder region. In the fine detection, the HOG feature is extracted and the SVM classifier is adopted to do the final confirmation, which can improve the accuracy of detection. The complete process of the framework is shown in Fig. 1. Among these, background modeling and foreground detection can be performed by current mainstream methods, such as Gaussian mixture modeling [11] and run-time background subtraction algorithm [8].

To reduce the influence of noise, foreground image is filtered by using a median filter with the size of 3×3. Then, morphological operations are applied to remove isolated noise and to fill the holes inside objects.

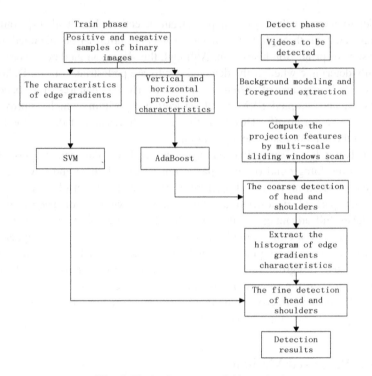

Fig. 1. The basic process of this method

According to different positions of the objects relative to the camera, pedestrians in the image also have different sizes. In order to detect the pedestrians in different scales as accurate as possible, we employ a multi-scale sliding window to scan foreground image. In this paper, we select three sizes of 24×24, 32×32and 48×48 pixels.

2.2   Feature Selection

(1) Projection Features

Since the projection-based features can be extracted easily, efficiently, and are robust to noise, in this paper, we apply both vertical projection features and horizontal projection features for the fast detection of head and shoulders of pedestrians. We obtain the vertical projection and horizontal projection of the samples in three scales respectively, and then map the projection values to an eight-dimension vector. The calculation method is described as follows.

$$Vertical[i] = \sum_{j=0}^{image->height-1} I(i,j), i \in [0, image \to width - 1] \tag{1}$$

The total number of foreground pixels in an image can be obtained from above data.

$$sum = \sum_{i=0}^{image->wdith-1} Vertical[i] \qquad (2)$$

Then we calculate the eight-dimensional vector in the corresponding direction.
The eight-dimensional vector of the vertical direction is as follows:

$$Ver[i] = \sum_{j=i\times image->width/8}^{j+image->width/8} Vertical[j] / sum, i \in [0,7] \qquad (3)$$

The eight-dimensional vector of the horizontal direction is as follows:

$$Hor[x] = \sum_{y=x\times image->heigth/8}^{y+image->heigth/8} Horizon[y] / sum, x \in [0,7] \qquad (4)$$

For low computation complexity and fast detection speed, we adopt the projection features in the coarse detection, by which the location of head and shoulders of a pedestrian can be obtained in a fast way.

(2) Edge Gradient Features
This approach is proposed by referring to the thinking of HOG features in reference [1]. In this method, the HOG features, called edge gradient characteristics, are extracted in the foreground image. The features extraction process can be described as follows: first of all, the edge information is extracted from the foreground image. Secondly, the histogram of the edge gradient direction is computed and regarded as the edge gradient features. The pixels used to compute the edge gradient features are fewer and the edge gradient can be used to calculate the direction of edge point accurately. The detailed calculation steps of the histogram of the statistical edge gradient direction are as follows.

①Edge detection. We can obtain the corresponding edge images of head and shoulders sample images, shown as Fig. 2 (a), by edge detection for training the classifier. Then further judgment is performed on the sliding window containing head and shoulders in pre-judgment by edge detection.

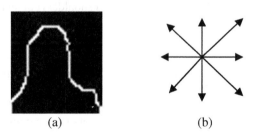

(a)   (b)

Fig. 2. Edge image and possible directions of the edge points

②Compute the gradients of edge pixels. In a binary edge image, there are eight directions for an edge point as Fig. 2 (b). Compared to that in reference [1], this method can further reduce the dimension size of the feature vectors. The gradient directions can be further mapped to the range from 0°to 180°, and the possible

number of directions of the gradient become five (0, π/4, π/2, 3π/4, π). The edge
gradient is calculated as follows:

$$G_x(x, y) = I(x+1, y) - I(x-1, y) \tag{5}$$
$$G_y(x, y) = I(x, y+1) - I(x, y-1) \tag{6}$$

$$G(x, y) = \sqrt{G_x(x, y)^2 + G_y(x, y)^2} \tag{7}$$

$$\theta(x, y) = \arccos(Gx(x, y) / G(x, y)) \tag{8}$$

In above equations, $G_x(x, y)$, $G_y(x, y)$, $G(x, y)$ and $\theta(x, y)$, are respectively the
horizontal gradient, vertical gradient, gradient magnitude and gradient direction of
edge pixel $I(x, y)$.

③Calculate the histogram of gradient direction in a cell. In this paper, the sliding
windows with sizes 24×24, 32×32 and 48×48 are divided into a number of 3×3, 4×4,
and 6×6 pixel cells. Four cells consist of a block. Firstly, we should judge whether
there are edge pixels in a block. If there are edge pixels in a block, the gradient
magnitudes of each cell and block is calculated by the gradient directions. Otherwise,
the gradient amplitude of that cell is set as zero. Because there are a relatively small
number of edge pixels, this step is necessary for reducing the calculation complexity
and improving the detection efficiency.

④Normalize the histogram. The gradient vector histogram in each cell is divided
by the gradient amplitude of each block.

⑤Obtain the features of the statistical edge gradient histogram. The edge gradient
characteristics of the sample or the sliding window can be obtained by combining the
above characteristics. The features' number of each window is 7×7×5=245
dimensions. The 7×7 is the number of overlapped blocks when the step sizes of the
sliding window are 3, 4 and 6 under three scales. And 5 is the number of directions.

In this paper, the edge gradient features are used for the fine classification to
implement the final judgment of the head and shoulders contents.

2.3   Object Classification

Currently, the most popular classifiers are AdaBoost algorithm-based classifier and
SVM classifier.

AdaBoost is an iterative algorithm, which is used to train different weak classifiers
in an identical training set. These weak classifiers is then combined together to form a
strong classifier. The specific steps of the algorithm are as follows.

①Obtain the training samples

$$S = \{(x_1, y_1),...,(x_n, y_n)\}, \quad y_i \in \{1, -1\}, \quad i = 1,...,n.$$

②Initialize each sample's weights, set as $D_j = 1/n$, j =1, . . . , n.

③In accordance with $t = 1,...,T$ weak classifiers, execute the following steps:

a) Normalize weights: $D_{t,i} = \dfrac{D_{t,i}}{\sum_{j=1}^{n} D_{t,j}}$

b) For each feature j, obtain the corresponding weak classifier h_j and the related

errors $\varepsilon_t = \sum_{i=1}^{n} D_{t,i} \left| h_j(x_i) - y_i \right|$

c) Choose the h_t corresponding to the minimum ε_t

d) Update the weight with

$$\beta_t = \dfrac{\varepsilon_t}{1 - \varepsilon_t}, \quad D_{t+1,i} = D_{t,i} \beta_t^{1-e_i} = \begin{cases} D_{t,i} \beta_t, & h_t(x_i) = y_i \\ D_{t,i}, & h_t(x_i) \neq y_i \end{cases}$$

When the classification is right, $h_t(x_i) = y_i, e_i = 0$, otherwise $h_t(x_i) \neq y_i, e_i = 1$.

④ Construct the final strong classifier: $H(x) = \begin{cases} 1, & \sum_{t=1}^{T} \alpha_t h_t(x) \geq \dfrac{1}{2} \sum_{t=1}^{T} \alpha_t \\ -1, & others \end{cases}$

Here $\alpha_t = \ln(\dfrac{1}{\beta_t}) = \ln(\dfrac{1 - \varepsilon_t}{\varepsilon_t})$.

The training process of the algorithm shows that the weights of samples classified correctly should decrease and those of samples classified incorrectly should increase. A stronger classifier can be constructed by combining multiple weak classifiers with different weights. We use AdaBoost classifier as a coarse detection classifier due to its detection efficiency, to classify the projection characteristics of a sliding window.

The obvious advantage of SVM classifier is Vapnik's structural risk minimization principle, which has many unique advantages to solve non-liner and high dimensional pattern recognition problem in a small number of samples. Therefore, SVM classifier has become a hot research topic in the field of machine learning. In addition, the SVM algorithm is a convex optimization problem, so the local optimal solution must be also the global optimal solution, which can avoid over learning. In this paper, we use SVM classifier for fine classification to obtain the final results.

3   Experimental Results and Analysis

In this paper, the experimental data is mainly obtained from PETS2006 [9] and CAVIAR [10] test case database, including our manual shooting samples. The scenes selected are mainly corridors and stairs for their relative stability. The positive and negative samples of the binary head and shoulders images in training sample images are from the images performed foreground detection in CAVIAR test database. The 2257 positive samples and 2084 negative samples are selected manually for classifier training. The sample size is 32×32 pixels. The other two sizes 24×24 and 48×48 pixels of a sample can be obtained by rescaling operations. The positive samples are the binary head and shoulders images of various postures of different pedestrians. The negative samples are the binary image of a body's other parts, like arms, legs, etc. Some examples are as follows.

Fig. 3. Some positive samples and negative samples of head and shoulders

From the input samples we can know the diversity of the binary images of the pedestrian's head and shoulders. However, it is obvious that the edge of head and shoulders image is similar to " Ω "shape.

The average accuracy of the method in three videos to be detected is listed in Table 1.

Table 1. The results of two classifiers

	Total	Possible	FtoT	TtoF	Accuracy (%)
Coarse detection(AdaBoost)	540	691	175	24	72.1
Fine detection(SVM)	516	526	28	18	91.5

In Table 1, "Total" is the total number of head and shoulders of pedestrian. "Possible" is the number of windows judged as head and shoulders. "FtoT" is the number of incorrect judgment from non-head-shoulder as head-shoulder. "TtoF" is the number of incorrect judgment from head-shoulder as non-head-shoulder. The accuracy in Table 1 is calculated using following equation.

$$Accuracy = (Total - TtoF) / (Total + FtoT) \times 100\% \qquad (9)$$

From Table 1, we can know that the accuracy is not very high if only the projection features combined with AdaBoost classifier is used to detect head and shoulders. This is because that the deformation of head and shoulders occurs when pedestrian is moving, which leads to incorrect judgment. When we use the SVM classifier trained by HOG features, the accuracy is much higher. Additionally, some misjudgments of the head and shoulders happened duo to the limitation of the number of training samples.

Table 2. The results of three videos to be detected

	The number of pedestrians	Correctly detected	Incorrectly detected	Accuracy (%)	The average detection time (s)
video1	123	112	11(+), 7(-)	86.1	0.064
video2	175	163	12(+), 9(-)	88.6	0.070
video3	242	223	19(+), 12(-)	87.8	0.078

Table 2 shows the results of pedestrian detection in the three test videos. Because the backgrounds of the test videos used are relatively stable, we choose the run-time background subtraction algorithm [8] to extract the foreground pixels. In Table 2, (+) represents the incorrect judgments from head and shoulders images to non-head and shoulders ones and (-) represents the incorrect judgments from non-head and shoulders images to head and shoulders ones. From Table 2, we can also know the efficiency of this method is still very high.

Some images samples of the test results are listed as follows.

Fig. 4. Some detection results

From the experimental results, we can know that the proposed algorithm has a good detection performance for in the cases with partial occlusion. For the cases without any occlusion, the head and shoulders images can be detected accurately if the size requirements of the basic sliding window are reached. However, the test results are affected greatly when the occlusion situations are serious. This is because the binary images of head and shoulders cannot be obtained correctly when the occlusions are serious or the deformations are serious, which leads to the incorrect classification.

4   Conclusions

A pedestrian detection method based on the characteristics of head and shoulders of pedestrian is proposed in this paper. By applying the projection characteristics combining them with AdaBoost classifier in the coarse detection, we can obtain quickly the rough locations of head–shoulder part of pedestrians. In fine detection process, the head and shoulders of pedestrians can be detected more accurately by using the trained SVM classifier combined with the characteristics of edge gradient. The experimental results show that our proposed method has a good detection performance even in the cases containing partial occlusions of pedestrians. However, if head and shoulders of a pedestrian are not obvious, or the occlusions are too serious, then the detection results are not satisfied, which is our future work to improve the method.

References

1. Dalal, N., Triggs, B.: Histograms of oriented gradients for human detection. In: Proceedings of IEEE Conference on Computer Vision and Pattern Recognition, San Diego, CA, USA, vol. 1, pp. 886–893 (2005)
2. Viola, P., Jones, M.: Detecting pedestrians using patterns of motion and appearance. In: Proceeding of the IEEE International Conference on Computer Vision, Nice France, pp. 734–741 (2003)
3. Mikolajczyk, K., Schmid, C., Zisserman, A.: Human Detection Based on a Probabilistic Assembly of Robust Part Detectors. In: Pajdla, T., Matas, J. (eds.) ECCV 2004. LNCS, vol. 3021, pp. 69–82. Springer, Heidelberg (2004)
4. Ma, H., Lu, H., Zhang, M.: A real-time effective system for tracking passing people using a single camera. In: Proceedings of World Congress on Publication Intelligent Control and Automation, pp. 6173–6177. IEEE Computer Society, Washington DC (2008)
5. Bo, W., Ram, N.: Detection of multiple, partially occluded humans in a single image by Bayesian combination of edgelet part detectors. In: Tenth IEEE International Conference on Computer Vision, vol. 1, pp. 90–97 (2005)
6. Zhe, L., Gang, H., Larry, S., Davis: Multiple instance features for robust part-based object detection. In: IEEE Conference on Computer Vision and Pattern Recognition, pp. 405–412 (2009)
7. Papageorgiou, C., Poggio, T.: A trainable system for object detection. International Journal of Computer Vision 38(1), 15–33 (2000)
8. Cucchiara, R., Grana, C., Piccardi, M., Prati, A.: Detecting moving objects, ghosts, and shadows in video streams. IEEE Transactions on Pattern Analysis and Machine Intelligence 25(10), 1337–1342 (2003)
9. D. T. e. Overview of the pets 2006 challenge. In: 9th IEEE International Workshop on PETS, pp. 47–50 (2006)
10. CAVIAR Benchmark Data,
    http://groups.inf.ed.ac.uk/vision/CAVIAR/CAVIARDATA1/
11. Stauffer, C., Grimson, W.E.L.: Learning patterns of activity using real-time tracking. IEEE Transactions on Pattern Analysis and Machine Intelligence 22(8), 747–757 (2000)

A New Electronic Image Stabilization Technology Based on Random Ferns for Fixed Scene

Hui Hu, Jie Ma[*], and Jinwen Tian

State Key Laboratory of Multi-spectral Information Processing Technology,
Huazhong University of Science and Technology,
Wuhan, China
majie.hust@sohu.com

Abstract. The paper propose a new electronic image stabilization based on Random Ferns algorithm for the fixed scene. We make an offline training after getting a view of the fixed scene to receive random ferns classifier for image matching and estimating motion. At last we remove the unintentional motion with kalman filter(KF) and make corrections to image sequence to get stable frames. This method is effective with scale, rotation, and shift. What's more, the method is real-time and with high-precision.

Keywords: image stabilization, motion estimation, feature matching, random ferns.

1 Introduction

People have paid high attention to the electronic image stabilization system which tends to be miniature, real-time and high-precision gradually. The basic process of traditional electronic image stabilization is as follows. First of all, estimate local motion and global motion according to the inter-frame. Secondly decide the desired motion after the comprehensive evaluation and motion smoothing, then compensate the current frame. mosaicing the missing image areas and output the stable image sequence finally. The basic flowing chart is shown in Fig. 1.

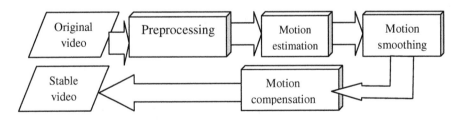

Fig. 1. The basic flow chart of video stabilization

---

[*] Corresponding author.

J. Lei et al. (Eds.): NCIS 2012, CCIS 345, pp. 501–508, 2012.
© Springer-Verlag Berlin Heidelberg 2012

The key of video stabilization is the phase of motion estimation. The main methods of motion estimation used in video stabilization are block-matching,optical flow model, gray projection algorithm and feature matching. The development of video stabilization can be traced back to the work of Ratakonda [1], who performed the profile matching and sub-sampling to produce a low resolution video stream in real time.Ting Chen [2] calculates the mainly movement (only including translation and rotation) of image sequence and processes motion vector based on block-matching and affine model in time. Chang [3] presents an approach to feature tracking and motion estimating based on optical flow, calculating on a fixed grid of point in the video. As the widely application of feature recognition, Rong Hu [4] puts forward the video stabilization algorithm based on SIFT to estimate the motion and reconstructs the missing image area by DP(Dynamic Programming) method. Matsushita [5] proposed an improved method for reconstructing undefined regions called Motion Inpainting and it was a practical motion deblurring method, but it was strongly relies on the result of global motion estimation. At present , the common defect of the above image stabilization technologies is the difficulty to be real-time and guarantee accuracy at the same time.

The paper proposes a new image stabilizing algorithm for motion estimation based on Random Ferns which is put forward by Vincent LEPETIT [6][7] .

2   A New Electronic Image Stabilizing Algorithm

2.1   Proposed Approach

Random Ferns is the algorithm trying to train a Semi-Naive Bayesian Classifier to recognize angular points in essence. Training and classifying the global view offline in advance, and then extracting angular points of the current frame for motion estimation. The electronic stabilization processing diagram is shown in Fig. 2.

2.2   Offline Training

Step 1:Building the training set. The training set is obtained by randomly deforming original view using an affine transformation and adding in random illumination and noise to enhance the robustness of classifier.

$$I_{rand} = A_{rand} I_o \tag{1}$$

Where I_0 is the original view and I_{rand} is one of the training views, A_{rand} is the random affine transformation.

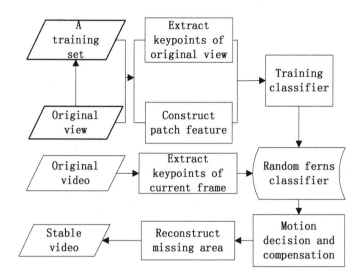

Fig. 2. The schematic diagram of the video stabilization

Step2:This paper adopts the FAST [8] (Features from Accelerated Segment Test) which was put forward by Edward Rosten and Tom Drummond in 2006 to recognize keypoints. The detector classifies k as a corner if there exists a set of n contiguous pixels in the circle which are all brighter than the intensity of the candidate pixel I_k plus a threshold t, or all darker than $I_k - t$, as illustrated in Fig. 3. FAST is many times faster than other existing corner detectors and is easy to implement. Fig. 4 shows the results of image matching using FAST.

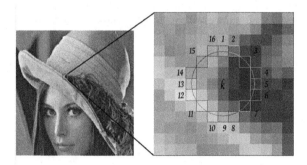

Fig. 3. FAST corner detector. The Fig. on the right is the enlarged view of the small block in the left Fig.. Point k will be detected with comparing the intensity of pixels around it as step 2.

Step 3: Selecting W interesting points which can be detected in the highest probability as the number of classes C_i. We treat the set of all training views of the image patch *Kpatch* ($L \times L$) surrounding a angular points as a class. Select $M \times S$ pairs of pixels d_{j1} and d_{j2} in the patch in according to the uniform distribution randomly.

$$f_j = \begin{cases} 1 & I_{d_{j1}} < I_{d_{j2}} \\ 0 & otherwise \end{cases} \tag{2}$$

$f_j, j = 1, \cdots, M \times S$ is the set of binary feature which is partitioned into M groups of size S. These groups are define as Ferns. The correlation between Ferns are ignored when computing the joint probability for features in each Fern $F_m (m = 1, \cdots, M)$ .With convention, we considering F_m to be equal to x is the base 2 exponential value. And the maximum of F_m is not more than 2^S . Assuming a uniform prior $P(C)$ and according to Semi-Naive Bayesian, we are looking for

$$\hat{c}_i = \arg\max_{c_i} P(C = c_i \mid f_1, f_2, \cdots, f_N) = \arg\max_{c_i} \prod_{m=1}^{M} P(F_m \mid C = c_i) \tag{3}$$

$$P_{x,c_i} = P(F_m \mid C = Ci) = P(F_m = x \mid C = Ci) \tag{4}$$

We would assign the maximum likelihood estimate to the $P_{x,c_i}, x = 1, 2, \cdots, x_{max}$ from the training samples under the constraint.

$$P_{x,c_i} = \frac{N_{x,c_i} + N_r}{N_{c_i} + x_{max} N_r} \tag{5}$$

$$\sum_{x=1}^{x_{max}} P_{x,c_i} = 1 \tag{6}$$

where N_{x,c_i} is the number of training samples of class c_i that evaluates to Fern value x and N_{c_i} is the total number of samples for class c_i and N_r is a constant.

Fig. 4. It's the results of image matching using FAST. Abstract keypoints on the right view size of 239×360 pixel and train that to obtain a classifier. Then detect the keypoints on the right Fig. classified and matched through the classifier.

2.3 Real-Time Image Stabilization

2.3.1 Motion Estimation

The first step of video stabilization algorithm is to estimate the global motion between sequential images. Considering the accuracy and real-time, the geometric transformation between two images can be described by a 2D affine motion model including six parameters. $p(x, y, 1)^T$ and $p'(x', y', 1)^T$ stand for the locations of interesting points in the reference frame and current frame. That is

$$\begin{pmatrix} x \\ y \\ 1 \end{pmatrix} = \begin{pmatrix} a_1 & a_2 & a_3 \\ a_4 & a_5 & a_6 \\ 0 & 0 & 1 \end{pmatrix} \begin{pmatrix} x' \\ y' \\ 1 \end{pmatrix} \tag{7}$$

First, matching the FAST features extracted in the original view and in each reference frames by employing the classifier obtained in the training phase. Then, eliminating the mistaking matching point by using RANSAC. At last, the verification of consistent motion parameters is performed through least-squares solution.

2.3.2 Motion Smoothing and Compensation

The idea of Kalman filter [9] (KF) is to construct the state and observation model of intentional motion using statistical method. The intentional motion in the video is usually slow and smooth, so a stabilized motion can be obtained by removing undesired motion fluctuation and high frequency component in the original video sequence. After estimating the global motion, KF calculates the intentional motion. The unintentional motion is finally computed by subtracting the intentional motion from the global one. It is essential to update the model through the global motion vector for calculating the next intentional motion.

Assuming that V_i is the motion vector from frame I_i to the original view and $\overline{V}_i$ is the intentional motion calculated by KF and each parameter of observation model is independent. The motion compensated frame I_i' can be warped from the current frame I_i by:

$$I_i' = \overline{V}_i^{-1} V_i I_i \tag{8}$$

The missing area appeared after compensating current frame is reconstructed by stitching .In general, PSNR is used to evaluate the stability objectively. That is

$$PSNR(S_0, S_1) = 10 \log_{10} \frac{255^2}{\dfrac{1}{M \times N} \displaystyle\sum_{i=1}^{N} \sum_{j=1}^{M} (S_0(i, j) - S_1(i, j))^2} \tag{9}$$

Where $S_0(x, y)$ and $S_1(x, y)$ represent the intensity of the pixel located in (i, j) from consecutive frames and $M \times N$ is the size of frame. The bigger the value of PSNR, the better the result of image stabilization.

3   Results

To evaluate the performance of the proposed method, we have conducted extensive experiments on many videos to cover different types of scenes. The computation speed of our current research implementation is more about 30 frames per second for a video of size 360×240 with a Core2 2.8 GHz CPU and 2G memory without any hardware acceleration.

Fig. 5. The original view size 640×480 pixel will be detected and trained and the video captured from the same scenario will be stabilized

Fig. 5 shows one of the original view to be trained. The first line of image sequence in Fig. 6 is the original video's screen shot containing random motion, the second line is the stable video's screen shot which still missing image areas after processing and the last line is the result after stabilizing and mosaicing. Fig. 7 shows the PSNR analysis results of both the original frames and stable frames. The blue curve and the red curve represents the values of PSNR before and after processing respectively. The PSNR of stable video reached 25.8 that is much higher than 19.5 before video stabilization on average.

Fig. 6. Result of video stabilization. Top row: original image sequence. Middle row: stabilized sequence which still has missing image areas. Bottom row: stabilized and mosaicing sequences.

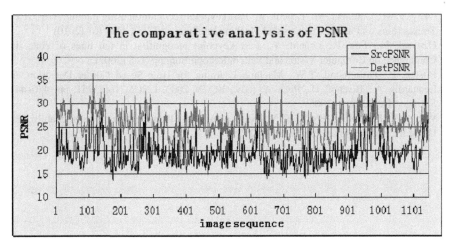

Fig. 7. The comparative analysis of PSNR from original video and stable video. The blue curve represents the PSNR of original image sequence and the red curve shows the PSNR after stabilizing.

4   Conclusion

This paper presents a new method for electronic image stabilization adopting FAST detector and random ferns classifier to estimate global motion in order to reach high accuracy and be real-time. Experiments results show that the method is robust for the video containing rotation, scaling and translation among image sequences obtained from a fixed view. It's a pity that the method is inapplicable when the video comes from a camera shifted in a large view.

Acknowledgements. This research was supported by Innovation Research Fund of Huazhong University of Science and Technology .

References

1. Ratakonda, K.: Real-time digital video stabilization for multi-media applications. In: Proceedings of the 1998 IEEE International Symposium on Circuits and Systems, ISCAS 1998, vol. 4, pp. 69–72 (May 1998)
2. Chen, T.: Video stabilization algorithm using a block-based parametric motion model [EB/OL] (2007)
3. Chang, H.C., Lai, S.H., Lu, K.R.: A robust and efficient video stabilization algorithm. In: IEEE International Conference no Multimedia and Expo., vol. 1(1), pp. 29–32 (June 2004)
4. Hu, R., Shi, R., Shen, I.-F., Chen, W.: Video Stabilization Using Scale-Invariant Features. In: IEEE 11th International Conference Information Visualization (2007)
5. Matsushita, Y., Ofek, E., Ge, W., Tang, X., Shum, H.-Y.: Full-frame video stabilization with motion inpainting. IEEE Transactions on Pattern Analysis and Machine Intelligence (PAMI) (7), 1150–1163 (2006)
6. Ozuysal, M., Calonder, M., Lepetit, V.: Fast keypoint recognition using random ferns. IEEE Transactions on Pattern Analysis and Machine Intelligence 32(3), 448–461 (2010)
7. Ozuysal, M., Fua, P., Lepetit, V.: Fast keypoint recognition in ten lines of code. In: Conference on Computer Vision and Pattern Recognition, pp. 1–8 (2007)
8. Rosten, E., Drummond, T.W.: Machine Learning for High-Speed Corner Detection. In: Leonardis, A., Bischof, H., Pinz, A. (eds.) ECCV 2006. LNCS, vol. 3951, pp. 430–443. Springer, Heidelberg (2006)
9. Wang, C., Jin-Hyung, Byun, K.-Y., Ni, J., Ko, S.-J.: Robust Digital Image Stabilization Using the Kalman Filter 55(1), 6–14 (2009)

A CPS Design Mode of Scheduling Management for Hydro-Junction Project

Zhen Zhang, Hui Feng, Zhenli Ma, Lizhong Xu, and Fengchen Huang[*]

College of Computer and Information Engineering, Hohai University, Nanjing, China
zz_hhuc@163.com, hhice@126.com

Abstract. Based on the concept of building cyber physical system (CPS), the present study analyzes the business process of hydro-junction information system, which leads to the concept of interaction between cyber and physical systems, and feedback control. The design model of hydro-junction CPS is proposed because its overall structure can solve the problems of "Information Isolated Island" and simple "Integration". In addition, we illustrate the advantage of this design model, and use it to design the software information platform for the example of the Cihuai River.

Keywords: hydro-junction, scheduling management, cyber physical system.

1 Introduction

Recently, research on hydro-junction's scheduling system is concentrated on information systems with single function, such as flood scheduling system, decision support system of water resources scheduling, and flood simulation system. These systems are independent of each other; therefore, data sharing and unified scheduling can not be achieved. Additionally, this requires more than one operator to manage different systems, which cause the wastage of resources, and "Information Isolated Island". In recent years, researchers have realized the interaction among these various subsystems because of the introduction of a contemporary integrated manufacturing system (CIMS), which is characterized by information integration and business optimization. Some hydro-junction information integrated systems have emerged, but they involve only the development of a single-process scheduling, and implementation of the best scheduling programs is difficult to achieve.

Cyber physical system (CPS) has been a hot research topic in Europe and America, which has been applied in medical, electrical, and other areas, and the results show that CPS is effective [1]. CPS is characterized by the concept of interaction between cyber and physical systems and feedback control [2], [3]. And it is also suitable for hydro-junction operation scheduling management system.

---

[*] Corresponding author.

J. Lei et al. (Eds.): NCIS 2012, CCIS 345, pp. 509–519, 2012.
© Springer-Verlag Berlin Heidelberg 2012

2   Overview of CPS

With the expansion and extension of internet of things (IOT), the concept of CPS was first proposed by the U.S. National Fund Committee in 2006. CPS changes the way of interaction between human and the physical world, which is expected to become the third wave of the world information technology following the computer and the internet. Its core is computation, communication, and control (3C) technology integration, that is, computing, communications, and control integration. Through the feedback loop between the calculation process and the physical processes, deep integration and real-time interaction, monitoring, and control of a physical entity in a safe, reliable, efficient, and real-time form are achieved.

CPS is a new interconnection system that integrates computing systems [4], [5], large-scale communication networks, large-scale sensor networks, control systems, and physical systems. CPS has real-time monitoring, simulation, analysis, and control functions for large-scale physical system, and its ultimate goal is to enable the physical system to have the capability of flexibility, autonomy, high efficiency, high reliability, and high security, among others. CPS is an integrated system of physical process, economic process, and calculation process, which describes the interaction of human and the physical world. Compared with existing physical and information systems, CPS has several important advantages, as follows.

1. Cyber systems and physical systems exist and change simultaneously [6]. Physical systems and virtual simulation systems are interrelated, affecting each other. This means that the change in physical system state will also change the simulation results of virtual simulation systems, which will in turn affect the behavior of physical systems by CPS.
2. The combination of centralized and decentralized control. Hydro-junction CPS can control the physical device partly through a variety of embedded control systems. Meanwhile, the control center can adjust the parameters of the control systems online and control the physical equipment directly to coordinate the whole system if necessary [7].
3. Real-time monitoring and comprehensive simulation. CPS can use sensor networks and communication networks to obtain comprehensive and detailed system information, which is translated to the control center for system analysis and simulation through different communication networks such as the internet, hydro-dedicated communication network, and wireless communication network, among others [8].

The advantages of CPS mentioned above provide hydro-junction running scheduling management system with the capacity of great flexibility and rapid response, which are greatly essential for the maintenance and expansion of hydro-junction. CPS emphasizes that the system is developed from the concept of the interaction between the "virtual" information platform and the "real" application of the physical system. This does not only achieve the integration of each business functions, but also pays attention to the concept of feedback control. One of the advantages is that it integrates cyber systems and physical systems, which is equivalent to creating the virtual mirrors of the physical system in computer virtual environment, in which the physical system and its virtual mirrors will change and affect each other simultaneously [9]. Therefore, changes in the physical process of hydro-junction will affect the scheduling program in the cyber system, and changes in the scheduling program of the cyber system will be feedback to control the physical process of hydro-junction until the best scheduling program is achieved.

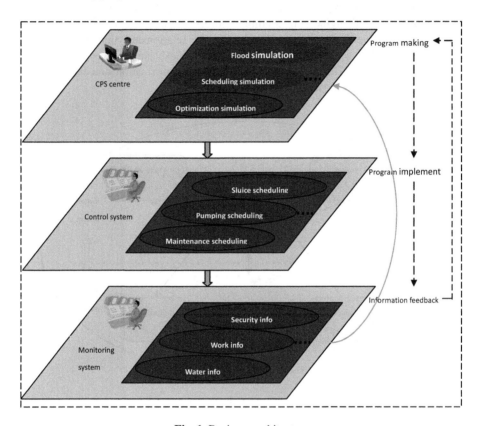

Fig. 1. Business architecture

3   Business Architecture

Business architecture is the prerequisite of and basis for overall architecture. On the basis of describing the functions and responsibilities of the existing hydro-junction schedule management system by analyzing the operation of business process and combining it with the concept of CPS, we further clarify the function of various modules and its interaction relationship, which lay a solid foundation for the overall architecture design.

Figure 1 shows the function of various modules and its interaction relationship of hydro-junction CPS. From the lateral view, each module realizes its business process functions. The responsibility of the CPS center is to make scheduling simulation with hydro-junction information, which means to simulate the hydro-junction's "virtual mirror". It then develops a management and scheduling plan, and makes simulation with feedback information circularly until the best scheduling plan is fixed. The control system's responsibility is to realize the control of physical devices such as sluices and pumping stations, maintenance scheduling, and other tasks. Meanwhile, the monitoring system's responsibility is to get feedback information, such as security information, real-time engineering conditions information, and real-time water information. From the vertical perspective, it shows the relationship among the various modules. The CPS center develops scheduling plans, and the control system implements the plans. The CPS center gets feedback information and modifies the scheduling plans so that it can realize feedback control.

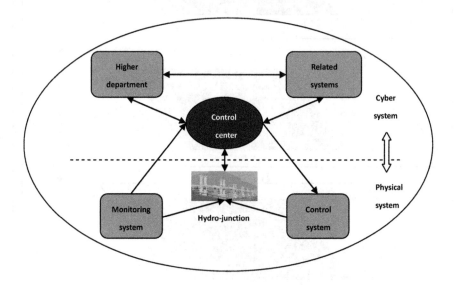

Fig. 2. Logic diagram of hydro-junction CPS

4   Framework Design

4.1   Logic Diagram

The key point of hydro-junction CPS is to realize the integration of physical and cyber systems. The cyber system manages and schedules hydro-junction while developing optimized management and scheduling plan with the change in hydro-junction state. In this system, a CPS control center is set up in the hydro-junction, which is connected with the control systems and other external related information systems. Therefore, it can manage the scheduling business comprehensively and at the same time will receive the scheduling requirement of the higher department. The logic diagram is shown in Figure 2.

In the system, the control center plays the role of a scheduling center, which is the core of entire hydro-junction CPS. Its main functions include the following: integrate all the information of the hydro-junction physical system from data acquisition and monitoring equipment, fix the system model and conduct analysis and simulation with the obtained system information, control the physical device on the basis of system simulation and analysis results. The control center is connected with the higher scheduling department to coordinate the scheduling command through the communication network. It is also sometimes connected with a number of data sources, such as a regional meteorological database, to obtain drought, water, rain, and other system-related information through the internet.

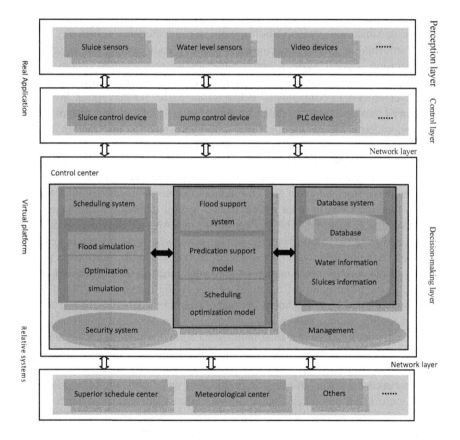

Fig. 3. Overall structure diagram

4.2   Overall Structure Diagram

The design of the overall structure should start from the concept of the realization of the feedback control process between the hydro-junction physical system and its "virtual mirror" information system. First, it uses the hydro-junction's real-time water, rain, and work information, to conduct flood model simulation computation and computer simulation based on flood and optimization of water resources targets, which are combined with water coming predication and water demand predication. Second, it develops the initial scheduling scheme. Third, it makes further computing and simulation with the returned feedback results of the implementation from the monitoring system. It therefore forms a closed loop structure system, and the best scheduling scheme will be developed.

The overall structure diagram is shown in Figure 3. Hydro-junction scheduling and management CPS is connected by a computer communication network and is based on the control and monitoring system. Its main responsibility is to finish the core task of flood control decision support and optimization of water resources, among others. System components are divided into three parts from the structure: (1) "Real" applications such as sluice and pump station monitoring, maintenance scheduling, etc. (2) "Virtual" information platform, including scheduling and management system, flood control decision support system, optimization of water resources system, security system, support system, external related systems, etc. (3) External relative systems

The layer of system components includes four parts: (1) Perception layer. It includes sensor devices such as sluice opening, water-level sensors, and monitoring equipment, which are used to collect real-time hydro-junction information. (2) Control layer. It includes sluice and pumping station control equipment, motor machine units, and PLC equipment. The function is to complete the implementation of the hydro-junction's scheduling decisions. (3) Communication network layer. The communication network is the cable and information transmission channel of each part of the hydro-junction CPS. In order to achieve the overall operation of the system, network connection is required, which is composed of LAN, wireless networks, optical networks, and field bus, among others. (4) Decision layer. It mainly refers to workers being able to develop reasonable scheduling decisions to use the information platform according to the dynamic information of the hydro-junction obtained by the sensing layer, and through the platform functions of scheduling management, flood control, decision support, and water resources optimal allocation.

The scheduling management module is based on the decision support and optimization model, which makes real-time multimedia computer simulation for multi-level control as well as scheduling command and management decisions. The returned implementation results will be used in feedback control. The flood decision support module is based on water information predication and flood support model, which achieves multimedia computer simulation for various schemes, in order to provide multi-level decision-making scheme and coordinate scheduling command. The optimization of water resources module is based on years of optimization and the scheduling and multi-objective analysis models; in order to maximize the development and rational use of limited water resources, it achieves optimization and scheduling of water resources of the entire control area. The security indemnity module is used to guarantee the security of hydro-junction with the monitoring information. The system management module can handle system configuration and system management services.

5   System Platform Development and Application

Software information platform is the most important part of hydro-junction CPS. It is the "virtual mirror" and performance form of the physical hydro-junction in the control center. A rational platform is the basis for realizing the feedback control of the hydro-junction's physical system and its "virtual mirror", which is also related to information processing, scheduling, and management schemes' development and optimization of the hydro-junction. It is the connection window between workers and the physical system of the hydro-junction, and all aspects of hydro-junction information is shown on the platform. Through the application of information platform, workers can keep abreast of the running, scheduling, and management situations of hydro-junction. Simulation functions will help in demonstrating the water level and flood, which provides reliable information for the development of scheduling decision. Its establishment is related to the effectiveness and efficiency of the operation and maintenance of hydro-junction.

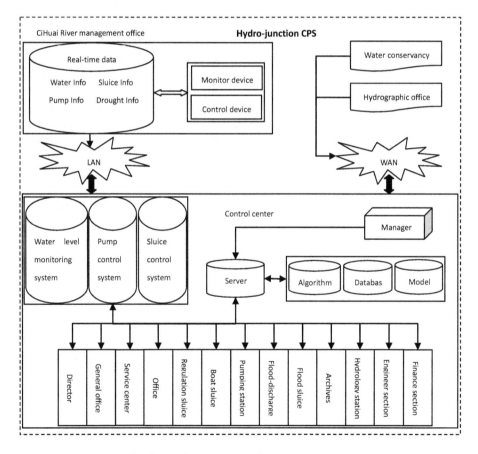

Fig. 4. Topology structure of hydro-junction CPS

5.1   System Topological Structure

Software information platform is designed and developed on the background of the Cihuai River Project, and it has been applied in Cihuai River Project conservancy. Its topology is shown in Figure 4, which reflects the network interconnection of the various departments, equipment, and staff of system.

The system topology diagram shows the components of hydro-junction CPS and their relationships. Through the interconnection of internal LAN, the decision control center can monitor the running situation of the Shangqiao hydro-junction by information transmission. Meanwhile, through the connection of internal WAN, the decision control center can make the best scheduling scheme according to the schedule target combined with the actual running situation.

Under the unified information platform, each department and working sector may achieve real-time information sharing, organic collaboration, and unified scheduling objectives.

5.2   Function Model

The platform mainly manages each function module of hydro-junction, in which different kinds of information are used in the analysis and simulation for better scheduling program. Through a unified database, subsystems are integrated to achieve information sharing and unified management. Different kinds of data from each subsystem are integrated into a comprehensive database according to a unified format by command and data interfaces. Moreover, it can provide analysis and prediction of information from the database. Therefore, on this platform, users can test, control, report, and debug online physical devices, and get historical and real-time information of each subsystem. Its function model is shown in Figure 5.

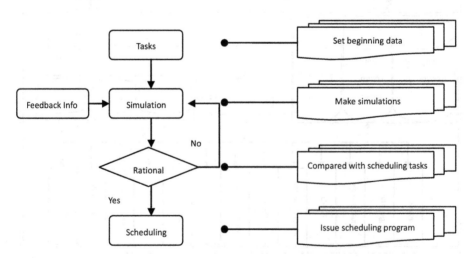

Fig. 5. Platform function model

5.3   System Scheduling and Simulation

The main page of the information platform is is simple and clear, aside from being easy to operate, as shown in Figure 6. The system's components are divided into six parts: office automation module, project scheduling module, OLAP data analysis module, remote video monitoring module, flood routing and simulation module, and GIS geographic information module.

1. The office automation module is used to improve the level and efficiency of office automation. The OLAP data analysis module helps to develop the scheduling scheme with the analysis of each department's information. The remote video monitoring module monitors the real-time information of a running hydro-junction. The GIS geographic information module helps to check the location information.
2. The project scheduling module includes project management, pumping station management, boat sluices management, flood-discharge reservoir sluices management, flood sluices management, and other parts. The concept of feedback control is used in management. The issue and implementation of scheduling scheme is realized in the form of operation and command tickets, and the feedback state of the operation and command tickets will be used in feedback control.
3. The flood routing and simulation module includes regulation sluices simulation, flood-discharge reservoir sluices simulation, flood sluices simulation, and flood simulation, among others. It provides reference for the decision of scheduling program with simulation and predication of information from hydro-junction. The flood routing model provides an abstract description of the flood running process. Using flash can show the process in chronological order so that dispatchers can intuitively understand the development of the flood situation, which is conducive to hydro-junction. Meanwhile, it can intuitively show the implementation of each sluice scheduling scheme with the simulation.

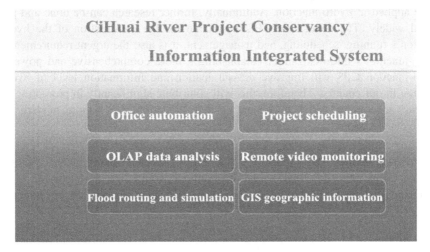

Fig. 6. Cihuai River conservancy CPS

Table 1 shows the simulation result of flood-discharge reservoir sluice. In the table, the end time represents the data acquisition time; sq_sy (unit: meter) represents the upstream water level of the hydro-junction; sq_xy (unit: meter) represents the downstream water level; and ch (unit: meter) represents the water level of the Cihuai River.

Table 1. Real-time data of hydro-junction

End time	sq_sy	sq_xy	ch
2011-10-27 0:00:00	21.17	18.11	18.15
2011-10-27 0:15:00	21.17	18.12	18.15
2011-10-27 0:30:00	21.17	18.11	18.15
2011-10-27 0:45:00	21.17	18.12	18.15
2011-10-27 1:00:00	21.16	18.12	18.15
……	……	……	……

6   Conclusion

Through the convergence of communication networks, hydro-junction CPS handles its running, scheduling, and management work by the interaction and feedback between the calculation process and the physical process. In this mode, all related resources are reasonably and comprehensively applied, and hydro-junction can achieve higher efficiency and bigger benefits. The system based on the Cihuai River has been applied in the Cihuai River conservancy and has yielded good results. The best implementation of hydro-junction scheduling and management program involves the process of integration of the physical and cyber systems, and the form of hydro-junction optimization will run from a single integration stage to a cyber and physical integration stage. This design mode can be referenced by other CPS mode applied in hydro-junction. Additionally, further research can be done and promoted widely. The concept of CPS is suitable for the construction of the hydro-junction's running, scheduling, and management, it is also the urgent requirement of hydro-junction's informatization. Establishing a more comprehensive and powerful hydro-junction CPS will improve the automation and information level of hydro-junction in our country. Therefore, this will contribute significantly in promoting the running, scheduling, and management of hydro-junction into a more modern and intelligent direction.

Acknowledgements. This paper was supported by National Natural Science Foundation of China (No. 51179047), and the authors would like to thank Mr. Zhao Keshuang of Hohai University for strong support in field work and data processing.

References

1. Zhong, L., Dongsheng, Y.: Cyber-Physical-Social Systems for Command and Control. IEEE Intelligent Systems 26(4), 92–96 (2011)
2. Chenming, L., Fengzhou, W., Xiaodong, W., Zhenli, M.: Measuring Concept Similarity of Heterogeneous Ontologist in Multi-agent Systems. Journal of Convergence Information Technogy 5(9), 246–256 (2010)
3. Wolf, W.: Cyber-physical Systems. Computer 3, 88–89 (2009)
4. Poovendran, R.: Cyber–Physical Systems: Close Encounters Between Two Parallel Worlds [Point of View]. Proceedings of the IEEE 98, 1363–1366 (2010)
5. Sztipanovits, J., Koutsoukos, X.: Toward a Science of Cyber–Physical System Integration. Proceedings of the IEEE 100, 29–44 (2012)
6. Edison, J.C., Lee, E.A.: Distributed Real-Time Software for Cyber–Physical Systems. Proceedings of the IEEE 100, 45–59 (2012)
7. Ragunathan, R., Insup, L., Liu, S., John, S.: Cyber-physical Systems: the Next Computing Revolutionized. In: 47th Design Automation Conference, California, USA, pp. 731–736 (2010)
8. Chenming, L., Fengzhou, W., Xiaodong, W., Zhenli, M.: Solution Method of Optimal Scheme Set for Water Resources Scheduling Group Decision-making Based on Multi-agent Computation. Intelligent Automation and Soft Computing 17, 871–883 (2011)
9. Lui, S., Sathish, G., Xue, L., Qixin, W.: Cyber-Physical Systems: A New Frontier. In: Machine Learning in Cyber Trust. Springer, US (2009)

Research on Framework of Information Security for Ship Electronic Information System

Ding-gang Wu

China Ship Development and Design Center, 268 Zhangzhidong Rd, Wuhan 430064, China
hbsandy79@163.com

Abstract. Technology of information security is developing rapidly, and to provides security for application requirement of the information, ensure the effective use of information. The application of The ship electronic information system has more difference compared to others, information security determines the system's normal running and completing task directly. This paper introduces the concept, features, and common security technology of information security firstly, then analyzes the characteristics of the ship electronic information system, combines with security requirements of the ship electronic information system, and proposed a security architecture oriented the ship electronic information system, describes implement of the main technology, improves the security of the ship electronic information system.

Keywords: information security, architecture, ship electronic information system.

1   Introduction

With the rapid development of network technology and modern communication technology, ways of information generation and information transmission has become more and more, and shared information more widely, information has become necessary resources with the current social development, been into the every corner in life. Security issues of computer information becomes increasingly prominent, the situation is increasingly complex, It is a small threat about personal privacy and private property but a large threat about the interests of the peoples and nations.

The development of information security technology has made considerable progress, generated a variety of security technologies and measures, and provided reliable protection for information security. Information security framework plays a vital role for the control of information systems security ,from the early stage of system design, beginning to design and control the security can reduce the potential safety hazards and proportional impact effectively. Information security architecture has become the essential issue that should be considered, it can support system design and running safely.

This paper analyzes the characteristics and needs of the ship electronic information system, proposes a security framework which is adapted to electronic information system in ship, and supports system design and implementation.

J. Lei et al. (Eds.): NCIS 2012, CCIS 345, pp. 520–527, 2012.
© Springer-Verlag Berlin Heidelberg 2012

2   Information Security

2.1   Concept[1]

Information security is a broad and abstract concept. information security is concerned about the security of the information itself, regardless of whether the application has used computer as information processing means. Task of information security is to protect the information assets and in order to prevent information disclosure, modification or destruction ,and making information not be reliable or not be handled, regardless of which means the intruder took, they have to attack several security features of information to achieve their goals. On a technical level, the meaning of information security is to ensure to put an end to threats against information security features objectively, make the information owner to assure security of information in the subjective.

2.2   Features[2]

Characteristics of information security are mainly as confidentiality, authenticity, integrity, reliability, availability, non-repudiation, auditability, controllability, operability and so on.

Confidentiality is a characteristics of information that should not be leaked to unauthorized persons and be against passive attacks, in order to ensure that confidential information is not leaked to unauthorized users.

Authenticity indicates that the user's identity is true, prevents the occurrence of camouflage and deception.

Integrity is a characteristics of information that should not be changed without warrant in the process of information stored or transmitted , can be against the active attacks, ensure data consistency, prevent data from modification and damage or loss by unauthorized users.

Reliability refers to the system can complete the specified functions in the time and the conditions provided. Reliability is one of the most basic requirements of network security and is the basic goal of the construction and operation of information system.

Availability is that the legitimate users should not be unreasonably refused on the use of information and resources. When attacking or destruction happens, the system can be resumed and put into use quickly.

Non-repudiation is convinced that the true identity of the participants; participants should not deny operation and commitment completed in communication.

Controllability refers to control features for transmission and content of information. Agency authorized may control the confidentiality of the information at any time, and monitor security of the information in real-time.

Auditability refers to provision of detection method and detection basis of information when security issues happened.

Operability is that can take advantage of some means or other measures of computer to control the dissemination and use of information.

2.3   Category

Information security can be classified from different aspects.

From the perspective of principal security object, information security can be divided into network security and computer security. Previous information security displays the individual's computer security, current information security performs security for the entire network of groups, with the greater size of the network, security issues are more prominent, prevention is more difficult.

From the perspective of expression form, information security can be divided into passive attacks, active leakage, virus invasion categories, these three forms are not existence independently, and sometimes is a combination of integration.

2.4   General Information Security Technology[3][4][5][6]

In order to ensure information security, There has generated a lot of technologies to process information security.

1) Firewall technology

The firewall technology is widely used in security protection. It can separate internal and external networks by a firewall, and prevent the external network users access to the internal network and internal network resources through illegal means, filter out unsafe network services and unauthorized users effectively, restrict accession to the internal network, prevent intruders being near defense facilities, reduce the likelihood of attack, protect operating environment and information security of the internal network. In accordance with the protective principle, It can be divided into four categories: application-level firewalls, network-level firewall, circuit-level firewall and state inspection firewall.

2) Intrusion detection technology

Intrusion detection is a technology of detecting for inviolation of security policy behavior in computer network, in order to ensure the safety of computer systems involving design and configuration of a timely detection of unauthorized or unusual phenomenon, can identify and make the appropriate treatment to the behavior of malicious use of network resources. Intrusion detection technology is a reasonable complement of firewall technology, can help to deal with a variety of network attacks, ensure the integrity of information, improve system security.

3) Vulnerability scanning technology

Vulnerability scanning is a technology that automated monitors host security of remote or local, inquiries communication port of service, records host response, collect useful information about specific projects, identifies the existing security weaknesses in a very short time, assists to obtain possible attack, support security analysis for information systems.

4) Anti-virus technology

Anti-virus technology is to detect virus by monitoring access files, and clear the virus timely, prevent destruction or tampering of information. Through installing virus filtering software in firewalls, proxy servers, web servers, groupware servers to prevent the spread of the virus; by installing virus monitoring and killing software on your computer to make virus check remove.

5) Data encryption

The data encryption technology is to process the information through the encryption algorithm and protect information safty. It can be divided into symmetric encryption and asymmetric encryption (digital signature). Data encryption can not only protect the computer network information not to be stolen, but be an important means of the overall system security for computer networks. In addition, It can protect the safety and reliability of the entire system by key management system which makes system encryption.

6) Data backup and recovery

Data damage or loss will bring us more impact, it is very difficult to completely rebuild a system destroyed. Making data backup on specialized equipment on a regular time is not only to ensure data integrity and availability of information, but be an effective remedial measure to restore data and systems quickly.

7) Access control technology

Access control technology gives a first access control for network access, controls and manages resources, access time, resources authorization of the access node, and audits user's access to determine the invasion of illegal users, gives alarm message.

3   Design for Information Security Architecture of Ship Electronic Information System

3.1   Characteristics of Ship Electronic Information System

Ship electronic information system utilizes Ethernet architecture to achieve a distributed deployment and management for ship business resources, carrys out the information exchange and applications between systems or equipments. Compared to the information systems based on public network, ship electronic information system has the following characteristics:

1) The network environment is independent and small relatively

Space of ship platform is relatively narrow, this determines the scale of the network platform, usually ship electronic information system has its own LAN on network design, complete a variety of information processing and transmission by LAN.

2) Information has higher real-time

Business processes of ship platform require more real-time, so the ship electronic information system will need to have high real-time, in order to meet the requirements of the internal real-time transmission of information, Due to the different mission requirements, different real-time requirements are not the same. The safety requirements of the different real-time information would be different too.

3) Information has a variety of types

Information types processed of ship electronic information system include the different formats of data information, graphics and image information and voice information, even involve in the processing of satellite data and other specialized formats, different types of information have special requirements about transport mechanism and bandwidth on the network, and different types of information orient to different users, so it's necessary to control security and access of information.

4) Information has a variety of processing Permissions

Specific tasks in the business process allocate different functions and different mission to distinct stations and persons, privilege of different operators behind the same station is not the same, different people has different control permissions to equipment and station, There must control permissions to the resource and equipment.

3.2   Information Security Architecture of Ships Electronic Information System

The development of ship electronic information system is from centralized control mode formerly to Ethernet-based distributed control mode currently, requirements for application and processing of information systems have greatly changed, combined with characteristics of ship electronic information system and emphasis of information security controls, information security of the ship electronic information systems can be divided into four levels[7][8][9], physical security, link security, data security and application security. These correspond to information protection from information gathering to information transmission, then to information processing and information using during the whole procedure. This basic structure as shown below:

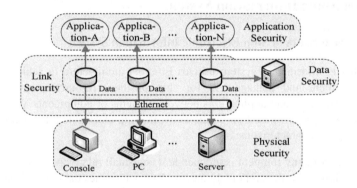

Fig. 1. Information Security Architecture

Physical security is to protect security for the physical entity on the platform of ship, such as business equipment, network facilities, storage media, to ensure the security of the ship electronic information system operating platform. At the same time, because of the special environment of ship, carrier-based physical entities also need to have some abilities to moisture-proof, vibration, corrosion protection, electromagnetic shielding, to ensure safety and availablity of equipment.

Link security is to protect information exchange within platform and communication link. And controls security of internal LAN in ship platform by control technology of network security, controls the safety of external wireless communication link of ships platform by wireless control testing technology and ensure the safety of the transmission of information by technologies of electromagnetic interference, shielding, data isolation and certification.

Data security is to achieve security of transmissing data, store data through data encryption and data disaster recovery or other technical means. to ensure confidentiality, integrity and usability of information data.

Application is to control the security to business and application which is running in equippments on ship platform via permissions distribution and access control policy, to ensure that specified services and applications can be used and operated by the authorized person. On the basic of separation of business applications and physical entities, complete control and implementation of application security.

3.3   Information Security Control for Ships Electronic Information Systems

Binding by four levels of security, there are some corresponding security control techniques,shown in table1:

Table 1. Common Technique for Security Control

Security level	Common technique
Physical security	Firewall technology, Virus protection,Intrusion detection technology, Physical isolation technology, Vulnerability scanning technology
Link security	Network security technology, Electromagnetic interference, Electromagnetic shielding technology, Data isolation and certification
Data security	Data encryption technology, Data isolation technology, Disaster recovery technology, Invasion and illegal access technology
Application Security	Permission control technology, Access control policy, Digital signature technology

Combined with the characteristics of the ship platform and the ship electronic information system, security threats from physical layer, link layer, data layer are relatively less and simple. By security protection measures as security status monitoring; establish a reasonable management mechanism to reduce the possible ways and opportunities between physical entities and the external environment to exchange information and control the safety of the equipment effectively. Application Security is the greatest security challenges which ship electronic information systems faced. most of the business of the system are all concentrated in, the information exchange between each other is frequently, function of different stations and control permission of different person are not the same, in order to ensure application security, assign permissions to role and control access right to the application. Make dipartition of roles and tasks, and identify their constraints. the principle shown in Figure 2:

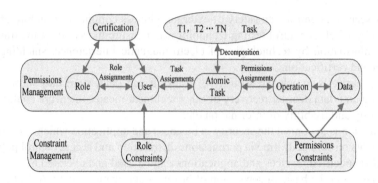

Fig. 2. Permission Distribution of the Role

Operator completes identity authentication on the authentication server through the console, then obtains corresponding information of permission distribution and tasks distribution on directory server, matchs information of allocation and task to user information and permissions assigned, completes the authorization of user roles to achieve role assignment and access management, controls access permissions of information, achieves security control, shown in Figure 3.

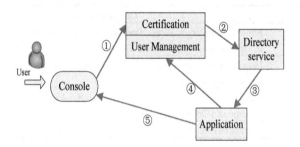

Fig. 3. Access Control Process

4   Conclusion

Information security of ship electronic information system directly determines the normal operation of the system and the execution of tasks. Information processed environment on ship platform is more different with the public network environment, resource limitation of the platform determines the participant, scale and network feature of the electronic information system. Builds LAN of the ship platform based on Ethernet, with security measures to physical entity, the transmission communication link, data processing and business application, establishes the role assignment and access control strategy, implements security controls for ship electronic information system, guarantee safe operation of the system effectively.

References

[1] Min, J., Ma, W., Hu, D.: The analysis of security requirements based on information security theory and model. Network Security Technology and Application, 58–60 (November 2004)

[2] Li, Y., Ba, D., Cheng, L.: Summary of network information security technology. Semiconductor Technology 27(10), 9–12 (2002)

[3] Lei, Z., Lu, W., Hao, L.: Network Security and Protection of Command and Control System on Ship. Ship Electronic Engineering (4), 29–32 (2003)

[4] Hu, S., Lan, H., Jin, J.: Military computer networks, information security and protection. Journal of Anhui Vocational College of Electronic and Information Technology (5-6), 97–98 (2004)

[5] Cao, Y., Yin, Y.: Research on network information security and countermeasures of military. Missile Test Technology (5), 49–53 (2003)

[6] Gong, J.: Discussion of computer network security policy. Fujian Computer (5), 18–19 (2004)

[7] Ellalif, S.A., Miloud, A.: Security and AAA Architecture for WIFIWIMAX mesh network. In: Conf. Rec. 2007 IEEE Int. Symposium on Wireless Communications Systems, Trondheim, Nowary, pp. 587–591 (2007)

[8] ISO/IEC7498-2, Security Architecture of OSI Reference Model, Part 2, Security, Architecture (1989)

[9] Common Data Security Architecture (CDSA) [EB/OL], Intel Architecture Lab (2005), http://www.intel.com

The Analysis of Influencing Factors of College Students' Learning Effect in Face-to-Face, Online and Blended Learning

Jun Tong, Jun Han[*], Jing Liu, Fan Yang, and Shuo Chen

Capital Normal University, Beijing 100048, China
{tongjun02.student,cskaoyandota}sina.com, jameshan@vip.sina.com
{fionaliujing,www.yangfan2007-47}@163.com

Abstract. This paper comparative analysis the characteristics of face-to-face learning, online learning and blended learning. Also, it comparative analysis students' learning affecting factors of three kinds of learning mode, which from student autonomy, enthusiasm for learning, degree of concentration of attention, learning communication, emotional communication, the efficiency of problem solving, learning resources and achievement evaluation. It explained the blended learning is the most effective way of learning. And it described the advantages of blended learning in college students' learning.

Keywords: blended learning, face-to-face learning, online learning, influence factors, learning effect.

1   Introduction

With the gradual improvement of college information instruction, the increasingly rich digital teaching resources, and the continuous improvement of students' information literacy, the major colleges and universities are eager to achieve the goal of cultivating talents through the extensive use of information technology in higher education.

Initially defined the characteristics of face-to-face, blended, online learning, we grasp of the law of the learning behavior of learners in the three learning by studying the effect of influencing factors in the different learning styles. It is contribute to the development of educational resources and organization of the curriculum. Also, it is conducive to make an effective evaluation on learners and learning resources, so as to promote students to improve learning effect.

2   The Comparative Analysis on Meanings and Characteristics of Face-to-Face Learning, Blended Learning and Online Learning

Through the comparative study of the characteristics of face-to-face learning, blended learning and network learning, the following discusses the advantages and the problems of three ways of learning. Learning characteristics of the three learning styles shown in Table 1.

---

[*] Corresponding author.

J. Lei et al. (Eds.): NCIS 2012, CCIS 345, pp. 528–538, 2012.
© Springer-Verlag Berlin Heidelberg 2012

Table 1. The comparative analysis on meanings and characteristics of face-to-face learning, blended learning and online learning

		Face-to-face Learning	Blended Learning	Online Learning
Definitions		Students passively accept knowledge. Its core is the "learning" to emphasize that the transfer of knowledge, including concepts, theories, methods, etc., passed from one person to another person.	It is a combination of online learning and face-to-face learning. Not only does it play the leading role of teachers in the classroom learning, but also reflects the principal role of students.	It is an educational way that teaching and learning in the physical space-time locations separated from each other. With information technology as a tool platform, it combines information technology and modern education thought organically.
Characteristics	Advantages	Easy to control Vividness	Flexibility Real-time Comprehensive Suitability	Freedom Subjectivity Personalized Cooperative
	Shortcomings	Passive Isolated Closed	Uncertainty	Uncontrollability Inefficiency

The comparative analysis on meanings and characteristics of face-to-face learning, blended Learning and online learning as follows:

2.1   Face-to-Face Learning

Face to face teaching is the main feature of the traditional classroom teaching. It is not only conducive to the emotional interaction between teachers and students, but also conducive to the imparting of the basic concepts, principles, laws, and factual knowledge. It is convenient for teachers to monitor the teaching process and students to master knowledge of the system.[1]

Advantages

- Easy to control: According to the training programs and syllabus, teachers develop teaching objectives and plans, and play its leading role strictly organizing and monitoring of the whole teaching process. With a clear goal, student can get a lot of system knowledge in a short period of time. When students have problems, the teachers can solve it as soon as possible.
- Vividness: Teachers can make the knowledge easier to understand by vividly explain. His words and actions have an impact on students, and it can improve students' learning effect.

---

[1] Zhan Zehui, Li. Xiaohua.: Blended learning: the definition , the strategy, the status and development trend. J. China. Educational. Technology , vol. 275, pp.1-5,(2009).

Shortcomings

- Passive: In the traditional classroom, teaching content and teaching methods arranged by the teachers. Student loss the dominant position, so that it had affected the students' enthusiasm. The interest in learning of students is reduced, so that it can affect learning outcomes.
- Isolated: In general, traditional classroom learning is independent of individual preparation before class, learn lessons, after-school review. Only more familiar companions were limited communication. Visible, the exchange of learning object is little, the scope is narrow.
- Closed: It includes the closed of the learning content and learning time and space closed. Teaching contents were prepared by teachers before class, students gain knowledge of pathway confined to textbooks. The class time of students is fixed.

2.2   Online Learning

Online learning, including real-time and non real-time online learning, can break through time and space constraints. It can provide learners with more abundant resources, for students to take the initiative to independent or cooperative inquiry, to cultivate the students' spirit of exploration and innovation ability.[2]

Advantages

- Freedom: Students are not restricted by time and space in the network environment. According to interests and needs, Students search on the Internet at any time to learn the information, and broaden their knowledge, as well as improve professional standards.
- Subjectivity: Students outstanding subjectivity. In the learning process, students can give full play to their enthusiasm and creativity to consciously learn.
- Personalized: According to their own circumstances, students make the formulation of learning objectives, learning content, the choice of methods in the learning process. Students independently identify problems, analyze problems and solve the problem. It can cultivate the students' ability to think independently.[3]
- Cooperative: During the online learning, if students meet difficulties, they can make use of the network interaction with their peers to learn, and work together to discuss and solve the problem, which can enhance the spirit of cooperation and teamwork of students.

---

[2] Peng Wenhui, Yang Zongkai, Tu Shanqing, Li Nian.: Survey of online learners' and learning behavior. J. China Educational.Technology, vol.251,(2007).

[3] Li Yubin, Yan Xuesong, Yao Qiaohong, Chu Yunyun, Nan Lilan.: Online learning behavior model building and empirical. J. The educational study, vol. 2,(2012).

Shortcomings

- Uncontrollability: Online learning is completely independent by the students. Due to the discrimination ability and cognitive level is not perfect, students is difficult to make the right choice when they select the learning resources facing of online multi-values. Because some students' self-control ability is relatively poor, students are easily addicted to Internet from reality, causes the student society sense of responsibility falls. Therefore, in the network environment, students' learning attitude and emotional factors are difficult to control.
- Inefficiency: Due to the students' self-control is insufficient and lack of social experience, they are vulnerable to interference with information unrelated to learning when they study online. In the selecting learning information, students easily information lost, resulting in reduced efficiency of online learning.

2.3   Blended Learning

Blended learning is the two organic combination, play to their strengths, and do learn from each other, complement each other rather than against each other, in order to achieve the best learning outcomes.[4]

Advantages

- Flexibility: In accordance with the needs, Learners can be used of a variety of styles: You can choose to learn in the classroom, followed by remote online review and practice; you can also choose to lectures in the classroom or to look at a teaching video online. You can be repeated to see the online learning resources, and repeated as needed to learn when no teacher in the class.
- Real-time: When learners encounter problems, they can be communicate with teachers and peers face to face or online learning, it enable the problem to be answered in time, to solve the problem of high efficiency, so it help to improve students' learning effect.
- Comprehensive: The "blended" refers to the combination or integration of multiple aspects of "teaching" and "learning". It is the organic combination of many different teaching methods, teaching environment, teaching media, teaching elements. Blended learning theory is a pluralistic, which is a mixture of many theories, including the behaviorist learning theory, cognitive learning theory, this ideology, constructivist learning theory, instructional system design theory, educational communication theory, principles of instruction, activity theory and the creation of educational theory.
- Suitability: By traditional teaching classroom impact, students tend to passively accept knowledge rather than actively engage in knowledge construction. So it is difficult to adapt to the autonomous mode of learning when students into the online

---

[4] Huang Lei, Yang Jiumin, and Li Wenhao.: Building blended learning model of the university based on the free internet service. J. The educational study, vol. 8,(2011).

teaching. Blended learning provides students with a good transition. Teachers play the main role, taking into account the students' learning autonomy of culture, to enable students to acquire knowledge.

Shortcomings

- Uncertainty: The proportion of face-to-face teaching and online learning cannot be determined. How should we be mixed? When do we use of face-to-face teaching? When do you need to use the virtual online environment teaching? How to blend them together in order to achieve the best results? Scale uncertainty of the blended learning: How many students in a blended learning could achieve better teaching? How do we distribute of blended learning resources so that each student can get the necessary attention?

These are very important issues of blended learning, which is urgent to our in-depth study.

3   The Analysis of Influencing Factors under Three Different Learning Styles of College Students' Learning Effect

Different learning styles have different characteristics. It will produce different effects and learning effects. Table 2 comparative analysis students' learning affecting factors of three kinds of learning mode, which from student autonomy, initiative, degree of concentration of attention, emotional communication, problem solving efficiency, learning resources, performance evaluation and other aspects. The article discusses the advantages of a blended learning model is more suitable for college students.

The analysis of influencing factors under three different learning styles of college students' learning effect as follows:

3.1   The Autonomy of Students

At present, China's universities are mostly taught education. The teacher arranged teaching content, methods, forms and others. The teacher taught in class, students seriously memorizing. When students have exams, they recite the content of teaching, repeating " taught" --" memory" --" retelling" teaching model, ignoring students' autonomy training and their ability to solve problems.

The autonomy of the online learning requires students to determine the learning objectives, develop a learning plan and prepare to learn before learning. Student should make self-monitoring, self-feedback and self-regulation to learning progress and methods in learning. Students can self-summary, evaluation and remediation after

Table 2. The analysis of influencing factors under three different learning styles of college students' learning effect

		Face-to-face Learning	Blended Learning	Online Learning
The Autonomy of Students		Low	High	High
Enthusiasm of Students		High	High	Low
Degree of Concentration of Attention		High	Low	Low
Learning Communication	Teachers	Much	Much	A little
	Classmates	A little	Much	Much
Emotional Communication		Much	Much	A little
Problem Solving Efficiency		Low	High	Low
Learning Resources	Type	A few	Many, targeted selection	Many
	Form	A little	Much	Much
Achievement Evaluation	Content	Examination	Examination; Formative evaluation	Formative evaluation
	Time	The final	The end of each chapter	The end of each chapter

learning.[5] Online learning train students to learn the information collection, analysis and judgment, able to independently acquire knowledge, apply knowledge to solve problems, give full play to the autonomy of the students, thereby it can enhance creative thinking ability.

But during online learning, learners are vulnerable to many factors interfere. Compared with the boring learning content, learners are more vulnerable to other more fresh and interesting content attract, led to an interest in transfer, do something unrelated to learning.

In contrast, blended learning can not only play the role of the student's autonomy, but also ensures the guidance of teachers. It can ensure that students in meaningful learning, and foster students' learning ability.

3.2   Enthusiasm of Students

In face-to-face learning, the teachers and students interact to stimulate students' enthusiasm. However, traditional class lack of interesting, so the majority of the teachers' evaluation feedback in the classroom to enable students to participate in learning activities.

In the early stages of online learning, with the increasing of network knowledge and interest, students learn with highly motivated and their grades rise. But in the late of online learning, the learners become familiar with the network learning mode, the interest in learning rapidly decline. Then the results will be significantly reduced.

[5] Yin Rui, Xu Danna.: Online learning environment and college students correlation of self-efficacy. J. China Distance Education, vol.10, pp.50 -96, (2011).

Such an "interest of fatigue" phenomenon of online learning, exists generally in the student population.[6]

In blended learning, rich and interesting content of their online classroom can stimulate students' interest. Also, when students' interested in fatigue, teachers can be evaluated feedback to stimulate the enthusiasm of students.

3.3   Degree of Concentration of Attention

Due to the dominant role of the teacher in traditional classroom, the students' degree of attention is highly concentrated.

In online learning, due to some network learning resources lack of interest and themselves difficult to understand, learners in the learning process easy sleepy or cannot concentrate.

In blended learning, students is prone to distracted, because the conversion of communication process of face to face and online learning is not compact.

3.4   Learning Communication

In face-to-face learning in the university classroom, teachers can be learned the students' mastery of new knowledge by the student's facial expressions, body language and the class answer. Contrast to online teaching, teachers and students together to exchange to jointly discuss and resolve issues. And teachers could inspire students to think, learning to explore and collaboration capabilities. The average of quantity of teachers and students in the classroom are higher than 1:30, so it is difficult to the teachers communicate with most of the students. Some students will be forgotten by the teachers, therefore, their learning active and will reduce. And in a simple face-to-face teaching, because of the limited classroom time, the learner will does not have enough time and opportunity to fully thinking and communicating.

Online learning includes two types of learning activities: 1. Student learning activities alone. 2. The interactions of students with others.[7] Compared to traditional teaching, online learning exchanges will be more between students. Students inspired by each other, learn to exchanges and cooperation in learning activities. But the exchange of learners and teachers is very little. The teacher is responsible for arranging the learning task and uploading learning materials. They communicate with students by replying or operating feedback. Because of distance in online learning, the learner will have a strong sense of loneliness, which is not conducive to communication.[8]

---

[6] Li Yongfan, Li Licheng,: Of affective computing and technical support the Web3D network of independent online learning model design and construction. J. China Distance Education, vol.295,(2011.8).

[7] Guo Xuepin, Chen Hongqing, Li Cuibai,Huang Cheng.: E-learning self-evaluation to explore. J. China Distance Education,. pp.70 -72, (2011).

[8] Liao Li.: The comparison of situated learning and traditional learning. N. Jiangxi Radio & TV University, vol.3,(2011).

In contrast, the blended learning has advantage. In blended learning, learners have more opportunities to communicate with teachers and students. They could have a dialogue with peer in the classroom, online forum, or posted a message in the course forum. In other words, learners can not only construct and exchange of knowledge in the classroom, but also re-organization and reflect on the content in the after-school learn through online, and they could reflect and construct knowledge collaborative with other learners.

3.5   Emotional Communication

In the online learning environment, emotional factors and cognitive factors of learners closely linked. Only students holding a sense of identity on the learning environment, they can be possible to take the initiative to learn by using learning resources and learning strategies. Learners will undermine its own effort on their learning environment in which the lack of emotion.

Different from the face-to-face learning, owing to learners communicating with others through the network platform, they not know each other emotes tone, etc. It can be caused the lack of students' emotional interaction, so that the learners have a sense of loneliness.[9]

And the autonomy of the online learning requires students to be able to determine their own learning goals, develop a learning plan, and timely self-monitoring, self-feedback and self-regulation. But this requirement is not every student can adapt. Students accustomed to traditional teaching mode, so the majority of students have a stronger sense of dependence to teachers. This is not only reflected in the knowledge itself, but also reflected in the various aspects of school life. Therefore, once the role of teachers weakening or missing, many students will feel lonely, helpless and perplexed because of the lack of the ability to solve problems independently.

Teachers cannot know the extent of absorption of new knowledge and the student's status in class. It is not conducive to teaching reflection if teachers lack the mastery of students' learning. Students' learning effect is greatly reduced.

Blended learning can be better because it overcomes this lack of emotional interaction.

3.6   Problem Solving Efficiency

In traditional classroom teaching, the learners discuss and solve problems timely with teachers or classmates face-to-face when they encounter problems. But after the lesson, learners have problems will not be able to promptly resolve.

In online learning, once students encounter problems, as the learner's time is not uniform, learners discuss only through a message or post.[10] The problem is not solved in time, so that learners will produce frustration and loneliness, motivation and enthusiasm for study weakened.

---

[9] Zhang Xiaoai, Wang Hong.: Online learning and learning factors.   N. Shandong Province Youth Institute, vol.1,(2006).

[10] Sun Ge.: Online learners behavior condition. J. China Education Information, vol.15,(2010).

In blended learning, students can be communicating face to face when they have a problem. After class, students can use the online questions. Relative to the other two learning modes, blended learning problem-solving is more efficient.

3.7   Learning Resources

In traditional classroom, learning resources prepared by the teacher before class, the types of resources is limited. Being not enthusiastic , student will feel dull and boring. It is not conducive to the cultivation of students' divergent thinking.[11]

The online learning is a multi-directional information exchange activities. It has extensive resources. Students can obtain a variety of learning resources to compared, in-depth understanding of the knowledge. So it can help students to construct the meaning of new knowledge. But on the other hand, the overload and free border of resources has become the factors that affect student learning.[12] Online resources is complicated, lacking of teacher guidance, students are vulnerable to interference with free resources, so it is difficult to select appropriate learning resources. And students are easy to produce feelings of fatigue in the process of selecting learning resources. It is not conducive to learning outcomes.

Blended learning learn from others' strong points and close the gap, make up the two disadvantages. Providing a rich online learning resources, teachers guide students to select learning resources, avoiding unnecessary wasting of time and generating boredom because of long time resource selection.

3.8   Achievement Evaluation

The teaching evaluation of traditional classroom is generally exists in the end of the semester. But by the end of the semester, the learning process has basically ended. Students are unable to make aware of their own learning and improve it during the semester.

In online learning, students can grasp their own learning at any time and make adjustments through assessment of each chapter. Teachers in accordance with the learners' online learning time, and replies number of learners to make formative evaluation, giving students a clear profit commitment (such as scores, reward, value, significance, etc.).[13] This can lead students to produce active learning needs and the power of action, to improve students' online learning enthusiasm. But on the other hand, this can lead to students showed a positive status, even if not interested in learning content, hanging on the platform but not practical and meaningful learning.

In blended learning, teachers can guarantee the authenticity of online formative evaluation by observing the learning status of students usually. And using a variety of comprehensive assessment will be more accurate, not just by the grades of final exam.

---

[11] Qi Liming.: The comparative study of college English online teaching and traditional teaching. N. Inner Mongolia University of Technology, vol.2, (2008).

[12] Liang Bin, Wang Xuankong.: The learner characteristic factors of behavior of network learning and traditional learning. N. Guangzhou University, vol.9, (2009).

[13] Gao Dan.: The surveys and research of students online learning behavior. J.   pp. 1-45,(2008).

3.9   Other Factors

The main form of online learning is independent learning, but learners are not subject to the various factors of the surrounding environment. Many factors will directly affect the quality of learners' attention and interest in learning, including radiation screen, visual fatigue, high temperature indoor, equipment defects, little computer knowledge, unskilled operation, as well as the words of neighbors and computer entertainment activities.[14,15]

4   Conclusion

In summary, blended learning is the most effective mode of learning for college students.

In the blended learning, at first, teachers explain the learning content, learning process, and requirements of learning activities to students, and then students learn online independently. In this way, students can clearly know their own learning content, the need to study the problem, how to find, study and listen to learning resource, so that students learn more targeted.

In the light of different teaching objectives and content, blended learning requires different forms.[16] This teaching activity is not necessarily full-face or online. We alternately arranged in a variety of environments, according to the characteristics of the event. In online learning, these problems are the key to the success of blended learning, including that teachers' ability to select appropriate tools platform and participate in a timely, whether a reasonable allocation of the proportion of face-to-face teaching and online teaching.

References

1. Zhan, Z., Li, X.: Blended learning: the definition, the strategy, the status and development trend. J. China Educational Technology 275, 1–5 (2009)
2. Peng, W., Yang, Z., Tu, S., Li, N.: Survey of online learners' and learning behavior. J. China EducationalTechnology 251 (2007)
3. Li, Y., Yan, X., Yao, Q., Chu, Y., Nan, L.: Online learning behavior model building and empirical. J. The Educational Study 2 (2012)
4. Huang, L., Yang, J., Li, W.: Building blended learning model of the university based on the free internet service. J. The Educational Study 8 (2011)
5. Yin, R., Xu, D.: Online learning environment and college students correlation of self-efficacy. J. China Distance Education 10, 50–96 (2011)

---

[14] Xu Hongcai.: In a survey of college students online learning behavior. J. Online Education and Distance Education, vol.6, pp.61-73, (2005).
[15] Xiao Aiping Jiang Chengfeng.: Network learners online learning situation, influencing factors and countermeasures. J. Open Education Research,vol.1, pp.75-80, (2009).
[16] Xu Mengya.: College learning support services for the design. D. vol.10, pp.1-60, (2010).

6. Li, Y., Li, L.: Of affective computing and technical support the Web3D network of independent online learning model design and construction. J. China Distance Education 295 (August 2011)

7. Guo, X., Chen, H., Li, C., Huang, C.: E-learning self-evaluation to explore. J. China Distance Education, 70–72 (2011)

8. Li, L.: The comparison of situated learning and traditional learning, vol. 3. Jiangxi Radio & TV University (2011)

9. Zhang, X., Wang, H.: Online learning and learning factors, vol. 1. Shandong Province Youth Institute (2006)

10. Sun, G.: Online learners behavior condition. J. China Education Information 15 (2010)

11. Qi, L.: The comparative study of college English online teaching and traditional teaching, vol. 2. Inner Mongolia University of Technology (2008)

12. Liang, B., Wang, X.: The learner characteristic factors of behavior of network learning and traditional learning, vol. 9. Guangzhou University (2009)

13. Gao, D.: The surveys and research of students online learning behavior. J., 1–45 (2008)

14. Xu, H.: In a survey of college students online learning behavior. J. Online Education and Distance Education 6, 61–73 (2005)

15. Xiao, A., Jiang, C.: Network learners online learning situation, influencing factors and countermeasures. J. Open Education Research 1, 75–80 (2009)

16. Xu, M.: College learning support services for the design.   10, 1–60 (2010)

DHT-Based Cross-Transmission Protocol Peer-to-Peer Resource Sharing Model

Xinyan Li, Huiying Zhang, and Chunxia Yin

Department of Information & Engineering, Ocean College of Hebei Agricultural University,
Qinghuangdao, China
lxyyongyuan@163.com, {zhy6465,xxgc_yin}@yahoo.com.cn

Abstract. In this paper, a DHT-based cross-transmission protocol P2P resource sharing model is proposed to address the interconnection and intercommunication problem in P2P systems, where the DHT network stores the resource information for each P2P system. Peer in the model can participate in multi P2P systems, intelligently finding out the same resources among them. Through parallel downloading file from multi P2P systems, the model can provide essential functions to original system, such as reducing user response latency, minimizing file download time and providing Quality of Services (QoS) guarantees. Simulation results demonstrate that the model has better system robustness, scalability and user experience compared with current P2P systems.

Keywords: Cross-transmission, Peer-to-Peer (P2P), Distributed Hash Table (DHT), Resource Sharing, Interconnection and Intercommunicatio.

1 Introduction

Peer-to-peer computing (Peer-to-Peer, P2P), from 1999 years of Napster [1] music sharing development so far, ten years still attracted people to the study and application of widespread concern. P2P network has a very high work efficiency and bandwidth resources utilization, and the system has the advantages of it can be expanded, fault tolerance strong, etc [2], The applications based on P2P technology are emerging one after another, and typically include file sharing class Bittorrent, Gnutalla and eDonkey, multimedia transmission class of PeerCast, PPLive and PPStream, instant communication class of Skype, Jabber and collaborative computing class SEIT @ Home and so on [3]. One recent study found that [4], P2P traffic has occupied 75% of the Internet traffic, and is expected in the next 5 years will increase of 400%. Speaking from the side, these data reflect the popularity of P2P applications. But, on the other hand we can see these questions, such as P2P application software number of rapid growth has brought the diversification of P2P protocol, different P2P system resources can not be shared, and user's QoS can not be protected and so on. Therefore, the P2P system optimization, especially between the interchange of P2P system, the problems were apparent.

J. Lei et al. (Eds.): NCIS 2012, CCIS 345, pp. 539–546, 2012.
© Springer-Verlag Berlin Heidelberg 2012

2   Research Progress

P2P file sharing application system with its unique technology advantage obtained a rapid development, but still exist in the following problems: (1) Between the P2P file sharing system cannot interconnected. P2P system of mutual independence brought in two aspects of the problem: on the one hand, the same resources in different P2P system are reduplicate exist,this caused the resources of information redundancy; On the other hand, different P2P system service requirements users install software on the corresponding P2P, increased operating responsible for degrees, reduce the user experience. (2) P2P systems lack of content integrity QoS guarantee. P2P network unconstrained work mode led to the lack of online trust. A lift, "public goods sorrow" problems and not reliable service and fraud greatly affected the QoS of P2P systems. At present, for the solutions to problems, mainly concentrated in the P2P cache and P2P system enhancement of the incentive mechanism, etc.

The basic idea is the P2P cache in network edge caches P2P content, use the cached content service subsequent P2P request, filter repeated P2P content, and at the same time, as P2P system of super service node, Lasting protection of system Sharing resources. In the aspect of theory, the literature [5] was put forward based on the user behavior characteristics of P2P proxy caching scheme, through a period of time the user behavior analysis, extraction hot downloaded data, proxy caching and provide service to users. Literature [6] put forward in P2P subdivision of HTTP logo way of increasing head, make full use of the Internet widespread Web cache server deploys of P2P traffic cache. Literature [7] through literature in output gateway on P2P traffic increased identification function, modeling and analyzing the flow rate, and provides cache service to the P2P traffic. However literature [8] is combined with physical topology perception technology, optimize the node neighbor choice, and the hot P2P content cache and provide service for downloading. Above solutions based on the single most of P2P systems flow caching optimization service, don't involve to cross protocol of P2P cache. Although literature [7] mention cross protocol cache concept, but no specific implementation. And the scheme based on serial access network of centralized gateway nodes of development, easy to cause the network single node bottleneck.

In the incentive mechanism, eMule and BitTorrent used similar "Tit-for-Tat" way to encourage nodes are Shared. Research progress including :literature [9] based on the credit mechanism improve contribution user's global reputation P2P, makes it gets a better service. Literature [10] from flow equilibrium and efficiency analysis of the performance of the payment mechanism, it is considered that the currency of the guarantee of proportion and the online user number, the network to achieve a balance of the highest efficiency. Literature [11] Proposes a game theory approach that provides incentives for network and distinguishs between services.Literature [12] put forward to join the selfless node to provide basic services guaranteed time so as to improve the P2P network availability.

The optimization above mentioned scheme for a single P2P system, is not very good solve we mention two questions. In this paper, a across the agreement P2P resource sharing model based on DHT technology, through the ground floor DHT networking to distributed storage each independent P2P system of information resources, and by using intelligent matching technology found the same as in the different network sharing resources, solve the basic problems about the P2P system interconnection. At the same time, the model can make full use of P2P rich system resources, guarantee the P2P resource download integrity, meets the user QoS requirements. In addition, the network technology based on DHT also fully guarantee the robustness and expansibility.

3   System Model

3.1   Framework Model

Model system working principle is: based on P2P system resources for the only mark ID_Unique (here and the contents of the documents using SHA-1 hash Value, to ensure that the documents the uniqueness of mark), shielding the file on the label of the differences inthe P2P systems, and to the only ID_Unique logo for DHT Key network, each P2P system identifier Set ID_X Set for Value, distributed storage in DHT system (hereinafter referred to as the network for Layer_Unique). For each of the P2P system, at the same time to form a ID_X for Key, ID_Unique Value for the DHT network (hereinafter referred to as the network for Layer_X). So, the system model is also provided from (ID_X-> ID_Unique) and (ID_Unique-> ID_X Set) mapping function. Through the search process of ID_X-> ID_Unique-> ID_X Set, model of the nodes can obtain the P2P systems for the same resource description identifier, dig out the different P2P system the same Sharing resources, by implementing cross protocol download, realize interconnection between the P2P systems.

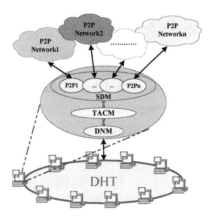

Fig. 1. System model

Fig. 1. shows a system block diagram of the model. The model uses distributed architecture network, each Peer network node consists of three main modules: DHT

Networking Model(DNM), Task Administrative Center Model(TACM),and Specific Downloading Model(SDM).

The functions of each module are as follows :

DNM: DHT overlay network based on the Chord protocol (including Multiple networks (ID_X, ID_Unique) and a network (ID_Unique, ID_X Set)). Distributed storage shared resource information, besides provide insert, delete, and query functions in DHT overlay network.

TACM: Responsible for global management of user downloads, including the download task onward slice SDM sub-modules, manage the global file in the download process.

SDM: Contains multiple sub-modules, each module proprietary P2P system protocol, responsible for the implementation of the slice to download and resource sharing tasks.

3.2   Resource Release Strategy

Two P2P systems, the following example of the resource to the publishing process. Assume that the P2P system at the same time a same storage resource. Resources in the P2P system 1 identified as ID_1,Resources in the P2P system B identified as ID_2.A unique identifier for resources is ID_Unique.The user in P2P system 1is Peer1, users in P2P system 2 is Peer2.The system works as follows:

(1)After download task of Peer1 finished, comute resourse unique identifier ID_Unique, execute Add(ID_1, ID_Unique), then insert data to Layer_1 DHT network.

(2)Peer1 execute Add(ID_1, ID_Unique) , and insert data to Layer_1 DHT network.

(3)After download task of Peer2 finished, comute resourse unique identifier ID_Unique, execute Add(ID_1, ID_Unique) , then insert data to Layer_1 DHT network.

(4)execute Add(ID_1, ID_Unique) , then insert data to Layer_1 DHT network.

(5)Layer_Unique DHT network discover existing ID_Unique record, and execute Update(ID_Unque, Value(ID_1, Info1), (ID_2, Info2)) update operation, then return to (5)

Operating the following pseudo code:

```
// P2P System 1 Download Complete  Compute ID_Unique
Compute_IDUnique(content, ID_Unique);
Layer1_Add(ID_1, ID_Unique);
LayerUnique_Add(ID_Unique, info_value_1);
// P2P System 2 Download Complete
Compute_IDUnique(content, ID_Unique);
Layer2_Add(ID_2, ID_Unique);
LayerUnique_Add(ID_Unique, info_value_2);
// Layer Unique Update
LayerUnique_Update(ID_Unique, info_value1,
info_value2,…);
```

After the operation finished, infranet will form the three layers of overlapping DHT network which are DHT network DHT Layer 1, DHT Layer 2 and DHT Layer Unique, and the network can store P2P system 1、P2P system 2 and ID_Unique resource information.

3.3   Resource Query and Download Policy

Assume that the P2P system 3, Peer3 node task to download the task and P2P systems, P2P systems 2 shared resources belong to the same content. The identifier of the content in the P2P system for ID_3. The system works as follows:

(1)Peer3 execute Layer3_FindUnique(ID_3, ID_Unique) operation, and obtain file unique identifier ID_Unique from DHT Layer3.

(2)Peer3 execute LayerUnique_FindIDSet(ID_Unique, ID_Set) operation, and obtain file resource information set of other P2P systems ID Set(ID_1,Info_1;ID2,Info_2);

(3)According to ID Set information scheduling SDM sub module 1 and 2, TACM module of Peer3 scheduling distribute the download task, and manage file whole download process.

(4)Each sub module in SDM of Peer3 download data-partition, and submit TACM module to combine the partition.

Operating the following pseudo code:

```
// P2P System 3   // Find ID_Unique
Layer3_FindUnique(ID3, ID_Unique);
// Find ID_X
LayerUnique_FindIDX(ID_Unique, ID_Set);
// File Download Management
SDM_M1_Download(piece_1);
SDM_M2_Download(piece_2);
……
SDM_Mn_Download(piece_n);
// TACM File Manage
TACM_FileManage(piece_1,piece_2,…);
```

Peer3 node basis identifier ID_3, through to the underlying DHT network ,query to obtain the set of identifiers ID of the Set of other P2P systems. At the same time, the scheduling of multiple SDM module sub-P2P module, parallel from multiple P2P networks to download data, thereby improving download speed and shorten the download time.

4   System Simulation

We assess the performance of the system in two ways: Node file download time and download integrity QoS guarantees. Experiment, we set up four independent

P2P systems, respectively, share the same 100M file. 10 Peer nodes, each P2P system contains one of the nodes as a seed node, 9 download node. In order to simplify the design of P2P protocols, we assume that each P2P system file fragmentation size for 2M/Piece, the download process is not complex P2P protocol interaction.

4.1   Download Time

Experiment, set up the run of the P2P system is stable, trouble-free node. We observed a fixed node in the P2P systems before and after the use of cross-protocol download, the download is complete contrast. Observational data using the average of many experimental results. The experimental results shown in Fig. 2.

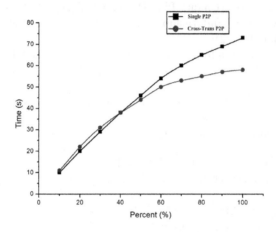

Fig. 2. Comparison chart of download completed

Can be seen from the figure, when the system is running for some time, with the increase of the number of seeds in other P2P networks, The cross-protocol download P2P model can download the data in parallel from multiple P2P networks, thereby reducing the file download completion time.

4.2   Download the Integrity Test

We will increase the number of nodes in each P2P system 100, and randomly select 10 nodes, respectively, share 10 different file. And every P2P system the sharing of 10 files are the same. For each P2P network, set up 10 seed random node failure. Experiments, we observed that the number of a fixed node in the P2P system to complete the download tasks before and after the use of cross-protocol. The experimental results shown in Figure 3:

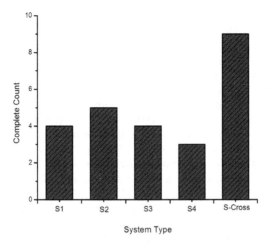

Fig. 3. Comparison of node download integrity in unrest network

From the chart you can see, the cross-protocol model in the case of P2P networks turbulent and still be able to maximize the completion of the user to download tasks for users, and so as to provide the users download integrity QoS guarantee.

5 Summary and Outlook

This paper put forward DHT-based cross-protocol P2P resource sharing model, through the resources of the logo to identify, realize interconnection between the P2P systems. At the same time, take full advantage of the richness of the system's resources, provide the download integrity QoS guarantee. In addition, distributed network based on DHT, also improve the robustness and expansibility.

The simulation results show that the model in the system robustness, scalability and user experience is existing P2P system. The next step will be to consider the traditional C/S network resources to join model system, by the stable resources really do users QoS guarantee, and research on this basis to provide a unified resource sharing platform.

References

1. Meshkova, E., Riihijärvi, J., Petrova, M., Mähönen, P.: A survey on resource discovery mechanisms, peer-to-peer and service discovery frameworks. Computer Networks 52(11), 2097–2128 (2008)
2. Chen, G., Li, Z.: P2P networks: architecture application and design, pp. 12–14. Tsinghua University Press (September 2007)
3. Chen, G., Li, Z.: P2P networks: architecture application and design, pp. 168–174. Tsinghua University Press (September 2007)
4. Dickson, F.: P2P: Content's "Bad Body": Tomorrow's Distribution Channel. Report (November 2008)

5. Shen, L., Luo, H.-Q., Tang, H., Zhou, X.: Research on P2P Proxy Cache Based on User's Character. Application Research of Computers 24(11), 106–108 (2007)
6. Shen, G., Wang, Y., Xiong, Y., Zhao, B.Y., Zhang, Z.-L.: HPTP: Relieving the Tension between ISPs and P2P. In: Sixth International Workshop on Peer-to-Peer Systems (IPTPS 2007), Bellevue, WA, US (February 2007)
7. Hefeeda, M., Hsu, C., Mokhtarian, K.: pCache: A Proxy Cache for Peer-to-Peer Traffic. In: ACM SIGCOMM 2008 Technical Demonstration, Seattle, WA (August 2008)
8. Xu, Z., Hui, T., Wei, Q., Chao, S., Nan, M.: DDP: A Novel P2P Taffic Management and Optimization Protocol. In: Third International Conference on Communications and Networking in China (ChinaCom 2008), August 25-27, pp. 208–212 (2008)
9. Li, X., Ling, L.: Peertrus: Supporting reputation-based trust for Peer-to-Peer electronic communities. IEEE Transactions on Knowledge and Data Engineering 16(7), 843–857 (2004)
10. Friedman, E.J., Halpern, J.Y., Kash, I.A.: Efficiency and nash equilibria in a scrip system for P2P networks. In: Proceedings of the 7th ACM Conference on Electronic Commerce, EC 2006, Ann Arbor, Michigan, USA, pp. 140–149 (2006)
11. Ma, R.T.B., Lee, S., Lui, J., Yau, D.K.Y.: A game theoretic approach to provide incentive and service differentiation in P2P networks. In: Proceedings of the International Conference on Measurements and Modeling of Cormputer Systems, SIGMETRICS 2004, New York, USA, pp. 189–198 (2004)
12. Peng, D., Lin, C., Liu, W.: Improving the Performance of Payment Mechanism Based P2P Application with Altruistic Nodes. Chinese Journal of Computers 6(30), 953–959 (2008)

Risk Assessment for Information Security Based on Fuzzy Membership Matrix

Yan Bai[1,*], Zhong Yao[1], Hong Li[1], and Yong-Qiang Zhang[2]

[1] School of Economics and Management, Beihang University, Beijing 100191, PRC
{Xiaoyoulang,lihong.buaa}@gmail.com, iszhyao@buaa.edu.cn
[2] Advent Software,Inc, No.3 Dongzhimen South Avenue, Beijing, 100007, PRC

Abstract. According to assets, threats and vulnerabilities and other factors in risk assessment model, this paper proposed an information security and risk calculation method on the basis of fuzzy membership matrix, besides, this work also designed an information security risk assessment system to implement the above method, which achieves risk assessment from three aspects-asset identification, risk calculation and risk results processing. The system improves objectivity and practicality of information security risk assessment. Also, it can generate a risk assessment report, which can be regarded as an indicator in evaluating the safety and security construction status of a company.

Keywords: risk assessment, fuzzy matrix, risk calculation.

1 Introduction

Convenience to the people, the rapid development of Internet has also brought a huge security risk at the same time. So information security has become the focus worldwide. Information security risk assessment is a process of computing and information systems security risks rating based on national standards, and it is also the basis for making security measures and building security system. This paper proposed an information security and risk calculation method on the basis of fuzzy membership matrix, besides, this work also designed an information security risk assessment system to implement the above method. Furthermore, this system analyzed the information security risk status of a company in Beijing. It successfully proved that using information technology means and newly proposed method could effectively and accurately accomplish risk assessment for information security.

This paper is organized as follows: section 2 gives a brief description of current researches on risk assessment for information security; risk assessment model is stated in detail in section 3; according to the risk assessment model in section 3, this paper gives a practical application in section 4. Last but not least, this paper conclude the results in section 5.

---

* This work was supported by National Natural Science Foundation of China (No.71271012 and No. 71071006).

J. Lei et al. (Eds.): NCIS 2012, CCIS 345, pp. 547–554, 2012.
© Springer-Verlag Berlin Heidelberg 2012

2   Related Work

Information security risk assessment derives from a threat report of the U.S. Department of Defense in June, 1996, in which the department stated that they hoped to reduce insider threat by lower cost and shorter period of time. Initiated by the U.S. military, the famous RAND (RAND) Corporation came forward to a series of Lander meeting on organization's internal threat which showed direction for the study of network security at that stage. In addition, Carnegie Mellon University (CMU), United States Secret Service (USSS) and U.S. Department of Defense Human Security Research Center (DoD) jointly in 2002 to study the internal threat, has launched a research project as CERT, MERIT which collected 150 cases of internal threats from those important infrastructure sectors in the United States from 1996 to 2002. And they researched from the aspects of the information technology and behavioral motivation.

The method for calculating the risk assessment is usually divided into three categories: qualitative method, a combination of quantitative, qualitative and quantitative methods. The qualitative method is over-reliant on the experience and knowledge of experts; quantitative method is not workable; so, most researches and engineers use a combination of qualitative and quantitative methods. At present, the commonly used assessment methods are: 1) The Analytic Hierarchy Process (AHP). Zhao uses AHP method to assess risk [6] and Qu [7] uses the improved AHP method, but these two method require that the data categories are evenly distributed and it is difficult to achieve. 2) Grey theory for risk assessment. Researches uses grey theory to assess risks, but failed to solve the uncertainty of assessing value. The most commonly used tools for risk assessment are: COBRA, CRAMM, ASSET and @Risk.

Due to the uncertainty of risk factors, Fuzzy computing can be a good application in the risk. Thus, researchers use fuzzy method [8, 9, 10] to solve the problem. Though fuzzy methods can compensate for the defects of the Analytic Hierarchy Process, risk assessment variables are relatively singles which can not fully describe the risks. Among the existing fuzzy comprehensive evaluating methods, most of the literatures regard the judge set membership as a determined value for assessment, which is strongly subjective and arbitrary. At the same time, others define weights of factors using experts' evaluation method or the entropy weight coefficient method, which is also very subjective.

3   Risk Assessment Model

3.1   Risk Calculation Model

The basic elements of risk assessment include assets, vulnerability and threat [2]. Managers should take full account of the value of the assets, security incidents, residual risks and those which are associated with the basic elements in the assessment process for these elements. On the basis of risk factors, we build up the risk calculation model, which is showed below.

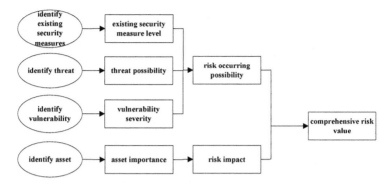

Fig. 1. Risk calculation model

Risk calculation model contains assets, vulnerabilities, threats, security measures and other key elements. Each element has its own properties, property of assets is asset criticality, property of the vulnerability is the severity of the impact of assets after the weakness is exploited by threats, the property of threats is the probability of the threat occurring, and the property of security measure is the likelihood of reducing the level of risk after the implementation.

When you submit your final version, after your paper has been accepted, send an e-mail with complete contact information for all authors. Include full mailing addresses, telephone numbers, fax numbers, and e-mail addresses. In addition, designate one author as the "corresponding author." This is the author to whom proofs of the paper and a complimentary copy of the issue in which the paper appears will be sent.

1. Identify Asset and assign assets values;
2. Analyze the threat, and assign a value for the probability of the threat occurring;
3. Identify the vulnerabilities of assets, and assign values for the severity of assets and vulnerabilities;
4. Identify security measures, and assign values fir security assignments;
5. Based on threats, vulnerabilities and security measures, calculate the probability of security events;
6. Combine the importance of assets and the possibility of security events occurring, calculate the asset value-at-risk.

3.2   Comprehensive Risk Value Calculation

According to the corresponding risk value calculated by the risk calculation model, risk value is most related to two factors: risk probability and risk impact value of the incident (also known as asset criticality). Comprehensive risk value calculation formula is as follows:

$$R = P \times I \tag{1}$$

Where R denotes the comprehensive value of risk, and P, I representatively denote possibility of risk occurring and risk impact value.

Obviously, the comprehensive risk measure must consider both factors. The more likelihood the risk event is, the higher the value-at-risk is; and the same as risk impact value: the higher risk impact value is the higher value-at-risk is. The threat model is designed to quantitatively calculate the probability and risk impact values stated in formula (1). Information security risk assessment specification [1] gives the formula for calculating the risk value, and it is stated as follows:

$$R = F\left(T, V, A\right) = F\left(P\left(Ta, Va\right), I\right)$$
(2)

Where *R, T, V, A, I, P* respectively represents risk value, threats, vulnerability, the asset security business impact on organization after the events occurred, possibilities of security incidents caused by threats using asset vulnerability.

3.3   Risk Calculation

In the formula (2), it is only to deal with risk of overall assets. However, there are different needs of confidentiality, security and integrity for some enterprises, and there are no security measures being used to analyze in the possibility of risk occurring. Based on the above deficiencies, this paper designed of fuzzy membership matrix of risk assessment for information security. The model analyzes the impact of every essential factor on risk assessment. , and uses the objective data to make risk calculation values scientific and more in line with the objective reality. The model as show in the figure 2.

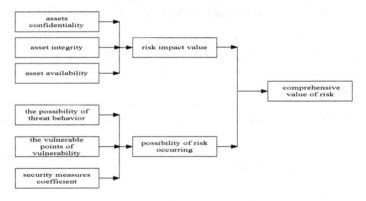

Fig. 2. Comprehensive value of risk model

The comprehensive value of risk is determined by possibility of risk occurring and risk impact value common decisions. The risk impact value include assets confidentiality, asset integrity, and asset availability; the possibility of risk occurring include the possibility of threat behavior and so on.

The new comprehensive risk value calculation formula is as follows:

$$R = F\left(T, V, A\right) = F\left(P\left(Ta, Va, C\right), I\left(I_1, I_2, I_3\right)\right)$$
(3)

In the formula(3), Impact value of risk I associated with confidentialityI_1, integrity I_2 and availability I_3 of assets; possibility of risk occurring P associated with vulnerability V_a, threat T_a and control measures C, Appropriate control measures can reduce the risk value. The calculation   method of the possibility value P and impact value I are use fuzzy membership matrix and factor weights, they are as follows:

(1)   Determine fuzzy membership matrix

The fuzzy membership matrix composed by the factor set $U:\{u_1,u_2,...u_m\}$ and evaluation objectives set $V:\{v_1,v_2, ...v_m\}$. According to the factors provided by the elements of the set, each element u_i belongs to the grade given according to the required standard set V, $v_j{\in}V$ .The number v_j reference to evaluation of u_i is f_{ij} in evaluation objectives set V, the statistics of the frequency f_{ij} of u_i affiliated with grade v_j,then use $\sum_{j=1}^{m} f_{ij}$ removal of each frequency. Obtains the index factor which belongs to evaluation grade of membership .

$$r_{ij} = f_{ij} / \sum_{j=1}^{n} f_{ij}, j = 1, 2, \cdots , n$$ From this, obtains the fuzzy appraisal vector of the preliminary factor.

$$R_i = (r_{i1}, r_{i2}, \cdots, r_{ij}, \cdots, r_{in}) \tag{4}$$

So, the fuzzy matrix of comprehensive evaluation indicators is

$$R = (R_1^T, R_2^T, \cdots, R_n^T) \tag{5}$$

Take U for a set of individual indicators, so $U = \{u_1,u_2,u_3\} =\{possibility\ of\ risk\ occurring\ ,\ asset\ vulnerability\ level,\ asset\ security\ level \}$.Take V for the level of the possible of risk event occur. Based on the construction of evaluation index system, $V = \{v_1, v_2, v_3, v_4, v_5\}= \{grade1, grade2, grade3, grade4, grade5\}$. Expert assessment of the indicator in U, through the membership function respectively derive the membership of individual indicators on the V at the five grade. So, the membership matrix is

$$\begin{pmatrix} \mu_{11} & \cdots & \mu_{1n} \\ \cdots & \cdots & \cdots \\ \mu_{m1} & \cdots & \mu_{mn} \end{pmatrix} \tag{6}$$

(2)   Determine the weight factors

Due to the different factors in the evaluation of different roles, refer to them as the appropriate weighting of the factors. Weighting reflects the function of various factors in integrated decision-making processes, it has a direct impact on the results. According to the factor U_i given by experts of the right weight, then take the average, form is as follows:

$$a_i = \frac{1}{k}\sum_{j=1}^{k} a_{ij} \quad (i=1,2,...,m)$$

(7)

In this formula ,a_i is the factor weighting value of U_i, and a_{ij} indicates that the *ith* expert to the *jth* factor weight value.

4   Application of Risk Assessment

4.1   Risk Assessment System

According to the above model of risk assessment which based on the fuzzy matrix, and since the complexity of risk assessment process, the information security risk assessment system which adopted design principle of level of system framework, was designed and applied. The system adopted B/S architecture, the Visual studio 2008 platform, and C# program language. The principle modules of system contain information identification, expert assessment, risk calculation and so on.

4.2   Risk Assessment Implementation

Within this system, this work launched risk assessment for information security on a company in Beijing, system input/output relationship is showed below.

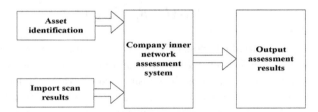

Fig. 3. System input/output relation

Step 1: identify assets, vulnerabilities, threats and security measures.

Table 1. Asset identification chart

Asset name	category	description
Intelligent analysis DSS	software	Management of intrusion detection system
MCX	software	Secure session management
Document access control server	software	Document access control rules
PCG	hardware	Fingerprints and IP telephone control
Total switch hardware	hardware	Packet forwarding
User(192.168.5.117)	hardware	Access to the terminal
User(192.168.5.112)	hardware	Access to the terminal

Assets identification includes hardware, software, data, documentation, personnel identification; vulnerability identification needs to identify technical vulnerabilities and vulnerability management; threat identification aims at environmental factors, accidents and so on; identification of security measures is composed of firewalls and other security devices identification

Step 2: Configure the network assessment environment of the evaluated company. In the information security assessment system, the evaluated network is divided into four categories: business network, internet, government affairs network and military industry network. Since the evaluated company belongs to the war industry network, the proportion of threat, vulnerability and existing measures weighs 0.25, 0.35 and 0.40 respectively, which come from the analysis and consultation of the experts; in the same way, make sure the weight of availability, confidentiality and integrality of hardware, software, services, document, equipment, data and others in the category of asset. The above values of weight are the key elements in the risk calculability formula.

Step 3: the expert assessments. By logging onto information assessment system, Experts evaluate the company's assets, vulnerabilities and threats.

Step 4: output the assessment results and further analysis. The system can obtain the risk distribution and risk level, and also gives further solution to deal with the risks. Figure 6 is the comparison chart of existing risk and security measures which has already been taken.

Table 2. assessment result

Asset name	grade	description
Intelligent analysis DSS	low	Application risk
MCX	mid	Turn on unnecessary network services
Document access control server	mid	Did not update the security vulnerabilities
PCG	mid	Fingerprint deception
Total switch hardware	low	Not running IGMP Snooping
User(192.168.5.117)	high	Remote logins, the weak password
User(192.168.5.112)	mid	Did not update the security vulnerabilities

Form the result table, because the system whose ip address is 192.168.5.117, opened the telnet service and used the weak password, which was easily utilized by intruder, the PC has a high risk grade. The document server is graded as middle since the highly security loopholes has not been updated. The evaluated company can take precaution measures according to the assessment results.

4.3   Risk Assessment Model Characteristics

(1)   In the assessment model, the existing security measures act as an important element to calculate risk in the model. The security measures of asset can properly reduce the risk value, and be more in line with the situation.

(2)   Since the assessment focal in the evaluated companies are different, the risk

assessment system can be active adjustment network environment and the weight of availability, confidentiality and integrity
(3)   The model uses fuzzy matrix to objectively evaluate the data objectively, making the assessment result more scientifically and precisely.

5   Conclusions

In the process of risk calculation, the subjectivity in the traditional risk assessment process has been reduced effectively by introducing the fuzzy matrix and weight coefficient. In this paper, the risk assessment system was designed and applied to evaluate information system of a company to verify the availability of risk calculation model. The network risk assessment is a development technology, the further job will contain the construction the security grade protect match along with the risk assessment, and the security advices will be automatically generated on the basis of the assessment result to raise the automation degree of assessment process.

References

1. GB/T 20984-2007,Information security technology— Risk assessment specification for information security. National Standardization Management Committee, Beijing (2007)
2. NIST-800-30, Special Publications Risk Management Guide. National Institute of Standards and Technology (2006)
3. Hong, F.: Information Security Risk Assessment Guide. The State Council informatization office, Beijing (2004)
4. Zhang, L., Xiang, D.Q.: Grey evaluation model and algorithm of security effectiveness of military information system. Journal of Air Force Engineering University: Natural Science Edition 8(1), 77–80 (2007)
5. Duan, J.L., Zhang, Q.S., Liu, W.J.: The model of information system's risk assessment based on analytic hierarchy process and grey theory. Journal of Guang-dong University of Technology 23(4), 12–16 (2006)
6. Zhao, D., Zhang, Y., Ma, J.F.: Comprehensive Risk Assessment of the Network Security. Computer Science 31(7), 66–69 (2004)
7. Qu, W., Zhang, D.Z.: Serurity metrics,models and application with SVM in information security management. In: Proceedings of the Sixth International Conference on Machine Learning and Cybernetics, pp. 3234–3238. IEEEPress, Hong Kong (2007)
8. Chen, S.J., Chen, S.M.: Fuzzy risk analysis based on similarity measures of generalized fuzzy numbers. IEEE Transactions on Fuzzy Systems 11(5), 45–55 (2003)
9. Zhao, D.-M., Wang, J.-H., Ma, J.-F.: Fuzzy risk assessment of network security. In: Proceedings of the 4th International Conference on Machine Learning and Cybernetics, Dalian, August 13-16, pp. 4400–4405 (2006)
10. Xiao, L., Qi, Y., Li, Q.-M.: Information security risk assessment based on AHP and fuzzy comprehensive evaluation. Computer Engineering and Applications 45(22), 82–85 (2009)

No-Reference Image Quality Assessment Based on SVM for Video Conferencing System[*]

Liangqiang Yu, Xin Tian[**], Tao Li, and Jinwen Tian

Institute for Pattern Recognition and Artificial Intelligence, Huazhong University
of Science and Technology, Wuhan 430074, China
tianxin@smail.hust.edu.cn

Abstract. Traditional image quality assessment method is mainly subjective assessment method, that is to say, the human eye is used to observe and judge the quality of the image. This paper proposes a no-reference image quality assessment method and introduces the support vector machine (SVM) into image quality assessment of the video conferencing system. A SVM classifier is employed to distinguish the image sequences of poor quality from the good ones. The experimental results show that the proposed method has good performance.

Keywords: No-reference, Video Conference, SVM, Image Quality Assessment.

1   Introduction

With the rapid development of information technology, video conferencing is gradually becoming an important means of company training and meeting. However, the issue of packet loss and delay in the internet should not be ignored, due to the bandwidth limitation of network. The image quality directly determines the quality of the video conferencing system, a timely and effective assessment method of image quality is needed for the video conferencing system. At present, the assessment methods of video/image are mainly divided into two categories: subjective assessment method and objective assessment method. In our daily life, the primary method of image quality assessment is subjective assessment method, that is to say, the human eye is used to judge the quality of the image. The subjective assessment method is the most effective and accurate method because that the ultimate recipient of the image information is human being. However, this subjective assessment method is vulnerable to the psychological state of the observer, background knowledge and observation environment. Above all, subjective assessment method is costly, difficult to be achieved. it is not only time consuming, but it is also not suitable for real-time systems [1].

The objective assessment methods can be divided into three categories: full-reference image quality assessment method, part of reference image quality assessment method and no-reference image quality assessment method. In the video

---

[*] This work was supported by grants from The National Natural Sciences Foundation of china (61102064).
[**] Corresponding author.

J. Lei et al. (Eds.): NCIS 2012, CCIS 345, pp. 555–560, 2012.
© Springer-Verlag Berlin Heidelberg 2012

conferencing system, it is difficult to get the reference image sequences. So, the no-reference assessment method will be a better choice.

At present, structural similarity [2], human visual system (HVS) [3], neural networks [4][5] and support vector machine (SVM) [6] have been used in image and video quality assessment[7].

This paper proposes a no-reference image quality assessment method based on SVM, in which LBP operator is used for the image texture analysis.

2   Texture Analysis with LBP

Mosaic effect, delay and fuzzy will occur during the video frame transmission, which will lead to great changes of local texture in the image. Local Binary Patterns (LBP) is a non-parametric 3*3 kernel, which was first introduced by Ojala et al, who showed the high discriminative power of this operator for texture classification [8]. It summarizes the local special structure of an image, and achieves good results in the field of face image for quality testing and analysis. In this paper, LBP operator is used to describe the image feature.

In practical applications, the LBP operator is defined as an ordered set of binary comparisons of pixel intensities between the center pixel and its eight surrounding pixels and considering the result as a binary number, as shown in Fig.1.

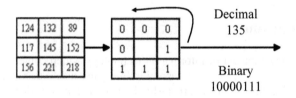

Fig. 1. The LBP Operator (3*3)

The binary number can be determined as:

$$\text{LBP}_{binary} = \sum_{i=0}^{7} B(x_i - x_e)2^{7-i} \tag{1}$$

Where xi corresponds to the grey value of the neighborhood pixels, xe to the grey value of the central pixel, B(x) is a simple function, which can be defined as

$$B(x) = \begin{cases} 1, x \geq 0 \\ 0. x < 0 \end{cases} \tag{2}$$

Converting to binary number of decimal number, the number is 135. The binary number reflects the distribution of the image pixel, and them the histogram of the labels can be used as a texture descriptor.

3   Quality Assessment Using SVM

3.1   Support Vector Machine

Support Vector Machine (SVM) is firstly put forward by Cortes and Vapink. It is a new type of learning machine derived from the VC dimension theory of statistical learning. It is also based on the theory of structural risk minimization in the feature space on construction of the optimal separating hyperplane. It shows a lot of advantages for solving the pattern recognition problems of small sample, nonlinear and high dimension.

SVM is linearly separable for analysis. Considering a binary classification problem with a training set consists of n sample, the basic idea of optimal separating hyperplane is described in Fig.2.

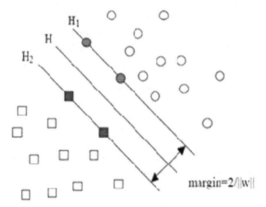

Fig. 2. The basic idea of Optimal Separating Hyperplane in linearly separable case

The hollow circles and the rectangle boxes in the figure are two types of sample points. H is the optimal separating hyperplane (OSH). Respectively, H1 and H2 are two support hyperplanes. The distance between H1 and H2 is called classification interval. Each sample is defined as a two-tuple (xi, yi) (i=1,2,...,n) yi∈(+1,-1). +1 represents positive class and -1 represents negative class. A classifier can be described as

$$w^T x + b = 0 \tag{3}$$

where W T and b are parameters of the classification model. The primal problem is to find the W T and b which minimize function

$$\phi(w) = \frac{1}{2} \| w \|^2 \tag{4}$$

under the conditions:

$$y_i[w^T x_i + b] - 1 \geq 0 , \; i = 1, 2, \ldots n \tag{5}$$

3.2   Quality Assessment Based on SVM

At present, maximum likelihood principle, SVM, and neural network model are widely used in the classifier design [9]. Among these algorithms, maximum likelihood principle is a probability-based algorithm, the probability of parameters should be known beforehand. And the neural network algorithm is complex and lots of parameters are needed. Considering feasibility and complexity of the algorithm, classifier based on SVM is proposed in this paper. The image quality based on SVM classification process is shown in Fig.3.

The classification steps are as follows:

1) Take a certain number of images of good quality and poor quality from a video sequences as a training set over which we trained the assessment algorithm. The choice and quantity make great influence on the SVM model.

2) The samples are processed with gray-scale transformation and feature extraction.

3) Select appropriate kernel function and training algorithm according to the extracted feature and start the training to get the classification model.

4) Use the model to evaluate each image in the testing set and determine its quality.

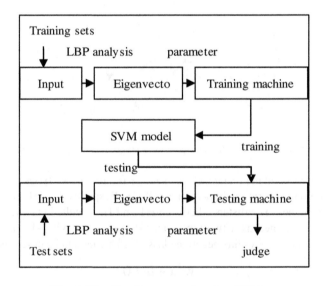

Fig. 3. Classification process based on SVM

4   Experimental Results and Analysis

The quality assessment of image classification based on SVM model in this paper is proposed to distinguish between the image sequences of poor quality and good quality. The examples of these image sequences are shown in Fig.4.

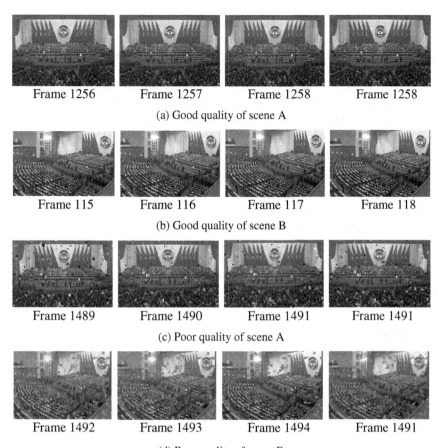

Frame 1256   Frame 1257   Frame 1258   Frame 1258

(a) Good quality of scene A

Frame 115   Frame 116   Frame 117   Frame 118

(b) Good quality of scene B

Frame 1489   Frame 1490   Frame 1491   Frame 1491

(c) Poor quality of scene A

Frame 1492   Frame 1493   Frame 1494   Frame 1491

(d) Poor quality of scene B

Fig. 4. Experimental image sequences

The experimental images are divided into two groups. Group A is composed of 250 images of good quality and 200 of poor quality, which are from a video sequences in a fixed background. Group B is composed of 220 images of good quality and 170 of poor quality, which are from a video sequences in an unstable background. The training sample set consists of 75 images of good quality and 60 of poor quality. The experimental results are shown in Table 1.

Table 1. Statistical data of the experiment

NO.	category	the number of test sample	classifier for good image quality	classifier for poor image quality	classification rate%
A1	good	175	161	14	92.0
A2	poor	140	128	12	91.4
B1	good	145	118	27	81.4
B2	poor	110	87	23	79.1

From the statistical data in table I we can see that the image quality assessment method proposed in this paper achieves a good performance with accurate classification rate of better than 90% when the background is relatively fixed. But for the unstable background, the accuracy rate is just about 80%.

The video sequences are not coherent most likely due to the narrow bandwidth. According to the image quality, a meaningful reference can be provided to the quality of the video conferencing system. Users must fully consider the environment of the network when they choose the equipment of video conferencing system.

5   Conclusions

There are only a few studies on blind image quality assessment. According to the unpredictability and the features of the image sequences of poor quality in the video conferencing system, this paper proposes a no-reference image quality assessment method based on support vector machine. The experimental results show that the method achieves a good effect on the identification under the situation that the image background is relatively stable.

References

1. Wang, Z., Bovik, A.C., Lu, L.: Why is image quality assessment so difficult? In: Proc. IEEE Int. Conf. Acoustics, Speech, and Signal Processing, Florida, USA, pp. 3313–3316 (2002)
2. Fei, X., Xiao, L., Sun, Y., Wei, Z.: Perceptual image quality assessment based on structural similarity and visual masking. Signal Processing: Image Communication (2012), http://dx.doi.org/10.1016/j.image.2012.04.005
3. Guo, B., Zhang, Z., He, Y.: Blind Image Quality Assessment Based on Property of Human Vision System. Journal of Military Communication Technology 30(1), 76–80 (2009)
4. Li, Q., Yang, J., He, L., Fan, S.: Reduced-Reference Video Quality Assessment Based on BP-Neural Network Model for Packet Networks. In: International Conference on Future Information Technology, pp. 500–503 (2010)
5. Gastaldo, P., Zunino, R., Heynderickx, I., Vicario, E.: Objective quality assessment of displayed images by using neural networks. Signal Processing: Image Communication 20, 643–661 (2005)
6. Ding, W., Tong, Y., Zhang, Q., Yang, D.: Image and Video Quality Assessment Using Neural Network and SVM. Tsinghua Science and Technology 13(1), 112–116 (2008)
7. Suresh, S., Venkatesh Babu, R., Kim, H.J.: No-reference image quality assessment using modified treme learning machine classifier. Applied Soft Computing 9, 541–552 (2009)
8. Ojala, T., Pietikainen, M., Harwood, D.: A comparative study of texture measures with classification based on feature distributions. Pattern Recognition 29, 51–59 (1996)
9. Huang, X., Ma, H., Yuan, H.: Video Mosaic Block Detection Based on Template Matching and SVM. In: The 9th International Conference for Young Computer Scientists, pp. 1082–1086 (2008)

Research on Mining Association Rules
in University Scientific Projects Management

Lijian Chen[1], Keji Mao[2], Yuefeng Zheng[2], Xue Zhou[1], and ChaoMing Zhu[1]

[1] Xiaoshan Campus of Zhejiang Radio and Television University, Hangzhou, Zhejiang, China
843120596@qq.com
[2] College of Computer, Zhejiang University of Technology, Hangzhou, Zhejiang, China
maokeji@zjut.edu.cn

Abstract. It is very necessary to find the association rules among a large set of data items, in order to support the applying and establishing scientific research projects, and also support subject teams forming and subjects syncretizing. The paper gave an improved Apriori Algorithm of association rules to mine university scientific research projects data items, and then provide the rules to executive officer support-aid. From the effect practical application shows that it is very useful to teams building and subjects constructing.

Keywords: Association Rule, Apriori Algorithm, Scientific Projects Management, Data Mining.

1 Introduction

Along with the constant development of information technology, especially the development of database technology, the information systems built on the foundation of database technology management are also widely used by businesses[1]. For the management of scientific research, which has been in urgent need of the original data by using various analytical tools to multi-angle analyze of the problem, reasoning, evaluation and judgments, and achieve the purpose of supporting decision-making. We use the improved Apriori algorithm to mine the projects of College of Information Engineering in the last ten years, draw the relevant conclusions, providing a reference in the formulation of policies and projects and encouraging teachers to carry out research projects declaration.

2 Mining Association Technology

2.1 The Concept of Association Mining

(1) Item and Item-set: Establishing I={i_1, i2, i_3, ..., i_n} is n collections of different projects, then each item i_k (k=1, 2, 3, ...n) is called item. I is item-set, n is the length of the item-set. The item-set whose length is n is called K-dimensional item-set, short as k-Item-sets.

J. Lei et al. (Eds.): NCIS 2012, CCIS 345, pp. 561–567, 2012.
© Springer-Verlag Berlin Heidelberg 2012

(2) Services: A service T(Transaction) is a collection of a group of project of the item-set I, that is T is concluded in I. Every service gives each one a unique identifier TID. All collections of the services is called service database D.

(3) Mining association rules: is digging out from the data to meet certain conditions dependent relationship. Data Services is the main target of Mining Association Rules, Association Rules is expressed as X→Y, in which both X and Y belong to I, and X∩Y=Φ.X is called the premise of the rules, Y is the result. In which the support is s%, confidence is c%.

(4) Confidence: in the services which support item-set X of the service database D, there are c% services support item-set Y at the same time, so c% is called the confidence of association rules X→Y, confidence show the strength of the rules, which is expressed as confidence (X→Y).The minimum confidence is written as minconf, users set association rules must meet the minimum confidence, that is the association rules confidence found by System is not less than the minimum confidence.

(5) Support: there are s% services in the service database D which both support the item-set X and Y, so s% is called the support of the association rules X→Y, Support shows the frequency of the rules, expresses as support(X). The minimum support is written as minsup, users set association rules must meet the minimum support that is the association rules support found by System is not less than the minimum support.

(6) High frequency item-set: the support(X) is not less than minsup, then we call X is a high frequency item-set. Both confidence and support are higher than the liminal given is called a strong rule, data mining is mainly about strong rule mining.

2.2   Apriori Algorithm

Mining Association Rules algorithm's main task is: give a service database D, work out all the association rules meeting min-sup and min-conf, The problems generally can be divided into two sub-problems:

(1)Work out all the high frequency item-sets meeting the min-sup;

(2)Using high frequency item-sets to develop all the association rules to meet the minconf. At first R.Agrawal[2] and others raised the classical algorithm of association mining-- Apriori Algorithm.

Apriori Algorithm's Description: Establishing L[K] is a big item-set whose length is K, C[K+1] is a candidate item-set whose length is K+1, the basic idea is as follows:

(1) First scan database and generate the big item-set whose length is 1

(2)Let L[K] self-link to generate the candidate item-set L[K+1].We can know from the previous basic tenets that, the candidate item-set C[K+1] can still be sure to conclude all the big item-set L[K+1].

(3)Use the service of the service database D to test the support of the C[K+1] to generate the big item-set whose length is K+1,calculate the support of each candidate item-set, if it is not less than minsup , then add it in the L[K+1](it's empty at first).

(4)If L[K+1] is empty ,then end, the requiring answer is Answer= UkL[K];else turn to step 2,and continue cycle. The description of the algorithm shown in Fig.1.

#1	L[1]={large 1-item-sets}
#2	For {k=1; L[K]! = ⊅; k++} do
#3	Begin
#4	Ct=apriori_gen(L[K]);
#5	For all transactions t ∈ D do
#6	Begin
#7	Ct=subset（C[k+1],t）;
#8	For all candidates c ∈ Ct do
#9	c.count++
#10	End
#11	L[K+1]={c ∈ C[K+1] | c.count>=minisup}
#12	End
#13	Answer=UkL[K]

Fig. 1. The description of the algorithm

In which:

#1 generating 1-dimensional big item-set;

#2-#12 cycling control until L[K] is empty so that generate K-dimensional candidate item-set C[K+1],it's completed by the function apriori gen;

#5-#10 look over all the services of the service database D, calculate every support of each candidate item c in candidate item-set C[K+1];

#7 to any service t in the service database D, find out all the item-set Ct supported by item t in the candidate item-set C[K+1];

#8-#9 count every candidate item c in the item-set Ct, until the end of cycle #5;

#11 when #5 ends, find out the candidate item whose support is more than minsup from the candidate item-set C[K+1] to build up a K+1-dimensional big item-set;

#13 when #2 ends, the union of all the L[K] is all the big item-sets.

We can know from the algorithm explanation above, the characteristic of Apriori Algorithm is taking advantage of L[K] self-link to generate candidate item-set C[K+1],it makes the full use of the basic principles of the big item-set, it not only have a high efficiency, but also make sure that all the C[K+1] is in the C[K+1]

Apriori Algorithm mainly has these two problems in the operation:

(1) Original candidate item-set is too big, but then can be smaller, the biggest problem is in the generation of two-dimensional candidate item-set, and thus we need to smaller the proportion of two-dimensional candidate item-set;

(2)In the affairs of each cycle the number of item-sets will also affect the efficiency of the algorithm, the problem is particularly conspicuous when in the large data, how to shorten the cycle time for each item-set of services also need to be further improved.

2.3 Improved Apriori Algorithm

Targeting Apriori Algorithm In the search space issues to improve, mainly in the production of the item-set every time in accordance with certain rules to reduce and deleted the size of data sets, thus greatly reducing the number of the data sets, effectively improve the efficiency of the algorithm, and to better applied to the portal log Mining.

Specific approach of improved Apriori Algorithm:

First calculate the frequency of all the items in Lk-1, find out items whose frequency is less than K-1, noted as I, then delete the frequency item-set concluding any items in I, and get a new and smaller K-1-dimensional frequency item-set Lk-1',then let Lk-1'self

```
Input: data set D, minsup, min_support_threshold;
Output: frequent item-sets L;
L1={large 1-item-sets};
for (k=2;Lk-1≠ ;k++)
    {Ck=Apriori_gen (Lk-1, minsup);
    for each t ∈ D          // Scan D for the candidate count
      {if t.delete=0 then
          {C1=subset(Ck,t);      //get the candidate pool generated by t
          if C1= then t.delete=1
              else
              for each c ∈ C1
              c.count++;  // count the candidate pool of candidates
              end;
      }
Lk={c ∈ Ck | c.count≥minsup}
}
return L=∪kLk
procedure Apriori_gen(Lk-1;frequent(k-1)_item-sets;minsup;
min_support_threshold)
for each item 1 ∈ Lk-1
for each i ∈ 1'
    if i ∈ 1
        i.count++;
for each item i ∈ 1'
    if i.count<k-1
        for each item-set i ∈ Lk-1
            if i ∈ 1
            L'K-1= Lk-1-{1};
        for each item-set 11 ∈ Lk-1
        for each item-set 12 ∈ Lk-1
C=11∪12;    // Joint
if has_infrequent_subset(c, Lk-1)
    then
    delete c;    // Pruning
    else add c to Ck
}
return Ck
procedure has_infrequent_subset(c:candidate k_item-set;
                    Lk-1:frequent(k-1)-item-set)
for each (k-1) subsets of c
if c  Lk-1 then
return TURE
else
return FALSE
```

Fig. 2. Steps of the improved Apriori Algorithm

link to generate candidate K-dimensional service database Ck'.This is because candidate K-dimensional service database generated by Lk-1'self-link can't be percolated by the own nature of frequent item-sets. Then in the process of calculating the support of Ck',note on services concluding any item-set in Ck', and no longer calculate in the later scanning of the number, therefore, in calculating the support designate options set by the number of records in the database will be far less than the actual number of records, and with the increase of K, the margin is growing, thus effectively reduce the computation speed of the item-sets, improve the efficiency of the algorithm.

Steps of the improved Apriori Algorithm as shown in Fig.2.

3   The Application of the Association Rule Mining in University Management of Scientific Projects

We use algorithms Mining Association Rules to mine the research data of the in-service teachers of Zhejiang University of Technology, Information Engineering College from 1997 to 2006. Used Improved Apriori Algorithm, execute the mining of the association rules between teachers' title, the highest academic qualifications of teachers and the level of commitment to the project of the teacher. To facilitate the description, we number teachers as 001、002、003、…, teachers' title sorted as main high, secondary high, middle level and junior, etc, the highest academic qualifications of teachers sorted as doctor, master, bachelor, etc, the level of the project sorted as National(including National 973 project, National 863 project, National Fund, etc) ,Provincial or ministerial (including The Ministry of Education project, Province funds, Technology UNOPS, etc) ,department or bureau(including Office of Education project, Technology Bureau projects throughout the city, School Fund, etc),and Transverse(Enterprise commissioned or Cooperation projects which has a Project research costs higher than 500,000). Through the collation of relevant data we received a total of 238 data(because space is limited only in part), format as Table 1.

Table 1. Title teacher qualifications list

number	teacher	title	academic qualifications	project
1	001	main high	master	National
2	001	main high	master	Provincial or ministerial
3	002	secondary high	doctor	Provincial or ministerial
4	003	middle level	master	Provincial or ministerial
5	003	middle level	master	department or bureau
…	…	…	…	…
238	175	junior	master	department or bureau

Through improved Apriori algorithms View Table 1 for all of the frequent-and we can get through the analysis set a candidate item-set 1, as Table 2.

When we finally set the minsup of 16%, Through improved Apriori algorithms can get frequent item-sets { main high, doctor, National } By the second set of the frequent mining, available following six association rules, calculated their degree of confidence is: Conf (main high→doctor, National) = 31.5 % , Conf (doctor→main high, National) = 30.6 %, Conf (National →main high, doctor) = 45.8 %, Conf (main high, doctor→National) = 68.5 %, Conf (main high, National →doctor) = 72.1% , Conf (doctor, National →main high) = 69.1 %。If we establish minconf = 70 % , can reach association rules(main high, National →doctor,support= 16 % ,confidence= 70 %) , The data on association rules shows: Teachers are senior titles and the highest academic qualifications and commitment Dr. national research projects of the total number of teachers 16%; And the number of teachers in the title is now senior national commitment to the project and the total number of 70%.

Table 2. Candidate item-set 1

item-set	number	support	item-set	number	support	item-set	number	support
main high	81	34%	doctor	117	49.2%	National	39	16.4%
secondary high	96	40.3%	master	103	43.3%	Provincial or ministerial	86	36.1%
middle level	42	17.6%	bachelor	18	7.5%	department or bureau	95	39.9%
junior	19	8.1%				Transverse	18	7.6%

We set the minsup of 16%, So from Table 2 can be a frequent item-sets 1.

Table 3. Frequent item-sets 1

item-set	number	support	item-set	number	support	item-set	number	support
main high	81	34%	doctor	117	49.2%	National	39	16.4%
secondary high	96	40.3%	master	103	43.3%	Provincial or ministerial	86	36.1%
middle level	42	17.6%				department or bureau	95	39.9%

If we set up different support and confidence can come to some other association rules,for example establish minsup = 10% ,minconf =55 % , then rules can be introduced: (secondary high, master→Provincial or ministerial, support = 10% , confidence

=55%), (secondary high, Provincial or ministerial→master, support = 10% , confidence = 55%), (main high, doctor→National , support =10% , confidence = 55%), (doctor, National →main high, support = 10% , confidence = 55%), (secondary high, doctor→National , support =10% , confidence = 55%), (secondary high, National→doctor, support =10% , confidence = 55%).

Through the above our association rules can be found:

(1) Project bearers at the national level, main high a doctorate titles and the highest proportion of teachers;

(2)Undertake projects at the provincial and ministerial level who have doctorate degrees accounting for a higher proportion of teachers, And the majority of these teachers has secondary high title.

Through these linkages, can help leadership to raise the overall level of scientific research in decision-making, in particular when encouraging teachers to declare projects, use as a basis, for example, to encourage teachers to actively apply for a doctorate in national and provincial-level issues, teachers who has the title of a high positive declaration of national projects. In the introduction of talent when more consideration with a doctorate in higher education teachers, encouraging teachers positively postgraduate in the qualifications.

4   Summary

Data Mining Association Rules as an important part of technology has been used In the college management of scientific research, Personnel Management, teaching Management. This paper used Improved Apriori Algorithm to mine the science research data, find some of the relevance of the data which can't come from the surface, played a supporting role in decision-making,such as helping the leadership to declare in research, and talent introduction,etc.

References

[1] Mao, K.J.: Government web log mining research and implementation. Zhejiang University of Technology (2005)
[2] Agrawal, R.: Parallel mining of association rules. IEEE Transactions on Knowledge and Data Engineering 8(6), 962–969 (1996)
[3] Toivonen, H.: Sampling large databases for association rules. In: VLDB 1995, Zurich, Switzerland, pp. 407–419 (September 1995)
[4] Ye, J., Zhou, R.L., Xie, K.L.: Data Mining Association Rules improvement and the achievement. Small Micro-computer System 23(3), 347–349 (2002)
[5] Deng, G., Tang, H.Y.: University research in the Decision Support System Application Mining Association Rules. Sheng Yang Teacher Training School Learned Journal(Natural Science Section) 22(1), 7–11 (2004)
[6] He, W., Qi, Y., Xin, Y., Xu, Y.W.: Mining association rules in the Medical research project management. Computer Engineering 31(4), 102–103 (2006)

Public Key Encryption with Multi-keyword Search

Chengyu Hu[1], Peng He[2], and Pengtao Liu[3]

[1] School of Computer Science and Technology, Shandong University, Jinan, P.R. China
[2] Xi'an Communications Institute, Xi'an, P.R. China
[3] Institute of Information Science and Technology, Shandong University
of Political Science and Law, Jinan, P.R. China
hcy@mail.sdu.edu.cn, {helix_win,ptwave}@163.com

Abstract. Since the notion of Public-Key Encryption with Keyword Search (PEKS) scheme was proposed, many revisions and extensions have been given. Public-Key Encryption with Multi-Keyword Search(PEMKS) is one of these extensions, which means that the receiver could query subset keywords of all the keywords embedded in the ciphertext. In this paper, we study the problem of multi-keyword search over encrypted data, and put forward a generic construction for public-key encryption with multi-keyword search scheme. We also give out the security analysis.

Keywords: searchable encryption, multi-keyword search, public key model.

1   Introduction

With the rapid developments of Internet technologies, the amount of sensitive data to be stored and managed on networked servers rapidly increases. To ensure the privacy and confidentiality of sensitive data from even inside attackers such as a malicious system administrator of a server, a user may encrypt the sensitive data before uploading the data into a database server. However, secure encryption transforms data into random strings that are not readable to anyone except the holder of the corresponding decryption key. In turn, this renders a server unable to perform searches for retrieving the data upon a query from a user. To resolve this problem, in 2004, Boneh et al.[1] proposed the concept of public key encryption with keyword search (PEKS) scheme to enable one to search encrypted keywords without compromising the security of the original data and proposed a universal transformation from anonymous identity-based encryption (IBE)[2, 3, 4] to PEKS. In a PEKS scheme, a sender generates encrypted data with an encrypted list of keywords. The sender can use a standard public key encryption scheme to encrypt the data and a PEKS scheme to encrypt each keyword in the list of keywords. This kind of encrypted data may be stored in a server. To search the encrypted data on the server, the user can give the server a certain trapdoor T_w of the searched keyword that enables the server to test whether one of the keywords associated with the data is identical to the keyword of the trapdoor without revealing any information about the list of keywords. Abdalla et al. presented an improved universal transformation from

J. Lei et al. (Eds.): NCIS 2012, CCIS 345, pp. 568–576, 2012.
© Springer-Verlag Berlin Heidelberg 2012

anonymous IBE to PEKS and a novel expansion of PEKS that public-key encryption with temporary keyword search (PETKS)[5]. If one trapdoor has only one keyword information, scheme in [1] could fully realize this function. However, if there are multiple keywords in the trapdoor and they are the subset of the given keywords, the PEKS scheme could do nothing about this. To cope with the problem, two schemes on public-key encryption with conjunctive keyword search (PECKS)[6, 7] were respectively proposed which achieve combinable multi-keyword search function. However, both of the schemes do not support subset keyword search which means that the receiver could query subset keywords of all the keywords embedded in the ciphertext. To cope with this problem, Boneh and Waters constructed public-key systems that support comparison queries on encrypted data as well as more general queries such as subset queries[8]. In paper [9], Zhang et al. gave out a more efficient construction of public-key encryption with conjunctive-subset keywords search (PECSK) scheme. Cao et al. define and solve the problem of multi-keyword ranked search over encrypted data while preserving strict system-wise privacy in the cloud computing paradigm[10]. However, it is not in public-key model.

In this paper, we put forward a generic construction for public-key encryption with multi-keyword search based on inner-product encryption[11] and prove its security. Our constructed scheme can allow the receiver to query subset keywords of all the keywords embedded in the ciphertext. Then, a concrete scheme is given out. The rest of this paper is organized as follows. In Section 2, we review some preliminaries. In Section 3, we give out the definition and security model of public-key encryption with multi-keyword search. In Section 4, we describe our generic construction and provide a security analysis. A concrete scheme is given in Section 5. Finally, we draw our conclusions in Section 6.

2   Preliminaries

2.1   Bilinear Pairings

Let $G1$ be a cyclic group generated *by* g, with a prime order p, and $G2$ be a cyclic group with the same prime order p. Let $e : G1 \times G1 \rightarrow G2$ be a map with the following properties[12]:

1) *Bilinearity*: for all $u, v \in G_1$ and any $a, b \in Z^*_p$ $e(u^a, v^b) = e(u, v)^{ab}$;
2) *Non*-degeneracy: $g_2 = e(g,g)$ is a generator of G_2, i.e., $g_2 \neq 1_{G2}$;
3) *Computability*: There is an efficient *algorithm* to compute $e(u,v)$ for all $u,v \in G_1$;

2.2   Inner-Product Encryption(IPE)

Let $\sum$ be the set of attributes involving vectors $\vec{v}$ of dimension n, and F be the class of predicates involving inner-products over vectors, i.e., $F = \{f_{\vec{x}} \mid \vec{x} \in \sum\}$ such that $f_{\vec{x}}(\vec{y}) = 1$ iff $<\vec{x}, \vec{y}> = 0$. An inner-product encryption (IPE)[11] scheme for the class of predicate F over the set of attributes $\sum$ consists of four algorithms as follows:

-Setup(λ,n): takes as input a security parameter λ, and the dimension n of vectors. It outputs a public/secret key pair (pk, sk).

-Encrypt(pk, $\vec{x}$, m): takes as input the public key pk, a vector $\vec{x} \in \Sigma$, and a message m. It outputs a ciphertext CT.

-KeyGen(sk, $\vec{v}$): takes as input the secret key sk and a vector $\vec{v} \in \Sigma$. It outputs a private key $sk_{\vec{v}}$.

-Decrypt($sk_{\vec{v}}$, CT): takes as input the private key $sk_{\vec{v}}$ and a ciphertext $CT = Encrypt(pk, \vec{x}, m)$. It outputs either a message m if $f_{\vec{x}}(\vec{v}) = 1$ ie., $< \vec{x}, \vec{v} >= 0$ or the distinguished symbol $\perp$ if $f_{\vec{x}}(\vec{v}) = 0$.

For correctness, it is required that for all n, all (pk, sk) generated by Setup(λ,n), all $\vec{x}, \vec{v} \in \Sigma$ and any private key $sk_{\vec{v}} \leftarrow KeyGen(sk, \vec{v})$:

(1) If $f_{\vec{x}}(\vec{v}) = 1$, then Decrypt($sk_{\vec{v}}$, Encrypt(pk, $\vec{x}$, m))=m.

(2) If $f_{\vec{x}}(\vec{v}) = 0$, then Decrypt($sk_{\vec{v}}$, Encrypt(pk, $\vec{x}$, m))= $\perp$ with all but negligible probability.

Security Model for IPE. In [11], attribute-hiding property of the IPE scheme is defined by the following game as follows:

-Init: A selects two target vectors $\vec{x}$ and $\vec{y}$, and sends them to the challenger C.

-Setup: The challenger takes a security parameter 1^{λ} and runs the Setup algorithm. The public key pk and the system parameters are given to A. The challenger C keeps the secret key sk to itself.

-Phase 1: A adaptively issues private key queries for any vectors, $\vec{v}_1, \vec{v}_2, \cdots \vec{v}_d$, subject to the restriction that, for all i, $< \vec{v}_i, \vec{x} >= 0$ if and only if $< \vec{v}_i, \vec{y} >= 0$. C responds with $sk_{\vec{v}_i} \leftarrow KeyGen(sk, \vec{v}_i)$.

-Challenge: A outputs two messages M_0 and M_1. If $M_0 \neq M_1$, it is required that $< \vec{v}_i, \vec{x} > \neq 0 \neq < \vec{v}_i, \vec{y} >$ for all queried vectors $\vec{v}_i$. The challenger picks a random bit $b \in \{0,1\}$. If $b=0$ then C gives $CT \leftarrow Encrypt(pk, \vec{x}, M_0)$ to A, and if $b=1$ then C gives $CT \leftarrow Encrypt(pk, \vec{y}, M_1)$ to A.

-Phase 2: A continues to issue private key queries for additional vectors, subject to the same restriction as before.

-Guess: Finally, A outputs a guess $b' \in \{0,1\}$. It wins the game if $b' = b$.

The advantage of the adversary A against the IPE scheme is defined as: $Adv_{IPE,A}^{AH}(1^{\lambda}) = |\Pr[b = b'] - \frac{1}{2}|$.

3   PEMKS Definition and Security Requirements

3.1   Definition

The definition and security requirements of PEMKS similar to that of public-key encryption with conjunctive-subset keywords search presented in paper [9] are given as follows:

Definition. Public key encryption with multi-keyword search scheme consists four algorithms, Setup, PEMKS, Trapdoor, Test:

1) Setup(λ,l): takes as input the security parameter λ and the max number of keywords in the ciphertext. It outputs public key pk, secret key sk and the keyword list L.

2) PEMKS(pk, w_{i1}, w_{i2},..., w_{it}): takes as input the public key pk and t ($t \leq l$) keywords which is associated with one document, where i_m ($m=1,...,t$) is the keyword order of w_{im} in the keyword list L. It outputs a ciphertext C of w_{i1}, w_{i2},..., w_{it} which will be used for test.

3) Trapdoor(sk, $w'_{j1}, w'_{j2}, \cdots, w'_{jk}$): takes as input the secret key sk and keywords $w'_{j1}, w'_{j2}, \cdots, w'_{jk}, k \leq t$, where j_n ($n=1,...,k$) is the keyword order of w'_{jn} in the keyword list L. It outputs the trapdoor $T_{w'_{j1}, w'_{j2}, \cdots, w'_{jk}}$.

4) Test(C, $T_{w'_{j1}, w'_{j2}, \cdots, w'_{jk}}$): takes as input ciphertext C and trapdoor $T_{w'_{j1}, w'_{j2}, \cdots, w'_{jk}}$. Then it outputs a bit b, which satisfies

(1)$b=1$, when $(w'_{j1}, w'_{j2}, \cdots, w'_{jk}) \subseteq (w_{i1}, w_{i2}, \cdots, w_{it})$

(2)$b=0$, otherwise.

3.2   Security Requirements

Based on the model of PEKS, the secure PEMKS scheme   should satisfy the anonymity of the ciphertext. This requirement means that no one could get the embedded keywords from the ciphertext. As the content was encrypted, the information is safe without the private key. This requests that the PEMKS ciphertext C cannot leak any information about the content, even the keywords. We call it the Anonymity of the ciphertext, i.e. the keywords can not be extracted directly from theciphertext.

Following [6], we define the security, i.e., indistinguishability of ciphertext from ciphertext (IND-CC-CKA), of the PEMKS scheme. The security is defined by the following game interacted between an attacker A and a challenger C. The IND-CC-CKA game is as follows:

-Init: A selects two target keyword sets W_0 and W_1, and sends them to the challenger C.

-Setup: The challenger takes a security parameter 1^λ and runs the Setup algorithm. The public key pk and the system parameters are given to A. The challenger C keeps the secret key sk to itself.

-Phase 1: A adaptively issues trapdoor queries for any keyword sets, $\vec{v}_1, \vec{v}_2, \cdots \vec{v}_d$. The challenger C responds with $T_{\vec{v}_i} \leftarrow$ Trapdoor($sk, \vec{v}_i$).The only restriction is that W_0 and W_1 should not be distinguished from trapdoors issued.

-Challenge: The challenger picks a random bit $b \in \{0,1\}$. And it sets $C_b =$ PEMKS(pk, W_b). Then send it to A.

-Phase 2: A continues to issue trapdoor queries for additional keyword sets, $\vec{v}_{d+1}, \cdots \vec{v}_\gamma$, subject to the restriction that $\vec{v}_i \neq W_0$ or W_1 . The challenger runs Trapdoor($sk, \vec{v}_i$) and generates the trapdoor $T_{\vec{v}_i}$. If $T_{\vec{v}_i}$ cannot distinguish for W_0 and W_1, then it responds $T_{\vec{v}_i}$ to A.

-Guess: Finally, A outputs a guess $b \in \{0,1\}$. It wins the game if $b'= b'$.

We define the advantage of the adversary A against the PEMKS scheme as the function of the security parameter 1^λ: $\mathrm{Adv}_{PEMKS,A}^{IND-CC-CKA}(1^\lambda) = |\Pr[b = b'] - \frac{1}{2}|$.

4   A Generic Construction for Public Key Encryption with Multi-keyword Search Scheme

4.1   Generic Construction

We suggest a generic construction using IPE and the keywords order should be fixed in our construction. We define our construction for PEMKS as follows.

1)Setup(λ,l): It runs IPE.Setup(λ,l) and sets pk=IPE.pk and sk=IPE.sk. The keyword list consists of l keyword, denoted as $W=(w_1, w_2,\ldots, w_l)$. Let $\tilde{m}$ be a fixed message which can be negotiated by the sender and the receiver.

2)PEMKS($pk, w_{i1}, w_{i2},\ldots, w_{it}$): Let $\vec{w}[h]$ be the hth element of vector $\vec{w}$. First, it builds the l dimension vector of keywords associated with the ciphertext $\vec{w}$, where $\vec{w}[i_h] = 0 (h = 1 \sim t)$ and $\vec{w}[h] = r \neq 0$ $h \notin \{i_1, i_2, \cdots, i_t\}$,r is a random value. Then it runs IPE.Encrypt($pk, \vec{w}, \tilde{m}$) and sets the ciphertext C=IPE.CT.

3)Trapdoor(sk, $w'_{j1}, w'_{j2}, \cdots, w'_{jk}$):   It   extends   the   search   keywords $w'_{j1}, w'_{j2}, \cdots, w'_{jk}$ to a l dimension vector of searched keywords $\vec{w}'$, where $\vec{w}'[j_z] = w'_{jz}(z = 1 \sim k)$ and $\vec{w}'[z] = 0$, $z \notin \{j_1, j_2, \cdots, j_k\}$. Then it runs IPE.KeyGen($sk, \overline{w}'$) and sets the trapdoor $T_{w'_{j1}, w'_{j2}, \cdots, w'_{jk}} =$ IPE.$sk_{\overline{w}'}$.

4)Test($C, T_{w'_{j1}, w'_{j2}, \cdots, w'_{jk}}$): It runs IPE.Decrypt($T_{w'_{j1}, w'_{j2}, \cdots, w'_{jk}}$,C) and sets $\tilde{m}'$ to the result value. If $\tilde{m}'= \tilde{m}$, then it outputs 1, otherwise it outputs 0.

Correctness. From PEMKS and Trapdoor algorithm, we can see that $<\vec{w}, \vec{w}'> = 0$ iff. $\{w'_{j1}, w'_{j2}, \cdots, w'_{jk}\} \subseteq \{w_{i1}, w_{i2}, \cdots, w_{it}\}$. So if the searched keywords are the subset of the keywords associated with the ciphertext, Test algorithm can get $\tilde{m}'= \tilde{m}$ from IPE.Decrypt and return 1. Otherwise, it outputs 0.

4.2   Security Analysis

The notion of inner-product encryption security is called *attribute hiding* which requires that the ciphertext associated with attribute I hides all information about the underlying message and the associated attribute I. That is, an adversary holding several private keys $sk_{\vec{v}_1}, sk_{\vec{v}_2}, \cdots, sk_{\vec{v}_l}$ learns only $<\vec{x}, \vec{v}_i> = 0$ and the message, where $\vec{x}$ is the corresponding vector of attribute I, but learns nothing else about I. In PEMKS of our construction, we take $\vec{w}$ as the attribute I of IPE, so if the IPE is attribute hiding, an adversary can learns nothing about $\vec{w}$. That is, the anonymity of the keywords associated with the ciphertext is guaranteed by the attribute hiding property of IPE.

Theorem 1. Assuming that IPE is attribute hiding, PEMKS as per the above construction is IND-CC-CKA secure.

Proof. Assume that A is an adversary with advantage ε in breaking PEMKS against IND-CC-CKA. Then we can construct an adversary B who attacks the attribute hiding property of IPE with advantage ε using A as described below.

-Init: B selects two target vectors sets $\vec{x}$ and $\vec{y}$, and sends them to A. A sets $W_0 = \vec{x}$ and $W_1 = \vec{y}$, and sends them to the challenger C.

-Setup: The challenger takes a security parameter 1^λ and runs the Setup algorithm. The public key PEMKS.pk is given to A. The challenger C keeps the secret key PEMKS.sk=IPE.sk to itself. A sends the public key PEMKS.pk to B as IPE.pk.

-Phase 1: B adaptively gives private key queries for any vectors, $\vec{v}_1, \vec{v}_2, \cdots \vec{v}_d$ to A, subject to the restriction that, for all i, $<\vec{v}_i, \vec{x}> = 0$ if and only if $<\vec{v}_i, \vec{y}> = 0$. A sends the queries to C and C responds with $T_{\vec{v}_i} \Leftarrow$ Trapdoor$(sk, \vec{v}_i)$ to A. Then A sends $T_{\vec{v}_i}$ to B as $sk_{\vec{v}_i}$.

-Challenge: B sends to A two messages M_0 and M_1. If $M_0 \neq M_1$, it is required that $<\vec{v}_i, \vec{x}> \neq 0 \neq <\vec{v}_i, \vec{y}>$ for all queried vectors $\vec{v}_i$. A sends M_0 and M_1 to the challenger. The challenger C picks a random bit $\beta \in \{0,1\}$. C sets $C_\beta = \text{PEMKS}(pk, W_\beta)$ (Note that the PEMKS algorithm should set $\tilde{m} = M_\beta$ to run IPE.Encrypt). C gives C_β to A, and A sends C_β to B as CT.

-Phase 2: B continues to send to A the private key queries for additional vectors, $\vec{v}_{d+1}, \cdots \vec{v}_\gamma$, subject to the same restriction as before. A just takes the vectors as the queries keyword sets and gives $\vec{v}_{d+1}, \cdots \vec{v}_\gamma$ to the challenger. The A obtains from challenger C the trapdoor $T_{\vec{v}_i}$ which are returned to B as $sk_{\vec{v}_i}$.

-Guess: Finally, A outputs a guess $\beta' \in \{0,1\}$ and gives β' to B. B outputs β'.

We can get $\text{Adv}_{\text{IPE,B}}^{\text{AH}}(1^\lambda) = \text{Adv}_{\text{PEMKS},A}^{\text{IND-CC-CKA}}(1^\lambda)$. So if A can break PEMKS scheme against IND-CC-CKA with advantage ε, then B can attacks the attribute hiding property of IPE with advantage ε.

5   An Instantiation of PEMKS under Standard Assumptions

We now consider a specific PEMKS scheme under standard assumptions as per our construction of section 4 using the inner-product encryption scheme in paper [11] which is attribute-hiding under Decision BDH and Decision Linear assumptions.

1) Setup(λ,l): Given a security parameter $\lambda \in Z^+$, the algorithm obtain a tuple (p,G_1,G_2,e). The algorithm picks a random generator $g \in G_1$, random exponents $\delta_1,\delta_2,\theta_1, \theta_2, \{a_{1,i}\}_{i=1}^l, \{b_{1,i}\}_{i=1}^l, \{f_{1,i},f_{2,i}\}_{i=1}^l, \{d_{1,i},d_{2,i}\}_{i=1}^l$ in Z_p. It also picks a random $g_2 \in G_1$. It picks a random $\Omega \in Z_p$ and obtains $\{a_{2,i}\}_{i=1}^l, \{b_{2,i}\}_{i=1}^l$ in Z_p under constraints that $\Omega = \delta_1 a_{2,i} - \delta_2 a_{1,i}$, $\Omega = \theta_1 b_{2,i} - \theta_2 b_{1,i}$.

For $i=1,\ldots,l$, the algorithm sets $A_{1,i} = g^{a_{1,i}}$, $A_{2,i} = g^{a_{2,i}}$, $B_{1,i} = g^{b_{1,i}}$, $B_{2,i} = g^{b_{2,i}}$, $F_{1,i} = g^{f_{1,i}}$, $F_{2,i} = g^{f_{2,i}}$, $D_{1,i} = g^{d_{1,i}}$, $D_{2,i} = g^{d_{2,i}}$. Next, it sets $U_1 = g^{\delta_1}$, $U_2 = g^{\delta_2}$, $V_1 = g^{\theta_1}$, $V_2 = g^{\theta_2}$, $g_1 = g^{\Omega}$, $\Lambda = e(g,g_2)$. The public key pk and secret key sk are set to be
$pk = (g, g_1, \{A_{1,i}, A_{2,i}, F_{1,i}, F_{2,i}\}_{i=1\sim l}, \{B_{1,i}, B_{2,i}, D_{1,i}, D_{2,i}\}_{i=1\sim l}, \{U_i, V_i\}_{i=1,2}, \Lambda)$,
$sk = (\{a_{1,i}, a_{2,i}, b_{1,i}, b_{2,i}, f_{1,i}, f_{2,i}, d_{1,i}, d_{2,i}\}_{i=1\sim l}, \delta_1, \delta_2, \theta_1, \theta_2, g_2)$.

The keyword list consists of l keyword, denoted as $W = (w_1, w_2, \ldots, w_l) \in Z_p^l$. Let $\tilde{m} \in G_2$ be a fixed message which can be negotiated by the sender and the receiver.

2) PEMKS($pk, w_{i1}, w_{i2}, \ldots, w_{it}$): Let $\vec{w}[h]$ be the hth element of vector $\vec{w}$. Let $\vec{w}$ be the l dimension vector of keywords associated with the ciphertext, where $\vec{w}[i_h] = 0 (h = 1 \sim t)$ and $\vec{w}[h] = r \neq 0$ $h \notin \{i_1, i_2, \cdots, i_t\}$, r is a random value. the algorithm picks random exponents $s_1, s_2, s_3, s_4 \in Z_p$ and computes the ciphertext $C = (C_A, C_B, \{C_{1,i}, C_{2,i}, C_{3,i}, C_{4,i}\}_{i=1\sim l}, C_D)$ as follows:

$$C_A = g^{s_2}, C_B = g_1^{s_1}, C_{1,i} = A_{1,i}^{s_1} \cdot F_{1,i}^{s_2} \cdot U_1^{\vec{w}[i]s_3}, C_{2,i} = A_{2,i}^{s_1} \cdot F_{2,i}^{s_2} \cdot U_2^{\vec{w}[i]s_3},$$

$$C_{3,i} = B_{1,i}^{s_1} \cdot D_{1,i}^{s_2} \cdot V_1^{\vec{w}[i]s_4}, C_{4,i} = B_{2,i}^{s_1} \cdot D_{2,i}^{s_2} \cdot V_2^{\vec{w}[i]s_4}, C_D = \Lambda^{-s_2}\tilde{m}$$

3) Trapdoor($sk, w'_{j1}, w'_{j2}, \cdots, w'_{jk}$): It extends the search keywords $w'_{j1}, w'_{j2}, \cdots, w'_{jk}$ to a l dimension vector of searched keywords $\vec{w}'$, where $\vec{w}'[j_z] = w'_{jz} (z = 1 \sim k)$ and $\vec{w}'[z] = 0, z \notin \{j_1, j_2, \cdots, j_k\}$. Then the algorithm picks random exponents $\lambda_1, \lambda_2, \{r_i\}_{i=1}^l, \{\phi_i\}_{i=1}^l \in Z_p$ and computes the trapdoor $T_{w'_{j1}, w'_{j2}, \cdots, w'_{jk}} = (K_A, K_B, \{K_{1,i}, K_{2,i}, K_{3,i}, K_{4,i}\}_{i=1\sim l})$ as:

$$K_{1,i} = g^{-\delta_2 r_i} g^{\lambda_1 \vec{w}'[i]a_{2,i}}, K_{2,i} = g^{\delta_1 r_i} g^{-\lambda_1 \vec{w}'[i]a_{1,i}}, K_{3,i} = g^{-\theta_2 \phi_i} g^{\lambda_2 \vec{w}'[i]b_{2,i}}, K_{4,i} = g^{\theta_1 \phi_i} g^{-\lambda_2 \vec{w}'[i]b_{1,i}},$$

$$K_A = g_2 \prod_{i=1}^l K_{1,i}^{-f_{1,i}} K_{2,i}^{-f_{2,i}} K_{3,i}^{-d_{1,i}} K_{4,i}^{-d_{2,i}}, K_B = \prod_{i=1}^l g^{-(r_i + \phi_i)}.$$

4) Test(C, $T_{w'_{j1},w'_{j2},\cdots,w'_{jk}}$): The algorithm outputs

$$\tilde{m}' \leftarrow C_0 \times e(C_A,K_A)e(C_B,K_B) \times \prod_{i=1\sim l} e(C_{1,i},K_{1,i})e(C_{2,i},K_{2,i})e(C_{3,i},K_{3,i})\ e(C_{4,i},K_{4,i})$$

If $\tilde{m}' = \tilde{m}$, then it outputs 1, otherwise it outputs 0.

Analysis. The correctness of the used IPE scheme is proved in paper [11], so it guarantees that the Test algorithm in our scheme is correct. From the analysis in section 4, we can get that 1) our scheme is trapdoor unforgeable for the unforgeability of private key in the IPE scheme[11] and 2) our scheme has the property of keyword anonymity because the IPE scheme in paper [11] is a attribute hiding.

6   Summary

We show how to generically implement public key encryption with multi-keyword search scheme using inner-product encryption scheme. We provide the security model of PEMKS scheme and also provide the security analysis of the construction. Based on a secure inner-product encryption scheme under standard assumptions, we give a concrete instantiation of our generic construction.

Acknowledgements. This project is supported by The Key Science Technology Project of Shandong Province(GrantNo. 2011GGX10124), Independent Innovation Foundation of Shandong University(Grant No.2012TS073).

References

1. Boneh, D., Di Crescenzo, G., Ostrovsky, R., Persiano, G.: Public Key Encryption with Keyword Search. In: Cachin, C., Camenisch, J.L. (eds.) EUROCRYPT 2004. LNCS, vol. 3027, pp. 506–522. Springer, Heidelberg (2004)
2. Boneh, D., Franklin, M.: Identity-Based Encryption from the Weil Pairing. In: Kilian, J. (ed.) CRYPTO 2001. LNCS, vol. 2139, pp. 213–239. Springer, Heidelberg (2001)
3. Boyen, X., Waters, B.: Anonymous Hierarchical Identity-Based Encryption (Without Random Oracles). In: Dwork, C. (ed.) CRYPTO 2006. LNCS, vol. 4117, pp. 290–307. Springer, Heidelberg (2006)
4. Ducas, L.: Anonymity from Asymmetry: New Constructions for Anonymous HIBE. In: Pieprzyk, J. (ed.) CT-RSA 2010. LNCS, vol. 5985, pp. 148–164. Springer, Heidelberg (2010)
5. Abdalla, M., Bellare, M., Catalano, D., Kiltz, E., Kohno, T., Lange, T., Malone-Lee, J., Neven, G., Paillier, P., Shi, H.: Searchable Encryption Revisited: Consistency Properties, Relation to Anonymous IBE, and Extensions. In: Shoup, V. (ed.) CRYPTO 2005. LNCS, vol. 3621, pp. 205–222. Springer, Heidelberg (2005)
6. Park, D.J., Kim, K., Lee, P.J.: Public Key Encryption with Conjunctive Field Keyword Search. In: Lim, C.H., Yung, M. (eds.) WISA 2004. LNCS, vol. 3325, pp. 73–86. Springer, Heidelberg (2005)
7. Hwang, Y.-H., Lee, P.J.: Public Key Encryption with Conjunctive Keyword Search and Its Extension to a Multi-user System. In: Takagi, T., Okamoto, T., Okamoto, E., Okamoto, T. (eds.) Pairing 2007. LNCS, vol. 4575, pp. 2–22. Springer, Heidelberg (2007)

8. Boneh, D., Waters, B.: Conjunctive, Subset, and Range Queries on Encrypted Data. In: Vadhan, S.P. (ed.) TCC 2007. LNCS, vol. 4392, pp. 535–554. Springer, Heidelberg (2007)
9. Zhang, B., Zhang, F.: An efficient public key encryption with conjunctive-subset keywords search. Journal of Network and Computer Applications 34, 262–267 (2011)
10. Cao, N., Wang, C., Li, M., Ren, K., Lou, W.: Privacy-Preserving Multi-keyword Ranked Search over Encrypted Cloud Data. In: Proc.of INFOCOM 2011, pp. 829–837 (2011)
11. Park, J.H.: Inner-product encryption under standard assumptions. Des. Codes Cryptogr. 58, 235–257 (2011)
12. Menezes, A.J., Okamoto, T., Vanstone, S.A.: Reducing elliptic curve logarithms to a finite field. IEEE Transactions on Information Theory 39(5), 1636–1646 (1993)

S&T Novelty Search and R&D of Removing Duplicate Software

XiaoDan Wang, Shen Li, and XueTing Li

Si ling Street No.17, Nan-gang District, Harbin, Harbin Institute
of Technology, China

Abstract. Science and technology(S&T) novelty search is a special information consultation service developed as part of the Chinese science and technology system. This paper briefly introduces the university library S&T novelty search. At the same time, it briefly describes the situation of the Harbin Institute of Technology library. It is focuses on research and development (R&D) of removing duplicate software that are used for S&T novelty search. The R&D of software includes three parts: research of requirement, design of software, testing and running of software.

Keywords: Science and Technology Novelty Search, Removing Duplicate, Research and Development, Software.

1   Introduction

1.1   S&T Novelty Search in Chinese University Libraries

With the development of the Chinese S&T system, S&T novelty search will further develop as a kind of special information consultation service [1]. During the 1980s, in order to make improvements in the way projects are set up and evaluated in terms of S&T research excellence, a series of management measures were established in China to promote the quality of S&T research. As one of these measures, a number of S&T information searching and evaluation centers were set up in Chinese university libraries. [1]

1.2   S&T Novelty Search in HITLIB

S&T novelty search plays an important role in university technology research. The Harbin Institute of Technology library（HITLIB）has been started in 1998 on the S&T novelty search [1] [2]. Up to now, seventy-eight S&T novelty search centers were established directly under the P.R.C. Ministry of Education [3]. According to the types of university, S&T novelty search are divided into four types [9]: comprehensive, science and engineering, agronomy, medicine. Now our HITLIB is the preparatory station of ministry of education, at the same time, it is S&T novelty search station of the former ministry of aerospace and ministry of construction.

HITLIB has a number of S&T Novelty Search consultant, they have rich professional knowledge and experience of retrieval technology. S&T novelty

J. Lei et al. (Eds.): NCIS 2012, CCIS 345, pp. 577–581, 2012.
© Springer-Verlag Berlin Heidelberg 2012

search has strict regulation and procedures. S&T novelty search is complex process, but there is some simple and repetitive work, such as removing duplicate document. Usually we retrieve the Chinese or foreign database, which achieve a large number of documents. There is a high repetition rate of document. In order to remove duplicate, we have developed a kind of software. The software can be achieved removing the duplicate function. The software can save work time consumedly, increase work efficiency. With using the software system, it makes novelty search service systematize, norm turn, automation, then attain exaltation purpose of the efficiency.

1.3   The Workflow of S&T Novelty Search in HIT

In general, the workflow of S&T novelty search has the same basic way in university libraries [1] [4]. Firstly, researchers identify one or more innovation points, keywords,

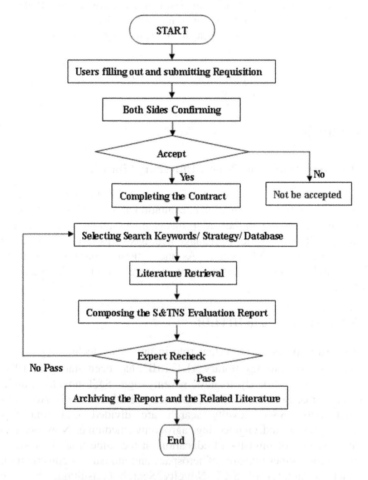

Fig. 1. The workflow is HITLIB novelty search service

technical points etc. Then staff in the S&T novelty search service search a variety of electronic databases and Dialog system around the innovation points[1] [5]. Secondly, the S&TNS staff will analyze the similarities and differences between the research and the corresponding literature [6] [7]. Finally, the S&TNS service gives a "Novelty Proof" according to the material retrieved. The following of workflow is HITLIB novelty search service [8] (Fig.1).

2   R&D of S&T Novelty Search Software

2.1   Research Contents

This research contents includes three following parts:

2.1.1   Research of Requirement

Document retrieval and removing duplicate is one of the most important aspects in S&T novelty search work. We often used CNKI database, WF database, CQWP database. These databases included a great quantity duplicate document. The same to foreign database, especially network database SCI, ISTP, EI, INSPEC etc. In the past, novelty-searching personnel have been using manual method in document duplicate, which wastes much time. Therefore, we desperately need the software of removing duplicate. More than anything, software can perform a particular required function, which removing duplicate and outputting standard format.

2.1.2   Design of Software

Software design should take into account the needs of many, including the Chinese and foreign database compatibility, different database output format, database update cycle. The end-users are novelty search personnel, therefore facing end-user, the software operation should be simple and software interface be friendly. When the database format changes, it will modify the corresponding program module. At the same time, the software can display removing duplicate amount and rest of document quantity. The software can export different report format as required.

2.1.3   Testing and Running of Software

In order to make use of software to achieve the best effect, all personnel of our novelty search center help to test. When find a few of problem in testing, we will timely adjust and perfect. After several tests and operations, the software that is running on our system will be the official software.

2.2   Research Methods

The software is developed based on Java. Java is a kind of object-oriented programming language as we usually know. It consists of multiple key technologies, including JVM, class loader, Java API and Java programming language. Java technology has excellent versatility, high efficiency, portability and safety of platform. It widely used in personal PC, data center, a game console, science super computer, mobile phone and Internet.

In this system scheme, the whole work is divided into five modules:

1. Based on language understanding rules module

For different databases derived in different document formats, this module uses a language understanding rules. It will be complete format unification, in order to facilitate the subsequent processing.

2. Automatic duplicate checking module

Based on the theme matching method, the core module of the system will complete the function of removing duplicate.

3. Based on the fuzzy matching sentence similarity module

According to different database samples might be slight difference, we will use sentence similarity measure.

4. Intelligent check processing module

Using the module 3 of the sentence similarity results, we performed two times check about high similarity results. By authors, journals and other information, we carry out new novelty search processing with module2 based on the subject matching method. We will get to the final results.

5 、 Result display module

The module is mainly for librarian convenient interface windows. In addition to display results, also undertake checking whether the right input and output effect management. The interface includes reading results number, removing duplicate number, the final output text and etc.

2.3   The Part of Code of the Program

The following code segments come from relative program. Firstly, the program calls a procedure called 'Converter' to identify all the literature in the different database, then it removes duplicate literature. Finally the literature is stored to the status information.

```
private Converter converter = new Converter();
  private Map<String, List<String>> dups = new
HashMap<String, List<String>>();
* @param inputDirectory
  * the input directory
* @param outputDirectory
* the output directory
* @throws IOException
* Signals that an I/O exception has occurred.
 */public void process(String inputDirectory, String
outputDirectory)
    throws IOException {
    converter.convert(inputDirectory);
    conferences = converter.getConferences();
    dissertations = converter.getDissertations();
    journals = converter.getJournals();
    dedup();
```

```
    writeInfo(outputDirectory);
    write(outputDirectory); }
  private void writeInfo(String outputDirectory)
throws IOException {
    String i = info();
  System.out.println(i);
  FileUtils.writeStringToFile(new
File(outputDirectory + "/status.txt"),
          i);
```

3   Summary

The software has passed through research, development, testing stage. Currently we have officially used this removing-duplicate software in our HITLIB. The effect is very ideal. The reason why the operation process is simple and accurate is that it is welcome by novelty retrieval personnel. We hope that the software can serve more university novelty search station. Thereby we should make contributions to our country university S&T novelty search institutions.

References

1. Li, A.G.: A Kind of Transformation of Information Service—Science and Technology Novelty Search in Chinese University Libraries. Journal of Academic Librarianship 33, 144–148 (2007)
2. Wu, L.C., Wu, L.H.: Service Engineering: An Interdisciplinary Franework. Journal of Computer Information System 51, 14–23 (2010)
3. Liu, H.J., Qin, X., Chen, T.: Mashup-the Combination of Sci-tech Novelty Search and Corporation Competitive Intelligence System. In: Proceedings of International Forum on Technological Innovation and Competitive Technical Intelligence 2008, pp. 331–337 (2009)
4. Wang, S.W.: Studies on New Service Model of Sci-tech Novelty Search in Technological Innovation. In: Proceedings of International Forum on Technological Innovation and Competitive Technical Intelligence 2008, pp. 357–362 (2009)
5. Wen, X.A.: Development Strategy of Technology Innovation-oriented Science and Technology Novelty Search. In: Proceedings of International Forum on Technological Innovation and Competitive Technical Intelligence 2008, pp. 363–372 (2009)
6. Zhang, W.: Sci-tech Innovation Analysis of Beijing Based on the Statistical Analysis of the Sci-tech Novelty Search Projects Finished by Beijing Academy of Science and Technology. In: Proceedings of International Forum on Technological Innovation and Competitive Technical Intelligence 2008, pp. 381–8572 (2009)
7. Li, M., Liu, B.S., Dan, W., Hu, Y.H.: Problems and Solutions of Company Competitive Intelligence Serving Government Decision-making Based on the Similarities and Differences between Novelty Search and Company Competitive Intelligence Service. In: Proceedings of International Forum on Technological Innovation and Competitive Technical Intelligence 2008, pp. 444–450 (2009)
8. Harbin Institute of technology library website, http://www.lib.hit.edu.cn/page/chaxin/gong-zuo-liu-cheng
9. Ministry of Education website, http://www.chaxin.edu.cn/

Optimization Model for Three-State Devices Networks Reliability and Its Particle Swarm Optimization Algorithm

WulanTuya, Dongkui Li, Xuebao Li, and Liping Yang

School of Information Science and Technology, Baotou Normal University,
Inner Mongolia, P.R.C. 014030
wl_bttc@sina.com

Abstract. In this paper, we deal with three- state device network system reliability model problem, by particle swarm optimization algorithm to seek the optimal solution of the problem. At first, classification is made for three- state device network system reliability optimization model, then, we construct two new three-state system reliability optimization model and design a discrete particle swarm optimization algorithm is used to solve the approximate optimal solution. Computer simulations show that the algorithm gives the approximate optimal solution of the model. New models and optimization algorithms for researching network system design and optimization problems are of theoretical and practical significance.

Keywords: Reliability optimization model, three-state device networks, PSO algorithm, optimum solution.

1 Introduction

System reliability must be considered performance indicators in system design, operation and maintenance process. The three- state system in the real world is also widely exist, the three - state device network reliability assessment and reliability optimization problem has aroused extensive attention [1-3]. Three- state device network is composed by the three-state device, and also shows a two failure mode; three-state devices and networks, in addition to the normal state, but also for the two failure modes, namely, open failure and shorted failure mode. Three-state network system has a more complex combination property, therefore, the assessment of the three-state device network system reliability and reliability optimization problem is more complicated, and some optimization problems are NP-HARD problem. Existing research results are also very limited.

Building process of three-state device network system, in addition to care about the reliability of the system, but also consider the component count, size, price and other factors [1-3], thus the reliability optimization model is divided into:

J. Lei et al. (Eds.): NCIS 2012, CCIS 345, pp. 582–591, 2012.
© Springer-Verlag Berlin Heidelberg 2012

(1) Constituting a system's component count, price, size does not exceed a certain quantitative limits and other constraints; the goal is to select the appropriate network topology, constructed from the system with maximum reliability [1-4];

(2) The network topology has a relatively fixed shape, and constituting the system's reliability to meet certain minimum conditions, the goal is to select the appropriate number of components, or the appropriate allocation of different reliability components, to get component amount minimum, or volume minimum or the lowest price.

Existing three-state device network reliability optimization problem results, mainly in type 1, and studying the network topology is a series-parallel structure or parallel-series of structural components to form a network have the same open failure probability of failure and shorted failure mode. Three- state device network reliability optimization model proposed in this paper are type 2, and to design a discrete particle swarm algorithm to solve the optimization model.

2   Three-State Device Network Reliability Optimization Model

2.1   Assumptions

(1) The network is a three-state device network. Network and form a network of device have and only have three states, namely, normal working mode, open failure mode and shorted failure mode.

(2) Network represented by a graph G = (V, E), where V is the collection of nodes, E is collection of edges. And the edge represents the connection of the device. s is the source node, t is a sink node.

(3) The node is completely reliable, and never failed.

(4) The network is Coherent.

(5) The device failures are statistically independent. The probability of a device in a certain state is known.

In the three-state device network G = (V, E), 2-terminal reliability refers to the probability of the system to work, under normal condition, only the failure probability can be calculated, that is the open probability of failure mode and shorted failure mode probability.

In this paper, P (G) the normal operation probability, Q (G) network open failure probability, S (G), the network shorted failure probability. p_i, q_i, s_i, respectively is the normal work probability, open failure and short failure probability of the device i. In order to calculate the reliability of the network, just find the Q (G), S (G).

The reduction formula:

$$S(G) = R(G)\big|_{r_i = s_i} \tag{1}$$

$$Q(G) = 1 - R(G)\big|_{r_i = 1 - q_i} \tag{2}$$

$$P(G) = 1 - Q(G) - S(G) \tag{3}$$

Which R (G) is a network of 2-state reliability expressions, r_i is the component i's 2 - state reliability.

2.2   Models

2.2.1   Series-Parallel of Optimization Model

Assumption that the system G=(V, E)   is made of by a series of n independent subsystems (see Fig. 1), use of the same three-state components in parallel in each subsystem, C_n is the total price of the system (here only consider the component costs), R indicates   the system reliability, c_i is the unit price of the i-th component, the number of the i-th component is x_i of the i sub-systems, $x_i >= 1$, R_0 is the system the desired reliability.

Then series-parallel of optimization model is:

$$\min \ C_n = \sum_{i=1}^{n} c_i x_i \tag{4}$$

$$s.t. \prod_{i=1}^{n} R_i(x_i) = \prod_{i=1}^{n}(1 - q_i^{x_i}) - \prod_{i=1}^{n}(1 - (1 - s_i)^{x_i}) \geq R_0 \tag{5}$$

Where equation (5) may be got by using the formula (1)-(3), the definition of three-state network system's open failure as well shorted failure mode. This is a redundancy optimization model [5], belong to NP-HARD problem, we can consider using smart algorithms developed in recent years to seek its approximate optimal solution [5, 6].

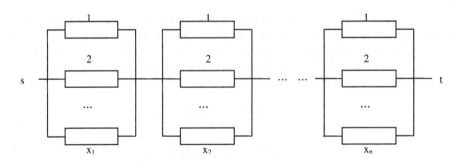

Fig. 1. Series-parallel of optimization model

2.2.2   Parallel-Series of Optimization Model

Assumption that the system $G = (V, E)$ consists of n independent subsystems in parallel (see Fig. 2), using the same three-state components in each subsystem is a series, C_n is the total price of the system (here only consider the component costs), R indicates that the system reliability, c_i is the unit price of the i-th component, the number of the i-th component is x_i of the i sub-systems, $x_i >= 1$, R_0 is the system to achieve the desired reliability.

Then parallel-series of optimization model is:

$$\min \ C_n = \sum_{i=1}^{n} c_i x_i \tag{6}$$

$$s.t. \prod_{i=1}^{n} R_i(x_i) = \prod_{i=1}^{n}(1 - s_i^{x_i}) - \prod_{i=1}^{n}(1 - (1 - q_i)^{x_i}) \geq R_0 \tag{7}$$

Where equation (7) may be got by using the formula (1)-(3), the definition of three-state network system's open failure as well shorted failure mode. This is a redundancy optimization model [5], belong to NP-HARD problem, we can consider using smart algorithms developed in recent years to seek its approximate optimal solution [5, 6].

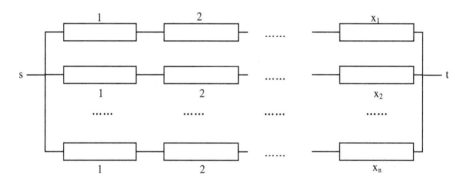

Fig. 2. Parallel-series of optimization model

3   Particle Swarm Optimization Algorithms

3.1   Continuous Particle Swarm Optimization Algorithm

Particle swarm optimization algorithm (Particle Swarm Optimization, PSO) was first proposed by Eberhart and Kennedy in 1995, it is the basic concept from the foraging behavior of birds. PSO algorithm is to be inspired from the behavior of these biological populations for solving optimization problems. In PSO, each potential solution of the optimization problem can be seen as a point on the D-dimensional search space, called "particles" (Particle), all the particles have an objective function determines the adaptation value (Fitness Value), each particle has a speed to determine the direction and distance they fly, and then the particles are following the current optimum particles in the solution space search. The particle swarm optimization is an iterative model-based optimization algorithm, was originally used for continuous space optimization. Continuous space coordinate system, the mathematical description of the particle swarm algorithm is as follows.

In the PSO algorithm, each particle is a solution of D-dimensional space, then the i-th particle state $X_i = (x_{i1}, x_{i2}, ..., x_{iD})$, each particle's velocity vector $V_i = (v_{i1}, v_{i2} ... v_{iD})$, the optimal state of each particle denoted $P_{besti} = (p_{i1}, p_{i2}, ..., p_{iD})$, the optimal state with groups experienced $P_{gbest} = (p_{g1}, p_{g2}, ..., p_{gD})$. The entire population particles by tracking the extreme value of the individual extreme as well groups to update their flight speed and position, finding the optimal solution in the solution space. PSO algorithm iteration formula is as follows:

$$v_{id}^{t+1} = w * v_{id}^{t} + c_1 * rand()(p_{id} - x_{id}^{t}) + c_2 * rand()(p_{gd} - x_{id}^{t}) \tag{8}$$

$$x_{id}^{t+1} = x_{id}^{t} + v_{id}^{t+1} \tag{9}$$

$$\begin{cases} v_{id}^{t} = v_{max} & \text{if } v_{id}^{t} \geq v_{max} \\ v_{id}^{t} = -v_{max} & \text{if } v_{id}^{t} \leq -v_{max} \end{cases} \tag{10}$$

Where, w is the inertia weight factor; c_1, c_2 are acceleration constants; t is evolution algebra. In formula (8), Part 1 is the speed of the particle inertia, reflecting the memory behavior of particles; Part 2 is the distance between the particle i with its own best location for the "cognitive" part of the particle; identify the particle's action from the part of their experience; part 3 is the distance between particle i the current position and the group best position the action of "social" part of the particle, marking particles from other particles in the group experience part of the knowledge sharing and cooperation.

3.2   Discrete Particle Swarm Optimization Algorithm

Particle swarm optimization algorithm was originally based on the real-valued continuous space optimization techniques, however, many practical engineering applications have characteristics of combinatorial optimization, particle swarm optimization algorithm will be in a binary space expanded, get a discrete binary arithmetic model.

In the binary space, the particles move is represented through the inverted position, the speed of particles described changing the number of bits per iteration, or a particle in the Hamming distance between t and t-1 times of the value. Consistent with the formulation in continuous space of particle swarm optimization, ignoring one of the time without changing the meaning of other parameters. Discrete binary model of particle velocity and position update equations as follows:

$$v_{id} = v_{id} + c_1 * rand1() * (p_{id} - x_{id}) + c_2 * rand2() * (p_{gd} - x_{id})$$

If (rand ()S(v_{id})) then x_{id}=1 else x_{id}=0. Where $S(v_{id}) = \dfrac{1}{1+\exp(-v_{id})}$ is Sigmoid

function, and rand () is random number on [0, 1].

3.3   New Particle Swarm Optimization Algorithm

Three-state device network system reliability optimization problem (Part 2 of model 1 and model 2) may use the discrete particle swarm optimization to seek the optimal solution; they can be transformed into the integer programming problem to get the optimal solution [7] also. We design a new algorithm using a flow chart as follows (see Fig. 3).

4   Simulation

4.1   Example of Series-Parallel Model

Assume that a series-parallel model (Fig.1) consists of five subsystems, components in each subsystem's normal work probability, open failure probability and shorted failure probability as follows:

$$\begin{cases} p_1=0.96, \\ q_1=0.03, \\ s_1=0.01, \end{cases} \begin{cases} p_2=0.93, \\ q_2=0.02, \\ s_2=0.05, \end{cases} \begin{cases} p_3=0.85, \\ q_3=0.1, \\ s_3=0.05, \end{cases} \begin{cases} p_4=0.80, \\ q_4=0.1, \\ s_4=0.1, \end{cases} \begin{cases} p_5=0.75 \\ q_5=0.1 \\ s_5=0.15 \end{cases}$$

$c_1 = 3\$$, $c_2 = 12\$$, $c_3, = 8\$$, $c_4 =5\$$, $c_5 = 10\$$, the system requirements for $R_0= 0.9$. Set population size is 20, the maximum number of iterations is 100, the acceleration constants $c_1 = c_2 = 1.4962$, the weights w reduced to 0.4 by 0.9 linear, that is, w = 0.9-0.5*(t-1)/99. Simulation by Matlab2009a programming in Lenovo's dual-core notebook (basic configuration is CPUT1400@1.73Ghz 1.73Ghz 1G memory, the Windows XP SP3 system).

Initialization: the population size N, the maximum number of iterations G_{max}; inertia weight w, the probability of open failure and shorted failure of the device vector Q,S, the cost of vector C, the initial velocity $V_{i,}$ (i = 1, ..., N), a global particle P; produce two sets of particle swarm X_i, X_i', calculated for each particle of reliability, judgment to satisfy the constraints ($\geq R_0$), if not to meet is to be adjusted until the meet. Calculating the objective function (price). When particle X_i not satisfy the constraint conditions, need for each bit of the particles to adjust .with d bits, for example, if rand()$\geq$0.5,then $X_{id} \leftarrow X_{id}+1$,otherwise $X_{id} \leftarrow X_{id}-1$

Update individual extreme and global extreme: If particle X_i of the objective function value is less than X_i 'of the objective function value, then the X_i instead of X_i', if X_i 'objective function value is less than P, then X_i' instead of P.

Update rate by (8), (9) is amended as $x_{id}^{t+1} = [x_{id}^t + v_{id}^t]$, where [x] the largest integer not exceeding x;In addition, the number of components in each subsystem can not be 0, when $x_{id}^{t+1} < 1$,set $x_{id}^{t+1} = 1$.

Calculate the reliability of each particle, to determine whether to satisfy the constraints, otherwise the adjustment, until satisfy the constraints; calculate for each particle corresponds to the objective function value.

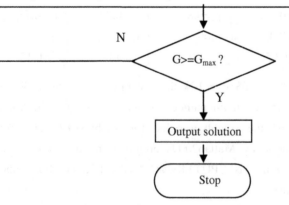

N

$G>=G_{max}$?

Y

Output solution

Stop

Fig. 3. Particle swarm algorithm for solving three-state device network reliability optimization model

Calculation 50 times, calculates the actual optimal solution is (1, 1, 2, 2, 2) and the system reliability is 0.9224, and a total cost is 61$. The overall situation is as follows: smallest solution is 61$, the maximal solution of 133$; average solution (approximate optimal solution) 109.88$, the total iteration time is 17.748508 seconds. Particle swarm algorithm convergence speed can converge to the minimal solution, the overall time-consuming is short, but the comparison with the simulated annealing algorithm, the average optimal solution cost is too large. During the execution of which the particle swarm algorithm to produce the best solution, the cost of - iterations relations, see Fig.4.

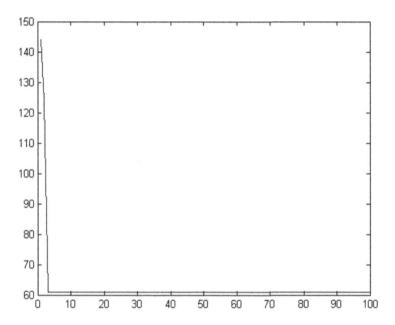

Fig. 4. The relationship between the number of iterations and cost of algorithm to generate the optimal solution (abscissa-number of iterations, vertical coordinates-cost)

4.2   Example of Parallel-Series Model

Parallel-series model of Figure 2, the probability of each subsystem components work properly, the open probability of failure and shorted failure probability is same with example 4.1.

Set $c_1 = 3\$$, $c_2 = 12\$$, c_3, $= 8\$$, $c_4 = 5\$$, $c_5 = 10\$$, the system requirements for $R_0 = 0.9$. Set population size is 20, the maximum number of iterations is 100, the acceleration constants $c_1 = c_2 = 1.4962$, the weights w reduced to 0.4 by 0.9 linear, that is, w = 0.9-0.5*(t-1)/99. Simulation by Matlab2009a programming in Lenovo's dual-core notebook (basic configuration is CPUT1400@1.73Ghz 1.73Ghz 1G memory, the Windows XP SP3 system).

Calculation 50 times, calculate the actual optimal solution for (1, 1, 2, 2, 2), then the system reliability is 0.9079 for a total cost of 61$. The overall situation is as follows: smallest solution is 61$, the maximal solution of 133$; average solution (approximate optimal solution) 107.48 $, the total iteration time is 11.998573 seconds. Particle swarm algorithm can converge to the minimal solution, the overall time-consuming short, but the comparison with the simulated annealing algorithm, the average optimal solution cost is too large. During the execution of which the particle swarm algorithm to produce the best solution, the cost of - iterations relations, see Fig. 5.

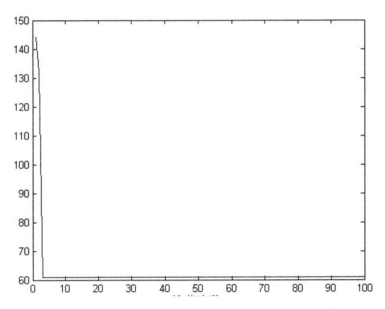

Fig. 5. The relationship between the number of iterations and cost of algorithm to generate the optimal solution (abscissa-number of iterations, vertical coordinates-cost)

5   Conclusions

On the basis of the three-state device network system reliability optimization model classified to construct two kind of new three-state device network system reliability optimization model; model belong to NP-HARD problem. According to the model characteristics, we design a particle swarm optimization algorithm to obtain the approximate optimal solution; simulation results show that the algorithm can quickly give the optimal solution. Three-state device network system reliability optimization problem, due to its optimal solution is affected by many factors, a variety of intelligent algorithm convergence conditions to be various, and thus, many problems worthy of further study.

References

1. Anzanello, M.J.: A Simplified Approach for Reliability Evaluation and Component Allocation in Three-state Series and Parallel Systems Composed of Non-identical Components. Gest. Prod. Sao Carlos 16, 54–62 (2009)
2. Page, L., Perry, J.: Optimal "Series-Parallel" Networks of 3-state Devices. IEEE Transations 37, 388–394 (1988)
3. Levitin, G.: Optimal series-parallel topology of multi-state system with two failure modes. Reliability Engineering & System Safety 77, 93–107 (2002a)
4. Gutjahr, W., Pflug, G.C., Ruszczynski, A.: Configurations of Series-Parallel Networks with Maximum Reliability. Microelectronic and Reliability 36, 247–253 (1996)
5. Gao, S., Yang, J., Wu, X., Liu, T.: Ant Colony Algorithm for Optimization of System Reliability. Computer Applications and Software 24, 94–96 (2004)
6. Luo, J., Liu, Y.: Application of Intelligent Algorithm in Optimization Design of All-terminal Networks Reliability. Computer Measurement & Control 14, 782–785 (2007)
7. Wang, Z., Li, W.: Optimization of System Reliability Based on Particle Group Algorithms. Journal of Taizhou University 28, 29–32 (2006)
8. Kang, Q., Zhang, Y., Wang, L., Wu, Q.: Intelligent Particle Swarm Optimization Algorithm. Metallurgical Industry Automation 30, 5–9 (2005)
9. Zhou, T., Meng, X., Wang, S., Li, Y.: The Reliability Optimization Method for Two Kinds of Three-state Systems. Journal of Natural Science of Heilongjiang University 32, 758–761 (2009)
10. Qi, R., Xie, L., Lin, H., Li, Y.: The Redundancy Design and Optimization for a Three-State System. Journal of Systems Engineering and Electronics 14, 1039–1041 (2003)

Application of the Webcam for High Voltage Transmission Towers Constructing and Building[*]

Siguo Zheng[1,**], Fanguang Li[2], Yugan You[2], and Gang Liu[2]

[1] Shanghai Electric Power Construction Co, Ltd., State Grid Corporation of China, 200010
lifanguang2008@126.com
[2] School of Electrical Power and Automation Engineering,
Shanghai University of Electrical Power, 200090

Abstract. From the current status quo of China's electric power construction, an improved coordination of wireless audio and video system is designed according to application of the webcam for high voltage transmission towers constructing and building in the paper. Field experiments proved that the system not only solves the deficiency of the traditional way that is through propaganda for coordination and communication during the construction process, it also could transmit the operation condition of high-voltage tower to the ground command and the remote terminal clearly and accurately. The information could be saved in the local computer or the TF card at the same time. The system can remove the interference of the video images online, enhance immunity to electromagnetic interference, improve work efficiency and reduce the risk of construction. The system is more convenient, simpler and has lower cost.

Keywords: Webcam, Audio and video system, Image processing, High-voltage tower.

1   Introduction

With the development of China's industrialization and urbanization and the increase of electric power construction scale gradually, high-voltage overhead lines in the application of power transmission and transformation aerial industry are becoming more and more. The approval of 1000kV UHV power transmission and transformation project and the high-voltage overhead line construction of 220kV, 500kV and above voltage have been quite common. However, the work in high-voltage line tower

---

[*] Project supported by National Natural Science Foundation of China(No.61203224/ F030307), the Science and Innovation Fund of shanghai Municipal Education Commission (No.13YZ101.) and Shanghai Electric Power Construction co, ltd (No.QWZHKJ[2012]243).
[**] Siguo Zheng(March 1963-), a engineer, has attended and been responsible for the infrastructure project management of nearly 20 about 500kV or 220kV substation in Shanghai Power Economic Research Institute, Shanghai Municipal Electric Power Company since1984.

J. Lei et al. (Eds.): NCIS 2012, CCIS 345, pp. 592–600, 2012.
© Springer-Verlag Berlin Heidelberg 2012

construction is still in the relatively backward state, and the degree of modernization of construction method and construction equipment is quite lower. There are in a number of accidents which can not be found and eliminated in the site of power constructions. These accidents lead to the security incidents, such as casualties, damage of power grid and loss of equipments etc.

The traditional audio and video coordinate system could monitor operation on the high-voltage tower remotely [1], but the system is limited in the use of electric power construction site due to its inconvenient to carry, poor immunity to electromagnetic interference and shorter transmission distance. A set of audio and video coordinate system with "remote viewing" for overhead operation on the high-voltage is designed in this paper. The system improves the intuitiveness of overhead operation, enhances the ability of anti-electromagnetic interference, reduces the risk of accidents and provides help for the accident identification. The informatization of electric power construction process is an important part of our smart grid vision. The audio and video operating system for the high-voltage transmission towers constructing and building will fill the gaps of the field, and accord with the development direction of smart grid and information.

2 A Wireless Audio and Video Coordinate System

The video surveillance system is a new technology developed in recent years [2]. It has been played an important role in the fields of aerospace, security, emergency and medical health. This paper uses the video surveillance system at the core of the embedded DSP system. Two types of digital audio and video surveillance system are used widely now. One is the digital video recording equipment which is as the core of the digital video surveillance systems. Another is video surveillance system based on the embedded video server.

The audio and video surveillance system consists of a webcam, a computer, a wireless router and some remote monitoring equipment such as PAD, NokiaE71 mobile phones and so on.

The overall structure of the wireless audio and video coordination system is shown in Figure 1. The operation area is divided into three parts: the work area in high altitude, the command area on the ground, and the monitoring area on the remote. Modified webcams are worn on the operators who distribute in different places of the high voltage tower. The video images collected by webcams are wirelessly transmitted to a computer which is as a local server. The local computer displays the split-screen video images of the construction site by accessing the IP address of camera. The video images could be transmitted from the local computer to the remotely monitoring devices with video playback, such as PAD, NokiaE71 phone etc. The commanding officers could view the pictures of the construction site by using the portable devices at anytime, anywhere. The commanding officers on the ground can issue instructions to the operator in high altitude if needed.

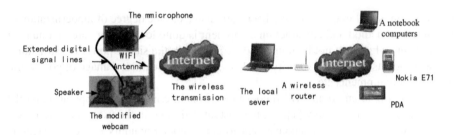

Fig. 1. The overall structure of the system

2.1   The Modified Webcam

The webcam is a combination of the traditional cameras and the network video technology. In addition to image capture function of the traditional camera, the webcam also has built-in digital compression controller and the operating system based on WEB.   The compressed and encrypted data of video is sent to the terminal Users via LAN, Internet or wireless network. Remote users could use a standard Web browser on a computer to access the webcam according to its IP address, to monitor the situation of the target site real-time, and to edit and storage the image data real-time.

In order to the need of the high-altitude operation of high voltage lines and to carry the webcam easily for operators, the traditional webcam is divided into that the lens, the launch and the speaker system, and the digital signal transmission lines between the lens and the transmitter are extended. The modified webcam is shown in figure 2.   The lens is fixed on the operator's helmets [3], and the speaker and the transmitter with a WIFI antenna are worn on the operator's waist. Due to the built-in digital compression controller which can convert analog signals into digital signals, the webcam reduces the electromagnetic interference from the high-voltage lines.

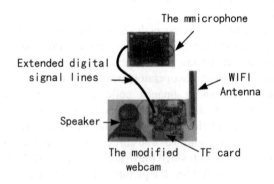

Fig. 2. The modified webcam

2.2   The Local Server and the Wireless Router

The operating performance of the webcam determines the local server and router should be configured below the high-voltage tower. A HP Touch Smart PC is used as the local sever in the system. The local computer could access the webcam and split-screen display the operating dynamics on the high-altitude tower, so that operators on the high-altitude tower and the command staff on the ground could coordinate and coordinate each other. The local computer could write the information into the hard disk and playback them, in order to check the occurrence of safety accidents or the important part of the construction, to identify the security responsibility for the accidents and the re-examine extent of the operating regulation. At the same time, it also can transfer information to the remote terminal for RMON (remote monitoring).

The wireless router should meet the following conditions:

(1) Complaints with IEEE802.11b standards;
(2) Supports IP broadband controlling, and allocate broadband networks reasonably and freely;
(3) Supports WDS, so that the wireless router could be WDL wirelessly, expand the wireless network, and across the distance barrier;
(4) The wireless transmission rate is up to 150Mbp;
(5) The operating frequency is 2.4GHz.

2.3   The Remote Monitoring Equipments

In order to understand the high-altitude operation of high voltage lines, some portable electronic devices, like PAD, NokiaE71 mobile phones, laptop computers and others should be equipped for commanding officers in the remote terminal. By itself with or installing the remote login software, these devices access to the wireless router's IP address. The video monitor screen could play after entering the password [4].

3   Removing the Interference of the Video Images Online

The audio and video coordination system is mainly used for the monitoring of the aerial work on the high-voltage transmission line tower. The environment of construction site is relatively poor. The magnetic leakage of overhead wires and high-voltage equipment in the high voltage lines, the digital interference of overhead communication lines and equipment and the ground potential differences among several webcams will cause the interferences of snows, textured, denim, stripes, distortions and upper and lower jitters in the video images. In order to monitor the aerial construction of high-voltage line more clearly, and to have better coordination and communication between the commanding officers and the operators, the video images with interfere processing should be processed.

There are many ways of image denoising such the mean filter, the median filtering and the wiener filtering.[5] The mean filter which is also known as the linear filter, mainly adopts the neighborhood average method to get the mean. The basic idea of the mean filter is that the average grays of several pixels instead the gray of each pixel. Mean filter can effectively suppress additive noise, but images will become blurred, and clarity is down.

The median filter is a signal processing technology of smoothing filter nonlinearly based on order statistics theory, which can suppress the noise effectively. The steps of median filtering are: Firstly, some pixel is as the center to determine a neighborhood which usually is the square, circle or cross neighborhood. Secondly, the pixel gray value of neighborhood is sorted, and the middle value is as the new value of the middle pixel gray, where the neighborhood is called the window. When the window moves, the image could be smoothed using the median filtering. The formula of the median filter is,

$$y_i = Med\left\{f_{i-v} \cdots, f_i \cdots, f_{i+v}\right\} \qquad i \in Z, v = \frac{m-1}{2} \tag{1}$$

Its algorithm is simple and the time complexity is low, but the image of points, lines and spire should not use the median filtering.

The wiener filtering is a restoration method which makes the mean-square error between the original image and the recovered image minimum. The wiener filtering is an adaptive filter, which could remove the Gaussian noise effectively.

Assuming that the true value of the useful signal is $s(n)$, the estimated value of the signal is $s'(n)$, and The error between the true value and estimated value is $e(n)$, then,

$$e(n) = s(n) - s'(n) \tag{2}$$

Where, $e(n)$ is a random variable. The minimum mean square of the wiener filter is,

$$E\left[e^2(n)\right] = E\left[\left(s(n) - s'(n)\right)^2\right] \tag{3}$$

A denoising method of wavelet packet transform based on the wiener filter is used in this paper.[5, 6] This method not only can effectively remove the additive white Gaussian noise, but it can effectively preserve the edge information, which greatly improves the visual quality of the image. Firstly, it processes the image with noise using the wiener filter, and calculates the standard deviation of the noise using the processed image. The standard deviation is as the threshold of the wavelet packet. Secondly, it decomposes the processed image using the wavelet packet, so that the low-frequency and the high-frequency part of the image are decomposed. The wavelet packet tree coefficients are processed with the soft threshold using the calculated threshold. Finally, it could access to the denoised image using the wavelet packet inverter transformation.

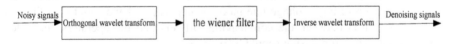

Fig. 3. The denoising process combining the wavelet transform with the wiener filter

The mathematical model of the image with the shot noise pollution is Eq (4).

$$f(i, j) = x(i, j) \cdot q(i, j) \qquad (4)$$

Where, $x(\bullet)$ is the unknown true image which should be restored; $f(\bullet)$ is the actually observed image with noise pollution; $q(\bullet)$ is the multiplicative shot noise; i,j are the spatial location of the pixels, $(i,j) \in R^2$.

In order to distinguish the shot noise $q(\bullet)$ and the true image $x(\bullet)$, and change the multiplicative noise of ultrasound images into the additive noise, we take logarithms of both sides of Eq(5), then ,

$$f'(i, j) = x'(i, j) + q'(i, j) \qquad (5)$$

Where, $f'(\bullet), x'(\bullet), q'(\bullet)$ are the logarithms of the $f(\bullet), x(\bullet), q(\bullet)$ respectively.

Assuming that the transformed $q'(\bullet)$ obeys the Gaussian Distribution $N(0, \sigma^2)$, and the Independent Identical Distribution, is independent of each other with $f'(\bullet)$.

After the wavelet transform for Eq(6), then,

$$W_f = W_x + W_q \qquad (6)$$

Where, w_f is the wavelet coefficients of the image with noise; w_x is the wavelet coefficients of the original image; w_q is the wavelet coefficients of the noise.

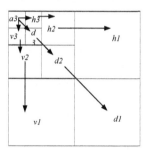

Fig. 4. The figure of wavelet decomposition

The original images are mostly the low-frequency signals or some relatively stable signals, while the noising images $q'(\bullet)$ are the high-frequency signals in the ultrasound images. So the following approach is adopted in the denoising process [7].

Firstly, to decompose $f'(\bullet)$ with the wavelet transform. The decomposition process is as shown in Figure 4.

Secondly, to reconstruct the signal, in order to achieve the purpose of removing the noise.

(a) The original image   (b) The processed image

Fig. 5. Comparison between the original image and the processed image

It could be seen through the comparison of two images that the processed image is clearer than the original one, which shows that the denoising method of wavelet packet transform based on the wiener filter is feasible and could be used for the interference removal of the video images online in figure 5.

4   Application of Modified Webcam in High-Voltage Monitoring System

The operators should complete the cable laying, the installation of high-voltage tower, insulators, the controlling and protective devices in high altitude. The commanders should monitor the operation and make orders on the ground. The coordination and communication should be timely and correct. Obviously, the traditional way of gestures and propaganda is not appropriate. The transmission system using analog signal also is not ideal due to the poor anti-electromagnetic interference and inconvenient carrying for commanders because of the receivers and the data acquisition card. To solve these problems, the modified webcam is adopted to monitor the operation of the high-voltage tower. The steps are as follows:

(1) The installation of webcam driver. The webcam driver software is installed on the local sever in order to configure the computer information and the webcam information. The IP address of webcam is 192.168.1.126 and the HTTP port is 81 when the IP address of the local computer is 192.168.1.100.

(2) Signing in the webcam system. By clicking directly the button "open" behind the on the internal address, or directly , entering directly the external address http://192.168.1.126:81 in the web address bar, we can sign in the webcam system, and then enter the username "admin" and password.

(3) Functional operation. Accessing to the main interface, we could set the operating information according to requirement. The monitoring screen is shown as in figure 6.

Fig. 6. The monitoring screen in the local sever

The system supports the mobile surveillance. The operating system of Windows Mobile system and the 2.0 smart phone systems which belong to the development platform of Symbian Series 60 could get the monitoring screen of the local computer by signing in the IP address of the local computer via the wireless router. NokiaE71 could get the screen as shown in Figure 7.

Fig. 7. The monitoring screen in NokiaE71

It is shown from the monitor screen that the commander on the ground could see clearly the operation and equipment of operators in high-altitude area, and make the right decision. At the same time, the audio and video could be saved in the computer.

5   Conclusion

This system is modified based on the wearable audio and video coordinate system. Unlike the analog camera, the convert webcam could c the transmission of analog signals to the transmission of digital signals, and improve the ability of anti-electromagnetic interference. Saving for the wireless receiver and the data acquisition card facilitates to carry the system for the commanders on the ground. The feature of removing interfere of the video images online improves the clarity of the video images. Through the wireless transmission, the data of voice and video is fed back to the commanders on the ground, which forms a different practice with the past system, greatly enhances the efficiency of construction, and reduce the risk of high-altitude operations, while the data could be real-time saved.

The following features are mainly achieved in the system:

a) The audio and video transmission remotely based on the 2.4G;
b) The audio and video network transmission wirelessly;
c) The split-screen monitoring of multi-browsers online;
d) The playback and the storage in local hard disk and TF card of video;
e) The function of two-way voice intercom;
f) The terminal monitoring via wireless phone.

The experiment shows that, the wireless audio and video system based on webcam can not only be used for the construction and installation of high voltage tower, it can also be used for the similarly aerial operations project. Such as the installation of fans in the wind farm, the high-altitude command operations of buildings and so on. The improved transmission and coordination system of wireless audio and video can also be used for the centralized control station, especially for the security, operations management and supervision in the unattended substation. This is in line with the development direction of China's intelligent network.

References

[1] Zheng, S., Li, F., Qian, H.: A Wireless Audio and Video Coordinate System for High Voltage Transmission Towers Constructing and Building. In: The International Conference on Computer and Management, March 2012 (to be published)
[2] Luo, S., Zuo, T., Zou, K.: Principle and maintenance of video surveillance systems, pp. 36–48. Electronic Industry Press, Beijing (2007)
[3] Feng, C., Jun, S.: Application of wearable mobile audio and video interactive system s to power production. East China Electric Power (37), 1514–1516 (2009)
[4] Zhou, C., Wang, Z., Tang, K., Jin, X.: Design and Implement of the Distributed Audio and Video digital Surveillance System Based on IP Multicast. Computer Systems & Applications (11), 48–51 (2004)
[5] Liu, J., Tan, Y., Wen, M.: Application of Wavelet Transform in Ultrasound Image. Coal Technology (30), 137–139 (2011)
[6] Tian, P., Li, Q., Ma, P.: A New Method Based on Wavelet Transform for Image Denoising. Journal of Image and Graphics 13(3), 394–399 (2008)
[7] Mihcak, M.K., Kozintsev, I., Ramchandran, K., et al.: Low-complexity image denoising based on statistical modeling of wavelet coefficients. IEEE Signal Processing Letters 6(12), 300–303 (1999)

The Remote Video Monitoring System Design and Development for Underground Substation Construction Process[*]

Siguo Zheng[1,**], Yugan You[2], Fanguang Li[2], and Gang Liu[2]

[1] Shanghai Power Economic Research Institute, Shanghai Municipal Electric
Power Company, State Grid, Shanghai 200010, China
274160071@qq.com
[2] School of Electrical Power and Automation Engineering, Shanghai University
of Electrical Power, Shanghai 200090, China

Abstract. From the current situation of underground substation construction in China, we design and development a remote video monitoring system. By using the web camera, power line carrier technology and image enhancement technology, the construction of underground substation can be clearly and accurately transmitted to the ground control station and real-time preservation. This system provides technical means for safety and quality management of power grid construction, improves the work efficiency and reduces hidden danger of construction work.

Keywords: Power line carrier, Video monitoring system, Web camera.

1   Introduction

Current,State Grid Corporation of China has entered a new stage of development, needed to improve the ability of controlling large power system, put a higher demand on professional and lean management. The core content is uniforming grid construction management process, technical specifications and construction standards; strengthening the control of construction's key link; strengthening the professional management of construction function, project and construction team; enhancing power grid construction safety quality and craft level; promote construction management efficiency and benefit. However, there are many problems in power grid construction process: power grid construction process involves project management, civil engineering, electrical and many other professionals; the construction environment is harsh; construction security risk is high and there are a lot

---

[*] Project supported by National Natural Science Foundation of China(No.61203224/F030307),
the Science and Innovation Fund of shanghai Municipal Education Commission.

[**] (No.13YZ101.) and Shanghai Electric Power Construction co, ltd (No.QWZHKJ[2012]243).
Siguo Zheng(March 1963-), a engineer, has attended and been responsible for the
infrastructure project management of nearly 20 about 500kV or 220kV substation in
Shanghai Power Economic Research Institute, Shanghai Municipal Electric Power Company
since1984.

J. Lei et al. (Eds.): NCIS 2012, CCIS 345, pp. 601–605, 2012.
© Springer-Verlag Berlin Heidelberg 2012

of construction hidden dangers. According to the city underground substation construction actual situation, this project is to build a power construction supervision system based on Video Wireless Sensor Network (VSWN) technology [1]. This system can realize the online accessing to the scene of construction site and off-line recording playback functions. It will provide technical means for power grid construction's safety and quality management, has application value.

2   Remote Video Supervision System

Video monitoring system is a new technology developed in recent years, it has played an important role in the aerospace, security emergency, medical and many other fields [2]. The widely used digital video surveillance system has two types. One is a digital video surveillance system using digital video equipment as the core, the other is a video monitoring system using the embedded video server as the core.

This remote video supervision system consists of the web camera, wireless transmitter, wireless router, power line carrier device and some remote monitoring equipment.

The overall structure of video surveillance system is shown in Figure1. The system uses the web cameras located in the underground substation to collect the scene screen, and it will transmit to the wireless receiver through the wireless transmitter. Then signal will returns on the local server computer on the ground through the power line carrier devices. The local server computer can use a wireless router to transmit pictures to the remote monitoring devices with video playback, such as mobile phones and notebook computers.

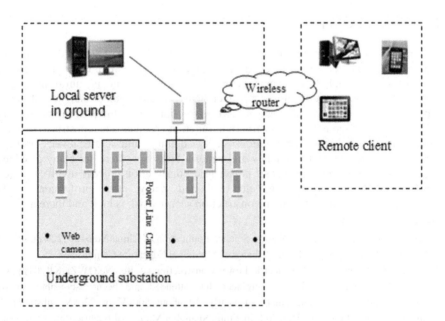

Fig. 1. The overall structure of video surveillance system

Local server can not only play audio and video, but also write these information into the hard disk. So that when a security incident in the construction process, we are able to review the accident process and identify the responsibility of the accident.

2.1   Web camera and Wireless Router

Active web camera [3] is a combination of traditional cameras and network video technology. In addition to the traditional camera image capture function, the machine also built-in digital compression controller and WEB-based operating system, and can be used in low-light environments. Video data, after compression and encryption, sent through the LAN, internet or wireless network to end users. can be used in low-light environments. Remote users can use a standard Web browser on a PC, according to the IP address of the network camera,to access network camera, then real-time monitoring the situation of the target site and edit image data.

Wireless router can receive and transmit signals, highest provide 150Mbps wireless transmission rate.Various devices can free communication through the wireless router bridge to cross the barrier of distance.

2.2   Power Line Carrier Device

Power line carrier communication [4-5] refers to the technology of using existing power lines to transmit analog or digital signals by the way of carrier. Its greatest feature is not required to set up a new network, as long as the wires it will be able to pass data. Underground substation is located in the underground10 meters deep, and is divided into several layers. Wireless signals underground can not penetrate the wall to the ground and the laying of the network line is not convenient. So we using power line carrier to realize communication between underground and ground. The project used lighting circuit in underground substation for carrier. Because in the underground substation construction, lighting system is one of the earliest completed and its load is low, the signal interference is relatively small. By the power line carrier equipments, we can transmit the signals received from wireless router to the ground through the lighting circuit, then the local server to receive these signals after switched.

2.3   The Local Server and Remote Client

Local server is responsible for receiving the signals, split-screen displaying them and storing them to disk. By accessing to the network camera' IP, local server is able to control the various functions of the web camera. Then local sever can broadcast the signals by wireless router, and remote clients can see the scene picture at the same time.

3   Video Images Online Enhancement

The construction environment is relatively poor, light is dim and visibility is low, the captured images may not be able to achieve a very good monitoring effect. So it is necessary to enhance the images online. Commonly used methods of image enhancement are histogram equalization, low-pass filter, high pass filter [6-7] and so on. The traditional image enhancement algorithm has its flaws, can not do the underground substation scene image enhancement work. The traditional image enhancement algorithms have their flaws, can not do the underground substation scene image enhancement work. This paper uses a Multiscale Retinex algorithm based on the Retinex theory to do image enhancement [8-9]. In Retinex model, image S (x, y) is composed of two parts: one is the brightness image L(x,y), determines the dynamic range of the image pixels; another part is the reflective image R(x,y), determines the nature of an image.

The imaging process can be expressed as:

$$S(x, y) = R(x, y) \cdot L(x, y) \tag{1}$$

Wanting to directly obtain the reflection image is not reality, so we can estimate the incident part first. S is known. Then we can get reflected part R through the equation(1). Gaussian function can well estimate the brightness image from the known image S, it can be expressed as:

$$G(x, y) = k \cdot e^{\frac{x^2+y^2}{c^2}} \tag{2}$$

So we can get enhanced model:

$$r(x, y) = \log[R(x, y)] = \log\frac{S(x, y)}{L(x, y)} = \log[S(x, y)] - \log[S(x, y) \cdot G(x, y)] \tag{3}$$

Multiscale Retinex is the result of multiple single-scale Retinex weighted sum. The equation is as follows:

$$R(x, y) = \sum_{1}^{n} \omega_n \{\log S(x, y) - \log[G_n(x, y) * S(x, y)]\} \tag{4}$$

In the equation(4), n is the number of scales, ω_n corresponds to the weight of a scale, G_n is the Gauss convolution function of corresponding weight.

According to the above method, we process the image collected on the underground substation processing, the results is as follows.

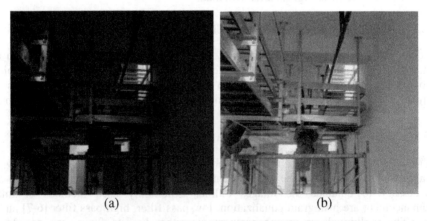

(a)   (b)

Fig. 2. A comparison chart of the image effect after using the MSR algorithm.(a) is the original image, (b) is the image after MSR processing

From the result of Figure 2, we can directly see the image being significantly brighter and visual effect enhanced.

Table 1. The mean, standard deviation and entropy contrast result before and after treatment

	Mean	Standard deviation	Entropy
The original image	14.6850	24.2065	5.1051
MSR	103.6952	45.5459	5.2643

From the data in the table, we can also see that the image mean and standard deviation are obviously increased after processing, the visual effects of the image is obviously enhanced, verified the conclusion of front.

4   Conclusion

By using the web camera, power line carrier technology and image enhancement technology, this paper design and development a remote video monitoring system so that the construction of underground substation can be clearly and accurately transmitted to the ground control station and real-time preservation.This monitoring system provides technical means for the standard operation of the power grid construction and monitoring of the site critical construction process, improves the safety operation level of the construction process in a certain extent and avoids project risks caused by human factors. The monitoring system can be used not only in the construction process of underground substation, but also can be used for similar underground engineering such as subway tunnel construction process, coal mining process and so on. It has a wide popularization value.

References

1. Tian, B., Zhao, X.L., Ya, Q.M.: Design and implementation of a wireless video sensor network. In: 2012 9th IEEE International Conference on Networking, Sensing and Control (ICNSC), Beijing, pp. 411–416 (2012)
2. Fallahi, A., Hossain, E.: QoS provisioning in wireless video sensor networks: a dynamic power management framework. IEEE Wireless Communications 14(6), 40–49 (2007)
3. Lin, Z.: Monitoring system development based on IP camera. Southeast University (2002)
4. Feng, C., Gang, Z.W., Jun, S.C.: Low voltage power line carrier communication technology and its application. Power System Protection and Control 37(22), 188–195 (2009)
5. Dong, G.W.: Intelligent automatic meter reading system based on low voltage power line carrier. Automation of Electric Power Systems 25(24), 48–52 (2001)
6. Kim, M., Min, C.: Recursively separated and weighted histogram equalization for brightness preservation and contrast enhancement. IEEE Transactions on Consumer Electronics 54(3), 1389–1397 (2008)
7. Hurley, N.V., Bolton, H.R.: High-performance low-pass filter utilising a mechanical energy store. Proceedings of the Institution of Electrical Engineers 124(1), 61–66 (1997)
8. Wen, F.G.: Image enhancement algorithm research and realization based on Retinex. Shanghai Jiaotong University (2011)
9. Jobson, D.J., Rahman, Z., Woodell, G.A.: A multiscale retinex for bridging the gap between color images and the human observation of scenes. IEEE Transactions on Image Processing 6(7), 965–976 (2002)

Modelling Emotional Agents Based on Graded BDI Architectures

Xiaojun Zhang

Department of Philosophy, Xiamen University, Xiamen 361005, China
Fujian Provincial Key Laboratory of Brain-Like Intelligent Systems
(Xiamen University)
zhangxj666@yahoo.cn

Abstract. In this paper I present an improved version of the emotional BDI logic and the graded BDI logic to model Emotional Graded BDI agent's behavior determined by the different measure of each context which is added by concrete conditions. I blend the infinite-valued Łukasiewicz Logic and Propositional Dynamic Logic to formulize the Emotional Graded BDI model which explicitly represents the uncertainty of mental attitudes and emotional states. This paper is to look for a possible axiomatic modelling of beliefs, desires, intensions, fear, anxiety and self-confidence, and to show how they influence the agent's behavior. After presenting the language and semantics for this model, I propose axioms and rules for the emotional graded BDI logic and prove its soundness and completeness. On the basis of illustrating relationship between/among contexts for the model, an application of an Emotional Graded BDI agent is given.

Keywords: emotional graded Belief-Desire-Intention (BDI) agents; uncertain reasoning, emotional states, actions, models.

1 Introduction

In the recent past, the most widely used in multi-agent systems is the BDI (Belief-Desire-Intention) agent architecture developed by Rao and Georgeff [1-3]. This architecture can give engineer complex distributed systems a formal support. After the BDI logic was proposed, researchers tried to extend and improve this theory using all sorts of means. For example, a formal model for emotional BDI agents developed by Pereira et al. illustrates that agents' behavior is guided not only by beliefs, desires and intentions, but also by the role of emotions in reasoning and decision-making [4-6], following Oliveira and Sarmento's model of emotional agent [7-9]. A general model for graded BDI agents presented by Casali et al. is able to model the graded mental attitudes in multi-context systems [10]. In this paper I present an improved version of the emotional BDI logic [6] and the graded BDI logic [10] to model the role of three emotions in Emotional Graded BDI agents (EGBDI agents for short): *fear, anxiety* and *self-confidence*. The aim of this paper is to show EGBDI logic has enough expressivity to model agents' uncertain behavior determined by the mental

J. Lei et al. (Eds.): NCIS 2012, CCIS 345, pp. 606–616, 2012.
© Springer-Verlag Berlin Heidelberg 2012

attitudes and emotions states, following Xiaojun Zhang et al.'s model of graded BDI agent [11] based on Propositional Dynamic Logic [12] and the infinite-valued Łukasiewicz Logic [13]. It is hoped that this study will make contributions to represent and reason under uncertainty, and to provide a formal support for distributed artificial intelligence.

This paper is organized as follows. In Section 2 I define the Emotional Graded BDI logic. The logic is based on the graded BDI logic developed by Xiaojun Zhang et al. [11] and I begin by presenting the new operators that were added. After giving the syntax and semantics of EGBDI logic, I present the axiom systems for the new modal operators, and then prove its soundness and completeness result. In Section 3 I use the EGBDI logic to illustrate relationship between/among contexts which are pre-requisites for defining how emotions are activated in Emotional Graded BDI agents and composite actions which are executed by the agent when it "feels" these emotions. In Section 4 I model the activation and effects of each of the emotions in Emotional Graded BDI agents using an example for buying houses. Finally, Section 5 I present some concluding remarks and point some topics for ongoing and future research in the EGBDI logic.

2   The Emotional Graded BDI Logic

The Emotional Graded BDI Logic is an extension of Pereira et al.'s emotional BDI logic [6], following Xiaojun Zhang et al.'s graded BDI logic [11]. In order to provide a more accurate notion of the importance of a desire to the decision-making process of an agent, in the line of the graded BDI logic developed by Casali et al.[10], this extension adds a notion of graded importance to the modal operators which represent the concepts of beliefs, desires, intentions and emotions. The formal semantics is based on Kripke models with accessibility relations between possible worlds which correspond to different mental attitudes and emotional states.

2.1   The Emotional Graded BDI Language

The Emotional Graded BDI Logic is a multi-modal logic which combines Propositional Dynamic Logic (PDL) [12] and infinite-valued Łukasiewicz Logic (LL) [13]. PDL can be used to model agents' actions. We define modal operators for representing the mental states of *belief* (B), *desire* (D) and *intention* (I) and emotional states of *fear*, *anxiety* and *self-confidence* in LL. The main idea behind LL is that probability values of crisp propositions can be viewed as truth-values of some suitable fuzzy propositions associated to the crisp ones. In the LL, we are interested in inference from partially true assumptions, admitting that the conclusion will also be partially true, truth values are real members from the unit interval [0, 1], and the provability degree equals to the truth degree. Hence, the infinite-valued Łukasiewicz Logic can be used to reason about uncertainty, in which truth functions are $\neg x = 1 - x$,

$x \rightarrow y = \min(1, 1-x+y)$, and two formulas are equivalent in Łukasiewicz Logic then they are classically equivalent.

Now I define the language L_{EGBDI} by adding action modalities of the form $[\alpha]$ where α is an action, and six fuzzy modal operator B, D, I, *Fear*, *Anx* and *SConf* to the classical propositional language L. $B\varphi$, $D\varphi$ and $I\varphi$ mean that "φ is believable", "φ is desired" and "φ is intended" , respectively, and their truth degrees refer to the agent's level of satisfaction would φ become true. The meanings of *Fear*φ, *Anx*φ and *SConf*φ are similar.

The language L_{EGBDI} has expressions of two sorts: propositions or formulae φ, ψ, ... and actions (or programs) α, β, ... In this paper, Φ_0 and Φ refer to the set of all atomic propositions and the set of all propositions, respectively. Π_0 and Π refer to the set of all atomic actions and the set of all actions (including atomic actions and plans which are in fact composite actions), respectively. Formulae are built inductively from the atomic ones using connectives (negation $\neg$, implication $\rightarrow$) and mixed operators [] (necessity) and ? (test). Other connectives are definable from $\neg$ and $\rightarrow$. Actions are built inductively from the atomic ones using the following action operators: ; (composition), $\cup$ (nondeterministic choice) and $*$ (iteration), and the mixed operator ? (test).

Definition 1: formulae can be defined inductively as follows:

$\varphi ::= \varphi \mid \neg\varphi \mid \varphi \rightarrow \psi \mid [\alpha]\varphi \mid B\varphi \mid D\varphi \mid I\varphi \mid Fear\varphi \mid Anx\varphi \mid SConf\varphi \mid$

Definition 2: actions can be defined inductively as the following:

$\alpha ::= \alpha^0 \mid \alpha; \beta \mid \alpha\cup\beta \mid \alpha* \mid \varphi? \mid$

Here $[\alpha]\varphi$ means that φ is necessarily true after executing α. Iterated actions α^n (with $n \geq 0$) are inductively defined by $\alpha^0 = id$, and $\alpha^{n+1} = \alpha; \alpha^n$.

In order to define a modal context language for ΣC (in which $\Sigma \in \{B, D, I, Fear, Anx, SConf\}$), we also need to use the connectives of Łukasiewicz many-valued Logic to build Σ-modal from elementary modal formulae and truth constants r_c, for each rational $r \in [0,1]$:

(1) if $\varphi \in L_{EGBDI}$, then φ, $\Sigma\varphi \in \Sigma C$
(2) if $r \in Q \cap [0,1]$, then $r_c \in \Sigma C$
(3) if $\Sigma\varphi$, $\Sigma\psi \in \Sigma C$, then $\Sigma\varphi \rightarrow_L \Sigma\psi \in \Sigma C$ and $\Sigma\varphi \& \Sigma\psi \in \Sigma C$

For example, if $\Sigma = Fear$ and $\varphi \in L_{EGBDI}$, then φ, $Fear\varphi \in FearC$ by clause (1). If $\Sigma = Fear$ and $Fear\varphi$, $Fear\psi \in FearC$, then $Fear\varphi \rightarrow_L Fear\psi \in FearC$ and $Fear\varphi \& Fear\psi \in FearC$. The other cases are similar. In clause (3), $\rightarrow_L$ and & correspond to the implication and conjunction of Łukasiewicz Logic. A formula $\Sigma\varphi \rightarrow_L \Sigma\psi$ is 1-ture if and only if the truth value of $\Sigma\varphi$ is greater or equal to that of $\Sigma\psi$. And modal formulae of the type $r_c \rightarrow_L \Sigma\varphi$ mean that the probability of φ is at least r_c. For simplicity's sake, formulae of the type $r_c \rightarrow_L \Sigma\varphi$ is denoted as $(\Sigma\varphi, r_c)$.

In order to formulize Emotional Graded BDI agents, I choose to use Łukasiewicz Logic extended with a new unary connective Δ (known as Baaz's connective). For any modal $\Sigma\varphi$, if $\Sigma\varphi$ has value < (smaller than) 1, then $\Delta\Sigma\varphi$ gets value 0; otherwise, if $\Sigma\varphi$ has value 1, then $\Delta\Sigma\varphi$ gets value 1 as well. Thus, $\Delta\Sigma\varphi$ becomes a two-valued Boolean formula.

2.2   The Emotional Graded BDI Semantics

EGBDI-formulae are interpreted in extended graded BDI models, called EGBDI-models. I follow Casali et al.'s approach to graded BDI logic [10], by considering possible worlds corresponding to mental attitudes and emotional states. As in usual in modal logics, adding to Kripke structure a τ function, a probability measure ρ and a preference distribution θ, a possibility distribution μ_w, as well as emotion distribution, such as *Fear* distribution ε, *Anx* distribution η and *SConf* distribution κ over possible worlds, I can define an Emotional Graded BDI model as a 9-tuple Kripke structure $K=\langle W, \upsilon, \rho, \tau, \theta, \{\mu_w\}_{w\in W}, \varepsilon, \eta, \kappa \rangle$ where:

(4) W is a non-empty set of possible worlds.

(5) $\upsilon: \Phi\times W \rightarrow \{0, 1\}$ assigns a two-valued Boolean evaluation to each $\varphi\in\Phi$ and $w\in W$, and $\upsilon(\varphi, w)\in\{0, 1\}$.

(6) $\rho: 2^W \rightarrow [0, 1]$ is a finitely additive probability measure on a Boolean algebra of subsets of W.

(7) $\tau: \Pi_0 \rightarrow 2^{W\times W}$ provides a set of pairs of worlds referring to world transitions for each atomic action.

(8) $\theta: W \rightarrow [0, 1]$ is a distribution of preferences over possible worlds, and $\theta(w) < \theta(w')$ means that w' is more preferred than w.

(9) $\mu_w: W\rightarrow[0, 1]$ is a possibility distribution, for each $w\in W$. Where $\mu_w(w')\in[0, 1]$ is the degree on which the agent may try to reach the world w' from the world w.

(10) $\varepsilon: W \rightarrow [0, 1]$ is a distribution of fear over possible worlds. And $\varepsilon(w) < \varepsilon(w')$ means that w' is more feared than w.

(11) $\eta: W \rightarrow [0, 1]$ is a distribution of anxiety over possible worlds. And $\eta(w) < \eta(w')$ means that w' is more anxious than w.

(12) $\kappa: W \rightarrow [0, 1]$ is a distribution of self-confidence over possible worlds. And $\kappa(w) < \kappa(w')$ means that w' is more self-confident than w.

As in graded BDI logic, L_{EGBDI} is defined by extending L using classical connectives and action modalities. And Σ-formulae (in which $\Sigma\in\{B, D, I, Fear, Anx$ and $SConf\}$ are defined by extending Łukasiewicz Logic as follows:

(13) $\upsilon(\Sigma\varphi, w) = \xi(\{w'\in W \mid \upsilon(\varphi, w')=1\}$, for each φ. Here $\xi \in \{\rho, \theta, \mu_w, \varepsilon, \eta, \kappa\}$

(14) $\upsilon(r_c, w) = r$, for all $r\in Q\cap[0,1]$

(15) $\upsilon(\Sigma\varphi\&\Sigma\psi, w) = \max(\upsilon(\Sigma\varphi)+\upsilon(\Sigma\psi)-1, 0)$

(16) $\upsilon(\Sigma\varphi \rightarrow_L \Sigma\psi, w) = \min(1-\upsilon(\Sigma\varphi)+\upsilon(\Sigma\psi), 1)$

(17) $\|\Sigma\varphi\|K = td_{w\in W}\upsilon(\Sigma\varphi, w)$, where $\|\Sigma\varphi\|^K$ is the truth degree of a formula $\Sigma\varphi$ in the Kripke structure $K=\langle W, \upsilon, \rho, \tau, \theta, \{\mu_w\}_{w\in W}, \varepsilon, \eta, \kappa \rangle$.

(18) $\upsilon(\Delta\Sigma\varphi, w) = 1$, if $\upsilon(\Sigma\varphi, w) = 1$

(19) $\upsilon(\Delta\Sigma\varphi, w) = 0$, if $\upsilon(\Sigma\varphi, w) \neq 1$

(20) $td\varnothing = 1$

(21) $\upsilon(\Sigma L, w) = 1$, for all $w \in W$

In clauses (17) and (20) *td* refers to the truth degree of a formula $\Sigma\varphi$ in the Kripke structure $K = \langle W, \upsilon, \rho, \tau, \theta, \{\mu_w\}_{w \in W}, \varepsilon, \eta, \kappa \rangle$. The evaluation of Σ-formulae only depends on the formula itself-represented in its corresponding measure over possible worlds where the agent is situated.

2.3   Axioms and Rules for the Emotional Graded BDI Logic

According to the Emotional Graded BDI semantics, Propositional Dynamic Logic ([12]) and Łukasiewicz Logic ([13]), axioms for Emotional Graded BDI logic are given as follows (22-34) (in this paper, $\Sigma \in \{B, D, I, Fear, Anx, SConf\}$):

(22) Axioms of classical Propositional Logic for the non-modal formulae

(23) Axioms of the Łukasiewicz Logic for modal formulae, for example, axioms of Hájek basic logic ([13]) plus the axiom schema: $\neg\neg\Sigma\varphi \rightarrow \Sigma\varphi$.

Axioms for Σ over Łukasiewicz Logic are as follows [13]:

(24) $\Sigma(\varphi \rightarrow \psi) \rightarrow_L (\Sigma\varphi \rightarrow \Sigma\psi)$.

(25) $\neg_L \Sigma(\varphi) \equiv \Sigma(\neg\varphi)$

(26) $\Sigma(\varphi) \equiv \neg_L\Sigma(\varphi \wedge \neg\psi) \rightarrow_L \Sigma(\varphi \wedge \psi)$

(27) $\neg\Sigma(\bot)$

Axioms for Σ over Propositional Dynamic Logic are the following:

(28) $[\alpha]\Sigma(\varphi \rightarrow \psi) \rightarrow ([\alpha]\Sigma\varphi \rightarrow [\alpha]\Sigma\psi)$

(29) $[\alpha]\Sigma(\varphi \wedge \psi) \leftrightarrow [\alpha]\Sigma\varphi \wedge [\alpha]\Sigma\psi$

(30) $[\alpha \cup \beta]\Sigma\varphi \leftrightarrow [\alpha]\Sigma\varphi \wedge [\beta]\Sigma\varphi$

(31) $[\alpha; \beta]\Sigma\varphi \leftrightarrow [\alpha][\beta]\Sigma\varphi$

(32) $[\Sigma\psi?]\Sigma\varphi \leftrightarrow (\Sigma\psi \rightarrow \Sigma\varphi)$

(33) $\Sigma\varphi \wedge [\alpha][\alpha*]\Sigma\varphi \leftrightarrow [\alpha*]\Sigma\varphi$

(34) $\Sigma\varphi \wedge [\alpha*](\Sigma\varphi \rightarrow [\alpha]\Sigma\varphi) \leftrightarrow [\alpha*]\Sigma\varphi$

Deduction rules for Emotional Graded BDI logic are given as follows:

(35) Modus Ponens (MP): from (φ, r_1) and $(\varphi \rightarrow \psi, r_2)$ derive $(\psi, r_1 \& r_2)$.

(36) Truth Constant Introduction: from (φ, r_1) derive $(r_c \rightarrow \varphi, r \rightarrow r_1)$.

2.4   Soundness and Completeness for the Emotional Graded BDI Logic

My Emotional Graded BDI Logic (EGBDIL) is the extension of Graded BDI Logic (GBDIL), and the latter is the extension of Propositional Dynamic Logic (PDL) and Łukasiewicz Logic (LL), which are sound and complete (cf. [12] and [13], respectively). Using other words, PDL⊂GBDIL⊂EGBDIL and LL⊂GBDIL⊂ EGBDIL. Thus, we can prove soundness and completeness for EGBDIL by embedding of EGBDIL into PDL or LL. Because embedding operations can preserve the structure of formulae and properties of logics [14]. For example, if L_1 is embeddable into a sound and complete logic L_2, then L_1 is also sound and complete. We are now in conditions to find an effective translation function Tr such that, for all formulae $\varphi \in$ EGBDIL if and only if $Tr(\varphi) \in$ PDL or $Tr(\varphi) \in$ LL. Let Tr be a map from EGBDIL to PDL or LL defined as follows:

Definition 1

(37) $Tr(p) = p$, if p is a PDL or LL formula

(38) $Tr(\neg\varphi) = \neg Tr(\varphi)$, if φ is a EGBDIL formula

(39) $Tr(\varphi\to\psi) = Tr(\varphi)\to Tr(\psi)$, for all EGBDIL formulae φ and ψ

(40) $Tr(\varphi\wedge\psi) = Tr(\varphi)\wedge Tr(\psi)$, for all EGBDIL formulae φ and ψ

(41) $Tr([\alpha]\Sigma\varphi) = Tr([\alpha]\varphi)$, if φ is a EGBDIL formula

(42) $Tr(\Sigma\varphi) = Tr(\varphi)$, if φ is a EGBDIL formula

According to the translation function Tr, the following theorem can be proved:

Theorem 1. The map Tr defined by definition 1 is an embedding of EGBDIL to PDL or LL.

Proof: We can easily show that: all formulae $\varphi \in$ EGBDIL if and only if $Tr(\varphi) \in$ PDL or $Tr(\varphi) \in$ LL. For instance, for clause (28), $[\alpha]\Sigma(\varphi\to\psi)\to([\alpha]\Sigma\varphi\to[\alpha]\Sigma\psi) \in$ EGBDIL, by definition 1, $Tr([\alpha]\Sigma(\varphi\to\psi)\to([\alpha]\Sigma\varphi\to[\alpha]\Sigma\psi))=Tr([\alpha]\Sigma(\varphi\to\psi))\to Tr([\alpha]\Sigma\varphi\to[\alpha]\Sigma\psi)$ $=Tr([\alpha](\varphi\to\psi))\to(Tr([\alpha]\Sigma\varphi)\to Tr([\alpha]\Sigma\psi))=[\alpha](\varphi\to\psi)\to(Tr([\alpha]\varphi)\to Tr([\alpha]\psi))=[\alpha](\varphi\to$ $\psi)\to([\alpha]\varphi\to[\alpha]\psi)\in$ PDL. Other clauses are similar to (28). Therefore, the translation function Tr is an embedding of EGBDIL to PDL or LL.

Propositional Dynamic Logic (PDL) and Łukasiewicz Logic (LL) are sound and complete, hence the Emotional Graded BDI logic (EGBDIL) is sound and complete by the properties of embedding operations. In fact, in terms of the soundness and completeness result of GBDIL [11], we can straightforwardly prove soundness and completeness for EGBDIL by embedding of EGBDIL into GBDIL.

3   Relationship between/among Contexts

In this section, I try to illustrate the relationship between/among contexts. From the mental attitudes and emotional states of the agent, and the possible transformations using actions, the planner can build plans generated from actions to fulfill desires. Relationships among D, B, *Fear*, *Anx*, *SConf*, and P contexts are the following:

(43) if D: $\neg\Delta\neg(D\varphi)$, B: $(B([\alpha]\varphi, r))$, *Fear*: $(Fear(\varphi, l))$, *Anx*: $(Anx(\varphi, m))$, *SConf*: $(SConf(\varphi, n))$ and P: $action(\alpha, Pre\text{-}, Cost_\alpha)$, then P: $plan(\varphi, action(\alpha, Pre\text{-}, Cost_\alpha), r)$ where:

$\alpha\in\Pi_0$ is an atomic action, *Pre-* are the preconditions of the action α, and $Cost_\alpha\in[0,1]$ is the associated cost according to the action α involved; r, l, m and $n\in[0,1]$ are respectively belief, fear, anxiety and self-confidence degree of actually achieving φ by performing α; $action(\alpha, Pre\text{-}, Cost_\alpha)$ is the special predicate which formally expresses an atomic action; *plan*(φ, *action*(α, *Pre-*, *Cost*$_\alpha$), r) the special predicate formally expressing a plan which is a composite action allowing the agent to move from its current world to another, where a given formula is satisfied.

In this paper, we assume that only one instance of this predicate is generated per formula and only one instance with the best plan is generated, and that the current state of the world must satisfy the preconditions and the plan must make true the desire that the plan is built for.

If we use the intention degree to trade off the benefit and the cost of achieving a goal, then for each composite action α that allows to reach the goal, the degree of *I*φ is deduced from the degree of *D*φ, *Fear*φ, *Anx*φ, *SConf*φ and the cost of a plan that satisfies the desire φ. In other words, the degree of *I*φ is calculated by a function *f* as follows:

(44) if D: (Dφ, d), Fear: (Fear([α]φ, m)), Anx: (Anx([α]φ, n)), SConf: (SConf([α]φ, t)) and P: plan(φ, action(α, Pre-, Cost$_\alpha$), r), I: (Iφ, f (d, m, n, t, r))

Different functions *f* (*d*, *m*, *n*, *t*, *r*) may model different individual behaviors. Given full belief in achieving φ after performing α, the degree of the intention to bring about φ mainly depend on the satisfaction and the degree of *D*φ, *Fear*φ, *Anx*φ, *SConf*φ that it bring the agent and in the cost. The key is to find what kind of the relationship between/among *f*, *d*, *m*, *n*, *t* and *r*. Rational agents always try to avoid or alleviate negative emotions such as fear, anxiety caused by the execution of an action α, and hope that the associated cost according to the actions involved as small as possible. Therefore, we should consider the complement to 1 of the degree of *Fear*φ, *Anx*φ and the normalized cost when we calculate the degree of the intention. That is, the function *f* (*d*, *m*, *n*, *t*, *r*) can be defined as follows:

$$(45)\ f(d, m, n, t, r) = r(d+(1-Cost_\alpha)+(1-m)+(1-n)+t)/5$$

This definition associates the agent's intention with the mental attitudes of belief, desire and emotional states of fear, anxiety and self-confidence. According to the definition, the degree of intention is the ultimate embodiment of the other mental attitudes and emotional states, and it makes the agent can determine whether she should take action or not and judge which action is more reasonable. If the agent intends φ at i_{max}, then the agent will focus on the best plan. That's the way of the agent's interactions with the environment. In other words:

(46) if I: (Iφ, i_{max}), and P: bestplan(φ, action(α, Pre-, Cost$_\alpha$), r), then C: C(does(α))

4   Applications

In this section, we consider to instruct an Emotional Graded BDI agent to look for a buying-houses package, and relate this section to the theoretical formalism and the abstract architecture of the previous sections. We instruct the agent with three desires: we firstly hope the house near a school; secondly hope the house near a subway; and thirdly the house from her workplace no more than 8 kilometers. At the same time, we assign to the agent the three emotions: she has the fear of the house in a noisy environment; she has the anxiety of that the shared building area is large; she has the self-confidence of the housing appreciation. To decide to buy a house the agent will have to take into consideration the benefit (with respect to near a school and a subway, and the housing appreciation), fear, anxiety and the cost of the buying. In this example, *BC*, *DC*, *FearC*, *AnxC*, *SConfC* and *PC* contexts are as follows:

Desire Contexts (*DC*): The agent has the following desires:

(47) (*D*(*near a school*), *d*=0.85)

(48) (*D*(*near a subway*), *d*=0.83)

(49) (*D*(*near a school* ∧ *near a subway*), *d*=0.94)

(50) (*D*(*distance* ≤ 8km), *d*=0.86)

In this case, the values of desire degree can take all real number from the unit interval [0, 1]. If the value is greater, then its corresponding desire is stronger. All of the other degrees in this paper are similar to this.

Belief Contexts (*BC*): The Emotional Graded BDI agent has knowledge about the relationship between /among possible actions that she can take and formulae made true by their execution. In this scenario, different actions are to buy different houses, and the chosen houses are as follows:

(51) Π_0 ={*House-A*, *House-B*, *House-C*, *House-D*, *House-E*}

The degree of *B*([α] *near a subway*) refers to the probability of near a subway after buying α. We assign to the agent the following belief:

(52) *B*([*House-A*]*near a subway*, r_1=0.96)

(53) *B*([*House-B*]*near a subway*, r_1=0.86)

(54) *B*([*House-C*]*near a subway*, r_1 =0.56)

(55) *B*([*House-D*]*near a subway*, r_1 =0.48)

(56) *B*([*House-E*]*near a subway*, r_1=0.42)

In this scenario, the degree of *B*([α] *near a school*) means the probability of near a school after buying α. The agent's beliefs about buying houses near a school are given as follows:

(57) *B*([*House-A*]*near a school*, r_2=0.88)

(58) *B*([*House-B*]*near a school*, r_2=0.81)

(59) *B*([*House-C*]*near a school*, r_2=0.52)

(60) *B*([*House-D*]*near a school*, r_2=0.72)

(61) *B*([*House-E*]*near a school*, r_2=0.64)

We assume that the desires are stochastically independent and add the following inference rule for *BC*:

(62) if *B*([α]*near a school*, r_1) and *B*([α]*near a subway*, r_2), then *B*([α]*near a school* ∧ *near a subway*, $r = (r_1+r_2)/2$)

Fear Contexts (*FearC*): In this example, we assign to the agent the following measure of fear:

(63) *Fear*([*House-A*]*in a noisy environment*, *m*=0.56)

(64) *Fear([House-B]in a noisy environment, m =0.78)*

(65) *Fear([House-C]in a noisy environment, m =0.66)*

(66) *Fear([House-D]in a noisy environment, m =0.32)*

(67) *Fear([House-E]in a noisy environment, m =0.91)*

Anxiety Contexts (*AnxC*): In this example, the agent has the following measure of anxiety:

(68) *Anx([House-A]shared building area is large, n=0.92)*

(69) *Anx([House-B]shared building area is large, n =0.42)*

(70) *Anx([House-C]shared building area is large, n =0.79)*

(71) *Anx([House-D]shared building area is large, n =0.68)*

(72) *Anx([House-E]shared building area is large, n =0.36)*

Self-confidence Contexts (*SConfC*): In this case, the agent has the following measure of self-confidence:

(73) *SConf([House-A]appreciation, t=0.88)*

(74) *SConf([House-B]appreciation, t =0.92)*

(75) *SConf([House-C]appreciation, t =0.72)*

(76) *SConf([House-D]appreciation, t =0.48)*

(77) *SConf([House-E]appreciation, t =0.66)*

Plan Contexts (*PC*): In this scenario, a series of atomic actions are the following:

(78) *action(House-A, {dist-=2km}, {cost=5millions}, $Cost_\alpha$=0.96)*

(79) *action(House-B, {dist-=3km}, {cost=4millions}, $Cost_\alpha$=0.81)*

(80) *action(House-C, {dist-=11km}, {cost=2millions}, $Cost_\alpha$=0.51)*

(81) *action(House-D, {dist-=12km}, {cost=1millions}, $Cost_\alpha$ =0.36)*

(82) *action(House-E, {dist-=5km}, {cost=3millions}, $Cost_\alpha$=0.66)*

The agent is now in conditions to determine which intention to adopt and which plan is associated with that intention. A brief schema of the steps in this process is as follows:

Firstly, the agent's desires are conveyed to plan contexts by desire contexts.

Secondly, within plan contexts, the agent finds plans for each desire.

The agent looks for a set of different buying house plans in terms of mental attitudes and emotional states, and takes into comprehensive consideration the various aspects of the contexts. Due to the restriction by the desire (50), that is, the distance no more than 8kms, the agent gives up plans (80) and (81), that is, the agent gives up to buy House-C and House-D. Hence, plans are generated for each desire by (43). For instance, for the most preferred desire, i.e. near a school ∧ near a subway, the generated plans are the following:

(83) *plan(near a school ∧ near a subway, action(House-A, {dist-=2km}, {cost= 5million}, $Cost_\alpha$=0.96), $(r_1+r_2)/2 = 0.92)$*

(84) *plan(near a school ∧ near a subway, action(House-B, {dist-=3km}, {cost= 4million}, $Cost_\alpha$=0.81), $(r_1+r_2)/2 = 0.835)$*

(85) *plan(near a school ∧ near a subway, action(House-E, {dist-=5km}, {cost= 3million}, $Cost_\alpha$=0.66), $(r_1+r_2)/2 = 0.53)$*

Thirdly, according to mental attitudes and emotional states, the plans determine the degree of intentions.

The function f is monotonically increasing with respect to d by (45). Therefore, it is enough to take into consideration the most preferred desire, i.e. near a school $\wedge$ near a subway, which is preferred to a degree 0.94. In terms of (45), using $f(d, m, n, t, r) = r(d+(1-Cost_\alpha)+(1-m)+(1-n)+t)/5=(r_1+r_2)/2\bullet(0.94+(1-Cost_\alpha)+(1-m)+(1-n)+t)/5$, we successively have for $\alpha\in\{House\text{-}A, House\text{-}B, House\text{-} E\}$ as the following:

(86) $I(near\ a\ school \wedge near\ a\ subway, (r_1+r_2)/2\bullet(0.94+(1-Cost_\alpha)+(1-m)+(1-n)+t)/5 = 0.43792)$

(87) $I(near\ a\ school\ l\wedge near\ a\ subway, (r_1+r_2)/2\bullet(0.94+(1-Cost_\alpha)+(1-m)+(1-n)+t)/5 = 0.47595)$

(88) $I(near\ a\ school \wedge near\ a\ subway, (r_1+r_2)/2\bullet(0.94+(1-Cost_\alpha)+(1-m)+(1-n)+t)/5 = 0.28302)$

The maximal degree of intention for near a school $\wedge$ near a subway by the plan House-B is 0.47595.

At last, the agent adopts the best plan and takes the corresponding action.

Now, the action α = buying House-B can be selected and passed to the communication context by (46).

5   Conclusions and Future Work

In this paper I have presented an improved version of the graded BDI logic to model the activation and effects of emotions in the behavior exhibited by an Emotional Graded BDI agent. The emotions analyzed were fear, anxiety and self-confidence, in the line of the work done by Pereira et al. in [6]. This formalization was based on the infinite-valued Łukasiewicz Logic and Propositional Dynamic Logic. In order to represent the uncertainty behavior by belief, desire, intention, fear, anxiety and self-confidence degree, the corresponding axioms are added to Łukasiewicz Logic. The Emotional Graded BDI agent's behavior is determined by the different measure of each context which is added by concrete conditions. This paper is to look for a possible axiomatic modelling of beliefs, desires, intensions, fear, anxiety and self-confidence, and to show how they influence the agent's behavior. This model can also easily be extended to include other mental attitudes and other emotional states.

As a future work, it would be interesting to extend my Emotional Graded BDI agent to a multi-agent scenario by introducing a social context in the agent architecture to deal with all aspects of social relations with other agents. I plan to equip this social context with a good logical model of trust which allows the agent to infer belief from other agents' information, in the line of the work done by Liau [15].

Acknowledgements. This research has been supported by the China Postdoctoral Science Foundation under Grant No. 2012M510167.

References

1. Rao, A., Georgeff, M.: Modeling rational agents within a BDI-architecture. In: Proceedings of the 2nd International Conference on Principles of Knowledge Representation and Reasoning (KR 1992), pp. 473–484 (1991)
2. Rao, A., Georgeff, M.: BDI agents: from theory to practice. In: Proceedings of the 1st International Conference on Multi-Agents Systems, pp. 312–319 (1995)
3. Rao, A., Georgeff, M.: Decision Procedures for BDI Logics. Journal of Logic and Computation 8(3), 293–342 (1998)
4. Pereira, D., et al.: Towards an architecture for emotional BDI agents. In: 12th Portuguese Conference on Artificial Intelligence, pp. 40–46 (2005)
5. Pereira, D., Oliveria, E., Moreira, N.: Modelling Emotional BDI Agents. In: Workshop on Formal Approaches to Multi-Agent Systems, Riva Del Garda, Italy (2006)
6. Pereira, D., Oliveira, E., Moreira, N.: Formal Modelling of Emotions in BDI Agents. In: Sadri, F., Satoh, K. (eds.) CLIMA VIII 2007. LNCS (LNAI), vol. 5056, pp. 62–81. Springer, Heidelberg (2008)
7. Oliveira, E., Sarmento, L.: Emotional Valence-Based Mechanisms and Agent Personality. In: Bittencourt, G., Ramalho, G.L. (eds.) SBIA 2002. LNCS (LNAI), vol. 2507, pp. 152–162. Springer, Heidelberg (2002)
8. Oliveira, E., Sarmento, L.: Emotional advantage for adaptability and autonomy. In: AAMAS, pp. 305–312 (2003)
9. Sarmento, L., Moura, D., Oliveira, E.: Fighting fire with fear. In: Proceeding of 2nd European Workshop on Multi-Agent Systems, EUMAS 2004 (2004)
10. Casali, A., Godo, L., Sierra, C.: Graded BDI Models for Agent Architectures. In: Leite, J., Torroni, P. (eds.) CLIMA 2004. LNCS (LNAI), vol. 3487, pp. 126–143. Springer, Heidelberg (2005)
11. Zhang, X., Jiang, M., Zhou, C., Hao, Y.: Graded BDI Models for Agent Architectures Based on Łukasiewicz Logic and Propositional Dynamic Logic. In: Wang, F.L., Lei, J., Gong, Z., Luo, X. (eds.) WISM 2012. LNCS, vol. 7529, pp. 439–450. Springer, Heidelberg (2012)
12. Harel, D., Kozen, D., Tiuryn, J.: Dynamic Logic. The MIT Press (2000)
13. Hájek, P.: Mathematics of Fuzzy Logic. Kluwer (1998)
14. Chagrov, A.: Zakharyaschev, M.: Modal Logic. Clarendon Press (1997)
15. Liau, C.J.: Belief, information acquisition, and trust in multiagent systems – a modal formulation. Artificial Intelligence 149, 31–60 (2003)

Instrument System of Airport Fire Engine Simulator Based on Parallel Simulation Technology

Lishan Jia[1,2], Liwen Wang[1,2], and Xi Chen[1,2]

[1] Tianjin Key Laboratory for Civil Aircraft Airworthiness and Maintenance of Civil Aviation University of China, Tianjin 300300, China
[2] Ground Support Equipments Research Base of Civil Aviation University of China, Tianjin 300300, China
jlshfd163@yeah.net

Abstract. To the high real-time quality requirement of instrument simulation system of airport fire engine simulator, a system base on parallel simulation technology was promoted. It uses PLC with fast pulses output function to control micro step motor to simulate the motion and indication of instrument of fire engine, and uses industrial personal computer to solve vehicle device model to simulate working of fire engine. PLC and industrial personal computer exchange data with each other through a RS-422 serial bus. PLC and industrial personal computer working in parallel, which promotes the response speed of instrument system. RS-422 serial bus transforms data fast, long and strong anti-jamming, which decreases system delay greatly and insures the reliable running of real-time simulation system. Experiment showed that it can be guaranteed of real-time and accuracy of the system and the system can meet the fire engine simulator instrument system requirements.

Keywords: parallel simulation, fire engine simulator, micro step motor, PLC, high speed pulses output, RS-422 serial bus.

1 Introduction

The fire safety of airport has always been the focus of attention. According to the International Civil Aviation Organization (ICAO) Statistics, 71% of the crashed aircraft caught fire and burned in the accident at the airport. ICAO clearly states: the response time of airport fire engines reaching any part of airport traffic area should be no more than three minutes [1]. So it is the top priority to control the fire of the airport security. Airport fire engine drivers need higher skill than ordinary fire engine drivers because of the special working environment of the airport fire engines. Whether the skilled manipulation of fire engines rushed to the scene of the accident and helped to evacuate the crew and control the fire or not is directly related to the safety of lives and property. Airport fire engine simulator is a simulation device designed precisely for training airport fire engine driver. The airport fire engine simulator generates virtual visual, audio and control force to provide high quality training environment and correct operation of the driving for the firefighters.

J. Lei et al. (Eds.): NCIS 2012, CCIS 345, pp. 617–625, 2012.
© Springer-Verlag Berlin Heidelberg 2012

Instrument simulation system is one of the sub system of airport fire engine simulator, which shows the information of vehicle speed, engine running speed, water pressure, and so on. Instrument system of fire engine being simulated is mechanical and electrical type. So the instrument simulation system adopted the same type. Micro step motor is used more and more widely in mechanical and electrical type instrument of vehicle recently, which has advantages of high precision and easy to control[2]. But running of micro step motor need continuous TTL pulses input of high frequency, and there are at least four instruments need to be controlled in real-time at the same time. Indication of instruments needs data from solving of mathematical model of vehicle device, which needs computer resource too.

Parallel simulation is a technology of making simulation work executing in different computer system. Parallel simulation can decrease running time of system and promote real-time quality of simulation system.

So instrument system based on parallel simulation technology was promoted. In the system, micro step motor was selected to be the driving unit of instrument pointer. Instrument system should show status of vehicle in real-time, but running of step motor need continuous pulses input, the generation of which would cost a lot of CPU time when using industrial personal computer and digital I/O card as controller, especially more than one step motor need different frequency pulses input at the same time. So PLC of Panasonic FP-C30T with function of 4 channels high speed pulses output was selected as controller of step motor, which can generate TTL pulse up to 100kHz, and which can satisfy the need of simulation of instrument running. One industrial personal computer was used to solve mathematical model of vehicle device, which simulates working of devices of fire engine according to input of control system. PLC takes instrument data from industrial computer through a RS-422 serial bus. And industrial computer queries status of PLC through the RS-422 serial bus too. Experiments showed that the parallel simulation system running fast and accurately, and having good real-time simulation quality.

2   Composition and Principle of the Airport Fire Engine Simulator

The airport fire engine simulator is composed of hardware part and software part. Hardware part include: the simulator cockpit devices, computer systems, visual display system and the interface device. Software part include: airport fire engine mathematical model, visual system, sound system, instructor system and data transmission control. The schematic of airport fire truck simulator is shown in Figure 1. Instructor system will transmit the information of training programs to the fire engine mathematic model and the visual system. Fire engines mathematic model calculates vehicle state parameters based on the firemen input and passes it to other systems. Visual system displays the virtual scene based on vehicle location, speed, acceleration, and other information in real time, the instrument system displays the current state of the vehicle, the sound system sound when the vehicle travel, control system collects control data from system driver. Firefighters experience the virtual environment provided by these systems through vision, hearing, feels and make the appropriate input into the training simulator. This creates the interactive environment of one person per car so that firefighters can be trained.

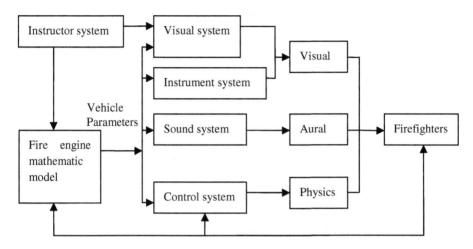

Fig. 1. Airport fire engine simulator principle

3   Simulation of Vehicle

The airport fire engine is divided into vehicle system and fire system according to the characteristics. Combined with object-oriented modeling approach, the system will be divided into relatively independent parts of the physical and functional. So the vehicle system is divided into: the engine object, the power train object, the steering system object, braking system object and driving system object. Taking fire protection system to two parts are the power divider and pump clutch object and fire pump and piping object.

The engine model includes engine characteristic data and the simulation. The engine simulation is the running process of simulation engine that based on access to the engine characteristic data and different input (throttle) and feedback (engine load) and output the simulation results.

Power train is composed of torque converter, automatic transmission control strategy, the gearbox and main gear.

Steering system is generally composed of steering operation agencies, steering gear and steering linkage. The relationship between the front wheel angle δ and the steering angle θ can be expressed as:

$$\delta = \theta / i_s \tag{1}$$

in which, i_s is steering transmission ratio, according to the manufacturer parameter i_s=28.

The braking system is the complex structure and different braking system structure varies. The physical modeling approach requires to consider the actual structure of the braking system. The relationship equation between braking torque T_b and brake pedal displacement L_b as follows:

$$T_b = T_{bmax} L_b / L_{bmax} \tag{2}$$

where L_{bmax} is the maximum stroke of the brake pedal; T_{bmax} is the maximum braking torque of the brake system[3-4].

Driving system model includes factors that affect vehicle movement, including the elements of the vehicle driving force, rolling resistance, aerodynamic drag, braking force and vehicle quality.

Power divider and pump clutch used to transfer power. Power divider passes the output torque of the engine to pump clutch. Pump clutch cut off or pass the engine output power.

The fire pump worked by torque drive transferring from the clutch. Pipe in the valve is controlled by the firemen, who can open and close the pipe leading to the main gun and secondary batteries, which will change the impedance of the pipe, affecting the flow of the fire pump.

4   Simulation of Instrument Running

Instrument system uses a combination of step motor driver and PLC with function of fast pulses output in the simulation of instrument running. The step motors are the motors that convert the electrical pulse signal into angular displacement or linear displacement by electromagnet principle. Each pulse input will make it rotate a certain angle or forward a step [5]. FP-C30T PLC has advantages of stability and high adaptability as well as the specified pulse output channels. It has five kinds of high-speed pulse output modes and can output 1.5Hz-100kHz frequency with high precision and small error. The PLC also has four high-speed pulse output terminals so that you can save space and easy to operate [6]. Here is the hardware design flow chart shown in Figure 2.

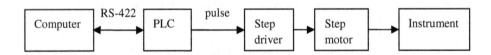

Fig. 2. Hardware design flow

1 PLC and 4 step motors are used on the structures of the instrument system, including tachometer, speedometer, oil temperature, water pressure and so on. The hardware circuit diagram of instrument system shown in Figure 3. Take a PLC and a step motor driver and four step motor for example because of the same principle to the other half. In the circuit, two 100nF capacitor protect the circuit from being destroyed. Fscx is pulse frequency, and CW / CCW control the motor rotation direction of step motor, the foot 26 is the reset pin.

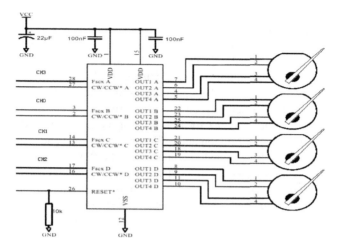

Fig. 3. System schematic

5   Communication of System

5.1   PLC Side

It can be seen in Figure 2 that the PC control the entire system and PLC system is the bond of system, so the communication between PC and PLC is particularly important. Serial communication was selected in the system. An extension module named AFPX-COM3 was added to the PLC, which support RS-422 serial communication using MEWTOCOL-COM communication protocol. Settings of serial port of PLC are: baud rate 115200bps; Odd parity; 8 data bits; 1 stop bit. The following is the software programming process of the PLC side. As the program is too long and follow the same principle, take one channel for example to illustrate [7-8]. Ladder program is shown in Figure 4.

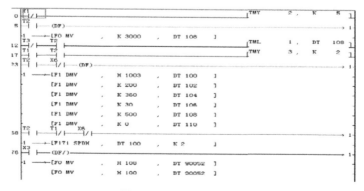

Fig. 4. Ladder program

Taking the start and stop frequency of the step motor into account to avoid steps lost [9], pulse output instruction of F171 (trapezoidal control commands) is used in control. The control code 1003 mean: Output pulse with duty cycle of 1/4, the pulse frequency range 1.5-9.8kHz and the relative PLS + SIGN; K200 is the initial speed (200Hz), K360 is the maximum speed (360Hz), K30 is the acceleration and deceleration time (30ms), K500 is the amount of movement (500Hz). K2 means that pulse output channel is 2. There are another three timers except the pulse output. Timer 2 is start time; timer 1 is the rotation time of motor through which the host computer to control the motor rotation angle; Timer 3 is for read and write serial port that can be set as needed. It is needed to comply with the PLC's MEWTOCOL-COM communication protocol to make the computer and the PLC communicate. It requires the industrial personal computer to send commands (main station) and the PLC response (slave), so industrial personal computer should send the command frame in accordance with the agreement to communication protocol. The format is shown in Table 1.

Table 1. Send command format

%or<	Station number	#	Command code	Text data	BCC	C_R

% or <code stands for the beginning code. The length of % at the beginning can reach single frame maximum of 118 bytes and < for 2048 bytes.

Station number is the PLC station number which composed of two bits and former in high, latter in low.

stands for the instruction code.

The command code typically includes 26 types of instructions. Such as the RCS (single read), the WCS (single point write) and the WD (write data area).

Text data is written for content, such as closure is 1 and open is 0.

BCC is block verification code, two bits, the specific algorithm is hexadecimal XOR operation from first bit to last bit.

C_R is frame terminator code.

PLC receives the command frame from the computer and answers the industrial personal computer according to the protocol of MEWTOCOM-COM, the response format is shown in Table 2.

Table 2. Receive reply format

%or<	Station number	$	Response code	Text data	BCC	C_R

$ is response frame code. Other code is the same meaning to send commands. Error response format is shown in Table 3.

Table 3. Error response

%or<	Station number	!	Error code	BCC	C_R

! is Error frame code. The error code mark the cause of the error, including a link to system errors, procedural errors, handling system errors, a total of 26 kinds of PLC error. The error code can help us find the wrong reasons and improve work efficiency.

Industrial personal computer uses a RS-422 to RS-232 converter on Physical connection to change 422 level of PLC to 232 level which the industrial personal computer can receive.

5.2   The Communication of Industrial Personal Computer Side

VC + + 6.0 was used in software programming on host computer side [10-11]. VC + + 6.0 is a Windows application development tools which has strong capabilities in the graphics processing and database management and use it to the bottom of the communication control has a faster speed.

SerialPort class is used to construct serial procedures of computer side. SerialPort class is a serial communication class using the Windows API technology development. This class is based on multi-serial port and multithreading, which only need to add this class to the framework of a program[12-13].

5.3   Serial Communication Test

When described communication protocol of the PLC side, the communication command frame format is given and only the correct command frame format can cause the response of the PLC. Test content: Host computer sends a command frame and detect whether the PLC response or not and the response is correct or not. The ComboBox control of MFC dialog will show the various parts of the command frame, which will ease visual observation and simplify command writing. So we only need to write text content in a send text box. Programming code as follows:

```
m_strSend="%"+m_strStaNum+"#"+m_strCmd+m_strDaa+ m_strSend +"**\x0d";
```

Set command of PLC timer process values test: Select Station No. 01 from the drop-down triangle in the (the rest of the operation is the same) MFC interface; the timer process value writing command is "WK"; register select "00000000"; "0001" is written in text box   "Send". PLC response is shown in Figure 5. The same step test data register written command: the same station number; the command select "WDD"; register select "0,003,000,030"; send text box setting "50". The tests above are the correct responses which indicate that the PC and PLC can communicate each other normally.

Fig. 5. MFC interface

6   Conclusion

Application of parallel simulation technology in instrument system of airport fire engine simulator makes simulation of running and indication of instrument pointer and simulation of working of fire engine in the same time, which enhances the real-time quality and accuracy of instrument system. RS-422 serial bus is used to exchange data between two simulation computer (PLC and industrial personal computer). With assistant of AFPX-COM3 extension module, MEWTOCOL-COM communication protocol and converter module between RS-422 and RS-232, the communication between two computers is reliable and in time, which assures the parallel simulation system working well.

References

1. He, F., Dong, S.: Basic performance requirements for airport fire engines. Fire Technique and Products Information 3(3), 61–62 (2004)
2. Duan, Y.-N., Lv, H.: The Controller of Step-Motor in Instrument based on FPGA. Electrical Measurement & Instrumentation 43(1), 33–34, 56 (2006)
3. Zhang, Y.: Vehicle dynamic parameters simulation based on car driving simulation system. Kunming University of Technology, Kunming (2008)
4. Bemard, J.E., Clover, C.L.: Validation of Computer Simulation of Vehicle Dynamics. SAE paper NO.940231
5. Liu, B., Cheng, S.: Step motor drive control system, 2nd edn. Harbin Institute of Technology Press, Haerbin (1997) (in Chinese)
6. Shi, J.: Step motor servo control technology, 1st edn. Science and Technology Press, Beijing (2006) (in Chinese)
7. Zhang, R., Hu, A., Zhang, C.: PC and PLC serial communication implementation based on VC + +. Manufacturing Technology & Machine Tool 09, 58–61 (2010)
8. Tian, B., Wang, W.: The PC and PLC serial communications programming implementation based on VC. NET. Process Automation Instrumentation 03, 20–22 (2008)
9. Li, G.: Step motor drive and control system design. Coal Mine Machinery 02, 114–116 (2008)

10. Zhao, J.: Using VC + 6.0 Serial communication between PC and PLC. Heilongjiang Science and Technology Information 07, 71 (2008)
11. Hui, H.: Using VC + 6.0 Serial communication between PLC and PC. Microcomputer Information 16, 55–57 (2006)
12. Wang, W.: Serial communication system implementation based on Serial Port. Science Mosaic 05, 21–23 (2011)
13. Chen, C., Li, C., Han, L.: SerialPort class in the radar serial communication. Computer Knowledge and Technology 24, 5921–5922, 5927 (2011)

Material Database Design and Realization
Based on the Metadata Management of Electric Power

HaiZhou Du[1,*], DaQuan Zhang[2], and ChongTian Wu[2]

[1] College of Computer & Information Engineering, Shanghai University of Electric Power,
China, 200090
[2] College of Energy & Environment, Shanghai University of Electric Power, China, 200090
duhaizhou@shiep.edu.cn

Abstract. The importance of materials database have been well aware of as requirements of engineering design, risk management and new materials design. The paper discusses the problems of power material complexity and lack of data model. The problems are often faced the designer of electric power material. At the same time, we propose metadata management-based data with the sharing way. We referred to the Dublin core metadata standards system, and established the metadata standards system which it has conformed to the characteristic of electric power material data. Thus it realized the metadata centralized storage, centralized management and carried on the strict quality control to the input data. In the process of whole system designing, we use the object-oriented pattern method to establish the electric power material database system.

Keywords: Meta-data management, Electric power materials database, Database design.

1 Introduction

The electric power industry is the important basis industry of the national economy and social development, the development and application of high new material are the important guarantees of electricity production safe economy. The electric power materials data is very important information in such field: the electric power project, power plant equipment design, manufacture and service security evaluation, the new material research and development and so on. It is also the basis of the engineering design and product design. The data is not only relates to the quality and cost of project and product, but also relates to the construction the service security, moreover relates to the accuracy of the failure analysis and life forecast of product. Our country currently did not have the perfect electric power energy material data service. The data related to electric power energy material mostly centralized in steel and iron material [1].

---

* Corresponding author.

J. Lei et al. (Eds.): NCIS 2012, CCIS 345, pp. 626–631, 2012.
© Springer-Verlag Berlin Heidelberg 2012

Since China has not suitable to the integrated resource sharing platform for the power company electric power energy material design at present. And we faced to such things as follows: without reference data to design, without the excellent communication of material data, without making the best of limited data resources, and in addition the electric power energy material data is very complexity. So all these causes the solutions of most power company projects to rely on the expert of rich knowledge and experience. And the expert also needs enough information to make the correct judgment. According to the sharing research in the electric power energy scientific data and with the metadata management-based way, we has used application with Jsp(Java Server Pages) and the Oracle database solution. And on the foundation of the collecting literature material data, we fully mined the domestic existing research results and data. That contains the boiler material, the steam-turbine material, auxiliary engine material, ultra-supercritical critical material and wind-powered electricity material five categories. It provides system's solution in the electric power energy material design and control for the user. And it will make the electric power energy material database to obtain the scientific and reasonable application in the engineering construction and modern manufacturing industry.

2   Metadata Management Technologies

With such a huge electric energy materials data resources, how to standardize the data so as to facilitate data sharing, exchange, integration and effectively using is an urgent issue. Yet the metadata theory is one of major means of achieving shared data. First of all it is necessary to conduct a rational and effective management of metadata. Metadata is data about data. It is to describe data sources, content, format, quality, status and structural features of information. Plain speaking, metadata is the data dictionary of database. Metadata is described object what can do, and how to get the basic issues. [2]

Good metadata can be easily made to the database administrator user management and maintenance, and more rapid and comprehensive, more effective discovery, access, and use of shared data resources.

Metadata management can be resolved by comprises three main aspects: Firstly, It is necessary to the large number of information resources in an effective Organization, and because of the existing URL way store has apparently do nothing with the current needs. Secondly, provide access to the methods and means. That is the question how to make it in the vast information ocean, and quick to retrieve the required information. At present the main method of searching through the search engine is a search engine. And the large number of useless information and also cannot be satisfied with the results of the query. Thirdly how to effective manage the large information resources. how to adapt to the changing world of information, timely updates and additions to existing information, which need to further strengthen data mining, expert systems, intelligent agents, such as the new support system. Therefore the function and role is mainly reflected in the description of the information content of the resource. It provides a convenient way to retrieve, maintain, supplement and update the original information. Thus that will contribute to the access, use and sharing of information resources.

At present the metadata also don't have the unified standard properties and uniform format. Its form is also very flexible. Different organizations have also developed a specific focus on different variety of metadata standards. such as Dublin core, and IAFA Template, CDF (Channel definition format), Web Collections. One of the most influential is Dublin core. And it has gradually become a universal standard. Therefore, if we want to multiple forms of data to the database for better focused, unified management, facilitate the search, we must be built the metadata based management and sharing the data-sharing first disciplines. Therefore, with reference to the current standard of Dublin core metadata standards, we will develop standards of electrical energy materials Data Metadata standard system. The metadata based in each data set corresponds to a globally unique identifier that can be interpreted as a meta-data corresponding to a record in a data-set on the datasets. The access is based on the visit of metadata records. In order to focus on the meta-data storage, centralized management has been gradually replaced by simply as the core data sets the traditional sharing mode.

Based on the above metadata standards, each record of the data of the above information will be in a detailed description of the contents. When a visitor access to the database, he will see the Data Metadata information in the first sight. Thus he can be immediately informed of all the basic information data, more quickly and easily from the needs and interest in the data. At the same time the standards will help to enforce a strict control over the quality of the data, and ensure that true data, reliable, and practical in the database.

3   Electrical Energy Materials Database Structure Design

Electric energy materials based on materials in accordance with the characteristics, uses a classification into boiler materials, gas turbine materials, auxiliary machine materials, Ultra (ultra-) critical materials and wind electric materials 5 major categories, and specific for boiler furnace steel pipes, boiler furnace and steel, gas turbine rotor, spindle, impeller with steel, generator rotor, annex with steel, turbine blades made of steel, copper alloy tubes, stainless steel heat exchanger tube heat exchangers, titanium alloy heat exchanger tube, low alloy steel, heat-resistant austenitic steel, heat-resistant austenitic stainless steel, heat-resistant steel, wind machine materials and leaf material in 13 categories. In accordance with this model for integrating effect is better, and mainly embodied in more than a user-friendly classification in accordance with demand for materials, conduct a search at the same time will help retrieve the material uses similar performance. The material classification is shown in Table 1.

Table 1. Material classification and the specific inclusion of data situation

system	Type	subcategory / material
Electrical energy materials	Boiler	boiler furnace steel pipes
		boiler furnace and steel
	gas turbine	gas turbine rotor, spindle, impeller with steel
		generator rotor, annex with steel
		turbine blades made of steel
	auxiliary machine materials	copper alloy tubes
		stainless steel heat exchanger tube heat exchangers
		titanium alloy heat exchanger tube
	Ultra (ultra-) critical	low alloy steel
		Ferritic heat resistant steel
		Austenitic steel
	wind electric	wind machine materials
		leaf material

The number of five major categories of grades of material classification of materials of a boiler, two steam turbine materials, three auxiliary materials, super (super) critical materials, wind power materials. 13 sub-class grade numbers to the largest category of number is the first number, sequentially numbered, such as boiler tubes of steel 11, boiler tube steel 12. Similarly to the sub - class number of 125 kinds of materials for the first number , then take the two as a sub- number , 1101 cases of boiler furnace tubes of steel 20G , 1102 boiler tubes Steel 20MnG 1103 boiler tubes Steel 25MnG.

Due to the importance of data in the power of Materials Science database does not recommend physically delete records, so each table is the addition of the "flag" field , normal data value of " 1" , when the execution of the delete operation will mark the position "0" , no longer show the so-called tombstone .

When added a new brand to the following 13 categories table, we should add to the material properties detailed table corresponding brand information. The categories tables are as follows: the boiler furnace tube with the steel table, boiler stove tube with the steel table, steam engine rotor table, main axle and impeller with the steel table, generator armature and appendix with the steel table, steam turbine leaf blade with the steel table, copper alloy heat change tube table, stainless steel heat change tube table, titanium alloy heat change tube table, low-alloy high-temperature steel table, ferrite high-temperature steel table, Austenite high-temperature steel table, the air blower bill of materials, the leaf blade bill of materials and other subgroup tables. The material properties detailed tables are as follows: mechanics performance table, the craft performance table, the physical performance table, the high-temperature performance table, welding and processing table. The specific data sharing platform onstage showed that contact surface as shown in Figure 1.

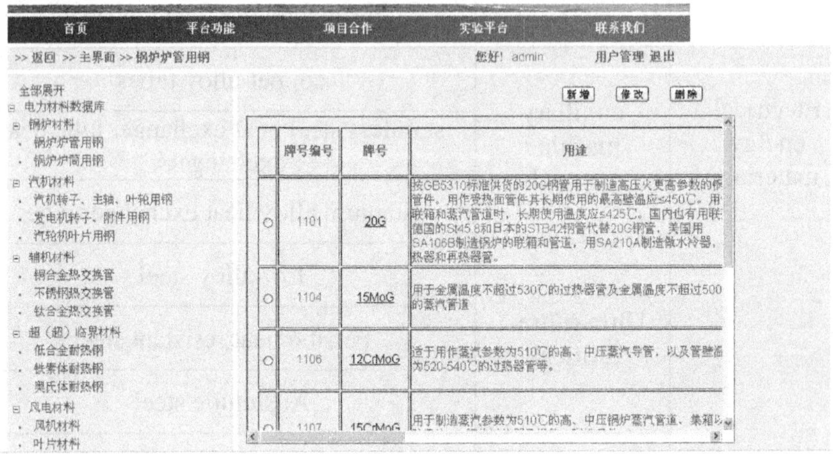

Fig. 1. Electric power energy material data platform onstage contact surface

4   Conclusions

The platform which is based on Metadata management of the electric power energy material data will become to a core of the sharing mechanism. And it will provide the service to more and more users. Along with the development of technology and the hi-tech material, the information that includes also unceasingly in the database increases to the data along with it the integrity. Meanwhile the platform may also act according to the user the special demand, provides the specialized service. Next step we will consummate further electric power energy material database platform plan and frame construction. And we will go on collecting the search and familiar domestic and foreign related electric power energy material data, integrating into the data sharing platform to carry on the sharing service. Through service the feedback promotion corresponding serviceability of platform operational aspect, we will continue investigate and develop the new service model. To improve the organization management system is our next task.

Acknowledgement. The authors express their appreciation for supports form the project of Shanghai Science and Technology Committee (11JC1404400) and the project of platforms of national basic scientific and technical conditions (2005DKA32800).

References

1. Ljungberg, L.V., Kevin, L.: Design materials selection and marketing of successful products. Materials and Design 24, 519–529 (2003)
2. Zhang, L.F., Xie, C.S.: The Current development of materials science database. Huazhong University of Science and Technology (4), 43–46 (1997)
3. Dan, W.: To several views of our country materials science data sharing. Chinese Society for Corrosion and Protection 27(12), 47–51 (2003)
4. Bruce, T.A.: Designing Quality Database with IDEFIX Information Models. Dorset House, New York (1992)
5. Zhang, X.J.: An Effective Design Method For Components Made of A Multiphase Perfect Material. The University of HongKong, Hongkong (2004)

A Strategy of Network Security Situation Autonomic Awareness

Ruijuan Zheng[*], Dan Zhang, Qingtao Wu, Mingchuan Zhang, and Chunlei Yang

Electronic and Information Engineering College, Henan University of Science
and Technology, Luoyang 471023, China
rjwo@163.com, dandan2006_1213@126.com

Abstract. To solve self-adaptation problem of network situation awareness process, a strategy of network security situation autonomic awareness (NSSAA) drawing on autonomic computing ideas was proposed in this paper. The policy can effectively extract situation information by analyzing the situation extraction in real time. On the basis of this, current network security situation is evaluated by employing hierarchical analysis method from two angles of attack and defense. Future network security situation is forecast by adopting based on likelihood BP to realize self-learning adjustment of the weight of the specified parameter. Test results show that the proposed policy could made self-adaptation ability of system effectively enhance.

Keywords: Autonomic computing, Autonomic awareness, Situation extraction, Situation assessment, Situation prediction.

1   Introduction

In recent years, with the increasing complexity of the network structure and the constant emergence of various new attack means, the network security issues are becoming more and more austere. At the same time, the network security technologies are constantly changing. For instance, the development of these technologies change from the traditional intrusion prevention and intrusion detection to intrusion tolerance and survivability, from the information privacy to availability and sustainability of information, from the attention of the solutions of a single security problem to the overall network security situation and variation trend. On the basis of this, the research on network security situation awareness (NSSA) technology is rapidly becoming a new hotspot.

However, the existing techniques of NSSA can be only simply and rough qualitative description on the risks of network in the past [1-2]. These techniques lack real-time quantitative perception ability in the risk of the system being attacked. They couldn't automatically adjust the defense strategy of the entire system according to the

[*] Project supported by the National Nature Science Foundation of China (No.61142002, U1204614,61003035).

J. Lei et al. (Eds.): NCIS 2012, CCIS 345, pp. 632–639, 2012.
© Springer-Verlag Berlin Heidelberg 2012

changes on network environment threat, lack of adaptability [3-4], and can't identify unknown attacks and keep away the serious network security threats. In the evaluation strategies, the current evaluation methods [5-8] assessed the entire network security situation only from the attack or vulnerability and did not consider the impact of the defensive measures on the whole network security situation.

Comprehensive comparative research found that although the research on NSSA has been widespreadly concerned at present and techniques and evaluation strategies of the situation awareness also have made constantly progress, from the angle of attack and defense, according to some changes such as the current state of the system, security and environmental parameters, and integrating self-regulatory characteristics, how dynamically adjusted to network security situational awareness system configuration and operating parameters to achieve a truly self-adaption network is the bottleneck to constraint study of network security situational awareness. Therefore, this paper proposed a strategy of network security situation autonomic awareness drawing on autonomic computing [9-10] ideas to make the system real-time autonomically perceive internal and external environment change and analyze and dynamically adjust the system parameters. Thus, the system self-adaption ability is effectively enhanced.

2   Modular System Architecture

NSSA is a new technology which meets the demands of network security monitoring and a process which gains, understands, evaluates and predicts to the dynamic change network security situation elements [11].

Thus, a network security situation autonomic awareness system is established according to the working mechanism of autonomic computing system [9]. The system consists of the managed resource, the Agent collaborative layer and autonomic manager, as show in Fig.1.

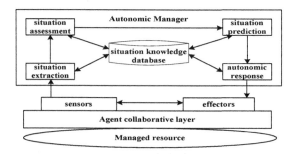

Fig. 1. Network security situation autonomic awareness

Managed Resource(MR): MR is physical resources and virtual resources which mainly include database, server, application modules, routers, Web server and host log, network packets and firewall alarm information, etc. These managed resources are uniformly dispatched and managed by Agent collaborative layer.

Agent Collaborative Layer (ACL): For different types of MR, ACL provides the data support for Autonomic Manager (AM) with different intelligence Agent. The main function of ACL is to receive AM information feedback and autonomic regulation system environment, which can dynamically adapt to the environment change in order to realize the dynamic configuration of the resource, the dynamic synthesis of the service and the dynamic calibration of the system parameters.

Autonomic Manager (AM): AM consists of the situation extraction, situation assessment, situation forecast, and autonomic response and knowledge base component. The situation extraction component extracts the aggressive behavior and stores it in the situation knowledge base [13] according to the data information provided by ACL. The situation assessment component views the attack as security elements, evaluates the current network security situation and then stores situation value information in situation knowledge base. Situation forecast component predicts the future network security situation on the basis of the past and current network security situation. Autonomic response component is mainly autonomic regulation situation values according to the strategy knowledge of situation knowledge base. Thus, the system is in a stable state.

3   Realization of Strategy of Network Security Situation Autonomic Awareness

3.1   Situation Extraction

Situation extraction is the foundation of NSSAA, which provides the real-time original data for situation awareness, as show in Fig.2. It mainly consists of the integration platform of data source of network security status, anomaly-based and autonomic association learning modules.

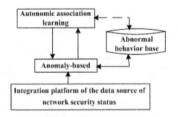

Fig. 2. Situation extraction

The data integration platform mainly realizes the integration of multi-heterogeneous data and unifies it as XML, which provides the upper module with data support. Anomaly-based module detects the possible various attacks in the network by employing signature-based technology on the base of the abnormal behavior library and the abnormal behavior library is updated in real time. Autonomic association learning module predicts the possible abnormal condition and early abnormal symptom. Using the method of the diagnosis forecast and intelligent decision-making realizes autonomic association learning, and the results are stored in the abnormal behavior library. Thus, it achieves the association learning on the unknown attack and rapidly extracts effective situation information, which prepares for situation assessment.

3.2   Situation Assessment

From the point of view of attack and defense, the whole network system which is divided into network layer, host layer and attack-defense layer top-down step by step is layered by employing hierarchical analysis method [12], as show in Fig.3.

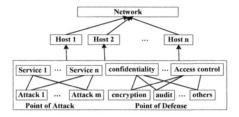

Fig. 3. Layered structure of network system

Definition 1. Function F_s is the service security situation status of the target network in t moment, noted for:

$$F_s(S, K, N, D, t) = N(t) \bullet 10^{D(t)} . (1) \tag{1}$$

In Eq. (1), S is some service which is provided by the current target network; K is the attack types in the service; N is the number of the attack in the service; D is the severity of the attack in the service; N (t) is the number of attacks in t moment; D (t) is the severity of the attack in t moment.

Definition 2. Function DF_H is the defense strength of host of the target network in t moment, noted for:

$$DF_H(W_s, SM, Ed, t) = W_s \bullet Ed(t) . \tag{2}$$

In Eq. (2), W_s is the importance weight of the security properties on the host; SM is the security measures running on a host; Ed is the effect degree that SM is relative to security attributes.

Definition 3. Function F_H is the host security situation status of the target network in t moment, denoted by:

$$F_H(H, W, F_s, t) = W \bullet F_s(t) / DF . \tag{3}$$

In Eq. (3), H is the host of the target network; W is the weight of the service in the host, DF is the defense strength.

Definition 4. Function F_L is the system security situation status of the target network in t moment, denoted by:

$$F_L(L,V,F_H,t)=V \bullet F_H(t). \qquad (4)$$

In Eq. (4), L is the system in the target network; V is the weight of the host in the local area network.

3.3   Situation Prediction

On the basis of assessment of the current network security status, the weights of the specified parameters are self-learning adjustment by adopting the likelihood of BP [13] to achieve the forecast of the future network security situation, specific steps as follows:

Step 1:According to the information of the value of past and current situation, the situation prediction function $F(\hat{y}_m^p|V)$ which is the multi-input single-output of service, host and system and the corresponding error function G (V) are defined as Eq. (5) and Eq. (6) in this paper.

$$F(\hat{y}_m^p|V) = (2\pi|Ky_m|)^{-1/2} \exp\{-\frac{(y_m^p - \hat{y}_m^p)^T(y_m^p - \hat{y}_m^p)}{2Ky_m}\}. \qquad (5)$$

$$G(V) = \sum_{m=1}^{N_p} \frac{(y_m^p - \hat{y}_m^p)^T(y_m^p - \hat{y}_m^p)}{Ky_m} \qquad (6)$$

In (5) and (6), K is the attack types in the service, $\hat{y}_m^p$ and y_m^p is respective the actual output and expected output of the m neurons of the p layer, corresponding to the situation prediction value; for flow parameters of each single point input in the propagation, V is respective attack severity D, services weights W and host importance weights V in situation assessment.

Step 2: Training the neural network is to make the fitting deviation $(y_m^p - \hat{y}_m^p)$ tend to zero. The weights of the specified parameters are self-learning adjustment to find the optimal combination of parameters. Finally, the curve of situation prediction after training is output.

4   Simulation Experiment

In order to verify the validity of the proposed strategy of NSSAA, the main equipments of the experimental environment are Gigabit Ethernet Switch, IDS Firewall and protected hosts (H1, H2, H3) in all which runs different services and security defense mechanisms. Part of the data of KDDCUP 99 from the laboratory of MIT LINCOLN is selected as the experimental data. Then the protected hosts are attacked by using the attack means, such as land, perl, spy, the imap, smurf, etc.

4.1   Result Analysis of Situation Assessment

In order to more objectively evaluate the importance of each service and the host, the service weight and the host weight are radicated by employing the IAHP [12]. The service weight on the host H1 is W1 = {0.2535, 0.1261 0.2236, 0.3968}. The service weight on the H2 is W2= {0.1739, 0.5843 0.2837, 0.1106, 0.2837, 0.1739}. The service weight on the H3 is W3 = {0.2789, 0.7211}. The weight of host is V = {0.1332, 0.5987, 0.2877}. It can be seen that the corresponding weight of host H2 is the largest, which is consistent with the actual situation.

According to (1), (2), (3) and (4), the security situation of the network in the experimental environment is calculated, as shown in Table 1. The status of network security situation is given in April, 2011. Trend of greater value is meant that the network security situation is more serious. It can be seen that the values in the days 6, 12, 21, 27 are larger, which means the threat degree of attack to network security is larger. At the moment, the automatic response components of the system will respond and automatically adjust system environment, which can made it dynamically adapt to the environmental change. The situation values in the days 18 and 24 are smaller, which suggests that the network is suffered less attack and network security situation is in good condition.

Table 1. Values of network security situation

Date	3	6	9	12
Situation Values	13.4	25.8	4.3	8.3
Date	18	21	24	27
Situation Values	4.6	37	3.7	13.5

In the actual process, self-adaption of the situational awareness process of the system which loads the strategy of NSSAA is tested by importing randomly attacks. During April, 2011, every three days sampling, it gets 10 sampling points.

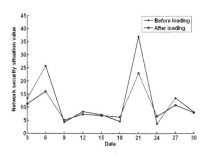

Fig. 4. Change circumstance of network security situation before and after loading the strategy

Change circumstance of the target network security situation is generated, showed in Figure 4.It can be clearly seen that the change of security situation of the target network which loads the strategy is relatively stable. The reason is that the system which loads the strategy possesses autonomic features. It possesses self-adaption on external attacks and can perceive internal and external environment changes of systems in real time and dynamically adjust the situation values according to the changes of internal external environment parameters in the system.

4.2   Process of Situation Prediction and Analysis of Results

According to the trend of assessment results, 90 continuous security situation values are taken, the former 55 of which are as the training sample, the later 35 of which are test samples. After pretreated, it is input likelihood BP network to train the network. The predetermined target error is 0.001. The rate of learning is LP.lr = 0.01 and maximum training times are 2000. It achieves the target error when training 475 times. The comparative analysis was also carried out using ordinary BP network to test samples and found that it has not yet reached the target error after training in 2000.

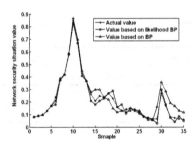

Fig. 5. Prediction Curves of Likelihood BP and BP

The predicted curves based on the likelihood BP and BP algorithms are shown in Fig.5. By a comparative analysis, BP method based on likelihood [14] whether convergence speed or running time is better than BP method.

5   Conclusions

Drawing on the idea of autonomic computing, a strategy of NSSAA was proposed and a system of NSSAA was established in this paper. Each functional components of the system are analyzed, the results show that the proposed strategy of autonomic awareness can made system identify the known and unknown aggression, acquire effectively the state information, understand accurately the current security situation of network, predict quickly future network security situation, and thus enhance self-adaption ability of the system. The simulation experiment results show that the autonomic perception strategy proposed can effectively enhance self-adaption ability of the system. Because it is still in exploration stage which autonomic computing is introduced to the study of the network security situation awareness, the related methods and theories need to be further researched and perfected.

Acknowledgments. This project is financially supported by the National Natural Science Foundation of China (NSFC 61003035 and 6142002).

References

1. Bass, T.: Intrusion detection systems & multisensory data fusion: Creating cyberspace situational awareness. Communications of the ACM4 43, 99–105 (2000)
2. Yin, X.X., Yurcik, W., Slagell, A.: The design of VisFlowConnect-IP: A link analysis for IP security situational awareness. In: IWIA 2005, Baltimore, USA (2005)
3. Batsel, S.G., Rao, N.S., Shankar, M.: Distributed intrusion detection and attack containment for organizational cyber security. IEEE Transactions on Computers 42(4), 447–553 (2007)
4. Shifflet, J.: A technique independent fusion model for network intrusion detection. In: Proceedings of the Midstates Conference on Undergraduate Research in Computer Science and Mathematics, pp. 13–19 (2005)
5. Zhang, Q.Y., Sun, N., Chi, N., Liu, Y.: Evaluation for security of networked system based on fuzzy information fusion. Computer Engineering 33(13), 182–184 (2007)
6. Liu, N., Liu, S.J., Liu, Y., Zhao, H.: Method of network security situation awareness based on artificial immune. Computer Science 37(1), 126–129 (2010)
7. Li, J.P., Wang, H.Q., Lu, A., Hao, H.L., Feng, G.S.: Quantification awareness method of network security situation based on conditional random field. Transducer and Microsystem Technologies 29(10), 83–86 (2010)
8. Zhang, Y., Tan, X.B., Cui, X.L., Xi, H.S.: Network security situation awareness approach based on Markov Game model. Journal of Software 22(3), 495–508 (2011)
9. Liao, B.S., Li, S.J., Yao, Y., Gao, J.: Conceptual model and realization methods of autonomic computing. Journal of Software 19(4), 779–802 (2008)
10. Wu, Q.T., Hua, B., Zheng, R.J., Wei, W.Y., Zhang, M.C.: Intrusion tolerance model based on autonomic computing. Journal of Computer Application 30(9), 2386–2388 (2010)
11. Lai, J.B., Wang, H.Q., Zhu, L.: Research on network security situation awareness. Journal of Computer Research and Development 43(2), 456–460 (2006)
12. Lai, J.B.: Research of a number of key technologies of network security situation awareness based on heterogeneous sensor Ph.D. Thesis, Harbin Engineering University, Harbin (2009)
13. Zhang, Y., Guo, S.Z., Huang, S.G., Wang, Y.Y.: Novel multi-heterogeneous sensor based network security situation awareness model. Application Research of Computers 29(1), 286–289 (2012)
14. Tang, C.H., Yu, S.Z.: Method of network security situation prediction based on Likelihood BP. Computer Science 36(11), 97–100 (2009)

Stuxnet Vulnerabilities Analysis of SCADA Systems[*]

Yong Wang[1], Dawu Gu[2], DaoGang Peng[1], Shuai Chen[1], and Heng Yang[1]

[1] Department of Computer Science and Technology, Shanghai University of Electric Power,
2103 Pingliang Road
Shanghai, 200090/Yangpu District, China
[2] Department of Computer Science and Engineering, Shanghai Jiao Tong University, 800
Dongchuan Road
Shanghai, 200240/Minhang District, China
wy616@126.com

Abstract. Stuxnet virus is a first discovered malware to damage nuclear power station in June 2010 and targets only Siemens supervisory control and data acquisition (SCADA) system via vulnerabilities. Through the static reverse and dynamic analysis of Stuxnet malware files, we researched on MS10-046 (CVE-2010-2772) shortcut vulnerability, MS10-061 (CVE-2010-2729) in print spooler service vulnerability and MS10-073 (CVE-2010-2743) keyboard layout elevation of privilege vulnerability. The paper illustrated internal details and the Stuxnet implemented methods.

Keywords: Stuxnet, Vulnerability, CVE, SCADA.

1 Introduction

Stuxnet is widely suspected to be used to damage uranium enrichment infrastructure in Iran, which is discovered in June 2010. The Iran nuclear program using Siemens equipment has been damaged by Stuxnet according to widely report. Stuxnet targets only Siemens supervisory control and data acquisition (SCADA) systems through PLCs by subverting the Siemens Step-7.

Stuxnet self-propagates via Windows some vulnerability. MS10-046 (CVE-2010-2772) shortcut vulnerability is in windows shell that could allow remote code execution. MS10-061 (CVE-2010-2729) in print spooler service could allow remote code execution. MS10-073 (CVE-2010-2743) keyboard layout vulnerability allows elevation of privilege.

---

[*] This work is supported by State Key Laboratory of Information Security (Institute of Software, Chinese Academy of Sciences) (04-02-1), Shanghai Education Commission Innovation Foundation (11YZ192), Shanghai Science and Technology Commission Key Program (11511504400) and National Nature Science Foundation of China under Grant (60903188). Natural science foundation of Shanghai City (NO.12ZR1411900).

J. Lei et al. (Eds.): NCIS 2012, CCIS 345, pp. 640–646, 2012.
© Springer-Verlag Berlin Heidelberg 2012

2   Stuxnet Files

Stuxnet from tuts4you.com has 7 files in root directory 2 subdirectory with 1,129,027 bytes.

2010/09/14	16:52		26,616 A0055521.sys
2010/08/25	20:15		4,171 Copy of Shortcut to.lnk
2010/07/18	01:07		40,960 dll.dll
2010/09/27	17:46		513,536 malware.exe
2010/07/22	09:03	\<DIR\>	signed drivers
2010/10/02	02:02	\<DIR\>	stuxnet core
2010/07/18	00:37		392 suckme.lnk_
2010/08/25	20:15		517,632 ~WTR4132.tmp
2010/08/25	20:15		25,720 ~WTR4141.tmp

There are dropper.exe_ and maindll.decrypted.unpacked. dll_ in the stuxnet core directory besides the files listed. In the signed drivers directory, files are "0d8c2bcb575378f6a88d17b5f6ce70e794a264cdc8556c8e812f0b5f9c709198", "1635ec04f069ccc8331d01fdf31132a4bc8f6fd3830ac94739df95ee093c555c", "63e6b8136058d7a06dfff4034b4ab17a261cdf398e63868a601f77ddd1b32802"   and 70f8789b03e38d07584f57581363afa848dd5c3a197f2483c6dfa4f3e7f78b9b.

3   Stuxnet Analysis

3.1   Dll.dll

The Dll.dll is a main module. Its size is 40,960 bytes. Section header of .text composed of 00006354h virtual size, 10001000h virtual address, 0006400h raw data, and 0000400h pointer to raw data.

_text_1000285C in .text with 96h length is the main program in dll.dll, which has procedures, such as _text_1000288E, _text_100028D4, _text_100028DF and _text_100028EE. The string in dll.dll file is shown in Table 1.

Table 1. String in Dll.dll by PE Explorer

Virtual Address	String
10008838	'Microsoft Visual C++ Runtime Library',0
10008120	SUCKM3 FROM EXPLORER.EXE MOTH4FUCKA #@!',0Ah,0
7783ADC1	'R6032',0Dh,0Ah,'- not enough space for locale information',0Dh,0Ah,0
1000830C	'DOMAIN error',0Dh,0Ah,0
100091D8	'GetProcessWindowStation',0

3.2   Malware.exe

Malware.exe released mrxcls.sys and mrxnet.sys files which located in %System32%\drivers\ directory. The sys files altered registry table with MrxCls and MrxNet value. Malware also released oem7A.PNF, mdmeric3.PNF, mdmcpq3.PNF and oem6v.PNF in %Windir%\inf\ directory [3,4].

Exports, imports and function name of Malware.exe is shown in Table 2.

Table 2. Exports, Imports and function name of Malware.exe by PE Explorer tools

Exports	Imports	Function name
CPlApplet	ExitProcess	DllEntryPoint
DllCanUnloadNow	FreeLibrary	DllCanUnloadNow
DllEntryPoint	GetModuleHandleW	DllGetClassObject
DllGetClassObject	GetVersionExW	DllRegisterServerEx
DllGetClassObjectEx	lstrcmpiA	CPlApplet
DllRegisterServer	GetProcAddress	
DllRegisterServerEx	DeleteFileA	
DllUnregisterServer	VirtualProtect	
DllUnregisterServerEx	GetCurrentProcess	
	GetCurrentThreadId	
	GetTickCount	
	lstrcpyW	
	lstrlenW	
	wsprintfW	
	lstrcmpiA	

3.3   ~WTR4141.tmp in Stuxnet

Timestamp in the ~wtr4141.tmp indicates the complication data was 03/02/2010 06:30:26 4B691802H using Microsoft Visual. Linker version 9.0 of ~wtr4141.tmp indicated the Stuxnet used Visual Studio 2008 [3]. Linker version 8.0 of A0055521.sys indicated Visual Studio 2005.   Malware.exe also complied by linker version with different Microsoft Visual C++ Private Version 1. The difference between files indicated the Stuxnet may developed by a group[3].

The ~wtr4141.tmp file also have signature from Realtek Semiconductor Corp valid from March-15-07 8:00:00 to June-12-2010 7:59:59.   The signature details is shown in Table 3.

Table 3. Signature details of ~wtr4141.tmp

Field	Value
Version	V3
Serial Number	5e 6d dc 87 37 50 82 84 58 14 f4 42 d1 d8 2a 25
Signature Algorithm	sha1RSA
Issuer	CN = VeriSign Class 3 Code Signing 2004 CA OU = Terms of use at https://www.verisign.com/rpa (c)04 OU = VeriSign Trust Network O = VeriSign, Inc. C = US
Valid From	March-15-07 8:00:00
Valid To	June-12-2010 7:59:59
Subject	CN = Realtek Semiconductor Corp OU = RTCN OU = Digital ID Class 3 - Microsoft Software Validation v2 O = Realtek Semiconductor Corp L = Hsinchu S = Taiwan C = TW
Public Key	30 81 89 02 81 81 00 b5 6c 5e 03 88 79 57 9a 4f ce 02 30 b9 05 1f 06 13 7a 57 17 4e ee 59 d6 b0 20 d0 7c e9 17 32 bb 03 e8 13 45 1a 3e 22 57 4c b4 bc b3 c5 3d 32 62 e8 a9 6c f2 03 d1 72 ee 1e f2 65 ce dd df 0f 6e 77 08 a7 b2 13 92 db 30 f3 d8 8e b9 53 46 d5 08 16 4f 6d 92 a5 f2 74 5e d9 42 d2 89 50 92 53 0a e6 ff 67 3f 14 59 fe 0d af e0 97 8e 1f f0 eb 6f c6 e1 93 3e 5e 50 a6 26 65 69 21 84 32 be a3 27 02 03 01 00 01
Subject Type	Subject Type=End Entity Path Length Constraint=None

CRL Distribution Point	CRL Distribution Point
	  Distribution Point Name:
	    Full Name:
	      URL=http://CSC3-2004-crl.verisign.com/CSC3-2004.crl

Certificate Policy	Certificate Policy:
	  Policy Identifier=2.16.840.1.113733.1.7.23.3
	  Policy Qualifier Info:
	    Policy Qualifier Id=CPS
	    Qualifier:
	      https://www.verisign.com/rpa

Advanced Key	Code Signature (1.3.6.1.5.5.7.3.3)

Table 3. (*continued*)

Authority Info Access	Authority Info Access
	    Access Method= Online Certificate Status Protocol (OCSP)
	(1.3.6.1.5.5.7.48.1)
	    Alternative Name:
	        URL=http://ocsp.verisign.com
	Authority Info Access
	    Access Method=Authority Issuer (1.3.6.1.5.5.7.48.2)
	    Alternative Name:
	        URL=http://CSC3-2004-aia.verisign.com/CSC3-2004-
	aia.cer

Authority Key ID	KeyID=08 f5 51 e8 fb fe 3d 3d 64 36 7c 68 cf 5b 78 a8 df b9 c5 37
Netscape Cert Type	Signature (10)
Spc Financial Criteria	Financial Information=Not Avaliable
Digital Signature	Digital Signature (80)
Fingerprint Algorithm	sha1
Fingerprint	68 41 39 3d 9a 1d 09 c9 f5 c6 39 c0 c7 14 fb 42 ad dd 7d d2

4   Vulnerabilities in Stuxnet

4.1   MS10-046 (CVE-2010-2772) Shortcut Vulnerability by Copy of Shortcut Oto.lnk

MS10-046 vulnerability is in windows shell that could allow remote code execution [1,2]. Shortcut file will search for the icon resource according to the file structure. If the icon resource is in the DLL file, the MS10-064 vulnerability can load the malware DLL file. When open an infected USB flash disk, the "copy of shortcut to.lnk" will load the ~WTR4141.tmp. The content of the link is shown in Fig. 1 as below [3,4].

Fig. 1. Attribute content of the "copy of shortcut to.lnk" is shown although the USB flash disk hasn't been infected

```
00000080  ...j..........\.\...\.S.T.O.R.A.G.E.#.V.o.l.u.m.e.#._.?.?._.U.S.
000000C0  B.S.T.O.R.#.D.i.s.k.&.V.e.n._.K.i.n.g.s.t.o.n.&.P.r.o.d._.D.a.t.
00000100  a.T.r.a.v.e.l.e.r._.2...0.&.R.e.v._.P.M.A.P.#.5.B.6.B.0.9.8.B.9.
00000140  7.B.E.&.0.#.{.5.3.f.5.6.3.0.7.-.b.6.b.f.-.1.1.d.0.-.9.4.f.2.-.0.
00000180  0.a.0.c.9.1.e.f.b.8.b.}.#.{.5.3.f.5.6.3.0.d.-.b.6.b.f.-.1.1.d.0.
000001C0  -.9.4.f.2.-.0.0.a.0.c.9.1.e.f.b.8.b.}.\.~.W.T.R.4.1.4.1...t.m.p.
```

Fig. 2. Sting contents of the copy of shortcut to.lnk file is shown when using the WinHex tools

The shortcut always find icon in the directory   %SystemRoot% \system32 \~wtr414.tmp once change the icon.

4.2   MS10-061 (CVE-2010-2729) Print Spooler Vulnerability by Dropper.exe and Maindll.decrypted.unpacked. dll

MS10-61 (CVE-2010-2729) vulnerability in print spooler service could allow remote code execution[1,2].

The report of "Stuxnet Under the Microscope" declare that "the worm copies the dropper and additional file into Windows\System32\winsta.exe and Windows\System32\wbem\mof\sysnullevnt.mof" [4]. The winsta.exe and sysnullevnt.mof are loaded with guest privileges.

Maindll.decrypted.unpacked. dll file check the system is STEP7 or not according to three strings "Step7\Example", "STEP7_Version" and "SOFTWARE\SIEMENS\STEP7".

4.3   MS10-073 (CVE-2010-2743) Keyboard Vulnerability in Stuxnet

MS10-073 (CVE-2010-2743) vulnerability in windows kernel-mode drivers could allow elevation of privilege, which allows local users to gain privileges via a crafted application using the NtUserLoadKeyboardLayoutEx function[1,2]. Stuxnet loads a keyboard layout file to elevate user privilege to system administration privilege. The MS10-073 (CVE-2010-2743) vulnerability is exploited in Stuxnet.

5   Conclusion

Stuxnet virus in nuclear power station exploits MS10-046 (CVE-2010-2772), MS10-061 (CVE-2010-2729) and MS10-073 (CVE-2010-2743) Vulnerabilities. Siemens Simatic WinCC and affected windows issued corresponding patch. Researches on Stuxnet virus in nuclear power station can improve the risk assessment of nuclear power station security from cyber. We had begun the continuing study on the related filed with my good friend Professor Da Ruan [5].

Greatis Software provides the free Stuxnet Remover Version 1.0.1.3 for Stuxnet/Tmphide removal tool. The software supported windows XP /2003/ Vista/Win7 32bit. Stuxnet Remover can detect and remove the active infection files such as mrxcls.sys, mrxnet.sys, mdmcpq3PNF, mdmeric3.PNF, oem6c.PNF and oem7A.PNF. Stuxnet Remover can also detect and remove "lnk" and "tmp" files on USB flash disk. And delete the ~ WTR4132.tmp, ~WTR4141.tmp, copy of shortcut to.lnk [9].

Anti-virus software is facing new challenges of Stuxnet Industrial control systems (ICS) malware [6]. Although the vulnerabilities used by Stuxnet malware have been updated by windows, Many potential vulnerabilities still exist in ICS. The threats from ICS demand the development of a security-positive environment [7]. How to find these in real time industrial control system is a big problem for Anti-virus software and intrusion prevention system.

References

1. Common Vulnerabilities and Exposures, `http://cve.mitre.org/`
2. Microsoft Security Bulletins, `http://technet.microsoft.com/en-us/security/bulletin/`
3. Matrosov, A., Rodionov, E., Harley, D., Malcho, J.: Stuxnet Under the Microscope Revision 1.31, `http://www.eset.com`
4. Antiy, Report on the Worm Stuxnet's Attack, `http://www.antiy.com`
5. Wang, Y., Ruan, D., Gu, D., et al.: Analysis of Smart Grid Security Standards. In: Proc. CSAE 2011, June 10-12, pp. 697–701 (2011)
6. Townsend, K.: Anti-virus: a technology update. Infosecurity 7(6), 28–31 (2010)
7. Durbin, S.: Tackling converged threats: building a security-positive environment. Network Security 2011(6), 5–8 (2011)
8. Stuxnet Remover, `http://greatis.com/security/stuxnet_remover.html`

Probe into Digital Resources Service Model in Web3.0

Hao Rao

Department of Computer Science, Shaoguan University, Shaoguan, China
gdrh@tom.com

Abstract. Web3.0 is a kind of tendency belonging to the Internet's development, and the result of all network techniques' advancement. This paper elaborate service patterns of digital resources. In the environment of Web3.0, the digital resources gradually tend to a assemble service model. The so called assemble service model can be seen in the collection of sources, the collecting of techniques and the collection of services. Users could choose their own digital resources according to their interest hobbies and needs.

Keywords: Digital Resources, Service Model, Web3.0.

1   Introduction

The Internet has been developed constantly. From web1.0 which was the era of surfing the webpage to web2.0, the times of which users create contents on their own. Then it comes to web3.0 centering on the services. All walls of the world haven't got a unified definition to it until now. The concept, web3.0 has been announced since 2005, Brian Solis, in a large sense, lays down a definition of the progress of all kinds of network techniques to web 3.0[1]. Nova Spivak holds the opinion that the web3.0 is a collection of statistics, linguistics, computer intelligence, wisdom of crowds and the content created by the users on the Internet[2]. Chinese scholars Hanhua Wu and Zizhou Wang consider that the nut-shell concept of web3.0 is turning to human nature, as well as intellectual ability, and it will stay with web2.0 and web 3.0 in a long run[3]. Wikipedia wrote that web3.0 is employed to describe different kinds of circumstances and characters, which may appear during Internet's development[4].

In general, web3.0 is a kind of tendency belonging to the Internet's development, and the result of all network techniques'advancement. Web3.0 owns the following characters.

- Painstaking Accuracy of the Information. The development of semantic network improves the describing accuracy of information and makes the information not difficult to combine accurate retrieval with effective polymer.
- Compatibility of Multi-network Multi-terminal. With the constant development and changes of the Internet correspondent techniques, the way to surf the Internet has been changed as well. The Internet formation of web3.0 will make different terminals be compatible. It means that equipments like PC, cell phone, PDA, Set-Top Box, and so on can surf the Internet through many kinds of communicational network[5].

J. Lei et al. (Eds.): NCIS 2012, CCIS 345, pp. 647–652, 2012.
© Springer-Verlag Berlin Heidelberg 2012

- Intellectual Network Platform: It bases on the web completely. That means in order to show its ability, the complex system took place by the browser[6]; its unit widget can compose freely and it can fit many terminals like PC, cell phone, and PDA, the network platform will be a filter and satisfy comprehensive needs. According to the users'needs, such platform can deal with the problems about reorganizing and consolidating the huge Internet information intellectually, so the users'needs would come together finally.

2   The Development of Digital Resources Website

Digital resources website is the website whose excellent illustrations texts are made and saved by the digital technique. In fact, it is a distributed digital information system with large scale. The system uses digital techniques to save information sources from all kinds of different carrier and different places through the connection with the Internet to make it convenient for network enquiry and spreading[7]. It concerns all process about information progressing, information storages, message retrieval, information transmission and use of information .Only owning network terminal and accordingly jurisdiction can enjoy the information sources which belonged to the digital resources website.

With the development of the techniques, the concept and connotation of "network terminal" enlarge widely. "Network terminal" not only concerns PC, notebook PC, smart mobile phone, but also contains telephone, TV, digital camera and many other handed equipment. In the same way, the network interface no longer turns towards a single terminal. But, it turns in the directions of different characteristics terminals.

The web3.0 technique bears many types of terminal equipment including PC, mobile phone, PDA. Users of digital resources will no longer contact with merely one terminal, but with a user-contacting environment formed by many terminals. The user-contacting environment with multi-terminals is composed by a series of different Internet terminal groups which can be tied or moved at any time. For instance, when the user of digital resources is out without taking a PC, but at the same time he is in a urgent need to surf the information sources, through the telephone reservation, he can use the mobile phone to receive and surf information (or download through digital set-top box), then he can edit the information by using the PDA and finally, sends it out by the mobile phone.

3   The service Pattern Under Digital Resources

From a lower rank to a higher one, the digital resources website develops without a stop. The core of digital resources service has experienced from centering on webmasters sources to users which is a widely-changed process. In the early period, the offered services are based on the need of website work. The servant of information leads an important role which has made the users have to accept the information products offered by the staff. In the developing period, it is the process information sources and producing services that attract the attentions. The needs were lead by the products. In a state of mature, the practice of services is based on the information's needs asked by the users. The information products are got by making or surfing a certain type of information. Also, in the service process, the users' temptation to participate and initiative are considered.

With the popularization and development of modern information technology, and under the qualifications of multi-network multi-terminals, the digital resource gradually tends to a assemble service model. The so called assemble service model can be seen in three parts, the collection of sources, the collecting of techniques and the collection of services.

3.1   The Collection of Resources

It is necessary for the service pattern of digital resources in the future to deeply consider the characteristics of information sources distribution under the condition of network environment, assembling the digital information sources with difference and subsection, technique, worker, organization and services to control the distracted digital sources effectively[8]. The pattern will make controlled information that is isomerism information products through assembling in order to offer the users information service platform inside a digital resources website with the ability to shield isomerism not only breaking the serious separation of former departments but also support the surfing and getting of isomerism information everywhere and there is a unified user interface to offer convenient service and dealing the computers in different websites.

- The collections between one website to another one. Each digital resources website owns its surfing system, knowledge and data storage. The way they contact with each other is working with each other public by using the Internet. Instead of restricting and depending on each other, the physic existence and logic one of information sources assemble the information sources, services, users and activities in the same digital space. All kinds of information dealing mechanism, basing on network, knowledge, co-working become mature gradually. It is possible for them to realize interlinkage, interchange, co-operation, co-working and assembling. Breaking the serious division between former departments, digital resources website turns to newly cooperating mechanism like website to website, website to user. It is able to surf and get distributed information, strengthening the usage and management over information service.
- The collection of isomerism data. Different types of digital sources are untied effectively by digital digital resources website to assemble the information sources. Under the differences of operation system, data storage, and the way to keep the information between one website and anther, by the assembling information service pattern, all sources needed by users are organized into a logical one to make the information be gotten by the users in one same way. Instead of facing the comprehensive data storage or system, the users get to use the information, forming a logical unified one. Information assembled services satisfy the needs of

being convenient for users to get digital network information. The services let users surf the digital sources inside a website by using one search method or word, at the same time, offer the search and inquiry that one same information source of thesis can directly be searched. All sets of instruments should be equipped by website to achieve the interlinkage of searching, collecting, analyzing, processing, offering information and effective collection of all kings of information.

3.2   The Collecting of Techniques

Digital resources website is the product of high technology and the collection of information techniques play a significant role in during the building of the website. Through applying to informational techniques, it can better realize the website individuality and intellectual power. The following part is talking about the main techniques involving users' services.

- Intellectual Agent service. Intellectual Agent is composed of users Agent and system Agent that is an intellectual construction. Users Agent spies on users deeds. Their time to surf the website、 time to surf、 keys works and so on would be gotten automatically by the Users Agent, and it studies and keeps the uses' interests in mind, thus it is able to build a distinctive information model. At the same time, the connection with users Agent is going on in the green room. Finally, individual information services will be offered to the users. Intellectual Agent can make such as managing personal data, informing information automatically, guiding browser, surfing intellectually individual pages come true.
- Polymerization RSS. RSS means a way to sharpen content from one web station to another. It is used for collecting information sources、 sharing、 sending、 subscribing and declaring issues. Users, with the help of bowers or reading software, can collect large amount of RSS Feeds information sources together instead of surfing websites one by one. In this way, they can access to information offered by websites, thus forming information gateway of them. By applying the RSS techniques, website improves its digital services level. Surfing and subscribing to different types of news、 programs data、 special subject data storage、 guiding course data can be found under RSS technique. In addition, RSS technique can apply to declare books and periodicals、 audio and videos、 electronic products. Subscribing RSS to surfing system of public lists can showing the latest sources of website to the users.
- Data mining technology. Data mining technology is also called the finding knowledge of data. They are gotten from large amount unknown data which is noisy、 blurry and random. Because of the rapid development of information sources, to users, the relative ability to collect and deal with information is slow. Thus, how to find useful knowledge from large amounts of data becomes a problem needed to be solved.   Data mining technology accompanies this usage.

3.3 The Collection of Services

The information services of the digital resources website must make its service in accordance with the users' needs, explore the unknown needs of the users, and try to satisfy users' needs with the help of a series of service patterns. Main patterns of information services include services which involve all process, distinctive service and initiative service.

- Service involving all process. Reorganizing and consolidating all services of website, it is convenient for users to use the information in the service entrance. Through this service entrance, users can search many strange construction information reach and get many information of the website and extra information such as comments and recommends, and take part in the organizing and controlling of sources, for example, sending digital sources, classifying sources distinctively. Making use of technique XML/RDF, all information would be shown in interface in one same pattern, and then a perfect connecting platform would be shown to the users.
- Distinctive service. Distinctive service is mainly performed in two following aspects. One is a distinctive interface, the other is information content and function according to the customs and needs of users. After previous rulers being made by users, system can automatically follow the using customs of users, thus choose the information which is the most attractive and interesting from large amount of information to the users. It makes full uses of information sources and users' needs be satisfied as widely as possible. The other one is to reorganize and explore the information sources according to the characteristics of users or groups of users, building a distinctive information environment. A reader can own a private collection by asking for a service system. By this way, website opens to more users and satisfies more needs, and its distinctive and intellectual service come into a winder use.
- Initiative service. It is a way of initiative service, being open to users by using the push technique. Firstly, users key to their own information needs including personal information, informational themes which attract their interests in the computer system, them the system would search in particular, regularly pushing related information to users' terminal. It changes "information finds persons" into "persons finds information". The way of pushing information is through email, channels, web pages and so on.

4   Concluding Remarks

What has been talked above is about service patterns of digital resources in theory. The application and practice of digital resources need practicing and researching. The appearing of Web3.0 changes the way which information is gotten by users. According to their interest hobbies and needs, users could choose their own digital sources, even collect other information from the Internet to build their private website. Centering on users, relying on Internet and basing on collected sources, techniques and services, it is clearly sure that digital resources website would offer more distinctive and intellectual service to users.

References

1. Web 3.0 is about Intelligence [EB/OL] (January 10, 2008),
   http://bub.blicio.us/?p=432
2. What is Web 3.0?It's Web 2.0 with a Brain [EBOL] (October 21, 2007) (January 10, 2008),
   http://venturebeat.com/2007/10/21/what-is-web-30-its-web-20-with-a-brain
3. Wu, H., Wang, Z.: Envisioning Library3.0 from Web3.0. Library Development (4), 66–70 (2008)
4. Web3.0 [EB/OL] (October 6, 2010), http://zh.wikipedia.org/zh-cn/Web_3.0
5. Web3.0 [EB/OL] (October 19, 2010),
   http://baike.baidu.com/view/269113.htm
6. Feng, W.: Library in the Web3.0 era. Journal of Southwest University for Nationalities (2), 274–277 (2010)
7. Digital Library [EB/OL] (June 5, 2010),
   http://baike.baidu.com/view/8181.html?wtp=tt
8. Guo, H., Liu, G.: Research on digital library service model development. Information Studies:Theory & Application 28(3), 251–254 (2005)

The Periodicity of Nonlinear Pseudo Random Sequence Based on Latin Squares

Jing Li and Yunqing Xu

Mathematics Department, Ningbo University, Ningbo 315211, China
xuyunqing@gmail.com

Abstract. Nonlinear pseudo random sequences based on Latin squares have important applications in cryptography. Nonlinear pseudo random sequences with large periods have more extensive applications. Different Latin squares have different properties with the period of the sequence it produced. There are many different experimental methods to determine which Latin square is suitable. In this paper, based on mathematical theory, we give the constructions of Latin squares with large period growth from Frobenius groups.

Keywords: Latin square, Frobenius group, pseudo random sequence.

1   Introduction

Pseudo random sequences play an important role in communication, automatic control, computer and cryptography. Pseudo random sequence generators (PRSG) are the production algorithm of pseudo random sequence. According to the different algorithms, it is divided into two categories. One category is linear pseudo random sequence generators, the other kind is nonlinear pseudo random sequence generators. Because nonlinear pseudo random sequence generators have arbitrary long cycle and unpredictability, they are more suitable for the field of cryptography.

On Latin squares pseudo random sequence generator is a nonlinear pseudo random sequence generator [1]. Edon80 derived from four Latin squares of order 4 which was submitted to the eSTREAM project is a nonlinear pseudo random sequence.

The number of Latin squares is huge. For example, there are approximately 10^{37} Latin squares of order 10. The quantity growth sharply when the order of the Latin squares increase. The number of all Latin squares of order n is no smaller than $(n!)^{2n} n^{-n^2}$, but not every Latin square is suitable for pseudo random sequence generators. For example, for pseudo random key sequence generators of Edon80, the increasing of the periods of string processed is very different. For some of them it is linear, for others it is exponential. The increasing of periods is the most important index in pseudo random key sequence generators algorithm of stream cipher. There are 576 Latin squares of order 4, and for Edon80, by Gligoroski's experiments, 384 of them are suitable, 64 of them are very suitable [3]. Latin squares of arbitrary order can be used to generate pseudo random sequence algorithm of sequence cipher system,

J. Lei et al. (Eds.): NCIS 2012, CCIS 345, pp. 653–660, 2012.
© Springer-Verlag Berlin Heidelberg 2012

the most convenient should be the Latin squares of order 256. But for higher order of Latin squares, their statistical tests are almost impossible, What's worse, the result of the experiment is not very accurate. So it is necessary to find a way to determine whether a Latin square is suitable for pseudo random sequence algorithm from mathematics theory. In this paper, we just to solve the problem from Frobenius groups since Frobenius groups have some special properties to construct Latin squares with large period growth.

2   Definitions and Theorems on Period Growth of Quasigroups

We will briefly mention the definition of the Latin square as it is defined in [4]. A Latin square of order n with entries from an n-set Q is an $n \times n$ array L in which every cell contains an element of Q such that every row of L is a permutation of Q and every column of L is a permutation of Q. Closely combinatorial structures to Latin squares are the so called quasigroups: A quasigroup $(Q,*)$ is a groupoid satisfying the law:

$$(\forall u, v \in Q)(\exists! x, y \in Q) \ u * x = v \ \& \ y * u = v \tag{1}$$

We use only finite quasigroup, i.e., Q is a finite set.

To any finite quasigroup $(Q,*)$ given by its multiplication table it is associated a Latin square L, consisting of the matrix formed by the main body of the table, and each Latin square L on a set Q define a quasigroup $(Q,*)$.

Consider a finite set $Q(|Q| \geq 2)$, and denote the set of all nonempty words (i.e., finite strings) by $Q^+ = \{x_1 x_2 \cdots x_k | x_i \in Q, k \geq 2\}$. For a fixed $\alpha \in Q$ we define an e-transformation of Q^+ based on the quasigroups operation $*$ as follows:

$E_{\alpha,*} : Q^+ \to Q^+ : E_{\alpha,*}(x_1 x_2 \cdots x_k) = y_1 y_2 \cdots y_k$ if   and only if

$$\begin{cases} y_1 = \alpha * x_1, \\ y_i = y_{i-1} * x_i, \quad (i = 2, 3, \cdots, k). \end{cases} \tag{2}$$

The function $E_{\alpha,*}$ is called an e-transformation of Q^+ based on the operation $*$ with leader α. Edon80 gets a non-linearity pseudo random sequence $y_{79,1} y_{79,3} \cdots$ as keystream sequence, which obtains through 80 e-transformations with the initial sequence 012301230123... as shown in Table 1. Particularly, $*_i$ is an operation on $Q=\{0, 1, 2, 3\}$.

Definition 1. Suppose $(Q, \circ)$ is a quasigroup. $\forall X \in Q^+$, $\alpha \in Q$, let $c(X)$ denotes the period of X and $c(E_\alpha(X))$ denotes the period of $E_\alpha(X)$. Define $\sum_{\alpha \in Q} P(\alpha) \dfrac{c(E_\alpha(X))}{c(X)}$ the period growth of quasigroup $(Q, \circ)$ on X ; define

$C(Q, \circ) = \sum_{X \in Q^+} P(X)(\sum_{\alpha \in Q} P(\alpha) \frac{c(E_\alpha(X))}{c(X)})$ the   period   growth   of   quasi-

group $(Q, \circ)$, where $P(\alpha)$ and $P(X)$ denote the probability of α and X respectively.

Table 1. Representation of quasigroup string e-transformations of Edon80

$*_i$	α	0	1	2	3	0	1	2	3	0	...
$*_0$	α_0	$y_{0,0}$	$y_{0,1}$	$y_{0,2}$	$y_{0,3}$	$y_{0,4}$	$y_{0,5}$	$y_{0,6}$	$y_{0,7}$	$y_{0,8}$	...
$*_1$	α_1	$y_{1,0}$	$y_{1,1}$	$y_{1,2}$	$y_{1,3}$	$y_{1,4}$	$y_{1,5}$	$y_{1,6}$	$y_{1,7}$	$y_{1,8}$	...
...	...	...	...	...	...	...	...	...	...	...	...
$*_{79}$	α_{79}	$y_{79,0}$	$y_{79,1}$	$y_{79,2}$	$y_{79,3}$	$y_{79,4}$	$y_{79,5}$	$y_{79,6}$	$y_{79,7}$	$y_{79,8}$	...

Let $Q = \{1, 2, \cdots n\}$ and suppose $(Q, \circ)$ is a quasigroup. $\forall i \in Q$, $1 \circ i$, $2 \circ i$, $\ldots, n \circ i$ is a permutation of Q. We call

$$\sigma_i = \begin{pmatrix} 1 & 2 & \cdots & n \\ 1 \circ i & 2 \circ i & \cdots & n \circ i \end{pmatrix}$$

the i-th column permutation of quasigroup $(Q, \circ)$ and the corresponding Latin square.

Definition 2. Suppose Q is a set and G is a permutation group on Q, $\forall \sigma \in G, \alpha \in Q$, the period of sequence $\alpha \sigma(\alpha) \cdots \sigma^k(\alpha)$ is called the period growth of σ of sequence $\alpha \alpha \cdots \alpha$, and denoted by $C_\alpha(\sigma)$. Define $C(\sigma) = \sum_{\alpha \in Q} P(\alpha) C_\alpha(\sigma)$ the period growth of the permutation σ ; define $C(G) = \sum_{\sigma \in G} P(\sigma) C(\sigma) = \sum_{\sigma \in G} P(\sigma) \cdot (\sum_{\alpha \in Q} P(\alpha) C_\alpha(\sigma))$ the period growth of permutation group G, where $P(\alpha)$ and $P(\sigma)$ denote the probability of α and σ respectively.

Quasigroups have many interesting properties, and for our purposes the most important ones are the following:

Theorem 1 [5, Theorem 2.2]. Suppose G is a permutation group generated by n column permutations σ_1, σ_2, $\cdots$, σ_n of a Latin square L, e.i., $G = \langle \sigma_1, \sigma_2, \cdots, \sigma_n \rangle$. Then the period growth of Latin square L equal to the period growth of permutation group G. That is, $C(L) = C(G)$.

From the theorem, we know that the period growth of a Latin square equal to the period growth of the permutation group which generated by column permutations of the Latin square. That is to say, the period growth of a Latin square depends on its column permutations.

Arbitrary permutation can be written as a product of disjoint cycles [6]. If a permutation has λ_i cycles of length i $(1 \leq i \leq n)$, we call $1^{\lambda_1} 2^{\lambda_2} \cdots n^{\lambda_n}$ as the type of the permutation. The following property holds:

Theorem 2 [5, Lemma 3.1]. Let $Q = \{1, 2, \cdots, n\}$. Suppose the probability distribution on Q is uniform, e.i., $\forall \alpha \in Q$, $P(\alpha) = \dfrac{1}{n}$. If σ is a permutation of Q with type $1^{\lambda_1} 2^{\lambda_2} \cdots n^{\lambda_n}$. then the period growth of σ is

$$C(\sigma) = \frac{1}{n} \sum_{i=1}^{n} i^2 \lambda_i. \tag{3}$$

Theorem 3. Suppose L is a Latin square of order n, then the period growth of L is no more than $\dfrac{n^2 - n + 1}{n}$.

Proof. We consider n as a prime number at first. For any column permutation σ of a Latin square L, σ can be written as a product of disjoint cycles, the sum of length of these disjoint cycles is no more than n. In these disjoint cycles, suppose the length of the longest cycle is m, then the subgroup G_1 generated by σ is $\{e, \sigma, \sigma^2, \cdots, \sigma^{m-1}\}$. The period growth of G_1 is no more than $\dfrac{m^2 - m + 1}{m}$. Obviously, $\dfrac{m^2 - m + 1}{m}$ is no more than $\dfrac{n^2 - n + 1}{n}$. For any two column permutations σ_1, σ_2 of the Latin square L, let $\sigma_1 \sigma_2 = \tau$, G_2 is the subgroup by τ, similarly, the period growth of G_2 is no more than $\dfrac{n^2 - n + 1}{n}$. From the above, the period growth of G which is generated by all column permutations of the Latin square L is no more than $\dfrac{n^2 - n + 1}{n}$, i.e., the period growth of L is no more than $\dfrac{n^2 - n + 1}{n}$. When n is not a prime number, situation is similar. In conclusion, the period growth of L is no more than $\dfrac{n^2 - n + 1}{n}$.

3   Period Growth of Latin Squares Base on Frobenius Groups

We will briefly mention the definition of Frobenius groups as it is defined in [7]. A Frobenius group is a transitive permutation group which is not regular, but in which only the identity has more than one fixed point. We can get a better conclusion about the definition:

Theorem 4 [7, Example 3.4.1]. Let G be a finite field and U be a subgroup of the group of units of F. Then

$$G = \{t_{\alpha\beta} : \xi \mapsto \alpha\xi + \beta | \ \alpha \in U, \beta \in F\} \tag{4}$$

is a Frobenius group.

Now, we give the method of constructing Latin squares from theorem 4.

Theorem 5. Let n be a prime number and $F = \{\beta_0, \beta_1, \cdots, \beta_{n-1}\}$ be a finite field of order n. 1 is the identity element of F, let $T = \{\sigma_i : \xi \mapsto \xi + \beta_i | \ i = 0, 1, \cdots, n-1\}$ be a set of permutations on F from G of Theorem 4. Let $L = (\sigma_{i_0}, \sigma_{i_1}, \cdots, \sigma_{i_{n-1}})$ be an $n \times n$ array with every column a permutation from T_α, where $i_0, i_1, \cdots, i_{n-1}$ is a permutation of $0, 1, \cdots, n-1$. Then L is a Latin square with period growth

$$C(L) = \frac{n^2 - n + 1}{n}. \tag{5}$$

Proof. If $i_j \neq i_j$, then $\xi + \beta_{i_j} \neq \xi + \beta_{i_k}$ for every $\xi \in F$. So, every row of L is a permutation of F and L is a Latin square on F. Let $K = \langle \sigma_{i_0}, \sigma_{i_1}, \cdots, \sigma_{i_{n-1}} \rangle$. Then $K \cong (F, +)$ of G. Apparently, these permutations of K as column permutations can constitute a Latin square L, what more, there are $n-1$ cycles of length n, the remaining is the identity. The period of the cycle of length n is $\frac{1}{n} \times n^2 = n$. According to   Theorem 2, we have

$$C(L) = C(K) = \sum P(\sigma)C(\sigma) = \frac{1}{n}[1 + (n-1) \times n] = \frac{n^2 - n + 1}{n}.$$

This completes the proof.

Theorem 6. Let U denote a subgroup of the group of units of a field F and the order of the field F be q^m. Suppose $q^m = n$ and G consisting of all permutations of F of the form $t_{\alpha\beta} : \xi \mapsto \alpha\xi + \beta$ with $\alpha \in U$, $\beta \in F$ is a Frobenius group on F. When $\alpha = 1$, β take over the field F, these permutations $t_{1\beta_1}, t_{1\beta_2}, \cdots, t_{1\beta_n}$ constitute a Latin square L of order n. The period growth of the Latin square L is:

$$C(L) = q - \frac{1}{n}. \tag{6}$$

In the following, we consider the finite field F of order q^n, where q is a prime number. At first we suppose that $q = 2$. We have the theorem:

Theorem 7. Let U denote a subgroup of the group of units of a field F and the order of field F is q^m. Let G consisting of all permutations of F of the form $t_{\alpha\beta} : \xi \mapsto \alpha\xi + \beta$ with $\alpha \in U$ be a Frobenius group on F. Suppose L is a Latin square base on the Frobenius group G, $t_{\alpha\beta_i} (\alpha \neq 1, i = 1, q, \cdots, q^m)$ is the i-th column permutation of the Latin square L, when α is generator of U, the permutation group generated by $t_{\alpha\beta_i} (\alpha \neq 1, i = 1, q, \cdots, q^m)$ is the Frobenius group G, i.e., $\langle t_{\alpha\beta_1}, t_{\alpha\beta_2}, \cdots, t_{\alpha\beta_{q^m}} \rangle = G$.

Proof. On one hand, $\langle t_{\alpha\beta_1}, t_{\alpha\beta_2}, \cdots, t_{\alpha\beta_{q^m}} \rangle$ is the subgroup of G because $t_{\alpha\beta_i}$ $(\alpha \neq 1, i = 1, q, \cdots, q^m)$ is a element of the Frobenius group G. On the other hand, for any element $t_{\alpha\beta_k}$ of the Frobenius group G, there is always $t_{\alpha\beta_1}, t_{\alpha\beta_2}, \cdots, t_{\alpha\beta_{l-1}},$ $t_{\alpha\beta_l}$, making $t_{\alpha\beta_l} t_{\alpha\beta_{l-1}} \cdots t_{\alpha\beta_2} t_{\alpha\beta_1}(\xi) = \alpha^l \xi + \alpha^{l-1}\beta_1 + \cdots + \alpha\beta_{l-1} + \beta_l = t_{\alpha\beta_k}(\xi) = \alpha\xi + \beta_k$ here $\alpha^l = \alpha, \beta_l = \beta_k - (\alpha^{l-1}\beta_1 + \cdots + \alpha\beta_{l-1})$, so G is the subgroup of $\langle t_{\alpha\beta_1}, t_{\alpha\beta_2}, \cdots,$ $t_{\alpha\beta_{q^m}} \rangle$. As a result, $\langle t_{\alpha\beta_1}, t_{\alpha\beta_2}, \cdots, t_{\alpha\beta_{2^m}} \rangle = G$.

In Frobenius group G, only the identity has more than one fixed point, when $2^m - 1$ is a prime number, the situation is better. We can get a conclusion as follow:

Theorem 8. Let U denote a subgroup of the group of units of a field F and G consisting of all permutations of F of the form $t_{\alpha\beta} : \xi \mapsto \alpha\xi + \beta$ with $\alpha \in U$ be a Frobenius group on F. Suppose the order of field F is 2^m and L is a Latin square of order 2^m based on Frobenius group G. Let $2^m = n$ and $t_{\alpha\beta_i} (\alpha \neq 1, i = 1, 2, \cdots, n)$ be the i-th column permutation of the Latin square L, when $n-1$ is a prime number, the period growth of the Latin L of order n is

$$C(L) = \frac{n^3 - 4n^2 + 8n - 5}{n(n-1)}. \tag{7}$$

Proof. Because the order of the field F is n, there are $n(n-1)$ permutations in Frobenius group G. When $n-1$ is a prime number, every element of U is its generator, from theorem 3.5, the permutation group generated by these column permutations of the Latin square L is the Frobenius group G and the distribution of the permutation in G is uniform. There is one identity, the period growth of the identity is 1. There are $n(n-2)$ cycles of length $n-1$ and the period growth of each one is $\frac{1+(n-1)^2}{n}$.

There are $n-1$ permutations whose type is $2^{\frac{n}{2}}$. Their Period growth is 2. So

$$C(L) = C(G) = \sum P(\sigma)C(\sigma)$$

$$= \frac{1}{n(n-1)}\{1+2(n-1)+\frac{1+(n-1)^2}{n}[n(n-2)]\}$$

$$= \frac{n^3-4n^2+8n-5}{n(n-1)}$$

When 2^m-1 is not a prime number, the period growth of Latin squares base on Frobenius group is not satisfied. For example, when $m = 4$, in other words, the finite field is $GF(2^4)$, $F = \{0,1,a,a^2,a^3,a^4,\cdots,a^{14}\}$, $U = \{1,a,a^2,a^3,a^4,\cdots,a^{14}\}$, the Frobenius group G has $2^4 \times (2^4-1) = 240$ permutations. Take $\alpha = a$, when β taking over the field F, we can get the following 16 permutations:

$$T_{a0} = (1\ a\ a^2 a^3 a^4 a^5 a^6 a^7 a^8 a^9 a^{10} a^{11} a^{12} a^{13} a^{14})$$

$$T_{a1} = (0\ 1\ a^4 a^{10} a^{12} a^6 a^9 a^5 a^{13} a^3\ a\ a^8 a^7 a^2 a^{14})$$

$$T_{aa} = (0\ a\ a^5 a^{11} a^{13} a^7 a^{10} a^6 a^{14} a^4 a^2 a^9 a^8 a^3\ 1)$$

$$T_{aa^2} = (0\ a^2 a^6 a^{12} a^{14} a^8 a^{11} a^7\ 1\ a^5 a^3 a^{10} a^9 a^4\ a)$$

$$T_{aa^3} = (0\ a^3 a^7 a^{13}\ 1\ a^9 a^{12} a^8\ a\ a^6 a^4 a^{11} a^{10} a^5 a^2)$$

$$T_{aa^4} = (0\ a^4 a^8 a^{14}\ a\ a^{10} a^{13} a^9 a^2 a^7 a^5 a^{12} a^{11} a^6 a^3)$$

$$T_{aa^5} = (0\ a^5 a^9\ 1\ a^2 a^{11} a^{14} a^{10} a^3 a^8 a^6 a^{13} a^{12} a^7 a^4)$$

$$T_{aa^6} = (0\ a^6 a^{10}\ a\ a^3 a^{12}\ 1\ a^{11} a^4 a^9 a^7 a^{14} a^{13} a^8 a^5)$$

$$T_{aa^7} = (0\ a^7 a^{11} a^2 a^4 a^{13}\ a\ a^{12} a^5 a^{10} a^8\ 1\ a^{14} a^9 a^6)$$

$$T_{aa^8} = (0\ a^8 a^{12} a^3 a^5 a^{14} a^2 a^{13} a^6 a^{11} a^9\ a\ 1\ a^{10} a^7)$$

$$T_{aa^9} = (0\ a^9 a^{13} a^4 a^6\ 1\ a^3 a^{14} a^7 a^{12} a^{10} a^2\ a\ a^{11} a^8)$$

$$T_{aa^{10}} = (0\ a^{10} a^{14} a^5 a^7\ a\ a^4\ 1\ a^8 a^{13} a^{11} a^3 a^2 a^{12} a^9)$$

$$T_{aa^{11}} = (0\ a^{11}\ 1\ a^6 a^8 a^2 a^5\ a\ a^9 a^{14} a^{12} a^4 a^3 a^{13} a^{10})$$

$$T_{aa^{12}} = (0\ a^{12}\ a\ a^7 a^9 a^3 a^6 a^2 a^{10}\ 1\ a^{13} a^5 a^4 a^{14} a^{11})$$

$$T_{aa^{13}} = (0\ a^{13} a^2 a^8 a^{10} a^4 a^7 a^3 a^{11}\ a\ a^{14} a^6 a^5\ 1\ a^{12})$$

$$T_{aa^{14}} = (0\ a^{14} a^3 a^9 a^{11} a^5 a^8 a^4 a^{12} a^2\ 1\ a^7 a^6\ a\ a^{13})$$

These 16 column permutations constitute a Latin square L of order 256. The permutation group generated by these 16 column permutations is the Frobenius group G. So we have

$$C(L) = C(G) = \frac{35746}{3840} \approx 9.31.$$

When the order of the field F is $q^m (q \neq 2)$ and q is a prime number, then $q^m - 1$ is not a prime number. The situation is similar.

4   Concluding Remarks

A Frobenius group is a transitive permutation, in which only the identity has more than one fixed point. Historically, finite Frobenius groups have play an important role in many areas in finite group theory. It was our inspiration for writing this paper. It is satisfying in the following two cases: 1) The order of field F is a prime number. The period growth of the Latin square which we constructed above is $\frac{n^2 - n + 1}{n}$; 2) The order of the field F is 2^n and $2^n - 1$ is a prime number. In this case, the period growth of the Latin square is $\frac{n^3 - 4n^2 + 8n - 5}{n(n-1)}$. The results we have obtained truly confirm the possibility of using the Latin squares in cryptography.

Acknowledgment. The authors would like to acknowledge the support of the National Natural Science Foundation of China under Grant No. 60873267.

References

1. Dimitrova, V., Markovski, J.: On quasigroup pseudo random sequence generator. In: Manolopoulos, Y., Spirakis, P. (eds.) Proc. of the 1-st Balkan Conference in Informatics, Thessaloniki, November 21-23, pp. 393–401 (2004)
2. van Lint, J.H., Wilson, R.M.: A course in combinatorics. Cambridge University Press, Cambridge (1992)
3. Gligoroski, D., Markovski, S., Knapskog, S.J.: The Stream Cipher Edon80. In: Robshaw, M., Billet, O. (eds.) New Stream Cipher Designs. LNCS, vol. 4986, pp. 152–169. Springer, Heidelberg (2008)
4. Stinson, D.R.: Combinatrial Designs: Constructions and Analysis, pp. 123–124. Springer-Verlag New York, Inc. (2004)
5. Li, Y.F., Xu, Y.Q.: The period study of pseudo random sequence based on quasigroups. Journal of Ning bo University 24(3), 41–44 (2011) (in Chinese)
6. Helmut, W.: Finite Permutation Groups, pp. 1–9. Academic Press Inc. (1964)
7. John, D.D., Brian, M.: Permutation Groups, pp. 85–91. Beijing World Publishing Corporation (1997)

Security Research on the Interfaces
of Information Appliances Described by XML

Shaojun Qu and Hong Liu

College of Mathematics and Computer Science,
Hunan Normal University, 410081, Changsha, China
powerhope@163.com, liuhong@hunnu.edu.cn

Abstract. At present, home network is one of the key research field, one of the important services that home network provides is remote control information appliances in home network. However, the remote control service causes various security threats. Therefore, home network should provide strong security services, particularly for remote user authentication and authorization. In this paper, we provide an effective solution to provide secure remote access in home network environment. It uses XML to describe the information appliances interfaces, which can effectively settle interoperability and plug and play problem. To provide the omni-directional safety protection for home network, uses soap to encapsulate xml standard message format, combines xml's encrypted mechanism and signature mechanism, uses authentication and access control technics to achieve the security of remote control.

Keywords: information appliances, security, xml, encryption, signature, authentication, access control, RBAC.

1   Introduction

With the continuous development of digital technology, many new fields combined with digital technology emerge such as information appliances and intelligent home network. The greatest advantage of intelligent home network lies in its remote control of home information appliances.

Intelligent home network has three important features, the device of ordinary objects, the network of autonomous terminal and intelligence of pervasive services. Intelligent home network will provide wider range of interconnection, more thorough information perception and more comprehensive information intelligence services, which need higher security for home network and information appliances. Intelligent home network faces more security threats in the aspects of 'perception', 'network', 'wisdom', 'control', and the threats not only from outside the home, but also from the inner family. Mainly are: hackers, malicious code execution, eavesdropping, spoofing, replay attacks, unauthorized access, offline dictionary attacks, information tampering, implants, denial of service attacks, mail intrusion and viruses, and the disclosure of privacy. Therefore, provide a safe, reliable and stable network environment for users is an urgent problem.

J. Lei et al. (Eds.): NCIS 2012, CCIS 345, pp. 661–668, 2012.
© Springer-Verlag Berlin Heidelberg 2012

Plain text based XML is information carrier that independent of software and hardware, it allows reading and processing data on any platform, moving data among different applications and communicating among different environments and operating systems. And it can solve the description problem of heterogeneous devices in home network environment. We worked [1-2] from the particularity of information appliances, designed XML-based information appliances interface definition language(XIAIDL). In this paper uses Simple Object Access Protocol(SOAP) to encapsulate xml standard message format, combines the XML encryption and signature mechanisms, combines xml's encrypted mechanism and signature mechanism, uses authentication and access control technics to achieve the security of remote control.

2   Related Work

The international research about information appliances and intelligence home network has mainly focus on the home network intelligent device's function of dynamic network, automatic discover, sharing resources and synergies services for a long time. Relevant home network security work mainly include.

IGRS' safety mechanism between devices proposed is based on the symmetric key system authentication and message of authentication mechanism, or the public-key system authentication, message transmission encryption and authentication mechanism, or the trusted third-party authentication, message transmission encryption and authentication mechanism. OSGi's Security Layer is an optional implementation which based on the security architecture of Java2. UPnP's design trend to based on industrial demand rather than family needs. Making their administration difficult and sometimes assuming the existence of both physical security and a group of on-call support professionals. Open Cable [3] developed two specifications: system security specification and copy protection 2.0 specification, which focus on the device authentication and copy protection.

Work [4] offer an extensive analysis on residential gateway security issues which aims at allocating Common Criteria protection configuration files in different using circumstance, and is based on providing a trust value chain. Work [5] use the service architecture of OSGi, and designed four security services for home gateway, safty control services, firewall service based on communication state, wireless LAN security services and user management services. Work [6] proposed an OSGi service platform based on RBAC [7] authorized strategy, compared RBAC model with other access control model, and described the advantages while using RBAC in home network. Work [8] proposed an OSGi authentication and authorization mechanism based on XACML, which is an statement type access control markup language with XML language implementation. Work [9] proposed an RBAC mechanism with OSGi compatible. use the "role" and "authority" of traditional RBAC instead of the concept of user groups and activities group which access conrol in OSGi environment. Work [10] extend the existing authorization mechanism of OSGi platform, so as to slove the limitations of its dynamic deployment. Add the concept of related role by the use of delegation model, and activate the access control.

Work [11] proposed the home network security framework, which based on authentication, authorized and security startegy, to ensure the reliability and availability of the home network. Work [12] proposed the function, which based on device authentication, registration of certificate of home device and issuing method of certificate of home device. The home device authentication framework has hierarchical PKI structure. This scheme lack of certificate schemes related to access control scheme. Work [13] proposed device authentication and access control mechanism, which based on two layers of PKI model. Work [14] proposed an user authentication mechanism which based on smart card. Work [15-16] proposed an information appliances authentication mechanism based on Kerberos. Some induatry advise a hardware fingerprint method , which extract confidential information by the single hardware fingerprints and verify it to trust device. Bouetooth and Zigbee provide an device authentication mechanism which based on the sharing symmetric key.

Work [17-19] proposed public key, which based on One-time password certification schemes.

Work [20] proposed a security mechanism, which based on the human trust ideas, Trust-based security mechanisms allow access rights to evolve among previously unknown principals, thus minimizing security configuration. The main idea is to integrate a trust establishment mechanism into the access control mechanism of intelligent device, so as to manage the interaction between users, which unknown previosly, and intelligent device. Other than establish an access control list for single entity. Before interacting with an angetroffen entity, what the owner of a device have to is merely set the trust degree needed.

Work [21] proposed an idea which restrict the operations that can be executed on a computer according to the physical location of the user who initiated the operation.

Current consumer electronics devices do not interoperate and are hard to use. Devices use proprietary, device-specific and inflexible protocols. If all the devices can be described by the same language and communicate with each other in a natural way, without man-made technical barriers, seamless application will be easily established to gather the ability all the electronic equipment. Interoperation will increase the value of all the equipment. Work [22] proves that XML and SOAP indeed can be useful in small devices, which Solutions to heterogeneous configuration, privacy and security issues, and real-time requirements. We proposed a security mechanism which based on XML to describe the information appliances interface.

3   The Security Mechanism Of Information Appliances Based On XML Description

We designed the XIAIDL based on XML. Because IAIDL have nothing to do with the specific information appliances' function and manufacturer, thus solved the problem of interoperability and plug and play among different manufacturers' information appliances. In the security architecture of home network, assuming all information appliances are using XIAIDL to describe the interface and state.

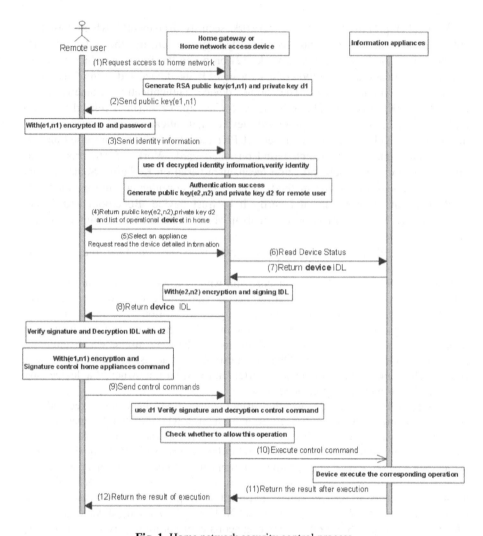

Fig. 1. Home network security control process

New purchase or new access in the home appliance must register in the home gateway or home network access devices(the following are referred to as the HNAD). HNAD have the strong computing power, with internet access, automatic identification device, user management, the key distribution and management functions. The home network security control process as shown in Fig. 1, Remote control information appliances including 12 steps.

(1)Remote user send the request of visit a home network through public network, HNAD produce the public key(e1 ,n1) and private key d1 with the remote user session, public key and private key is only used in the current remote user communication, and have the timeliness, to ensure the confidentiality and integrity of the information.

(2) HNAD send public key (e1, n1) to remote users.

(3)Remote users use public key (e1, n1) encryption own ID and password, send identity information to HNAD, HNAD use private key d1 to decrypt identity information, check ID and password, if identity authentication successfully, then for remote users produce a public key (e2, n2) and a private key d2, and record the remote users' corresponding public key, when remote users quit home network connection the key will become invalid.

(4)HNAD extract device list which can be operated. Return device list, the public key (e2, n2) and the private key d2 to the remote user together.

(5)Remote users select home appliance device, send requirement to HNAD to read device's detail information.

(6)HNAD read device's detail information and running state from the device.

(7)Device returns to the IDL.

(8)HNAD use the remote user's public key (e2, n2) to encrypt and signature IDL, and send to remote user. Fig. 2 is air-conditioning's IDL before encryption and signature. Fig. 3 is the IDL document after encryption and signature.

```
...................
<condition>
   <attributelist name="Appliance Information">
       <attribute name="Type">Air-conditioning</attribute>
       <attribute name="Produced No">101:234:90:100</attribute>
       <attribute name="Production company">Haier</attribute>
       <attribute name="Model">KCD-46(4620)</attribute>
   </attributelist>
   <actionlist name="Function operation">
       <action name="Running" datatype="boolean" allowevalue="On|Off">Off</action>
       <action name="Temperature control" datatype="int"    allowevalue="16|38">20</action>
       <action name="Running Mode" datatype="string" allowevalue="Hot|cold|mild">mild</action>
   </actionlist>
</condition>
```

Fig. 2. Air-conditioning IDL

```
...................
<EncryptedData Type="http://www.w3.org/2001/04/xmlenc#Element"  xmlns="http://www.w3.org/2001/04/xmlenc#">
   <EncryptionMethod Algorithm="http://www.w3.org/2001/04/xmlenc#aes256-cbc"  />
   <CipherData>
<CipherValue>on+qxMAFTsJRMHl4cyJEhCRDnLaZ/7pcOh6ua0q5BsEOgRabcBrvUjyZvuCbdxeh4/CSYb2ENDVp+qGlD7ebyOMO
TCkXVgokQfuQ6EkXOjc5NJRm8afrMvPx9cGG4cd7QhOY1NscIV6Grh0AiwRlZc2svXyRyvFXsIMp8QGg······
</CipherValue>
   </CipherData>
   <Signature xmlns="http://www.w3.org/2000/09/xmldsig#">
   <SignedInfo>
   <CanonicalizationMethod Algorithm="http://www.w3.org/TR/2001/REC-xml-c14n-20010315"  />
   <SignatureMethod Algorithm="http://www.w3.org/2000/09/xmldsig#rsa-sha1"  />
       <Reference    URI=""><Transforms><Transform    Algorithm="http://www.w3.org/2000/09/xmldsig#enveloped-signature"
/></Transforms>
   <DigestMethod Algorithm="http://www.w3.org/2000/09/xmldsig#sha1"  />
   <DigestValue>JQWo4DKymXiAZC2G9/E0IqP5cY0=</DigestValue></Reference></SignedInfo>
<SignatureValue>OeMHmT1vuTtR1+toVW5FuGxS28BSWbUmBu+BGT1Hz7Ec6K7MJuAd3acovBKqHeyJoWG+5wFP5hdW72b3
beuRllWrwho5YqXzQvY2pXdM3j8AFKtktdzaxnWQKkDL0Ctus6JLx5mo8BP2HP7YT9FrA+kp6ZThb7hKdWjcLwUCew=
</SignatureValue></Signature>
</EncryptedData>
```

Fig. 3. Encryption and signature air-conditioning IDL

(9)Remote users use d2 to check the correctness of signature, if signature is right, it will decrypt IDL, and select the operation of information appliances. Use HNAD's public key(e1,n1) encrypt and signature the order of home appliances operation. Send to HNAD.

(10)HNAD use private key d1 to check the correctness of signature, if signature is right, it will decrypt information, and check the remote user operation is allowed or not, here adopt RBAC, if be allowed, it will send operation command to the corresponding information appliances.

(11)After execute the order, information appliances return the state to the HNAD.

(12)HNAD returns the result to remote user.

In the remote user and HNAD communication process using SOAP, the information is being sealed in the SOAP during the transfer. The encryption and signature mechanism adopt XML encryption, signature and verify the signature mechanism. During the information transfer, only do encryption and signature operation for key and important information, in order to improve the communication efficiency.

4   Role-Based Access Control

In the remote user authorization to visit, the RBAC is adopted, considering the particularity of the home network and the stationary of the home network users, satisfying the security needs and simplify the operation, home network remote user will be divided into three categories: administrator, general users and guests. The home network according to their level of security divide information appliances into four levels: danger level, high level of security, the medium level of security and basic security level. Danger level (such as: open gas stoves, close family safety control system) prohibited from remote control. Administrator (usually parents) has all the operation except danger level permissions. The general user (usually child) with partial high level of security, all medium level of security and basic security control privileges. The guest has only part of the basic level of security control permissions. RBAC model shown in Fig. 4.

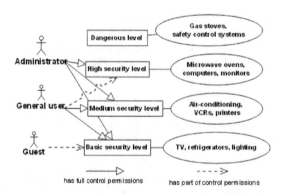

Fig. 4. Encryption and signature air-conditioning IDL

5   Conclusion And Future Work

We based on XIAIDL to study information appliances and home network security. XIAIDL is unrelated to the realization of the function of the specific information appliances, thus it solves the problem of information appliance's interoperability and plug and play. HNAD adopted the random key distribution scheme to provide secret key to XML's encryption and signature. The secret key will be ineffective at the end of this communication. So it can prevent the menace of the offline dictionary attacks and password leak. Combine the system of XML's encryption and signature with home network communication, will protects data's integrity and confidentiality in network communication. The process of secret key distribution, encryption and signature will all be done automatically, it doesn't need users to intervene, simplifies the use of home user and provides the safe and reliable home network environment.

Existing scheme is mostly considerate by industrial demand. Its structure is much complex and it needs much strong ability of calculate. It relies on public CA or home CA or PKI, or excessive dependence on unique platform or programming languages, needs special safety management personnel and so on. It doesn't consider the characteristics of home network users. Most home network users don't have enough professional knowledge background. It doesn't have the full-time and skilled administrators likes in enterprise. It does not quite suitable for residents used in intelligent home network. Moreover it doesn't combine system structure with security in lot of work. Research in home network security is still in its primary stage, we have quite a distance from we can real apply it. We also have a lot of research work to do.

In the current work, the emphasis of our next research is combining cooperation security in information appliances with the home network privacy protection, and providing easy-to-use and more safety home network environment.

Acknowledgments. The work presented in this paper has been supported by Scientific Research Fund of Hunan Provincial Education Department(11C0812).

References

1. Qu, S., Liu, H.: Architecture Research of Information Appliances. Computer Technology and Development 17, 224–227 (2007)
2. Yuan, C., Jiang, Y., Xiao, J., Qu, S.: Research of Information Appliance and Remote Management System. Computer Knowledge and Technology 6, 8682–9684 (2010)
3. OpenCable Security Specification,
   http://www.opencable.com/specifications
4. Trialog.: E-protection of appliances through secure and trusted access. E-Pasta IST Project Final Report 2000-26086 (2002)
5. Jiang, Z., Lee, K., Bae, H., Kim, S.: Security Service Framework for Home Network. In: The Fourth Annual ACIS International Conference on Computer and Information Science, pp. 233–238. IEEE Computer Society, South Korea (2005)
6. Cho, E.-A., Moon, C.-J., Park, D.-H., Baik, D.-K.: Access control policy management framework based on RBAC in OSGi service platform. In: Sixth IEEE International Conference on Computer and Information Technology, pp. 161–166. IEEE Computer Society, Korea (2006)

7. Ferraiolo, D.F., Richard Kuhn, D.: Role based access control. In: 15th National Computer Security Conference, Baltimore, pp. 554–563 (1992)
8. Cho, E.-A., Moon, C.-J., Park, D.-H., Baik, D.-K.: An effective policy management framework using RBAC model for service platform based on components. In: SERA 2006, pp. 281–288. IEEE Computer Society, Washington (2006)
9. Lim, H.-Y., Kim, Y.-G., Moon, C.-J., Baik, D.-K.: Bundle authentication and authorization using XML security in the OSGi service platform. In: Fourth Annual ACIS International Conference on Computer and Information Science, pp. 502–507. IEEE Computer Society, Washington (2005)
10. Kim, I., Lee, D., Kim, K.J., Lee, J.: Flexible authorization in home network environments. Cluster Computing 15, 3–15 (2012)
11. Kim, G.W., Lee, D.-G., Han, J.-W., Kim, S.-C., Kim, S.-W.: Security Framework for Home Network: Authentication, Authorization, and Security Policy. In: Washio, T., Zhou, Z.-H., Huang, J.Z., Hu, X., Li, J., Xie, C., He, J., Zou, D., Li, K.-C., Freire, M.M. (eds.) PAKDD 2007. LNCS (LNAI), vol. 4819, pp. 621–628. Springer, Heidelberg (2007)
12. Lee, D.-G., Lee, Y.-k., Han, J.-W., Park, J.-H., Lee, I.-Y.: Intelligent Home Network Authentication: Home Device Authentication Using Device Certification. In: Meersman, R. (ed.) OTM 2007, Part II. LNCS, vol. 4804, pp. 1688–1700. Springer, Heidelberg (2007)
13. Hwang, J.-B., Lee, H.-K., Han, J.-W.: Efficient and User Friendly Inter-domain Device Authentication/Access Control for Home Networks. In: Sha, E., Han, S.-K., Xu, C.-Z., Kim, M.-H., Yang, L.T., Xiao, B. (eds.) EUC 2006. LNCS, vol. 4096, pp. 131–140. Springer, Heidelberg (2006)
14. Hea, D., Mab, M., Zhangc, Y., Chena, C., Bua, J.: A strong user authentication scheme with smart cards for wireless communications. Computer Communications 34, 367–374 (2011)
15. Qu, S., Liu, H.: Research of Family Network'S Security. Aeronautical Computing Techniquel 37, 112–115 (2007)
16. Shrestha, A.P., Choi, D.-Y., Kwon, G.R., Han, S.-J.: Kerberos based authentication for inter-domain roaming in wireless heterogeneous network. Computers and Mathematics with Applications 60, 245–255 (2010)
17. You, I.: A One-Time Password Authentication Scheme for Secure Remote Access in Intelligent Home Networks. Knowledge-Based Intelligent Information and Engineering Systems 4252, 785–792 (2006)
18. Park, J.-O., Jun, M.-S., Kim, S.-G.: A Study on Home Network User Authentication Using Token-Based OTP. In: Kim, T.-H., Stoica, A., Chang, R.-S. (eds.) SUComS 2010. CCIS, vol. 78, pp. 59–64. Springer, Heidelberg (2010)
19. Vaidya, B., Park, J.H., Yeo, S.-S., Rodrigues, J.J.P.C.: Robust one-time password authentication scheme using smart card for home network environment. Computer Communications 34, 326–336 (2011)
20. Colin, E., Nixon, P., Terzis, S.: Security Models for Trusting Network Appliances. In: The 5th IEEE International Workshop on Networked Appliances, pp. 39–44. IEEE Press, Liverpool (2002)
21. Mortensen, K.H., Schougaard, K.R., Schultz, U.P.: Distance-Based Access Modifiers Applied to Safety in Home Networks. In: Markopoulos, P., Eggen, B., Aarts, E., Crowley, J.L. (eds.) EUSAI 2004. LNCS, vol. 3295, pp. 315–326. Springer, Heidelberg (2004)
22. Helander, J.: Deeply Embedded XML Communication Towards an Interoperable and Seamless World. In: Proceedings of the 5th ACM International Conference on Embedded Software, pp. 62–67. ACM Press, New York (2005)

Research on Flexible Trusted Terminal Model

Chaowen Chang[*] and Xi Qin

#307, Information Engineering University, Zhengzhou, Henan, 450004, China
{ccw,qx}@xdja.com

Abstract. The specification of Trusted Computing requires that all the components running on trusted computing platform should be trusted, which has seriously hampered the application of trusted computing platform. This paper presents a flexible trusted terminal model of tolerance non-trusted components. Compared with the existing trusted computing platform, the model allows the existence of non-trusted components, in the mean time it can also guarantee the predictable and controllable of security result. The model is divided into trusted domain and non-trusted domain of tolerance non-trusted components. Based on the noninterference theory of information flow and the noninterference theory of interdomain, the paper presents the tolerance mechanism of non-trusted components and derives the sufficient condition that the trusted terminal should meet. On this basis, the specific physical model design is given and the model is proved to be a trusted terminal model.

Keywords: trusted terminal model, non-trusted components, noninterference, embedded trusted system.

1 Introduction

In the TNC [1] architecture, it requires that the computing platform of access requester should be trusted [2-3]. From the current view of trusted computing platform solutions, Intel's LaGrande [4] technology and Microsoft's NGSCB [5],with security operating systems, are based on hardware security chip to provide users with a high security strength operating environment. Some domestic trusted computing platform solutions [6] also use reliable security chip with dedicated motherboard and enhance the security of BIOS and operating system to construct the trusted computing terminal. Therefore, in order to construct trusted computing platform, not only the support of trusted hardware security chip, but also the cooperation of I/O devices, operating system and related software is needed. In view of this, it is difficult to construct the trusted computing environment in the traditional computing platforms.

This paper presents a flexible trusted terminal model of tolerance non-trusted component. Without changing the existing terminal hardware structure and the upper operating system, the model ensures that the existence of non-trusted component in the terminal will not cause serious information security threats.

---

[*] Corresponding author.

J. Lei et al. (Eds.): NCIS 2012, CCIS 345, pp. 669–679, 2012.
© Springer-Verlag Berlin Heidelberg 2012

2   Trusted Computing and Noninterference Theory of Information Flow

2.1   TCG Trusted Platform Specifications and Its Limitations

Shen Chang-xiang [7], Zhang Huan-guo [8]and other scholars argue that since the PC software and hardware structure is simplified, resources in PC is arbitrary use, especially the implementation codes can be modified, and malicious programs can be implanted. More seriously, the legitimate users are not being taken strict access controls, as a result of unauthorized access and insecurity incidents. And these problems using traditional security technologies cannot be resolved fundamentally. It should be resolved by taking the implementations of high-grade defend from the client operating platform, so that the source of insecurity can be controlled in the terminal. In fact, based on the source of trusted of terminal, security has been regarded for a long time. Researchers have gradually realized that a software system cannot guarantee the security of information systems fundamentally, and this is the background of trusted computing [9, 10].

According to the basic concepts of TCG trusted computing [11-12], a component is trusted if and only if it passed the integrity assessment. Based on this view, if a measurement result of component is inconsistent with the reference value, the component is sentenced to "non-trusted" and cannot be started and loaded. But in fact, the non-trusted component does not mean that it had to be compromised, such as upgrades new components. In this case, the component judged non-trusted is perhaps trust. If the platform adds new hardware or upgrades critical system components, the reference values of TPM integrity measurement of trusted computing platform must be rewritten, which is complicated and lengthy. Just because of the processing mechanism of TCG, the application of trusted computing platform is seriously restricted and questioned by the parties [13].

2.2   The Noninterference Theory of Information Flow and Trusted Model

Goguen and Meseguer [14] proposed the noninterference theory of information flow. The theory points out that if an operation u1 will change the security status of the security domain which is u1 in, but the operation not taking impact to the observed system status of another security domain u2, it is considered that the domain u1 is noninterference to u2. On this basis RUSHBY [15], adopting the noninterference model of state machine, gave the definition that a system on the noninterference policy of transfer and non-transfer is security and gave three properties of noninterference model: single-step coherence, result consistency and local consistency in 1992.

In the field of trusted computing, the noninterference theory of information flow is often used to establish a secure terminal model by many researchers. The model of trusted chain based on noninterference theory is established from the perspective of the dynamic by Zhao Jia et al [16]. Referring to noninterference theory of information flow, using process algebra and logical reasoning, Zhang Xing et al [17] gives the conditions and nature under which the process is running credibly. Zhao Yong [18] proposed an isolation model for trusted application environment. However, the trusted component and the interaction only with trusted components are required to ensure the credibility of system in above research, which is difficult to overcome the limitations of the application of TCG Trusted Platform.

3   A Flexible Trusted Terminal Model of Tolerance Non-trust Components

3.1   Model Elements

Definition 3-1: Let terminal $M = \{S, D, A, C, O, F, R\}$, and $M \in$ TNC. Of which:

S is identified as the set of terminal states, initial state $s_0 \in S$. The terminal state can be denoted a limited number of objects with N (the set of object name n) and its value V (the set of object values v), namely $S \times N \rightarrow V$.

D is the set of terminal In Field, including the trusted domain D_T and non-trusted domain D_N.

A is the set of terminal operations. $A = \{r, w\}$ is the model of component to access the resource. r denotes a read operation and w denotes a write operation.

Λ denotes nothing operation. $\circ$ indicates an action cascaded relationship. s is the state. a represents a single operation. α is the sequence of operations. A^* represents the closure of the set of operations.

C is the set of terminal components, and the element is denoted as c. Component C includes two subsets of C_T and C_N. C_N is the set of components of non-trusted domains. C_T is the set of components of trusted domains.

O is the object resources of terminal.

F is terminal system function. $F = \{step, output, run, domain, component, seal, unseal\}$, F has 7 functions, namely:

1) The transfer function *step:* $S \times A^* \rightarrow S$, $step(s, a)$ represents that the operation of a changes the terminal from the state s into another state.

2) The system output function *output:* $S \times A \rightarrow O$ represents the output of terminal is only related to state and operation.

3) State multi-step transition function *run:* $S \times A^* \rightarrow S$ represents the terminal state transition taken by the operating sequence of A^*, meeting the $run(s, \Lambda) = s$ and $run(s, a \circ \alpha) = run(step(s, a), \alpha)$.

4) Domain subjection function *domain:* $C \rightarrow D$ is the domain where component is located.

5) Mapping function of operation and component *component:* $A \rightarrow C$, *component* $(a) = c$ means that the action a is implemented by the component c.

6) The sealing function *seal:* $C \times V \rightarrow V$, *seal* (c, v) represents that the component c takes a sealing operation on the object value v.

7) The unsealing function *unseal:* $C \times V \rightarrow V$, *unseal* (c, v) represents that the component c takes a unsealing operation on the object value v.

R represents the relationship on the set of terminal components, including equivalence relationship and interference relationship.

1) Equivalence $\overset{c}{=}$ represents the relationship of the set of state on component *c*.

2) Interference ~> on the set of components *C* is with reflexivity. When the component *c* in the implementation of operation, system changes can be observed from the perspective of component *d*, it is called that the component *c* is interference with the component *d*, denoted as *c* ~> *d*. Otherwise, it is called the component *c* is noninterference with the components *d*, denoted as *c* $\overset{+}{>}$ *d*.

Definition 3-2: Filter function *filtrate: A* × D→V, filtrate(α,c)* represents that all the operation sequences with noninterference with *c* are filtered from the operation sequence α, α∈*A**, *c*∈ *C*.

$$filtrate\ (\Lambda, c) = \Lambda$$

$$filtrate(a \circ \alpha, c) = \begin{cases} a \circ filtrate(\alpha, c), if\ component(a) \sim> c \\ filtrate(\alpha, c), otherwise \end{cases}$$

Definition 3-3: Trusted component *(Tc)* is the component of which the integrity has not been destroyed. T_C ∈ *C*, a component is trusted if:

iff Hash *(c)* = *c₀| c* ∈ *C* (*c₀* is the expectation of integrity of the component *c*).

Definition 3-4: Non-trusted component *(MC)* is the component of which integrity has been damaged. *MC* ∈ *C*, a component is not non-trusted if:

iff Hash *(c)* ≠ *c₀| c* ∈ *C* (*c₀* is the expectation of integrity of the component *c*).

Definition 3-5: If ∃α makes *run(s₀,α)* = *s*, *s*∈ *S*, *S* is called the reachable state, denoted as a tuple *(c,α)* (*c* is the component which is implemented when terminal is in state *s*).

3.2   Noninterference Trusted Domain Based on Trusted Components

According to the definition of the first part, in the trusted domain D_T of the terminal, all the components (indicated by tc) are static trusted, that is:

tc ∈ T_C domain (tc) = D_T, T_C ∈ C.

In [11] and [12], it is proposed that the condition of trusted running of component *c* = *component (a)* can be expressed as:

$$output(run(s_0,\alpha), a) = output(run(s_0, filtrate(\alpha, component(a))), a) \qquad (3\text{-}1)$$

The condition could be interpreted as: If there is no potential components interference with the implementation of this component or the component is influenced only by the predicted components. Based on these considerations, the trust of component running is defined as:

Definition 3-6: The condition of trusted running of component $c = component\ (a)$ can be expressed as:

$$output(run(s_0,\alpha),a) = output(run(s_0, filtrate(\alpha,component(a))), a) \wedge component(a) \in T_C$$

According to the definition of 3.1 model elements, the component of trusted domain is static trusted, so in the terminal trusted domain, Definition 3-6 and Formula (3-1) are defined equivalently.

Definition 3-7: From the property of equivalence, for $\forall t_c \in C$, there is always an observation equivalence on the terminal state, denoted $\overset{tc}{=}$ That is, if $s \overset{tc}{=} t$, from the view of component tc, the terminal state s and t are the same.

It can be proved that in the trusted domain with the property of the observation equivalent, if a component tc with the property of output isolation meets:

$$run(s_0,\alpha) \overset{tc}{=} run(s_0,\ filtrate(\alpha,component(a))$$

the component running is trusted[15-16].

Definition 3-8: The condition of the executable component tc meeting the property of output isolation is:

$$s \overset{tc}{=} t \Rightarrow output(s, a) = output(t, a), tc = component(a)$$

The property shows that if $s \overset{tc}{=} t$, when the execution of operation a, whether the terminal is in the state s or t, the system output is the same after performing the same operation after a.

Definition 3-9: The condition of the executable component tc meeting the property of noninterference isolation is:

$$Domain\ (a) \overset{+>}{} tc \Rightarrow s \overset{tc}{=} step(s, a), tc = component(a)$$

The property shows that, if an operation a does not interfere with the running of component tc, for the component tc, from the view of component tc, the system states before and after the implementation of operation a are the same.

Definition 3-10: The condition of the executable component tc meeting the property of single-step isolation is:

$$s \overset{tc}{=} t \Rightarrow step(s, a) \overset{tc}{=} step(t, a), tc = component(a)$$

The property shows that if $s \overset{tc}{=} t$, when the operation a performed, whether the terminal is in state s or t, the system states are the same after performing the same operation a.

In [11] and [12], it is shown that the trusted decision theorem of system running is:

Theorem 3-1: IF the following three conditions are met, the system M is trusted:

1) M starts to run from the root of trust.

2) All the components of M ($\forall tc \in C$) satisfy the condition of single-step and output isolation.

3) Components meet the trusted test, stating that:

if $run\ (s_0, \alpha) \xrightarrow[component(b)]{component(a)} run(s_0,\ filtrate(\alpha, component(a)) \Rightarrow run(s_0, \alpha)$
$\xrightarrow{component(b)} run(s_0, filtrate(\alpha, component(b)))$.

Based on Theorem 3-1, it can be obtained:

Theorem 3-2: The necessary condition of trusted running in trusted domain of terminal M is:

1) The trusted domain starts to run from the trusted root.

2) All components of the domain are static integrated, and all the components of the domain are loaded order.

3) All components of the domain are taken the integrity measurement when loaded.

Proof: Let trusted domain satisfy the above conditions.

According to the conditions 2) of this theorem, all components of the domain are integrated and loaded order. That is, the system state is unique, determined and predictable when component t_c is loaded and the system does not exist the possibility of the second state when t_c is loaded. Under such conditions, if there is

$\forall tc(s \overset{tc}{=} t)$, $tc \in T_C$, it must have $s = t$. Then there is:

$s \overset{tc}{=} t \Rightarrow output(s, a) = output(t, a)$, $s \overset{tc}{=} t \Rightarrow step(s, a) \overset{tc}{=} step(t, a)$

By the definition of 3-8 and 3-10, all components of D_T ($\forall tc \in C$) satisfy the output and single-step isolation. It satisfies the Condition 2) of Theorem 3-1.

According to the conditions 3) of the theorem, all components of the domain are loaded based on integrity measurement. It is supposed that t_{ci} is the component of trusted running. By definition 3-6, there is:

$run(s0, \alpha) \xrightarrow{component(a)} run(s0, filtrate(\alpha, component(a)))$, $tci = component(a)$ (3-2)

It is supposed that t_{cj} is the component loaded after tci ($j = i + 1$), tci measures the integrity of t_{cj}. The conditions which are determined whether established are as follows:

Hash $(t_{cj}) = t_{cj0}$ (t_{cj0} is the expectation of integrity of component t_{cj})   (3-3)

If the formula (3-3) holds, t_{cj} passes the integrity measurement. t_{cj} is determinate from the perspective of t_{ci} is, and further that, which components affecting t_{cj} when loaded are known with certainty.

Also: t_{ci} is trusted running, without potential interference with t_{ci} and t_{ci} is certain that t_{cj} is determined and loaded according to the determined manner. There is no potential interference with the running of component t_{cj}. t_{ci} pass the property of trust to t_{cj}, so t_{cj} is trusted running, namely:

$run(s_0, \alpha) \xrightarrow{component(b)} run(s_0, filtrate(\alpha, component(b)))$, $t_{cj} = component(b)$ (3-4)

It can be seen, Formula (3-4) must be established:

if $run(s0, \alpha) \xrightarrow{component(a)} run(s0, filtrate(\alpha, component(a))) \Rightarrow$
$run(s0, \alpha) \xrightarrow{component(b)} run(s0, filtrate(\alpha, component(b)))$ (3-5)

Formula (3-5) satisfies the condition 3) of Theorem 3-1, that is, components meet the trusted verification. So, the trusted domain running is trusted.

3.3   Tolerance Mechanism of Non-trusted Components

Definition 3-11: All components not belonging to terminal trusted domain D_T compose the terminal non-trusted domains D_N., namely:

  if (domain(c)$\in$D) $\wedge$ (domain(c) $\notin$ D_T) then domain(c)$\in D_N$

Definition 3-12: The object set which Domain u $\in$ D can access is denoted Nu=$\{n_1,$ $n_2,..., n_k\}$ (k is the number of objects). Nu is called the set of objects which Domain u can see. The value of Nu is $V_{Nu}= \{v_{n1}, v_{n2},..., v_{nk}\}$, which is called the view of Domain u.

Definition 3-13: The terminal view is $S\times(N_T\cup N_N\cup N_{IO}) \rightarrow (V_{NT}\cup V_{NN}\cup V_{NIO})$. N_T is the set of objects which trusted domain can see. N_N is the set of objects which non-trusted domain can see. N_{IO} is the set of objects with which terminals exchange with other external entities. V_{NT}, V_{NN} and V_{NIO} are respectively the object values of N_T, N_N, N_{IO}, called the trusted domain view, the non-trusted domain view and input and output view of terminal.

Definition 3-14: Function write: D $\rightarrow$P (Nu) represents the set of objects the Domain u can write. P (N) is the subset of N. Function read: D $\rightarrow$P(Nu) represents the set of objects Domain u can read.

Definition 3-15: w represents that a component c of non-trusted domain takes part in and completes a work of exporting information to an external entity and to complete the work w, terminal implements an operation sequence α. The system view before w executed is view1=$\{V_{NT1}, V_{NN1}, V_{NIO1}\}$. While w is completed, the system view is view2=$\{V_{NT2}, V_{NN2}, V_{NIO2}\}$. If the following are satisfied, the output information flow of component c is secure and controlled.

  if $V_{NIO1} \neq V_{NIO2} \Rightarrow$(a1$\circ$ a2$\in \alpha$) $\wedge$ V_{NIO2} = seal(c_T, f(V_{NN2})), component(a1) = $c_T \in D_T$,
    component(a2) = c$\in D_N$ (f is the business rule function, varying with w.) (3-6)

Formula (3-6) shows that, if V_{NIO2} is changed when w exports information to external entities, an operation a1 taken by trusted domain components must be included in the operation sequence α of this work. a1 seals the output of work. Namely: when the component c sends information to external entities, the information must be sealed security by trusted domain component c_T.

Definition 3-16: r represents that non-trusted domain component c completes a work of reading information from the external entity. a2 is an operation that the component c reads a set of entity object V_{NN}. The system view before r executed is view1=$\{ V_{NT1}$, $V_{NN1}, V_{NIO1}\}$, and the system view after r completed is view2=$\{ V_{NT2}, V_{NN2},$ $V_{NIO2}\}$. α is an operation sequence through which terminal implements to complete r. If the following conditions are satisfied, the input information flow of the component c is secure and controlled.

$$\exists a1 \ ((a_2{}^\circ \ a_1 \in \alpha) \wedge (V_{NN2} = \text{unseal}(c_T, g(V_{NIO2}))))\text{, component}(a1) = c_T \in D_T \quad (3\text{-}7)$$

In Formula (3-7), g is the business rule function, varying with r. Formula (3-7) shows that if the input information flow of component c is the secure and controlled, when the work r reads information from external entities, an operation a1 sent by D_T must be included in the operation sequence α of this work. When the component receives information from external entities, the information must be unsealed and verified by component D_T.

Theorem 3-3: The components of a terminal M ∈ TNC can be divided into the non-empty trusted domain D_T and non-trusted domain D_N. When M satisfies the following conditions, M is the trusted terminal in the TNC architecture.

1) D_T is the trusted running, namely: to meet the requirements of the sufficient conditions of Theorem 3-2;

2) $(N_{IO} \subset N_T) \wedge (N_{IO} \not\subset N_N)$;

3) $N_T \cap \text{write}(D_N) = \phi$;

4) The terminal writing and reading to N_{IO} are based on the security sealing of TNC protocol specification.

Proof: From Condition 3): $N_T \cap \text{write}(D_N) = \phi$

By the definition of 3-13 and 3-14, write (D_N) represents the set of objects that non-trusted domains D_N can write (modify) the object. N_T is the set of objects that trusted domain D_T can access. There is no intersection of N_T and D_T. It is shown that the operation of the trust domain DN have no impact on the value of the set of object the trusted domain D_T can access. According to Goguen's definition of information flow noninterference, it is shown that:

$$D_N \not\rightarrow D_T \ (D_N \text{ is noninterference with } D_T.) \quad (3\text{-}8)$$

By the right part of Condition 2), $N_{IO} \not\subset N_N$, so, $N_N \cap N_{IO} = \phi$

By the definition of 3-13, N_N is the set of object non-trusted domain can see. N_{IO} is the set of object that the terminal exchanges with other external entities. The intersection of N_N and N_{IO} is empty. It is indicated that the operations in non-trusted domain D_N does not have impact on the state of other external entities outside the terminal. According to Goguen's definition of information flow noninterference, it is shown that:

$$D_N \not\rightarrow D_{IO} \quad (D_{IO} \text{ is the input and output domain outside the terminal.}) \quad (3\text{-}9)$$

By the left part of Condition 2), $N_{IO} \subset N_T$, so, $N_T \cap N_{IO} \neq \phi$

The set of objects that trusted domain D_T and external input and output domains can access together is not empty. This condition allows the trusted domain D_T of the terminal to exchange information with external entities.

Combining Formula (3-8) and (3-9), it is shown that the non-trusted domain can exchange information with external entities only through the middle layer D_T, and the components of non-trusted domain can exchange information with D_T only by read mode.

United Condition 2) and Condition 3), there is:

($N_T \cap$ write $(D_N) = \phi$)$\wedge$($N_{IO} \not\subset N_N$)

It is shown that D_N can access N_{IO} only by D_T. By Condition 1) it is shown that D_T is trusted running. With Condition 4), the terminal write and read to NIO are based on security sealing of TNC protocol specification. According to the definitions of 3-15 and 3-16, it can be seen that the input/output information flow of non-trusted components c is secure and controllable.

4   The Design of Flexible Trusted Terminal

Based on formal theoretical model in Section 3, the specific physical design and implementation of the model is given, as shown in Fig.1.

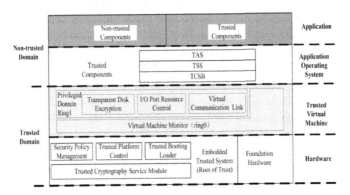

Fig. 1. The trusted terminal of tolerance non-trusted components

1) Trusted Domain
The domain is made up from hardware layer embedded trusted system and trusted virtual machine.

Embedded trusted system is the trusted root of the terminal. The trusted cryptographic service module provides the trusted supports for the terminal, including the trusted measurement, trusted storage and trusted reports. In this respect, it corresponds to the TPM of TCG. Virtual Machine (VM) is a system which supports multiple operating systems to run in parallel on a single physical server, providing more effective use of the underlying hardware. Trusted virtual machine can control the hardware resources through virtualization technology.

2) Non-trusted Domain
Non-trusted domain is composed of the application layer operating system and application layer components. The application layer components allow non-trusted components to exist.

Compared with the trusted computing platform with theoretical model, the trusted terminal model of tolerance non-trusted components has the following advantages:

(1) In the precondition that the platform is trusted and secure results are controllable and predictable, the terminal allows for the existence of non-trusted components. (2) The level of embedded trusted system is introduced. Embedded trusted system itself is a system on chip (SOC) of independence and completeness, not impacted and controlled by the upper operating system.(3) The introduction of the embedded trusted system can solve the problem that the current terminal is lack the support of TPM. The terminal has a better implementation.(4) In the trusted terminal model, the level of virtual machine is introduced, to achieve isolation between tasks and transparent security control of hardware resources.

5   Conclusions

The model of flexible trusted terminal is proposed. The model is different from the existing trusted computing platforms. The model allows non-trusted components to load, but the secure results can be guaranteed predictable and controllable. Based on noninterference theory of information flow, the formal analysis of trusted domain is implemented. Based on the ideology of interdomain noninterference, the tolerance mechanism of non-trusted component is given and the sufficient condition which the trusted terminal should meet is derived. Then the formal theoretic model is put forward.

References

1. Trusted Computing Group. TNC Architecture for Interoperability (2003), http://www.trustedcomputinggroup.org/resources/ tnc_architecture_for_interoperability_version_13
2. Li, X.Y., Zuo, X.D., Shen, C.X.: System Behavior Based Trustworthiness Attestation for Computing Platform. Acta Electronica Sinica 35(7), 1234–1239 (2007) (in Chinese)
3. Wang, S.H., Li, X.Y.: Policy Based Trustworthiness Attestation for Computing Platform. Acta Electronica Sinica 37(4), 900–904 (2009) (in Chinese)
4. Intel. Intel Trusted Execution Technology (2007), http://www.intel.com/ technology/security/downloads/TrustedExec_Overview.pdf
5. Microsoft Coporation, Next-Generation Secure Computing Base (2003), http://www.microsoft.com/res-ources/ngscb/default.mspx
6. Liu, F.Y.: JetWay trusted computing platform. Netinfo Security 11, 23–25 (2006)
7. Shen, C.X.: Building up Active-defending Infsec Assurance Framework Based on Trusted Platform. Information Secruity and Communications Privacy 9, 17–19 (2004)
8. Zhang, H.G., Luo, J., Jin, G.: Development of Trusted Computing Research. Journal of Whuan University (Natural Science Edition) 52, 513–518 (2006)
9. Department of Defense Computer Security Center.DoD 5200. 282STD. Department of Defense Trusted Computer System Evaluation Criteria. USA:DOD (1985)
10. Abrams, M.D., Joyce, M.V.: Trusted system concepts. Computers & Security 14, 45–56 (1995)
11. Trusted Computing Group. TCG Specification Architecture Overview (2011), http://www.trustedcomputinggroup.org/ resourcestcg_architecture_overview_version_14

12. Trusted Computing Group. Infrastructure Work Group Integrity Report Schema Specification (2011), `http://www.trustedcomputinggroup.org/resources/` `infrastructure_work_group_integrity_report_schema_` `specification_version_10`
13. Zhou, M.H., Mei, H.: Research and development of Trusted Computing. Computer Science 31, 5–8 (2004)
14. Goguan, J.A., Meseguern, J.: Security Policies and Security Model. In: The 1982 IEEE Symposium on Security and Privacy, Qakland, California, pp. 11–20 (1982)
15. Noninterference, R.J.: Transitivity, and Channel-Control Security Policies. CSL-92-02. Stanford Research Institute, Menlo Park (1992)
16. Zhao, J., Shen, C.X., Liu, J.Q.: A Noninterference-Based Trusted chain Model. Journal of Computer Research and Development 45, 974–980 (2008)
17. Zhang, X., Chen, Y.L., Shen, C.X.: Non-interference Trusted Model Based on Processes. Journal of Communications 30, 6–11 (2009)
18. Zhao, Y.: The Security Architecture and practical Model for Important Information System. Beijing Jiaotong University, Beijing (2008)
19. Beijing University of Technology, IWNCOMM, TOPSEC, Trusted Computing Specification—Part 5: The Architecture of Trusted Network Connection (V1.03) (2007)

Secure Obfuscation of a Two-Step Oblivious Signature*

Chao Li[1,2], Zheng Yuan[1,2,**], and Ming Mao[1,2]

[1] Beijing Electronic Science & Technology Institute, Beijing 100070, China
yuanzheng@besti.edu.cn, zyuan@tsinghua.edu.cn
[2] School of Telecommunications Engineering, Xidian University,
Shanxi 710071, China

Abstract. Although obfuscation in cryptography is one of the most intriguing and attractive open problems, only a few positive results have been proposed after impossibility results[1,9]. Hohenberger et al.[13] proposed an obfuscation for re-encryption functionality and Hada[11] gave a secure obfuscator of encrypted signature(ES). Both of them contained a and a public operation, the secret operation was guaranteed without revealing by an obfuscator. Inspired by their works, we first construct a secure obfuscation of a special functionality of oblivious signature (OS) in this paper, which contains two-step verifying processions. The obfuscation of our functionality is certain equal to a application of oblivious transfer protocol, which is based on Zero Knowledge Proof(ZKP). We start with a basic model of oblivious transfer, then discuss its functionality and security by structuring an obfuscation of OS. Moreover, some security definitions of obfuscation can be extended to ZKP.

Keywords: Obfuscation, Oblivious Signature, Zero Knowledge, ACVBP.

1 Introduction

Since the obfuscation has been brought into the field of cryptography, it preserves its ideology in code obfuscation: making code elusive while keeping the original functionality. In CRYPTO'01, Barak et al.[1] proposed some concepts of obfuscation and a well-known impossibility obfuscation result. Defining a obfuscator to be a compiler which converts a program P into a new program $\mathcal{O}(P)$, their black-box obfuscation concept means that a secure obfuscator should satisfy three requirements: (1)Functionality Preserved: $\mathcal{O}(P)$ computes the same function as P; (2)Polynomial Slow-down: the execution time of the obfuscated program should not exceed the polynomial of the execution time of the original program; (3) Virtual Black-box Property(VBP): anything that can be efficiently computed from

---

* This work is supported by the National Natural Science Foundation of China(No. 61070250), Foundation of State Key Laboratory of Information Security(Nos.01-01, 01-02-6), and Foundation of Key Laboratory of Information Security of BESTI(Nos.YZDJ0905).
** To whom correspondence should be addressed.

J. Lei et al. (Eds.): NCIS 2012, CCIS 345, pp. 680–688, 2012.
© Springer-Verlag Berlin Heidelberg 2012

$\mathcal{O}(P)$ can be efficiently computed given oracle access to P. They proved that there existed no obfuscation for general functionalities and deterministic functions by constructing a family of functions that inherently cannot be securely obfuscated. Goldwasser et al.[9] also showed impossibility result of obfuscation with auxiliary input. They also present that there would be many useful applications if an efficient obfuscator really exits. For example, homomorphic encryption, removing random oracles, software protection and transforming private-key encryption into public-key encryption. So how to design special functionalities in a probabilistic way under some relaxed security requirement become methods of structure secure obfuscations[10]. In TCC'07, Hohenberger et al.[13] proposed a secure obfuscator for a re-encryption functionality, which takes a ciphertext for a message encrypted under Alice's public key and transforms it into a ciphertext for the same message under Bob's public key. This is the first positive obfuscation result for a traditional cryptographic functionality. They also proposed a significant definition of secure obfuscation called Average-Case Virtual Black-box property (ACVBP): *If a cryptographic scheme is secure when the adversary is given black-box access to a program, then it remains secure when the adversary is given the obfuscated program.* This is another way to explain any third party who has the obfuscated program learns no more from the re-encryption program than it does from interaction with a black-box oracle that provides the same functionality. In this case, a third party could execute this program without revealing any secret information which would imply many useful applications. Later, Hada[11] proposed a secure obfuscator of encrypted signatures (ES), which signs a message under an encrypted signing key. Both of them conceal a secret operation and then take a public encryption. Obviously, an appropriate obfuscation guarantees the secret operation cannot be acquired by any executor.

Oblivious transfer (OT) model[16] is very useful for constructing secure protocols, which has been widely used in Internet shopping, banking and other online-commercial trade. An oblivious transfer protocol makes the sender sends information to the receiver, but remains oblivious as to what is received, it guarantees the personal information cannot be revealed to any other one in the communication. The first oblivious transfer was introduced by Rabin[15], later Even et al.[7] developed the 1-out-of -2 oblivious transfer.

This paper considers a kind of oblivious signatures, which contain a more complicated encrypting process and a special signing process. We construct a two-step ES functionality with the oblivious property, then obfuscating our two-step ES functionality enable it equal to a certain application of oblivious transfer based on ZKP. Thus we first present an obfuscation of a two-step oblivious signature. Under SDHI Assumption and DL Assumption, our obfuscation scheme is proved security according to ACVBP w.r.t dependent Oracles.

This paper is organized as follows. Section 2 is Preliminaries. Section 3 gives our double-locked system. In section 4 we describe the detailed construction of our two-steps obfuscation program. and analyze its security in section 5. Conclusion in section 6.

2   Preliminaries

2.1   Bilinear Maps

Let $\mathbb{G}_1$ and $\mathbb{G}_2$ be two (multiplicative) cyclic groups of prime order p, and g be a generator of $\mathbb{G}_1$. A computable Bilinear map $e : \mathbb{G}_1 \times \mathbb{G}_2 \rightarrow \mathbb{G}_2$ has the following properties:

1. Bilinearity: For all $\mu, \nu \in \mathbb{G}_1$ and $a, b \in \mathbb{Z}_p$, $e(\mu^a, \nu^b) = e(\mu, \nu)^{ab}$.
2. Non-degeneracy: $e(g, g) \neq 1$. $\mathbb{G}_1$ is a bilinear group if the group operation in $\mathbb{G}_1$, and $\mathbb{G}_1$ is efficiently computable. Notice that the map e is symmetric since $e(g^a, g^b) = e(g, g)^{ab} = e(g^b, g^a)$.

2.2   Pedersen's VSS Scheme[5,6]

Set $< g >$ as a cyclic group with prime order p, $h \in< g > \backslash\{1\}$, $\log_g h$ is kept secret, $s \in \mathbb{Z}_p$ is the shared secret. Pedersen's VSS scheme contains two parts:
1. Secret distributing protocol

(a) The distributor D chooses two random $a(x), b(x)$: $a(x) = \alpha_0 + \alpha_1 x + \ldots + \alpha_{t-1}x^{t-1}$, and $b(x) = \beta_0 + \beta_1 x + \ldots + \beta_{t-1}x^{t-1}$.
For $i \in [1, n], j \in [0, t)$, D give the chip $s_i := (s_{i1}, s_{i2}) = (a(i), b(i))$ to the participant P_i secretly, and broadcast the value $C_j = g^{\alpha_j}h^{\beta_j}$.
(b) Receiving their own chip s_i, P_i check the validity: $g^{s_{i1}}h^{s_{i2}} = \prod_{j=0}^{t-1} C_j^{ij}$.
-If satisfied, accept it as the valid chip, else P_i ask D for the right ones.

2. Secret recovers protocol: If the entire participants get valid chips, t-out-of-n of them can recover the secret using Shamir's (t,n)-secret sharing method.

3   The Double-locked System

We present a basic OT model called double-locked system, and prove that there exist some special structures, having the property of oblivious transfer, can be obfuscated:

– The sender Alice locked all the n similar boxes with the her own keys, and then sends them to receiver Bob.
– Bob randomly chooses $k(k < n)$ boxes out of them, also locks them with his own keys and returns them back to Alice.
– Alice unlocks the k boxes using her keys, then returns them to Bob. Bob unlocks the k boxes and obtains their secrets at last.

Clearly, Alice cannot know which boxes is chosen by Bob, and Bob cannot obtain the secrets of the rest $n - k$ boxes. In this process, the following three requirements should be satisfied:

1. Both distributions of the Alice's n keys and the Bob's k keys, used to lock the boxes, should be indistingsuihable (respectively).

2. The result distribution of ciphertexts should be uniform.
3. There must be an efficient decryption algorithm.

Similar to Hohenberger's re-encryption functionality[13], our double-locked system contains a secret decryption operation and then a public encryption operation. To make both of sender and recipient only decrypt what they locked, the message are always encrypted. We put forward heuristic study of an obfuscation of this instructive, the obfuscation is an encryption based on oblivious transfer. The arm is to construct the obfuscation on 1-out-of-n oblivious signature (OS_1^n), and to analysis three requirements above.

4   Structure of Our Special Functionality and Obfuscation

In this section, we structure a special two-step oblivious signature functionality, then make a secure obfuscation of it based on the ACVBP definition and complexity assumptions.

4.1   Security Assumption and Complexity Assumption

Definition 1 (Strong Diffie Hellman Indistingshuishability (SDHI) Assumption)[13]. Let $\mathbb{G}$ be a group of order q where q is a k-bit prime, $g \xleftarrow{r} \mathbb{G}$ and $a, b, c, d \xleftarrow{r} \mathbb{Z}_q$. Then the following two distributions are computationally indistinguishable: $\{g, g^a, g^b, g^c, e(g,g)^{abc}\}_k \overset{c}{\approx} \{g, g^a, g^b, g_c, e(g,g)^d\}_k$

Definition 2 (Decision Linear (DL) Assumption)[2]. Let $\mathbb{G}$ be a group of k-bit prime order q, $f, g, h \xleftarrow{r} \mathbb{G}$ and $a, b, c \xleftarrow{r} \mathbb{Z}_q$. Then the following two distributions are computationally indistinguishable:

$$\left\{f, g, h, f^a, g^b, h^{a+b}\right\}_k \overset{c}{\approx} \left\{f, g, h.f^a, g^b, h^c\right\}_k$$

Definition 3 (ACVBP w.r.t Dependent Oracles)[11]. Let $T(C)$ be a set of oracles dependent on the circuit C. A circuit obfuscator obf for C satisfies the ACVBP w.r.t dependent oracle set T if the following condition holds: There exists a PPT oracle machine S (simulator) such that, for every PPT oracle machine D (distinguisher), every polynomial $p(\cdot)$, all sufficiently large $n \in \mathbb{N}$, and every $z \in \{0,1\}^{poly(n)}$,

$$\left| Pr \begin{bmatrix} C \leftarrow C_n; \\ C' \leftarrow Obf(C); b = 1 \\ b \leftarrow D^{\ll C, T(C) \gg}(C', z) \end{bmatrix} - \begin{bmatrix} C \leftarrow C_n; \\ C'' \leftarrow S^{\ll C \gg}(1^n, z); b = 1 \\ b \leftarrow D^{\ll C, T(C) \gg}(C'', z) \end{bmatrix} \right| < \frac{1}{p(n)}$$

4.2   Construct the Two-Step ES Functionality with the Oblivious Property

Combining the Waters's signature scheme[19] and Boneh's linear encryption scheme[2], we present a special encrypted signature. As the essence of R.Tso's scheme is the well-know Pedersen's VSS protocol, we are aiming to prove the appropriate obfuscation structure could achieve the oblivious property and preserve the functionality as the OS scheme. Our structure is dividing into two steps: the verifying of oblivious property and the verifying of signature.

4.3   The Construction of Special Functionality

In the special two-step ES functionality, we adopt Tso's idea of verifying the oblivious signature[17], choose the algorithm based on Pedersen's VSS schema, and construct a bilinear map to verify the oblivious property. The construction is as follows:

1. The sender S, randomly chooses $g_1, g_2 \in \mathbb{G}$, $u' \leftarrow \mathbb{G}$, $U = \{u_i\}(i \in [1, n])$, sets $sk = (g_2^\alpha, u', U), pk = (g_1, g_2, g^{g_2^\alpha})$, $g_1 = g^\alpha$, $\alpha \in \mathbb{Z}_q$, computes $y = g^{g_2^\alpha}$ and make it public.
2. The recipient R randomly chooses $r \in \mathbb{Z}_q^*$, computes $c = g^r h^l$, then sends $M = \{m_1, \ldots, m_n\}$ and c to S, in which $m_l \in M$ be the signed message.
3. S randomly chooses k_i, computes $K_i \leftarrow g^{k_i} modp$, $Q \leftarrow k_i c/(gh)^i modp$, $s_i \leftarrow k_i - g_2^\alpha Q modq$. Meanwhile the signature $\sigma = (\sigma_1, \sigma_2)$ is generated as Waters's Signature scheme[19], where $x \in \mathbb{Z}_q$, $\sigma_1 = g_2^\alpha (u' \Pi u_i)^x$, $\sigma_2 = g^x$
4. Receiving (Q, s_i, σ), R computes $\varrho_i \leftarrow g^{(r-i)} h^{(l-i)} modp$, $e_i \leftarrow g^{s_i} y^Q \varrho_i modp$
   -if $e_i = Q$, R sets $s = r - l$, $e = e_i$, gets $\Delta = (e(g^s, y^{e_l}), \sigma)$, goto step 5.
   -else halt and R ask for the other $m_l' \neq m_l$.
5. Verify the oblivious property:

$$e(g^s, y^{e_l}) \overset{?}{=} e(g^{s_l} \varrho_l, y^{e_l}) \tag{1}$$

6. Verify the validity of the signature:

$$e(\sigma_1, g)/e(\sigma_2, u' \Pi_{i \in M} u_i) \overset{?}{=} e(g_1, g_2) \tag{2}$$

If both (1) and (2) are satisfied, accept it as the signature of m_l.

4.4   The Obfuscation of Our Two-Step ES Functionality

Here we make a secure obfuscation of the special two-step ES functionality above. One of our obfuscation purposes is to keep the $s_i \leftarrow k_i - g_2^\alpha Q modq$ safe when it is transferred, since the secret key g_2^α exists potential risk of being revealed. Thus how to obfuscate this functionality and keep the oblivious property becomes the emphasis of our construction. We use bilinear map instead of hash function and encrypt the signing key for two reasons: First, Both the Waters's signature scheme and Boneh's linear encryption use bilinear map as their building block. Second, most important, it has being proposed that there exists a secure obfuscation via combining the Waters's signature scheme and Boneh's linear encryption scheme[13,11]. It has been proved that it is the only feasible and efficient obfuscation for encryption signature. Following is the obfuscation:

1. Set $params$:$g_1, g_2 \in \mathbb{G}$, $u' \leftarrow \mathbb{G}$, $U = \{u_i\}_{i \in M}$, $sk_e = (a, b)$, $pk_e = (g^a, g^b)$, $a, b \in \mathbb{Z}_q^*$, $g_1 = g^\alpha, i \in \{1, \dots, n\}$, $\alpha \in \mathbb{Z}_q$.
2. Following Boneh's linear encryption schema[2], the sender S use pk_e to encrypt the secret signing key: $(c_1, c_2, c_3) = ((g^a)^t, (g^b)^s, g^{t+s}g_2^\alpha) \leftarrow Enc(p, pk_e, g_2^\alpha)$, obtain the new signing key $sk' = (c_3, u', U)$, then compute $pk' = (g_1, g_2 \cdot g^{g^{t+z}}g_2^\alpha)$.
3. The recipient R randomly chooses $r \in \mathbb{Z}_q^*$, compute $c = g^r h^l$, assume m_l is just what R wants to sign, then sends $M = \{m_1, \dots, m_n\}$ and c to S.
4. S randomly choosen k_i, compute:

$$K_i \leftarrow g^{k_i} mod p, Q \leftarrow k_i c/(gh)^i mod p, \tilde{s}' \leftarrow k_i - g^{t+s} g_2^\alpha Q mod q.$$

Generate the signature:

$$\sigma = (\sigma_1, \sigma_2, \sigma_3) = ((g^a)^t, (g^b)^s, g^{t+s} g_2^\alpha (u' \Pi_{i \in M} u_i)^x), x \in \mathbb{Z}_q.$$

Then ReRandom $\sigma = (\sigma_1, \sigma_2, \sigma_3)$, and get the random signature:

$$\sigma' = (\sigma_1', \sigma_2', \sigma_3') = ((g^a)^{t+t'}, (g^b)^{s+s'}, g^{t+s+t'+s'} g_2^\alpha (u' \Pi_{i \in M} u_i)^x), (t', s' \in \mathbb{Z}_q)$$

5. When received $(Q, \tilde{s}_i', \sigma')$, R compute $\varrho_i \leftarrow g^{(r-i)} h^{(l-i)} mod p$ and $\tilde{e}' = g^{\tilde{s}_i} y^Q \varrho_i mod p$, $(1 \le i \le n)$,
   -if $\tilde{e}' = Q$, set $s = r - l + \tilde{s}_i'$, $e = \tilde{e}_i'$, get $\Delta' = (e(g^{\tilde{s}_i} \varrho_l), y^{\tilde{e}_l}, \sigma')$, goto step 6;
   -else halt and ask for the other $m_l' \neq m_l$
6. Verify the oblivious property:

$$e(g^s, y^{\tilde{e}_l}) \overset{?}{=} e(g^{\tilde{s}_i} \varrho_l, y^{\tilde{e}_l}) \tag{3}$$

7. Decrypt: $\sigma = c_3'/c_1'^{1/a} \cdot c_2'^{1/b} = g_2^\alpha (u' \Pi_{i \in M} u_i)^x = \sigma_1$
8. Verify the validity of the signature, Similar to [11]:

$$e(\sigma_1, g)/e(\sigma_2, u' \Pi_{i \in M} u_i) \overset{?}{=} e(g_1, g_2) \tag{4}$$

If Equ.(3) and (4) passed, accept it as the signature of message m_l.

5   Analyse the Security of Our Obfuscation Scheme

R.Tso[17] proposed three propertis of oblivious signature security: the complete of the scheme (Game A), the unforgeability for signers and ambiguity in selected messages which against signers for recipients (Game B).

Lemma 1. The proposed obfuscation scheme is complete.

Proof. First, prove the completeness of the oblivious property.
Given $(Q, \tilde{s_i'}, \sigma')$ and $\varrho_i \leftarrow g^{(r-i)}h^{(l-i)} mod p$. For $m \in \{m_1, \ldots, m_n\}$, the scheme is completeness if the following equation is established, :

$$\tilde{e_i'} = g^{\tilde{s_i'}} y^Q \varrho_i mod p = g^{k_i - g^{t+s} g_2^\alpha} g^{g^{t+s} Q} g^{(r-i)} h^{(l-i)} mod p$$
$$= g^{k_i} g^{(r-i)} h^{(l-i)} mod p = g^{k_i} (g^r h^l)/(gh)^i mod p = K_i c/(gh)^i mod p = Q$$

Our structure is different from the $Tso's$ structure[17]. Here we only prove the oblivious property, and the verifying of signature directly is equivalent to verifying the structure based on the Pedersen's protocol. We find out that $Tso's$ signature, with Hash function, only verifies right part of the tuple[17]. If above is satisfied, we accept it as the element in our oblivious proving system:

When accepted, we set $s = r - l + \tilde{s_i'}, e = \tilde{e'}$

Second, verify $e(g^s, y^{\tilde{e_l}}) = e(g^{\tilde{s_i'}} \varrho_i, y^{\tilde{e_l}}) = e(K_l g^{r-l}, g)$ if and only if $i = l$. $\square$

Theorem 1. An adversary $\mathcal{A}$ can break this scheme is equal to solve the DL problem.

Proof. We adopt the R.Tso's proving method[17] and give some changes. Assume $\mathcal{A}$ utilizes β as a black-box. To get the black-box β running properly, $\mathcal{A}$ simulates the environments of the proposed OS_1^n (1-out-of-n oblivious signature) scheme. The hash function H is regard as a random oracle. While as the definition of the virtual black-box property (VBP)[13], β can also be viewed as a simulator S, which has oracle access to our obfuscated circuit $C_{Q, \tilde{s_i'}, \varrho_i}$. Assume S is well-behaved who always queries the random oracle on the message , for each $M_i = \{m_{i_1}, \ldots, m_{i_n}\}$ and $c_i = g^{r_i} h^{l_i}$ chosen by S, S simulate the obfuscated program in a random way via the interactive way with $\mathcal{A}$ in order to obtain the $\tilde{s_i'}$, and Q is public issued. $\mathcal{A}$ dose the following steps:

- For each $j = 1, \ldots, n$, $\mathcal{A}$ picks a random number $k_{i_j} \in \mathbb{Z}_q^*$ and
  - Computes $C_{Q, \tilde{s_i'}, \varrho_i}$,
  - Picks $Q \leftarrow k_{ij} c/(gh)^{ij} mod p$,
  - Computes $g_2^\alpha = \frac{\tilde{s'} - \tilde{s'*}}{(g^{t+s} - g^z)Q} mod p$
- $\mathcal{A}$ returns $(Q, \tilde{s'*})$ to S, who get $\tilde{s'} \leftarrow k_i - g^{t+s} g_2^\alpha Q mod p$ and $\tilde{s'*} \leftarrow k_{i_j} - g^z g_2^\alpha Q mod p$, $(z \in \mathbb{Z}_p^*)$.

Our obfuscated circuit, $C_{Q, \tilde{s_i'}, \varrho_i, pk_e, sk_e}$, satisfies $c = g^r h^l = g^{r_1} h^{l_1} = \ldots = g^{r_i} h^{l_i} = \ldots = g^{r_n} h^{l_n} mod p$, $g_2^\alpha = \frac{\tilde{s'} - \tilde{s'*}}{(g^{t+s} - g^z)Q}$, and

$$\left| Pr \left[\begin{array}{c} C \leftarrow C_n; \\ \tilde{s'} \leftarrow g^{t+s} g_2^\alpha Q mod q; b = 1 \\ b \leftarrow D^{\ll C, S \gg} \left(Q, \tilde{s_i'}, \varrho_i, pk_e, sk_e \right); \end{array} \right] - Pr \left[\begin{array}{c} C \leftarrow C_n; \\ \tilde{s'*} \leftarrow g^z g_2^\alpha Q mod q; b = 1 \\ b \leftarrow D^{\ll C, S \gg} \left(Q, \tilde{s_i'*}, \varrho_i, pk_e, sk_e \right); \end{array} \right] \right| \leq \frac{1}{p(n)}.$$

Recall the definition 2 above, solution to the circuit $C_{Q, \tilde{s_i'}, \varrho_i, pk_e, sk_e}$ is the DL problem. That is to say it is hard to distinguish which message is signed by S.

Meanwhile any distinguisher D cannot check out between using a simulator S running the random oracle queries to the obfuscated program.   □

Theorem 2. Under the SDHI assumption and the DL assumption, our scheme provides the oblivious property in computational sense.

Proof. Theorem 1 has proved that an adversary $\mathcal{A}$ distinguishing $\tilde{s}'$ from $\tilde{s}'^*$ is equal to solve the DL problem, and Hohenberger et al.[13] proposed that $D_{C_{Q,\tilde{s}'_i,\varrho_i,pk_e,sk_e}}$ and $D_{C_{Q,\tilde{s}'^*_i,\varrho_i,pk_e,sk_e}}$ satisfies the indistinguishability under the SDHI assumption. For our obfuscation scheme, this indistinguishability provide the oblivious property of the signer. Upon the Pedersen's protocol, we construct the obfuscation which could preserve this property, so we view the g^{t+s} as a random key and use KEM encryption algorithm, which has the scalar homomrphic property, to strengthen its security, for more detail consult to papers[8,11].   □

Theorem 3. This scheme provides unconditional security on the ambiguity of the selected message for recipients.

Proof. [17]For $l \in \{1,\ldots,n\}$, the recipient R choose c, we have:

$$c = g^r h^l = g^{r_1} h^{l_1} = \ldots = g^{r_i} h^{l_i} = \ldots = g^{r_n} h^{l_n} mod p, r_i \in \mathbb{Z}_q.$$

□

Theorem 4. Under the SDHI assumption and the DL assumption, the obfuscation of our special two-steps oblivious signature scheme satisfies ACVBP w.r.t. dependent oracle set T.

Proof. As we discussed above, we have give out that the functionality is preserved and the distribution of secret signing key is indistinguishable. The oblivious signature scheme is constructed as $\Delta' = (e(g^{\tilde{s}'_l}\varrho_i, y^{\tilde{e}_l}), \sigma')$, we have proved under the DL assumption and the SDHI assumption, the security of unforgeability for signers is satisfied and signers cannot distinguish which verifying part they produced. Meanwhile the functionality of verifying the oblivious property is preserved and its obfuscation provide the stronger security. From definition 3 above, our scheme satisfies ACVBP *w.r.t.* dependent oracle set T.   □

6   Conclusion

This paper first study the possibility of obfuscate an OT model, we propose a special two-steps ES functionality of OS_1^n model based on Tso's scheme, and give its obfuscation. We analyze the relation of ACVBP and the property of oblivious, which indicates some positive potentials obfuscation using an appropriate structure under some security assumption and certain virtual black-box property. Because there exist a relationship between distinguishability and oblivious property, ACVBP of obfuscation implies sense of oblivious in concept. We insist this would contain a lot of applications such as the certifications distribution by CA, and other incredible delegations. The oblivious property provides anonymity of both sender and recipient. More important, without using hash function suggest a new proof system without random oracle.

References

1. Barak, B., Goldreich, O., Impagliazzo, R., Rudich, S., Sahai, A., Vadhan, S.P., Yang, K.: On the (Im)possibility of Obfuscating Programs. In: Kilian, J. (ed.) CRYPTO 2001. LNCS, vol. 2139, pp. 1–18. Springer, Heidelberg (2001)
2. Boneh, D., Boyen, X., Shacham, H.: Short Group Signatures. In: Franklin, M. (ed.) CRYPTO 2004. LNCS, vol. 3152, pp. 41–55. Springer, Heidelberg (2004)
3. Canetti, R., Dakdouk, R.R.: Obfuscating Point Functions with Multibit Output. In: Smart, N.P. (ed.) EUROCRYPT 2008. LNCS, vol. 4965, pp. 489–508. Springer, Heidelberg (2008)
4. Catalano, D., Gennaro, R.: New Efficient and Secure Protocols for Verifiable Signature Sharing and Other Applications. In: Krawczyk, H. (ed.) CRYPTO 1998. LNCS, vol. 1462, pp. 105–120. Springer, Heidelberg (1998)
5. Chen, L.: Oblivious Signatures. In: Gollmann, D. (ed.) ESORICS 1994. LNCS, vol. 875, pp. 161–172. Springer, Heidelberg (1994)
6. Chen, L., Pedersen, T.P.: New Group Signature Schemes. In: De Santis, A. (ed.) EUROCRYPT 1994. LNCS, vol. 950, pp. 171–181. Springer, Heidelberg (1995)
7. Even, S., Goldreich, O., Lempel, A.: A randomized protocol for signing contracts. Communication of the ACM 28(6), 637–647 (1985)
8. Gentry, C.: A fully homomorphic encryption scheme, PhD Thesis (2009)
9. Goldwasser, S., Kalai, Y.T.: On the Impossibility of Obfuscation with Auxiliary Input. In: FOCS 2005, pp. 553–562 (2005)
10. Goldwasser, S., Rothblum, G.N.: On Best-Possible Obfuscation. In: Vadhan, S.P. (ed.) TCC 2007. LNCS, vol. 4392, pp. 194–213. Springer, Heidelberg (2007)
11. Hada, S.: Secure Obfuscation for Encrypted Signatures. In: Gilbert, H. (ed.) EUROCRYPT 2010. LNCS, vol. 6110, pp. 92–112. Springer, Heidelberg (2010)
12. Hada, S.: Zero-Knowledge and Code Obfuscation. In: Okamoto, T. (ed.) ASIACRYPT 2000. LNCS, vol. 1976, pp. 443–457. Springer, Heidelberg (2000)
13. Hohenberger, S., Rothblum, G.N., Shelat, A., Vaikuntanathan, V.: Securely Obfuscating Re-encryption. In: Vadhan, S.P. (ed.) TCC 2007. LNCS, vol. 4392, pp. 233–252. Springer, Heidelberg (2007)
14. Lynn, B.Y.S., Prabhakaran, M., Sahai, A.: Positive Results and Techniques for Obfuscation. In: Cachin, C., Camenisch, J.L. (eds.) EUROCRYPT 2004. LNCS, vol. 3027, pp. 20–39. Springer, Heidelberg (2004)
15. Rabin, M.O.: How to exchange secrets by oblivious transfer. Technical Report TR-81, Aiken Computation Laboratory, Harvard University (1981), http://eprint.iacr.org/2005/187.pdf
16. Schnorr, C.P.: Efficient signature generation by smart cards. Journal of Cryptology 4(3), 161–174 (1991)
17. Tso, R., Okamoto, T., Okamoto, E.: 1-out-of-n Oblivious Signatures. In: Chen, L., Mu, Y., Susilo, W. (eds.) ISPEC 2008. LNCS, vol. 4991, pp. 45–55. Springer, Heidelberg (2008)
18. Tzeng, W.: Efficient 1-out-of-n oblivious transfer schemes with universally usable parameters. IEEE Trans. on Computers 53(2), 232–240 (2004)
19. Waters, B.: Efficient Identity-Based Encryption Without Random Oracles. In: Cramer, R. (ed.) EUROCRYPT 2005. LNCS, vol. 3494, pp. 114–127. Springer, Heidelberg (2005)
20. Wee, H.: On obfuscation point functions. In: STOC 2005, pp. 523–532. ACM (2005)

A Formal Description for Multi-owner Privacy

Yi Ren and Zhi-Ting Xiao

Network Management Center, PLA Academy of National Defense Information,
JieFang Park Road No. 45, WuHan, HuBei, China
rwxing_zh@yahoo.com.cn, xzting@163.com

Abstract. The current privacy-preserving researches focus on single-owner privacy. However, multi-owner privacy is also a type of widespread privacy. In order to research the privacy-preserving method for multi-owner privacy, it is necessary to find a formal description, which is not concerned by the current researches. In this paper, a privacy definition is proposed, as well as a class hierarchy of privacy type for clarification of the relationship between single-owner privacy and multi-owner privacy. The characteristics of multi-owner privacy and a formal description based on these characteristics are introduced.

Keywords: Privacy Concept Model, Multi-owner Privacy, Privacy Protection.

1 Introduction

It is widespread concerned for information security how to protect the personal privacy [1]. The current privacy-preserving researches [2-10] focus on the protection of the single-owner privacy data, which is related to personal information, such as one's salary, preference and so on. Usually, it is easy to store and use such privacy data in relational data schema. However, in real world, there is another type of privacy data, which is related to multiple persons. The type of privacy, named as "multi-owner privacy", is proposed in [11]. A multi-owner privacy includes several individual privacy objects and relationships among these objects. Compared with single privacy, the relationship is also a type of privacy and must be protected. However, the relationships are not considered in the current privacy-preserving researches. The current researches did not provide a means how to indicate personal privacy and how to describe them. In the paper, a graph-based formal description method is proposed in order to indicate and model privacy.

The main contribution of this paper is to propose a new modelling approach for multi-owner privacy, which is based on Graph theory. In the approach, a multi-owner privacy object is described as a directed graph, whose vertex represents an owner of privacy object and whose edge represents a relationship between two single-owner privacy objects. The single-owner privacy can be considered a special case of multi-owner privacy.

The rest of this paper is organized as follows. Section 2 discusses previous related works. Section 3 introduces a new privacy definition and a class hierarchy of privacy type according to the owner's number and the complexity of privacy object that is

J. Lei et al. (Eds.): NCIS 2012, CCIS 345, pp. 689–695, 2012.
© Springer-Verlag Berlin Heidelberg 2012

used to represent personal privacy. Section 4 presents the graph-based formal description for multi-owner privacy. Finally, we propose the future research intention in section 5.

2   Related Works

In the current researches, privacy is defined as "the right of individuals to determine for themselves when, how and to what extent information about them is communicated to others"[1]. In order to protect personal privacy, the concept of Hippocratic database is proposed [12]. The Hippocratic database incorporates the privacy protection in RDBMS firstly. In the database, privacy policies represent the data administrator's policies; privacy preferences represent the data provider's intention. When a user tries to access the privacy data, he must satisfy both privacy policies and privacy preferences.

Currently, the evolution and complexity of privacy have been considered by some researchers. In order to research the evolution of privacy, a composite privacy object model is proposed [13]. The paper proposes a privacy data model based on deputy mechanism to depict the generalization relationship among different privacy objects and provide a stronger hiding capability that IS-A relationship. In order to protect the privacy known by multiple individuals, the concept of multi-owner privacy is propose in [11]. In the paper, a privacy policy conflict detection method based on sub-graph isomorphic is proposed for protect the multi-owner privacy. However, the paper is not proposed a formal description method for multi-owner privacy. The multi-owner privacy is identified by defining privacy policy. So the operation and evolution algorithm for multi-owner privacy is difficult to define and use.

3   The Definition and Classification of Privacy

In the current researches, it is a consensus view that privacy is not equivalent to personal information, and privacy is a kind of personal information that be concerned by owner. So, a new privacy definition is proposed as follows.

Definition 1 (Privacy). Privacy is a usage view of personal information, which is assigned by information owner and is restricted by usage context.

From the definition, it is clear that privacy consists of three elements:
(1) *The Owner*. The owner is the subject of personal information, which includes privacy information;
(2) *The personal information*. The personal information is the carrier of privacy.
(3) *Context*. The context is the environment of privacy assignment and usage, which includes privacy recipient, usage purpose, retention, and so on.
The definition 1 can be described as follows figure 1.

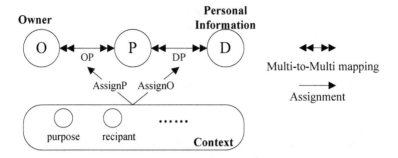

Fig. 1. The privacy definition

In the figure 1, the mapping OP $\subseteq$ O × P represents a multiple-to-multiple mapping between the owner and its privacy, the mapping DP $\subseteq$ D × P represents a multiple-to-multiple mapping between the privacy and the personal information, which includes privacy, *AssignP*: E → OP represents an assignment function, which is used to restrict that an owner defines a privacy assignment according special context, *AssignO*: E → DP represents an assignment function, which is used to restrict the operation that makes a new privacy object by composing of several privacy objects.

It is indicated by current researches that there isn't a mechanism to protect privacy perfectly. The effectiveness of a mechanism depends on the type of special privacy data. In the paper, according to the complexity of privacy data, they can be classified as single privacy object and composite privacy object [13], and according to the owners' number of privacy object, they can be classified as single-owner privacy object and multi-owner privacy object, shown as Figure 2.

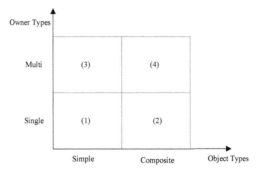

Fig. 2. The classification of privacy object

Definition 2 (Privacy type). Each type of privacy can be defined as follows:

(1) **Single-owner, Single-object privacy type.** The privacy type is used to represent a kind of privacy information, which can be expressed by predefined standard data types and is related with a single individual, such as personal ID, e-mail address, etc. In the privacy type, the OP is a one-to-one mapping and the DP is also a one-to-one mapping.

(2) ***Single-owner, Composite-object privacy type.*** The privacy type is used to represent a kind of privacy information, which can be expressed by composite data types and is related with a single individual, such as personal curriculum vitae. In the privacy type, the OP is a one-to-one mapping and the DP is also a multiple-to-multiple mapping.

(3) ***Multi-owner, Single-object privacy type.*** The privacy type is used to represent a kind of privacy information, which can be expressed by predefined standard data types and is related with multiple individual, such as marriage status, employment relationship, etc. In the privacy type, the OP is a multiple-to-multiple mapping and the DP is a one-to-one mapping.

(4) ***Multi-owner, Composite-object privacy type.*** The privacy type is used to represent a kind of privacy information, which can be expressed by composite data types and is related with multiple individual, such as discussion content, information interaction between the two individual, etc. In the privacy type, the OP is a multiple-to-multiple mapping and the DP is also a multiple-to-multiple mapping.

The four types of privacy data are not dependable. The relationship among the four privacy type can be shown as Figure 3.

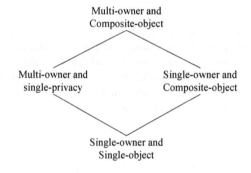

Fig. 3. The relationship of four types of privacy data

The hierarchy shown in Figure 3 denotes that the characteristics of lower privacy data type can be inherited by upper privacy data type. So a privacy protection method, which can protect the senior privacy data type, can also protect the junior privacy data type. In order to find a method to protect multi-owner privacy, the description method for multi-owner privacy must be proposed firstly.

4   The Formal Description of Multi-owner Privacy

E-mail is a typical multi-owner privacy data. An E-mail between two individuals is a common privacy data of the two individuals. Without the consent of the another party, any party should not publish the contents of the e-mail. However, both sender and receiver are owners of the e-mail, each of them can forward the e-mail independently. The forwarding process may cause leakage of another owner's private information.

The multi-owner privacy is created by the interaction among multiple individuals, such as marry, talk, learn, etc. These interactions can be induced as follows.

(1) Aggregating privacy information of multiple owners. Multiple owners integrate their privacy information into new privacy information, which can be known by each owner. Fox example, "Family property" privacy information is created by "marry" action, and both husband and wife can know this information. The multi-owner privacy object can be created by joining multiple privacy objects in the Hippocratic database.

(2) Extending privacy information by adding privacy information of other owner. An owner extends his privacy information by importing other owner's privacy information. For example, an e-mail can include the extension when it is forwarded or replied. The forwarded or replied e-mail can be known by the sender and the receiver. The multi-owner privacy object can be created by union operation in the Hippocratic database.

According to the generation process of multi-owner privacy, three factors must be considered when a multi-owner privacy object is expressed. The three factors are privacy owner, privacy data and interaction. So the formal definition of multi-owner privacy can be defined as follows.

Definition 3. The multi-owner privacy can be described as a tuple $(U, D, \rightleftharpoons)$,

> **Where:** $U=\{u_i \mid i \in N\}$ represents the set of privacy owners;
> $D=\{data_{i\text{-}j} \mid data_{i\text{-}j}$ is the privacy known both u_i and $u_j\}$ represents the set of privacy data;
> $\rightleftharpoons = \{(Direction_i, Function_i) \mid i \in N\}$ represents the relationship among the elements of D. $Direction_i$ denotes the relationship direction between two privacy objects; $Function_i$ denotes the composite operation.

According to above definition, a multi-owner privacy object can be represented as a weighted directed graph G=<V, E, Weight>. Here, V denotes the owner set; E denotes relationship direction between two privacy objects, and Weight denotes the privacy data.

For example, user A sends an e-mail to user B. Obviously, both user A and user B can disseminate the e-mail, so they are the owner of the e-mail. With the mail forwarding, the owner set of the e-mail is also increasing. If user A sends the e-mail to user C and user B forwards the e-mail to user D, the set of the e-mail owner will be extended to contain user C and user D. All of e-mail copies will be considered as a multi-owner privacy object and each copy will be considered as a part of the multi-owner privacy object. Furthermore, if user B reply the e-mail to user A, then the replied e-mail is also considered a part of the multi-owner privacy object, because the e-mail and its replied e-mail express the full semantic together. The multi-owner privacy object shown in above example can be modelled as Figure 4.

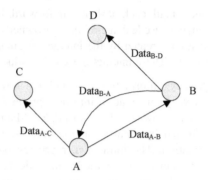

Fig. 4. The description example of multi-owner privacy

In the example, the multi-owner privacy object can be denoted as follows:

$$Privacy_{multi-owner} = (U, D, \rightleftharpoons)$$

Where:

$$U = \{A, B, C, D\}$$

$$D_{set} = \{Data_{A-B}, Data_{B-D}, Data_{A-C}, Data_{A-D}\}$$

$$\rightleftharpoons = \left\{ \left(Direction_{D_{A-B}}, Function_{D_{A-B}} \right) \left(Direction_{D_{B-C}}, Function_{D_{B-C}} \right), \right.$$
$$\left. \left(Direction_{D_{A-C}}, Function_{D_{A-C}} \right) \left(Direction_{D_{A-D}}, Function_{D_{A-D}} \right) \right\}$$

In our description method, the single-owner privacy type is considered as a special case of the multi-owner privacy type. For example, a single-owner privacy object, the salary of user A, its formal description can be denoted as following equation and its graph description can be shown in Figure 5.

$$Privacy_{Single-owner} = (U, D, \rightleftharpoons) = (\{A\}, \{data_{A-A}\}, \{Direction_A, Function_{data_{A-A}}\})$$

$$Function_{DataA}$$

Fig. 5. The description example of single-owner privacy

It is noted that the symbol Function in the multi-owner definition can represent not only a special function, but also a function family. It is assigned by the owner of privacy $data_i$ and its result is the usage view of privacy. By the function (or function family), different recipient can read different version of a privacy object. This is an implementation mechanism of Polymorphism.

5   Conclusions

With the development of information society, privacy on the internet is increasing rapidly and the structure of privacy becomes more complex. In the paper, a formal description mechanism for complex privacy is proposed. Furthermore, the operation semantic for complex privacy will be researched based on the mechanism.

Reference

1. Bertino, E., Sandhu, R.: Database Security-—Concepts, Approached, and Challenge. IEEE Transaction on Dependable and Secure Computing 2(1)
2. Xiao, X., Tao, Y.: Personalized Privacy Preservation. In: Proceedings of the 2006 ACM SIGMOD International Conference on Management of Data (2006)
3. Byun, J.-W., Bertino, E., Li, N.: Micro-views, or on how to protect privacy while enhancing data usability – Concepts and Challenges. SIGMOD Record 35(1)
4. Byun, J.-W., Bertino, E., Li, N.: Purpose Based Access Control of Complex Data for Privacy Protection. In: SACMAT 2005 (2005)
5. Bayardo, R., Agrawal, R.: Data privacy through optimal k-anonymization. In: ICDE, pp. 217–228
6. Yao, C., Wang, L., Wang, X.S., Jajodia, S.: Indistinguishability: The Other Aspect of Privacy. Journal of Secure Data Management, 1–17
7. Samarati, P., Sweeney, L.: Protecting privacy when disclosing information: k-anonymity and its enforcement through generalization and suppression Technical Report Technical Report, SRI International
8. Sweeney, L.: k-anonymity: A Model For Protecting Privacy. International Journal on Uncertainty, Fuzziness and Knowledge-based Systems 10 (5), 557–570
9. LeFevre, K., DeWitt, D.J., Ramakrishnan, R.: Mondrian multidimensional k-anonymity. In: ICDE 2006 (2006)
10. Machanavajjhala, A., Gehrke, J., Kifer, D.: l-diversity: Privacy beyond k-anonymity. In: ICDE 2006 (2006)
11. Ren, Y., Cheng, F., Peng, Z., Huang, X., Song, W.: A Privacy Policy Conflict Detection Method for Multi-owner Privacy Data Protection. Journal of Electronic Commerce Research, 23–39
12. Agrawal, R., Kiernan, J., Srikant, R., Xu, Y.: Hippocratic Databases. In: Proc. 28th Int'l Conf. on Very Large Data Bases
13. Ren, Y., Luo, M., Tang, Z., Ye, L.: A Composite Privacy Protection Model. In: Second International Workshop in Information and Computer Security, Nara, Japan (2007)

A Novel Multi-channel MAC Protocol
for Cluster Based Wireless Multimedia Sensor Networks

Longmei Zhang[1] and Wei Lu[2]

[1] Department of Communication Engineering, Xi'an University of Science and Technology,
Xi'an, 710072, China
[2] Department of Software and Microelectronics, Northwestern Polytechnical University,
Xi'an, 710072, China
longmei.zhang@gmail.com, luweinpu@nwpu.edu.cn

Abstract. A light weight, scalable and collision free MAC protocol, DTFMM, is presented in this paper, which combines frequency and time division principles for medium sharing. Based on clustered network topology, the protocol employs a distributed local coordinate algorithm for assigning channels among clusters to enable simultaneous non-interfering data collection. Intra-cluster transmissions are scheduled by cluster head (CH) based on time slot. CHs aggregate the gathered data and forward it over inter-CH paths to the base-station based on minimum spanning tree routing. Simulation demonstrated superiority of DTFMM in terms of convergent rate, throughput and delay performance when compared with well-known protocol MMSN.

Keywords: Wireless multimedia sensor networks, distributed coordination, TDMA/FDMA, multi-channel MAC.

1 Introduction

The availability of low-cost hardware, for instance, CMOS cameras, has resulted in fast growth of Wireless Multimedia Sensor Networks (WMSNs) with their applications in remote environment monitoring, video surveillance and image-based tracking to name a few [1]. Different from traditional sensor networks, WMSNs usually require much higher bandwidth and larger throughput to transmit mass of multimedia data to base station (BS) rapidly. However, data rates provided by existing commercial products, e.g., 250Kbps in MICAz, are not sufficient to support such requirements. Current sensor nodes, such as MICAz and Telos that use CC2420 radio, already support multiple frequencies. Though some popular wireless network protocols, such as 802.11 and Zigbee standard, allow using multiple frequency channels at the physical layer, their MAC protocol doesn't provide multiple channels scheme. This limited some single-channel MAC protocols to perform well in the multi-channel environment. Therefore, multi-channel MAC protocols are needed in order to take full advantage of multi-channel parallel transmission mechanisms and meet high data rate demand for multimedia applications.

J. Lei et al. (Eds.): NCIS 2012, CCIS 345, pp. 696–704, 2012.
© Springer-Verlag Berlin Heidelberg 2012

In order to maximize the network throughput with enhanced energy efficiency, a light weight distributed time/frequency division multi-channel MAC protocol (DTFMM) is proposed in this paper.

In the remaining of the paper, relevant work is reviewed in Section 2. Design of DTFMM is presented in Section 3 and its evaluation is presented in Section 4 through simulation. Finally Section 5 summarizes the paper.

2   Related Works

Research on Ad Hoc network and multi-channel MAC protocol are mainly focused on competition-based [2-4] and coordinator-based multi-channel protocol [5, 6]. DCA[2] divides the overall bandwidth into one control channel and n data channels. Each mobile host is equipped with two half-duplex transceivers, with one operating on the control channel to exchange control packets with other mobile hosts and obtaining rights to access data channels. However, two transceivers per mobile host increases cost. In addition, one channel being used for control will cause resource waste when only a few channels are available, while result in insufficient usage of data channels when too much data channels are available. MMAC[3] built on top of the IEEE 802.11 power-saving mechanism. It is a time-slotted protocol in which bandwidth is divided into time slots comprising beacon period, ATIM window and data window. Because MMAC requires network-wide temporal synchronization, frequent synchronization introduces an additional power overhead. MMSN[4] is the first multi-channel MAC protocol that takes into account the restrictions imposed by WSNs. The protocol suggests four strategies for assigning different frequencies to the nodes. With the assigned frequencies, nodes operate to maximize parallel transmission among neighboring space. It achieves high throughput with enough channels. However, the same channel can be assigned to multiple nodes when channels are limited, which can cause collision hence reduce channel usage. A multi-channel MAC protocol was proposed by Xun et. al. [5], within which all the nodes in the network are clustered and cluster heads collect request messages from the cluster members, and then assign channels to both the source and the destination nodes. Although this coordinator-based mechanism is able to increase the total sleeping time of the nodes, the maximum network throughput is limited by the number of request packets which can be managed by the cluster head. COM-MAC[6] is another coordinator-based multi-channel protocol for WMSNs, within which all the nodes in the network are also clustered and each cluster head is equipped with N half-duplex transceivers. The protocol solved nodes communication within cluster but did not consider channel assignment of the whole network. In addition, N transceivers per cluster head increased cost enormously.

3   DTFMM Protocol Design

3.1   Network Topology

A set of homogeneous sensors is randomly distributed in an area under monitoring. Sensors are grouped into disjoint clusters by applying a distributed randomized clustering algorithm such as HEED [7]. One sensor in each cluster acts as cluster head (CH), responsible for cluster management and intra-cluster access schedule. The others acquire useful information from surroundings and then transmit to the CH in their cluster. Minimum spanning tree routing is adopted by CHs to forward collected data over inter-CH paths to the base-station (BS). Each node can only join one cluster. The network topology is illustrated in Fig. 1, within which arrows represent shortest route from CHs to BS.

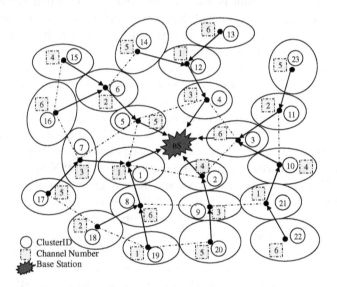

Fig. 1. Cluster ID and channel assignment

3.2   Assumptions

(1) There are N different channels available for use, which have the same bandwidth.

(2) All multimedia sensor nodes are identical and quasi-stationary. Each of them is equipped with a single half-duplex transceiver.

(3) BS is equipped with N half-duplex transceivers and can send or receive on N channels simultaneously. In addition, BS has sufficient power supply and processing capacity. It lies in the center of the monitoring area and its radio range can cover the whole area.

(4) Each node can only join one cluster and communicate with its CH directly. The CH's sending capacity is 1.5 times of other nodes, which ensures inter-CH connection and they can forward collected data to BS.

(5) Each cluster has an ID that is sequentially numbered from 0. The ID of BS is 0.

3.3   Protocol Design of DTFMM

DTFMM will work in three stages, Distributed channel assignment, Intra-cluster communication, and Inter-cluster communication.

(1) Distributed channel assignment: Following setting up of clustered network, each cluster has a unique ID, and IDs of all clusters form a sequential list starts from 0. Each CH knows its own as well as its neighbor CHs' ID. Each node maintains an NL, a list of its neighbor clusters information including their IDs and assigned channels. The channel assignment is based on cluster ID, a cluster with lower ID selects channel with higher priority. By checking NL before selecting channels, it is ensured that a CH does not select channels until all other CHs with lower ID have selected their channels. The CH broadcasts its channel information after the selection through public channel, so that its neighbor CHs could update their NL. In the meantime, other member nodes in the same cluster tune their transceivers to the same channel selected by the CH. The channel assignment stage ends after the CH with the lowest priority selects its channel. The public channel is selected during network establishment by network coordinator, such as BS. Fig. 1 shows one possible process of channel selection. In this example, the ID of clusters are given sequentially from inside to outside of the network. Dash line indicates neighbor clusters that can be reached within one hop.

In Fig. 1, channel assignment starts from CH1. It selects channel 1 and propagates the information to its neighbor clusters 2, 5, 7 and 8. Because CH2 has the highest priority, it selects channel 4 and propagates the information to CH3 and CH9 so that they update their NL. It was then followed by CH3 selecting channel 6, CH4 selecting channel 3, and CH5 selecting channel 5. After this round, clusters 6, 7, 8, 10, and 12 have highest priority in their NL hence can select channels based on the principle that neighbor clusters use different and also non-adjacent channels. By using this method, only 6 channels are used in Fig. 1 by the 23 clusters that enable simultaneous intra-cluster non-interference communication.

The above algorithm has the following three features:

① The message overhead used for channel assignment is very small. All message exchange takes place only among neighbors.

② The channel assignment can be carried out in parallel. It can be started for any CH if it has the lowest ID in its NL.

③ The maximum iteration of channel assignment is N, which is the number of clusters.

(2) Intra-cluster communication stage: After channel assignment, each CH tunes its transceiver to the assigned channel. Non-interference communication can be carried out with different and non-adjacent channels chosen by neighbor clusters. To meet communication requirements of the cluster with most nodes, the BS broadcasts the maximum time slots of intra-cluster communication within each channel. Frame length of intra-cluster communication is determined by the cluster with most nodes. Therefore, cluster with only a few nodes can sleep until its intra-cluster communication starts.

In the intra-cluster communication stage, CH collects data from its member nodes. To avoid collision caused by multi nodes sending data to CH at the same time, TDMA is adopted within cluster for channel access. The time frame structure of each cluster in the intra-cluster communication stage is shown in Fig. 2. As can be seen, they are composed of Synchronous beacon, Request phase, Schedule phase, Data transmission, and Sleep phase. At first, CH broadcasts synchronous beacon within its cluster channel, and synchronizes with its member nodes. Nodes with data to be sent send requests to CH with CSMA method, which include node ID and the size of data to be sent. On receiving requests from its member nodes, CH schedules the time for node members based on priority and broadcasts time slots to them. Each member node sends data within its assigned time slot, and turns off the transceiver and sleeps in other time slots. The length of request, data transmission and sleeping time are different for clusters with different numbers of nodes. CH of the cluster has most nodes enter inter-cluster communication stage immediately after its intra-cluster communication.

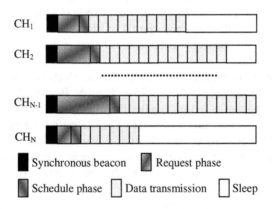

Fig. 2. Time slot structure of each cluster's intra-cluster communication

(3) Inter-cluster communication phase: After aggregating the sensor readings in its cluster, a CH forwards the data to the BS over an inter-CH path. It is assumed that the clustering process has been completed and routing tree has been created as shown in Fig. 1. The BS is the root of the tree that has multiple independent non-crossing paths, which has limited depth. After intra-cluster communication, each CH is still on its own frequency channel. However, they have to switch to the same channel in order to communicate between clusters along the path. Therefore, different channels need to be assigned to different paths to ensure non-interference communication between them. A simple but effective algorithm is used here. That is, each path uses the channel used by the cluster nearest to the BS. Because the channel assignment process ensures neighbor clusters use different and non-adjacent channels, the channel assignment for different paths is also non-interfering. The CHs on the same path then use TDMA to access the channel, and the time slots are scheduled in depth-first ordering, of which the deepest CH has the highest priority. Therefore, the delay of inter-cluster communication is proportional to the depth of the routing tree.

4   Evaluation

The performance of the DTFMM protocol was evaluated through simulations on GloMoSim, in terms of convergence rate of the channel assignment algorithm, aggregate MAC throughput, and average package delay. The last two aspects were also compared with the even-selection of channel assignment of MMSN protocol.

4.1   Simulation Environment

In each simulation, a number of sensors, ranging from 100 to 600, were distributed in an area with size of 400m*400m. BS was located in the center of the area. A sensor's communication can reach 50m diameter (maximum 100m) and BS's communication can cover the whole area. Channels were set to 8, with each bandwidth 250kbps. The maximum nodes within each cluster were 20, and the maximum depth (or hop) of each path was 6. It was supposed that each sensor randomly requested sending 0-500B data with probability P $(0<P\leq1)$. A higher P represents larger data rate to be sent and heavier network load. Different clusters were formed for each simulation by using different random seeds algorithm. The final value of each experiment is the average of 20 calculations.

4.2   Simulation Results

(1) Convergence rate of distributed channel assignment algorithm: The convergence rate represents the average number of iterations needed for all clusters being assigned distinct channels for transmissions. Fig. 3 illustrates relationship between the total sensors number, the average number of iterations, and the number of clusters. It can be seen from the figure, as the number of sensors increased from 100 to 600, the number of clusters increased from 22 to 45, and the average number of iterations slightly grew from 5 to 8. While the scale of network increased largely, the iteration of channel assignment ended after limited numbers due to the parallelism of the algorithm. Therefore, it can be concluded that the algorithm has good convergence rate and scalability for large scale network.

(2) Aggregate MAC throughput: The throughputs of networks with different numbers of sensors by using DTFMM and MMSN are compared in Fig. 4. As can be seen, when the network load was comparatively low (the nodes number was below 200), the throughputs of the two protocols were similar. However, as the number of nodes grows, the superiority of DTFMM is more obvious because the collisions among nodes increased when using MMSN. In MMSN, channels become inadequate with increased nodes, which results in the same channel being assigned to multiple nodes and causes channel access collision. The collisions deteriorate with increased network nodes, which resulted in decreased network throughputs eventually in MMSN.

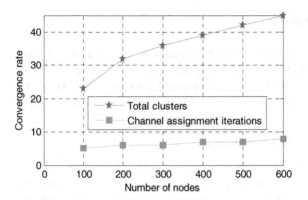

Fig. 3. Convergence rate of distributed channel assignment algorithm

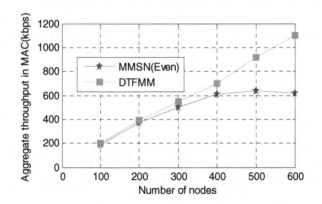

Fig. 4. Comparison of aggregate MAC throughput

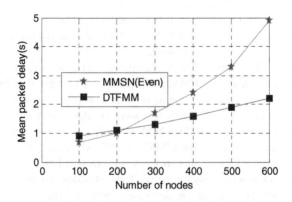

Fig. 5. Comparison of average package delay

(3) Package delay: The relationship of package delay and nodes number by using DTFMM and MMSN are compared in Fig. 5. It can be seen that when the nodes number was 100, the delay of MMSN was slightly shorter than DTFMM. It was because DTFMM uses TDMA for intra-cluster communication and nodes can only send data during their own time slots, which resulted package delay. MMSN uses randomly assigned channel, hence nodes can send data immediately when they are assigned channel. However, competition increases with increased nodes number, which results in increased collisions, hence longer delay existed for MMSN. Though nodes within a cluster also increased with increased network nodes, which increased package delay slightly in DTFMM, the delay was not serious with the constraint of maximum nodes, which was set to 20 in the simulation.

It can be seen from the evaluation that DTFMM has good convergence rate. Compare to MMSN, DTFMM performs better in terms of MAC throughputs and package delay. Especially with increased sensor nodes, DTFMM shows its superiority over MMSN.

5   Conclusions and Future Works

A novel hybrid time/frequency division multi-channel MAC protocol, DTFMM, is presented in this paper. The protocol requires only one transceiver for each node, hence reduces hardware cost. Frequency resources are maximized used by adopting FDMA among clusters. The TDMA used within cluster avoided access collisions among nodes, which resulted in improved throughput and package delay. DTFMM allows nodes to stay in sleeping mode for the longest duration and thus minimizes energy consumption. The channel assignment can finish after a limited number of iterations, even with high number of sensor nodes. Hence the channel assignment algorithm has good scalability. Simulations showed that the protocol has better throughputs and package delay compare to MMSN.

Acknowledgment. This work is partially supported by Aviation Science Foundation of China #2010ZD53047 to Lu Wei.

References

[1] Sharif, A., Potdar, V., Chang, E.: Wireless multimedia sensor network technology: A survey. In: 7th IEEE International Conference on Industrial Informatics, INDIN 2009, pp. 606–613 (June 2009)
[2] Shih-Lin, W., Chih-Yu, L., Yu-Chee, T., Jang-Laing, S.: A new multi-channel MAC protocol with on-demand channel assignment for multi-hop mobile ad hoc networks. In: Proceedings of International Symposium on Parallel Architectures, Algorithms and Networks, I-SPAN 2000, pp. 232–237 (2000)
[3] So, J., Vaidya, N.: Multi-channel mac for ad hoc networks: handling multi-channel hidden terminals using a single transceiver. In: Proceedings of the 5th ACM International Symposium on Mobile Ad Hoc Networking and Computing, MobiHoc 2004, pp. 222–233 (2004)

[4] Zhou, G., Huang, C., Yan, T., He, T., Stankovic, J.A., Abdelzaher, T.F.: MMSN: Multi-Frequency Media Access Control for Wireless Sensor Networks. In: Proceedings of 25th IEEE International Conference on Computer Communications, INFOCOM 2006, pp. 1–13 (2006)

[5] Xun, C., Peng, H., Qiu-Sheng, H., Shi-liang, T., Zhang-Long, C.: A Multi-Channel MAC Protocol for Wireless Sensor Networks. In: The Sixth IEEE International Conference on Computer and Information Technology, CIT 2006, pp. 224–224 (September 2006)

[6] Cheng, L., Pu, W., Hsiao-Hwa, C., Guizani, M.: A Cluster Based On-demand Multi-Channel MAC Protocol for Wireless Multimedia Sensor Networks. In: IEEE International Conference on Communications, ICC 2008, pp. 2371–2376 (May 2008)

[7] Younis, O., Fahmy, S.: HEED: a hybrid, energy-efficient, distributed clustering approach for ad hoc sensor networks. IEEE Transactions on Mobile Computing 3, 366–379 (2004)

The Design of Wireless Medical Monitoring Network Based on ZigBee

Minghui Wu[1,2] and Qing Xie[1,2]

[1] School of Computer Science and Technology, Zhejiang University, Hangzhou 310027, China
[2] School of Computer and Computing Science, Zhejiang University City College,
Hangzhou 310015, China
mhwu@zucc.edu.cn

Abstract. In order to solve the problems of wiring complexity, high cost, poor mobility and high energy consumption, which are occurred in current medical monitoring devices. In the basis of analyzing the devices and topologies of ZigBee network, a novel wireless medical monitoring network is designed based on ZigBee technology in this paper. The wireless network nodes are constructed by CC2530 ZigBee modules and the wireless medical monitoring network is formed by way of Ad Hoc network based on ZigBee. The hardware platforms and software of the network nodes are designed. The body's pulse signal is monitored in time by the monitoring network and the implementation results indicate that the novel wireless healthcare monitoring network has the advantages of low power consumption, low cost, good instantaneity and strong expandability.

Keywords: ZigBee, wireless medical monitoring network, CC2530.

1 Introduction

With the approach of the aging society, resolving the monitoring of the long-term chronic diseases has become an important problem [1]. Some acute illness and family care, such as cardiovascular disease, the daily care of the elderly, the health monitoring of the pregnant women, fetuses and infants, also need the assistance of monitoring system.

Existing medical care system, most of which use fixed medical monitors, complex equipments and wired data transmission systems, would result in the patient's psychological stress and tension; affect the correctness of collected data and diagnosis of the disease [2].

Especially in the ward care, a variety of connections not only make the patients feel uncomfortable, but also make the wards appear disorganized, affecting the patients' mood. Therefore, an effective medical monitoring system needs a low-cost, high reliability wireless transmission scheme instead of the traditional wired approach. The emergence of ZigBee wireless sensor network and its applications in the medical field have injected new vitality into the study of wireless medical monitoring system.

J. Lei et al. (Eds.): NCIS 2012, CCIS 345, pp. 705–713, 2012.
© Springer-Verlag Berlin Heidelberg 2012

ZigBee is a new type of short-range wireless communications technology. Compared with other short-range wireless communications technologies, ZigBee protocol has the characteristics of low power, low cost, high reliability, flexible networking, low complexity, and network capacity [3]. In this paper, a wireless medical monitoring network based on ZigBee technology is designed. The transferring of physiological parameters is used by ZigBee technology, which reduces the connections between the monitoring equipment and medical sensors, making the patients to have more free space. The monitoring network is not only able to obtain an accurate measurement, and has characteristics of low power consumption, low cost, strong scalability and strong anti-interference.

2   The Devices in ZigBee Network and Network Topologies

2.1   The Devices in ZigBee Network

Depending on the function, the devices in ZigBee network are divided into two types: full function devices (FFD) and Reduced Function Devices (RFD), by the group of IEEE 802.15.4 [4]. FFD achieve the complete works of the IEEE 802.15.4 protocol, while RFD only implement part of the IEEE 802.15.4 complete agreement based on the specific application needs. According to the roles of devices in the network, three kinds of devices are defined: coordinator (FFD), router (FFD) and end device (FFD or RFD).

The coordinator is the heart of the ZigBee network, and there is only one network coordinator in a ZigBee network. The main functions of the coordinator are establishing a network, sending web beacons, managing network nodes and storing information of network nodes. The router's main functions are message routing and forwarding. The main functions of the end device are the collection and control of information, and it can only be in the position of the leaf nodes in the tree network.

2.2   Network Topologies

The above three devices has the flexibility to constitute three types of network topologies: star, tree and network structure, as shown in Fig. 1. A ZigBee device has a unique 64-bit IEEE address, which can be used to communicate in the PAN (Personal Area Network). However, after establishing a connection with end device or router, the network coordinator will assign it a 16-bit short address, which will be used to communicate in the PAN thereafter [4]. The 64-bit IEEE address of device is an absolute address, which is analogous to the computer's MAC address; while the 16–bit short address is a relative address, which is similar to the IP address in TCP / IP.

The characteristics of these network topologies are as follows:

(a) Star network: There is a coordinator and a number of end devices in the network. The coordinator is responsible for initiating and maintaining the network works properly, and maintaining communications with end devices.

(b) Tree network: The network consists of a coordinator, a number of routers and end devices. The routers can't communicate with each other directly. If a router is excluded in the network because of an error, the corresponding end device and coordinator would be de-linked. The data of end devices can route by extending tree network;

(c) Mesh network: The network consists of a coordinator, a number of routers and end devices on the basis of tree topology, while the routers can communicate with each other directly. The structure of the network is complicated and the data of end devices can be transmitted through the optimal path of the mesh network.

The wireless medical monitoring network designed in the paper employ mesh topology, because using mesh topology can make the wireless network more robust and flexible. Even if some router nodes fail and exit the network, it will not affect the entire wireless network because the end nodes can also get in touch with the nearest router node, and then get in touch with the coordinator by the way of multi-hop routing, and ultimately join the wireless network. This is the self-healing feature of the ZigBee wireless network [5]. It can also easily expanded the entire wireless network through the networking of multi-hop routing.

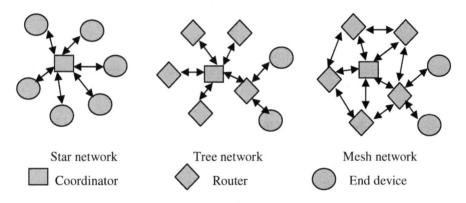

| Star network | Tree network | Mesh network |

■ Coordinator   ◆ Router   ● End device

Fig. 1. The topologies of ZigBee network

3 The Overall Design of the Wireless Medical Monitoring Network

The entire wireless medical monitoring network consists of a number of end nodes which integrate physiological parameters sensors, a number of router nodes (RFD) and a network coordinator node (FFD). After the physiological parameters sensors of the end nodes complete data collection, the data can be sent directly to the network coordinator by way of ZigBee wireless communication; it can also be sent to a router node, and then to a coordinator through the router node. The network coordinator connects with PC via a RS-232 serial cable, and the monitoring software in PC can achieve real-time display of human's physiological signals data, storage, data playback and alarm function, and thus achieve real-time monitoring of patients. Furthermore, the data can be sent to a remote medical monitoring center through the Internet network, and can be observed statistically by medical professionals to provide the necessary consulting services, thus achieve remote medical treatment. The overall framework of the system is shown in Fig. 2.

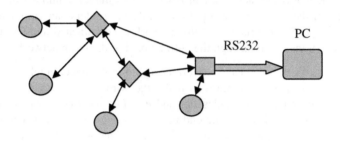

Fig. 2. The overall framework of the system

4   The Design of Wireless Network Nodes

As the convenient, flexible, low-cost and low power consumption characteristics of the System-on-Chip ZigBee node development program in implementation. The System-on-Chip solution—CC2530 ZigBee module is used to design wireless medical monitoring network nodes in this paper.

4.1   The Introduction of CC2530 Chip

CC2530 chip is TI's next-generation SOC solution which supports for the ZigBee protocol stack. It includes a high-performance 2.4GHz DSSS (direct sequence spread spectrum) RF transceiver core and a high-performance and low-power 8051 microcontroller core, as well as other strong support function and peripherals[6].

CC2530 chip provides 101dB link quality, excellent receiver sensitivity and robust anti-jamming, as well as an extensive set of peripherals - including two USARTs, a 12-bit ADC and 21 general-purpose I/O interfaces. CC2530 chip supports five operating modes. Its current consumption differs in different modes, for example, 24mA in receiving mode and 29 mA in transmitting mode. Under the sleep mode current consumption is only 1mA; power consumption of the others is 0.2mA and 0.4uA. The time of mode conversion is very short, which can satisfy the requirements of ultra low-power system and suit for applications that require very long battery life. Therefore, the wireless medical monitoring network that uses CC2530 modules has the advantages of low power consumption.

4.2   The Construction of Hardware Platforms of Nodes

(1) Coordinator node: Coordinator is a full-function device (FFD), as shown in Fig. 3 and it is composed by a microprocessor, a transceiver module, power, interfaces of communication module and other components. The CC2530 single-chip solution integrates a microprocessor and a transceiver module, uses DC power supply or battery to power [6]. Coordinator connects with computer through the RS232 serial interface, so that the physiological parameters data of coordinate node can be transferred to a computer, and be observed dynamically by monitoring software in computer to conduct more flexible management.

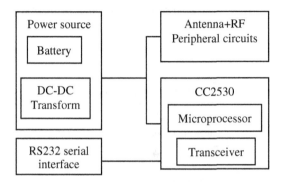

Fig. 3. The hardware structure of coordinator node

(2) End node: End node is generally a reduced function device (RFD). It's main function is to make sensors begin to collect physiological parameters data of human body, then send the physiological parameters data (after A/D conversion) into CC2530, finally send the data to router node or coordinator node through the wireless communication module. It does not participate in routing. Under normal circumstances, this node is in sleep state and the power consumption of it is low, so it can be powered by batteries. The hardware structure of end node is shown in Fig. 4.

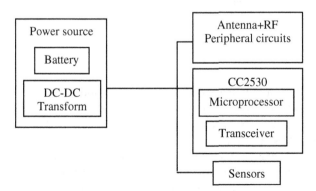

Fig. 4. The hardware structure of end node

(3) Router node: Router is a full function device (FFD). Its hardware structure is basically the same as end node. In addition, the router can choose to have sensors, if so, it can also realize data collection.

4.3   The Design of Software of Nodes

4.3.1   The Design of Software of End Node

After powering on, the end node firstly initializes the CC2530 chip, and then seeks to join the network. After joining the network successfully, if end node receives a data collection instruction sent by the coordinator, it will begin data collection, and conduct A/D conversion by using the ADC CC2530 comes with, and then send the data packets to a router node or directly to the coordination node. The program flow chart of end node is shown in Fig. 5.

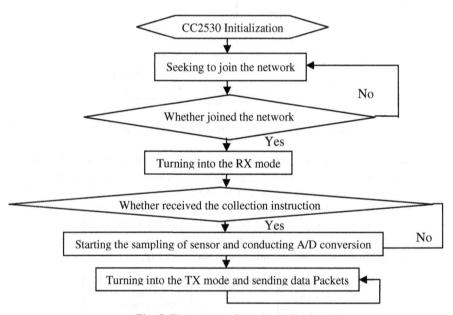

Fig. 5. The program flow chart of end node

4.3.2   The Design of Software of Coordinator Node

After powering on, coordinator node firstly initializes the CC2530 chip, and then scans all the channels specified by the DEFAULT_CHANLIST, and select the best channel to establish a wireless network. When an end node or a router node seeks to join the network, the coordinator node assigns a 16-bit network address to the end node or the router node. After the identification of end node and router node according to the IEEE address, the coordinator node send a collection instruction to the end node, then the coordinator begin to receive collected data packets and send them to a

PC through the RS-232 serial interface. At last, the data is monitored in real time by the monitoring software in the PC. The program flow chart of coordinator node is shown in Fig. 6.

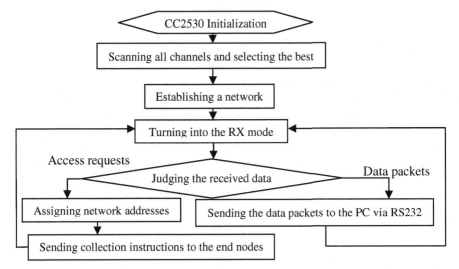

Fig. 6. The program flow chart of coordinator node

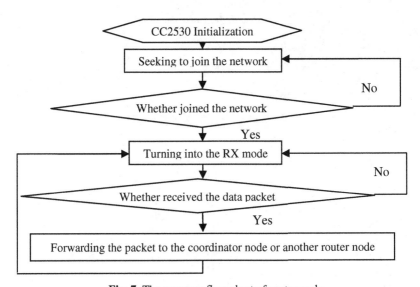

Fig. 7. The program flow chart of router node

4.3.3   The Design of Software of Router Node
The router node considered here doesn't carry physiological parameters sensors. After powering on, router node firstly initializes the CC2530 chip, and then seeks to join the

network. After joining the network successfully, the router node enters into the RX mode, if it receives the collected data packages sent by a end node or another router node, it will send packages to another router node or the coordinator node. The program flow char of router node is shown in Fig. 7.

5   The Experiment of Pulse Monitoring

According to the ZigBee wireless medical monitoring network introduced above, the end nodes integrate photoelectric pulse sensors, employ the 12-bit single-channel A/D conversion and set the resolution to 512. Because the frequency energy of the pulse signal is 99% concentrated in 0.3HZ ~ 15HZ, so it can basically detects the whole pulse signal waveform by setting the sampling rate of end node to 50HZ in this system. By using the way of system software timing, making a end node sends a 75-byte data packet to a router node or the coordinator node by the way of ZigBee wireless transmission every 1.5 seconds to achieve the sampling rate of 50HZ. When an end node receives the collection instruction sent by coordinate node, it starts continuous collection of pulse signals of human, and then the coordinator node sends the signal data to a PC via the RS-232 serial interface, finally, the signal data is displayed in the PC. The picture of the experiment is shown in Fig. 8.

Fig. 8. The picture of the experiment

6   Conclusion and Future Work

WSN based medical monitoring system is the trend of medical monitoring equipment at home and abroad. The wireless medical monitoring network based on ZigBee technology in this paper has the characteristics of low power consumption, small size, strong scalability, and strong anti-jamming and so on, but there are still many other problems need further research, such as routing algorithm, integration of sensors and end node, node localization, availability and stability of the system, intelligent analysis algorithms of signals and the research of related software. With the development of wireless communication technology, the wireless sensor networks based on ZigBee technology with the advantages of low cost, low power, high flexibility will have a broad application prospect in the health care services of hospitals and communities [7].

Acknowledgements. This work is partly supported by the Science Foundation of Zhejiang Province under Grand No. 2011C33015 and 2010R50009, and the Major Projects on Control and Rectification of Water Body Pollution of China (No. 2009ZX07424-001).

References

1. Chang, W.W., Sung, T.J., Huang, H.W., Hsu, W.C., Kuo, C.W., Chang, J.J., Hou, Y.T., Lan, Y.C., Kuo, W.C., Lin, Y.Y., Yang, Y.J.: A smart medication system using wireless sensor network technologies. Sensors and Actuators A-Physical 172, 315–321 (2011)
2. Vijayalakshmi, S.R., Muruganand, S.: Real-time monitoring of ubiquitous wireless ECG sensor node for medical care using ZigBee. International Journal of Electronics 99(1), 79–89 (2012)
3. De Schatz, C., Medeiros, H.P., Schneider, F.K., Abatti, P.J.: Wireless Medical Sensor Networks: Design Requirements and Enabling Technologies. Telemedicine and E-Health 18(5), 394–399 (2012)
4. ZigBee, A.: ZigBee Specification Version 1.0 (2004)
5. Du, Y.C., Lee, Y.Y., Lu, Y.Y., Lin, C.H., Wu, M.J., Chen, C.L., Chen, T.S.: Development of a Telecare System Based on ZigBee Mesh Network for Monitoring Blood Pressure of Patients with Hemodialysis in Health Care Centers. Journal of Medical Systems. 35, 877–883 (2011)
6. CC2530 Datasheet, http://www.ti.com/lit/ds/symlink/cc2530.pdf
7. Grgic, K., Zagar, D., Krizanovic, V.: Medical applications of wireless sensor networks - curre nt status and future directions. Medicinski Glasnik 9, 23–31 (2012)

Design and Application of ZigBee Locating and Transparent Transmission Serial Port Module for Tele-health Monitoring

Minghui Wu[1,2], Wei Zhou[1,2], and Honglun Hou[1,2,*]

[1] School of Computer Science and Technology, Zhejiang University, Hangzhou 310027, China
[2] School of Computer and Computing Science, Zhejiang University City College, Hangzhou 310015, China
houhl@cs.zju.edu.cn

Abstract. Traditional patient monitoring equipment has the capability of real-time monitoring, but now the tele-health equipment in the aged community service needs not only real-time monitoring but person locating in the communities for mobile applications. The paper presents a new WSN solution for tele-health equipment that can transmit the real-time monitoring and locating data by improving ZigBee module. The method does not change the transition of traditional signal detection module, let the detection module transmit the real-time data by UART to ZigBee router, and the ZigBee locating router module gets the data and packs the data and locating information together, and transmit the whole package by ZigBee stack's wireless protocol to ZigBee coordinator, and the coordinator convert the application level protocol data to RS-232 port for web-based tele-health management platform. The method makes the ZigBee locating module not only a main controller but a locating node by the modified ZigBee application level protocol, which avoids using a new controller for getting the locating data and real-time detection data by two separate UART. This approach decreases the equipment components to two core modules, not three modules. And the cost and power consumption is to be reduced.

Keywords: ZigBee, RSSI locating, Transparent Transmission Serial Port, Tele-health.

1   Introduction

With the level of ageing continuing to increase, the traditional social institutes for the aged have far less met the demands of social development [1]. Currently, the socialized elderly support community has become an emerging industry in China, it undertakes the life services, health promotion and health service. Based on the requirements driven by above demands, it is required to offer the service objects (especially old people) a portable device. Within the scope of community services, the device can provide better dynamic services. It has some functions, for example, measuring pulses and counting step dynamically, and judging abnormally tumbling or

---

* Corresponding author.

J. Lei et al. (Eds.): NCIS 2012, CCIS 345, pp. 714–721, 2012.
© Springer-Verlag Berlin Heidelberg 2012

not. In addition, users can give out the emergency request by it, and its terminal transmits the measured data to the service management platform and the terminal equipment of service administrative personnel in the aging community, so as to realize dynamic safe tele-care and related services for middle-aged and aged people in the community. With the ever-increasing aging communities, corresponding tele-care means should be improved for high-standard management requirements [2]. For example, not only do the aged people send out actively the data of requests for a help by pressing keys to the service center, but also a timely related active state and physiological information is required to transmit to the service center as a relevant assistant method. In some cases, the aged can not judge something correctly and have no ability to actively provide information, and they need to be positioned in the community, which facilitates to receive first aid quickly on the site. In particular, in the event of emergency, the possible medical assistance may exert the crucial effect.

Currently, some existing wireless monitoring terminals are made up of several data testing sensor modules and a wireless data transmission module [3]. The data testing module for heart rate, tumbling and movement can complete the data transmission by connecting serial communication with wireless transparent transmission module and addressing communication. In addition, some portable wireless testing terminals are required to increase related positioning and data transmission abilities. The traditional solution is to increase independent positioning modules within original wireless monitoring terminals, and provide data to the original controller by positioning the serial port of the module [4]. The original mode is still used for the wireless channel. The solution is simple but there are great technical obstacles and the cost is expensive. Due to characteristics of the aging community, the original communication protocol is modified in our project based on original ZigBee's RSSI positioning, so as to realize the transparent transmission of serial data at the same time of transmission of positioning data.

2   The System Framework

2.1   Integration of Detection Equipment and ZigBee Positioning Equipment

In order to integrate the equipment for detection and positioning, there are the two traditional solutions as followed. The first one is to transmit the data of positioning and detection equipments independently. The second one is to transmit the location data to main CPU of the detection equipment through serial port by the positioning module, then return the data to the service end together.

The cost for above two solutions is very high. Aiming at high cost for the traditional solutions, the paper is intended to transform the original communication protocol on the basis of positioning by applying the ZigBee network's own RSSI positioning ability, so as to realize the transparent transmission of the serial data for the positioning module at the same time of transmission of positioning data. We integrate the detection module and positioning wireless ZigBee module. The detection module transmits the detected data to ZigBee module, and then the location information and detection data were transmitted to the service end by modifying the instruction format of ZigBee protocol stack as shown in Fig. 1.

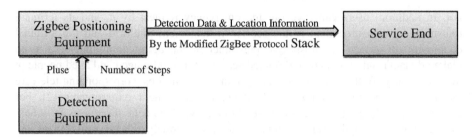

Fig. 1. Integration of detection equipment and ZigBee positioning equipment

2.2 Wireless Sensor Network Framework

As shown in Fig. 2, the framework of the Wireless Sensor Network (WSN) is made up of three ZigBee module nodes [5].

(1) Synergistic point: the only one control node in the entire wireless network. It is responsible for establishing and managing the wireless network. It can transmit data (including instructions) interactively between serial port and service end, and it needs to be in the active state all the time.

(2) Reference node: it has fixed coordinate, responsible for routes and participate in the positioning. Because it is fixed, the power supply is available by power line. In the reference node, the ZigBee module's CC2430 chip is used.

(3) Blind point: the mobile terminal equipment. It is responsible for positioning and transparent transmission of data. As battery is used, the blind node is in the sleeping state in most of time. In the node, the ZigBee module's CC2431 chip is used.

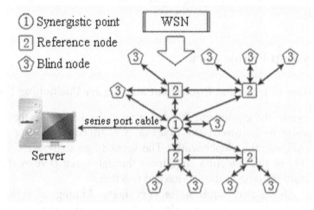

Fig. 2. Framework map of wireless sensor network

ZigBee can support network topology of three communication equipments, i.e., star-based, tree-based and network-based. The system's wireless sensor network is the network based topology can ensure the wireless sensor network is more robust and flexible. Even if some reference nodes fail and quit the network, it doesn't affect the entire wireless network.

The transmit information for all nodes in the wireless sensor network should exchange with service end through synergistic point. Now simply introduce module design of the service end as follows. There are four main modules in the service end: UART, Packet, database and Servlet. The UART module is responsible for task of serial communication and monitoring serial port to take and transmit serial data; the Packet module is responsible for analyzing and packing serial data; the database module is used for interaction of database; and Servlet module is mainly used for page display of Web, in convenience for guardians to check relevant data in real time. The Servlet module may obtain the real-time information from Packet module, and also obtain the historical information from database, as shown in Fig. 3.

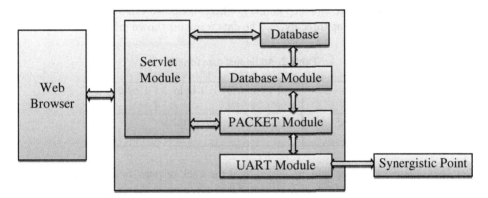

Fig. 3. Module design of the service end

3   Instruction Set Design for ZigBee Protocol Stack

In order to realize data transparent transmission of the location information with the detection information such as pulse and step number, the data in the instructional data format should be modified aiming at ZigBee serial application layer.

3.1   Data Format of Instructions for ZigBee Serial Application Layer

The data format of serial instructions for interaction between the server and synergistic point is shown in Table 1.

Table 1. ZigBee serial instruction data format

SOP	HI_CMD	LO_CMD	D_LEN	DATA	CHECK

SOP: start of packet, and its value is 0x02, representing data packet starting;
HI_CMD-LO_CMD: operating instruction number. The ZigBee instruction distinguishes different instructions by the instruction. For the instruction of

application layer, the instruction number sent out to the synergistic point by the server is 0x0018, and the instruction number sent out by the synergistic point to the server is 0x1018;

D_LEN: data length. If the data length is less than 7, it indicates this frame of data is only a simple ACK frame;

DATA: application data, detailed in section 3.2;

CHECK: check sum; starting from HI-CMD field to the end of DATA field, the entire field perform the exclusive-or operation, and result is CHECK field value.

The design about above application layer instruction format can pack the information such pulse and step number and location information to the service end. So, some supplement data field ADD-DATA need to be added to store the information such as pulse and step number, where, the pulse value takes up one byte, and step number makes up three bytes. The data format is shown in Table 2.

Table 2. Additional data format

1 byte	1 byte	1 byte	1 byte
Pulse	Step number		

Then, these additional data are added to at the back of pure data DATA field, and the data format of the additional ZigBee serial instructions is shown in Table 3.

Table 3. Improved ZigBee serial instruction data format

SOP	HI_CMD	LO_CMD	D_LEN	DATA	ADD_DATA	CHECK

3.2   Design of Application Data Format

In order to understand, DATA and ADD_DAA field in the improved ZigBee serial instruction data format is regarded as a new DATA field, and the following involved application data format DATA fields should be the improved DATA fields.

The DATA domain in the data format of ZigBee serial layer instruction should include the application data. And the specific application data format can be shown in Table 4.

Table 4. Serial instruction application data format

ENDP	LO_ADDR	HI_ADDR	EP	LO_ID	HI_ID	LEN	DATA

ENDP: Mark number of the terminal node, and designated as 0xCB;

LO_ADDR-HI_ADDR: Short address, and 0xFFFF stands for broadcast instruction;

EP : Mark number of the terminal node;

LO_ID-HI_ID : Mark number of the cluster ID;

LEN : Data load length;

DATA : Data load, where, data format changes with different instructions. Only data load format is given for the following instructions.

3.3 Instruction Sets for Reference Node

In addition, the server may receive all kinds of instructions at the same time in ZigBee's networking. For example, when the server configures blind and reference nodes, it is in the state of full duplex. As a result, the returned instructions include not only the configuring information of the reference nodes but also identifying information of the blind nodes or other uncorrelated instructions when the server requests the configuring information of the reference nodes at a certain moment. These instructions will be mixed together, and the server is required to identify them. So, it is necessary to introduce the instruction formats related to nodes in the ZigBee protocol stack. In order to realize transparent transmission of the data, the instruction formats related to the nodes should be modified accordingly.

Configuring Reference Node Instructions

When configuring reference nodes, the server only configures the static coordinates of the reference nodes, where, X stands for horizontal ordinate of the reference nodes, and Y is vertical coordinate of the reference nodes. No return information occurs when configuring reference nodes.

Return Instruction of Configuring Information for Reference Nodes

When the service end program requests or a new reference node joins the network, it will send out its own configuring information to the service end program, and its default coordinate is (0xFF, oxFF). The specific instruction data load format is the same as the configuring reference node instruction.

3.4 Instruction Sets for Blind Node

Configuring Blind Node Instruction

The service end program mainly configures the working parameters of blind nodes, including positioning parameters A and N values, working mode, working time, periodic time, and target node address and terminal number in automatic mode, as well as minimum needed reference node number in positioning. The specific instruction formats are shown in Table 5.

Table 5. Data format for configuring blind node instructions

A	N	MODE	CT	CYCLE	REPaddr	REPEP	MRN

A : Positioning parameter a;

N : Positioning parameter n;

MODE : Working mode for blind node identification, 1 stands for auto mode (auto), and the blind node returns a piece of identification information per second in this mode; 0 stands for poll mode, and when the service end program requests, the blind node can return the identification information, and defaulted as auto mode. What is discussed in the paper is that the work mode for the blind node is automatic.

CT : Collect time, and the working time for the blind node collects RSSI info;

CYCLE : Periodic time for blind node. When CYCLE–CT=SLEEP TIME, most of time for blind node is in sleeping state. By this way, consumption is avoided. Because the blind node is moving and needs to battery supply feed, so it is noted specially avoiding power consumption;

REPaddr : The short address of target node when reporting identification information in the auto mode;

REPEP : The target node Endpoint when reporting identification information;

MRN : Min ref nodes, where the minimum needed reference node number should be positioned correctly.

Return Instruction Configuring Information for Blind Node

It is required to return the blind node configuring information only when the service end program requests. The specific instruction data load format is the same as the instruction format configuring blind node as shown in Table 5

Response Instruction for the Blind Node Identification Information

As the blind nodes discussed in the paper are in the auto mode, the blind nodes can send out the identification information to the server per second. The instruction data load format for the identification information is shown in Table 6.

Table 6. Instruction data load format for the blind node return identification information

STAT	X	Y	NORN	Raddr	RX	RY	RRSSI

STAT : Blind node status, where 1 stands for if there is no enough reference node to position, the following X and Y will be 0; 0 stands for the successful positioning;

X : x coordinate to identify blind node;

Y : y coordinate to identify blind node;

NORN : Num of ref node, and number of the reference nodes;

Raddr : Short address for the reference nodes;

RX : x coordinate information returned by the reference nodes;
RY : y coordinate information returned by the reference nodes;
RRSSI : RSSI information returned by the reference nodes.

Above identification information instruction format only includes the location information of blind nodes and not includes the information such as pulse and step number. Thus, the instruction for the improved identification information should be added finally with two fields, which are pulse value (PULSE) and step number (STEP). The specific format is shown in Table 7.

Table 7. Instruction format of identification information returned by the improved blind nodes

STAT	X	Y	NORN	Raddr	RX	RY	RRSSI	PULSE	STEP

4   Conclusion

The method for equipment integration provides the new WSN integrated model for data detection and locating. Some application level protocols based stack V1.4.3 is modified. We have proposed the integrated router module for ZigBee Locating and transparent transmission serial port package. But the prototype only provide the basic ZigBee application level wireless communication, some modified instruction format have not enough robust, securities and flexibility. Next, some works must be done, such as configuration for short address of ZigBee coordinator and router, change the baud of router and coordinator separately, and so on.

Acknowledgements. This work is partly supported the Science Foundation of Zhejiang Province under Grand No. 2011C33015 and 2010R50009, and the Major Projects on Control and Rectification of Water Body Pollution of China (No. 2009ZX07424-001).

References

1. Chen, X., Hou, H., Wu, M., Huo, M.: Wrist wearable physiological signal detection equipment with biochemical materials. Advanced Materials Research 459, 293–297 (2012)
2. Chai, J.: Patient Positioning System in Hospital Based on Zigbee. In: 2011 International Conference on Intelligent Computation and Bio-Medical Instrumentation (ICBMI), pp. 159–162 (2011)
3. Gutierrez, R., Fernandez, S., Jesus Garcia, J., Carlos Garcia, J., Marnane, L.: Monitoring vital signs and location of patients by using ZigBee wireless sensor networks. In: 2011 IEEE Sensors, pp. 1221–1224 (2011)
4. Tso-Cho, C.: Fall detection and location using ZigBee sensor network. In: 2011 Cross Strait Quad-Regional Radio Science and Wireless Technology Conference (CSQRWC), vol. 2, pp. 937–941 (2011)
5. Li, X.: RSS-Based Location Estimation with Unknown Pathloss Model. IEEE Transactions on Wireless Communications 5, 3626–3633 (2006)

Power Line Short Circuit Fault Orientation System Based on Wireless Sensor Network

Lu Cao, Junjie Yang, Xiangwen Wang, and Wei Jiang

ShangHai University of Electric Power, 200090, Shanghai, China
caolu1988@126.com, iamyjj@163.com

Abstract. The article introduces the advantages and features of wireless sensor network used in power line short circuit fault localization, and puts forward the plan of power line short circuit fault localization that based on wireless sensor network, also it designs the topology of wireless sensor note and wireless sensor network.

Keywords: wireless sensor network, sensor note, power grid line fault monitoring.

1 Introduction

The construction of smart grid puts forward higher requirements to the reliability of the grid lines.When there are some faults occur on the grid lines,it has become the hot spot of the research of the smart grid that how to fast and accurate find and locate the fault point.At present,there are many technology researches achivements on the grid lines short circuit fault location,but most of them are according to 110KV and above transmission lines,there are very little researches on the low voltage distribution net-work.The reason is that high voltage grid use effective neutral grouding methed,which belongs to large current grouding system,the circuit structure is simple,the fault signal is obvious,and it is easy to discriminant and extract. 35 kV, 66 kV medium voltage distribution network use the uneffective neutral grounding way, the fault signal is relatively weak when the one-phase fault earthing occurs,at present there are not good fault location metheds[1].Usually the power network line fault location needs adopt to the physical method to apply a signal to the grid lines,the signal reflects and refracts at the fault point,it can calculate the accurate results through analysis of the reflected signal,this communication methed generally use the power line carrier and optical communications, But this kind of traditional cable monitoring network wiring and engineering line undesirable,easy to be damaged,cannot move.In some cases,such as complex working place,uncertainly working place,not enough original obligate port,sudden accident scence,the application is limited in some degree.In recent years, the progress of the ZigBee[2] wireless sensor network technology puts forward a new solution for the grid short circuit fault monitoring.The commonly used ZigBee wire-less sensor network technology is a kind of low distance、 low complexity、 low power consumption 、 low rate、 low costs of the two-way wireless communication

J. Lei et al. (Eds.): NCIS 2012, CCIS 345, pp. 722–730, 2012.
© Springer-Verlag Berlin Heidelberg 2012

technology,it is mainly used for short distance、 low power consumption and low rate electronic equipments data transmission and application of transmiss typical periodic data、 intermittent data and low reaction time data. It integrates information acquisition, data processing and wireless communications, and other functions ,which can quickly and reliably acquist weak fault signal,and fast and accurately judge the fault location.Wireless sensor network as a large-scale self-organised network,it can ensure users in any place send commands to any equipment with wireless communication inererace, at the same time wireless sensor network have the characteristics of low energy consumption,making wireless sensor networ aplly in the grid line fault possible.Therefore,it gets more and more attention in the medium voltage distribution network fault location.

This paper applies ZigBee wireless sensor network technology into grid line short circuit fault analysis,and puts forward a grid line short circuit fault orientation system which based on the technology,then design and introduce each part.

2 The Grid Line Short Circuit Fault Orientation System Structure Based on Wireless Sensor Network

The grid line short circuit fault orientation system structure schematic diagram based on wireless sensor network is shown as figure 1.This program divides the system structure into three parts,they are respectively grid line fault signal acquisition system,wireless sensor communication network and monitoring center control system.

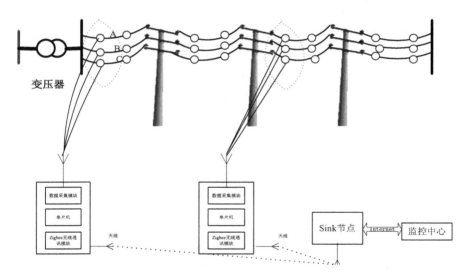

Fig. 1. The grid line short circuit fault orientation system structure schematic diagram based on wireless sensor network

In this system,the wireless sensor nodes on the grid lines can perceive the current through the nodes real-time through the current sensor,and prosess the current signal,then transfer useful information into the monitoring center through the communication module based on ZigBee technology,the monitoring center then determines the type and the location of the fault by analysising the current amplitude changes through each node and adjacent nodes.

2.1   The Fault Signal Acquisition Module

In this scheme, to avoid node battery energy loss too fast,at the same time to ensure the accuracy of the signal, the rapidity, synchronicity and reliability,we decorate a node for every 100 meters.Wireless sensor node as the test information carrier, it can not only percept of the change of the current flows through the nodes,also it can process acquisited current signal,then extracts useful data,and at the same time transfer the processed data.

This system analysises the current flowed through the nodes to analysis the type of the short circuit fault,if it is two phase fault,the current signal of the node before the fault point will much higher than that of the node after the fault point in the fault phase;if it is single phase fault, the current signal of the node before the fault point will much higher than that of the node in other two phases.

2.2   Wireless Sensor Communication Network

In order to realize the current signal realiable transmission,this system uses the IEEE 802.15.4/ZigBee agreement based on the wireless sensor network,the nodes laid on the grid line are mainly divided into 3 categories: the first kind is common information collection node,mainly acquisition the current signal of the nodes and wireless transfer,etc;the other one is a routing,trunk relay node,mainly complete relay each acquisition sensor,in order to extend the transmission distance;the last one is the Sink gathering node,which is usede to complete coordinating function and gather and process all nodes' information from all the monitoring area,then send the information to the background monitoring center though Internet.

The wireless network based on the ZigBee technology is a self-organizing network,to a large extent ,the formation and operation of wireless network is finished independent by several network node,which does not need to undertake artificial configuration.There are three main network topology structure: Star network topology structure, net form network topology structure, tree form network topology structure[3].

2.3   Monitoring Center Control System

The monitoring center is mainly consist of computer and analysis software component.The monitoring center computer analysises the received information from the Sink nodes real time,if the fault information,then the system need confirm the fault position 、 the fault line 、 the fault tower 、 the fault type 、 and the voltage,current,phase,frequency,etc,and then store all the fault information into database,finally,send the information to the power system management personnel on the phone by GPRS,guarantee the fault information transission in real time. This module fault display function can display the fault position on the monitor view with red reverse phase,and display the number of the power tower and phase in the thumbnail of the remark column as character.If the information is useless,it will be regarded as invalid information, , this information is only saved in already receiving information data table, no such information for secondary processing.

3   Short Circuit Fault Orientation

The most common power system fault is the grid line short circuit fault,short circuit faults are divided into interphase short circuit and single phase grounding short circuit.In view of these two short circuit fault,we adopt the following detection positioning method.[4]

3.1   Two Phase Short Circuit Fault Orientation

As shown in figure 2,the black dots are the wireless sensor nodes installed in power transmission line,the power transmission direction from left to right.T stands for industrial frequency cycle,M stands for sampling frequency,i(t) stands for the current samples at moment t, Sampling get i(t), i (t-(M-1) t) according to advanced first out way storage. Because the relay protection unit has disconnect the circuit breaker,that is when the current value of a power frequency sampling period is zero.it can judge faults occure at this time.

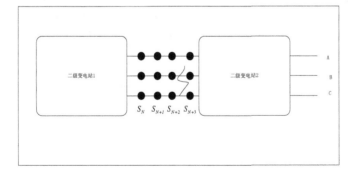

Fig. 2. Wireless sensor node involved in positioning level 2 substation two phase short-circuit fault schemes

Assume that between the level 2 Substation Secondary Substation 1 and level 2 Substation Secondary Substation 2,phase B and phase C short circuit fault occurred,as is shown in figure 2. P_{sk}(P=A,B,C;k=N,N+1,N+2,N+3)represents the wireless sensor notes at position S_k in phase P. i(P_{sk}) represents the sampling current of wireless sensor note P_{sk}.Then we can get

$$\begin{cases} i\left(B_{S_{N+2}}\right) \gg i\left(A_{S_{N+2}}\right) \\ i\left(C_{S_{N+2}}\right) \gg i\left(A_{S_{N+2}}\right) \\ i\left(B_{S_{N+2}}\right) \gg i\left(B_{S_{N+3}}\right) \\ i\left(C_{S_{N+2}}\right) \gg i\left(C_{S_{N+3}}\right) \end{cases} \tag{1}$$

At the same time, the substation 1 supervisor section sampling current and substation the subordinate section 2 sampling current approximately equal.From the equations (1) we can position the faulty section between the node S_{N+2} and the node S_{N+3} in phase B and phase C.The fault orientation accuracy is related to the configuration interval of nodes.We use ε represents repeatability,R represents the configuration interval of nodes,we can get

$$\varepsilon \ll R \tag{2}$$

3.2   Single Phase Short Circuit Fault Orientation

The zero sequence equivalent network as shown in figure 3 when a single-phase short circuit occurs in grid lines. In the figure switch K decided to network belongs to neutral grounding system or not by the coil of arc extinction grounding system. The black dots are the wireless sensor nodes installed in power transmission line.Line of wireless sensor node is the fault line.The current of single phase grounding fault is lower than that of two-phase short circuit fault,especially the system with coil of arc extinction.Then we can determine the fault point by comparing the fault current along to the fault line.Suppose phase A grounding fault occurs between node 1 and 2,the current value of the fault point on the left is always larger than that of the fault point on the right, P_j represents the wireless sensor node at position j in phase P. $i_x(P_j)$ represents the sampling current of sensor node P_j before fault. $i_y(P_j)$ represents the sampling current of sensor node P_j when the fault occur.α represents the phase angle of the current before fault and fault occur,we can get the value of the fault current $i(P_j)$:

$$i(P_j) = \sqrt{i_x^2(P_j) + i_y^2(P_j) - 2i_x(P_j)i_y(P_j)\cos\alpha} \tag{3}$$

Thus,we can get the different value of different nodes in phase A:

$$\begin{cases} \Delta(A_1, A_2) = |i(A_1) - (iA_2)| \\ \Delta(A_2, A_3) = |i(A_2) - i(A_3)| \end{cases} \tag{4}$$

When fault occurs in phase A:

$$\begin{cases} \Delta(A_2, A_3) \approx \Delta(B_2, B_3) \approx \Delta(C_2, C_3) \\ \Delta(A_1, A_2) \geq \Delta(B_1, B_2) \\ \Delta(A_1, A_2) \geq \Delta(C_1, C_2) \end{cases} \tag{5}$$

From equations (5)we can define the fault occurs between node 1 and 2.

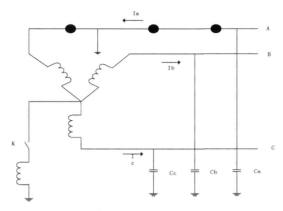

Fig. 3. Single-phase grounding fault orientation scheme

4 Wireless Sensor Network Design

Communication part is an important part of this system, so we must ensure the accuracy and speed of communication, synchronicity and reliability.

In order to reduce the sensor node energy loss,this system divides the urban distribution network into several monitoring areas,in every area, a single power tower detection range is regard as a small network model,in this model the sensor nodes use simple star networking method;in every area the power tower nodes use chain networking method to transfer its data into the Sink node through chain of data networking method,then send the monitor data through Internet into monitoring center from Sink nodes,and then analysis the fault type and position by means of software.However, for the whole city distribution network topology need to be adopted by the different area connection,suppose each area is a cluster,so we should connect adjacent clusters that achieve the long distance of the linear network communication, Connection scheme as shown in figure 4.

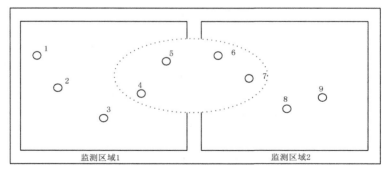

Fig. 4. The adjacent area network scheme

For monitoring area 1 (node 1-5) and monitoring area 2 (node 6-9) respectively set up a corresponding cluster,adopt the star nerwork structure,for the overall monitoring area 3,node 4-7 form a new network to constitute a long distance of linear network communication. Considering the development cost and node rf communications system stability,the system uses wireless sensor node with Xbee module[5] which produced by MaxStream company and compatible with ZigBee, Freescale MCl319x chipset with as the core to construct wireless sensor network. Xbee module integration conform with the standards of the agreement ZigBee rf transceiver and microprocessors,which has advantages of long distance communication、 strong anti-interference、 network flexible、 reliable and steady performance. This module USES a 3.3 V power supply, send power for 100 mW; the transmission distance of indoor and outdoor respectively for 300 m and 1500 m, Xbee Pro modules of the transmission distance is farther;receive high sensitivity;good network character.

Xbee module intergrations a UART interface—DIN and DOUT, modules can be through the UART interface directly link with the controller UART interface ,its hardware interface is simple and practical.In the system,communication module uses 51 single-chip microcomputer to control, Xbee module in this part and single-chip microcomputer interface circuit shown as shown in figure 5,RXD,TXD represent MCU pins.

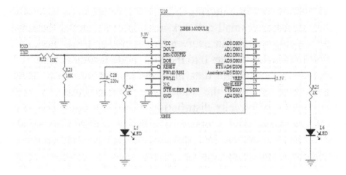

Fig. 5. Xbee module and single-chip microcomputer interface scheme

The communication process between two Xbee module as shown in figure 6.There are send buffer(RFTX) and receive buffer(RFRX) in Xbee module. In figure 7 we can see .The data ready to send is from the MCU serial part,through the DIN pins into module,and stored in DI buffer,finally into send buffer waiting to send;the data to receive is from the antenna,receive by the receivebuffer,finally into DO buffer,and read by MCU.The two buffer data arrive at the same time,but, Only 100 bytes each buffer temporarily stopped place.Usually,data from send buffer through antenna to another Xbee module;and receive buffer transfer data through serial port to host.In order to avoid the receive buffer overflow problem because of large data input,we use CTS to suppress data communication.

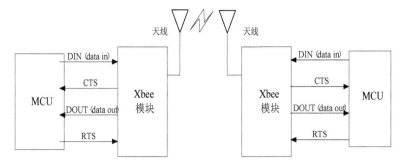

Fig. 6. The communication process between two Xbee module

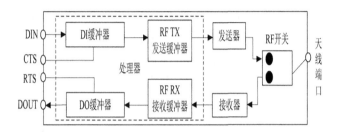

Fig. 7. The Xbee UART internal data control process

5   Conclution

This paper first introduce the advantage of apllying the wireless sensor network in grid line fault orientation,and then put forward a system based on wireless sensor network. This program is mainly consist of three parts,they are respectively grid line fault signal acquisition system,wireless sensor communication network and monitoring center control system,then plan and introduce each module respectively,we use a kind of common single-phase grounding fault and alternate phase fault oreintation principle.Finally introduce the design of the wireless sensor network.

Wireless network is inevitable result of the development of communication technology，especially in recent years,communication、computer、microelectronics technology develop rapidly,lay a solid foundation for wireless sensor network and accelerating the process.The wireless sensor network combine with data accquisition、process、wireless communication，which greatly expand the cognitive and processing ability of electric power system,extensive configuration node can let us understand the power system process details more subtle.At the same time,because the wireless sensor network is cheap、easily network、low power loss and comprehensive many new technology,such as the node low-power sensor technology, embedded technology, wireless network technology ,etc,it has been widely used in medical care、industry、transportation areas.

Acknowledgement. This paper was supported by Shanghai Technology Innovation Project (10110502200,11510500900), Innovation Program of Shanghai Municipal Education Commission (09ZZ185,09YZ337,12ZZ176), Project of Science and Technology Commission of Shanghai Municipality(10PJ1404500), and Leading Academic Discipline Project of Shanghai Municipal Education Commission(J51303).

References

[1] Huang, X., Liu, P., Miao, S., et al.: Applicationof sensor networks in power monitoring system. Automation of Electric Power Systems 31(7), 99–103 (2007)

[2] Zhao, J., Li, Y., Xu, C.: Introduction of ZigBee technology. Power System Communication 27(165), 54–56 (2006)

[3] Hnang, X.Y., Lju, P.: A discrete distributed topology—control algorithm of wireless sensor network. In: 3rd Annual International Conference on Mobile and UbiquitousSysten Networking and Services, San Jose, pp. 17–21 (2006)

[4] Xu, B., Li, T., Xue, Y.: Intelligent distribution network and power distribution automation. Automation of Power Systems 33(17), 38–41 (2009)

[5] Introduction of Xbee,
http://wenku.baidu.com/view/ce490222aaea998fcc220e90.html

Multidimensional LDPC for the Reconciliation of the Continuous Variables Quantum Key Distribution System[*]

Chun-Hui Huang

College of Physics and Information Engineering, Fuzhou University, Fuzhou 350108, PRC
hchfzu@163.com

Abstract. Reconciliation is one of the most important technology in continuous variables quantum key distribution. In this paper, we implement multidimensional reconciliation, which can realize reconciliation without quantizing continuous variables, that greatly reduces the computational complexity of continuous variable reconciliation. Applying a linear group code of LDPC, the encoding and decoding was simple and has the performance of near to shannon's limit. LDPC is used in multidimensional reconciliation algorithm for correction. The results show that the key error rate approaches zero when noise-signal ratio comes to 5.2dB..

Keywords: reconciliation, continuous-variable quantum key, multidimensional LDPC code.

1   Introduction

Most quantum key distribution (QKD) protocols encode information on discrete variables such as the phase or the polarization of single photons and are currently facing technological challenges, especially the performance limits of photodetectors in terms of speed and efficiency in the single-photon regime. The continuous variable QKD (CV-QKD) [1,2], due to its strong signal, suitable for long distance transmission and the advantages of high rate of key generation, has the attention of the people. CV-QKD is facing technology challenges of the classical information post-processing, more exactly on the reconciliation [3]. In QKD system, Alice converts the key words into quantum states, and transmit them to Bob through the quantum channel, Bob measures quantum states and recoveries them to the classic information. Then Alice and Bob carry out classic error correction by public classic channel. The processing is said reconciliation.

Because of the variables in CV-QKD are continuous variation, the reconciliation of QKD can't be directly used to the CV-QKD, it need to be discretized into continuous variables. Assche proposed the slice reconciliation method [4], which was designed for Gaussian distribution of continuous variables, but the calculation method

---

[*] This work was supported by the National Natural Science Foundation of China under Grant No. 61177072.

© Springer-Verlag Berlin Heidelberg 2012

is too complex, which procedure involved in the interval differentiate, and each interval differentiate often needs to carry multi-time iteration, every iterative process needed to calculate a double integral, speed very slowly. Leverrier propose firstly multidimensional (MD) reconciliation theory [5], the key advantage of the MD reconciliation is continuous variables without discretization. However Leverrier mainly elaborated in the theory of information process, but not implemented the concrete application. In this paper, we make a further study of this algorithm, and propose the specific implementation procedure which is LDPC code used in MD reconciliation to realize error correction. The simulation analysis shows that our scheme is feasible and efficient.

2   Multidimensional Reconciliation Algorithm

2.1   General Reconciliation Method

Wyner first proposed the method of side informational reconciliation, the basic setups are: Assume two correlated random variables U and X, and white noise ε. Alice creates a code word $U \in C$ randomly, then she send ($X - U$), as a side information, to Bob. Alternative Bob distillates his information and has $X + \varepsilon$, furtherly calculated $U + \varepsilon$ and decoded the codes U [6]. The implementation is presented as figure 1.

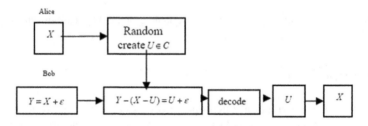

Fig. 1. A general reconciliation method

2.2   M Operator

Similar to a general reconciliation scheme, the MD reconciliation also used a side information from original key to correct the error codes. A key work is to find a special side information for the continuous variables without quantitative reconci-liation. In MD reconciliation scheme, we can construct a M operator that satisfying above side information condition. We state the procedure as follow:

Theorem 1. [3] If there exists a continuous operator $M : S^{n-1} \times S^{n-1} \to O_n$ $(x, y) \mapsto M(x, y)$, such that $M(x, y) \cdot x = y$. for all $x, y \in S^{n-1}$, then $n = 1, 2, 4, or 8$.

It was said that if Alice chooses randomly one vertices u on the canonical cube of R^n and send it to Bob, Bob mapp x to u by the orthogonal transformation $M(x, u)$. This transformation defines the cube QX. Alice has chosen u among an appropriate binary code C, then Bob can recover u from the knowledge of y

and $M(x,u)$. There are many such mappings M, but one needs a mapping easy to describe and to compute.

Unfortunately, such an orthogonal transformation leaks some information about x and u because the distribution of x given by $M(x,u)$ is not uniform for n > 2 due to the phenomenon of the concentration of the measurement for spheres in dimensions n > 2, therefore cannot be used by Alice in a QKD protocol[7]. If use u replace y, we have :

$$M(x,u) \cdot x = u \tag{1}$$

$$M(x,u) \cdot y = u' \tag{2}$$

If making x, u, y corresponding to Alice's variables, choice of code words and Bob's variables, respectively. When Bob knows M operator, he can apply formula (2) to decode a code words $u' = u + \varepsilon$ with the noise, and obtain the result that is corresponding to the correct code words u. Bob use the inverse function of the code words u, again using formula (3), Bob can obtain the data same as Alice's value x:

$$x = M^{-1}(x,u) \cdot u \tag{3}$$

Theorem 2. [3] $M(x,y) = \sum_{i=1...n} \alpha_i(x,y) A_i$ With $\alpha_i(x,y) = (A_i x | y)$ is a continuous mapping from $S^{n-1} \times S^{n-1}$ to $O(n)$, such that $M(x,y) \cdot x = y$.

Theorem 2 is a coset formula of M operator. Assuming A_i is a $n \times n$ matrix, A_i has n components which form a orthogonal group $A_n = (A_1, ..., A_n)$. Leverrier gave the examples of these families. For $i, j > 1$, A_i and A_j satisfy the anti-commutation property $\{A_i, A_j\} = -2\delta_{i,j} 1_n$. The $(A_1 x, A_2 x, ..., A_n x)$ is an orthogonal basis of R^n for any $x, y \in S^{n-1}$, $(\alpha_1(x,y), ..., \alpha_n(x,y))$ is coordinates of y in the orthogonal basis $(A_1 x, A_2 x, ..., A_n x)$. So that $M(x,y) \cdot x = y$. Therefore, $(\alpha_1(x,y), ..., \alpha_n(x,y))$ is sufficient to describe $M(x,u)$ operator. If use u replace y, then we obtain a M operator replace side information:

$$M(x,u) = \sum_{i=1...n} \alpha_i(x,u) A_i \tag{4}$$

In the QKD protocol, Alice chooses randomly u in a finite code and gives the value of $\alpha(x,u)$ to Bob, then Bob is able to compute $M(x,u) \cdot y$ which is a noisy version of u'. One should note that the final noise is just a "rotated" version of the Bob's noise on x: in particular, both noises are Gaussian with the same variance,.and the Gaussian distribution of the noise is invariant under orthogonal transformations. To solve a system of linear equations, we selected the gaussian elimination method; the computation complexity is moderate, compared with other methods and guarantees the numerical stability. The procedure is described as follow:

```
function b = mat_inv2(a)
% Find dimensions of input matrix
[r,c] = size(a);
% If input matrix is not square, stop function
if [r ~= c
disp('Only Square Matrices, please')
    b = [];
    return ];
% Target identity matrix to be transformed into the output
% inverse matrix
b = eye(r);
%The following code actually performs the matrix inversion
for [j = 1 : r
for [i = j : r
    if [a(i,j) ~= 0
        for [k = 1 : r
            s = a(j,k); a(j,k) = a(i,k); a(i,k) = s;
            s = b(j,k); b(j,k) = b(i,k); b(i,k) = s; ];

        t = 1/a(j,j);
        for [k = 1 : r
            a(j,k) = t * a(j,k);
            b(j,k) = t * b(j,k); ];
        for [L = 1 : r
            if [L ~= j
                t = -a(L,j);
                for [k = 1 : r
                    a(L,k) = a(L,k) + t * a(j,k);
                    b(L,k) = b(L,k) + t * b(j,k); ];];];];
    break
    ]
% Display warning if a row full of zeros is found
    if [a(i,j) == 0
        disp('Warning: Singular Matrix')
        b = 'error';
        return ] ]
```

Fig. 2. Flow chart of multi-dimension reconciliation

1. Write the augmented matrix of the system.

2. Use row operations to transform the augmented matrix in the form described below, which is called the reduced row echelon form (RREF).

(a) The rows (if any) consisting entirely of zeros are grouped together at the bottom of the matrix.

(b) In each row that does not consist entirely of zeros, the leftmost nonzero element is a 1 (called a leading 1 or a pivot).

(c) Each column that contains a leading 1 has zeros in all other entries.

(d) The leading 1 in any row is to the left of any leading 1's in the rows below it.

3. Stop process in step 2 if you obtain a row whose elements are all zeros except the last one on the right. In that case, the system is inconsistent and has no solutions. Otherwise, finish step 2 and read the solutions of the system from the final matrix.

Note: When doing step 2, row operations can be performed in any order. Try to choose row operations so that as few fractions as possible are carried through the computation.

3   Application LDPC Code to MD Reconciliation

LDPC code [9] can be described as one type of sparse check-up matrix or binary chart of the definition of the linear group code, the first discovered by Gallager. LDPC code has simply describe, low complexity of decode, and it is suitable for high-speed parallel etc. In theory, the reconciliation scheme based on LDPC code can achieve optimal performance.

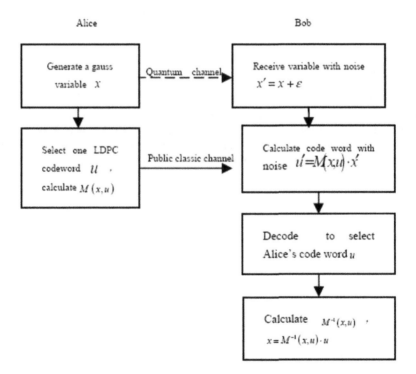

Fig. 3. Flow chart of MD reconciliation

LDPC code according to deliver the message of the different decoding, divided into hard decision decoding and soft decision decode. The former in decoding process transfer message is bit, the latter transmission is a posteriori probability confidence.

We improved algorithm based on the latter-logarithm likelihood BP decoding algorithm [9,10]. The figure 3 shows the flow chart of MD reconciliation Based on the LDPC scheme, the steps are discribed as follow:

1. Alice sent a bunch of original signal (key) with a gaussian distribution to Bob, Bob then received the signal with noise. Both of them treated their continuous variables as multidimensional vector and normalization.

2. Alice randomly chooses a LDPC code $u \in S^{n-1}$ as code words, calculated $M(x,u)$, and sent it to Bob as a side information.

3. Using $M(x,u)$, Bob computed $M(x,u) \cdot y = u'$, u' is code words with the noise. The LDPC logarithm-likelihood of BP algorithm used to calculated the primary code words u.

4. Bob judge the correct or not. If code words u was a correct decode, Bob take the next step. Otherwise the communication is invalid, turned back to the first step reconciliated the next group data.

5. Bob solution the inverse operator of $M(x,u)$, applying $x = M^{-1}(x,u) \cdot u$ to calculated x same as Alice's value. After privacy amplified x, Alice and Bob share x as final key.

4   Simulation Results

In the simulation, generated random numbers accuracy to 10^{-6}; because the elements of matrix were floating random values, and account to the precision of the computer. We calculated the element values of the inverse operator in 10^{-5}, the key was accuracy to 10^{-4} now. By changing the signal-to-noise ratio, adjust the iteration times of decode, statistical error rates. The error correction performance of key as shown in figure 4 .

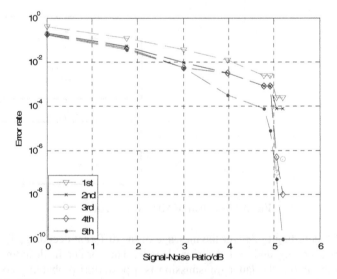

Fig. 4. The MD reconciliation error correction algorithm performance based on LDPC code

The iterative times given by 1~5 times, the performance curve by figure known that the error rate of key could be reduced when the iteration times was increased. In data test process, when iteration times greater than 5 times, the performance improvement to decode is not significant. And increases the decoding iteration times will surely increase decode delay, the comprehensive consideration, and set the iteration times for 5 times.

For a certain iteration times, as increasing of the signal-to-noise ratio, the lower of the error rate. Observe the curves of iteration times$\leq$5: We known that when SNR is less than 1 dB, the key error rates began to greater than 10^{-1}; When the signal-to-noise ratio greater than 5.2 dB, error rate near 0.

5   Conclusions

This paper present one CV-QKD reconciliation scheme which compact a complicated process. The reconciliation was a simple, fast method based on the multidimensional LDPC. The algorithm implemented a error correction, dosen't need to discrete the continuous variable, only by constructing a special kind of side information, combined with LDPC. The MD reconciliation has been analyzed, including construct the operator of side information, solves the inverse operator; Then proposed MD reconciliation based LDPC algorithm, finally simulating this scheme and analysis quantum key ratio. The simulation results show that, when the signal-to-noise ratio larger than 5.2 dB, tending to zero error.

Using the MD reconciliation scheme LDPC substitute the complex quantitative process, the computation complexity is moderate, and LDPC can effectively achieve the continuous variables quantum key.

Acknowledgements. The author thanks Lin Li-ping and Zheng Ping-yin for helpful discussions. He also acknowledges support from the National Natural Science Foundation of China (NSFC project 61177072).

References

1. Mehrdads, Sharbaf: Quantum cryptography: a new generation of the information technology security system. The Information Technology: New Generations 27-29, 1644–1648 (2009)
2. Ma, R.: Quantum cryptography communication, pp. 120–135. Science Press, Beijing (2006)
3. Grosshans, F., Grangier, P.: Continuous Variable-Quantum Cryptography Coherent States. Put Physical Review 88(5), 579021–579024 (2002)
4. Van Assche, G., Cardinal, J., Cerf, N.J.: Reconciliation of the quantum Gaussian distributed a key specific. IEEE 50(2), 394–400 (2002)
5. Leverrier, A., Alleaume, R., Boutros, J.: Multidimensional reconciliation for a continuous-variable quantum key distribution. In: IEEE International Symposium on Information Theory, July 6-11, pp. 1020–1024 (2008)

6. Liveris, A.D., Xiong, Z., Georghiades, C.N.: Compression of binary sources with side information at the decoder using LDPC codes. IEEE Communication Letters 6, 440–442 (2002)
7. Adans, J.: Vector fields on spheres. Annals of Math. 75, 603–632 (1962)
8. Li, Q.-Y., Wang, N.-C., Yu, D.-Y.: Numerical analysis, pp. 165–178. Tsinghua University Press, Beijing (2001)
9. Lu, W.-M.: Research on LDPC Codes and Applications.: [Ph.D. Thesis]. Huazhong University of science and technology, Wuhan (2006)
10. Yuan, D.-F., Zhang, H.-G., et al.: LDPC code theory and application, pp. 72–80. People's posts and telecommunications press, Beijing (2008)

A New Hybrid Semantic Similarity Measure Based on WordNet[*]

Lingling Meng[1], Junzhong Gu[2], and Zili Zhou[3]

[1] Computer Science and Technology Department, Department of Educational Information Technology, East China Normal University, Shanghai, 200062, China
[2] Computer Science and Technology Department, East China Normal University, Shanghai, 200062, China
[3] College of Physics and Engineering, Qufu Normal University, Qufu, 273165, China
{mengzero,zlzhou999}@163.com,
jzgu@ica.stc.sh.cn,

Abstract. Semantic similarity between words is a general issue in many applications, such as word sense disambiguation, information extraction, ontology construction and so on. Accurate measurement of semantic similarity between words is crucial. It is necessary to design accurate methods for improving the performance of the bulk of applications relying on it. The paper presents a new hybrid method based on WordNet for measuring word sense similarity. Different from related works, both information content and path have been taken into considerate. We evaluate the new measure on the data set of Rubenstein and Goodenough. Experiments show that the coefficient of our proposed measure with human judgment is 0.8817, which demonstrates that the new measure significantly outperformed than related works.

Keywords: hybrid measure, semantic similarity, information content, WordNet.

1   Introduction

Accessing semantic similarity is a hot topic for many years in many research areas such as Linguistics, Cognitive Science, and Artificial Intelligence. It has shown its talents in word sense disambiguation [1], information extraction [2], semantic annotation, summarization [3], question answering [4], and so on. Therefore it is mandatory to design accurate methods for improving the performance of the bulk of applications relying on it. Some measures have been proposed, which can be classified into two categories on the basis of the source of information they exploit. One is path based measures, which assess semantic similarity by counting the number of edges separating two concepts. The methods are intuitive, but they suffer from the limitation of that ontology between general concepts and that between specific ones have the same

---

[*] The work in the paper was supported by Shanghai Scientific Development Foundation (Grant No. 11530700300) and Shandong Excellent Young Scientist Award Fund (Grant No. BS2010DX012).

J. Lei et al. (Eds.): NCIS 2012, CCIS 345, pp. 739–744, 2012.
© Springer-Verlag Berlin Heidelberg 2012

interpretation. The other is Information Content(IC) based measures, which exploit the notion of Information Content (IC) of concepts defined as a measure. The methods are simple, but they can't distinguish different concepts pairs. The purpose of this paper is to solve the shortcomings of existing approaches. Hence a new model is presented, which combines information content and paths separating concepts. Experiments demonstrate that our new method significantly outperformed related works.

The rest of the paper is as follows: we discuss related works of word sense similarity measure in section 2. In Section 3 a novel semantic similarity measure based on WordNet is proposed. The performance of our measure is evaluated and compared to others in Section 4. Conclusion and future work are described in Section 5.

2   Related Work

The measures in the following are all based on WordNet. WordNet is the product of a research project at Princeton University which has attempted to model the lexical knowledge of a native speaker of English [5]. In WordNet concepts are represented by a synonym set or synset and organized into taxonomic hierarchies via a variety of semantic relations. In the taxonomy the deeper concept is more specific and the upper concept is more abstract. These semantic relations for nouns include hyponym/hypernym (is-a), part meronym/part holonym (part-of), member meronym/member holonym (member-of), substance meronym/substance holonym (substance-of) and so on. Hyponym/hypernym (is-a) is the most common relations. Fig.1 illustrates a fragment of is-a hierarchy in WordNet.

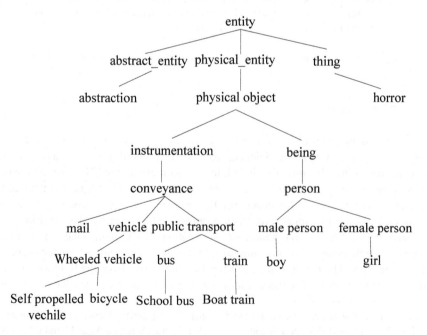

Fig. 1. A fragment is-a hierarchy taxonomy in WordNet

In this paper, we are only concerned about the similarity measure based on nouns and is-a relations of WordNet. Generally the typical measure based on WordNet can be grouped into two categories: path-based approaches and information-based approaches. Next, we will introduce these measures briefly.

Definition of related concept in the following measures as follows :

(1) len(c_i,c_j): the length of the shortest path from synset c_i to synset c_j in WordNet.
(2) lso(c_i,c_j): the most specific common subsumer of c_i and c_j
(3) depth(c_i): the length of the path to synset c_i from the global root entity.
(4) deep_max: the max depth(c_i) of the taxonomy
(5) hypo(c): the number of hyponyms for a given concept c.
(6) node_max: the maximum number of concepts that exist in the taxonomy.

2.1   Path Based Measures

Wu and Palmer assumed that the similarity between two concepts is the function of path length and depth [6].

$$sim_{W\&P}(c_1,c_2) = \frac{2*depth(lso(c_1,c_2))}{len(c_1,c_2)+2*depth(lso((c_1,c_2))} \tag{1}$$

Leakcock and Chodorow took the maximum depth of taxonomy into account and proposed the following measure [7]:

$$sim_{L\&C}(c_1,c_2) = -\log\frac{len(c_1,c_2)}{2*deep\_max} \tag{2}$$

2.2   Information Content Based Measures

Information content based measures assumed that each concept includes much information in WordNet. The more common information two concepts share, the more similar the concepts are. In 1995 Resnik proposed information content based similarity measure [8]. It is based on the assumption that for two given concepts, similarity is depended on the information content that subsumes them in the taxonomy.

$$sim_{Resnik}(c_1,c_2) = -\log p(lso(c_1,c_2)) = IC(lso(c_1,c_2)) \tag{3}$$

We can see that the values only rely on concept pairs' lowest subsumer in the taxonomy. Lin and Jiang took the IC of compared concepts into account respectively and proposed another two methods for similarity measure from different view [9]:

$$sim_{Lin}(c_1,c_2) = \frac{2*IC(lso(c_1,c_2)))}{IC\ (c_1)+IC\ (c_2)} \tag{4}$$

$$dis_{Jiang}(c_1, c_2) = (IC(c_1) + IC(c_2)) - 2IC(lso(c_1, c_2)) \tag{5}$$

Jiang calculated semantic distance to obtain semantic similarity [10]. Semantic simi-larity is the opposite of the distance.

It is noted that the IC is crucial. One commonly used measure was proposed by Nuno, which is hyponyms-based. It assumed that in WordNet a concept with more hyponyms expresses less information than the concepts with less ones, which is de-fined as [11]:

$$IC(c) = 1 - \frac{\log(hypo(c) + 1)}{\log(node\_max)} \tag{6}$$

According to formula (6), two concepts with the same number of hyponyms will have the same IC values.

3   A New Semantic Similarity Measure Based on WordNet

Let's take Fig.1 as example and discuss the measures stated above. The IC is com-puted with formula (6).

We find that, len (mail, bicycle) and len (wheeled vehicle, bus) are both equal to 4. For a specific version of WordNet, deep_max is a fixed value. Therefore, the two pairs will have the same similarity value with L&C's measure. Another fact must be noted that, both lso (mail, bicycle) and lso (wheeled vehicle, bus) are conveyance. This fact make the two pairs will have the same similarity value with Wu&Palmer's measure and Resnik's measure, too.

Next, let's analyze Lin's measure and Jiang's measurse. The two measures have taken the IC of compared concepts into account respectively. If the summary of IC of compared two pairs with the same lowest subsumer is equal, they will have the same similarity values. For example, in Fig.1 the IC value of all the leaves is equal to 1 according to formula (6), which makes the similarity values of pairs (mail, bicycle) and pairs (bicycle, school bus) are equal.

Based on stated above, it is noted that the similarity measure could not distinguish different concepts pairs effectively. Here a new model is presented, which combines information content and paths of concepts. It is expressed by:

$$sim_{new}(c_1, c_2) = \left(\frac{2 * IC(lso))}{IC(c_1) + IC(c_2)}\right)^{\left(\frac{1 - e^{-k*len(c_1, c_2)}}{e^{-k*len(c_1, c_2)}}\right)} \tag{6}$$

Where k is a factor, which can be adapted manually to make the method to get good performance. $Sim_{new}(c_1, c_2)$ is inversely proportional to $len(c_1, c_2)$. If $len(c_1, c_2)$ is 0, $sim_{new}(c_1, c_2)$ get the maximum value of 1.As $len(c_1, c_2)$ increases to ∞, $sim_{new}(c_1, c_2)$ is close to 0. Therefore the values of sim_{new} are range from 0 to 1.

4   Evaluation

In this section, we evaluated the results by correlating our similarity values with that of human judgments provided by Rubenstein and Goodenough (1965) [12]. In their study, 51 undergraduate subjects were given 65 pairs of words, which ranged from "highly synonymous" to "semantically unrelated". Subjects were asked to rate them on the scale of 0.0 to 4.0. In formula (7), the k value is very important, which decides the performance of the algorithm. We compute different correlation coefficients between proposed measure and human judgments corresponding to different k values. Experiments show that when k is 0.08, the correlation gets the maximum value 0.8817.

Next, we compare the five chosen methods listed in section 2 with our new method. The chosen algorithms and their correlation coefficient are illustrated in Table1. For the convenience of comparison intuitively, the compared graph are presented in Fig.2.

Table 1. Coefficients of correlation between human ratings of similarity

Similarity algorithm	coefficients of correlation (R&G)
Wu & Palmer	0.7767
Leacock & Chodorow	0.8535
Resnik	0.8400
Lin	0.8643
Jiang	-0.8569
New Measure	0.8817

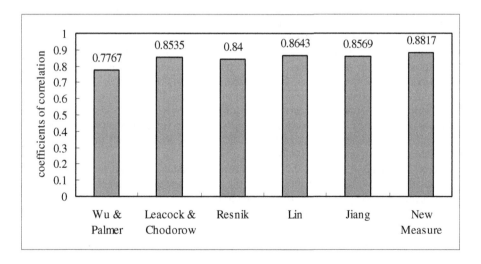

Fig. 2. The compared results of our proposed measure with other five measures

5   Conclusion and Future Work

This paper presents a new hybrid similarity measure to calculate semantic similarity between word pairs, which combines path based measure and information content based measure. We evaluate our model on the data set of Rubenstein and Goodenough (1965), and compare the results of our proposed measure with Wu&palmer's method, Leacock&Chodorow' method, Resnik's method, Lin's method and Jiang's method. Experiments show that the correlation with human judgment is 0.8817 in proposed measure, which outperforms other classical semantic similarity measures. In future work, we will put the measure into practical application, such as ontology construction, big data analysis and so on.

References

1. Patwardhan, S., Banerjee, S., Pedersen, T.: Using measures of semantic relatedness for word sense disambiguation. In: 4th International Conference on Computational Linguistics and Intelligent Text Processing and Computational Linguistics, Mexico City, Mexico, pp. 241–257 (2003)
2. Atkinson, J., Ferreira, A., Aravena, E.: Discovering implicit intention-level knowledge from natural-language texts. Knowlege-Based System 22(7), 502–508 (2009)
3. Sánchez, D., Isern, D., Millán, M.: Content annotation for the Semantic Web: an automatic web-based approach. Knowl. Inf. System. 27(3) (2011)
4. Tapeh, A.G., Rahgozar, M.: A knowledge-based question answering system for B2C eCommerce. Knowledge-Based System 21(8), 946–950 (2008)
5. Fellbaum, C. (ed.): WordNet: An electronic lexical database. MIT Press (1998)
6. Wu, Z., Palmer, M.: Verb Semantics and Lexical Selection. In: Annual Meeting of the Associations for Computational Linguistics, pp. 133–138. Morgan Kaufmann Publishers, Las Cruces (1994)
7. Leacock, C., Chodorow, M.: Combining Local Context and WordNet Similarity for Word Sense Identification in WordNet. In: Fellbaum, C. (ed.) An Electronic Lexical Database, pp. 265–283. MIT Press (1998)
8. Resnik, P.: Using information content to evaluate semantic similarity in a taxonomy. In: Proceedings of the 14th International Joint Conference on Artificial Intelligence, Montréal Québec (1995)
9. Lin, D.: An information-theoretic definition of similarity. In: Proceedings of the 15th International Conference on Machine Learning, Madison, Wisconsin, pp. 296–304 (1998)
10. Jiang, J.J., Conrath, D.W.: Semantic similarity based on corpus statistics and lexical taxonomy. In: Proceedings of International Conference on Research in Computational Linguistics, TaiWan, pp. 19–33 (1997)
11. Seco, N., Veale, T., Hayes, J.: An intrinsic information content metric for semantic similarity in WordNet. In: Proceedings of the 16th European Conference on Artificial Intelligence, Valencia, Spain, pp. 1089–1090 (2004)
12. Rubenstein, H., Goodenough, J.B.: Contextual correlates of synonymy. Communications of the ACM 8(10), 627–633 (1965)

Research of Dynamic Axle Load Truck Scale Sampling Data Selection Method

Jun Liu[1] and Li-hong Li[2]

[1] Bureau of Quality and Technical Supervision of Shanxi Province, Taiyuan, China
sxzjlj@163.com
[2] College of Information Engineering Taiyuan University of Technology, Taiyuan, China
Hong6301@163.com

Abstract. In order to improve the weighing accuracy of the dynamic axle load truck scale, this article carries the static and dynamic tests on the dynamic truck scale and analyzes the test data. From the list, mapping, analysis and calculation of a serial of sampled values of the rear axle ,we can concluded that on computing axle load by the sampled values, we should all select valid weighing platform data if some of sampled values are from transition section, inaccuracy of weight value greaten, the more sampled values from transition section, the more inaccuracy of the weight value. The test results prove that the selection of the sampled values is an important factor that influence the accuracy of the dynamic axle truck scale, In the design of the dynamic axle truck scale, We should take effective processing method, guarantee as far as possible to select sampled values of valid weighing section and avoid using the transition section.

Keywords: Dynamic Axle, Truck Scale, Sample Data, Error.

1   Introduction

The dynamic axle load truck scale is important equipment for the highway fee by weight system. The accuracy of weighing a vehicle is much Influenced by its speed. For Many of the dynamic axle load truck scale products, there is a phenomenon that the faster the greater of the weighing negative error. That is, the faster of the vehicle is, the smaller of its weighing value is. IT is a bottleneck of improving the dynamic axle load truck scale accuracy. Therefore, the study of the speed factor on the dynamic weighing error influence mechanism, and Find out an effective way to reduce the influence of the speed factor on the weighing error, can improve the dynamic axle load truck scale weighing accuracy.

2   The Composition and Principle of Dynamic Axle Load Truck Scale

The dynamic axle load truck scale is composed of the following four parts,load weighing platform,weighing sensors (4), a junction box and a weighing display instrument. When the truck axle onto the scale platform,the load weighing platform will

J. Lei et al. (Eds.): NCIS 2012, CCIS 345, pp. 745–750, 2012.
© Springer-Verlag Berlin Heidelberg 2012

send the Signal of the weight of the truck as far as possible without distortion to the weighing sensor, The truck axle load is linearly converted to a millivolt signal corresponding to the axle load by weighing sensor, then after transmitted through the junction box circuit to Parallel and be superimposed, then into the weighing display instrument. In the weighing display instrument,the signal is amplified and filtered, then afte A/D converting and digital processing, it is converted to a corresponding digital signal of the axle load and then display output. For the convenience of processing signal, the two sensors which the truck axle press on first are connected in parallel into a group(Hereinafter referred to as the front sensors), the two sensors which the truck axle press on later are connected in parallel into another group(Hereinafter referred to as the rear sensors).

When the truck axle through the load weighing platform, The relationship between the first and the rear sensors output signals, the total output signal and A/D sampling location shown in Figure 2.The output signals of the front sensors such as curve 1, the output signals of the rear sensors such as curve 2, curve 1 and curve 2 are superimposed to the total output signal of the 4 sensors output signals such as curve 3. The Sample values between the maximum value of Curve 1 and the maximum value of Curve 2 are the total value of an axle all press on the load weighing platform ,These numbers are valid sample values.

3   Test Methods and Data

The test vehicle using a dual axle truck, the Static measurement method is both the front and the rear axles are staying on the weighing platform, Read the weight value after the display numbers are stable. Static weighing in the truck, the measured values of the front and the rear axles are 4700 and 8640, respectively. The total value of the two axles measured values is 13340.The dynamic measurement method is the truck with a uniform speed that is less than 30km/h through the weighing platform, after the front and the rear axles are passed through, there are two groups of sampled values respectively, the number of each group of sampled values ranges from tens to hundreds, according to the length of time that its axles are on the weighing platform. Each group of sampled values are calculated in the weighing display instrument within the set of algorithms to the corresponding dynamic axle measurement. The whole truck measured values is the total value of the two axles measured values. Table 1 below is the rear axle sampled values in a test statistical measurement.

Table 1. The rear axle sampled values in a test statistical measurement

Serial number	Sampled values	Serial number	Sampled values	Serial number	Sampled values	Serial number	Sampled values	Serial number	Sampled values
1	2053	18	7730	35	8536	52	8325	69	7001
2	2598	19	7743	36	8574	53	8326	70	6570
3	3300	20	7743	37	8631	54	8302	71	6161
4	3886	21	7766	38	8641	55	8323	72	5726

Table 1. (*continued*)

5	4464	22	7797	39	8667	56	8318	73	5312
6	4973	23	7878	40	8637	57	8330	74	4853
7	5498	24	7899	41	8658	58	8299	75	4433
8	6039	25	7966	42	8652	59	8318	76	4002
9	6593	26	8019	43	8694	60	8331	77	3609
10	7072	27	8144	44	8655	61	8390	78	3197
11	7445	28	8215	45	8631	62	8407	79	2833
12	7628	29	8316	46	8560	63	8424	80	2455
13	7781	30	8389	47	8543	64	8349	81	2134
14	7800	31	8458	48	8500	65	8258		
15	7781	32	8472	49	8488	66	8054		
16	7778	33	8486	50	8421	67	7766		
17	7779	34	8479	51	8385	68	7396		

4   Analysis and Results

Figure 1 shows the waveform of the sampled values based on the data listed in Table 1. According to the waveform shape, the figure data is divided into three sections: the section of AB is the former transition section, that is the Sampled values when the wheels traveling from the road to the weighing platform transition; the section of BC is valid weighing section, that is the sampled values when the wheels is completely pressing onn the weighing platform; the section of CD is the later transition section, that is the Sampled values when the wheels traveling from the weighing platform to the road transition. A=0,B=15,C=63,D=81, A'=5 ,A''=10.

Assumed that the length of the weighing platform is L, The average speed of the measured truck axle through the weighing platform is v, The A/D converter sampling frequency is f, Then the relationship between the number of samples N and vehicle speed V is:

$$N = \frac{fL}{v} \tag{1}$$

For the selected dynamic axle truck scale product, its weighing platform length L and the A/D converter sampling frequency f are fixed values, Therefore, the sampling number N and weighing speed V are inversely proportional relationship, when weighing faster, the fewer number of samples values got, and the number of sample value not only directly affect the selection of samples values for the measured value calculation, but also can affect the accuracy of the measured value.

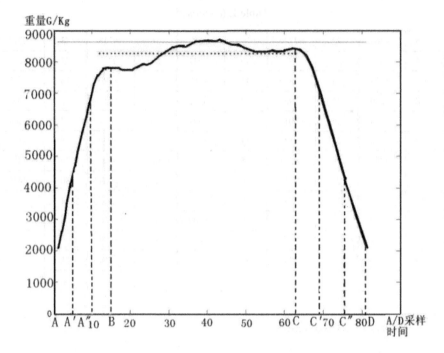

Fig. 1. The Waveform of the rear axle sampled values in a test of statistical measurement

In order to facilitate analysis, We take the averaging method to calculate weight. Thos sampling values of the front and the final section of the transitional, where the axle is not completely on the platform, can't be used to calculation. At the same time, that sampling values of the effective section, where the axle is all loaded on the platform, should be effective to the calculation As far as possible. Calculate the measured value is:

$$G = \frac{\sum_{i=B}^{C} G_i}{C - B} = 8546 \tag{2}$$

The relative error of measured value:

$$r_G = \frac{G - G_0}{G_0} * 100\% = -1.1\% \tag{3}$$

If the calculation error take the samples value of transition section A " B, calculate the measured value is:

$$G' = \frac{\sum_{i=A''}^{C} G_i}{C - A''} = 7311 \qquad (4)$$

The relative error of measured value:

$$r_G' = \frac{G' - G_0}{G_0} * 100\% = 15.4\% \qquad (5)$$

According to the above methods, repeated 15 measured times to get samples values, calculate the measured values in different sections, which are selected according to above formula, and Obtain the corresponding measured value and relative error, As shown in the Table2.

As the data of table2 displays, sampling value should guarantee that all the effective values have been selected. It would cause the measurement accuracy of the measured value declines, that select the sampling value transition section when calculating the weight. the more data of transition section be selected, the more rapidly the error of the measured value increases.

Table 2. The measured values and error values of selected a different section of the sampled values

Serial number	Static values	All select valid weighing platform data		Select transition section 1/3 data		Select transition section 2/3 data	
		Measured values	error values %	Measured values	error values %	Measured values	error values %
1		8546	-1.10	7311	-15.40	6634	-23.20
2		8201	-5.10	7224	16.40	5523	-36.10
3		8535	-1.20	7594	-12.00	6148	-28.80
4		8351	-3.30	6735	-22.00	5160	-40.30
5		8651	0.12	7916	-8.30	7311	-15.40
6		8550	-1.10	8019	-7.20	7048	-18.50
7		8180	-5.30	7792	-9.80	7040	-18.50
8	8640	8375	-3.10	7579	-12.30	6917	-19.90
9		8615	-0.30	8327	-3.60	7430	-13.90
10		8645	0.05	7995	-7.50	7009	-18.90
11		8628	-0.15	7982	-7.60	7295	-15.60
12		8406	-2.70	7788	-9.80	7460	-13.70
13		8285	-4.00	7680	-11.10	7225	-16.40
14		8344	-3.40	7382	-14.60	6955	-19.50
15		8369	-3.10	7326	-15.20	5916	-31.50

5   Conclusion

From the test and the analysis above, we can concluded that, the selection of the sampled values is an important factor that influence the accuracy of the dynamic axle truck scale, In the design of the dynamic axle truck scale, We should take effective processing method, to ensure as much as possible to select sampled values of valid weighing section and avoid using the transition section.

References

1. Xu, K.-J., Ma, X.-S., Li, X.-L.: Sensor and Detection Technology. Publishing House of Electronics Industry, Beijing (2008)
2. Ruan, S.-Y.: MATLAB Program Design. Publishing House of Electronics Industry, Beijing (2004)
3. Yang, G.-B., Jian, Q.-H.: The Hardware Connection between 24-bit A/D Converter AD7714 and 80C51 Microcontroller and Software Programming. China Instrumentation 6, 29–32 (2000)
4. Fang, G.-Z., Chi, H.-J., Chen, B.-Y.: Application of MSC1210 to the Dynamic Weighing System. Journal of Harbin University of Science and Technology 12(2), 94–96 (2007)
5. Ma, X.-J., Zhang, Z., Zhu, S.-L.: Mathematical model establishment of dynamic electronic truck scale weighing system. Journal of Jiamusi University 24(3), 379–381 (2006)
6. Wan, L.-Q.: Application of Dynamic Weighing Technology in the Highway fee by weight system and Relevant Requirements. Weighing Apparatus (5), 39–41 (2006)
7. Wang, J.-G.: Dynamic Road Vehicles Automatic Weighing Apparatus. China Metrology Press, Beijing (2006)
8. Wang, J.-J.: Detection Technology and Instruments. Wuhan University of Technology Press, Wuhan (2002)
9. Hu, G.-S.: Digital Signal Processing—Theory, Algorithms and Implementation. Tsinghua University Press, Beijing (1997)
10. Shi, C.-Y.: Status and Development Trend of Dynamic Weighing technology of the dynamometer. Metrology and Measurement Technique 1, 18–20 (2000)

A New Method of Smoothing of Boolean Operations of Surfaces

Haining Mou

Department of Computational and Applied Mathematics, College of Science,
China University of Petroleum, Qingdao, Shandong 266555, China
hainingmou@yahoo.com.cn

Abstract. In this paper, we present a new method to construct the smooth transitional surfaces of boolean operations of convex objects which based on algebraic splines. This method is more effective and easier to implement. Examples are provided to demonstrate the smoothing effects.

Keywords: Surface smoothing, Boolean operations of surfaces, Algebraic splines.

1 Introduction

Boolean operations of surfaces are useful tools in geometric modeling for constructing solid objects from simple primitives. Any New objects can be defined as the union, intersection, or subtraction of several objects. A large proportion of computer graphics scenes are modeled with polyhedra, even the natural objects being modeled are themselves curved. However, the edges and corners of models remain sharp when we use boolean operations of polyhedra to approximate curved surfaces. In CAD/CAM, it is a common and important issue to smooth the intersection, union or subtraction of polyhedra.

As we know, the boolean combination of two objects through a union, intersection or subtraction is complex and time consuming. Such surface blending is difficult and hard to implement. Many researches have studied this subject [1, 2, 3, 4, 5, 7].

In this paper, we present a method to smooth the union, intersection or subtraction of polyhedra which based on algebraic splines. This method is easy to implement. For each polyhedron, we first construct its smooth transitional surface by algebraic spline inside or outside. The blending surfaces of the union, intersection, subtract of polyhedra can be obtained by defining the corresponding algebraic operations between blending surfaces of each polyhedron.

The rest of the paper is organized as follows. In section 2, we introduce some preliminary knowledge about algebraic splines, which is a basic and useful tool to construct the smooth transitional surfaces. In section 3, we propose the smoothing method of boolean operations. And some examples are provided to show the smoothing

J. Lei et al. (Eds.): NCIS 2012, CCIS 345, pp. 751–758, 2012.
© Springer-Verlag Berlin Heidelberg 2012

effect. Finally in section 4, we conclude the paper and point out the future research problems.

2   Preliminary of Multivariate Algebraic Spline

We give a brief introduction of multivariate splines. References [8, 9] are the sources for most of the material on multivariate splines in this section.

Let D be a bounded polyhedral domain of R^3 which is partitioned with irreducible algebraic surfaces into cells Δ_i, $i=1,2,\cdots N$. The partition is denoted by Δ. A function $f(x)$ defined on D is a spline function if $f(x) \in C^r(D)$ and $f(x)|_{\Delta_i} = p_i \in P_k$ (P_k is the set of all the polynomials of degree k), which is expressed for short as follows:

$$f(x) \in S_k^r(D,\Delta) \tag{1}$$

[8] established the following results:

Theorem 1[8] Let Δ_i and Δ_j be two adjacent cells with partitioning plane $p_{ij}=0$. Suppose the degree of p_{ij} is d_{ij}. $f(x) \in C^r\left(\Delta_i \cup \Delta_j\right)$ if and only if

$$p_i - p_j = p_{ij}^{r+1} \cdot g_{ij} \tag{2}$$

where $g_{ij} \in P_{k-(r+1)d_{ij}}$ is called a smooth cofactor of $f(x)$ on the partitioning plane p_{ij}.

Further, $f(x) \in S_r^k(D,\Delta)$ if and only if there exists a smooth cofactor on each interior partitioning plane and

$$\sum_{p_{ij}L_k} p_{ij}^{r+1} \cdot g_{ij} = 0 \tag{3}$$

where L_k is the set of partitioning planes sharing the common interior line.

For any spline function $f(x)$, the inverse image $f^{-1}(0)$ is called an algebraic spline, that is, the inverse image of a bivariate spline is called an algebraic spline curve or piecewise algebraic curve; the inverse image of a trivariate spline is called an algebraic spline surface or piecewise algebraic surface.

3   Construction of Smoothing Surfaces of a Polyhedron

Suppose P_1, P_2 are two given polyhedra. In order to blend $P_1 \cup P_2$, $P_1 \cap P_2$, $P_1 \setminus P_2$, we construct the blending surface of each polyhedron first.

3.1   Simultaneous Smoothing of a Polyhedron

Given a polyhedron P with vertices $v_1, v_2, \cdots, v_m$, suppose its boundary faces be $T_i^{-1}(0)$, $i = 1, 2, \cdots, m$. We Smooth the polyhedron P according to following steps:

1.   Space partition.

Construct a polyhedron Q with surfaces $T_i - d = 0$, $i = 1, 2, \cdots, m$, outside P, where $d > 0$ is a constant. Suppose the vertices of Q be $t_1, t_2, \cdots, t_m$. Let

$$r_i = (1 - m\alpha)v_i + \alpha \sum_{j=1}^{m} v_j \tag{4}$$

where $\dfrac{1}{m} < \alpha < \dfrac{1}{m-1}$, $i = 1, 2, \cdots, m$. Denote R be a polyhedron with vertices $r_1, r_2, \cdots, r_m$, then R is inside P. Fig. 1 shows the position relations of tetrahedra P, Q, R.

Partition R^3 such that each cell has the form of

$$\Delta_{\{i_1, i_2, \cdots, i_k\}} = t_{i_{k+1}} \cdots t_{i_m} r_{i_1} \cdots r_{i_k} \tag{5}$$

where $i_1, i_2, \cdots, i_m$ are the elements of the set $N_m = \{1, 2, \cdots, m\}$, $1 \le k \le m$.

2.   Construct the spline surface defined on the partition introduced above.

Compute the blending surface by use of algebraic spline. Since the spline outside the cell $t_{i_1}, t_{i_2}, \cdots, t_{i_m}$ is zero, we can deduce the surface patch defined on the cell Δ_{i_1} by use of the smoothly connecting condition Eq. 2.

Suppose we have obtained the algebraic spline surface patch defined on the cell $\Delta_{\{i_1, i_2, \cdots, i_k\}}$, the algebraic spline surface patch on the cell $\Delta_{\{i_1, i_2, \cdots, i_k, i_{k+1}\}}$ can be gotten by use of Eq.2. Thus, we get the spline surface $S_p^{-1}(0)$. The blending surface expression of polyhedron P is $S_p - d = 0$.

Readers can refer to [6] for the detailed computation processes of this step.

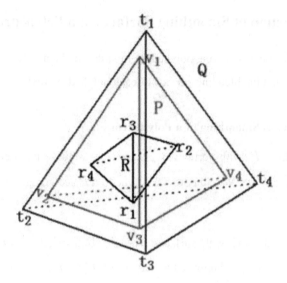

Fig. 1. Space partition when smoothing outside

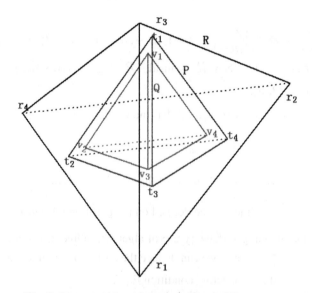

Fig. 2. Space partition when smoothing inside

We call this type smoothing method be smoothing outside. Similar surfaces can be smoothed inside, the partition of which is shown in Fig. 2. The inside smoothing surface can be obtained similar to the method of outside smoothing. Fig.3 and Fig.4 show smoothing of a polyhedron outside and inside.

Fig. 3. Smooth the polyhedron outside

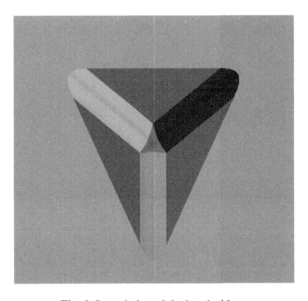

Fig. 4. Smooth the polyhedron inside

3.2   Smoothing of Boolean Operations of Polyhedra

In this section, we present the method of smoothing boolean operations, such as union, intersection and straction of convex polyhedra. By use of above smoothing method, we can get smooth transitional surfaces of polyhedra P, Q which are denoted by p_i or p_e and q_i or q_e, where the subscripts i and e mean smoothing inside and smoothing outside respectively.

The intersection of two polyhedra $P \cap Q$ can be smoothed by surface $s^{-1}(0)$, where $s = p_i \oplus q_i$. The union $P \cup Q$ can be smoothed by surface $s^{-1}(0)$, where $s = p_e \oplus q_e$. The subtraction $P \backslash Q$ can be smoothed by surface $s^{-1}(0)$, where $s = p_i \oplus q_e$. The operation $\oplus$ is defined by

$$p_a + p_b = \sum_i c_i \cdot g_i^n + \sum_i k_i \cdot h_i^n - d \qquad (6)$$

where g_i and h_i are equations of flow lines[8].

Fig.5, Fig.6 and Fig.7 show smoothing of intersection, union, and subtraction of two polyhedra respectively.

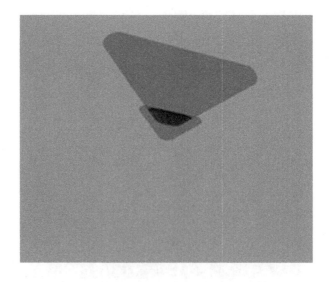

Fig. 5. Smoothing of intersection of two polyhedra

Fig. 6. Smoothing of union of two polyhedra

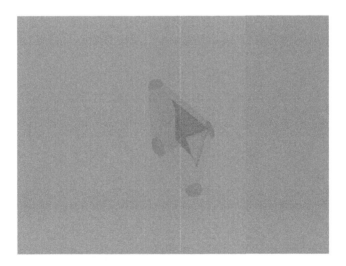

Fig. 7. Smoothing of subtraction of two polyhedra

4   Conclusion

In this paper, we present a method to smooth the union, intersection and subtraction of polyhedra. This method is intuitionistic and easy to implement since it only constitutes of algebraic computation. However, how to smooth the boolean operations of concave surface remain unsolved and will be our future work.

References

1. Chen, C., Chen, F., Feng, Y.: Blending quadric surfaces with piecewise algebraic surfaces. Graphical Models 63(4), 212–227 (2001)
2. Farin, G.: Curves and Surfaces for Computer Aided Geometric Design: A Practical Guide. Academic Press Inc., New York (1990)
3. Holmström, L.: Piecewise quadric blending of implicitly defined surfaces. Computer Aided Geometric Design (4), 171–189 (1987)
4. Liming, R.A.: Practical analytic geometry with applications to aircraft. Macmillan, New York (1994)
5. Middleditch, A.E., Sears, K.H.: Blending surfaces for set theoretic volume modeling system. Comput. Graphics (19), 161–170 (1985)
6. Mou, H.N., Zhao, G.H., Wang, Z.R., Su, Z.X.: Simultaneous Blending of Convex Polyhedra by S^2_3 Algebraic Splines. Computer Aided Design (39), 1003–1011 (2007)
7. Rockwood, A., Owen, J.: Blending surfaces in solid modeling. In: Farin, G. (ed.) Geometric Modeling: Algorithm and New Trends. SIAM, Philadelphia (1985)
8. Wang, R.: The Structural Characterization and Interpolation for Multivariate Splines. Acta Math. Sinica (10), 91–106 (1975)
9. Sederberg, T.W.: Piecewise algebraic surface patches. Comput. Aided Geom. Design (2), 53–60 (1985)

Performance Evaluation of Virtualization Technologies for Windows Programs Running on Linux Operating System

Conghui Huang, Jing Chen, Li Zhang, and Qiao Luo

College of Information and Navigation, Air Force Engineering University, XiAn, China
{huangdoubleten,zhangli614,lq1008}@126.com,
jingchen0803@gmail.com

Abstract. System virtual machine, kernel virtualization in kernel space and kernel virtualization in user space are the three virtualization technologies for Windows programs running on Linux operating system. System virtual machine technology can support Linux operating system to install and run Windows operating system and its programs by simulating the complete or a subnet of hardware. However, the other two virtualization technologies respectively emulate the function of Windows kernel in the Linux kernel space and in Linux user space. Because the three virtualization technologies have different principles and methods of realization, the same Windows programs running on them have different performance under the same condition. In this paper, we evaluate the performance of the system virtual machine, kernel virtualization in kernel space and kernel virtualization in user space. Using VMware Workstation, Longene and Wine as the typical representative of the three virtualization technologies, we measure the performance of the three virtualization technologies by the method of benchmark application, and compare them with the test results on the native Windows XP. And the experimental results demonstrate that Wine has the better performance, compared with Windows programs running on the VMware Workstation and Longene.

Keywords: Binary Compatibility, Virtualization, VMware Workstation, Longene, Wine.

1 Introduction

As the most popular open source operating system, Linux operating system has a high market share in embedded devices, servers and high performance computing. But in the mainstream field of desktop, Linux market share has a big gap compared with the market share of Windows. According to the data collected from Wikipedia, Windows held about 80% market share in the desktop field, while Linux took about 2% market share. The reason why Linux market share is so low in the desktop field is that the user-friendly graphic user interface of Windows has become the habit of the people and the de facto industry standard, which prevent the popularity of Linux. In addition, the most software and hardware providers prefer to provide applications, drivers, and high

J. Lei et al. (Eds.): NCIS 2012, CCIS 345, pp. 759–766, 2012.
© Springer-Verlag Berlin Heidelberg 2012

quality service for Windows rather than those for Linux, as a result, Linux lacks enough application, drivers, and does not meet the various needs of users.

The challenge faced by Linux on the desktop area can be solved by making Windows programs to run on Linux operating system. The solution not only takes care of people's habit, but also enriches applications for Linux. And system virtual machine [1], kernel virtualization in kernel space, kernel virtualization in user space are the three virtualization technologies for running Windows programs on Linux operating system. Because the three virtualization technologies have different principles and methods of realization, the same Windows programs running on them have different performance under the same condition. And the performance of the three virtualization technologies is the important reason for Linux users to choose the right virtualization technology to run Windows programs on Linux operating system, so we select the VMware Workstation [2], Longene and Wine respectively as the typical representative of the three virtualization technology for testing their performance.

The rest of the paper is organized as follows. Section 2 summarizes the related work. Section 3 analyzes the advantages and disadvantages of the three virtualization technologies. Section 4 describes the benchmark applications and common applications used in our performance test. Section 5 presents performance measurement setup and methodology. Section 6 gives the performance measurement results and analysis. Section 7 concludes the paper.

2   Related Work

As far as we know, there are a lot of literatures about performance analysis of system virtual machine technology, but there is no performance evaluation study on virtualization technologies for Windows programs running on Linux operating system in the literature.

Andrew et al. [3] analyzed and compared the performance of Xen, KVM and Virtual Box in high performance computing environment, and pointed out that the KVM hypervisor was the best choice for supporting high performance computing applications in cloud computing environment.

Pradeep et al. [4] evaluated Xen and OpenVZ in terms of application performance, resource consumption, scalability, low-level system metrics and virtualization-specific metrics, and indicated OpenVZ had better performance than Xen in server consolidation, because the OpenVZ had a higher L2 cache hit rate and instruction hit rate.

Benjamin et al. [5] evaluated the performance and usability of Vserver, Xen, UML and VMware in large scale grid and P2P simulation environment in terms of availability, scalability, resource consumption and isolation, which help users select the appropriate technology according to their application characteristics.

Todd Deshane et al. [6] present initial results from and quantitative analysis of two leading open source hypervisors, Xen and KVM. They found the overall performance results were mixed with Xen outperforming KVM on a kernel compile test and KVM outperforming Xen on I/O-intensive tests.

3   Virtualization Technology

Currently the three virtualization technologies for Windows programs running on Linux operating system are respectively system virtual machine, kernel virtualization in kernel space and kernel virtualization in user space, which are shown in Figure 1.

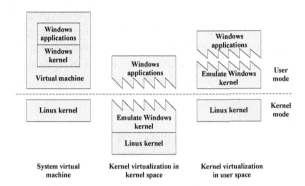

Fig. 1. Three virtualization technologies for Windows programs running on Linux operating system

System virtual machine technology emulates the entire instruction set architecture or the hardware abstraction layer, which supports the installation and running of the Windows operating system and its programs. This technology separates the execute environment of Windows applications from the Linux operating system by virtual machine monitor, which avoids damaging the security of the Linux operating system and makes Windows programs run perfectly and steadily in the virtual machine environment. However, the disadvantage is that the overload of virtual machine monitor causes the performance degradation of Windows applications, incurs much start-up time and needs to install the Windows operating system for running Windows programs. Examples of system virtual machine technology are VMware Workstation, Xen, KVM, Virtual Box and so on.

Kernel virtualization in kernel space technology provides system call service and virtual environment for running Windows programs by simulating the Windows operating system kernel in the kernel space of Linux operating system. The advantage of this technology is that theoretically Windows programs can run with high efficiency in Linux operating system, but the disadvantages are obviously that this technology is difficult to develop, damages the security and stability of Linux operating system and has poor portability. Examples of kernel virtualization in kernel space technology are Linux Unified Kernel which also named Longene, NDISwrapper and so on.

Kernel virtualization in user space technology provides system call service and virtual environment for running Windows programs by simulating the Windows operating system kernel in the user space of Linux operating system. The advantages of this technology are that it is easy to develop, and has high portability and adaptability. The disadvantage is that theoretically Windows applications run slowly with this technology. Examples of kernel virtualization in user space are Wine[7], Wabi and so on.

4   Benchmark Applications

Benchmark applications are a set of programs which are specially developed for measuring the overall performance of computer systems or for the performance of computer certain components. Usually the overall performance of computer is determined by the performance of CPU, disk, memory, graphics subsystem and network. Most computer users use benchmark applications for mutual virtualization technologies performance comparison. So we use various industry-recognized benchmark applications and common applications to analyze the performance of Windows programs running on the three virtualization technologies of system virtual machine, kernel virtualization in kernel space and kernel virtualization in user space. Benchmark applications and common applications are described as follows:

(1) Super PI mod 1.5
Super PI [8] is a benchmark program that calculates pi to a specified number of digits after the decimal point, which can reach a maximum of 32 million. We measured the time to compute pi after the decimal point 1 million and 32 million digits. The result is given in seconds, and the shorter the time, the better the performance.

(2) CPU Free BenchMark 2.2
CPU Free BenchMark is a benchmark program to measure the performance of CPU registers, floating point unit, arithmetic logic unit. The result is given in seconds, and the shorter the time, the better the performance.

(3) 3DMark03
3DMark is a benchmark application for testing computer 3D graphics rendering and CPU processing capabilities, which was developed by Futuremark corporation. In our measurement the 3DMark score indicates the performance of the selected virtualization technologies. And the test result is shown with number of points, and the higher the result, the better the performance of computer graphics subsystem.

(4) Passmark Performance Test 7
PassMark Performance Test [9] is a tool designed to test the performance of computer. It contains twenty-eight standard benchmark tests in test suites and seven advanced testing windows for custom benchmarking.In our performance measurement we used the CPU, memory and disk test suites. The test results are shown with number of points, and the higher the result, the better the performance.

(5) PCMark04
PCMark is a benchmark program to evaluate the overall computer performance as well as the performance of CPU, memory, graphics, disk subsystem, which was developed by Futuremark corporation. In our performance measurement we used the memory, graphics and hard disk test suites. The test results are shown with number of points, and the higher the result, the better the performance.

(6) Netperf 2.4.3
Netperf [10] is a benchmark program to evaluate the performance of network, especially for the transport of TCP and UDP. In our performance measurement we used the TCP_Stream mode of Netperf to test the throughput of network. The test result is shown by Mbit/s, and the higher the result, the better the performance of network.

(7) Total Video Converter 3.61

Total Video Converter is a converter for files with various video and audio formats, which is developed by Effect Matrix corporation and used frequently in the application of video encoding. In our performance measurement we measured the time by using this program to convert a 400M AVI file to MPEG1 format. The result is given in seconds, and the shorter the encoding time, the better the performance.

(8) WinRAR 4.01

WinRAR is a common used data decompression program, which can decompress RAR, ZIP and other format file. In our performance measurement we use the program's own test for performance and hardware. The test result is shown in KB/sec, and the higher the result, the better the performance. At the same time we measured the time by using the program to compress a 400M AVI file. The result is given in seconds, and the shorter the time, the better the performance.

5   Performance Measurement Setup and Methodology

We did the experiment on a dell desktop computer whose model named vstro 230. Hardware and software configurations used in our performance measurement are shown in Table 1. For comparative analysis, we also measured the performance of the host operating system, namely Windows XP SP3.

Table 1. Hardware and software configurations

hardware configuration	host operating system	the tested virtualization software	guest operating system
CPU: Intel Core 2 E7500 2.93 GHz	Ubuntu 10.10 32 bit	VMware Workstation 7.1.4 for Linux	Windows XP SP3 32 bit
Memory: DDR3 2 GB	Windows XP SP3 32bit	Wine 1.3.17	
Graphic Card: nVIDIA GeForce 310		Longene 0.3.1	
Disk: Hitachi 320 GB			

Before the test, we updated the device drivers of the host operating system and guest operating system to the latest state, because the device drivers affect the performance of the computer. In order to avoid measurement errors and irrelevant factors, our experimental steps were performed as follows:

1. Install Windows XP SP3 operating system and update it to the latest status.

2. Install the benchmark application, and then restart the operating system.

3. Run the benchmark application, and record the results.

4. Uninstall the benchmark application, and then restart.

5. Format the hard disk, install Ubuntu 10.10 Linux operating system, and then update it to the latest status.

6. Install VMware Workstation 7.1.4 for Linux version.

7. Create VMware virtual machine, install the guest operating system of Windows XP SP3 in the VMware virtual machine and then update it to the latest status.

8. Repeat steps 2-4 in order.

9. Repeat step 5, and then install the Wine 1.3.17.

10. Repeat steps 2-4 in order.

11. Repeat step 5, and then install Longene 0.3.1.

12. Repeat steps 2-4 in order.

In order to ensure the accuracy of the measurement results we repeated steps 3 three times for each benchmark application, and then calculated the arithmetic mean of the results. For avoiding affecting the measurement results, we did not install other application on the host operating systems and guest operating systems except the applications bound with the operating system and required for the experiment.

6   Results and Analysis

We measured the performance of the computer components with benchmark applications. And the analysis of the experimental results are shown in figure 2 from the perspective of CPU, memory, disk, graphics subsystem and the computer overall performance. One thing needed to explain is that Longene only has the test results of the Super PI and WinRAR in figure 2, because other benchmark applications cannot be installed and run on the Longene.

The measurement results from Super PI, CPU Free BenchMark and Passmark Performance Test show that the CPU performance on the Longene, Wine and VMware Workstation is very similar, and close to the performance on the native Windows XP operating system.

From the memory performance test results of the Passmark Performance Test and PCMark, we can conclude that the highest of memory performance is the Wine, followed by the Windows XP, and finally the VMware Workstation.

From the disk performance test results of Passmark Performance Test and PCMark, we can conclude that the highest of the disk performance is the Wine, followed by the VMware Workstation, and finally the Windows XP.

From the graphics subsystem performance test results of PCMark and 3DMark, we can conclude that the highest of the graphics subsystem performance is the Windows XP, followed by the Wine, and finally the VMware Workstation.

From the network performance test results of Netperf, we can conclude that the highest of the network performance is the wine, followed by the VMware Workstation, and finally the Windows XP.

From the test results of common application, We can find out that when converting the video formats of file by running total video convertor, the longest time required is on the VMware Workstation (18.3% longer than the execution time required on the native Windows XP), followed by the Wine (3.3% longer than the execution time required on the native Windows XP). When doing data compression, the longest time required is on the Longene (61.3% longer than the execution time required on the native Windows XP), followed by the VMware Workstation (33.7% longer than the execution time required on the native Windows XP), and finally on the Wine (12.9% longer than the execution time required on the native Windows XP). From the test results of common application, we can conclude that for the real-world usage the Wine is also the best choice to run Windows programs on Linux operating system from the perspective of performance.

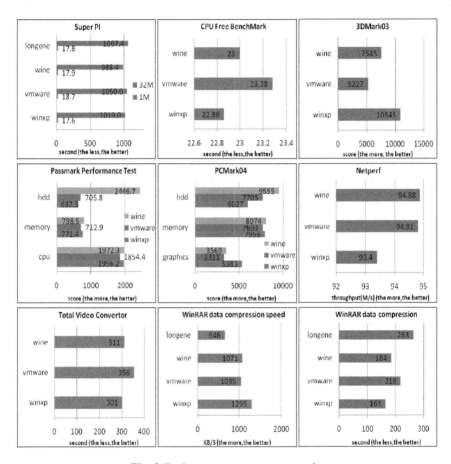

Fig. 2. Performance measurement results

7   Conclusion

This paper attempts to evaluate the performance of the system virtual machine, kernel virtualization in kernel space and kernel virtualization in user space, which are the three virtualization technologies for Windows programs running on Linux operating system. And we used benchmark applications to evaluate the performance of the VMware Workstation, Longene and Wine, which are respectively the representative of the three virtualization technologies.

The test results show that under the same condition the performance of the Wine is comprehensive superior to the performance of the VMware Workstation and Longene. And in terms of CPU performance, the efficiency of Windows program running on Wine is close to the efficiency on the native Windows XP. From the performance perspective of the Memory, disk and network, the efficiency of Windows programs running on Wine is superior to the efficiency on the naive Windows XP. But in the graphics subsystem, the efficiency of Windows program running on Wine is much lower than the efficiency on the native Windows XP. In the end if you do not consider the stability of Windows programs running in Linux operating system, Wine will be a better choice for running Windows programs on Linux operating systems because of its good performance.

References

1. Smith, J.E., Nair, R.: The architecture of virtual machines. Computer 38(5), 32–38 (2005)
2. Sugerman, J., Venkitachalam, G., Lim, B.-H.: Virtualizing I/O Devices on VMware Workstation's Hosted Virtual Machine Monitor. In: Proceedings of the 2001 USENIX Annual Technical Conference (2001)
3. Younge, A.J., Henschel, R., Brown, J.T., von Laszewski, G., Qiu, J., Fox, G.C.: Analysis of Virtualization Technologies for High Performance Computing Environments. In: Proceedings of IEEE CLOUD, pp. 9–16 (2011)
4. Padala, P., Zhu, X., Wang, Z., Singhal, S., Shin, K.G.: Performance Evaluation of Virtualization Technologies for Server Consolidation. HP Labs Technical Report, HPL-2007-59R1 (2008)
5. Quetier, B., Neri, V., Cappello, F.: Selecting A Virtualization System For Grid/P2P Large Scale Emulation. In: Proc. of the Workshop on Experimental Grid Testbeds for the Assessment of Large-Scale Distributed Applications and Tools (2006)
6. Deshane, T., Shepherd, Z., Matthews, J.N., et al.: Quantitative Comparison of Xen and KVM. Xen Summit (2008)
7. Nanda, S., Chiueh, T.-C.: A Survey on Virtualization Technologies. ECSL, USA (2005)
8. Horalek, J., Hatas, M., Sobeslav, V.: Comparison of Software Virtualization Hypervisors. Recent Researches in Circuits, Systems, Communications and Computers, 118–124 (2011)
9. Martinović, G., Balen, J., Rimac-Drlje, S.: Impact of the Host Operating Systems on Virtual Machine Performance. In: Proceedings of MIPRO 2010, pp. 613–618 (2010)
10. Menon, A., Cox, A.L., Zwaenepoel, W.: Optimizing Network Virtualization in Xen. In: Proceedings of 2006 USENIX Annual Technical Conference, pp. 15–28 (2006)

A Replica Management Strategy of Hybrid P2P Network for Massive Terrain Data

Xiaoxia Lu[1,2] and Sikun Li[1]

[1] College of Computer, National University of Defense Technology, ChangSha 410073
[2] School of Computer, ZhongYuan University of Technology, ZhengZhou, 450007
lxxwl2008@163.com

Abstract. To satisfy the requirements of massive data management for rendering terrain scene, a hybrid structure p2p network consisting of fundamental storage sites and application sites is presented. Further, the application sites are divided two types considering their capability and QOS requirement. On these bases, a replica placement method named selective caching along road and corresponding consistency management method are designed. To improve the effectiveness of replica, an new replica deleting method is proposed based on competitive learning. The simulation results show the strategy can control effectively the quantity of both total replicas and replicas in single site, guarantee the stability of searching and hitting target and avoid invalid deletion.

Keywords: massive terrain data, hybrid p2p network, replica management, selective, competitive learning.

1 Introduction

In the task of rendering terrain scene of virtual battle field, one of the key technology is how to storage and manage massive terrain data such as texture image, elevation etc. For real-time rendering, it is highly required of searching, locating and downloading those sharing terrain data. In recent years, the data are increased explosively with the development of data acquirement technology, which make distributed storage system adopted to deal with the problem. And if not considering terrain change caused by battle's explosion etc, terrain data are mostly read-only data. Furthermore, the terminals for executing rendering task are variable including many types especially some handheld devices. So, all different types rendering devices shall be managed effectively and supported by the data storage system. Lastly, the storage system shall optimized its performance to satisfy the QOS requirement of requesting site [1].

Currently, the p2p network for distributed storage has been the focus in this field. According to the topology type, it can be divided as 4 p2p networks of centralized topology, decentralized unstructured topology, partially decentralized topology and decentralized structured topology. [2] uses centralized topology and supports downloading tile terrain data by searching central site to response a given site's request. It needs memory a large mount of catching information and has many problems such as

J. Lei et al. (Eds.): NCIS 2012, CCIS 345, pp. 767–774, 2012.
© Springer-Verlag Berlin Heidelberg 2012

weak stability, low extensibility and performance bottle etc. [3] presents a hybrid structure p2p massive terrain navigation search model called group flooding based on the buffer map info and group peer map info, which supports searching quickly peers to get the tiles. [4] designs a terrain data storage system based on unstructured p2p network, keeps load balance by dynamical reassignment and avoids the performance decrease caused by concentrated load in central structure network.

Replica technology is important of p2p network for data storage and management. It can effectively shorten response time, reduce long distance data transfer and decrease network traffic etc. Replica management includes multiple technologies such as placement, replacement, deletion and consistency maintains. Especially the QOS replica placement problem (QRPP) has been the focus recently [5]. In structured p2p network with sites organized by DHT or tree, for replica management strategy, it abstracts the RPP as a optimization problem to satisfy load balance, traffic, delay and QOS of requesting site [6,7]. Whereas, unstructured p2p network represented by Gnutella has characters such as a variety of site types and scales, also disperse locations etc. Thereby, many replica management strategies solve its replica placement problem using the methods of catching all sites along road or catching at origin site, while searching by flooding algorithm and using FIFO or least accessed recently based on trend prediction (hot file) as its replacing strategy [8].

In view of the characters of massive data and application system in the task of rendering terrain scene, it's not suitable to adopt central or structured p2p network because of the variation of scales and users. While if unstructured topology adopted, searching has more delay by flooding algorithm going against real-time rendering. Therefore, this paper considers comprehensively rendering task requirement and characters of all types of p2p network, designs a hybrid p2p network combined with structured fundamental storage sites and unstructured application sites. Those application sites are also divided two types as fat and thin. Accordingly, an new selective caching along road method is presented for replica placement. Based on competitive learning, an new replica deleting method is also proposed. The remainder of this paper is organized as follows. Section 2 describes the replica management strategy on the hybrid p2p network in detail. Tests and evaluations on the strategy are shown in Section 3 from several aspects, and concludes in Section 4.

2   Replica Management Based on Selectivity and Learning

Considering the characters of massive terrain data and its application, this paper sets a determined mount of fundamental sites, which adopt fully-connected structured topology and have high performance, are used to storage terrain data initially and maintain the index information of all fundamental sites to support searching and locating quickly. This design can satisfy the hypothesis of strong site of steady storage. Its details of structure, maintenance and load balance etc can be found in other paper. In addition, other sites are called application sites, which are not limited of scale and ability (including some handheld devices) and adopt unstructured topology. This paper mainly focuses on the problem of replica management in the unstructured p2p network constituted by application sites.

2.1   Replica Placement of Application Sites

Application sites working for rendering have various types, which are divided two types: fat and thin, according to the performance relevant to replica management in this paper. To define the fat and thin sites, the performance of sites is defined firstly.

Definition 1. Performance of sites: Given undirected network G=(V,E), site $r \in V$, define the performance of site r as P(r) described by formula (1).

$$P(r) = \frac{1}{2}S(r)Q(r)(T(r) + D(r)) \qquad\qquad (1)$$

Here, $S(r)$ is the storage performance of site r, $S(r) \in [0,1]$, which is defined as

$$S(r) = \begin{cases} 0, SA(r) \le 2G \\ SA(r) - SU(r) \Big/ SA(r), else \end{cases}$$, $SA(r)$ represents the total volume of site r, $SU(r)$

represents the used storage of site r.

$Q(r)$ is the QOS benefit of site r, that is how many sites can be satisfied for their QOS requirements if replica is placed at site r, $Q(r) \in [0,1]$. It is defined as $Q(r) = 1 - \frac{1}{QOS(r)+1}$, $QOS(r)$ represents the number of sites satisfied for its QOS constraint if replica is placed at site r. The adding 1 of denominator is for avoiding divide by 0.

$T(r)$ is the performance of stable service, that is the on-line time of site r, $T(r) \in [0,1]$. It's defined as $T(r) = \frac{t(r)}{T\_month}$, $t(r)$ represents the average on-line time monthly (hour), T_month representing the total time of one month equals to 30*24=720 (hours).

$D(r)$ is the location performance of site r, that is the distance between fundamental sites and site r, $D(r) \in [0,1]$. If it has longer distance, the replica are placed dispersed relatively, which can improve the ratio of hitting target of replica. It is defined as $D(r) = 1 - \frac{1}{d(r,f)}$, and $d(r,f) = hops(r,f)$ that is the shortest hops between fundamental site f and site r.

Definition 2. Fat and thin sites: if a given site r has performance $P(r) \ge T_{Fat}$, the site r is defined as application fat site; if $P(r) \le T_{Thin}$, it is defined as application thin site; if $T_{Tine} \le P(r) \le T_{Fat}$, the site is defined pseudo fat site, which means starting replica deletion.

Based on the division of fat and thin sites the replica placement process can be described as:

Firstly, the shared files are placed at those fundamental sites. It's needed to consider the fundamental sites amount and load balance. It is assumed that the files have been placed at suitable fundamental site, and the load balance is described in other paper.

The start of replica placement: when the site placed shared files receives a request and accept for downloading, the replica placement algorithm starts. That is, when the file is transferred from resource site to requesting site, the replica are placed at the sites along the road.

If multiple sites request the same shared file simultaneously, the site nearest to fundamental sites is preferentially responded for downloading according to the location performance of requesting site.

Selective caching along road: those unstructured p2p network represented by Gnutella adopt caching all sites along road as replica placement strategy, which causes a large mount of replica difficult to be maintained and managed. This paper considers not only the storage performance of site but also on-line time, distance and specially QOS constraint of requesting site completely, selects only fat sites placed replica with two abilities of rendering and storage, then thin only for rendering, which avoids the resource waste caused by placing replica at all sites along road.

The replica placement algorithm of application fat site:

(1) If the request file exists at this site, consistency with the file transferred is checked. If coincide, it's transferred to requesting site; if not, the local file is replaced by the file from fundamental sites, then transferred to requesting site. After the replica placed here, the request can be satisfied at this site instead of fundamental sites. Certainly , consistency shall be checked before downloading.

(2) If the request file does not exist at this site, the replica placement is start and supports forwarding.

The division of fat and thin is not invariable but changes constantly in the whole network. If the performance of fat site has bigger changes, it could turn to thin site.

2.2   Replica Deletion

The deletion is executed at the fat sites. Competitive learning is used for deleting some not often request replica.

Learning start: while the request of file received each time, the learning is start.

Initially each replica file are set the same hot value $w_i = \frac{1}{N}$, N is the total amount of replicas in this site. Then, there are two circumstances to trigger the learning: one is that a request is received; the other a replica accepted. The learning process is:

For the jth replica file, let

$$w_j = w_j + \eta .\tag{2}$$

Then the hot value of all replica files are normalized as

$$w_i = \frac{w_i}{\sum w_j} .\tag{3}$$

η is defined as $\eta = k_1 A - k_2 T_{last}$ according to availability A and duration T_{last}. More availability, higher η; longer duration, lower η. Here, A represents the total times of downloading, and T_{last} represents the duration of storage the replication file at this site.

When there exist these situations described below, replica deletion is needed to clear those replicas with the lowest hot value.

2.3   Consistency Maintenance and Searching of Replica

Consistency check is executed only after current fat site received a request of shared file. It checks the local replica with the fundamental sites. If not coincide, the replica is updated then transferred to the request site.

This hybrid p2p network supports both index searching at fundamental sites and flooding searching at unstructured sites. Firstly requesting site sends connection message to fundamental site. Then the hop number arrived at fundamental site is obtained, which is set the TTL of the requesting site to support its flooding searching. For this, if some replicas are searched among TTL value except for fundamental sites downloading is executed. Otherwise, requesting site shall connect to those fundamental sites and fulfill downloading. So, flooding searching message can be controlled in a certain range, which can avoid a large mount of invalid flooding searching. The method also guarantees searching and obtaining the request shared data. And fail searching does not exist.

3   Performance Evaluation

Optorsim2.1 is adopted to evaluate the replica management strategy presented above. Firstly, 16 sites are built as fundamental sites with characters of both CE and SE, storage volume 500G, fully connected and bandwidth 1000Mbps. Then 1000 application sites are built with connected matrix made randomly (including connecting the 16 fundamental sites), 3 types sites (both SE and CE, only SE, only CE), storage volume set randomly among [80G, 500G], bandwidth randomly 100Mbps or 1000Mbps. The application sites only with CE ability resemble the hand-held devices, which used only for rendering. The terrain files are divided 4 types with sizes 5G, 10G, 20G,40G, totally 4800G (256 files), which are placed uniformly at 16 fundamental sites initially (with hypothesis of load balance).

For it is not considered of terrain changes such as crater in this paper, terrain files are nearly not needed of write operation. So, 4 read operations are designed with a given probability according to file size as shown in Table 1.

Table 1. Schedule of read access

Type	Size(GB)	Probability
R1	5	20%
R2	10	20%
R3	20	30%
R4	40	30%

3.1   Controlling Total Amount of Replicas

Replica placement has two key problems: the amount of replicas and location. In an unstructured p2p network, two methods are generally adopted including catching all sites along road and catching at origin site. And the methods of FIFO or least accessed recently are generally used for replica replacement. To test the effectiveness of our replica management strategy including selective catching along road, deletion based on learning etc, comparisons are made with those general methods of catching all sites along road for placement and least accessed recently for deletion.

For each 10 seconds, 500 external read access requests are submitted. Suppose there are no occurrences with site failures or network partitions during simulator running. Total replica amount of each site is recorded. Experimental results show total replica amount increases form 0 up to 1015 with the passage of time, then decreases at about 870 stably with the effect of learning. Compared with this, total amount of replicas of the general replica placement method increase from 0 up to 1240. Then it decreases at about 1080 with the management of deleting the files with least hot value. Therefore, the strategy has better performance than general methods.

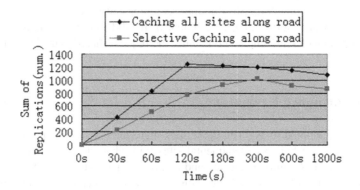

Fig. 1. Comparison of total replica amount

3.2   Searching Time and Ratio of Hitting Target

The objectives of p2p distributed storage are presenting shared file searching and downloading steadily and quickly. For this, ratio of hitting target is an important performance index. Because of the hybrid structure in this paper, each data request has response from at least fundamental sites. That is, the ratio of hitting target can receive 100%, though maybe needs longer searching time. Therefore, it's mainly test in this simulations how many time a shared file request costs.

For each 10 seconds, 500 external read access requests are submitted. The type of response site and hops are recorded for each request. Experiments show that the hops of hitting target decrease at about 2-3 stably with the passage of time, which can also satisfy thoroughly the QOS constraint of requesting site.

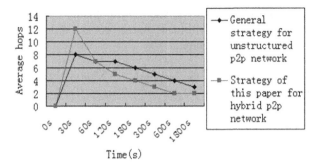

Fig. 2. Time of searching

3.3   Performance of Replica Storage at Each Site

The performance has relation with the storage capability of site itself and bandwidth etc. In this paper, learning is used to delete those invalid replicas, which make the replica amount of fat sites keeping in a reasonable range. To evaluate the replica storage of each site, the maximum and minimum replica amount of each site are recorded in the experiments above and shown as Figure 3.

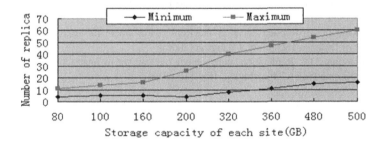

Fig. 3. Distribution of replica

At the sites with better storage capability both the maximum and minimum replica amounts increase at the same time. Generally all sites control its replica amount at 50%-70% of total storage volume. Experimental results show that the strategy in this paper has not excellent performance in load balance though can guarantee effort storage of each site.

4   Conclusions

This paper presents a hybrid p2p network of distributed storage terrain data and its replica management strategy. Experimental results show that the replica placement of selective catching along road can reduce total amount of replicas. At the mean time the stability of searching and ratio of hitting target can be guaranteed. And the competitive learning controls effectively the replica amount of each site and avoids invalid deletion. Further research will focus on the problem of load balance, which is the deficiency of this strategy currently.

Acknowledgement. Thanks for the support of National (China) 863 Project 2006AA01Z309.

References

1. Feiyan, S.: Research on replica optimization in data-intensive computing. Wuhan University of Technology, Wuhan (2011)
2. Jing, X., Chunhua, L., Tianzi, C.: GIS data transportation based on P2P. Computer Engineering and Design (China) 28(12), 2851–2853 (2007)
3. Shaoming, P., Zhanwu, Y., et al.: Massive terrain navigation search model based on P2P. Application Research of Computers (China) 26(5), 1659–1662 (2009)
4. Zhengquan, X., Lu, G., et al.: A terrain data storage model based on an unstructured P2P network. Geomatics and Information Science of Wuhan University (China) 35(1), 122–125 (2010)
5. Wei, F., Nong, X., Xicheng, L.: A survey for QoS-aware replica placement problem. Journal of Computer Research and Development (China) 46(suppl.), 36–43 (2009)
6. Xiong, F., Ruchuan, W.: Study on replica placement algorithm in tree-based data grid environments. Journal of Nanjing University of Posts and Telecommunications (Natural Science) (China) 31(3), 72–78 (2011)
7. Wei, R.: Research of Replica Location and Replica Placement for Massive Data. National University of Defense Technolgy, Changsha (2006)
8. Yu, C., Jianquan, D.: Replication management mechanism in unstructured P2P network. Computer Engineering (China) 34(18), 108–110 (2008)

The Application of LBS Based on Android

Wei Li[1] and Dongxin Lu[2]

[1] Software College, Nanchang University, Nanchang, China
Jane_liwei@qq.com
[2] Software College, Nanchang University, Nanchang, China
Lu.dongxin@zte.com.cn

Abstract. LBS (Location Based Service) is a service which is provided to mobile users according to their location and the support of GIS (Geographic Information System). LBS can get the users' location though the wireless communication network (i.e. GSM, CDMA) of Mobile telecommunications operators or external positioning (i.e. GPS). As the development of travelling, people are urgent to have LBS apps to help them to be familiar to a new place. And Android platform is free and open to provide interrelated functions. This paper summary the concepts of LBS including the component and characteristics. In this paper also introduces Android, including the architecture and component models of Android. At last the paper illustrates the application of LBS based on android.

Keywords: LBS, Android, GIS, location.

1 Introduction of LBS

1.1 The Definition of LBS

Location Based Services includes two meaning: The first is making sure the location of the mobile user; the second is providing kinds of information services with the users' location [1]. It is a system of services related with location. People also called it "MAPS-Mobile Position Services".

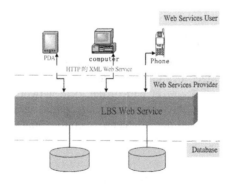

Fig. 1. LBS

J. Lei et al. (Eds.): NCIS 2012, CCIS 345, pp. 775–782, 2012.
© Springer-Verlag Berlin Heidelberg 2012

For example, we can use LBS to find hotels, cinemas, libraries, gas stations and so on in 1 km radius of current location. So LBS can be defined as completing two functions ---- location and service with the Internet or wireless network between fixed users and mobile users.

1.2 The Component of LBS

Overall, LBS is integrated the mobile communication network and the computer network. The two networks interact though the gateway. The mobile terminal send requests via mobile communication network and send them to LBS platform though gateway. The service platform will deal with the requests according to the location of the user. Then the platform will send the result to the user though the gateway.

The mobile terminal can be mobile phones, PDA (Personal Digital Assistant), pocket PC and desktop PC which can communicate via Internet. The service platform includes web server, location server and LDAP (Lightweight Directory Access Protocol) server.

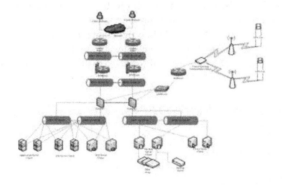

Fig. 2. The component of LBS

1.3 The Characteristics of LBS

There are two main characteristics in this paper we just introduce as fellow:

- High coverage

On the one hand, the covered area is required large enough; On the other hand, the indoor should be included. Users use this function indoor mostly. The high buildings and the underground facilities both must be guaranteed to cover every corner. According to the scope of coverage, location-based services can be divided into three types: in the entire local network, to cover part of the local network and the roaming network In addition to coverage, the network structure and dynamics of changes in environmental factors may also lead that a telecom operator cannot guarantee the services in the local network or roaming net-work.

- Positioning accuracy

Mobile location should provide different accuracy depending on the user demand for services and can provide the right to select precision to the user. Positioning accuracy is not only depending on the positioning technology, but also is depending on business external environment, including radio propagation environment, the density and location of the base station and positioning equipment.

2   Android

Along with the rapid development of Mobile Internet, a new time has coming. "Mobile Internet" refers to access to the Internet from a mobile device, such as a smartphone or laptop via integrated abilities. The smartphone is an iconic client tool of Mobile Internet era. Android is open source mobile phone operating system developed by Google based on the Linux platform. It includes all the software that required by mobile phone, such as operating systems, user interface and applications. And there are no obstacles of innovation exclusive right in the mobile industry as past.

2.1   Architecture

Android uses a layered architecture as other operating systems. There are four layers in Android architecture. From the top to the lower are applications, application framework, libraries and Linux kernel [2].

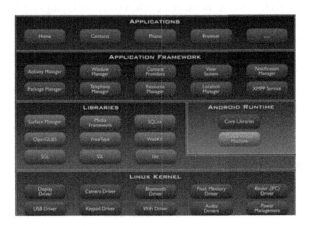

Fig. 3. Android Architecture [3]

A set of core applications are on the top level in the framework, including an email client, a SMS app, a calendar, web browser and so on. All apps are written using the Java programming language.

2.2   The Component of Android Application

There are four building blocks to an Android application: Activity, Intent Receiver, Service and Content Provider [4]. They are introduced as fellow:

1.   Activity

A activity usually is a user interface screen. An application can define one or more activities to handle the different tasks at different stage. As a part of life circle of applications, every activity needs to save their own state in case of restoring the state in the future.

2.   Intent Receiver

Intent receiver is a description of the mechanism of specific action [5]. For example, take a photo, make a call or listen to music. In Android system, almost everything need to go through intent. Thus, there are many opportunities to replace or reuse many components.

For example, now you want to send an e-mail. If the application needs to send the mail, it will use the intention. Or you are writing a new email program, you can register a activity to handle the intention instead of using the traditional email application. When others want to send an email, they will use your app.

3.   Service

Service is the task which runs in the background. There is no need for users to contact with it. It is something like the progress daemon in UNIX [6].

Take an example: when we use mobile phone to listen to music, we hope we can keep on listening even when we are using other apps. So the codes which are for playing music should be in one service. Then the service maybe binds together with another activity, which is to tell the service when to stop playing. Android installs lots of services and APIs inside. Hence we can use them easily.

4.   Content Provider

Content provider is a set of data which implements in self-defined APIs. And we can read or write data in the API. This is the best way to share the data with other applications. A good example is contact application. Google use a content provider in contact. Any application which wants to use the information of contacts can share all the messages, such as name, address, telephone and so on.

3   An Application of LBS Based on Android

Before 2007, it is very complex and difficult to write a LBS application. People need to pay a big mount of copyright fee to the map maker [7]. But now it is not a problem. Flexible map display and control functions and location support are provided in Android. What's more, android is totally free and open. You can develop a LBS application as you want based on android.

3.1   Get a Google Map API Key

Before you use GoogleMaps in your Android application, you should first get a Google Map API key. The API key can be used in many applications but not every application needs to apply a API key.

Before applying the API Key, we should first get the MD5 of keystore in the computer of the developing environment. We can enter the direction where the keytool of JDK at through DOS. Then we can write fellow codes:

Keytool-alias android debugkey –keytool C:\user\jane\.android\debug.keystore –storepass android –keypass android

Then we can get such information:

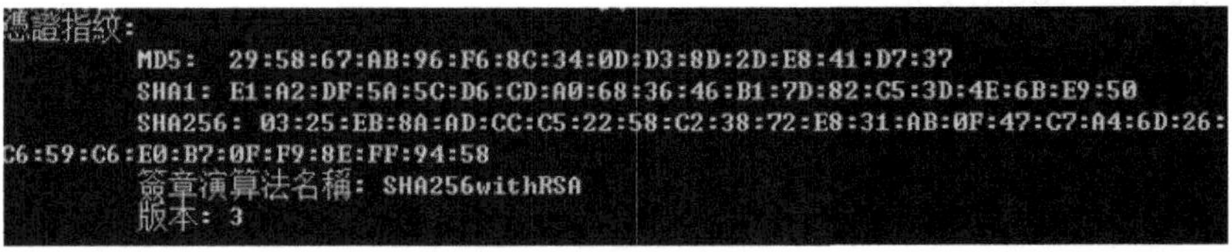

Fig. 4. MD5

Next we can go to http://code.google.com/android/maps-api-signup.html, enter the MD5 in the MD5 fingerprint. Thus we get the Google Map API Key. Last but not least, we should declare the authority in the AndroidManifiest.xml as follow:

```
<user-permission andro-
id:name="android.permission.INTERNET"/>
<user-library android:name="com.google.android.maps"/>
```

Then we can display the map in the application.

3.2   MapView

MapView is used to play a view of map. We can zoom in and out of the map by the MapView. It also supports the map movement. Thus we can see wherever we want to get with simple operations. What's more we can also draw strings or circles on the map. It supports multi-layer overlay. MapView need to be added into the layout as follow:

```
<com.google.android.maps.MapView
  android:id="@+id/myMap"
  android:layout_width="wrap_content"
  android:layout_height="wrap_content"
  android:enabled="true"
  android:clickable="true"
 android:apiKey="application apikey"/>
```

3.3   Location

We can simply know that we should get location first through the name-Location Based Service. In Android, the two important classes for location are LocationManager and LocationProvider. LocationManager provides the methods that can be access to location. LocationProvider defines the ways that how we get the location. [8] We can use the android Location-Based API to collect user current position and display the current user location on the phone.

```
locationManager=(LocationManager) getSystemSer-
vice(Context.LOCATION_SERVICE);
String provider=LocationManager.GPS_PROVIDER;
Location location=
locationManager.getLastKnownLocation(provider);

double lat=0.0;
double lng=0.0;
if (location!=null){
lat=location.getLatitude();
lng=location.getLongitude();
    }
GeoPoint point=new Geo-
Point((int)(lat*1E6),(int)(lng*1E6));
controller.animateTo(point);
```

Thus we can get the location in the map.

Fig. 5. Show location

3.4   Get Services

After we get user's recent location, we can get some information such as the canteens, parks or ATMs around the user through Internet with Android APIs.

```
resultString = MapsHttpUtil.getGetRoundPlace(
Tools.getLocation(getApplicationContext()), parame-
ters[0].split(",")[0],parameters[0].split(",")[1] );
```
Then we can show these information in your application to
the users.
```
String localDetailString = MapsHttpU-
til.getGetdPlaceDetailMessage(refranceString);
JSONObject jsonObject = new JSONOb-
ject(localDetailString);
JSONObject resultJsonObject = new JSONOb-
ject(jsonObject.getString("result"));
placeName.setText("名称:" + resultJsonOb-
ject.getString("name"));
placeAddress.setText("地址 :" + resultJsonOb-
ject.getString("formatted_address"));
phoneNumber.setText("电话:" + resultJsonOb-
ject.getString("formatted_phone_number"));
  mapURL = resultJsonObject.getString("url");
```

Users can get follow information:

Fig. 6. Show canteen around the user

If user want to know more about one canteen, he just need to click it then the browser
will get the detailed information from the Internet to him.

In developing and testing, using simulating machine is very convenient. We can use DDMS tool of Eclipse to send different geographical coordinates to simulate the application in Emulator Control.

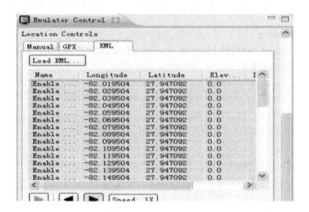

Fig. 7. Location Control

4   Conclusion

Android platform is very convenient for developers to develop a LBS application. It integrates zoom and map movement by just a few lines of java codes and XML codes. Through the research on LBS and Android, from this paper, it also shows that the user can easily get useful service information from the android application. And the application achieves high performance. With the development of mobile internet, Android will become more and more strong and bring us more convenient. In the future, we will keep on working more powerful LBS application based on Android.

References

1. Baidu Baike, http://www.baike.baidu.com/
2. Shu, X., Du, Z., Chen, R.: Researh on Mobile Location Service Design Based on Android. Dalian, China
3. Android Developers, http://www.androidin.com/
4. Open Hanset Alliance, http://www.openhandsetalliance.com/
5. DiMarzio, J.F.: Android: A Programmer's Guide. McGraw-Hill, Chicago (July 2008)
6. Haseman, C.: Android Essentials. PDF Electronic Book (2008), http://androidos.cc/dev/index.php
7. Gramlich, N.: Android Programming, PDF Electronic Book (2008), http://androidos.cc/dev/index.php
8. Burnette, E.: Hello, Android: Introducing Google's Mobile Development Platform, pp. 11–19 (2008)

Research on 3G Application with NFC

JunWu Xu[1] and JunLing Liang[2]

[1] Hubei Provincial Key Laboratory of Intelligent Robot,
Wuhan Institute of Technology, 430073, China
[2] School of Automation, Wuhan University of Technology 430074, China

Abstract. This paper describes research in the use of NFC to develop 3G applications. This paper introduces the structure of NFC library and describes the implementation of algorithms in our library.. NFC is a standards-based, short-range wireless connectivity technology that enables simple and intuitive two-way interactions between electronic devices. With NFC technology, consumers can perform contactless transactions, access digital content and connect NFC-enabled devices with a single touch.

Keywords: NFC ,Tag ,RFID, GSM.

1   What Is NFC?

Near Field Communication (NFC) is a short-range wireless connectivity technology (also known as ISO 18092) that provides intuitive, simple, and safe communication between electronic devices. Communication occurs when two NFC-compatible devices are brought within four centimeters of one another.   NFC operates at 13.56 MHz and transfers data at up to 424 Kbits/second.

Because the transmission range is so short, NFC-enabled transactions are inherently secure. NFC is distinguished by its intuitive interface and its ability to enable largely proprietary wireless networking   platforms to interoperate in a seamless manner.

The following chart shows how NFC compares in range and speed with other wireless technologies that can be used in a mobile phone. Communication occurs when two NFC-compatible devices are brought within about four centimeters of each other. By design, NFC requires close proximity and it offers instant connectivity, which provides an intuitive consumer experience that can be readily applied to the transit environment.

Smart Poster is the name given by the NFC Forum to small writer RF tags, which Arnold says can be embedded "almost anywhere, from a magazine to a poster or a statue, or on the wall". You can then tap this with an NFC device, such as a suitably equipped phone, and see whatever information has been included. It could be a short description of what you're looking at, or a film poster could give you the showing times at your local cinema and directions to it, or an advert in a magazine might give you a coupon.

It could have more important uses, too. Arnold gives the example of a prescription bottle with more safety and usage information available using an embedded Smart Poster than you could fit on the label.

J. Lei et al. (Eds.): NCIS 2012, CCIS 345, pp. 783–790, 2012.
© Springer-Verlag Berlin Heidelberg 2012

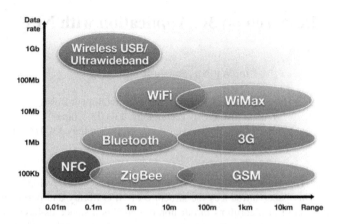

Fig. 1. NFC Compared with Other Wireless Technologies

With two powered devices, peer-to-peer data transfer similar to Bluetooth is possible. Although it's slower than Bluetooth and has a much more limited range, it consumes less power. There are also no set-up passwords or codes required, as there is with Bluetooth and secure Wi-Fi. You could simply place your digital camera next to your TV to send photos across for viewing.

NFC was approved as an ISO/IEC standard on December 8, 2003 and later as an ECMA standard.

NFC is an open platform technology standardized in ECMA-340 and ISO/IEC 18092. These standards specify the modulation schemes, coding, transfer speeds and frame format of the RF interface of NFC devices, as well as initialization schemes and conditions required for data collision-control during initialization for both passive and active NFC modes. Furthermore, they also define the transport protocol, including protocol activation and data-exchange methods. The air interface for NFC is standardized in:

ISO/IEC 18092 / ECMA-340
    Near Field Communication Interface and Protocol-1 (NFCIP-1)
ISO/IEC 21481 / ECMA-352
    Near Field Communication Interface and Protocol-2 (NFCIP-2)

2   NFC Applications

2.1   Transit and Ticketing

Contactless tickets have already begun to revolutionize the speed and ease with which all consumers can use public transport and access controlled environments like parking garages. Users praise NFC transactions for their speed, security, and fexibility. With NFC-enabled mobile phones, you can buy tickets, receive them electronically, use them for seamless traveling (such as "Park and Ride"), and then go through fast track turnstiles while others wait.Later, you can check your balance or update your tickets remotely.

The cost of providing transport or event ticketing will be driven down because NFC- based systems reduce the cost of card issuance andmanagement. Commuter transit systems in Europe and a number of Asia Pacifc countries already use NFC-compatible contactless technologies to speedtravelers through to their destinations.

Fig. 2. Using NFC to Pay for Parking

2.2   "Amazing NFC"–Oulu,Finland

The Oulu Region is in northwest Finland and has over 200,000 inhabitants. It is the fastest-growing region in Finland, and it boasts world-class standards in information technology networks and services. Its high-tech industries are famous for their high growth.

"Amazing NFC" is a city orienteering course for educational purposes, which has two routes: a civic track and a cultural/historical track. On the civic, or "survival," track, pupils get to know Oulu's offces and institutions. On the cultural/historical track, students become familiar with Oulu's culture and history.

The pedagogical goals of the NFC-based Urban Orienteering project were to teach secondary school students skills and knowledge for coping with everyday life, and to familiarize students with the culture and history of their own city. By transferring the educational setting from the classroom to the actual contextual environment, the project aimed to infuence the students' motivation to learn and build life-management skills, with the idea that school is part of the surrounding society and we learn from life in general.

By touching the NFC Smart Posters, the students would receive text, video, or audio tracks relating to each checkpoint. They would also receive a map to the next checkpoint. The teachers could also monitor the student's progress, as the checkpoint information was sent back to a central system that the teacher could access via computer.

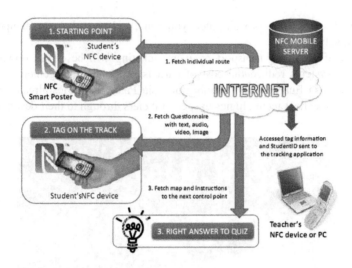

Fig. 3. "Amazing NFC" Urban Orienteering

2.3   Opt-in forTimely Couponing–Kuwait

In Kuwait, a shopping mall adds value for its retailers by using NFC Smart Posters placed in the entrances of the mall. Users touch their NFC-enabled handsets to NFC Smart Posters to opt in and receive the day's special offers. The relevant special offers are matched to the user's profle so that each shopper receives pertinent and attractive offers. This is particularly benefcial to the businesses advertised, as it drives pre-qualifed (more motivated) customers to their establishments. Not only the retailer but also the payment processor benefts, as these incentives are also tied to a specifc mode of payment used in this case.Contributors: ViVOtech, National Bank of Kuwait, Zain, Visa, The Avenues

Fig. 4. Opt-in for Timely

3   Develop 3G Application with NFC

3.1   NFC Technology

This section describes the NFC Mobile Framework, based on the essential recommendations in this white paper . It helps players in the NFC Mobile Ecosystem to envision a generic and balanced end-to-end system. It shows how the pieces of technology are put together to provide successful NFC mobile services, and how existing and future systems and services are constructed.

This framework can be a reference for standardization work, but will not dictate what needs to be standardized by the NFC Forum. It will help audiences understand the relationships with other technology providers such as standards development organizations and industry forums.

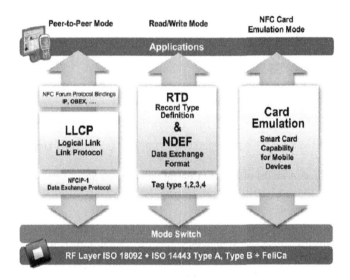

Fig. 5. Functional Framework Overview

3.2   Service and Content Providers

A service provider, such as an advertising agency, provides a communications, storage, or processing service, or any combination of the three, in a platform as an enabler to a content provider, such as a retailer that wants to promote its products to consumers.

In practice, an advertising agency that offers an NFC Smart Poster platform would be engaged by a retail chain to process, store, and communicate its messages to its target customers. In this case, consumers would access the content of the retail chain, but it would be provided via the agency's presentation platform.

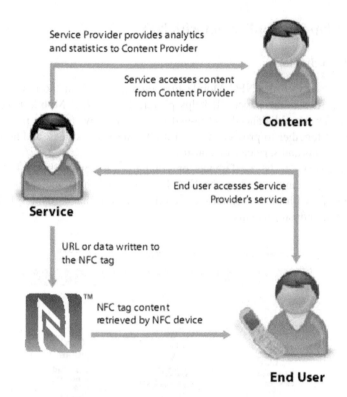

Fig. 6. A model of how the Content Provider and Service Provider

3.3   JSR-257

This specification defines the Contactless Communication API, a Java ME optional package containing anapplication programming interface that allows applications to access information on contactless targets, such as RFID tags and bar codes.

Listing 1 NFC code

```
import java.io.IOException;
import javax.microedition.contactless.*;
import javax.microedition.contactless.ndef.*;
import javax.microedition.io.Connector;
/**
* Example class of how to discover targets using
* JSR 257 Contactless Communication API
*/
public class CCAPIExample implements TargetListener {
private DiscoveryManager dm;
public CCAPIExample()
```

```
{
registerTargetToDiscovery();
}
public void registerTargetToDiscovery()
{
// Check that NDEF_TAG target is supported
TargetType[] targets = DiscoveryManager.getSupportedTargetTypes();
boolean supported = false;
for (int i=0; i<targets.length; i++)
  {
     if (targets[i].equals(TargetType.NDEF_TAG))
       {
         supported = true;
         }
     }
  if (supported)
  {
  // Get DiscoveryManager instance and
  // set TargetListener for NDEF_TAG target
     dm = DiscoveryManager.getInstance();
  try {
     dm.addTargetListener(this, TargetType.NDEF_TAG);
     }
     catch (ContactlessException ce) {
     // handle exception
     }
   }
}
```

4   Conclusion

In this article, we can use the NFC to develop application for 3G . The mobile NFC ecosystem represents a convergence of differing business cultures. This presents an opportunity to develop new businesses and markets. The variety of ecosystem players involved will stimulate the development of new NFC mobile services and the intent of this white paper is to contribute to this activity.

References

[1] ECMA International Standard ECMA-340, Near Field Communication Interface and Protocol (NFCIP-1), 2nd edn. (December 2004)
[2] Catrysse, M., Hermans, B., Puers, R.: An inductive power system with integrated bi-directional data-transmission. Sensors and Actuators A: Physical 115(2-3), 221–229 (2004)

[3] Wireless Power Consortium, System Description Wireless Power Transfer, vol.1: Low Power, Part 1: Interface Definition, Version 1.0 (July 2010)

[4] Strömmer, E., Kaartinen, J., Pärkkä, J., Ylisaukko-oja, A., Korhonen, I.: Application of near field communication for health monitoring in daily life. In: Proc. 28th IEEE EMBS Annual International Conference, New York City, pp. 3246–3249 (2006)

[5] NFC Activity Specification. Technical Specification. NFCForum-TSActivity- 1.0. NFC Forum (November 18, 2010)

[6] NFC: When Will Be the Real Start? Frost&Sullivan (January 11, 2011)

[7] Technical Specification, Smart Poster Record Type Definition. NFC Forum (2006)

[8] Bluetooth Specification plus EDR, Master Table of Contents & Compliance Requirements. Bluetooth SIG, version 2.1 (2007)

[9] Mulliner, C.: Vulnerability Analysis and Attacks on NFC-enabled Mobile Phones. In: Proceedings of the 1st International Workshop on Sensor Security (IWSS) at ARES, Fukuoka, Japan, pp. 695–700 (March 2009)

[10] Identification cards — contactless integrated circuit(s) cards — vicinity cards (ISO/IEC 15693), ISO/IEC (2000)

[11] Specification of implementation for integrated circuit(s) cards (JICSAP/ JSA jis x 6319). JICSAP/JSA (2005)

[12] Information technology — telecommunications and information exchange between systems — near field communication interface and protocol 1 (NFCIP-1) (ISO/IEC 18092), ISO/IEC (2004)

[13] Technical Specification, NFC Record Type Definition (RTD). NFC Forum, rTD 1.0 (2006)

[14] Simple pairing whitepaper. Bluetooth SIG, revision V10r00 (2006)

[15] Collins, J.: Rfid-zapper shoots to kill. RFID Journal (2006),
http://www.rfidjournal.com/article/print/2098

[16] Near Field Communication (NFC) controller — Product data sheet. NXP Semiconductors, rev. 3.2 (2007)

[17] Technical Specification, NFC Data Exchange Format (NDEF). NFC Forum, nDEF 1.0 (2006)

Short-Term BF Research on TD-LTE System

Xiaotao Xu[*] and Wenbing Jin

Zhejiang Institute of Mechanical and Electrical Engineering, Hangzhou 310053, China

Abstract. The beamforming used in TD-LTE systems is a somewhat more complex proposition. Eigenvalue-based beamforming (EBB) is based on Singular value decomposition. It's included short-term BF and Long-term BF two methods and applied in different channel knowledge. In this paper, firstly, it described short-term BF algorithm, especially focused on the method how to apply for OFDM and TD-LTE system. And then make a SW designing implementation for short-term BF, too. It is involved in some basic idea of implementation, SRS combiner and MAC layer designing. Finally, the paper gives the detailed simulation for different performance index and gets some technical conclusion.

Keywords: TD-LTE, beamforming, EBB algorithm, performance simulation, SRS combiner, temporal correlation.

1 Introduction

Beamforming is supported by LTE release 8 with transmission mode 7 and dedicated reference signals. In release 9, after request from CMCC service provider, a new transmission mode for dual layer beamforming is introduced. Standard is ready except for some RAN4 (Radio Area Networks) requirements, and optimized to work with dual polar antenna arrays. Dedicated reference signal for DL MIMO (multiple input multiple output) is becoming default for beyond rel8.

DL beamforming isn't critical for neither the link budget nor the system performance. It can provide gains by improving the user signal and reducing the inter cell interference but implementation complexity is nonegligble. DL beamforming produces interference flashlight effect which makes inter-cell interference very unstable. This reduces the performance and makes a network with beamforming less robust than one without. It uses arrays of antenna elements at the base station to improve user bit rate, too. Its antenna weights were determined by measuring uplink channel and every UE has specific beam. In same way DL beamforming reduces coverage of DL control channels, in certain cases these channels could be limiting the coverage and/or capacity. DL beamforming relies on correspondence between signals measured from the UEs UL transmission and transmitted by base station in DL. This requires accurate calibration between transmitter and receiver in base station (calibration in the UE does not

---

[*] Corresponding author.

J. Lei et al. (Eds.): NCIS 2012, CCIS 345, pp. 791–797, 2012.
© Springer-Verlag Berlin Heidelberg 2012

make a big difference). Calibration is a complex, expensive and nonstandard function which needs hardware support in the RF parts of the base station.

The rest of this paper is organized as follows; section 2 gives simple introduction of short-term algorithm. Especially has some details explanation how to apply for OFDM or TD-LTE system. Section 3 gives the software designing of short-term BF, for example, basic implementation idea, SRS combiner, Mac layer designing etc. Section 4 simulate and analyze short-term BF performance: frequency granularity, performance benchmark and temporal correlation etc.

2   Short-Term Algorithm Overview

2.1   Algorithm Assumption

System model:

$$y = H \cdot x + n, \quad where \ H = U\Sigma V^{H}$$

Assuming perfect channel state information at the transmitter and receiver we could apply perfect Tx and Rx beam-forming to transfer signal model to diagonal:

$$\tilde{y} = U^{H} \cdot H \cdot V \cdot x + U^{H} \cdot n = \Sigma \cdot x + n'$$

Where the beamforming matrix UH and V can be determined as the eigenvectors of the channel correlation matrix

$$R_{RX} = HH^{H} = U\Lambda_{RX}U^{H} \quad and \quad R_{TX} = H^{H}H = V\Lambda_{TX}V^{H}$$

For multiple beamformer instantaneous water-filling based on eigen-value is performed to maximize the channel capacity. The above equation assumes instantaneous CSI at TX, e.g. for each transmission the channel is known perfectly.

2.2   Applied to OFDM

Multipath MIMO channel with path delay (i-RX; j-TX):

$$h_{i,j}(t) = \sum_{k=1}^{L} h_{i,j}^{(k)}(t) \cdot \delta(\tau - \tau_{k}) = [0...0 \ h_{i,j}^{(1)}(t)...h_{i,j}^{(L)}(t) \ 0...0]^{T}$$

With cyclic prefixed OFDM the frequency selective channel evolves into N frequency flat channel (k is subcarrier index)

$$H_{i,j}(k) = FFT\{h_{i,j}(t)\} = \sum_{l=1}^{L} h_{i,j}^{(l)} \cdot \exp\left(-j2\pi \frac{\tau_{l}}{T_{c}} \frac{k}{N}\right)$$

The receiver covariance matrix can be written as

$$R_{i,j}(k) = \sum_{m=1}^{N_{TX}} H_{i,m}(k) \cdot H_{m,j}^{H}(k)$$

It can be seen that the instantaneous spatial correlation matrix is frequency selective and different for each freq bin/subcarrier. For implementation simplicity we can perform short-term EBB on subband basis instead of subcarrier by assuming channel flat within the subband.

2.3 Applied to TD-LTE

Short-term BF is need for SRS hopping, time-consuming, tens of TTIs (Transmission Time Intervals) to scan full bandwidth. CSI quickly out-dated in case of fast changing channels. For SRS hopping, it's impossible due to limited UE Tx power and SRS capacity (UE multiplexing). Antenna in short-term BF is imbalance with UE. There are 2 Rx antennas but only 1 Tx antenna, and alternating sounding from both Tx antennas of the UE. Antenna switching is optional in 3GPP R8 (not supported by most terminals). Only half of channel state information (CSI) is obtained in 1Tx Antenna sounding.

For subband SINR, short term EBB is updated when new sounding received in the subband. For sub band eigenvector of channel covariance matrix, short term EBB is updated when new sounding received in the subband. Especially, for dual stream two vectors is needed in short term EBB. On the other hand, Short term EBB with dual antenna sounding can enable the generation of dual antenna sounding measurements, can be used for generating precoder both for first and second stream, and then support increased sounding bandwidth of 16 PRB, too.

3 Software Designing Description

3.1 Basic Idea of Implementation

Short-term BF uses the instantaneous channel vector to calculate the weighting factor. Assuming the freq granularity of short-term BF is S PRBs, then the spatial covariance matrix at current sub-frame is computed by averaging over the subband size.

If the suband size is equal to one PRB then we can avoid EVD calculation because the channel h_i is a column vector due to one TX antenna in the uplink and R_s has rank=1 so the principle eigenvector is equal to the normalized channel vector h_i.

3.2 SRS Combiner

Short term BF weight calculation is $W_i = \dfrac{S_i}{\sqrt{\sum_{i=1}^{8} S_i}} * 1.414$. Si is the value sent by

SRS receiver, which is an average result over 4PRB after SRS derogate and Rx calibration compensation. And the weight for the 4 PRB in one PRB group has same value.

SRS combiner needs to save weight for each PRB to 256k bytes DDR circular buffer. The maximum space to store short term BF weight is 8*96*4 = 3k bytes, SRS combiner need to allocate 256k byte which means it is able to save over 85 TTI, if CDM is 3, and this buffer should be good enough to hold over 28 TTI. SRS should write weight in order of ant 1, 5,2,6,3,7,4,8. SRS combiner sends Message to MAC, too.

3.3   MAC Layer Designing

MAC is new interface to DL PHY, too. It forwards the weight address and additional info to DL PHY in SDlTbFormat. The SW designing add a new parameter to MAC, too. The purpose is switching between long term BF and short term BF, if R&D parameter is set to enable LT BF weight, MAC has the following value in SDlTbFormat (stWeight   = NULL). When DL PHY detect the address is NULL, then it will use Long term BF weight.

For DL PHY layer, there is may be a chance that, the SRS bandwidth do not cover all PRB, that mean not every PRB got a short term BF weight, a quick solution is for those PRB without short term BF weight use the long term.

MAC only passes the short-term beamforming weight pointer from UL PHY to DL PHY. For this purpose, a transparent pointer of stBFWeight is added to both PHY_SRS_RECEIVE_RESP_U_MSG and PHY_PDSCH_SEND_REQ_MSG.

4   Performance Simulation and Analysis

4.1   Simulation Assumption

They are several types of algorithms for the beamforming, such as EBB, DOA, EqualGain .... Before the EBB link level performance evaluation, we should make clear which channel model should be used, how to define the simulation parameters and the basic assumption for this feasibility study.

For the beamforming feasibility study iteration1, we assume it is the single user under low mobility, PDSCH only, no PBCH, no Control Channels and Synchronization Signals. For the baseline, we used 1Tx1Rx SISO and 1Tx2Rx SIMO (MRC).

4.2   Performance Simulation

4.2.1   Short Term Frequency Granularity

We set different subbands to check the frequency granularity for the STBF. x PRBs means x PRBs have the same BF vector.

In Figure 1, obviously, for the STBF, in frequency selective channel, less subband sizes have better performances. But per the current SRS channel estimation algorithm limitation; we just support at least 4 PRBs for one subband. It is one open issue for the further work.

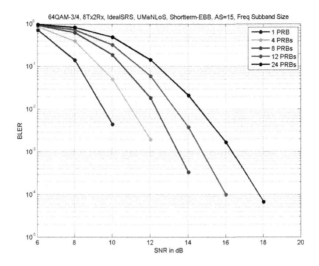

Fig. 1. Performance simulation under different subband

4.2.2   Short Term Performance Benchmark

Figure 2 show the performances for different scenarios. From the results, we can see that short-term BF can provide about 6~7.5 dB gain at UE 2Rx, and 9~12 dB gain at UE 1Rx. For overall, it has better results at large angular spread. It is quite sensitive with the SRS noise power, especially at small angular spread.

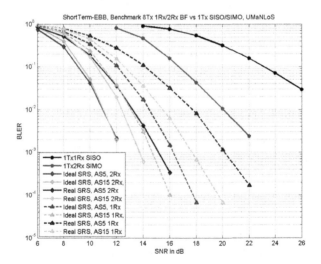

Fig. 2. Performance benchmark with SRS noise power

4.2.3   Short Term Temporal Correlation

Figure 3 gives the results at different BF vector feedback delay and different UE moving speeds. Regarding the BF feedback delay, we can see that for 19 TTIs, the performances are still acceptable. So we can get the important information: as long as the SRS is within 20 ms, the CSI acquired from the SRS is still useful for DL beamforming. This is very useful for the SRS configuration and DL scheduler.

For the Short term BF, since it used the instantaneous channel statistics, it is also sensitive with the UE moving speeds. Low moving speed has the better performance. This is verified at Figure 3. But even in 120kmh, it is still better than the SIMO in 3kmh.

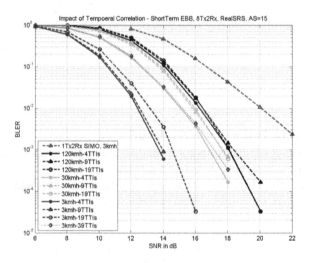

Fig. 3. Performance impact of temporary correlation

Acknowledgment. Short term BF fit for the scenarios with increased multipath (high angular spread) and low UE mobility. It is much sensitive to frequency resolution and fast channel variation. We can increase SRS bandwidth and decrease periodicity (12 PRB, 2ms SRS periodicity) to maintain good BF performance. As long as the delay between SRS and PDSCH is within 20ms, the instantaneous channel state from SRS is still useful for DL beamforming.

References

1. Gaudes, C.C., Santamaria, I., Via, J., Masgrau, E., Sese, T.: Roubust array beamforming with sidelobe control, using support vector machines. IEEE Trans. Sig. Proc. 55(2), 654–672 (2007)
2. Li, J., Stoica, P., Wang, Z.: On robust Capon beamforming and diagonal loading. IEEE Trans. Sig. Proc. 51(7), 1502–1514 (2003)

3. Li, G., Yan, G., Ning, L.: A fast convergence DOA estimation algorithm. In: International Conference in Communications and Networking in China 2006 (CHINACOM 2006), Beijing, China, October 25-27 (2006)
4. Singh, H., Singh, S.: Smart-802.11b MAC protocol for use with smart antennas. In: IEEE International Conference on Communications (ICC 2004), Paris, France, June 20-24, vol. 6, pp. 2684–2688 (2004)
5. Zhao, R., Yu, F., Yang, L.: Relay-Assisted Cooperative Communication Networks. ZTE Communications 6(3), 21–23 (2008)
6. 3GPP R1-090193. Aspects of Joint Processing in Downlink CoMP (2009)

Building M-Learning System Based
on Wireless Network in Colleges

Yan-Qun Xiao

Department of Information Engineering
Yangzhou Polytechnic College
Yangzhou, China
yzxiaoyanqun@yahoo.com.cn

Abstract. With the fast development of wireless communication technology, the brand-new m-learning plays an important role in the education of colleges. This paper describes the design plan of campus wireless network, and studies the learning mode,system structure and platform building of m-learning system based on WLAN. Moreover, this paper makes an active discussion of the application of m-learning in the education of colleges.

Keywords: M-Learning, Education of Colleges, Wireless Network, Campus Network.

1   Introduction

M-Learning is an extension of digital learning and a brand-new learning mode after E-Learning. Relying on mobile communication technology and mobile communication terminals, m-learning provides personalized and open learning anywhere at any time.

With the fast development of mobile communication technology, campus wireless network technology has become increasingly well-developed, thus laying a solid foundation for the application of m-learning in the education of colleges. With campus wireless network, students and teachers can have access to campus network or internet via wireless terminals like laptop or PDA, which will enable them to share information resources with more convenience and efficiency. The combination of campus wireless network and m-learning platforms enriches teaching methods and cultural life on campus, and improves the level of teaching, scientific research and administration.

2   Building Campus Wireless Network

2.1   The Necessity of Building Campus Wireless Network

With the further building of information campus, many colleges have been equipped with campus network – a major channel for students and teachers to obtain

J. Lei et al. (Eds.): NCIS 2012, CCIS 345, pp. 798–803, 2012.
© Springer-Verlag Berlin Heidelberg 2012

information and resources. Nowadays, most of campus network is LAN. Recent years have seen the increasing expansion of college size and the surge in the number of students and teachers. Campus wireless network has exhibited its shortcomings like high construction cost, difficulty in network node expansion and limited coverage. So, it has become a must to build wireless network on campus.

Campus wireless network is an important part of building information campus, an extension and supplement of campus wired network. Breaking through the limit of traditional wired network, campus wireless network is more flexible and can achieve maximum compatibility with the existing backbone network on campus in building an all-pervasive campus network in colleges.

The building of campus wireless network mainly uses WLAN technology . Compared to wired local area network, WLAN is characterized by high mobility, long transmission distance, good network privacy, low cost of development and operation, good extension, minimum subjection to natural environment, flexible networking and easy maintenance. These characteristics make up for the deficiency of traditional wired local area network [1].

2.2   Plans to Build Campus Wireless Network

2.2.1 Topological Structure of Campus Wireless Network
Based on the design of existing wired network, campus wireless network acts as an important supplement and extension of the existing network. The general target of such building is to make sure campus network can reach every inch of campus space and realize high-speed visit of all on-campus areas to the campus network or internet based on the existing campus network and IEEE802.11 WLAN criterion. The building of campus wireless network also aims to solve the issue of inadequate points of information on campus and enable students and teachers to use campus network and internet with efficiency and convenience anywhere at any time, thus satisfying their needs to study and communicate on campus.

Building campus wireless network can use the wireless-AP-centered system structure, where the communication of all base stations needs to be directed via AP which enables the seamless connection to the wired network. We can be flexible in setting the access points (AP) according to the school need and actual conditions. Using multiple coverage, thorough wireless coverage on campus can be achieved. After the completion of coverage via AP, any device supporting WiFi can access the campus network and then internet at every place on campus.

Refer to Figure 1 of WLAN structure plan for the topological structure of campus wireless network [2].

2.2.2 Technical Standard of Campus Wireless Network
WLAN has Bluetooth, IEEE 802.11 series, HiperLAN and HomeRF Technology, among which IEEE 802.11 series have been widely applied. The IEEE 802.11 series

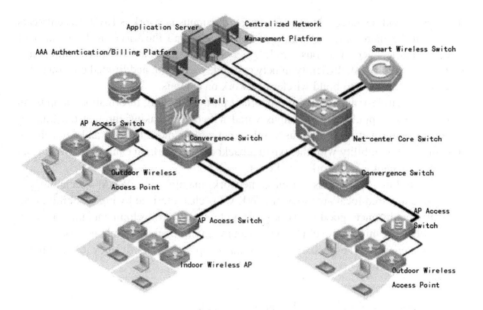

Fig. 1. Topological Structure of Campus Wireless Network

have three criteria: 802.11a, 802.11b and 802.11g. IEEE802.11b can support the shared access rate of 11Mbps, using the frequency range of 2.4GHzISM; IEEE 802.11a uses the frequency range of 5GHz, with a maximum rate of 54Mbps; IEEE 802.11g is a mixed criterion, suitable for the criteria of both IEEE 802.11b and IEEE 802.11a. It isn't so well developed. Now, IEEE 802.11b is the most advantageous of all three in terms of both transmission distance and rate. Therefore, we suggest that IEEE 802.11b be used in building campus wireless network.

2.2.3 The Composition of Campus Wireless Network

Campus wireless network is made up of WLAN card and AP. Using the common local area network (like 10M/100M/1000M Ethernet) and interconnection devices (router and switch) as backbone supporting network, WLAN relies on AP to support the mobility and roaming of MT (mobile terminals). Desktop computers, notebook computers or other hand-held mobile terminals equipped with WLAN card can all connect to wireless network.

WLAN card is a port connecting client to wireless network and a high-frequency (2.4GHz), broad-band (11Mbps or 54Mbps) wireless networking device. WLAN card can be a built-in PCMCIA card for laptop computers or a built-in PCI+PCMCIA card for desktop computers, or external USB adapters suitable for both types of computers.

Used as the wireless switch for wireless network, wireless AP is the core of wireless network. Wireless AP receives, buffers memory and transmits data between WLAN and wired network. It is a device that supports a group of wireless network users and the bridge between WLAN and LAN.

3 Building M-Learning System Based on Campus Wireless Network

3.1 M-Learning Mode Based on Campus Wireless Network

M-learning is a brand-new form of learning that obtains educational information, educational resource and service by using wireless mobile communication technology and devices of wireless mobile communication (like mobile phone, PDA and Pocket PC). M-learning is the combined outgrowth of mobile computing technology and digital learning technology and represents the trend of future learning [3]. M-learning is characterized by convenience in learning, personalized teaching, abundant interaction and situational relevance, which will enable people to study anywhere at any time as one likes.

M-learning has 3 learning modes: learning based on short messages, learning based on connected browse and learning based on campus wireless network [4].

Apart from voice service, m-learning based on short messages also offers SMS. Via short messages, a limited number of characters can be sent from students to students or network servers. Via learning terminals like cellphone, MP3 and MP4, short messages can be sent to the teaching server which will analyze the user message and transform it into data request, followed by data processing and forwarding to student. M-learning mode based on short messages is intermittent and doesn't support real-time connection. It doesn't permit the browse of learning websites, transmit or display the multimedia teaching resources.

M-learning mode based on connected browse refers to students using mobile learning terminals, going through gateways to connect to network, visiting the teaching server, browsing and searching the teaching resources. This mode can transmit not only texts but also images.

M-learning based on campus wireless network adopts mixed connection. Centered on campus network, this mode can connect a variety of wireless mobile learning regions and realize mobile learning within the campus. As campus m-learning is only restricted to the campus and adopts advanced WLAN technology, it has a high transmission efficiency. It supports the transmission of texts, images and dynamic multimedia teaching material (like video), thus providing more comprehensive and convenient learning channels for students.

3.2 Structure of M-Learning System Based on Campus Wireless Network

The structure of m-learning system based on campus wireless network has 3 layers: presentation layer, service logic layer and data service layer, as shown in Figure 2 [5].

Presentation layer is located in the client side. As the interface for interaction between user and system, presentation layer processes the communication between system and user. At the client side, presentation layer realizes the communication between user and service logic processing result, and provides different interfaces for different users, including student interface, teacher interface and administrator interface.

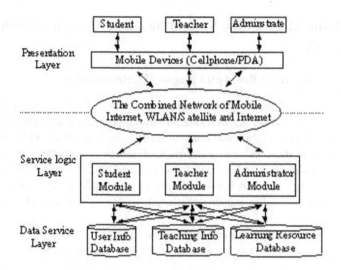

Fig. 2. Structure of M-Learning System

Service logic layer is located in the server side. Used for service of packaging system, it is the core of the system. It receives application requests from the presentation layer and conducts logic judgment of service processing.

Data service layer is also located in the server side and provides data sources. Data service layer includes user information database, teaching information database and learning resource database. User information database is used for recording the basic information of teachers and students, students' learning process information and teachers' teaching process information; teaching information database is used for recording teaching information, teaching status and Public course information; learning resource database is used for recording information like course resource, student question and teacher answer.

4   Building M-Learning Platform Based on Campus Wireless Network

4.1   Functional Module Design of M-Learning Platform

In module partitioning, according to user type, m-learning system has three modules: student module, teacher module and administrator module. According to service logic, the system has the following modules: teaching management module, curriculum management module, course learning module, course test module, teaching resource management module and user information management module.

4.2   Teaching Resource Design of M-Learning Platform

Building a mobile learning resource database is the foundation for commencing m-earning and needs to take into account the characteristics of m-learning like small screen, limited memory and bandwidth of the terminal device. Diversified, multiple learning resources like texts, audio, video and FLASH animations should be available, sometimes with combined representation.

M-learning curriculum offers 3 major types of teaching resources: 1. teaching description documents of a course, like course introduction, teaching syllabus, experiment syllabus, course implementation plan and performance evaluation; 2. learning resources of course content, like PPT courseware, multimedia courseware, course recording or video; 3. tutorial material for a course, like the analysis of difficult or key points in each chapter, case database and test database.

5   Conclusion

M-learning is a new type of learning mode and acts as a new direction for developing modern educational technology. Campus wireless network will gradually change the access to educational resources, as well as how students study and interact with teachers. With the fast development and widespread application of wireless communication technology, especially the application of 3G/4G mobile communication technology and three-network convergence, m-learning based on campus wireless work and mobile terminal devices will have a greater prospect of application.

References

1. Yan, H.: On the Design and Building of Campus Wireless Network. J. Career Horizon 8, 36 (2008)
2. Lei, L., Kai, Z.: The Planning and Design of Campus Wireless Network. J. Computer & Telecommunication 7, 71–73 (2011)
3. Ye, C., Xu, F., Xu, J.: M-Learning Research Review. J. E-education Research 3, 12–19 (2004)
4. Ting, Z., Lina, R.: A Study of M-Learning Mode from the Perspective of Multiple Intelligence Theory. J. Oversea English 8, 481–482 (2010)
5. Wei, H., Di, J., Sun, H.: Theoretical Research and Practice of M-Learning. J. Computer Engineering & Science 9, 135–137 (2009)

Mobility Support in OLSR Routing Protocol

Lakrami Fatima and Elkamoun Najib

STIC Laboratory, Chouaib Doukkali Universtity
Eljadida, Morroco
{fatima.lakrami,elkamoun}@gmail.com

Abstract. We present in this paper a new mechanism for supporting the mobility in OLSR routing protocol. We use the nodes speed combined with the signal strength of received hello packets to decide about nodes ability to become MPRs. The speed will control the willingness of nodes while the signal strength will give an idea about the traveling direction. Our approach aims in the first hand to enhance the auxiliary functioning of OLSR , making it "mobility aware" without the need of adding any supplement traffic to control messages. In the second hand the standard MPRs selection algorithm is preserved in order to guarantee the optimum number of MPRs selected.

Keywords: Adhoc networks, OLSR,mobility.

1 Introduction

An ad hoc network is a set of mobile nodes that are dynamically and arbitrarily scattered in a way where the interconnection between nodes may change at any time. In most cases, the destination unit is not necessarily within the scope of the source unit which means that data flowing between any two nodes must be performed by intermediate stations. The management of data forwarding involves establishing some overall architecture where we must consider the mobility of units and the versatility of the physical medium. In this context, routing protocol for MANETs is used in order to discover paths between the nodes. The main purpose of such a strategy is the establishment of roads that are correct and effective between any pair of units, which ensures the exchange of messages in a continuous manner.

The fact that mobile nodes are not controlled by a single entity means that their movement is very difficult to predict and therefore the radio connectivity changes over time. Accordingly, we are in the presence of networks with dynamic topology and where nodes have limited resources. Hence it is necessary to develop methods for making routing protocols in MANETs aware about such constraints and enable them, in a dynamic process, to adapt their functioning to the continuous variations of the topology.

OLSR is a proactive link state protocol and non-uniform since it relies on a distinction based on the neighborhood to establish a hierarchy between nodes. In fact, OLSR tries to limit the amount of control messages, optimizing their number and broadcast within the entire network. For this, it uses a multipoint relays technique

J. Lei et al. (Eds.): NCIS 2012, CCIS 345, pp. 804–812, 2012.
© Springer-Verlag Berlin Heidelberg 2012

(or MultiPoint Relays, MPR) that consists of selecting among the neighbors of each node in the network, a set of small number of symmetric neighbors capable of relaying broadcast traffic. We propose in this paper a new mechanism for supporting the mobility in OLSR; by combining node's speed with the signal strength to select stable nodes as MPRs. Nodes will get their speed value thanks to their GPS receiver. Unless the speed does not give a real idea about the traveling direction, we add the signal strength of hello packets received from neighbors to be informed if the node is moving in or out the transmission range. We demonstrate through simulations the efficiency of our contribution, unless it requires no add to traffic control, besides the preservation of the standard MPR selection algorithm, proved to be optimal in term of complexity.

The rest of this paper is organized as follows : Section 2describes the OLSR routing protocol and MPR issues, in section 3 we present and explain our approach .Section 4 discusses performance of our extension with results of simulation experiments, while section 5 concludes the paper.

2   OLSR Overview and MPR Selection Issues

2.1   Introduction

OLSR is a proactive routing protocol[1], designed to operate in a mobile environment with absolutely no central device for controlling and responding to the mobility (Ad hoc networks)[2]. It is frequently used in dense networks with low mobility rate[1]. OLSR introduces the concept of MPRs in order to minimize control traffic and reduce redundant messages in a broadcast to all nodes in the network. Each node selects its MPRs among its 1-hop-neighbors to cover all of its 2-hop neighbors. In order to reduce control traffic flooding over the network, MPRs are the only nodes authorized to relay broadcast traffic issued from their selectors. Besides that, MPRs are also used to form routes from their selectors to the rest of the network.

The double role associated to MPRs, implies the necessity to choose those nodes in a way to meet certain criteria, related to their physicals features, and also the quality of the link established with their selectors. For example: nodes with a high residual energy level will be able to relay traffic and maintain the path available longer. A number of heuristics were proposed by the literature for the MPR selection, in order to define certain criteria to select a specific node instead of another. Two major algorithms have appeared: the first one selects nodes with the highest coverage degree in term of the two-hop neighborhood [3]. The second one introduces a new parameter called "the willingness" that expresses nodes ability to perform the relaying task[1]. We offer in the next paragraph a brief overview of those two basics heuristics for MPRs selection.

2.2   Simple Greedy

This algorithm consists on selecting form the 1-hop-neighbors set, nodes that covers the largest number of 2-hop-neighbors. This idea enables to cover the maximum number of the second hop neighbors, which enable a wider network coverage.

2.3   The RFC 3626 Heuristic

This heuristic is a variant of the simple greedy. The particularity of this heuristic is that it introduces a new weight called Willingness on the nodes. The Willingness reflects the ability of a node to relay traffic in the MANET. This specification remains open about the role that we can affect to the Willingness. An example is provided by representing the residual capacity of the battery node on a scale of 0-7, 0 being the lowest value and 7 the highest [4]. So, it aims to choose as MPRs, nodes with longer energy autonomy to guarantee a longer stability of the structure built in the MANET based on the MPRs. Our approach takes advantage of this feature to introduce a new parameter related to mobility, to control nodes willingness.

3   MA-OLSR (Mobility Aware OLSR)

3.1   Mobility Impact on MPR Selection

OLSR was initially developed for large and fixed networks. Nodes and links discovery is based on HELLO packets exchange. Once connections are established, their status is maintained active for a fixed period. If a link is lost, nodes will have to wait to detect the successive loss of two hello packet, to be able to confirm it. In the case of mobile network, nodes need imperatively to detect rapidly links breaking, or in a better way to predict it. Frequent disconnections due to nodes travelling, impacts mostly The MPR selection process in OLSR, considering the double functionality associated to MPR nodes, in term of relaying traffic and forming routes between communicating nodes.

A several works were proposed to resolve the mobility problem in OLSR protocol, to reduce losses and maintain communication as longer as possible. Authors in [5] propose a new extension called fast-OLSR, where the auxiliary functioning of OLSR is lightly modified to differentiate the behavior of fixed nodes and fast-mobile nodes. However its performance, the fixed values attributed to mobile nodes doesn't expose the mobility level (high, medium...). Another solution is proposed in [6][7] that uses an indirect mobility metric based on measuring the neighboring change rate, nodes will then exchange information about their mobile status to enable other nodes to select MPR nodes based on their stability, this idea is very useful , firstly with a non-uniform distribution of mobile nodes, and secondly, if the added data supposed to carry information about mobility is not too heavy to overload the network with an important number of mobile nodes .

3.2   Proposed Algorithm

Based on the speed value, we define three mobility classes that correspond to three willingness levels: low, normal, high. Nodes can inform their neighbors about their mobility rate, by reducing the weight affected to the willingness. We demonstrate in a previous work the efficiency of this contribution [6], in a controlled topology where the number of mobile nodes and their trajectory is already defined. We succeed to enhance network performance, in term of loss rate and delay, since our approach enables to select stable nodes as MPRs, which preserves the stability of the MPR neighborhood and also guarantees a longer lifetime for the routes built based on those MPRs, without the need to add any supplement traffic at packet control level.

In order to expand the validity contour of this previous proposition, we propose to use another metric related to a physical characteristic of links with 1-hop neighbors, it is the signal strength of hello packets. This information must be transferred from the physical layer to the routing protocol, to be stocked in the 1-hop neighbor set. We use the algorithm defined in [7] which accumulate the signal variation in order to keep a trace of node position, taking as reference the node performing the MPRs selection.

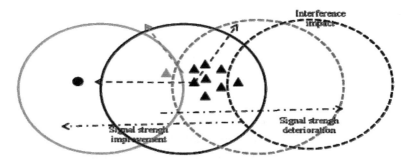

Fig. 1. Impact of node travelling and interference on radio signal strength

The problem with the use of speed as unique mobility metric is the absence of any knowledge about the direction of nodes movement. In the case where a node is traveling inside the transmission range towards its expected selector, there is no need of excluding it from the MPRs primitive list, regardless his mobility since the signal strength of hello packet is improving. Besides, the combination of mobility metric and the signal strength will avoid erroneous decision about the deterioration of the link quality, further to the signal attenuation because of a multitude factors (obstacle, Absorption losses, diffraction, scattering, interference ....), specialy when nodes is in a fixed state and the communication is affected by one of the previous cited factors .

The algorithm relatd to the willingness is presented as follow:

```
if (mobility_speed = 0)
   willingness=willigness_high;
if (0    <   mobility_speed <= mobility_threshol)
   willingness=willigness_default
if (mobility_speed > mobility_threshold)
   willingness=willigness_low
   END.
```

We define the link quality as a logical function that depends on the signal strength of the received hello packet, and the willingness of the competitive node. At the beginning of the process, node must select neighbors with high signal strength value, it is an assurance that those 1-hop-neighbors are closer to it, so if they start to move after, the node will have enough time to detect their mobility and to accumulate the signal strength variation. This will avoid unexpected links breaking. The new algorithm is presented as follow:

```
If(willingness=high     && signal_strenght is improving
(Δ>0 ))
Link_quality= 1
If((willingness=high    && signal_strenght is deterioring
(Δ<0))   ||   ((willingness=low    && signal_strenght is
improving (Δ>0 ) )
Link_Quality=0.5;
If((willingness=low     && signal_strenght is deterioring
(Δ>0))
Link_quality=0
   END.
```

The basic core of the RFC3626 MPR selection algorithm is preserved. In the proposed heuristic nodes selects firstly MPRs with high willingness value (stable ones), since the second neighboring is not yet entirely covered, nodes will take into consideration the second criterion which is link quality associated to signal strength variation. Both willingness and link quality are deployed in this second stage. The signal strength is recorded for every HELLO packet received.

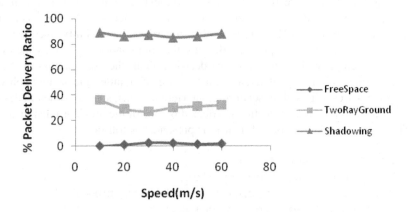

Fig. 2. The percentage of Loss Rate in function of nodes speed for different propagation models: FreeSpace, TwoRayGround and Shadowing

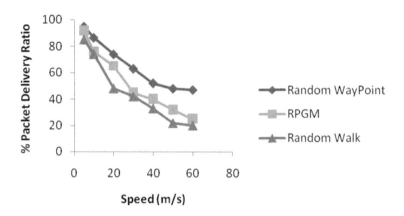

Fig. 3. The percentage of Packet Delivery Ratio in function of nodes speed for different propagation models: FreeSpace, TwoRayGround and Shadowing

It is important to notice the impact of the environment characteristics on the network performance. For different propagation models, different attenuation factors are recorded. The same remark is noticed about the speed impact for different mobility models. Figure1 and 2 presents respectively the percentage of packet delivery ratio in function of nodes speed first for different propagation models and second for different mobility models:

The ideal combination implies the use of the FreeSpace and Random Waypoint successively as propagation and mobility model. They give both the best PDR values even with high speed values. In this work we focus principally on the signal strength deterioration due to wireless channel physical properties so we choose the deploy the TwoRayGround as propagation model, proved to give more accurate prediction for large-scale topologies, and the Random WayPoint for modeling the mobility, due to its large global used .

4   Simulation and Results

We use network simulator NS2.34 [7], to validate our approach. Scenarios consist of 75 nodes moving in a 1000 × 1000 m area. 40% of nodes are moving following a waypoint random model, with a speed that varies from 5m/s to 60 m/s with no pause time. The duration of each simulation is 500 seconds. We use the IEEE 802.11 MAC protocol. The channel data rate is set to 5.5Mbps. Packets size is set to 512 bytes with a transmission range of 250m. For the propagation model, TwoRayGround model is used. We choose to compare the performance of our approach, compared with the standard OLSR using the following metrics: Loss Rate, Average Delay and the average number of MPRs selected, of which the results are represented respectively by figures 4,5 and 6.

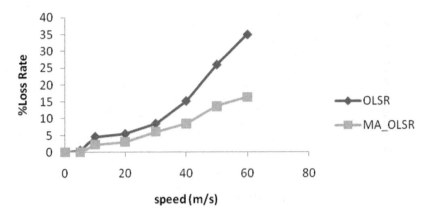

Fig. 4. The percentage of Loss Rate in function of nodes speed for different propagation models :FreeSpace, TwoRayGround and Shadowing

Figure4 illustrate the loss rate corresponding to the OLSR and our approach MA_OLSR (mobility aware OLS), for different nodes speed. As shown MA_OLSR reduce the loss rate percentage. It enables a given node to select among its 1-hop-neighbors stable MPRs (with high willingness), OR mobile nodes that's move toward the node (signal strength is improving). The packet delivery ratio is improved by 30% in the case of MA_OLSR compared with native OLSR. As known, MPRs are used to build paths from their selector to the rest of the networks. Hence, whichever the case, paths formed by stable nodes, will be maintained for a lifetime longer than those built by the native OLSR , which considers the coverage degree as the only criteria for selecting MPRs, which reduce considerably the loss rate caused by the frequent link breakage .

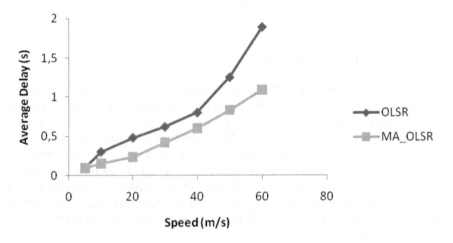

Fig. 5. The Average Delay for OLSR and "mobility aware OLSR"

By referring to Figure 5, the average delay is enhanced for the MA_OLSR(mobility aware OLSR). Smaller values are recorded for different speeds compared with the original OLSR. This can be explained by the fact, that reducing the loss rate by maintaining the connections longer in plus of expecting links corruption, will reduce the number of retransmissions required to achieve correct packet delivery which has as result delay enhancement.

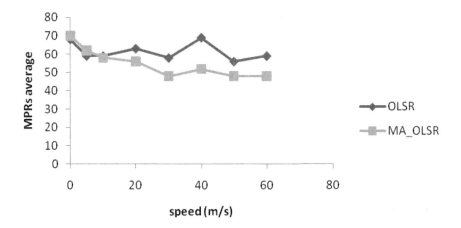

Fig. 6. Average MPRs number for OLSR and "mobility aware OLSR"

As shown in figure 6, OLSR and MA_OLSR give approximately the same average number of MPRs selected, except for high speed value , where the criteria of mobility occurs in a more persistent manner , in term of reducing nodes willingness. In plus the hello refreshing interval is 2 seconds, which means , that for nodes moving faster towards a node before changing the direction , won't be counted in MPRs selection process as long as their deviation happened faster than hello sensing process.

5   Conclusion

We present in this work a new mechanism for mobility support in OLSR routing protocol. Our approach aims to enhance network performance in presence of mobility, without any modification in the core functioning of the protocol, or the need of exchanging any additional traffic between nodes. The speed will inform neighbors about the moving status of a node by reducing its willingness while signal strength measure will help out to know if the node is travelling inside or outside the transmission range of its expected selector. We succeed to demonstrate the efficiency of this proposition through different performance metrics. We work actually on developing a new mobility metric, to detect the movement for nodes that don't have a GPS receiver. It will be interesting to perform the same process based on locations for example, considering as reference the node performing the selection.

References

1. Jacquet, P., Laouiti, A., Minet, P., Muhlethaler, P., Qayyum, A., Viennot, L.: Optimized Link State Routing Protocol. RFC 3626, IETF (2003)
2. Bansal, N., Liu, Z.: Capacity, Delay and Mobility in Wireless Ad-Hoc Networks (2003)
3. Busson, A., Mitton, N., Fleury, E.: Analysis of the Multipoint Relays selection in OLSR and Implications (2010)
4. De Rango, F., Fotino, M., Marano, S.: Ee-Olsr: Energy Efficient Olsr Routing Protocol for Mobile Ad-Hoc Networks (2008)
5. Benzaid, M., Minet, P., Al Agha, K.: Analysis and simulation of Fast-OLSR. In: International Workshop on Mobile and Wireless Communications Network (December 2002)
6. Oudidi, K., Hajjami, A., Elkoutbi, M.: A New Composite Metric For QOS Satisfying Both Mobility an Bandwidth Constraints in Manets. In: Proceedings of African Conference on Research in Computer Science and Applied Mathematics CARI 2010, Yamoussoukro-2010, Rabat, Côte d'Ivoire (2010)
7. Oudidi, K., Elkoutbi, M.: A Mobility Based Metric For Qos In Mobile Ad Hoc Netwoks. In: Proceedings of the IASTED International Conference on Wireless and Optical Communications (WOC 2009), Banff, Canada, July 6-8, pp. 11–18 (2009) ISBN: 978-0-88986-793-2
8. Lakrami, F., Elkamoun, N.: Energy and mobility in OLSR routing protocol. Cyber Journals: Multidisciplinary Journals in Science and Technology, Journal of Selected Areas in Telecommunications, JSAT (March Edition 2012)
9. Mansoor Ali, H., Busson, A., Meraihi Naimi, A.: Un Algorithme de Gestion des Adjacences basé sur la Puissance du Signal (March 2008)
10. The network simulator, http://www.isi.edu/nsnam/ns/ (cited July 2011)

An Efficient and Rapid Address Assignment Algorithm for LR-WPAN Meshes

Zhi Ren, Yan Liu, Jianlin Cao, and Hongjiang Lei

Chongqing Key Lab of Mobile Communications Technology, Chongqing University of Posts and Telecommunications, Chongqing, China 400065
renzhi@cqupt.edu.cn,
liuyan_0413@163.com

Abstract. The IEEE 802.15.5 standard provides an address assignment algorithm for low-rate wireless personal area (LR-WPAN) mesh networks, which can reduce the need of route discovery. In our study, however, we found that the algorithm contains some redundancy in control overhead and allocation time. In this paper, we propose an effective and rapid address assignment algorithm (ERAA) for LR-WPAN meshes, which compresses the address assignment frame and changes the condition of address allocation to reduce control overhead and to speed address assignment. Simulation results show that ERAA can reduce control overhead and shorten allocation time, as compared to the address assignment algorithm defined by the IEEE 802.15.5 Standard.

Keywords: LR-WPAN meshes, address assignment algorithms, delay, compression.

1 Introduction

The IEEE 802.15.5 standard [1] is developed to support both LR-WPAN meshes and high rate WPAN meshes. By binding logic addresses to the network topology, IEEE 802.15.5 obviates the need for route discovery which eliminates the initial route discovery latency, saves storage space compared to routing table, and reduces the communication overhead and energy consumption [2-5]. LR-WPAN mesh supports mesh functions on top of IEEE 802.15.4 [6].

Currently, ZigBee [7] is based on cluster tree [8] structure and built on IEEE 802.15.4 MAC [6]. In the Distributed Address Assignment Mechanism (DAAM) for ZigBee [7], three default parameters have been confirmed before address assignment: the maximum number of children a parent may have, (C_m); the maximum depth in the network, (L_m); and the maximum number of routers a parent may have as children, (R_m). According to these three parameters and a node's depth, d, we compute the function, $Cskip(d)$. With the $Cskip(d)$ and the sequence number of the children, we work out the addresses and send.them to devices. Without the procedure of children number report, allocation time and overhead in DAAM are less than those in LR-WPAN mesh address assignment algorithm. However, default parameters cannot correspond with the topology of the network, some orphan nodes [9] may come out.

J. Lei et al. (Eds.): NCIS 2012, CCIS 345, pp. 813–820, 2012.
© Springer-Verlag Berlin Heidelberg 2012

In LR-WPAN mesh address assignment algorithm, root can receive the imformation of the topology.

In LR-WPAN mesh address assignment algorithm, the tree formation starts with the first node in the network designating itself as the root and beginning to accept association requests from other nodes. After a node is successfully associated, it determines whether to become a parent node which allows other nodes to join the network through it. After a branch reaches its bottom, that is, no more devices waiting for joining the networks, a bottom-up procedure shall be used to calculate the number of devices along each branch. After the root receives the information from all the branches, it should begin to assign addresses. During the address assigning stage, a top-down procedure is used [5].

However, in LR-WPAN meshes, there is some redundancy in address assignment frame. Meanwhile, an amount of addresses can be confirmed before the root node receives the information from all the branches which will lead to some extra delay. At the same time, if one of children number report frames cannot be received, address assignment would fail.

To solve the above problems, in this paper we propose ERAA (Effective and Rapid Address Assignment), a novel algorithm for LR-WPAN Meshes. In ERAA, the redundancy of address assignment frame has been removed. The condition of address assignment has also been changed to reduce the allocation time and the probability of assignment failure. The rest of this paper is organized as follows.

2   ERAA Algorithm

ERAA consists of two stages: association and address assignment. Moreover, ERAA has two new mechanisms: compressing the address assignment frame to reduce the overhead of address assignment frame, and changing the condition of address allocation to allocate address in advance in the address assignment stage. The address assignment result is shown in Fig.1.

2.1   New Mechanisms of ERAA

Compressing the Address Assignment Frame. Ending Address is calculated by Beginning Address and the number of children of itself. Ending Address and Beginning Address compose an address block. Address assignment frame only includes Beginning Address field.

We assume that the Beginning Address of parent node is 'j' and the Beginning Address to be assigned to child is 'k'. Beginning Address compression needs satisfying the following formula:

$$|k - j| \leq (0xff - 0x18)/2 \tag{1}$$

$0x18$ and $0xff$ are hexadecimal. Using the reserved command frame identifier $0x18$-$0xff$ in LR-WPAN mesh, we define $0x18$-$0x7f$ as 1-104 increments and $0x80$-$0xff$ as

1-104 decrements both according to the Beginning Address of parent node. As a result, there is no address field in the address assignment command. MC will not operate this compression process and just uses *0x18* and *0x80* to inform Increase Decrease Attribute of Address (IDA) to child. With the Increase Attribute of Address (IA), Beginning Address which the node later allocates to its branches is greater than its own. With the Decrease Attribute of Address (DA), Beginning Address which the node later allocates to its branches is less than its own. MD can get the IDA from the command frame identifier or the relationship between its Beginning Address and its parent's.

Changing the Condition of Address Allocation. MC and Mesh Device (MD) with routing capability are given the operation of allocation below.

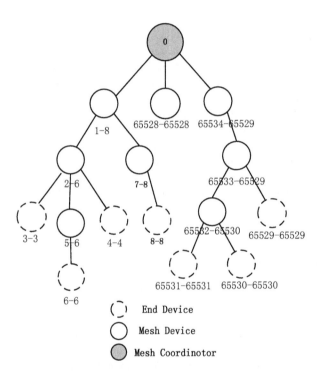

Fig. 1. Calculation of number of devices along each branch

Receiving associate request. MC transmits the address assignment frames with Beginning Address *0x0001* and *0xfffe* to the first and second devices which join the MC and informs them IDA. Having Beginning Address, MD transmits the address assignment frame to first child which joins MD. The value of allocated address is one greater or less than its own according to its IDA.

Receiving children number report. When MD receives the children number report frame transmitted by the node which has Beginning Address, it shall immediately transmit   the address assignment frame to some other branches according to its IDA and existing children number report. Meanwhile, we ensure the continuity of the address block in these branches. When MC receives the children number report frame transmitted by the node which has Beginning Address, it shall immediately   transmit the address assignment frame to some other branches according to IDA of the sender and existing children number report. Meanwhile, we ensure the continuity of the address block in these branches.

Receiving address assignment. When MD receives address assignment frame, it shall immediately transmit address assignment frame to some of its children according to its IDA and existing children number report.

2.2   Basic Operations of ERAA

Association. After the initialization of the mesh coordinator (MC), MC chooses *0x0000* as its own short address, and constructs beacon to allow new devices to join. When a mesh device joins the network, it constructs beacon to allow new devices to join and starts a timer. The device becomes a leaf device if no other devices join it before the time (T_{cnr}) expires. A leaf device should immediately send a children number report frame to its parent. If non-leaf device receives children number report frame from each of its children, it shall report the number of children to its parent.

Address Assignment. When the node receives associate request, children number report, or address assignment, it transmits address assignment frame to its children according to the new mechanism of changing the condition of address allocation.

2.3   Theoretical Analysis

Lemma 1. ERAA has less control overhead than the existing algorithm in the IEEE 802.15.5 standard.

Proof: The control overhead in two algorithms includes: beacon (BC), associate request command (AR), children number report frame (CR) and address assignment frame (AA). The n indicates the number of MDs in network. The control overhead of the existing algorithm, C_o, is described by following formula.

$$C_o = \sum_i^n BC_i + \sum_i^n AR_i + \sum_i^n CR_i + \sum_i^n AA_i \qquad (2)$$

In ERAA, because some short addresses can be allocated to some nodes in advance, these nodes use short address to transmit beacons and children number reports. We assume that the number of these nodes is m and the average number of beacons which has been transmitted after allocated address is b. The sum of bits reduced by beacons (BC) and children number reports (CR) can be described by the following formula.

$$B_{bc} = (64 - 16) \cdot m \cdot b + (64 - 16) \cdot m \qquad (3)$$

Address assignment frame only includes Beginning Address field. We assume that the number of Beginning Address which can be compressed is k. The sum of bits reduced by address assignment frame (AA) can be described by the following formula.

$$B_{aa} = 16 \cdot (n + k) \ . \qquad (4)$$

When the overhead of associate request command in two algorithms is the same, the overhead of beacon, children number report frame and address assignment frame has been reduced in ERAA, so we have:

$$C_{ERAA} = C_o - B_{bc} - B_{aa} < C_o \ . \qquad (5)$$

C_{ERAA} is the control overhead of ERAA. Therefore, ERAA has less control overhead than the existing algorithm in the IEEE 802.15.5 standard.

3 Numerical Results

We use OPNET14.5 as the simulation platform and quantitatively compare our algorithm with LR-WPAN mesh address assignment algorithm.

3.1 Settings of Key Simulation Parameters

There are five simulation scenes in a rectangular. Side length of rectangular is $400m$. The number of fixed MDs is N, $N \in \{100, 200, 300, 400, 500\}$. There is a MC in the center of rectangular, and MDs are randomly distributed in rectangular. To ensure most of the nodes included in the connected domain and associated successfully, the transmitted power is set as $0.6mw$, $0.45mw$, $0.43mw$, $0.4mw$ and $0.39mw$ in different scenes. T_{cnr} is set to $0.2s$. We use 128, 130, 132 and 134 four random seeds in five scenes to calculate the average.

3.2 Simulation Results and Analysis

Control Overhead. Fig. 2 shows that the control overhead in ERAA in each scene is smaller than that in the existing algorithm, respectively. That is because ERAA removes the redundancy of the address assignment command and uses the short address to communicate in advance.

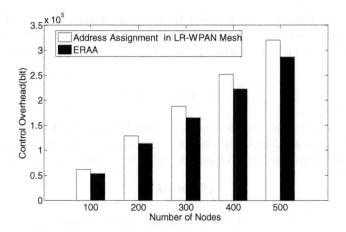

Fig. 2. Control overhead

Allocation Time. Fig. 3 shows that the allocation time in ERAA in each scene is shorter than that in the existing algorithm, respectively. The reason is that some short addresses allocated to the nodes in advance in ERAA can improve bandwidth utilization rate, shorten the Allocation time.

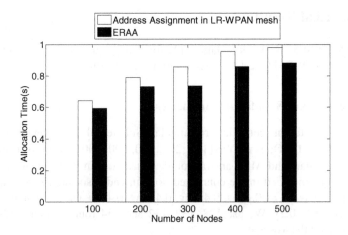

Fig. 3. Allocation time

Success Rate. As shown in Fig. 4, the success rate reaches above 97% and there is little different in two algorithms. ERAA does not change the principle that address assignment depends on the association and children report. With the same suitable value of transmit power and T_{cnr}, only packet loss can lead to the failure.

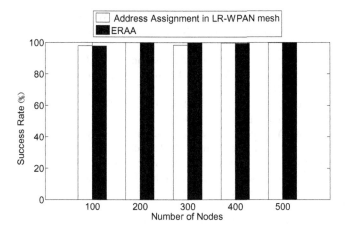

Fig. 4. Success rate of address assignment

4   Conclusions

In this paper, we proposed a new algorithm called ERAA for LR-WPAN meshes. By compressing the address assignment frame and changing the condition of address assignment, ERAA has less control overhead and shorter allocation time than the existing algorithm defined in IEEE802.15.5. In future, we plan to investigate the address assignment in dynamic network topologies.

Acknowledgments. This work was supported in part by the National Natural Science Foundation of China under Grant No. 60972068, the Scientific Research Starting Foundation for Returned Overseas Chinese Scholars, Ministry of Education of China under Grant No. 2010-1561, the open project of Emergency Communication Laboratory of Chongqing under Grant No. 201201, and the special fund of Chongqing key laboratory (CSTC) under Grant No. D2011-24.

References

1. IEEE 802.15.5: Mesh Topology Capability in Wireless Personal Area Networks (WPANs). IEEE Standard. 802.15.5 (2009)
2. Lee, M., Zhang, R., Zhu, C.-H., et al.: Meshing Wireless Personal Area Networks: Introducing IEEE 802.15.5. IEEE Communication Magazine, 54–61 (2010)
3. Zhu, C.-H., Zheng, J.-L., Ngo, C., et al.: Low-Rate WPAN Mesh Network - An Enabling Technology for Ubiquitous Networks. In: Wireless Communications and Networking Conference, pp. 1–6 (2009)
4. Zhang, R., Park, T.R., Lee, M., et al.: Testbed Experimentation of a Meshed Tree Routing with Local Link State for Wireless PAN Mesh. In: IEEE International Conference on Communications, pp. 3060–3065 (2008)

5. Lee, M.J., Zhang, R., Zheng, J.-L., et al.: IEEE 802.15.5 WPAN Mesh Standard-Low Rate Part: Meshing the Wireless Sensor Networks. IEEE Journal on Selected Areas in Communications 28(7), 973–983 (2010)
6. IEEE 802.15.4: Wireless LAN Medium Access Control (MAC) and Physical Layer (PHY) Specifications for Low-Rate Wireless Personal Area Networks (LR-WPANs). IEEE Standard. 802.15.4 (2006)
7. ZigBee Alliance, ZigBee Document 053474r17, ZigBee Specification Version 2006. ZigBee Alliance Board of Directors (2006)
8. Hester, L., Huang, Y., Andric, O., et al.: NeuRon^{TM} netform: a self-organizing wireless sensor network. In: 11th International Conference on Computer Communications and Networks, Motorola Labs, Plantation, FL, USA, pp. 364–369 (October 2002)
9. Pan, M.-S., Tsai, C.H., Tseng, Y.C.: The Orphan Problem in ZigBee Wireless Networks. IEEE Transactions on Mobile Computing 8(11), 1573–1584 (2009)
10. Ahn, W.S., Hwang, D.Y., Kim, K.H.: A joining mechanism for efficient address management in low-rate WPAN mesh. In: International Conference on Advanced Communication Technology, pp. 67–70 (2011)
11. Yen, L.H., Tsai, W.T.: Flexible Address Configurations for Tree-Based ZigBee/IEEE 802.15.4Wireless Networks. In: The 22nd International Conference on Advanced Information Networking and Applications, pp. 395–402 (2008)

A RF Repeater for Low Data Rate Communication

Yuan-yuan Chen, Jun-jie Peng[*], and Sheng Luo

School of Computer Engineering and Science, Shanghai University
No.99, Shangda Rd, Shanghai 200444, China
juneboa@gmail.com,
jjie.peng@shu.edu.cn

Abstract. In the field of wireless communication, the repeater is mainly used for extending the communication range between transmitting node and receiving node. In some applications, the data rate of communication is not high, but the requirement of power consumption and node size is relatively strict. Based on this situation, we design a radio frequency repeater and present the hardware and software solutions. It is reliable, suitable for the situation with low data transmission rate. It's the advantages of the repeater are small in size and low power consumption. The results of experiment show that the repeater can forward signal without interferes, and meet the need of a wide range of data communication.

Keywords: Radio frequency, low data rate, low energy consumption, repeater.

1 Introduction

The signal of wireless communication applications in industrial and civilian areas mainly work in VHF and UHF band, so the path of signal transmission is almost linear and has significant path loss when signal pass obstacles. This greatly affects the range of communication. In order to solve this problem, increasing the signal transmitting power and receiving sensitivity and reducing data rate are adopted. However these ways increase power consumption of the node, they can't meet the future higher requirements of low power consumption and high data rate of wireless communication.

One widely adopted solution is to use the wireless repeater, repeater can receive signal, then enlarge and send the signal in a suitable location. Many studies have focused on wireless repeater, which include forwarding mode, the establishment and storage of forwarding path and the compatible of different communication protocols, etc. Literature [1] presents an intelligent lighting wireless repeater which includes power module, signal receiving module, signal processing module and signal transmitting module. Power module has two voltage output ports, one connects to transmitting module, and the other connects to the processing module and receiving module. The receiving module and transmitting module are controlled by the processing module. The repeater solves the issue that communication range of remote

---

[*] Corresponding author.

J. Lei et al. (Eds.): NCIS 2012, CCIS 345, pp. 821–826, 2012.
© Springer-Verlag Berlin Heidelberg 2012

control is short. It forwards the signal from the remote sources. Thus it realizes the wide range of data communication in the household intelligent lighting. Literature [2] describes a wireless sensor network repeater system. This system makes up of pairs of repeater. Its feature is that wireless sensor network can collect and send different sensor data, repeater processes data information received transparently, then sends processed data information to the wireless sensor network. This system can be compatible with different kinds of communication protocols. It extends communication range of wireless sensor network and be helpful for mass deployment of wireless sensor network applications due to low cost, communication efficiency and reliability.

The repeaters mentioned above are designed according to the actual demand for certain applications. With the popular of wireless communication applications, the requirements of system are more strict than before, such as miniaturization, low power consumption. How to achieve the wider range of wireless communication with lower power consumption and works efficiently is a hot topic that attracts many researchers. Based on the real case that the existing applications of wireless communication don't need too much communication traffic, we design a radio frequency repeater and give the hardware and software solutions.

2   Design of the Hardware

The repeater we designed is made up of data processing module and RF module. After comprehensive comparison of the current chips, we select STC51 microcontroller as the processor. For RF chip we select TI-CC1101 transceiver chip. Figure 1 shows the schematic circuit diagram of RF module and processing module. The repeater is designed as continuous power supply module. The repeater is connected by 220V power supply. The AC/DC converts 220V Alternating Current (AC) power into 3.3V Direct Current (DC) to meet the requirement of the working voltage of the modules. Processing module connects RF module by SPI bus. CC1101 works with FSK modulation, 433MHz radio frequency and forward error correction(FEC). And the RF module supports different transmission power. Compared with the other frequency and modulation, the choices support a lower bit error rate (BER) under the same conditions so that node can receives signal correctly at very low signal-to-noise ratio(SNR)[3]. The antenna which connects RF module is a quarter wave whip copper antenna. It is set up in parallel with the ground and the diameter is 0.5mm so that it can increase antenna gain[4]. It has been placed 1m above the ground in the experiment. When RF module receives and identifies signal, it will send out an interrupt signal from GDO0 pin after the signal is demodulated. The interrupt wakes up sleeping processing module so that it can process and forward the received signal. Processing module gets received signal by SPI. The repeater is shown in figure 2.

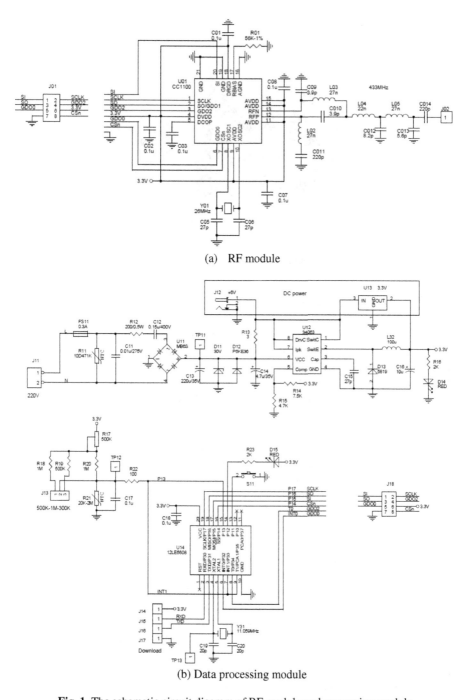

(a) RF module

(b) Data processing module

Fig. 1. The schematic circuit diagram of RF module and processing module

Fig. 2. The repeater designed

3   Design of the Software

The repeater we designed can process the received data packet transparently, and then send the processed data packet. Processing module maintains a configuration table, which storages device ID, packet type and the kind of forwarding. The configuration table is set up as follows: when the repeater is initialized, the repeater turns into sleeping. If the repeater receives a signal in 10s, an item is added to the configuration table.

Figure 3 illustrates the working flow chart of the repeater. At the beginning, processing module and RF module begin to initialize. Processing module determines whether the initialization button is pressed to perform corresponding operations, then determines whether it receive signal, if not, processing module and RF module are in sleeping state. When RF module receives signal, processing module checks the preamble field and synchronization field. If they are right, it will decode the packet and search the configuration table according to the device ID of the received signal. Otherwise, the data packet will be abandoned without any processing, and the processing module continues to be in sleeping state. When the module in sleeping receives correct transmission signal, it will be awaked immediately with WOR[5] method, and enters the normal working state to process the received signal. If the processing module detects the item successfully, it indicates that the data packet is allowed to forward, and then obtain the packet type and the kind of forwarding. At the same time the flag of forwarding is set to 1, which means the data packet has been repeated once. And then the flag is set to 0 after 200ms, if the repeater receives a data packet with same device ID again in 200ms after the repeater receives the data packet, the data packet will be abandoned without any processing. These methods try to solve the problem that the data packet might be repeated in loop in many repeaters. This can much avoid waste resources. The repeater turns into sleeping state after the signal is forwarded successfully.

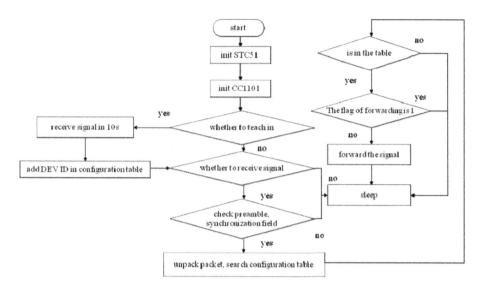

Fig. 3. The working flow chart of the repeater

4   Experiment and Analysis

In order to verify the efficiency and reliability of the repeater, we design the wireless transmitting and receiving terminal node. Their RF modules are based on CC1101, CC1101 can support data rate of 500Kbps at most. So the repeater we design is suitable for the situation in which requirement of data payload is low, such as a wireless sensor network which has limited power supply and low data rate requirement. In the experiment, we make CC1101 work in 433.92MHz band, the transmit power for 5dBm, data rate for 125Kbps, and channel space for 320KHz[6]. We test the transmission distance between transmitting node and receiving node under different conditions. We test the max transmission distance between transmitting node and receiving node when there are different number of repeaters between transmitting node and receiving node in open ground environment and indoor environment. Detailed data is as shown in Table 1.

Table 1. The transmission distance under different conditions

	No repeater	One repeater	Two repeaters
Open ground	200m	370m	550m
Indoor(more than 2 ~ 3 walls)	30m	55m	75m

From the comparison, it can easily find that in different environments, the repeater we designed extends the communication range of transmitting node and receiving node. And it avoids loop repeat in many repeaters. It achieves the wide range of wireless communication with lower power consumption.

5   Conclusion

Based on the real case that the existing applications of wireless communication have strict requirements of miniaturization and low power consumption, but don't need too much communication traffic. We design a radio frequency repeater. It can be embedded well in buildings and trees. The experimental results show that the repeater achieves the wide range of wireless communication and works efficiently. So it will be very promising for some applications.

Acknowledgments. This work is supported by Natural Science Foundation of China (No.61103054), Shanghai Leading Academic Discipline Project (No.J50103) and the innovation project of Shanghai Municipal Education Commission (11YZ09).

References

1. A intelligent lighting wireless repeater, http://www.bfb-100.com
2. A wireless sensor network repeater system, http://www.mambotek.com
3. Dessales, D., Poussard, A., Vauzelle, R., Richard, N., Gaudaire, F., Martinsons, C.: Physical layer study in a goal of robustness and energy efficiency for wireless sensor networks. In: 2010 Conference on Design and Architectures for Signal and Image Processing (DASIP), pp. 214–221 (2010)
4. Li, B.P., Yao, J.: Microwave and satellite communications. Xian electronic science and technology university press, Xi'an (2006)
5. STC12C5628AD, http://www.stcmcu.com/datasheet/stc/STC-AD-PDF/STC12C5628AD.pdf
6. CC1101, http://www.ti.com/lit/ds/symlink/cc1101.pdf

Author Index